CRACOW
photographed
by JANUSZ PODLECKI
Introduction
by GRAŻYNA ROTTER

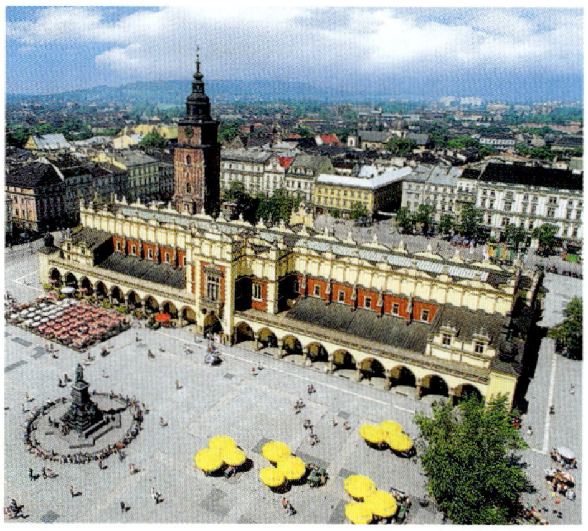

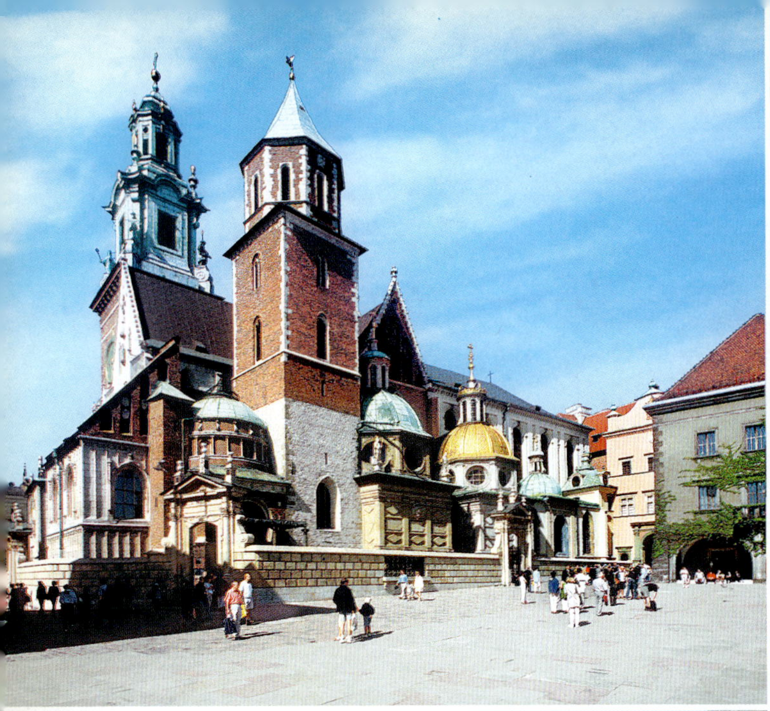

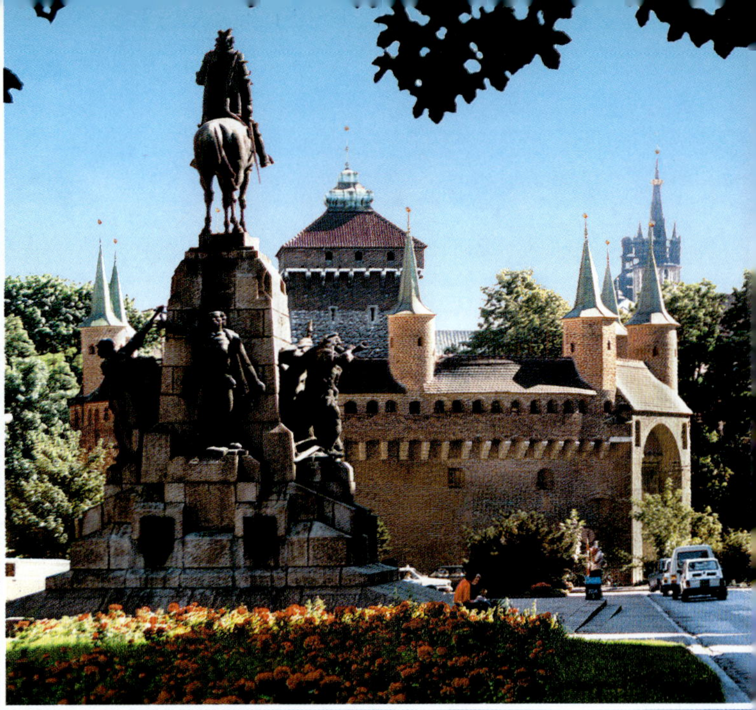

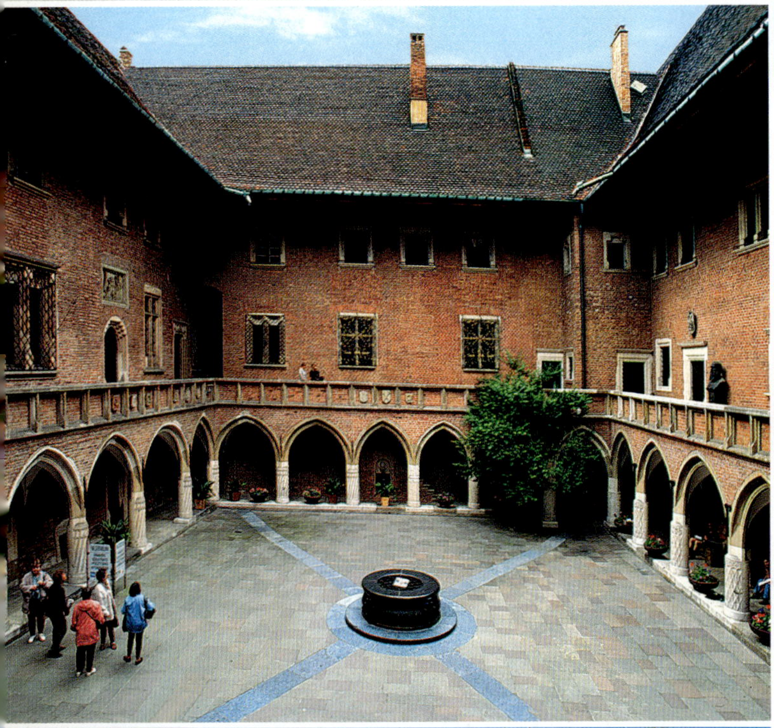

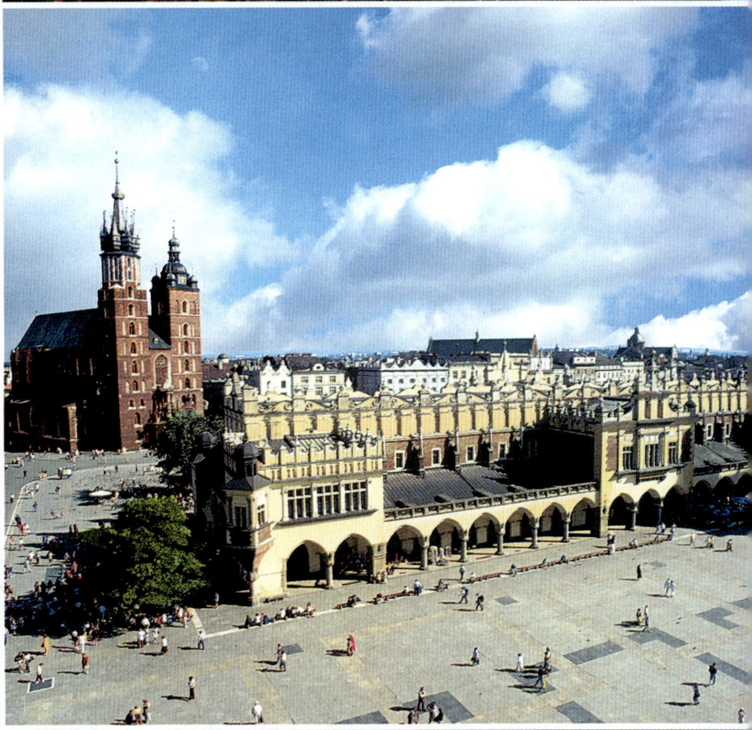

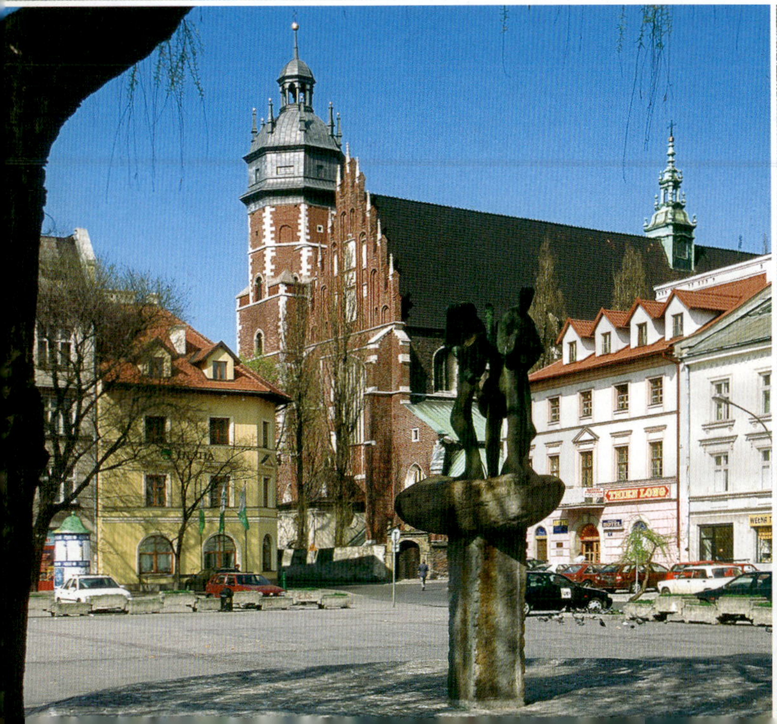

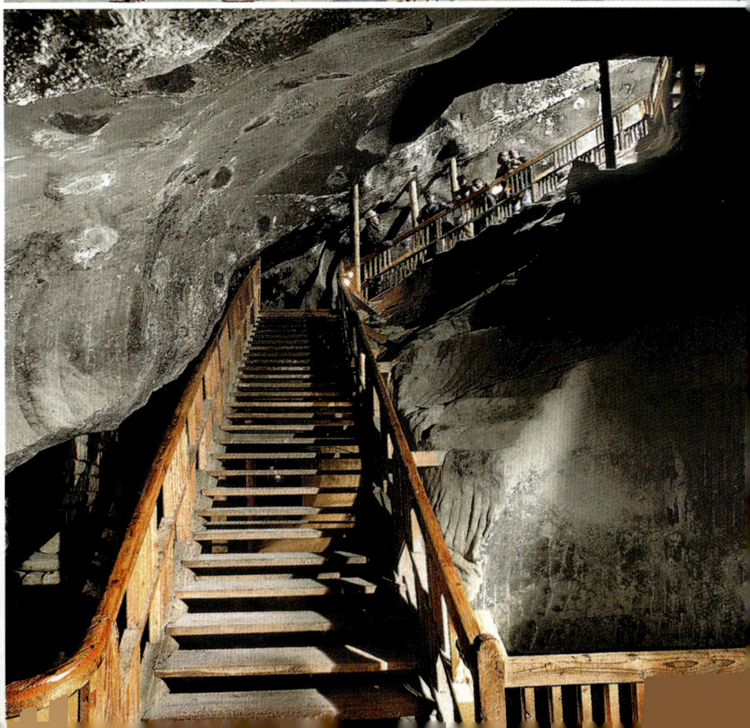

CRACOW

photographed
by JANUSZ PODLECKI

Introduction
by GRAŻYNA ROTTER

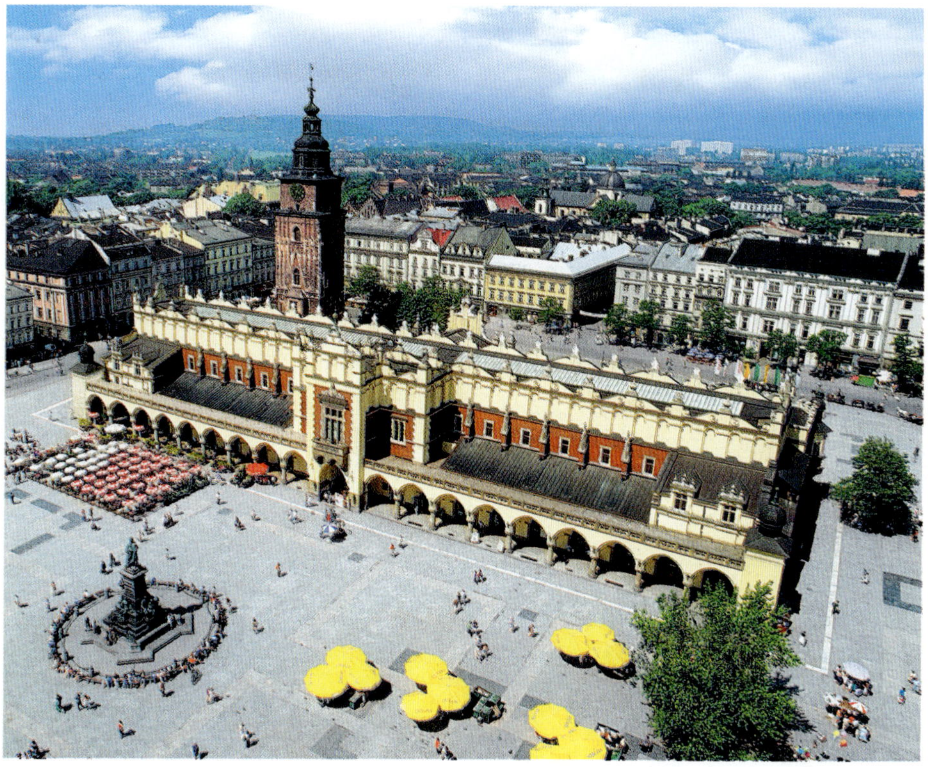

PUBLISHING HOUSE „KARPATY" – ANDRZEJ ŁĄCZYŃSKI
KRAKÓW 2001

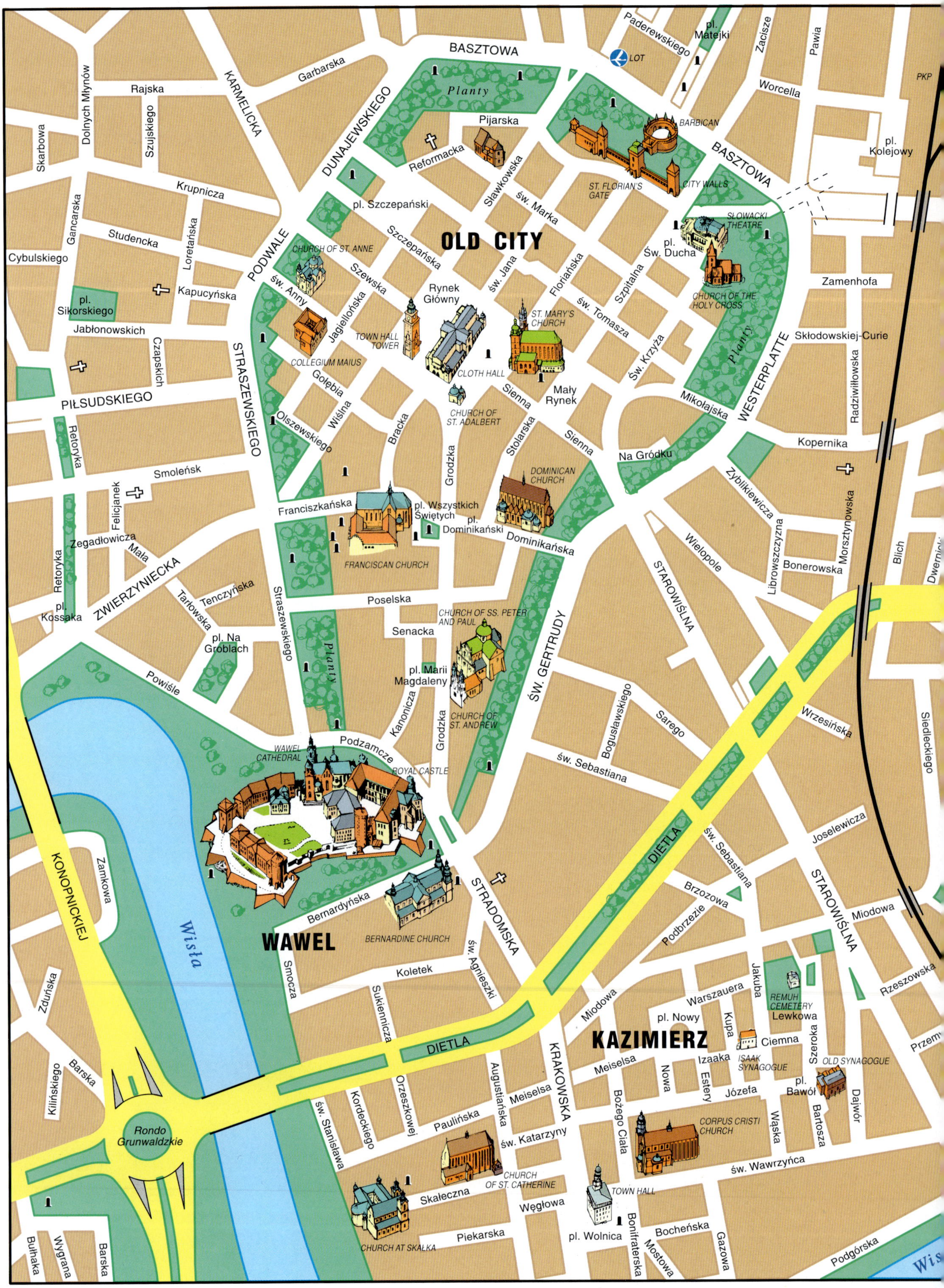
OLD CITY
WAWEL
KAZIMIERZ
BASZTOWA
Garbarska
Rajska
KARMELICKA
DUNAJEWSKIEGO
Planty
Paderewskiego
pl. Matejki
LOT
Zacisze
Pawia
PKP
Worcella
pl. Kolejowy
Dolnych Młynów
Szujskiego
Skarbowa
Pijarska
Reformacka
BARBICAN
CITY WALLS
ST. FLORIAN'S GATE
Sławkowska
Krupnicza
pl. Szczepański
św. Marka
SŁOWACKI THEATRE
pl. Św. Ducha
Gancarska
Loretańska
Studencka
Cybulskiego
PODWALE
CHURCH OF ST. ANNE
Szczepańska
Szewska
św. Anny
św. Jana
Floriańska
Szpitalna
Zamenhofa
CHURCH OF THE HOLY CROSS
Kapucyńska
pl. Sikorskiego
Jabłonowskich
Jagiellońska
Rynek Główny
TOWN HALL TOWER
ST. MARY'S CHURCH
św. Tomasza
Św. Krzyża
WESTERPLATTE
Skłodowskiej-Curie
Czapskich
STRASZEWSKIEGO
COLLEGIUM MAIUS
CLOTH HALL
PIŁSUDSKIEGO
Gołębia
Sienna
Mały Rynek
Mikołajska
Radziwiłłowska
Retoryka
Olszewskiego
Wiślna
CHURCH OF ST. ADALBERT
Bracka
Stolarska
Kopernika
Grodzka
Na Gródku
Smoleńsk
DOMINICAN CHURCH
Zyblikiewicza
Felicjanek
Franciszkańska
pl. Wszystkich Świętych
pl. Dominikański
Dominikańska
FRANCISCAN CHURCH
Zegadłowicza
Mała
ZWIERZYNIECKA
Wielopole
STAROWIŚLNA
Librowszczyzna
Bonerowska
Morsztynowska
Blich
Dwernickiego
Tenczyńska
Tarłowska
pl. Kossaka
Poselska
CHURCH OF SS. PETER AND PAUL
Senacka
pl. Na Groblach
Straszewskiego
ŚW. GERTRUDY
pl. Marii Magdaleny
Powiśle
Kanonicza
CHURCH OF ST. ANDREW
Bogusławskiego
Sarego
Wrzesińska
Siedleckiego
Podzamcze
WAWEL CATHEDRAL
ROYAL CASTLE
św. Sebastiana
Joselewicza
DIETLA
KONOPNICKIEJ
Zamkowa
STRADOMSKA
Brzozowa
Miodowa
Bernardyńska
BERNARDINE CHURCH
Podbrzezie
Wisła
Smocza
św. Agnieszki
Jakuba
REMUH CEMETERY
Koletek
Warszauera
Rzeszowska
Zduńska
Sukiennicza
pl. Nowy
Kupa
Lewkowa
Ciemna
Przemyska
Miodowa
Barska
Kilińskiego
Orzeszkowej
Kordeckiego
Augustiańska
KRAKOWSKA
Meiselsa
Nowa
Izaaka
Estery
ISAAK SYNAGOGUE
Szeroka
OLD SYNAGOGUE
pl. Bawół
Dajwór
Bartosza
Wąska
Józefa
Paulińska
św. Katarzyny
Bożego Ciała
CORPUS CRISTI CHURCH
Rondo Grunwaldzkie
św. Stanisława
CHURCH OF ST. CATHERINE
TOWN HALL
św. Wawrzyńca
Skałeczna
Węglowa
Piekarska
CHURCH AT SKAŁKA
pl. Wolnica
Bonifraterska
Mostowa
Bocheńska
Gazowa
Podgórska
Bułhaka
Wygrana
Barska
Wis

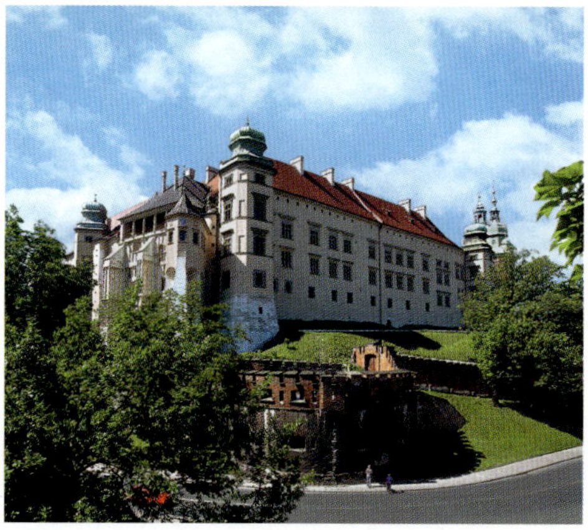

CRACOW with its 750 thousand inhabitants, is among the largest Polish cities. Yet its renown, which has reached beyond Poland and Europe, is based neither on its size nor on its economic significance. The city on the Vistula, the cradle and centre of Polish statehood, has been known predominantly as the nucleus of Polish national culture, as a city of thousands of unique old buildings which have survived numerous wars unscathed, and as a dynamic centre of science, its tradition dating back six centuries.

In the early Middle Ages Cracow was the main seat of the Slav tribe of the Vistulanians, and it was probably then, in the 7th century, that the two mounds, of Krak and Wanda, were erected. In the late 10th century Prince Mieszko I annexed Cracow and the land of the Vistulanians to the lands controlled by the Piast dynasty. In 1000 a bishopric was established in Cracow and the construction of the first cathedral was begun. Ca 1038 Prince Casimir the Restorer made Cracow his capital.

After the ravages by the Tartars in 1241, Prince Boleslaus the Chaste granted a charter to Cracow in 1257, and drew the city plan which has survived unchanged, with a regular grid of streets and a central square market place. From the 13th to the 14th century the stone and brick City Walls were built, encompassing the city and joining it with Wawel Castle.

In the reign of King Casimir the Great (1333-1370) the city and Wawel were thoroughly rebuilt in the Gothic style. The king established the borough of Kazimierz to the south of Cracow, and in 1364 founded Cracow Academy, the predecessor of the oldest Polish university, the Jagellonian University.

The city flourished in the 16th century under the last kings of the Jagellon dynasty, when a number of fine Renaissance buildings were erected. The period of the Vasa dynasty, particularly the reign of King Sigismund III Vasa, was marked by the lavish proliferation of the Baroque.

In 1609 Sigismund III Vasa moved the royal seat to Warsaw, yet Cracow remained the place of the coronation of the Polish kings and of their burial; it retained the title of the royal capital city. In the mid-17th century, and then again in the early 18th century, Cracow was sacked by Swedish troops. In 1734 the last coronation in Wawel Cathedral took place, of Augustus III of the Saxon Wettin dynasty.

After the First Partition of Poland (1772) Cracow found itself near the country's southern border. After the Second Partition, in 1794, a national insurrection started in Cracow, and its leader, Tadeusz Kościuszko, took an oath to the nation in the Market Square. After the suppression of the Insurrection and the Third Partition, the city was taken over by Austria. After the defeat of Napoleon, the Congress of Vienna proclaimed Cracow a free city (1815). In that period of limited autonomy, the remains of the national heroes, Tadeusz Kościuszko and Prince Józef Poniatowski, were buried at Wawel, and a mound in honour of the Insurrection leader was erected at St Bronisława's Hill. After Cracow's autonomy was abolished in 1846, the Austrians turned Wawel Castle into military barracks, encircled Wawel Hill with fortifications and built a line of defenses around the city. In 1918 Cracow, and Poland, regained independence.

The years of World War II were marked by harsh repressions of the Poles by the Nazis, the destruction of Polish culture and science, and the extermination of the Jews in Kazimierz.

In the post-war period, the city grew fast, and its industry developed, sometimes causing environmental degradation.

In 1978 the UNESCO entered the Cracow urban complex and the salt mine in nearby Wieliczka on

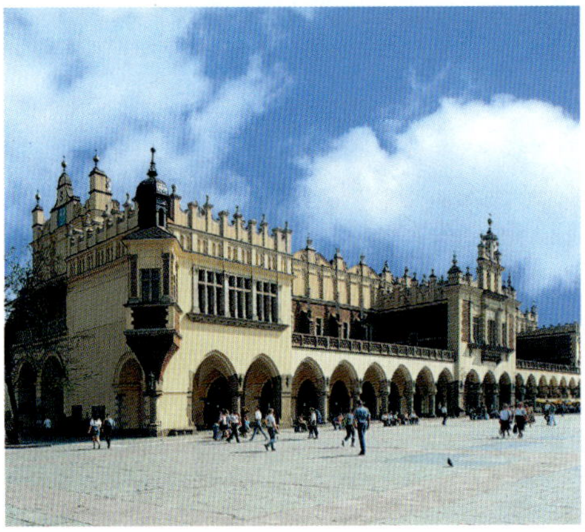

the first List of the World Cultural and Natural Heritage. In 1995 the Ministers of Culture of the European Union granted to Cracow and to eight other European cities the title of the European City of Culture 2000. Alone among them, it started a five-year cultural programme – Festival Cracow 2000, and secured the co-operation of the most outstanding art-ists, such as the composer Krzysztof Penderecki, the film director Andrzej Wajda, and the writers and Nobel Prize winners Wisława Szymborska and Czesław Miłosz.

The first traces of human settlement on Wawel Hill go back 50 thousand years. Until the late 16th century it was the residence of the Polish kings. The Royal Castle, of predominantly Renaissance character, was commissioned by King Sigismund the Elder and built by Italian architects in the years 1502--1536. Some of the rooms are furnished in the Renaissance style, some in the Baroque style. The northeast part of the Castle contains the Treasury and the Armoury, and in its west part a collection of Oriental art is exhibited.

The Gothic Cathedral is another fine building on Wawel Hill. It is encircled by chapels, with the pearl of Renaissance art, the Sigismund Chapel. Almost all Polish kings, from Ladislaus the Short (d. 1333), were crowned in the Cathedral. It was also the place of royal funerals and burials, and later received the remains of national heroes and great poets.

The vestiges of the oldest constructions on Wawel Hill can be seen at the unique exhibition „The Lost Wawel". The Cathedral Museum presents mainly items from the Cathedral Treasury.

In the Wawel fortifications, the most impressive are the Senators' Tower, the Sandomierska Tower and the Thieves' Tower, as well as the brick walls which run along the hill perimeter; they were built, together with the bastions and gates, by the Austrians in the 19th century.

At the west part of the Hill is the entrance leading down to the Dragon's Den, which features in the ancient legend about the dragon which once lived at the foot of Wawel.

The Old City contains most of the finest monuments and museums in Cracow. The oldest part of the city is outlined by the Planty – a four-kilometer-long green belt which in the 19th century replaced the demolished medieval city walls and moat. Some elements of those fortifications have survived: the unique 15th-century Barbican and a section of the walls with four towers and St Florian's Gate.

The Market Square is particularly remarkable; this largest (200 m x 200 m) and most beautiful square in Cracow for seven centuries, witnessed a number of historic events, including the homage paid to Sigismund the Elder by Duke Albert of Prussia, and the oath sworn by Kościuszko. Among the most important buildings are: the Gothic St Mary's Church, with the High Altar carved by Wit Stwosz (Veit Stoss), the Cloth Hall, a busy trading centre which dates from the reign of Casimir the Great and was later rebuilt in the Renaissance style, the 13th-century Town Hall Tower, as well as many mainly Renaissance and Baroque houses and palaces. Other famous historic buildings in the Old Town are the 15th-century Collegium Maius, the oldest seat of the Jagellonian University, and St Anne's Church, the finest Baroque church in Cracow.

Among the many museums in the Old Town the most recommended are: the Czartoryski Museum, with its fine collections of paintings, artefacts which once belonged to monarchs, and ancient art; the

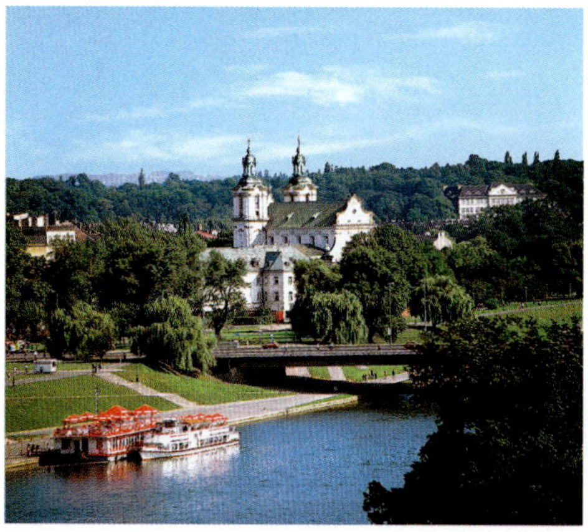

Gallery of Polish Painting and Sculpture in the Cloth Hall, with a rich collection of Polish, mainly 19th-century painting; the Historical Museum of the City of Cracow, whose exhibits tell the story of the city and its culture; the Jagellonian University Museum in Collegium Maius, with an unique collection which presents the history of the oldest Polish university.

The old borough of Kazimierz, now within the city centre, was founded in 1335 by King Casimir the Great. Its focus was a vast market square, not much smaller than the one in Cracow, and the borough was encircled by walls, which have partly survived. In the late 15th century Jews were moved from Cracow to Kazimierz; they lived there, in an autonomous community, for centuries, until World War II. Therefore, apart from the heritage of Polish history and culture, Kazimierz contains a rich heritage of the specific and unique Jewish material and spiritual culture.

Polish history and tradition is best symbolized in the Church na Skałce (the present 18th-century church was built on the site of the old Romanesque one). According to legend, Stanislaus, Bishop of Cracow, was killed there by King Boleslaus the Bold. The Polish kings used to make pilgrimage to that church before their coronation. In its crypt eminent Poles have been buried.

Particularly remarkable are two 14th-century churches, St Catherine's and Corpus Christi.

The most important Jewish buildings are the Old Synagogue, the oldest in Poland (now it houses the Judaic Museum), and the 16th-century Remuh Synagogue, with the adjacent cemetery.

Also in the outskirts of Cracow, beyond the typical urban landscape, noteworthy buildings can be found. West of the city centre, near the suburb of Bielany, on the wooded Silver Hill, stand the fine 17th-century Camaldolese church and monastery. In the old village of Tyniec, now within the city limits, rises above the Vistula Valley the picturesque Benedictine Abbey; of defensive character, built on a limestone rock, it dates back to the 11th century.

To the south of Cracow, at the Carpathian foothills, is the small town of Wieliczka, with the famous salt mine, where salt was extracted for over 700 years, from the late 13th century. The tourist route which runs through galleries and chambers (with lakes and rock-salt sculptures) attracts tourists from all over the world. Also, a section of the Salt Mine Museum can be seen underground. The mine, with its underground sanatoriums, is now a health centre as well.

To the east of Cracow is the town of Niepołomice, with the 14th -century castle, rebuilt in the Renaissance style, which for centuries was a royal hunting lodge. The kings went hunting in the nearby Niepołomicki Forest, a wild woodland, some of which has survived.

To the north-west and west of Cracow lies a limestone upland (Wyżyna Krakowsko-Wieluńska). Its area is cut by a number of picturesque rocky valleys, known as the Cracow Jurassic valleys. Particularly attractive are numerous karst caves; in the Kluczwoda Valley, tourists can visit one of the largest and most remarkable caves (Wierzchowska Górna), its corridors measuring 975 m. The largest among the Jurassic valleys is the Prądnik Valley. A part of it, with the most attractive landscape and nature, is now the Ojców National Park. In the Park, at Pieskowa Skała, stands high above the valley an impressive castle, rebuilt in the 16th century in the Renaissance style, and furnished in defenses in the 17th century; it is now a museum.

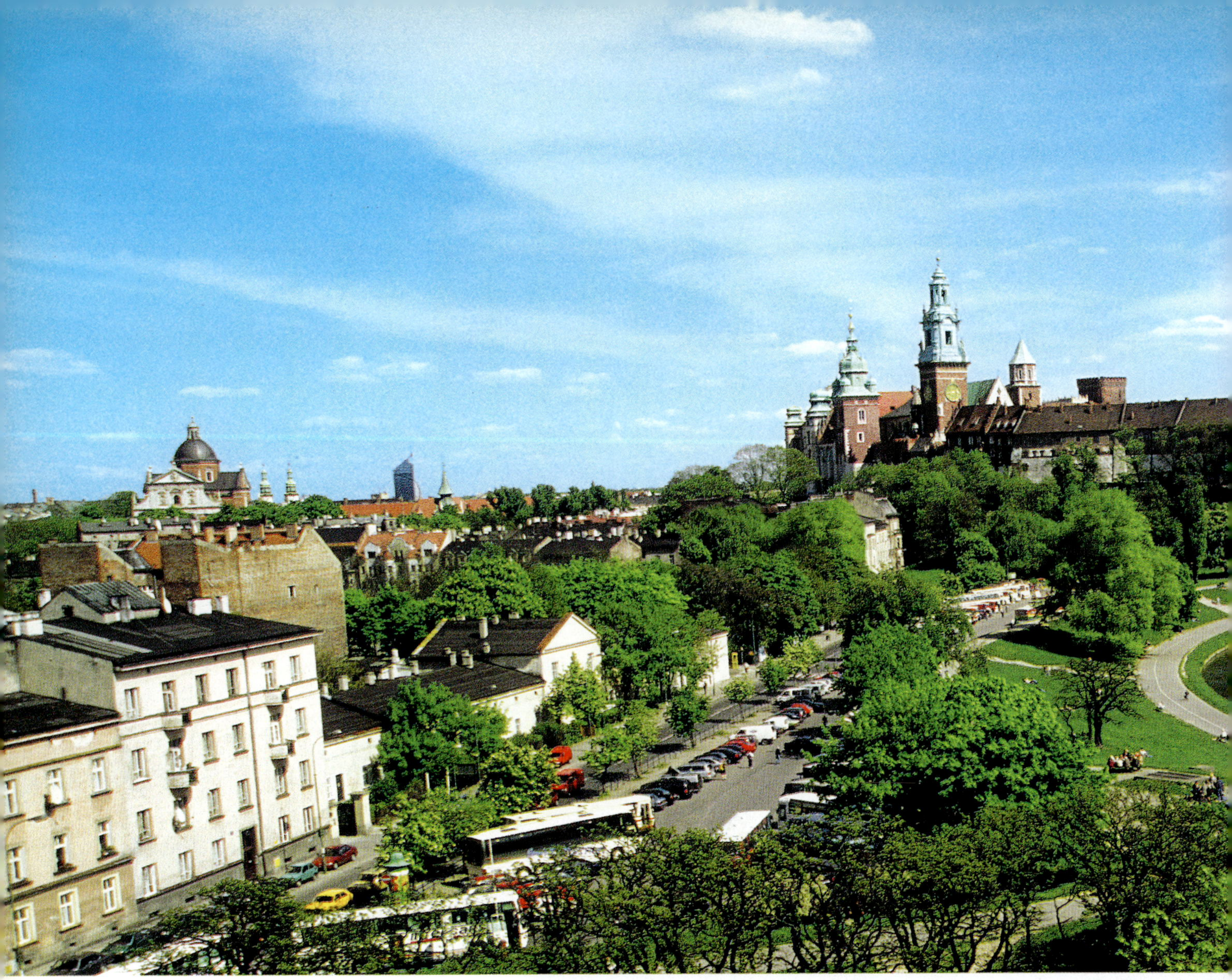

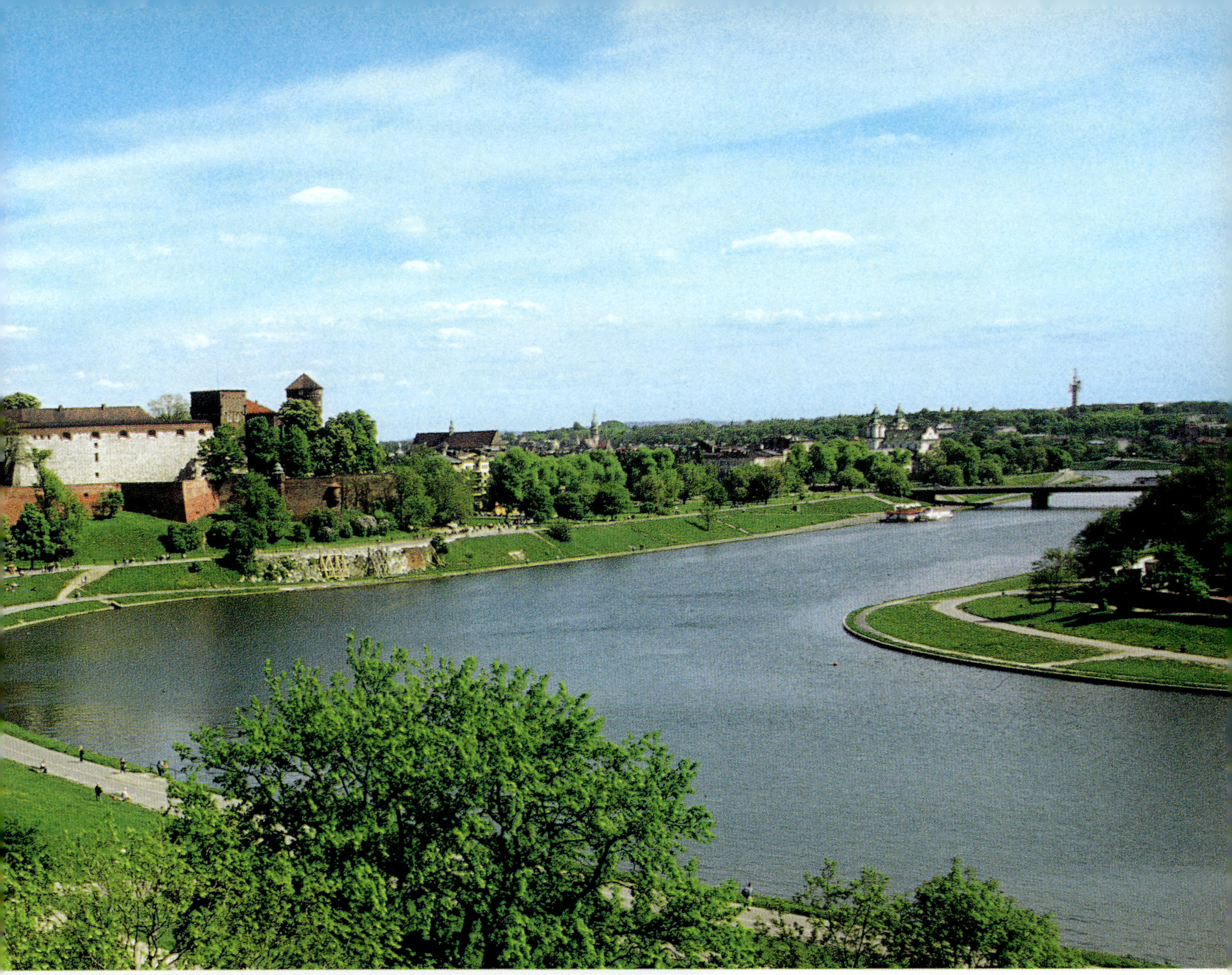

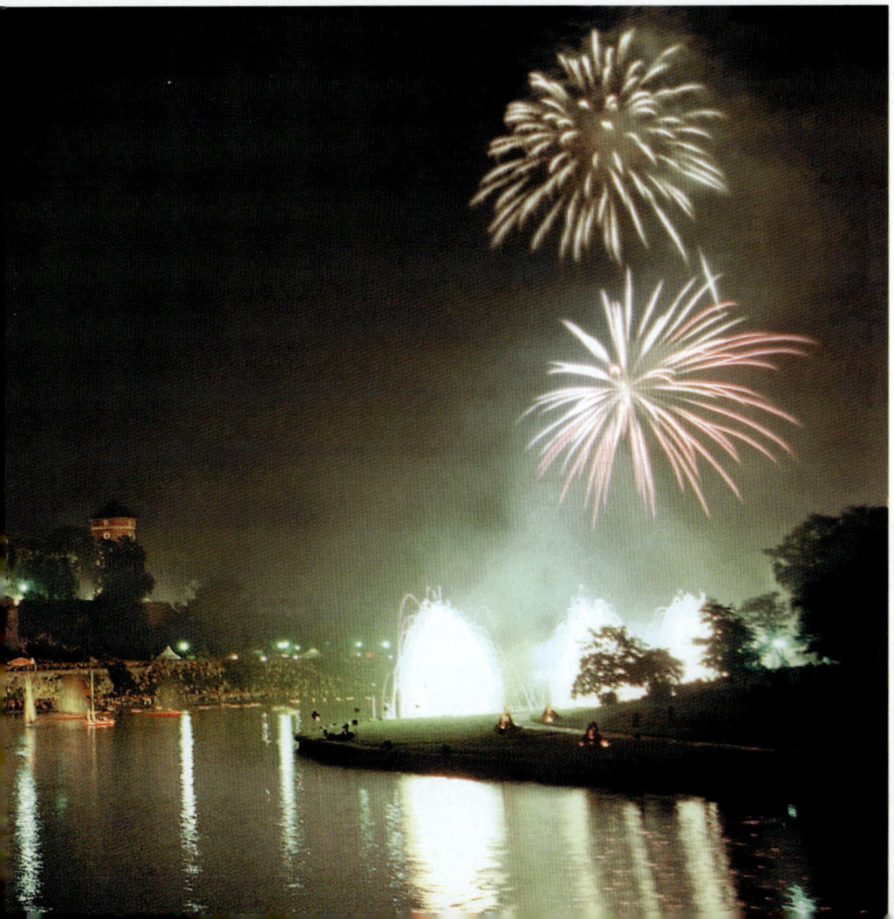

1-2. Wawel Hill, high above the Vistula and Old Cracow, the seat of the Polish princes and kings from the mid-11th to the early 17th c.; a night view, at the traditional 'Wreaths' ceremony; a view from the north-west, with a bend of the Vistula

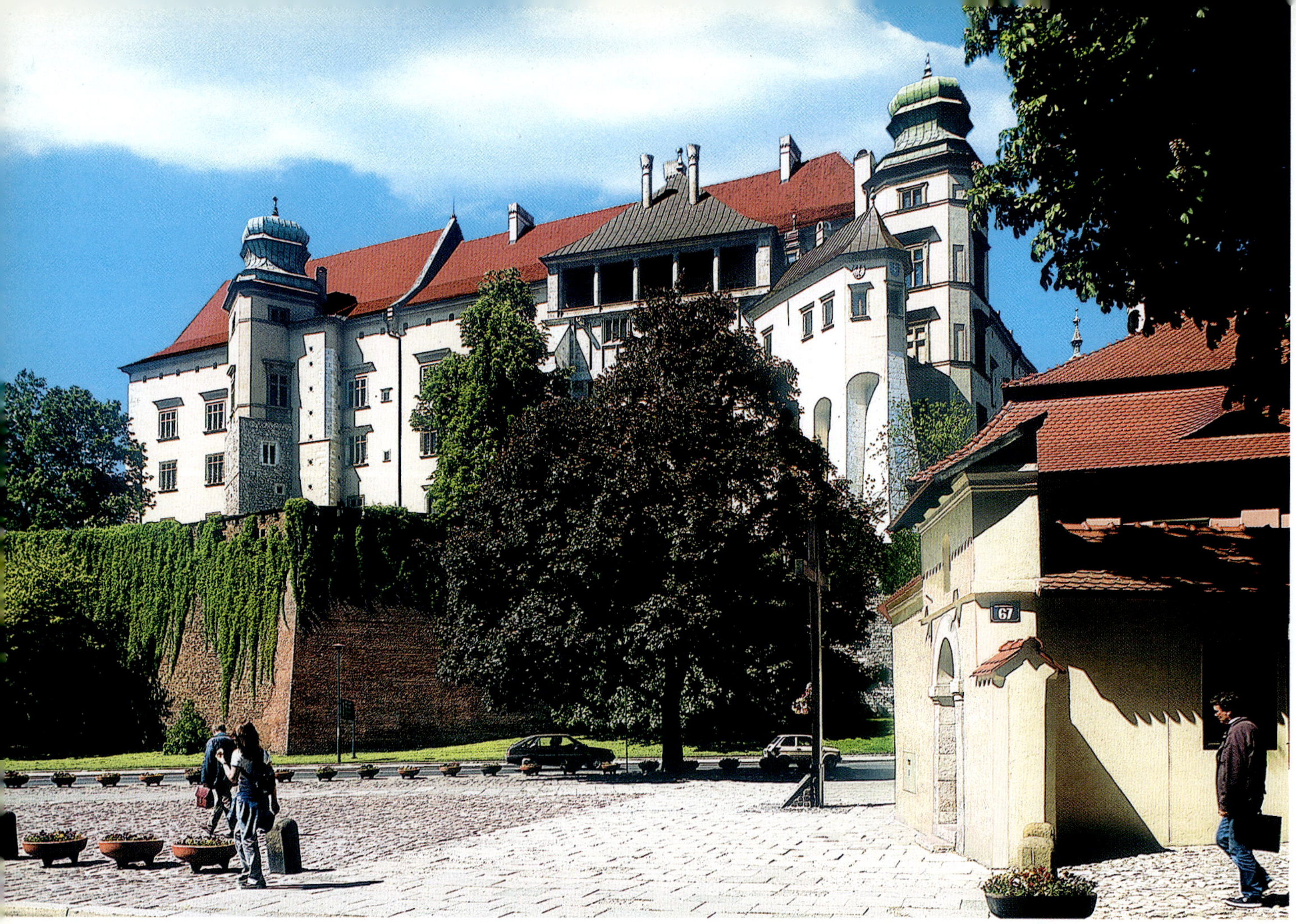

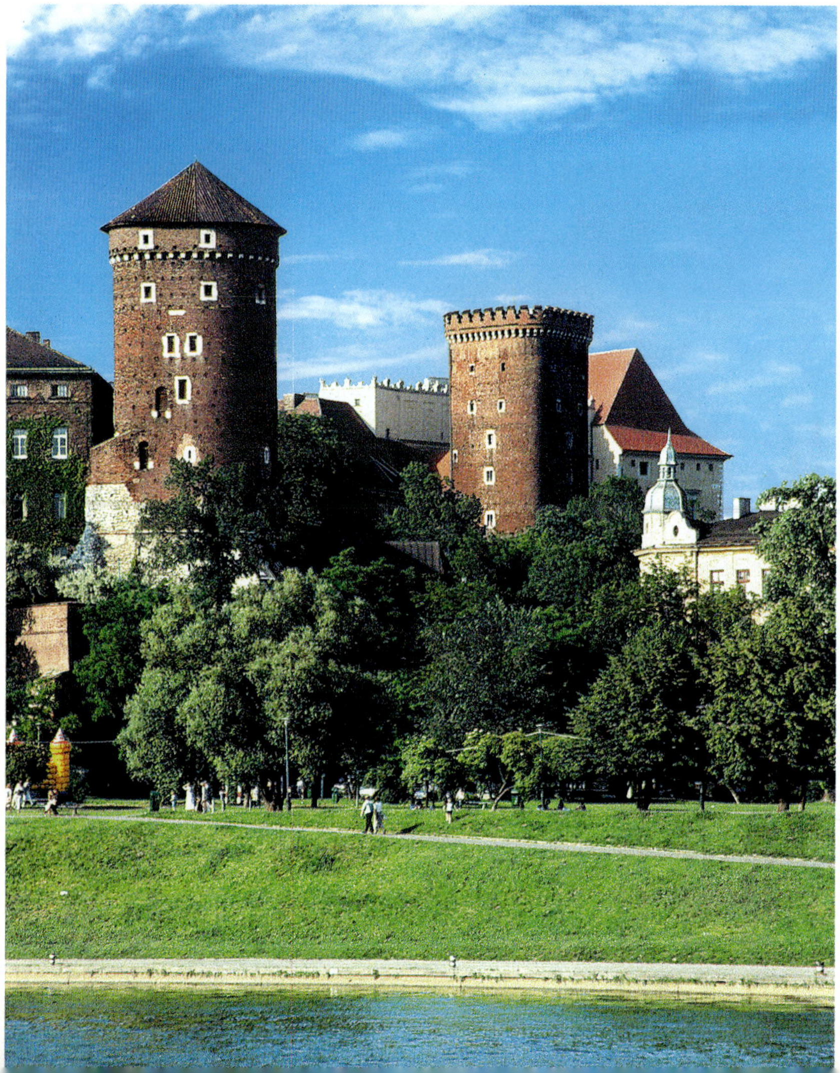

3. The Royal Castle at Wawel, originally Gothic (14th and 15th c.), rebuilt after a fire in the Renaissance style in the first half of the 16th c. – a view from the church and street of St Giles: the Jordanka Tower (left), further on the Danish Tower, the characteristic Hen's Foot Tower, and Sigismund III's Tower

5. Facing page: the cathedral on Wawel Hill goes back to the mid-11th c.; repeatedly restored and rebuilt, it is a fine historic building – a view from Podzamcze Street to the Sigismund Tower (left) and the Clock Tower, in the background the Sobieski Tower in the Royal Castle

4. The Sandomierska Tower (left) and the Senators' Tower (the tallest on the Hill) date from the mid-15th c.; in the background, a section of the Royal Castle

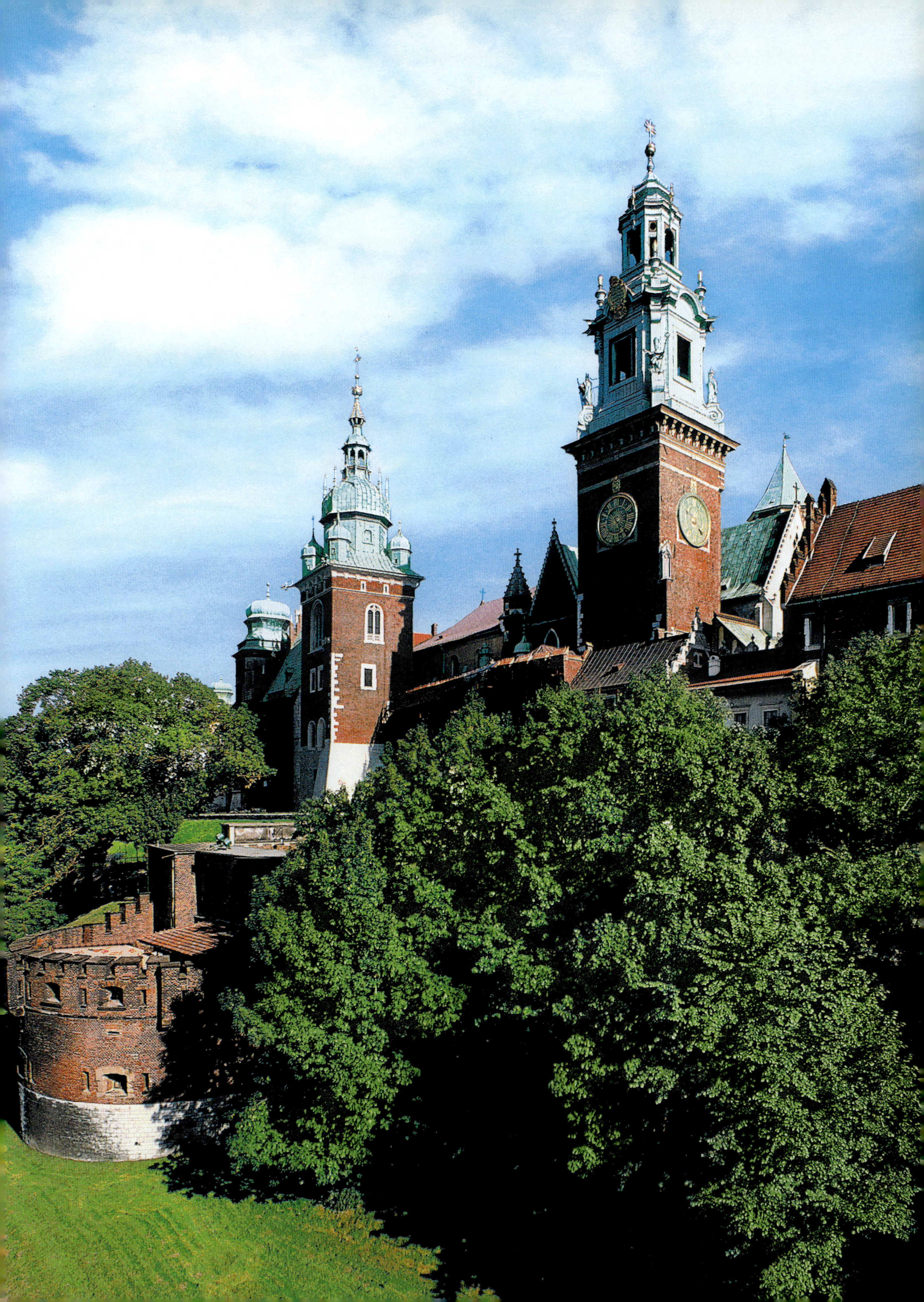

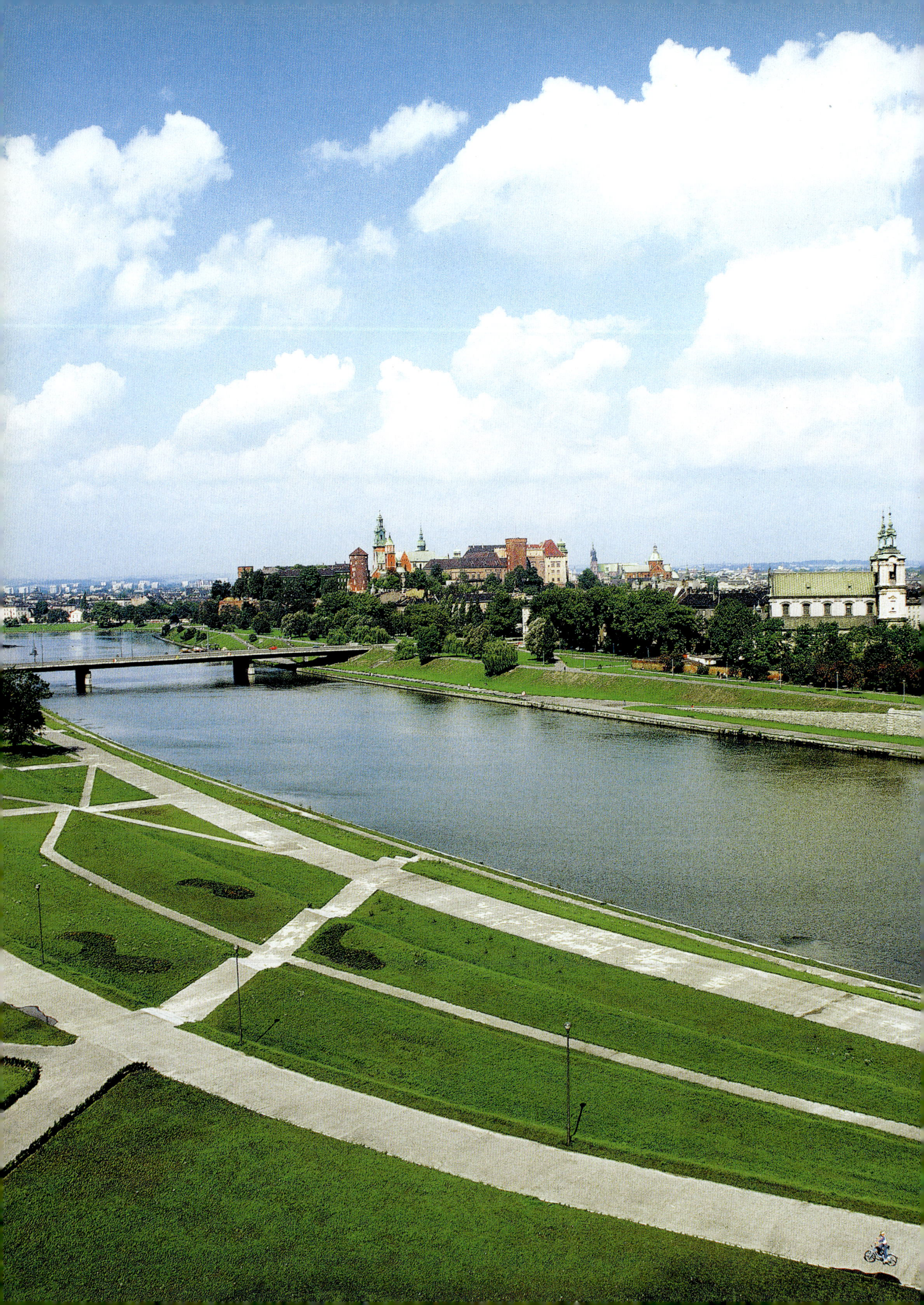

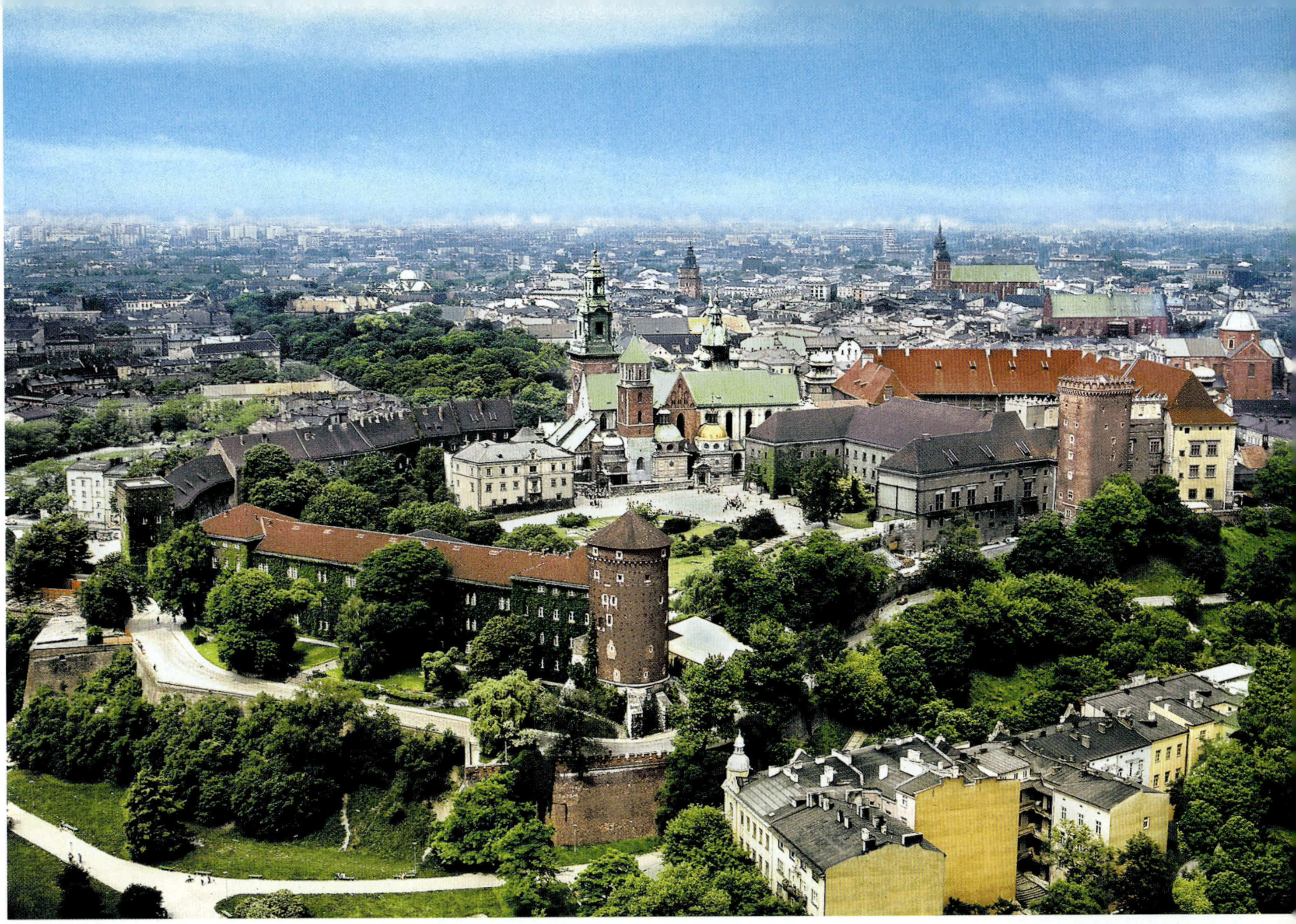

7. An aerial view of Wawel Hill – in the foreground the Sandomierska Tower (mid-15th c.), on the left the Thieves' Tower (14th – 15th c.), in the centre Wawel Cathedral, on the right the Royal Castle and the Senators' Tower (mid-15th c.) In the background the tower of the Town Hall and St Mary's Church, and the Dominican Church and the Church of SS Peter and Paul (right)

6. Facing page: a view from the south to Wawel Hill on the Vistula and to the Church of SS Michael the Archangel and Stanislaus at Skałka (right), in the background the tower of St Mary' Church and the dome of the Church of SS Peter and Paul

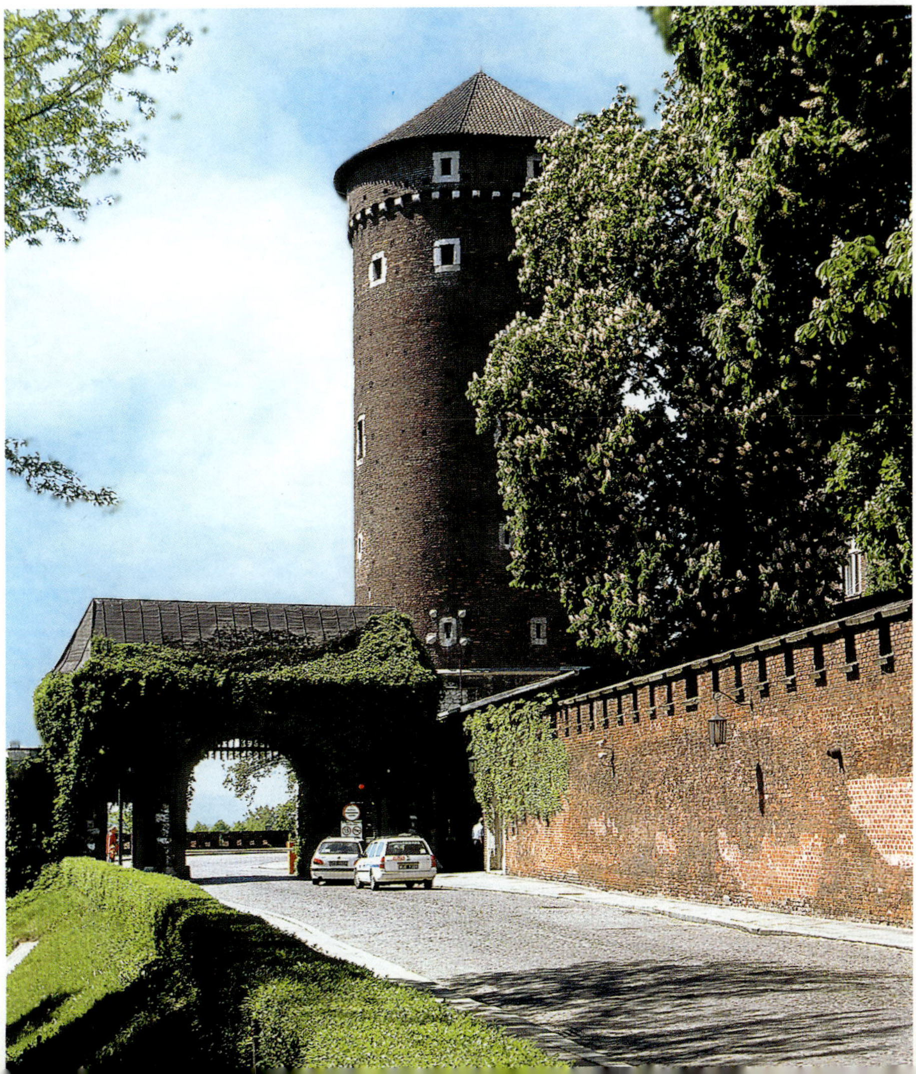

8. The Bernardine Gate leading to Wawel Hill, on the right the Sandomierska Tower (mid-15th c.)

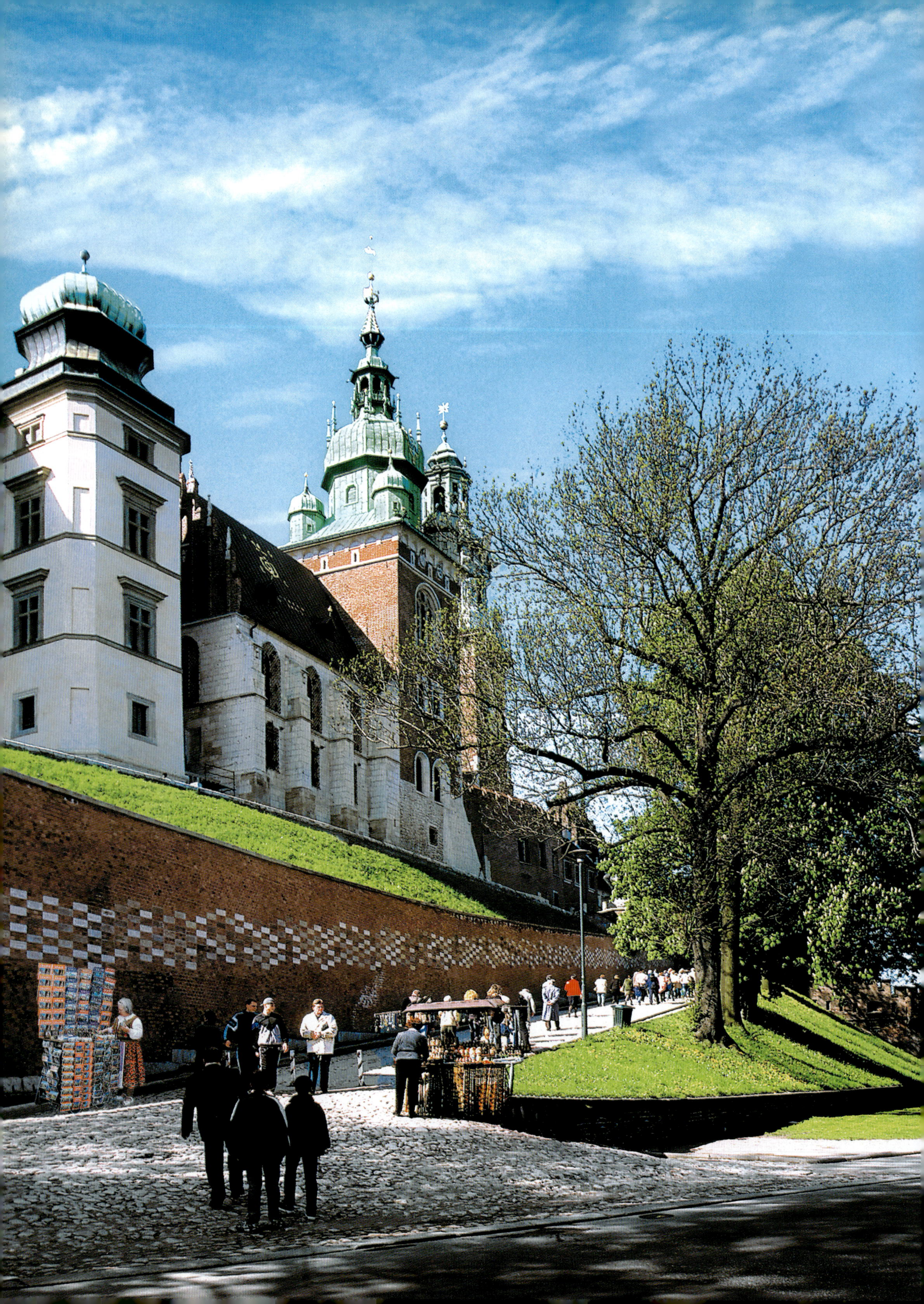

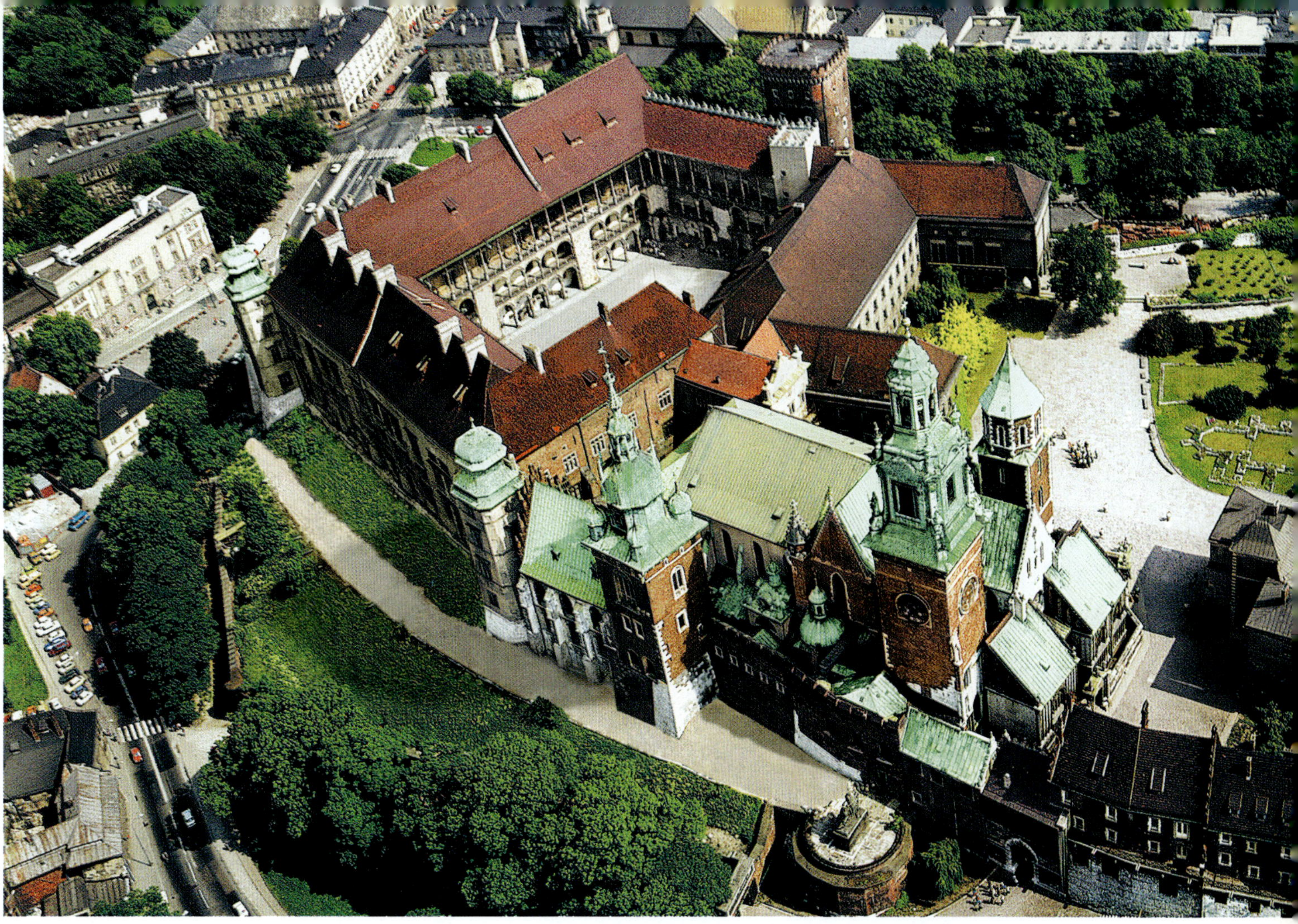

10. An aerial view of the Royal Castle, with the arcaded court, and of Wawel Cathedral (right)

9. Facing page: the north approach to Wawel Hill; in the wall the plaques commemorating the people and institutions – contributors of funds for the restoration of the Castle in the years 1921-1934. Above the Sobieski Tower (c. 1620) in the Castle, and Wawel Cathedral with the Sigismund Tower (14th c.), which was a part of the castle fortifications, and after 1520 became a belfry, with the famous Sigismund Bell

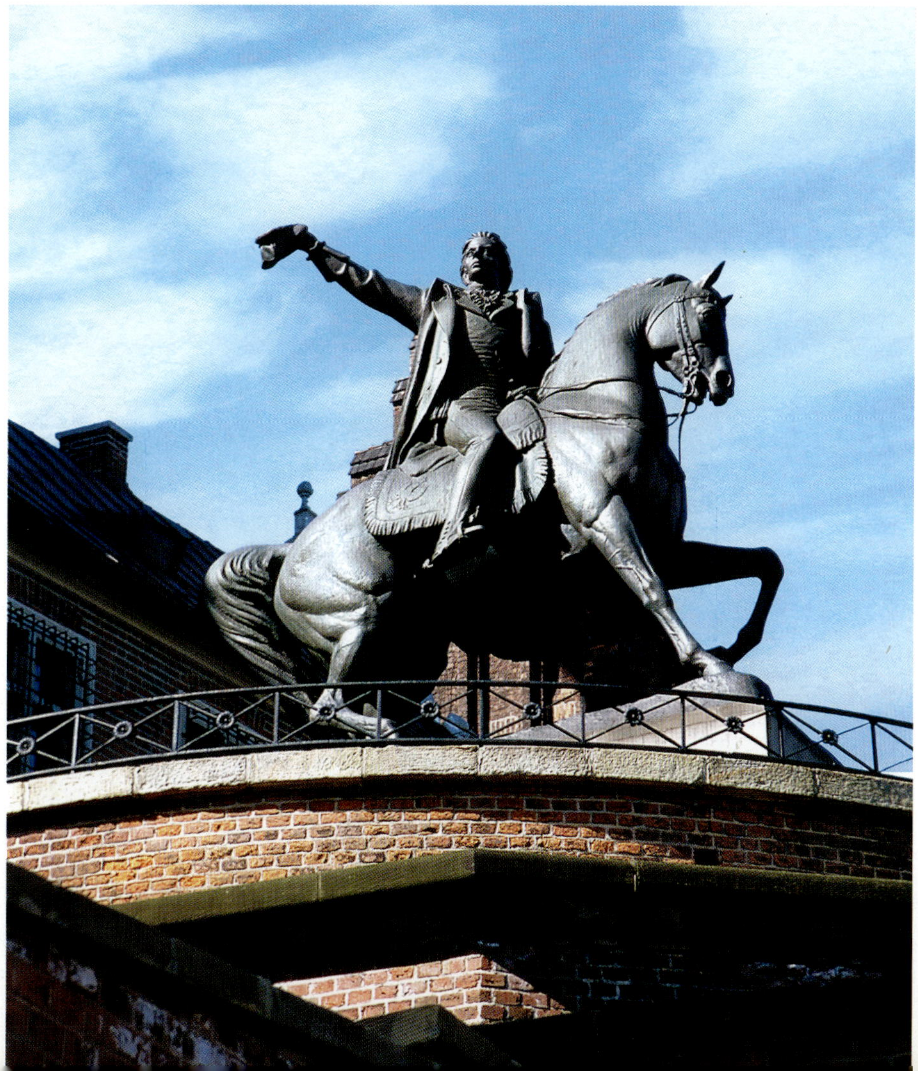

11. The monument of General Tadeusz Kościuszko, Commander of the insurrection against the Russians in 1794, who also fought in the American War of Independence in 1776-1783

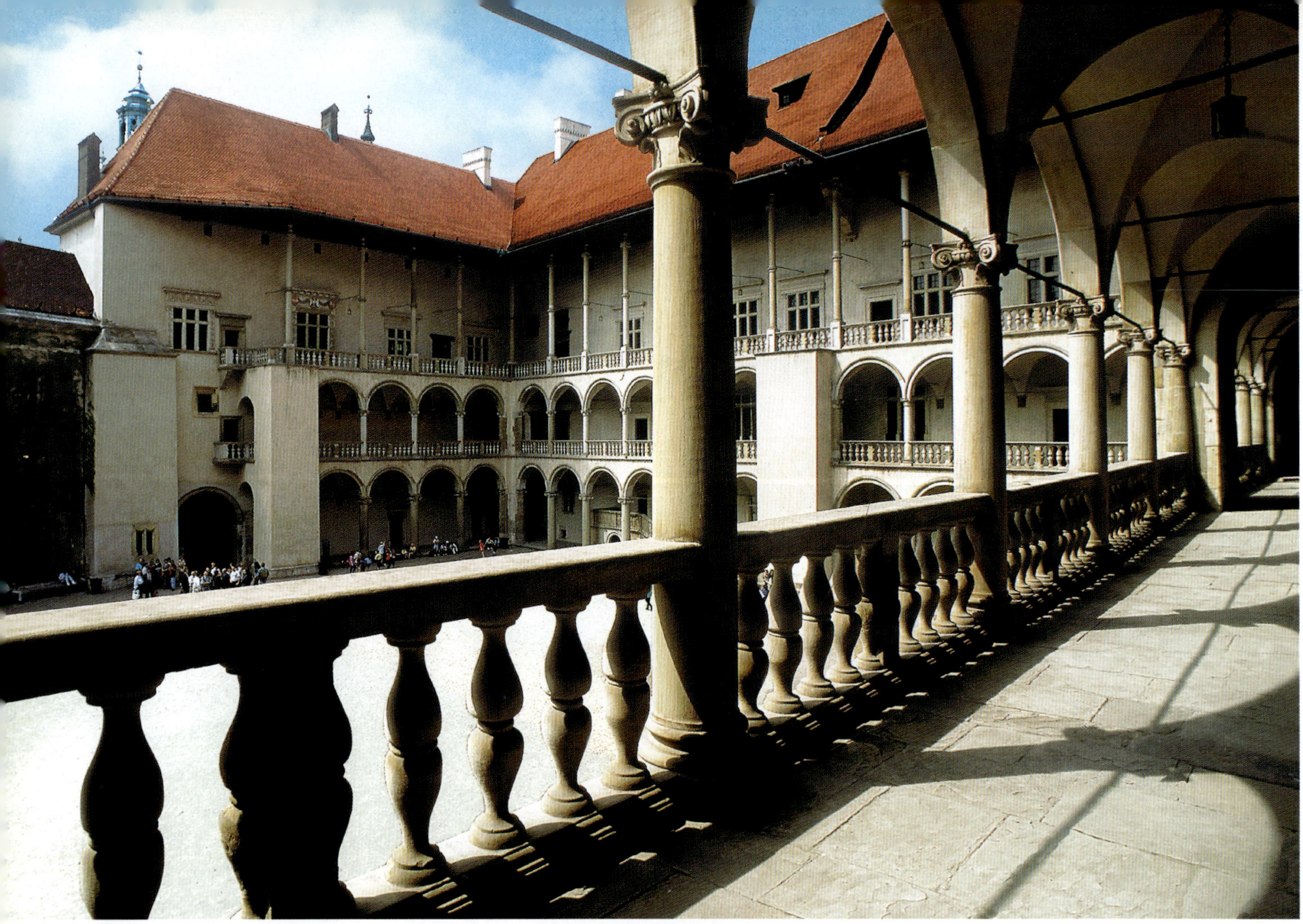

12. The court of the Royal Castle, with Renaissance arcades (first half of the 16th c.)

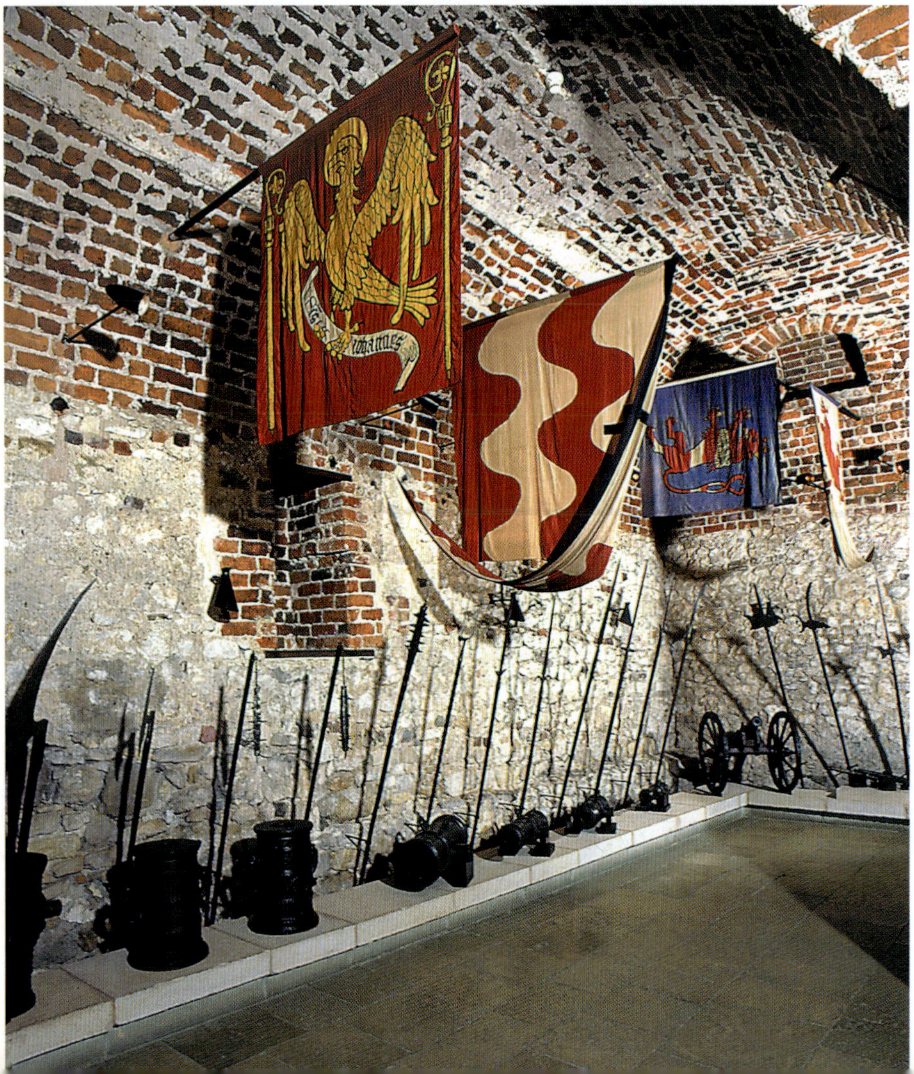

13. A section of the exhibition in the Armoury, in the basement of Ladislaus the Short's Tower in the Royal Castle

14-15. The Envoys' Room in the Royal Castle; the place where the kings received foreign envoys, and where the meetings of the Seym were held in the 16th c. Behind the throne is an armorial arras tapestry (1560), and above the frieze 'The History of Human Life'. Right: the ceiling with human heads in the Envoys' Room

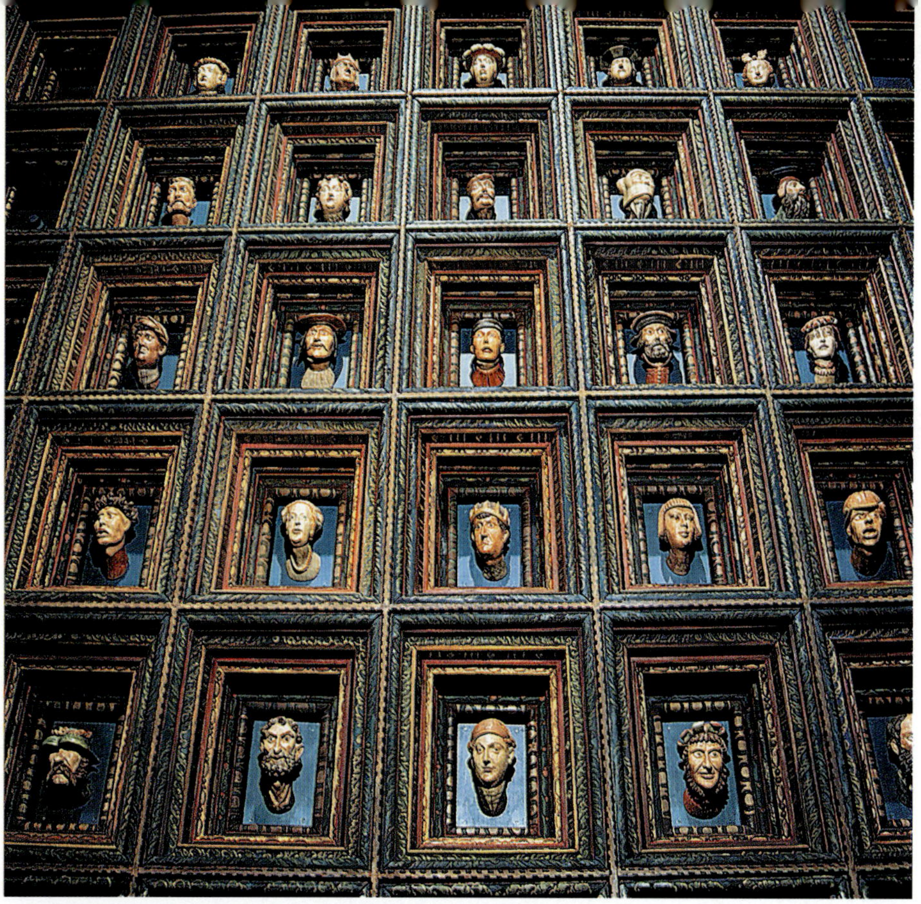

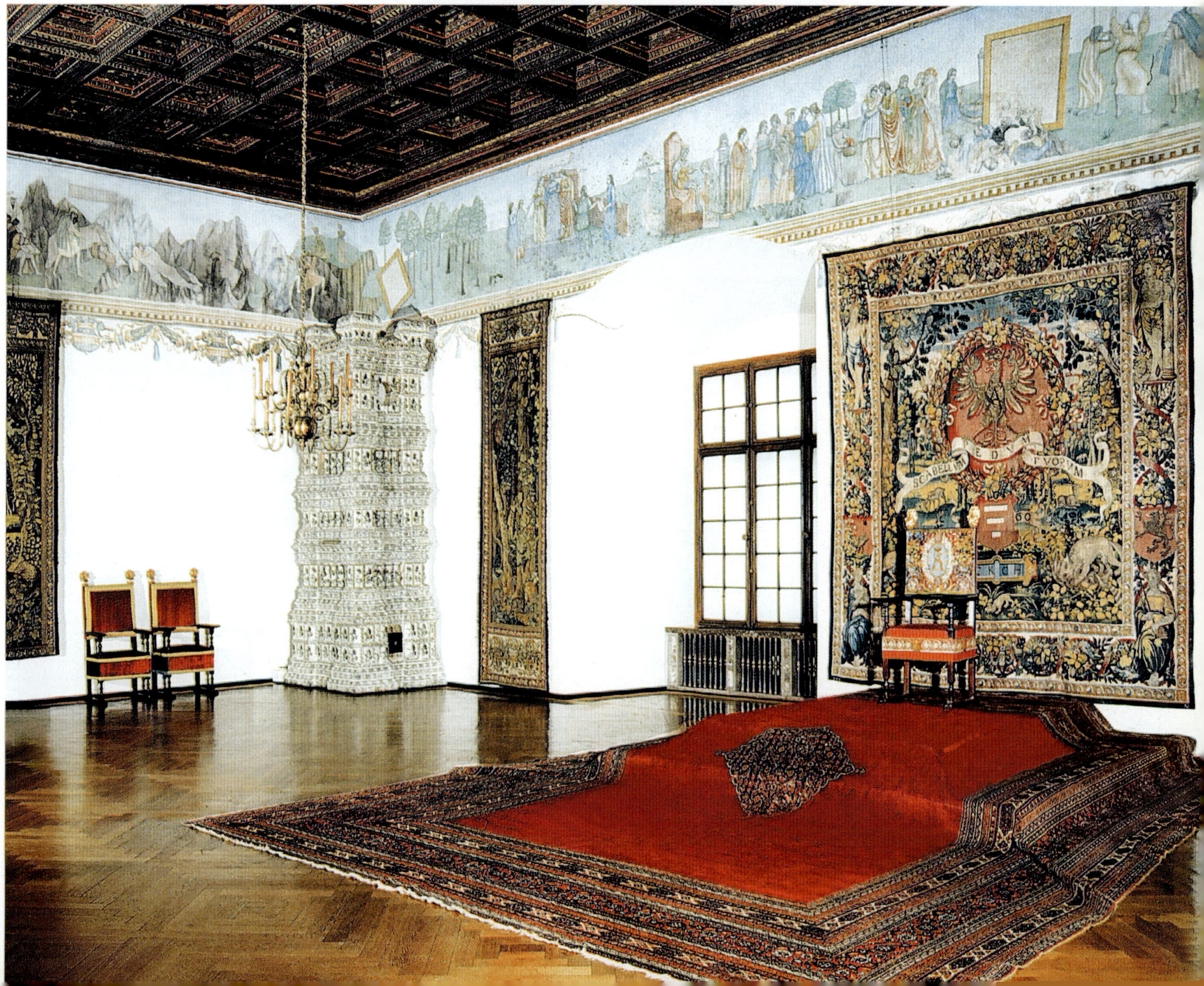

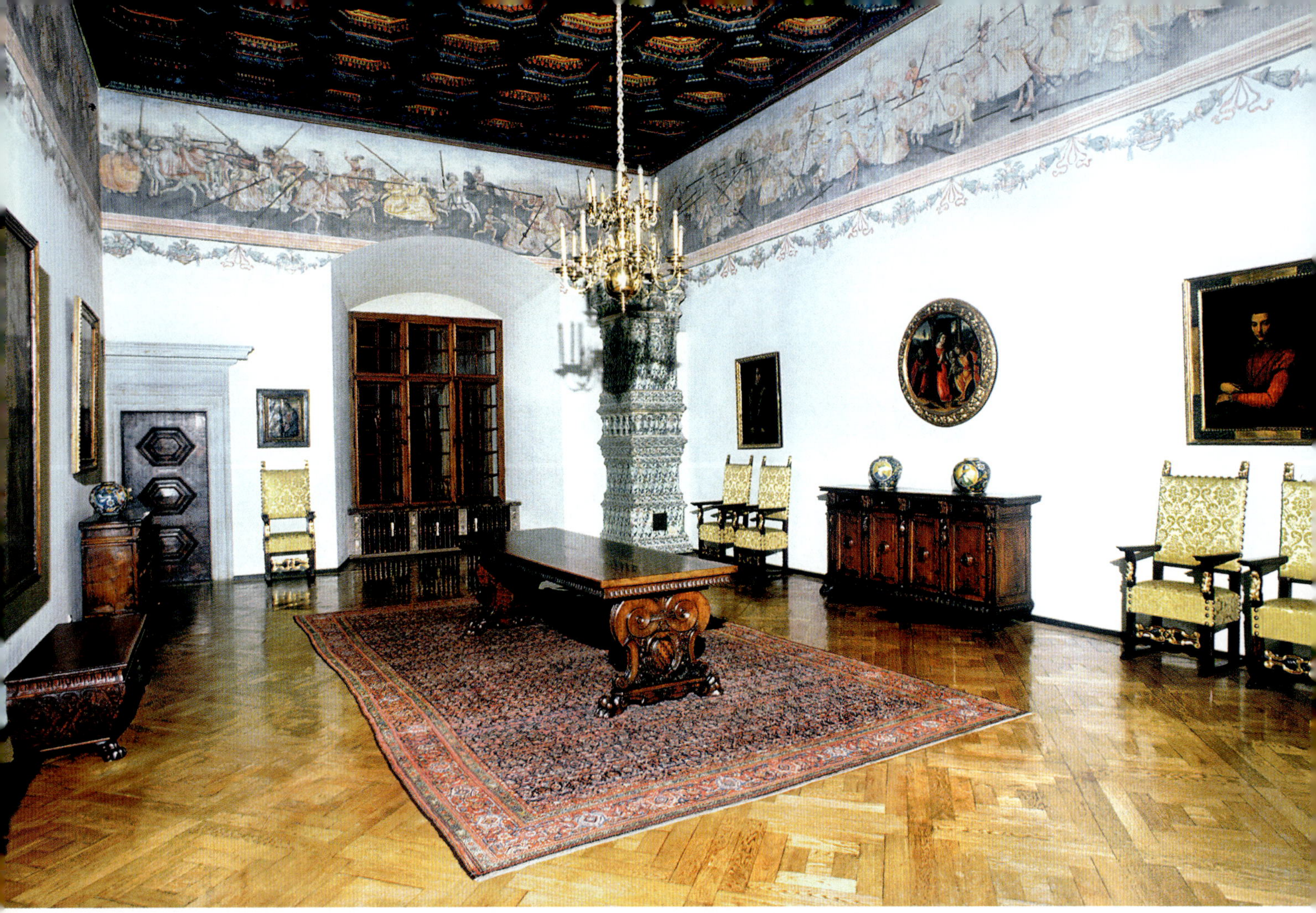

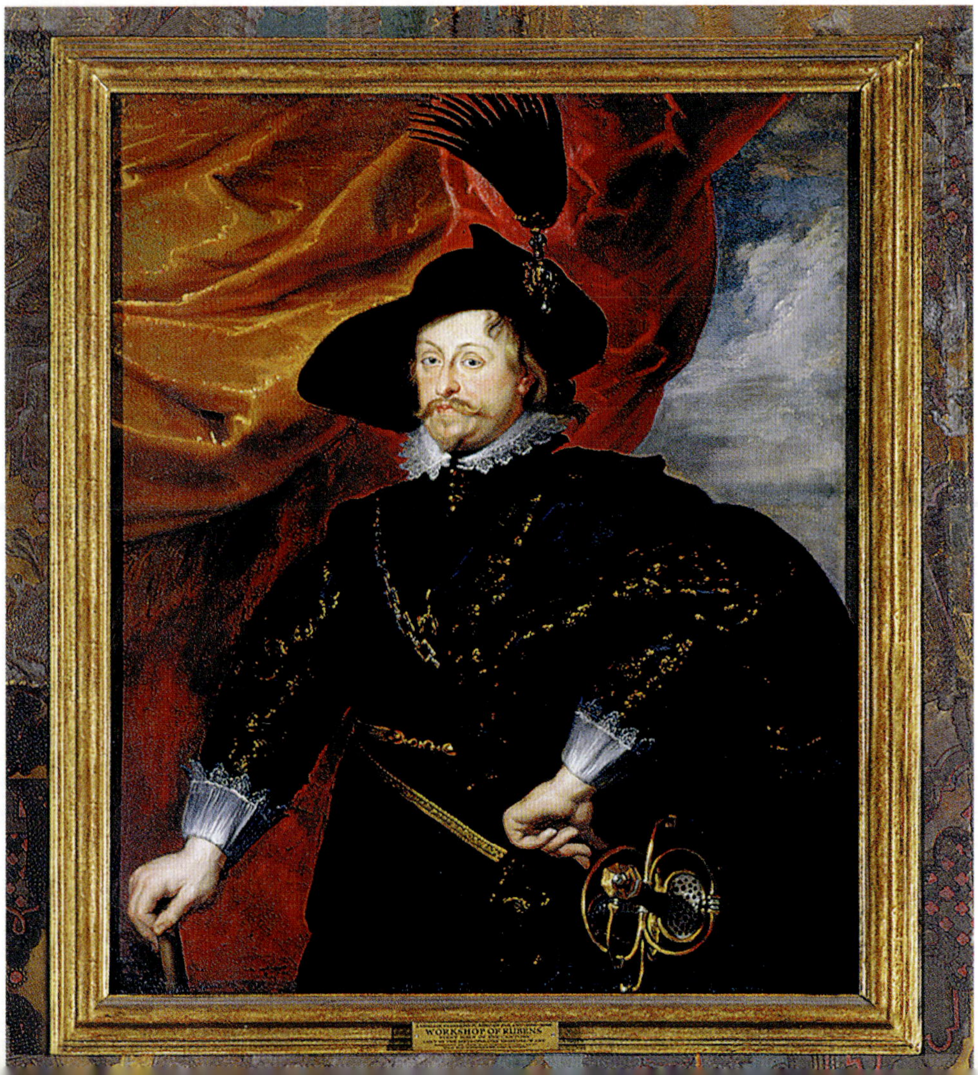

16. The Tournament Room in the Royal Castle; the frieze showing tournaments is partly the work of Hans Dürer (first half of the 16th c.)

17. The Birds Room in the Castle: the portrait of Prince Ladislaus Sigismund Vasa (later King Ladislaus IV), the work of Peter Paul Rubens and his workshop (1624)

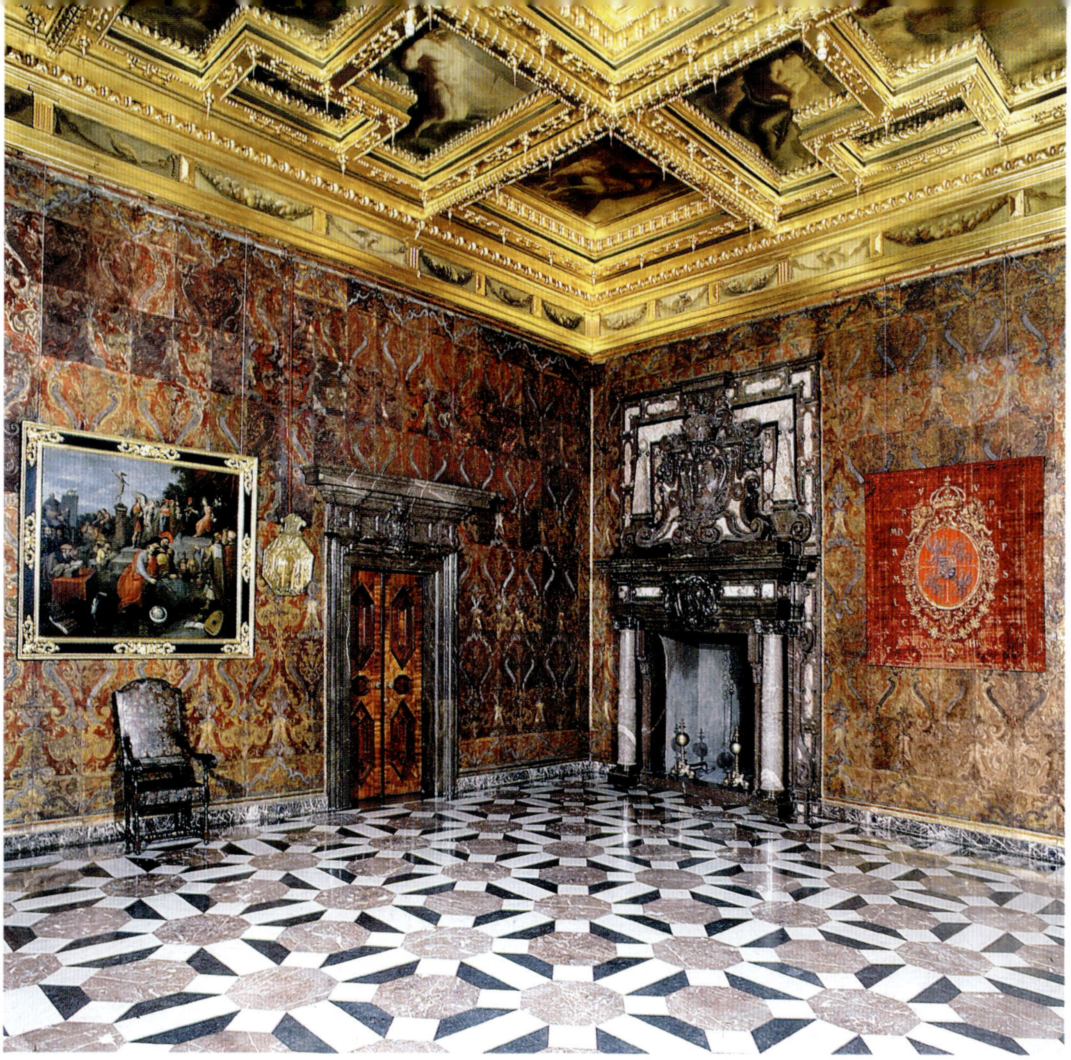

18. The Birds Room was furnished in the first half of the 16th c., and c. 1600 was refashioned as the grand reception room

19. The Senators' Room is the largest room in the Castle; meetings of the Senate took place there, as well as state and court ceremonies; on the walls are the arras tapestries from the collection of King Sigismund Augustus, showing Noah's story (second half of the 16th c.)

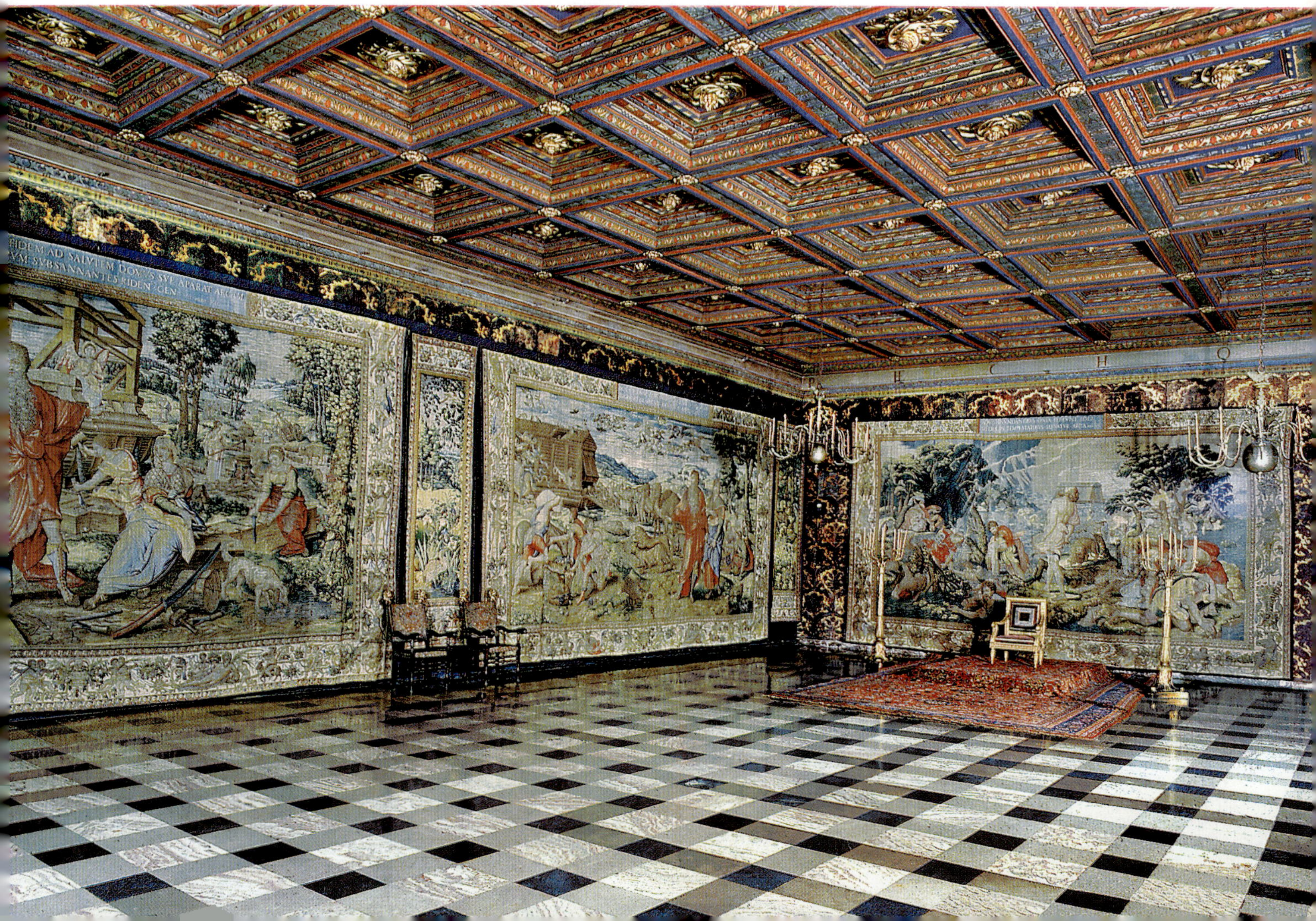

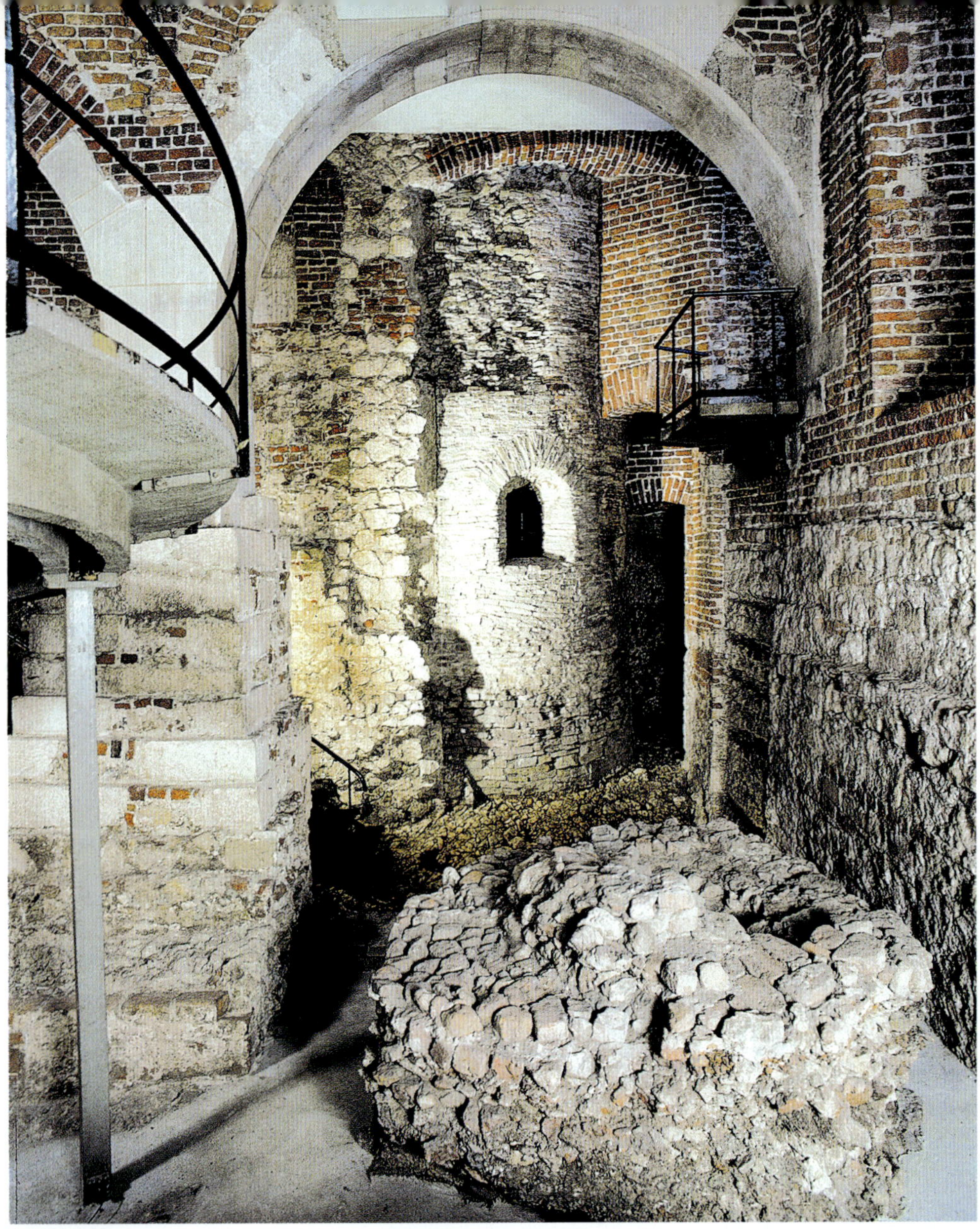

20. A section of 'The Lost Wawel' exhibition, an architectural reserve, the Rotunda of the Blessed Virgin Mary (or SS Felix and Adauctus), probably from the early 11th c.

22. Facing page: a view from the south-west to Wawel Cathedral, with the Clock Tower (left, early 15th c.) and the Silver Bells Tower (extended in the late 14th c.), on the right the Sigismund Chapel with the gilded dome (1518-1534)

21. Wawel Cathedral and the Vicar House (left), the buildings of the former royal kitchens and the Senators' Tower (right), in the foreground the outlines of the foundations of Gothic churches (14th c.)

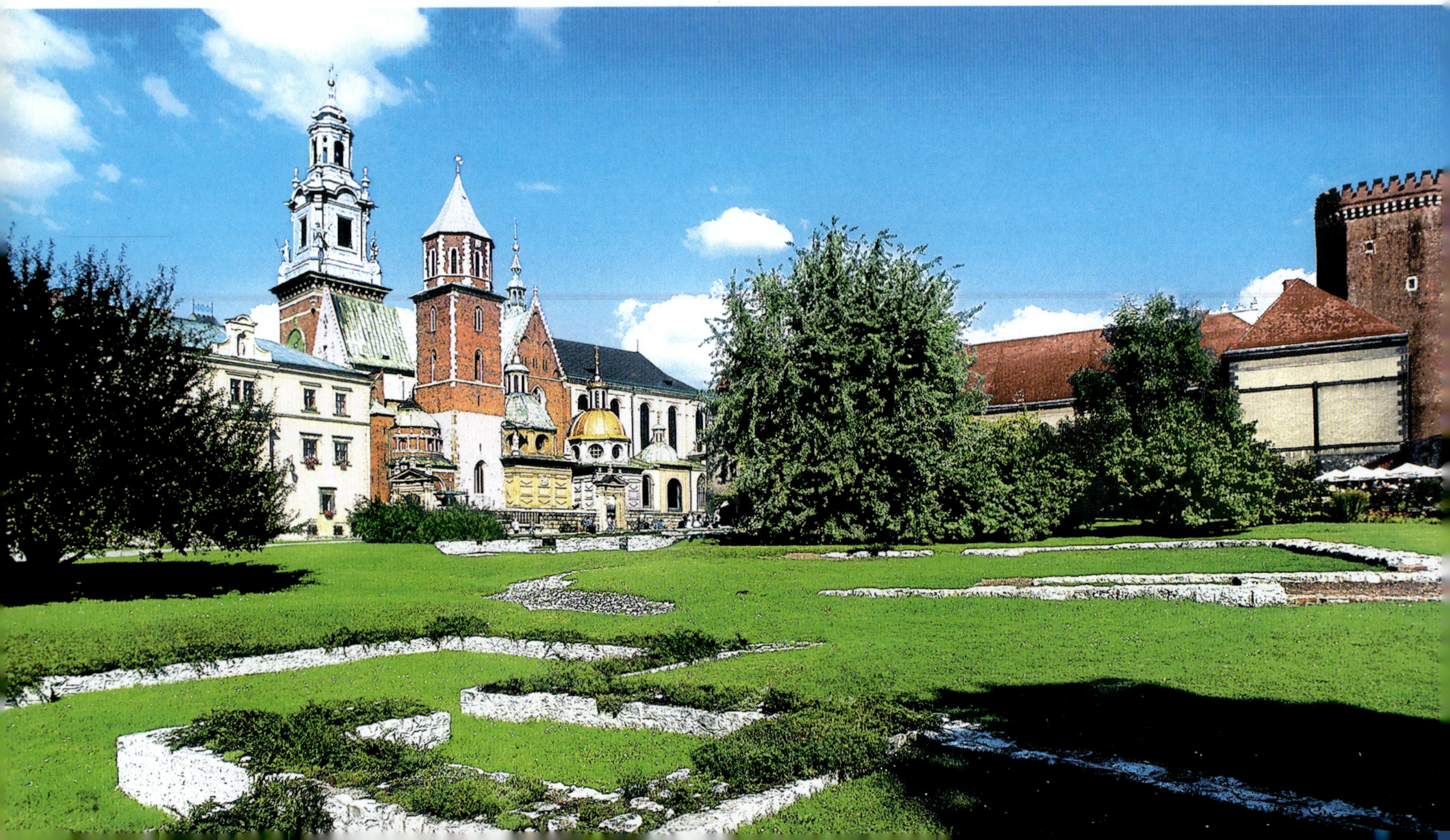

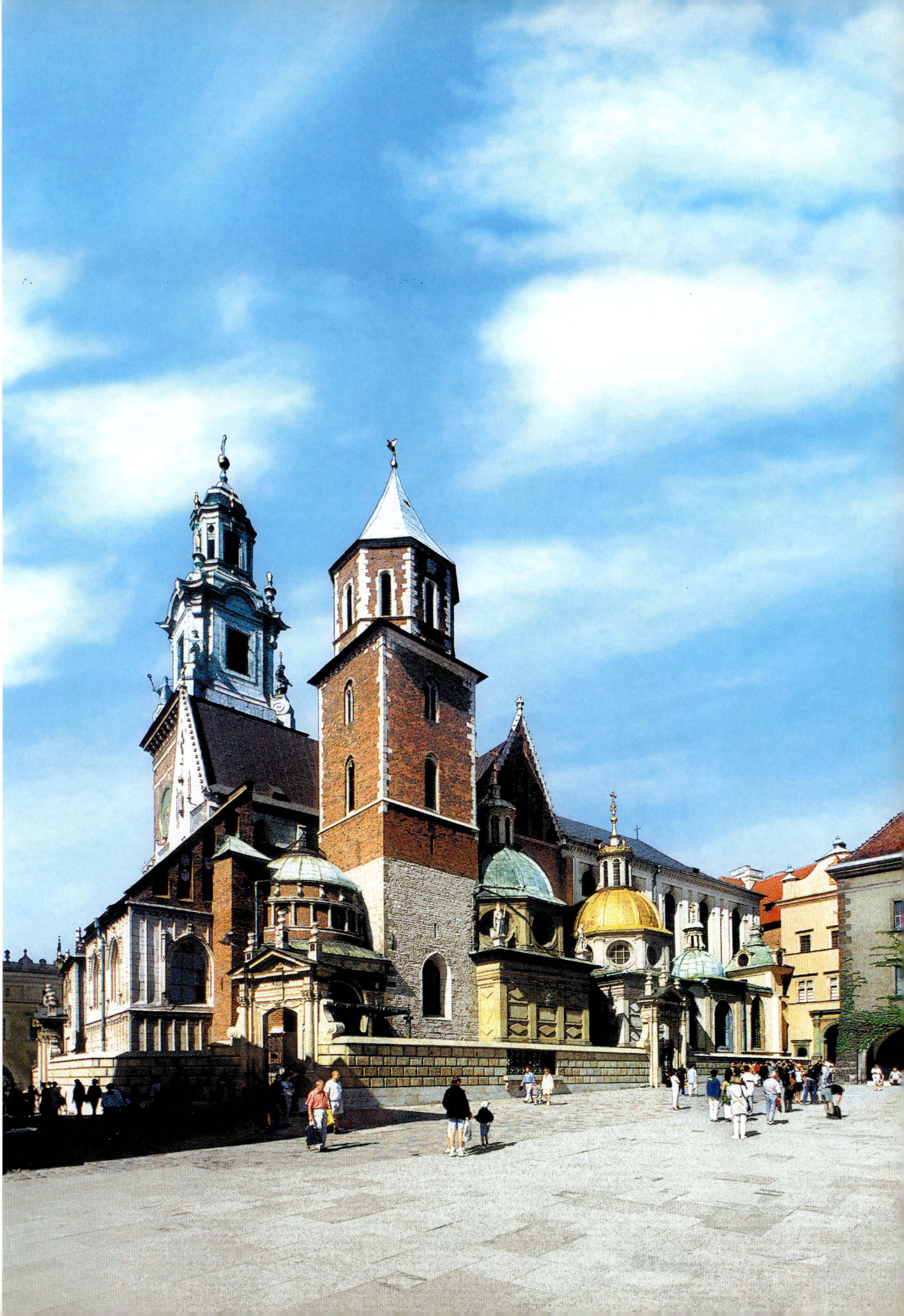

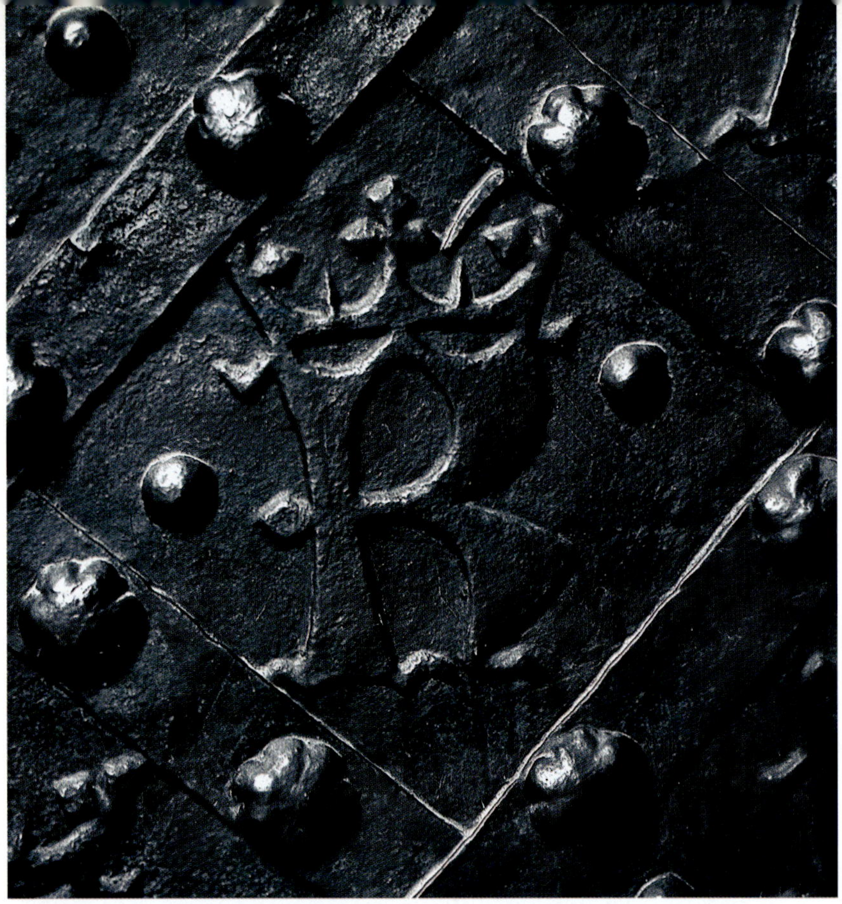

23. Wawel Cathedral, a section of the great door with the monogram of King Casimir the Great (second half of the 14th c.)

24. Wawel Cathedral, a view from the south-west to the Vasa Chapel (left, second half of the 17th c.), the Sigisnund Chapel with the gilded dome (1518-1534), and the chapels of Bishop Konarski (16th c.), Bishop Zadzik (17th c.) and King John Albert (16th c.)

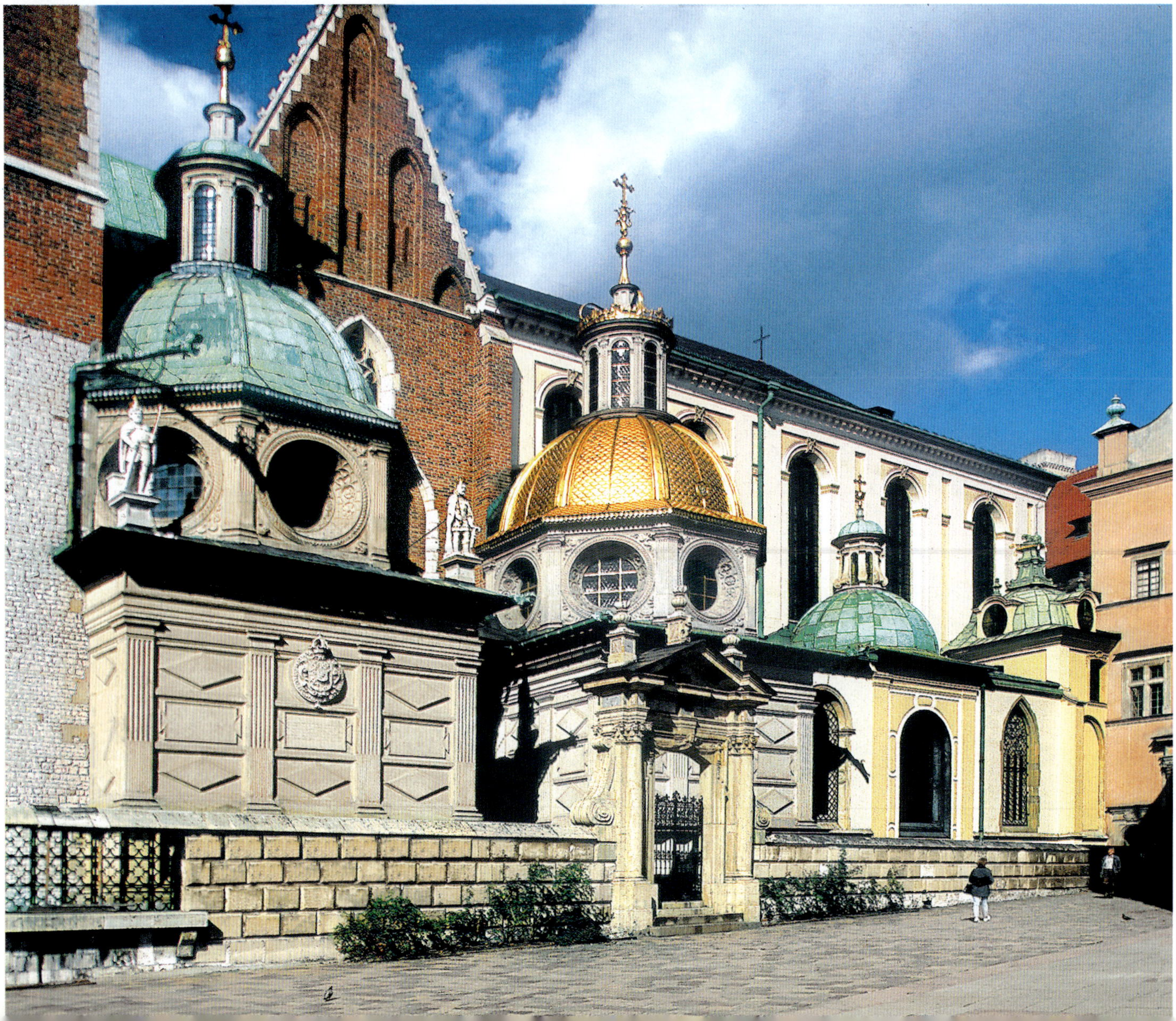

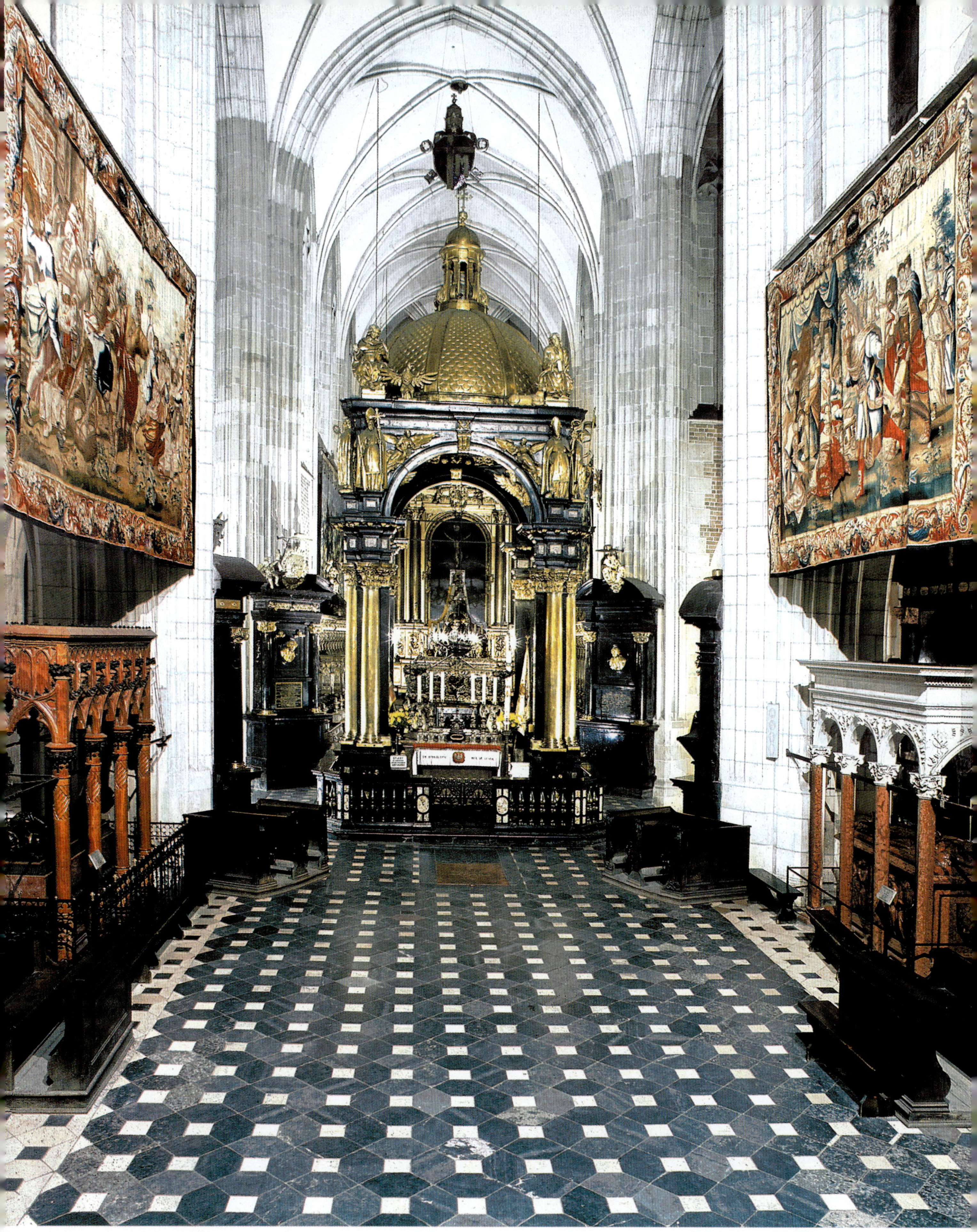

25. The nave of Wawel Cathedral, with the shrine of St Stanislaus in the centre (1626-1629) and the partly visible tombs of King Ladislaus III (left, a symbolic tomb, 1906) and King Ladislaus Jagiełło (right, first half of the 15th c., with the Renaissance sandstone canopy, 1524)

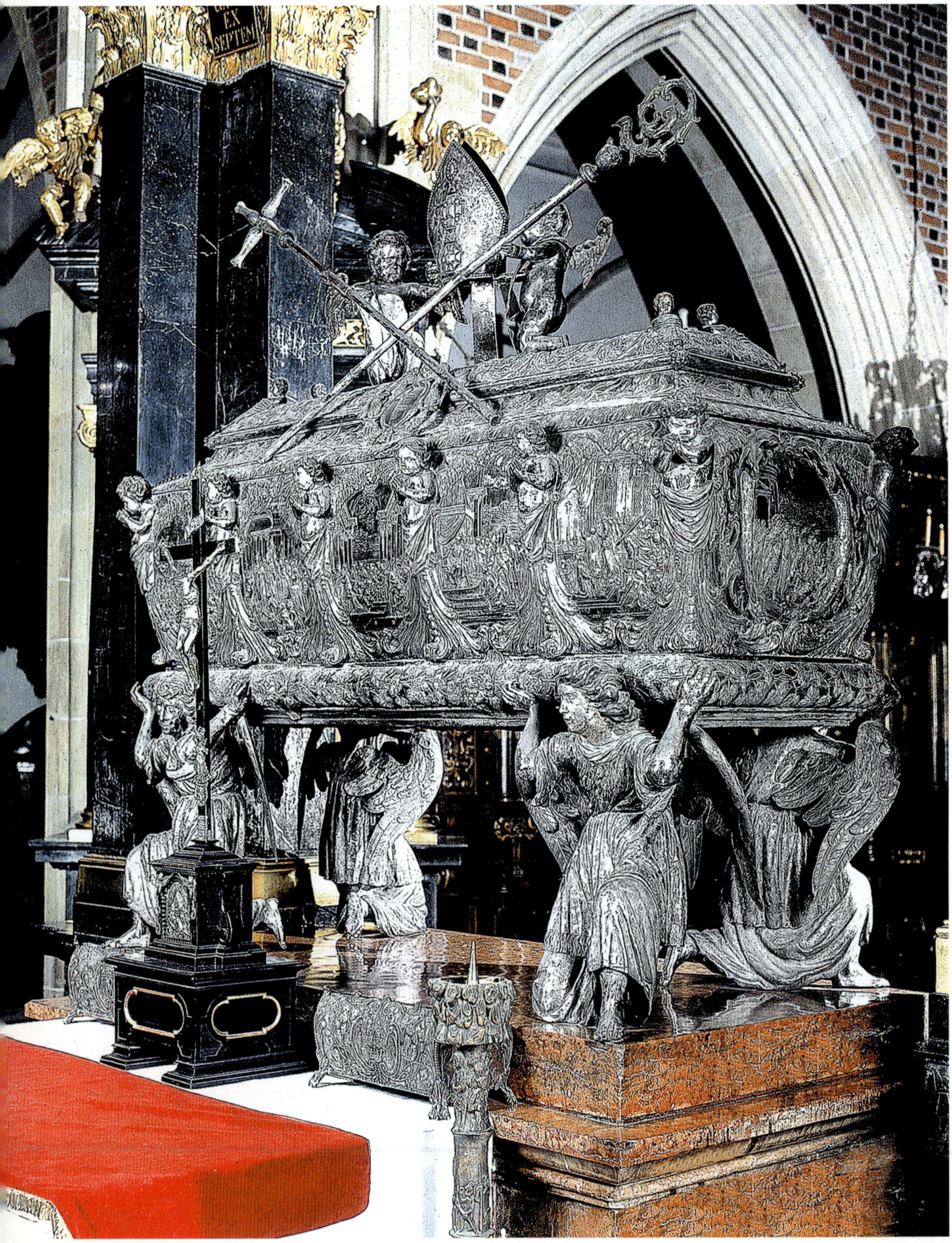

26-27. A section of the shrine of St Stanisalaus in Wawel Cathedral; the silver coffin by Peter van der Rennen, goldsmith from Gdańsk (1661-1671), decorated with twelve reliefs showing the scenes from the Saint's life. Facing page: the Sigismund Chapel, the finest work of Renaissance architecture and sculpture in Poland (1518-1534), with the monuments of King Sigismund the Elder and Sigismund Augustus (right), and Queen Anne (left)

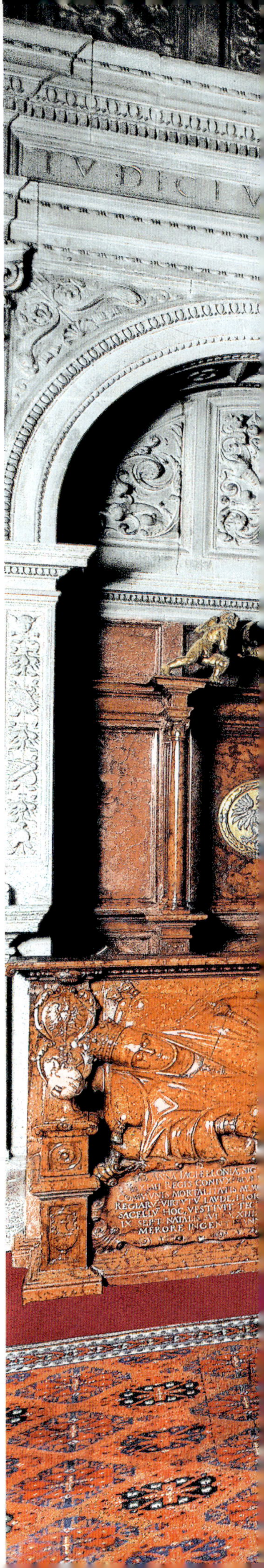

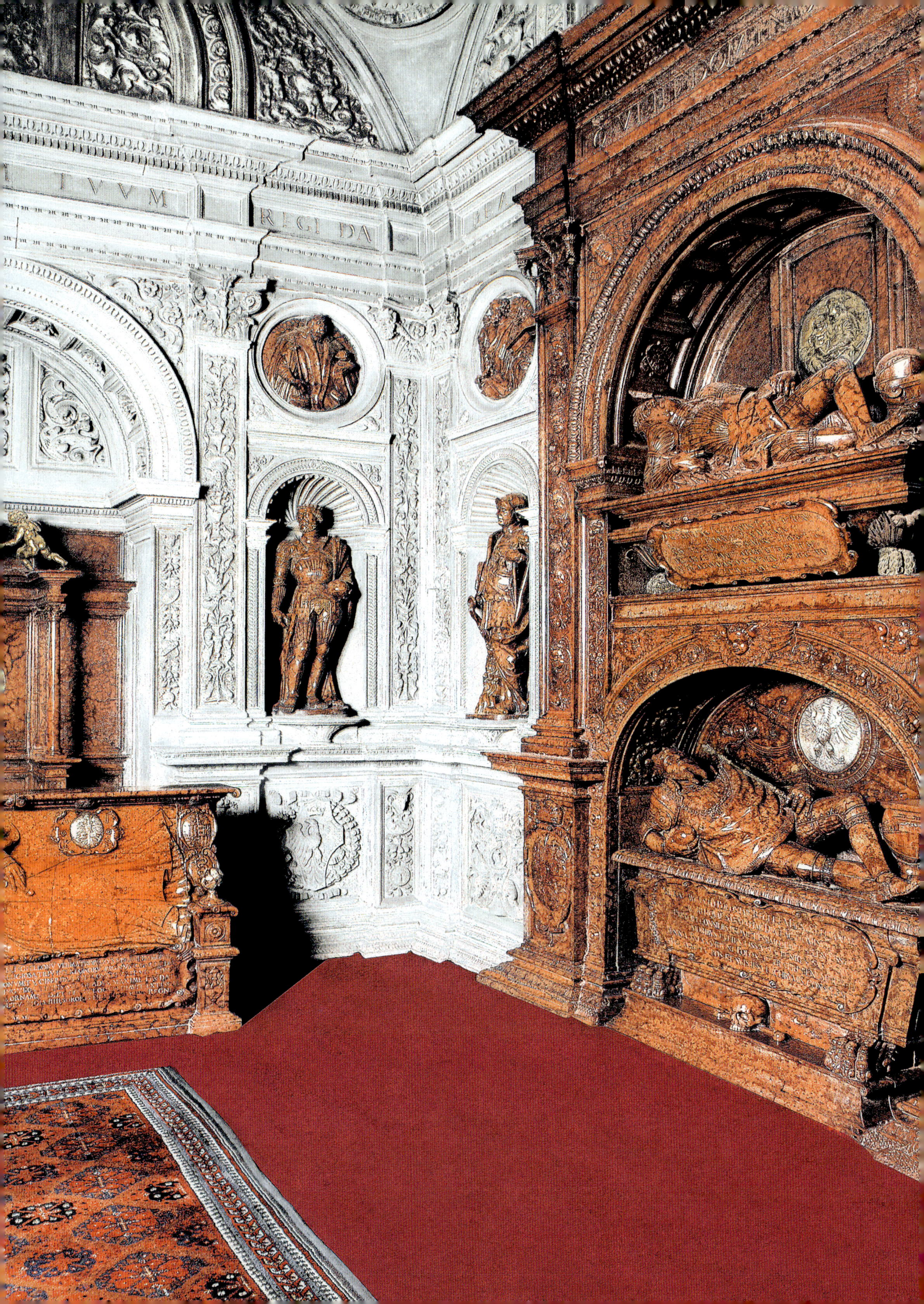

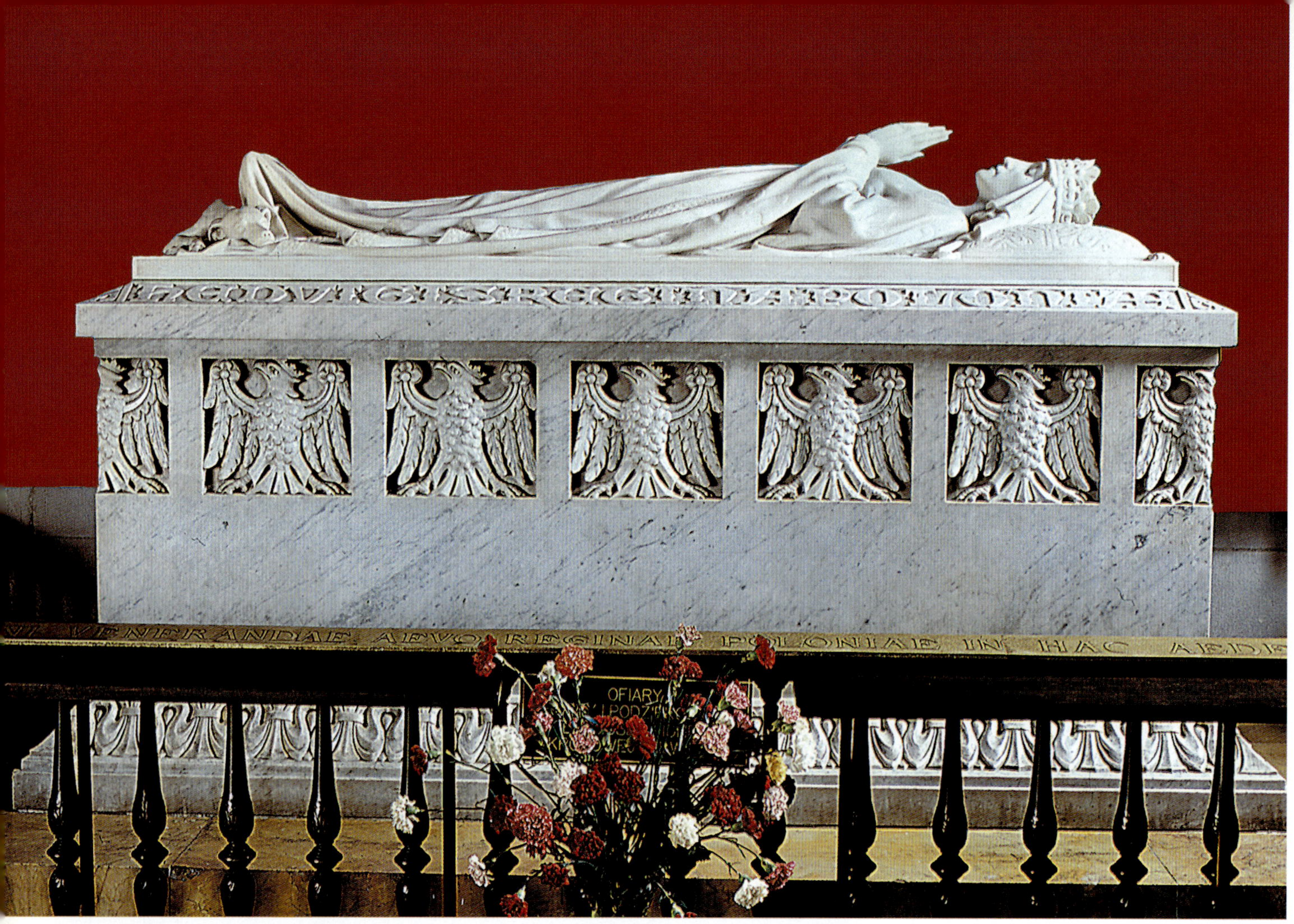

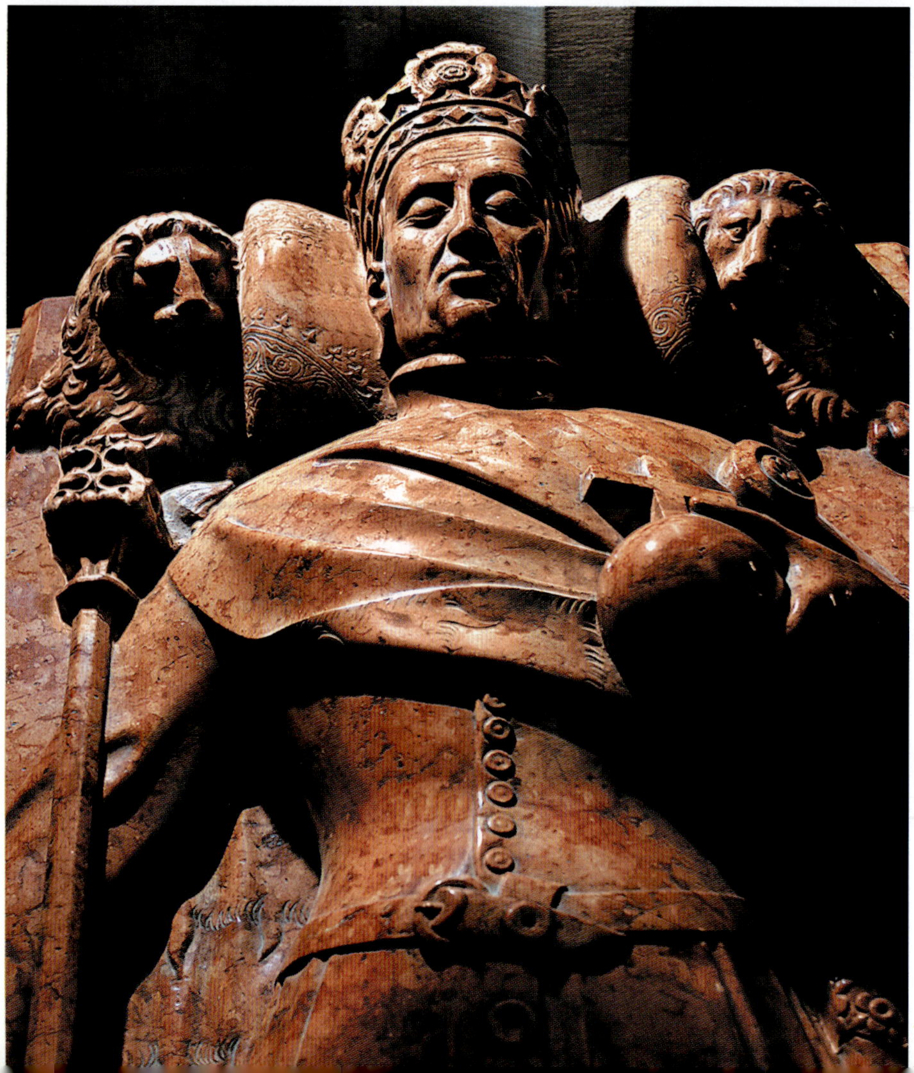

28. Wawel Cathedral: the tomb of Queen Jadwiga, daughter of King Louis of Hungary, wife of King Ladislaus Jagiełło (d. 1399), canonized in Cracow in 1997 by Pope John Paul II

30. Facing page: St Leonard's Crypt in Wawel Cathedral (before 1100), one of the finest Romanesque interiors surviving in Poland

29. Wawel Cathedral: a detail of the effigy of King Ladislaus Jagiełło, on the tomb of red Hungarian marble, one of the finest Gothic sculptures in Poland (first half of the 15th c.)

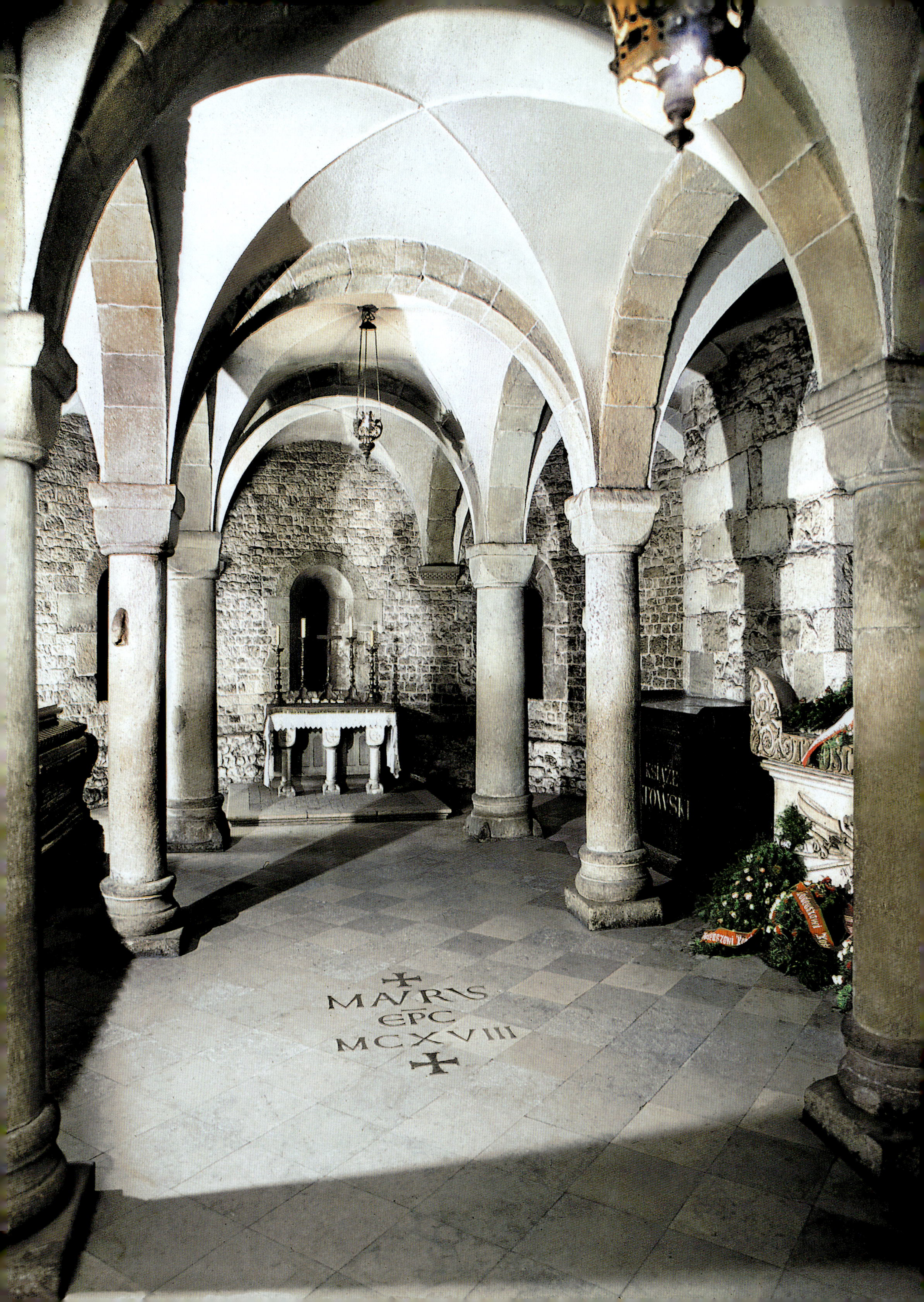
MAVRUS
EPC
MCXVIII

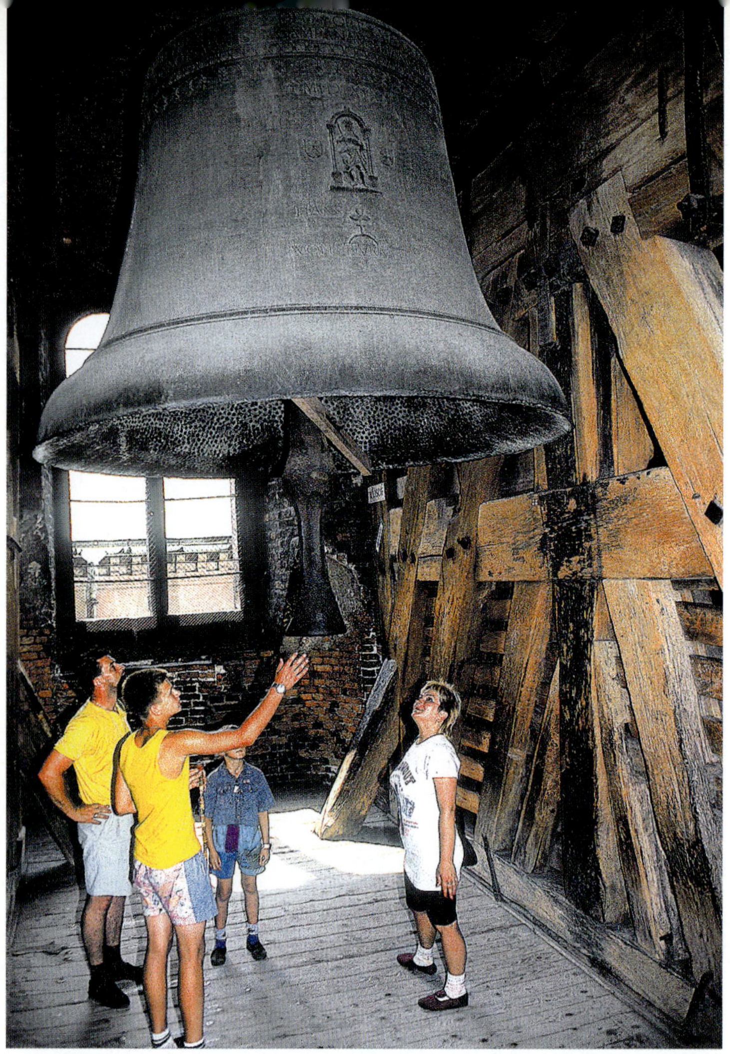

31. Wawel Cathedral, the Sigismund Bell (1520), one of the largest and the most famous bells in Poland, weighs c. 13 tons and its circumference is 8 m

33. Facing page: Jan Matejko Square, with the monument of King Ladislaus Jagiełło, also known as the Grunwald Monument, which was founded by Ignacy Jan Paderewski (in 1910), on the 500th anniversary of King Ladislaus' victory over the Teutonic Knights at Grunwald. In the background a section of the medieval City Walls, with the Barbican (late 15th c.) and the tower of St Florian's Gate visible beyond it (turn of the 13th and 14th c.)

32. The John Paul II Cathedral Museum at Wawel, the copies of the royal insignia found in the tomb of Casimir the Great

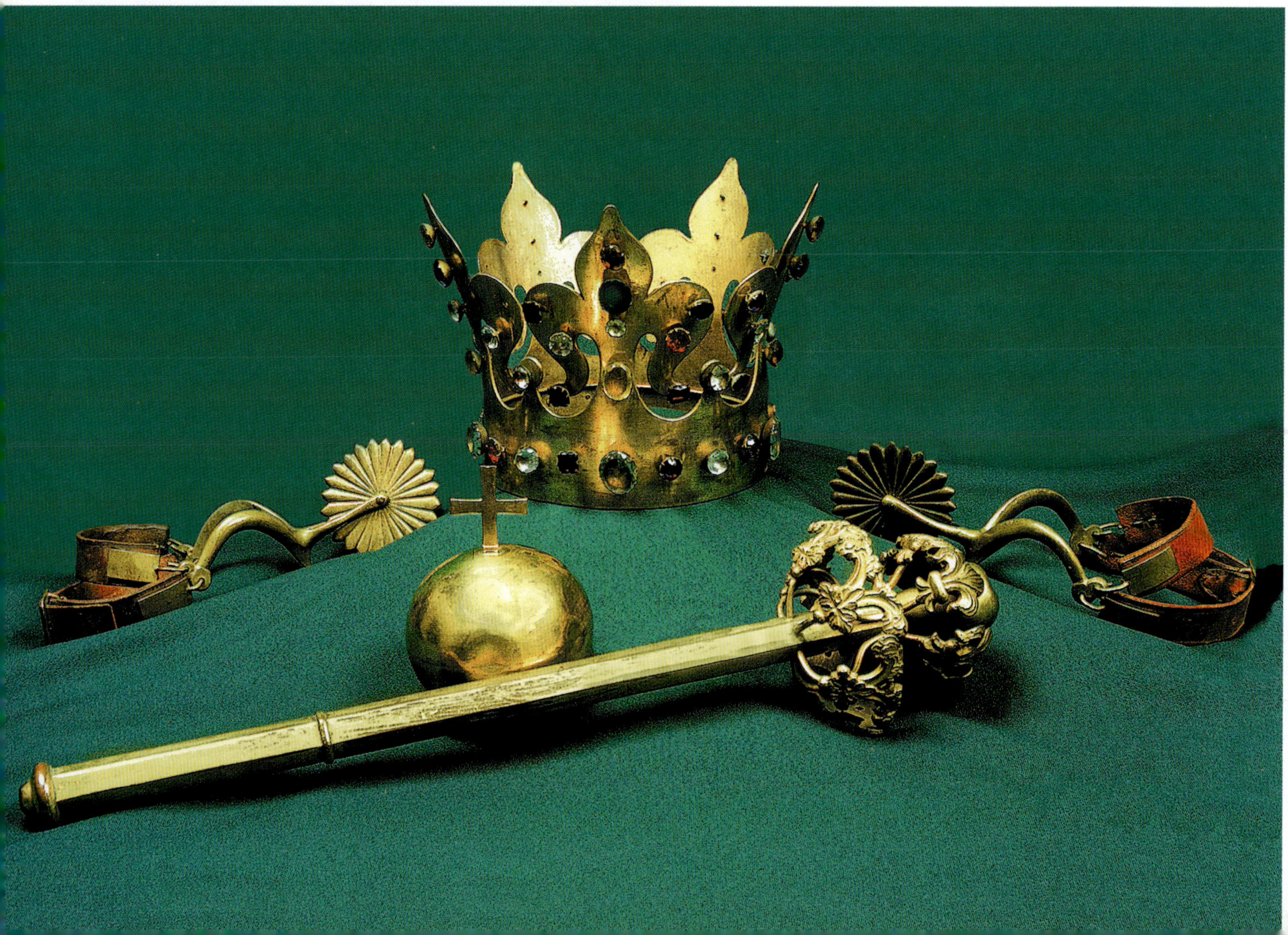

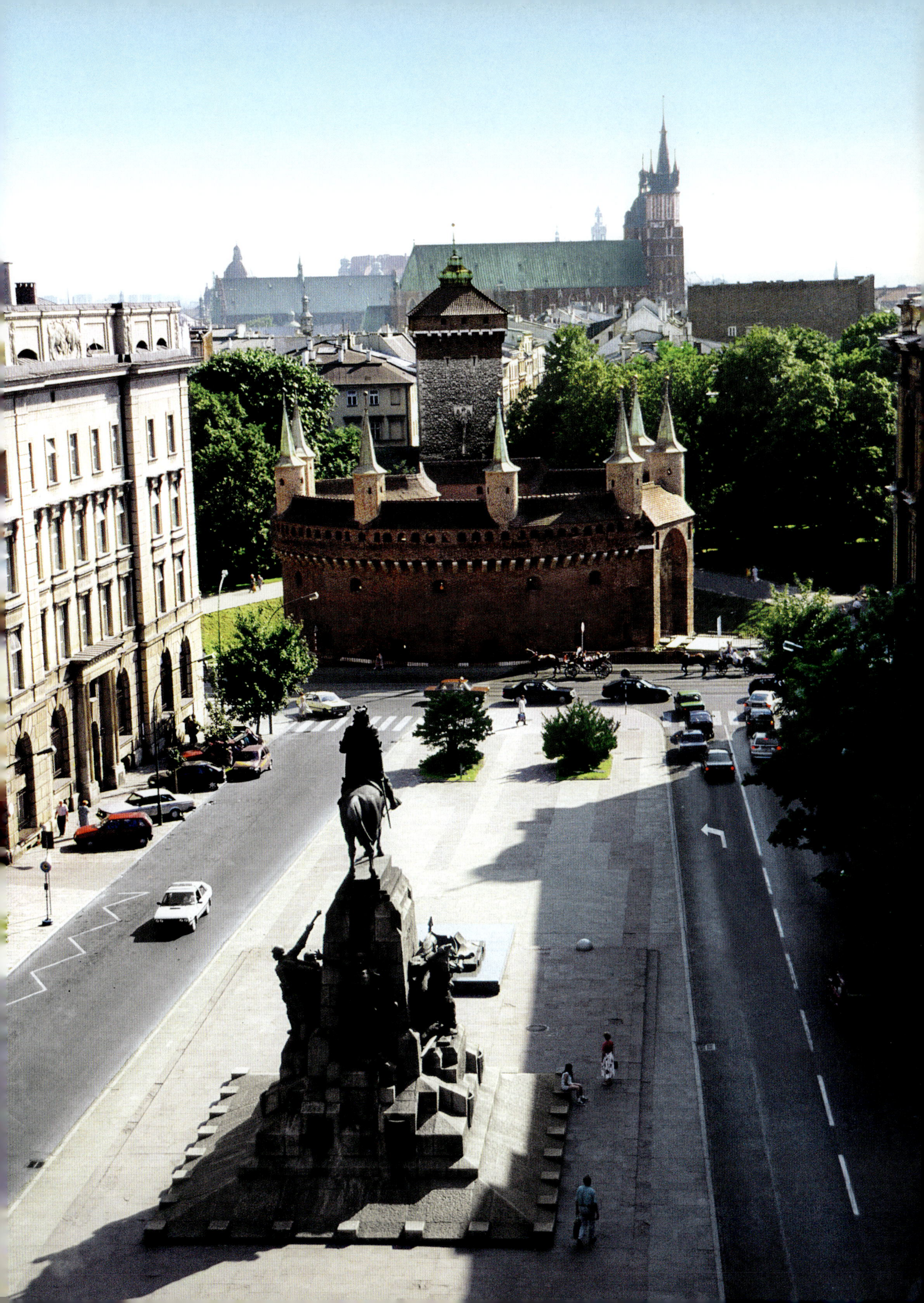

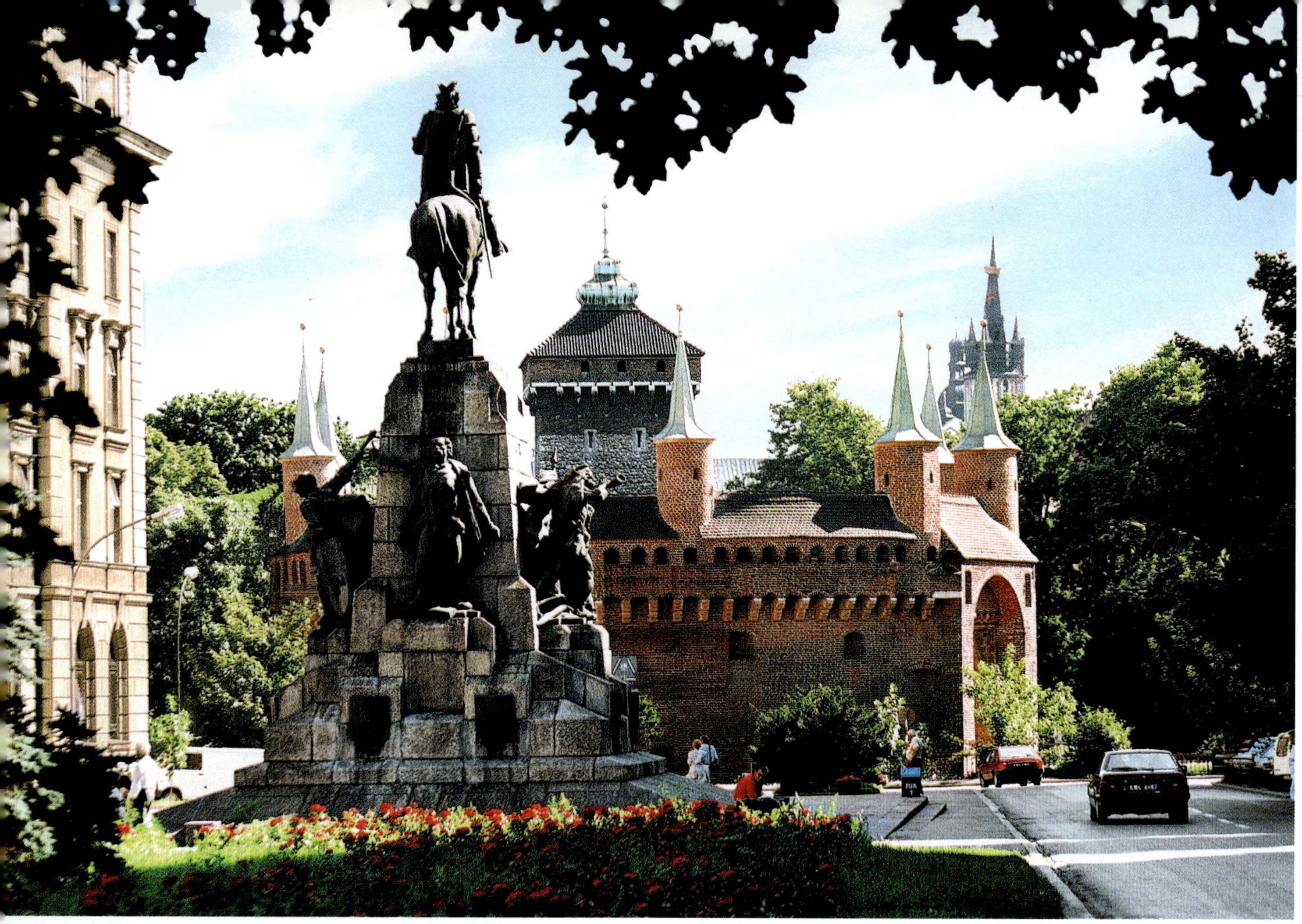

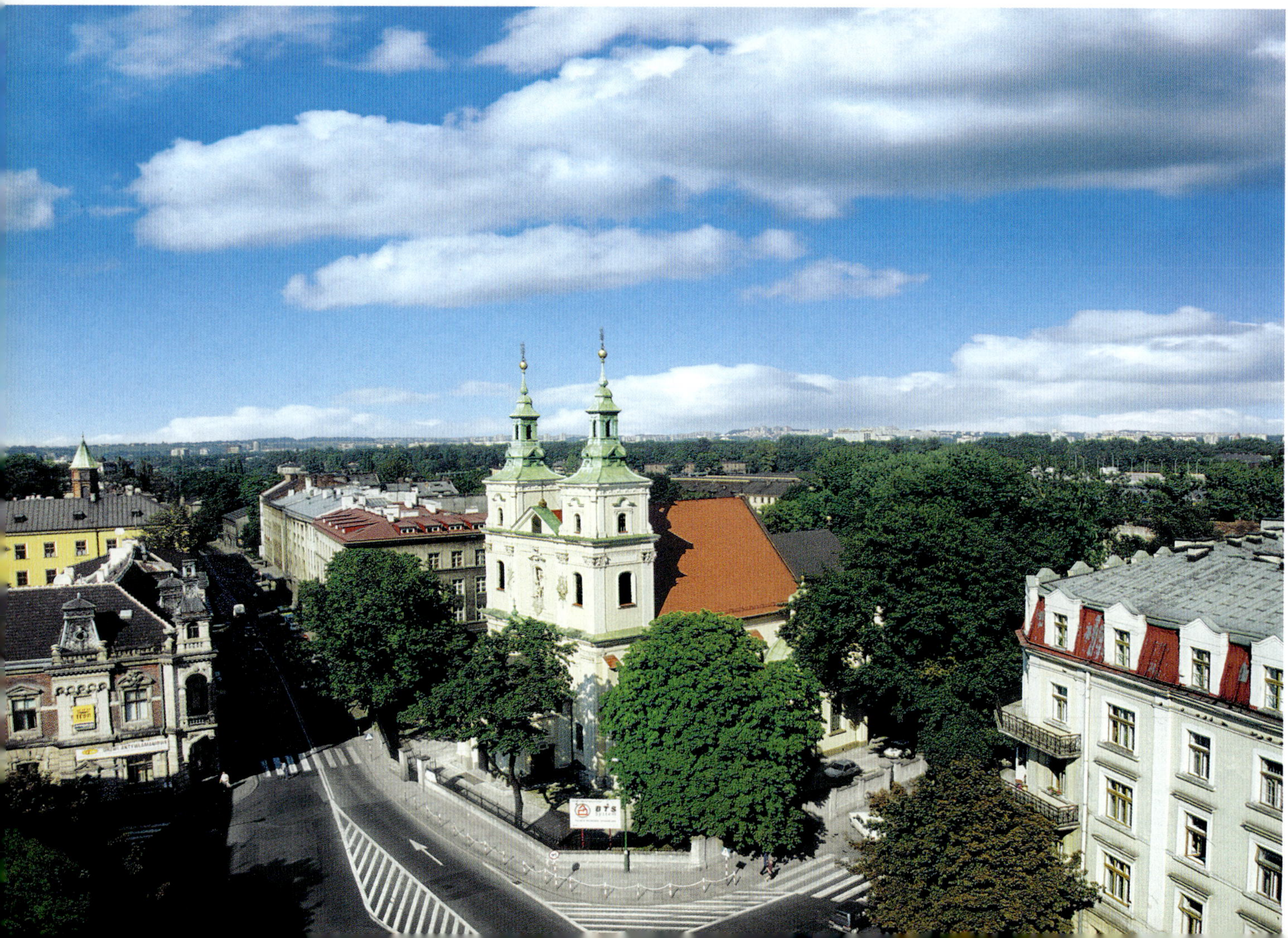

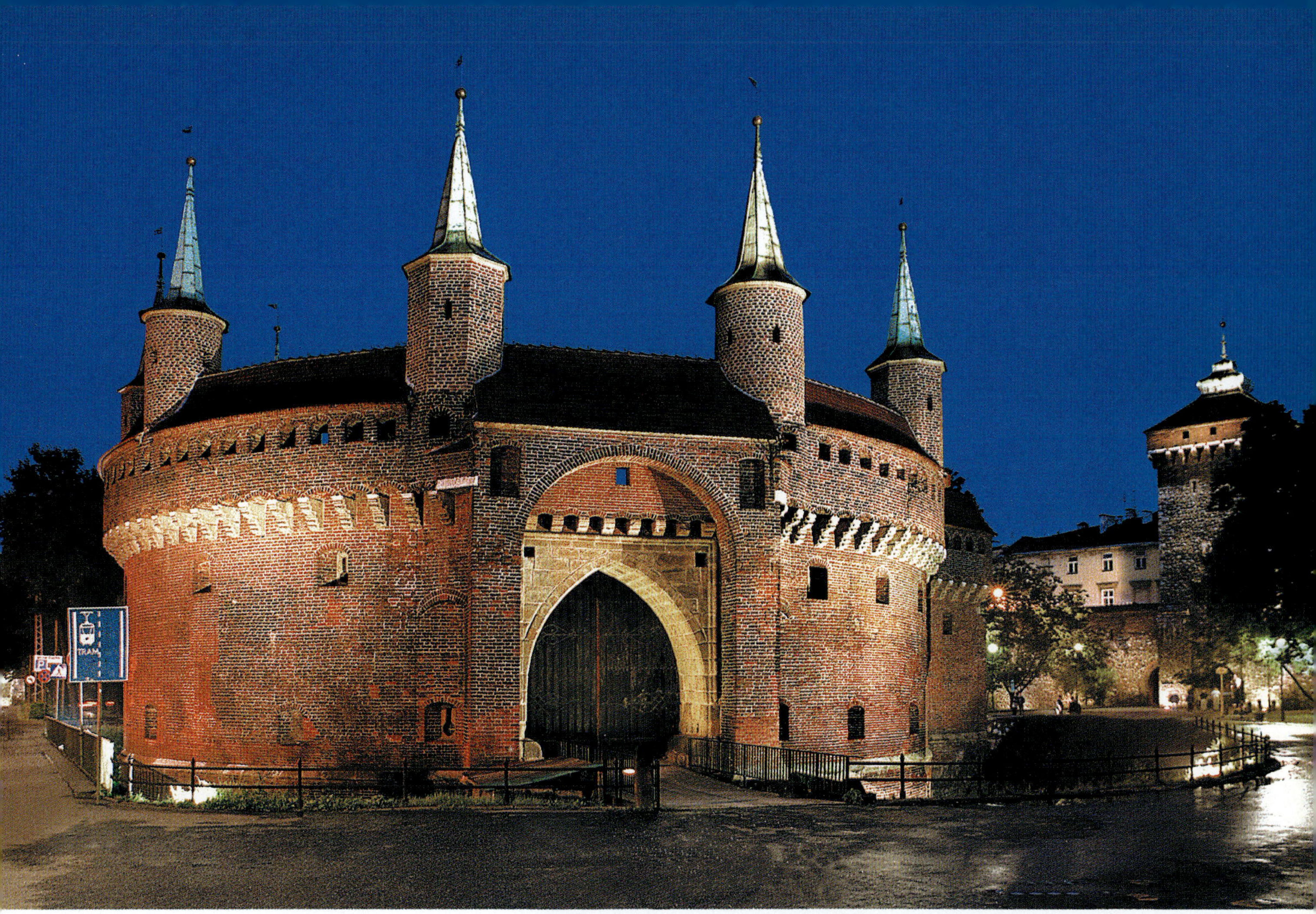

36-37. The Barbican (late 15th c.), the most impressive survival of the Cracow fortifications, one of the few of its kind extant in Europe, it was once connected by 'the Neck' with the City Walls. Bottom: St Florian's Gate (turn of the 13th and 14th c.), once the main city gate

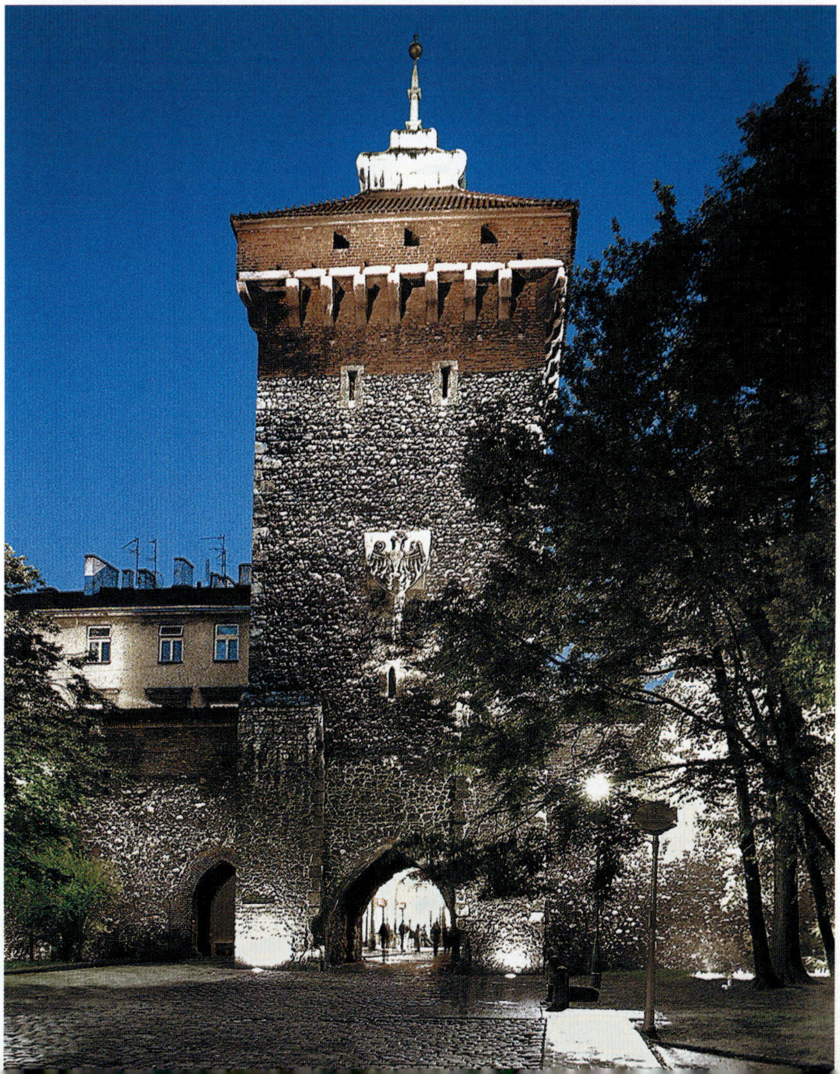

34-35. Facing page: the Grunwald Monument, beyond it the Barbican (later 15th c.), the tower of St Florian's Gate (turn of the 13th and 14th c.), and in the background, the late-Gothic spire (1478) crowning the steeple of St Mary's Church. Bottom: Jan Matejko Square, St Florian's Church, rebuilt in the Baroque style in the second half of the 17th c.

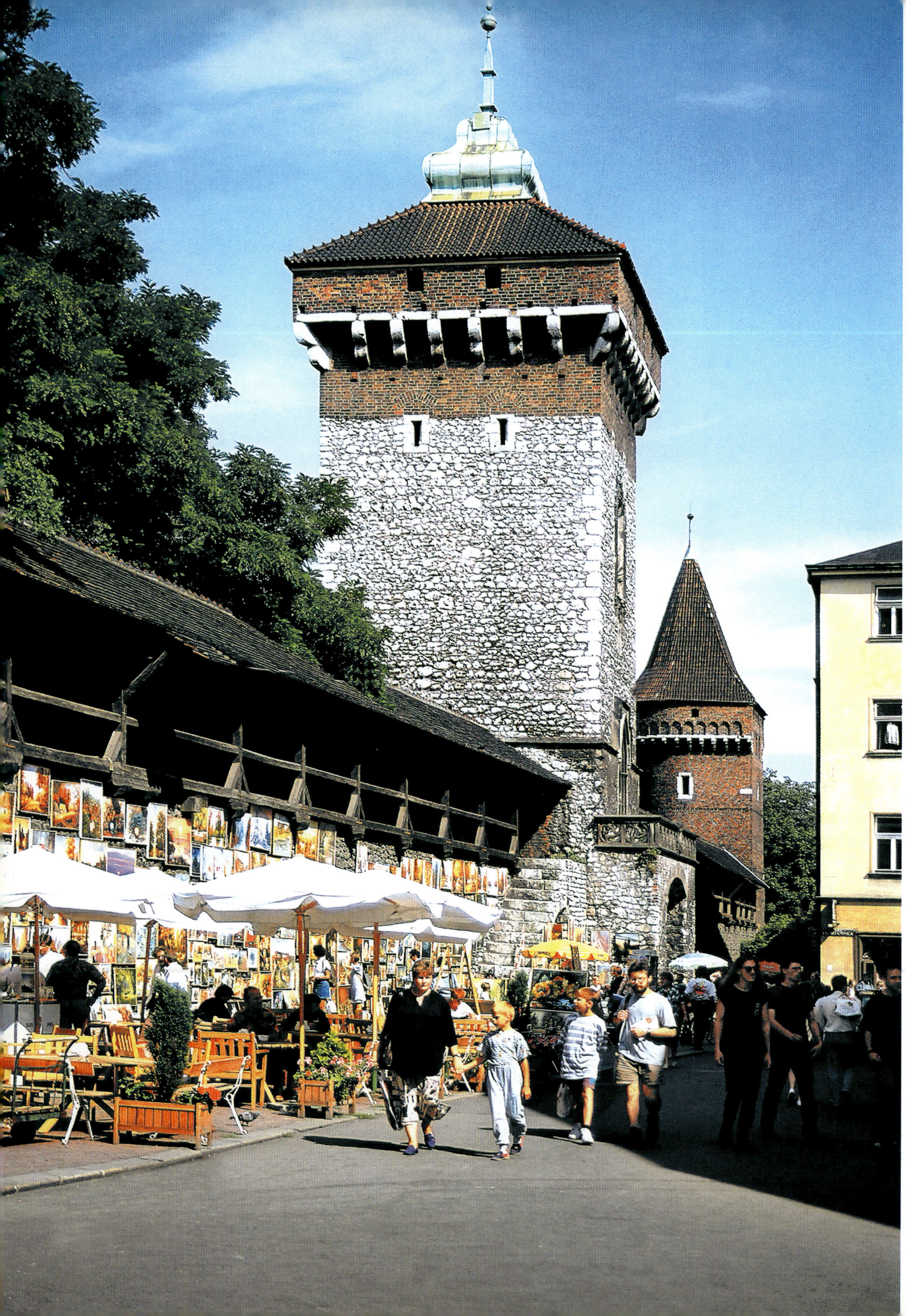

38. Facing page: a section of the medieval City Walls, with St Florian's Gate (turn of the 13th and 14th c.) and the Haberdashers' Tower (right, 15th c.). The reconstructed galleries for the guards, in the upper part pf the walls on the inner side, connected St Florian's Gate with the Carpenters' Tower and the Haberdashers' Tower. On the walls is a display of paintings and sculptures

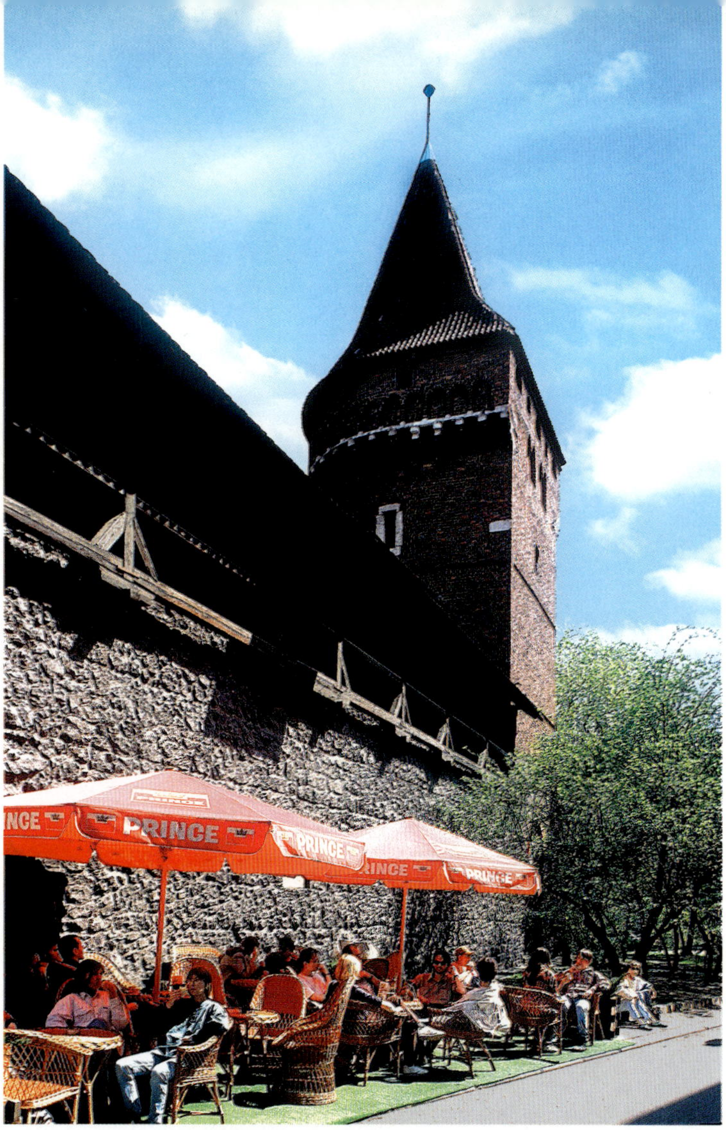

39-40. Sections of the City Walls, with the Haberdashers' Tower (15th c.) and the Joiners' Tower (bottom, 14th c.), and the adjacent building of the former City Arsenal (turn of the 16th and 17th c.)

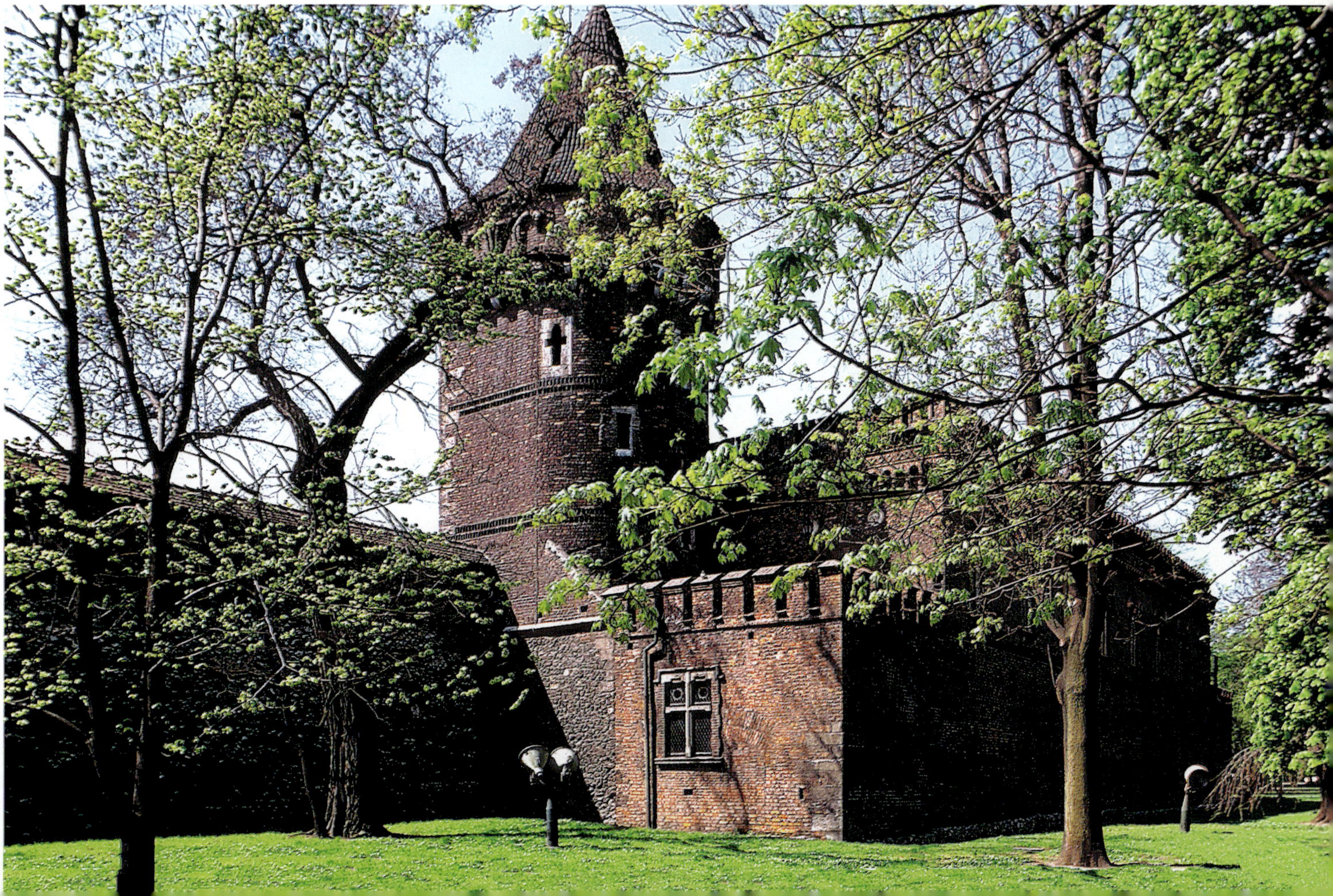

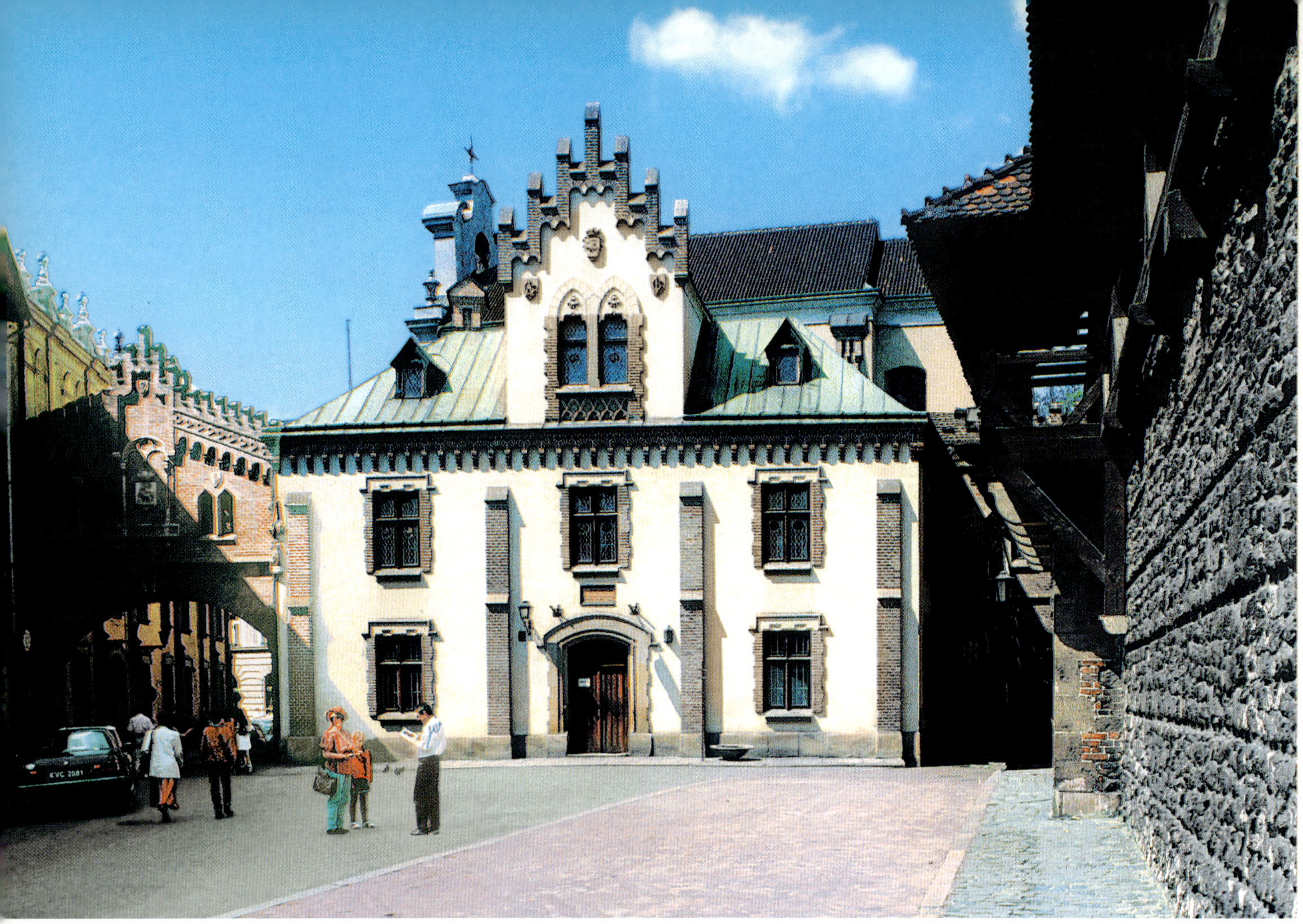

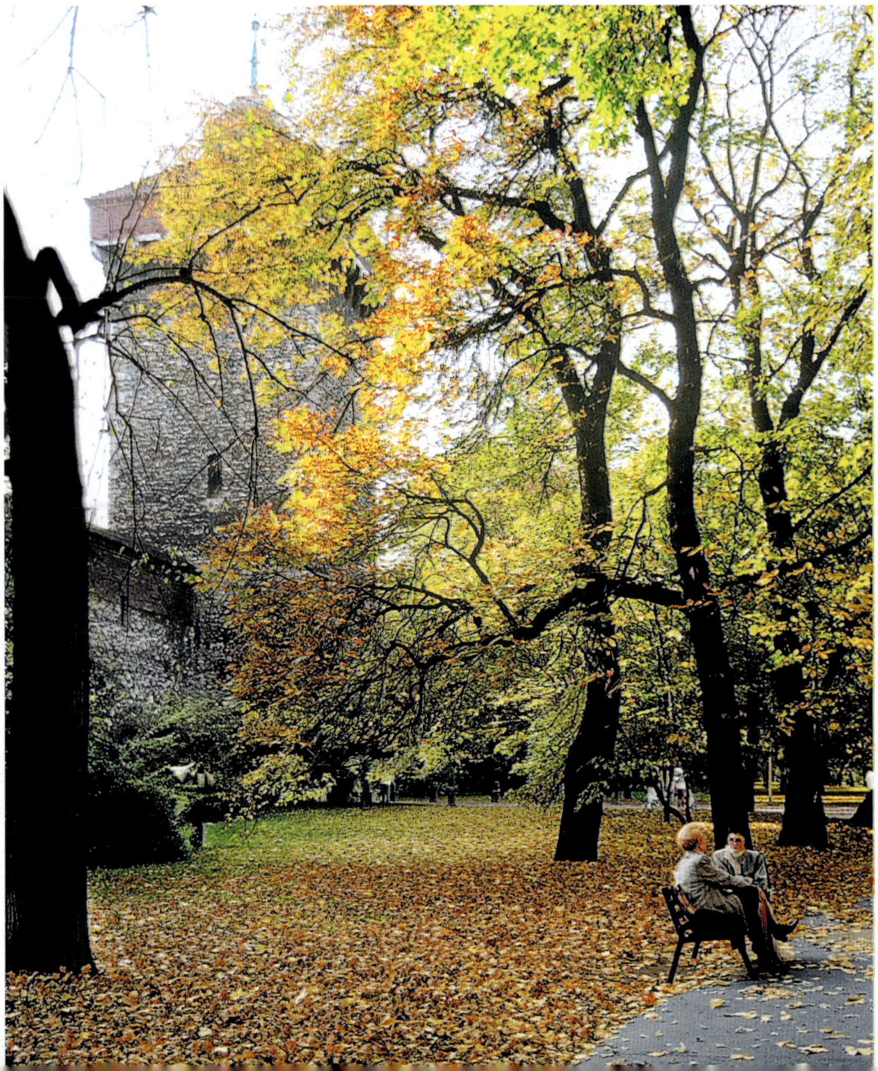

41. The Small Monastery, a part of the complex of the Czartoryski Museum, one of the oldest museums of art and historical memorabilia in Poland

43. Facing page: the Czartoryski Museum, 'Lady with an Ermine' by Leonardo da Vinci (c. 1490)

42. A section of the Planty Gardens, a green belt c. 4 km long and 40-120 m wide, surrounding the old part of the city, planted in 1810-1814 on the site of the demolished city fortifications

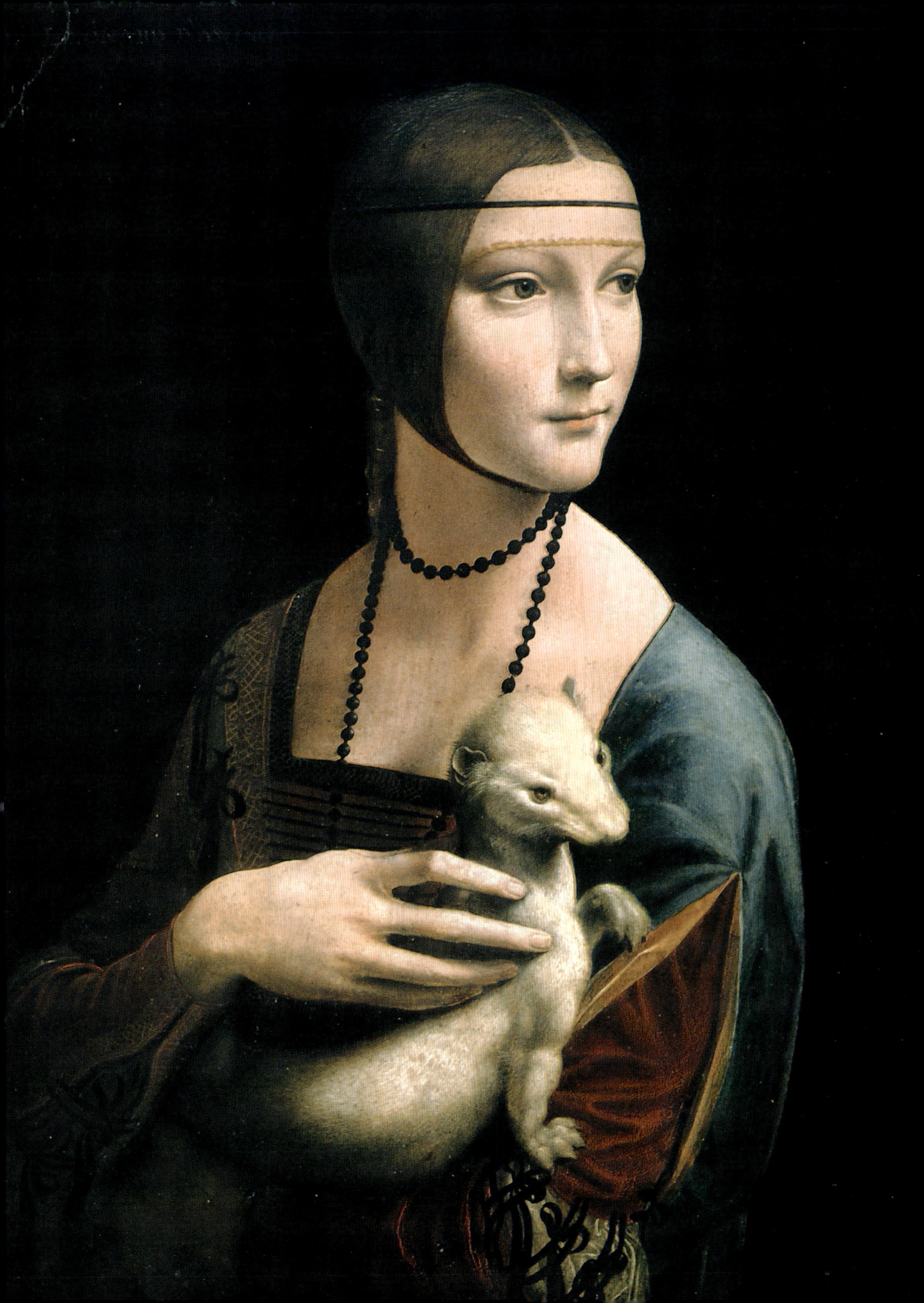

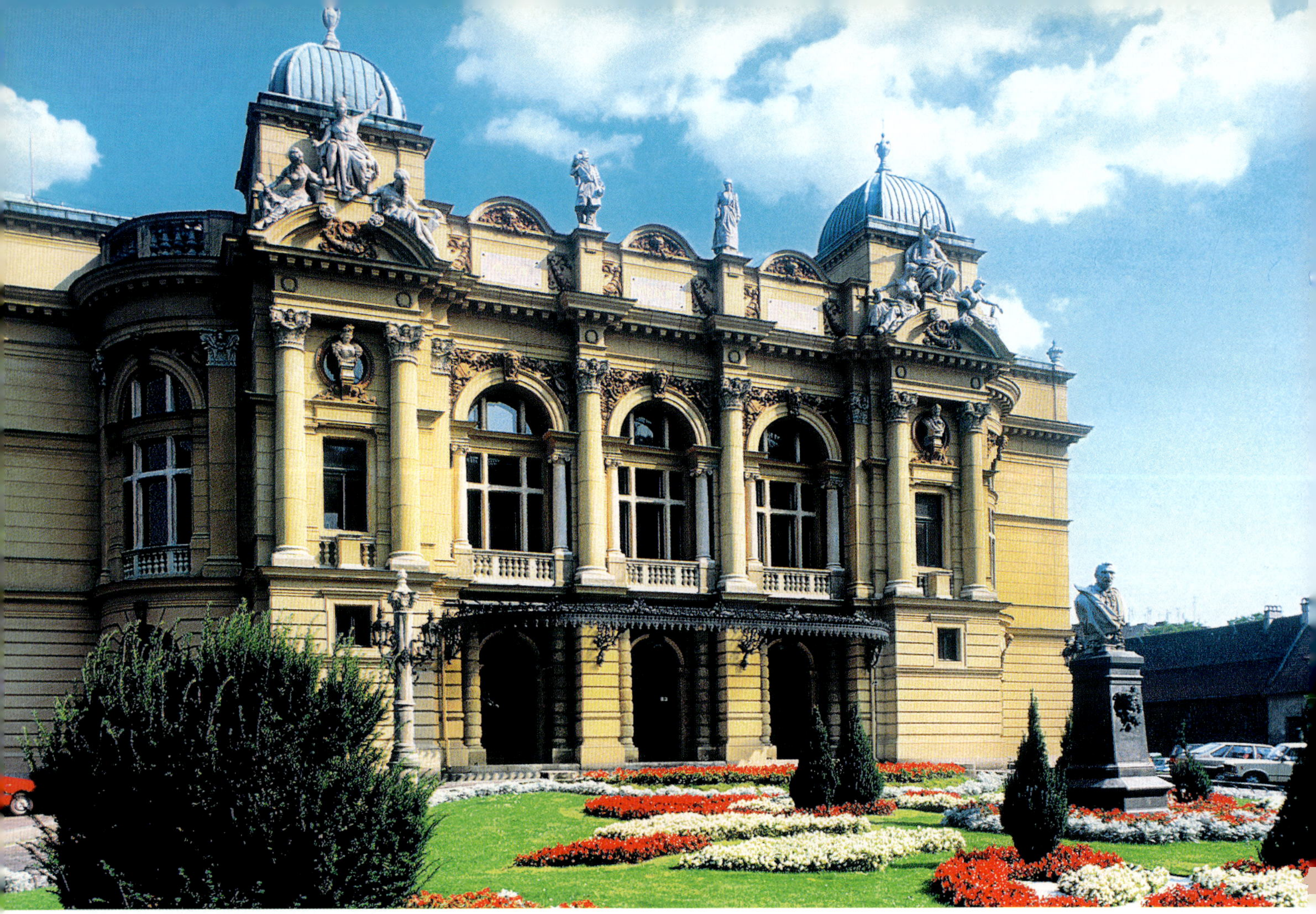

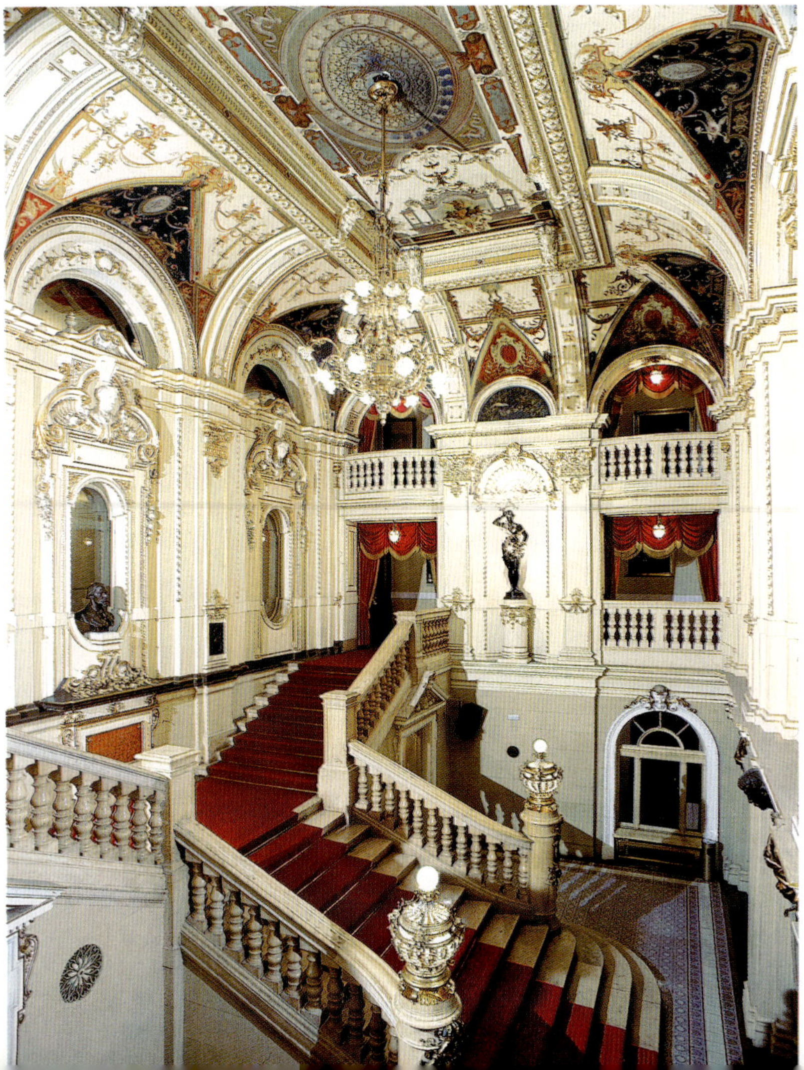

44-45. The Juliusz Słowacki Theatre (1893), the theatre front, and the sumptuous foyer (bottom). The theatre is also a venue for concerts, important events, conferences and congresses

46-47. Facing page: the Juliusz Słowacki Theatre, the curtain (1893-1894) by Henryk Siemiradzki; it depicts allegorical and symbolic figures connected with theatre. Bottom: the building of the Juliusz Słowacki Theatre and the nearby Gothic Church of the Holy Cross (14th c.)

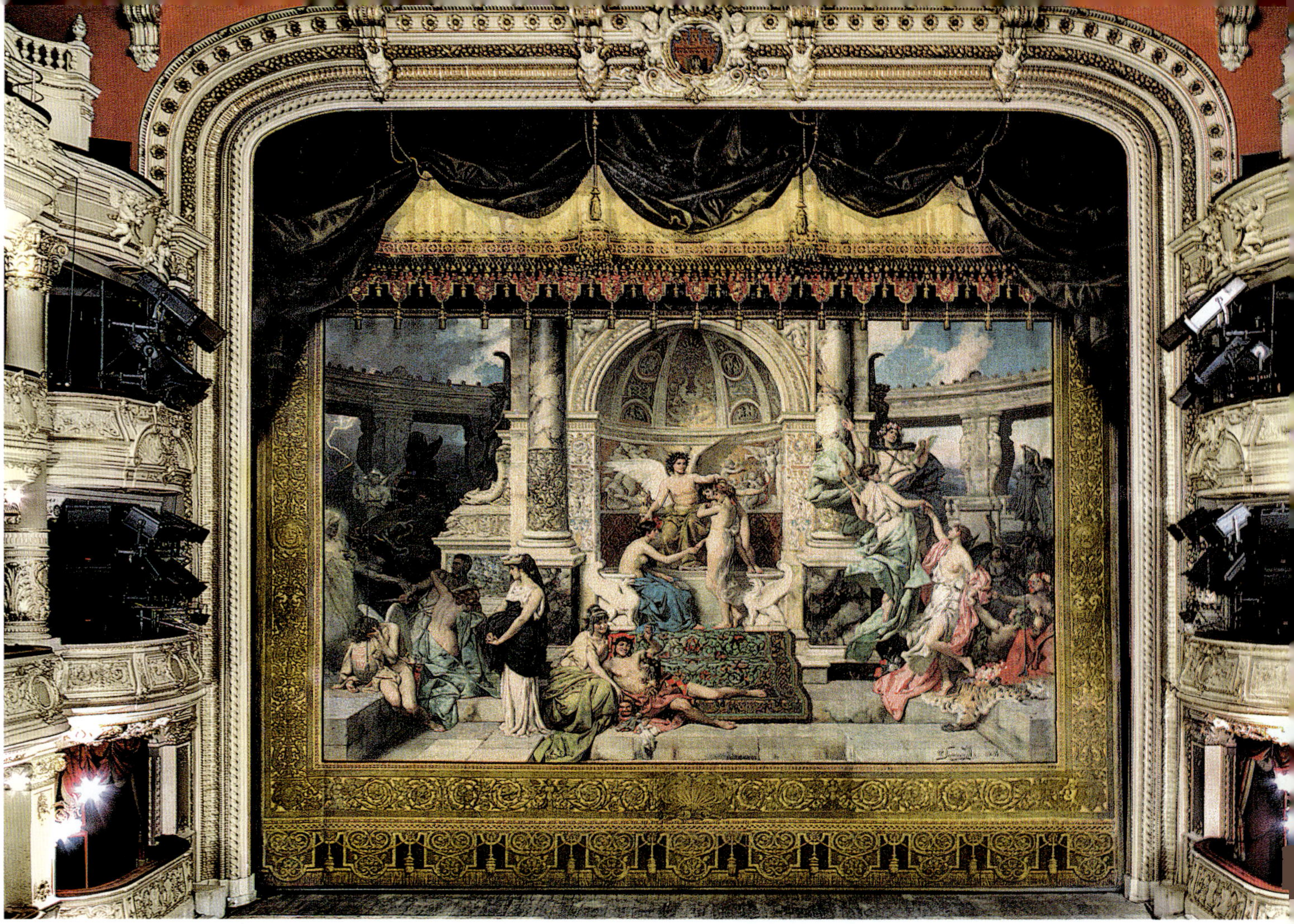

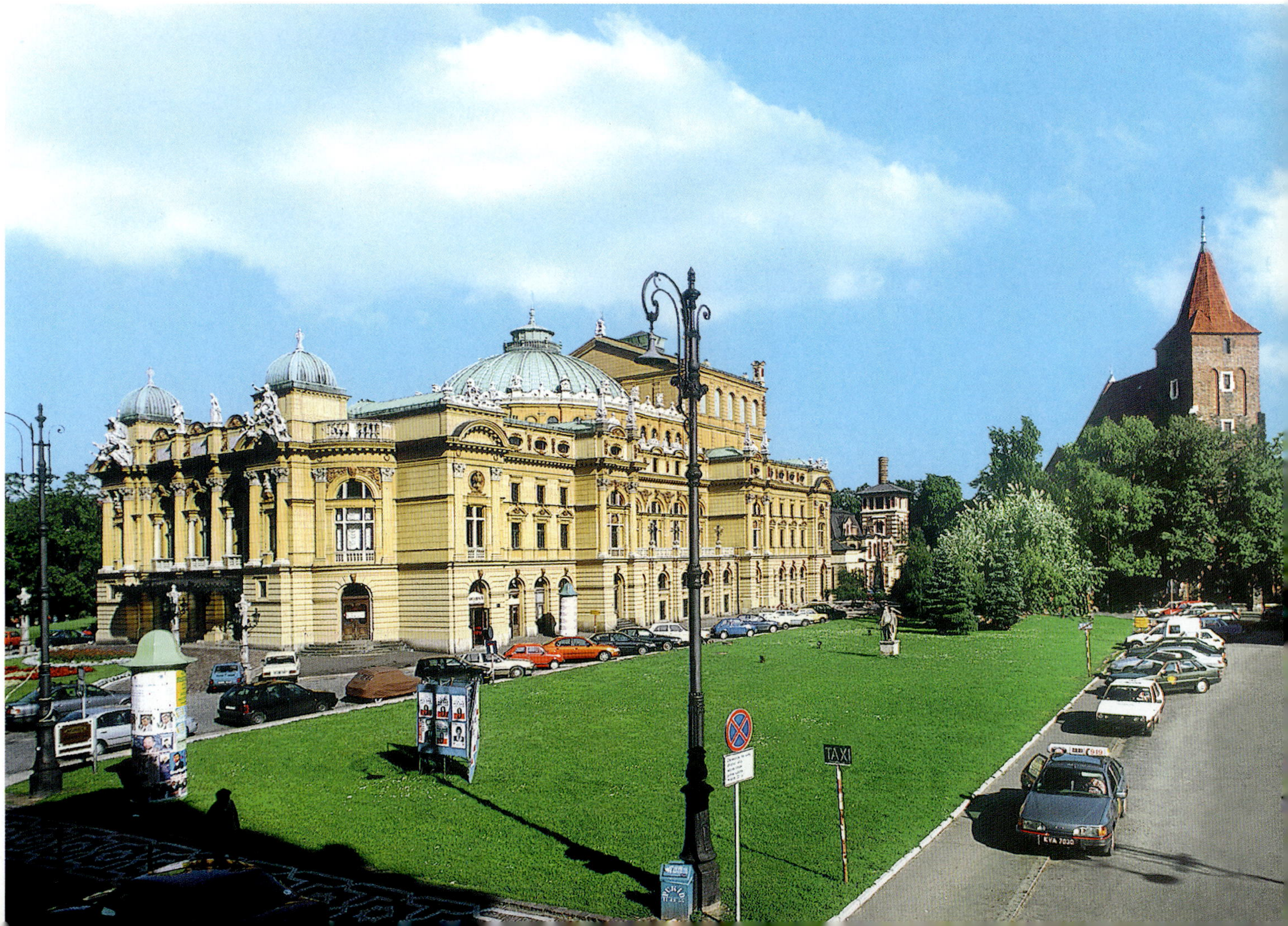
TAXI

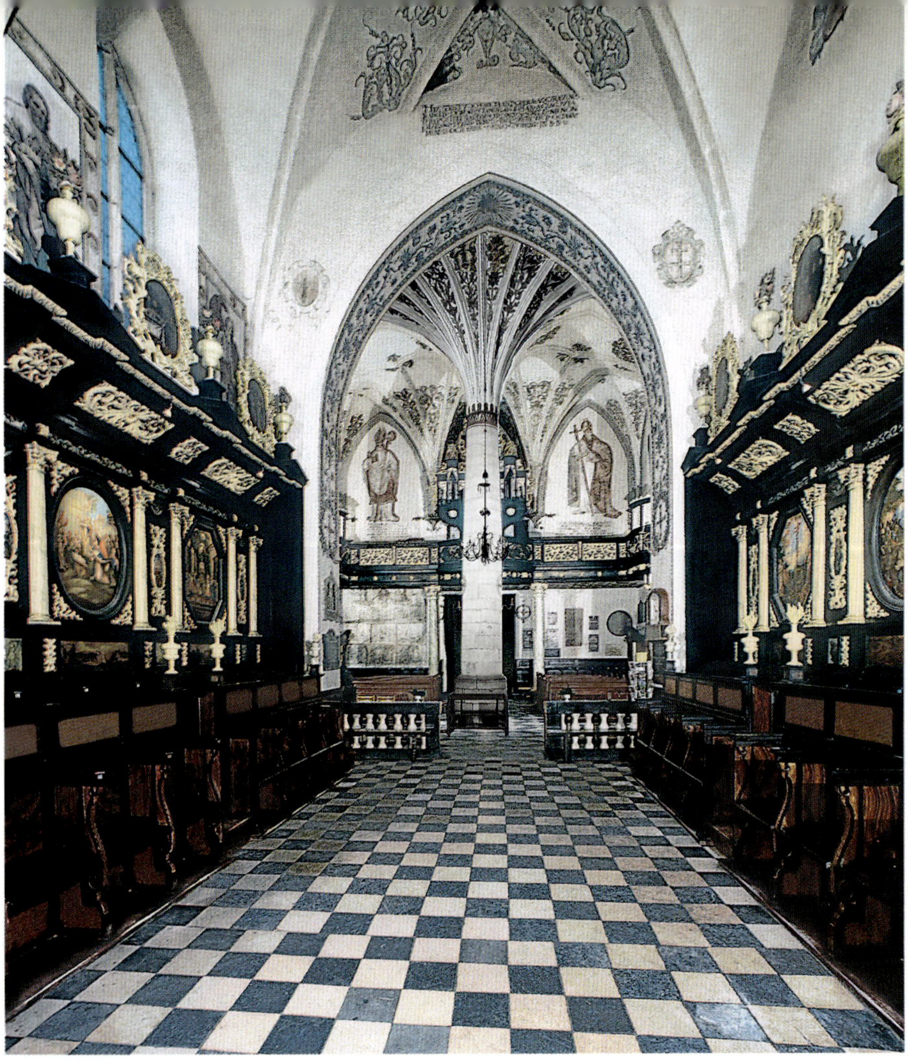

48-50. The Church of the Holy Cross, a section of the presbytery, with the stalls (17th c.), and the nave, its Gothic vault supported by a single pillar. Bottom: the stalls at the north wall of the nave (first half of the 17th c.). Right, facing page: the late-Renaissance pulpit with the figures of Christ and the four Evangelists carved in relief (early 17th c.)

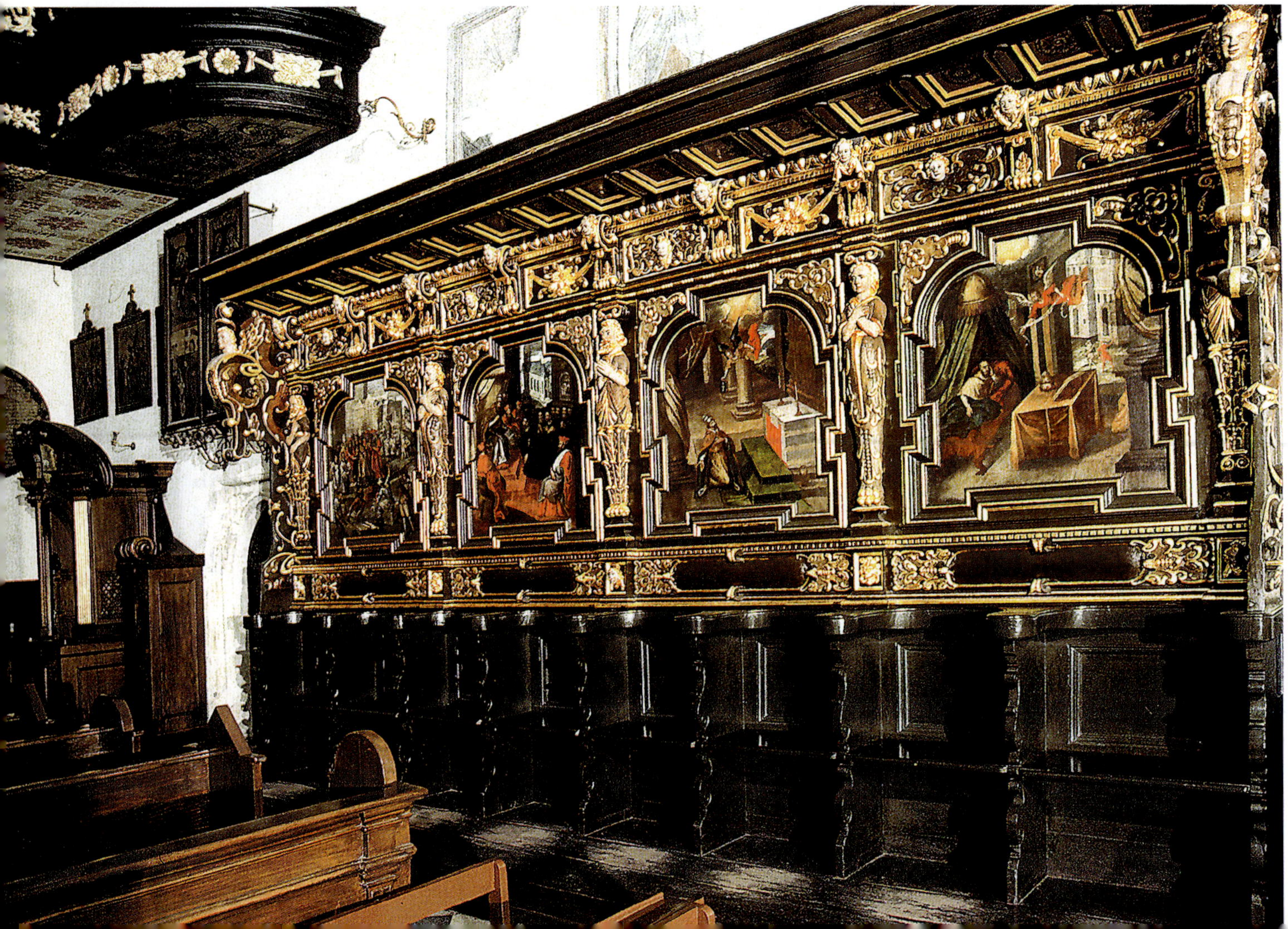

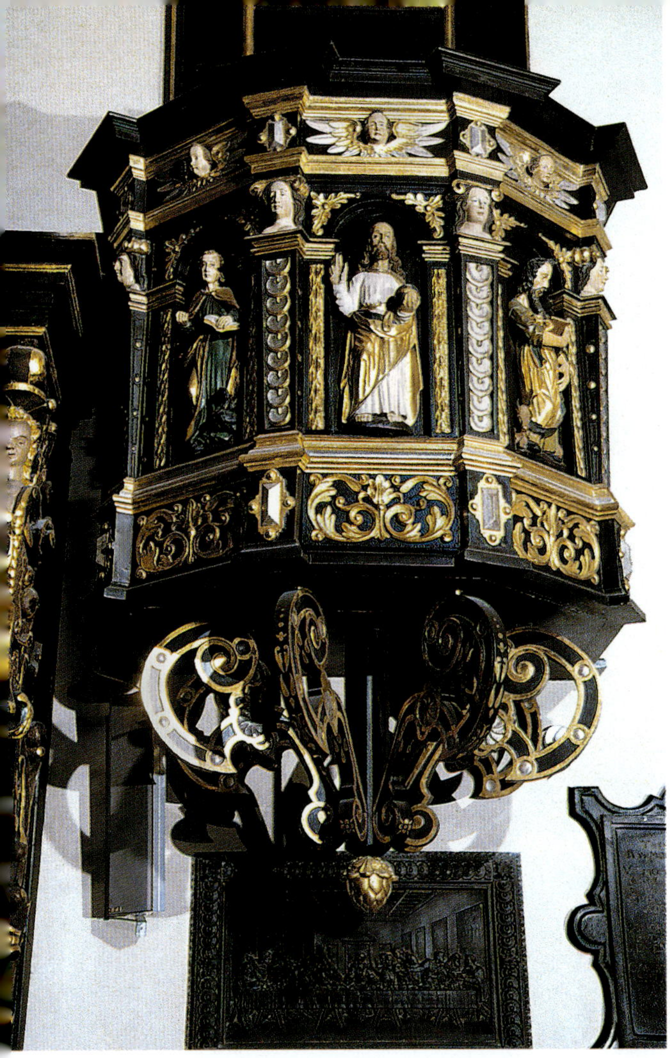

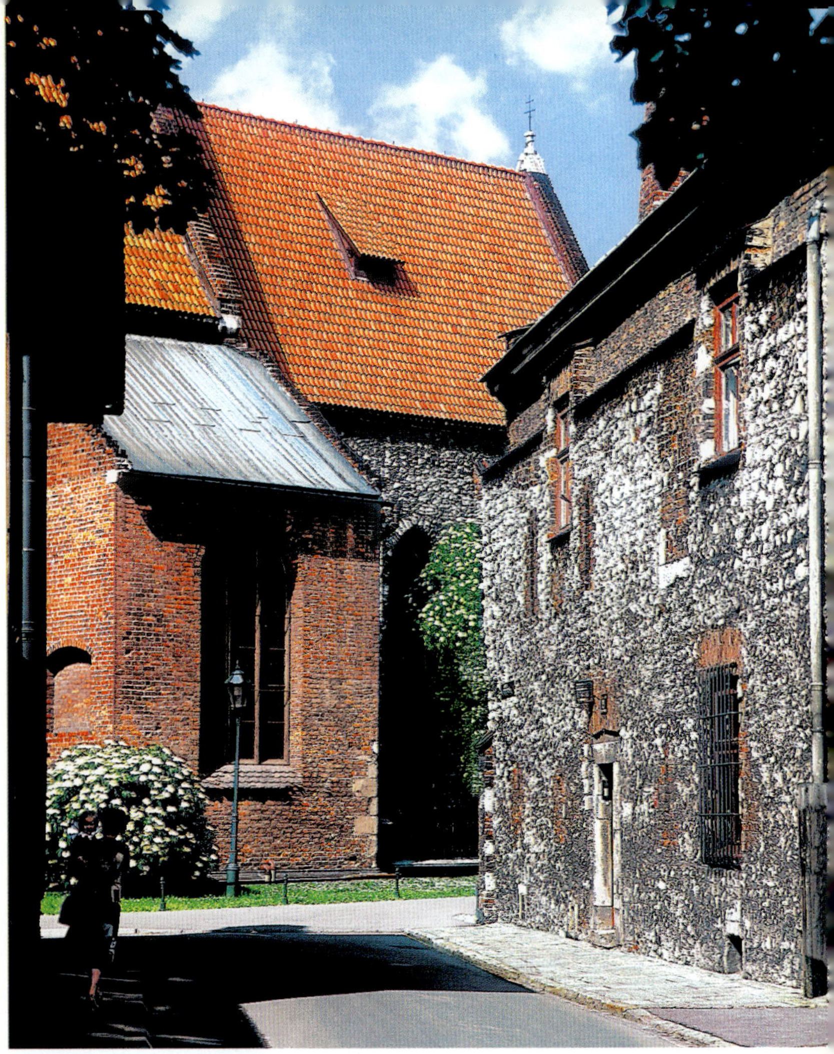

51. The picturesque alley near the Church of the Holy Cross, on the right the house of the medieval parish of the Holy Cross, fortified, built of rough stone and brick (c. 1300)

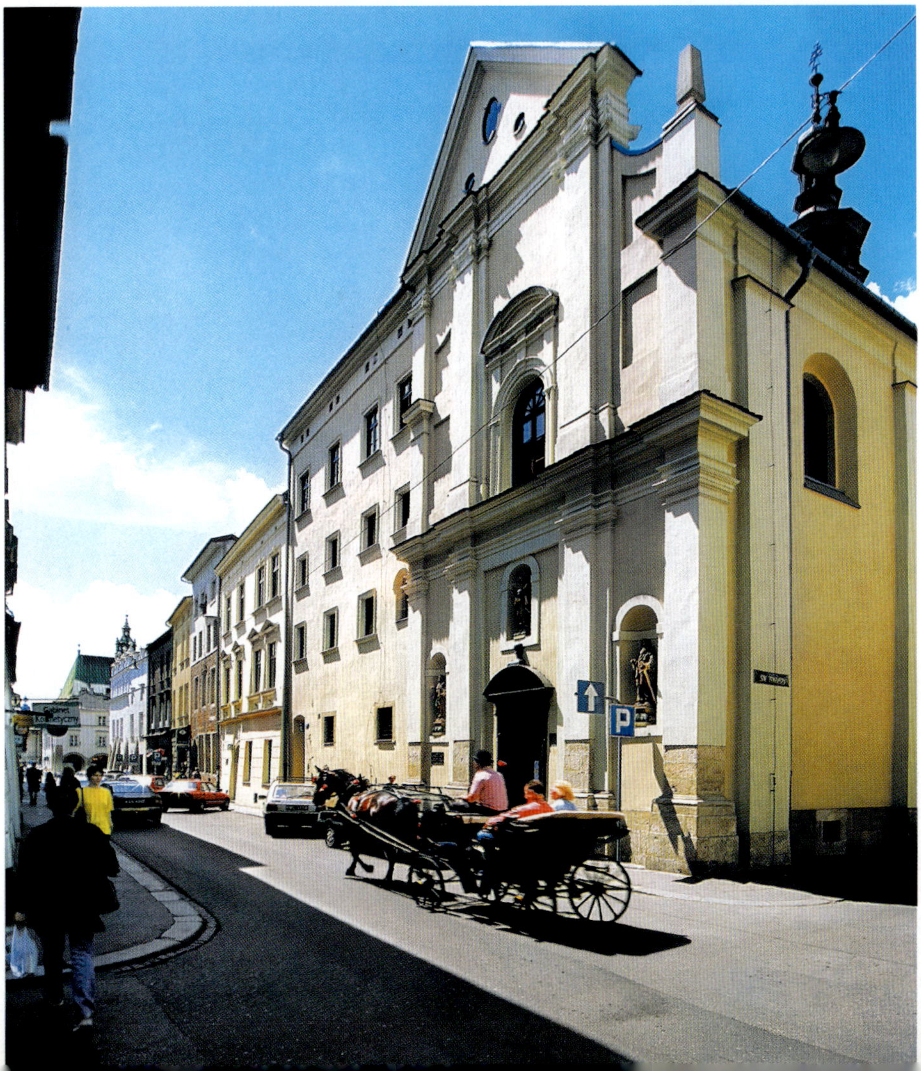

52. Szpitalna Street, one of the oldest Cracow streets, laid out at the time of the city foundation by the Duke of Cracow, Boleslaus V the Chaste (1257). On the right, the Church of St Thomas the Apostle (early 17th c.)

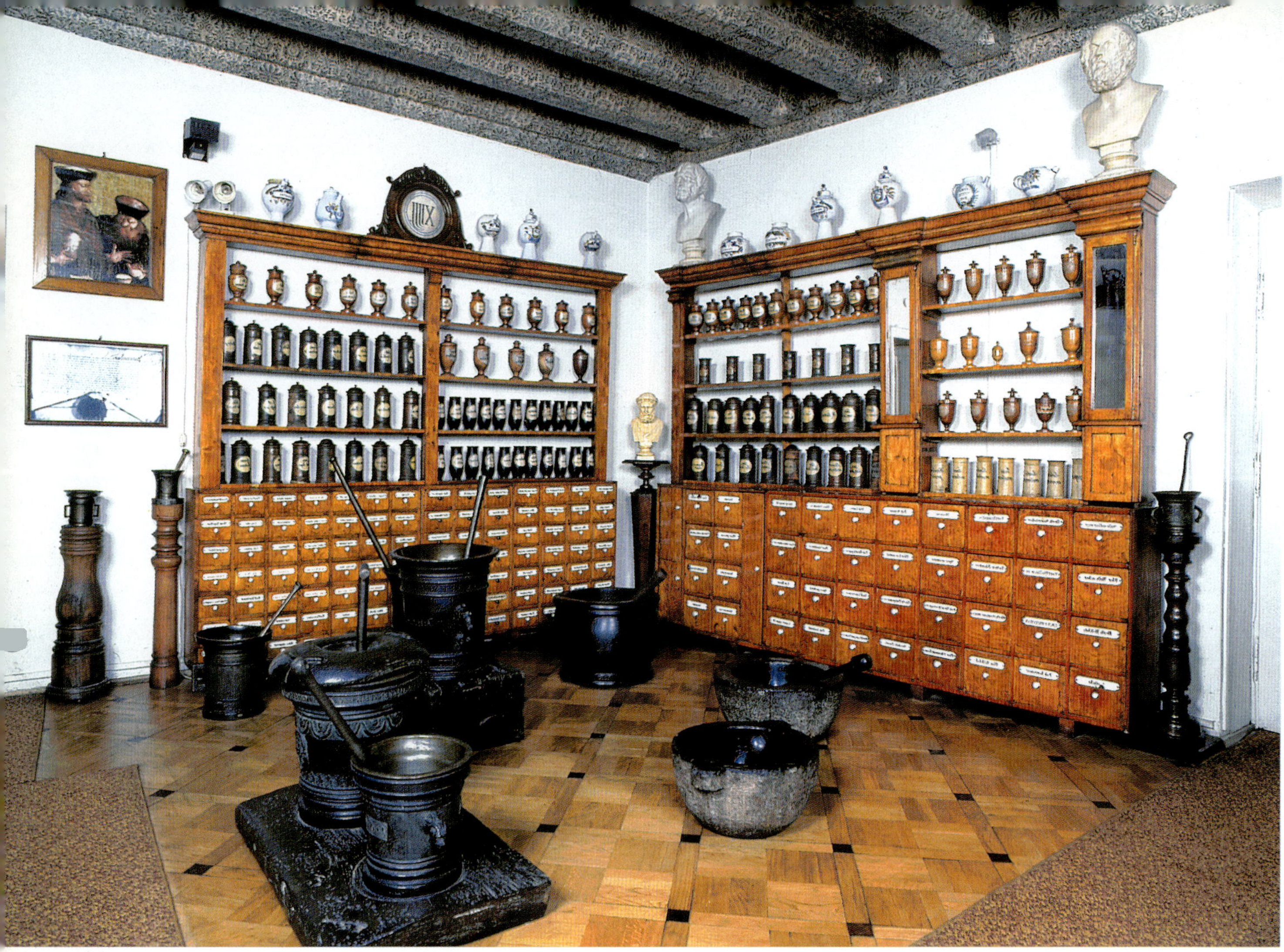

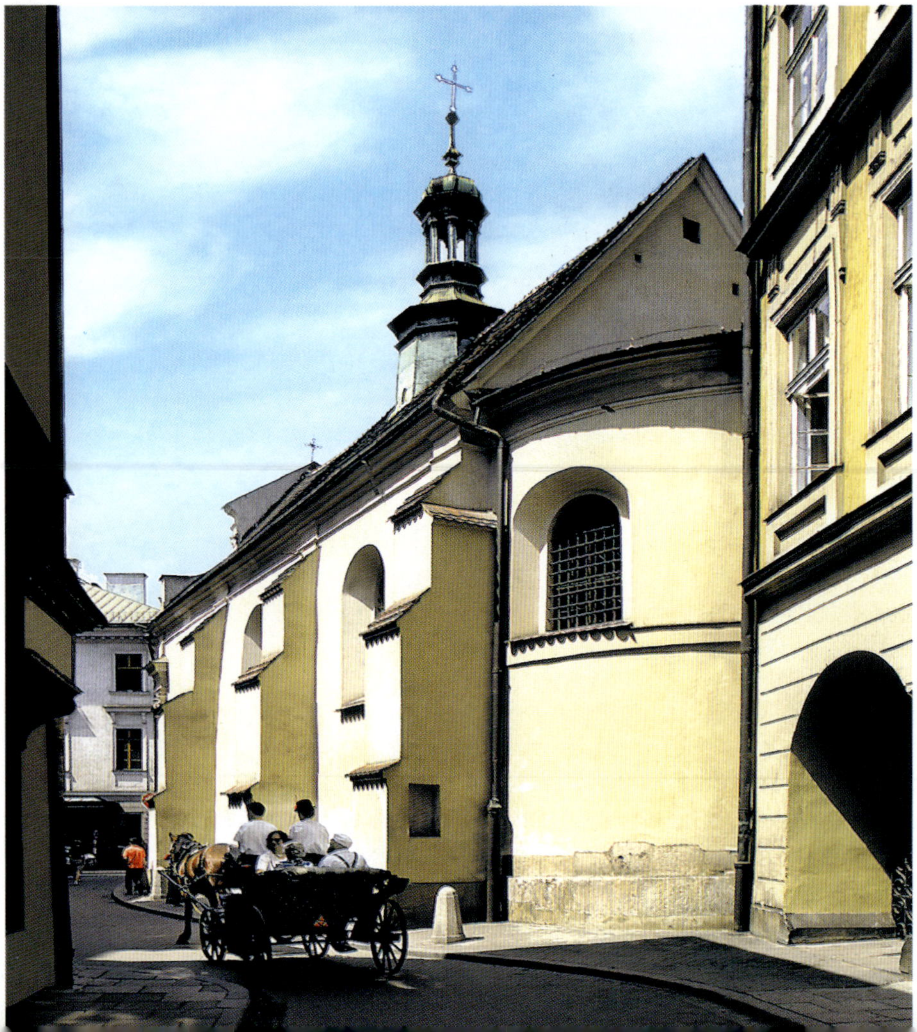

53. Floriańska Street, the Jagellonian University Pharmacy Museum, with over 20,000 items, the largest such museum in Poland and one of a few of its kind in the world

55. Facing page: Floriańska Street, Branch of the National Museum in Cracow – the Jan Matejko House, the museum of the life and work of the eminent Polish 19th-century historical painter

54. St Thomas' Street, one of the streets laid out in the city foundation plan (1257), with the Church of SS John the Baptist and John the Evangelist, originally Romanesque (first half of the 12th c.), rebuilt in the 14th c. and extended in the 17th and 18th c.

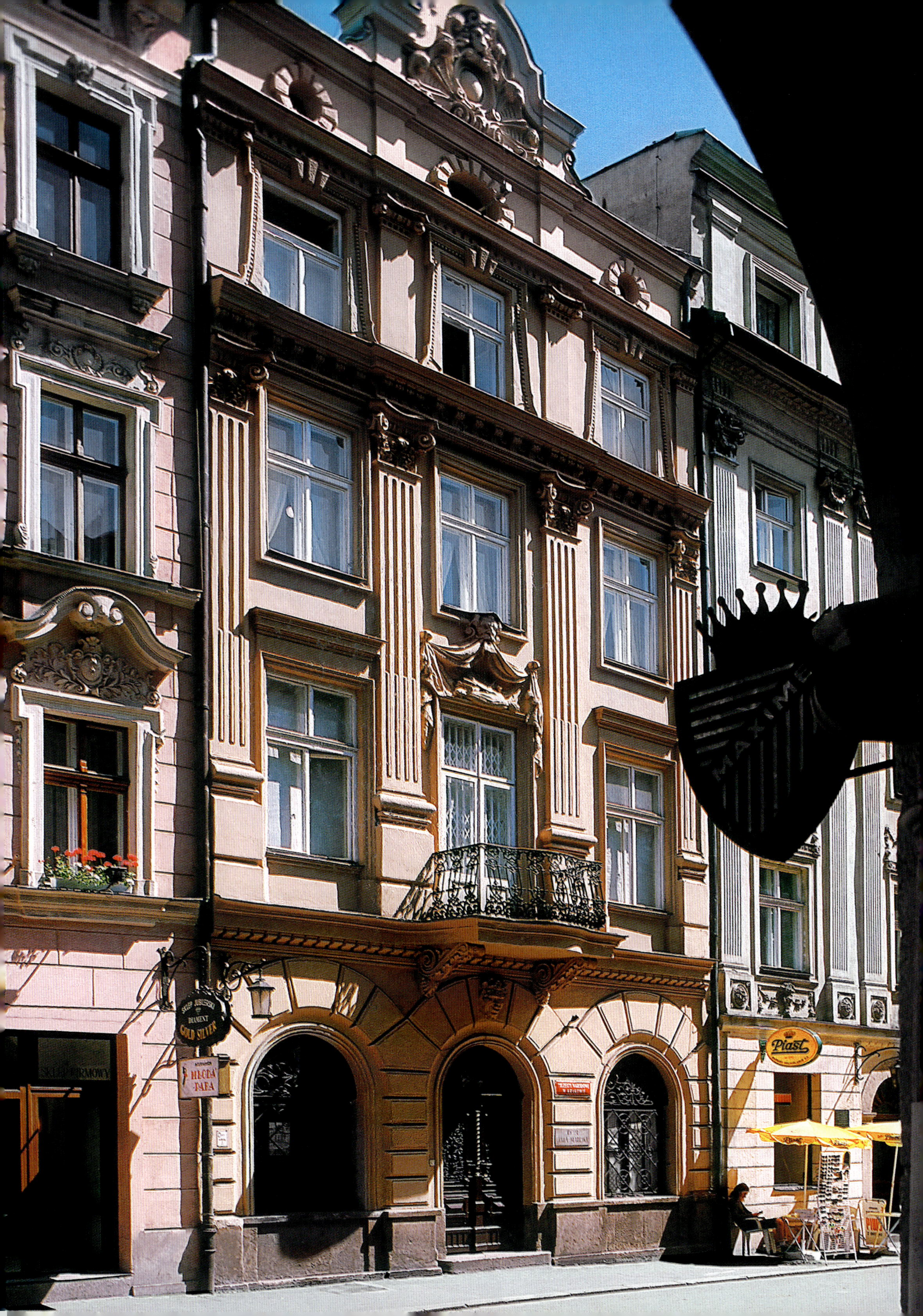
DIAMENT
GOLD SILVER
Piast

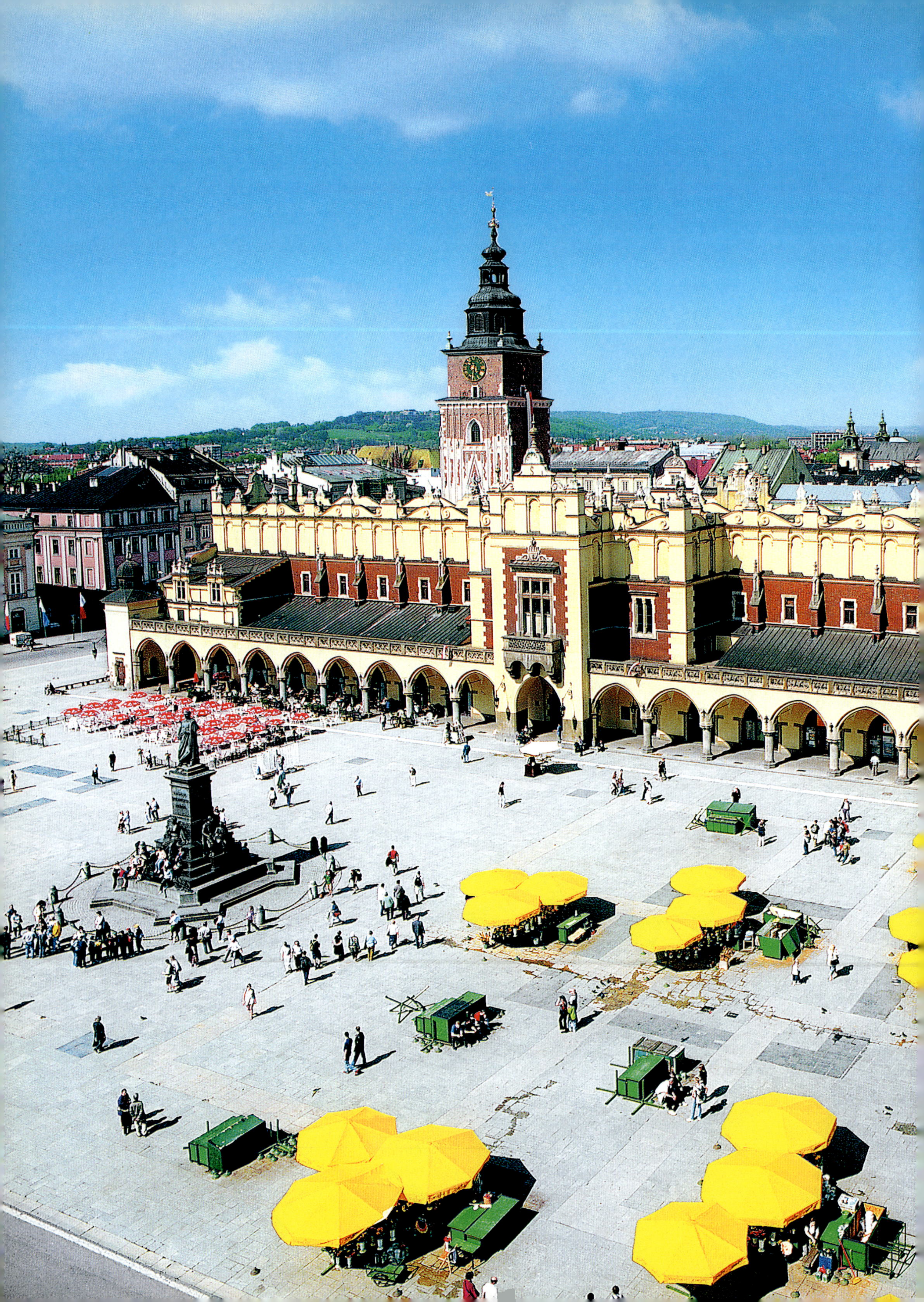

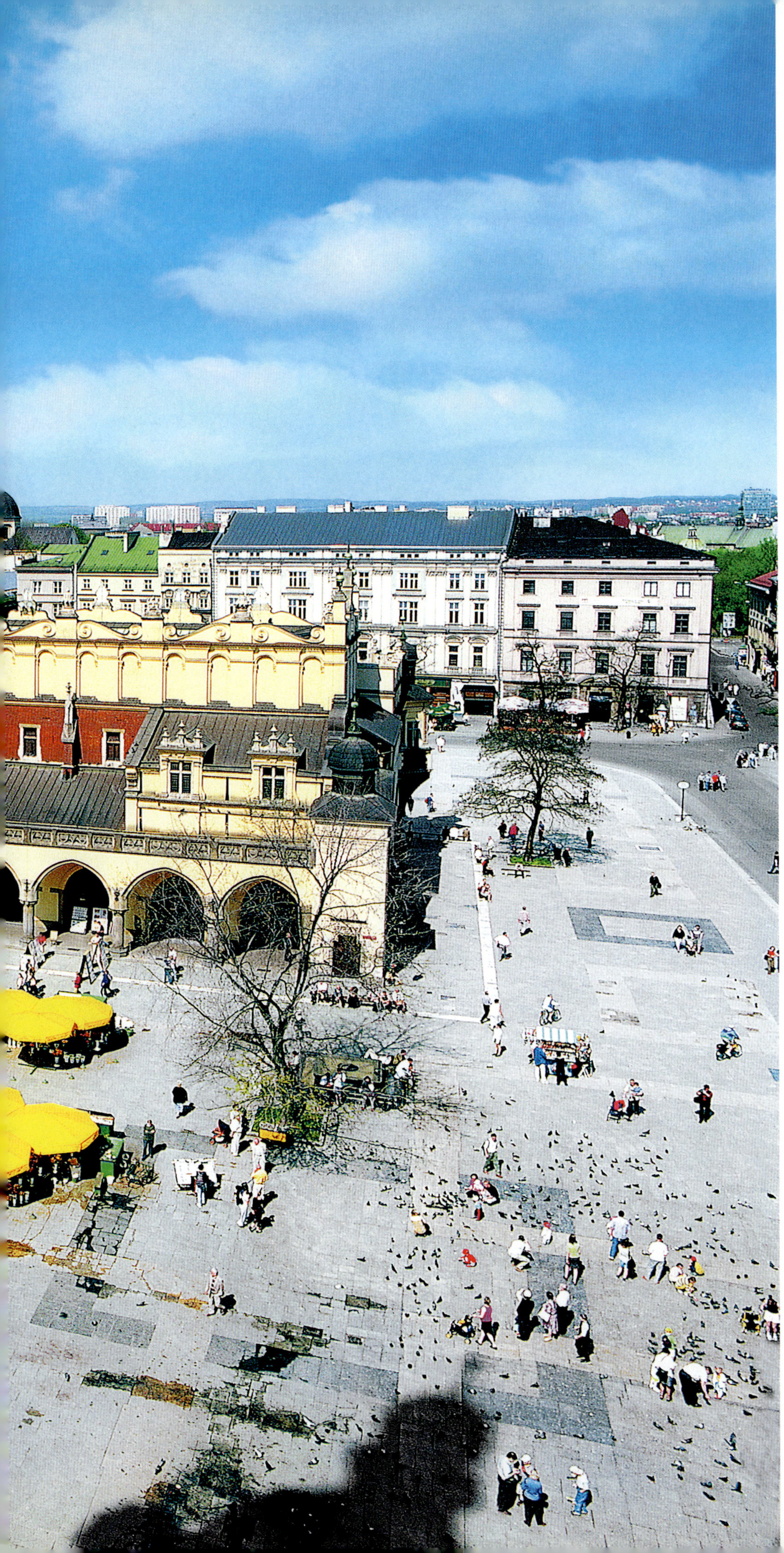

56. The Market Square, one of the largest squares in Europe (200 x 200 m), laid out at the time of the city foundation in 1257. In its centre is the Cloth Hall, with trading stalls, built about 1358 by King Casimir the Great. It was repeatedly rebuilt, its present shape being the result of the latest reconstruction in 1875-1879. In the background is the tower of the former Town Hall, one of the finest historic buildings in Cracow (acknowledged in 1383)

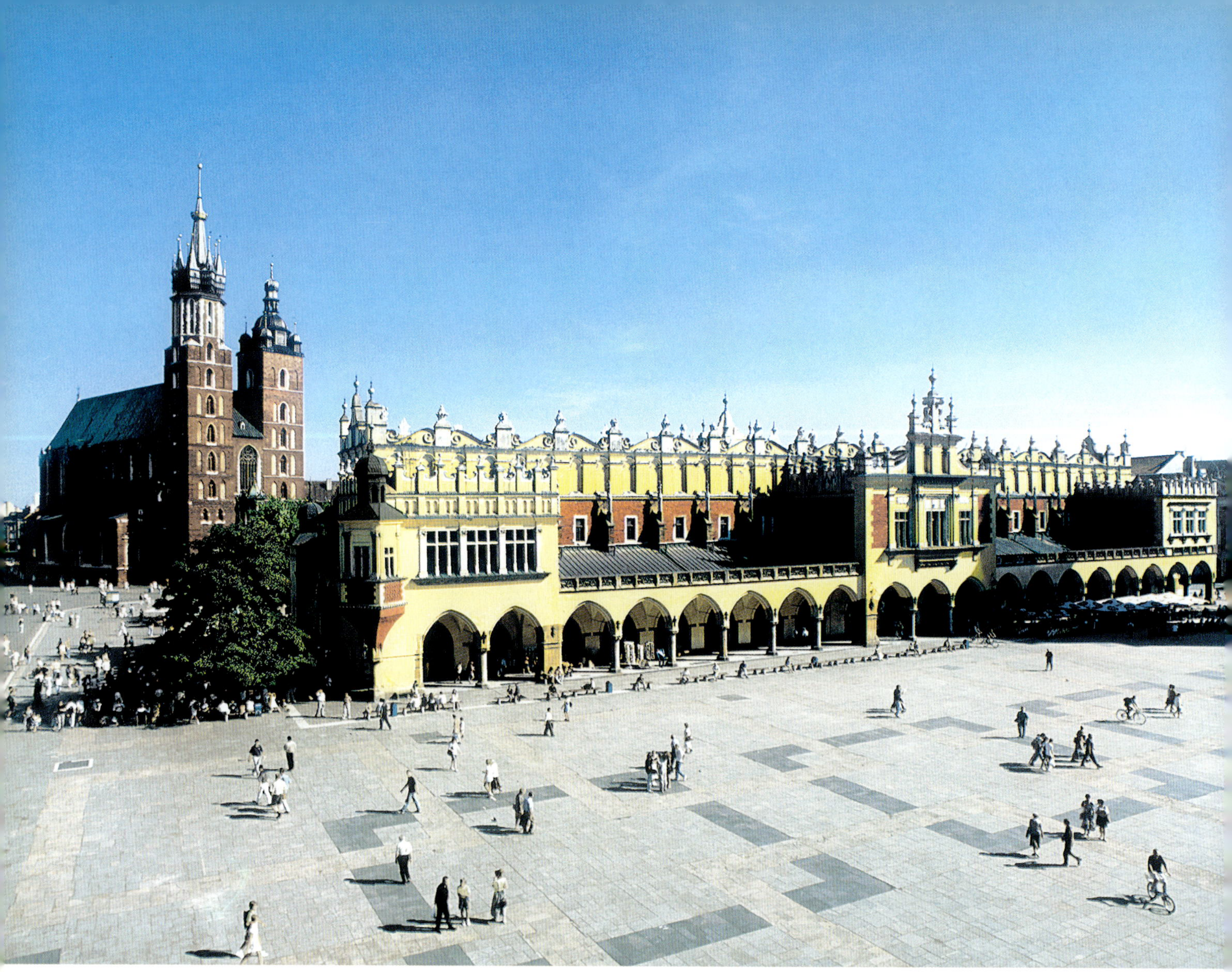

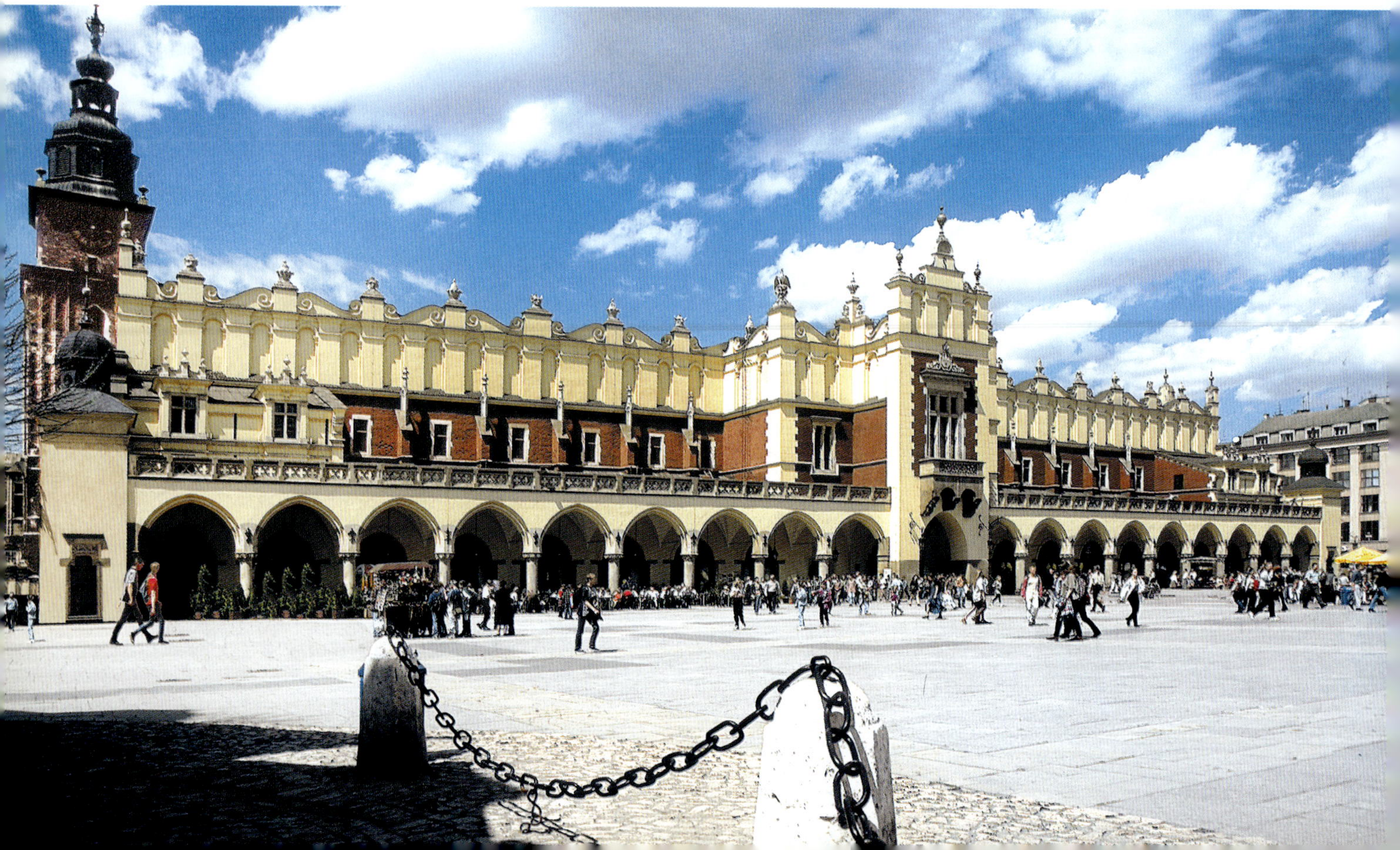

59. The Market Square, the monument of the great poet Adam Mickiewicz (unveiled in 1898), the Cloth Hall in the background

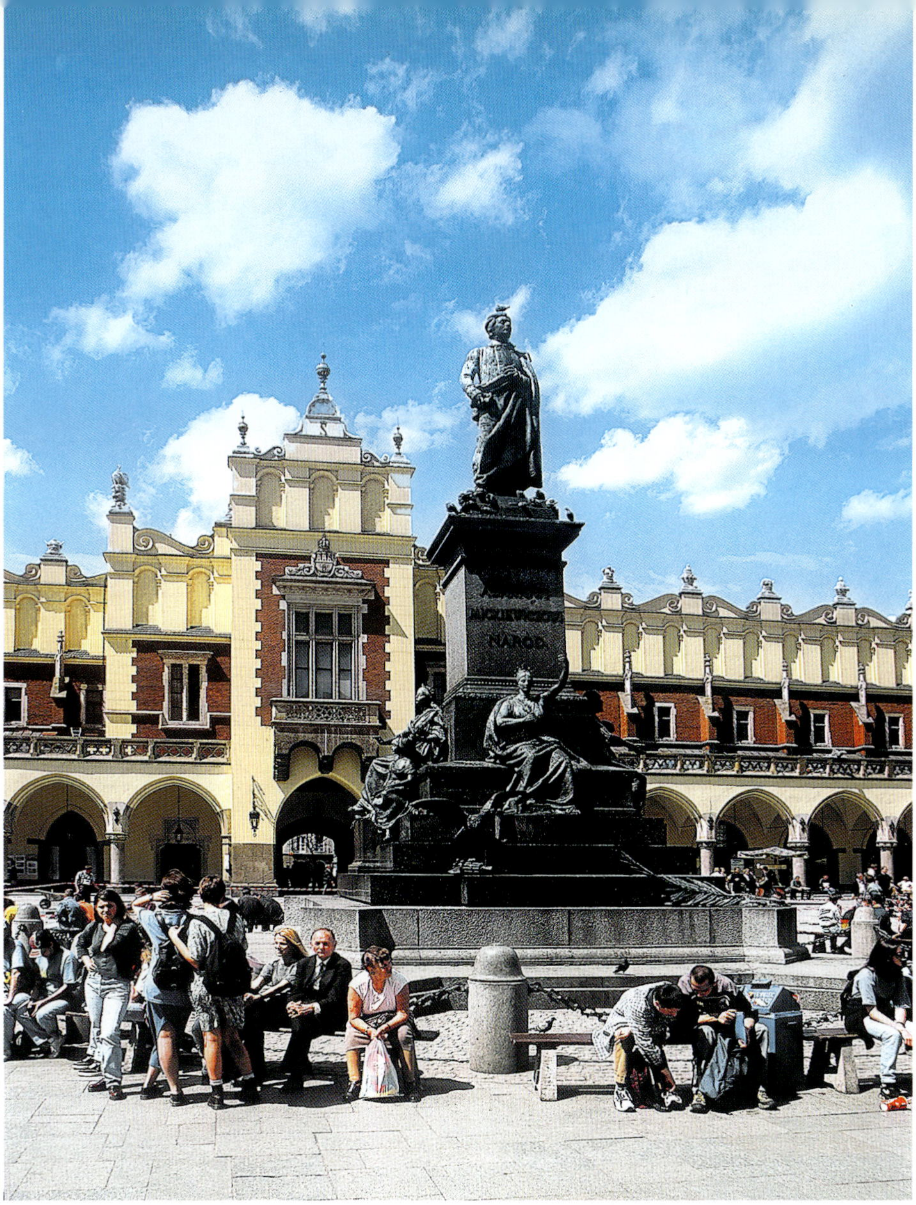

57-58. Facing page: a view from the north-west to the Market Square and the Cloth Hall , in the background the Gothic St Mary's Church (second half of the 14th c.). Bottom: a view from the south-east to the Market Square, in the background the tower of the former Town Hall (14th c.)

60. The Market Square, the Cloth Hall; its upper floor houses a branch of the National Museum in Cracow, the Gallery of the Polish 19th-century Painting and Sculpture, which exhibits the work of such artists as Jan Matejko, Jacek Malczewski, Henryk Siemiradzki, Józef Chełmoński, Artur Grottger, Aleksander Gierymski, and Leon Wyczółkowski

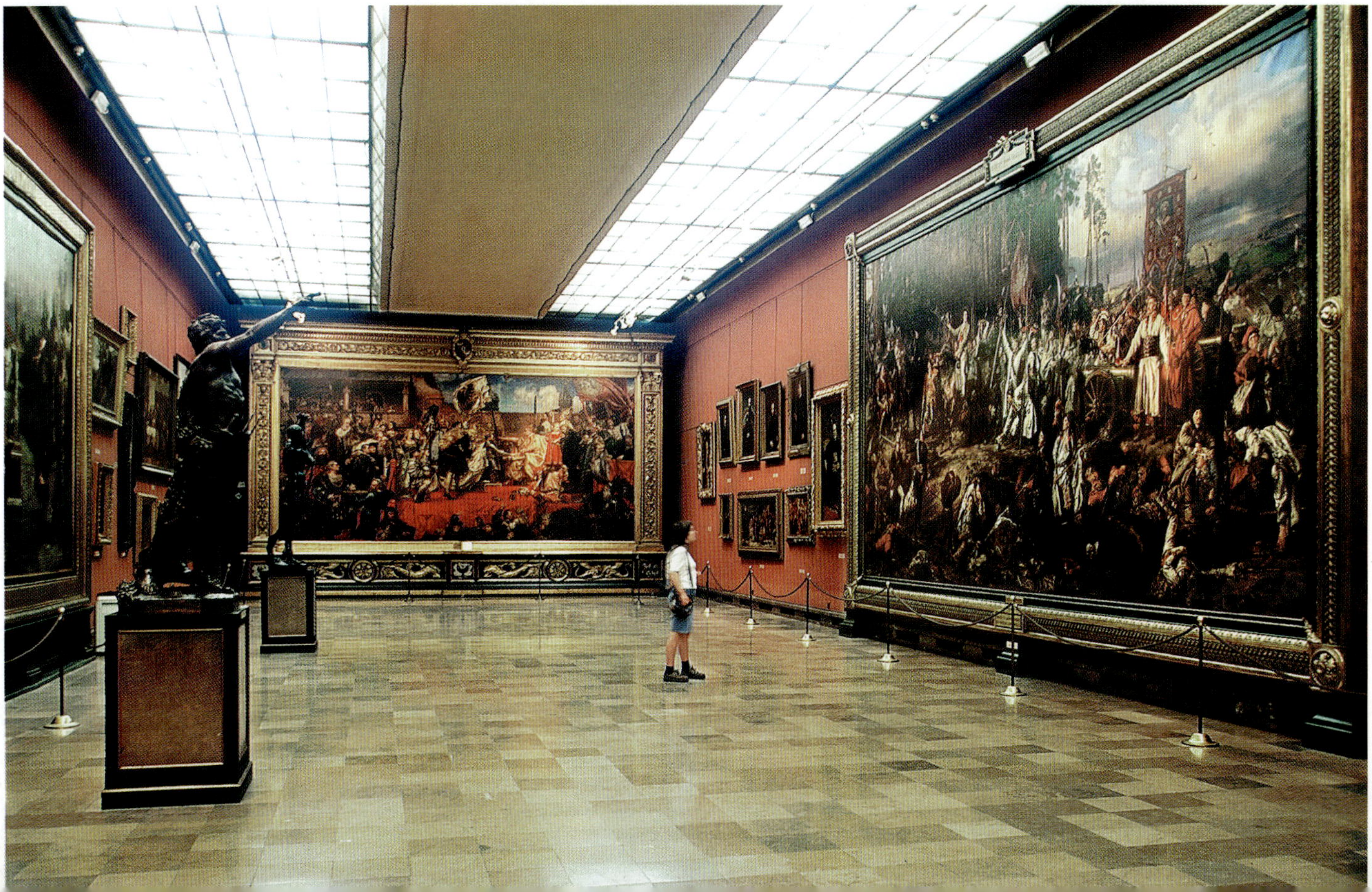

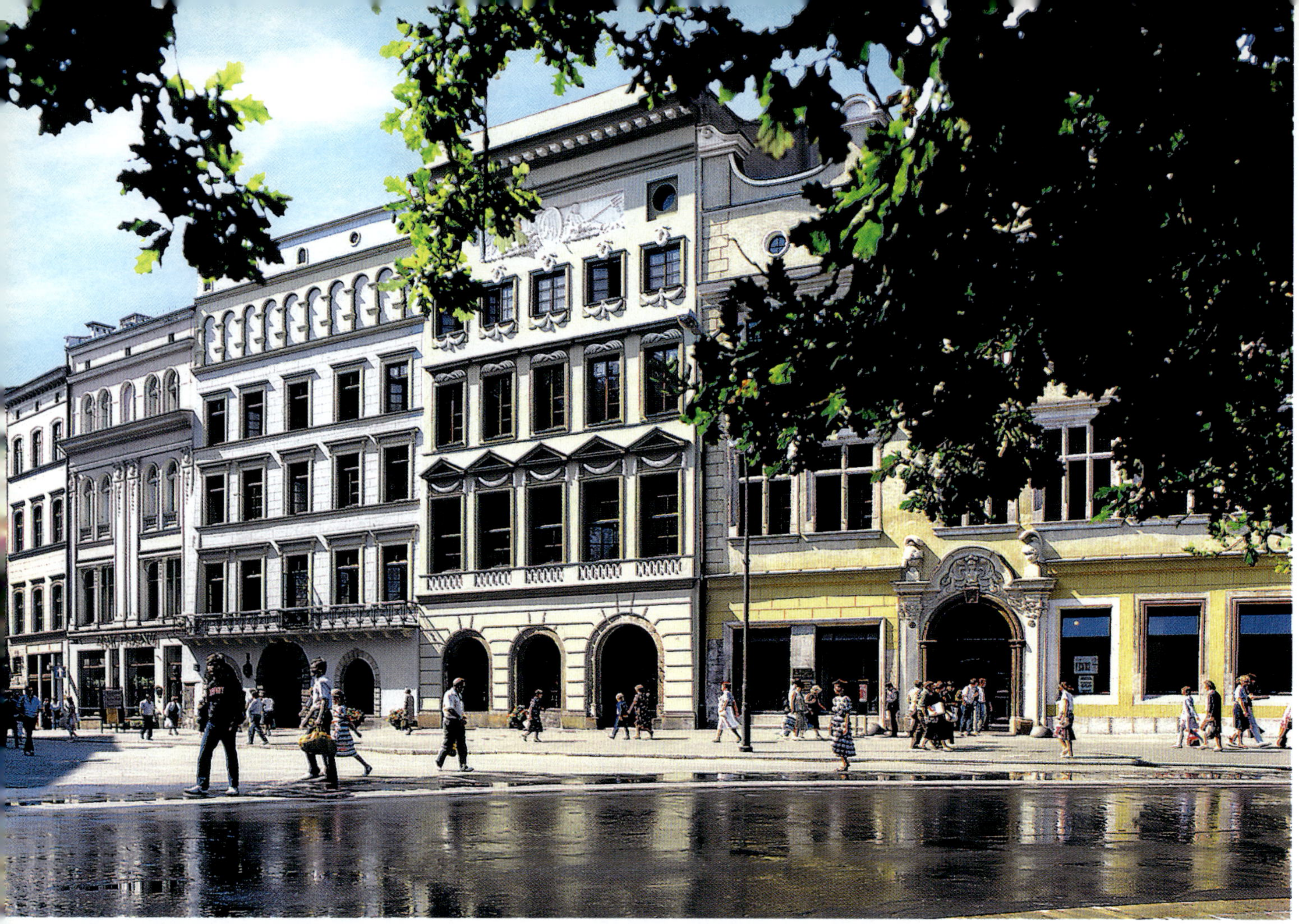

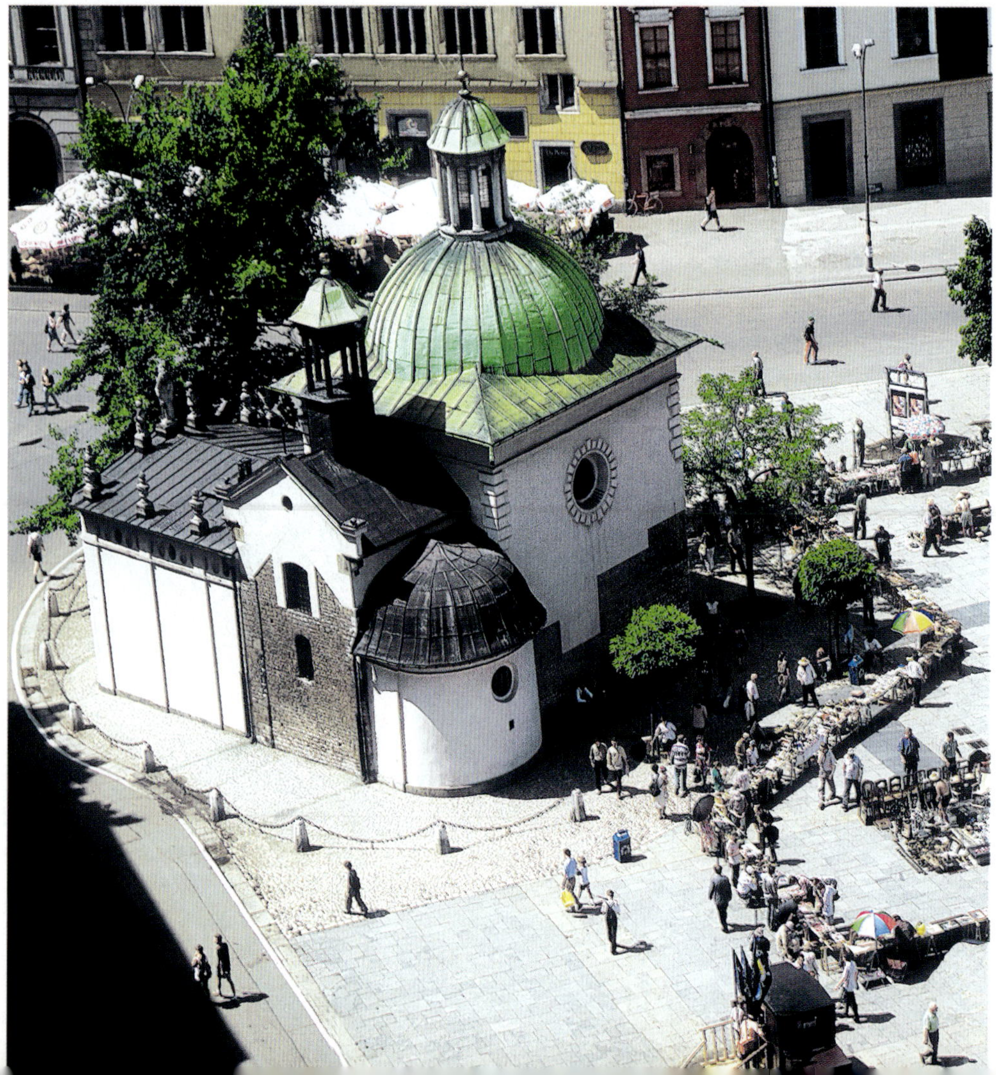

61-62. The Market Square is fringed with fine historic houses and mansions. In the 16th and 17th c. they were the residences of the wealthiest aristocratic and middle-class families. Bottom: St Adalbert's Church in the Market Square; Romanesque, built at the turn of the 11th and 12th c., and thoroughly rebuilt in the 17th and 18th c. Its undercroft houses the exhibition of archaeological finds in the church and the Market Square

63. Facing page: the Market Square, the tower of the former Town Hall (14th c.), one of the finest historic buildings in Cracow. On its second floor is a branch of the Historical Museum of the City of Cracow, which exhibits historical items from its past

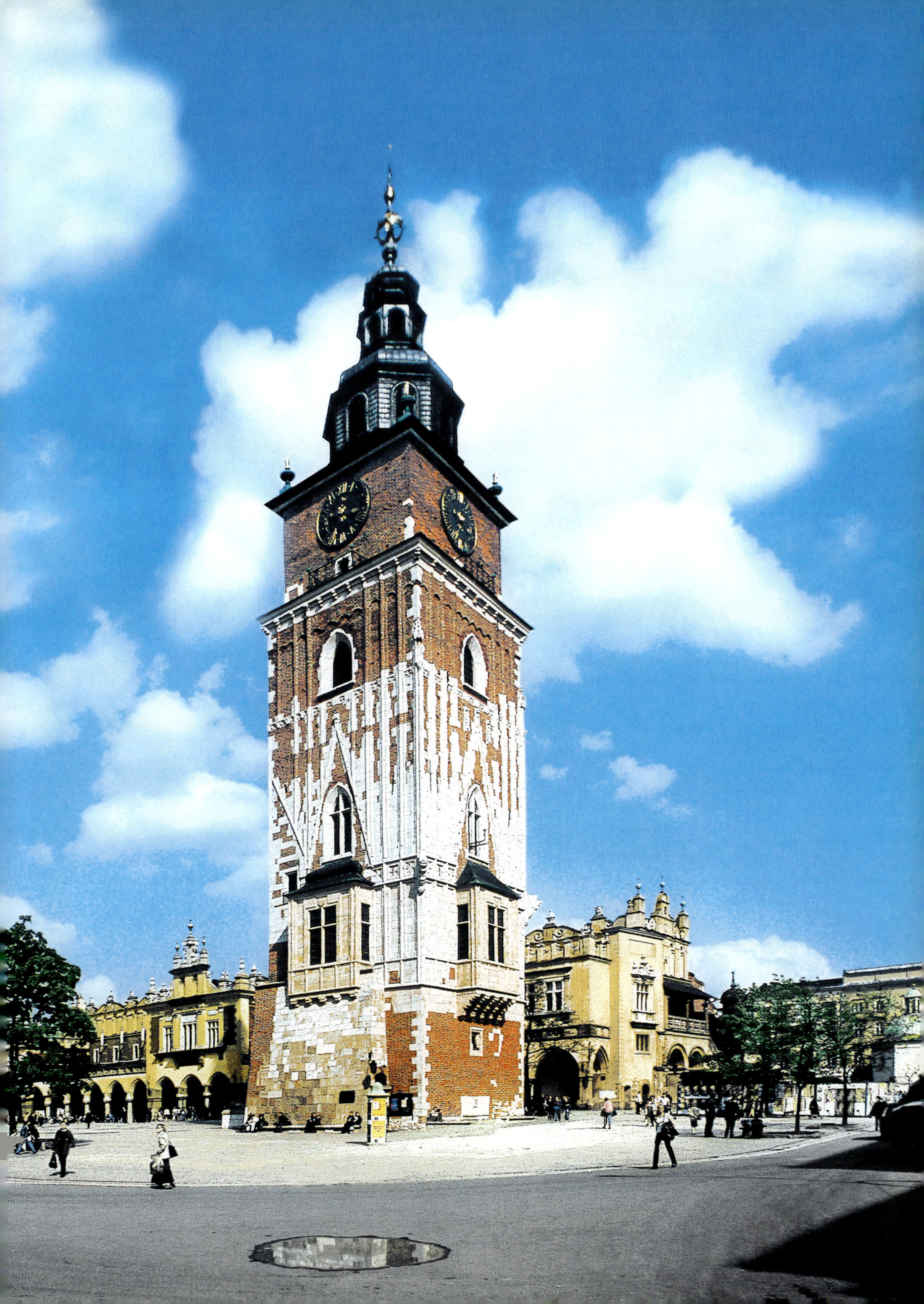

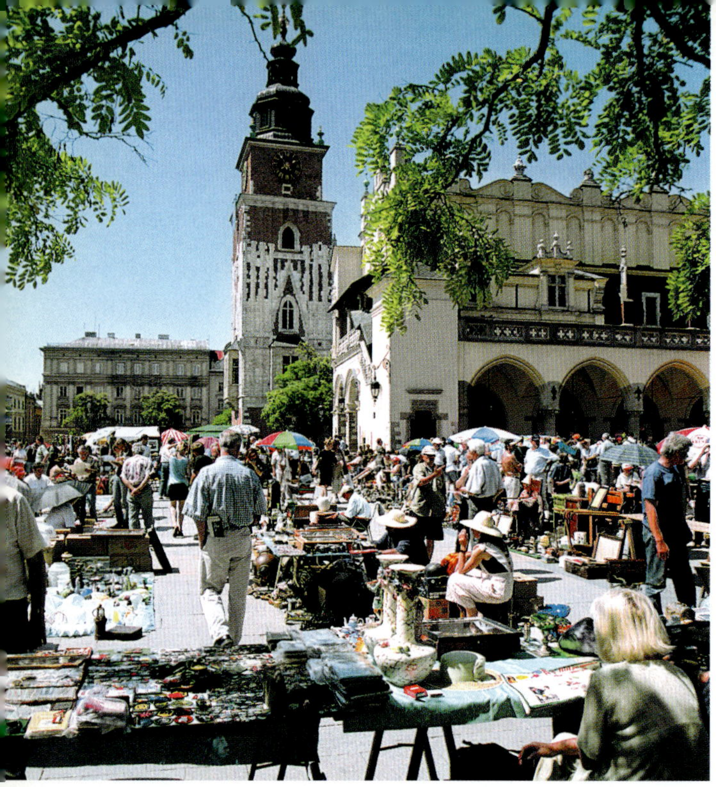
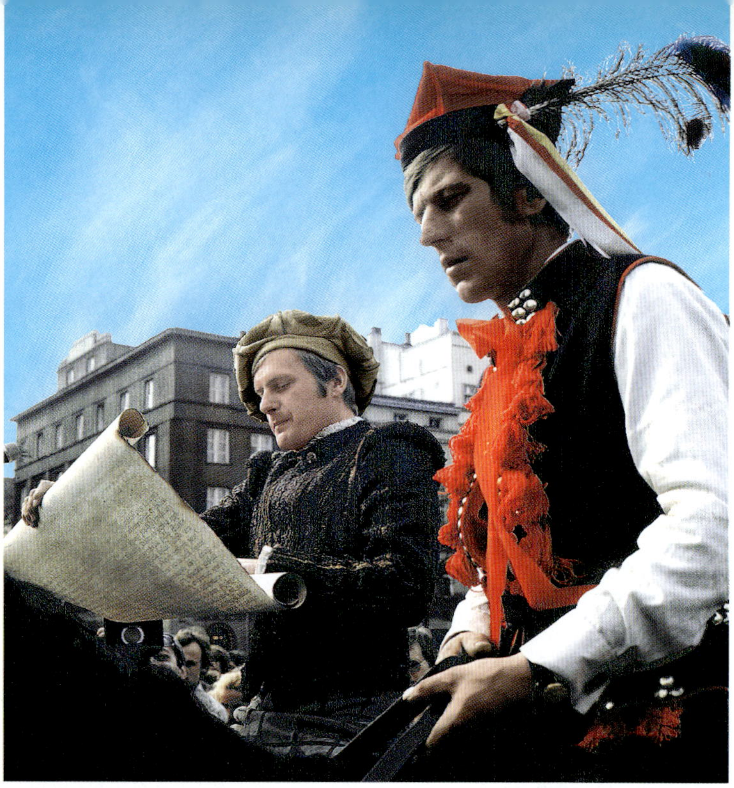
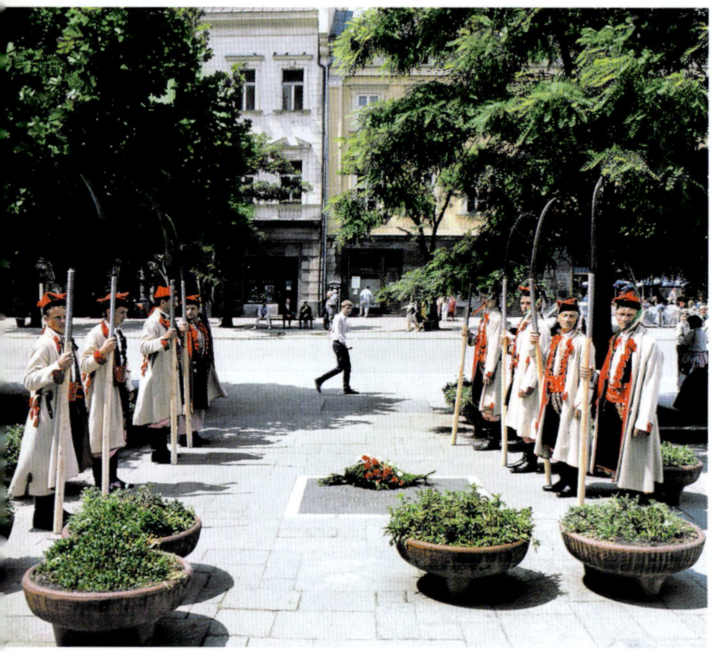
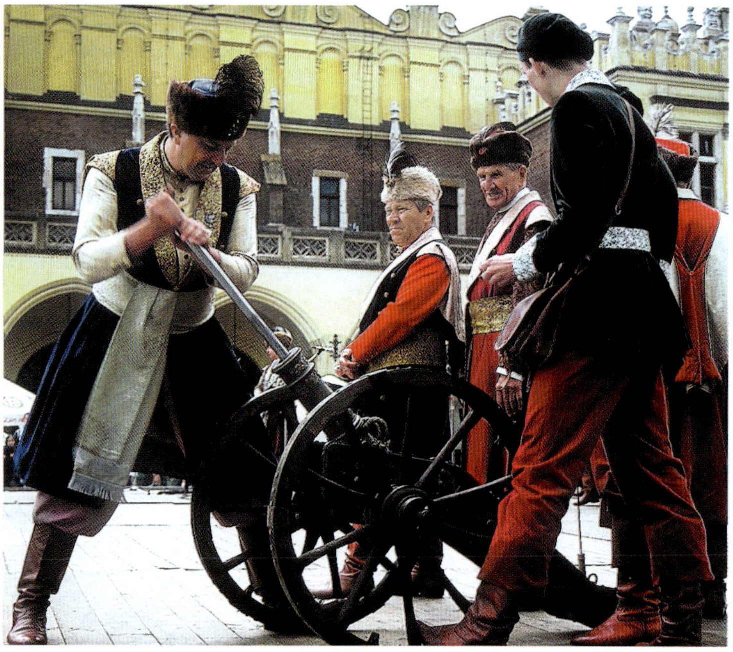
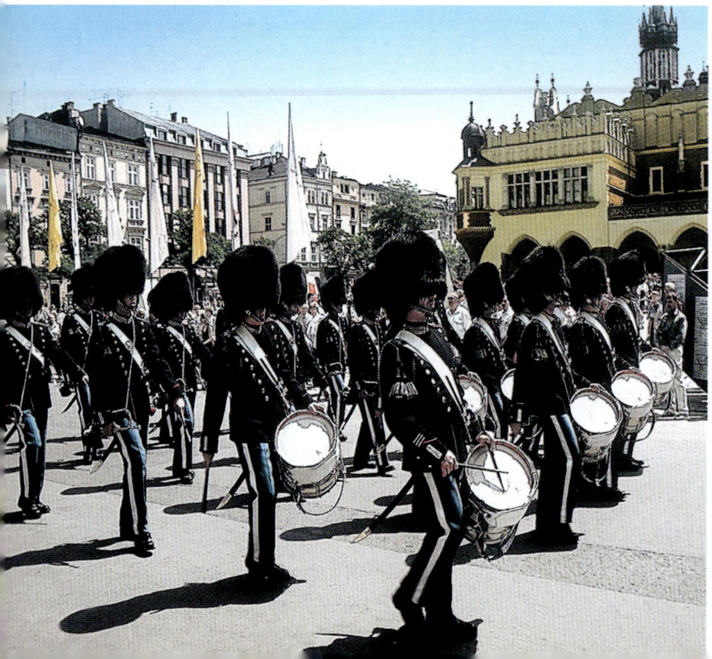
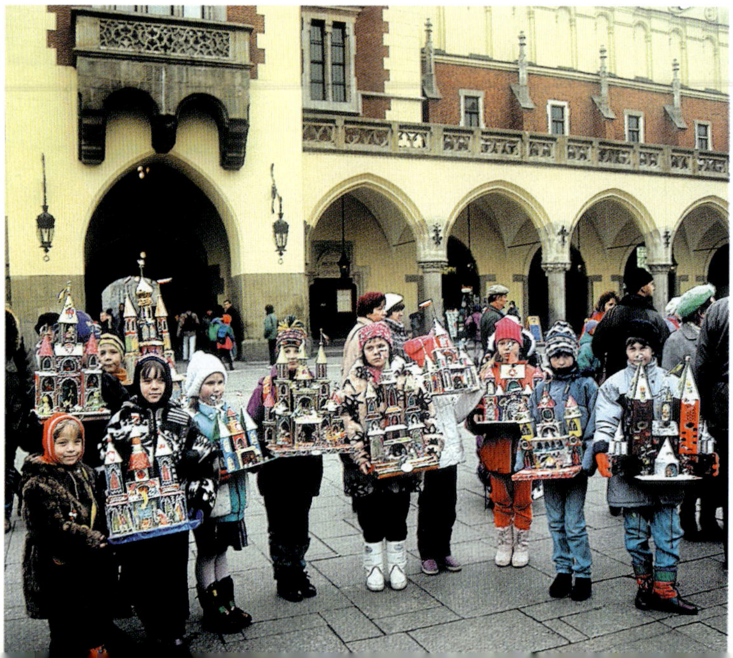

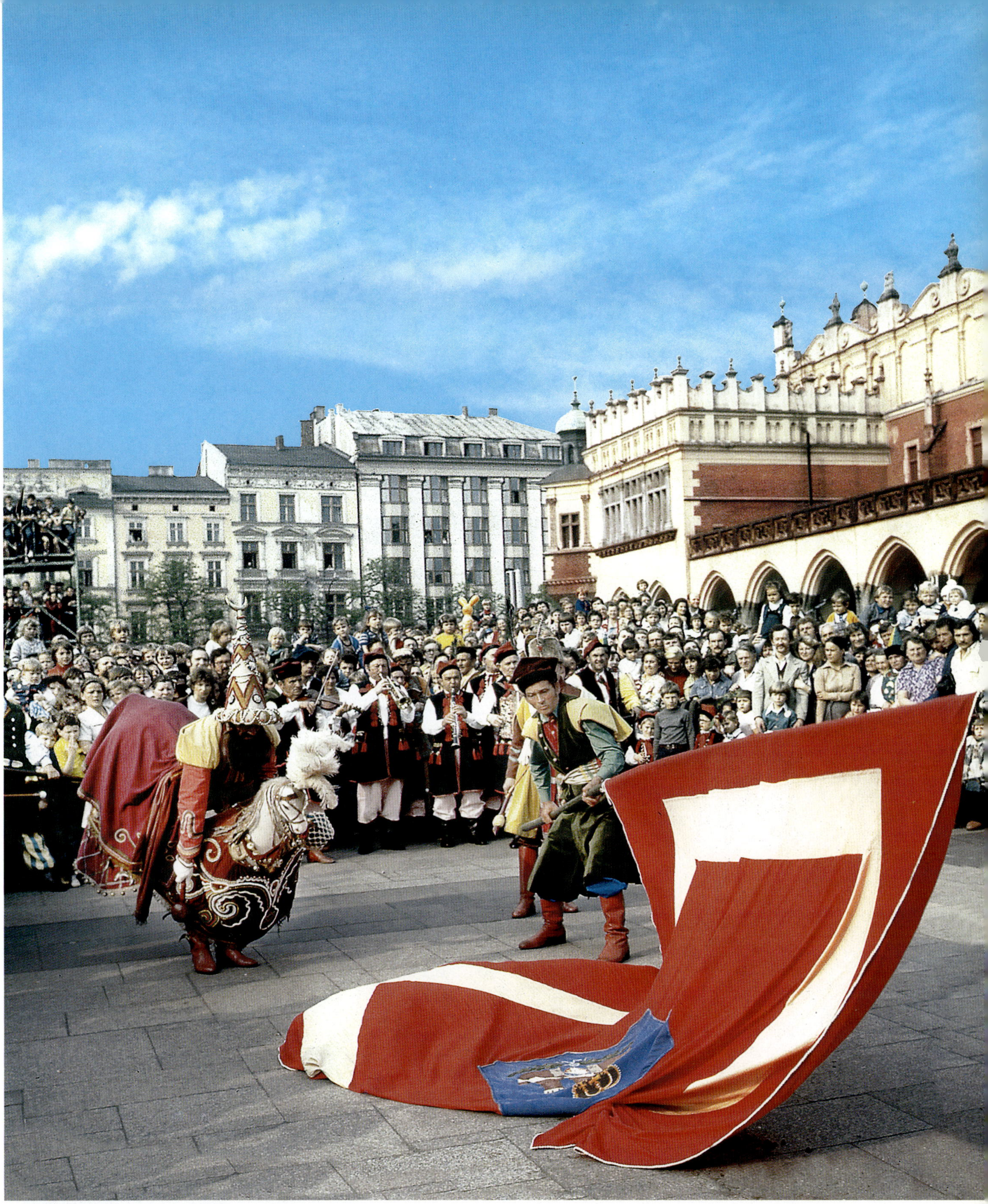

64-70. The Market Square is the venue for traditional ceremonies and festivities. Facing page: jumble sales take place there and the student feast of Juvenalia (top); anniversary ceremonies at the plaque commemorating General Tadeusz Kościuszko, and inaugurations of the king of the 400-years-old Rooster Brotherhood (centre); parades at the meetings of military bands, and contests for the best Cracow Christmas Cradle in December (bottom). Above: the pranks of Lajkonik, the annual custom dating back probably to the Middle Ages

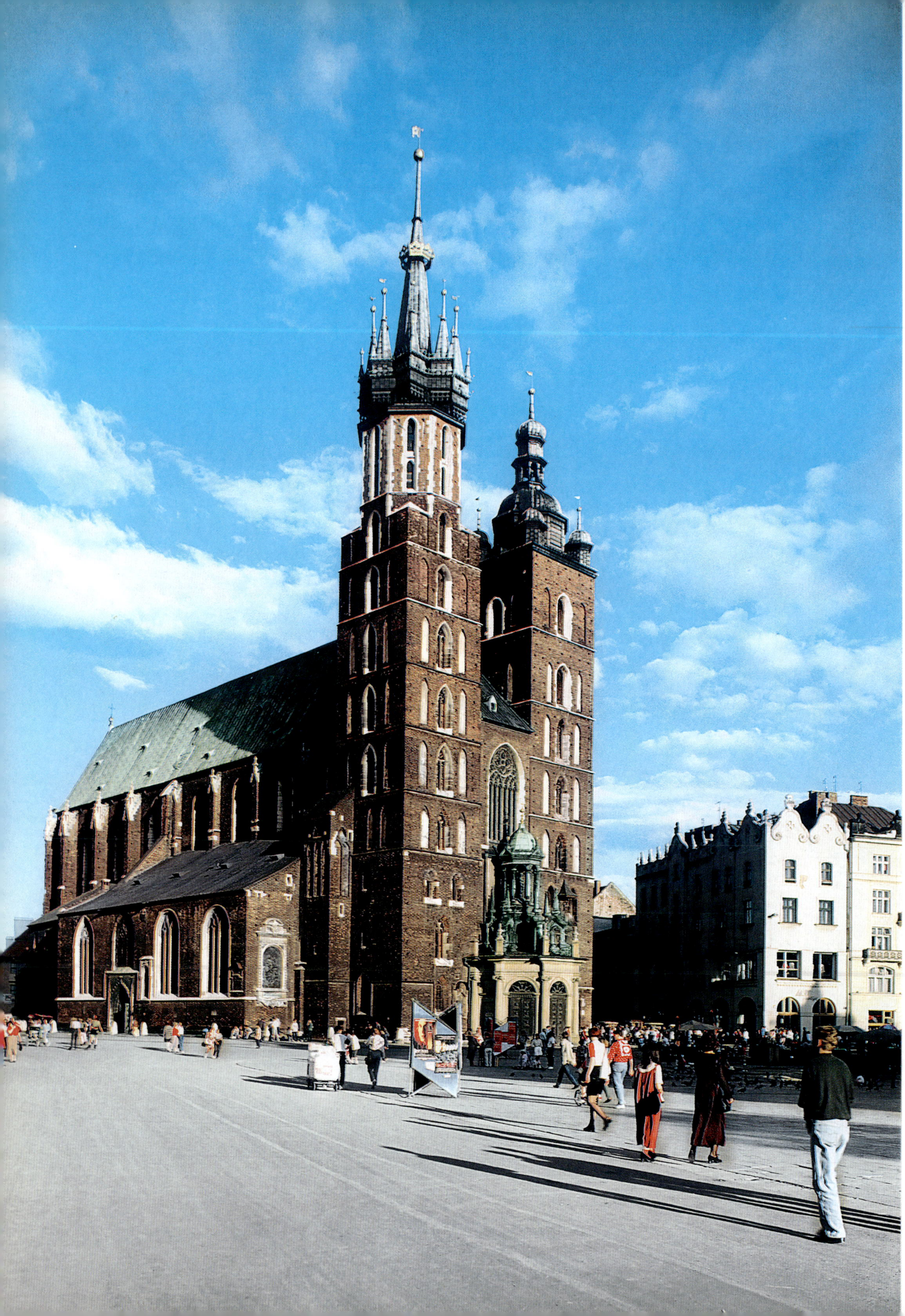

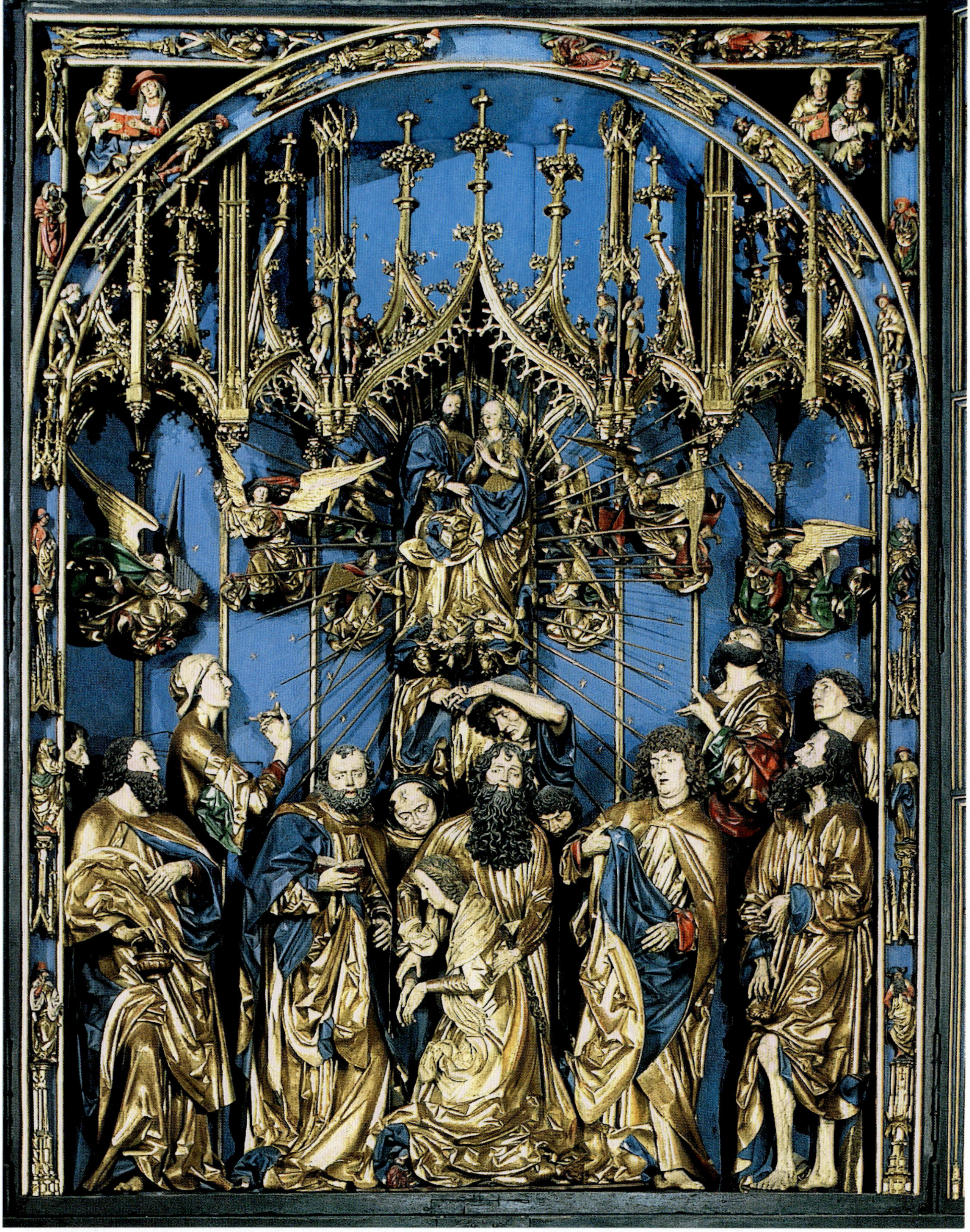

71-72. Facing page: the Gothic St Mary's Church (second half of the 14th c.), in 1962 raised to the rank of basilica minor by Pope John XXIII. Repeatedly rebuilt and extended, with fine furnishings, it is among the finest historic buildings in Cracow. Above: the central part of the High Altar, masterfully carved in linden in 1477-1489 by Wit Stwosz (Veit Stoss) and his disciples

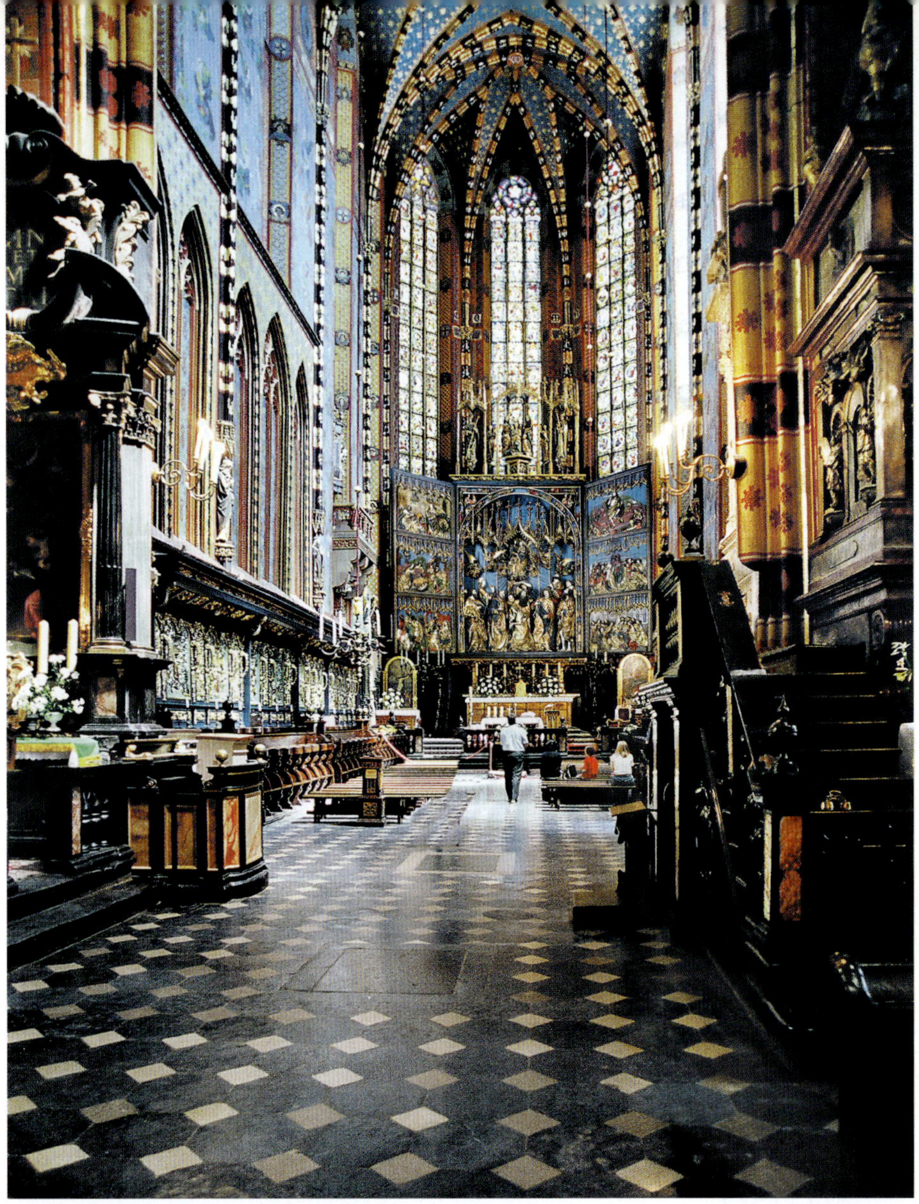

73. St Mary's Church, a view to the open High Altar carved by Wit Stwosz (Veit Stoss) and his disciples (1477-1489)

74-75. Bottom: St Mary's Church, the nave, the late-Gothic crucifix (left), much influenced by the work of Wit Stwosz (Veit Stoss, c.1520), and the monumental memorial to the Cellari family in the presbytery, one of the wealthiest and most powerful middle-class families in the 16th and 17th c. (right)

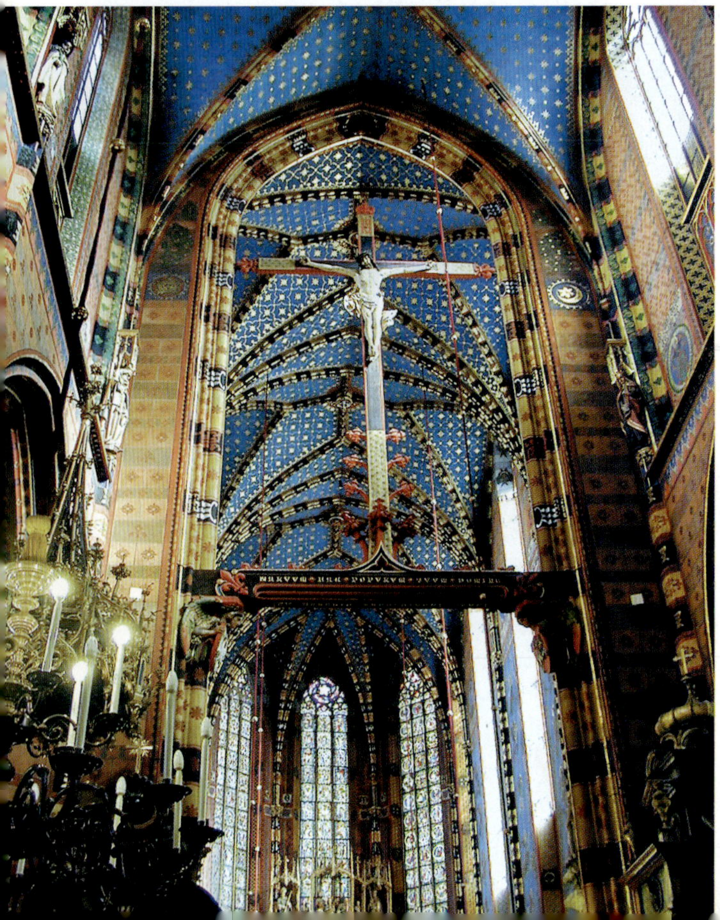

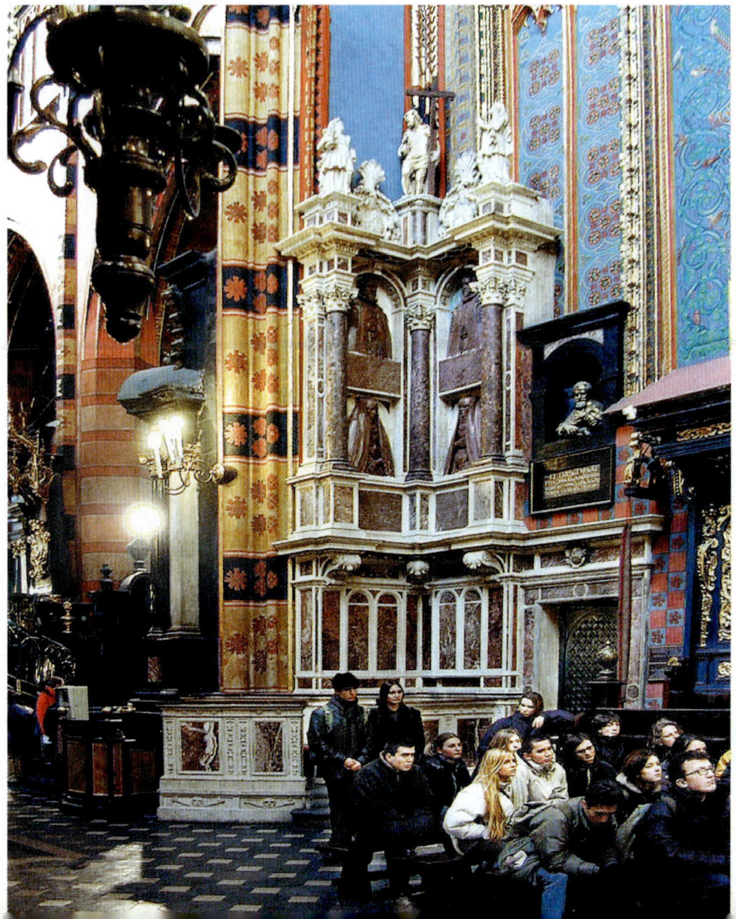

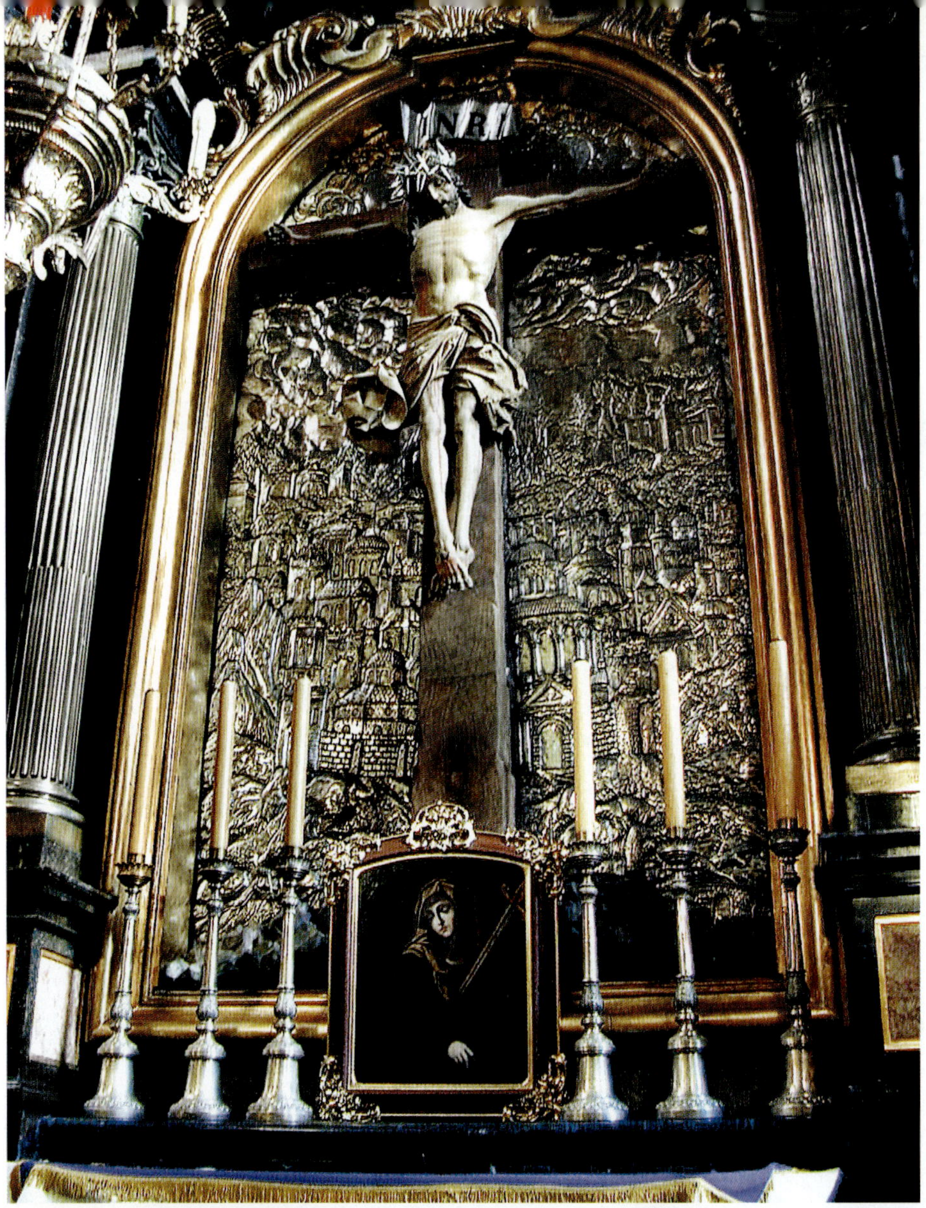

76. St Mary's Church, the south aisle, the late-Baroque altar (first half of the 18th c.), with the crucifix carved by Wit Stwosz (Veit Stoss, before 1496) and placed against the background of silver foil depicting Jerusalem.

77-78. Bottom: from the taller tower of St Mary's Church, which from the Middle Ages used to be a watch-tower, a bugle call is played, now every hour, to the four sides of the world (left). A view from the south to St Mary's Church (right)

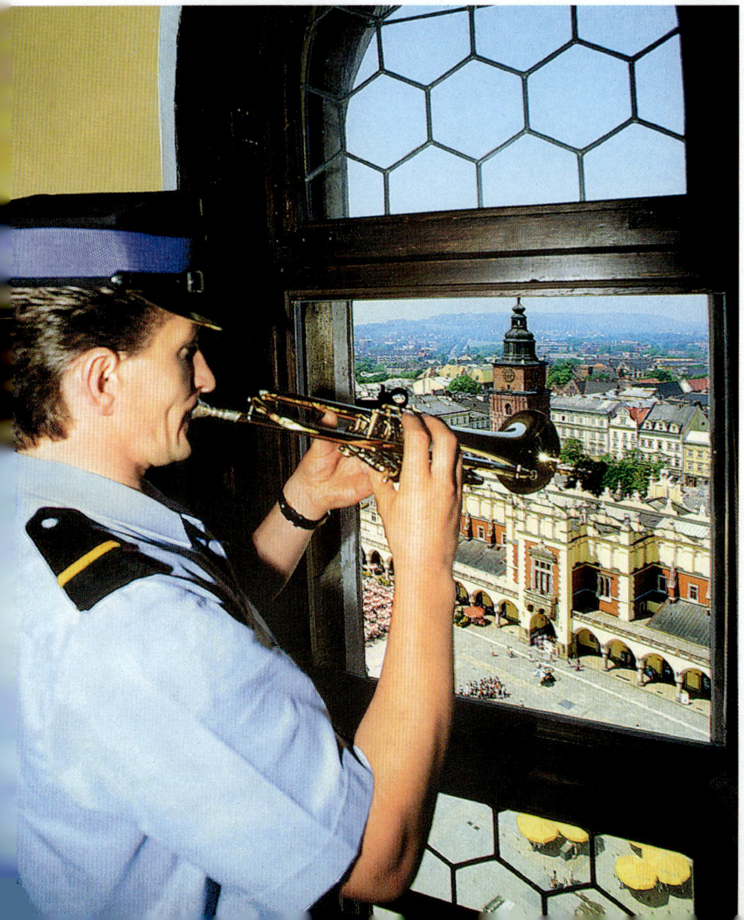

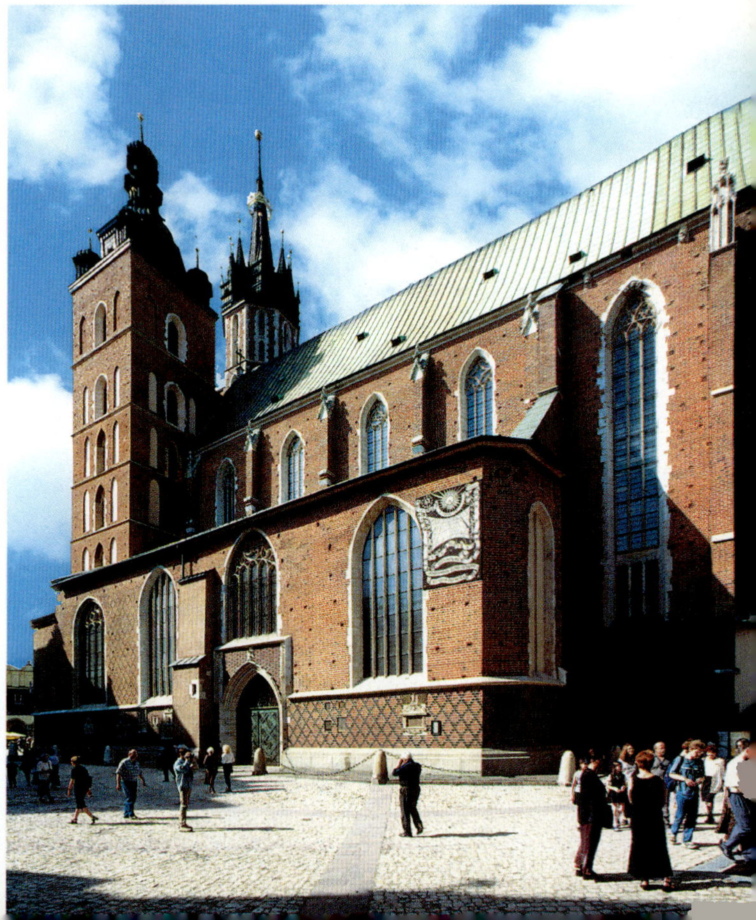

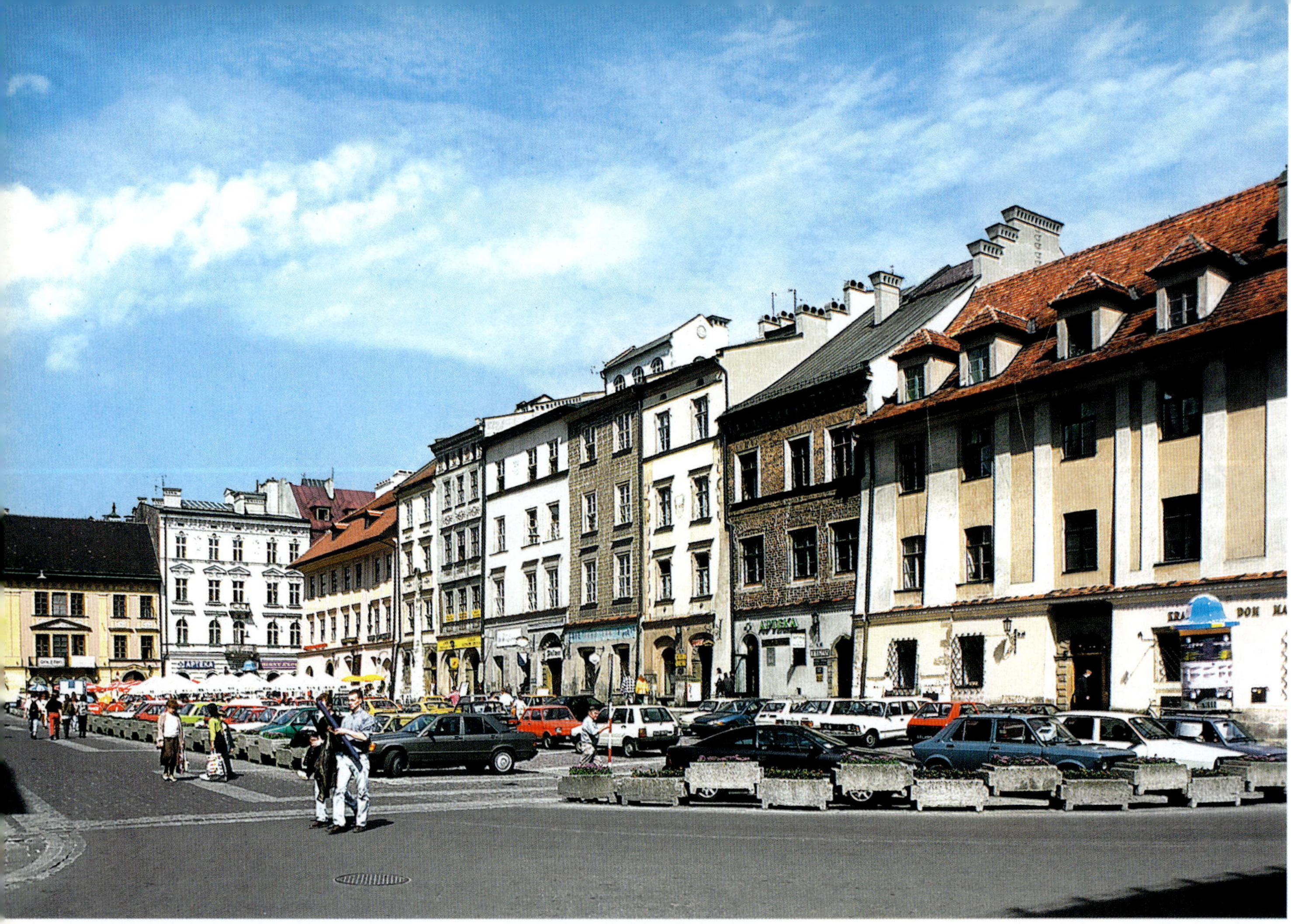

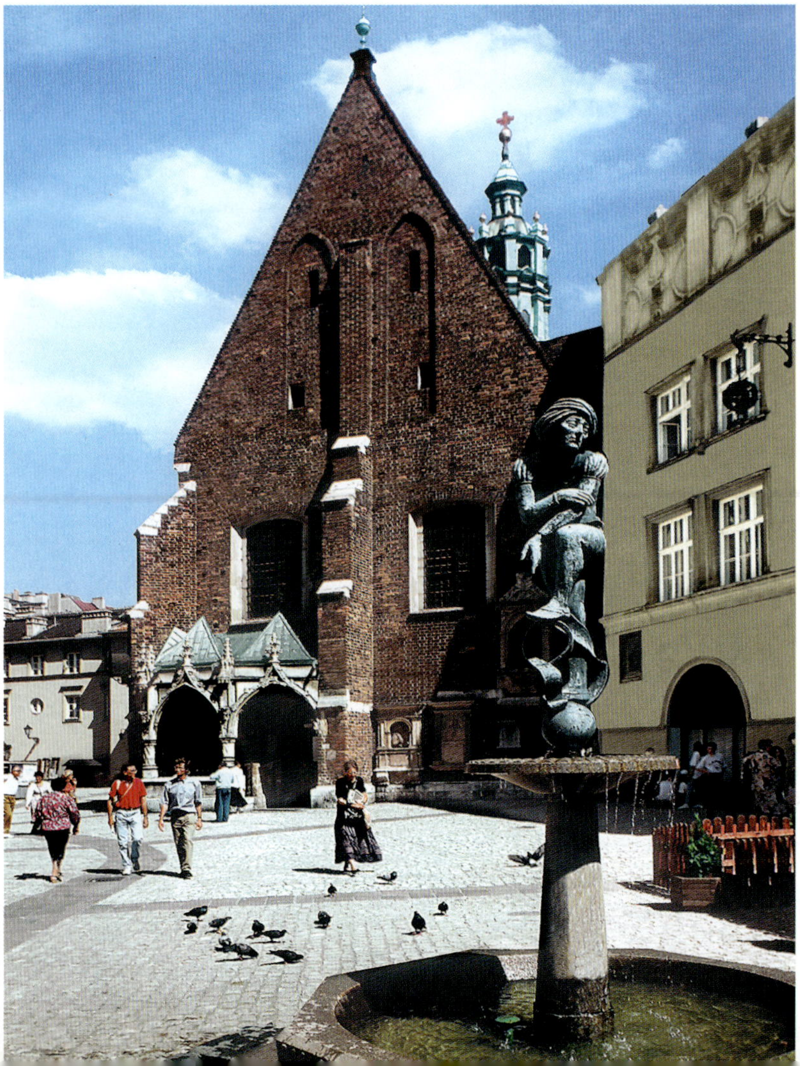

79. The Small Market Square, at the city foundation (1257) designed as a supplementary area for the Market Square; the east front, with the middle-class houses from the 17th and 18th c.

81. Facing page: Jagiellońska Street, Collegium Maius, the oldest building of the Jagellonian University. First lectures were held there in 1400. Now it houses the Jagellonian University Museum

80. St Mary's Square, the Gothic St Barbara's Church (14th c.), in the foreground the fountain with the figure modelled on the one in the High Altar by Wit Stwosz (Veit Stoss), founded by the Cracow craftsmen as a gift to the city in 1958.

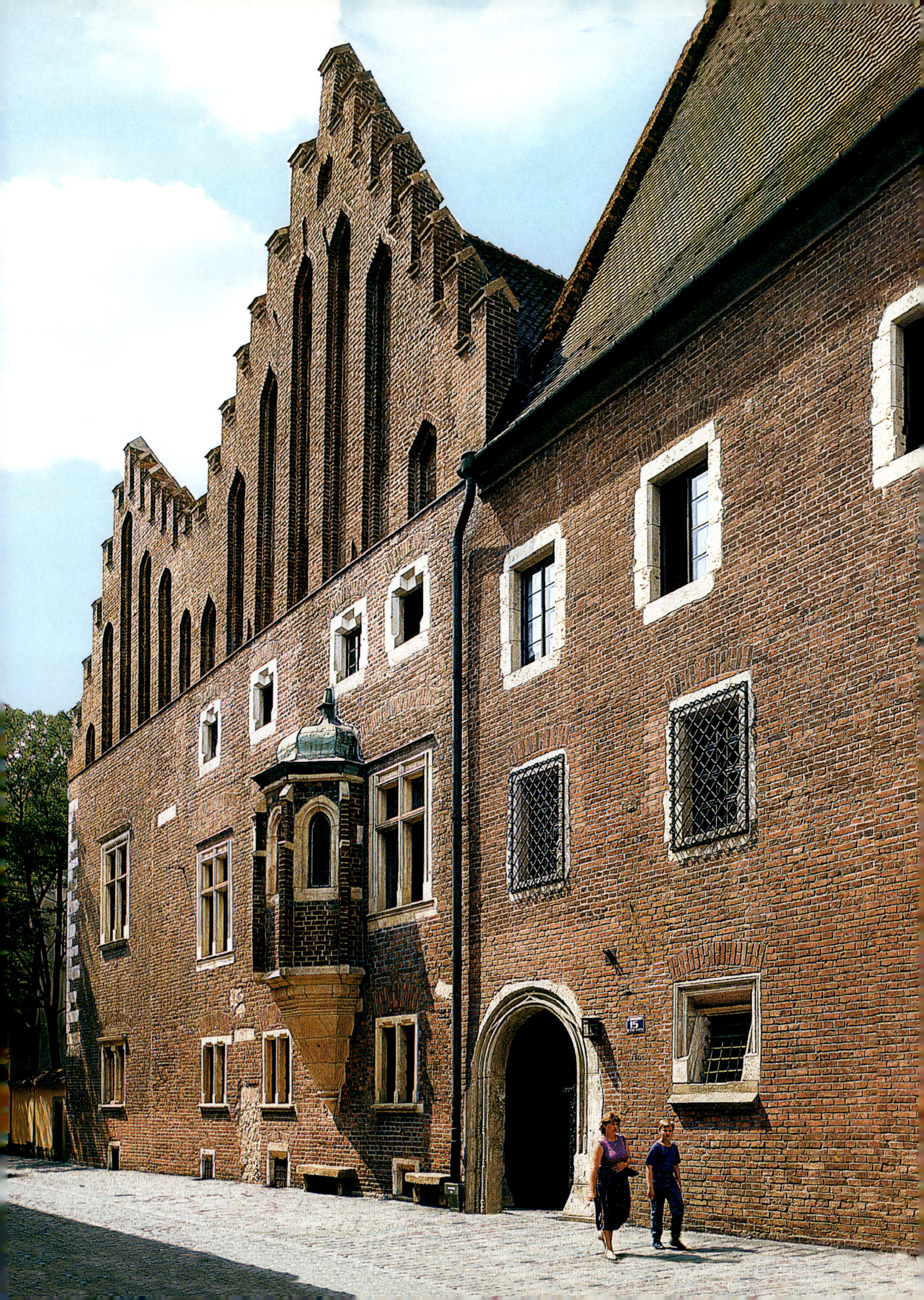
15

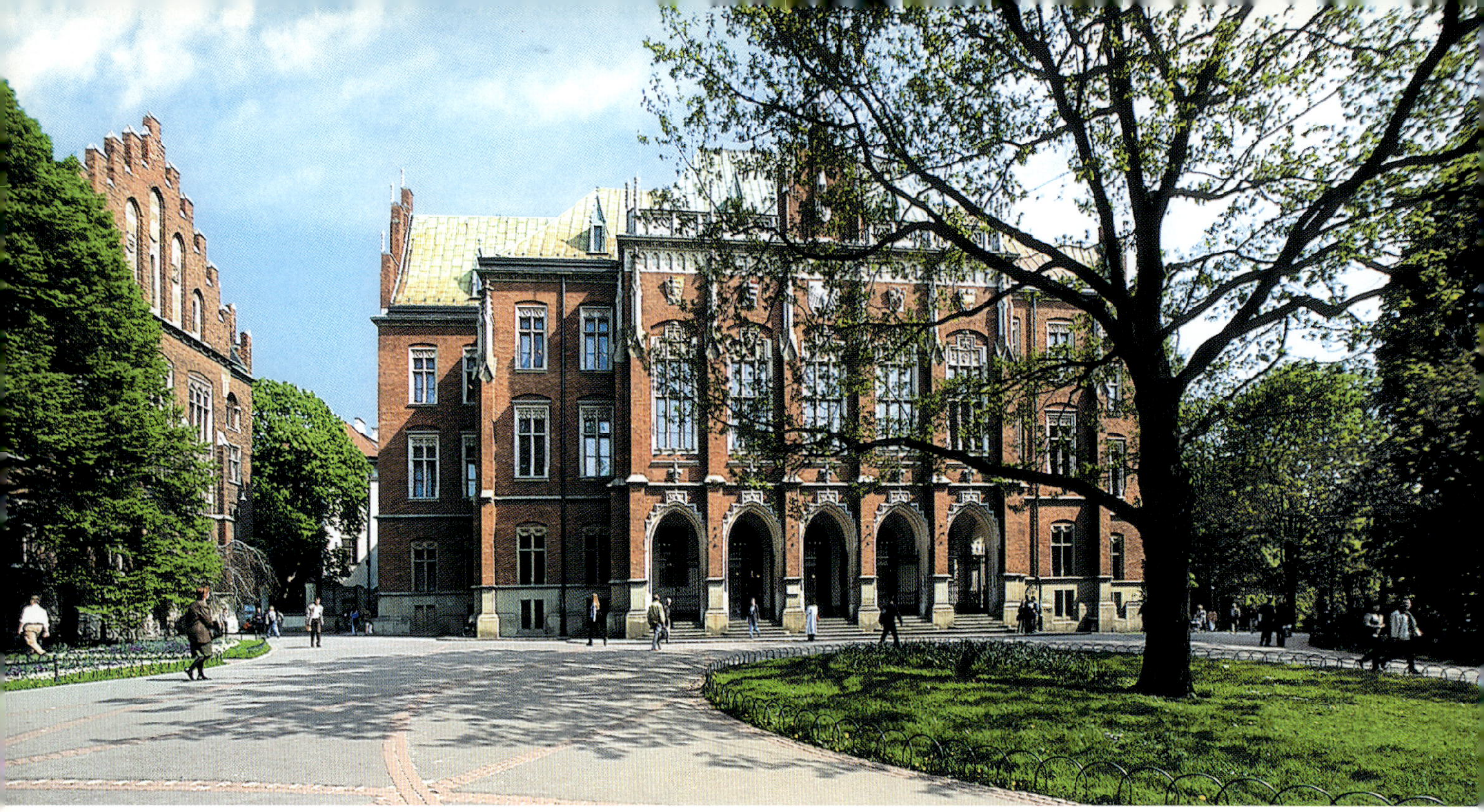

82-83. Top: the neo-Gothic building of Collegium Novum, Jagellonian University (1883-1887). In the Great Hall on the second floor the ceremonies of inaugurating a new academic year take place, as well as academic conferences, and honorary doctorates are conferred. Also, the Rector of the Jagellonian University has his office there. Bottom: the arcaded court of Collegium Maius (1493-1497)

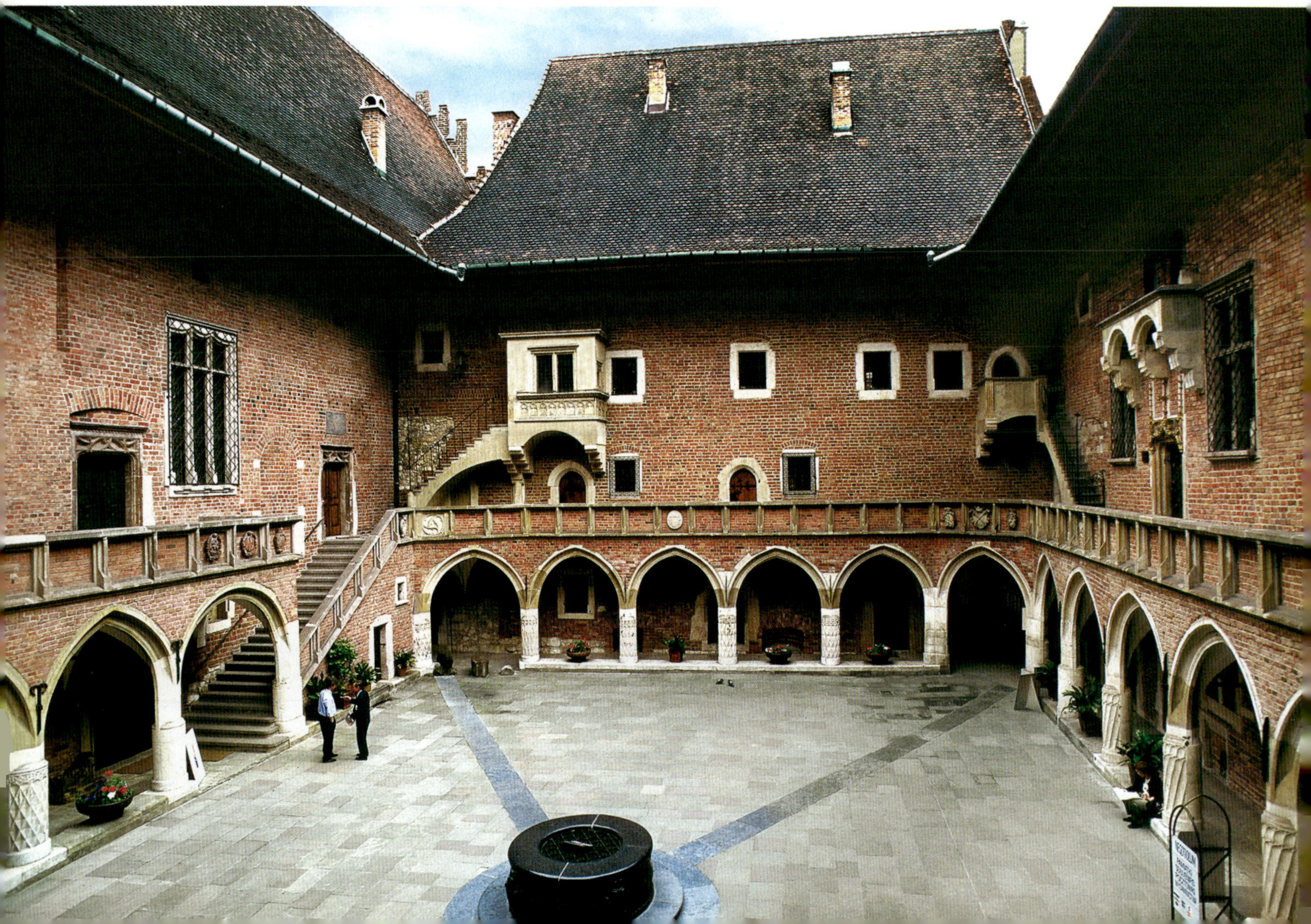

84. Collegium Maius, the Jagellonian University Museum, the Jagellonian Globe (first half of the 16th c.), the first globe to show America

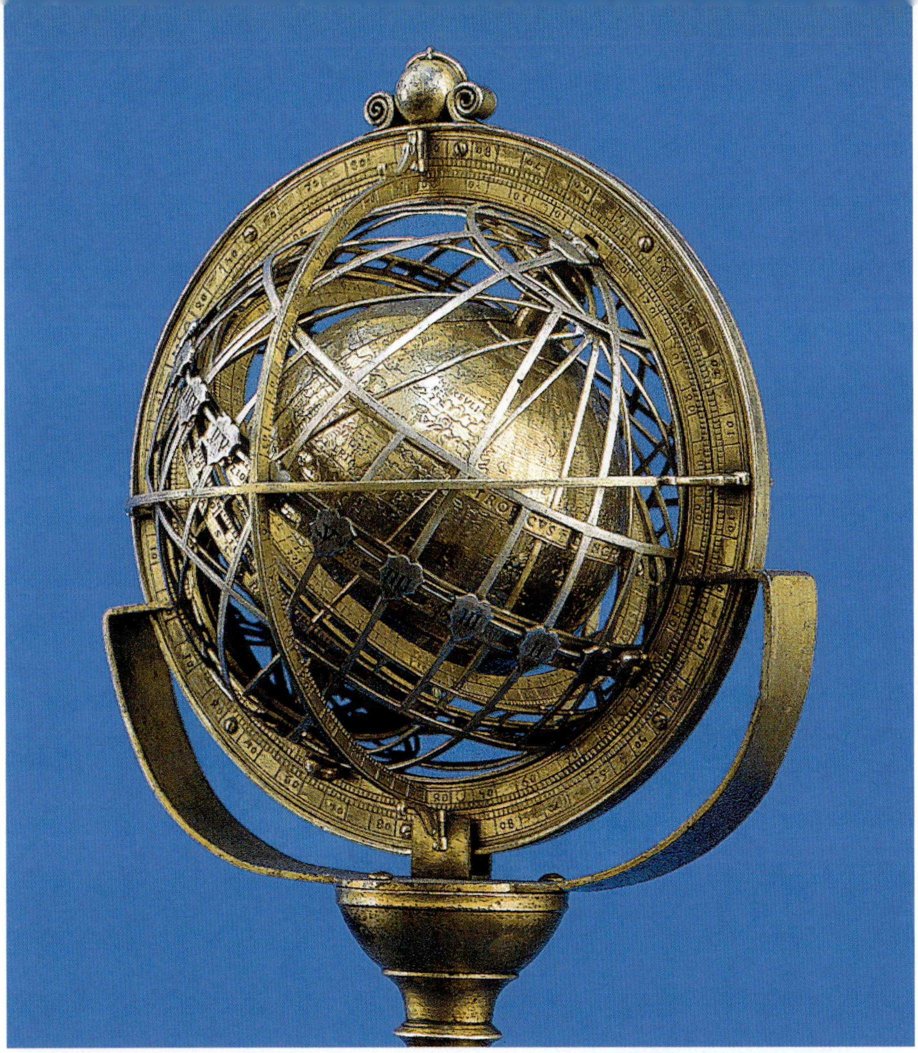

85. Collegium Maius, the Hall in its present shape goes back to the early 16th c. Great University ceremonies used to take place there, and Polish kings were welcomed. On the right are the stalls of the Senate members, and above them is the Rector's chair. On the walls are portraits of kings, bishops of Cracow, and University professors

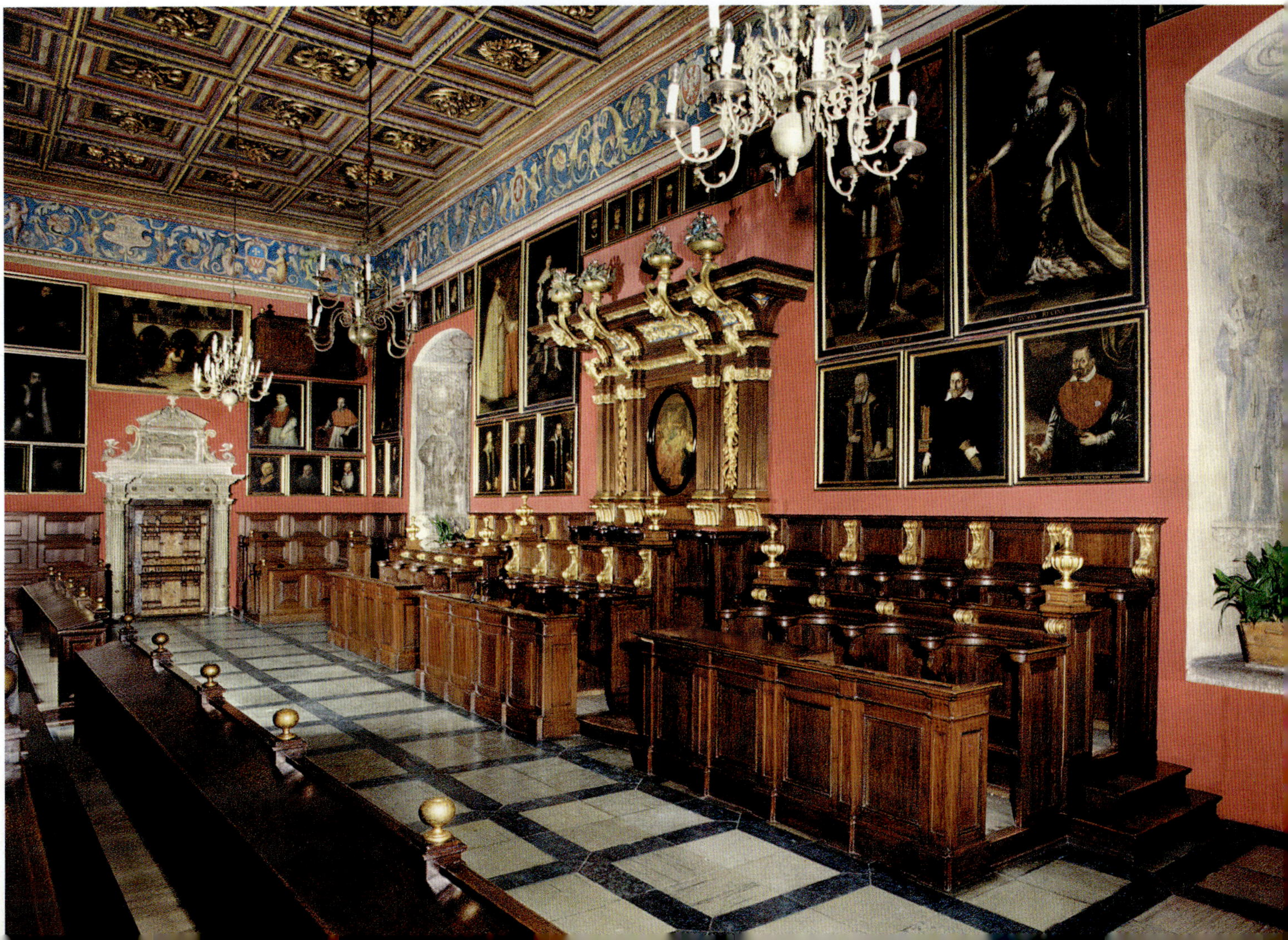

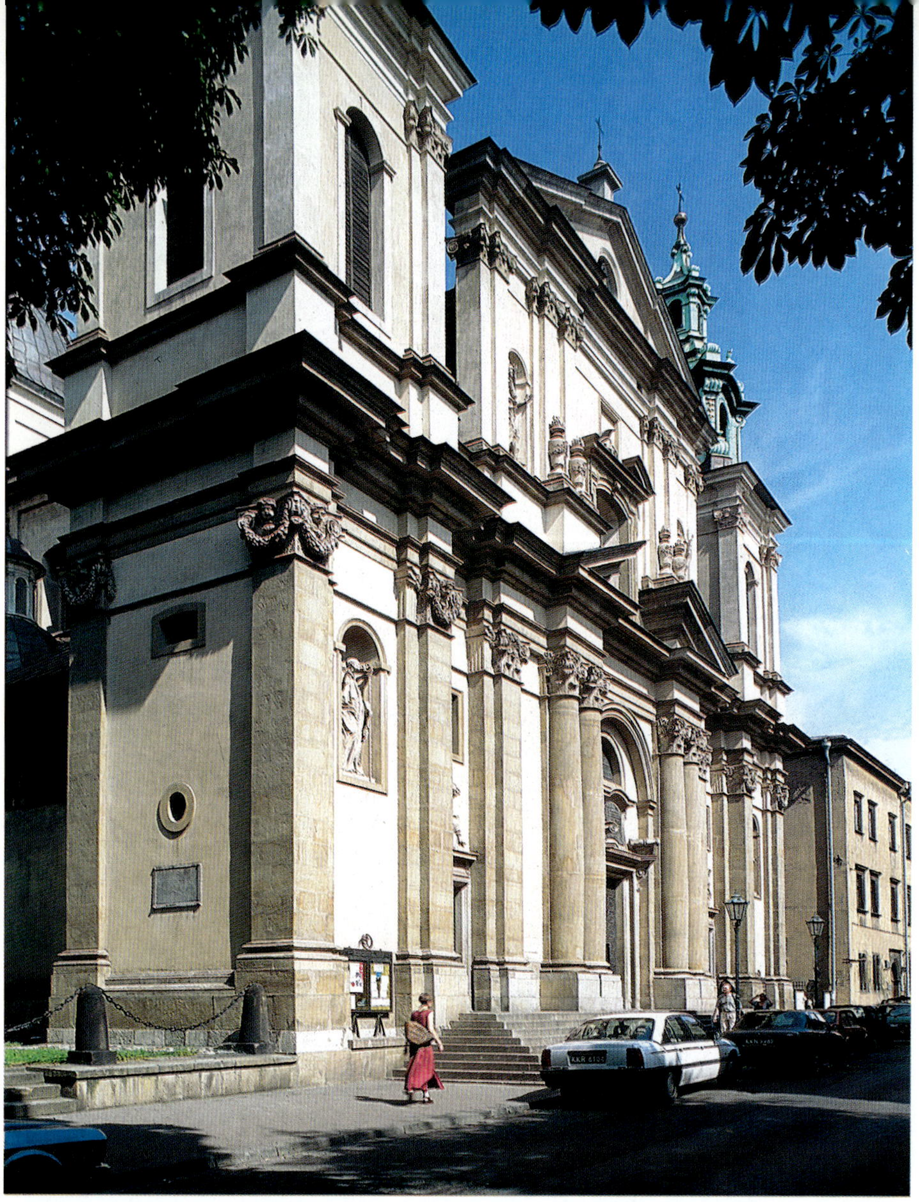

86. St Anne's Street, the University collegiate Church of St Anne, built in the present shape at the turn of the 17th and 18th c., is among the finest Baroque buildings in Poland. It contains the shrine of St John of Kanti, the patron saint of the Jagellonian University, canonized in 1767

87. All Saints' Square was the trading centre of the ancient settlement before the city foundation, located between the Franciscan Church and the Dominican Church. On the left, the former Wielopolski Mansion (mid-16th c.), now the seat of the President and the Council of Cracow; in the background the Gothic Franciscan Church, which together with the adjacent monastery is among the oldest buildings in the city (13th c., extended or restored after damage in the following centuries), with splendid historic furnishings

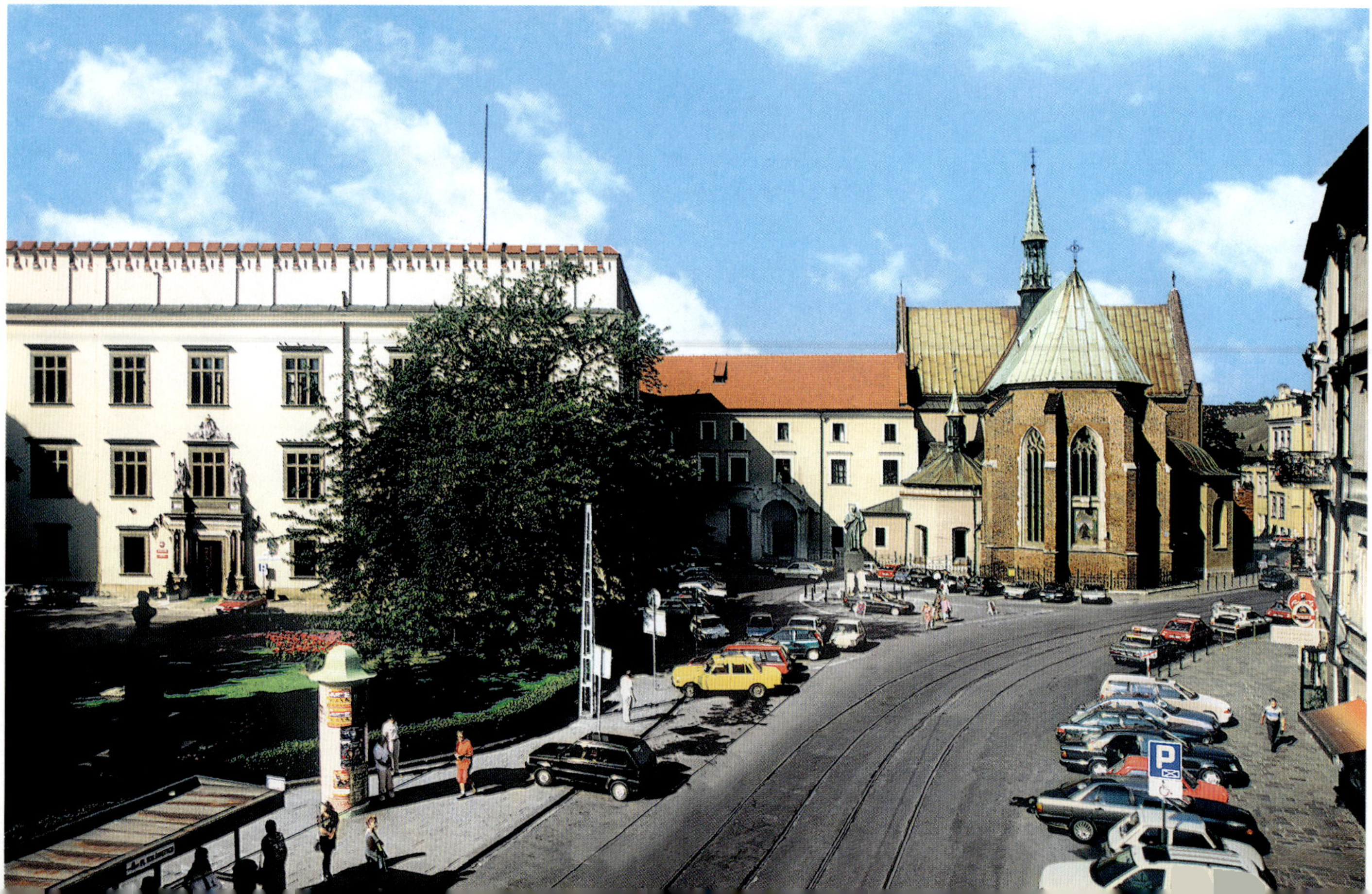

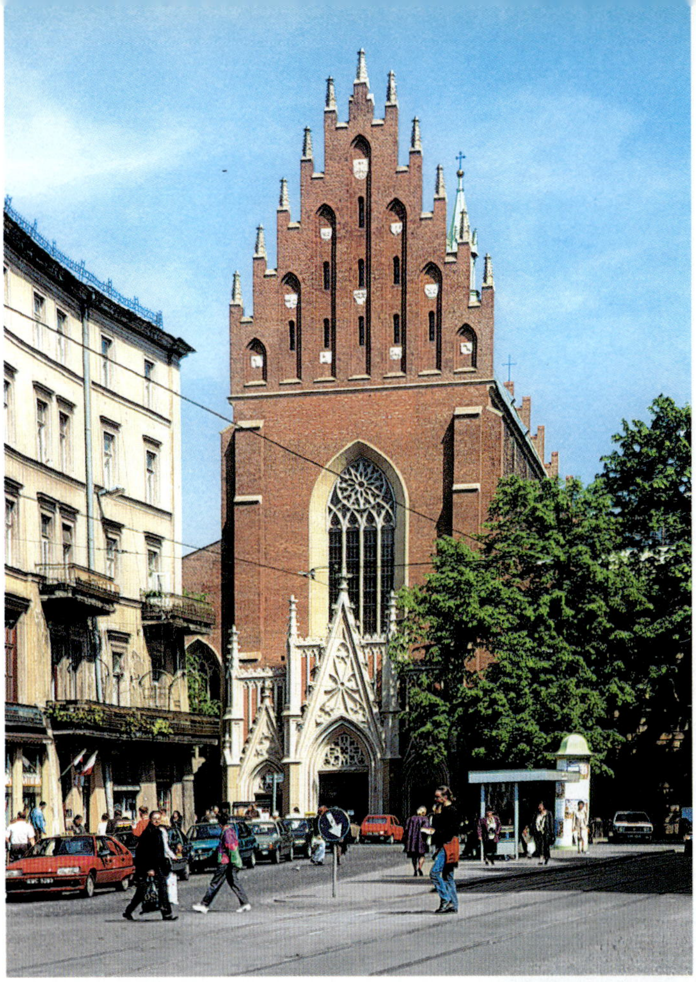

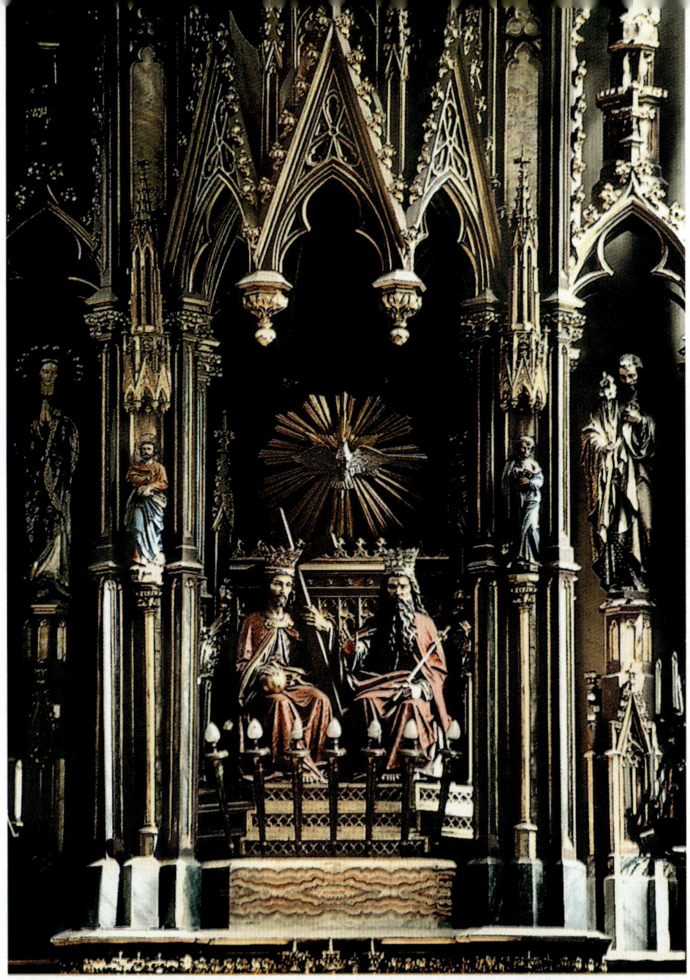

88-89. Dominican Square, the Dominican Church of the Holy Trinity; its construction was started about 1250, and extended or restored after damage in the following centuries. Right: a detail of the neo-Gothic High Altar (second half of the 19th c.), the work of the sculptor Wit Wisz

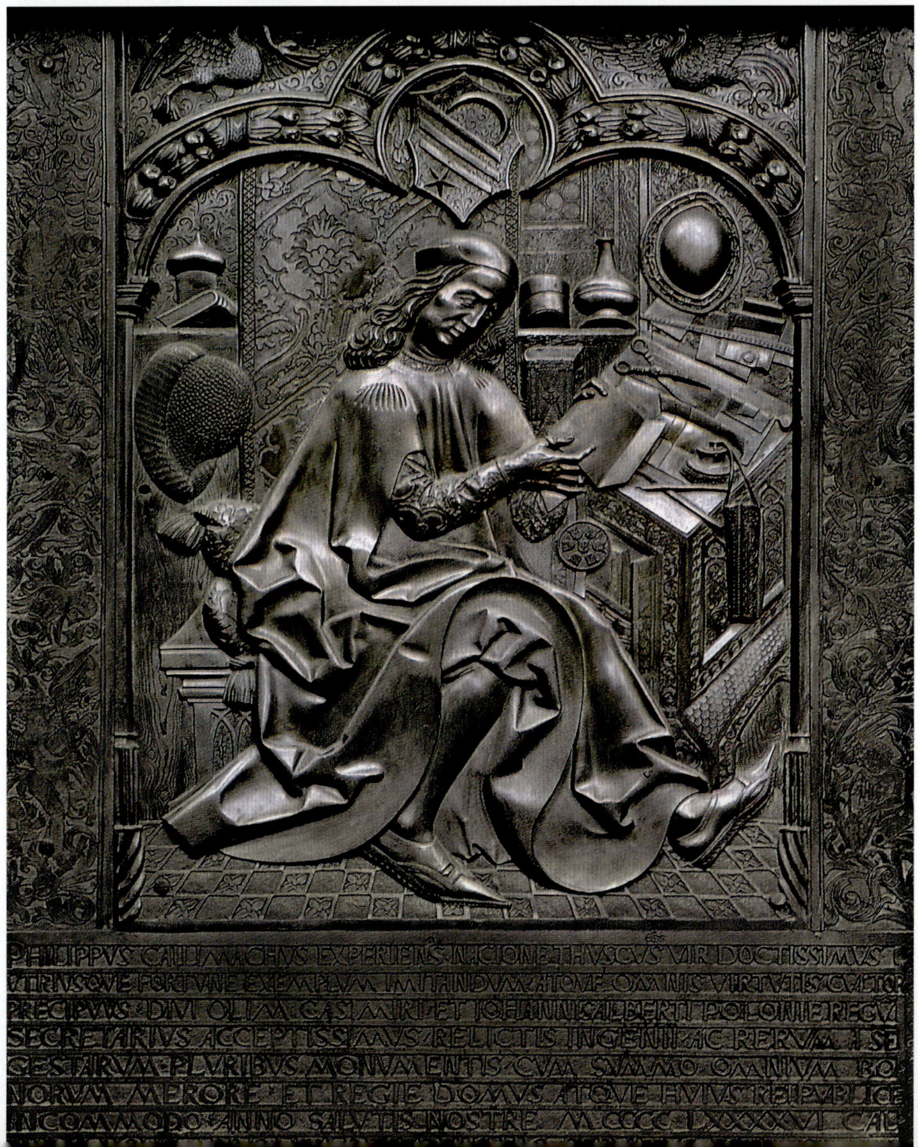

90. Dominican Square, the Dominican Church of the Holy Trinity, the tombstone of the eminent humanist Philip Callimachus, closely connected with the royal court, made after the design by Wit Stwosz (Veit Stoss, early 16th c.)

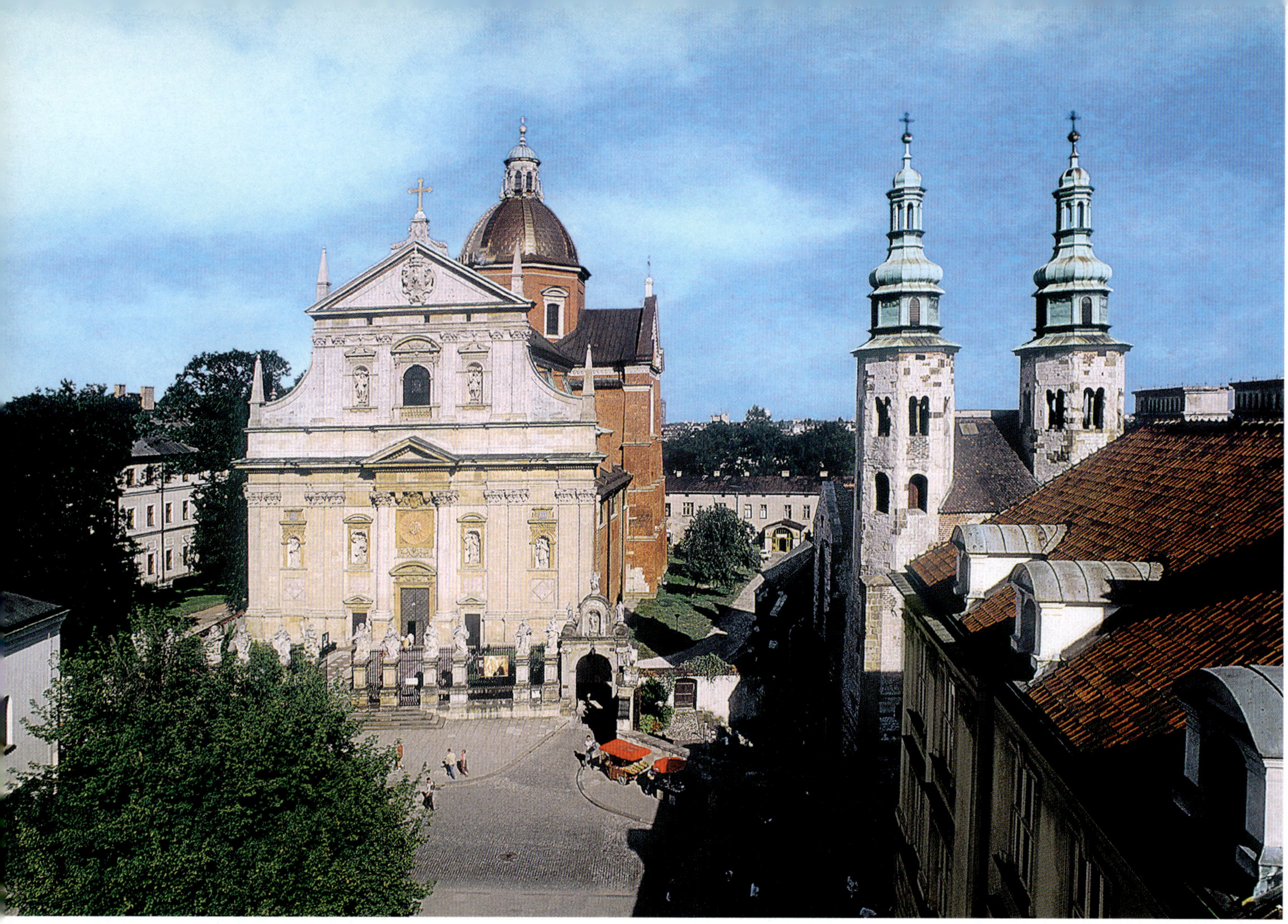

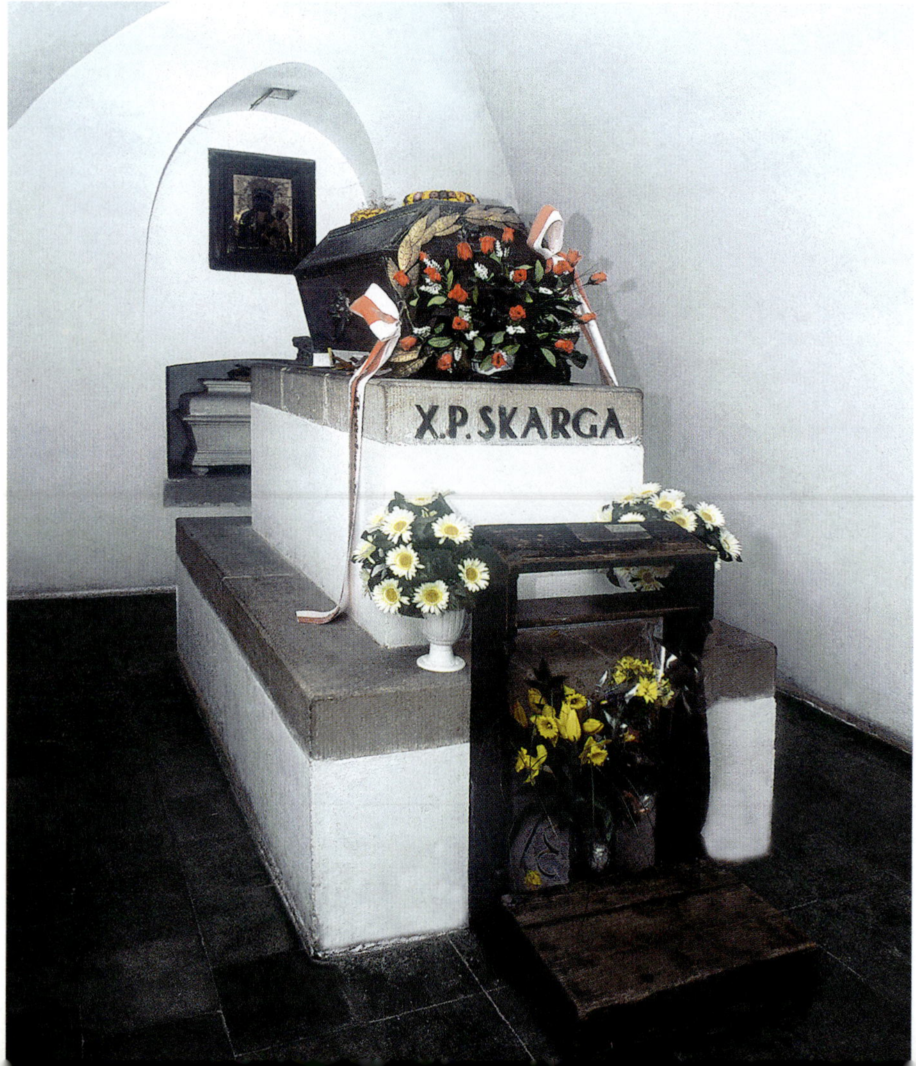

91. Grodzka Street, the Church of SS Peter and Paul (left), Baroque, from the turn of the 16th and 17th c., and the Church of St Andrew (right), Romanesque and fortified (late 11th c.), rebuilt and restored after damage in the following centuries

93. Facing page: Grodzka Street, the figures of the Apostles (left) in front of the Church of SS Peter and Paul are copies of the original figures carved by David Heel (1721-1723), in the background the Romanesque Church of St Andrew (late 11th c.)

92. The Church of SS Peter and Paul, in the crypt beneath the presbytery is the tomb of the eminent Jesuit, Fr Piotr Skarga (1536-1612), preacher to King Sigismund III Vasa, famous for his patriotic sermons, also at the Seym meetings

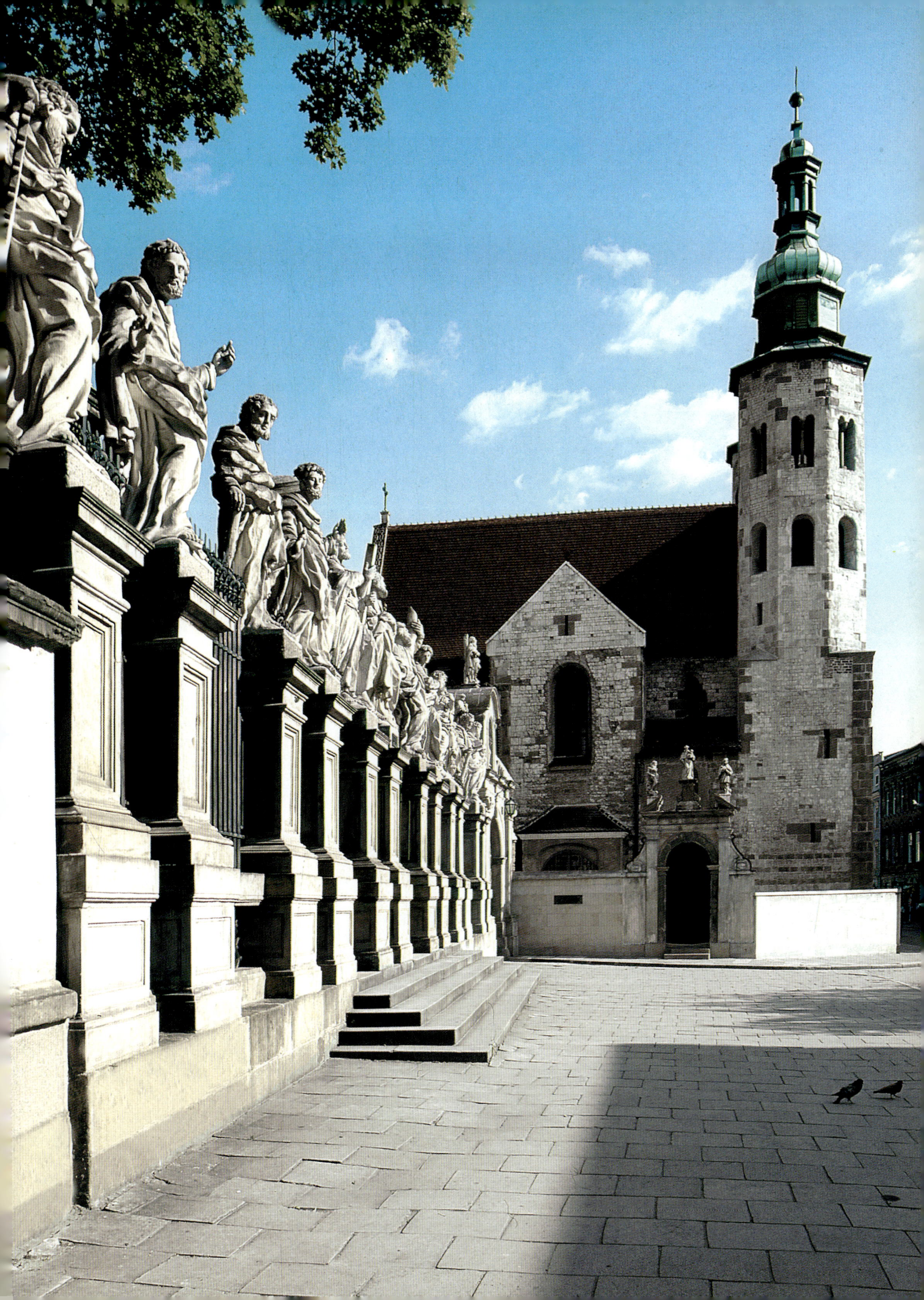

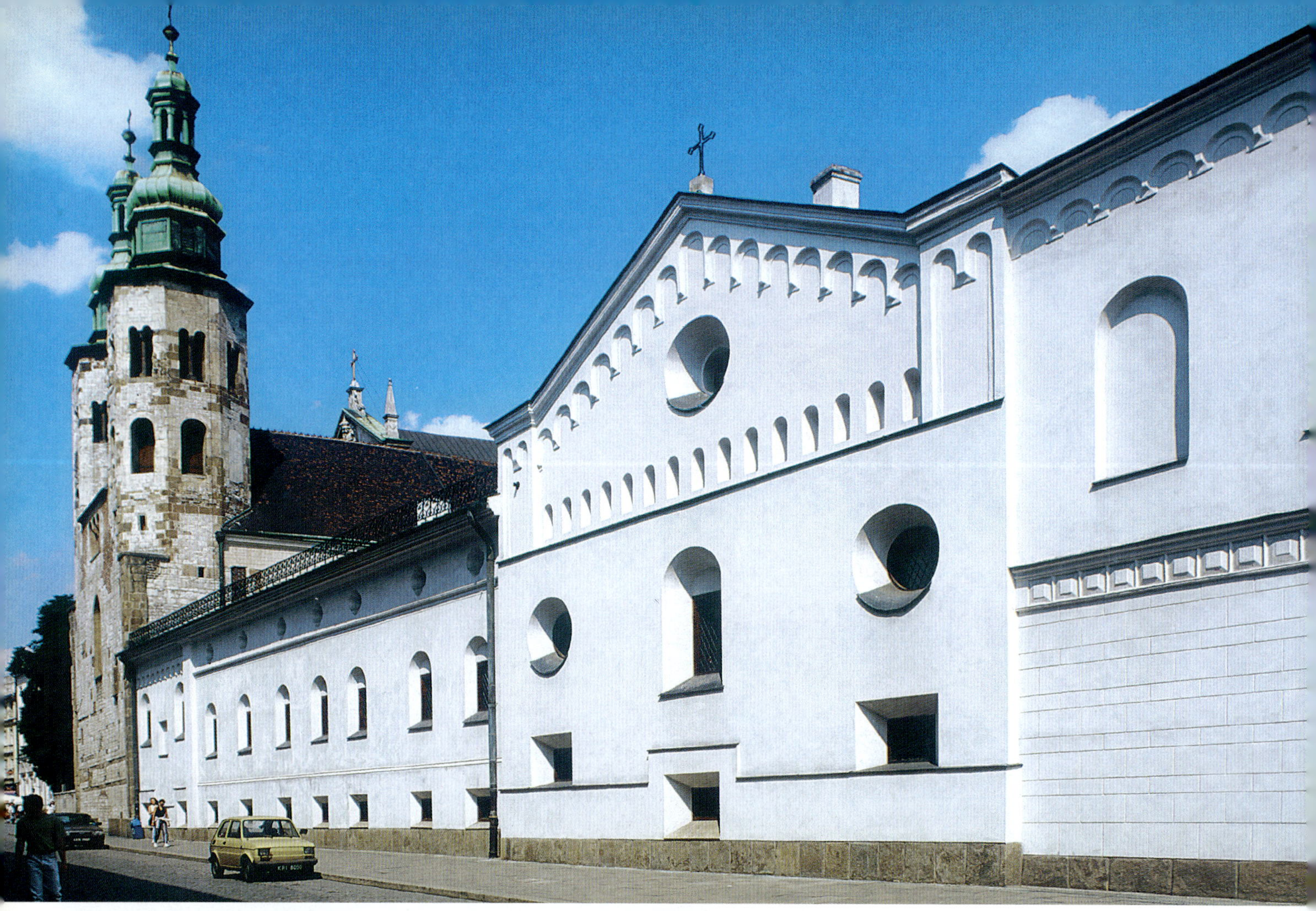

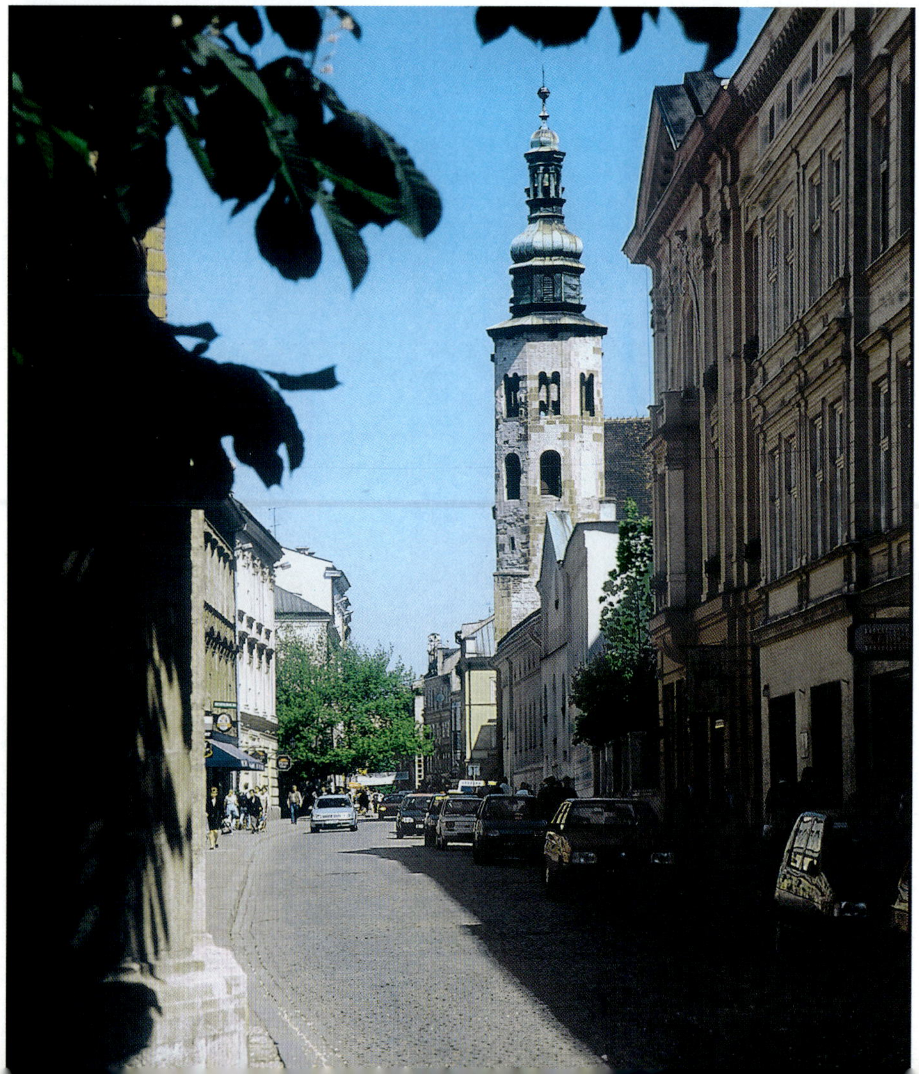

94. Grodzka Street, the convent of the Poor Clares, who settled there in the years 1316-1320. The convent building, destroyed by fire in 1455, was restored and then rebuilt at the turn of the16th and 17th c. In the background the Romanesque Church of St Andrew (late 11th c.)

95. Grodzka Street, one of the oldest roads in the city area, connected the Royal Castle at Wawel with the nearby settlement. It was a part of the so called Royal Way, which extended from the collegiate Church of St Florian at Kleparz to Wawel, and ran past the Barbican and St Florian's Gate, along Floriańska Street, across the Market Square (near St Mary's Church), and along Grodzka, Senacka and Kanonicza Streets

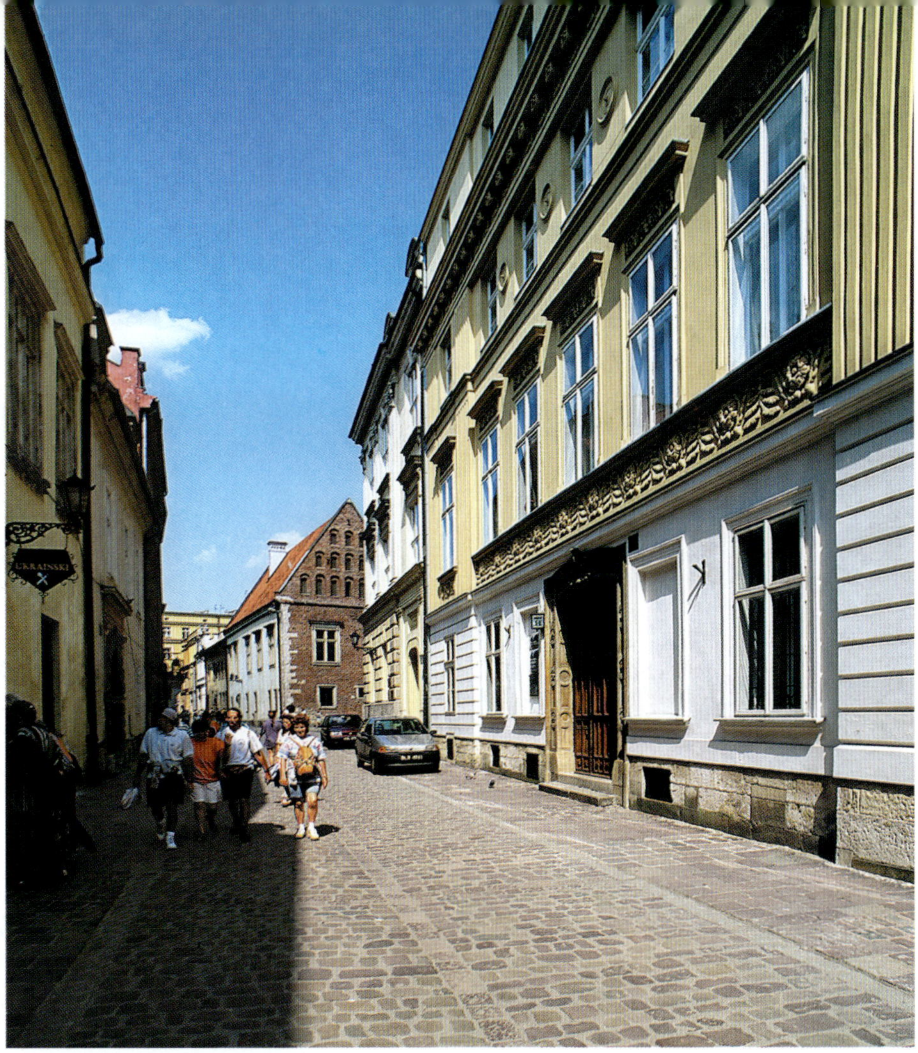

96. A section of Kanonicza Street, one of the finest streets in the city, which in the early Middle Ages was the main approach to Wawel Castle. From the second half of the14th c. the canons of the Cracow Chapter built their residences there; the original Gothic houses were rebuilt in the Renaissance style in the 16th c.

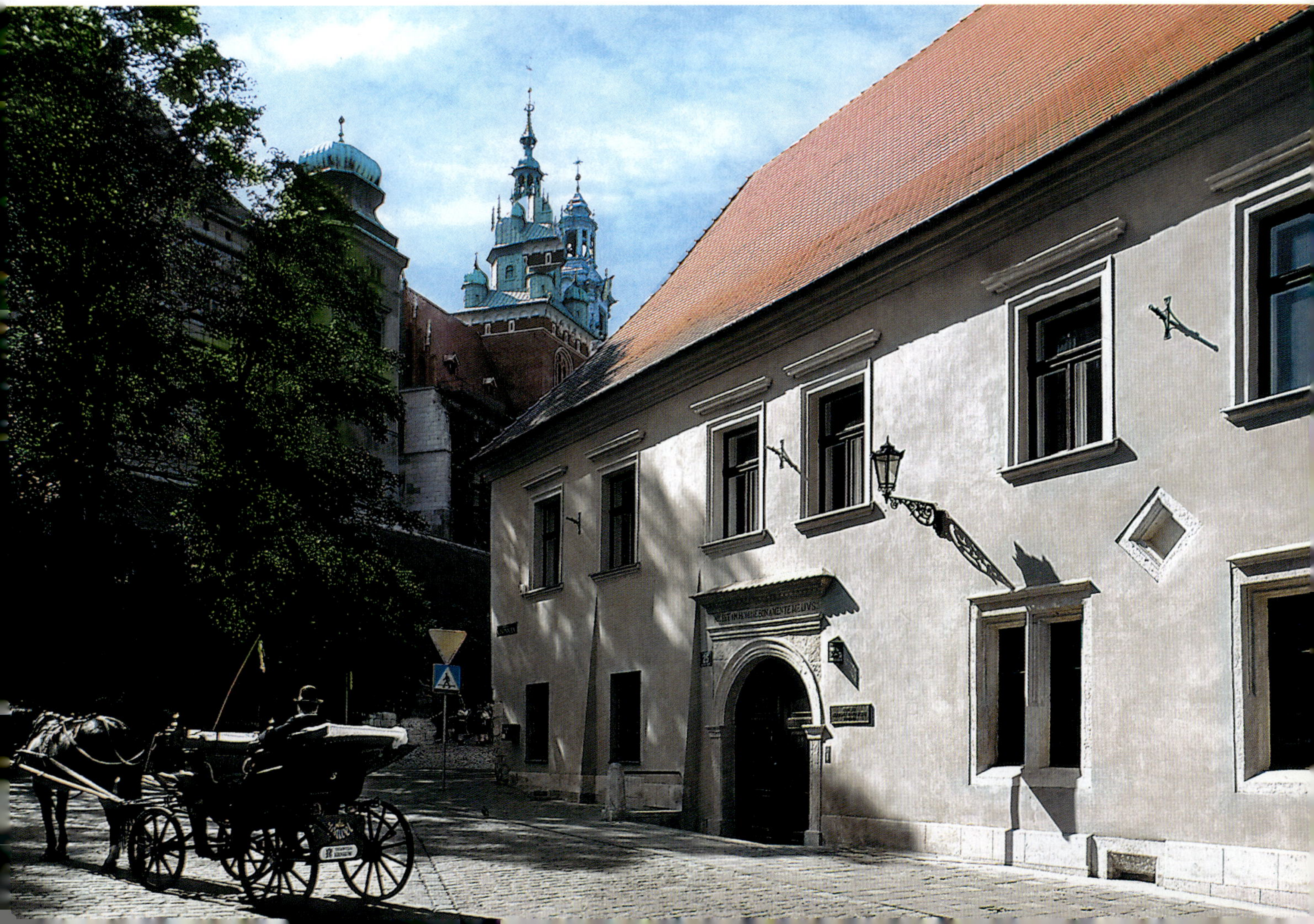

97. Kanonicza Street, the Długosz House, located at the place where Kanonicza meets Podzamcze Street, at the foot of Wawel Hill. It dates back to the first half of the 14th c.; in 1450-1480 it was the house of the eminent historian and diplomat, Jan Długosz (Longinus), the author of the work *Annals, or the Chronicles of the Illustrious Polish Kingdom*, which presents in 12 books the history of Poland, from the legendary period to 1480

98. Podzamcze Street, along the bottom of Wawel Hill, was a part of the early-medieval road to the crossing of the Vistula. In the foreground the Długosz House (first half of the 14th c.), in the background the upper storeys of the towers of St Andrew's Church and the dome of the Church of SS Peter and Paul

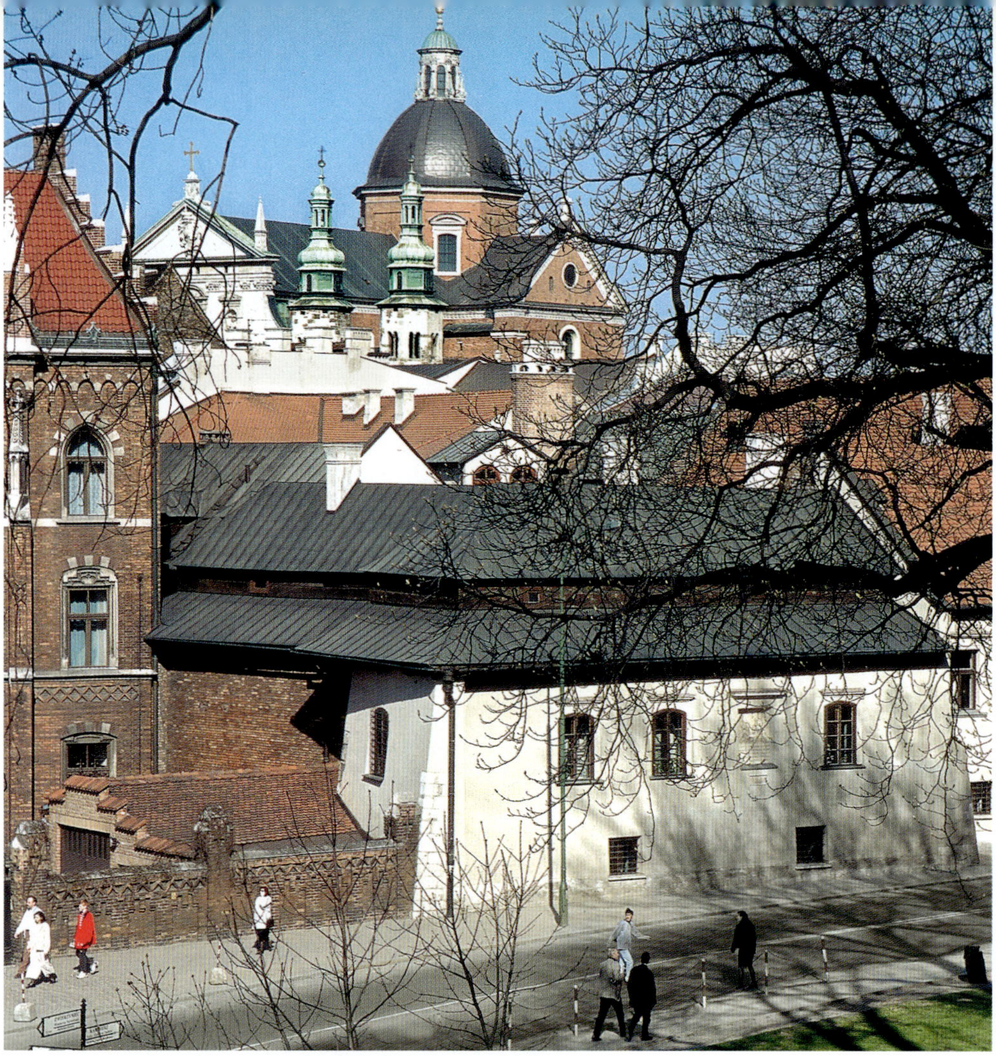

99. Kanonicza Street, the arcaded court of the Dean's House (second half of the 16th c.), in the background the Baroque figure of St Stanislaus (18th c.)

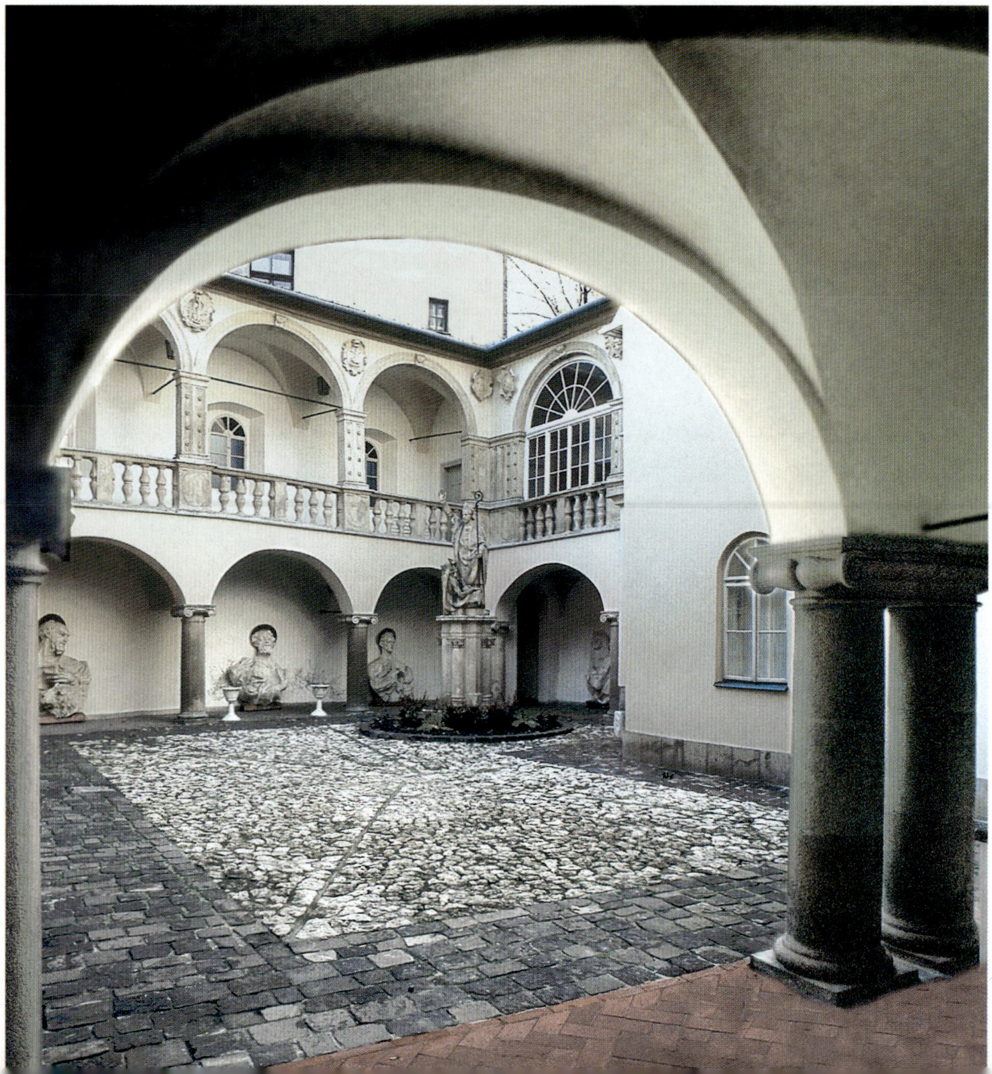

100-101. Facing page: the Baroque Church of SS Michael the Archangel and Stanislaus at Skałka on the Vistula (first half of the 18th c.). The site is traditionally associated with the death of St Sranislaus, killed by King Boleslaus the Bold. Under the church, in the Crypt of Eminent Poles, are the tombs of people important for Polish culture: the historian Jan Długosz, the poets Wincenty Pol, Teofil Lenartowicz and Adam Asnyk, the novelist Józef Ignacy Kraszewski, the painters Henryk Siemiradzki and Jacek Malczewski, the poet, painter, playwright and theatre reformer Stanisław Wyspiański, and the actor Ludwik Solski

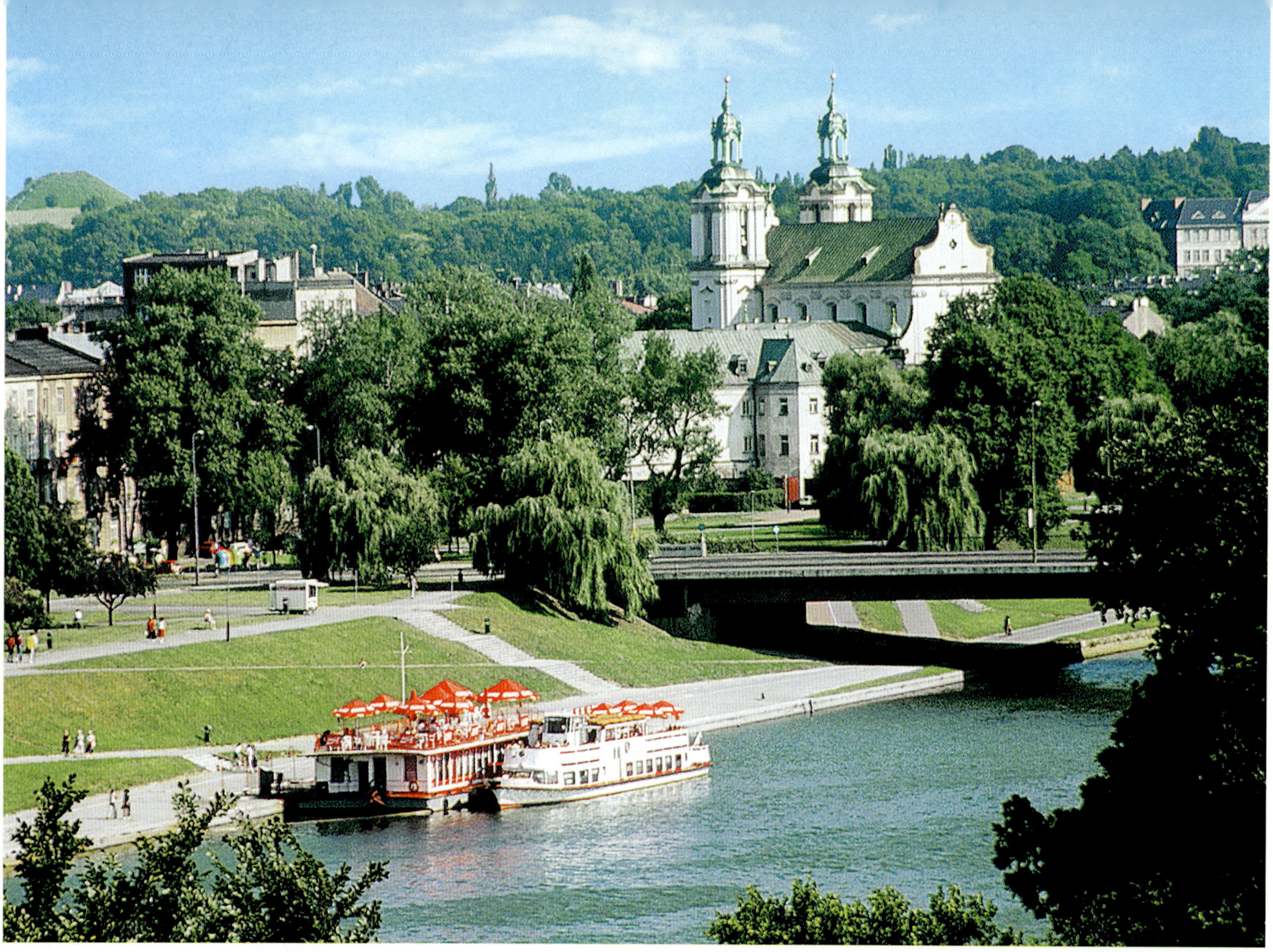

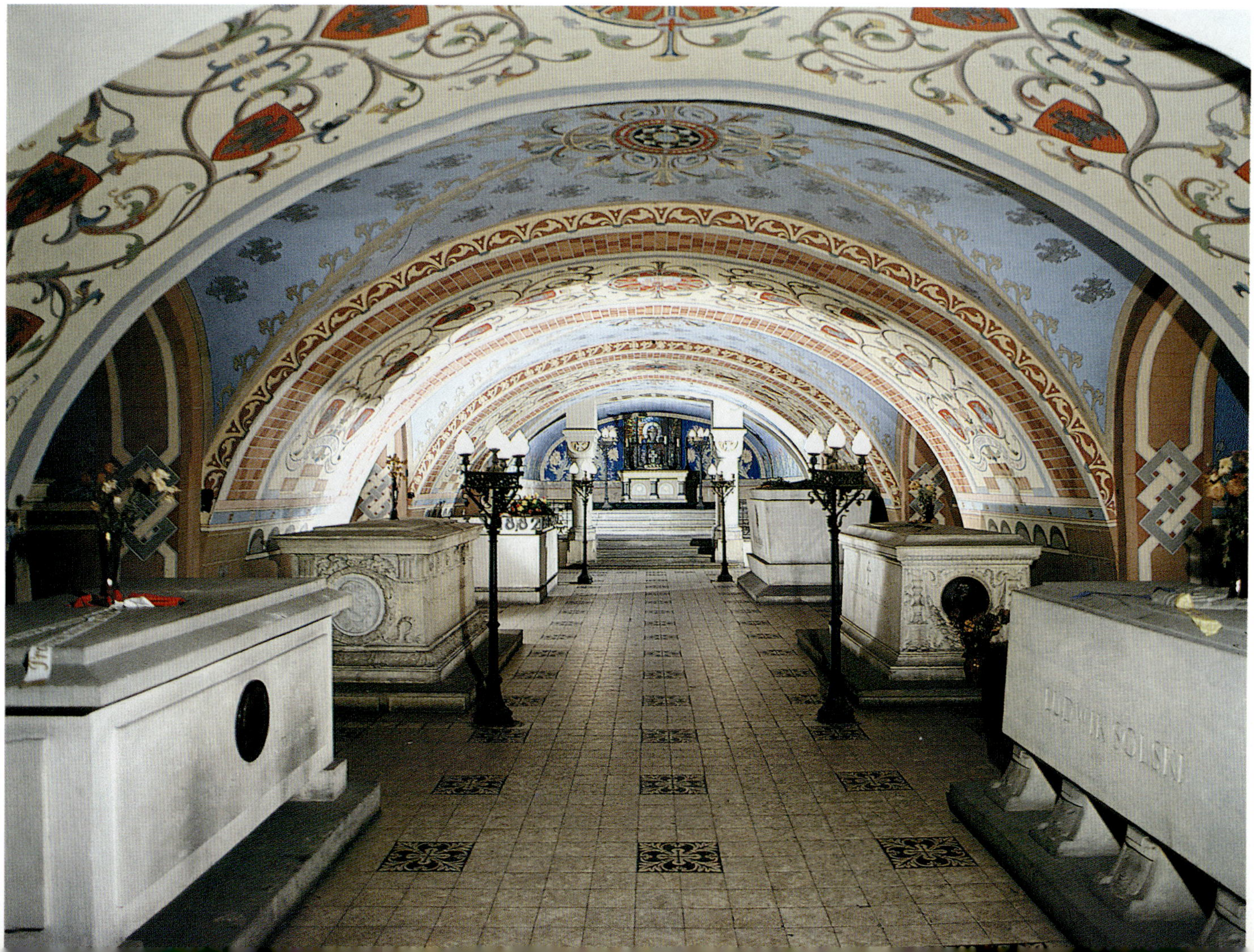

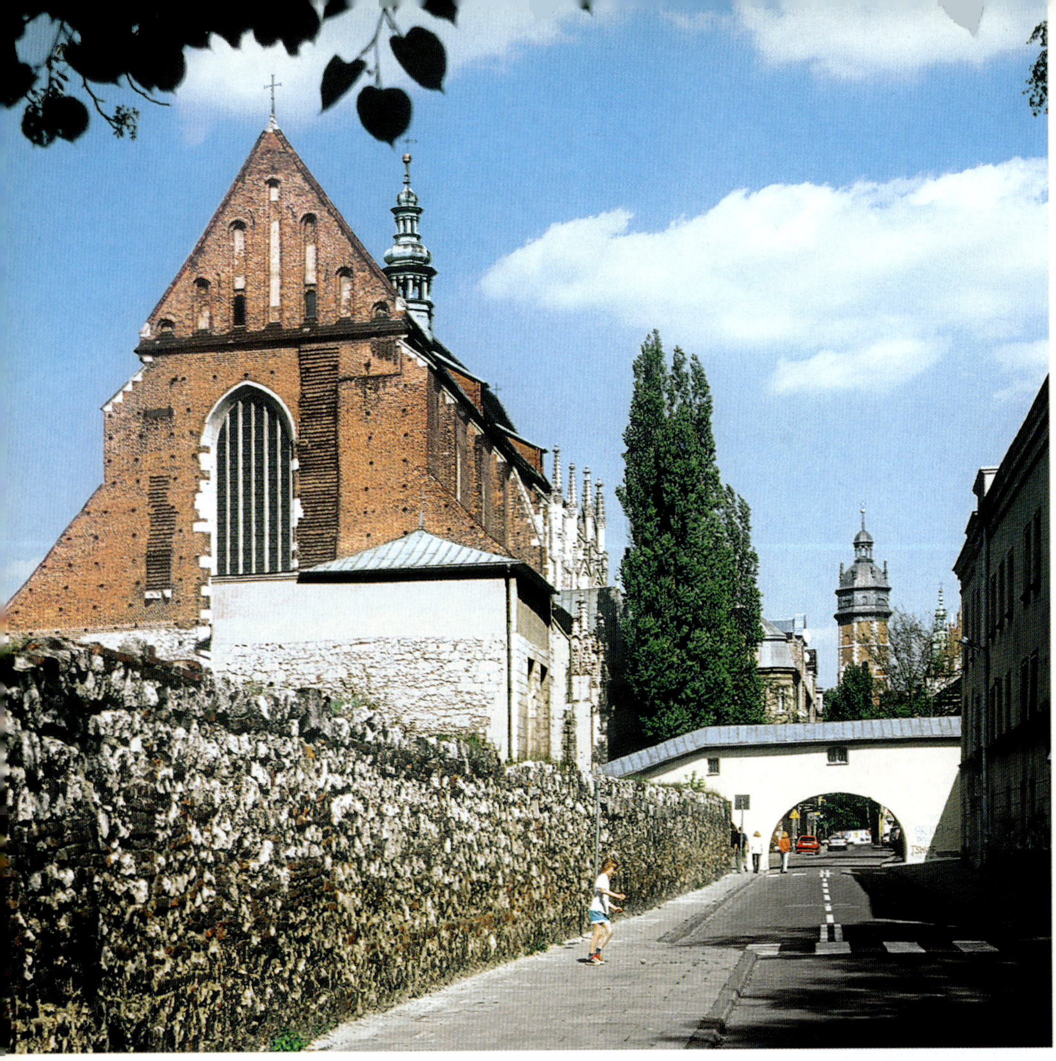

102-103. Skałeczna Street, the Church of SS Catherine and Margaret in Kazimierz, one of the most beautiful churches in the city (second half of the 14th c.). A covered gallery connects the church, above Skałeczna Street, with the Augustinian convent, in the background the tower of the Gothic Corpus Christi Church (turn of the 14th and 15th c.). Bottom left: the presbytery of the Church of SS Catherine and Margaret, with the multi-storey High Altar (1634); at the walls of the presbytery are the neo-Gothic stalls (second half of the 19th c.

104. Augustiańska Street, the cloisters in the Augustinian monastery (second half of the 14th c.), adjacent to the Church of SS Catherine and Margaret

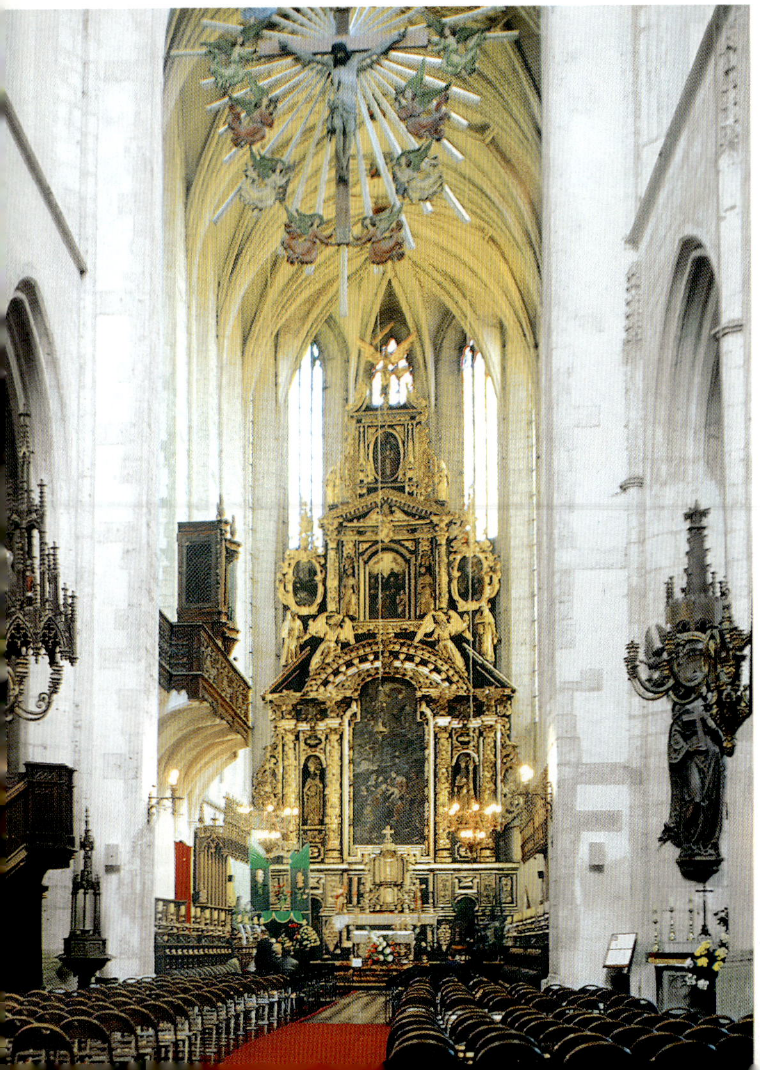

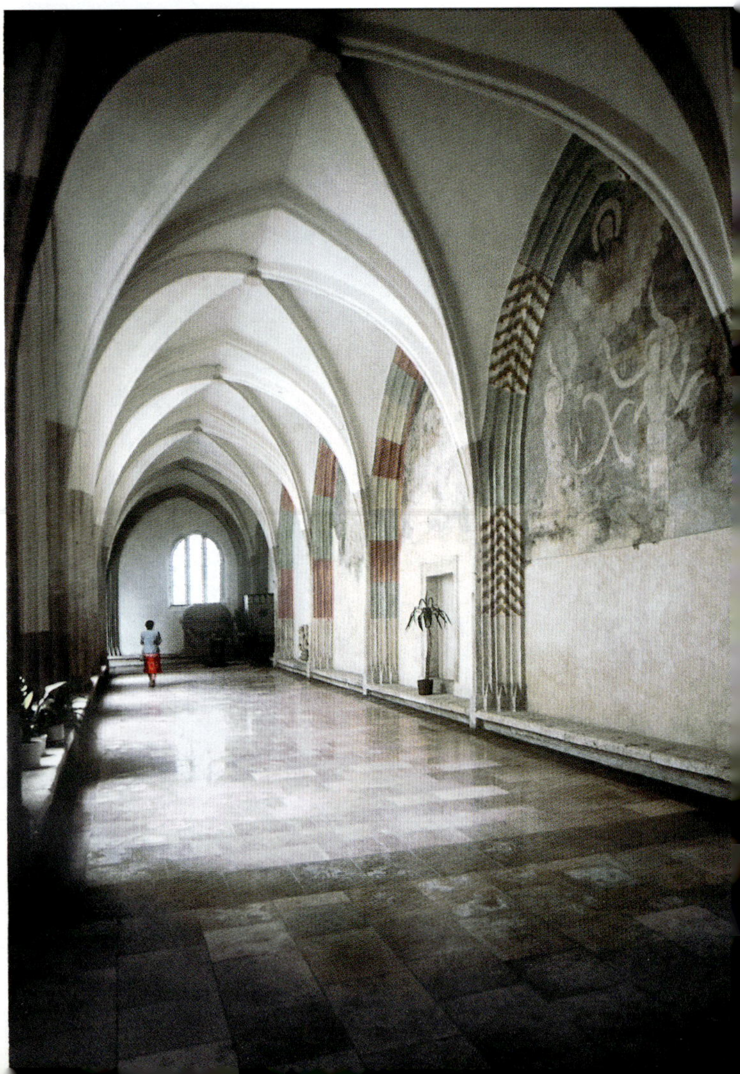

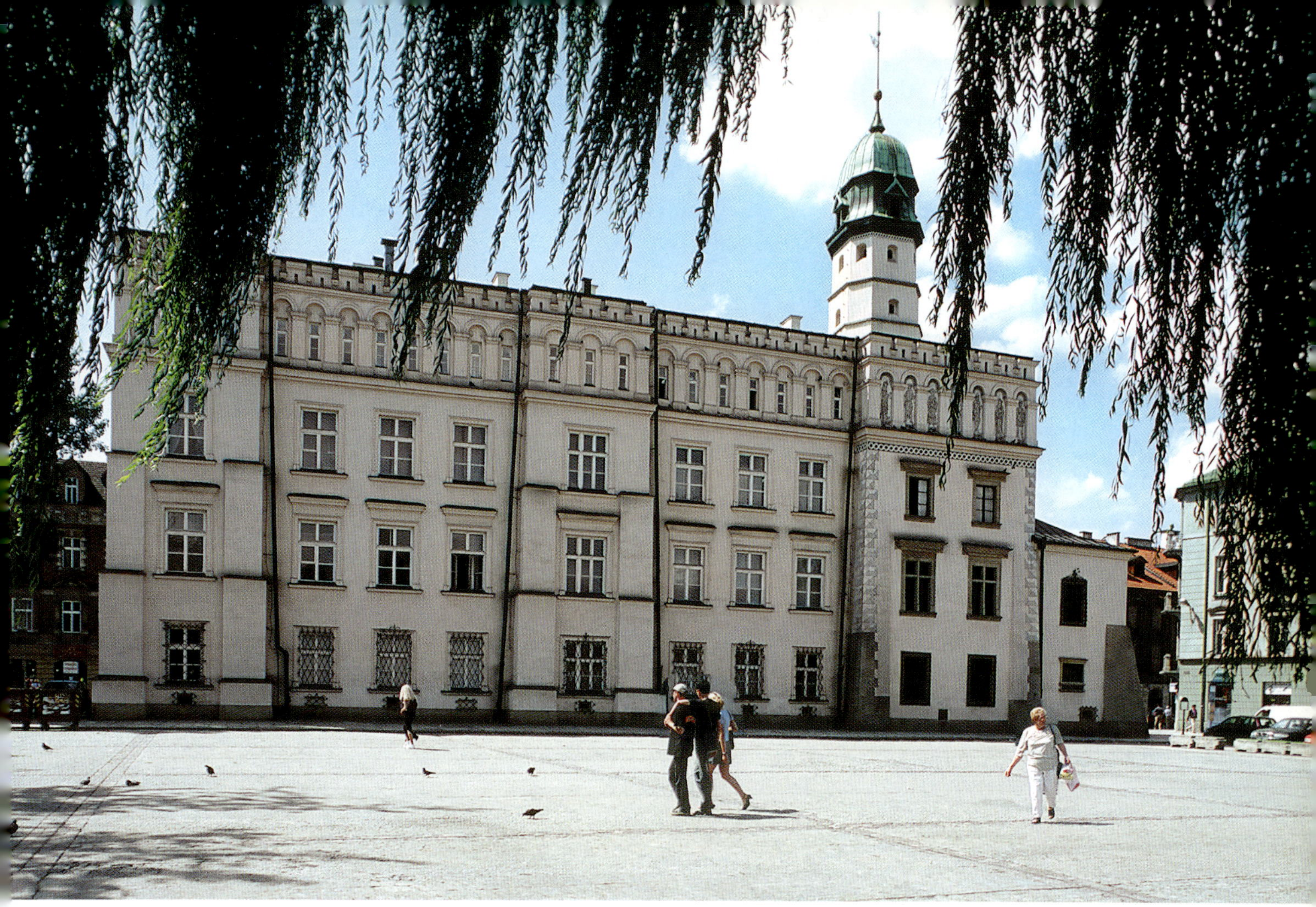

105. Wolnica Square, the Town Hall of the former borough of Kazimierz, dating back to the 15th c., repeatedly rebuilt in the following centuries. Since 1911 it has housed the Ethnographic Museum, its collection of Polish folk art being among the largest ones in Poland

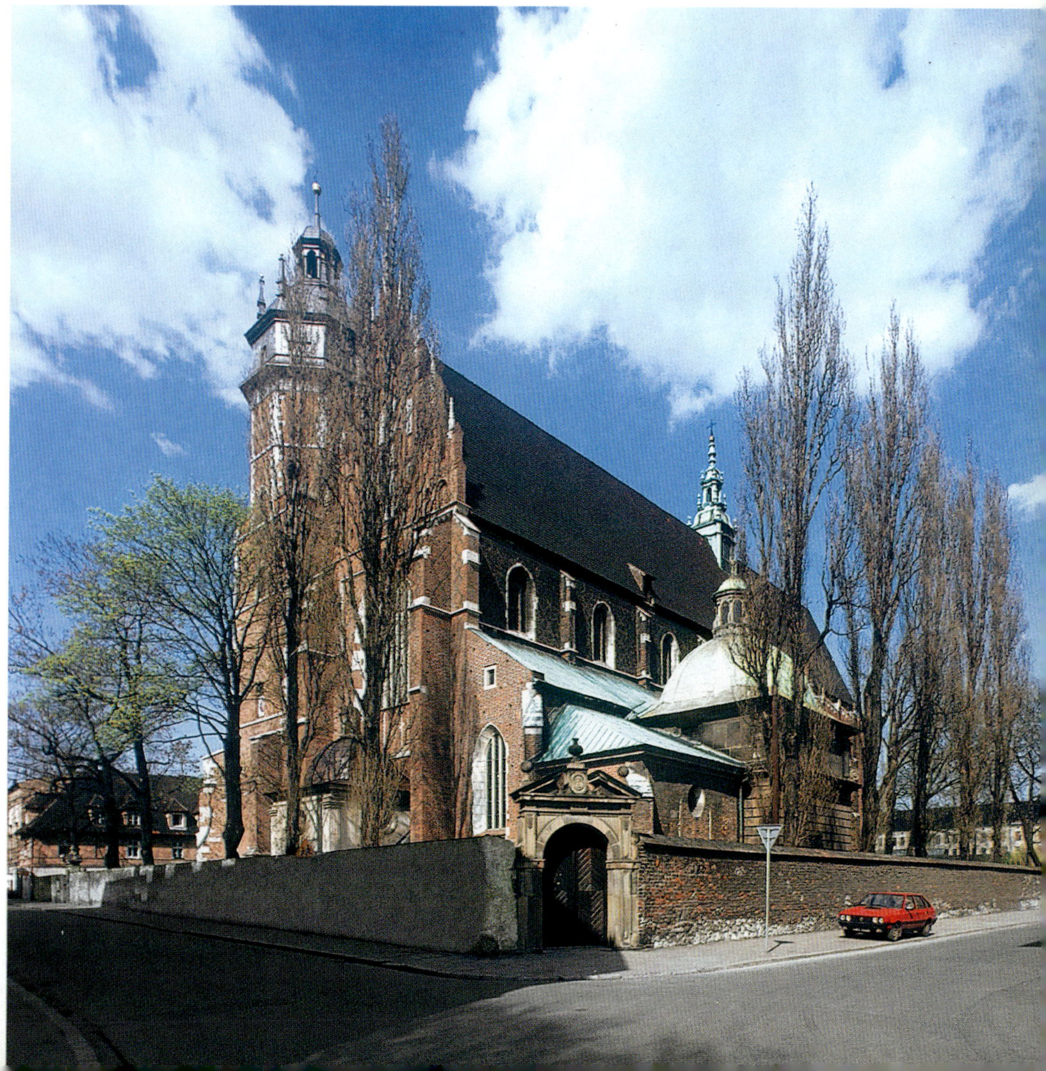

106. The Corpus Christi Church in Kazimierz, Gothic (turn of the 14th and 15th c.), founded by King Casimir the Great as the parish church for the new borough. The church interior is splendidly decorated in the Baroque style

107. The Corpus Christi Church, a section of the nave and the presbytery, in the background the High Altar (1634-1637)

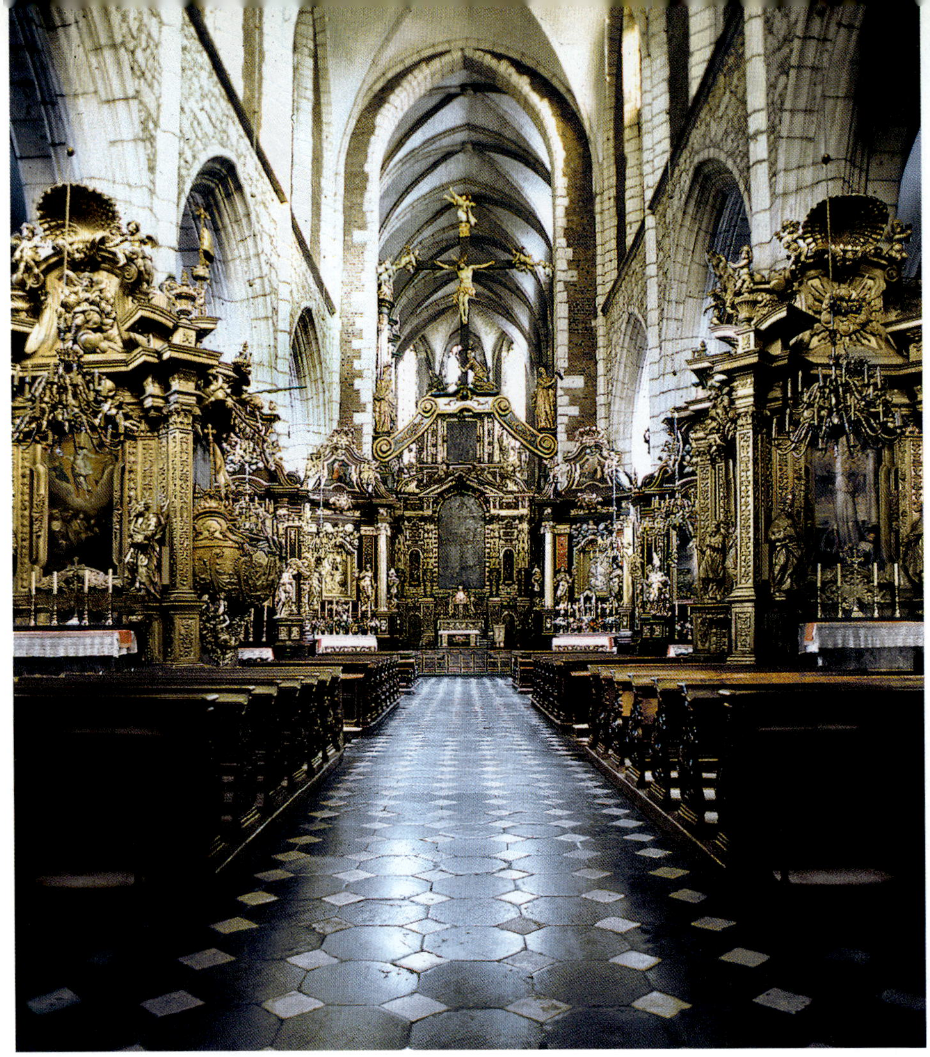

108. The Corpus Christi Church, the pulpit in the shape of a boat (mid-18th c.)

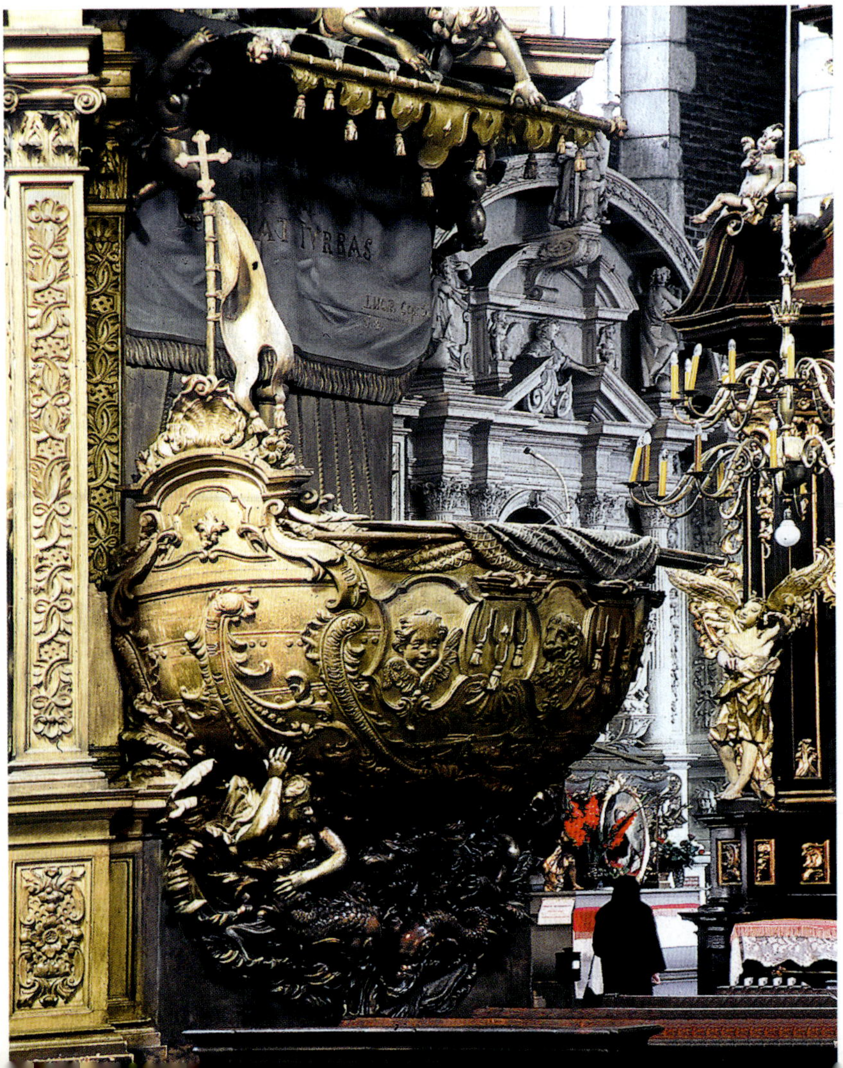

109. Facing page: The Corpus Christi Church from Wolnica Square

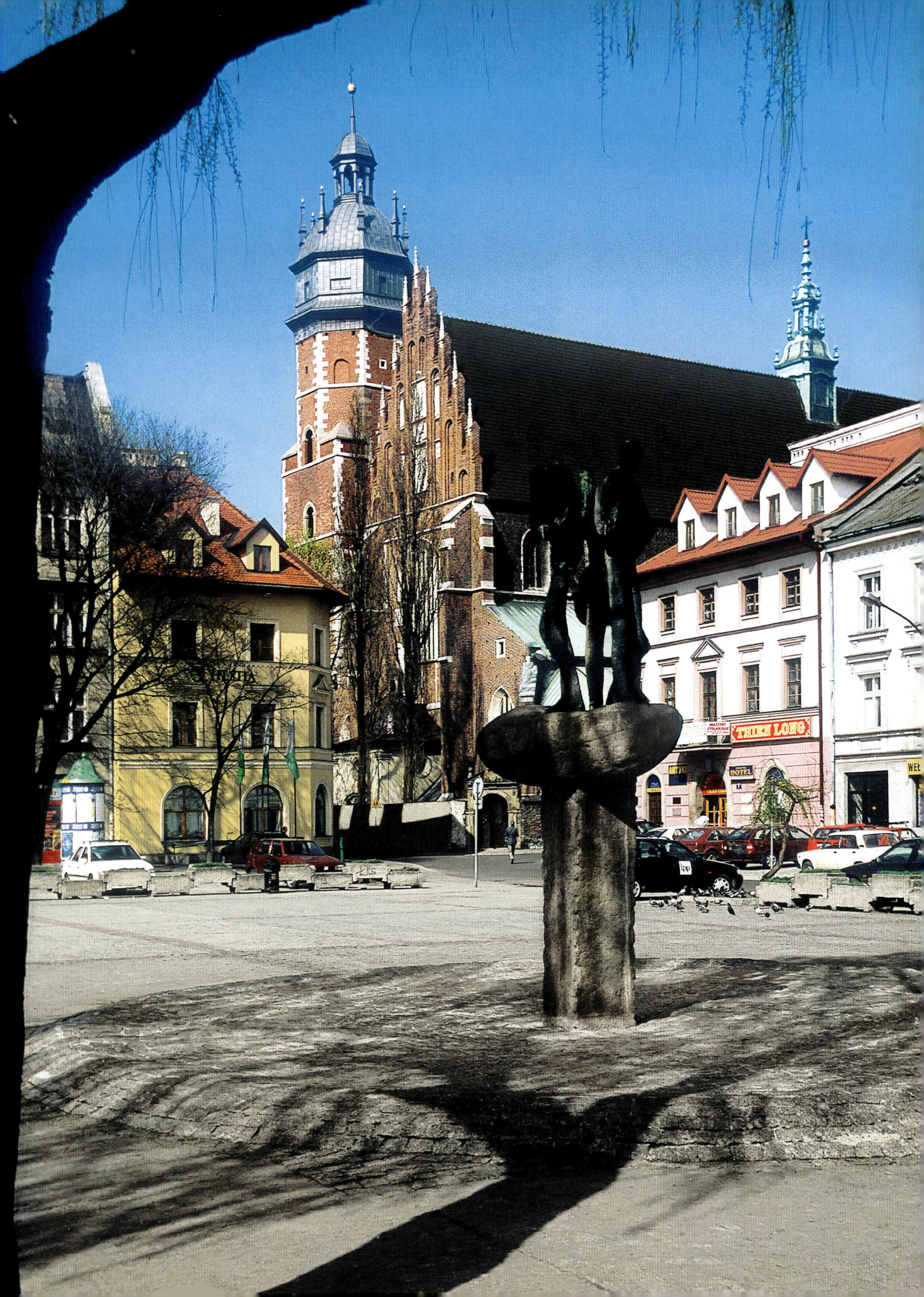
THIEN LONG
HOTEL

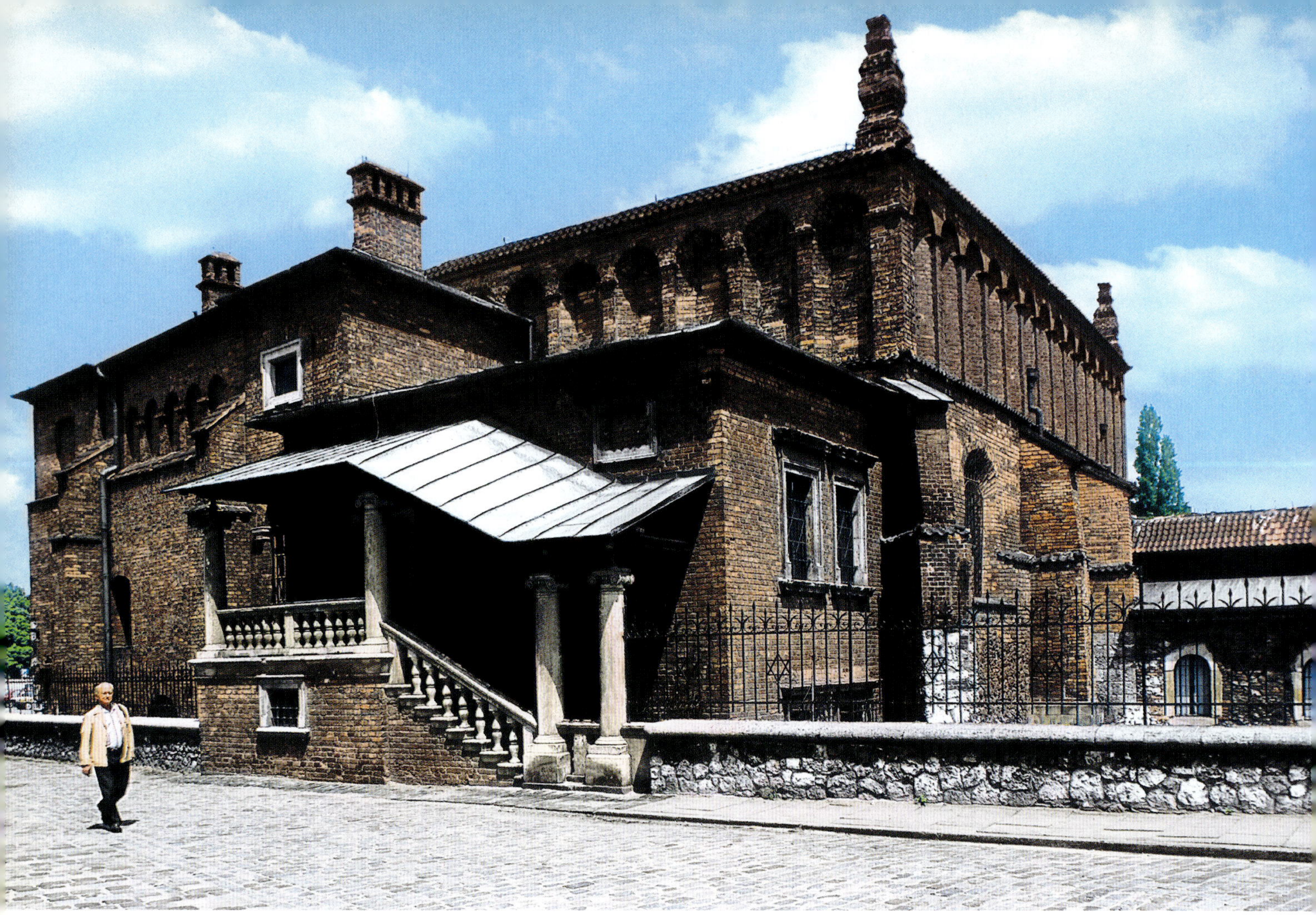

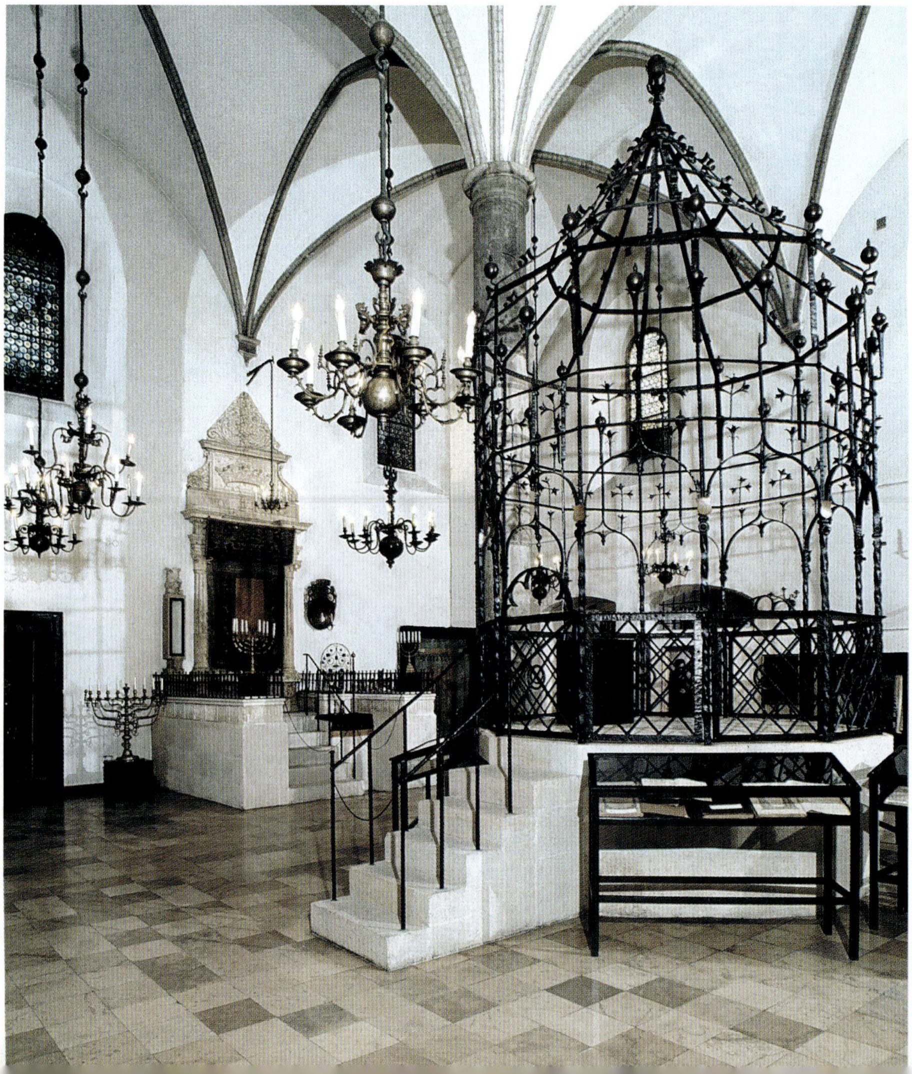

110-111. Szeroka Street, the Old Synagogue in Kazimierz, the oldest one in the city (late 15th c.) Now it houses a branch of the Historical Museum of the City of Cracow, with a collection of judaica. Since 1979 it has presented the exhibition of 'The history and Culture of the Cracow Jews'. Left: a section of the interior of the Old Synagogue

112-113. Facing page: Szeroka Street, a section of the Jewish Remuh Cemetery, next to the famous Remuh Synagogue (second half of the 16th c.) The cemetery is among the oldest ones in Poland and Europe. The name of both the cemetery and synagogue derives from Rabbi Mojżesz Isserles, known as Rabbi Moses-Remuh (d. 1572). Bottom: a detail of the so-called Wailing Wall in the Remuh Cemetery

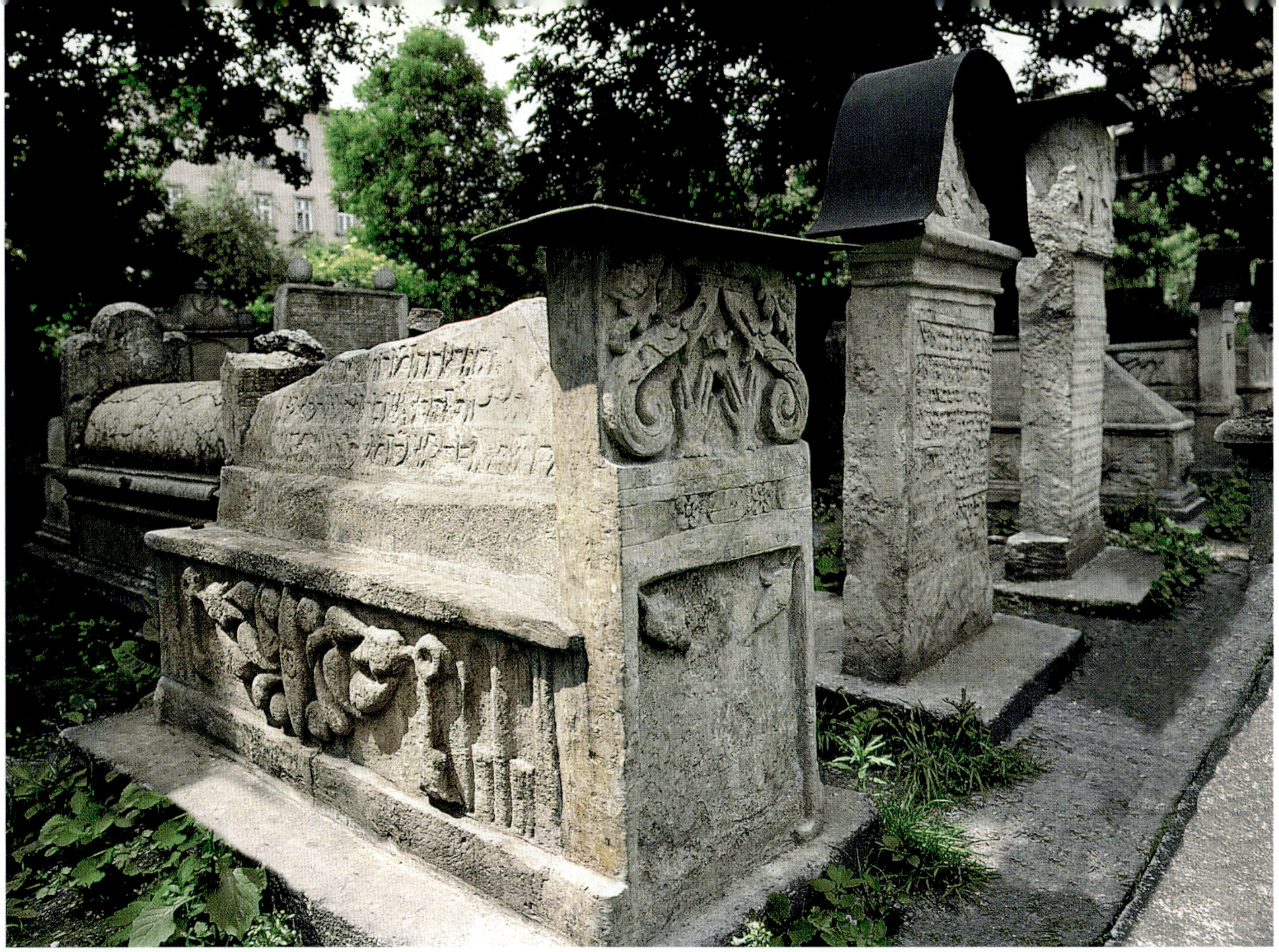

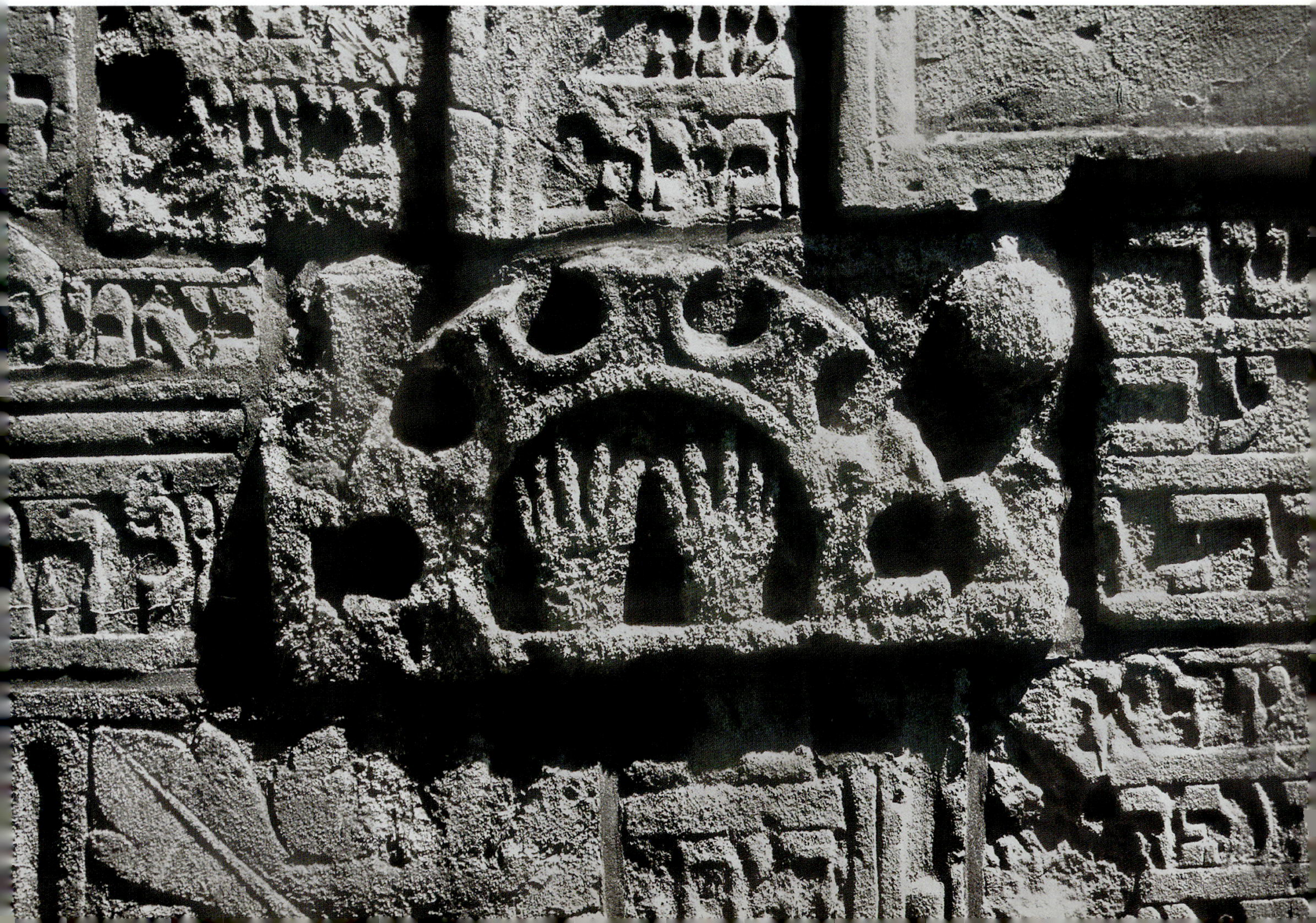

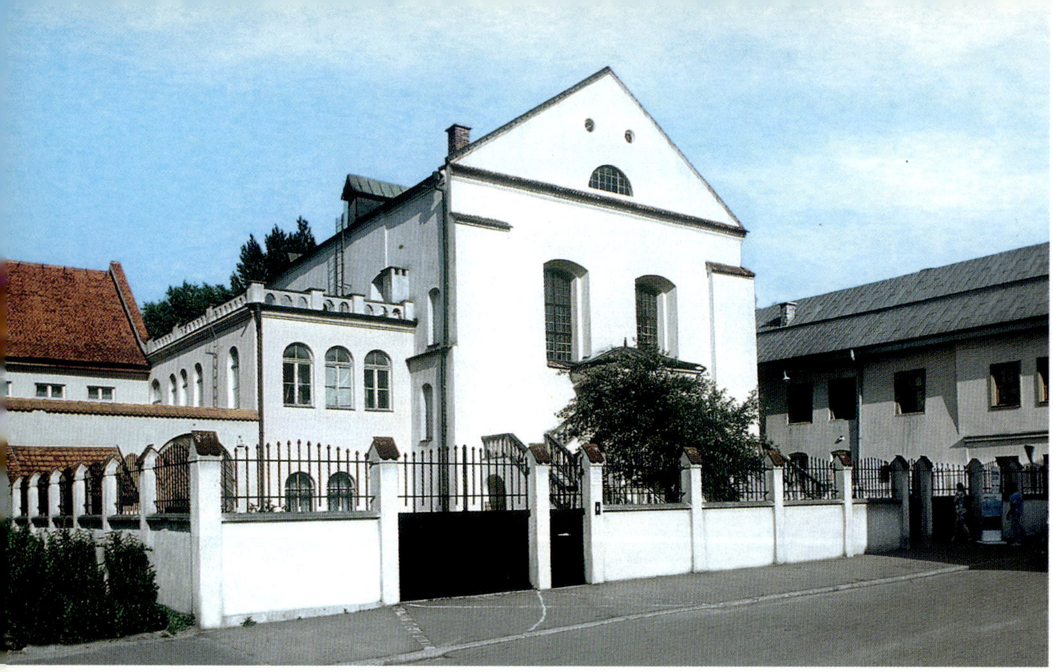

114. Jakuba Street in Kazimierz, the Isaac (Ajzyk) Synagogue, founded in the first half of the 17th c. by the merchant Isaac Jakubowicz, the senior member of the Jewish commune and a respected banker

115. Miodowa Street in Kazimierz, the Tempel Synagogue (second half of the 19th c.), one of the synagogues open in the city

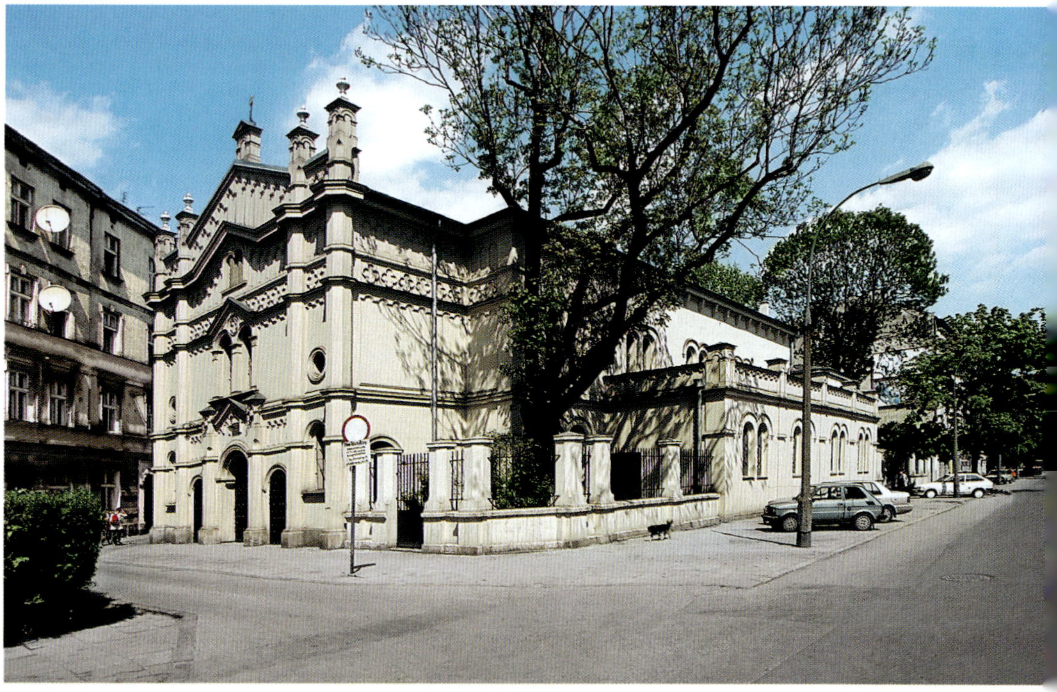

116. Szeroka Street in Kazimierz, the building of the *mykwa* (ritual bath) for men and women. It was built in the 16th c., rebuilt in the 17th c., and in 1997 reconstructed after damage in World War II (the old bathing pool has survived intact)

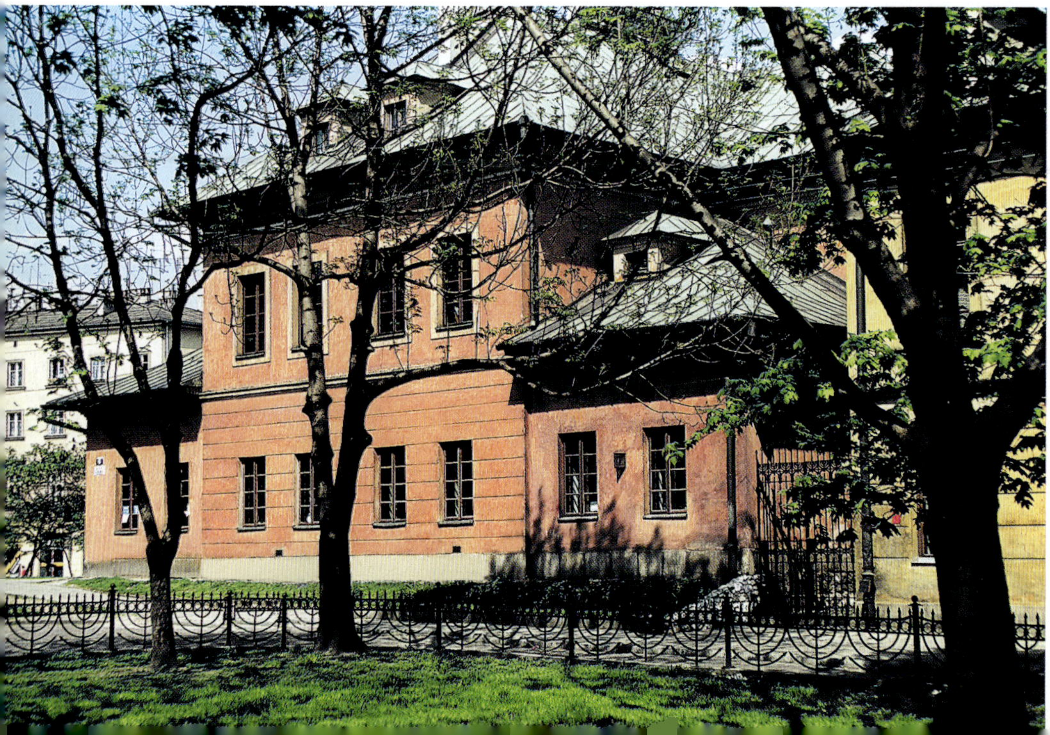

117-118. Facing page: a view to the Royal Castle on Wawel Hill from Wawrzyńca Street in Kazimierz. Bottom: Konopnickiej Street, the Centre of Japanese Art and Technology 'Manggha', built in the years 1993-1994, on the initiative of the film director Andrzej Wajda; it exhibits the Japanese art collection owned by the National Museum in Cracow

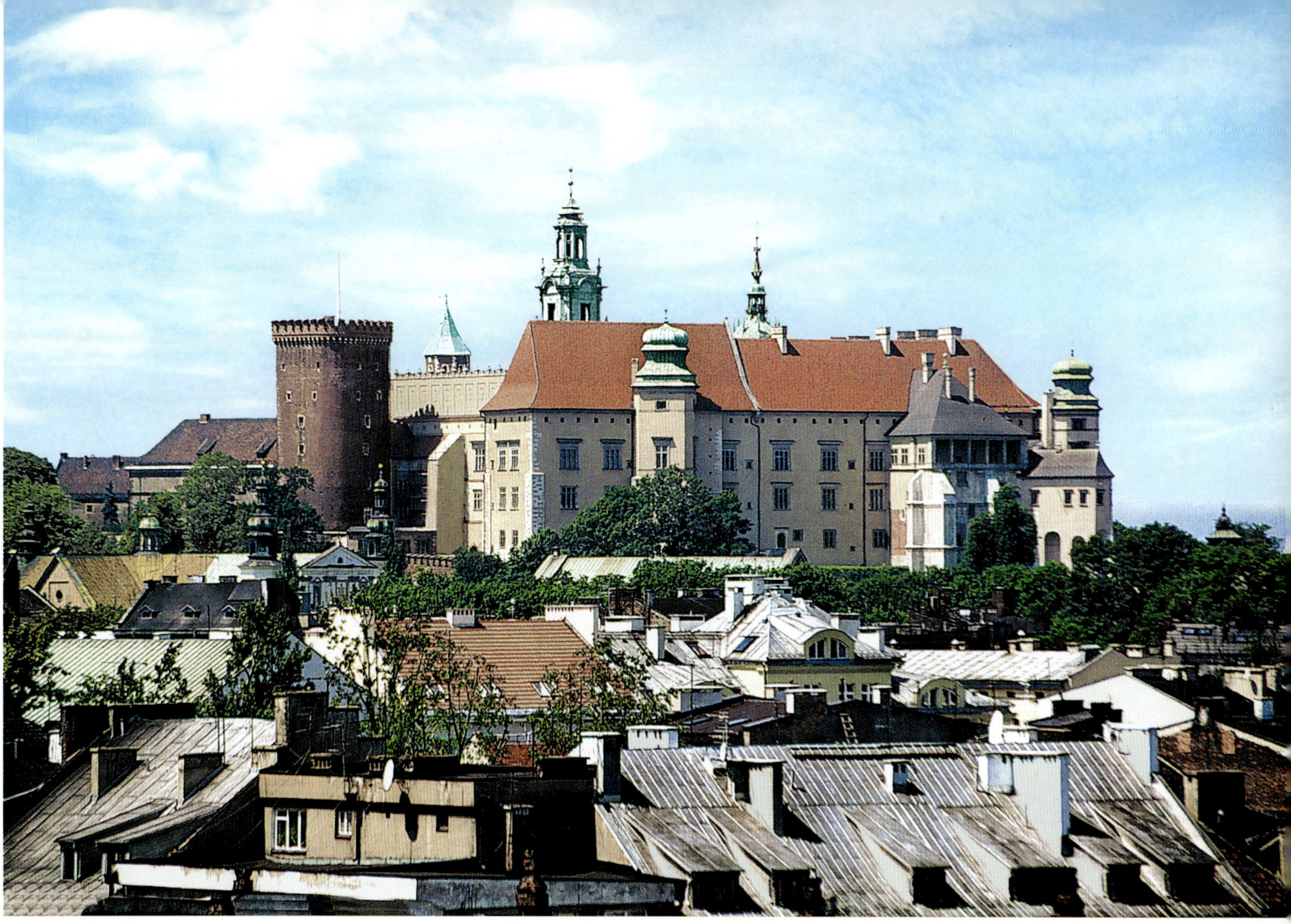

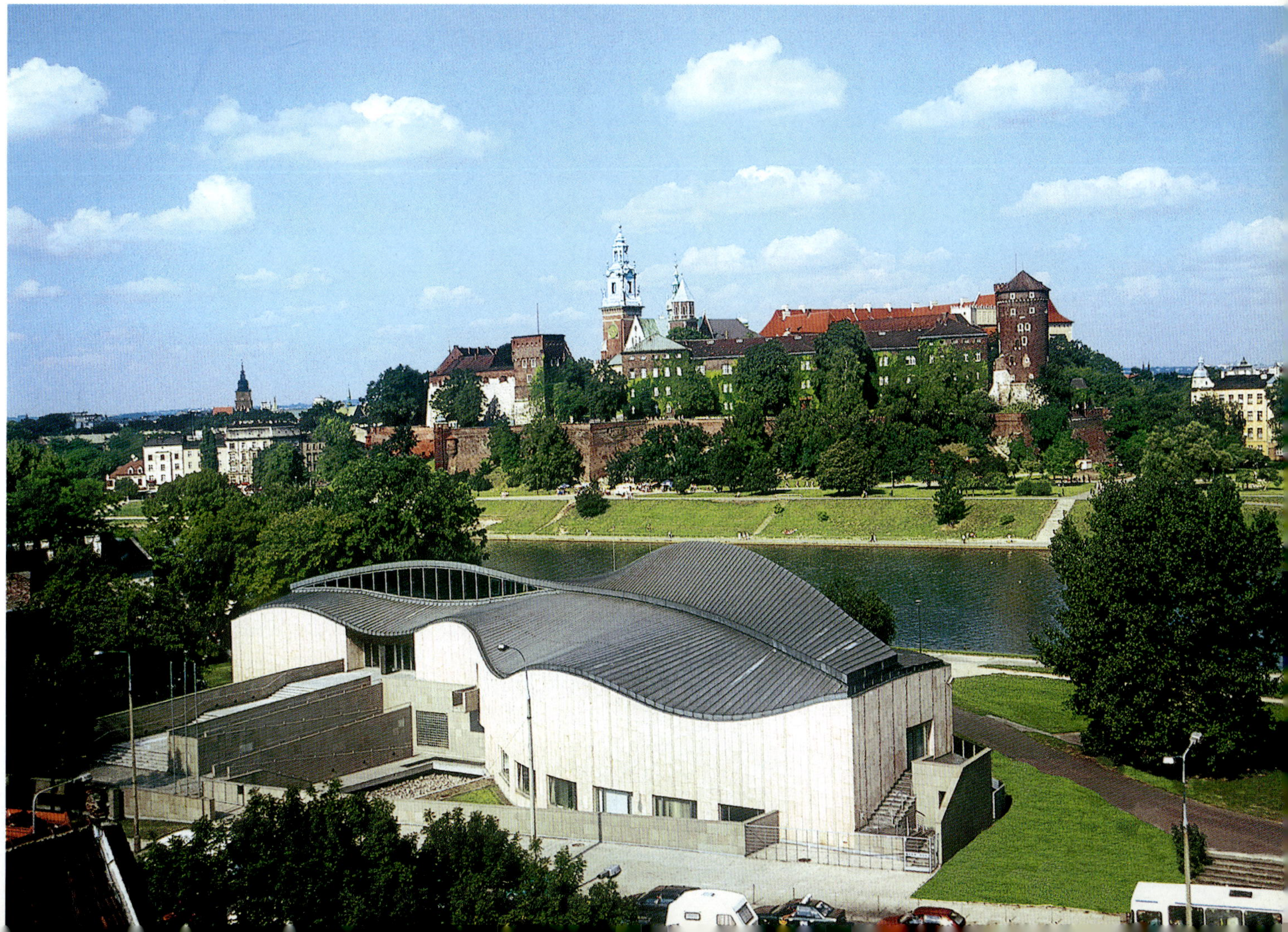

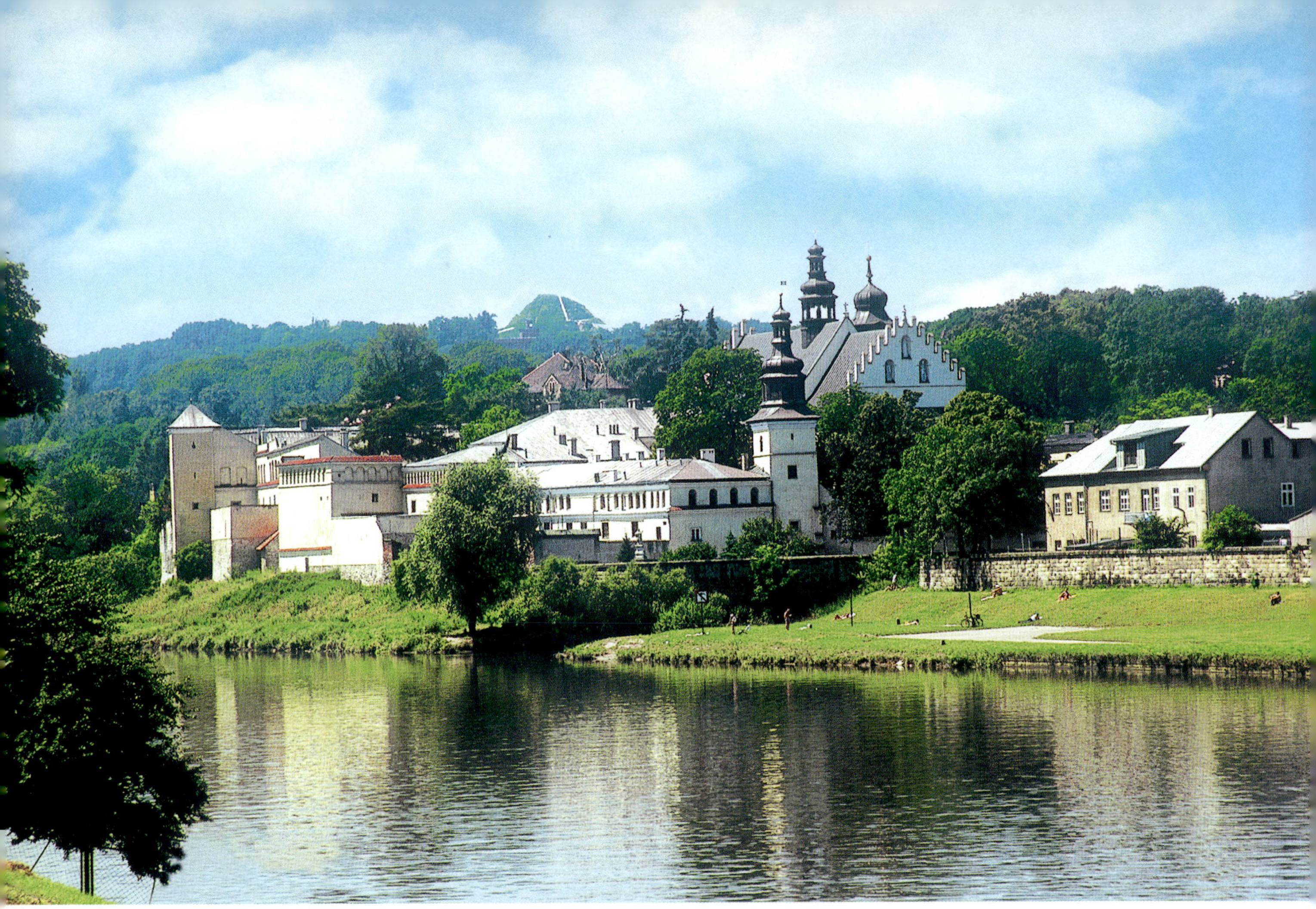

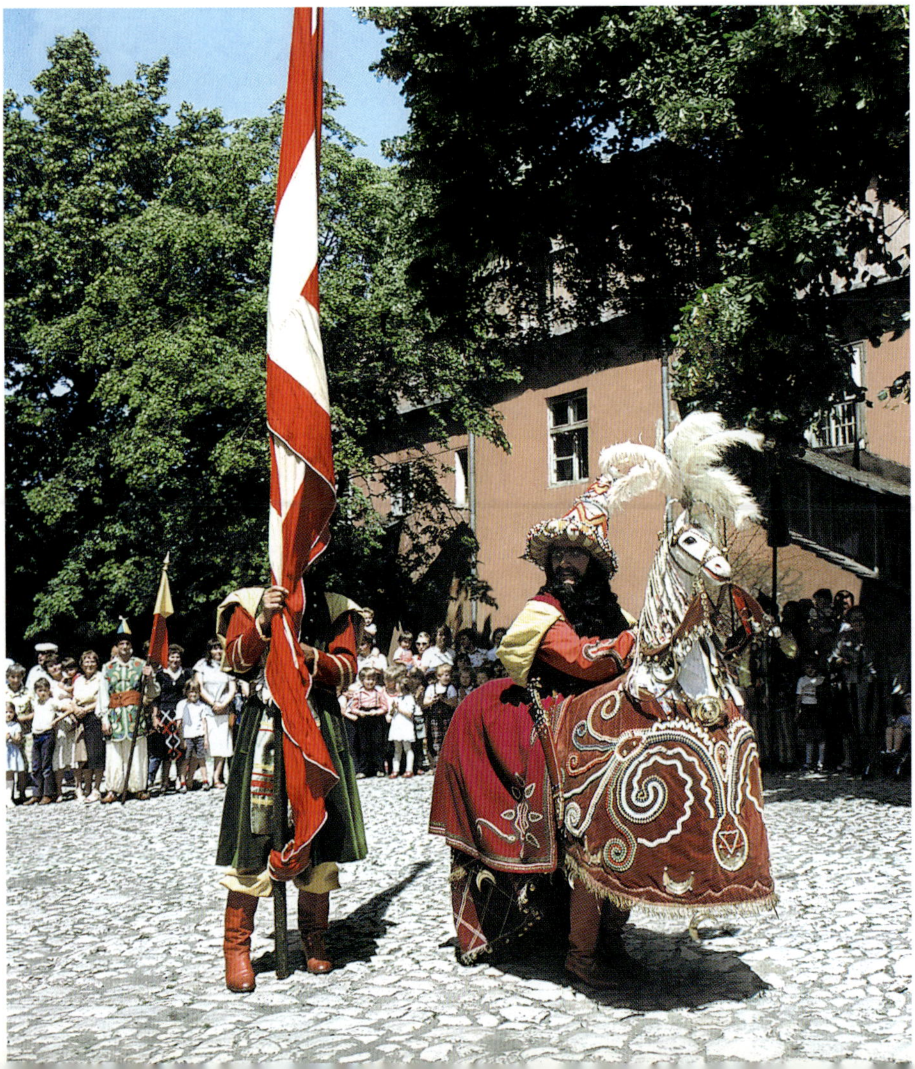

119. Salwator, the Church of SS Augustin and John the Baptist, and the complex of the Norbertine convent, situated picturesquely on the Vistula and its tributary, the Rudawa. It dates back to the 13th c., and its present shape was established in the mid-17th c. In the background the Kościuszko Mound on St Bronisława's Hill

120. The Norbertine convent; from its court the traditional procession of the Lajkonik starts each year, the custom followed probably since the Middle Ages

121. Bielany, the Camaldolese church and monastery on Silver Hill (first half of the 17th c.), Mannerist with a Baroque interior

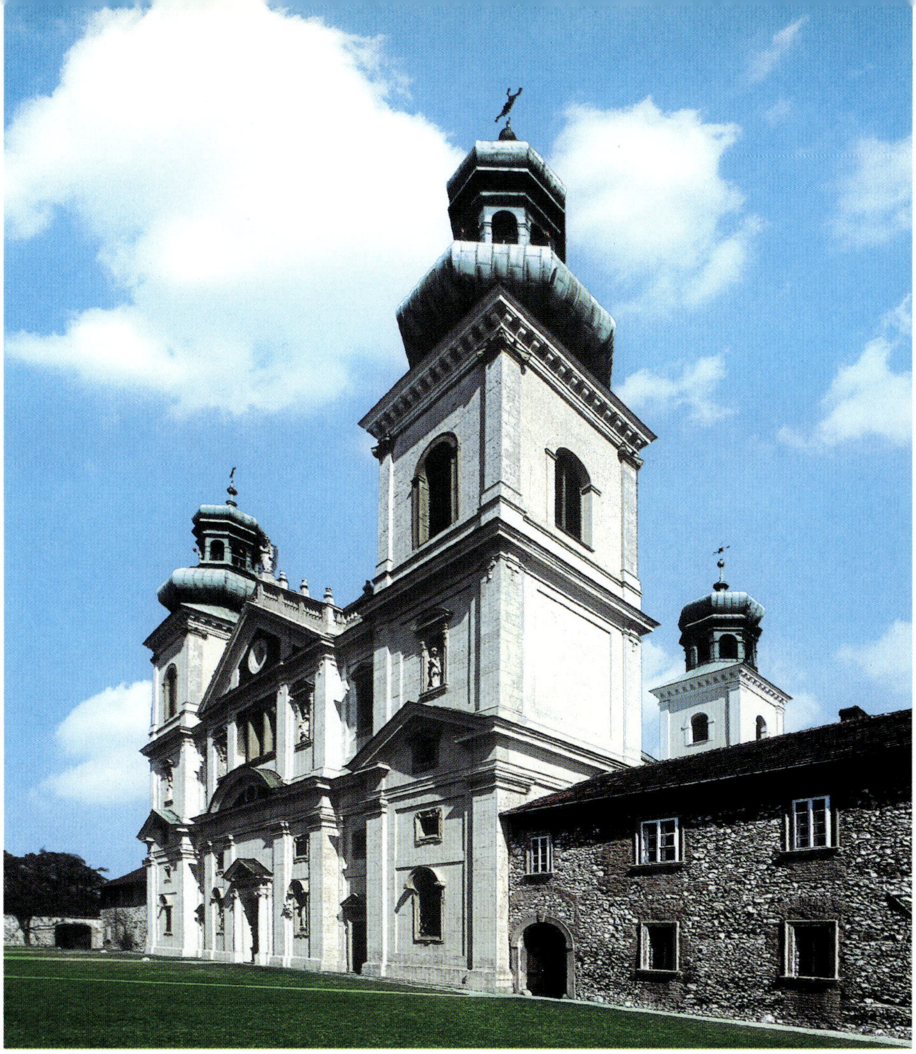

122. Tyniec, the Benedictine monastery, attractively situated on Jurassic rocks on the Vistula, founded by King Casimir the Restorer or King Boleslaus the Bold in the mid-11th c. Rebuilt after a Tartar raid in the 13th c., and surrounded with a wall with towers in the second half of the 15th c. At that time the Gothic Church of SS Peter and Paul the Apostles was built. In the second half of the 16th c. the monastery was rebuilt in the Renaissance style

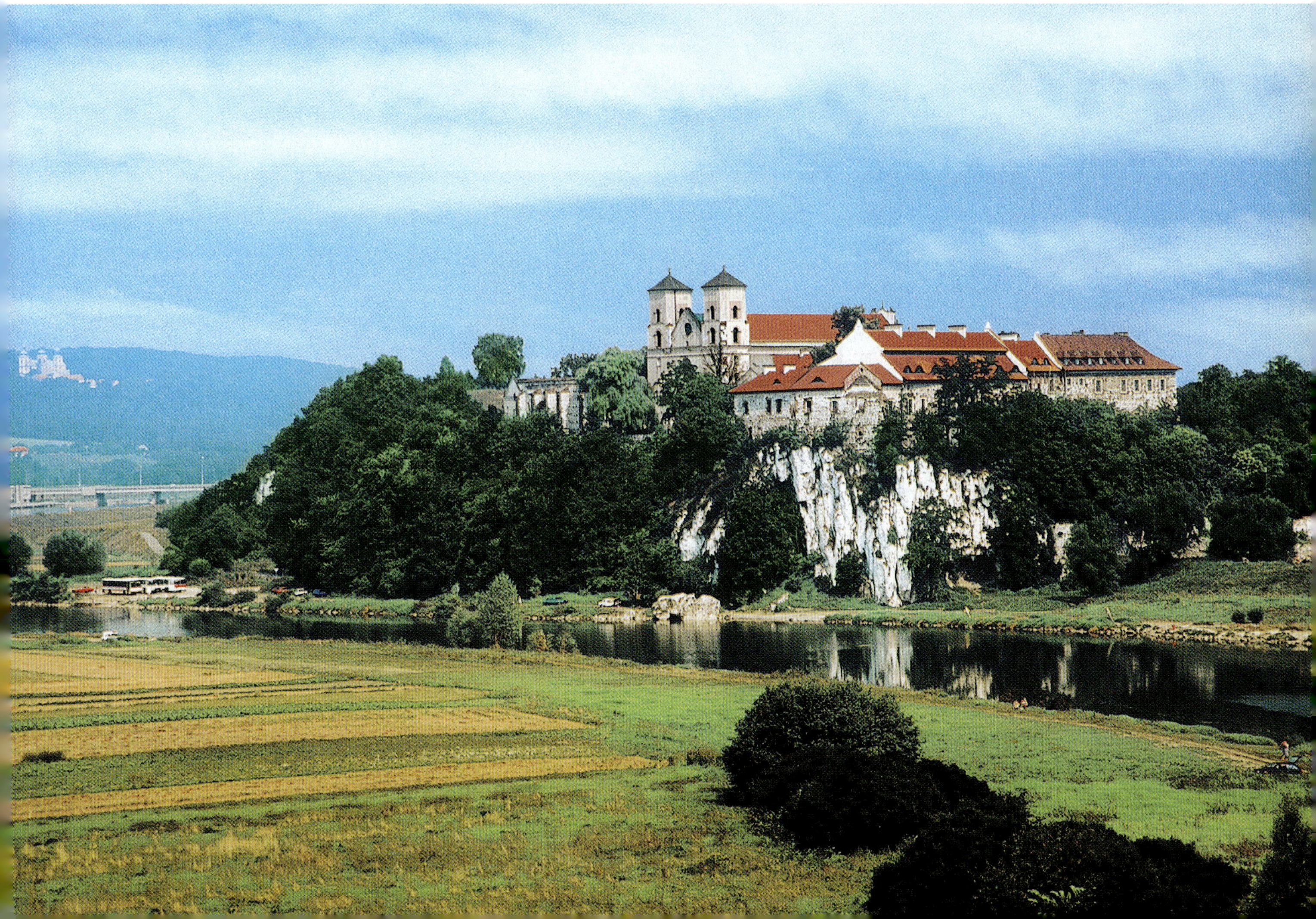

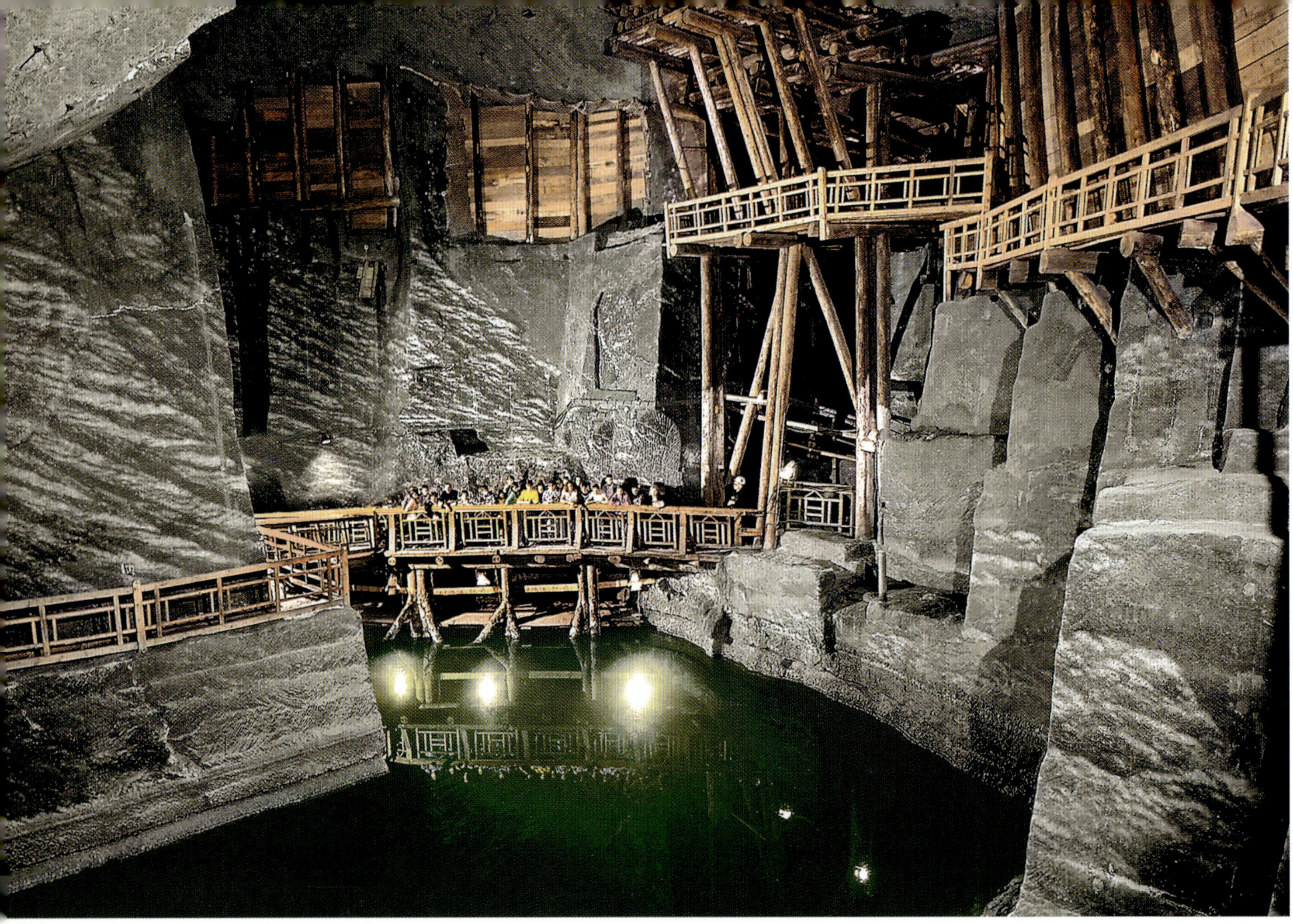

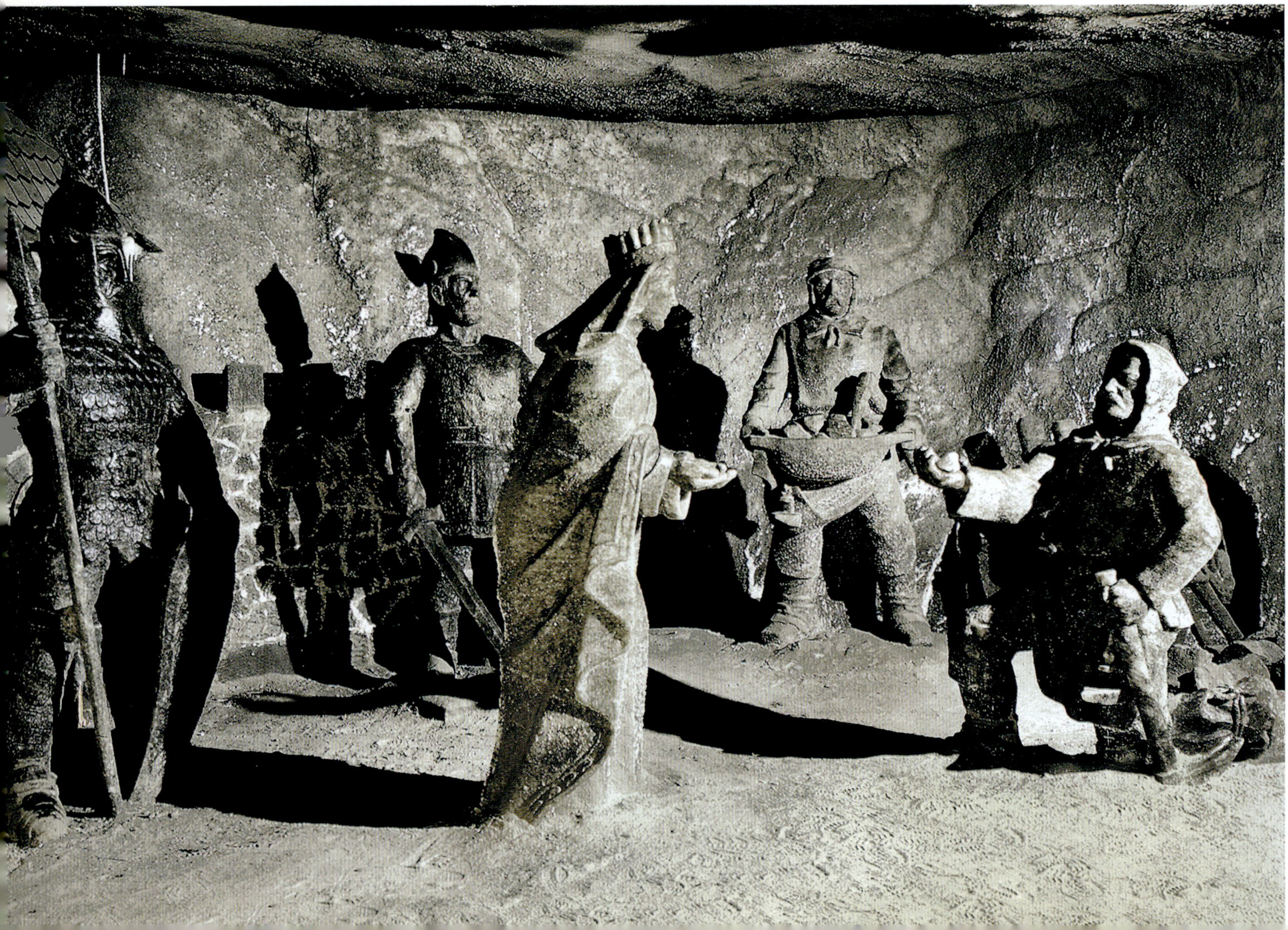

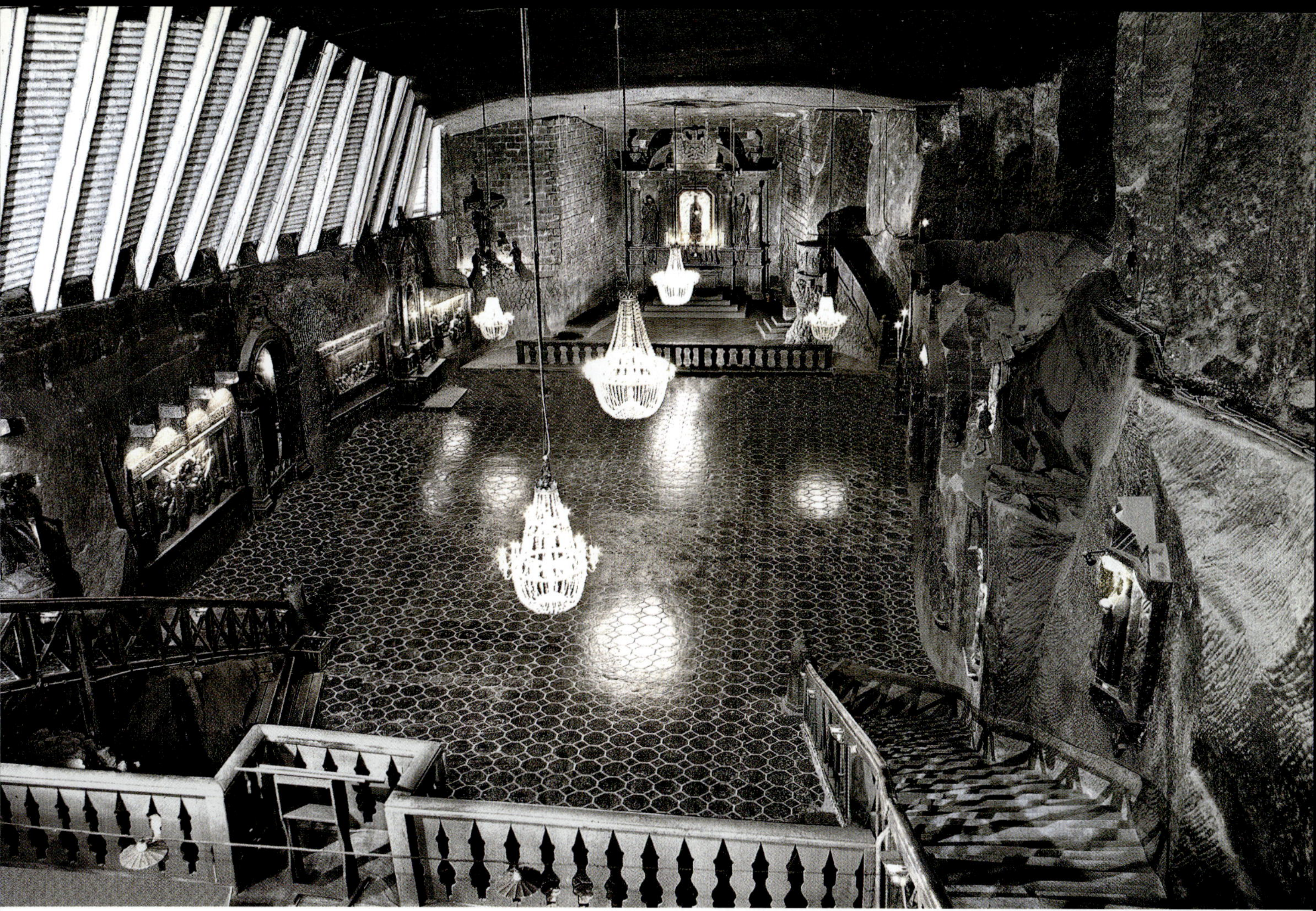

123-126. The Royal Salt Mine in Wieliczka near Cracow, where salt was mined already in the second half of the 13th c., was entered by the UNESCO on the first World List of Cultural and Natural Heritage in 1978. It may be visited by the Tourist Route, which runs along galleries, across chambers and past underground lakes as deep as 125 m underground. The impressive sculptures carved by miners in rock-salt, to be found in chambers on the route, as well as the natural beauty of the place, attract several hundred thousands of visitors each year. Facing page: the Erazm Barącz Chamber, exploited in the 19th c., with a salt lake, and 'The Great Legend', rock-salt sculpture by a miner sculptor Mieczysław Kluzek, in the Janowice Chamber (mined in the first half of the 17th c.); the sculpture shows the legendary scene of finding the ring of St Kinga, which had travelled together with salt from Hungary to Poland. This page: St Kinga's Chapel (101 m underground), a masterpiece carved in rock-salt by the local miner sculptors, the brothers Józef and Tomasz Markowski, and Antoni Wyrodek. Bottom: the Pieskowa Skała Chamber, one of the most beautiful in the mine

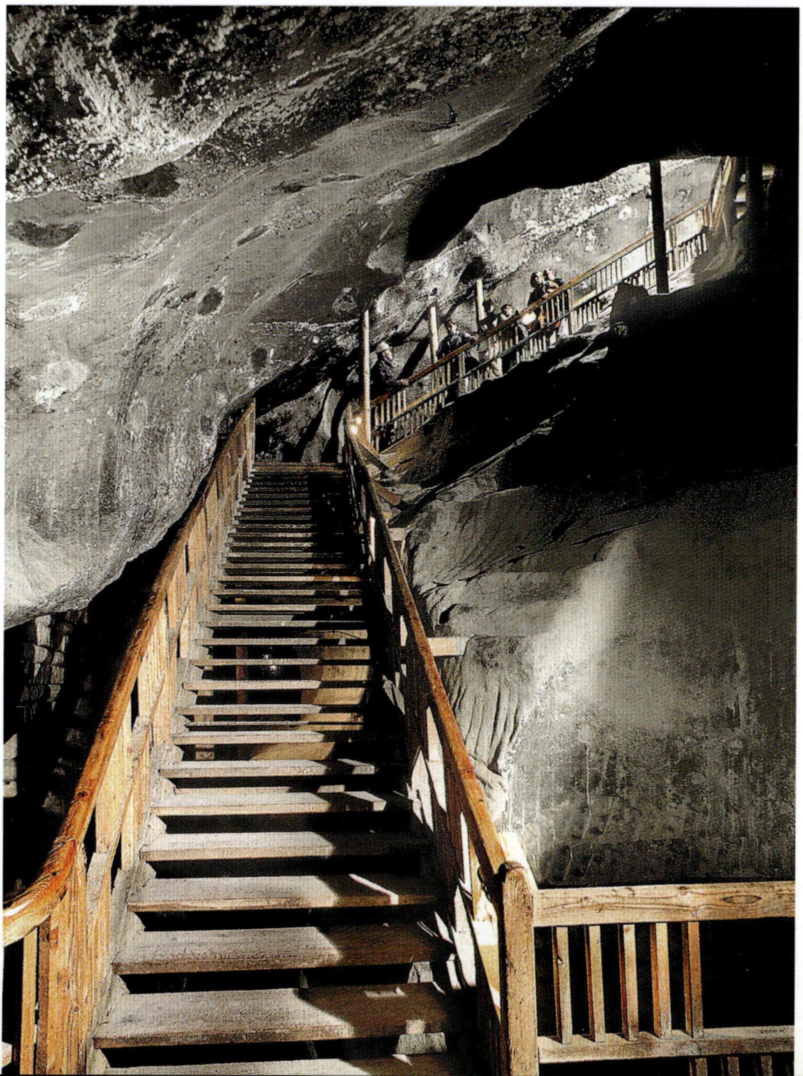

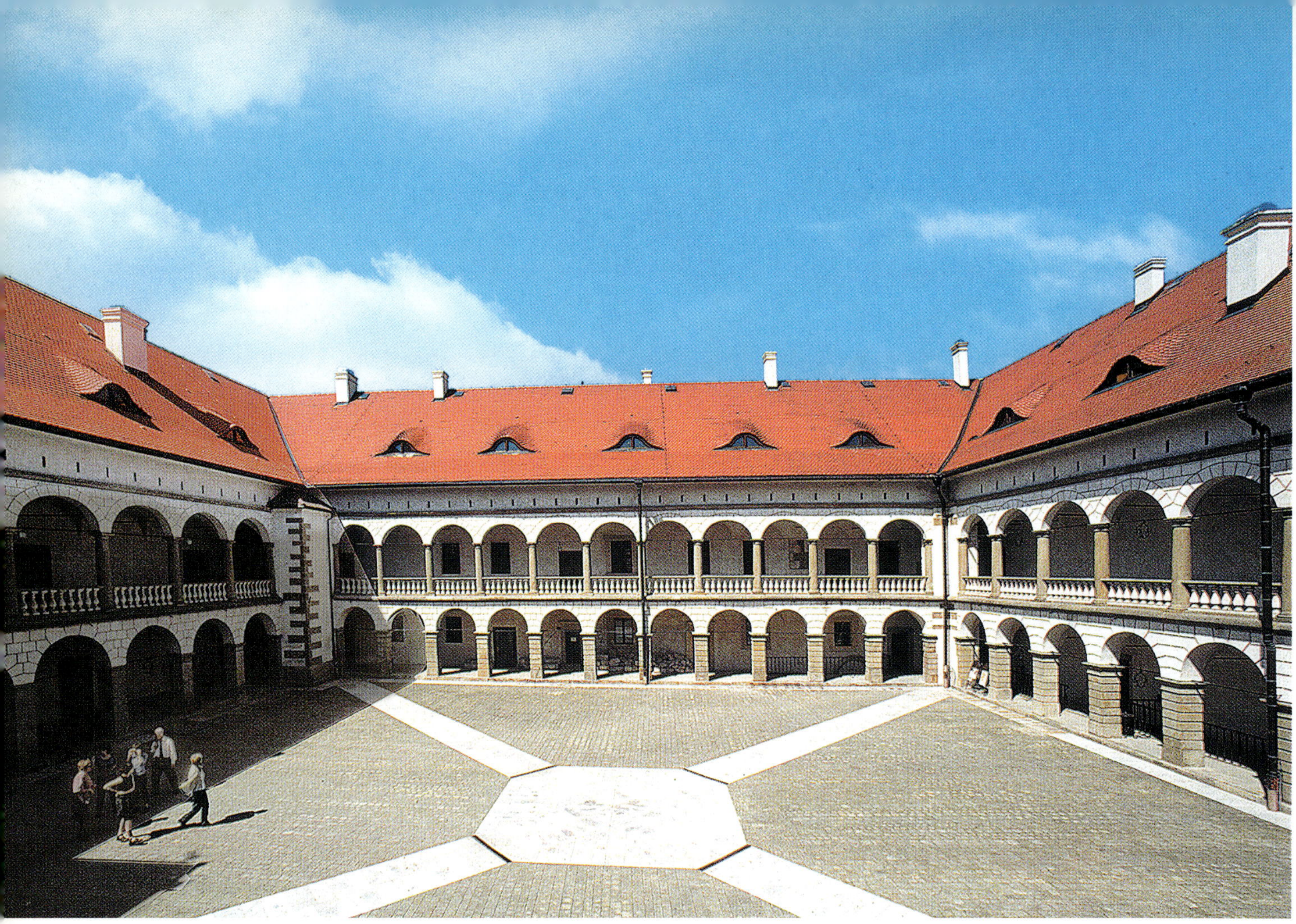

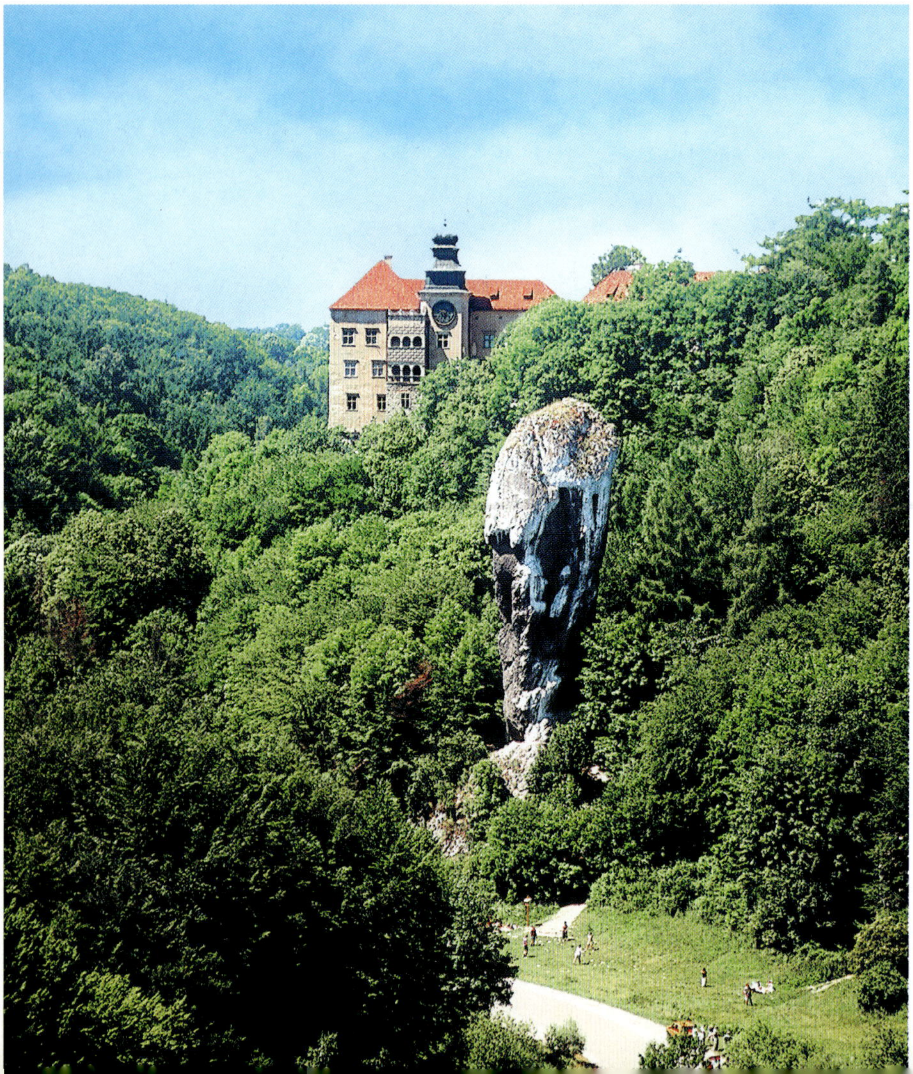

127. Niepołomice, east of Cracow, at the edge of the Niepołomicki Forest, the arcaded court of the castle, built in the 14th c. and rebuilt in the Renaissance style, which used to be the royal hunting lodge

128. Pieskowa Skała, the impressive castle, rebuilt in the 16th c. in the Renaissance style, with the 17th-century forticantions, situated high above the Prądnik Valley; it is now a museum. In the foreground one of the most attractive rocks, Hercules' Mace

129-130. Facing page: the Ojców National Park, in the most beautiful part of the Prądnik Valley, with unspoiled natural environment (north of Cracow). Bottom: a Jurassic cave (Wierzchowska Górna) in the Kluczwoda Valley (near the Ojców National Park), one of the largest and most remarkable caves in the limestone upland (Wyżyna Krakowsko-Wieluńska), its corridors are 975 m long

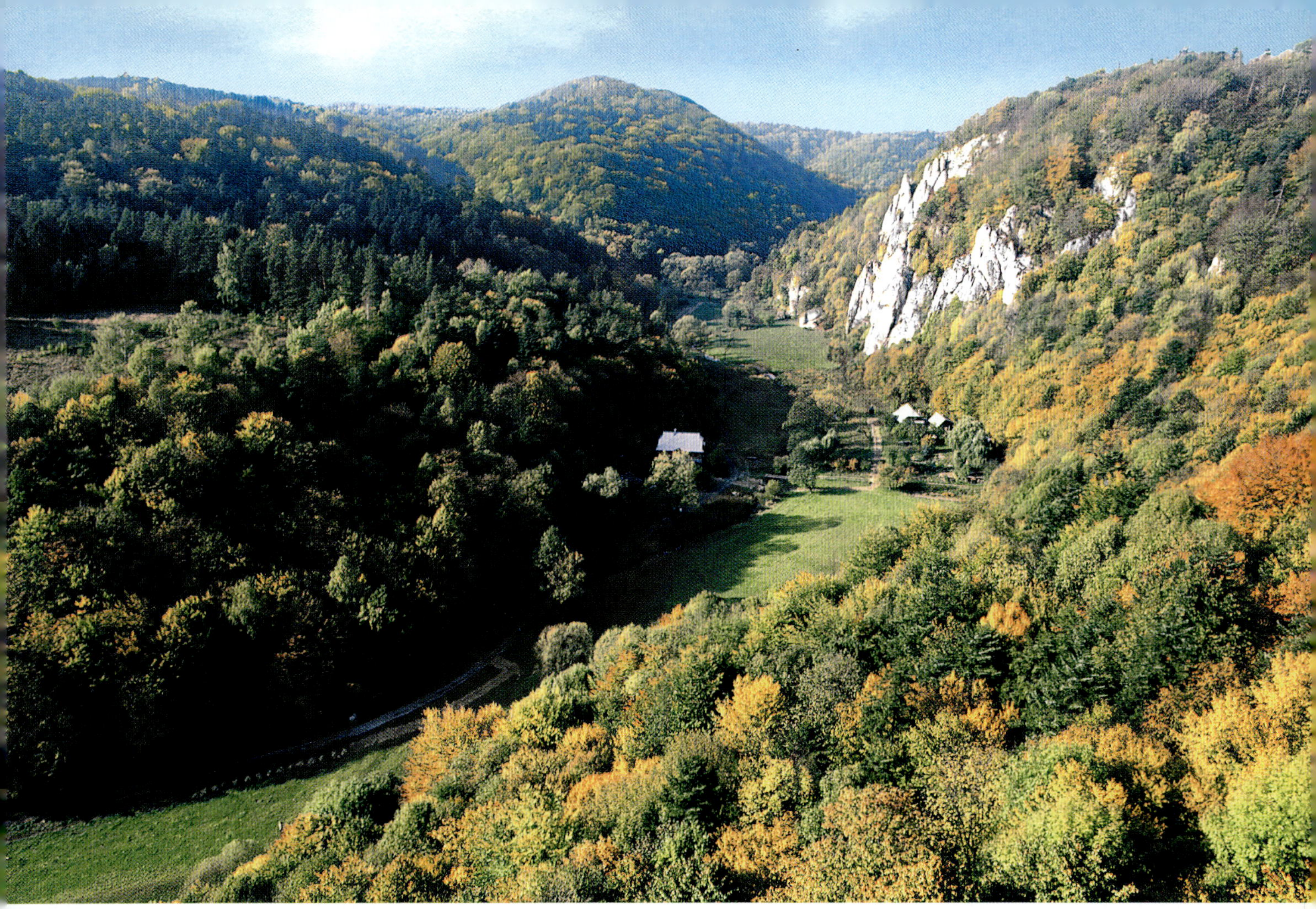

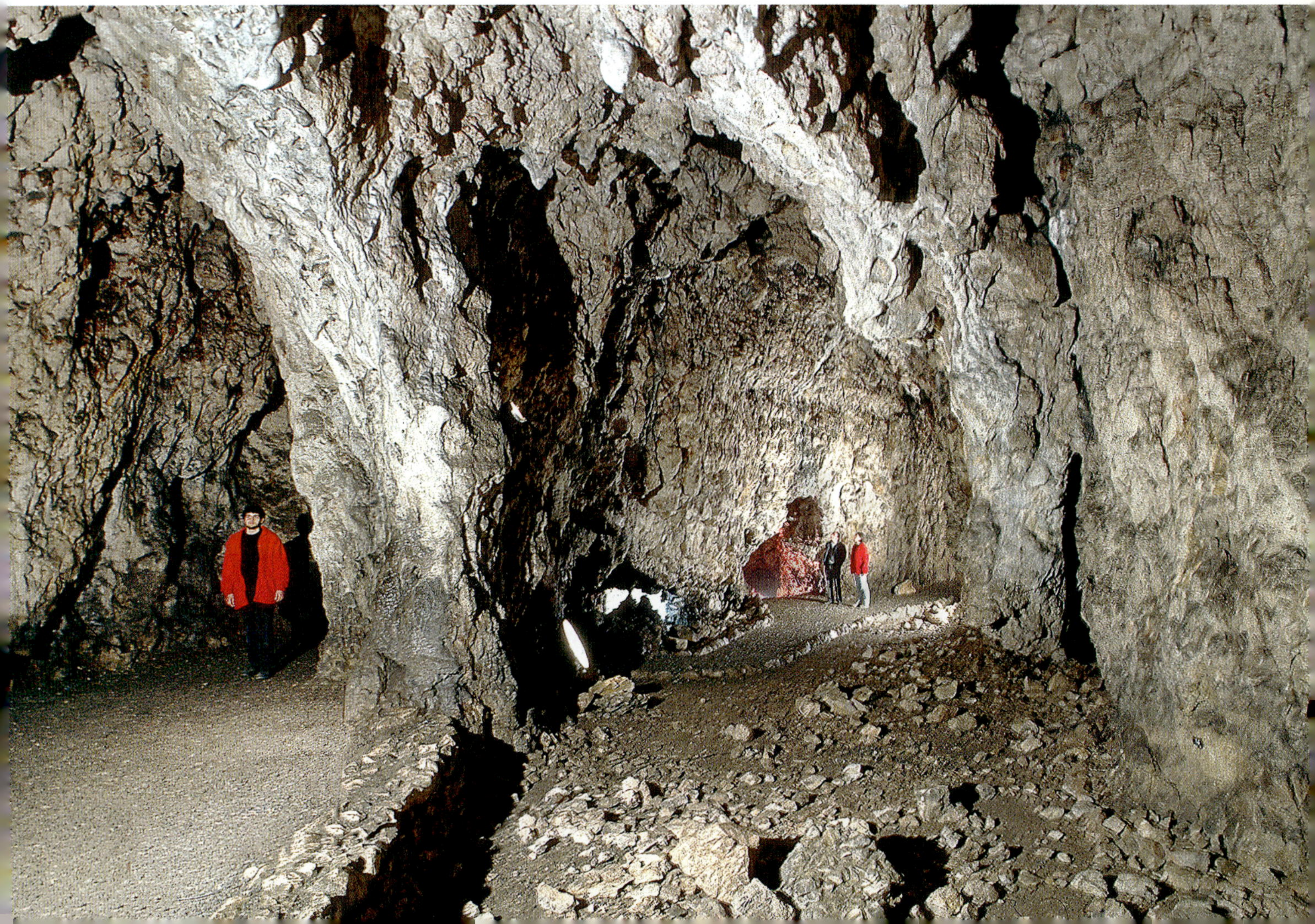

Photographs
© JANUSZ PODLECKI

Computer processing of photographs
© JANUSZ PODLECKI
In co-operation with „Lettra-Graphic", Cracow

Introduction
© GRAŻYNA ROTTER

Translated by
© JADWIGA PIĄTKOWSKA

Graphic design
© MAGDALENA MICHALSKA

Setting and plan
DESIGN FIRM „SZELEREWICZ", Cracow

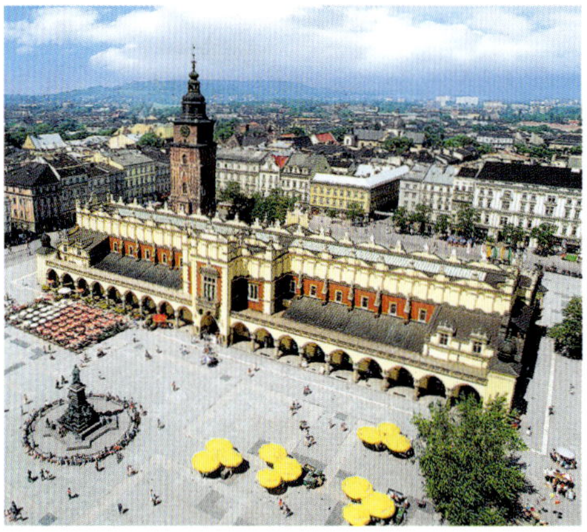

Printed by
FINIDR Ltd.

3rd edition, extended and modified

ISBN 83-88553-13-5

WYDAWNICTWO „KARPATY" – ANDRZEJ ŁĄCZYŃSKI
30-074 Kraków, ul. Kazimierza Wielkiego 21, tel./fax (48-12) 634-31-05

Published for
OXFORD INTE
AQA EXAMINA

International GCSE
COMBINED SCIENCES
Chemistry

Lawrie Ryan
Patrick Fullick
Editor: Lawrie Ryan

OXFORD
UNIVERSITY PRESS

OXFORD
UNIVERSITY PRESS

Great Clarendon Street, Oxford, OX2 6DP, United Kingdom

Oxford University Press is a department of the University of Oxford. It furthers the University's objective of excellence in research, scholarship, and education by publishing worldwide. Oxford is a registered trade mark of Oxford University Press in the UK and in certain other countries

First published in 2016

British Library Cataloguing in Publication Data
Data available

978-0-19-840794-2

10 9 8 7 6 5 4 3 2 1

Paper used in the production of this book is a natural, recyclable product made from wood grown in sustainable forests.
The manufacturing process conforms to the environmental regulations of the country of origin.

Printed in United Kingdom.

Acknowledgements
The publishers would like to thank the following for permissions to use copyright material:

Cover: Charles D. Winters/Science Photo Library

p7: sciencephotos/Alamy; p10: luismmolina/iStockphoto; **p17:** Martyn F. Chillmaid/Science Photo Library; **p26:** Leonard Lee Rue/Science Photo Library; **p27:** Dirk Wiersma/Science Photo Library; **p28:** Martyn F. Chillmaid; **p34:** Olga D. van de Veer/Fotolia.com; **p36:** Bloomberg via Getty Images; **p37t:** Joe Gough/Fotolia.com; **p37m:** iStockphoto; **p37b:** Pascal Goetgheluck/Science Photo Library; **p42:** Martyn F. Chillmaid/Science Photo Library; **p43:** Martyn F. Chillmaid; **p48l:** RosaIreneBetancourt 1/Alamy Stock Photo; **p48r** & **p49t:** iStockphoto; **p49b:** michellepix/fotolia.com; **p50:** Luis Veiga/Getty Images; **p51t:** Ton Kinsbergen/Science Photo Library; **p51:** iStockphoto; **p56l:** Britain on View/Photolibrary/Getty Images; **p56r:** iStockphoto; **p62t:** Peter Arnold Images/Photolibrary/Getty Images; **p62b:** DYK/iStockphoto; **p63:** Andrew Lambert Photography/Science Photo Library; **p66** & **p73:** iStockphoto; **p74t:** iStockphoto; **p74b:** aberenyi/fotolia.com; **p80:** Martyn F. Chillmaid; **p84t:** David Taylor/Science Photo Library; **p84b** & **p86:** Andrew Lambert Photography/Science Photo Library; **p87:** Charles D. Winters/Science Photo Library; **p90t:** Andrew Lambert Photography/Science Photo Library; **p90b:** Martyn F. Chillmaid/Science Photo Library; **p94:** Adrian Sherratt/Alamy; **p95:** iStockphoto; **p102t:** Michelle Lester/Fotolia.com; **p102b:** iStockphoto; **p104t:** Photolibrary/Getty Images; **p104b:** iStockphoto; **p105:** Phil Degginger/AlamyStock Photo; **p106:** Cordelia Molloy/Science Photo Library; **p108l:** Dr Keith Wheeler/Science Photo Library; **p108r:** Sheila Terry/Science Photo Library; **p112l:** Nina Ryan; **p112r:** iStockphoto; **p113:** Photolibrary/Getty Images; **p114:** Martyn F.Chillmaid; **p115:** Fuse/Getty Images; **p116:** Martyn F. Chillmaid/Science Photo Library; **p117:** Andrew Lambert Photography/Science Photo Library; **p124:** Tim Graham/Getty Images; **p127:** iStockphoto; **p128:** John Millar/Getty Images; **p129:** Photolibrary/Getty Images; **p130:** USDA; **p131:** Bloomberg/Getty Images; **p134:** Paul Rapson/Science Photo Library; **p136t:** Cordelia Molloy/Science Photo Library; **p136b:** Charles D. Winters/Science Photo Library; **p138:** fotomatrix/Fotolia.com; **p139:** Innershadows/Fotolia.com; **p140:** Image Source/Alamy; **p142:** iStockphoto; **p143:** AP Photo/Josh Reynolds; **p147:** Martyn F. Chillmaid/Science Photo Library; **p148:** OUP; **p149:** Andrew Lambert Photography/Science Photo Library; **p150:** Craig Lovell/Agstockusa/Science Photo Library.

Although we have made every effort to trace and contact all copyright holders before publication this has not been possible in all cases. If notified, the publisher will rectify any errors or omissions at the earliest opportunity.

Links to third party websites are provided by Oxford in good faith and for information only. Oxford disclaims any responsibility for the materials contained in any third party website referenced in this work.

With special thanks to Emma Gadsden for her editing and management of the project.

Chemistry

Contents

How to use this book

This book has been written for you by experienced teachers and subject experts. It covers the information you need to know for your exams and is packed full of features to help you achieve the very best that you can.

Figure 1 Many diagrams are as important for you to learn as the text, so make sure you revise them carefully

Key words are highlighted in the text. You can look them up in the glossary at the back of the book if you are not sure what they mean.

Required practical

This feature helps you become familiar with key practicals. It may be a simple introduction, a reminder or the basis for a practical in the laboratory.

Summary questions

These questions give you the chance to test whether you have learned and understood everything in the topic. If you get any wrong, go back and have another look. They are designed to be increasingly challenging.

And at the end of each chapter you will find …

Chapter summary questions

These will test you on what you have learned throughout the whole chapter, helping you to work out what you have understood and where you need to go back and revise.

Practice questions

These questions are examples of the types of questions you may encounter in your exam, so you can get lots of practice during your course.

Ext Extension Tier material is shown with this label. This will not be included in the Core Tier exams.

Learning objectives

Each topic begins with key statements that you should know by the end of the lesson.

Study tip

Hints that give you important advice on things to remember and what to watch out for.

Did you know … ?

There are lots of interesting and often strange facts about science. This feature tells you about many of them.

links

Links will tell you where you can find more information about what you are learning and how different topics link up.

Activity

An activity is linked to a main lesson and could be a discussion or task in pairs, groups or by yourself.

Key points

At the end of each topic are the important points that you must remember. They can be used to help with revision and summarising your knowledge.

Practical skills

During this course, you will develop your understanding of the scientific process and the skills associated with scientific enquiry. Practical work is an important part of this as it develops these skills and also reinforces concepts and knowledge developed during the course.

As part of this course, all students are expected to undertake practical work in many topics and are required to carry out the three required practicals listed below:

Required Practicals

1. Identify the metal ion in an unknown compound using flame testing techniques. (3.10.1) [Topic 6.3]

2. Determination of the reacting volumes of solutions of a strong acid and a strong alkali by titration. (3.11.1) [Topic 7.4]

3. Investigate factors affecting the rate of a reaction. (3.13.1) [Topics 8.3 and 8.4]

In Paper 2, you will be assessed on aspects of the practical skills listed below, and may be required to read and interpret information from scales given in diagrams and charts, present data in appropriate formats, design investigations and evaluate information that is presented to them.

Designing a practical procedure

- Design a practical procedure to answer a question, solve a problem or test a hypothesis.
- Comment on/evaluate plans for practical procedures.
- Select suitable apparatus for carrying out experiments accurately and safely.

Control

- Appreciate that, unless certain variables are controlled, experimental results may not be valid.
- Recognise the need to choose appropriate sample sizes, and study control groups where necessary.

Risk assessment

- Identify possible hazards in practical situations, the risks associated with these hazards, and methods of minimising the risks.

Collecting data

- Make and record observations and measurements with appropriate precision and record data collected in an appropriate format (such as a table, chart or graph).

Analysing data

- Recognise and identify the cause of anomalous results and suggest what should be done about them.
- Appreciate when it is appropriate to calculate a mean, calculate a mean from a set of at least three results and recognise when it is appropriate to ignore anomalous results in calculating a mean.
- Recognise and identify the causes of random errors and systematic errors.
- Recognise patterns in data, form hypotheses and deduce relationships.
- Use and interpret tabular and graphical representations of data.

Making conclusions

- Draw conclusions that are consistent with the evidence obtained and support them with scientific explanations.

Evaluation

- Evaluate data, considering its repeatability, reproducibility and validity in presenting and justifying conclusions.
- Evaluate methods of data collection and appreciate that the evidence obtained may not allow a conclusion to be made with confidence.
- Suggest ways of improving an investigation or practical procedure to obtain extra evidence to allow a conclusion to be made.

1.1 States of matter

Learning objectives

After this topic, you should know:

- there are three states of matter
- the arrangement and motion of the particles in each state of matter
- the names of the processes and energy changes involved in changing state.

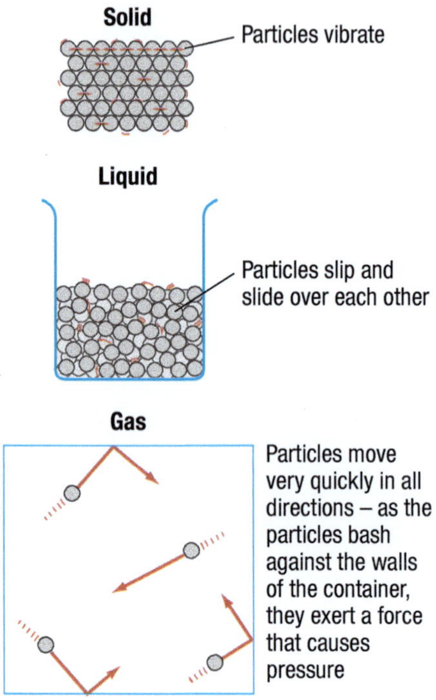

Figure 1 *The particles in the three states of matter*

You can classify the majority of substances as solids, liquids, or gases. These are called the three **states of matter**.

Solids have a fixed shape and volume. They cannot be compressed. **Liquids** have a fixed volume, but they can flow and change their shape. Liquids occupy just slightly more space than when solid (water and ice are exceptions). **Gases** have no fixed shape or volume. They can be compressed easily.

To explain the properties of solids, liquids, and gases you use the kinetic theory of matter. It is based on the fact that all matter is made up of tiny particles and describes:

- the movement of the particles, and
- the average distance between particles

within each state of matter.

Look at the diagrams to the left that represent the three states of matter.

Each particle in a solid is touching its nearest neighbours and they remain in this fixed arrangement. They cannot move around, but they do vibrate constantly.

The particles in a liquid are also very close together but they can move past each other. This results in a constantly changing, random arrangement of particles.

The particles in a gas have much more space, on average, between them. They can move around at high speeds and in any direction. This means the particles have a random arrangement. The hotter the gas is, the faster the particles move. The pressure of a gas is caused by the particles colliding with the sides of the container. The more frequent and energetic the collisions are, the higher the pressure of the gas. So, in a sealed container, the pressure of the gas increases with temperature.

Changing state

If a solid is heated and changes directly to a gas without melting, that is, it does not pass through the liquid phase, the change of state is called sublimation.

Look at the changes of state that occur when water is heated and cooled:

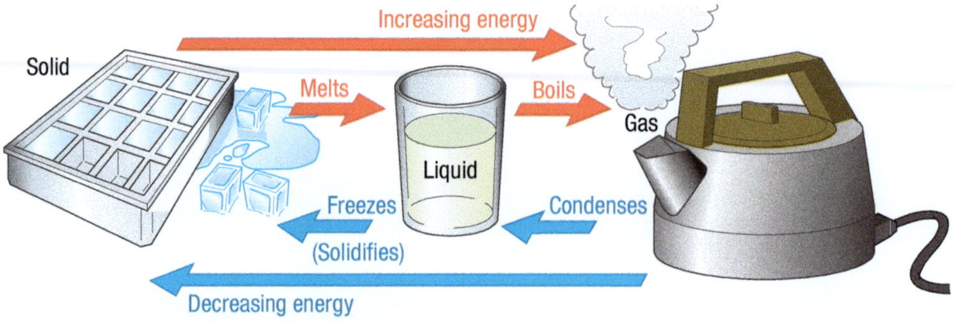

Figure 2 *The changes of state in water*

The hotter a solid is, the faster its particles vibrate. Eventually, the vibrations will be so strong that the particles begin to break free from their neighbours. At this point the solid starts to melt and become a liquid.

links

To find out how to indicate a substance's state in a balanced symbol equation, see Topic 1.5 Chemical equations.

The hotter a liquid is, the faster its particles move around. As the temperature rises, more and more particles gain enough energy to escape from the surface of the liquid. Its rate of evaporation increases. Eventually, the liquid boils and bubbles of gas rise and escape from within the liquid.

Each change of state is reversible. They are examples of physical changes. No new substances are formed in changes of state. For example, water molecules (H_2O) are the same in ice as they are in liquid water or in water vapour.

Energy changes during changes of state

When you monitor the temperature of a solid as you heat it to beyond its melting point, the results are surprising. The temperature stops rising at the solid's melting point. It remains constant until all the solid has melted, and only then starts to rise again.

At its melting point, the energy provided in heating the solid is being absorbed to break the forces between the particles in the solid. Once all the solid has melted, the energy from the heat source raises the temperature of the liquid as expected.

Changes of state which involve particles becoming closer together, that is, condensing and freezing (solidifying), transfer energy to the surroundings as stronger forces form between particles.

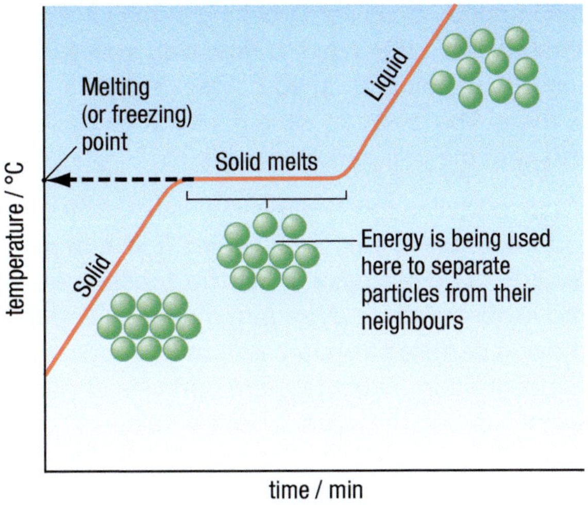

Figure 3 *The heating curve of a solid*

Practical

Cooling curve

Heat a test tube of stearic acid clamped in a water bath until its temperature reaches about 75 °C. Then remove the test tube from the hot water and monitor the temperature as it falls. Plot or print off a graph of the results.

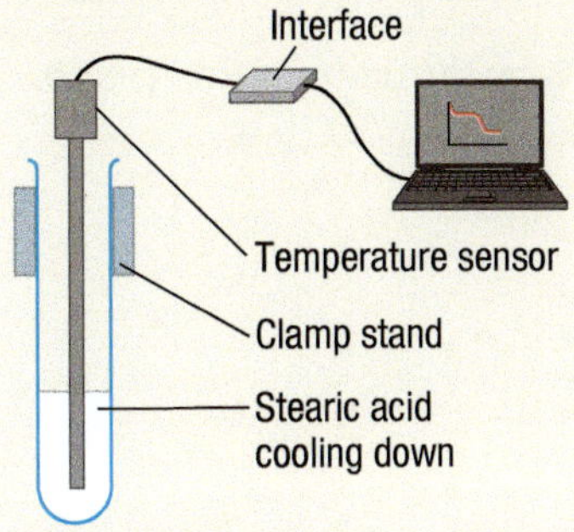

- What is the melting point of stearic acid?
- Explain the shape of the line on your graph.

Safety: Wear eye protection.

Summary questions

1 Draw a table to summarise the general properties of solids, liquids, and gases, as well as the average distance, arrangement, and movement of their particles.

2 Describe the changes that occur to the particles as a gas is cooled down to a temperature below its freezing point.

3 Name the following changes:
a liquid → solid **b** gas → liquid **c** solid → liquid
d liquid → gas **e** solid → gas (in a single step)

4 Using the kinetic theory of matter, predict how temperature and pressure affect the density of a fixed mass of gas.

5 Explain why substances have different melting points in terms of their particles.

6 Evaporation is the change of state that occurs when a liquid changes to a gas below its boiling point. You can investigate the factors that affect the rate of evaporation using a wet paper towel on a high resolution electronic balance.
Plan an investigation into one factor that might affect the rate of evaporation of water from the paper towel, writing a brief method.

Key points

- **The three states of matter are solids, liquids, and gases.**
- **The particles in a solid are packed closely together, fixed in their positions and vibrate.**
- **The particles in a liquid are also close together but can slip and slide over each other in random motion.**
- **The particles in a gas have, on average, lots of space between them and zoom around randomly.**
- **Melting and boiling take in energy from the surroundings as they take place, whereas freezing and condensing transfer energy to the surroundings when they occur.**

1.2 Evidence for particles

Learning objectives

After this topic, you should know:

- some evidence for the existence of particles in matter
- why diffusion takes place.

All the substances that make up our world are made of tiny particles. These particles are too small to see, although nowadays the latest powerful microscopes can show us images of particles. Scientists have developed special probes that can measure very small forces. These probes can be used to detect particles, and even position them where you want. However, long before the invention of these microscopes, people, such as the ancient Greeks, had proposed particle models to explain the properties of materials.

Diffusion

If somebody does some baking in the kitchen, the smell quickly spreads through into other rooms. However, you don't ***see*** any particles moving through the air and up your nose. Yet your sense of smell tells you that it really is there. The bread or cake gives off invisible particles of itself. These particles mix with the gas particles in the air.

When particles mix like this it is called **diffusion**. Diffusion happens automatically in mixtures that include substances which are liquids and gases. You don't need to mix or stir the substances. The particles in liquids and gases move constantly in a random manner. Gradually, this has the overall effect of moving particles from an area of ***high*** concentration to an area of ***low*** concentration. Eventually the particles of gas in a closed container will be evenly spread throughout the container.

Diffusion in liquids

Practical

Diffusion through a liquid

Use tweezers to pick up a few potassium manganate(VII) crystals.

Gently place them at the bottom of a beaker of water.

Observe the beaker for a few minutes.

- What do you see happen?

Leave your beaker until your next lesson.

Draw a diagram to show your results.

- Explain what you think happens to the purple particles.

Use the words **particles** and **diffuse** in your answer.

Safety: Wear eye protection. The crystals are harmful and will stain clothing and skin.

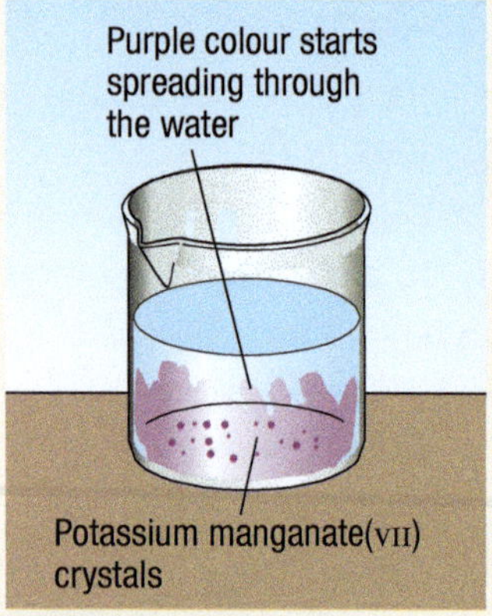

Figure 1 *Diffusion of potassium manganate(VII) through water*

Practical

Does temperature affect the rate of diffusion?

Plan an investigation to see how temperature affects the rate of diffusion through a liquid.

Let your teacher check your plan before you start any practical work.

Diffusion in gases

As in liquids, the random motion of particles in a gas enables diffusion to take place.

You can show this using a coloured gas, just as you used coloured particles dissolved in water in the first practical to demonstrate diffusion in a liquid. A little bromine liquid is placed in a gas jar with a lid. Bromine vapour evaporates from the volatile liquid and fills the gas jar. Then a second gas jar of air is placed upside down on top of the original bromine-filled gas jar and the lid is removed, linking the jars together. Even though bromine vapour is much more dense than air, the bromine gas gets distributed evenly between the two gas jars after a time. The rapid, random movement of air and bromine particles (molecules) ensure complete mixing takes place.

Diffusion takes place more quickly through gases than through liquids. That is because the particles of gas are moving much more rapidly, on average, than the particles in a liquid.

You find that lighter particles of gas move faster, on average, than heavy ones at the same temperature. Therefore small, light particles diffuse faster than large, heavy ones.

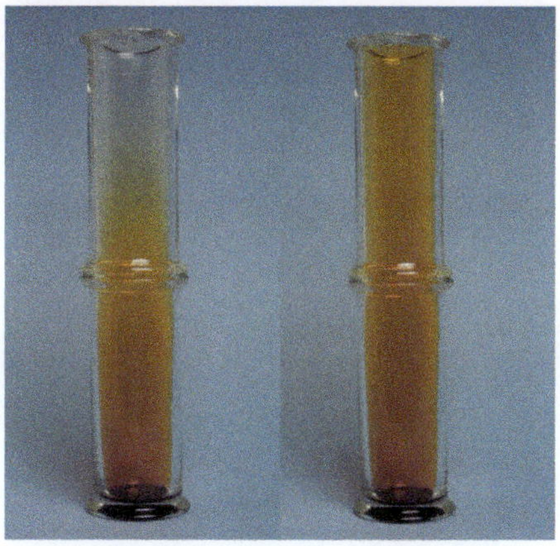

Figure 2 *Bromine vapour diffuses and mixes thoroughly with the air*

Demonstration

Diffusion through a gas

Watch what happens when the stoppers from bottles of concentrated ammonia solution and hydrochloric acid are brought near each other.

The reaction is:

ammonia + hydrogen chloride → ammonium chloride

$NH_3(g)$ + $HCl(g)$ → $NH_4Cl(s)$
(seen as white 'smoke')

Your teacher will set up the apparatus as shown below:

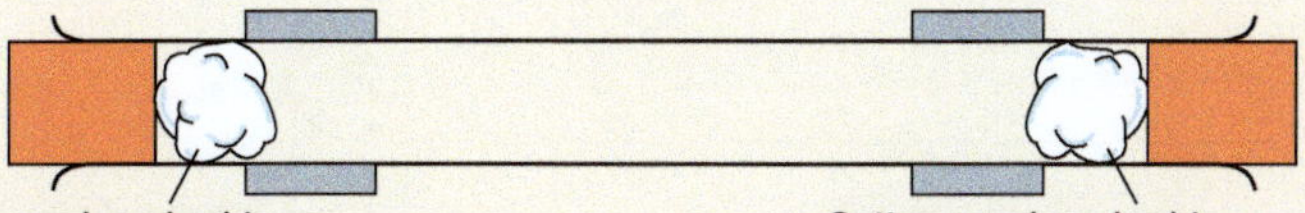

Figure 3 *Diffusion of $NH_3(g)$ and $HCl(g)$ through air*

- What do you see in the long tube where the HCl(g) and $NH_3(g)$ particles meet?
- Which particles diffuse faster, $NH_3(g)$ or HCl(g)? How can you tell?

In this experiment, the particles meet nearer the acid end of the tube.

- Which particles are lighter, the HCl(g) or $NH_3(g)$?

Safety: Do not inhale the gases. If you are asthmatic take particular care.

Summary questions

1. Explain each of the statements below in terms of particles:
   - **a** You can smell a fish and chip shop from across the road.
   - **b** Sugar dissolves faster in hot water than cold water.
   - **c** Condensation forms on the inside of your bathroom windows in winter.
   - **d** It is dangerous to smoke or strike a match in a petrol station.
2. **a** Define the word 'diffusion'.
   - **b** Explain why diffusion takes place more quickly in a gas than in a liquid.
3. When pollen grains in water are viewed under a microscope, the grains are seen to be moving in a haphazard, jittery manner. This is called Brownian motion, after the scientist who first observed it. Explain how Brownian motion gives us evidence for the existence of particles in matter.
4. Hydrogen bromide (HBr) is a similar gas to hydrogen chloride (HCl) but its particles (molecules) are more than twice as heavy. If the demonstration 'Diffusion through a gas' in Figure 3 was done with HBr(g) instead of HCl(g), explain what you would expect to see happen.

Key points

- **All substances are made up of particles.**
- **In liquids and gases, the random movement of particles mixes substances in a process called diffusion.**
- **Diffusion takes place faster in a gas than in a liquid.**
- **Small, light particles diffuse faster than large, heavy ones.**

1.3 History of the atom

Learning objectives

After this topic, you should know:

- how and why the atomic model has changed over time
- that scientific theories are revised or replaced by new ones in the light of new evidence.

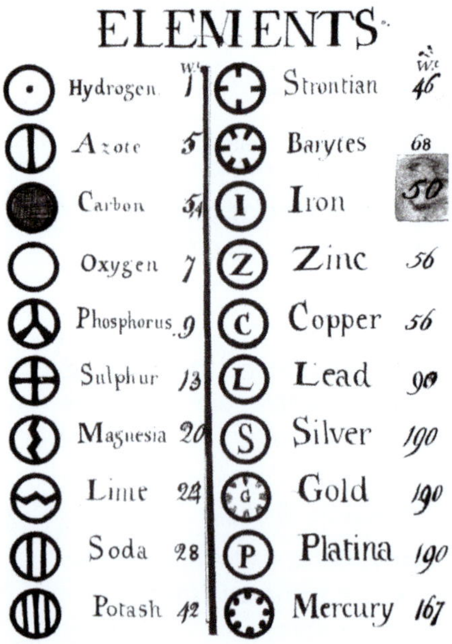

Figure 1 *Dalton made a list of substances that he believed were elements*

Early ideas about atoms

The ancient Greeks were the first to have ideas about particles and atoms. However, it was not until the early 1800s that these ideas became linked to strong experimental evidence when John Dalton put forward his ideas about atoms. From his experiments, he suggested that substances were made up of atoms that were like tiny, hard spheres. He also suggested that each chemical element had its own atoms that differed from others in their mass (Figure 1). Dalton believed that these atoms could not be divided or split. They were the fundamental building blocks of nature.

In chemical reactions, he suggested that the atoms re-arranged themselves and combined with other atoms in new ways. In many ways, Dalton's ideas are still useful today. For example, they help to visualise elements, compounds, and molecules, as well as the models still used to describe the different arrangement and movement of particles in solids, liquids, and gases.

Evidence for electrons in atoms

At the end of the 1800s, a scientist called J. J. Thomson discovered the **electron**. This is a tiny, negatively charged particle that was found to have a mass about 2000 times smaller than the lightest atom. Thomson was experimenting by applying high voltages to gases at low pressure (Figure 2).

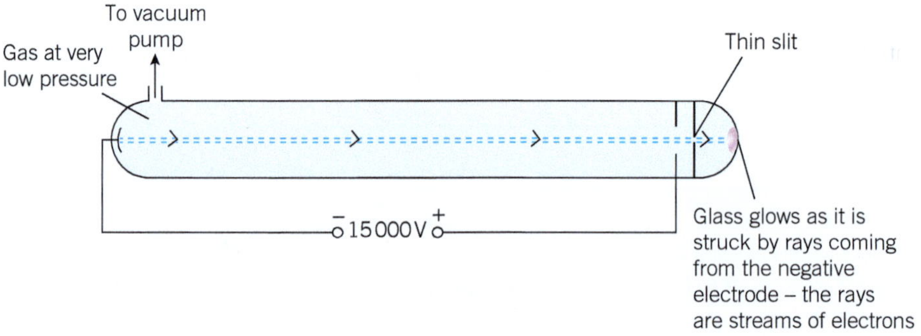

Figure 2 *Thomson's experimental evidence for the existence of electrons*

Thomson did experiments on the beams of particles. They were attracted to a positive charge, showing they must be negatively charged themselves. He called the tiny, negatively charged particles electrons. These electrons must have come from inside atoms in the tube. So Dalton's idea that atoms could not be divided or split had to be revised. Thomson proposed a different model for the atom. He said that the tiny, negatively charged electrons must be embedded in a cloud of positive charge. He knew that atoms themselves carry no overall charge so any charges in an atom must balance out. He imagined the electrons as the bits of plum in a plum pudding (Figure 3).

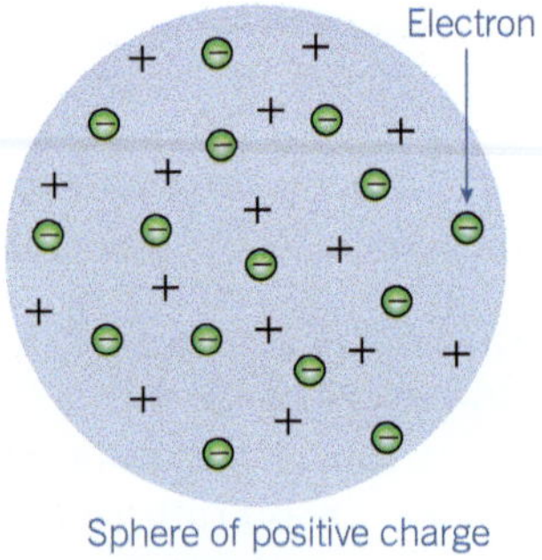

Figure 3 *Thomson's 'plum pudding' model of the atom*

Evidence for the nucleus

The next breakthrough in understanding the atom came about 10 years later. Two of Ernest Rutherford's students were doing an experiment with radioactive particles. They were firing dense, positively charged particles (called alpha particles) at the thinnest piece of gold foil they could make (see Figure 4). They expected the particles to pass straight through the gold atoms with their diffuse cloud of positive charge (as in Thomson's plum-pudding model). However, their results shocked them (Figure 4) as some particles came back towards the source.

In 1911, Ernest Rutherford interpreted their results and suggested a new model for the atom (Figure 5). He said that Thomson's atomic model was not possible. The positive charge must be concentrated at a tiny spot in the centre of the atom. Otherwise the large, positive particles fired at the foil could never be repelled back towards their source. He proposed that the electrons must be orbiting around this **nucleus** (centre of the atom), which contains very dense positively charged **protons** (Figure 5).

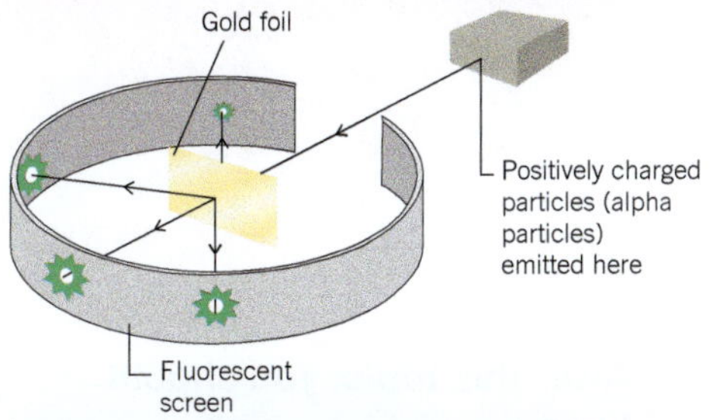

Figure 4 *The alpha particle scattering experiment that changed the* 'plum pudding' *theory*

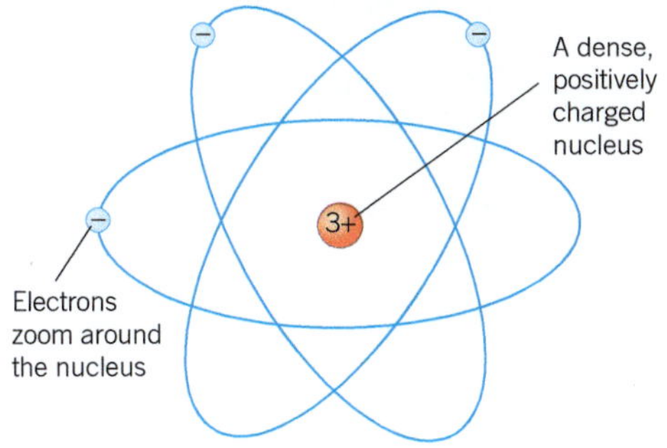

Figure 5 *Rutherford's nuclear model of the atom*

Evidence for electrons in shells (energy levels)

The next important development came in 1914, when Niels Bohr revised the atomic model again (Figure 6). He noticed that the light given out when atoms were heated only had specific amounts of energy. He suggested that the electrons must be orbiting the nucleus at set distances, in certain fixed energy levels (or shells). The energy must be given out when 'excited' electrons fall from a high to a low energy level. Bohr matched his model to the energy values observed (see Figure 6).

Evidence for neutrons in the nucleus

Scientists at the time speculated that there were two types of sub-atomic particles inside the nucleus. They had evidence of protons, but a second sub-atomic particle in the nucleus was also proposed to explain the missing mass that had been noticed in atoms. These **neutrons** must have no charge and have the same mass as a proton.

Because neutrons have no charge, it was very difficult to detect them in experiments. It was not until 1932 that James Chadwick did an experiment that could only be explained by the existence of neutrons!

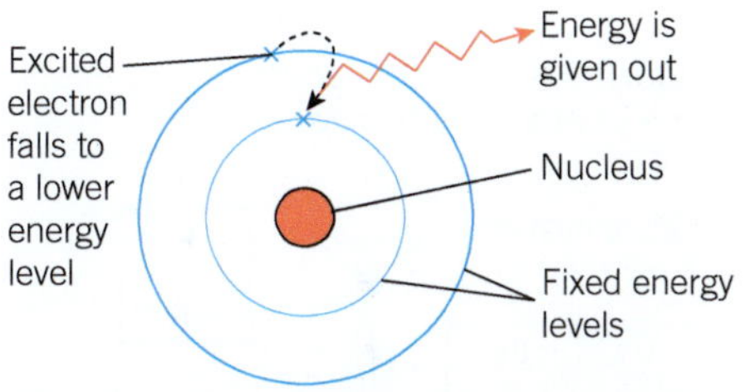

Figure 6 *Bohr's model of the atom*

Summary questions

1 a Which one of Dalton's ideas listed below about atoms do scientists no longer believe?

A Elements contain only one type of atom.

B Atoms get re-arranged in chemical reactions.

C Atoms are solid spheres that cannot be split into simpler particles.

b Which of the following substances from Dalton's list of elements (Figure 1) are not actually chemical elements?

soda oxygen carbon gold lime

2 a Which sub-atomic particle did J. J. Thomson discover?

b Describe J. J. Thomson's 'plum pudding' model of the atom.

3 State two ways in which Rutherford changed Thomson's model of the atom.

4 Explain why Bohr revised Rutherford's model of the atom.

Key points

- The ideas about atoms have changed over time.
- New evidence has been gathered from the experiments of scientists who have used their model of the atom to explain their observations and calculations.
- Key ideas were proposed successively by Dalton, Thomson, Rutherford, and Bohr, before arriving at the model of the atom you use at GCSE level today.

1.4 Atoms

Learning objectives

After this topic, you should know:

- the definition of an element
- that each type of atom has a chemical symbol
- the basic structure of the periodic table
- the basic structure of an atom.

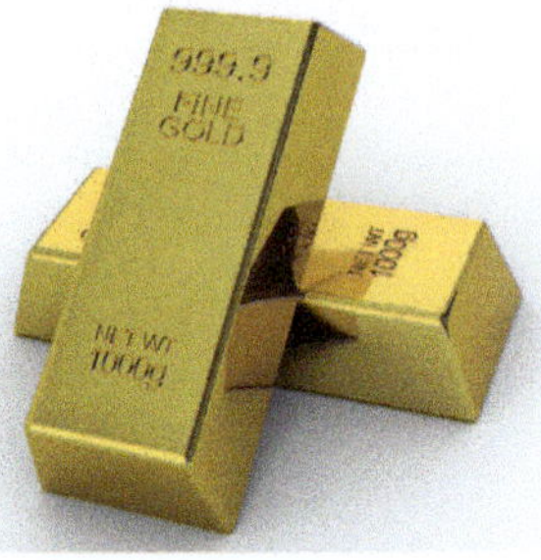

Figure 1 *An element contains only one type of atom – in this case gold*

Look at the things around you and the substances that they are made from. You will find wood, metal, plastic, glass ... the list is almost endless. Look further and the number of different substances is mind-boggling.

All substances are made of **atoms**. There are about 100 different types of atom found naturally on Earth. These can combine in a huge variety of ways, giving us all those different substances.

Some substances are made up of only one type of atom. These substances are called **elements**. It follows that as there are only about 100 different types of atom, there are only about 100 different elements.

Elements can have very different properties. Elements such as silver, copper, and gold are shiny, solid metals. Other elements such as oxygen, nitrogen, and chlorine are non-metals, and are gases at room temperature.

Chemical symbols

The name given to each different element depends on the language being spoken. For example, the element sulfur is called *schwefel* in German and *azufre* in Spanish. However, the scientific community communicates globally so it is important to have symbols for elements that all nationalities can understand. These symbols are shown in the **periodic table**.

- The symbols in the periodic table represent atoms. For example, O represents an atom of oxygen, Na represents an atom of sodium.

Group numbers

1	2											3	4	5	6	7	0
			H 1 Hydrogen														He 2 Helium
Li 3 Lithium	Be 4 Beryllium											B 5 Boron	C 6 Carbon	N 7 Nitrogen	O 8 Oxygen	F 9 Fluorine	Ne 10 Neon
Na 11 Sodium	Mg 12 Magnesium											Al 13 Aluminium	Si 14 Silicon	P 15 Phosphorus	S 16 Sulfur	Cl 17 Chlorine	Ar 18 Argon
K 19 Potassium	Ca 20 Calcium	Sc 21 Scandium	Ti 22 Titanium	V 23 Vanadium	Cr 24 Chromium	Mn 25 Manganese	Fe 26 Iron	Co 27 Cobalt	Ni 28 Nickel	Cu 29 Copper	Zn 30 Zinc	Ga 31 Gallium	Ge 32 Germanium	As 33 Arsenic	Se 34 Selenium	Br 35 Bromine	Kr 36 Krypton
Rb 37 Rubidium	Sr 38 Strontium	Y 39 Yttrium	Zr 40 Zirconium	Nb 41 Niobium	Mo 42 Molybdenum	Tc 43 Technetium	Ru 44 Ruthenium	Rh 45 Rhodium	Pd 46 Palladium	Ag 47 Silver	Cd 48 Cadmium	In 49 Indium	Sn 50 Tin	Sb 51 Antimony	Te 52 Tellurium	I 53 Iodine	Xe 54 Xenon
Cs 55 Caesium	Ba 56 Barium	Lanthanum see below	Hf 72 Hafnium	Ta 73 Tantalum	W 74 Tungsten	Re 75 Rhenium	Os 76 Osmium	Ir 77 Iridium	Pt 78 Platinum	Au 79 Gold	Hg 80 Mercury	Tl 81 Thallium	Pb 82 Lead	Bi 83 Bismuth	Po 84 Polonium	At 85 Astatine	Rn 86 Radon
Fr 87 Francium	Ra 88 Radium	Actinium see below															

The alkali metals (group 1); The alkaline earth metals (group 2); The transition metals; The halogens (group 7); The noble gases (group 0)

Lanthanides	La 57 Lanthanium	Ce 58 Cerium	Pr 59 Praseodymium	Nd 60 Neodymium	Pm 61 Promethium	Sm 62 Samarium	Eu 63 Europium	Gd 64 Gadolinium	Tb 65 Terbium	Dy 66 Dysprosium	Ho 67 Holmium	Er 68 Erbium	Tm 69 Thulium	Yb 70 Ytterbium	Lu 71 Lutetium
Actinides	Ac 89 Actinium	Th 90 Thorium	Pa 91 Protactinium	U 92 Uranium	Np 93 Neptunium	Pu 94 Plutonium	Am 95 Americium	Cm 96 Curium	Bk 97 Berkelium	Cf 98 Californium	Es 99 Einsteinium	Fm 100 Fermium	Md 101 Mendelevium	No 102 Nobelium	Lr 103 Lawrencium

Figure 2 *The periodic table shows the symbols for each type of atom*

- The elements in the table are arranged in columns, called **groups**. Each group contains elements with similar chemical properties.
- The 'staircase' drawn in bold black is the dividing line between metals and non-metals. The elements to the left of the line are metals. Those on the right of the line are non-metals. However, a few elements lying next to the dividing line are called metalloids or semi-metals as they have some metallic and some non-metallic characteristics. Examples include silicon (Si) and germanium (Ge) from Group 4.

Atoms, elements, and compounds

Most substances you encounter are not elements. They are made up of different types of atom joined together and are called **compounds**. Chemical bonds hold the atoms tightly together in compounds. Some compounds are made from just two types of atom (e.g., water, made from atoms of hydrogen and oxygen). However, most compounds consist of more than two different types of atom.

An atom is made up of a tiny central nucleus with electrons around it.

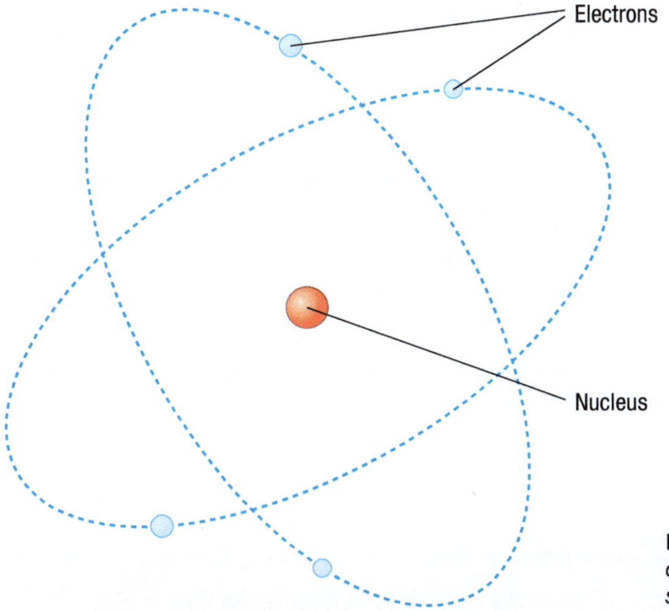

Figure 3 *Each atom consists of a tiny nucleus surrounded by electrons*

Summary questions

1 a Arrange these elements into a table showing metals and non-metals: phosphorus (P), barium (Ba), vanadium (V), mercury (Hg), krypton (Kr), potassium (K), and uranium (U).
b Would you classify hydrogen as a metal or a non-metal. Why?

2 Explain why, when you mix two elements together, you can often separate them again quite easily by physical means, but when two elements are chemically combined in a compound they are usually very difficult to separate.

3 Draw diagrams to explain the difference between an element and a compound.

4 Describe the basic structure of an atom.

5 Find out the Latin words from which the symbols of the following metallic elements are derived:
a sodium, Na **b** gold, Au **c** lead, Pb **d** potassium, K

links

For more information on the periodic table of elements, see 3.1 The periodic table.

Did you know ... ?

Only 92 elements occur naturally on Earth. The other heavier elements in the periodic table have to be made artificially and might only exist for fractions of a second before they decay into other, lighter elements.

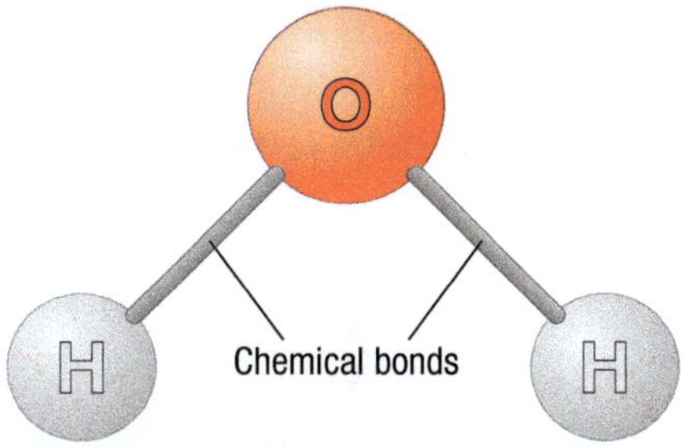

Figure 4 *A grouping of two or more atoms bonded together is called a* ***molecule****. Chemical bonds hold the hydrogen and oxygen atoms together in the water molecule. Water is an example of a compound.*

links

For more information on what is inside an atom, see 1.6 Atomic structure and 1.7 The arrangement of electrons in atoms.

Key points

- **All substances are made up of atoms.**
- **The periodic table lists all the chemical elements, with eight main groups each containing elements with similar chemical properties.**
- **Elements contain only one type of atom.**
- **Compounds contain more than one type of atom.**
- **An atom has a tiny nucleus at its centre, surrounded by electrons.**

1.5 Chemical equations

Learning objectives

After this topic, you should know:

- what happens to the atoms in a chemical reaction
- how the mass of reactants compares with the mass of products in a chemical reaction
- how to write balanced symbol equations, including state symbols, to represent reactions.

Chemical equations show the **reactants** (the substances you start with) and the **products** (the new substances made) in a reaction.

The test for hydrogen gas can be represented using a **word equation**:

hydrogen + oxygen → water
(reactants) (product)

In chemical reactions the atoms get rearranged. Now you can investigate what happens to the mass of reactants compared with the mass of products in a reaction.

Using **symbol equations** helps us to see how much of each substance is involved in a reaction.

For example, calcium carbonate decomposes (breaks down) on heating. You can show the reaction using a symbol equation like this:

$$CaCO_3 \rightarrow CaO + CO_2$$

This equation is **balanced** – there is the same number of each type of atom on both sides of the equation. This is very important, because atoms cannot be created or destroyed in a chemical reaction. This also means that:

The total mass of the products formed in a reaction is equal to the total mass of the reactants.

You can check if an equation is balanced by counting the number of each type of atom on either side of the equation. If the numbers are equal, then the equation is balanced.

You can also add **state symbols** to a balanced symbol equation to give extra information. The state symbols used are:

- (s) for solids
- (l) for liquids
- (g) for gases
- (aq) for substances dissolved in water, that is, **aqueous solutions**.

So the balanced symbol equation, including state symbols, for the decomposition of calcium carbonate is:

$$CaCO_3(s) \rightarrow CaO(s) + CO_2(g)$$

links

For more information on the decomposition of calcium carbonate, see 4.8 Metal carbonates.

Practical

Investigating the mass of reactants and products

You are given solutions of lead nitrate (toxic) and potassium iodide.

Wearing chemical splashproof eye protection, add a small volume of each solution together in a test tube.

- What do you see happen?

The formula of lead nitrate is $Pb(NO_3)_2$ and of potassium iodide is KI.

The precipitate (a solid formed in the reaction between two solutions) is lead iodide, PbI_2 (which is toxic).

- Predict a word equation and a balanced symbol equation, including state symbols, for the reaction.
- How do you think that the mass of the reactants compares with the mass of the products?

Now plan an experiment to test your answer to this question. Your teacher must check your plan before you start the practical work. Wash your hands after the experiment.

Making an equation balance

In the case of hydrogen reacting with oxygen it is not so easy to balance the equation. Firstly, we write the formula of each reactant and product:

$$H_2 + O_2 \rightarrow H_2O$$

Count the atoms on either side of the equation:

Reactants	**Products**
2 H atoms, 2 O atoms	2 H atoms, 1 O atom

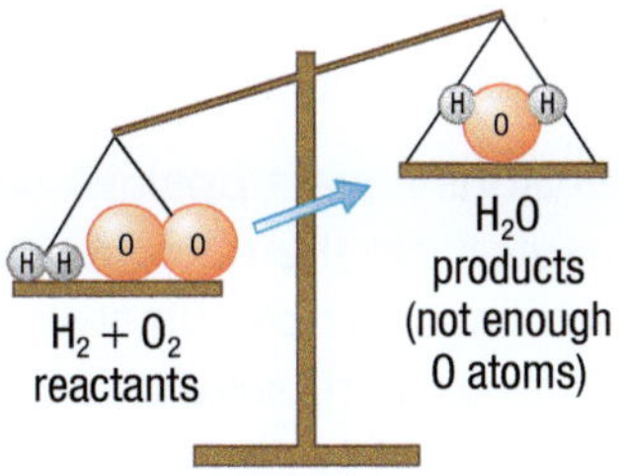

Not balanced

So you need another oxygen atom on the product side of the equation. You cannot simply change the formula of H_2O to H_2O_2. (H_2O_2 – hydrogen peroxide – is a bleaching agent which is certainly not suitable to drink!) But you can have **2 water molecules** in the reaction – this is shown in a symbol equation as:

$$H_2 + O_2 \rightarrow \mathbf{2}H_2O$$

Again, count the atoms on either side of the equation:

Reactants	**Products**
2 H atoms, 2 O atoms	4 H atoms, 2 O atoms

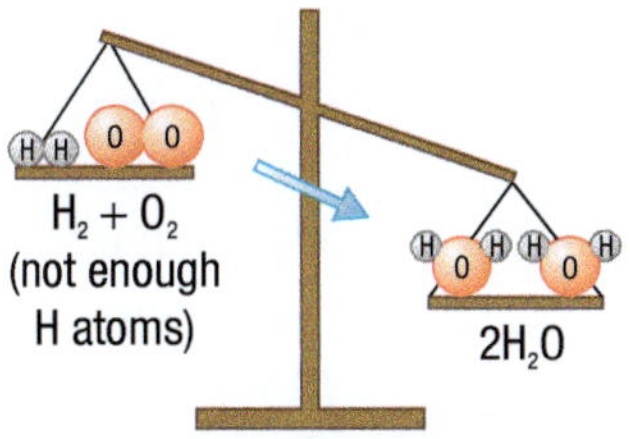

Still not balanced!

Although the oxygen atoms are balanced, you now need two more hydrogen atoms on the reactant side. You do this by putting 2 in front of H_2:

$$\mathbf{2}H_2 + O_2 \rightarrow 2H_2O$$

Now you have:

Reactants	**Products**
4 H atoms, 2 O atoms	4 H atoms, 2 O atoms

… and the equation is balanced.

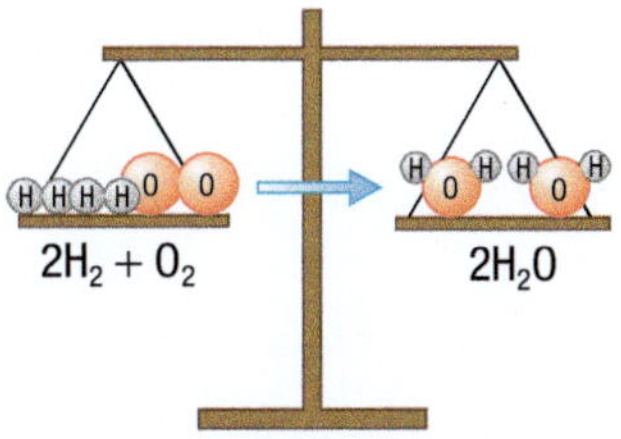

Balanced at last!

Look at the chemical equation on the previous page. You can work out the mass of $CaCO_3$, CaO, or CO_2 given the masses of the other two compounds.

Because the total mass of the products formed in a reaction is equal to the total mass of the reactants, you can write:

$$CaCO_3 \rightarrow CaO + CO_2$$
$$\text{Mass} = a = b + c$$

So if the mass of CaO formed is 2.8 g (*b* above) and the mass of CO_2 is 2.2 g (*c* above), then the mass of $CaCO_3$ (*a* above) that you start with must be 2.8 + 2.2 (*b*+*c*) which equals **5.0 g**.

Rearranging the equation for *a*, *b*, and *c* you get $a - c = b$.

So if the reaction started with 100 tonnes of $CaCO_3$ (*a*) and it gave off 44 tonnes of CO_2 (*c*), then the mass of CaO (*b*) made is 100 – 44 ($a - c$) = **56 tonnes**.

Summary questions

1 a Why must all symbol equations be balanced?
  b Copy this equation and balance it: $H_2 + Cl_2 \rightarrow HCl$

2 a A mass of 33.6 g of magnesium carbonate ($MgCO_3$) completely decomposed when it was heated. It made 16.0 g of magnesium oxide (MgO). What mass of carbon dioxide (CO_2) was produced in this reaction?
  b Write a word equation and a balanced symbol equation, including state symbols, to show the reaction in part **a**.

3 Copy these symbol equations and balance them:
  a $KNO_3 \rightarrow KNO_2 + O_2$ **b** $Li + O_2 \rightarrow Li_2O$ **c** $Fe + O_2 \rightarrow Fe_2O_3$

4 Sodium metal, Na, reacts with water to form a solution of sodium hydroxide, NaOH, and gives off hydrogen gas, H_2.
Write a balanced symbol equation, including state symbols, for this reaction.

Key points

- **No new atoms are ever created or destroyed in a chemical reaction:**

  the total mass of reactants = the total mass of products

- **There is the same number of each type of atom on each side of a balanced symbol equation.**

- **You can include state symbols to give extra information in balanced symbol equations. These are (s) for solids, (l) for liquids, (g) for gases, and (aq) for aqueous solutions.**

1.6 Atomic structure

Learning objectives

After this topic, you should know:

- the location and relative charge of the protons, neutrons, and electrons in an atom
- what the 'atomic number' and 'mass number' of an atom represent
- why atoms have no overall charge
- that atoms of a particular element have the same number of protons.

In the centre of every atom there is a very small nucleus. This contains two types of sub-atomic particle, called protons and neutrons. A third type of sub-atomic particle orbits the nucleus. These really tiny particles are called electrons.

Protons have a positive charge. Neutrons have no charge, that is, they are neutral. So the nucleus itself has an overall positive charge. The electrons orbiting the nucleus are negatively charged. The relative charge on a proton is +1 and the relative charge on an electron is –1.

Type of sub-atomic particle	Relative charge
Proton	+1
Neutron	0
Electron	–1

Because every atom contains equal numbers of protons and electrons, the positive and negative charges cancel out and its charge is zero. So, there is no overall charge on any atom. For example, a carbon atom is neutral. It has six protons, so therefore it must have six electrons.

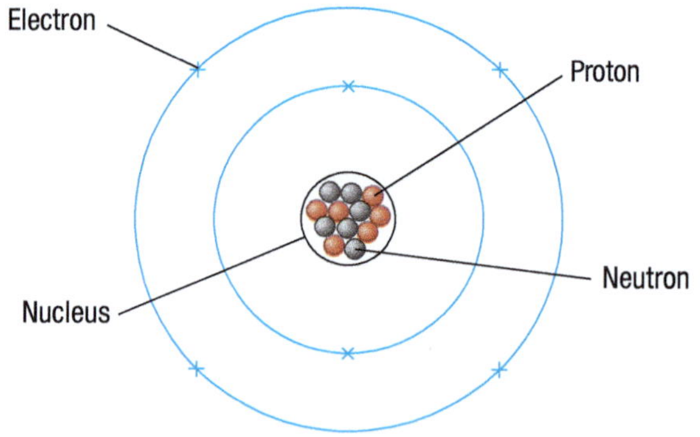

Figure 1 *Understanding the structure of an atom gives us important clues to the way chemicals react together. If you look carefully, this atom of carbon has six protons and six neutrons in its nucleus, and six electrons orbiting the nucleus. Note that although the number of protons and electrons are always equal in an atom, the number of neutrons can differ (but in this case they are the same).*

Did you know ...?

In 1808, a chemist called John Dalton published a theory of atoms. It explained how atoms joined together to form new substances (compounds). Not everyone liked his theory though – one person wrote 'Atoms are round bits of wood invented by Mr Dalton!'

Atomic number and the periodic table of elements

All the atoms of a particular element have the same number of protons. For example, hydrogen has 1 proton in its nucleus, carbon has 6 protons in its nucleus, and sodium has 11 protons in its nucleus.

The **number of protons** in each atom of an element is called the **atomic number** of that element.

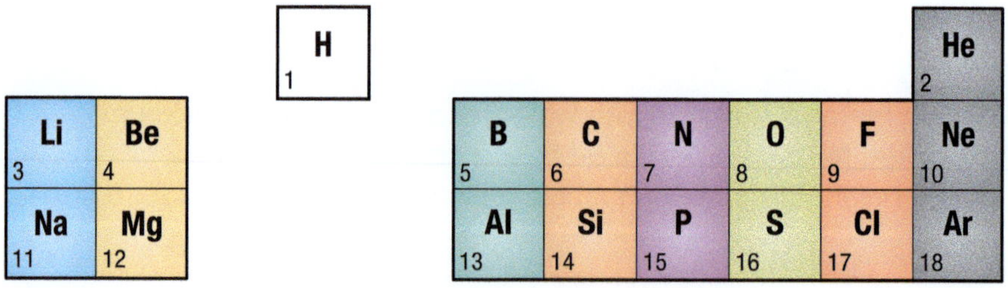

Figure 2 *You read the periodic table from left to right, and from the top down – just like reading a page of writing. This is an abbreviated version of the start of the periodic table, showing the first 18 elements. The elements in the periodic table are arranged in order of their atomic number.*

The elements in the periodic table are arranged in order of their atomic number (number of protons). If you are told that the atomic number of an element is 8, you can identify it using the periodic table. It will be the eighth element listed, that is, oxygen.

Mass number

The **number of protons plus the number of neutrons** in the nucleus of an atom is called its **mass number**. So, if an atom has four protons and five neutrons, its mass number will be 4 + 5 = **9**.

Given the atomic number and mass number, you can work out how many protons, electrons and neutrons are in an atom. For example, an argon atom has an atomic number of 18 and a mass number of 40.

- Its atomic number is 18 so it has **18 protons**. Remember that atoms have an equal number of protons and electrons. So argon also has **18 electrons**.
- The mass number is 40, so you know that:

18 (the number of protons) + the number of neutrons = 40

- Therefore, argon must have **22 neutrons** (as 18 + 22 = 40).

You can summarise the last part of the calculation as:

number of neutrons = mass number – atomic number

Study tip

In an atom, the number of protons is always equal to the number of electrons. You can find out the number of protons and electrons in an atom by looking up its atomic number in the periodic table.

links

For more information on the patterns in the periodic table, see 1.7 The arrangement of electrons in atoms.

Summary questions

1 Draw a table showing the location and relative charge of the three sub-atomic particles.

2 Look at the abbreviated periodic table in Figure 2.
  a How does the number of electrons in each atom vary going across each row (called a period) in the table?
  b What pattern do you notice in the number of protons going down Group 0?
  c Sort out the elements in the table into metals, non-metals, and metalloids.

3 Explain why all atoms are neutral.

4 An atom has 27 protons and 32 neutrons. Use the periodic table in Topic 1.4 to name this element, and give its symbol, atomic number, and mass number.

5 How many protons, electrons, and neutrons do the following atoms contain?
  a A nitrogen atom whose atomic number is 7 and whose mass number is 14.
  b A chlorine atom whose atomic number is 17 and whose mass number is 35.
  c A silver atom whose atomic number is 47 and whose mass number is 108.
  d A uranium atom whose atomic number is 92 and whose mass number is 235.

Key points

- **Atoms are made of protons, neutrons, and electrons.**
- **Protons have a relative charge of +1, and electrons have a relative charge of –1. Neutrons have no electric charge. They are neutral.**
- **Atoms contain an equal number of protons and electrons so carry no overall charge.**
- **Atomic number = number of protons (= number of electrons)**
- **Mass number = number of protons + number of neutrons**
- **Atoms of the same element have the same number of protons (and therefore electrons) in their atoms.**

1.7

The arrangement of electrons in atoms

Learning objectives

After this topic, you should know:

- how the electrons are arranged in an atom
- the electronic structures of the first 20 elements in the periodic table
- how to represent electronic structures in diagrams and by using standard notation.

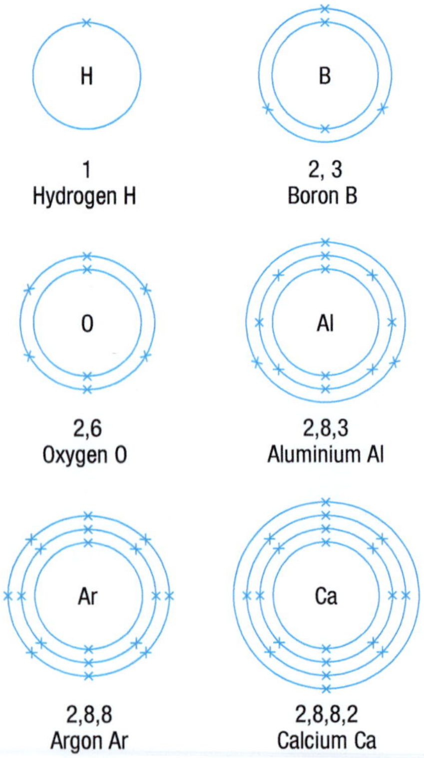

Figure 2 *Once you know the pattern, you should be able to draw the energy levels (shells) and electrons in the atoms of any of the first 20 elements (given their atomic number)*

The model of the atom which you use at this level has electrons arranged around the nucleus in **shells**, rather like the layers of an onion. Each shell represents a different **energy level**.

The lowest energy level is shown by the shell which is nearest to the nucleus. The electrons in an atom occupy the lowest available energy level (the shell closest to the nucleus).

Electron shell diagrams

An energy level (or shell) can only hold a certain number of electrons.

- The first, and lowest, energy level (nearest the nucleus) can hold up to 2 electrons.
- The second energy level can hold up to 8 electrons.
- Once there are 8 electrons in the third energy level, the fourth begins to fill up.

Beyond this point, that is, after the first 20 elements in the periodic table, the situation gets more complex so is covered in higher level courses. You only need to know the arrangement of electrons in atoms of the first 20 elements.

You can draw diagrams to show the arrangement of electrons in an atom. For example, a sodium atom has an atomic number of 11 so it has 11 protons, which means it also has 11 electrons. Figure 1 shows how you can represent an atom of sodium.

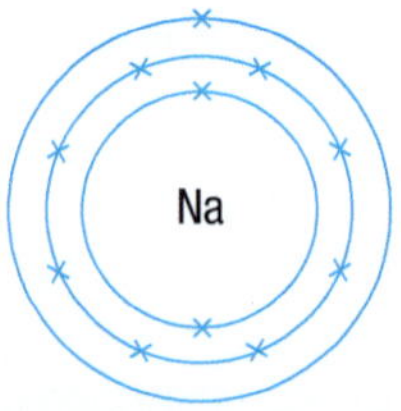

Figure 1 *A simple way of representing the arrangement of electrons in the energy levels (shells) of a sodium atom*

To save drawing atoms all the time, you can write down the number of electrons in each energy level. This is called an **electronic structure**. For example, the sodium atom in Figure 1 has an electronic structure of 2,8,1. You start at the lowest energy level (innermost or first shell), recording the numbers in each successive energy level or shell.

Silicon, whose atoms have 14 electrons, is in Group 4 of the periodic table. It has the electronic structure 2,8,4. This represents 2 electrons in the lowest energy level (first shell), then 8 in the next energy level or shell. There are 4 in the highest energy level (its outermost shell).

The best way to understand these arrangements is to look at the examples in Figure 2.

Study tip

Make sure that you can draw the electronic structure of the atoms for all of the first 20 elements. You will always be given their atomic number or their position in the periodic table (which tells you the number of electrons) – so you don't have to memorise these numbers.

Electrons and the periodic table

Look at the elements in any one of the main groups of the periodic table. Their atoms will all have the same number of electrons in their highest energy level. These electrons are often called the outer electrons because they are in the outermost shell. Therefore, all the elements in Group 1 have one electron in their highest energy level.

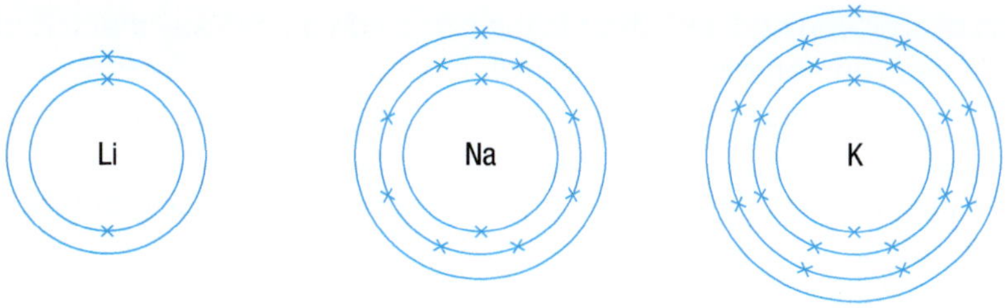

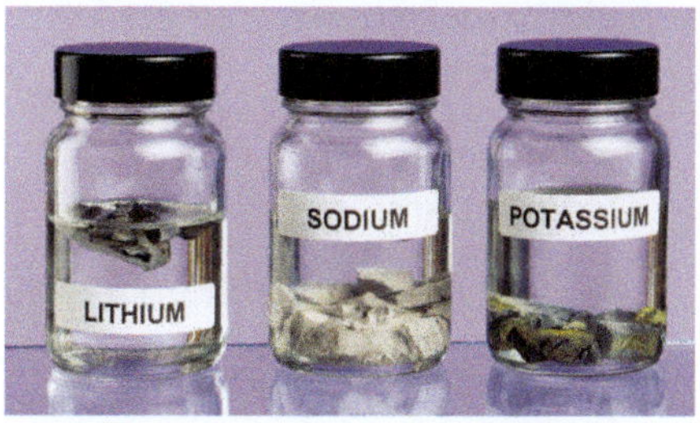

Figure 3 *The Group 1 metals are all reactive metals, shown here stored under oil*

The chemical properties of an element depend on how many electrons it has. The way an element reacts is determined by the number of electrons in its highest energy level (or outermost shell). So because the elements in a particular group all have the same number of electrons in their highest energy level, they all react in a similar way.

For example:

lithium + water → lithium hydroxide + hydrogen
sodium + water → sodium hydroxide + hydrogen
potassium + water → potassium hydroxide + hydrogen

The elements in Group 0 of the periodic table are called the **noble gases** because they are unreactive. Their atoms have a very stable arrangement of electrons. All the Group 0 elements have eight electrons in their outermost shell, except for helium, which has only two electrons.

links

For more information on the reactions of elements and their electronic structures, see Chapter 3 The periodic table.

Summary questions

1 a Which shell represents the lowest energy level in an atom?
b How many electrons can each of the lowest two energy levels hold?

2 Using the periodic table, draw the arrangement of electrons in the following atoms and label each one with its electronic structure.
a He b Be c Cl d Ar

3 a Write the electronic structure of potassium (atomic number 19).
b How many electrons does a potassium atom have in its highest energy level (outermost shell)?

4 Give the name and symbol of the atom shown:

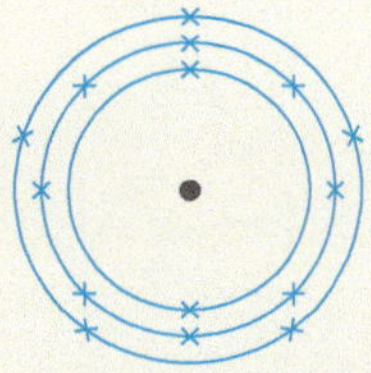

5 a Why do the Group 1 metals all react in a similar way with oxygen?
b Write word equations for the reactions of lithium, sodium, and potassium with oxygen to form their oxides.

Key points

- The electrons in an atom are arranged in energy levels or shells.
- The lowest energy level (1st shell) can hold up to 2 electrons and the next energy level (the 2nd shell) can hold up 8 electrons.
- The 4th shell starts to fill after 8 electrons occupy the 3rd shell.
- The number of electrons in the outermost shell of an element's atoms determines the way in which that element reacts.

1.8 Atoms and isotopes

Learning objectives

After this topic, you should know:

- the relative masses of protons, neutrons, and electrons
- how to represent an atom's atomic number and mass number
- what isotopes of an element are
- Ext: what is meant by the 'relative atomic mass' of an element.

Did you know ... ?

The volume of the nucleus of an atom can be between 10 000 and 100 000 times smaller than the volume of the atom itself.

As you have seen, an atom consists of a tiny nucleus containing positively charged protons, together with neutrons which have no charge. The negatively charged electrons are arranged in energy levels (shells) around the nucleus.

The mass of a proton and a neutron is the same so you can say that the 'relative mass' of a neutron compared with a proton is 1. Electrons are much, much lighter than protons and neutrons. They have a mass of about $\frac{1}{2000}$ of a proton or neutron. Because of this, the mass of an atom is concentrated in its nucleus and you can ignore the tiny mass of the electrons when working out the relative mass of an atom.

Type of sub-atomic particle	Relative mass
Proton	1
Neutron	1
Electron	very small

Representing the atomic number and mass number

Remember that:

- the number of protons in an atom is its atomic number, and
- the total number of protons and neutrons in an atom is its mass number.

You can show the atomic number and mass number of an atom like this:

Mass number

$^{12}_{6}C$ (carbon) $^{23}_{11}Na$ (sodium)

Atomic number

Given this information, you can work out the number of neutrons in the nucleus of an atom by subtracting its atomic number from its mass number. (See page 15).

number of neutrons = mass number – atomic number

For the two examples above:

Carbon has 6 protons and a mass number of 12.
So the number of neutrons in a carbon atom is (12 – 6) = 6.

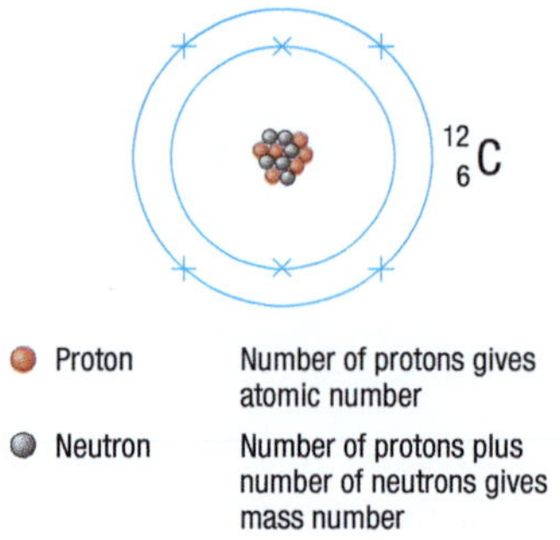

Figure 1 *An atom of carbon, which can be written showing its mass number as 'carbon-12'*

Sodium has an atomic number of 11 and the mass number is 23.
So a sodium atom has (23 – 11) = 12 neutrons.
In its nucleus there are 11 protons and 12 neutrons.

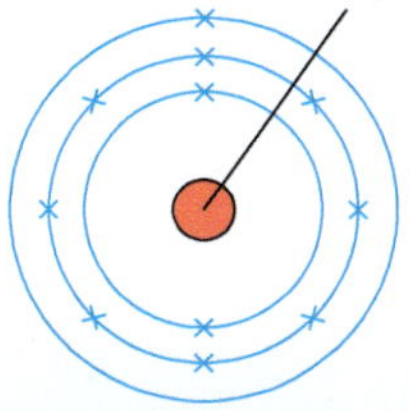

Figure 2 *An atom of sodium (sodium-23)*

Isotopes of elements

All atoms of an element have the same number of protons (and therefore electrons). However, an element can have atoms with different numbers of neutrons. These are called **isotopes** of the element.

The isotopes of an element will have the same atomic number but different mass numbers. Look at the three isotopes of hydrogen in Figure 3.

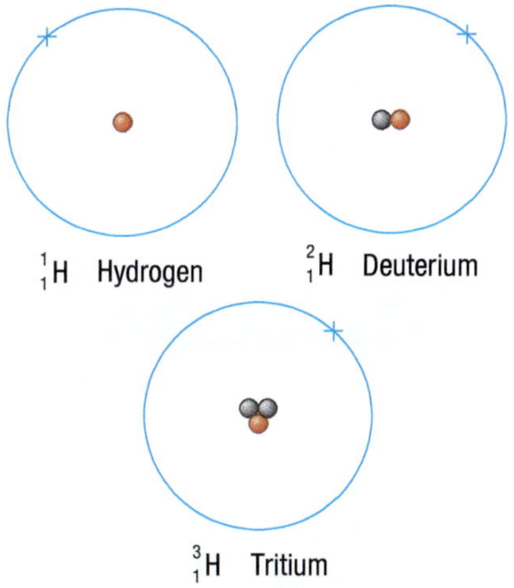

Figure 3 *The isotopes of hydrogen – they have identical chemical properties but different physical properties, such as density*

Ext

Relative atomic mass, A_r

Chemists define the **relative atomic mass** of an element as:

the ***average mass*** of the atoms of an element compared with carbon-12 (which is given a relative mass of exactly 12). This average mass must take into account the proportions of the naturally occurring isotopes of the element.

This is why relative atomic masses can be decimal numbers – for example the A_r of chlorine is 35.5 – whereas mass numbers are always whole numbers.

Note that '***relative*** atomic masses' have no units.'

Summary questions

1 Draw a table to summarise the relative mass and charge of the three sub-atomic particles.

2 State how many protons and how many neutrons there are in the nucleus of each of the following elements:

a $^{11}_{5}B$ **b** $^{14}_{7}N$ **c** $^{24}_{12}Mg$ **d** $^{37}_{17}Cl$ **e** $^{127}_{53}I$

3 A copper atom (Cu) has 29 protons and has a mass number of 64.

a How many electrons does the copper atom have?

b Choose which shell (energy level) copper's outer shell electrons will occupy:

A 1st shell **C** 3rd shell

B 2nd shell **D** 4th shell

c How many neutrons does the copper atom have?

d Write down the standard notation of this copper atom showing its atomic number and mass number.

e Copper is mixed with gold (Au) to make jewellery. In the gold atom $^{197}_{79}Au$, how many:

i protons,

ii neutrons, and

iii electrons

does this atom of gold contain.

4 Define what isotopes of an element are.

Ext **5** Define 'relative atomic mass'.

Key points

- The relative mass of protons and neutrons is 1.
- You can represent the atomic number and mass number of an atom using the notation: $^{24}_{12}Mg$, where magnesium's atomic number is 12 and its mass number is 24.
- Isotopes are atoms of the same element with different numbers of neutrons.
- Ext The relative atomic mass of an element is the average mass of the atoms of an element, on a scale which assigns carbon-12 atoms a relative mass of exactly 12. This average mass must take into account the proportions of the naturally occurring isotopes of the element.

Chapter summary questions

1 Arsenic (As) is a solid element that sublimes at 613 °C.

a What is sublimation?

b Assuming arsenic exists as atoms, draw a diagram to show the arrangement of some of its particles in boxes like the ones below:

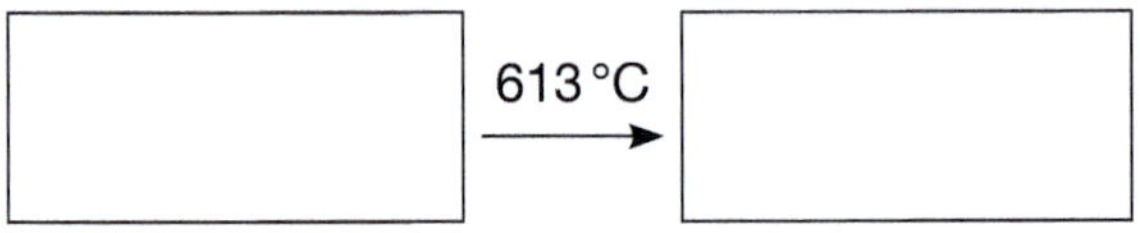

c Which of these processes take in energy from the surroundings?

boiling melting freezing condensation sublimation

2 Look at the experiment below:

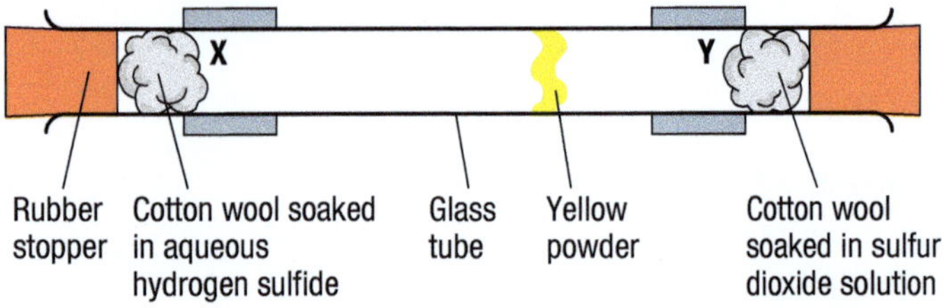

Hydrogen sulfide gas is released from the cotton wool at X and sulfur dioxide gas from the cotton wool at Y.

a The yellow powder inside the glass tube forms after 10 minutes. Explain how the yellow powder forms using the kinetic theory of matter.

b Name the physical process that this experiment demonstrates.

c Why is the yellow powder formed nearer to end Y of the tube?

d Draw a long tube and show the possible path of a hydrogen sulfide particle (molecule) travelling down the tube.

e The original experiment was carried out at 18 °C. Predict any difference you might notice if the experiment was repeated at 25 °C.

3 Look at the data in the table below:

Chemical element	Melting point (°C)	Boiling point (°C)	Density (g/cm^3)
Bromine	−7	59	3.12
Caesium	29	669	1.88
Fluorine	−220	−188	0.00158
Strontium	769	1384	2.6
Xenon	−112	−108	0.0055

a What is the physical state of each element in the table at 25 °C?

b Which element exists as a liquid over the widest range of temperature?

c Explain the large differences in the densities of the elements in the table using the kinetic theory of matter.

d What is the chemical symbol for atoms of each element in the table?

e Classify each element in the table as a metal or a non-metal.

4 **a** **i** Which sub-atomic particles are found in the nucleus?

ii What is the maximum number of electrons that can occupy each of the first two energy levels or shells?

b **i** Explain the overall charge on any atom.

ii Define 'atomic number' and 'mass number'.

5 This question is about some of the elements in the periodic table.

You will need to use the periodic table to help you answer some parts of the question. See page 41.

a Neon (Ne) is the 10th element in the periodic table.

i Is neon a metal or a non-metal?

ii Are there more metals or non-metals in the periodic table?

iii How many protons does an neon atom contain?

iv The mass number of a neon atom is 20. How many neutrons does it contain?

v State the name and number of the group to which neon belongs.

vi Name two other elements in the same group as neon.

vii Write the electronic structure of a neon atom.

viii What is special about the electronic structure of neon and the other elements in its group?

b The element radium (Ra) has 88 electrons.

i How many protons are in the nucleus of each radium atom?

ii How many electrons does a radium atom have in its highest energy level (outermost shell)? How did you decide on your answer?

iii Is radium a metal or a non-metal?

iv Calcium is in the same group as radium. Its atomic number is 20. Write down its electronic structure.

Practice questions

1 Use words from the list to complete the table to show the state of matter described.

gas liquid solid

Description	State
particles close together but not moving around	
particles very far apart	
particles close together but continuously moving around	

(3)

2 **a** Explain the difference between an element and a compound. (2)

b Why is ammonia classified as a compound but air is classified as a mixture? (2)

c Name the change of state in each of these processes.

i $H_2O(g) \rightarrow H_2O(l)$ (1)

ii $H_2O(l) \rightarrow H_2O(g)$ (1)

iii $I_2(s) \rightarrow I_2(g)$ (1)

3 A crystal of copper(II) sulfate is placed at the bottom of a beaker of water and left for a few days.

a Describe the appearance of the liquid in the beaker after a few days. (2)

b How does the appearance of the crystal change during the experiment? (1)

c Name **two** processes that occur during the experiment. (2)

4 The diagram shows the apparatus used in a teacher demonstration.

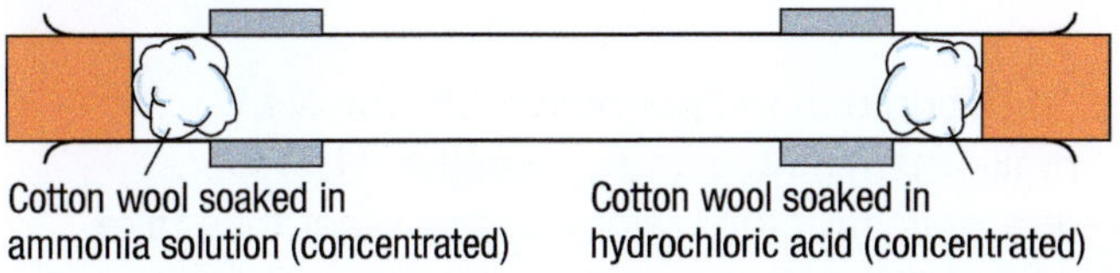

a Describe the observations you would make after a few minutes. (2)

b Use state symbols to complete the symbol equation for the reaction that occurs.

$NH_3(...) + HCl(...) \rightarrow NH_4Cl(...)$ (1)

c Explain how this experiment shows that ammonia molecules have a smaller mass than hydrogen chloride molecules. (1)

5 Electrons in atoms are arranged in energy levels (or shells) at different distances from the nucleus. Copy these statements and use numbers to complete them.

a The maximum number of electrons in the first shell is .... (1)

b The maximum number of electrons in the second shell is .... (1)

c Atoms of sodium have electrons in .... shells. (1)

d The number of electrons in the third shell of an atom of phosphorus is .... (1)

e The atomic number of an atom with the electronic structure 2,8,6 is .... (1)

f Copy these statements and use numbers to complete them.

i The number of protons in an atom of $^{20}_{10}Ne$ is .... (1)

ii The number of electrons in an atom of $^{22}_{10}Ne$ is .... (1)

iii The number of neutrons in an atom of $^{20}_{10}Ne$ is .... (1)

iv The mass number of $^{22}_{10}Ne$ is .... (1)

2.1 Atoms into ions

Learning objectives

After this topic, you should know:
- what a chemical compound is
- how elements form compounds
- how atoms can form either positive or negative ions
- how the elements in Group 1 bond with the elements in Group 7.

You already know that it is possible to mix two substances together without either of them changing. For example, you can mix sand and salt together and then separate them again. No change will have taken place. But in chemical reactions the situation is very different.

When the atoms of two or more elements react they make a compound.

A compound contains two or more elements which are chemically combined.

The compound formed is different from the elements and you cannot get the elements back again easily. You can also react compounds together to form other compounds. However, the reaction of elements is easier to understand as a starting point.

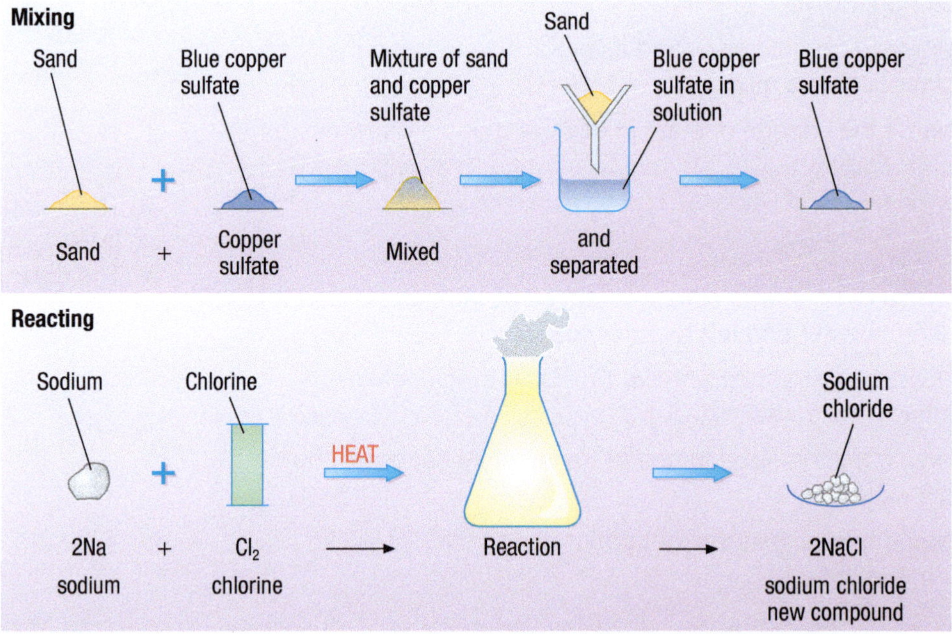

Figure 1 *The difference between mixing and reacting. Separating mixtures is usually quite easy, but separating the elements from compounds once they have reacted can be difficult.*

The atoms of the noble gases, in Group 0 of the periodic table, have an arrangement of electrons that make them stable and unreactive. However, most atoms do not have this electronic structure. When atoms react they take part in changes which give them a stable arrangement of electrons. They may do this either:

- by sharing electrons, which is called **covalent bonding**, or
- by transferring electrons, which is called **ionic bonding**.

Losing electrons to form positive ions

In ionic bonding the atoms involved lose or gain electrons to form charged particles called **ions**. The ions have the electronic structure of a noble gas. So, for example, if sodium (2,8,1), from Group 1 in the periodic table, loses one electron, it is left with the stable electronic structure of neon (2,8).

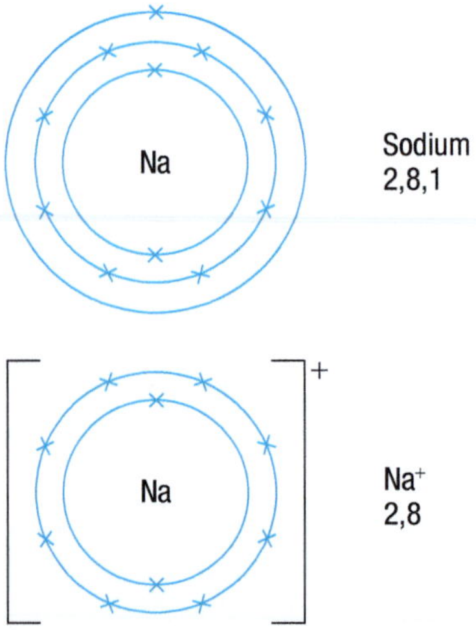

Figure 2 *A positive sodium ion (Na^+) is formed when a sodium atom loses an electron during ionic bonding*

However, it is also left with one more proton in its nucleus than there are electrons around the nucleus. The proton has a positive charge so the sodium atom has now become a positively charged ion. The sodium ion has a single positive charge. You write the formula of a sodium ion as Na^+. The electronic structure of the Na^+ ion is 2,8. This is shown in Figure 2.

Gaining electrons to form negative ions

When non-metals react with metals, the non-metal atoms gain electrons to achieve a stable noble gas structure. Chlorine, for example, has the electronic structure 2,8,7. It is in Group 7 of the periodic table. By gaining a single electron, it gets the stable electronic structure of argon (2,8,8).

In this case, there is now one more electron than there are positive protons in the nucleus. So the chlorine atom becomes a negatively charged ion. This carries a single negative charge. You write the formula of the chloride ion as Cl^-. Its electronic structure is 2,8,8. This is shown in Figure 3.

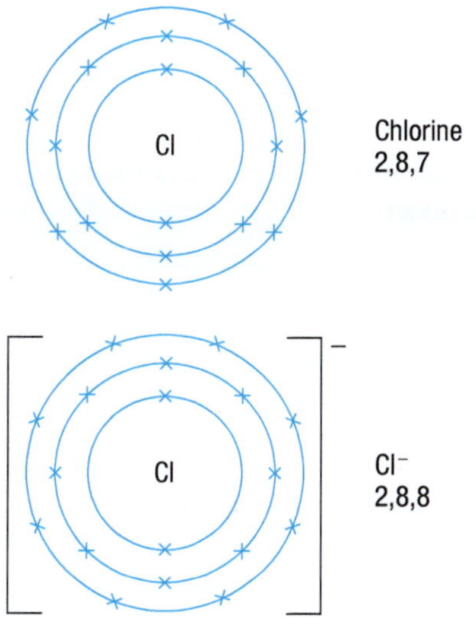

Figure 3 *A negative chloride ion (Cl^-) is formed when a chlorine atom gains an electron during ionic bonding*

Representing ionic bonding

Metal atoms, which tend to lose electrons, react with non-metal atoms, which tend to gain electrons. So when sodium reacts with chlorine, each sodium atom loses an electron and each chlorine atom gains an electron. They both form stable ions. The electrostatic attraction between the oppositely charged Na^+ ions and Cl^- ions is called ionic bonding.

You can show what happens in a diagram. The electrons of one atom are represented by dots, and the electrons of the other atom are represented by crosses. This is shown in Figure 4.

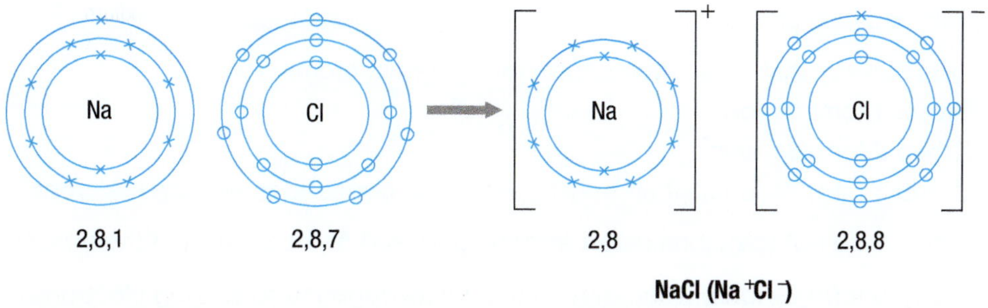

Figure 4 *The formation of sodium chloride (NaCl) – an example of ion formation by transferring an electron*

Summary questions

1 **a** When atoms bond together by *sharing* electrons, what type of bond is formed?

b When ions bond together as a result of *gaining* or *losing* electrons, what type of bond is this?

2 Explain how and why atoms of Group 1 and Group 7 elements react with each other, in terms of their electronic structures.

3 Write electron structures to show the ions that would be formed when the following atoms are involved in ionic bonding. For each one, state how many electrons have been lost or gained and show the charge on the ions formed.

a aluminium (Al) **b** fluorine (F)

c potassium (K) **d** oxygen (O)

Key points

- **Elements react together to form compounds by gaining or losing electrons or by sharing electrons.**
- **The elements in Group 1 react with the elements in Group 7. As they react, atoms of Group 1 elements can each lose one electron to gain the stable electronic structure of a noble gas. This electron can be given to an atom from Group 7, which then also achieves the stable electronic structure of a noble gas.**

2.2 Ionic bonding

Learning objectives

After this topic, you should know:

- **how ionic compounds are held together**
- **which elements, as well as those in Groups 1 and 7, form ions**
- **how the charges on ions are related to group numbers in the periodic table.**

You have seen how positive and negative ions form during some reactions. Ionic compounds are usually formed when metals react with non-metals. It is the metals that form positive ions and the non-metals that form negative ions.

The ions formed are held next to each other by very strong forces of attraction between the oppositely charged ions. This electrostatic force of attraction, which acts in all directions, is called ionic bonding.

The **ionic bonds** between the charged particles result in an arrangement of ions that is known as a **giant structure** (or a **giant lattice**). If you could stand among the ions they would seem to go on in all directions forever.

Ions and the periodic table

You have seen how atoms in Group 1 of the periodic table have 1 electron in their outermost shell (or highest energy level) and form 1+ ions. Group 7 atoms have 7 electrons in their outermost shell and form 1– ions. The group number gives us the number of electrons in the outermost shell. So how does the group number relate to the charges on the ions formed from atoms?

Sometimes the atoms reacting need to gain or lose two electrons to gain the stable electronic structure of a noble gas. An example is when magnesium (2,8,2), from Group 2, reacts with oxygen (2,6), from Group 6. When these two elements react they form magnesium oxide (MgO). This is made up of magnesium ions with a double positive charge (Mg^{2+}) and oxide ions with a double negative charge (O^{2-}).

So you can say that when atoms form **ionic** bonds, atoms from

- Group 1 form 1+ ions
- Group 2 form 2+ ions
- Group 3 form 3+ ions, when they form ions as opposed to sharing electrons
- Group 4 do not form ions (apart from tin and lead at the bottom of the group)
- Group 5 form 3– ions, when they form ions as opposed to sharing electrons
- Group 6 form 2– ions, when they form ions as opposed to sharing electrons
- Group 7 form 1– ions, when they form ions as opposed to sharing electrons
- Group 0 never form ions in compounds.

Figure 1 shows how the electrons are transferred between a magnesium atom and an oxygen atom.

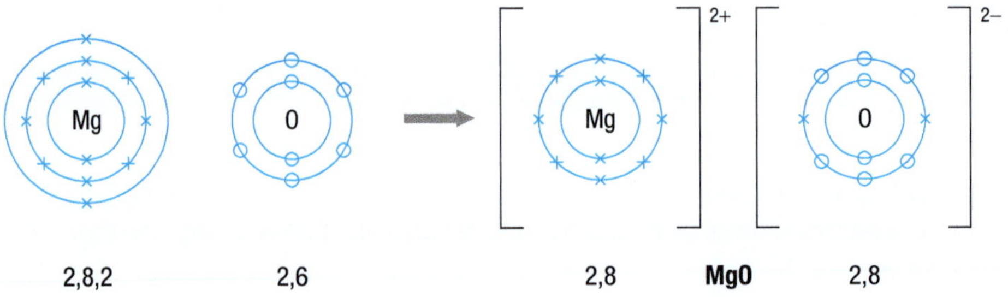

Figure 1 *When magnesium oxide (MgO) is formed, the reacting magnesium atoms lose two electrons and the oxygen atoms gain two electrons*

Another example of an ionic compound is calcium chloride. Each calcium atom (2,8,8,2) needs to lose two electrons but each chlorine atom (2,8,7) needs to gain only one electron. This means that two chlorine atoms react with every one calcium atom to form calcium chloride. So the formula of calcium chloride is $CaCl_2$.

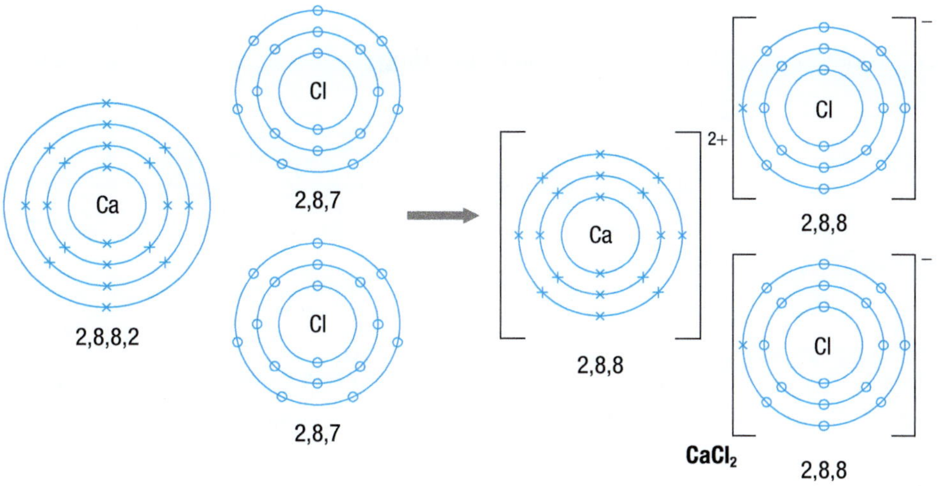

Figure 2 *The formation of calcium chloride ($CaCl_2$)*

Notice that the charges in the formula of an ionic compound cancel each other out as the overall charge on the compound is zero. So aluminium oxide, made up of aluminium ions, Al^{3+}, and oxide ions, O^{2-}, has the formula Al_2O_3 (total charges of 6+ on the aluminium ions cancelling out 6– on the oxide ions).

Did you know ... ?

The structure of ionic lattices is investigated by passing X-rays through them.

Summary questions

1 Copy and complete the table:

Atomic number	Atom	Electronic structure of atom	Ion	Electronic structure of ion
9	F			2,8
3		2,1	Li^+	
16	S		S^{2-}	
20		2,8,8,2		

2 Why do metal atoms form positively charged ions and non-metal atoms form negatively charged ions?

3 Think of rules to follow to remember the charge on any ions formed by elements in:

a Groups 1, 2, and 3

b Groups 5, 6, and 7.

4 a Explain why potassium bromide is KBr but potassium oxide is K_2O.

b Explain why magnesium oxide is MgO but magnesium chloride is $MgCl_2$.

5 Draw diagrams to show how you would expect the following elements to form ions together:

a potassium and oxygen

b aluminium and fluorine

Key points

- Ionic compounds are held together by strong forces of attraction between their oppositely charged ions. This is called ionic bonding.
- Besides the elements in Groups 1 and 7, other elements that can form ionic compounds include those from Groups 2 and 6.

2.3 Covalent bonding

Learning objectives

After this topic, you should know:

- how covalent bonds are formed
- what types of substances contain covalent bonds.

Reactions between metals and non-metals usually result in compounds with ionic bonding. However, many more compounds are formed in a very different way. When non-metals react together their atoms share pairs of electrons to form molecules. This is called covalent bonding.

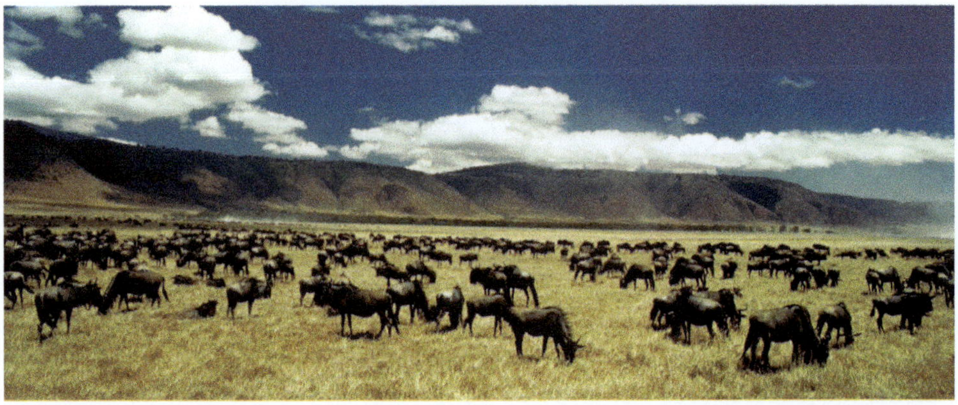

Figure 1 *Most of the molecules in substances which make up living things are held together by covalent bonds between non-metal atoms*

Simple molecules

The atoms of non-metals generally need to gain electrons to achieve stable electron structures. When they react together neither atom can give away electrons. So they get the electronic structure of a noble gas by sharing electrons. The atoms in the molecules are then held together by the shared pairs of electrons. These strong bonds between the atoms are called **covalent bonds**.

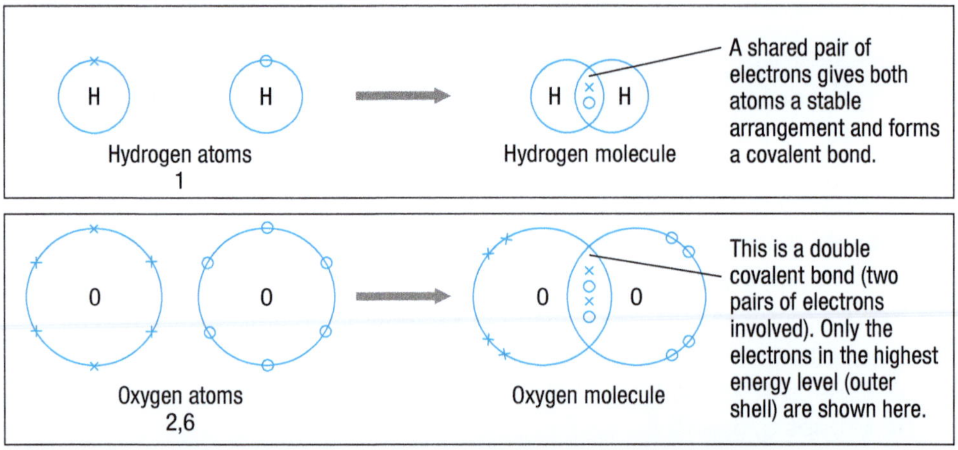

Figure 2 *Atoms of hydrogen and oxygen join together to form stable molecules. The atoms in H_2 and O_2 molecules are held together by strong covalent bonds.*

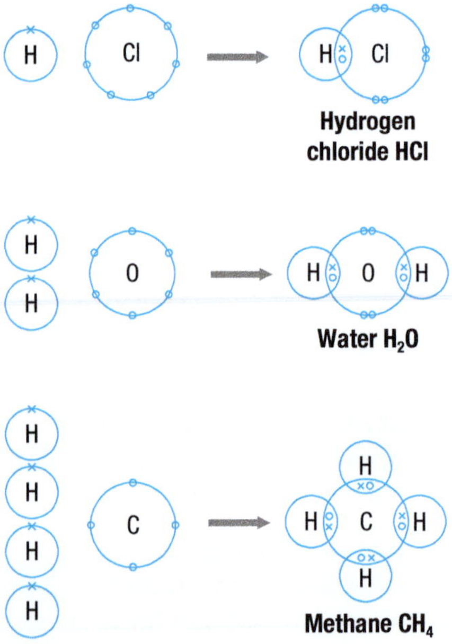

Figure 3 *The principles of covalent bonding remain the same however many atoms are involved*

Sometimes in covalent bonding each atom has the same number of electrons to share. But this is not always the case. Sometimes the atoms of one element will need several electrons, whilst those of the other element only needs one more electron for each atom to get a stable electron structure. In this case, more atoms become involved in forming the molecule, such as in water, H_2O, and methane, CH_4 (see Figure 3).

You can represent the covalent bonds in substances such as water, ammonia and methane in a number of ways. Each way represents the same thing. The method you should choose depends on what you want to show.

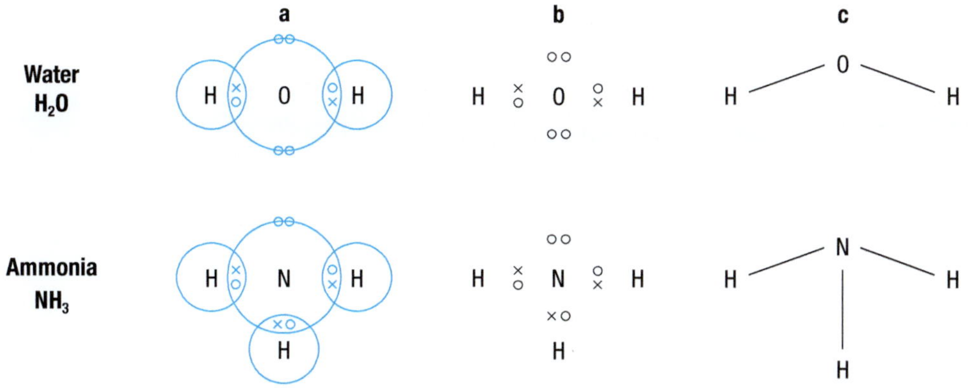

Figure 4 *You should represent a covalent compound by showing* **a** *the highest energy levels (or outer shells),* **b** *the outer electrons in a dot and cross diagram, or* **c** *the number of covalent bonds. Double bonds are shown by two lines, for example, O=O in an oxygen molecule*

Giant covalent structures

Many substances containing covalent bonds consist of small molecules, for example, H_2O. However, some covalently-bonded substances are very different. They have giant structures where huge numbers of atoms are held together by a network of covalent bonds. These are sometimes referred to as macromolecules.

Diamond has a giant covalent structure. In diamond, each carbon atom forms four covalent bonds with its neighbours. This results in a rigid giant covalent lattice.

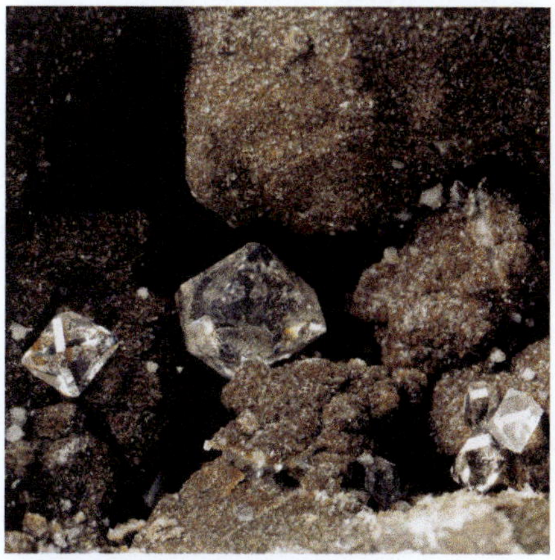

Figure 5 *Diamonds owe their hardness to the way the carbon atoms are arranged in a giant covalent structure*

links

For more information about diamond, see 2.8 Giant covalent structures.

Summary questions

1 Which of these compounds will contain covalent bonds? How did you decide?

hydrogen iodide, iron(II) chloride, lithium oxide, sulfur dioxide, nitrogen(III) chloride, magnesium nitride

2 Draw diagrams, showing all the electrons, to represent the covalent bonding between the following atoms:

- **a** two hydrogen atoms
- **b** two chlorine atoms
- **c** a hydrogen atom and a fluorine atom

3 Draw dot and cross diagrams to show the covalent bonds when:

- **a** a phosphorus atom bonds with three hydrogen atoms
- **b** a carbon atom bonds with two oxygen atoms.

4 Which noble gas electron structures do the atoms in a molecule of hydrogen chloride attain?

5 A covalent bond consists of a pair of electrons which occupy a space mainly between the nuclei of the two atoms bonded together. Explain how this pair of electrons bonds the atoms to each other. (Hint: think of the electrostatic forces of attraction between oppositely charged particles.)

Key points

- **Covalent bonds are formed when atoms of non-metals share pairs of electrons with each other.**
- **Each shared pair of electrons is a covalent bond.**
- **Many substances containing covalent bonds consist of simple molecules, but some have giant covalent structures.**

2.4 Bonding in metals

Learning objectives

After this topic, you should know:

- how the atoms in metals are arranged
- Ext how the atoms in metals are bonded to each other.

links

For more information on protecting iron from rusting, see Topic 5.5 Electroplating.

Metal crystals

The atoms in metals are built up layer upon layer in a regular pattern (see Figure 1).

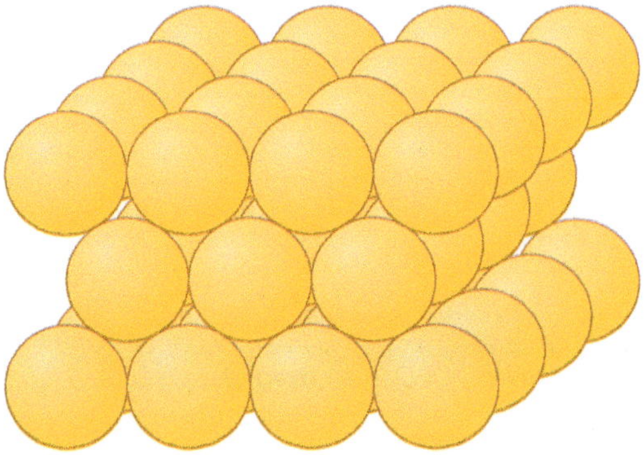

Figure 1 *The close-packed arrangement of copper atoms in copper metal*

This means that they form crystals, although these are not always obvious to the naked eye. However, sometimes you can see them. You can see zinc crystals on the surface of some steel that has been dipped into molten zinc to prevent it from rusting. This is called galvanised steel. For example, look at the surface of galvanised lamp posts and commercial wheelie bins (see Figure 3).

Practical

Growing silver crystals

You can grow crystals of silver metal by suspending a length of copper wire in silver nitrate solution. The crystals of silver will appear on the wire quite quickly. However, for the best results the experimental set-up needs to be left for several hours.

- Explain your observations.

Safety: Wear eye protection.

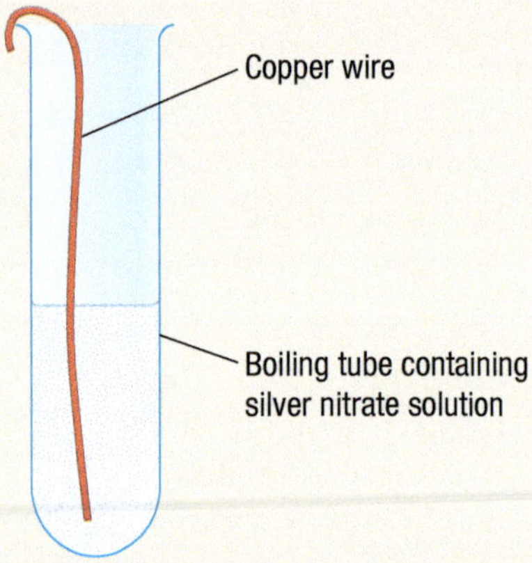

Figure 2 Growing silver crystals

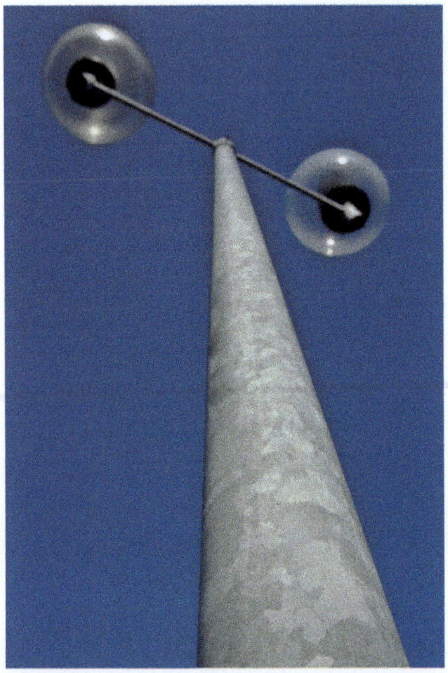

Figure 3 *Metal crystals, such as the zinc ones shown on this galvanised lamp post, give us evidence that metals are made up of atoms arranged in regular patterns*

Practical

Survey of metallic crystals

Take a look around your school or college to see if you can find any galvanised steel. See if you can spot the metal crystals. You can also look for crystals on brass fittings that have been left outside and not polished.

Ext

Metallic bonding

Metals are another example of giant structures. You can think of a metal as a lattice of positively charged ions. The metal ions are arranged in regular layers, one on top of another.

The outer electrons from each metal atom can easily move throughout the giant structure. The outer electrons (in the highest occupied energy level) form a 'sea' of free-moving electrons surrounding the positively charged metal ions. Strong electrostatic attraction between the negatively charged electrons and positively charged ions bonds the metal ions to each other.

The electrons in the 'sea' of free-moving electrons are called **delocalised electrons**. They are no longer linked with any particular metal ion in the giant metallic structure. These delocalised electrons help us explain the properties of metals. (See 2.8 'Giant metallic structures'.)

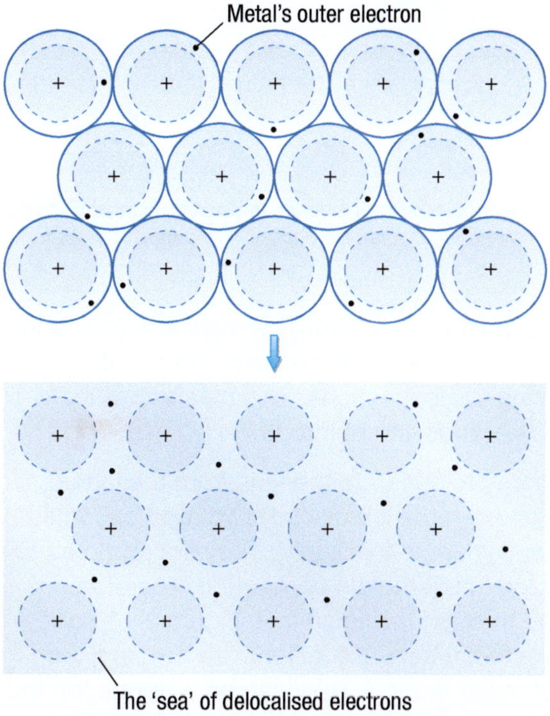

Figure 4 *A metal consists of positively charged metal ions surrounded by a 'sea' of delocalised electrons. This diagram shows us a model of metallic bonding.*

links

For more information about the properties of metals, see 2.8 Giant metallic structures.

Summary questions

Ext

1 What can you deduce about the arrangement of the particles in a metal from the fact that metals form crystals?

2 a Why are the particles that make up a metal described as positively charged ions?
  b What are delocalised electrons?

3 Use the theory of metallic bonding to explain the bonding in magnesium metal. Make sure you mention delocalised electrons. (The atomic number of magnesium is 12.)

4 Using a model to explain metallic bonding, delocalised electrons could be thought of as a 'glue'.
Explain why thinking of delocalised electrons in a metal as a glue is a useful model but one which has a major drawback.

Key points

- The atoms in metals are closely packed together and arranged in regular layers.
- Ext You can think of metallic bonding as positively charged metal ions which are held together by electrons from the outermost shell of each metal atom. These delocalised electrons are free to move throughout the giant metallic lattice.

2.5 Giant ionic structures

Learning objectives

After this topic, you should know:

- why ionic compounds have high melting points
- why ionic compounds conduct electricity when they are melted or dissolved in water.

In Topic 2.2 *Ionic bonding*, you have already seen that an ionic compound consists of a giant structure of ions arranged in a lattice. The attractive electrostatic forces between the oppositely charged ions act in all directions and are very strong. This holds the ions in the lattice together very tightly. Look at Figure 1.

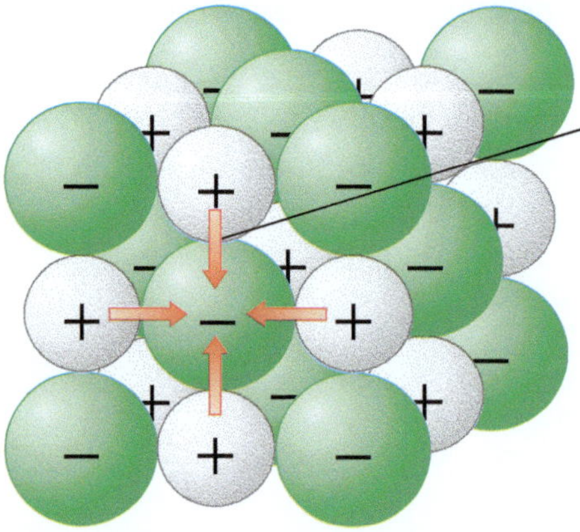

Figure 1 *The attractive forces between the oppositely charged ions in an ionic compound are very strong. The regular arrangement of ions in the giant lattice enables ionic compounds to form crystals.*

links

For more information on the movement and arrangement of particles in solids and liquids, look back to 1.1 States of matter.

It takes a lot of energy to break up a giant ionic lattice. There are lots of strong ionic bonds to break. To separate the ions you have to overcome all those electrostatic forces of attraction acting in all directions. This means that ionic compounds have high melting points and boiling points.

Once you have supplied enough energy to separate the ions from the lattice, they are free to move around. That is when the ionic solid melts and becomes a liquid. The ions are free to move anywhere in this liquid. They are attracted to oppositely charged electrodes dipping in the molten compound. Therefore, they can carry their electrical charge through the liquid (see Figure 2). A solid ionic compound cannot conduct electricity because its ions are held in fixed positions in the lattice. They cannot move around. They can only vibrate 'on the spot' when in the solid state.

Study tip

Remember that every ionic compound has a giant structure. The oppositely charged ions in these structures are held together by strong electrostatic forces of attraction. These act in all directions.

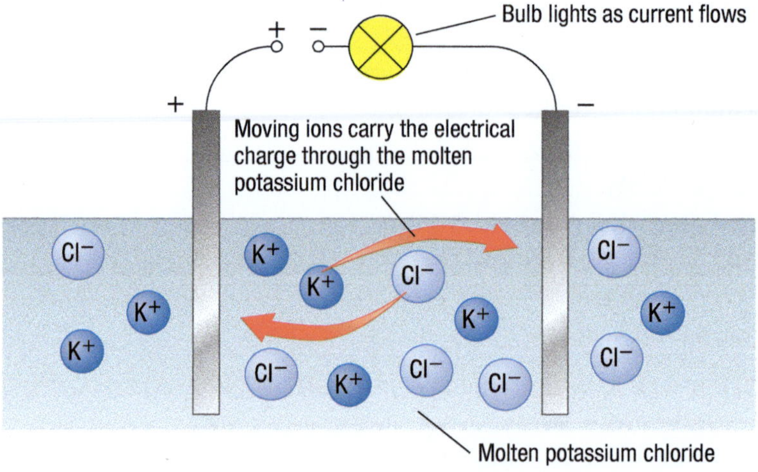

Figure 2 *Because the ions are free to move, a molten ionic compound can conduct electricity*

Many ionic compounds will dissolve in water. When you dissolve an ionic compound in water, the lattice is split up by the water molecules. Then the ions are free to move around in the solution formed. They can carry their charge to oppositely charged electrodes in the solution. Just as molten ionic compounds will conduct electricity, solutions of ionic compounds will also conduct electricity. The ions are able to move to an oppositely charged electrode dipped in the solution.

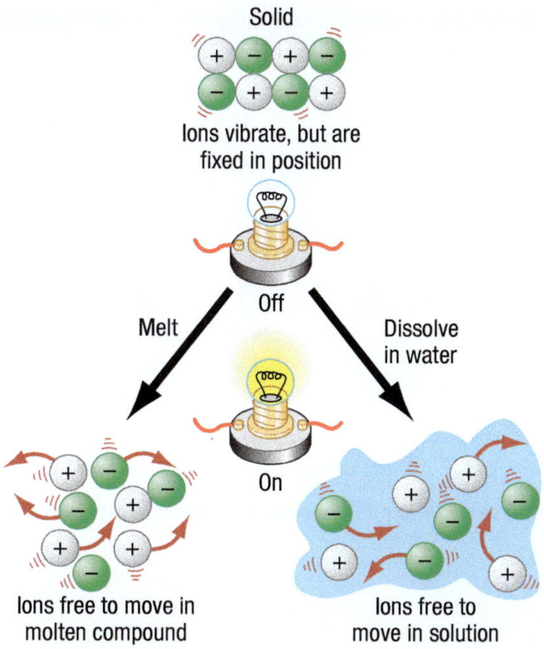

Figure 3 *Ionic compounds do not conduct electricity in the solid state but do when molten or when dissolved in water*

Ionic solid	Molten ionic compound	Ionic compound in solution
Ions are fixed in a giant lattice. They vibrate but cannot move around – it does not conduct electricity.	High temperature provides enough energy to overcome the many strong attractive forces between ions. Ions are free to move around within the molten compound – it does conduct electricity.	Water molecules separate ions from the lattice. Ions are free to move around within the solution – it does conduct electricity.

Summary questions

1 Explain why ionic compounds have high melting points.

2 Explain why ionic compounds conduct electricity only when they are molten or dissolved in water.

3 Why is seawater a better conductor of electricity than water from a freshwater lake?

4 Which of these ions will move to the positive electrode and which will move to the negative electrode in a circuit as shown in Figure 2?
lithium ions, chloride ions, bromide ions, calcium ions, sodium ions, zinc ions, oxide ions, iodide ions, barium ions

5 Predict which of these two ionic compounds has the higher melting point – sodium oxide or aluminium oxide. Explain your reasoning.

Practical

Testing conductivity

Using a circuit as shown in Figure 2, dip a pair of electrodes into a 1 cm depth of sodium chloride crystals. What happens?

Now slowly add water.

- What happens to the bulb?

Repeat the experiment using potassium chloride.

- Explain your observations.

Key points

- It takes a lot of energy to break the many strong ionic bonds that hold a giant ionic lattice together. So, ionic compounds have high melting points. They are all solids at room temperature.
- Ionic compounds will conduct electricity when they are melted or dissolved in water. That is because their ions can then move freely around and can carry charge through the liquid.

2.6 Simple molecules

Learning objectives

After this topic, you should know:

- that substances made up of simple molecules have relatively low melting points and boiling points
- Ext why substances made of simple molecules have low melting points and boiling points
- why these substances do not conduct electricity.

Many substances made up of simple covalently-bonded molecules have low melting points and boiling points. Look at the graph in Figure 1.

This means that many substances made up of simple molecules are liquids or gases at room temperature. Others are solids with quite low melting points, such as iodine (I_2) and sulfur (S_8).

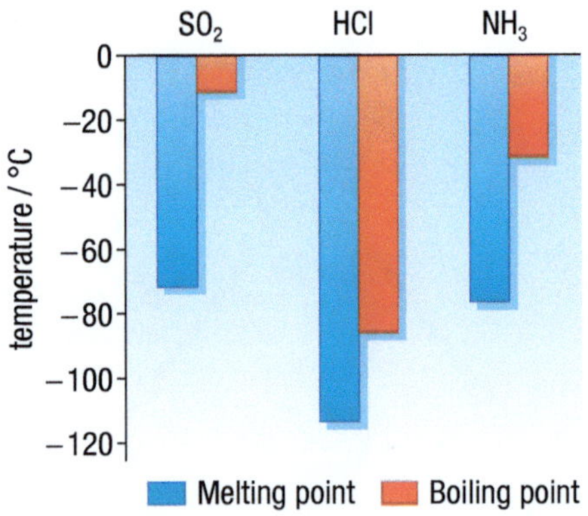

Figure 1 *Substances made of simple molecules usually have low melting points and boiling points*

Ext

Intermolecular forces

Covalent bonds are very strong so the atoms within each molecule are held very tightly together. However, each molecule tends to be quite separate from its neighbouring molecules. The force of attraction between the individual molecules in a covalent substance is relatively small. Scientists say that there are weak **intermolecular forces** between molecules. Overcoming these forces does not take much energy.

Look at the molecules in a sample of chlorine gas (Figure 2).

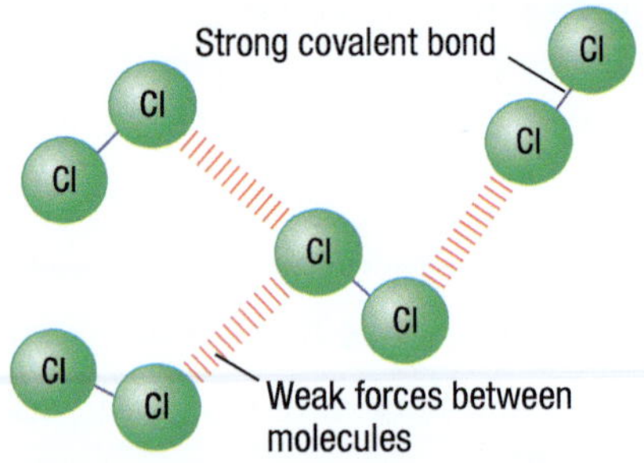

Figure 2 *Covalent bonds and the weak forces between molecules in chlorine gas. It is the weak intermolecular forces that are overcome when substances made of simple molecules melt or boil. The covalent bonds are not broken.*

You have seen that ionic compounds will conduct electricity when they are liquids. But although a substance that is made up of simple molecules may be a liquid at room temperature, it will not conduct electricity. Look at the demonstration below.

Demonstration

Conductivity

- What happens?

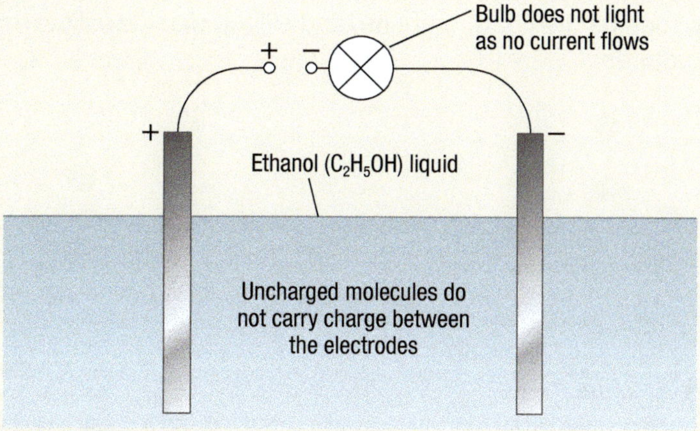

Figure 3 *Compounds made of simple molecules do not conduct electricity*

Safety: Ethanol is highly flammable so no naked flames.

There is no overall charge on the simple molecules in a compound like ethanol. So their neutral molecules cannot carry electrical charge. This makes it impossible for substances made up of simple molecules to conduct electricity.

Study tip

Although the covalent bonds in molecules are strong, the forces between molecules are weak.

links

For information on ionic compounds conducting electricity, look back at 2.5 Giant ionic structures.

Summary questions

Ext 1 Describe what is meant by the term 'intermolecular forces'?

2 Which of the following substances from each group of three will have relatively low melting points and boiling points?
   a aluminium oxide, aluminium, oxygen
   b magnesium chloride, magnesium, chlorine
   c hydrogen sulfide, hydrogen, sulfur

3 a Diamond has a very high melting point. Explain why.
   Ext b Nitrogen gas has a very strong triple covalent bond holding the nitrogen atoms together in diatomic molecules (N_2). Explain its boiling point of −196 °C.

4 A compound called sulfur hexafluoride (SF_6) is used to stop sparks forming inside electrical switches designed to control large currents. Explain why the properties of this compound make it particularly useful in electrical switches.

Ext 5 Explain why the melting point of hydrogen chloride is −115 °C but the melting point of sodium chloride is 801 °C.

Key points

- Substances made up of simple molecules have low melting points and boiling points.
- Ext The forces between simple molecules are weak. These weak intermolecular forces explain why substances made of simple molecules have low melting points and boiling points.
- Simple molecules have no overall charge, so they cannot carry electrical charge. Therefore, substances made of simple molecules do not conduct electricity.

2.7 Giant covalent structures

Learning objectives

After this topic, you should know:

- the general properties of substances with giant covalent structures
- why diamond is hard and graphite is slippery
- Ext why graphite can conduct electricity
- what fullerenes are made of and some of their uses.

Most covalently-bonded substances are made up of individual molecules. However, a few form very different structures. These do not have relatively small numbers of atoms arranged in simple molecules. They form huge networks of atoms held together by covalent bonds in **giant covalent structures**. They are sometimes called **macromolecules**.

Substances such as diamond, graphite, and silicon dioxide (silica) have giant covalent structures.

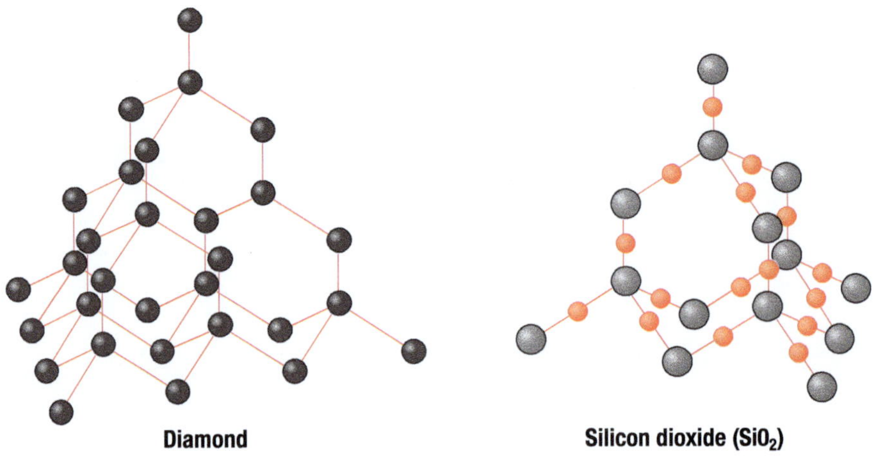

Figure 1 *The structures of diamond and silicon dioxide (silica) continue on in all directions*

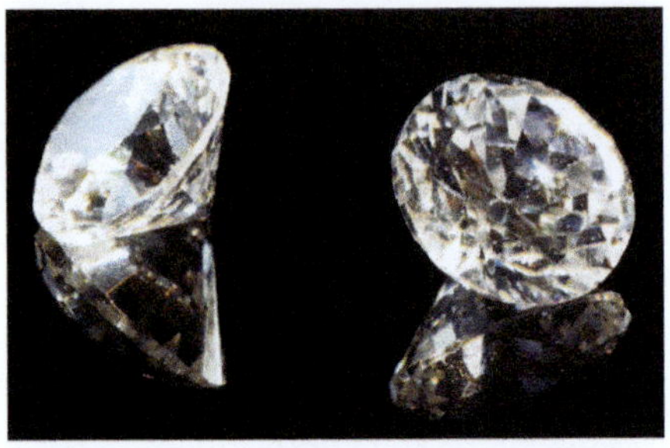

Figure 2 *Hard, shiny, and transparent – diamonds make beautiful jewellery*

All the atoms in these giant lattices are held in position by strong covalent bonds, as in diamond and silicon dioxide shown above. This gives them some very special properties. They have very high melting points and boiling points and are insoluble in water. Apart from graphite, they are hard and do not conduct electricity. Diamond is exceptionally hard and boils at 4827 °C. All its carbon atoms each form four strong covalent bonds, arranged in a perfectly symmetrical giant lattice.

Carbon isn't only found in the form of diamonds. Another form is graphite (well known for its use in pencil 'lead'). In graphite, carbon atoms are only bonded to three other carbon atoms. They form hexagons which are arranged in giant layers. There are no covalent bonds between the layers, only weak intermolecular forces. So the layers can slide over each other easily. It is a bit like playing cards sliding off a pack of cards. This makes graphite a soft material that feels slippery.

Study tip

Giant covalent structures are held together by covalent bonds throughout the lattice.

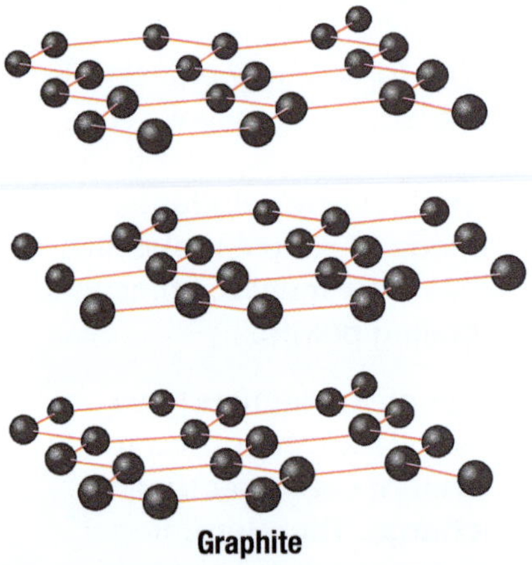

Ext **Figure 3** *The giant structure of graphite. There are strong covalent bonds* ***within*** *its layers but only weak intermolecular forces* ***between*** *the layers.*

Did you know ...?

Diamond is the hardest known natural substance. Artificial diamonds can be made by heating pure carbon to very high temperatures under enormous pressures. 'Industrial diamonds' made like this are embedded in the drill bits used by oil companies when drilling for oil.

Bonding in graphite

The carbon atoms in graphite's layers are arranged in hexagons so each carbon atom forms three strong covalent bonds (see Figure 3). Carbon atoms have four electrons in their outer shell available for bonding. This leaves one spare outer electron on each carbon atom.

Ext

This electron is free to move along the layers of carbon atoms. The free electrons found in graphite are called **delocalised electrons**. They behave rather like the electrons in a metallic structure.

These free electrons allow graphite to conduct electricity and heat along its layers of carbon atoms. Diamond – and most other covalently-bonded substances – cannot conduct electricity. This is because their atoms have no free electrons as all the outer shell electrons are involved in covalent bonding.

links

For information about delocalised electrons, look at 2.4 Bonding in metals.

Fullerenes

Apart from diamond and graphite, there are other structures that carbon atoms can form. In these structures the carbon atoms join together to make large cages which can have all sorts of shapes. Chemists have made shapes looking like balls, onions, tubes, doughnuts, corkscrews, and cones! They are based on *hexagonal rings of carbon atoms*.

The large carbon molecules containing these cage-like structures are called **fullerenes**. Scientists can now place other molecules inside these carbon cages. This has exciting possibilities, including the delivery of drugs to specific parts of the body. They are sure to become very important in **nanoscience** applications, for example, as catalysts and lubricants and are already used as nanotubes for reinforcing materials, eg in tennis racquets.

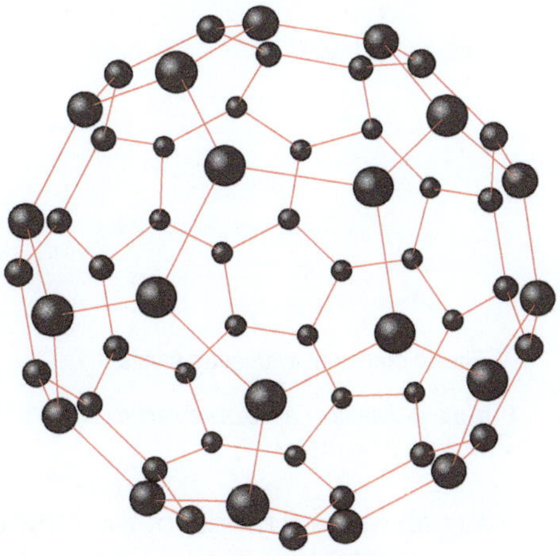

Figure 4 *The first fullerene to be discovered contained 60 carbon atoms, but chemists can now make giant fullerenes which contain many thousands of carbon atoms*

Summary questions

1 a Name three forms of the element carbon.
  b Find out what chemists call different forms of the same element in the same state.

2 List the general properties of a substance with a typical giant covalent structure.

Ext

3 a State a possible medical application of fullerene cages.
  b Give the shape of the fullerene molecules used to reinforce materials.
  c Give two other uses of fullerenes.

4 Graphite is sometimes used to reduce the friction between two surfaces that are rubbing together. Explain how it does this.

Ext

5 Explain in detail why graphite can conduct electricity but diamond cannot.

Key points

- Some covalently-bonded substances have giant structures. These substances have very high melting points and boiling points.
- Graphite contains giant layers of covalently-bonded carbon atoms. However, there are no covalent bonds between the layers, just weak intermolecular forces. This means they can slide over each other, making graphite soft and slippery. The carbon atoms in diamond have a rigid giant covalent structure, making it a very hard substance.
- Ext Graphite can conduct electricity and heat because of the delocalised electrons along its layers.
- As well as diamond and graphite, carbon also exists as fullerenes which can form large cage-like structures and tubes, based on hexagonal rings of carbon atoms.

2.8 Giant metallic structures

Learning objectives

After this topic, you should know:

- why metals can be bent and shaped without breaking
- why alloys are harder than pure metals
- Ext why metals conduct electricity and heat
- what 'shape memory alloys' are.

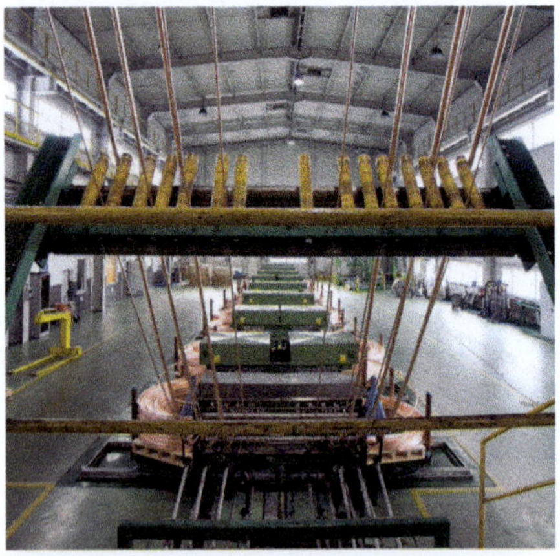

Figure 1 *Drawing copper out into wires depends on being able to make the layers of metal atoms slide easily over each other, without breaking the metal*

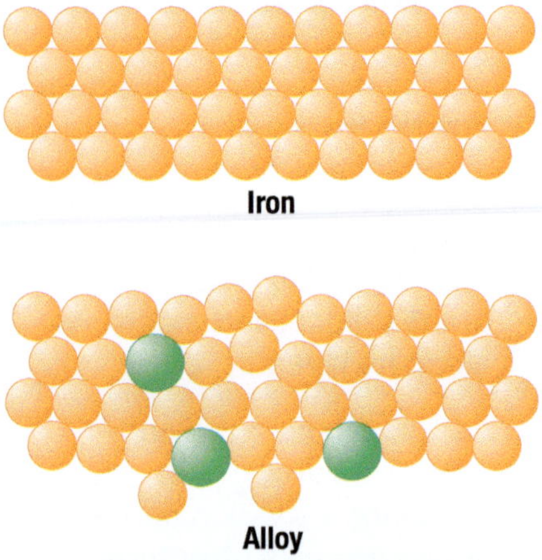

Figure 2 *The atoms in pure iron are arranged in layers which can easily slide over each other. In alloys the layers cannot slide so easily because atoms of other elements distort the layers.*

Metals can be hammered and bent into different shapes, and drawn out into wires. This is because the layers of atoms in a pure metal are able to slide easily over each other.

The atoms in a pure metal, such as iron, are held together in a giant metallic structure. The atoms are arranged in closely-packed layers. This regular arrangement allows the atoms to slide over one another quite easily. This is why pure iron is relatively soft and easily bent and shaped.

Alloys are usually mixtures of two or more elements, at least one of which is a metal. However, most steels contain iron with controlled amounts of carbon, a non-metal, mixed in its structure. The carbon atoms are a different size to the iron atoms. This makes it more difficult for the layers in the metal's giant structure to slide over each other. So, alloys are harder than the pure metals used to make them. This is shown in Figure 2.

Practical

Making models of metals

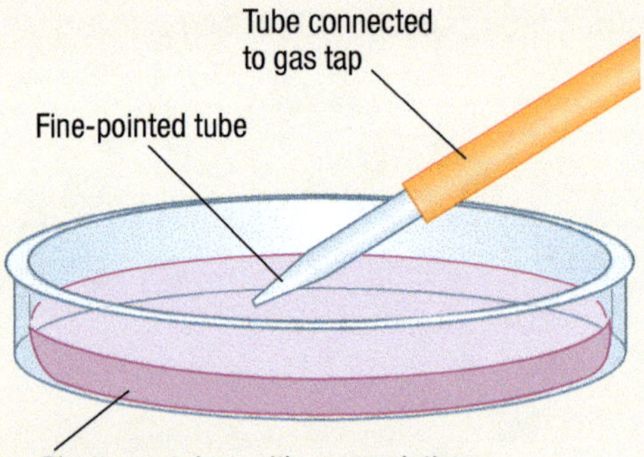

Figure 3 *Making a bubble raft to model the structure of a metal*

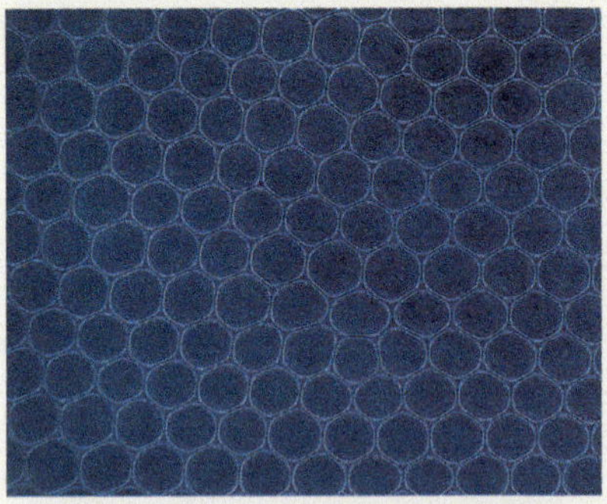

A regular arrangement of bubble 'atoms'

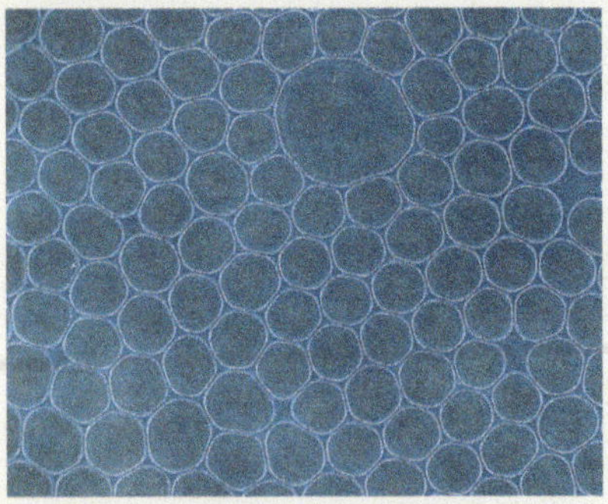

A larger bubble 'atom' disrupts the regular arrangement around it

You can make a model of the structure of a metal by blowing small bubbles of gas on the surface of soap solution to represent atoms.

- Why are models useful in science?

- Metal cooking utensils are used all over the world, because metals are good conductors of heat.
- Wherever electricity is generated, it passes through metal wires (usually made of copper) to get to where it is needed because metals are also good conductors of electricity.

Ext

Explaining the properties of metals

The positive ions in a metal's giant structure are held together by a sea of delocalised electrons. These electrons are a bit like 'glue'. Their negative charge between the positively charged ions holds the metal ions in position.

However, unlike glue, the electrons are able to move throughout the whole giant lattice. Because they can move around and hold the metal ions together at the same time, the delocalised electrons enable the lattice to distort. When struck, the metal atoms can slip past one another without breaking up the metal's structure.

Metals are good conductors of heat and electricity because the delocalised electrons can readily flow through the giant metallic lattice. The heat energy and electrical current are transferred quickly through the metal by the free-moving electrons.

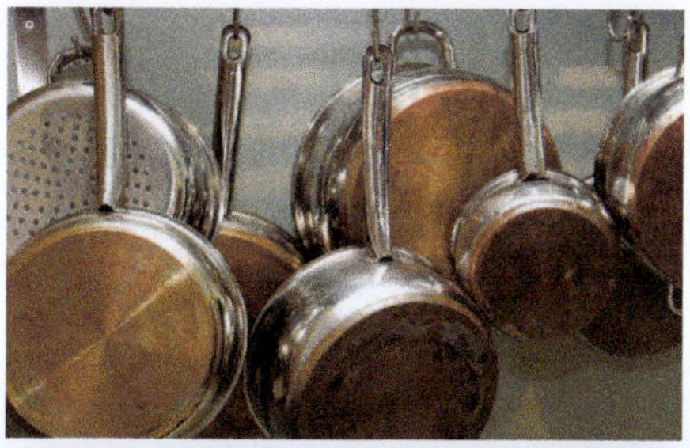

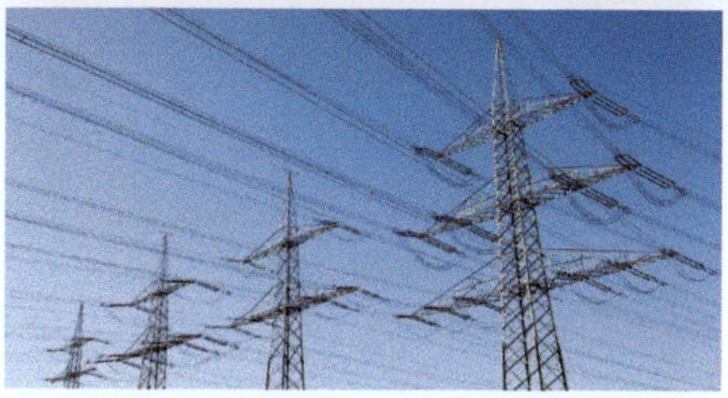

Figure 4 *Metals are essential in our lives – the delocalised electrons mean that they are good conductors of both heat and electricity*

links

For more about metalic bonding, look back at 2.4 Bonding in metals.

Shape memory alloys

Some alloys have a very special property. Like all metals they can be bent (or **deformed**) into different shapes. The difference comes when you heat them up and they return to their original shape automatically. These metals are called **shape memory alloys**, which describes the way they behave. They seem to 'remember' their original shape!

Shape memory alloys are used in many ways, for example, in health-care. Doctors treating a badly broken bone can use alloys to hold the bones in place whilst they heal. They cool the alloy before it is wrapped around the broken bone. When it heats up again the alloy goes back to its original shape. This pulls the bones together and holds them in place whilst they heal.

Dentists can also make braces to pull teeth into the right position using this technique (see Figure 5).

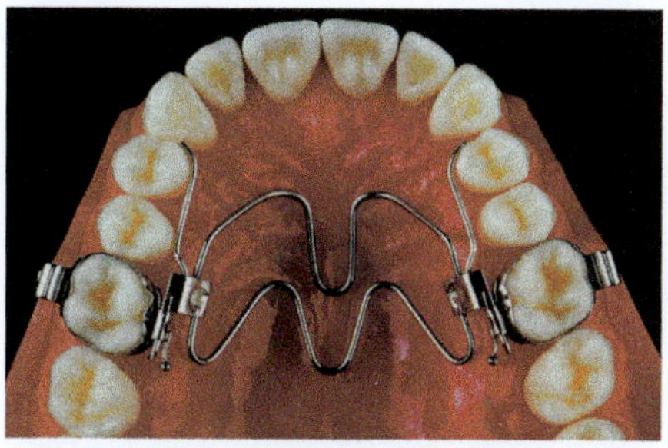

Figure 5 *This dental brace pulls the teeth into the right position as it warms up. It is made of a shape memory alloy called nitinol. It is an alloy of nickel and titanium.*

Summary questions

1 a Why can metals be bent, shaped and pulled out into wires when forces are applied?

b Find out the word used to describe a material, such as a metal, that can be:

i hammered into shapes **ii** drawn out into a wire.

2 a Use your knowledge of metal structures to explain why alloying a metal can make the metal harder.

b What is a shape memory alloy?

3 Explain how a dental brace made out of nitinol is more effective than a brace made out of a traditional alloy.

Ext **4** Explain why metals are good conductors of heat and electricity in terms of their structure and bonding.

Key points

- Metals can be bent and shaped because the layers of atoms (or positively charged ions) in a giant metallic structure can slide over each other.
- Alloys are harder than pure metals because the regular layers in a pure metal are distorted by differently-sized atoms in an alloy.
- Ext Delocalised electrons in metals enable electricity and heat to pass through a metal easily.
- If a shape memory alloy is deformed, it can return to its original shape on heating.

Chapter summary questions

1 Copy each sentence and write a number to fill in the blanks in **a** to **e**:

- **a** The elements in Group .... in the periodic table all form ions with a charge of 1+.
- **b** The elements in Group .... in the periodic table all form ions with a charge of 2+.
- **c** The elements in Group .... in the periodic table all form ions with a charge of 1–.
- **d** The elements in Group .... in the periodic table all form ions with a charge of 2–.
- **e** The elements in Group 4 in the periodic table have atoms which can form .... covalent bonds.

2 This table contains data about some different substances:

Substance	Melting point (°C)	Boiling point (°C)	Electrical conductor
ammonia	–78	–33	solid – poor liquid – poor
magnesium oxide	2852	3600	solid – poor liquid – good
lithium chloride	605	1340	solid – poor liquid – good
silicon dioxide	1610	2230	solid – poor liquid – poor
hydrogen bromide	–88	–67	solid – poor liquid – poor
graphite	3652	4827	solid – good liquid – good

- **a** Make a table with the following headings:

  Giant covalent, Giant ionic, Simple molecules

  Now write the name of each substance from the table above in the correct column.
- **b** Which substances are gases at 25 °C?
- **c** One of these substances behaves in a surprising way. Which one and why?
- **d** Draw a diagram to show the electron structures of a lithium atom and a chlorine atom and their ions in lithium chloride. (Atomic number of Li = 3, Cl = 17)

3 **a** Which of the following substances will have covalent bonding?

hydrogen iodide
chlorine(VII) oxide
silver chloride
phosphorus(V) fluoride
calcium bromide
silver nitrate

- **b** Explain how you decided on your answers in part **a**.
- **c** What type of bonding will the remaining substances in the list have?
- **d** What is the formula of:
  - **i** hydrogen iodide?
  - **ii** calcium bromide?

4 Copy and complete the following table with the formula of each ionic compound formed.
(The first one is done for you.)

	chloride, Cl^-	oxide, O^{2-}	sulfate, SO_4^{2-}	phosphate(V), PO_4^{3-}
potassium, K^+	KCl			
magnesium, Mg^{2+}				
iron(III), Fe^{3+}				

5 Draw a diagram which shows the bonding in:

- **a** hydrogen, H_2
- **b** carbon dioxide, CO_2.

Practice questions

1 Lithium and oxygen combine to form lithium oxide, an ionic compound.

The diagrams show the electronic structures of a lithium atom and an oxygen atom.

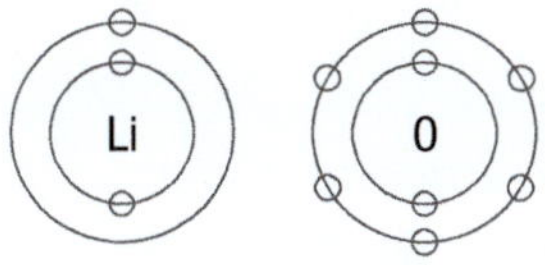

a Describe, in terms of electrons, what happens when a lithium atom combines with an oxygen atom. (3)

b The electronic structures of lithium and oxygen can be shown as follows:

Li 2,1 O 2,6

Write the charge of each of the ions formed in lithium oxide. (2)

c Explain why lithium oxide has a high melting point. (2)

d Explain why lithium oxide does not conduct electricity when solid but does when molten. (2)

2 Hydrogen and fluorine atoms combine to form the compound hydrogen fluoride.

The diagrams show the electronic structures of a hydrogen atom and a fluorine atom.

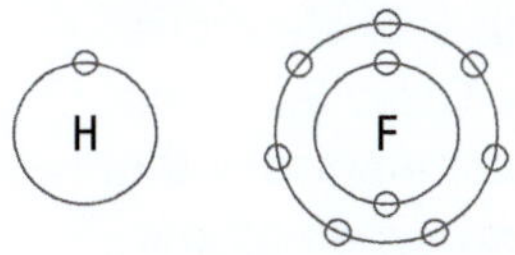

a Draw a diagram to show how the electrons are arranged in a hydrogen fluoride molecule. (2)

b What is the name of the bond in a hydrogen fluoride molecule? (1)

Ext **c** The bond in a hydrogen fluoride molecule is strong.

Explain why hydrogen fluoride is a gas at room temperature. (2)

d Hydrogen bromide has the same type of bonding as hydrogen fluoride.

A bond in a molecule can be represented by a straight line.

Show the hydrogen bromide molecule in this way. (1)

3 Silicon dioxide has a giant structure.

a Explain why silicon dioxide has a very high melting point. (3)

b Explain why molten silicon dioxide does not conduct electricity. (2)

4 Fullerenes and nanoscience may become more important in the future.

a One type of fullerene exists as molecules containing sixty atoms.

State the element in this molecule and how the atoms are arranged. (2)

Ext **b** Suggest **one** use of fullerenes in medicine. (1)

5 Copper is a useful metal.

a The diagram represents the structure of copper.

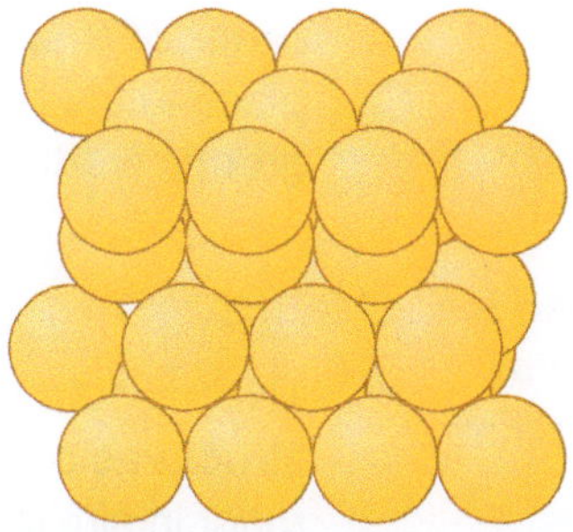

i Use this diagram to explain why copper can be easily shaped. (2)

Ext **ii** Explain why copper is a good conductor of electricity. (2)

b Pure copper is very soft and is made harder by adding other metals.

i What name is used for a mixture of metals? (1)

ii Explain how the other metals make copper harder. (2)

3.1 The periodic table

Learning objectives

After this topic, you should know:

- how atomic structure is linked to the periodic table
- why the noble gases are so unreactive.

The periodic table was first developed by a Russian chemist called Dmitri Mendeleev and published in 1869. He put elements in order of their atomic masses and started new rows to produce groups of similar elements. The word 'periodic' means repeated at regular intervals.

However, not all elements fit in with the pattern. For example, argon atoms have a greater average mass than potassium atoms. Ordering by atomic mass would result in argon (a **noble gas**) being in the same group as reactive metals such as sodium and lithium, and would group potassium (an extremely reactive metal) with the unreactive noble gases. So argon must be put before potassium in the periodic table to maintain the periodic pattern, even though the average mass of its atoms is heavier than that of potassium's atoms. Look at Figure 1 to check this out.

At the start of the 20th century scientists began to find out more about the structure of the atom. Only then could they solve this problem of certain elements breaking the periodic pattern. The elements are now arranged ***in order of their atomic (proton) number***. This puts them all in exactly the right place in the periodic table. It arranges the elements so that they line up in groups (vertical columns) with similar properties.

Did you know ...?

The alkali metal caesium reacts explosively with cold water, and will even react with ice at temperatures above –116 °C.

Mendeleev's predictions

When Mendeleev published his periodic table in 1869, not all scientists were convinced that he had it right. However, Mendeleev's brilliant idea was to leave gaps in his table for elements that had not yet been discovered. Then he used his table to predict what their properties should be, based on elements in the same group.

A few years later, new elements were discovered with properties that closely matched Mendeleev's predictions. Then there were few doubts that his table was a great breakthrough in scientific understanding.

Electronic structures and the periodic table

The periodic table also gives you an important summary of the electronic structures of all the elements. Elements in the same group of the periodic table react in similar ways because their atoms have the same number of electrons in the highest occupied energy level (outer shell). You saw in Topic 2.2 *Ionic bonding*, and Topic 2.3 *Covalent bonding*, how it is these outer electrons that are transferred (in ionic bonding) or shared (in covalent bonding) when atoms combine with each other.

In Chapter 2, you learnt that **the group number in the periodic table tells you the number of electrons in the outermost shell (highest occupied energy level) of an atom.**

For example, all the atoms of Group 2 elements have 2 electrons in their outermost shell (highest energy level) and those in Group 6 have 6 electrons in their outermost shell.

You also saw in Chapter 2 how atoms transfer or share electrons when bonding in order to attain the stable electronic structures of the noble gases. Look at the Group 0 noble gases, shaded purple in Figure 1. You can see how atoms of elements in Group 6 and 7 can gain electrons to form negative ions. These then have the electronic structure of the noble gas at the end of their row (called a period). Elements in Groups 1, 2, or 3 lose electrons and their positive ions attain the electronic structure of the noble gas at the end of the period one row above them.

The atoms of noble gases have eight electrons in their outermost shell, making the atoms very stable. The exception is the first of the noble gases, helium, which has just two electrons, but this complete first shell is also a very stable electronic structure.

Did you know ...?

Radon is a radioactive noble gas, produced in some rocks by the nuclear decay of radium. In some areas it is monitored as a health hazard as it can be released from the rocks and collect in the lower parts of buildings.

The stable electronic structures of the noble gases explains why they exist as single atoms. They are monatomic gases. They have no tendency to react to form molecules. However, chemists have managed to make a few compounds of the larger noble gases. These contain the most reactive non-metallic elements, fluorine and oxygen, for instance in the compounds XeF_6 and XeO_4.

Relative atomic mass 1, **H**, Atomic (proton) number 1

Group numbers

1	2											3	4	5	6	7	0
																	4 **He** 2
7 **Li** 3	9 **Be** 4											11 **B** 5	12 **C** 6	14 **N** 7	16 **O** 8	19 **F** 9	20 **Ne** 10
23 **Na** 11	24 **Mg** 12											27 **Al** 13	28 **Si** 14	31 **P** 15	32 **S** 16	35.5 **Cl** 17	40 **Ar** 18
39 **K** 19	40 **Ca** 20	45 **Sc** 21	48 **Ti** 22	51 **V** 23	52 **Cr** 24	55 **Mn** 25	56 **Fe** 26	59 **Co** 27	59 **Ni** 28	63.5 **Cu** 29	65 **Zn** 30	70 **Ga** 31	73 **Ge** 32	75 **As** 33	79 **Se** 34	80 **Br** 35	84 **Kr** 36
85 **Rb** 37	88 **Sr** 38	89 **Y** 39	91 **Zr** 40	93 **Nb** 41	96 **Mo** 42	98 **Tc** 43	101 **Ru** 44	103 **Rh** 45	106 **Pd** 46	108 **Ag** 47	112 **Cd** 48	115 **In** 49	119 **Sn** 50	122 **Sb** 51	128 **Te** 52	127 **I** 53	131 **Xe** 54
133 **Cs** 55	137 **Ba** 56	139 **La** 57	178 **Hf** 72	181 **Ta** 73	184 **W** 74	186 **Re** 75	190 **Os** 76	192 **Ir** 77	195 **Pt** 78	197 **Au** 79	201 **Hg** 80	204 **Tl** 81	207 **Pb** 82	209 **Bi** 83	209 **Po** 84	210 **At** 85	222 **Rn** 86
223 **Fr** 87	226 **Ra** 88	227 **Ac** 89															

Elements 58–71 and 90–103 (all metals) have been omitted

Key

Reactive metals These metals react vigorously with other elements like oxygen or chlorine, and with water. They are all soft – some of them can even be cut with a knife, like cheese!

Transition elements This group contains the elements that most people probably think of when the word 'metal' is mentioned, like iron, copper, silver, and gold. These metals are not usually very reactive – some, like silver and gold, are very unreactive.

Non-metals These elements have low melting and boiling points, and many are gases at room temperature and pressure.

Noble gases These (non-metal) elements are very unreactive, and it is very difficult to get them to combine with other elements.

Figure 1 *The modern periodic table. The upper number on the left of a symbol is the element's relative atomic mass. The lower number is its atomic number (or proton number) – the number of protons in the nucleus. The elements are arranged in order of atomic number.*

Study tip

Metals react by losing electrons. Non-metals react with metals by gaining electrons.

Summary questions

1 **a** What does 'periodic' mean in the term 'periodic table'?
b In the periodic table, what is:
i a group? **ii** a period?

2 In the periodic table, how does the number of metallic elements compare with the number of non-metal elements?

3 Explain why elements in many groups of the periodic table have similar chemical properties.

4 How many electrons do atoms of the following elements have in their highest energy level (outermost shell)?
a beryllium, Be **b** boron, B **c** potassium, K **d** helium, He
e argon, Ar **f** radium, Ra **g** radon, Rn **h** iodine, I

5 Why are the noble gases so unreactive?

Key points

- The atomic (proton) number of an element determines its position in the periodic table.
- The number of electrons in the outermost shell (highest energy level) of an atom determines its chemical properties.
- The group number in the periodic table equals the number of electrons in the outermost shell.
- The noble gases in Group 0 are unreactive because of their very stable electron arrangements.

3.2 Group 1 – the alkali metals

Learning objectives

After this topic, you should know:

- how the Group 1 elements behave
- how the properties of the Group 1 elements change going down the group.

Mass number	Symbol	Atomic number
7	**Li**	3
23	**Na**	11
39	**K**	19
85	**Rb**	37
133	**Cs**	55
223	**Fr**	87

Figure 1 *The alkali metals (Group 1)*

The first group (Group 1) on the left-hand side of the periodic table is called the **alkali metals**. This group consists of the metals lithium (Li), sodium (Na), potassium (K), rubidium (Rb), caesium (Cs), and francium (Fr) (Figure 1). You will probably only see the first three of these as the others are too reactive to use in schools.

Properties of the alkali metals

All the alkali metals are very reactive. They have to be stored in oil (see Figure 2). This stops them reacting with oxygen in the air. Their reactivity increases as you go down the group. So lithium is the least reactive alkali metal and francium is the most reactive.

All the alkali metals have a very low density compared with other metals. In fact lithium, sodium, and potassium all float on water. The alkali metals are also all very soft. They can be cut with a knife. They have a silvery, shiny surface when you first cut them. However, this quickly goes dull as the metal reacts with oxygen in the air. This forms a layer of oxide on the shiny surface.

The properties of this unusual group of metals result from their electronic structure. The atoms of alkali metals all have one electron in their outermost shell (highest energy level). This gives them similar properties. It also makes them very reactive. This is because they need to lose just one electron to get a stable (noble gas) electronic structure.

They react with non-metals, losing their single outer electron. They form a metal ion carrying a 1+ charge, for example, Na^+ and K^+. They always form ionic compounds.

Melting points and boiling points

The Group 1 metals melt and boil at relatively low temperatures for metals. Going down the group, the melting points and boiling points get lower and lower. In fact, caesium turns into a liquid at just 29 °C.

Reaction with water

When you add lithium, sodium, or potassium to water the metal floats on the water, moving around and fizzing. The fizzing happens because the metal reacts with the water to form hydrogen gas. Potassium reacts so vigorously with the water that the hydrogen produced catches fire. It burns with a lilac flame.

The reaction between an alkali metal and water also produces a metal hydroxide, which explains the name 'alkali metals'.

The hydroxides of the alkali metals are all soluble in water. The solution is colourless with a high pH. (**Universal indicator** turns purple.)

$$\text{sodium} + \text{water} \rightarrow \text{sodium hydroxide} + \text{hydrogen}$$
$$2Na(s) + 2H_2O(l) \rightarrow 2NaOH(aq) + H_2(g)$$

$$\text{potassium} + \text{water} \rightarrow \text{potassium hydroxide} + \text{hydrogen}$$
$$2K(s) + 2H_2O(l) \rightarrow 2KOH(aq) + H_2(g)$$

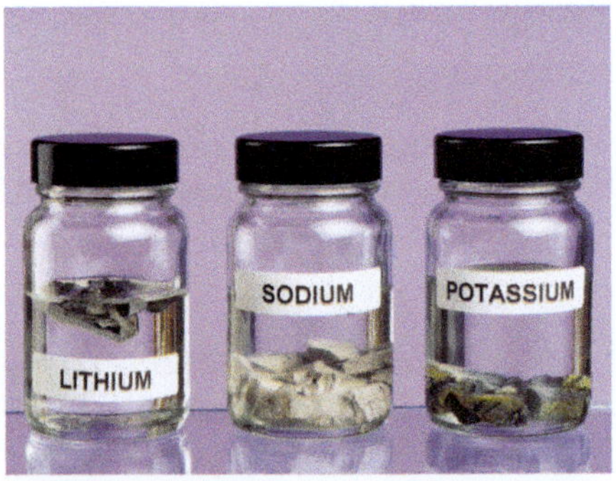

Figure 2 *The alkali metals have to be stored in oil because they are so reactive*

Demonstration

Reactions of alkali metals with water

The reaction of the alkali metals with water can be demonstrated by dropping a small piece of the metal into a trough of water. This must be done with great care. The reactions are vigorous, releasing a lot of energy. Hydrogen gas is also given off.

- Describe your observations in detail.

Safety: Wear your safety goggles when watching this demonstration.

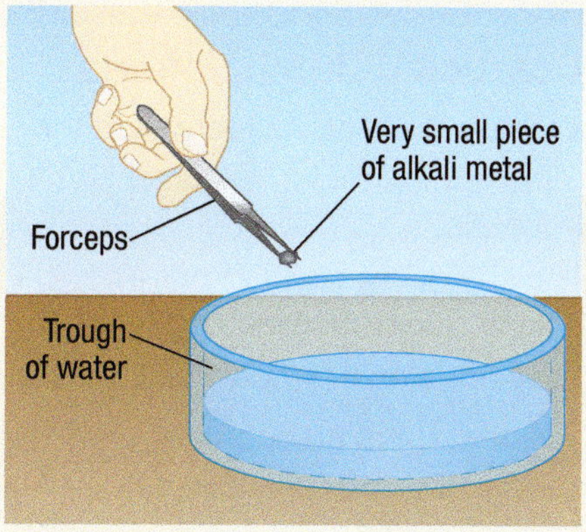

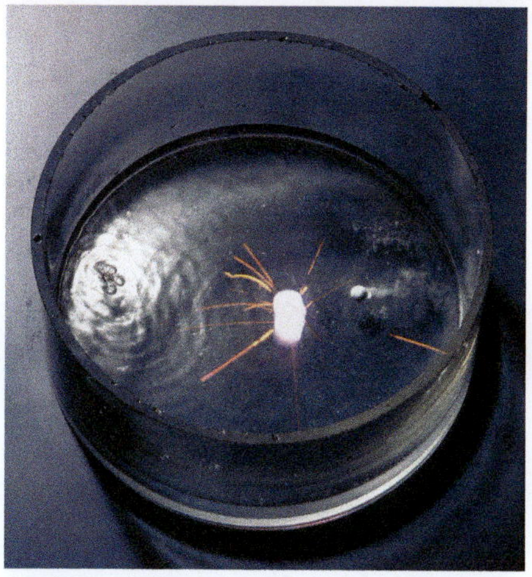

Figure 3 *Lithium, sodium, and potassium reacting with water (the lithium is on the left of the trough, the potassium has burning hydrogen above it, and the sodium is the molten silvery ball on the right)*

Other reactions

The alkali metals also react vigorously with non-metals such as chlorine gas. They produce metal chlorides, which are white solids. Their chlorides all dissolve readily in water to form colourless solutions.

The reactions get more and more vigorous as you go down the group. This is because it becomes easier to lose the single electron in the outer shell to form ions with a 1+ charge.

sodium + chlorine → sodium chloride

$$2Na(s) + Cl_2(g) \rightarrow 2NaCl(s)$$

They react in a similar way with fluorine, bromine, and iodine.

All of these ionic compounds of the alkali metals and non-metals are also white and dissolve easily in water. The solutions formed are all colourless.

Summary questions

1 Why are the alkali metals stored under oil?

2 What is the trend in the melting points of the alkali metals as their atomic number increases?

3 Explain why the alkali metals form ions with a 1+ charge.

4 Caesium is near the bottom of Group 1 in the periodic table. What do you think would happen if it was dropped into water? Include an explanation of your observations and a balanced symbol equation with state symbols in your answer.

5 Write a balanced symbol equation, including state symbols, for the reaction of caesium (Cs) with:
  a iodine
  b bromine.

Key points

- The elements in Group 1 of the periodic table are called the alkali metals.
- Their melting points and boiling points decrease going down the group.
- The metals all react with water to produce hydrogen and an alkaline solution containing the metal hydroxide.
- They form 1+ ions in reactions to make ionic compounds. These are generally white and dissolve in water, giving colourless solutions.
- The reactivity of the alkali metals increases going down the group.

3.3 Group 7 – the halogens

Learning objectives

After this topic, you should know:

- how the Group 7 elements behave
- how the properties of the Group 7 elements change going down the group.

19	**F** 9
35.5	**Cl** 17
80	**Br** 35
127	**I** 53
210	**At** 85

Figure 1 *The Group 7 elements*

Properties of the halogens

The Group 7 elements are called the **halogens**. They are a group of poisonous non-metals that have coloured vapours. They have fairly typical properties of non-metals.

- They have low melting points and boiling points. Their melting points and boiling points increase going down the group (see Figure 2).
- They are also poor conductors of heat and electricity.

As elements, the halogens all exist as molecules made up of pairs of atoms. The atoms in each pair are joined to each other by a covalent bond.

	Melting point (°C)	Boiling point (°C)
F—F (F_2)	−220	−188
Cl—Cl (Cl_2)	−101	−35
Br—Br (Br_2)	−7	59
I—I (I_2)	114	184

Figure 2 *The halogens all form molecules made up of a pair of atoms, joined by a covalent bond. This type of molecule is called a 'diatomic molecule'.*

Reactions of the halogens

The electronic structure of the halogens determines the way they react with other elements. They all have seven electrons in their outermost shell (highest energy level). So they need to gain just one more electron to achieve the stable electronic structure of a noble gas. This means that the halogens take part in both ionic and covalent bonding.

	How the halogens react with hydrogen
$F_2(g) + H_2(g) \rightarrow 2HF(g)$	Explosive even at −200 °C and in the dark
$Cl_2(g) + H_2(g) \rightarrow 2HCl(g)$	Explosive in sunlight, but slow in the dark
$Br_2(g) + H_2(g) \rightarrow 2HBr(g)$	300 °C + platinum catalyst
$I_2(g) + H_2(g) \rightleftharpoons 2HI(g)$	300 °C + platinum catalyst (very slow, reversible)

Look at the table of reactions of the halogens with hydrogen gas. It shows a general trend that you find in Group 7 – **the elements get less reactive going down the group**.

The halogens also all react with metals. They gain a single electron to give them a stable arrangement of electrons. They form ions with a 1– charge, for example, F^-, Cl^-, Br^-. Examples of their ionic compounds include sodium chloride, NaCl, and iron(III) bromide, $FeBr_3$.

Study tip

In Group 7, reactivity *decreases* as you go down the group. However, in Group 1, reactivity *increases* going down the group.

Look at the diagram of the ions in calcium chloride, $CaCl_2$, below:

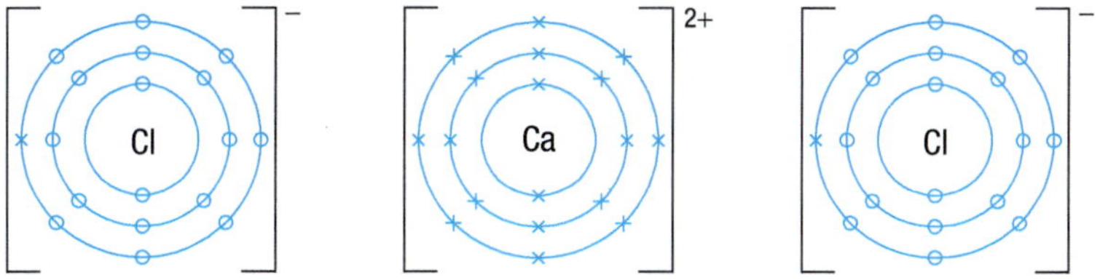

When a halogen reacts with another non-metal, the atoms of the halogen ***share electrons*** with the atoms of the other element. This gives the atoms of both elements the stable electronic structure of one of the noble gases. Therefore, the compounds of halogens with non-metals contain covalent bonds.

Look at the **dot and cross diagram** of hydrogen chloride, HCl, below, showing only the outer shell electrons:

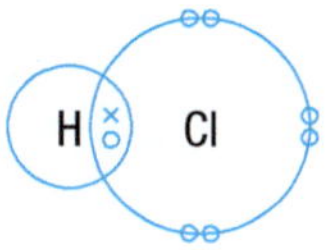

(Note that the circles need not be shown in dot and cross diagrams.)

Did you know ... ?

Many early chemists were badly hurt or even killed as they tried to make pure fluorine. They called it 'the gas of Lucifer'. It was finally produced by the French chemist Henri Moissan, who died aged just 55. His life was almost certainly shortened by his work with fluorine.

Summary questions

1 In the Group 7 elements, what is the trend going down the group in:
a their melting points? **b** their reactivity?

2 a Using the data in the table in Figure 2, give the state of each Group 7 element at 20 °C.
b What is the general name given to the Group 7 elements?

3 a Show the ions in lithium fluoride, LiF, in a diagram showing all the electrons.
b Draw a dot and cross diagram, showing only the outer shell electrons, of a molecule of hydrogen iodide.

4 Write a word equation for the reaction of lithium with bromine.

5 Write a balanced symbol equation, including state symbols, for the reaction of:
sodium metal with iodine vapour.

links

To remind yourself about ionic and covalent bonding, as well as dot and cross diagrams, look back to Chapter 2 Structure and bonding.

Key points

- The halogens all form ions with a single negative charge in their ionic compounds with metals.
- The halogens form covalent compounds by sharing electrons with other non-metals.
- The reactivity of the halogens decreases going down the group.

Chapter summary questions

1 **a** Where in the periodic table will you find:
  i the halogens?
  ii the noble gases?
  iii the alkali metals?

b In which groups would you find the four elements described in **i**, **ii**, and **iii** below?
  i This is a metal that can be cut with a knife and is stored under oil. It reacts violently with water and forms ions with a 1+ charge.
  ii This is a very unreactive, monatomic gas.
  iii This toxic gas is the most reactive of the all the non-metallic elements. It forms ions with a 1– charge and will also form covalent compounds.

2 Astatine (At) is a halogen whose atomic number is 85. It lies at the bottom of Group 7.

a How many electrons occupy its outermost shell (highest energy level)? How did you work out the answer?

b Predict the state of astatine at 20 °C.

c For the compound ***sodium astatide***, predict:
  i its type of bonding
  ii its colour
  iii its chemical formula
  iv the balanced symbol equation for its formation from its elements

3 Rubidium (Rb) is in Group 1 of the periodic table, lying directly beneath potassium.

a Predict the physical properties of rubidium, to include:
  i its hardness
  ii its electrical conductivity
  iii its melting point.

b **i** What will be the charge on a rubidium ion?
  ii Copy and complete the table below:

Rubidium compound	Chemical formula
Rubidium iodide	
Rubidium fluoride	
Rubidium hydroxide	

  iii What is the colour of the rubidium compounds in the table in part **ii**? Comment on their solubility in water.

c Write down word equations and balanced symbol equations, including state symbols, for the following reactions:
  i rubidium and water
  ii rubidium and chlorine.

d Will the reactions of rubidium in part **c** be more or less vigorous than the same reactions using potassium? Explain your answer.

4 **a** Draw dot and cross diagrams to show the bonding in the following substances. (Draw only the outer shell electrons.)
  i hydrogen bromide
  ii iodine

b Draw a diagram showing all the electrons in lithium chloride.

5 **a** Here are the Group 1 elements in order of their atomic number, with lowest atomic number listed first:
lithium (Li)
sodium (Na)
potassium (K)
rubidium (Rb)
caesium (Cs)
francium (Fr)
  i Name the three alkali metals with a density less than 1 g/cm^3 so will float on water.
  ii Which alkali metal will react most slowly with water?

b Here are the halogens in order of their atomic number:
fluorine (F)
chlorine (Cl)
bromine (...)
iodine (I)
astatine (At)
  i What is the chemical symbol of bromine?
  ii Which one of the halogens has the lowest boiling point?

Practice questions

1 The metals in Group 1 of the periodic table are chemically very reactive but have physical properties very different from most other metals.

a State **two** physical properties whose values are much lower for Group 1 metals than for most other metals. (2)

b A small piece of lithium is added to a large trough of water. A similar piece of potassium is added to a different trough of water. A reaction occurs in both troughs.

i State **two** observations that could be made in the lithium reaction. (2)

ii State **two** observations that could be made in the potassium reaction that would **not** be made in the lithium reaction. (2)

iii A piece of litmus paper was dipped in the solution formed in the lithium reaction.
State and explain the final colour of the litmus. (2)

iv Write a balanced symbol equation for the reaction between potassium and water. (2)

c A student wrote the following notes about the compounds of the Group 1 metal, sodium (Na):

'Sodium is a reactive alkali metal, forming a solution of sodium hydroxide, $NaOH_2$, when it reacts with water. Like most sodium compounds this is a pale yellow compound that is insoluble in water. The gas given off in the reaction is oxygen from the water.'

Explain how you would correct this piece of writing, saying what is wrong and how it should be corrected. (4)

d Describe the solution made when potassium nitrate dissolves in water. (1)

2 The elements in Group 7 of the periodic table are called halogens. They form salts called halides.

a Write a balanced symbol equation for the salt formation when calcium reacts with chlorine. (2)

b Using the trend in the boiling points of the halogens, match the halogen to its boiling point:

Halogen	Boiling point in °C
iodine	59
fluorine	184
bromine	–34
chlorine	–188

(2)

c i Suggest with a reason, which one of the halogens will react most vigorously with hydrogen gas. (2)

ii Name the compound formed in part i. (1)

iii Draw a dot and cross diagram, showing outer shell electrons only, to represent the bonding in the halide compound formed in part i during the reaction with hydrogen. (3)

d Explain why the chemical formula of lithium fluoride is LiF, in terms of the charges on ions. (4)

4.1 Useful metals

Learning objectives

After this topic, you should know:
- what transition metals are and why they are so useful
- why copper is such a useful metal
- why alloys are often more useful than pure metals.

Transition metals

In the centre of the periodic table there is a large block of metallic elements. Most are called transition metals and have similar properties. Like all metals, the transition metals are very good conductors of electricity and heat. They are strong but can also be bent or hammered into useful shapes.

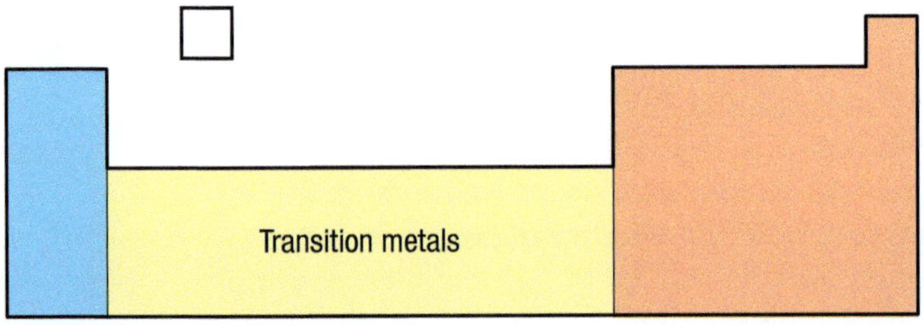

Figure 1 *The transition metals are found in the yellow block of the periodic table shown here*

The properties of the transition metals mean that they can be used in many different ways. You will find them in buildings and in cars, trains, and other types of transport. Their strength makes them useful as building materials. They are used in heating systems and for electrical wiring because heat energy and electricity pass through them easily.

Copper is a very useful transition metal. It can be bent but is still hard enough for plumbers to use as water tanks or pipes and it does not react with water. Copper also conducts electricity and heat very well. So it is ideal where we need:

- pipes that will carry water, or
- wires that will conduct electricity.

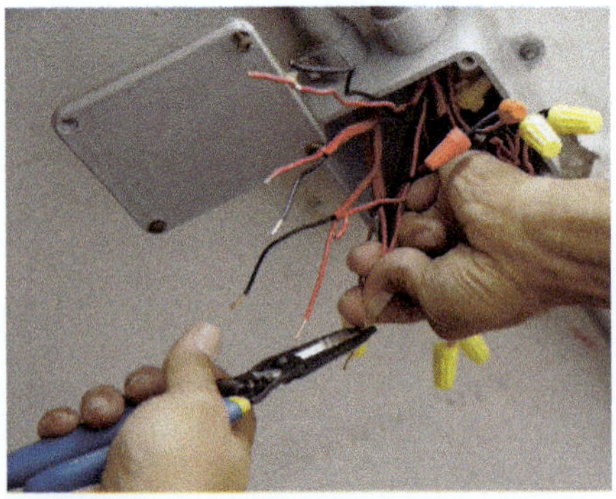

Figure 2 *Copper is particularly useful because it is such a good conductor of electricity*

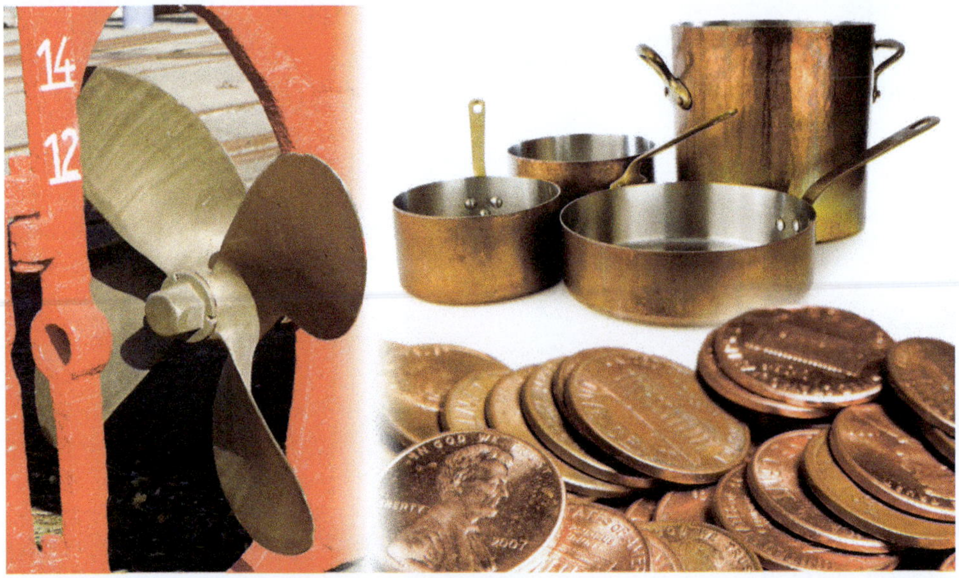

Figure 3 *Transition metals are used in many different ways because of their useful properties*

Copper alloys

Bronze was probably the first alloy made by humans, about 5500 years ago. It is usually made by mixing copper with tin. It is used to make ship's propellers because of its toughness and resistance to corrosion.

Brass is made by alloying copper with zinc. Brass is much harder than copper but it is workable. It can be hammered into sheets and pressed into intricate shapes. This property is used to make musical instruments, such as trumpets.

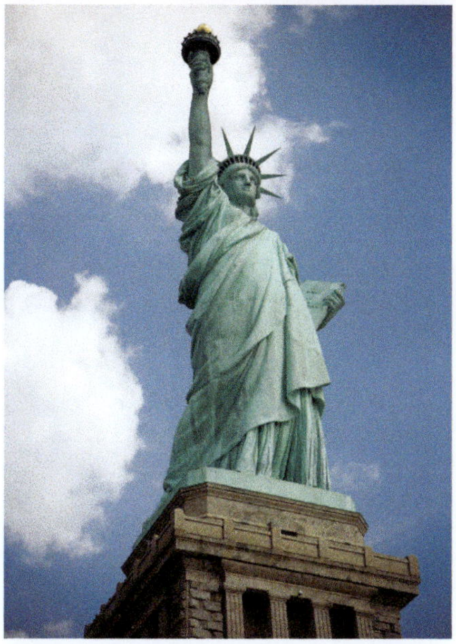

Figure 4 *The Statue of Liberty in New York contains over 80 tonnes of copper*

Aluminium alloys

Aluminium has a low density for a metal. It can be alloyed with a wide range of other elements. There are over 300 alloys of aluminium available. These alloys have very different properties. Engineers use 'light-weight', but strong, aluminium alloys to build aircraft whilst others can be used as armour-plating on tanks and other military vehicles.

Gold alloys

As with copper and iron, gold and aluminium can be made harder by adding other elements. Gold is usually alloyed with copper when used to make jewellery. Pure gold wears away more easily than its alloy with copper. By varying the proportions of the two metals you also get different shades of 'gold' objects.

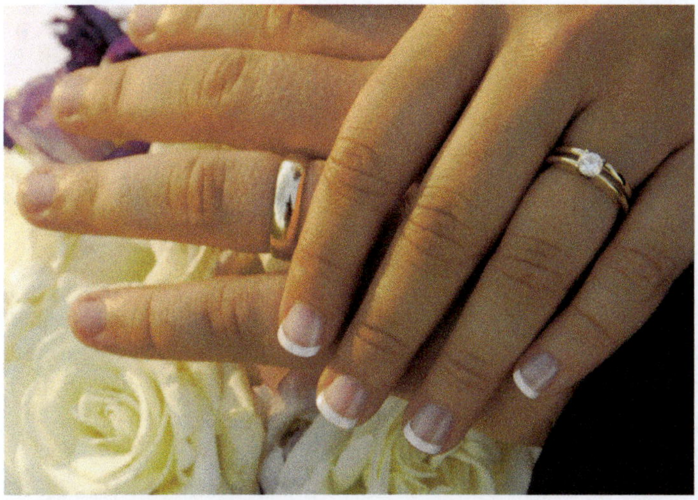

Figure 5 *Alloying with copper makes gold more hardwearing. This is especially important in wedding rings, which many married people wear most of the time.*

Did you know ... ?

The purity of gold is often expressed in 'carats', where 24-carat gold is almost pure gold (99.9%). If you divide the carat number by 24, you get the fraction of gold in your jewellery. So an 18-carat gold ring will contain $\frac{3}{4}$ (75%) gold.

Summary questions

1 a Write a list of the properties of a typical transition metal.
  b Where in the periodic table will you find the transition metals?
  c Which metal mentioned on this page is **not** a transition metal?

2 a Why is copper used so much in plumbing?
  b Why is gold alloyed with copper in many wedding rings?

3 Silver and gold are transition metals that are better conductors of electricity than copper. Why is copper used to make electric cables instead of either of these metals?

4 Why are aluminium alloys used extensively in the aircraft industry?

5 Explain in detail why copper alloys are more suitable for making coins than pure copper metal.

Key points

- **The transition metals are found in the central block of elements in the periodic table.**
- **Transition metals have properties that make them useful for building and making things. For example, copper is used in wiring because of its high electrical conductivity.**
- **Copper, gold, and aluminium are all alloyed with other metals to make them harder.**

4.2 Iron and steels

Learning objectives

After this topic, you should know:

- how iron ore is reduced
- how to explain oxidation and reduction in terms of the addition and removal of oxygen
- the main types and uses of steels.

Iron ore (the rock from which iron is extracted) contains iron combined with oxygen in iron(III) oxide along with rocky impurities. Iron is less reactive than carbon. So, iron can be extracted by using carbon to remove oxygen from the iron(III) oxide in the ore. Iron is extracted in a **blast furnace**. The raw materials fed into the furnace, which is run continuously, are:

- iron ore (called haematite)
- coke (a cheap form of carbon made from coal)
- air
- limestone (used to remove impurities by reacting with them to form slag).

The reaction which happens in the blast furnace to remove the oxygen is:

carbon + oxygen → carbon dioxide

$$C(s) + O_2(g) \rightarrow CO_2(g)$$

In this reaction, the carbon has been oxidised. It has had oxygen added to it to form carbon dioxide. One way that chemists define **oxidation** is 'the addition of oxygen'.

Another reaction inside a blast furnace is:

carbon dioxide + carbon → carbon monoxide

$$CO_2(g) + C(s) \rightarrow 2CO(g)$$

In this reaction, carbon dioxide is **reduced**, as it loses an oxygen atom to form carbon monoxide. One way that chemists define **reduction** is 'the removal of oxygen'. (Note also that carbon is oxidised in this reaction; forming carbon monoxide). The carbon monoxide then reduces the iron(III) oxide:

iron(III) oxide + carbon monoxide → iron + carbon dioxide

$$Fe_2O_3(s) + 3CO(g) \rightarrow 2Fe(l) + 3CO_2(g)$$

The molten iron is tapped off from the bottom of the furnace.

Iron straight from the blast furnace has limited uses. It contains about 96% iron and contains impurities, mainly carbon. This makes the iron brittle, although it is very hard and cannot be easily compressed. When molten it can be run into moulds and cast into different shapes. This **cast iron** is used to make wood-burning stoves, man-hole covers on roads, and engines. Despite being brittle, cast iron can withstand high forces of compression without breaking. This is why it is used in man-hole covers.

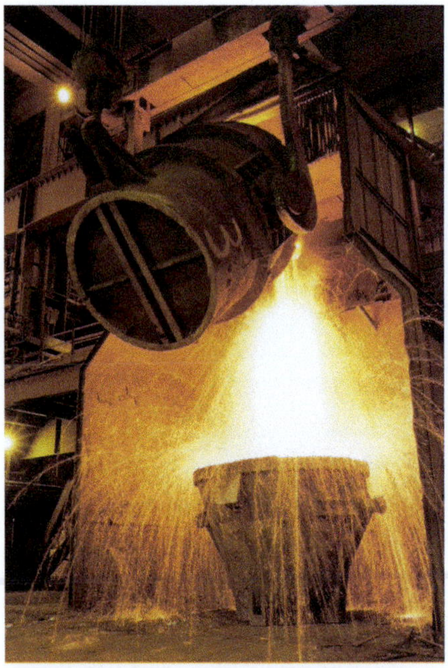

Figure 1 *The iron which has just come out of a blast furnace contains about 96% iron. The main impurity is carbon.*

The iron from the blast furnace can be treated to remove some of the carbon.

Removing all the carbon and other impurities from cast iron gives us pure iron. This is relatively soft and easily-shaped. However, it is too soft for most uses. If you want to make iron really useful you have to make sure that it contains tiny amounts of other elements. These include carbon and metals, such as nickel and chromium. A metal that is mixed with other elements is called an alloy.

Steels

Steels are alloys of iron. By adding elements in carefully controlled amounts, scientists can change the properties of the steels.

Steel is not a single substance. Like all alloys, it is a mixture. There are lots of different types of steel. All of them are alloys of iron with carbon and/or other elements.

Study tip

You need to know how the hardness of steels is related to their carbon content.

Carbon steels

The simplest steels are the **carbon steels**. These are made by removing most of the carbon from cast iron, just leaving small amounts of carbon (from 0.03% to 1.5%). These are the cheapest steels to make. They are used in many products, such as the bodies of cars, knives, machinery, ships, containers, and structural steel for buildings.

Often these carbon steels have small amounts of other elements in them as well. High carbon steel, with a relatively high carbon content, is very strong but brittle. On the other hand, low carbon steel is soft and easily shaped. It is not as strong, but is much less likely to shatter on impact with a hard object.

Mild steel is one type of low carbon steel. It contains less than 0.1% carbon. It is very easily pressed into shapes. This makes it particularly useful in mass production, such as making car bodies.

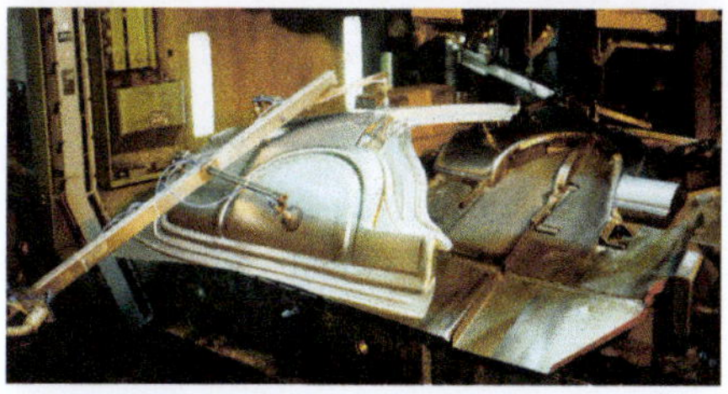

Figure 2 *Low carbon steel called mild steel is easily pressed into shapes*

Alloy steels

Low-alloy steels are more expensive than carbon steels because they contain between 1% and 5% of other metals. Each of these metals produces a steel that is well-suited for a particular use.

Even more expensive are the **high-alloy steels**. These contain a much higher percentage of other metals. The chromium–nickel steels are known as **stainless steels**. They are used to make cooking utensils and cutlery. They are also used to make chemical reaction vessels. This is because they combine hardness and strength with great resistance to corrosion. Unlike most other steels, they do not rust!

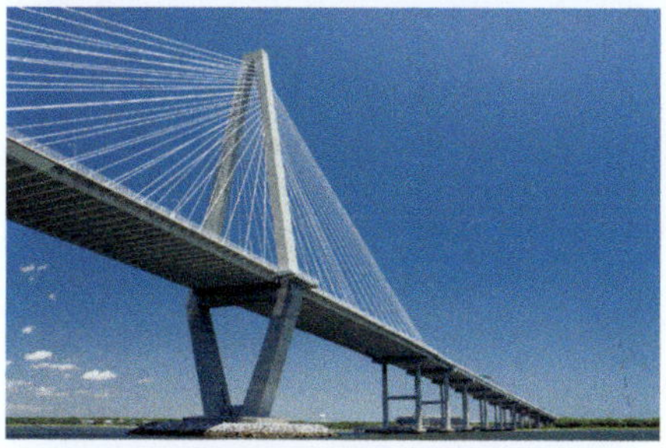

Figure 3 *The properties of alloy steels make them ideal for use in bridges*

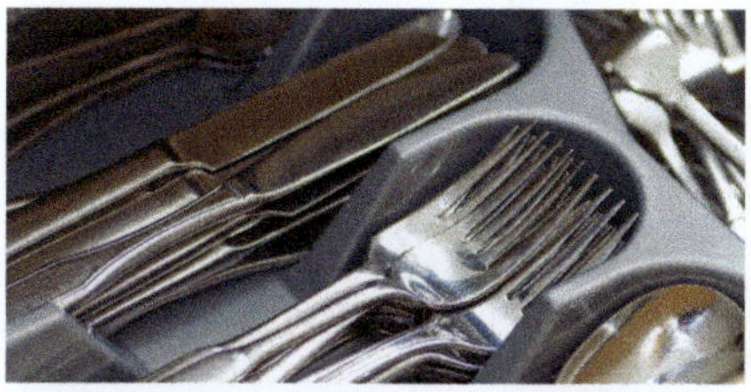

Figure 4 *The resistance of stainless steels to rusting make them ideal for making utensils and cutlery*

Did you know ... ?

Nickel–steel alloys are used to build long-span bridges, bicycle chains and military armour-plating. This is because they are very resistant to stretching forces. Tungsten steel operates well under very hot conditions so it is used to make high-speed tools such as drill bits.

Summary questions

1. **a** Why is iron from a blast furnace very brittle?
   b How does cast iron differ from pure iron in its composition and properties?
   c Give one use of cast iron which relies on its high strength in compression.
2. **a** Name the raw materials used in a blast furnace for the extraction of iron.
   b Name the main reducing agent in the blast furnace and write a balanced symbol equation for its formation. Include state symbols.
   c A small amount of iron(III) oxide is reduced by solid carbon in the blast furnace. Write a word equation and a balanced symbol equation with state symbols for this reaction.
   d Explain why carbon monoxide, as opposed to solid carbon, reduces most of the iron(III) oxide in the blast furnace.
3. Make a table to summarise the main useful properties of low carbon steel, high carbon steel, and chromium–nickel steel.
4. **a** Why are surgical instruments made from steel containing chromium and nickel?
   b Explain which type of steel is used to make:
   i car bodies **ii** railway tracks.

Key points

- Iron is extracted from iron ore by reducing it using carbon in a blast furnace. The main reducing agent is carbon monoxide gas.
- Pure iron is too soft for it to be very useful.
- Carefully controlled quantities of carbon and other elements are added to iron to make steel alloys with different properties.
- Important examples of steels are:
  - low carbon steels which are easily shaped
  - high carbon steels which are very hard
  - stainless steels which are resistant to corrosion.

4.3 The reactivity series

Learning objectives

After this topic, you should know:

- what the reactivity series is
- how some common metals react with water and with dilute acid.

Metals are important in all our lives. For example, in transport metals are used to make bicycles, cars, ships, trains, and aeroplanes. In this chapter you will look at the chemistry involved in getting these metals from their raw materials, **ores**. Ores are rocks from which it is economical to extract the metals that they contain. With new techniques, scientists can now extract metals from rock once thought of as waste.

Most metals in ores are chemically bonded to other elements in compounds. So, how can the metals be extracted from their ores? To answer this you must understand the **reactivity series** of metals. The reactivity series is a list of metals in order of their reactivity, with the most reactive metals at the top and the least reactive ones at the bottom (see Table 1 on the next page).

Metals plus water

You can start putting the metals in order of reactivity by looking at their reactions with water. Most metals do not react vigorously with water. Metals such as copper, which does not react at all with water, can be used to make water pipes. However, there is a great range in reactivity between different metals. For example, you have seen how the alkali metals in Group 1 react with water in Topic 3.2 *Group 1 – the alkali metals*. They react vigorously, giving off hydrogen gas and leaving alkaline solutions. The reactivity increases going down Group 1, so of the metals you observed, the order of reactivity is **1** potassium (most reactive), **2** sodium, and **3** lithium (least reactive).

Magnesium lies somewhere between lithium and copper in the reactivity series. If magnesium is left in a beaker of water, it takes several days to collect enough gas to test with a lighted spill. The resulting 'pop' shows that the gas is hydrogen.

Although magnesium reacts very slowly with water, you can speed up the reaction by heating and reacting the metal with steam.

Practical

Predicting reactions

Calcium is a metal that is more reactive than magnesium, but less reactive than lithium.

- Predict what you will see when a piece of calcium is added to a beaker of water and name any products that might be formed.

Try out the reaction in a large beaker (or trough) of water. Have an inverted test tube full of water ready to collect any gas given off and test the solution left with universal indicator paper. Test if the gas collected is hydrogen, using a lighted spill.

- Evaluate your prediction by comparing your observations with your ideas before trying out the experiment.
- Write a word and balanced symbol equation for the reaction between calcium and water.

Safety: Do not touch calcium metal or the solution formed in the reaction. Wear eye protection. Calcium is highly flammable.

Demonstration

Magnesium and steam

Watch your teacher demonstrate the reaction below:

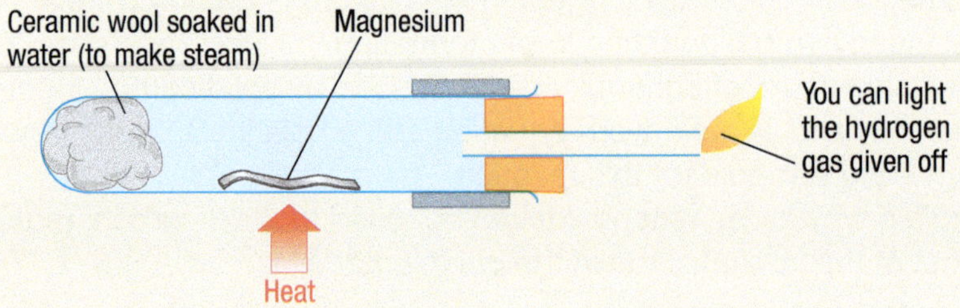

- Describe what happens as the magnesium reacts with the steam.
- Which gas burns off at the end of the tube?
- The white solid left in the test tube is magnesium oxide (MgO). Write a word equation and a balanced symbol equation, including state symbols, for the reaction of magnesium and steam.

Metals plus dilute acid

You have now seen how a range of metals react with water, and that you can use your observations of these reactions to place the metals into an order of reactivity. However, where the reactions are very slow, the task of ordering the metals is difficult. With these metals, look at their reactions with dilute acid to arrive at an order of reactivity.

Here is a table that summarises the reactions of some important metals with water and dilute acid:

Table 1 *The reactivity series*
Note: Aluminium is protected by a layer of aluminium oxide so will not undergo the reactions above unless the oxide layer is removed. This is why this fairly reactive metal can be used outside, for example in sliding patio doors, without corroding.

<table>
<tr><th>Order of reactivity</th><th>Reaction with water</th><th>Reaction with dilute acid</th></tr>
<tr><td>potassium</td><td rowspan="4">fizz, giving off hydrogen, leaving an alkaline solution of metal hydroxide</td><td rowspan="3">explode</td></tr>
<tr><td>sodium</td></tr>
<tr><td>lithium</td></tr>
<tr><td>calcium</td><td rowspan="5">fizz, giving off hydrogen and forming a salt</td></tr>
<tr><td>magnesium</td><td rowspan="4">react with steam, giving off hydrogen and forming the metal oxide</td></tr>
<tr><td>aluminium</td></tr>
<tr><td>zinc</td></tr>
<tr><td>iron</td></tr>
<tr><td>tin</td><td rowspan="2">slight reaction with steam</td><td rowspan="2">react slowly with warm acid</td></tr>
<tr><td>lead</td></tr>
<tr><td>copper</td><td rowspan="3">no reaction, even with steam</td><td rowspan="3">no reaction</td></tr>
<tr><td>silver</td></tr>
<tr><td>gold</td></tr>
</table>

Summary questions

1 Write the word equation and balanced symbol equation, including state symbols, for the reaction between:
  a lithium and water
  b zinc and steam.

2 A student added a piece of magnesium ribbon to dilute sulfuric acid.
  a List three ways she could tell that a chemical reaction was taking place.
  b Write down the general equation that describes the reaction between a metal and an acid. (See Topic 7.2.)
  c Write the word equation and balanced symbol equation, including state symbols, for the reaction between magnesium and dilute sulfuric acid.

3 Explain these facts in terms of chemical reactivity:
  a Gold, silver, and platinum are used to make jewellery.
  b Potassium, lithium, and sodium are stored in jars of oil.
  c Food cans are plated with tin, but not zinc.

4 Explain why aluminium can be used outdoors, for example, as window frames, even though it is quite high in the reactivity series.

Practical

Metals and acid

You are given coarse-grained filings of the metals copper, aluminium, zinc, iron, and magnesium to put into an order of reactivity according to their reactions with dilute hydrochloric acid.

Plan a test to put the metals in order of reactivity based on your observations. Your plan should include the quantities of reactants you intend to use. (You will have access to a balance and measuring cylinders.)

Let your teacher check your plan before you start your tests.

- Give a brief outline of your method, including how you will make it as fair a test as possible.
- Record your results in a suitable table.
- Put the metals in order of reactivity according to your observations.
- Identify any hazards.

links

For more about the reaction of metals with dilute acid, see 7.2 Making soluble salts from metals or insoluble bases.

Key points

- **The metals can be placed in order of reactivity by their reactions with water and dilute acid.**
- **Hydrogen gas is given off if metals react with water or dilute acids. The gas 'pops' with a lighted spill.**

4.4 Displacement reactions

Learning objectives

After this topic, you should know:

- how displacement reactions take place
- the position of hydrogen in the reactivity series
- the definitions of reduction and oxidation in terms of electron transfer.

In Topic 4.3 *The reactivity series*, you have seen how to use the reactions of metals with water and dilute acid to get an order of reactivity. You can also judge reactivity by putting the metals 'into competition' with each other. One metal starts off as the element and the other metal as an ion in a solution of one of its salts. For example, you might have magnesium metal, Mg(s), and copper(II) ions, Cu^{2+}(aq), in a solution of copper(II) sulfate.

A more reactive metal will displace a less reactive metal from an aqueous solution of one of its salts.

In this case, magnesium is more reactive than copper. Therefore the copper ions will be displaced from solution to form copper metal, Cu(s). In this reaction, the magnesium metal forms aqueous magnesium ions, Mg^{2+}(aq), and dissolves into the solution (see Figure 1). This is a **displacement reaction**.

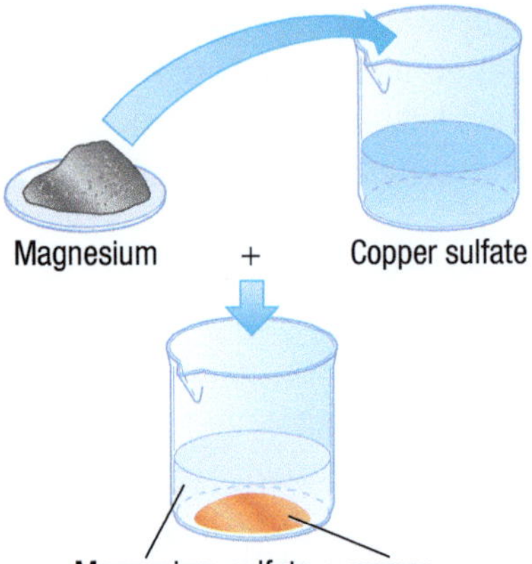

Figure 1 *Magnesium displaces copper from copper(II) sulfate solution*

The word equation is:

magnesium + copper(II) sulfate → magnesium sulfate + copper

The balanced symbol equation is:

$$Mg(s) + CuSO_4(aq) \rightarrow MgSO_4(aq) + Cu(s)$$

The **ionic equation** (showing only the atoms and ions that change in the reaction):

$$Mg(s) + Cu^{2+}(aq) \rightarrow Mg^{2+}(aq) + Cu(s)$$

This shows that magnesium atoms have a greater tendency to form positive ions than copper atoms.

Zinc is more reactive than lead – it is higher up the reactivity series. Therefore, zinc displaces lead from its solution:

zinc + lead nitrate → zinc nitrate + lead

$$Zn(s) + Pb(NO_3)_2(aq) \rightarrow Zn(NO_3)_2(aq) + Pb(s)$$

You will see the lead metal forming as crystals on the zinc.

Practical

Displacing a metal from solution

Set up the test tube as shown:

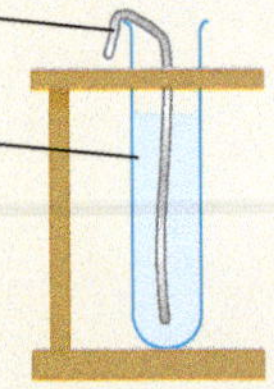

Leave the tube until you see metal crystals on the surface of the zinc sheet.

- What do the crystals look like?
- Explain what happens.

Safety: Lead compounds are toxic. Wear chemical splash-proof eye protection.

Practical

Predicting reactions

Copy and fill in the table below.

Solution \ Metal	Magnesium	Copper	Zinc	Iron
Magnesium sulfate	✗			
Copper sulfate		✗		
Zinc sulfate			✗	
Iron sulfate				✗

Predict which will react (enter a tick in your table), and which won't (enter a cross).

Try out the reactions on a spotting tile.

Safety: Wear eye protection. Some chemicals are harmful.

Hydrogen in the reactivity series

The positions of the non-metals hydrogen and carbon in the reactivity series can be determined using displacement reactions. You can think of the metal plus acid reactions as displacement of hydrogen ions, $H^{+}(aq)$, from solution. Copper cannot displace the hydrogen from an acid, whereas lead can. So hydrogen is positioned between copper and lead.

Oxidation and reduction

Oxidation can be defined as the chemical addition of oxygen, and **reduction** as the removal of oxygen. A wider definition involves the transfer of electrons rather than oxygen atoms.

Oxidation is the loss of electrons. **Reduction is the gain of electrons.**

You can apply these definitions to displacement reactions in solution. Take as an example, the displacement of copper by iron. This reaction is used in industry to extract copper metal from copper sulfate:

$$Fe(s) + Cu^{2+}(aq) \rightarrow Fe^{2+}(aq) + Cu(s)$$

The iron added to the copper sulfate solution is cheap scrap iron. Consider what happens to each reactant in the ionic equation above:

$$Fe(s) \rightarrow Fe^{2+}(aq) + 2e^{-}$$

This is called a **half equation** - you can see more examples on page 68. Iron atoms lose two electrons to form iron(II) ions. This is oxidation (the loss of electrons). We say that iron atoms have been **oxidised**.

These two electrons from iron are gained by the copper(II) ions as they form copper atoms:

$$Cu^{2+}(aq) + 2e^{-} \rightarrow Cu(s)$$

This is reduction (the gain of electrons). The copper(II) ions have been reduced.

This is why these displacement reactions are also known as redox reactions (**red**uction–**ox**idation).

Using displacement in industry

In industry, copper can be extracted from copper sulfate solution by adding scrap iron. Iron is more reactive than copper, so it can displace copper from its solutions, for example, from copper(II) sulfate solution:

iron + copper(II) sulfate →
iron(II) sulfate + copper

Did you know ... ?

The copper(II) sulfate solution used in the extraction of copper from its ores can be obtained by treating low-grade copper ores with bacteria, in a process called bioleaching.

Summary questions

1 Which of the following pairs of metals and solutions will result in a reaction? If a reaction is predicted, write a balanced symbol equation, including state symbols.
 a iron + zinc sulfate b zinc + copper sulfate
 c magnesium + iron(II) chloride

2 Hydrogen gas is used in the reduction of tungsten oxide, WO_3, to extract tungsten metal.
 a What does this tell you about the position of tungsten in the reactivity series?
 b Write a balanced symbol equation for the reduction of tungsten oxide by hydrogen.

3 a Write the ionic equation, including state symbols, for the reaction between zinc and iron(II) sulfate.
 b Explain in terms of the transfer of electrons which species (atom, molecule, or ion) is oxidised and which is reduced in this reaction.

Key points

- A more reactive metal will displace a less reactive metal from its aqueous solution.
- Hydrogen can be given a position in the reactivity series on the basis of displacement reactions.
- Oxidation is the loss of electrons.
- Reduction is the gain of electrons.

4.5 Extracting metals

Learning objectives

After this topic, you should know:

- where metals come from
- how metals can be extracted from their ores.

Metals have been important to people for thousands of years. You can follow the course of history by the materials people used. Starting from the Stone Age, we go to the Bronze Age (copper/tin) and then on to the Iron Age.

Where do we get metals from?

Metals are found in the Earth's crust. We find most metals combined chemically with other chemical elements, often with oxygen or sulfur. This means that the metal must be chemically separated from its compounds before it can be used.

When there is enough of a metal or metal compound in a rock to make it worth extracting the metal, we call the rock a **metal ore**. Ores are mined from the ground. Some need to be concentrated before the metal is extracted and purified. For example, copper ores are ground up into a powder. Then they are mixed with water and a chemical that makes the copper compound repel water. Air is then bubbled through the mixture and the copper compound floats on top as a froth. The rocky bits sink and the concentrated copper compound is scraped off the top. It is then ready to have its copper extracted.

Whether it is worth extracting a particular metal depends on:

- how easy it is to extract it from its ore
- how much metal the ore contains.

These two factors can change over time. For example, a new, cheaper method might be discovered for extracting a metal. We might also discover a new way to extract a metal efficiently from rock which contains only small amounts of a metal ore. An ore that was once thought of as 'low grade' could then become an economic source of a metal.

A few metals, such as gold and silver, are so unreactive that they are found in the Earth as the metals (elements) themselves. We say that they exist in their native state.

Sometimes a nugget of gold is so large it can simply be picked up. At other times tiny flakes have to be physically separated from sand and rocks by panning.

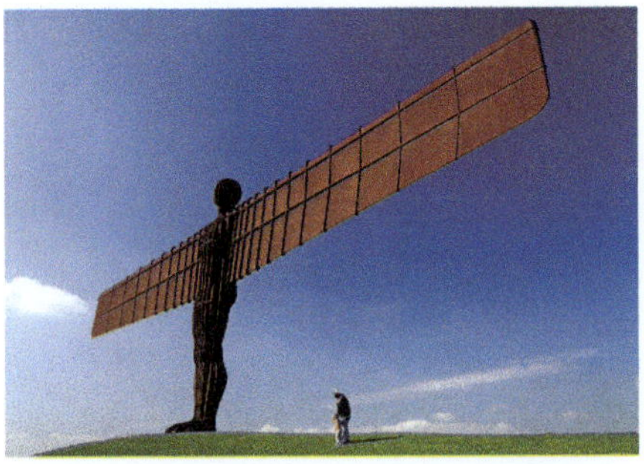

Figure 1 *The Angel of the North stands 20 metres tall. It is made of steel which contains a small amount of copper.*

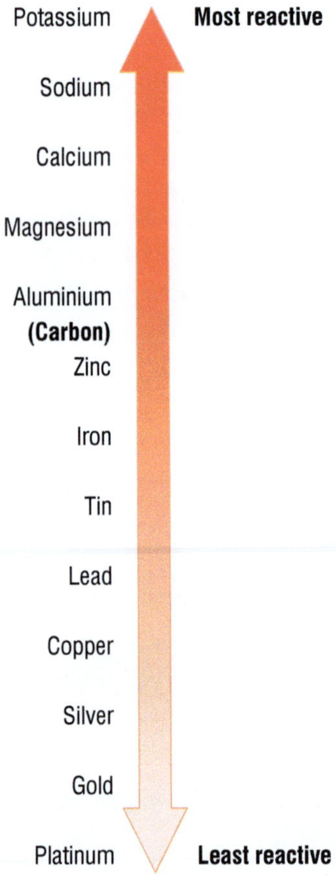

Figure 2 *This reactivity series shows the position of the non-metal carbon in the series*

Did you know ... ?

Gold in Wales is found in seams, just like coal – although not as thick, unfortunately! Gold jewellery was worn by early Welsh princes as a badge of rank. Welsh gold has been used in modern times to make the wedding rings of royal brides.

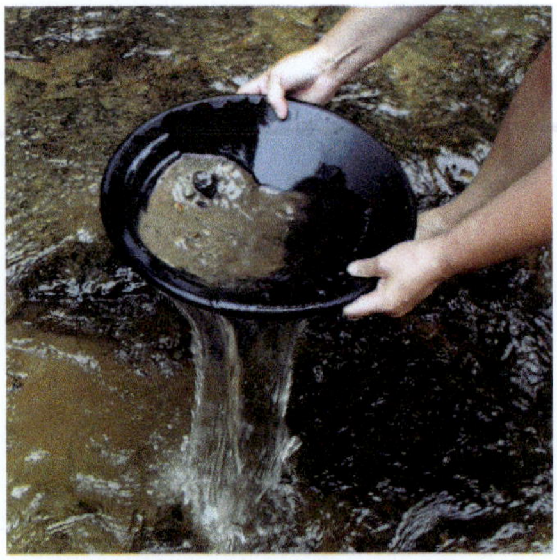

Figure 3 *Panning for gold. Mud and stones are washed away while the dense gold remains in the pan.*

How do we extract metals?

The way that we extract a metal depends on its place in the reactivity series. The reactivity series lists the metals in order of their reactivity (see Figure 2 which includes the non-metal carbon). As we have seen in 4.4, a more reactive metal will displace a less reactive metal from its compounds. Carbon (a non-metal) will also displace less reactive metals from their oxides. We use carbon to extract some metals from their ores in industry.

We can find many metals, such as copper, lead, iron and zinc, combined with oxygen as metal oxides. Because carbon is more reactive than each of these metals, we can use carbon to extract the metals from their oxides.

We must heat the metal oxide with carbon. The carbon removes the oxygen from the metal oxide to form carbon dioxide. The metal is also formed, as the element:

metal oxide + carbon → metal + carbon dioxide

For example:

$$\text{lead oxide} + \text{carbon} \xrightarrow{\text{heat}} \text{lead} + \text{carbon dioxide}$$

$$2PbO(s) + C(s) \rightarrow 2Pb(l) + CO_2(g)$$

The removal of oxygen from a compound is called chemical reduction. You can see how iron(III) oxide is reduced to extract iron on page 50.

The metals that are more reactive than carbon are not extracted from their ores by reduction with carbon. Instead they are extracted by **electrolysis** of the molten metal compound (see Chapter 5).

Summary questions

1 Define the term 'metal ore'.

2 Why is gold found as the metal rather than combined with other elements in compounds?

3 Platinum is found native. What does this tell you about its reactivity? Give a use of platinum that depends on this chemical property.

4 Zinc oxide (ZnO) can be reduced to zinc by heating it in a furnace with carbon. Carbon monoxide (CO) gas is given off in the reaction. The zinc formed is molten at the temperature in the furnace.
   - **a** Write a word equation for the reduction of zinc oxide by carbon in the furnace.
   - **b** Now write a balanced symbol equation, including state symbols, for the reaction in part a.

5 Lead is often found in the ore called galena which contains lead sulfide (PbS). Before reduction with carbon, the lead sulfide must be converted into lead oxide (PbO) by roasting the ore. This reaction with oxygen from the air also produces sulfur dioxide gas.
   - **a** Write a word equation for the roasting of lead sulfide.
   - **b** Now write a balanced symbol equation, including state symbols, for the reaction in part a.
   - **c** Lead oxide is reduced by heating with carbon. Write a balanced symbol equation for this reaction, assuming carbon dioxide is one of the products.

Practical

Reduction by carbon

Heat some copper oxide (harmful) with carbon powder in a test tube, gently at first, then more strongly.

Empty the contents into an evaporating dish.

You can repeat the experiment with lead oxide (toxic) and carbon if you have a fume cupboard to work in. Wear chemical splash proof eye protection. Wash hands after experiments.

- Explain your observations. Include a word equation and a balanced symbol equation with state symbols.

links

To find out more about the use of electrolysis to extract reactive metals, see 5.3 The extraction of aluminium.

Key points

- **A metal ore contains enough of the metal to make it economic to extract the metal. Ores are mined and might need to be concentrated before the metal is extracted and purified.**
- **We can find gold and other unreactive metals in their native state.**
- **The reactivity series helps us decide the best way to extract a metal from its ore. The oxides of metals below carbon in the series can be reduced by carbon to give the metal element.**
- **Metals more reactive than carbon *cannot* be extracted from their ores using carbon. They are extracted by electrolysing the molten metal compound.**

4.6 Extracting copper

Learning objectives

After this topic, you should know:

- how copper is obtained from copper-rich ores
- the methods used to obtain copper from low-grade ores
- how copper is purified.

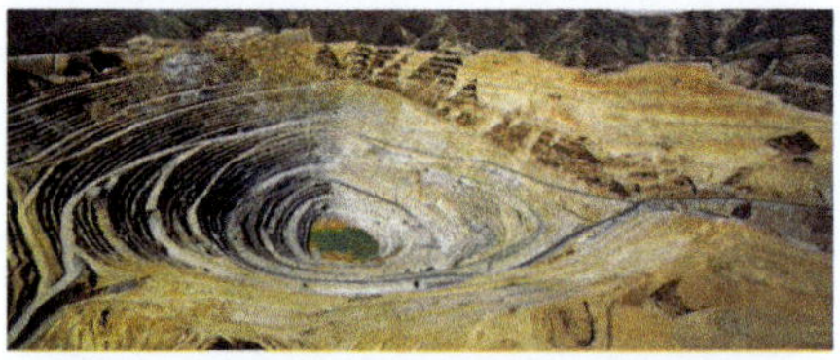

Figure 1 *Mining copper ores can leave huge scars on the landscape. This is called open-cast mining. About 90% of copper comes from open-cast mines. Our supplies of copper-rich ores are a limited resource.*

Extracting copper from copper-rich ores

We extract most of our copper from **copper-rich ores**. These are a limited resource and are in danger of running out.

There are two main methods used to obtain the copper metal from the ore.

- In one method we use sulfuric acid to produce copper sulfate solution, before extracting the copper metal.
- The other process is called **smelting** (roasting). We heat copper ore very strongly in a furnace with air to produce crude copper metal.

For example, copper can be found in an ore called chalcocite. This contains copper(I) sulfide, Cu_2S. If we roast the copper(I) sulfide in air, it decomposes to give copper metal:

copper(I) sulfide + oxygen → copper + sulfur dioxide

$$Cu_2S(s) + O_2(g) \rightarrow 2Cu(s) + SO_2(g)$$

Care has to be taken to avoid letting sulfur dioxide gas into the atmosphere. This gas causes acid rain. So chimneys are fitted with basic 'scrubbers' to neutralise the acidic gas or it is used to make sulfuric acid.

Then we use the impure copper as the positive electrode in electrolysis cells to make pure copper. About 80% of copper is still produced by smelting. Smelting and purifying copper ore uses huge amounts of heat and electricity. This costs a lot of money and will cause pollution in the environment.

Practical

Extracting copper from malachite

Malachite is a copper ore containing copper carbonate (harmful). To extract the copper we first heat the copper carbonate in a boiling tube. **Thermal decomposition** takes place. Copper oxide is left in the tube.

- Which gas is given off?

We then add dilute sulfuric acid to the copper oxide (harmful). Stopper and shake the tube. This makes copper sulfate solution (harmful). Filter off any excess black copper oxide in the solution.

To extract the copper metal, either:

1 Put an iron nail into the copper sulfate solution (harmful). What happens to the iron nail?

or;

2 Collect some extra copper sulfate solution (harmful) and place it in a small beaker. Set up the circuit as shown in Figure 2. Turn the power on until you see copper metal collecting. Which electrode – the positive or the negative – does the copper metal form on?

Safety: Wear eye protection. Chemicals used in this practical are harmful.

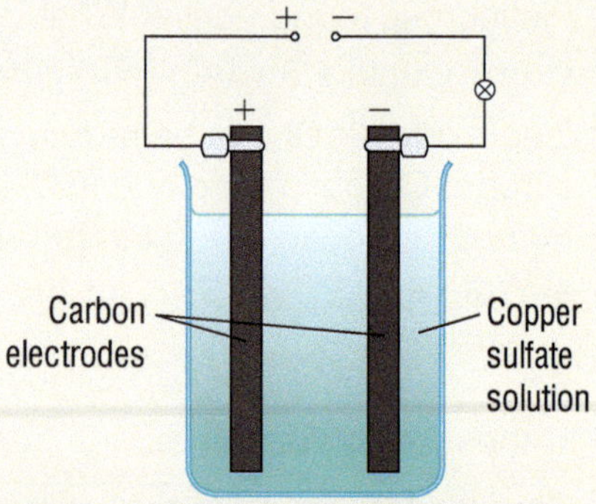

Figure 2 *Extracting copper metal using electrolysis. In industry, copper electrodes are used to obtain very pure copper metal at the negative electrode.*

Metal ions are always positively charged. Therefore, in electrolysis they are attracted to the negative electrode. So, metals are always deposited at the negative electrode. In industry the electrolysis is carried out in many cells running at once. This method gives the very pure copper needed to make electrical wiring. Electrolysis is also used to purify the impure copper extracted by smelting. In the industrial process, the electrolysis cells use copper electrodes.

Look at Figure 3. We can show what happens with the ionic half equations shown below. At the negative copper electrode (cathode) we get reduction:

$$Cu^{2+}(aq) + 2e^- \rightarrow Cu(s)$$

At the positive copper electrode (anode) we get oxidation:

$$Cu(s) \rightarrow Cu^{2+}(aq) + 2e^-$$

The copper can also be extracted from copper sulfate solution in industry by adding scrap iron. Iron is more reactive than copper, so it can displace copper from its solutions:

iron + copper(II) sulfate → iron(II) sulfate + copper

Extracting copper from low-grade copper ores

Instead of extracting copper from our limited copper-rich ores, scientists are developing new ways to get copper from low-grade ores. This would be uneconomical using traditional methods. We can now use bacteria (**bioleaching**) and even plants (**phytomining**) to help extract copper.

In phytomining, plants can absorb copper ions from low-grade copper ore as they grow. This could be on slag heaps of previously discarded waste from the processing of copper-rich ores. Then the plants are burned and the metals can be extracted from the ash. The copper ions can be 'leached' (dissolved) from the ash by adding sulfuric acid. This makes a solution (leachate) of copper sulfate. Then we can use displacement by scrap iron and electrolysis to extract pure copper metal.

In bioleaching, bacteria feed on low-grade metal ores. By a combination of biological and chemical processes, we can get a solution of copper ions (leachate) from waste copper ore. Once again, we use scrap iron and electrolysis to extract the copper from the leachate.

About 20% of our copper comes from bioleaching. This is likely to increase as sources of copper-rich ores run out. Bioleaching is a slow process so scientists are researching ways to speed it up. At present it can take years to extract 50% of the metal from a low-grade ore.

Summary questions

1 Why is copper an important metal in our technological society?

2 **a** Explain briefly two traditional ways of extracting copper metal.
b State an advantage of extracting copper using bacteria rather than traditional methods.
c Why can copper occasionally be found native?
d When copper is purified by electrolysis, which electrode do you think the pure copper collects at? Explain your answer.

3 Write a balanced chemical equation, including state symbols, for the extraction of copper:
a from copper(II) sulfide by smelting
b from copper sulfate solution by displacement.

4 **a** Write ionic half equations for the reactions at each copper electrode in the electrolysis of copper sulfate solution.
b Explain where reduction and oxidation takes place in the electrolysis cell in part **a**.

5 Explain how copper is extracted by phytomining and why this method will become increasingly important.

links
For information on the half equations at electrodes in electrolysis, see 5.2 Changes at the electrodes.

links
For information on the displacement (redox) reaction between copper ions in solution and iron metal, look back to 4.4 Displacement reactions.

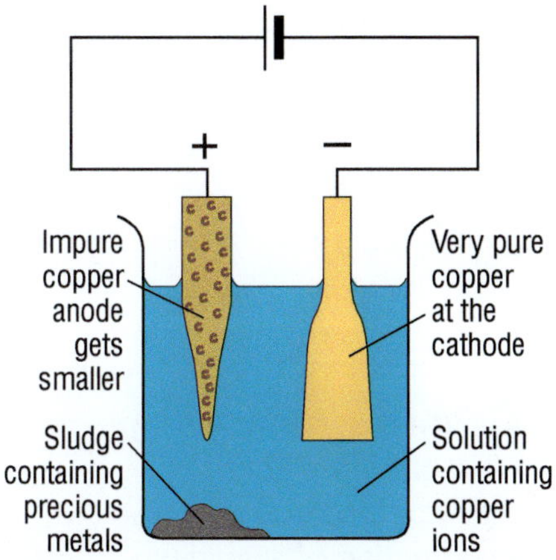

Figure 3 *Many of these cells operate at the same time in industry. The cathodes are removed about every two weeks.*

Key points

- **Most copper is extracted by smelting (roasting) copper-rich ores, although our limited supplies of ores are becoming more scarce.**
- **Copper can be extracted from copper solutions by electrolysis or by displacement using scrap iron. Electrolysis is also used to purify impure copper, e.g. the copper metal obtained from smelting.**
- **Scientists are developing ways to extract copper that use low-grade copper ores. Bacteria are used in bioleaching and plants in phytomining.**

4.7 Recycling metals

Learning objectives

After this topic, you should know:

- why we should recycle metals in terms of the Earth's natural resources, the use of energy and the effects on the environment.

Recycling aluminium

In the UK each person uses on average around 8 kg of aluminium every year. This is why it is important to **recycle** aluminium to help conserve the Earth's reserves of aluminium ore. Aluminium is extracted from molten aluminium oxide at high temperatures using electrolysis. The process requires huge amounts of electrical energy. Recycling saves energy, and therefore money, since recycling aluminium does not involve electrolysis. Comparing recycled aluminium with aluminium extracted from its ore, there is a 95% energy saving.

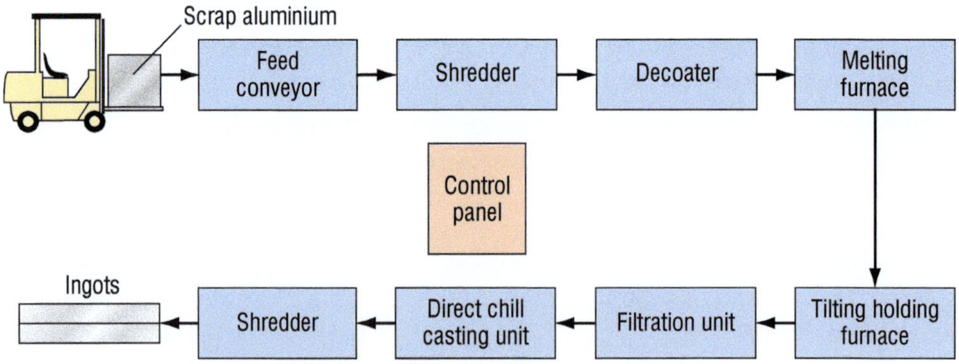

Figure 1 *The recycling of aluminium involves melting the scrap metal but still uses a lot less energy than extracting aluminium from its ore, bauxite*

links

To find out more about the production of aluminium, see 5.3 The extraction of aluminium.

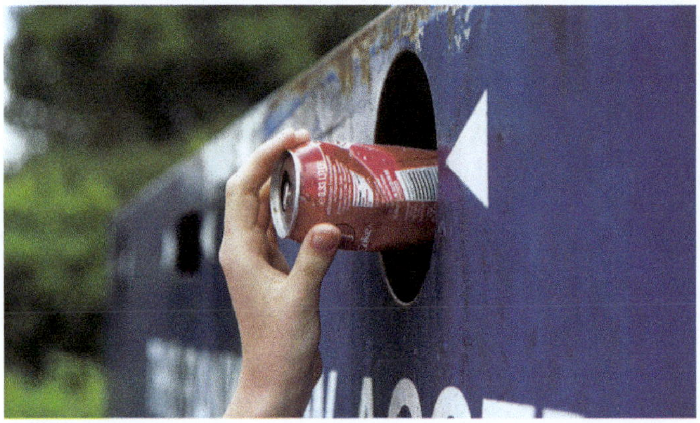

Figure 2 *Recycling cans saves energy, as well as our limited supplies of metal ores. It also reduces pollution.*

Did you know ... ?

It has been estimated that aluminium production uses 5% of the electricity generated in the United States.

Recycling iron and steel

We also recycle iron and steel, for example from the bodywork and engines of scrap cars. 'Tin cans' are another source of scrap iron. These are usually steel cans with a very thin coating of tin to prevent rusting. The cans are easy to separate from other domestic rubbish as they are magnetic.

Using recycled steel saves about 50% of the energy used to extract iron and turn it into steel. Much of the energy in the production of steel from iron ore is supplied by burning fossil fuels, such as natural gas used to heat the air entering a blast furnace. Therefore recycling helps save our dwindling supplies of the **non-renewable** fuels. There are also pollution problems that arise whenever we burn fossil fuels so using less energy helps reduce these effects. The pollutants produced by fossil fuels include sulfur dioxide, carbon dioxide, carbon monoxide, unburnt hydrocarbons and particulates.

links

For more information on the extraction of iron and production of steel, see 4.2 Iron and steels, and about the pollution caused by fossil fuels, see 10.3 Burning fuels.

Recycling copper

Copper is also recycled but this is difficult as it is often alloyed with other metals, e.g. in brass where copper is mixed with zinc. Therefore, the impure copper from recycling would need to be purified for use in electrical wiring unless it was reclaimed solely from old electricity wires. High quality copper from wires can be recycled by melting and/or re-using it.

However, with a lot of old copper, which is mixed with other metals in alloys, it has to be analysed to find the percentages of each metal present. Then there is the option of just melting the mixture of metals and re-using as the alloy.

With just a few impurities, a copper alloy can be made the anode and purified by electrolysis but if the percentage of copper is low, this method of purification does not work. The percentages of metals might be able to be adjusted to get another useful alloy. Alternatively, more copper can be added to the impure copper by melting them together. This raises the percentage of copper in the alloy so then you can purify it electrically. However, this makes the copper more expensive to recycle.

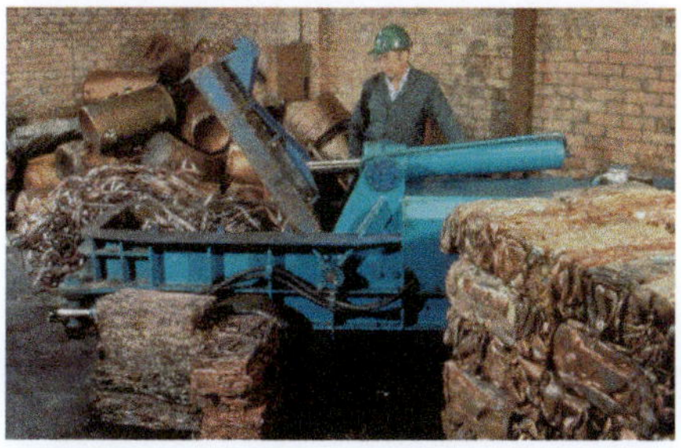

Figure 3 *The recycling of copper is made more difficult by the presence of other metals in copper alloys*

Environmental considerations

Recycling metals reduces the need to mine the metal ore and conserves the Earth's limited reserves of metal ores. It also prevents any pollution problems that arise from extracting the metal from its ore. For example, whenever we mine metal ores from the Earth's crust there are consequences for our environment. You have seen that open-cast mining is often used to get copper ore from the ground. The ores of iron and aluminium are also mainly mined like this. Huge pits that scar the landscape are made, creating noise and dust and destroying the habitats of plants and animals. The mines also leave large heaps of waste rock. The water in an area subjected to the mining of metal ores can also be affected. As rain drains through exposed ores and slag heaps of waste, the groundwater can become acidic.

Having mined the ores, then they must be processed to extract the metals. For example, sulfide ores are heated strongly in smelting. Any sulfur dioxide gas that escapes into the air will cause acid rain. In the extraction of iron, carbon dioxide is given off which can contribute to the enhanced greenhouse effect and global warming issues. Reducing these factors are why recycling metals is so important.

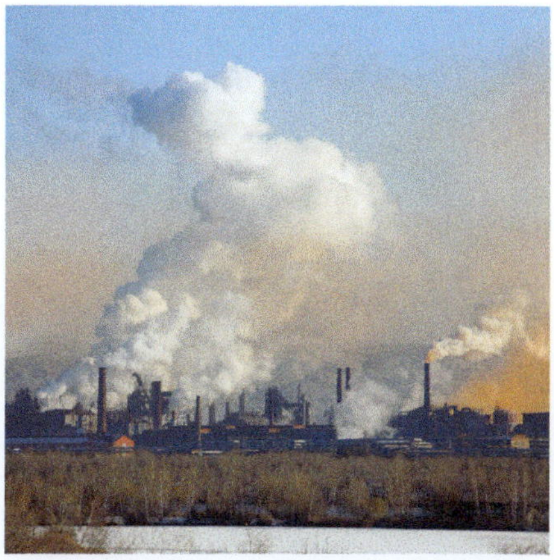

Figure 4 *Recycling helps to reduce the pollution problems arising from extracting metals*

Summary questions

1. What can a mining company do to help the environment when an open-cast mine is no longer economic?
2. Each person in the UK uses about 8 kg of aluminium each year. Recycling 1 kg of aluminium saves about enough energy to run a small electric fire for 14 hours. If you recycle 50% of the aluminium you use in one year, how long could you run a small electric fire on the energy you have saved?
3. Explain why the energy savings are so great when recycling aluminium compared with extracting aluminium from its ore.
4. Explain why it is difficult to recycle some metals, such as copper, and how this can be overcome.
5. Explain how a range of pollution problems are reduced by recycling metals.

Key points

- There are social, economic and environmental issues associated with exploiting metal ores.
- Recycling metals saves energy and our limited, non-renewable metal ores (and fossil fuels). The pollution caused by the mining and extraction of metals is also reduced by recycling.

4.8 Metal carbonates

Learning objectives

After this topic, you should know:

- what happens when dilute acid is added to a metal carbonate
- how the test for carbon dioxide gas works
- what happens in the thermal decomposition of metal carbonates
- some uses of limestone.

Buildings and statues made of limestone suffer badly from damage by acid rain. You might have noticed statues where the fine features have been lost. Limestone, which is quarried from the ground, is mostly calcium carbonate. This reacts with acid, giving off carbon dioxide gas in the reaction.

Metal carbonates react with acids to give a salt, water, and carbon dioxide. For calcium carbonate the reaction with hydrochloric acid is:

calcium carbonate + hydrochloric acid → calcium chloride + water + carbon dioxide

The balanced symbol equation, including state symbols, is:

$$CaCO_3(s) + 2HCl(aq) \rightarrow CaCl_2(aq) + H_2O(l) + CO_2(g)$$

Powdered limestone is used to raise the pH of acidic soils or lakes affected by acid rain, making use of the reaction between calcium carbonate and acid.

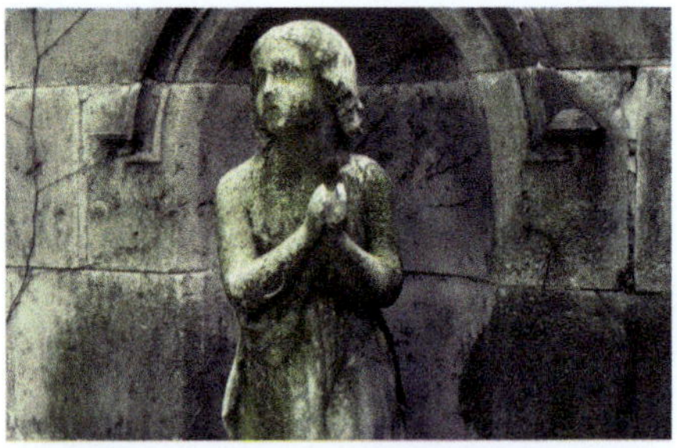

Figure 1 *Limestone, made up mainly of calcium carbonate, is attacked and damaged by acids*

Testing for carbon dioxide

You can use a simple test to verify that the gas given off is carbon dioxide. Carbon dioxide turns **limewater** solution cloudy. The test works as follows:

- Limewater is a solution of calcium hydroxide. It is alkaline.
- Carbon dioxide is a weakly acidic gas so it reacts with the alkaline limewater.
- In this reaction tiny solid particles of insoluble calcium carbonate are formed as a precipitate.
- The reaction is:

calcium hydroxide (limewater) + carbon dioxide → calcium carbonate (an insoluble white precipitate) + water

$$Ca(OH)_2(aq) + CO_2(g) \rightarrow CaCO_3(s) + H_2O(l)$$

- This precipitate of calcium carbonate makes the limewater turn cloudy. This is because light can no longer pass through the solution with the particles of white solid calcium carbonate suspended in it.

Practical

Acid plus metal carbonates

Set up the apparatus as shown.

Try the test with some other carbonates, such as those of magnesium, copper, zinc, and sodium.

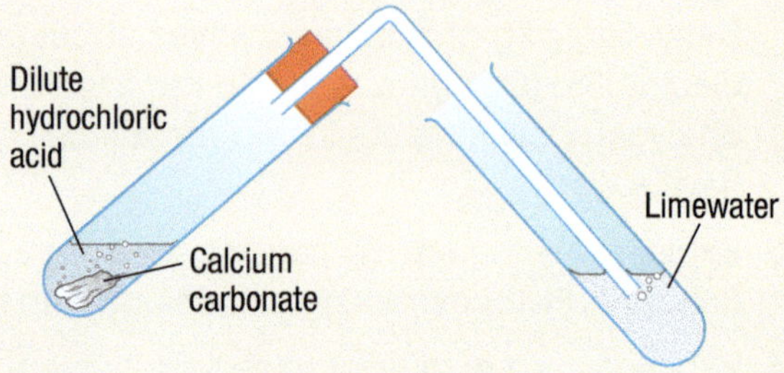

Record your observations.

- What conclusion can you draw?

Safety: Wear eye protection. Some of the chemicals are harmful.

Did you know ... ?

Sculptures from the Parthenon (a temple), built by the ancient Greeks in Athens, have had to be removed and replaced by copies to avoid any more damage from acid pollution from vehicle exhausts.

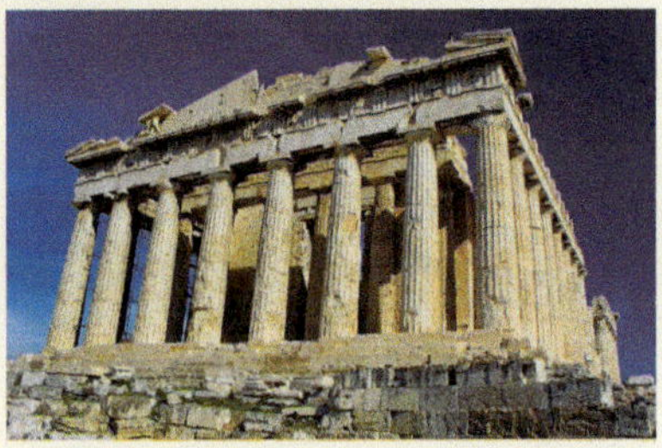

Thermal decomposition of carbonates

The calcium carbonate in limestone decomposes when it is heated. The reaction produces calcium oxide and carbon dioxide:

$$CaCO_3(s) \rightarrow CaO(s) + CO_2(g)$$

(lime or quicklime)

This reaction takes place in industry in a lime kiln. The calcium oxide made can be reacted with water to make a cheap alkali, calcium hydroxide. The **thermal decomposition** reaction shown above is also important when limestone is used in making **cement** and glass, as well as in the extraction of iron in a blast furnace.

So do other metal carbonates also decompose when heated?

Practical

Investigating carbonates

You can investigate the thermal decomposition of carbonates by heating samples in a Bunsen flame. You will have samples of the carbonates listed below.

Powdered carbonate samples: sodium carbonate, potassium carbonate, calcium carbonate, magnesium carbonate, zinc carbonate, copper carbonate

- What observations might tell you if a sample decomposes when you heat it?
- How could you test any gas given off?

Safety: It is important to remove the delivery tube from the limewater before you stop heating the carbonate. If you don't, the cold limewater will be 'sucked back' into the hot boiling tube causing it to smash.
You must wear eye protection when doing this practical.
Some chemicals will be harmful.

Investigations like this show that many metal carbonates decompose when they are heated in a Bunsen flame. They form the metal oxide and carbon dioxide – just as calcium carbonate does. Sodium and potassium carbonate do not decompose at the temperature of the Bunsen flame. They need a higher temperature.

Magnesium carbonate decomposes like this:

$$MgCO_3(s) \rightarrow MgO(s) + CO_2(g)$$

Summary questions

1 Give a general word equation for:

a the reaction of a metal carbonate plus an acid,

b the thermal decomposition of a metal carbonate.

2 Write a word equation plus a balanced symbol equation, including state symbols, for the reaction of sodium carbonate powder with dilute hydrochloric acid.

3 Copper(II) carbonate, $CuCO_3$, undergoes thermal decomposition. Write the balanced symbol equation, including state symbols, for this reaction.

4 Write the balanced symbol equation for the reaction of copper carbonate with dilute nitric acid.

5 Explain in detail why limewater turns cloudy in the test for carbon dioxide.

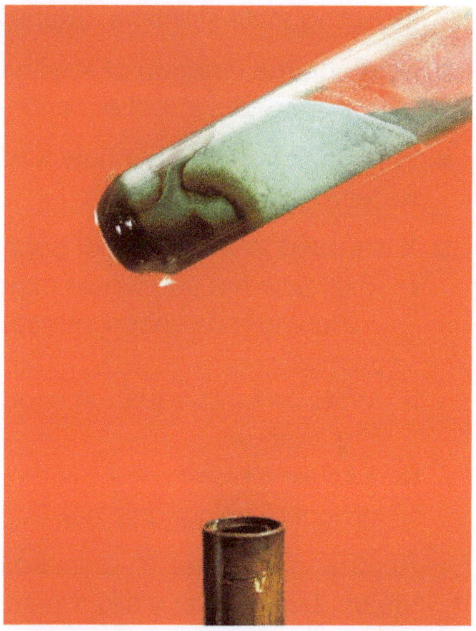

Figure 2 *The thermal decomposition of copper(II) carbonate*

Key points

- Carbonates react with dilute acid to form a salt, water, and carbon dioxide.
- Limewater turns cloudy in the test for carbon dioxide gas. A precipitate of insoluble calcium carbonate causes the cloudiness.
- Metal carbonates decompose on heating to form the metal oxide and carbon dioxide.
- Limestone, containing mainly calcium carbonate ($CaCO_3$), is quarried and can be used as a building material, or powdered and used to control acidity in the soil. It can also be used in the manufacture of cement, glass, and iron, as well as producing calcium oxide (lime) when heated.

Chapter summary questions

1 Imagine that a new metal, given the symbol X, has been discovered. It lies between calcium and magnesium in the reactivity series.

a Describe its reaction when heated in steam and give a word equation and a balanced symbol equation, including state symbols. (Metal X forms 2+ ions.)

b Describe the reaction of X with dilute sulfuric acid and give word and symbol equations.

c Why can't you be sure how X will react with cold water?

d X is added to a solution of copper(II) nitrate.
- **i** Explain what you would expect to see happen, including a balanced symbol equation with state symbols.
- **ii** Write an ionic equation showing what happens in the change.
- **iii** Explain which species is oxidised and which is reduced, using ionic half equations.

e Another new metal, Y, does not react with water or steam, but there is a slight reaction with warm dilute acid.
- **i** Where would you place metal Y in the reactivity series?
- **ii** Explain what you would expect to happen if metal Y was added to magnesium sulfate solution.

2 Decide which of the pairs below will react. If they do react, complete the word equations and balanced symbol equations, including state symbols:

a zinc + copper(II) oxide

b iron + zinc nitrate

c iron + magnesium oxide

d magnesium + copper(II) sulfate

3 The reaction between aluminium powder and iron(III) oxide is used in the rail industry.

a **i** Write a word equation and a balanced symbol equation for the reaction that takes place.
- **ii** What is the name for this type of reaction?

b Compare the reaction described above with the reaction you would expect to see between powdered aluminium and copper(II) oxide.

c Predict what would happen if you heated a mixture of aluminium oxide and iron.

d Explain why the uses of aluminium metal are surprising given its position in the reactivity series.

4 Choose from this list to name the metal described in **a** to **e**.

chromium

gold

aluminium
copper

magnesium

a A precious metal, often alloyed with copper to make it more hard-wearing.

b A metal that is alloyed with nickel and iron in stainless steel.

c A low density metal used to make alloys for the aircraft industry.

d A metal that is extracted from its solution using scrap iron.

e A metal that reacts very slowly with cold water but reacts vigorously when heated in steam, forming a white basic oxide.

5 **a** What name is given to the method of extracting copper from an ore:
- **i** using bacteria
- **ii** using plants
- **iii** using high temperatures
- **iv** using electricity?

b Which methods in part **a** are being developed to extract copper from low-grade copper ores?

Practice questions

1 One way to compare the reactivities of metals is to add them to acids. Some students added samples of five metals to separate tubes containing dilute hydrochloric acid. The teacher provided the metal labelled X. The amount of metal was the same in each experiment.

a To make the comparison fair, some other factors should be the same in each experiment.

i State **two** properties/factors applying to the acid that should be the same. (2)

ii State **one** other factor applying to the metal that should be the same. (1)

b The students recorded their observations in a table.

Metal	Observation
copper	nothing happened
iron	very few bubbles
magnesium	very large numbers of bubbles
X	very few bubbles
zinc	quite a lot of bubbles

i Which metal in the table is the most reactive? (1)

ii Why is it not possible to deduce that iron is the least reactive metal in the table? (1)

c The teacher suggested that a better method to compare the reactivities of the metals is to see how long it takes to collect a certain volume of the gas formed.

Name **two** pieces of apparatus needed in the suggested method. (2)

2 The reactivities of metals can be compared by using displacement reactions.

a A more reactive metal will displace a less reactive metal from its salt in solution. An equation for a displacement reaction is:

zinc + copper(II) sulfate → zinc sulfate + copper

Write a symbol equation for this reaction. (2)

b The equation for another displacement reaction is:

$Fe + CuCl_2 \rightarrow FeCl_2 + Cu$

Write the simplest ionic equation for this reaction. (1)

c The reaction in **b** is a redox reaction.

i State the meaning of the term 'redox'. (1)

ii State and explain, in terms of redox and electrons, what happens to the iron in this reaction. (2)

3 Aluminium is in Group 3 of the periodic table. It is a metal with very useful properties, and is often used as one of its many alloys.

a Aluminium alloys are used extensively in the manufacture of aeroplanes. Explain why aluminium alloys are used instead of pure aluminium metal to make the wings and body of an aeroplane. (3)

b Aluminium has also been used to make pans. Give two useful properties that make it suitable for this use. (2)

c i What is the charge on an aluminium ion? Explain your reasoning. (1)

ii Predict the chemical formula of aluminum sulfide. (1)

iii Using your answer to part i, explain why aluminum is such a good conductor of electricity. (3)

5.1 Electrolysis

Learning objectives

After this topic, you should know:

- what happens in electrolysis
- the type of substances that can be electrolysed
- the products of electrolysis.

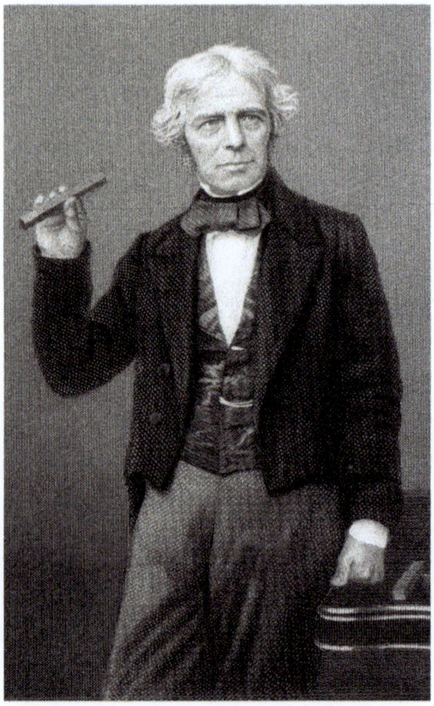

Figure 1 *The first person to explain electrolysis was Michael Faraday. He worked on this and many other problems in science nearly 200 years ago.*

The word **electrolysis** means 'breaking down using electricity'. In electrolysis, an electric current is used to break down an ionic substance. The substance that is broken down by electrolysis is called the **electrolyte**.

To set up an electrical circuit for electrolysis, there are two electrodes which dip into the electrolyte. The electrodes are conducting rods. One of these is connected to the positive terminal of a power supply. This positive electrode is called the **anode**. The other electrode is connected to the negative terminal and is called the **cathode**.

The electrodes are often made of an unreactive (or **inert**) substance. This is often graphite or sometimes platinum. This is so the electrodes do not react with the electrolyte or the products made in electrolysis.

During electrolysis, positively charged ions move to the cathode (negative electrode). At the same time, the negative ions move to the anode (positive electrode).

When the ions reach the electrodes they lose their charge and become elements. Gases may be given off or metals deposited at the electrodes. This depends on the compound used and whether it is molten or dissolved in water.

Demonstration

The electrolysis of molten lead bromide

- This demonstration needs a fume cupboard because bromine is toxic and corrosive.
- When does the bulb light up?
- What is observed at each electrode?

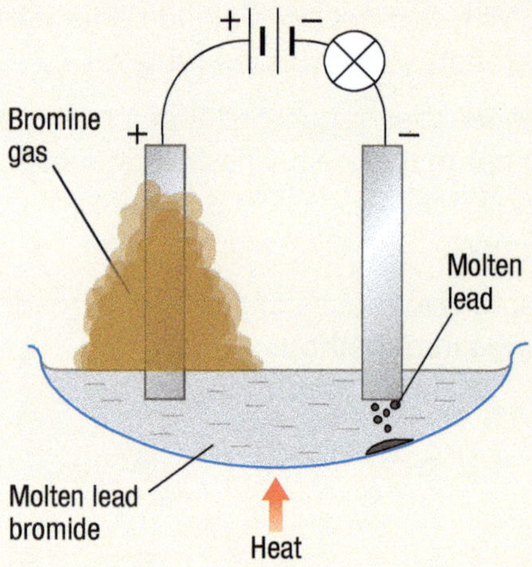

Figure 2 *Passing electricity through molten lead bromide. It forms molten lead and brown bromine gas as the electrolyte is broken down by the electricity.*

Safety: Warn asthmatics. Wear chemical splashproof eye protection. Lead bromide and bromine are toxic.

Figure 2 above shows how electricity breaks down lead bromide into lead and bromine. The reaction that is happening is:

lead bromide → lead + bromine

$$PbBr_2(l) \rightarrow Pb(l) + Br_2(g)$$

Lead bromide is an ionic substance. Ionic substances do not conduct electricity when they are solid as their ions are in fixed positions in their giant lattice. But once they are melted, the ions are free to move around within the liquid and carry their charge towards the electrodes.

The positive lead ions (Pb^{2+}) move towards the cathode (negative electrode). At the same time, the negatively charged bromide ions (Br^-) move towards the anode (positive electrode).

Notice the state symbols in the equation. They tell us that the lead bromide and the lead are molten at the temperature in the dish. The bromine is given off as a gas.

Electrolysis of solutions

Many ionic substances have very high melting points so it takes a lot of energy to melt them and free the ions to move to electrodes in electrolysis. However, some ionic substances dissolve in water and when this happens the ions also become free to move around.

When electrolysing ionic compounds in solution, and not as molten compounds, it is more difficult to predict what will be formed. This is because water also forms ions so the products at each electrode are not always exactly what you would expect (see Topic 5.2 *Changes at the electrodes*). Only metals of very low reactivity, below hydrogen in the reactivity series, are deposited from their aqueous solutions in electrolysis.

When you electrolyse an aqueous solution of copper(II) bromide, copper ions (Cu^{2+}) move to the cathode (negative electrode). The bromide ions (Br^-) move to the anode (positive electrode). Copper(II) bromide is split into its elements at the electrodes (see Figure 3):

copper(II) bromide → copper + bromine

$CuBr_2(aq) \rightarrow Cu(s) + Br_2(aq)$

The state symbols in the equation tell us that the copper bromide is dissolved in water, the copper is formed as a solid, and the bromine formed dissolves in the water.

Covalent compounds cannot usually be electrolysed unless they react (or ionise) in water to form ions. For example, acids in water always contain $H^+(aq)$ ions plus negatively charged aqueous ions.

Summary questions

1. **a** What is electrolysis?
   b What is the name of the substance broken down by electrolysis?
   c What type of bonding is present in compounds that can be electrolysed?
2. Predict the products formed at the cathode and anode when the following compounds are melted and then electrolysed:
   a zinc iodide
   b lithium bromide
   c iron(III) fluoride
   d sodium oxide
   e potassium chloride
3. Write a balanced symbol equation, including state symbols, for the electrolytic decomposition of molten sodium chloride.
4. **a** Which of the following solutions would deposit a metal at the cathode during electrolysis?

   $KBr(aq)$, $CaCl_2(aq)$, $FeBr_2(aq)$, $CuCl_2(aq)$, $Na_2SO_4(aq)$, $AgNO_3(aq)$

   b How did you decide on your answer to part **a**?
5. Solid ionic substances do not conduct electricity. Using words and diagrams, explain why they conduct electricity when molten or in aqueous solution, but not when solid.

links

Remind yourself of the relative reactivity of metals and hydrogen in 4.3 The reactivity series and 4.4 Displacement reactions.

links

For more information about the effect of water in electrolysis, see 5.2 Changes at the electrodes and 5.4 Electrolysis of brine.

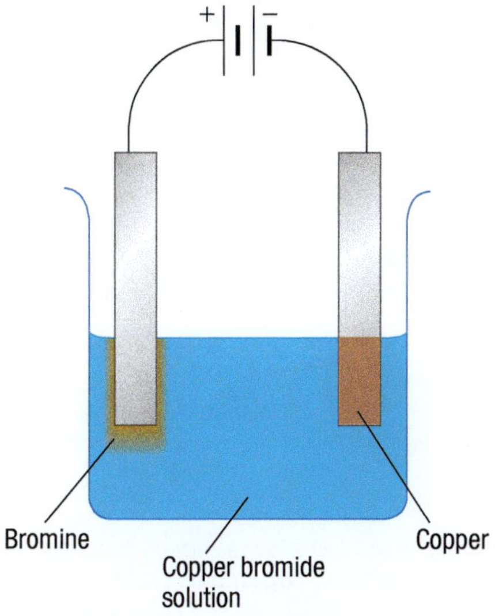

Figure 3 *If we dissolve copper bromide in water, we can decompose it by electrolysis. Copper metal is formed at the cathode (negative electrode). Brown bromine appears in solution around the anode (positive electrode).*

Key points

- Electrolysis breaks down a substance using electricity.
- Ionic compounds can only be electrolysed when they are molten or dissolved in water. This is because their ions are then free to move and carry their charge to the electrodes.
- In electrolysis, positive ions move to the cathode (negative electrode) whilst negative ions move to the anode (positive electrode).

5.2 Changes at the electrodes

Learning objectives

After this topic, you should know:

- what happens to the ions during electrolysis
- how to represent what happens at each electrode
- how water affects the products of electrolysis.

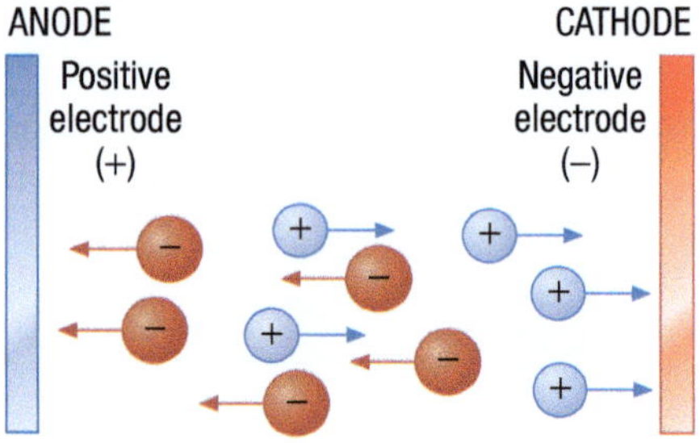

Figure 1 *An ion always moves towards the oppositely charged electrode*

During electrolysis, mobile ions move towards the electrodes. The direction they move in depends on their charge. As you saw in Topic 5.1, positive ions move towards the cathode (negative electrode). Negative ions move towards the anode (positive electrode).

When ions reach an electrode, they either lose or gain electrons, depending on their charge.

Negatively charged ions *lose* electrons to become neutral atoms. Positively charged ions *gain* electrons to become neutral atoms.

The easiest way to think about this is to look at an example.

Think back to the electrolysis of molten lead bromide. The lead ions (Pb^{2+}) move towards the negative electrode. When they get there, each ion gains two electrons to become a neutral lead atom.

Gaining electrons is called **reduction**. You say that the lead ions are **reduced**. 'Reduction' is simply another way of saying 'gaining electrons'.

The negatively charged bromide ions (Br^-) move towards the positive electrode. Once there, each ion loses its one extra electron to become a neutral bromine atom. Two bromine atoms then form a covalent bond to make a bromine molecule, Br_2.

Losing electrons is called **oxidation**. You say that the bromide ions are **oxidised**. 'Oxidation' is another way of saying 'losing electrons'.

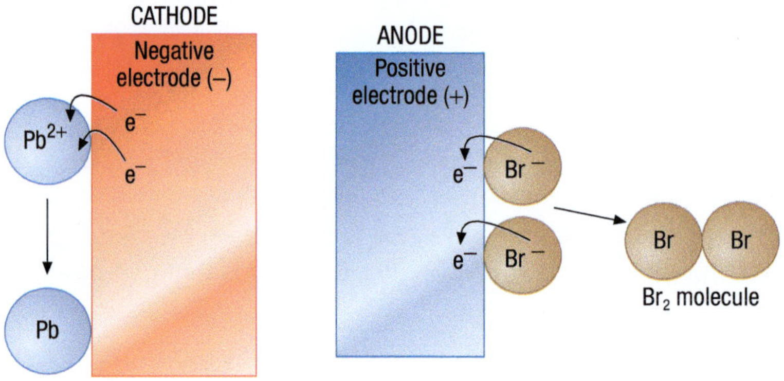

links

For more information on reduction and oxidation in terms of electron transfer, look back to 4.4 Displacement reactions.

Half equations

You can represent what is happening at each electrode using **half equations**.

At the cathode (negative electrode) you get reduction of a positive ion:

$$Pb^{2+} + 2e^- \rightarrow Pb$$

At the anode (positive electrode) you get oxidation of a negative ion:

$$2Br^- \rightarrow Br_2 + 2e^-$$

Sometimes half equations at the anode can show the electrons being removed from negative ions, like this:

$$2Br^- - 2e^- \rightarrow Br_2$$

You can write the half equation for negative ions either way. They both show the same oxidation of the negatively charged ions.

Study tip

Oxidation and reduction reactions do not have to involve oxygen. More generally they involve the transfer of electrons.

Remember **OILRIG** – **O**xidation **I**s **L**oss (of electrons), **R**eduction **I**s **G**ain (of electrons).

The effect of water

In aqueous solutions, electrolysis is more complex because of the ions formed by water as it ionises:

$$H_2O(l) \rightleftharpoons H^+(aq) + OH^-(aq)$$

hydrogen ions   hydroxide ions

There is a rule for working out what will happen. Remember that if two elements can be produced at an electrode, the less reactive element will usually be formed. In solutions, you will usually have positively charged metal ions and H^+ ions (from water) attracted to the cathode (negative electrode).

Look at Figure 2. It shows what happens in the electrolysis of a solution of a potassium compound. Hydrogen is less reactive than potassium, so hydrogen is produced at the cathode rather than potassium.

At cathode (–):

$$2H^+(aq) + 2e^- \rightarrow H_2(g)$$

So what happens at the anode in the electrolysis of aqueous solutions?

Hydroxide ions, $OH^-(aq)$, from water are often discharged. When hydroxide ions are discharged, you see oxygen gas given off at the anode (positive electrode).

At anode (+):

$$4OH^-(aq) \rightarrow 2H_2O(l) + O_2(g) + 4e^-$$

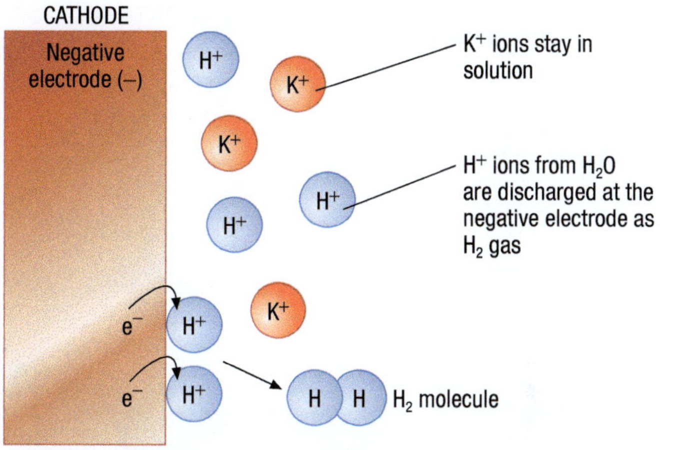

Figure 2 *Here is the cathode in the electrolysis of a solution of a potassium compound. Hydrogen is less reactive than potassium, so hydrogen gas is given off at the electrode.*

This happens unless the solution contains a reasonably high concentration of a halide ion, that is, Group 7 ions, such as $Cl^-(aq)$. In this case, the halide ion is discharged and the halogen is formed:

$$2Cl^-(aq) \rightarrow Cl_2(g) + 2e^-$$

So the 'order of discharge' (starting with the easiest) at the anode is:

halide ion > hydroxide > all other negatively charged ions.

Summary questions

1 a i How do negatively charged ions become neutral atoms in electrolysis?
ii Is this reduction or oxidation of the negatively charged ion?
b i How do positively charged ions become neutral atoms in electrolysis?
ii Is this reduction or oxidation of the positively charged ion?

2 Predict what is formed at each electrode in the electrolysis of:
a molten lithium oxide
b copper chloride solution
c sodium sulfate solution.

3 Copy and balance the following half equations where necessary:
a $Cl^- \rightarrow Cl_2 + e^-$
b $Br^- \rightarrow Br_2 + e^-$
c $Mg^{2+} + e^- \rightarrow Mg$
d $Al^{3+} + e^- \rightarrow Al$
e $K^+ + e^- \rightarrow K$
f $H^+ + e^- \rightarrow H_2$
g $O^{2-} \rightarrow O_2 + e^-$
h $OH^- \rightarrow O_2 + H_2O + e^-$

Key points

- In electrolysis, the ions move towards the oppositely charged electrodes.
- At the electrodes, negative ions are oxidised (at the anode) whilst positive ions are reduced (at the cathode).
- When electrolysis happens in aqueous solution, the less reactive element, either hydrogen or the metal, is usually produced at the cathode. At the anode, you often get oxygen gas given off from discharged hydroxide ions produced from water.

5.3 The extraction of aluminium

Learning objectives

After this topic, you should know:

- how aluminium is obtained from aluminium oxide
- why cryolite is used in the process
- what happens at each electrode in the process.

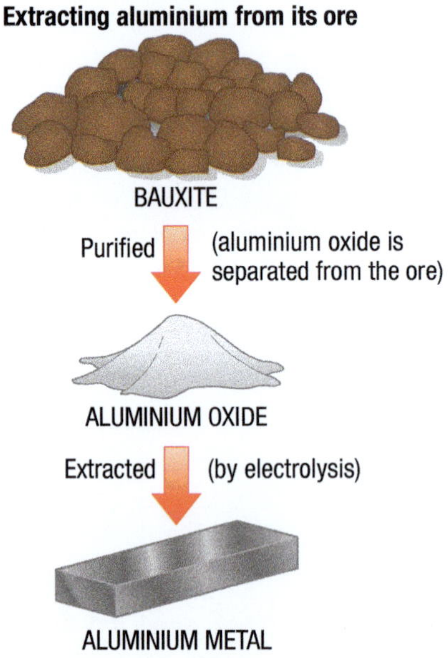

Figure 2 *Extracting aluminium from its ore. This process requires a lot of energy. The energy is needed for melting and electrolysing the oxide.*

You already know that aluminium is a very important metal. The uses of the metal or its alloys include:

- pans
- overhead power cables
- aeroplanes
- cooking foil
- drink cans
- window and patio door frames
- bicycle frames and car bodies.

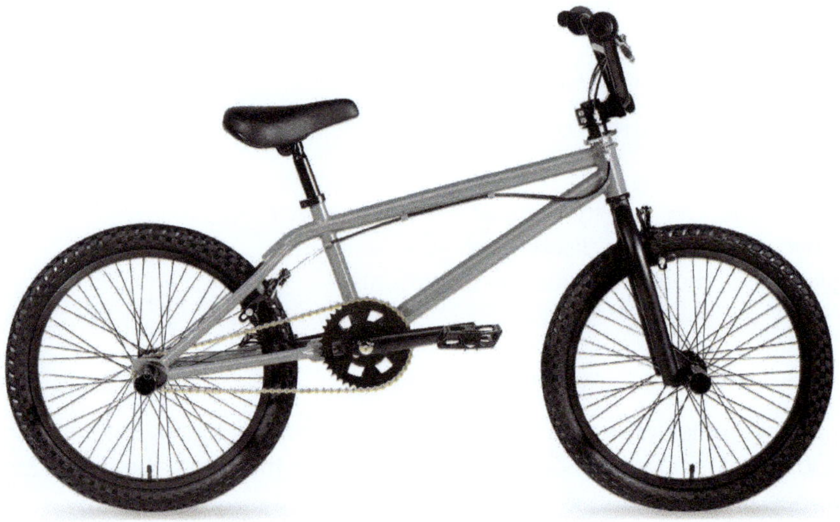

Figure 1 *Aluminium alloys have a low density but are very strong*

Aluminium is quite a reactive metal. It is less reactive than magnesium but more reactive than zinc or iron. Carbon is not reactive enough to use in its extraction so you must use electrolysis. The compound electrolysed is aluminium oxide, Al_2O_3.

Aluminium oxide is extracted from the ore called bauxite. The ore is mined by open- cast mining. Bauxite contains mainly aluminium oxide. However, it is mixed with other rocky impurities. So the first step is to separate aluminium oxide from the ore. The impurities contain a lot of iron(III) oxide. This colours the waste solution from the separation process rusty brown. The brown wastewater has to be stored in large lagoons.

Electrolysis of aluminium oxide

To electrolyse the aluminium oxide it must first be melted. This enables the ions to move to the electrodes.

Unfortunately aluminium oxide has a very high melting point of 2050 °C. However, chemists have found a way of saving at least some energy. This is done by mixing the aluminium oxide with molten cryolite. Cryolite is another ionic compound. The molten mixture can be electrolysed at about 850 °C. The electrical energy transferred to the electrolysis cells keeps the mixture molten (see Figure 3).

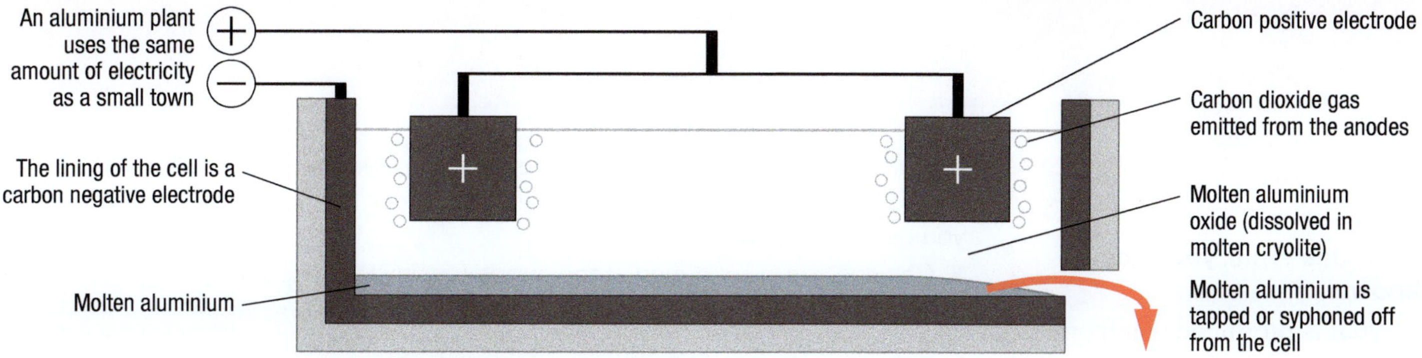

Figure 3 *A cell used in the extraction of aluminium by electrolysis*

The overall reaction in the electrolysis cell is:

$$\text{aluminium oxide} \xrightarrow{\text{electrolysis}} \text{aluminium} + \text{oxygen}$$
$$2Al_2O_3(l) \longrightarrow 4Al(l) + 3O_2(g)$$

At the cathodes (negative electrodes):

Each aluminium ion (Al^{3+}) gains three electrons. The ions turn into aluminium atoms. We say that the Al^{3+} ions are reduced (as they gain electrons) to form Al atoms:

$$Al^{3+}(l) + 3e^- \rightarrow Al(l)$$

The aluminium metal formed is molten at the temperature of the cell and collects at the bottom. It is siphoned or tapped off.

At the anodes (positive electrodes):

Each oxide ion (O^{2-}) loses two electrons. The ions turn into oxygen atoms. We say that the O^{2-} ions are oxidised (as they lose electrons) to form oxygen atoms. These bond in pairs to form molecules of oxygen gas (O_2):

$$2O^{2-}(l) \rightarrow O_2(g) + 4e^-$$

The oxygen reacts with the hot carbon anodes, making carbon dioxide gas:

$$C(s) + O_2(g) \rightarrow CO_2(g)$$

So the carbon anodes gradually burn away. They need to be replaced in the cells regularly.

Summary questions

1 a Explain why aluminium oxide must be molten for electrolysis to take place.
  b Why is aluminium oxide dissolved in molten cryolite in the extraction of aluminium?

2 Why are the carbon anodes replaced regularly in the industrial electrolysis of aluminium oxide?

3 a Write half equations for the changes at each electrode in the electrolysis of molten aluminium oxide.
  b Explain which ions are oxidised and which ions are reduced in the electrolysis of molten aluminium oxide.

4 a Explain why the extraction of aluminium requires so much energy.
  b Explain why aluminium metal was only discovered in the early 1800s despite it being the most common metallic element in the Earth's crust.

Did you know ... ?

Recycling one aluminium can can save enough energy to run a TV for about 3 hours.

Key points

- **Aluminium oxide, from the ore bauxite, is electrolysed in the manufacture of aluminium metal.**
- **The aluminium oxide is mixed with molten cryolite to lower its melting point.**
- **Aluminium forms at the cathode (negative electrode) and oxygen forms at the anode (positive electrode).**
- **The carbon anodes are replaced regularly as they gradually burn away.**

5.4 Electrolysis of brine

Learning objectives

After this topic, you should know:

- what is produced when brine is electrolysed
- how these products are used.

The electrolysis of **brine** (concentrated sodium chloride solution) is a very important industrial process. When an electric current is passed through brine you get three products:

- Chlorine gas is produced at the anode (positive electrode).
- Hydrogen gas is produced at the cathode (negative electrode).
- Sodium hydroxide solution is also formed.

You can summarise the electrolysis of brine as:

$$\text{sodium chloride solution} \xrightarrow{\text{electrolysis}} \text{hydrogen gas} + \text{chlorine gas} + \text{sodium hydroxide solution}$$

At the anode (+):

The negative chloride ions (Cl^-) are attracted to the positive electrode. When they get there, they each lose one electron. The chloride ions are oxidised, as they lose electrons. The chlorine atoms bond together in pairs and are given off as chlorine gas (Cl_2). The half equation at the anode is:

$$2Cl^-(aq) \rightarrow Cl_2(g) + 2e^-$$

[This can also be written as: $2Cl^-(aq) - 2e^- \rightarrow Cl_2(g)$]

At the cathode (–):

There are H^+ ions in brine, formed when water breaks down:

$$H_2O(l) \rightleftharpoons H^+(aq) + OH^-(aq)$$

These positive hydrogen ions are attracted to the negative electrode. The sodium ions (Na^+) are also attracted to the same electrode. But remember in Topic 5.2, you saw what happens when two different ions are attracted to an electrode. It is the less reactive element that gets discharged. In this case, hydrogen ions are discharged and sodium ions stay in solution.

When the H^+ ions get to the negative electrode, they each gain one electron. The hydrogen ions are reduced, as they each gain an electron. The hydrogen atoms formed bond together in pairs and are given off as hydrogen gas (H_2). The half equation at the cathode is:

$$2H^+(aq) + 2e^- \rightarrow H_2(g)$$

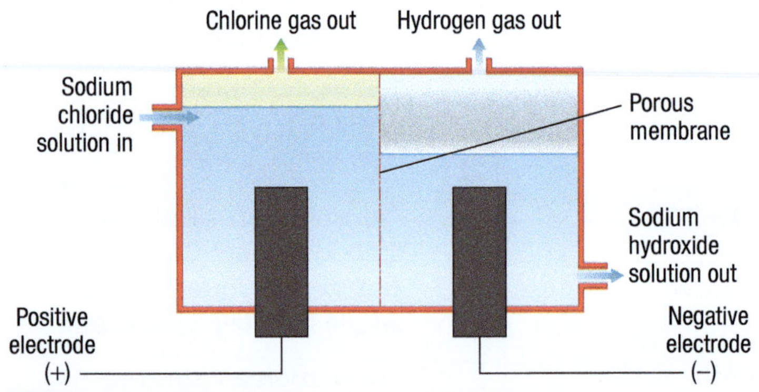

Figure 1 *In industry, brine can be electrolysed in a cell in which the two electrodes are separated by a porous membrane. This is called a diaphragm cell.*

The remaining solution:

You can test the solution around the cathode (negative electrode) with indicator. It shows that the solution is alkaline. This is because you can think of brine as containing aqueous ions of Na^+ and Cl^- (from salt) and H^+ and OH^- (from water). The $Cl^-(aq)$ and $H^+(aq)$ ions are removed during electrolysis. So this leaves a solution containing $Na^+(aq)$ and $OH^-(aq)$ ions, that is, a solution of sodium hydroxide, NaOH(aq).

Look at the way brine is electrolysed in industry in Figure 1.

Practical

Electrolysing brine in the lab

Turn off the electricity once the tubes are nearly full of gas to avoid inhaling chlorine gas (toxic).

- How can you positively test for the gases collected?

Test the solution near the cathode (negative electrode) with universal indicator solution.

- What does the indicator tell us?

Safety: Wear eye protection. Do not smell the gas.

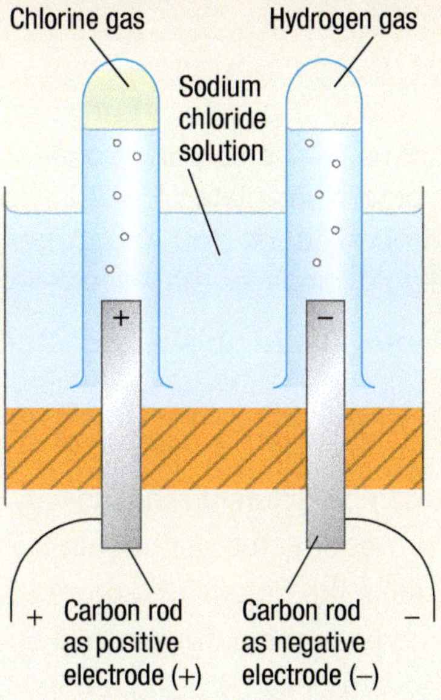

Using chlorine

You can react chlorine with the sodium hydroxide produced in the electrolysis of brine. This makes a solution of bleach. Bleach is very good at killing bacteria.

Chlorine is also important in making many other disinfectants, as well as plastics such as PVC.

Using hydrogen

The hydrogen made by electrolysing brine is particularly pure. This makes it very useful in the food industry. Margarine is made by reacting hydrogen with vegetable oils.

Using sodium hydroxide

The sodium hydroxide from the electrolysis of brine is an important alkali in industry. It is used to make soap and paper, as well as bleach (see above).

Summary questions

1 a What are the **three** products made when brine is electrolysed?
  b What are they used for?

2 For the electrolysis of brine, write half equations, including state symbols, for the reactions:
  a at the anode
  b at the cathode.

3 It is also possible to electrolyse *molten* sodium chloride.
  a Compare the products formed with those from the electrolysis of sodium chloride solution.
  b Explain any differences.

links

For information about what happens when two ions are attracted to an electrode, look back to 5.2 Changes at the electrodes.

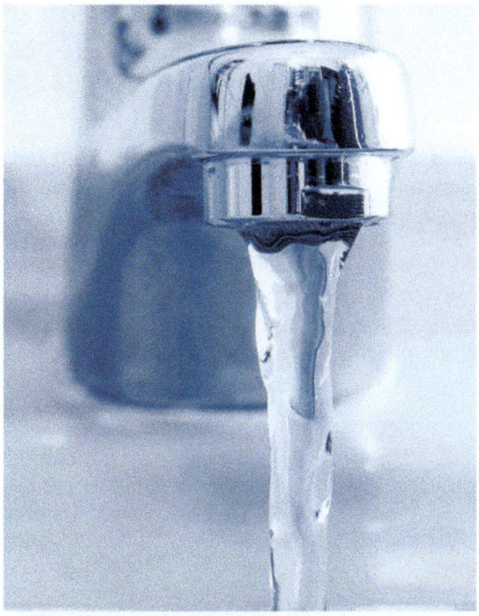

Figure 2 *The chlorine made when we electrolyse brine is used to kill bacteria in drinking water, and also in swimming pools*

Key points

- When brine is electrolysed, three products are formed – chlorine gas, hydrogen gas, and sodium hydroxide solution (an alkali).
- Chlorine is used to make bleach, which kills bacteria, and to make plastics.
- Hydrogen is used to make margarine.
- Sodium hydroxide is used to make bleach, paper, and soap.

5.5 Electroplating

Learning objectives

After this topic, you should know:

- why objects are electroplated
- how to electroplate a metal object.

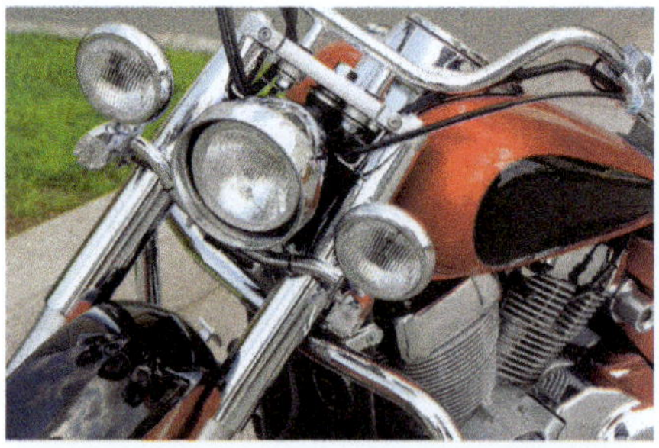

Figure 1 *Chromium-plated objects look very shiny and attractive. The chromium layer does not corrode away so it protects the steel beneath from rusting.*

Most of us will use an electroplated object at some time each day. You might use a chromium-plated kettle to boil water or ride a bicycle with chromium-plated handlebars. You could open a tin-plated steel can for a meal or put on some gold- or silver-plated jewellery.

An electroplated object is coated with a thin layer of metal by electrolysis.

Why are objects electroplated?

There can be different reasons why scientists electroplate objects. These include:

- to protect the metal beneath from corroding
- to make the object look more attractive
- to increase the hardness of a surface and its resistance to scratching
- to save money by using a thin layer of a precious metal instead of the pure expensive metal. This also helps people who are allergic to nickel – a metal often used to make cheap jewellery.

Electroplating saves money by making cheaper jewellery. However, using electroplating to protect large metal surfaces against rusting and damage makes things more expensive. In the long term, though, this can still make economic sense for some objects because they don't have to be replaced so often.

Electroplating a metal object

You can try to zinc-plate some copper foil in the experiment below.

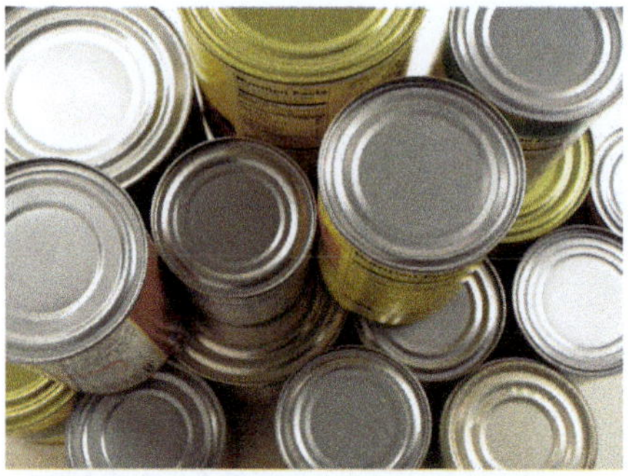

Figure 2 *So-called 'tin' cans actually contain very little tin. The layer on the steel can be only a few thousandths of a millimetre thick! The tin keeps air and water away from the iron in steel and stops it rusting – at least until the tin gets scratched! Tin is quite a soft metal, unlike chromium.*

Practical

Zinc-plating copper metal

Your teacher will melt some wax in a metal tray. Using tongs you can dip in a cleaned piece of copper foil.

Let the wax set. Then scratch a simple design in the wax. You want the design to be plated with zinc so get this area as free from wax as possible.

Set up the apparatus as shown in the diagram. The zinc-plating solution is made by adding 30 cm^3 of 0.4 mol/dm^3 sodium hydroxide solution to 5 cm^3 of 0.1 mol/dm^3 zinc sulfate solution and stirring. Using a small current for a long time will give best results.

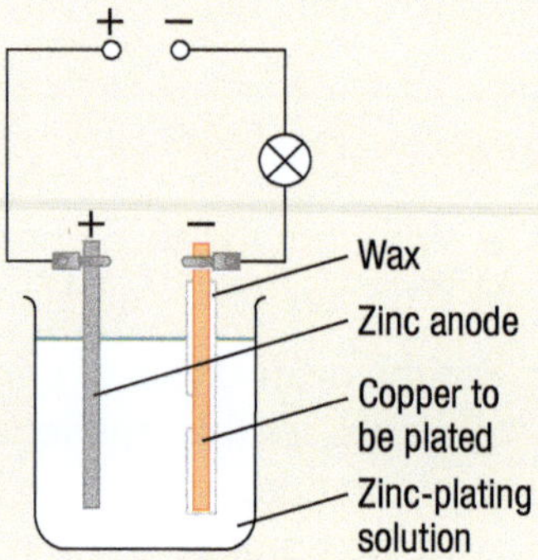

When you have finished, rinse the copper foil in water, dry, then scrape off the rest of the wax.

- What happens at the negative electrode?

Safety: Wear gloves and eye protection. Sodium hydroxide solution is an irritant.

Explaining the zinc-plating experiment

The metal object to be plated (the copper foil in this case) is used as the cathode (negative electrode). The anode (positive electrode) is made from the plating metal (in this case zinc). The electrolysis takes place in a solution containing ions of the plating metal. In the previous experiment you used zinc ions in the solution.

At the anode (+) made of the plating metal:

Zinc atoms in the electrode are oxidised. They lose two electrons each and form zinc (Zn^{2+}) ions which leave the anode and go into the solution. The half equation is:

$$Zn(s) \rightarrow Zn^{2+}(aq) + 2e^-$$

At the cathode (–) to be plated:

Zinc ions (Zn^{2+}) from the solution are reduced. They gain two electrons and form zinc atoms which are deposited on the copper cathode. The half equation is:

$$Zn^{2+}(aq) + 2e^- \rightarrow Zn(s)$$

Copper plating

Here are the half equations at each electrode if an object is electroplated by copper:

At the anode (positive electrode): $Cu(s) \rightarrow Cu^{2+}(aq) + 2e^-$

At the cathode (negative electrode) to be plated: $Cu^{2+}(aq) + 2e^- \rightarrow Cu(s)$

The electrolyte used contains copper(II) ions, such as a solution of copper(II) sulfate.

Did you know ... ?

It is not only metal objects that can be electroplated. Scientists can now electroplate plastic objects as well. The object to be plated is first coated in a 'paint' containing tiny particles of graphite. Once dry, the object has a layer of graphite that will conduct electricity. It can then be electroplated.

Summary questions

1 Name **four** metals that are used to electroplate objects.

2 List the reasons why objects get electroplated.

3 Look at the experiment described in the Practical box on the previous page.
  a Where are zinc atoms oxidised?
  b What is formed when zinc atoms are oxidised?

4 Draw a simple electrical circuit that could be used to copper-plate a steel ball.

5 In making 'chrome' objects, chromium metal is used to electroplate a steel object. The steel is first electroplated with nickel because chromium does not stick well on steel.
  a Give the half equation at the cathode for the nickel-plating process. Include state symbols in your answer. (The formula of a nickel ion is Ni^{2+}.)
  b Give the half equation at the cathode for the chromium-plating process, including state symbols. (The formula of a chromium ion is Cr^{3+}.)

Key points

- **Objects can be electroplated to improve their appearance, to protect their surface, and to use smaller amounts of precious metals.**
- **The object to be electroplated is made the cathode (negative electrode) in an electrolysis cell. The plating metal is made the anode (positive electrode). The electrolyte contains ions of the plating metal.**

5.6 Electrolysing copper sulfate solution

Learning objectives

After this topic, you should know:

- what happens at the electrodes in the electrolysis of copper(II) sulfate solution using inert and active electrodes
- the half equations at the electrodes in the electrolysis of copper(II) sulfate solution
- how to investigate the electrolysis of copper(II) sulfate solution.

You have now seen how electrolysis can be used to extract highly reactive metals, like aluminium. The other uses of electrolysis, such as electroplating, depend on electrodes which react – active electrodes.

In some of the experiments in this chapter, you have used carbon electrodes. These are called 'inert' electrodes. They take no part in the electrolysis. The hot carbon electrodes just carry electrons to and from the electrolyte. (Note that carbon electrodes can react with oxygen produced at an anode, forming carbon dioxide gas, as in the extraction of aluminium – see Topic 5.3 *The extraction of aluminium*.)

However, some metal electrodes do take part in electrolysis. These are called active electrodes. Let's look at copper as an example of an active electrode. You will electrolyse copper sulfate solution.

Practical

Investigate the electrolysis of copper sulfate solution with graphite and copper electrodes

Make sure your copper electrodes are clean and shiny.

Use a pencil to mark one electrode + and the other –.

Weigh them with an accurate balance.

Set up the apparatus as shown in Figure 1.

- What do you observe?

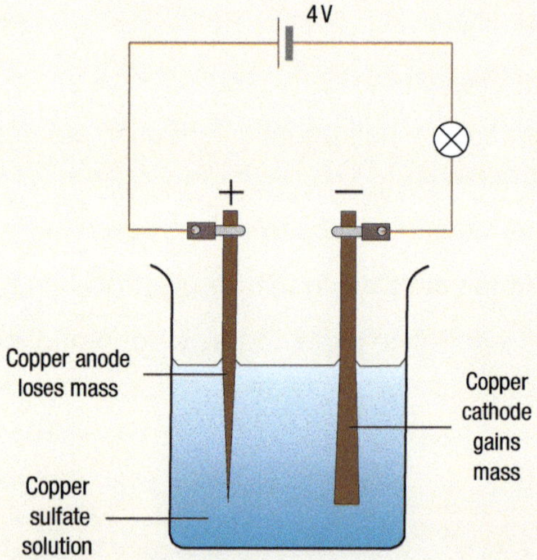

Figure 1 *The electrolysis of copper(II)* sulfate solution with copper electrodes

After 10 minutes, rinse the electrodes with distilled water.

Dry them by dipping them in propanone and letting it evaporate.

Re-weigh the electrodes when they are dry.

- What do you find?
- Why would it be a good idea to repeat your experiment?

Now carry out the electrolysis of copper sulfate solution, but this time using carbon electrodes.

- What difference do you notice at the anode (positive electrode)?

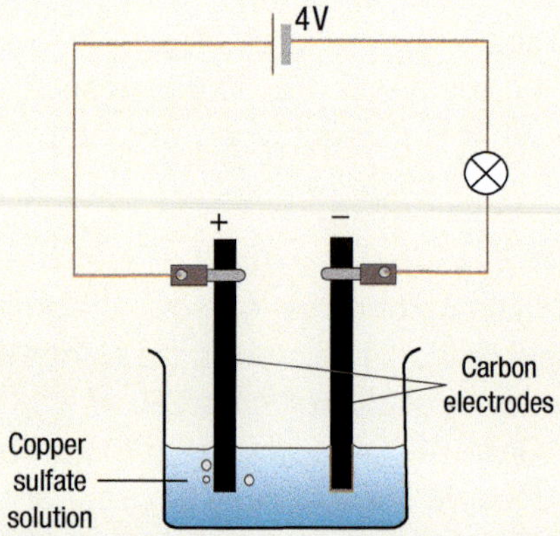

Figure 2 *The electrolysis of copper(II) sulfate solution with carbon electrodes*

Safety: Wear eye protection. Propanone is flammable.

Silver plating

Cheap metal objects can be plated with the expensive metal silver to improve their appearance.

At the silver anode (+):

$Ag(s) \rightarrow Ag^+(aq) + e^-$

At the cathode (object to be plated) (–):

$Ag^+(aq) + e^- \rightarrow Ag(s)$

The metal object is first coated in nickel metal to help the silver stick to the object to be plated You may see 'EPNS' marked on the object (standing for 'Electro-plated nickel silver')

When copper sulfate solution is electrolysed using copper electrodes, the mass of both electrodes changes. Remember that metals are always formed at the cathode (negative electrode). So not surprisingly, the cathode gets heavier.

The strange thing is that the anode loses mass. The copper anode is an active electrode. You will find that:

loss in mass of active electrode at the anode = gain in mass of active electrode at the cathode

Comparing inert and active electrodes

Let's compare the half equations at each electrode in the electrolysis of copper sulfate solution using carbon and copper electrodes:

Table 1 *Comparing the reactions at the cathode and anode in the electrolysis of copper(II) sulfate solution using different electrodes*

	Carbon electrodes	**Copper electrodes**
At the cathode (–)	$Cu^{2+}(aq) + 2e^- \longrightarrow Cu(s)$	$Cu^{2+}(aq) + 2e^- \longrightarrow Cu(s)$
	the reactions are the same	
At the anode (+)	$4OH^-(aq) \longrightarrow 2H_2O(l) + O_2(g) + 4e^-$ Oxygen gas is given off.	$Cu(s) \longrightarrow Cu^{2+}(aq) + 2e^-$ No oxygen is seen. Copper atoms on the anode lose 2 electrons and enter the solution as Cu^{2+} ions.

The copper anode is an active electrode. As copper atoms form on the cathode, copper atoms are lost from the anode. As copper ions leave the solution at the cathode, they are replaced in the solution at the anode.

Copper ions, $Cu^{2+}(aq)$, make copper sulfate solution blue.

- What do you think would happen to the colour of the copper sulfate solution using carbon electrodes?
- Why won't the blue colour fade using copper electrodes?

Did you know ... ?

Copper electrodes are used in a solution of copper(II) ions to purify copper. The impurities that collect as sludge at the bottom of the electrolysis cells contain the precious metals silver and gold.

Summary questions

1 Draw a table to compare the observations made at each electrode when copper(II) sulfate is electrolysed using copper electrodes and using carbon electrodes.

2 Explain why the copper electrodes in the practical in this topic are called 'active' electrodes whereas the carbon electrodes are called 'inert' electrodes.

3 a Write the half equations for the changes at each electrode in the electrolysis of copper(II) sulfate using copper electrodes.

b Explain in terms of oxidation and reduction the changes that occur at each electrode in part **a**.

Key points

- **The electrolysis of copper(II) sulfate solution using copper electrodes results in the copper anode (+) losing the same mass as the copper cathode (–) gains.**
- **In the electrolysis of copper (II) sulfate solution using carbon electrodes, copper is still deposited at the cathode (–). However, at the anode (+) oxygen gas is given off from hydroxide ions that come from the water in the copper(II) sulfate solution.**

Chapter summary questions

1 Select **A** or **B** to describe correctly the anode and cathode in electrolysis for statements **a–f**.

A Anode (+) **B** Cathode (–)

a Positive ions move towards this.

b Oxidation happens here.

c This is connected to the negative terminal of the power supply.

d This is connected to the positive terminal of the power supply.

e Reduction happens here.

f Negative ions move towards this.

2 **a** Which of the following ions would move towards the anode (+) and which towards the cathode (–) during electrolysis?

potassium iodide calcium fluoride
oxide magnesium aluminium bromide

b Write a half equation for the discharge of:

i magnesium ions

ii bromide ions.

3 The diagram shows the electrolysis of sodium chloride solution in the laboratory.

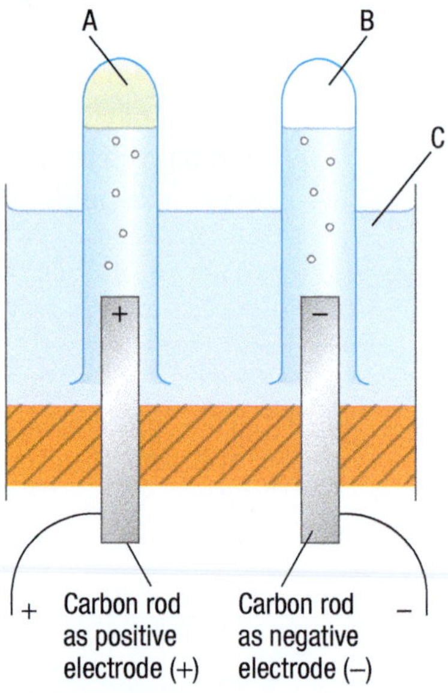

a Identify the products **A**, **B**, and **C** on the diagram.

b Give two uses for substance **A**.

c What would be the pH of the solution around the cathode?

d How would you carry out a positive test on product **B**?

e Write the half equations, including state symbols, for the changes at the anode and cathode.

4 Water can be slightly acidified and broken down into hydrogen and oxygen using electrolysis. The word equation for this reaction is:

water → hydrogen + oxygen

a Write a balanced symbol equation for this reaction, including state symbols.

b In water, a small percentage of molecules ionise (split up). Write a balanced symbol equation, including state symbols, for the ionisation of water molecules.

c Write half equations to show what happens at the positive and negative electrodes in the electrolysis of water.

d Where does the energy needed to split water into hydrogen and oxygen come from during electrolysis?

5 Copy and complete the following half equations:

a $Li^+ \rightarrow Li$

b $Sr^{2+} \rightarrow Sr$

c $F^- \rightarrow F_2$

d $O^{2-} \rightarrow O_2$

6 Electrolysis can be used to produce a thin layer of metal on the surface of a metal object.

Using words and diagrams, describe how you would cover a small piece of iron with tin using an electrolyte of tin(II) nitrate. Make sure that you write down the half equations that describe the changes at the anode and cathode, and include the words 'oxidation' and 'reduction'.

7 A student half-filled two small beakers with copper(II) sulfate solution and labelled them **A** and **B**. He electrolysed solution **A** using copper electrodes, and solution **B** using carbon electrodes.

a Describe what would happen at each electrode in each of the solutions.

b Write the half equations at each electrode in:

i beaker **A**

ii beaker **B**.

c If the electrolysis cells were left running for long enough, eventually the current would stop in both circuits.

Explain why the current stops in each of the two beakers.

Practice questions

1 The diagram shows apparatus for the electrolysis of lead bromide.

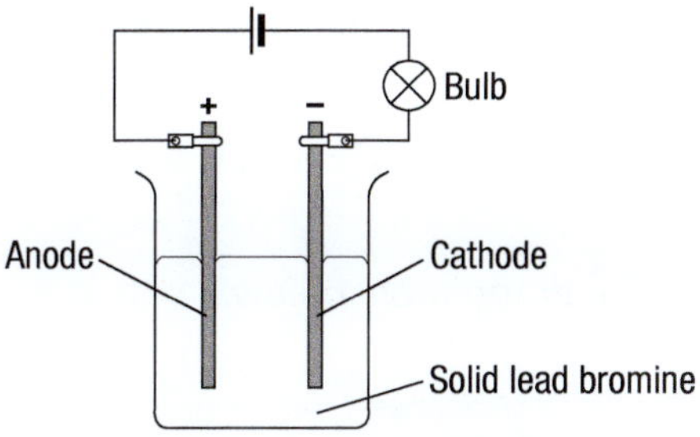

When the lead bromide is heated, it melts and observations can be recorded.

a A brown gas is seen at the anode. Name this gas and write a symbol equation for its formation. (3)

b Silvery globules are seen at the cathode. Name the substance in the globules and write a symbol equation for its formation. (3)

c The bulb does not light until the lead bromide is molten. What happens in the connecting wires when the bulb is lit? (1)

d Why does no electrolysis occur until the lead bromide has melted? (1)

e Why is the reaction at the cathode described as reduction? (1)

2 A student used the following apparatus to electrolyse dilute sulfuric acid.

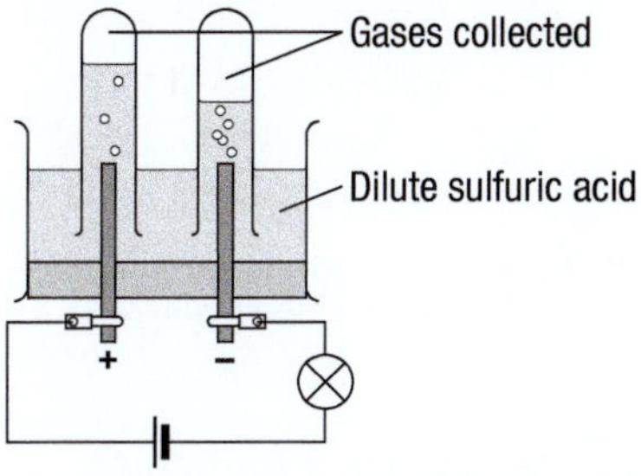

a What is the formula of the only positive ion in dilute sulfuric acid? (1)

b Write the equation for the reaction of the OH^- ion that occurs at the anode. (2)

c Which ion in dilute sulfuric acid is attracted to an electrode but is not discharged? (1)

d Predict what happens to the concentration of the sulfuric acid as electrolysis occurs. (1)

e Why is the volume of hydrogen gas collected approximately double the volume of the oxygen gas? (1)

3 The electrolysis of sodium chloride solution is used to manufacture hydrogen and chlorine.

a Why is the H^+ ion discharged in preference to the Na^+ ion at the cathode? (1)

b Why is the Cl^- ion discharged in preference to the OH^- ion at the anode? (1)

c Name the solution formed in this process. (1)

d i State **one** use for the hydrogen formed. (1)

ii State **one** use for the chlorine formed. (1)

4 Objects can be electroplated. For example, a copper spoon can be plated with nickel.

a i What should be used as the anode and cathode in this process? (1)

ii Suggest the name of a solution that could be used as the electrolyte. (1)

iii Write the half equation for the reaction at the anode. (1)

b Suggest **one** physical property of an object that would change when it is electroplated. (1)

c Objects made of plastic can be electroplated. Why are they coated with graphite before they are electroplated? (1)

5 Aluminium is made by the electrolysis of aluminium oxide.

Aluminium oxide is an ionic compound containing aluminium ions (Al^{3+}) and oxide ions (O^{2-}).

The diagram below shows the apparatus used to electrolyse aluminium oxide.

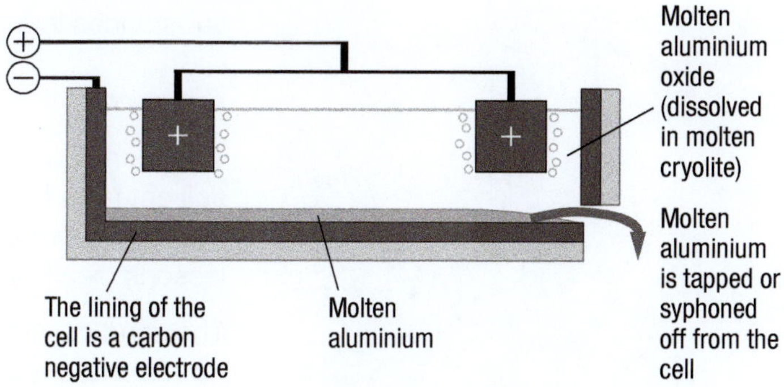

Use information in the diagram and your knowledge and understanding of this extraction to explain, as fully as you can, how aluminium and carbon dioxide are formed in this process. (6)

6.1 Separating mixtures

Learning objectives

After this topic, you should know:
- what a mixture is
- how to separate the components in a range of mixtures by:
  - filtration
  - distillation
  - crystallisation.

When analytical chemists are given an unknown sample to identify, it is often a mixture of different substances.

A mixture is made up of two or more elements or compounds which are not chemically combined together.

Mixtures are different to chemical compounds. Look at the table below:

Compounds	Mixtures
Compounds have a fixed composition (the ratio of elements present is always the same in any particular compound).	Mixtures have no fixed composition (the proportions vary depending on the amount of each substance mixed together).
Need chemical reactions to separate the elements in a compound.	The different elements or compounds in a mixture can be separated again more easily (by physical means using the differences in properties of each substance in the mixture).
There are chemical bonds between atoms of the different elements in the compound.	There are no chemical bonds between atoms of the different substances in a mixture.

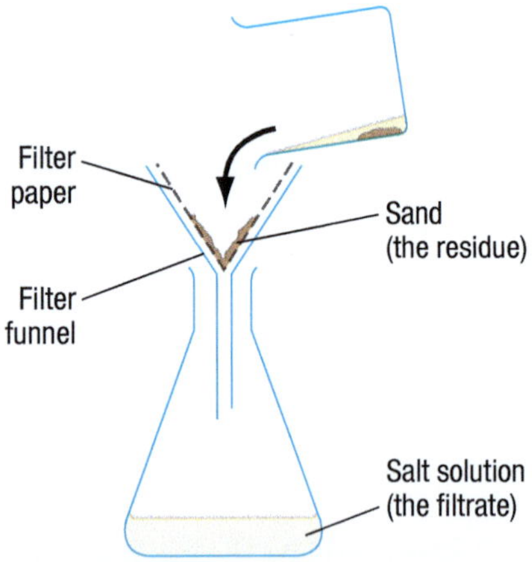

Figure 1 *Filtering a mixture of sand, salt, and water in the lab*

Before the substances in a mixture are identified, they are separated from each other. As it states in the table, scientists can use physical means to achieve the separation. The techniques available include:
- filtration
- crystallisation
- distillation
- chromatography (see Topic 6.2).

These techniques all rely on differences in the physical properties of the substances in the mixture, such as solubilities or boiling points.

Filtration

This technique is used to separate substances that are insoluble in a particular solvent from those that are soluble. For example, you have probably previously tried to separate a mixture of sand and salt (sodium chloride) in science lessons (see Figure 1).

The sand collected on the filter paper can be washed with distilled water (to remove any salt left in solution on it) and dried in a warm oven to obtain the pure sand.

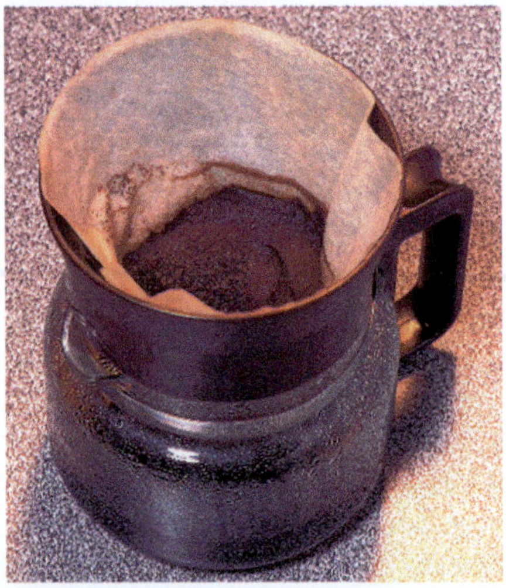

Figure 2 *Filtering in the home – some people like filter coffee made from ground-up coffee beans. The solid bits that are insoluble in water get left on filter paper as a residue.*

Crystallisation

To obtain a sample of pure salt from the sand/salt mixture, following filtration, you would need to get the sodium chloride from the solution in water (called the filtrate). The water is evaporated from the sodium chloride solution by heating in an evaporating dish on a water bath. The water bath is a gentler way of heating than heating the evaporating dish directly on a tripod and gauze.

Heating should be stopped when the solution is at the point of crystallisation, that is, when small crystals first appear around the edge of the solution or when crystals appear in a drop of solution extracted from the dish with a glass rod. Look at Figure 3. The rest of the water is then left to evaporate off the saturated solution at room temperature to get a good sample of crystals. A flat-bottomed crystallisation dish or Petri dish can be used for this final step to give a large surface area for the water to evaporate from.

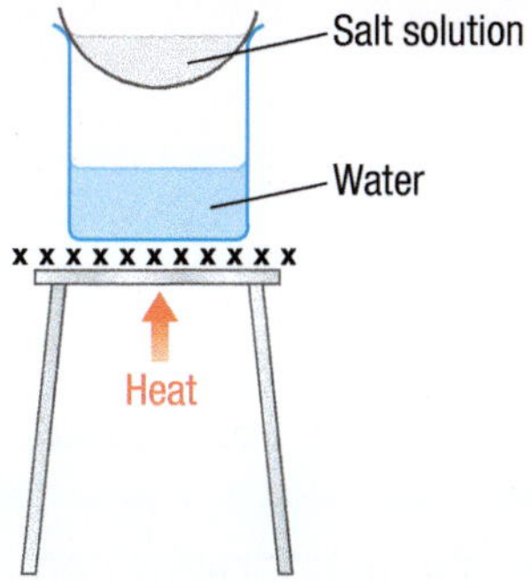

Figure 3 *Crystallising sodium chloride from its solution in water*

links

To see crystallisation in action, see 7.2 Making soluble salts from metals or insoluble bases and 7.3 Making salts by neutralisation or precipitation.

Distillation

Crystallisation separates a soluble solid from a solvent but sometimes people need to collect the solvent itself instead of just letting it evaporate off into the air. For example, some countries with a lack of freshwater sources purify seawater to obtain usable water. Distillation allows us to do this.

In distillation a solution is heated and boiled to evaporate the solvent. The vapour given off is then cooled and condensed back into a liquid for collection (see Figure 4). The dissolved solids remain in the heated flask.

Distillation can also be used to separate mixtures of miscible liquids, such as ethanol and water. Miscible refers to liquids that dissolve in each other – they do not form separate layers as in immiscible liquids. The liquids will have different boiling points, so this property can be used to distil off and collect the liquid with the lowest boiling point first.

However, it is difficult to get pure liquids from mixtures of liquids by simple distillation, as vapour is given off from liquids before they actually reach their boiling point. This is especially the case where the liquids in the mixture have similar boiling points. So to aid separation you can add a fractionating column to the apparatus in Figure 4. This is usually a tall glass column filled with glass beads, fitted vertically on top of the flask being heated. The vapours must pass over and between the glass beads before they reach the condenser. The substance with the higher boiling point will condense more readily on the glass beads and drop back down into the flask beneath.

Simple distillation

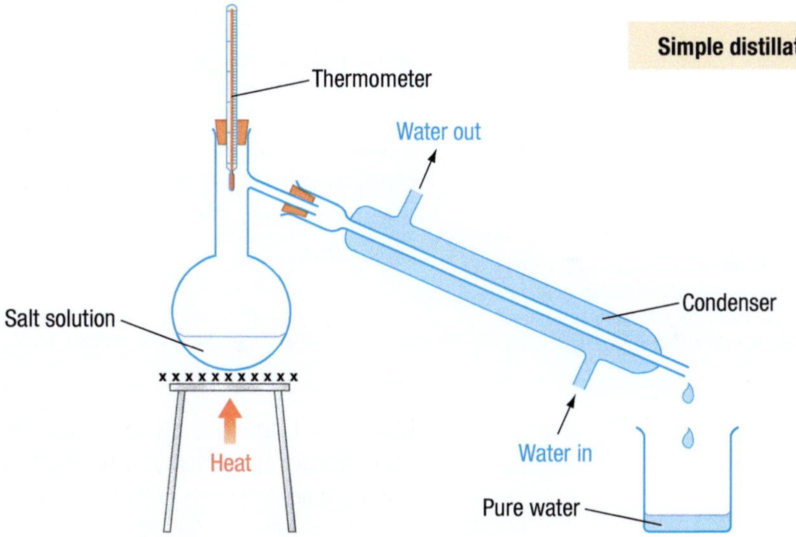

Figure 4 *Distilling pure water from a salt solution*

Summary questions

1 Define what a mixture is.

2 A mixture has 'no fixed composition'. What does this mean?

3 a Draw the apparatus you could use to separate ethanol and water.
b Explain why you would be able to collect a more pure sample of ethanol using this apparatus than by using simple distillation.

4 Sulfur is soluble in the flammable liquid xylene but not in water. Sodium nitrate is soluble in water but not in xylene.
Describe **two** ways to separate a mixture of sulfur powder and sodium nitrate to collect pure samples of each solid.

Key points

- A mixture is made up of two or more elements or compounds which are not chemically combined together.
- Mixtures can be separated by physical means, such as filtration, crystallisation, and distillation.

6.2 Paper chromatography

Learning objectives

After this topic, you should know:

- how chromatography can be used to distinguish pure substances from impure substances
- how to interpret chromatograms
- Ext how to determine R_f values from chromatograms.

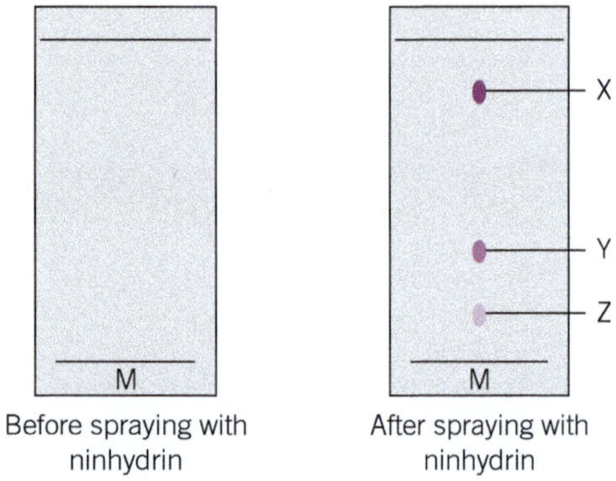

Figure 1 *A chromatogram produced by a mixture of amino acids. The spots are made by different amino acids forming coloured compounds with the locating agent (ninhydrin).*

Scientists have many instruments that they can use to identify unknown compounds. Many of these are more sensitive, automated versions of the techniques, such as paper chromatography, that you use in school labs. For example, **chromatography** can be used to separate and identify mixtures of amino acids. The amino acids are colourless, but appear as purple spots on the paper when sprayed with a locating agent and dried, as shown in Figure 1.

You will have tried paper chromatography before, and probably used it to separate dyes in inks or food colourings (see Figure 2).

Chromatography always involves a mobile phase and a stationary phase. The mobile phase moves through the stationary phase, carrying with it the components of the mixture under investigation. Each component in the mixture will have a different attraction for the mobile phase and the stationary phase. A substance with stronger forces of attraction between itself and the mobile phase, than between itself and the stationary phase, will be carried a greater distance in a given time. A substance with a stronger force of attraction to the stationary phase will not travel as far in the same time.

So in paper chromatography the mobile phase is the solvent chosen, and the stationary phase is the paper. In Figure 1, amino acid X from the mixture M has the strongest attraction to the solvent, and amino acid Z has the strongest attraction to the paper.

Given an unknown organic solution, chromatography can usually tell you if it is a single compound or a mixture. If the unknown sample is a mixture of compounds, there will probably be more than one spot formed on the chromatogram. On the other hand, a single spot indicates the possibility of a pure substance.

Identifying unknown substances using chromatography

Once the compounds in a mixture have been separated using chromatography, they can be identified. You can compare spots on the chromatogram with others obtained from known substances:

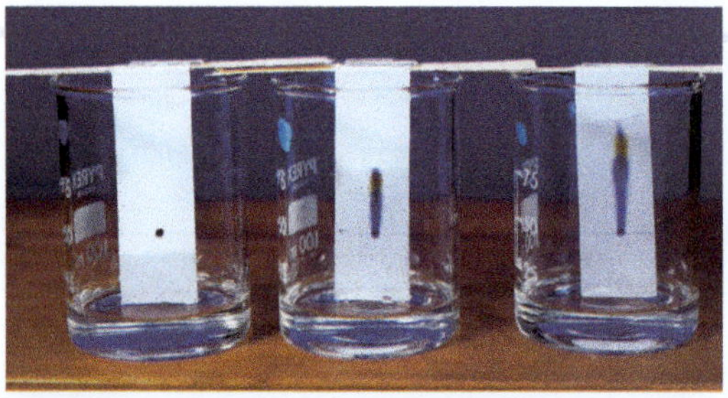

Figure 2 *Black ink can be separated out into its different colours on a chromatogram*

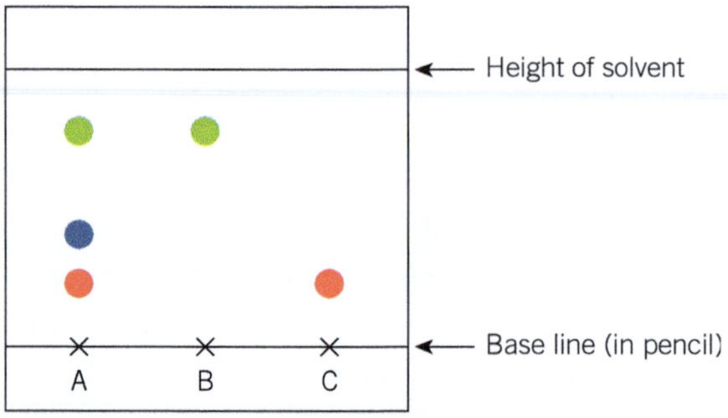

Figure 3 *This chromatogram shows that A is a mixture of three substances, B and C plus one other unknown substance*

Following the chromatography in Figure 3, mixture A still has one substance left unknown. A scientist making the chromatogram often does not know which pure compounds to include in their experiment to make a positive identification. It is also not practical to store actual chromatograms or their images, even on a computer. To make valid comparisons, every variable that affects a chromatogram would need to be exactly the same in all the chromatograms.

It is far more effective to measure data taken from any chromatogram of the unknown sample, then match it against a database. So the data is presented as an **R_f (retention factor)** value. This is a numeric value between 0 and 1, calculated by dividing the distance a spot travels up the paper (measured to the centre of the spot) by the distance the solvent front travels:

$$R_f = \frac{\text{distance moved by substance}}{\text{distance moved by solvent}}$$

As the number generated in the calculation is a ratio, it does not matter how long you run your chromatography experiment or what quantities you use. For comparisons against an R_f database to be valid, you just have to ensure that the solvent and the temperature used are the same as those quoted in the database or databook. Look at Figure 4 to see how to get the measurements to calculate R_f values.

Practical

Finding R_f values

Using a capillary tube, pencil, pipette, water, boiling tube, and a narrow strip of chromatography paper, find out the R_f values of the different dyes in the mixture of food colourings provided.

Present your evidence clearly. Include your dried chromatogram, calculations, and an evaluation.

Summary questions

1 Describe in detail how you can positively identify the dyes mixed to make a food colouring from its chromatogram.

2 What is the R_f value of this substance X?

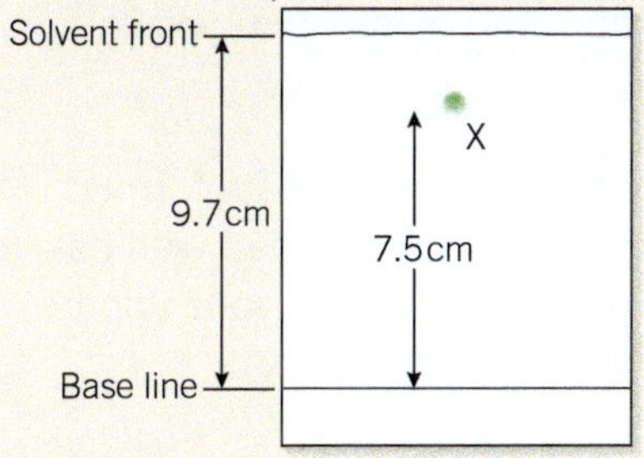

3 The R_f values of two substances, Y and Z, were taken from a chromatogram run in 50% water and 50% ethanol solvent at 20 °C. The R_f value of Y was 0.54 and of Z was 0.79.

What can you deduce about Y and Z from these values, and how could you use them to identify Y and Z?

4 In order to positively identify a compound from a chromatogram, explain why the solvent and temperature must be the same as those used to generate the R_f values in a database.

Worked example

Find the R_f value of compounds A and B using the chromatogram below.

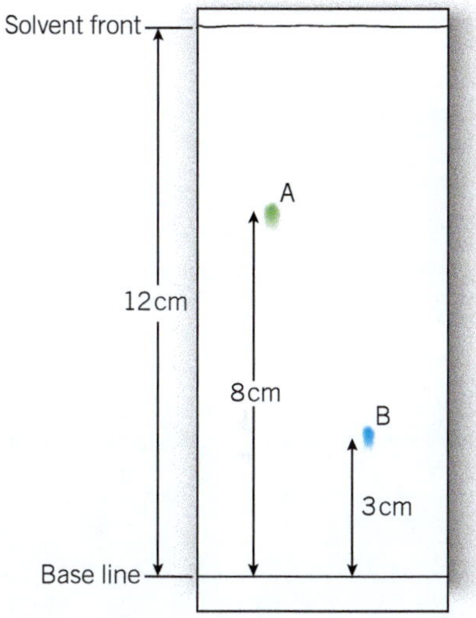

Figure 4 *The R_f value of an unknown substance, in a particular solvent at a given temperature, can be compared with values in a database to identify the substance*

Solution

The R_f value of A $= \frac{8}{12} = 0.67$ (2 s.f.)

The R_f value of B $= \frac{3}{12} = 0.25$

Key points

- **Scientists can analyse unknown substances in solution by using paper chromatography.**
- **R_f values can be measured and matched against databases to identify specific substances.**
- $R_f = \frac{\text{distance moved by substance}}{\text{distance moved by solvent}}$

6.3 Tests for positive ions

Learning objectives

After this topic, you should know:

- how to identify different positive ions by:
  - flame tests
  - precipitation reactions.

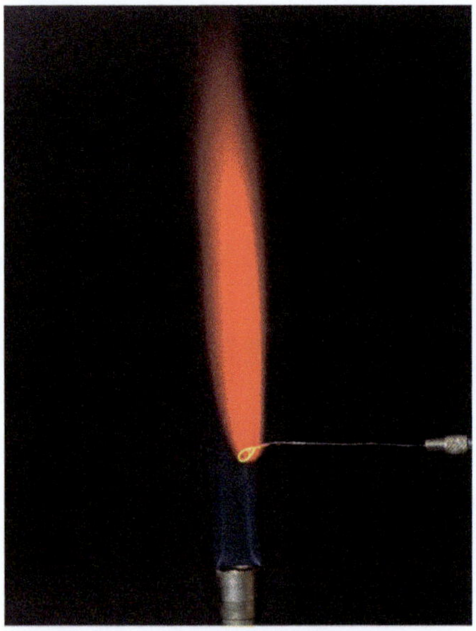

Figure 1 *A flame test can identify most Group 1 or Group 2 metals in a compound*

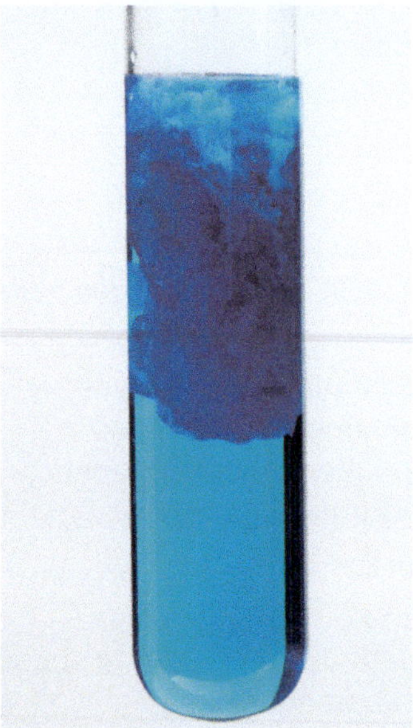

Figure 2 *This distinctive precipitate that forms when you add sodium hydroxide solution tells us that Cu^{2+} ions are present*

Scientists working in environmental monitoring, industry, medicine, and forensic science need to analyse and identify substances. To identify unknown substances, there are a variety of different chemical tests.

Flame tests

Some metal ions produce flames with a characteristic colour. To carry out a flame test you do the following:

- Put a small amount of the compound to be tested in a nichrome wire loop. (The wire loop should be dipped in concentrated hydrochloric acid and heated to clean it first. Then it should be dipped in the acid again before dipping in the metal compound.)
- Then hold the loop in the roaring blue flame of a Bunsen burner.
- Use the colour of the Bunsen flame to identify the metal ion in the compound.

Metal ion	Flame colour
Lithium (Li^+)	crimson
Sodium (Na^+)	yellow
Potassium (K^+)	lilac
Calcium (Ca^{2+})	red
Barium (Ba^{2+})	green

Reactions with sodium hydroxide

The reactions with sodium hydroxide solution can also help us identify some positive ions. Aluminium ions, calcium ions, and magnesium ions all form *white precipitates* with sodium hydroxide solution. So, if a white precipitate forms you know an unknown compound contains either Al^{3+}, Ca^{2+}, or Mg^{2+} ions.

For example, the ionic equation for the reaction with aluminium ions is:

$$Al^{3+}(aq) + 3OH^-(aq) \rightarrow Al(OH)_3(s)$$

If you add more and more sodium hydroxide then the precipitate formed with aluminium ions dissolves. However, the white precipitate formed with calcium or magnesium ions will not dissolve. Calcium and magnesium ions can be distinguished by a flame test. Calcium ions give a brick-red flame but magnesium ions produce no colour at all.

Some metal ions form *coloured precipitates* with sodium hydroxide.

If you add sodium hydroxide solution to a substance containing:

- copper(II) ions, a blue precipitate is formed
- iron(II) ions, a green precipitate is formed
- iron(III) ions, a brown precipitate is formed.

For example, adding sodium hydroxide solution to iron(II) ions gives the ionic equation:

$$Fe^{2+}(aq) + 2OH^-(aq) \rightarrow Fe(OH)_2(s)$$

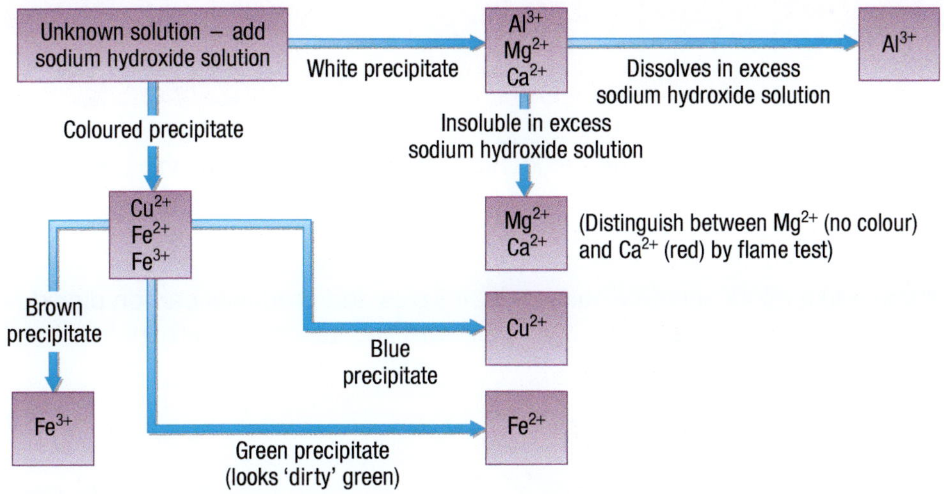

Figure 3 *Sodium hydroxide solution provides a very useful test for many positive ions*

Required practical

Identifying positive ions

Try to identify the metal ions in some unknown compounds provided for you.

Safety: Wear chemical splashproof eye protection.

Summary questions

1 a What colour precipitate does dilute sodium hydroxide produce with aluminium, calcium, and magnesium ions?
b How can you distinguish between these three metal ions?
c Write an ionic equation, including state symbols, for the precipitation of magnesium ions from solution by aqueous hydroxide ions.

2 a Draw a flow chart to describe how to carry out a flame test.
b If the flame test was carried out on barium chloride, describe what you would see.

3 Copy the table below and complete the missing cells **a** to **j**:

Add sodium hydroxide solution	Flame test	Metal ion
nothing observed	lilac	**f**
white precipitate	red	**g**
a	**d**	Fe^{3+}
white precipitate which dissolves in excess sodium hydroxide solution	nothing observed	**h**
green precipitate which slowly turns reddish-brown	nothing observed	**i**
b	**e**	Na^{+}
c	crimson	**j**

Key points

- Most Group 1 and Group 2 metal ions can be identified in their compounds using flame tests.
- Sodium hydroxide solution can be used to identify different metal ions, depending on the precipitate that is formed.

6.4 Tests for negative ions

Learning objectives

After this topic, you should know:

- how to identify different negative ions, in particular:
  - carbonates
  - halides
  - sulfates.

You can also do chemical tests to identify some negative ions in ionic compounds.

Carbonates

If you add a dilute acid to a carbonate, it fizzes and produces carbon dioxide gas. This is a good test to see if an unknown substance is a carbonate.

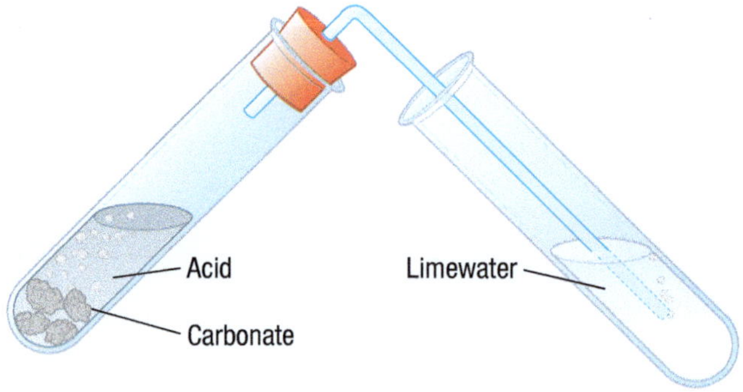

Figure 1 *The test for a carbonate*

links
For more information on carbonates, look back to 4.8 Metal carbonates.

If the carbonate is sodium carbonate, the reaction you get is:

$$Na_2CO_3(s) + 2HCl(aq) \rightarrow 2NaCl(aq) + H_2O(l) + CO_2(g)$$

You can represent the reaction by just showing the ions that change in the reaction in an ionic equation:

$$\underset{\text{acid}}{2H^+(aq)} + \underset{\text{carbonate ion}}{CO_3^{2-}(s)} \rightarrow CO_2(g) + H_2O(l)$$

In limewater, the carbon dioxide reacts with calcium hydroxide. It forms a white precipitate of calcium carbonate which turns the limewater cloudy white.

Halide ions (chlorides, bromides, and iodides)

A very simple test shows whether chloride, bromide, or iodide ions are present in a compound. First you add dilute nitric acid, and then add silver nitrate solution. If a precipitate forms, there are halide ions present.

(You add the nitric acid to dissolve the compound and to remove any carbonate ions as they would also form a precipitate with the silver ions, and so interfere with the test.)

Study tip

In the test for a halide ion: add dilute **nitric** acid before the silver **nitrate**. Do not add any other acid as they will produce precipitates with silver nitrate solution.

The colour of the precipitate tells us which halide ion is present:

- Chloride ions (Cl^-) give a white precipitate of silver chloride.
- Bromide ions (Br^-) give a cream precipitate of silver bromide.
- Iodide ions (I^-) give a yellow precipitate of silver iodide.

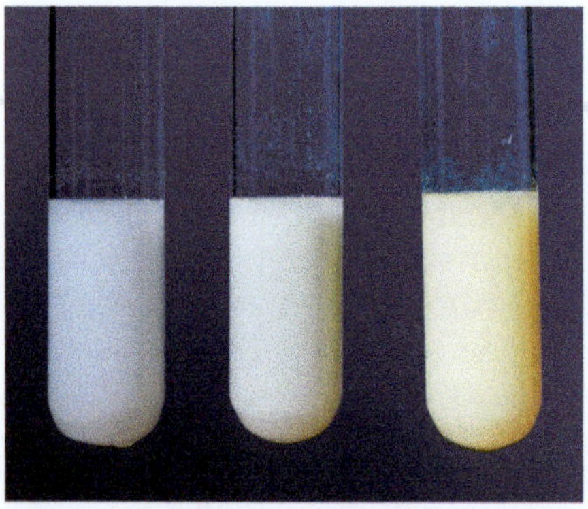

Figure 2 *One simple test with silver nitrate solution can tell us if an unknown substance contains chloride, bromide, or iodide ions*

If the unknown halide was sodium chloride, the precipitation reaction would be:

$$NaCl(aq) + AgNO_3(aq) \rightarrow NaNO_3(aq) + AgCl(s)$$

Here is the ionic equation, where X^- is the halide ion:

$$Ag^+(aq) + X^-(aq) \rightarrow AgX(s)$$

Did you know ... ?

Silver compounds are sensitive to light. If a silver halide precipitate is left for a few minutes in bright sunlight it slowly darkens as silver metal is formed.

Sulfates

You can test for sulfate ions by adding dilute hydrochloric acid, followed by barium chloride solution. (Add the dilute hydrochloric acid first to remove carbonate ions that would form a precipitate with the barium ions.) A white precipitate tells us sulfate ions are present. The white precipitate is the insoluble salt barium sulfate, $BaSO_4$.

If the unknown compound was potassium sulfate, then the equation for the precipitation reaction would be:

$$K_2SO_4(aq) + BaCl_2(aq) \rightarrow 2KCl(aq) + BaSO_4(s)$$

Here is the ionic equation for this reaction:

$$Ba^{2+}(aq) + SO_4^{2-}(aq) \rightarrow BaSO_4(s)$$

Practical

Identifying unknown ionic compounds

Now you know the tests for some positive and negative ions, you can try to identify some unknown compounds.

Safety: Wear chemical splashproof eye protection.

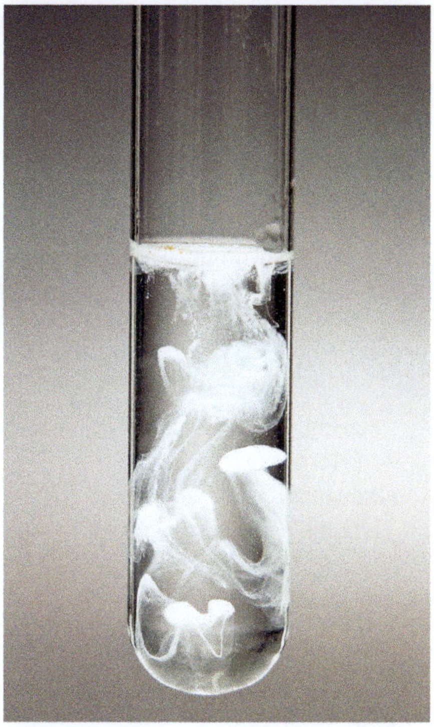

Figure 3 *The white precipitate of barium sulfate forming*

Study tip

In the test for the sulfate ion: add **hydrochloric** acid before the barium **chloride**. Do not add sulfuric acid – it contains sulfate ions!

Summary questions

1. List the reagents you would need to assemble in a lab to test a sample of an unknown substance for carbonate, halide, and sulfate ions.
2. An unknown compound is a white solid which dissolves in water to produce a colourless solution. When this solution is acidified with nitric acid and then silver nitrate is added, a yellow precipitate is produced. A flame test on the unknown compound produces a lilac flame. Deduce the name of the unknown compound and give your reasoning.
3. Write a word equation and a balanced symbol equation, including state symbols, for the following reactions:
   a magnesium chloride solution + silver nitrate solution
   b potassium carbonate powder + hydrochloric acid
   c aluminium sulfate solution + barium chloride solution
4. Write ionic equations, including state symbols, to summarise the reactions that help identify:
   a bromide ions
   b sulfate ions
   c carbonate ions.
5. In the test for halide ions, explain why nitric acid (rather than other acids) is added to a sample before you add silver nitrate solution.

Key points

- You identify carbonates by adding dilute acid, which produces carbon dioxide gas. The gas turns limewater cloudy.
- You identify halides by adding nitric acid, then silver nitrate solution. This produces a precipitate of silver halide (chloride = white, bromide = cream, iodide = yellow).
- You identify sulfates by adding hydrochloric acid, then barium chloride solution. This produces a white precipitate of barium sulfate.

Chapter summary questions

1 What would be entered in **a** to **f** to complete the table?

Add dilute acid	Add sodium hydroxide solution	Add dilute nitric acid followed by silver nitrate solution	Flame test	Substance
Nothing observed	Nothing observed	Yellow precipitate	Yellow	**e**
Fizzing – gas turns limewater cloudy	Pale blue precipitate formed	Not needed	Nothing observed	**f**
a	**b**	**c**	**d**	Calcium chloride

2 An unknown compound gave the following positive tests when analysed:

- The Bunsen flame turned crimson in a flame test.
- When dissolved in dilute hydrochloric acid and barium chloride solution was added, a white precipitate was formed.

Name the unknown compound.

3 The label on a jar of white crystals has been damaged by water and cannot be read. A science technician thinks it is probably a jar of potassium bromide.

a Describe how the technician could positively identify the crystals as potassium bromide.

b Give the formula of potassium bromide.

c What type of bonding will be found in potassium bromide?

4 a What are the differences between a mixture and a compound?

b Name the technique you would use to separate and collect:

i hydrated copper(II) sulfate, $CuSO_4{\cdot}5H_2O$, from its aqueous solution

ii a precipitate of lead iodide from the solution formed when aqueous solutions of lead nitrate and sodium iodide are mixed

iii water from a solution of potassium chloride

iv ethanol from a mixture of water and ethanol.

c Write a balanced symbol equation, including state symbols, for the reaction in part **b ii** above.

5 a Draw a table to record the flame colours for:

i sodium,

ii potassium,

iii calcium,

iv barium.

b i What do you see when you add sodium hydroxide solution to both calcium chloride and magnesium chloride?

ii Write a balanced symbol equation for each reaction.

iii What do we call this type of reaction?

iv Write an ionic equation, including state symbols, to describe each reaction.

v How could you carry out a test to distinguish between calcium and magnesium in the chlorides tested?

Ext

6 a You can use paper chromatography to identify solutes using R_f values from a database. Look at the chromatogram below and calculate the R_f value of the unknown substances X and Y.

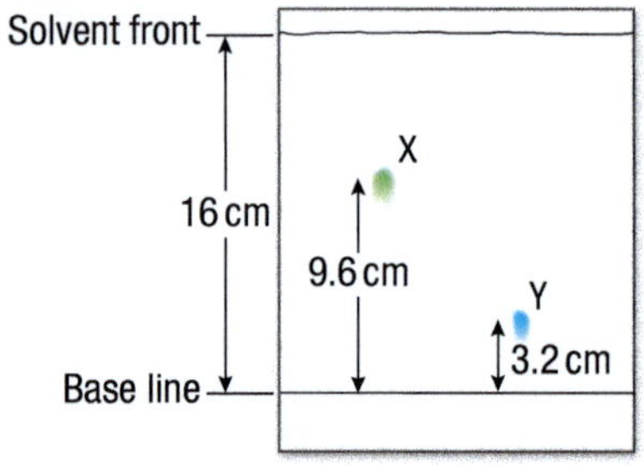

b The solvent used to obtain the chromatogram above was ethanol.

Explain the different R_f values of substance X and substance Y.

c In a database, apart from the solvent used, what other variable is quoted to ensure that R_f values are standardised?

Practice questions

1 Potash alum is a compound with the formula $KAl(SO_4)_2$

A student dissolved some potash alum in water and did some tests on the solution.

a Some of the solution was sprayed into a bunsen flame.

i State the colour of the flame. (1)

ii Write the formula of the ion responsible for this colour. (1)

b The student added a small amount of some sodium hydroxide solution to some potash alum solution.

i State the observation that could be made. (1)

ii Write the name of the compound responsible for this observation. (1)

c Another student added some sodium hydroxide solution to some potash alum solution and recorded his observation as a colourless solution.

Explain why he did not make the same observation as the student in part **b**. (2)

d Describe how the student should do a test to show that the potash alum contains sulfate ions. (3)

2 A solution contains dissolved sodium carbonate, iron(II) chloride, and iron(III) chloride.

a After some dilute nitric acid is added, bubbles are seen.

i Name the gas that forms. (1)

ii Describe how you could test for this gas. (2)

b Next, some silver nitrate solution is added. A white precipitate forms.

i Name the white precipitate. (1)

ii Write the simplest ionic equation for the formation of the white precipitate. (2)

c A student adds some sodium hydroxide solution to test for positive ions.

Why will this test not clearly identify the three positive ions in the solution? (3)

3 Many methods of separation depend on a property that is different for each substance in a mixture.

For each of the mixtures in this question, suggest a suitable method of obtaining the first substance from the mixture and state the property that the method depends on.

a Water from a mixture with sodium chloride (2)

b Calcium carbonate from a mixture with sodium chloride solution (2)

c Blue ink from a mixture with red ink (2)

4 A scientist used chromatography to identify the artificial colours in a flavoured drink.

The result of the experiment is shown in the diagram.

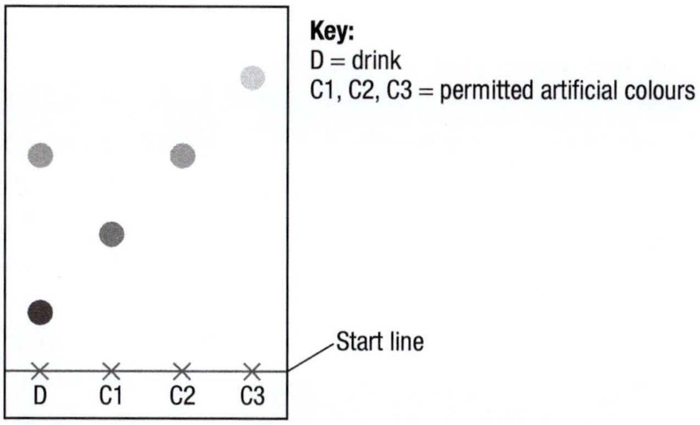

Describe how to do the experiment that gave this result. (6)

5 A student carried out a paper chromatography experiment on a mixture of the food colourings used to coat a chocolate-centred sweet

a What would the student use to mark the baseline on the chromatogram? (1)

b Suggest how the student could effectively spot the mixture on the baseline before standing the paper in the solvent. (3)

c The student ran the experiment and found that when the solvent front had almost reached the top of the paper, the food colourings had hardly moved from the baseline so there was poor separation of the different colours. Suggest a way in which the student could try to improve the results on the chromatogram (1)

7.1 Acids and alkalis

Learning objectives

After this topic, you should know:

- why solutions are acidic or alkaline
- what bases and alkalis are
- how to measure acidity.

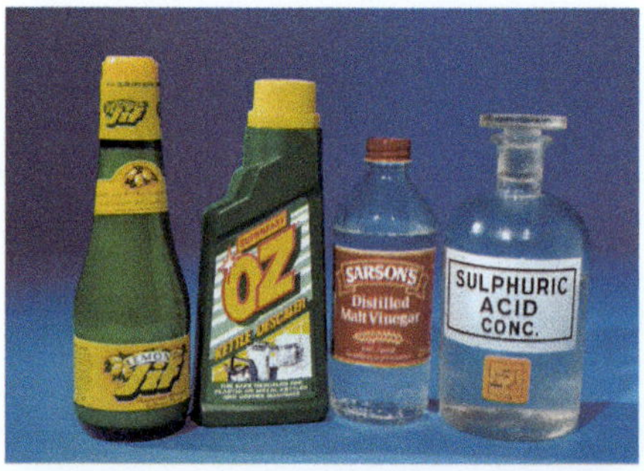

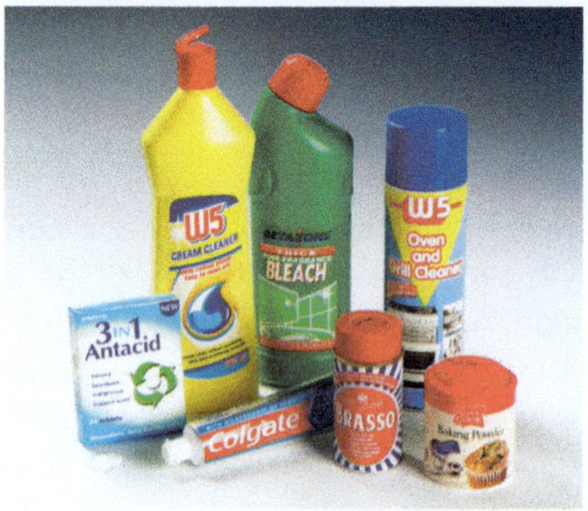

Figure 1 *Acids and bases are all around us, in many of the things you buy at the shops, in our schools and factories – and in our bodies too*

Acids and bases are an important part of our understanding of chemistry. They play an important part inside us and all other living things.

What are acids and bases?

When you dissolve a substance in water you make an aqueous solution. Whether the solution formed is acidic, alkaline, or neutral depends on which substance has been dissolved.

- Soluble hydroxides are called **alkalis**. Their solutions are alkaline. An example is sodium hydroxide solution.
- **Bases**, which include alkalis, are substances that can neutralise acids. Metal oxides and metal hydroxides are bases. Examples include iron oxide and copper hydroxide.
- **Acids** include citric acid, sulfuric acid, and ethanoic acid. All acids taste very sour, although many acids are far too dangerous to put in your mouth. Ethanoic acid (in vinegar) and citric acid (in citrus fruit and fizzy drinks) are acids that are edible.
- Pure water is **neutral**.

One acid used in science labs is hydrochloric acid. This is formed when the gas hydrogen chloride (HCl) dissolves in water:

$$HCl(g) \xrightarrow{\text{water}} H^+(aq) + Cl^-(aq)$$

All acids form H^+ ions when added to water. It is these $H^+(aq)$ ions that make a solution acidic.

Because alkalis are bases that dissolve in water and form solutions, they are the bases that are often used in experiments. Sodium hydroxide solution is often found in school labs. You get sodium hydroxide solution when you dissolve solid sodium hydroxide in water:

$$NaOH(s) \xrightarrow{\text{water}} Na^+(aq) + OH^-(aq)$$

All alkalis form hydroxide ions (OH^-) when added to water. It is these aqueous hydroxide ions, $OH^-(aq)$, that make a solution alkaline.

Measuring acidity or alkalinity

Indicators are substances which change colour when added to acids and alkalis. Litmus paper is a well-known indicator, but there are many more.

Scientists use the **pH scale** to show how acidic or alkaline a solution is. The scale runs from 0 (most acidic) to 14 (most alkaline). You can use universal indicator (UI) to find the pH of a solution. It is a special indicator made from a number of dyes. It turns a range of colours as the pH changes. Anything in the middle of the pH scale (pH 7) is neutral, that is, neither acidic nor alkaline.

You can use the mathematical symbols '>' (read as 'is greater than') and '<' ('is less than') when interpreting pH values.

You can say:

pH <7 indicates an acidic solution – that is, pH values less than 7 are acidic.

pH >7 indicates an alkaline solution – that is, pH values greater than 7 are alkaline.

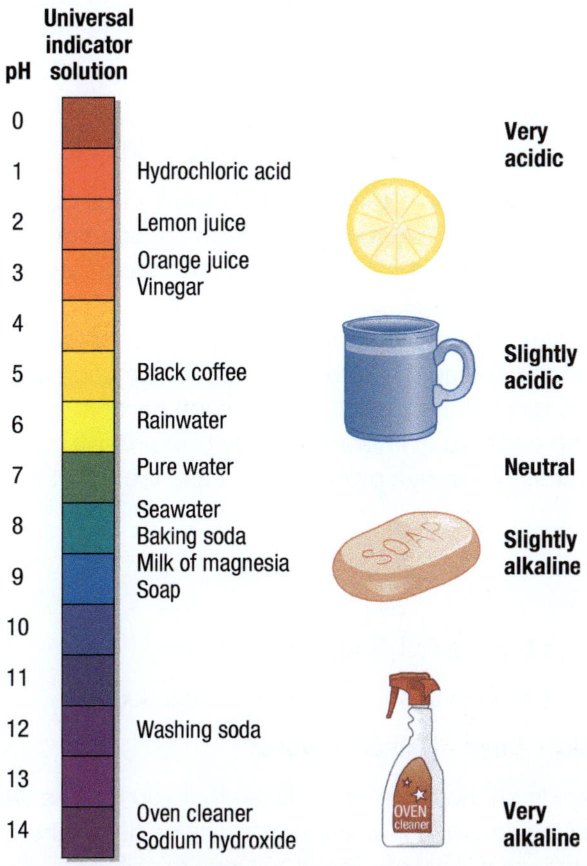

Figure 2 *The pH scale tells us how acidic or alkaline a solution is*

Practical

Which is the most alkaline cleaning product?

Compare the alkalinity of various cleaning products.

You can test washing-up liquids, shampoos, soaps, hand-washing liquids, washing powders/liquids, and dishwasher powders/tablets.

You could use a pH sensor and data logger to collect your data.

- What are the advantages of using a pH sensor instead of universal indicator solution or paper?

Safety: Wear chemical splash-proof eye protection and disposable gloves.

Summary questions

1 **a** What distinguishes alkalis from other bases?
b What do all alkalis have in common?
c Show the change that happens when potassium hydroxide (KOH) dissolves in water using an equation, including state symbols.

2 **a** What ions do all acids produce in aqueous solution?
b Show the change that happens when hydroiodic acid (HI) dissolves in water, including state symbols.

3 How could you use universal indicator paper as a way of distinguishing between distilled water, sodium hydroxide solution, and ethanoic acid solution?

4 Which would be the more accurate way of finding the pH of a solution, using universal indicator paper or a pH sensor and datalogger? Why?

Key points

- **Acids are substances which produce $H^+(aq)$ ions when added to water.**
- **Bases are substances that will neutralise acids.**
- **An alkali is a soluble hydroxide. Alkalis produce $OH^-(aq)$ ions when added to water.**
- **You can use the pH scale to show how acidic or alkaline a solution is.**

7.2 Making soluble salts from metals or insoluble bases

Learning objectives

After this topic, you should know:

- the products made when acids react with metals
- the products made when acids react with bases
- how to prepare crystals of salts from their solutions.

Acids + metals

A **salt** is a compound formed when the hydrogen in an acid is wholly or partially replaced by a metal or ammonium ions. One way to make salts is to react acids directly with metals. This is only possible if the metal is more reactive than hydrogen. If it is, then the metal will react with an acid to form a salt plus hydrogen gas:

acid	**+**	**metal**	$\rightarrow$	**a salt**	**+**	**hydrogen**
$2HCl(aq)$	+	$Mg(s)$	$\rightarrow$	$MgCl_2(aq)$	+	$H_2(g)$
hydrochloric acid	+	magnesium	$\rightarrow$	magnesium chloride	+	hydrogen

Note: If the metal is very reactive, the reaction with acid is too violent to carry out safely. So metals such as sodium or potassium are never added to acid.

Crystals of a salt (magnesium chloride in the equation above) can be obtained from the solution. Some of the water is evaporated off from the solution until the point of crystallisation. At this point, the solution becomes saturated and crystals will appear at the edge of a salt solution being heated in an evaporating dish. This point can also be tested by dipping a glass rod into the hot salt solution, removing it and seeing if crystals form on the solution left on the rod as it cools down. The salt solution should then be left at room temperature for the remaining water to evaporate off slowly in order to prepare the best samples of salt crystals. Wear eye protection in case the solution 'spits'.

Acid + insoluble base

When you react an acid with a base, a salt, and water is formed.

The general equation which describes this **neutralisation** reaction is:

acid + base → a salt + water

The salt that you make depends on the metal or the base that you use, as well as the acid. So bases that contain sodium ions will always make sodium salts. Those that contain potassium ions will always make potassium salts.

In terms of the acid used:

- the salts formed when neutralising hydrochloric acid (HCl) are always **chlorides** (containing Cl^- ions)
- sulfuric acid (H_2SO_4) makes salts which are **sulfates** (containing SO_4^{2-} ions)
- nitric acid (HNO_3) always makes **nitrates** (containing NO_3^- ions).

The oxide of a transition metal, such as iron(III) oxide, is an example of a base that can be used to make a salt in this way:

acid	+	base	$\rightarrow$	a salt	+	water
$6HCl(aq)$	**+**	**$Fe_2O_3(s)$**	$\rightarrow$	**$2FeCl_3(aq)$**	**+**	**$3H_2O(l)$**
hydrochloric acid	+	solid iron(III) oxide	$\rightarrow$	iron(III) chloride solution	+	water

links

For more information on neutralisation reactions, see 7.3 Making salts by neutralisation or precipitation.

Practical

Making a copper salt

You can make copper sulfate crystals from copper(II) oxide (an insoluble base) and sulfuric acid. The equation for the reaction is:

acid + base → a salt + water

$H_2SO_4(aq) + CuO(s) \rightarrow CuSO_4(aq) + H_2O(l)$

sulfuric acid + copper(II) oxide → copper(II) sulfate + water

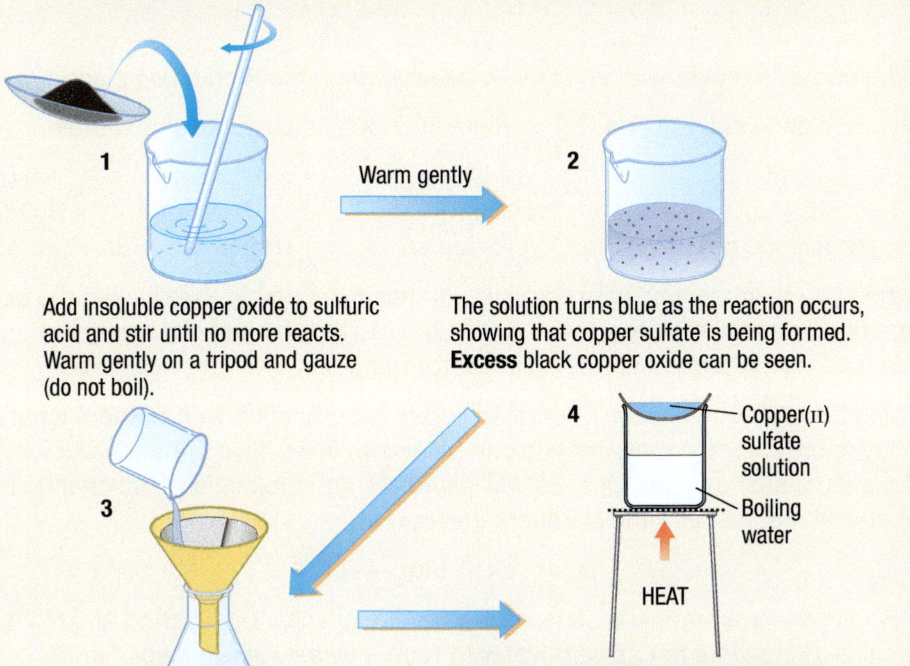

1 Add insoluble copper oxide to sulfuric acid and stir until no more reacts. Warm gently on a tripod and gauze (do not boil).

2 The solution turns blue as the reaction occurs, showing that copper sulfate is being formed. **Excess** black copper oxide can be seen.

3 When the reaction is complete, filter the solution to remove excess copper oxide

4 Evaporate the water so that crystals of copper sulfate start to form. Stop heating when you see the first crystals appear at the edge of the solution. Then leave for the rest of the water to evaporate off slowly. This will give you larger crystals.

■ What does the copper sulfate look like? Draw a diagram if necessary.

Safety: Wear eye protection. Chemicals in this practical are harmful.

Summary questions

1 Write the general word equation for the reaction between an acid and:
a a base **b** a metal.

2 Describe in detail how you could prepare a sample of copper sulfate crystals from its solution.

3 **a** Why can't copper sulfate be prepared by adding copper metal to dilute sulfuric acid?
b Why is potassium chloride never prepared by reacting potassium metal and dilute hydrochloric acid together?

4 Write balanced symbol equations, including state symbols, for the following reactions:
a magnesium + hydrochloric acid
b lithium oxide (in excess) + sulfuric acid

Key points

- A salt is a compound formed when the hydrogen in an acid is wholly or partially replaced by metal or ammonium ions.
- When you react an acid with a base a neutralisation reaction occurs.
- The reaction between an acid and a base produces a salt and water.
- Salts can also be made by reacting a suitable metal with an acid. This reaction produces hydrogen gas as well as a salt. A sample of the salt made can then be crystallised out of solution by evaporating off the water.

7.3 Making salts by neutralisation or precipitation

Learning objectives

After this topic, you should know:

- the ionic equation to describe neutralisation
- how to prepare salts from an acid and an alkali
- how to prepare insoluble salts.

There are two other important ways of making salts from solutions.

- You can react an acid and an alkali together to form a soluble salt.
- You can make an *insoluble* salt by reacting solutions of two soluble salts together.

Acid + alkali

When an acid reacts with an alkali, a neutralisation reaction takes place.

Hydrochloric acid reacting with sodium hydroxide solution is an example:

acid	+	alkali	→	a salt	+	water
HCl(aq)	**+**	**NaOH(aq)**	**→**	**NaCl(aq)**	**+**	**$H_2O(l)$**
hydrochloric acid	+	sodium hydroxide solution	→	sodium chloride	+	water

When you react an acid with an alkali you need to be able to tell when the acid and alkali have completely reacted. It is not obvious by just observing the reaction – so you need to use an indicator to help.

Think about neutralisation in terms of $H^+(aq)$ ions reacting with $OH^-(aq)$ ions. They react to form water and this can be shown in an ionic equation. An ionic equation just shows the ions, as well as atoms and molecules, that change in a chemical reaction and the products they form:

$$H^+(aq) + OH^-(aq) \rightarrow H_2O(l)$$

You can make ammonium salts, as well as metal salts, by reacting an acid with an alkali. Ammonia reacts with water to form a weakly alkaline solution:

$$NH_3(aq) + H_2O(l) \rightleftharpoons NH_4^+(aq) + OH^-(aq)$$

Ammonia solution reacts with an acid (e.g., nitric acid):

acid	+	ammonia solution	→	an ammonium salt	+	water
$HNO_3(aq)$	**+**	**$NH_4^+(aq) + OH^-(aq)$**	**→**	**$NH_4NO_3(aq)$**	**+**	**$H_2O(l)$**
nitric acid	+	ammonia solution	→	ammonium nitrate	+	water

Ammonium nitrate contains a high proportion of nitrogen, and it is very soluble in water. This makes it ideal as a source of nitrogen for plants to take up through their roots. It replaces the nitrogen taken up from the soil by plants as they grow (see Figure 1).

Ammonium salts are made by adding ammonia solution to an acid until there is a small excess of ammonia. You can detect the excess ammonia by using universal indicator paper which will turn blue. You then crystallise the ammonium salt from its solution. The excess ammonia evaporates off.

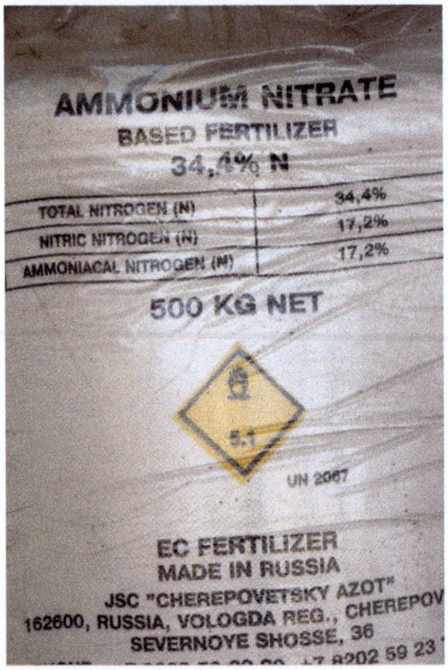

Figure 1 *Ammonium nitrate (NH_4NO_3) made from ammonia and nitric acid is used as a fertiliser*

Making insoluble salts

Scientists can sometimes make salts by combining two solutions that contain different soluble salts. When the soluble salts react to make an insoluble salt, we call the reaction a precipitation reaction. This is because the insoluble solid formed in the reaction mixture is called a **precipitate**.

$Pb(NO_3)_2(aq)$	**+**	**2KI(aq)**	**→**	**$PbI_2(s)$**	**+**	**$2KNO_3(aq)$**
lead nitrate solution	+	potassium iodide solution	→	lead iodide precipitate	+	potassium nitrate solution

Each of the reactant solutions contains one of the ions that make up the insoluble salt. In this case, they are lead ions in lead nitrate and iodide ions in potassium iodide. Lead iodide forms a yellow precipitate that you can filter off from the solution.

Practical

Making an insoluble salt

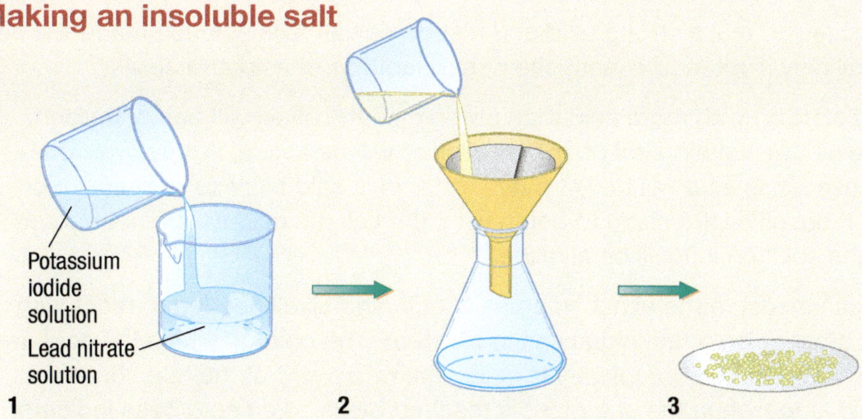

Make the salt lead iodide from lead nitrate solution and potassium iodide solution. The equation for the reaction is shown at the bottom of the previous page.

- Why is the precipitate of lead iodide washed with distilled water?

Safety: Wear chemical splashproof eye protection. Lead compounds are toxic.

Summary questions

1 **a** Write down a general equation for the neutralisation reaction between an acid and an alkali.
b Write an ionic equation to show what happens in this neutralisation reaction.

2 **a** Name the salt made when ammonia solution neutralises dilute nitric acid.
b Why is this salt important?
c Write a balanced symbol equation for the reaction to make this salt.

3 Write a balanced symbol equation, including state symbols, and a method to show how to make lithium chloride (a soluble salt – look ahead to Topic 8.6 for help if necessary).

4 Lead chloride, $PbCl_2$, is an insoluble salt.
a Suggest a method to prepare a sample of lead chloride. (Hint: all nitrates are soluble in water.)
b Write a balanced symbol equation, including state symbols, for the reaction used in part **a**.
c What type of bonding will be present in the lead chloride?

5 A chemical factory produces aqueous chromium(III) ions as a by-product. Suggest how the chemical company can remove the chromium ions from the wastewater before it is discharged from the factory.

Using precipitation

Precipitation reactions are used to remove pollutants from the wastewater produced by factories. The effluent must be treated before it is discharged into rivers and the sea.

Precipitation is used in the removal of metal ions from industrial wastewater. By raising the pH of the water, engineers can make insoluble metal hydroxides precipitate out. This produces a sludge which can easily be removed from the solution.

The cleaned-up water can then be discharged safely into a river or the sea.

Precipitation can be also used to remove unwanted ions from drinking water.

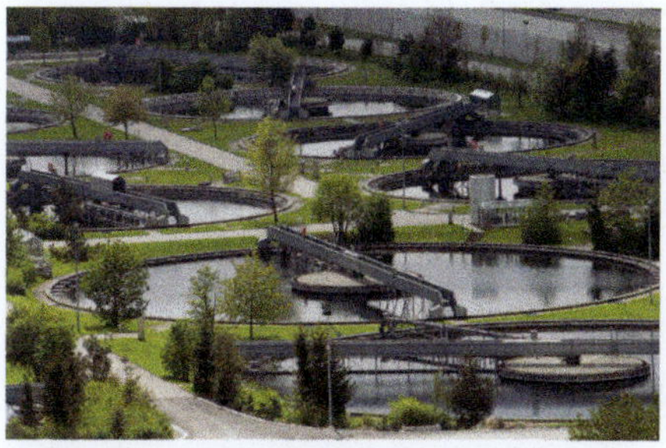

Figure 2 *Water treatment plants use chemical treatments, such as adding lime, to precipitate out metal compounds which can then be removed by filtering*

Key points

- An indicator is needed when a soluble salt is prepared by reacting an alkali with an acid.
- Insoluble salts can be made by reacting two solutions to produce a precipitate.
- Precipitation is an important way of removing some metal ions from industrial wastewater.

7.4 Titrations

Learning objectives

After this topic, you should know:

- how to measure accurately the amount of acid and alkali that react together completely
- how to determine when the reaction is complete.

links

For information about strong and weak acids see 12.3 Carboxylic acids.

links

For more information on neutralisation reactions, look back at 7.2 Making soluble salts from metals or insoluble bases and 7.3 Making salts by neutralisation or precipitation.

Study tip

Use a pipette to measure out a fixed volume of solution.

Use a burette to measure the volume of the solution added.

An acid and an alkali (a soluble base) react together and neutralise each other. They form a salt (plus water) in the process.

Suppose you mix a strong acid and a strong alkali. The solution made will be neutral only if you add exactly the right quantities of acid and alkali.

If you start off with more acid than alkali, then the alkali will be neutralised. However, the solution left after the reaction will be acidic, not neutral. This is because some acid will be left over. The acid is said to be ***in excess***. If you have more alkali than acid to begin with, then all the acid will be neutralised and the solution left will be alkaline.

You can measure the exact volumes of acid and alkali needed to react with each other using a technique called **titration**. The point at which the acid and alkali have reacted completely is called the **end point** of the reaction. You should judge when the end point is reached by using an acid/base indicator.

Required practical

Carrying out a titration

In this experiment you can carry out a titration. You will find out how much acid is needed to completely react with an alkali.

1 Measure a known volume of alkali into a conical flask using a volumetric **pipette**. Before doing this, you should first wash the pipette with distilled water, and then with some of the alkali.

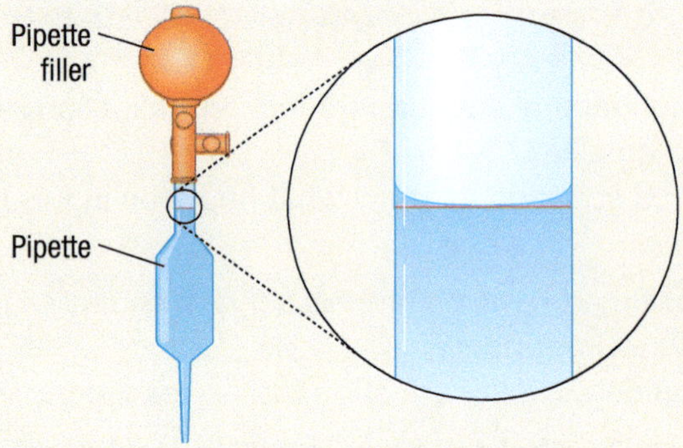

Figure 1 *A volumetric pipette and pipette filler. Fill the pipette until the bottom of the meniscus (curved surface of the solution) coincides with the mark. Allow the liquid to run out of the pipette and touch the tip on the side of the flask to drain out the solution. It is normal for a tiny amount of solution to remain in the pipette.*

2 Now add a few drops of acid/base indicator to the solution in the flask and swirl. Commonly used examples are methyl orange or phenolphthalein.

3 Pour the acid you are going to use into a **burette**. This is a long tube with a tap on one end. The tube has markings on it to enable you to measure volumes accurately (often to the nearest 0.05 cm^3). Before doing this, you should first wash the burette with distilled water, and then with some of the acid.

4 Record the reading on the burette. Then open the tap to release a small amount of acid into the flask. Swirl the flask to make sure that the two solutions are mixed.

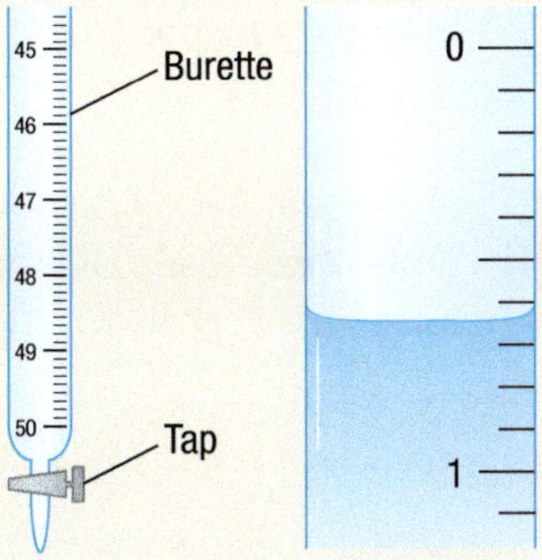

Figure 2 *A burette – use the bottom of the meniscus to read the scale. The reading here is 0.65 cm³.*

5 Keep on repeating step 4 until the indicator in the flask changes colour. This shows when the alkali in the flask has completely reacted with the acid added from the burette. Record the reading on the burette and work out the volume of acid run into the flask. (On your first go at doing this you will probably run too much acid into the flask, so treat this as a rough estimate of how much acid is needed.)

6 Repeat the whole process at least three times. Discard any anomalous results. Then calculate an average (mean) value to give the most accurate results possible. Alternatively, repeat the titration until you get two consecutive identical results. These are called concordant results. In practice, aim for two results within 0.10 cm^3 of each other and take their average.

Safety: Wear eye protection. Chemicals in this practical may be harmful or irritant.

Summary questions

1 What word do scientists use for a set of repeat readings with a very narrow range? (Hint: see pages 156–157 in the 'Experimental data handling' section.)

2 a What word is used for the curved surface of a liquid in a measuring cylinder?
  b i Name two measuring instruments used to measure volumes of liquid in a titration.
    ii What is the correct way to read the volume from the level of liquid in one of these measuring instruments.

3 a Describe how to carry out a titration between dilute nitric acid of known concentration and sodium hydroxide solution of unknown concentration.
  b Write a balanced symbol equation, including state symbols, for the reaction in part **a**.

4 a Name two acid/base indicators that can be used in the titration between dilute hydrochloric acid and sodium hydroxide solution.
  b Explain what makes a good indicator for a titration between an acid and an alkali.

Key points

- **Titration is used to measure accurately how much acid and alkali react together completely.**
- **The point at which an acid–alkali reaction is complete is called the end point of the reaction.**
- **Use an acid/base indicator to show the end point of the reaction between an acid and an alkali.**

Chapter summary questions

1 Nickel(II) sulfate crystals can be made from an insoluble oxide base and sulfuric acid.

a **i** Name the insoluble base that can be used to make nickel(II) sulfate.

ii Write a balanced symbol equation, including state symbols, to show the reaction.

iii What type of reaction is shown in the equation?

b Describe how you could obtain crystals of nickel(II) sulfate from the reaction in part **a ii**.

2 Write balanced symbol equations, including state symbols, to describe the reactions below. (Each reaction forms a salt.)

a Lithium hydroxide solution (in excess) and dilute sulfuric acid

b Iron(III) oxide (an insoluble base) and dilute nitric acid

c Zinc metal and dilute hydrochloric acid

d Barium nitrate solution and potassium sulfate solution (this reaction produces an insoluble salt)

3 **a** What is the chemical formula of calcium carbonate – the main compound in limestone?

b Calcium carbonate reacts with dilute hydrochloric acid, giving off a gas.

i Write a balanced symbol equation, including state symbols, for this reaction.

ii Draw a diagram of the apparatus you would use to give a positive test for the gas given off.

iii Write a word equation and a balanced symbol equation for the change that happens in a positive test for the gas in part **ii**.

c This is a lime kiln for roasting limestone:

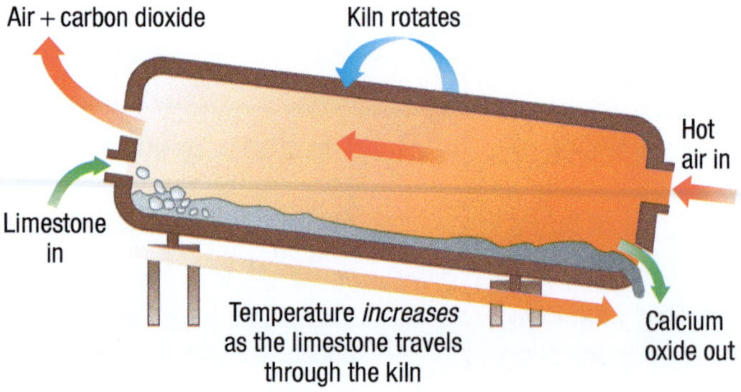

i Write a word equation and a balanced symbol equation, including state symbols, for the reaction in the lime kiln.

ii What do you call the type of reaction that takes place in a lime kiln?

iii What mass of the gas would be produced if 12.5 tonnes of limestone was roasted in a lime kiln, assuming all the limestone was composed of calcium carbonate and there was 100% conversion to calcium oxide? (See Topic 8.2).
(A_r values: Ca = 40, O = 16, C = 12)

iv State **three** uses of limestone not mentioned in this question.

Practice questions

1 Three solutions are made by dissolving equal amounts of compounds in water. The pH values of these solutions are 2, 7, and 12.

Solution 1 contains hydrochloric acid.
Solution 2 contains sodium chloride.
Solution 3 contains sodium hydroxide.

a Write the appropriate pH value for each solution shown above. (1)

b Name **one** indicator that could be used to identify each solution and explain why it is better than using litmus. (2)

c Solution 4 has a pH value of 9. Solution 5 has a pH value of 11.

Which solution contains more H^+ ions? (1)

2 One way to prepare soluble salts involves adding a metal or a metal compound to a dilute acid.

a Copy and complete the following word equations that show the reactions used to make three salts.

i magnesium + hydrochloric acid →
ii zinc oxide + nitric acid →
iii copper(II) carbonate + sulfuric acid → (6)

b What would you observe in reactions **i** and **iii** but not in reaction **ii**? (1)

c Why should an excess of metal or metal compound be used in each case? (1)

d After each reaction is complete, filtration is used.

i State the name of the substance in solution when reaction **i** is filtered. (1)
ii What does the residue in reaction **ii** contain? (1)
iii What is the colour of the filtrate in reaction **iii**? (1)

e The method used for all the reactions above produces a dilute solution of the salt. Describe how crystallisation is used to obtain a pure dry sample of the salt produced in reaction **iii**. (4)

3 Insoluble salts are made by the precipitation method.

a The word equation for a reaction used to make an insoluble salt is:

magnesium chloride + sodium fluoride → magnesium fluoride + sodium chloride

Write a symbol equation, including state symbols, for this reaction. (3)

b **i** Name **two** compounds that could be used to make the insoluble salt lead sulfate. (2)

ii When lead sulfate is made the reaction mixture is filtered. Lead sulfate is in the residue.
Why should the residue be washed with distilled water before it is dried? (1)

8.1 How fast?

Learning objectives

After this topic, you should know:

- what is meant by the rate of a chemical reaction
- how to find out the rate of a chemical reaction.

The rate of a chemical reaction tells us how fast reactants turn into products. In our bodies, there are lots of reactions taking place all the time. They happen at the correct rate to supply our cells with what they need, whenever required.

Reaction rate is also very important in the chemical industry. Any industrial process has to make money by producing useful products. This means the right amount of product needed must be made as cheaply as possible. If it takes too long to produce, it will be hard to make a profit when it is sold. The rate of the reaction must be fast enough to make it quickly but safely.

How can you determine the rate of reactions?

Reactions happen at all sorts of different rates. Some are really fast, such as the combustion of chemicals inside a firework exploding. Others are very slow, such as an old piece of iron rusting.

There are two ways to work out the rate of a chemical reaction. You can measure how quickly:

- the reactants are used up as they make products, or
- the products of the reaction are made.

Here are three ways you can make these kinds of measurement in experiments.

Practical

Measuring the decreasing mass of a reaction mixture

You can measure the rate at which the *mass* of a reaction mixture changes if the reaction gives off a gas. As the reaction takes place, the mass of the reaction mixture decreases. You can measure and record the mass at time intervals which you decide.

Some balances can be attached to a computer to monitor the loss in mass continuously.

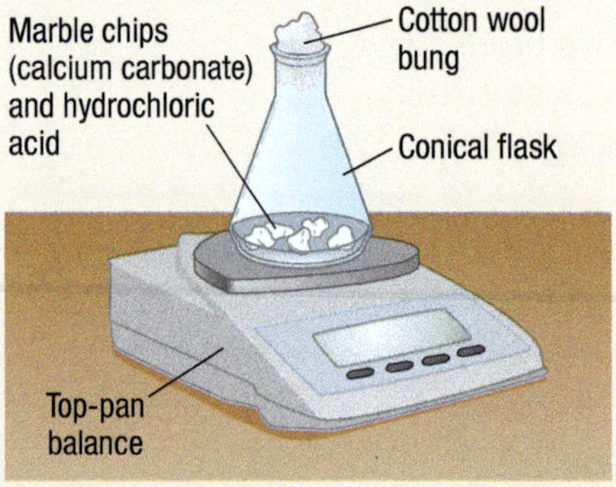

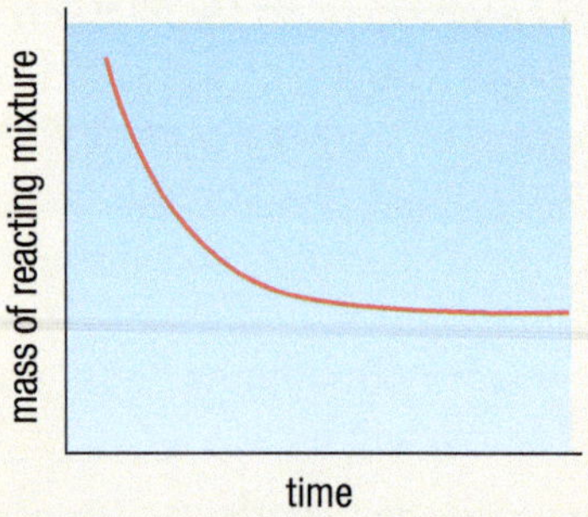

- Why is the cotton wool placed in the neck of the conical flask?
- How would the line on the graph differ if you plot 'Loss in mass' on the vertical axis?

Safety: Wear eye protection. Dilute hydrochloric acid is an irritant.

Study tip

The steeper the line on the graph, the faster the rate of reaction.

Practical

Measuring the increasing volume of gas given off

If a reaction produces a gas, you can use the gas to find out the rate of reaction. You do this by collecting the gas and measuring the volume given off at time intervals.

- What are the sources of error when measuring the volume of gas?

Safety: Wear eye protection. Dilute hydrochloric acid is an irritant.

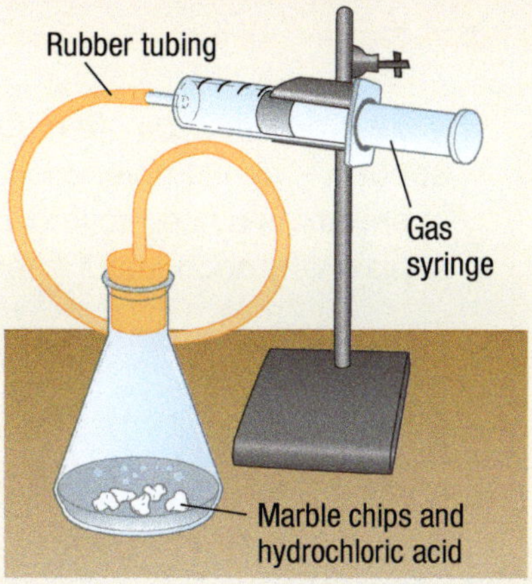

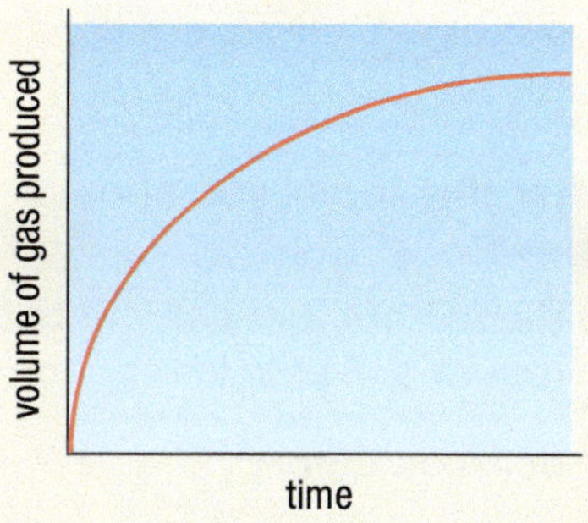

Practical

Measuring the decreasing light passing through a solution

Some reactions in solution make a suspension of an insoluble solid (precipitate). This makes the solution go cloudy. You can use this to measure the rate at which the precipitate appears.

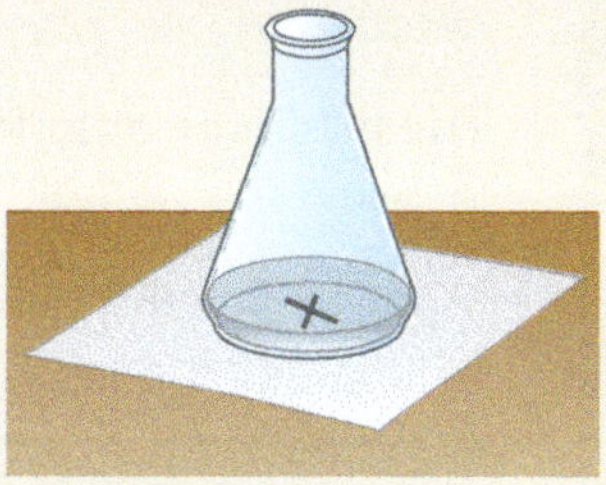

The reaction is set up in a flask. Under the flask, put a piece of paper marked with a cross. Then we can record the time taken for the cross to disappear. The shorter the time is, the faster the reaction rate.

Alternatively, you can use a light sensor and data logger. Then measure the amount of light passing through the solution over time, as the graph shows.

- What are the advantages of using a light sensor rather than the 'disappearing cross' method?

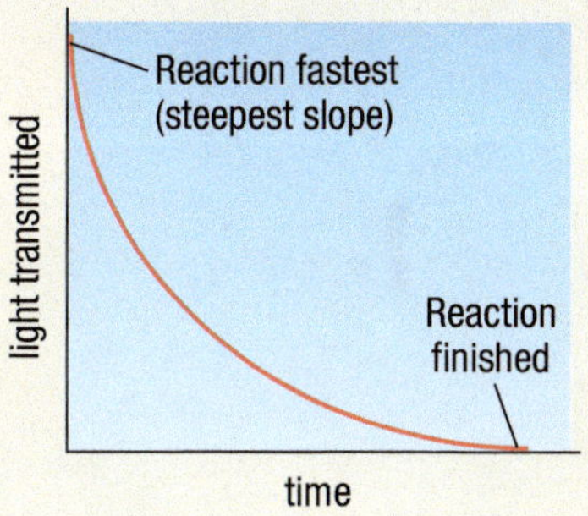

We can summarise these methods of working out the rate of a reaction using this equation:

$$\textbf{rate of reaction} = \frac{\left[\begin{array}{c}\textbf{amount of reactant used or}\\ \textbf{amount of product formed}\end{array}\right]}{\textbf{time}}$$

Summary questions

1 a Write a word equation and a balanced symbol equation, including state symbols, for the reaction taking place in the practical box on the previous page.

b In the same experiment, there were some marble chips left when the fizzing stopped. Why was no more gas given off?

c How can you tell from a graph of the experimental results when the reaction had finished?

2 a Sketch graphs to show the results of:

i measuring the mass of products formed in a reaction over time

ii measuring the mass of reactants remaining in a reaction over time.

b What does the slope of the line at any particular time on the graphs in part **a** tell us about the reaction?

Key points

- **You can determine the rate of a chemical reaction by measuring the amount of reactants used up over time.**
- **Alternatively, you can measure the rate of reaction by following the amount of products made over time.**
- **The slope of the line at any given time on the graphs drawn from such experiments tells us the rate of reaction at that time: the steeper the slope, the faster the reaction.**

8.2 Collision theory and surface area

Learning objectives

After this topic, you should know:

- the factors that can affect the rate of a chemical reaction
- collision theory
- how to use collision theory to explain the effect of surface area on reaction rate.

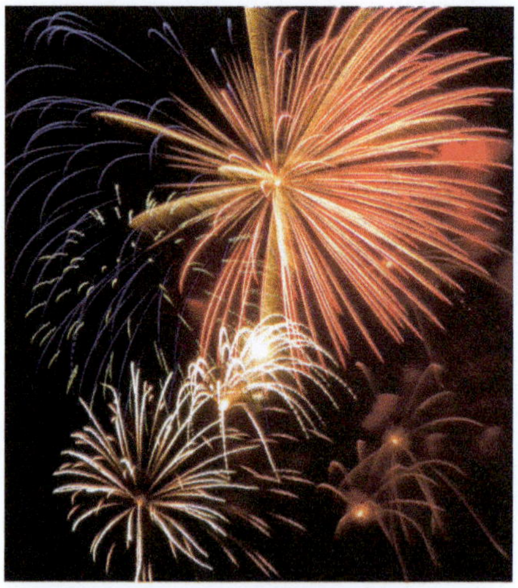

Figure 1 *There is no doubt that the chemicals in these fireworks have reacted. But how can you explain what happens in a chemical reaction?*

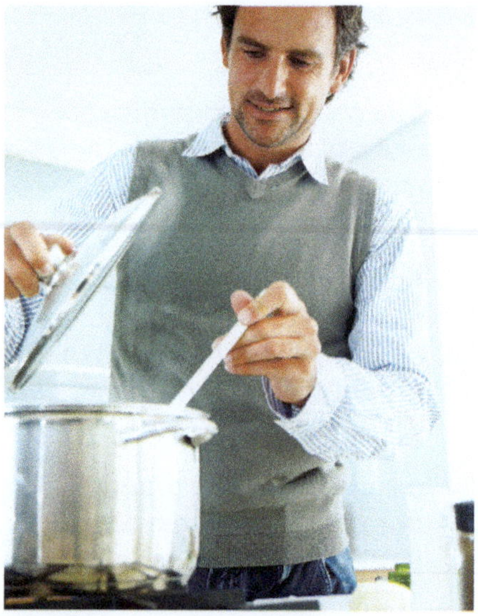

Figure 2 *Cooking – an excellent example of controlling reaction rates!*

In everyday life, you often control the rates of chemical reactions without thinking about it – for example, cooking cakes in an oven or revving up a car engine. In chemistry you need to know what affects the rate of reactions. You also need to explain why each factor affects the rate of a reaction.

There are four main factors which affect the rate of chemical reactions:

- temperature
- surface area
- concentration of solutions or pressure of gases
- presence of a catalyst.

Reactions can only take place when the particles (atoms, ions, or molecules) of reactants come together. But the reacting particles do not just have to collide with each other. They also need to collide with sufficient energy to cause a reaction to take place. This is known as **collision theory**.

The minimum amount of energy that particles must have before they can react is called the **activation energy**.

So reactions are more likely to happen between reactant particles if you:

- increase the frequency of reacting particles colliding with each other
- increase the energy they have when they collide.

If you increase the chance of particles reacting, you will also increase the rate of reaction.

Surface area and reaction rate

Imagine lighting a campfire. It is not a good idea to pile large logs together and try to set them alight. You use small pieces of wood to begin with. Doing this increases the surface area of the wood. This results in more wood being exposed to react with oxygen in the air.

When a solid reacts in a solution, the size of the pieces of solid affects the rate of the reaction. The particles inside a large lump of solid are not in contact with the reactant particles in the solution, so they cannot react. The particles inside the solid have to wait for the particles on the surface to react first before they have a chance to react.

In smaller lumps, or in a powder, each tiny piece of solid is surrounded by solution. Many more particles of the solid are exposed to attack at a given time. This means that reactions can take place much more quickly.

Practical

Which burns faster?

Using tongs, try igniting a 2 cm length of magnesium ribbon and time how long it takes to burn.

Take a small spatula tip of magnesium powder and sprinkle it into the Bunsen flame.

- Write a balanced symbol equation, including state symbols, for the reaction.
- Explain your observations.

Safety: Make sure you have a heatproof mat under the Bunsen burner and you must wear eye protection.

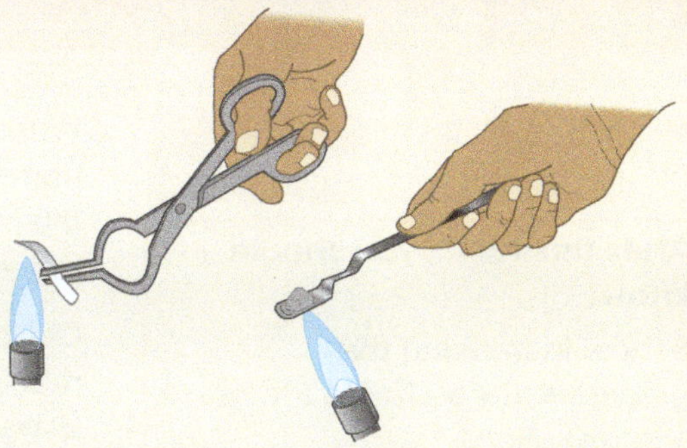

Required practical

Investigating the effect of surface area

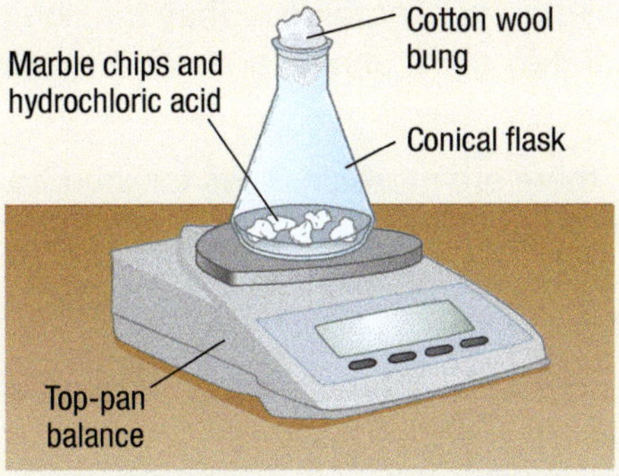

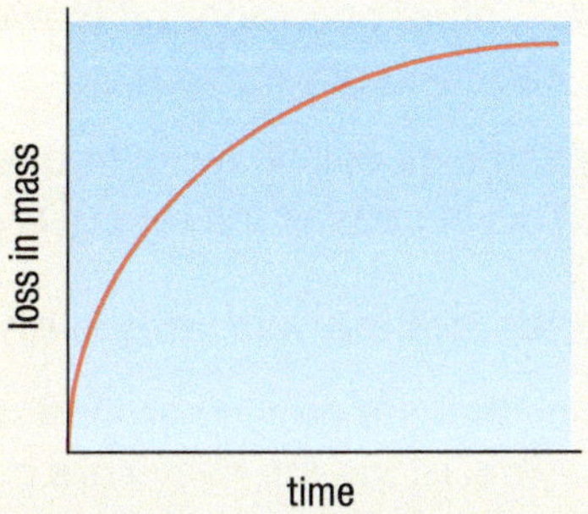

In this investigation you will be measuring the mass lost against time for different sizes of marble (calcium carbonate) chips. You need at least two different sizes of marble chips in order to vary the surface area.

- What variables should you control to make this a fair test?
- Why does this method of finding out the rate of reaction work?
- Use the data collected to draw a graph. Explain what the graph shows. (A data logger would help to plot a graph of the results.)

Safety: Wear eye protection.

Study tip

Particles collide all the time, but only some collisions lead to reactions.

Increasing the number of collisions in a certain time and the energy of collisions produces faster rates of reaction.

Larger surface area does not result in collisions with more energy but does increase the frequency of collisions.

Summary questions

1 List the factors that can affect the rate of a chemical reaction.

2 **a** Draw a diagram to explain why it is easier for an iron nail that has been cut into small pieces to rust than for a whole iron nail to rust under the same conditions.

b Why is the term 'under the same conditions' used in part **a**?

3 Explain why the idea of 'activation energy' is an important part of the collision theory used to explain rates of reaction.

4 Explain why the acid in your stomach can help you digest your food more quickly if you chew your food well before you swallow it.

Key points

- **Particles must collide with a certain minimum amount of energy before they can react.**
- **The minimum amount of energy that particles must have in order to react is called the 'activation energy' of a reaction.**
- **The rate of a chemical reaction increases if the surface area of any solid reactants is increased. This increases the frequency of collisions between reacting particles.**

8.3 The effect of temperature

Learning objectives

After this topic, you should know:

- how increasing the temperature affects the rate of reactions
- how to use collision theory to explain this effect.

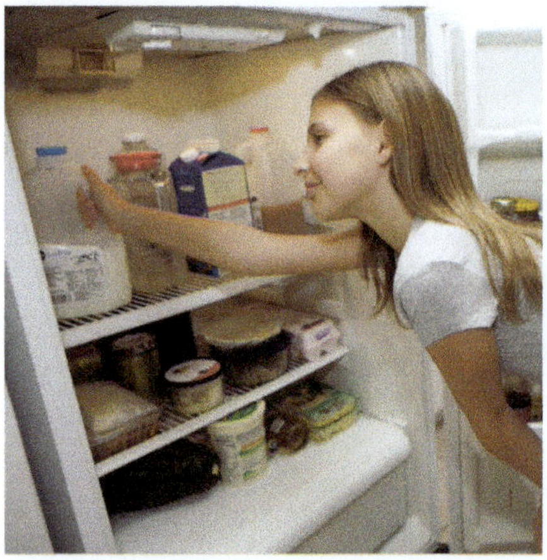

Figure 1 *Lowering the temperature will slow down the reactions that make foods go off*

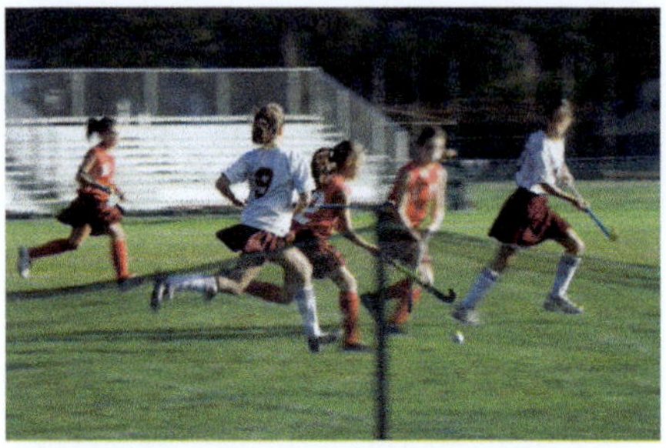

Figure 2 *Moving faster means it is more likely that you'll bump into someone else – and the collision will be harder too!*

When the temperature is increased, it increases the rate of reaction. In our homes, we use fridges and freezers to reduce the temperature and slow down the rate of reactions. When food goes off it is because of chemical reactions, so reducing the temperature slows down these unwanted reactions.

Collision theory tells us why raising the temperature increases the rate of a reaction. There are two reasons:

- Particles collide more frequently.
- Particles collide with more energy.

Particles collide more frequently

When you heat up a substance, energy is transferred to its particles. In solutions and in gases, this means that the particles move around faster. And when particles move around faster they collide more often. Imagine a lot of people walking around in the school playground blindfolded. They may bump into each other occasionally. However, if they start running around, they will bump into each other much more often.

When particles collide more frequently, there are more chances for them to react. This increases the rate of reaction.

Particles collide with more energy

Particles that are moving around more quickly have more energy. This means that any collisions they have are much more energetic. It is like two people colliding when they are running rather than when they are walking.

When you increase the temperature of a reacting mixture, a higher proportion of the collisions will result in a reaction taking place. This is because a higher proportion of particles have energy greater than the activation energy. **This second factor has a greater effect on rate of reaction than the increased frequency of collisions.**

Around room temperature, increasing the temperature of a reaction by 10 °C will cause the rate of the reaction roughly to double.

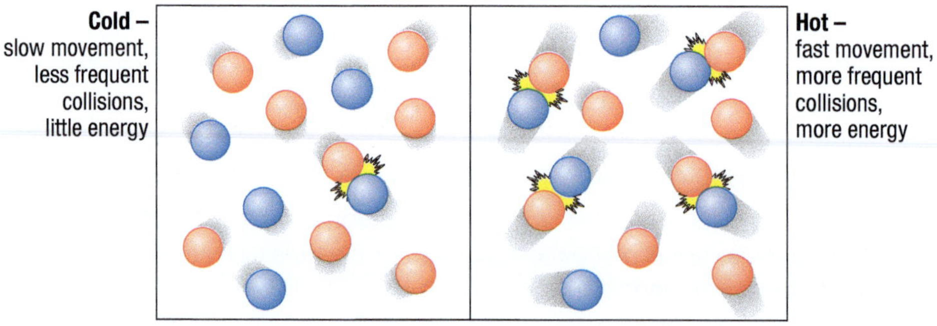

Figure 3 *More frequent collisions, with more energy – both of these factors lead to the increase in the rate of a chemical reaction that is caused by increasing the temperature*

Required practical

The effect of temperature on rate of reaction

Alka-Seltzer tablets are a well-known indigestion remedy. They fizz when added to water. The fizzing is caused by carbon dioxide gas, produced by the reaction of sodium hydrogen carbonate and citric acid, both contained in the tablets. These compounds can come into contact once the tablet is added to water. By varying the temperature of the water, you can measure its effect on the rate of reaction.

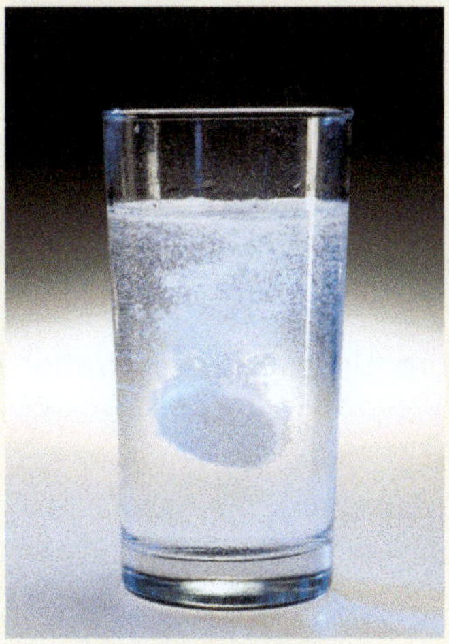

- How could you vary the temperature in the investigation?
- How could you measure the mean rate at different temperatures?

Check your ideas with your teacher before you start your investigation.

- Which variables do you have to control to make this a fair test?
- Why is it difficult to get accurate timings in this investigation?
- How can you improve the **precision**, and therefore the accuracy in this case, of any data which has random measurement errors?

Safety: Wear eye protection. Do not raise the temperature above 50 °C

The effect of temperature on the rate of reaction

As one goes up, the other comes down

In the experiment opposite you can measure the time for a cross to disappear as a precipitate forms.

This means that the longer the time, the slower the rate of reaction. There is an inverse relationship between time and rate. So as time increases, rate decreases.

The rate is proportional to $\frac{1}{\text{time}}$ (also written as time^{-1}). Therefore, you can plot a graph of temperature against $\frac{1}{\text{time}}$ to investigate the effect of temperature on rate of reaction.

The results of an investigation like this can be plotted on a graph (see right).

The graph shows how the time for the reaction to be completed changes with temperature. You could also measure the mean rate of this reaction by measuring either how long it takes to collect a set volume of gas, or the time for the reaction mixture to lose a set mass.

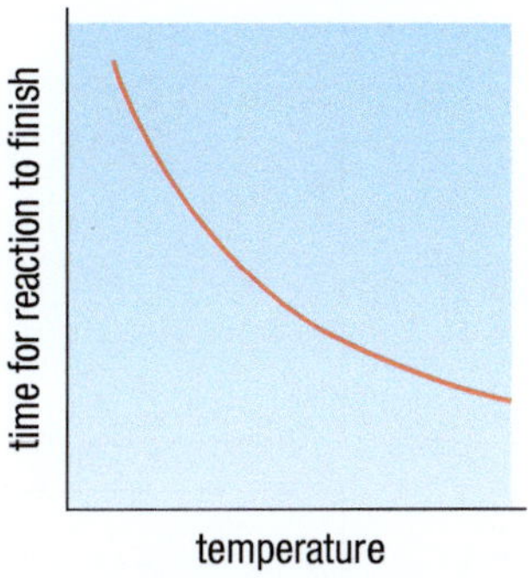

Summary questions

1 a Why does increasing the temperature increase the rate of a reaction?
  b By how much does a 10 °C rise in temperature increase reaction rate at room temperature?

2 Look at the experiment in the Practical box above.
  a Name the gas given off in the reaction.
  b Describe what happens to the time it takes for the reaction to finish as the temperature increases.
  c Explain your answer to part **b** in detail using collision theory.

3 Water in a pressure cooker boils at a much higher temperature than water in a saucepan because it is under pressure. Explain why food takes longer to cook in a pan than it does in a pressure cooker.

Key points

- **Reactions happen more quickly as the temperature increases.**
- **Increasing the temperature increases the rate of reaction because particles collide more frequently and more energetically. More of the collisions result in a reaction because a higher proportion of particles have energy greater than the activation energy.**

8.4 The effect of concentration or pressure

Learning objectives

After this topic, you should know:

- how, and why, increasing the concentration of reactants in solutions affects the rate of reaction
- how, and why, increasing the pressure of reacting gases affects the rate of reaction.

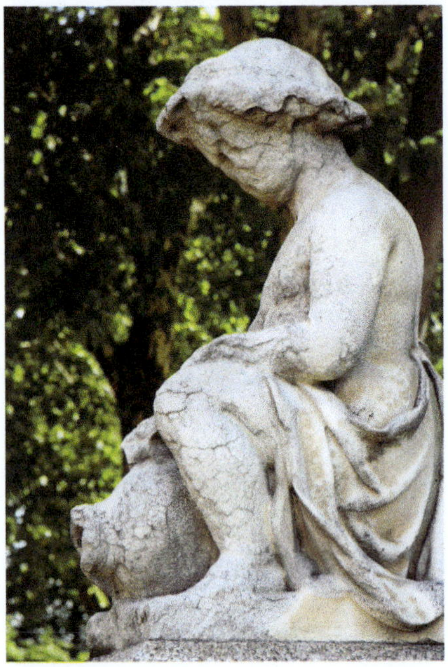

Figure 1 *Limestone statues are damaged by acid rain. This damage happens more quickly as the concentration of the acids in rainwater increases.*

Some of the world's most beautiful buildings are made of limestone or marble. These buildings have stood for centuries. However, they are now crumbling away at a greater rate than before. This is because both limestone and marble are mainly calcium carbonate. This reacts with acids, leaving the stone soft and crumbly. The rate of this reaction has speeded up because the concentration of acids in rainwater has increased.

Increasing the concentration of reactants in a solution increases the rate of reaction because there are more particles of the reactants moving around in the same volume of solution. The more 'crowded' together the reactant particles are, the more likely it is that they will collide. So the more frequent collisions result in a faster reaction.

Increasing the pressure of reacting gases has the same effect. Increased pressure squashes the gas particles more closely together. There are more particles of gas in a given space. This increases the chance that they will collide and react. So, increasing the pressure produces more frequent collisions which speeds up the rate of the reaction.

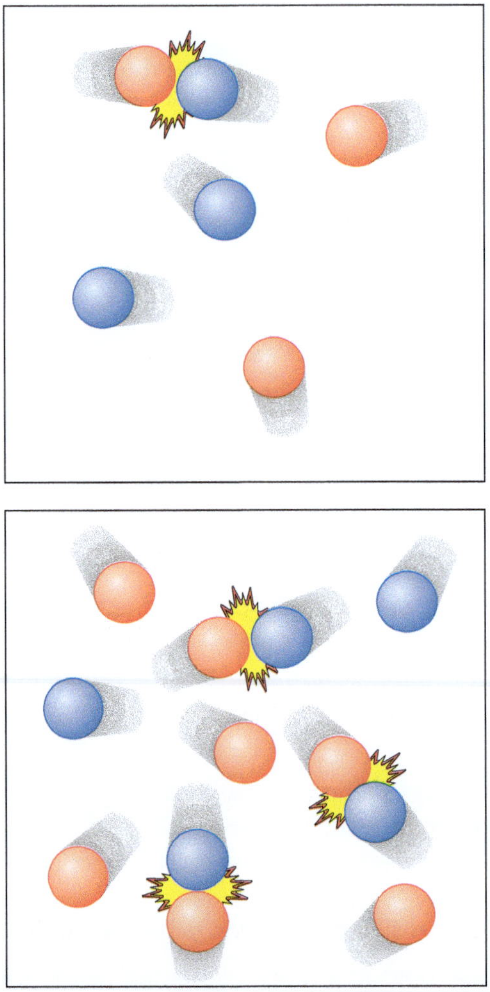

Figure 2 *Increasing concentration and pressure both mean that particles are closer together. This increases the frequency of collisions between particles, so the reaction rate increases.*

Required practical

Investigating the effect of concentration on rate of reaction

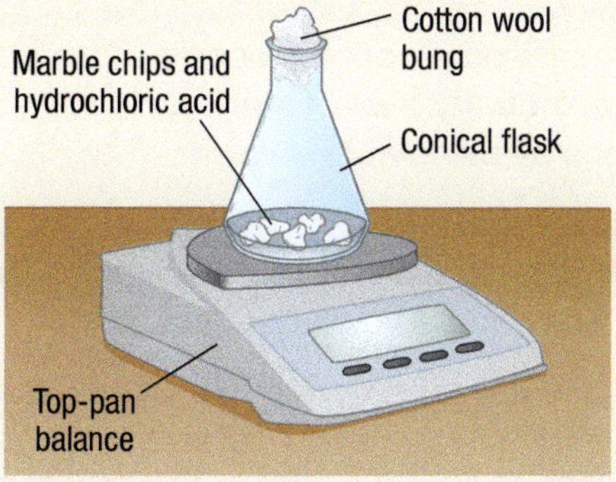

You can investigate the effect of changing concentration by reacting marble chips with different concentrations of hydrochloric acid:

$$CaCO_3(s) + 2HCl(aq) \rightarrow CaCl_2(aq) + CO_2(g) + H_2O(l)$$

Find the rate of reaction by plotting the mass of the reaction mixture over time. The mass will decrease as carbon dioxide gas is given off in the reaction.

- How do you make this a fair test?
- What conclusion can you draw from your results?

Safety: Wear eye protection.

Study tip

Increasing concentration or pressure does not increase the energy with which the particles collide. However, it does increase the frequency of collisions.

If you plot the results of an investigation like the one above on a graph they look like Figure 3.

The graph shows how the mass of the reaction mixture decreases over time at three different concentrations of acid.

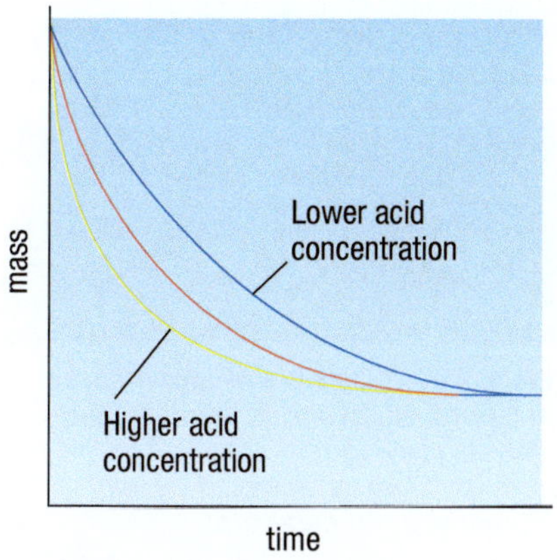

Figure 3 *Investigating the effect of concentration on reaction rate*

Summary questions

1 Look at the graph in Figure 3.
  a Which line on the graph shows the fastest reaction? How can you tell from the data displayed?
  b Why is the cotton wool bung used in the Practical above?
  c The electronic balance used in the experiment needs a 'high resolution'. What does this mean?

2 You could also follow the reaction described in the Practical above by measuring the volume of gas given off over time. Sketch a graph of volume of gas against time for three different concentrations. Label the three lines as high, medium and low concentration.

3 Explain, in terms of its particles, why the concentration of a gas is proportional to its pressure.

4 Acidic cleaners are designed to remove limescale (calcium carbonate) when they are used neat, that is, undiluted. They do not work as well when they are diluted. Using your knowledge of collision theory, explain why this is.

Key points

- **Increasing the concentration of reactants in solutions increases the frequency of collisions between particles, and so increases the rate of reaction.**
- **Increasing the pressure of reacting gases also increases the frequency of collisions and so increases the rate of reaction.**

8.5 The effect of catalysts

Learning objectives

After this topic, you should know:

- what a catalyst is
- why catalysts are important in industry.

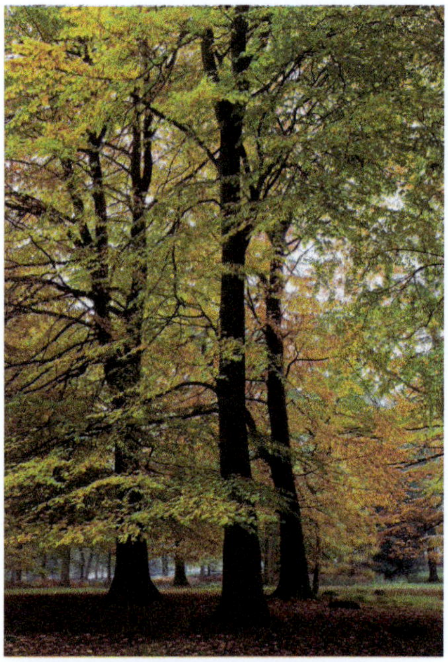

Figure 1 *Catalysts are all around us, in the natural world and in industry. The catalysts in living things are called enzymes. Our planet would be very different without catalysts.*

Sometimes a reaction might only work if it occurs at very high temperatures or pressures. This can cost industry a lot of money. However, it is possible to speed up some reactions by using **catalysts**.

A catalyst is a substance which increases the rate of a reaction. However, it is not changed chemically itself at the end of the reaction. A catalyst is not used up in the reaction so it can be used over and over again.

Different catalysts are needed for different reactions. Many of the catalysts used in industry involve transition metals. Examples include iron, used to make ammonia, and platinum, used to make nitric acid. Catalysts are usually in the form of powders, pellets, or fine gauzes. This gives them the biggest possible surface area and makes them as effective as possible as the reactions they catalyse often involve gases reacting on their surfaces.

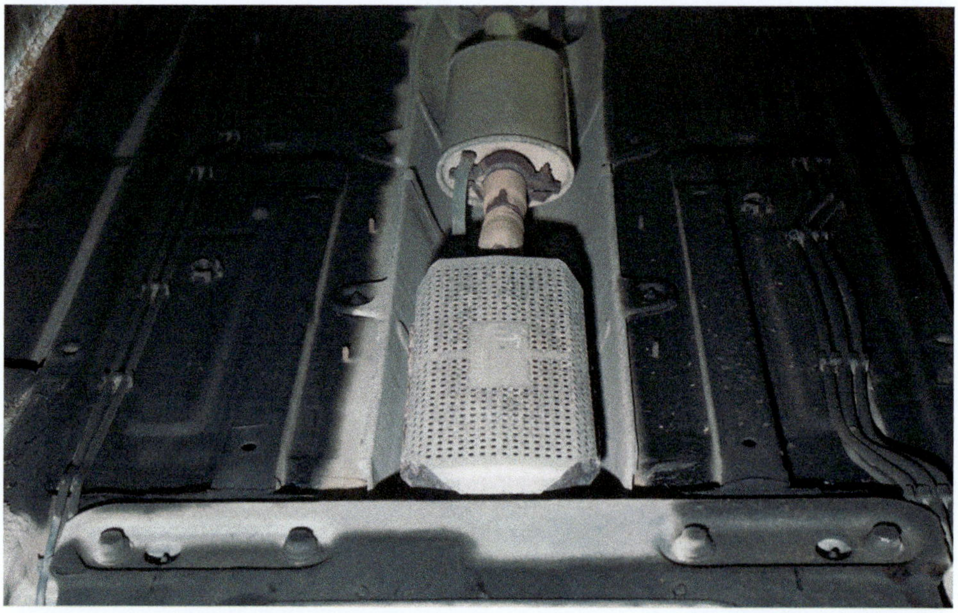

Figure 2 *The transition metals platinum and palladium are used in the* ***catalytic converters*** *in cars*

Advantages of catalysts in industry

Catalysts are often very expensive precious metals. Gold, platinum, and palladium are all costly but are the most effective catalysts for particular reactions. However, it is often cheaper to use a catalyst than to pay for the extra energy needed without one. To get the same rate of reaction without a catalyst would require higher temperatures and/or pressures.

So catalysts save money and help the environment. This is because using high temperatures and pressures often involves burning fossil fuels. So operating at lower temperatures and pressures conserves these **non-renewable** resources. It also stops more carbon dioxide entering the atmosphere, helping to combat climate change.

Not only does a catalyst speed up a reaction, but also it does not get used up in the reaction, so a tiny amount of catalyst can be used to speed up a reaction over and over again.

Practical

Investigating catalysis

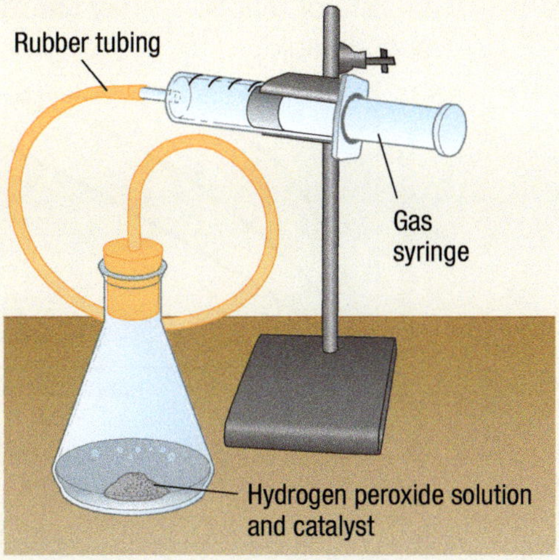

You can investigate the effect of different catalysts on the rate of a reaction. You will look at hydrogen peroxide solution decomposing:

$$2H_2O_2(aq) \rightarrow 2H_2O(l) + O_2(g)$$

The reaction produces oxygen gas. Collect this in a gas syringe using the apparatus shown above.

You can investigate the effect of many different substances on the rate of this reaction. Examples include manganese(IV) oxide, MnO_2, and potassium iodide, KI.

- State the independent variable in this investigation.

A table of the time taken to produce a certain volume of oxygen can then tell us which catalyst makes the reaction go fastest.

- What type of graph would you use to show the results of your investigation? Why?

Safety: Wear eye protection. If the syringe is glass take care to not expel the piston. Manganese(IV) oxide is harmful.

Did you know ...?

The catalysts used in chemical plants eventually become 'poisoned' so that they don't work any more. This happens because impurities in the reaction mixture combine with the catalyst and stop it working properly.

Study tip

Catalysts change only the rate of reactions. They do not change the products.

Summary questions

1 How is a catalyst affected by a chemical reaction it speeds up?

2 Solid catalysts used in chemical processes are often shaped as tiny beads or cylinders with holes through them. Why are they made in these shapes?

3 Why is the number of moles of catalyst needed to speed up a chemical reaction very small compared with the number of moles of reactants?

4 Do some research to find out four industrial processes that make products using catalysts. Write a word equation for each reaction and name the catalyst used.

5 Explain why catalysts are so useful in the chemical industry.

Key points

- **A catalyst speeds up the rate of a chemical reaction but is not used up itself during the reaction. It remains chemically unchanged.**
- **Different catalysts are needed for different reactions.**
- **Catalysts are used whenever possible in industry to increase rates of reaction and reduce energy costs.**

Chapter summary questions

1 A student investigated the reaction between magnesium and dilute hydrochloric acid. He started by reacting a piece of magnesium ribbon in 1.0 mol/dm^3 hydrochloric acid.

a Describe **one** method the student could use to measure the rate of this reaction.

b Suggest **three** ways in which the student could increase the rate of this reaction.

c i The student decided to investigate the effect of ***temperature*** on rate of reaction. Write an outline plan of how he should set up his investigation.

ii What would you expect the student to find out from the data he collected?

iii Explain the expected pattern in his results using collision theory.

2 Two students investigated the reaction of some marble chips with dilute nitric acid.

Time (minutes)	Investigation A Mass of gas produced (g)	Investigation B Mass of gas produced (g)
0.0	0.00	0.00
0.5	0.56	0.28
1.0	0.73	0.36
1.5	0.80	0.39
2.0	0.82	0.41
2.5	0.82	0.41

a Which gas was produced in the reaction? What is the test for this gas?

b i Marble chips contain calcium carbonate. Write a word equation for the reaction investigated.

ii Now write a balanced symbol equation, including state symbols, for the reaction.

c The students were investigating the effect of concentration on rate of reaction. How do you think the students got the data for their table above?

d Plot a graph of these results, with time on the *x*-axis.

e After 30 seconds, how does the rate of reaction in Investigation B compare with the rate of reaction in Investigation A?

f How does the final mass of gas produced in Investigation B compare with that produced in Investigation A?

g From the results, what can you say about the initial concentration of the acids in Investigations A and B?

h Explain the data obtained using collision theory.

3 A pair of students are studying the effect of surface area on rate of reaction. They use zinc foil reacting with dilute sulfuric acid.

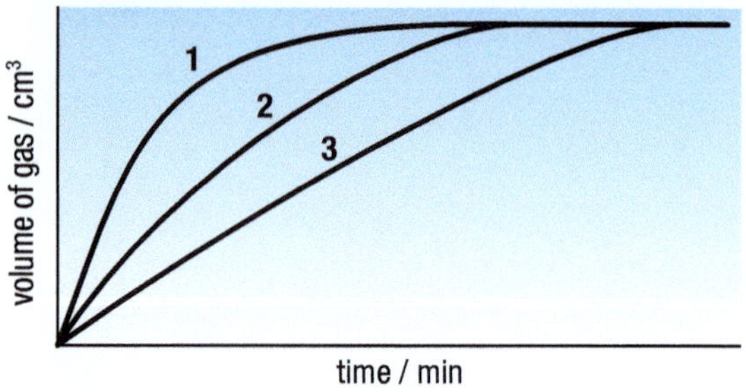

a What did the students investigating the reaction have to do to make it a *fair test*?

b Which gas was given off in the reaction? How could you test for this gas?

c Write a balanced symbol equation, including state symbols, for the reaction under investigation.

d Which line (1, 2, or 3) shows results for the zinc with the largest surface area (given the same mass of zinc in each test)?

e Which sized pieces of zinc would react most slowly?

f The students doing the experiments also tried reacting the same mass of *powdered* zinc with the acid. Describe what their results would look like on the graph above.

g Use collision theory to explain the results in this investigation.

4 a Define the word 'catalyst'.

b Hydrogen peroxide (H_2O_2) solution decomposes to form water and oxygen gas.
Write a balanced symbol equation, including state symbols, for this reaction.

c The reaction is catalysed by some metal oxides. You are provided with oxides of copper, lead, manganese, and iron. Describe how you can test which is the best catalyst for the decomposition of hydrogen peroxide, collecting quantitative (measured) data to support your conclusion.

d How can you get a pure dry sample of the metal oxides from the mixture left at the end of the reaction?

Practice questions

1 Some students investigated the reaction between calcium carbonate and nitric acid. They used this apparatus to collect the gas given off when dilute nitric acid was added to marble chips of different sizes.

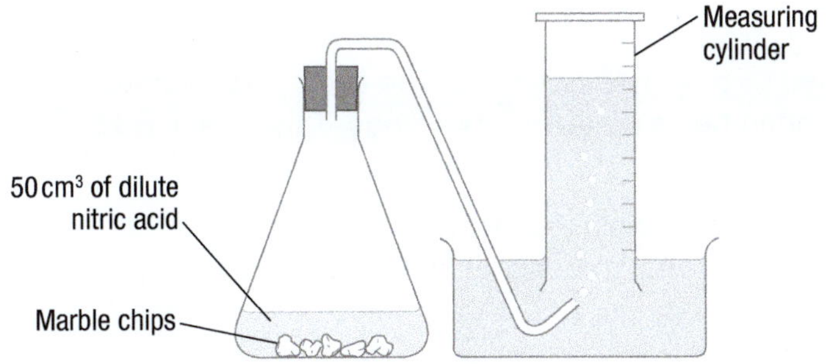

They recorded the volume of gas every 10 seconds until no more gas was collected.

The graph of their results is shown below.

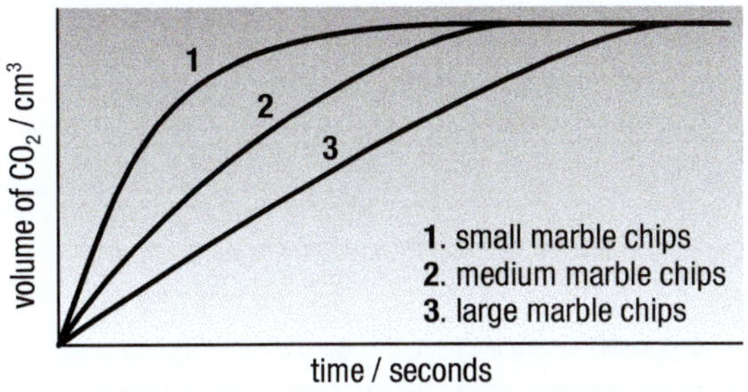

a The students all used the same mass of marble chips.

State **two** other factors that should have been kept constant to ensure a fair test. (2)

b Reaction 1 was the fastest of the three reactions. State how the graph shows this. (2)

c Why do small marble chips react faster than large marble chips? (1)

d Another group of students investigated the same reaction using equal masses of medium marble chips but using different concentrations of dilute nitric acid in each experiment. Student 1 used the original nitric acid. The other students added water to decrease the concentrations of the acid in their experiments. They recorded the time taken to collect 100 cm^3 of gas.

The table shows their results.

Student	Acid concentration	Time in seconds
1	100%	11
2	80%	16
3	60%	22
4	40%	32
5	20%	61

i Suggest which student's recorded results are least likely to be accurate. Give a reason for your choice. (2)

ii One student calculated the rate of reaction using the expression

$$\text{rate} = \frac{1}{\text{time}}$$

What is the rate of the experiment carried out by student 1? (2)

iii Another student plotted a graph of rate against concentration. She drew a straight line of best fit through the origin.
State the relationship between rate and concentration shown by this line. (2)

iv Explain why the rate of student 2's reaction was double that of student 4's reaction. (3)

2 The reaction between sodium thiosulfate and hydrochloric acid can be used to investigate reaction rates. The equation for the reaction is:

$Na_2S_2O_3(aq) + 2HCl(aq) \rightarrow 2NaCl(aq) + H_2O(l) + SO_2(aq) + S(s)$

a Identify the product that is used in measuring the rate, giving a reason for your choice. (2)

b Some students measured the rate of this reaction in a series of experiments. All the experiments were done in the same way, except that the temperatures were different. The students noticed that the rate was a lot faster at higher temperatures.

One student suggested that this was because there were more frequent collisions between the particles.

i Why do the particles collide more frequently? (1)

ii What is the other reason why the rate is faster at higher temperatures? (1)

3 Many reactions in industry are carried out at high temperatures and using catalysts.

a What is a catalyst? (2)

b Some expensive metals, such as platinum, are used as catalysts.

Explain why it is worthwhile to use expensive metals as catalysts. (1)

c Platinum is used as a catalyst in car exhausts.

Suggest why it is used in thin layers rather than as lumps. (1)

9.1 Exothermic and endothermic reactions

Learning objectives

After this topic, you should know:

- that energy is transferred to or from the surroundings in chemical reactions
- some examples of exothermic and endothermic reactions.

Whenever chemical reactions take place, energy is always transferred as chemical bonds are broken and new ones are made.

Some reactions transfer energy **from** the reacting chemicals **to** their surroundings. These are called **exothermic** reactions. The energy transferred from the reacting chemicals often heats up the surroundings. This means that you can measure a rise in temperature as the reaction happens.

Some reactions transfer energy **from** the surroundings **to** the reacting chemicals. These are called **endothermic** reactions. As they take in energy from their surroundings, these reactions cause a drop in temperature as they happen.

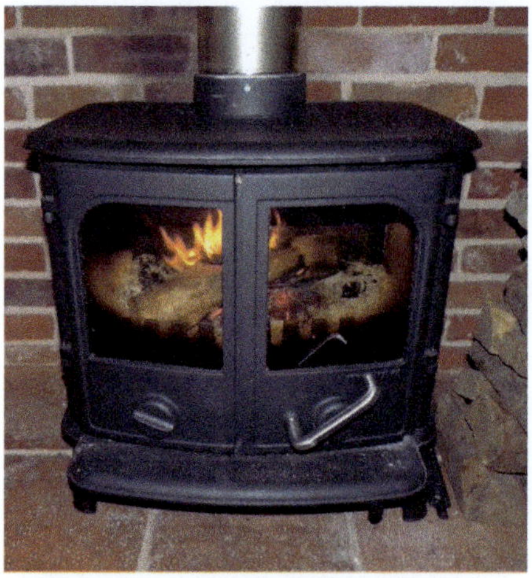

Figure 1 *When a fuel burns in oxygen, energy is transferred to the surroundings. You usually don't need a thermometer to know that there is a temperature change!*

Exothermic reactions

Burning fuels are an obvious example of exothermic reactions. For example, when methane (in natural gas) burns it gets oxidised and releases energy.

Neutralisation reactions between acids and alkalis are also exothermic. You can easily measure the rise in temperature using simple apparatus (see the experiment on the next page).

Scientists use the term 'enthalpy change' to describe the transfer of energy in chemical reactions at constant pressure. As the reactions carried out in the lab are at constant pressure, the energy we are considering in these reactions is enthalpy, symbol H. Any temperature change measured when a reaction takes place is a result of enthalpy changes between the reactants and products of the reaction. The enthalpy change is given the symbol ΔH. The products of exothermic reactions have less enthalpy content than the reactants so numerical values, measured in kilojoules per mole, are given a negative sign. For example:

$$CH_4(g) + 2O_2(g) \rightarrow CO_2(g) + 2H_2O(l) \qquad \Delta H = -890\,\text{kJ/mol}$$

links

For more information about enthalpy changes and how to represent them, see 9.4 Energy level diagrams.

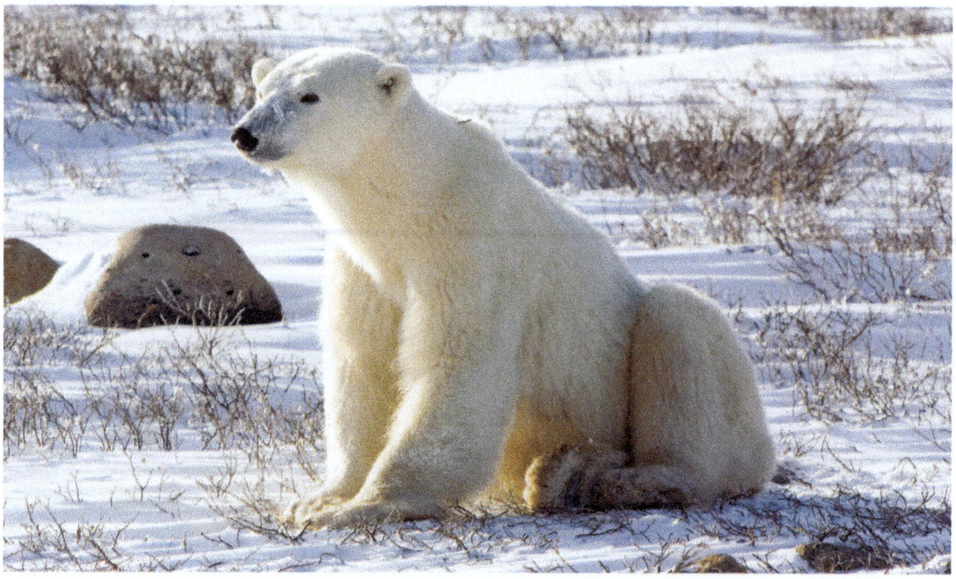

Figure 2 *All warm-blooded animals rely on exothermic reactions in* ***respiration*** *to keep their body temperatures steady*

Endothermic reactions

Endothermic reactions are much less common than exothermic ones.

Thermal decomposition reactions are endothermic. An example is the decomposition of calcium carbonate. When heated, it forms calcium oxide and carbon dioxide. This reaction only takes place if you keep heating the calcium carbonate strongly. The calcium carbonate needs to absorb energy from the surroundings to be broken down.

The products have more enthalpy content than the reactants in endothermic reactions, so numerical values are given a positive sign. For example:

$$CaCO_3(s) \rightarrow CaO(s) + CO_2(g) \qquad \Delta H = +178\,kJ/mol$$

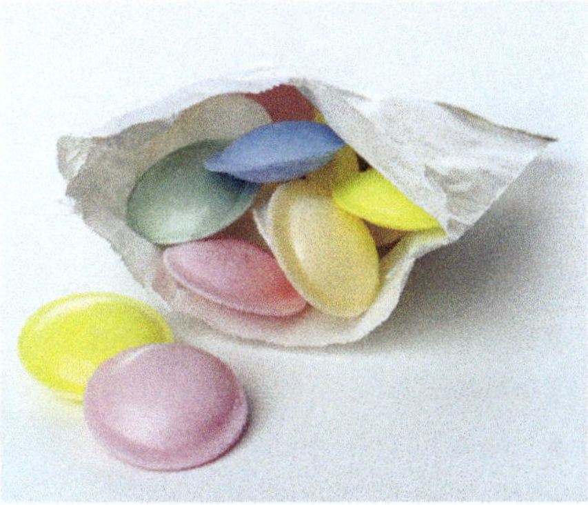

Figure 3 *When you eat sherbet you can feel an endothermic reaction. Sherbet dissolving in the water in your mouth takes in energy. It provides a slight cooling effect.*

Practical

Investigating energy changes

You can use very simple apparatus to investigate the energy changes in reactions. Often you do not need to use anything more complicated than a polystyrene cup and a thermometer.

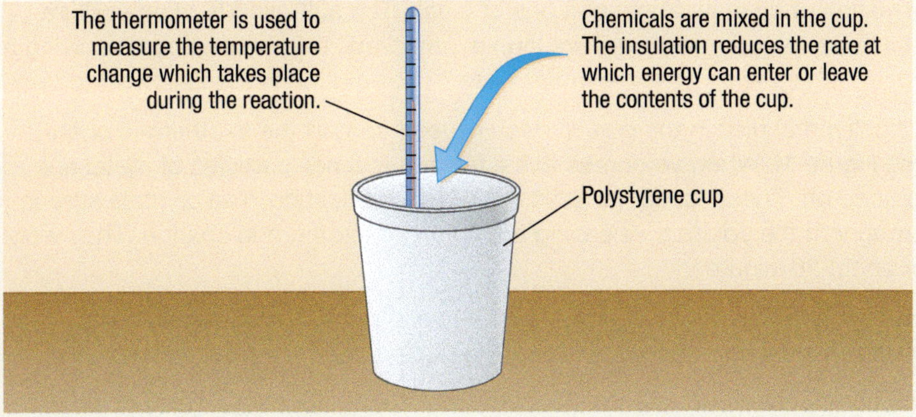

- State two ways in which you could make the data you collect more accurate.

Safety: Wear eye protection.

Study tip

Remember that exothermic reactions involve energy EXiting (leaving) the reacting chemicals, so the surroundings get hotter.

In endothermic reactions energy is transferred INTO (sounds like 'endo'!) the reacting chemicals, so the surroundings get colder.

Summary questions

1 a What do you call a reaction that releases energy to its surroundings?

b What do you call a reaction that absorbs energy from its surroundings?

c Give **two** examples of exothermic reactions.

d Give an example of an endothermic reaction.

2 Potassium nitrate dissolving in water is an endothermic process. Explain what you would feel if you held a beaker of water in your hand as you stirred in potassium nitrate.

3 Two solutions are added together and the temperature changes from 19 °C to 27 °C. Explain what you can say about the enthalpy change in this reaction, including the sign given to ΔH.

4 The enthalpy change for the thermal decomposition of 16.8 g of magnesium carbonate is +23.4 kJ. (A_r values: C = 12, O = 16, Mg = 24)

a Write a balanced symbol equation, including state symbols, for the reaction.

b Calculate the value of ΔH for the thermal decomposition in kilojoules per mole.

Key points

- **Energy may be transferred to or from the reacting substances in a chemical reaction.**
- **A reaction in which energy is transferred from the reacting substances to their surroundings is called an exothermic reaction.**
- **In exothermic reactions, the change in enthalpy, ΔH, has a negative value.**
- **A reaction in which energy is transferred to the reacting substances from their surroundings is called an endothermic reaction.**
- **In endothermic reactions, the change in enthalpy, ΔH, has a positive value.**

9.2 Using energy transfers from reactions

Learning objectives

After this topic, you should know:

- how to make use of the energy from exothermic reactions
- how to use the cooling effect of endothermic reactions.

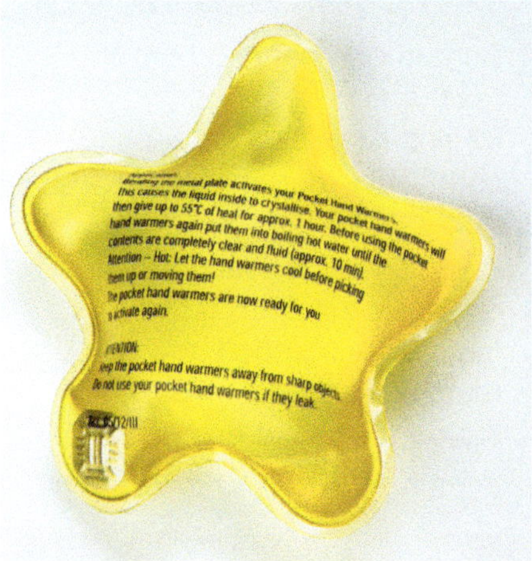

Figure 1 *Here is a hand warmer based on the recrystallisation of sodium ethanoate*

Warming up

Chemical hand and body warmers can be very useful. These products use exothermic reactions to warm you up. People can take hand warmers to places where they know they will get very cold. For example, spectators at outdoor sporting events in winter can warm their hands up. People usually use the body warmers to help ease aches and pains.

Some hand warmers can only be used once. An example of this type uses the energy released in the oxidation of iron. Iron turns into hydrated iron(III) oxide in an exothermic reaction. The reaction is similar to rusting. Sodium chloride (common salt) is used as a catalyst. This type of hand warmer is disposable. It can be used only once but it lasts for hours.

Other hand warmers can be reused many times. These are based on the formation of crystals from solutions of a salt. The salt used is often sodium ethanoate. A supersaturated solution is prepared. This is done by dissolving as much of the salt as possible in hot water. The solution is then allowed to cool.

A small metal disc in the plastic pack is used to start the exothermic change (see Figure 1). When you press this a few times small particles of metal are scraped off. These 'seed' (or start off) the crystallisation. The crystals spread throughout the solution, releasing energy in an exothermic change. They work for about 30 minutes.

To reuse the warmer, you simply put the solid pack into boiling water to re-dissolve the crystals. When cool, the pack is ready to be activated again.

Exothermic reactions are also used in self-heating cans (see Figure 2 on the next page). The reaction used to release the energy is usually:

$$\text{calcium oxide} + \text{water} \rightarrow \text{calcium hydroxide}$$

You press a button in the base of the can. This breaks a seal and lets the water and calcium oxide mix. Coffee is available in these self-heating cans.

Development took years and cost millions of pounds. Even then, over a third of the can was taken up with the reactants to release energy. Also, in some early versions, the temperature of the coffee did not rise high enough in cold conditions.

Activity

Hot food

Mountaineers and explorers can take 'self-heating' foods with them on their journeys. One example uses the energy released when calcium oxide reacts with water to heat the food.

Design a self-heating, disposable food container for stew.

- Draw a labelled diagram of your container and explain how it works.
- What are the safety issues involved in using your product?

Cooling down

Endothermic processes can be used to cool things down. For example, chemical cold packs usually contain ammonium nitrate and water (see Figure 3). When ammonium nitrate dissolves it absorbs energy from its surroundings, making them colder. These cold packs are used as emergency treatment for sports injuries. The coldness reduces swelling and numbs pain.

The ammonium nitrate and water (sometimes present in a gel) are kept separate in the pack. When squeezed or struck the bag inside the water pack breaks releasing ammonium nitrate. The instant cold packs work for about 20 minutes.

They can only be used once but are ideal where there is no ice available to treat a knock or strain.

The same endothermic change can also be used to chill cans of drinks.

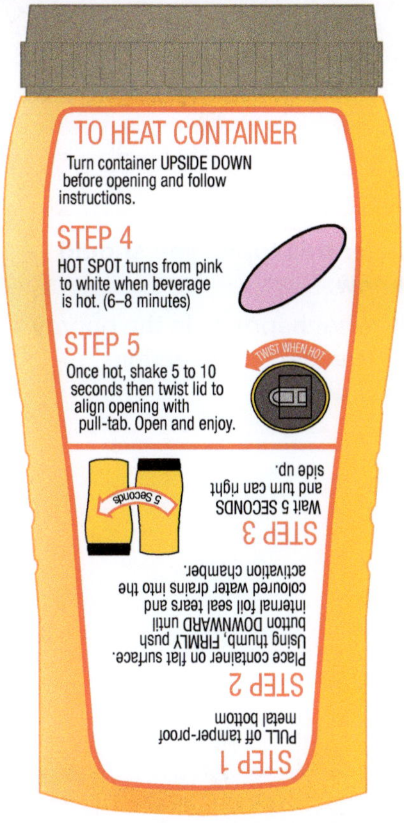

Figure 2 *Development of this self-heating can in the USA took about 10 years*

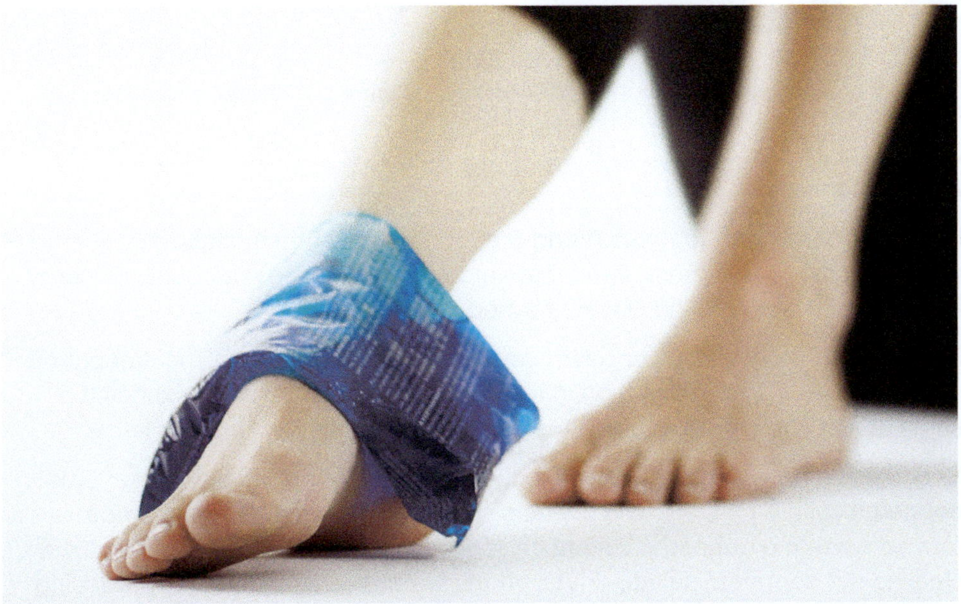

Figure 3 *Instant cold packs can be applied as soon as an injury occurs to minimise damage*

Summary questions

1 a Describe the chemical reaction which takes place in a disposable hand warmer.
b Describe how a re-usable hand warmer works.
c Give an advantage and a disadvantage of each type of hand warmer.
d Name **one** use of an exothermic reaction in the food industry.

2 a Give **two** uses of endothermic changes.
b Which endothermic change is often used in cold packs?
c The solid used in cold packs is often ammonium nitrate.
i Give the formula of ammonium nitrate.
ii State another use of ammonium nitrate.

3 a Which solid is usually used in the base of self-heating coffee cans?
b Write a balanced symbol equation, including state symbols, for the reaction of water with the solid in part **a**.
c Why is it essential that the coffee stays out of contact with the solid in part **a**?

Key points

- **Exothermic changes can be used in hand warmers and self-heating cans. Crystallisation of a supersaturated solution is used in reusable warmers. However, disposable, one-off warmers can give off heat for longer.**
- **Endothermic changes can be used in instant cold packs for sports injuries.**

9.3 Energy and reversible reactions

Learning objectives

After this topic, you should know:

- **what happens in the energy transfers in reversible reactions.**

Energy changes are involved in reversible reactions too. Let's consider an example.

Figure 1 shows a reversible reaction where A and B react to form C and D. The products of this reaction (C and D) can also react to form A and B again.

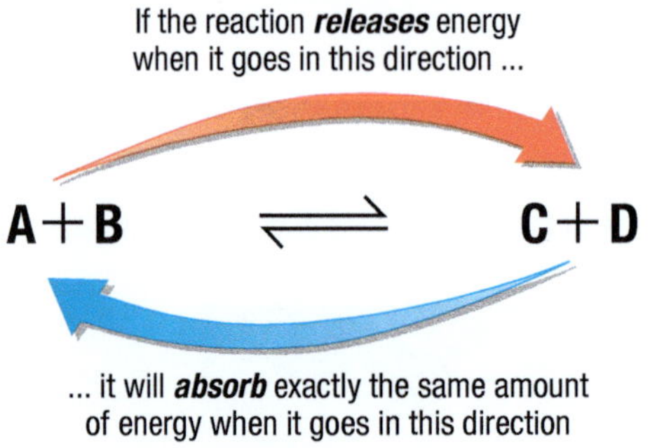

Figure 1 *A reversible reaction*

If the reaction between A and B is exothermic, energy will be released when the reaction forms C and D.

If C and D then react to make A and B again, the reaction must be endothermic. What's more, it must absorb exactly the same amount of energy as it released when C and D were formed from A and B.

Energy cannot be created or destroyed in a chemical reaction. The amount of energy released in one direction in a reversible reaction must be exactly the same as the energy absorbed in the opposite direction.

You can see how this works if you look at what happens when you heat blue copper(II) sulfate crystals. The crystals contain water as part of the lattice formed when the copper(II) sulfate crystallised. The copper sulfate is **hydrated**. Heating the copper(II) sulfate drives off the water from the crystals, producing white **anhydrous** ('without water') copper(II) sulfate. This is an endothermic reaction.

$CuSO_4.5H_2O$	$\rightleftharpoons$	$CuSO_4$	$+\ 5H_2O$
hydrated	$\rightleftharpoons$	anhydrous	+ water
copper(II) sulfate (blue)		copper(II) sulfate (white)	

When water is added to anhydrous copper(II) sulfate it forms hydrated copper(II) sulfate. The colour change in the reaction, from white to blue, is a useful test for the presence of water. The reaction in this direction is exothermic. In fact, so much energy may be produced that you may see steam rising as the water boils.

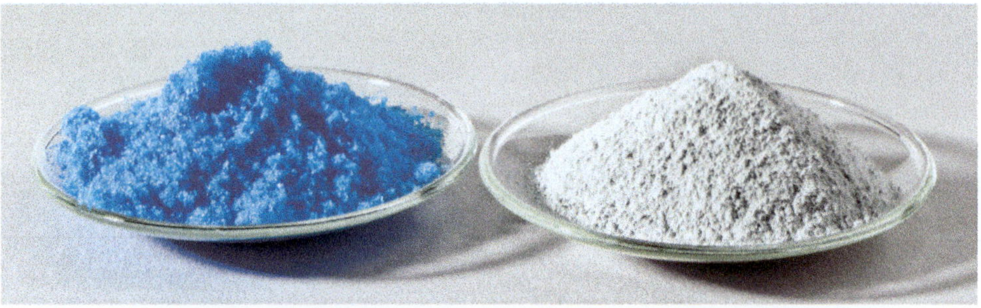

Figure 2 *Hydrated copper(II) sulfate and white anhydrous copper(II) sulfate*

Practical

Energy changes in a reversible reaction

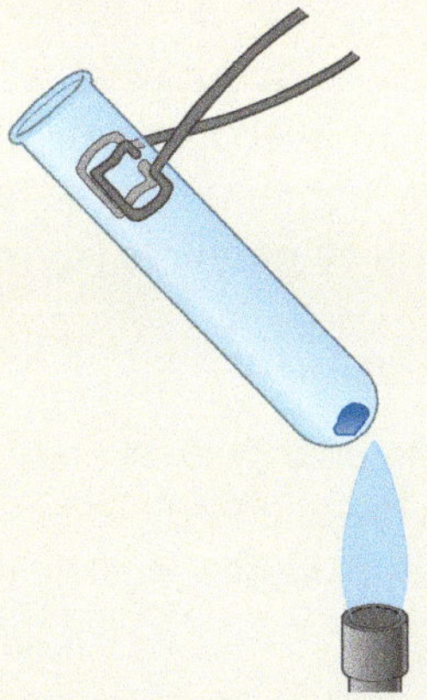

Figure 3 *Heating hydrated copper(II) sulfate*

Gently heat a few copper(II) sulfate crystals in a test tube. Observe the changes. When the crystals are completely white allow the tube to cool to room temperature (this takes several minutes). Add two or three drops of water from a dropper and observe the changes. Carefully feel the bottom of the test tube.

- Explain the changes you have observed.

You can repeat this with the same solid, as it is a reversible reaction, or try with other hydrated crystals, such as cobalt(II) chloride. Some are not so colourful but the changes are similar.

Safety: Wear eye protection. Avoid skin contact with cobalt(II) chloride (toxic). Copper salts are harmful.

You can soak filter paper in cobalt(II) chloride solution and allow it to dry in an oven. The blue paper that is produced is called cobalt(II) chloride paper. The paper turns pale pink when water is added to it, so it can be used as an indicator for water.

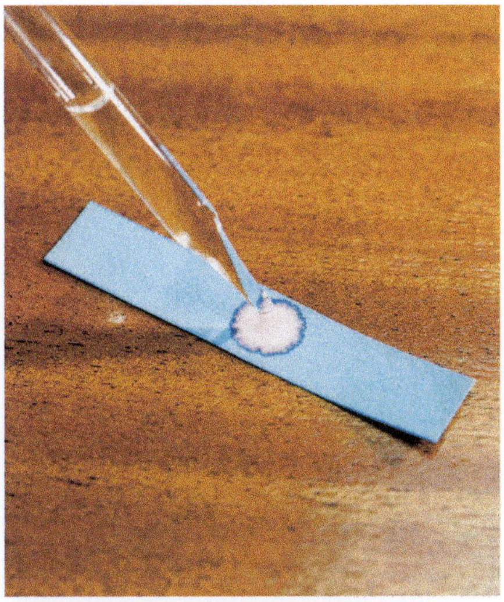

Figure 4 *Blue cobalt(II) chloride paper turns pink when water is added*

Summary questions

1 a How does the enthalpy change for a reversible reaction in one direction compare with the enthalpy change for the reaction in the opposite direction?

b What can anhydrous copper(II) sulfate be used to test for?

c Why does blue cobalt(II) chloride turn pink if left out in the open air?

d When water is added to blue cobalt(II) chloride is energy released or absorbed?

2 A reversible reaction gives out 50 kilojoules (kJ) of energy in the forward reaction. In this reaction W and X react to give Y and Z.

a Write an equation to show the reversible reaction.

b What can you say about the energy transfer in the reverse reaction?

3 Blue cobalt(II) chloride crystals turn pink when they become damp. The formula for the two forms can be written as $CoCl_2.2H_2O$ and $CoCl_2.6H_2O$.

a How many moles of water will combine with 1 mole of $CoCl_2.2H_2O$?

b Write a balanced chemical equation for the reaction, which is reversible.

c How can pink cobalt(II) chloride crystals be changed back to blue cobalt(II) chloride crystals?

Key points

- In reversible reactions, one reaction is exothermic and the other is endothermic.
- In any reversible reaction, the amount of energy released when the reaction goes in one direction is exactly equal to the energy absorbed when the reaction goes in the opposite direction.

9.4 Energy level diagrams

Learning objectives

After this topic, you should know:

- what energy level diagrams show us
- how catalysts affect the activation energy of a reaction
- the energy changes when bonds are broken
- the energy changes when bonds are made.

You can find out more about what is happening in a particular reaction by looking at its energy level diagram. These diagrams show us the relative amounts of energy contained in the reactants and the products. This energy is measured in kilojoules per mole (kJ/mol).

Exothermic reactions

Figure 1 shows the energy level diagram for an exothermic reaction. The products are at a lower energy level than the reactants. Therefore when the reactants form the products, energy is released.

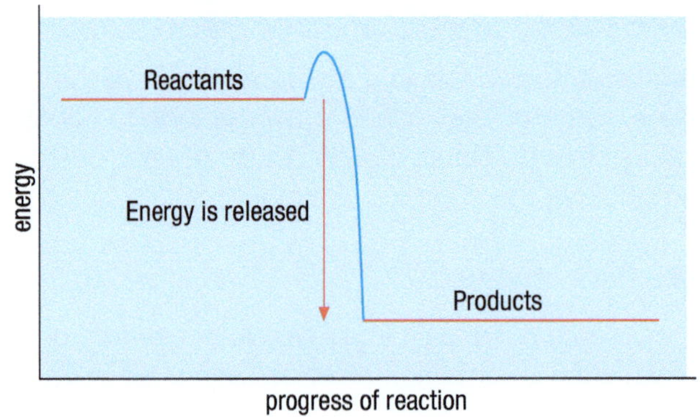

Figure 1 *The energy level diagram for an exothermic reaction*

The difference between the energy levels of the reactants and the products is the energy change during the reaction, measured in kJ/mol.

The difference in energy between the products and the reactants is released to the surroundings. Therefore in exothermic reactions the temperature of the surroundings increases. The surroundings get hotter and the value of ΔH for the reaction has a negative sign.

links

For more information about the enthalpy change, ΔH, in chemical reactions, look back at 9.1 Exothermic and endothermic reactions.

Endothermic reactions

Figure 2 shows the energy level diagram for an endothermic reaction.

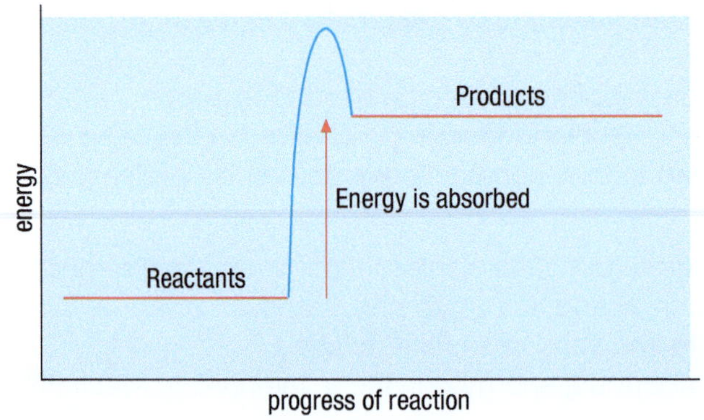

Figure 2 *The energy level diagram for an endothermic reaction*

Here the products are at a higher energy level than the reactants. As the reactants react to form products, energy is absorbed from the surroundings. The temperature of the surroundings decreases because energy is taken in during the reaction. The surroundings get colder. The products are at a higher energy level than the reactants, and the value of ΔH for the reaction is given a positive sign.

Activation energy and catalysis

Think back to your work on rates of reaction in Chapter 8. There you learnt about the collision theory of reactions. This stated that there is a minimum amount of energy needed before colliding particles can react. This energy needed to start a reaction is called the activation energy. This can be shown on the energy level diagrams. Look at Figure 3.

Catalysts can increase the rate of a reaction. The way they do this is to provide an alternative pathway to the products, which has a lower activation energy. This is shown on the energy level diagram in Figure 4. This means that a higher proportion of reactant particles now have enough energy to react when they collide.

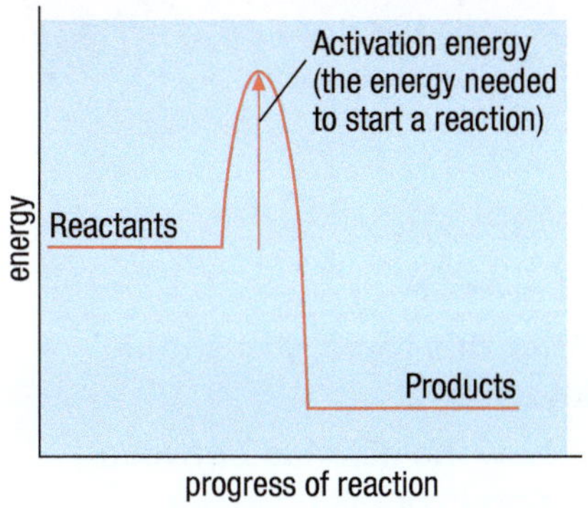

Figure 3 *The minimum amount of energy needed to start a reaction is called its activation energy*

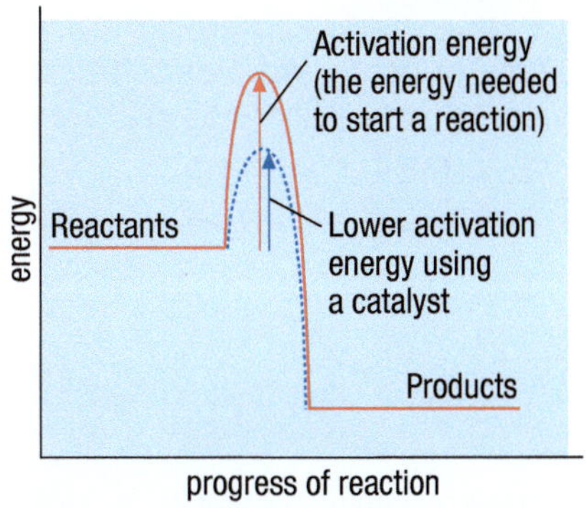

Figure 4 *A catalyst provides a different reaction pathway with a lower activation energy, so that a higher proportion of reactant particles have enough energy to react*

Bond breaking and bond making

Think about what happens as a chemical reaction takes place. You can think of the chemical bonds between the atoms or ions in the reactants being broken. Then new chemical bonds can be formed to make the products.

- Energy has to be supplied to break chemical bonds. This means that breaking bonds is an **endothermic** process. Energy is taken in from the surroundings.
- But, when new bonds are formed, energy is released. Making bonds is an **exothermic** process.

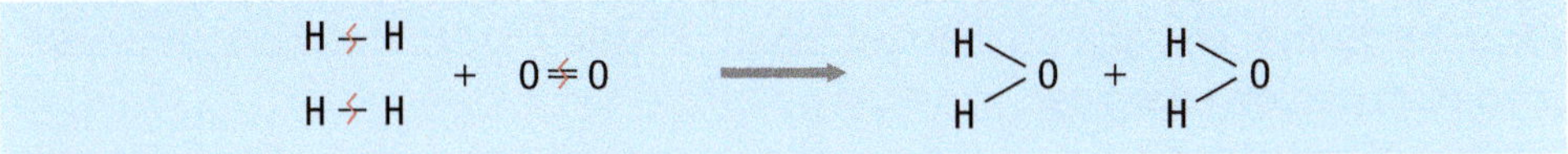

Figure 5 *Hydrogen and oxygen react to make water. The bonds between hydrogen atoms and between oxygen atoms have to be broken so that bonds between oxygen atoms and hydrogen atoms in water can be formed.*

Study tip

Remember that **B**reaking bonds a**B**sorbs energy, fo**R**ming bonds **R**eleases energy.

Summary questions

1 Draw energy level diagrams for the following reactions:

a $H_2(g) + Cl_2(g) \rightarrow 2HCl(g)$
ΔH for the reaction is -184 kJ/mol.

b $H_2(g) + I_2(g) \rightarrow 2HI(g)$
ΔH for the reaction $+26.5$ kJ/mol.

2 **a** Draw an energy level diagram for an endothermic reaction, $X \rightarrow Y + Z$, including its activation energy.

b Now show, on your energy level diagram drawn in part **a**, the effect of adding a catalyst.

c Explain how a catalyst increases the rate of a reaction.

3 **a** Explain why bond breaking is an endothermic process.

b Using a diagram like Figure 5 above, show the bonds being broken and new bonds made in the reaction between methane (CH_4) and oxygen which produces carbon dioxide and water.

c List the number and type of each bond broken and formed in your answer to part **b**.

Key points

- You can show the relative difference in the energy of reactants and products on energy level diagrams.
- Catalysts lower the activation energy so a greater proportion of reactant particles have enough energy to react.
- Bond breaking is endothermic, whereas bond making is exothermic.

9.5 Bond dissociation energy calculations

Learning objectives

After this topic, you should know:

- how the balance between bonds breaking in the reactants and bonds being made in the products affect the overall energy change of a reaction
- how to use bond dissociation energies to calculate energy changes in reactions.

Making and breaking bonds

There is always a balance between the energy needed to break bonds and the energy released when new bonds are made in a reaction. This is what decides whether the reaction is endothermic or exothermic.

- In some reactions the energy released when new bonds are formed (as the products are made) is more than the energy needed to break the bonds in the reactants. These reactions transfer energy to the surroundings. They are **exothermic**.
- In other reactions the energy needed to break the bonds in the reactants is more than the energy released when new bonds are formed in the products. These reactions transfer energy from the surroundings to the reacting chemicals. They are **endothermic**.

Bond dissociation energy

The energy needed to break the bond between two atoms is called the **bond dissociation energy** for that bond.

Bond dissociation energies are measured in kJ/mol. You can use bond dissociation energies to work out the enthalpy change (ΔH) for many chemical reactions. Before you can do this, you need to have a list of the most common bond dissociation energies:

Bond	Bond dissociation energy (kJ/mol)	Bond	Bond dissociation energy (kJ/mol)
C–C	347	H–Cl	432
C–O	358	H–O	464
C–H	413	H–N	391
C–N	286	H–H	436
C–Cl	346	O=O	498
Cl–Cl	243	N≡N	945

To calculate the energy change for a chemical reaction you need to work out:

1 how much energy is needed to break the chemical bonds in the reactants
2 how much energy is released when the new bonds are formed in the products.

It is very important to remember that the data in the table is the energy required for *breaking* bonds. However, the energy released as these bonds are formed is the same (see Figure 1).

For example, the bond dissociation energy for a C—C bond is +347 kJ/mol (an endothermic change). This means that the energy released *forming* a C—C bond is –347 kJ/mol (an exothermic change).

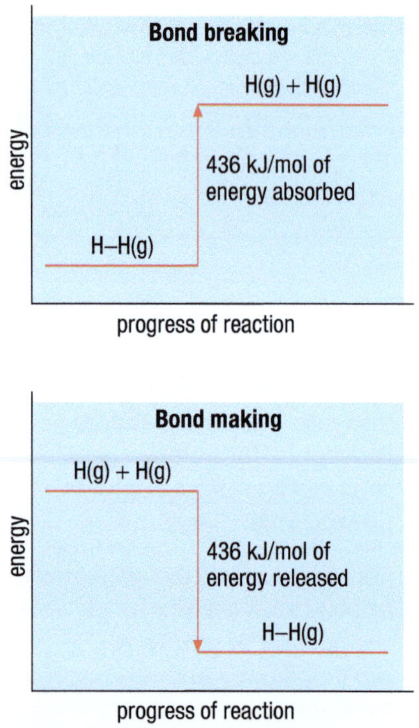

Figure 1 *Breaking and making a particular bond always involves the same amount of energy, but the change in enthalpy will have opposite signs (+ for bond breaking and – for bond making)*

Worked example

Ammonia is made from nitrogen and hydrogen in the Haber process. The balanced symbol equation for this reaction is:

$$N_2(g) + 3H_2(g) \rightleftharpoons 2NH_3(g)$$

Calculate the overall energy change for the forward reaction using bond dissociation energies.

Solution

This equation tells us that you need to break the bonds in 1 mole of nitrogen molecules and three moles of hydrogen molecules in this reaction. Look at Figure 2.

N≡N H—H H—H H—H

Figure 2 *These bonds are broken in the forward reaction*

Nitrogen molecules are held together by a triple bond (written like this: N≡N). This bond is very strong. Using data from the table, its bond energy is 945 kJ/mol.

Hydrogen molecules are held together by a single bond (written like this: H—H). From the table, the bond energy for this bond is 436 kJ/mol.
The energy needed to break 1 mole of N≡N and 3 moles of H—H bonds is
945 + (3 × 436) kJ = **+2253 kJ** (given a plus sign as this is an endothermic process).

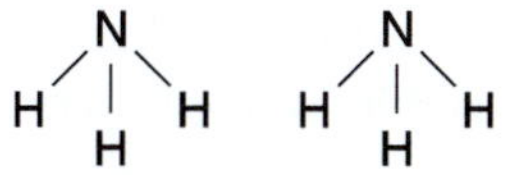

Figure 3 *These bonds are made in the forward reaction*

When these atoms form ammonia (NH_3), six new N—H bonds are made as two moles of NH_3 are formed (see Figure 3). The bond energy of the N—H bond is 391 kJ/mol.

Energy released when six moles of N—H bonds are made = 6 × 391 kJ = **–2346 kJ** (given a minus sign as this is an exothermic process).

Figure 4 shows the overall energy change for the forward reaction, as written.

So *the overall enthalpy change* (ΔH)
= (+2253 kJ) + (–2346 kJ)
= **–93 kJ** (This is the energy *released* in the forward reaction as written above.)

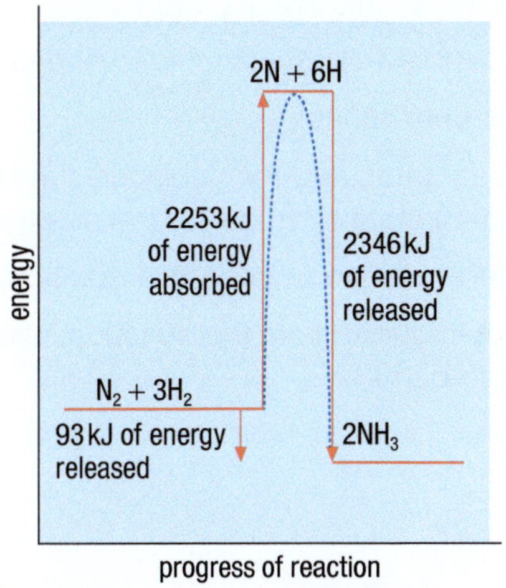

Figure 4 *The formation of ammonia. The energy released, 93 kJ, is for the formation of 2 moles of ammonia as shown in the balanced equation. So if you wanted to know the energy change for the reaction per mole of ammonia formed, it would release exactly half this, that is, 46.5 kJ/mol.*

Summary questions

1 If the energy required to break bonds is greater than the energy released when bonds are made, will the reaction be exothermic or endothermic?

2 What is meant by the 'bond dissociation energy' of a chemical bond?

3 Write balanced symbol equations and calculate the energy changes for the following chemical reactions:

a hydrogen + chlorine → hydrogen chloride

b hydrogen + oxygen → water

(Use the bond energies supplied in the table on the previous page.)

Key points

- In chemical reactions, energy must be supplied to break the bonds between atoms in the reactants.
- When new bonds are formed between atoms in a chemical reaction, energy is released.
- In an exothermic reaction, the energy released when new bonds are formed is greater than the energy absorbed when bonds are broken.
- In an endothermic reaction, the energy released when new bonds are formed is less than the energy absorbed when bonds are broken.
- You can calculate the overall energy change in a chemical reaction using bond energies.

Chapter summary questions

1 Two solutions are mixed and react in an endothermic reaction. When the reaction has finished, the reaction mixture is allowed to stand until it has returned to its starting temperature.

a Sketch a graph of temperature (*y*-axis) against time (*x*-axis) to show how the temperature of the reaction mixture changes.

b Label the graph clearly and explain what is happening wherever you have shown that the temperature is changing.

2 a Draw an energy level diagram to show the exothermic reaction between nitric acid and sodium hydroxide, including its activation energy.

b Draw an energy level diagram to show the endothermic change when ammonium nitrate dissolves in water, including its activation energy.

c Show an energy level diagram, including its activation energy, for the exothermic breakdown of hydrogen peroxide into water and oxygen. Then add to your diagram to show what happens when the same reaction is catalysed by manganese(IV) oxide.

3 When you eat sugar you break it down eventually to produce water and carbon dioxide.

a Copy and complete the balanced symbol equation:

$$C_{12}H_{22}O_{11} + O_2 \rightarrow$$

b Why must your body *supply* energy in order to break down a sugar molecule?

c When you break down sugar in your body, energy is released. Explain where this energy comes from in terms of the bonds in molecules.

d A person can get about 1700 kJ of energy by breaking down 100 g of sugar.
If a heaped teaspoon contains 5 g of sugar, how much energy does this release when broken down by their body?

4 Hydrogen peroxide has the structure H—O—O—H. It decomposes slowly to form water and oxygen.

$$2H_2O_2(aq) \rightarrow 2H_2O(l) + O_2(g)$$

The table shows the bond dissociation energies for different types of bond.

Bond	Bond dissociation energy (kJ/mol)
H—O	464
H—H	436
O—O	144
O=O	498

a Use the bond dissociation energies to calculate the enthalpy change, ΔH, for the decomposition of hydrogen peroxide as shown above.

b Explain the sign (+ or –) in your answer to part **a** in terms of bond breaking and making.

5 A student decided to investigate the energy transferred to the surroundings when iron reacts with copper(II) sulfate solution. She wanted to find out how the volume of copper(II) sulfate would affect the temperature change in the reaction, using excess copper(II) sulfate solution.

a Write a hypothesis for this investigation.

b Name the independent variable in this investigation.

c Name the dependent variable.

d Write the word equation and the balanced symbol equation, including state symbols for the reaction.

e i Will the temperature rise or fall in this reaction.

ii What piece of information in the question informed your answer to part **i**?

Practice questions

1 Most chemical reactions are exothermic. Some are endothermic.

Some equations are shown with a ΔH value.

a i What is the difference between these types of reaction? (2)

ii What is the meaning of ΔH? (1)

iii How can you decide from the ΔH value whether a reaction is exothermic or endothermic? (1)

b The progress of a reaction can be represented on an energy level diagram.

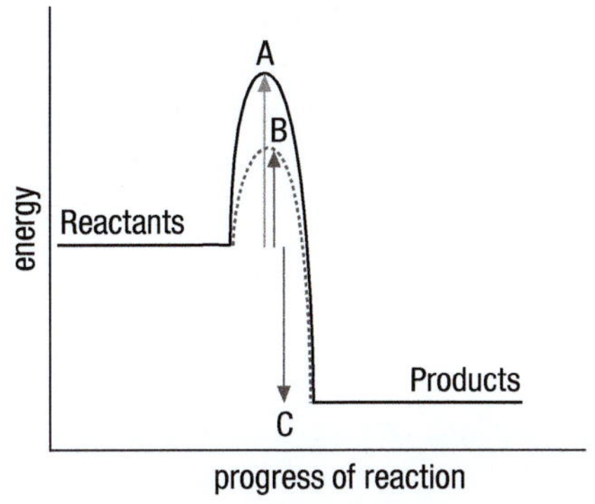

The diagram represents a reaction that can be done with or without a catalyst.

i How can you decide from this diagram that the reaction is exothermic? (1)

ii What name is used for the energies represented by arrows A and B? (1)

iii Why is arrow B shorter than arrow A? (1)

iv What is the enthalpy change for the reaction? (1)

c The following equation represents a reversible reaction.

$A + B \rightleftharpoons C + D \qquad \Delta H = +31$ kJ/mole

What is the value of ΔH for the following reaction?

$C + D \rightleftharpoons A + B$ (1)

2 A student carried out an investigation into the temperature changes when different combinations of chemicals were mixed together. The results were recorded in a table:

Reactants	Initial temperature of each reactant in °C	Maximum or minimum temperature recorded after mixing in °C
A. dilute hydrochloric acid + sodium hydroxide solution	18.2	22.3
B. magnesium + iron(II) sulfate	18.3	28.8
C. sodium hydrogencarbonate + citric acid	18.3	16.2
D. zinc + iron(II) sulfate	18.4	23.0

a i What is the scientific name given to the reaction vessel used in experiments investigating the energy transferred during chemical reactions? (1)

ii Name and explain the choice of material for the reaction vessel. (3)

iii Suggest the interval between the scale division marks on the thermometer used in this experiment. Give a reason for your choice. (2)

b Classify reactions A to D as exothermic or endothermic. (2)

c Which reaction involved the largest transfer of energy? (2)

d i Write a balanced symbol equation, including state symbols, for Reaction A. (3)

ii Predict the temperature change when dilute nitric acid reacts with potassium hydroxide solution (using reactants of the same concentration as those used in Reaction A). Explain your answer, including an ionic equation. (3)

e i What type of reaction is taking place in Reactions B and D? (1)

ii Explain what the results of the experiment indicate about the relative reactivity of magnesium, iron and zinc. (3)

3 The energy change in a reaction can be calculated using values of bond energy. The combustion of methane can be represented as follows:

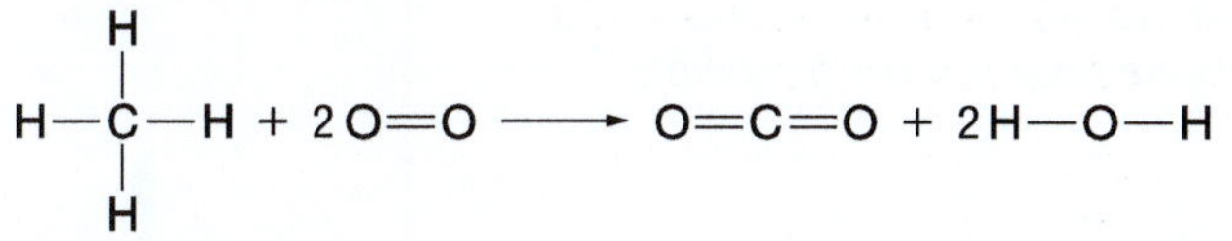

Use bond energy values from the tables in your calculations.

Bond	Bond energy in kJ/mole
C–H	412
O=O	496

Bond	Bond energy in kJ/mole
C=O	743
H–O	463

a Calculate the energy needed to break the bonds in the reactants. (2)

b Calculate the energy given out when the bonds in the products are formed. (2)

c What is the enthalpy change for the combustion of methane? (1)

10.1 Hydrocarbons

Learning objectives

After this topic, you should know:

- what crude oil is made up of
- what alkanes are
- how to represent alkanes.

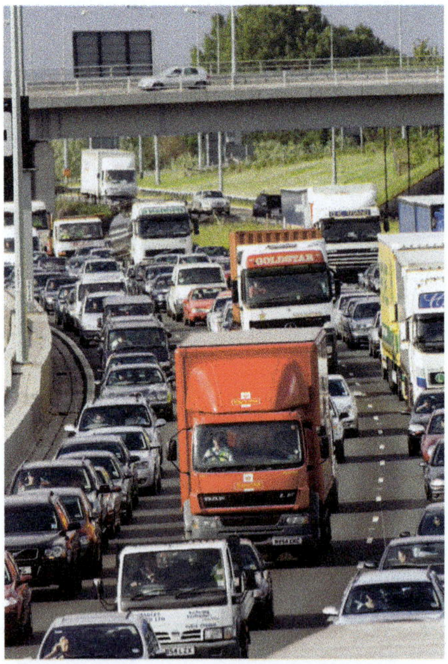

Figure 1 *The price of nearly everything you buy is affected by oil because the cost of moving goods to the shops affects the price you pay for them*

So far, some of the 21st century's most important chemicals come from crude oil. These chemicals play a major part in our lives. We use them as fuels to run our cars, to warm our homes, and to make electricity.

Fuels are important because they keep us warm and on the move. So when oil prices rise, it affects us all. Countries that produce crude oil can affect the whole world economy by the price they charge for their oil.

Crude oil

Crude oil is a dark, smelly liquid. It is a **mixture** of many different chemical compounds. A mixture contains two or more elements or compounds that are not chemically combined together. Nearly all of the compounds in crude oil are compounds containing only hydrogen and carbon atoms. These compounds are called **hydrocarbons**.

Crude oil straight from the ground is not much use. There are too many substances in it, all with different boiling points. Before we can use crude oil, it must be separated into different substances which contain molecules with a similar number of carbon atoms and have similar boiling points. These are known as **fractions**. Because the properties of substances do not change when they are mixed (as opposed to reacted), engineers can separate mixtures of substances in crude oil by **fractional distillation**. Fractional distillation separates liquids with different boiling points.

Demonstration

Fractional distillation of crude oil

Mixtures of liquids can be separated using fractional distillation. This can be done in the lab on a small scale. Heat the crude oil mixture so that it boils. The different fractions vaporise between different ranges of temperature. Collect the vapours by cooling and condensing them.

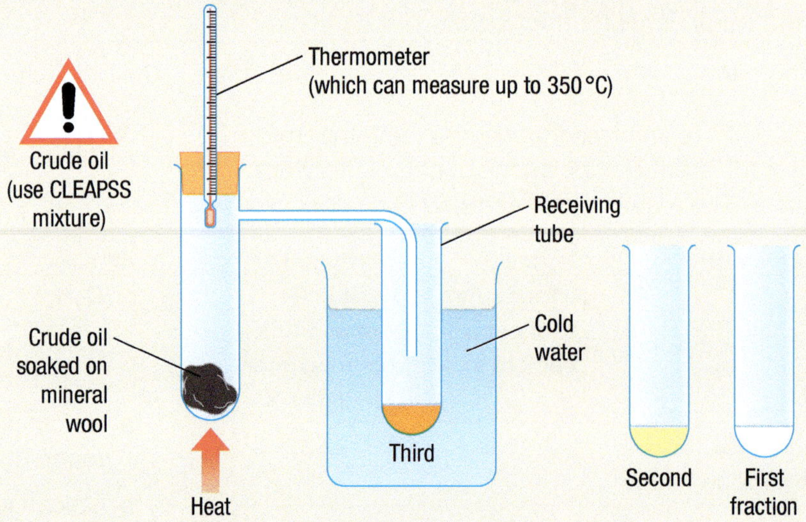

Figure 2 *The fractional distillation of crude oil in the lab*

- What colour are the first few drops of liquid collected?

Alkanes

Alkanes are **saturated hydrocarbons**. All the carbon–carbon bonds are single covalent bonds. This means that they contain as many hydrogen atoms as possible in each molecule. No more hydrogen atoms can be added.

Most of the hydrocarbons in crude oil are **alkanes**. You can see some examples of alkane molecules in Figure 3. Notice how all their names end in '–ane'. The first part of their names tells you how many carbon atoms are in their molecules.

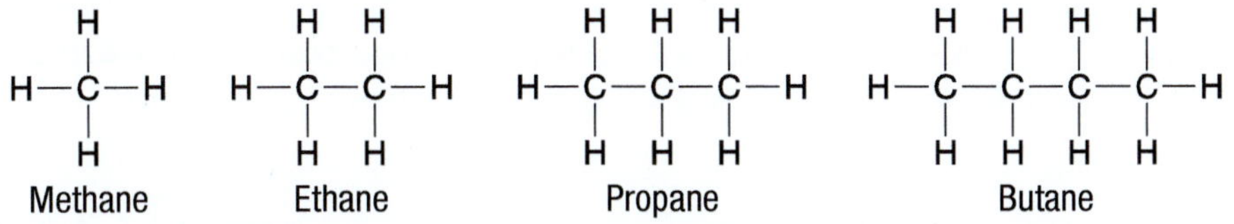

Figure 3 *You can represent alkanes like this, showing all of the atoms in the molecule. They are called 'displayed formulae'. The line drawn between two atoms in a molecule e.g. C – H or C – C, as shown above, represents a single covalent bond.*

links

For information on covalent bonding, look back at 2.3 Covalent bonding.

Look at the molecular formulae of the first five alkane molecules below:

$\mathbf{CH_4}$ (methane)

$\mathbf{C_2H_6}$ (ethane)

$\mathbf{C_3H_8}$ (propane)

$\mathbf{C_4H_{10}}$ (butane)

$\mathbf{C_5H_{12}}$ (pentane)

Can you see a pattern in the molecular formulae of the alkanes? You can write the general formula for alkane molecules like this:

$$\mathbf{C_nH_{2n+2}}$$

This means that 'for every n carbon atoms there are $(2n + 2)$ hydrogen atoms' in an alkane molecule. For example, if an alkane molecule contains 12 carbon atoms its formula will be $\mathbf{C_{12}H_{26}}$.

Summary questions

1 a What is crude oil?
b Why is oil so important to society?
c Why can crude oil be separated using distillation?

2 Engineers drill crude oil from beneath the ground or seabed. Why is this crude oil not very useful as a product itself?

3 a Write the general formula of the alkanes.
b Write the molecular formulae of the alkanes which have six to ten carbon atoms. Then find out their names.

4 a Draw the displayed formula of octane, whose molecules have eight carbon atoms.
b How many hydrogen atoms are there in an alkane molecule which has 22 carbon atoms?
c How many carbon atoms are there in an alkane molecule which has 32 hydrogen atoms?
d Why are alkanes described as 'saturated hydrocarbons'?

Key points

- **Crude oil is a mixture of many different compounds.**
- **Most of the compounds in crude oil are hydrocarbons – they contain only hydrogen and carbon atoms.**
- **Alkanes are saturated hydrocarbons. They contain as many hydrogen atoms as possible in their molecules.**
- **The general formula of an alkane is:**

$$C_nH_{2n+2}$$

10.2 Fractional distillation of crude oil

Learning objectives

After this topic, you should know:

- how the volatility, viscosity, and flammability of hydrocarbons are affected by the size of their molecules
- how to separate crude oil into fractions
- the properties that make a fraction useful as a fuel.

The properties of hydrocarbons

The properties of hydrocarbons depend on the size of their molecules. Some have molecules that are quite small, with relatively few carbon atoms in short chains. These short-chain molecules make up the hydrocarbons that tend to be most useful. These hydrocarbons make good fuels as they ignite easily and burn well, with less smoky flames than hydrocarbons made up of larger molecules. They are very **flammable** (see Figure 1 below). Other hydrocarbons have lots of carbon atoms in their molecules, and may have branches or side-chains.

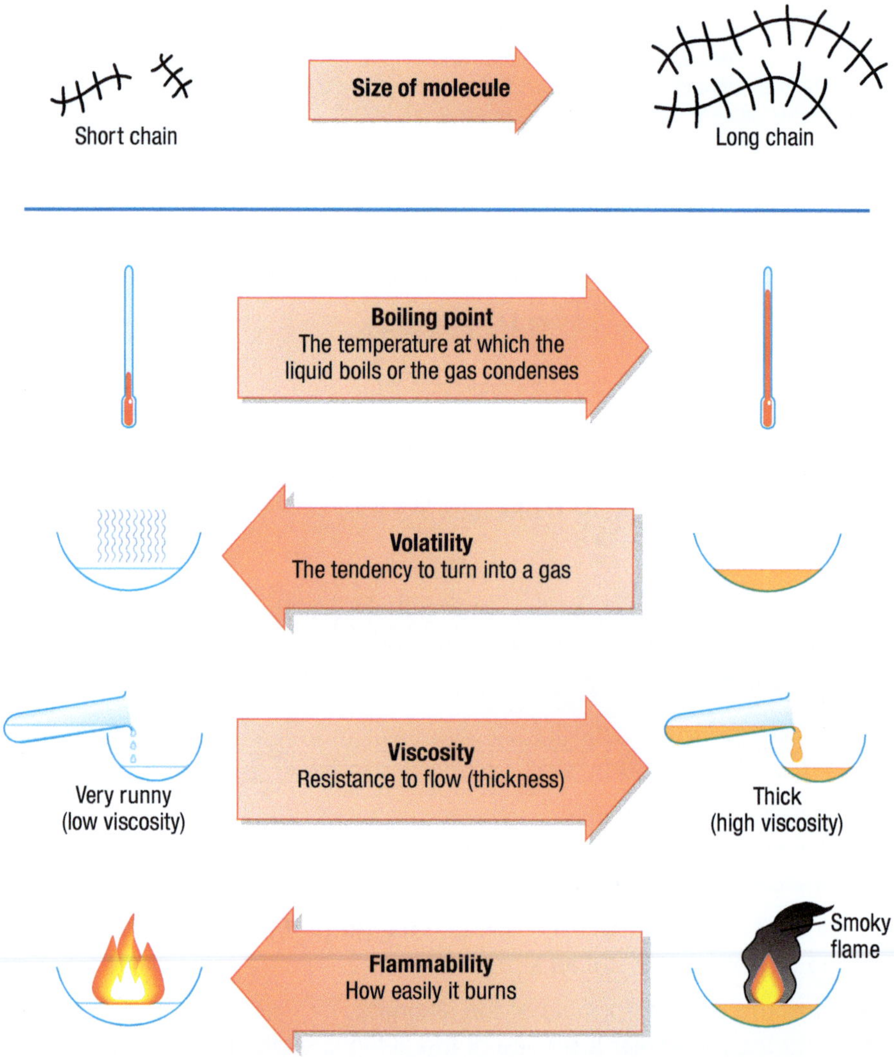

Figure 1 *The properties of hydrocarbons depend on the chain-length of their molecules*

Demonstration

Comparing fractions

Your teacher might compare the **viscosity** and flammability of some fractions (mixtures of hydrocarbons with similar boiling points) that are obtained from crude oil.

The boiling point of a hydrocarbon depends on the size of its molecules. Engineers can use the differences in boiling points in fractional distillation to separate the hydrocarbons in crude oil into fractions.

Fractional distillation of crude oil

Engineers separate out crude oil into hydrocarbons with similar boiling points, called fractions. This process is called **fractional distillation**. Each hydrocarbon fraction contains molecules with similar numbers of carbon atoms. Each of these fractions boils at a different temperature range because of the different sizes of the molecules in it.

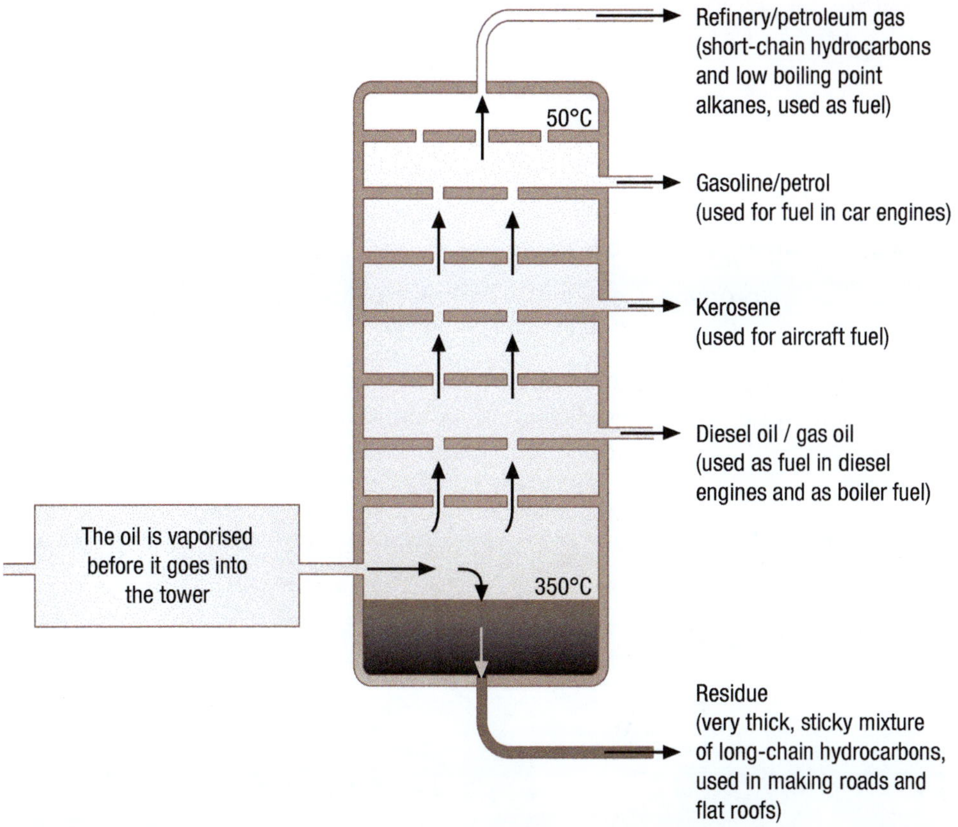

Figure 2 *Scientists and engineers use fractional distillation to separate the mixture of hydrocarbons in crude oil into fractions. Each fraction contains hydrocarbons with similar boiling points.*

Crude oil is heated and fed in near the bottom of a tall tower (a fractionating column) as hot vapour. The column is kept very hot at the bottom and much cooler at the top. The temperature decreases going up the column. The gases condense when they reach the temperature of their boiling points. The different fractions are collected as liquids at different levels. The fractions are collected from the column in a continuous process.

Hydrocarbons with the smallest molecules have the lowest boiling points. They are collected at the cool top of the column. At the bottom of the column, the fractions have high boiling points. They cool to form very thick liquids or solids at room temperature.

Once collected, the fractions need more processing before they can be used.

Summary questions

1 a How does the size of a hydrocarbon molecule affect:
 i the boiling point?
 ii the volatility?
 iii the viscosity (thickness) of a hydrocarbon?
 b A hydrocarbon catches fire very easily. Is it likely to have molecules with long hydrocarbon chains or short ones? Will it give off lots of black smoke when it burns?

2 Make a table to summarise how the properties of hydrocarbons depend on the size of their molecules.

3 Explain the steps involved in the fractional distillation of crude oil.

Did you know ... ?

2014 figures show that Venezuela contains 17.5% of the world's crude oil reserves, with Saudi Arabia containing 15.7% of total proved resources.

There are many different types of crude oil. For example, crude oil from Venezuela contains many long-chain hydrocarbons. It is very dark and thick and is called 'heavy' crude. Other countries, such as Nigeria and Saudi Arabia, produce crude oil which is much paler in colour and runnier. This is 'light' crude.

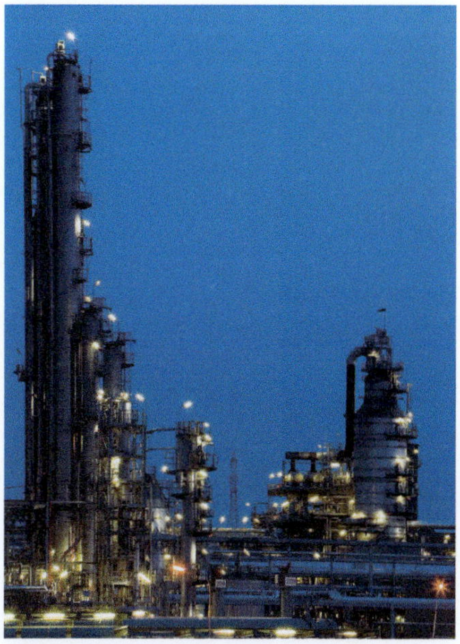

Figure 3 *An oil refinery at night*

Key points

- Crude oil is separated into fractions using fractional distillation.
- The properties of each fraction depend on the size of the hydrocarbon molecules in it.
- Lighter fractions make better fuels as they ignite more easily and burn well, with cleaner (less smoky) flames.

10.3 Burning fuels

Learning objectives

After this topic, you should know:

- the products of combustion when fuels are burnt in a good supply of air, or in a limited supply of air
- the pollutants produced when fuels are burnt.

The lighter fractions from crude oil are very useful as fuels. When hydrocarbons burn in plenty of air they release lots of energy.

For example, when propane burns:

$$\text{propane} + \text{oxygen} \rightarrow \text{carbon dioxide} + \text{water}$$
$$C_3H_8 + 5O_2 \rightarrow 3CO_2 + 4H_2O$$

The carbon and hydrogen in the fuel are **oxidised** completely when they burn like this. Remember that one definition of 'oxidation' means adding oxygen in a chemical reaction. The products of complete combustion are carbon dioxide and water.

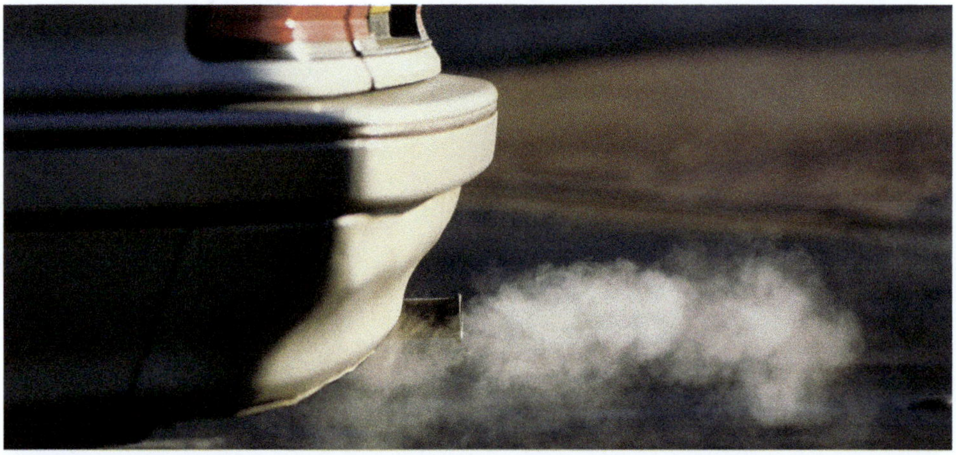

Figure 1 *On a cold day you can often see the water produced when fossil fuels burn*

Practical

Products of combustion

You can test the products given off when a hydrocarbon burns as shown in Figure 2.

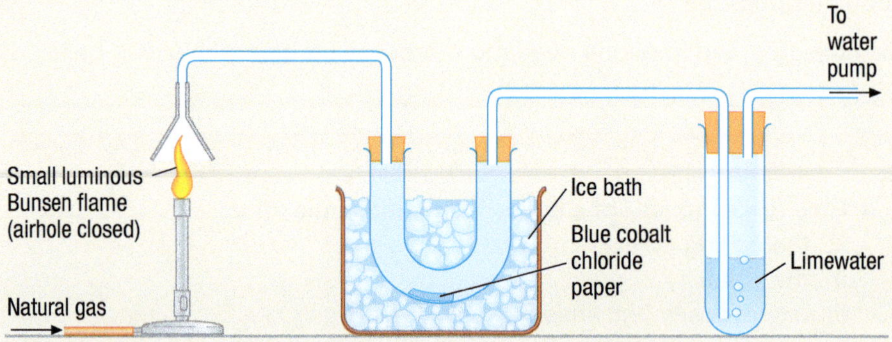

Figure 2 *Testing the products formed when a hydrocarbon burns*

- What happens in the U-tube? Which substance is present?
- What happens to the limewater? Which gas is given off?

Safety: Wear eye protection. Handle cobalt chloride papers as little as possible.

Pollution from fuels

All fossil fuels – oil, coal, and natural gas – produce carbon dioxide and water (vapour) when they burn in plenty of air. But as well as hydrocarbons, these fuels also contain other substances. Impurities containing sulfur found in fuels cause us major problems.

All fossil fuels contain at least some sulfur. This reacts with oxygen when the fuel is burnt. It forms a gas called **sulfur dioxide** (SO_2). This acidic gas is toxic. It is bad for the environment, as it is a cause of acid rain which damages trees, as well as killing animal life in lakes. The sulfur impurities can be removed from a fuel ***before*** the fuel is burnt. This happens in petrol and diesel for cars. In power stations, sulfur dioxide is also removed from the waste or 'flue' gases by reacting it with basic calcium oxide or calcium hydroxide.

When fuel is burnt in a car engine, even more pollution can be produced.

- When any fuel containing carbon is burnt, it makes carbon dioxide. Carbon dioxide is the main greenhouse gas in the air. It absorbs energy released as radiation from the surface of the Earth. Most scientists think that this is causing **climate change**, which affects temperatures around the world and might result in more severe weather events and the flooding of low-lying land as sea levels rise.
- When there is not enough oxygen inside an engine, it results in **incomplete** (or partial) **combustion**. Instead of all the carbon in the fuel turning into carbon dioxide, **carbon monoxide** gas (CO) is also formed. Carbon monoxide is a toxic gas. It is colourless and odourless. Your red blood cells pick up this gas and carry it around in your blood instead of oxygen.
- The high temperature inside an engine also allows the nitrogen and oxygen in the air to react together. This reaction makes **nitrogen oxides**. These are toxic and can trigger some people's asthma. They also cause acid rain.
- Diesel engines burn hydrocarbons with bigger molecules than petrol engines. When these large molecules react with oxygen in an engine they do not always burn completely. Tiny solid particles containing carbon (soot) and unburnt hydrocarbons are produced. These **particulates** get carried into the air. They travel into the upper atmosphere, reflecting sunlight back into space, causing **global dimming**. Scientists also think that they may damage the cells in our lungs and even cause cancer.

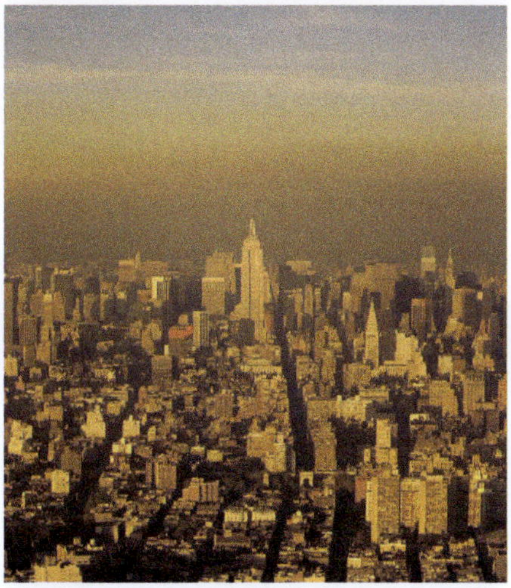

Figure 3 *A combination of many cars in a small area and the right weather conditions can cause smog to be formed. This is a mixture of SMoke and fOG.*

Summary questions

1 a What are the products of the complete combustion of a hydrocarbon?
  b When fossil fuels burn, which element present in impurities can produce sulfur dioxide?

2 a Which pollution problem does sulfur dioxide gas contribute to?
  b Which other non-metal oxides released from cars also cause this pollution problem?

3 Explain how **a** sulfur dioxide, **b** nitrogen oxides, and **c** particulates, are produced when fuels burn in vehicles.

4 a Natural gas is mainly methane (CH_4). Write a balanced symbol equation, including state symbols, for the complete combustion of methane.
  b When natural gas burns in a faulty gas heater it can produce carbon monoxide (and water). Write a balanced symbol equation, including state symbols, to show this reaction.
  c Why is carbon monoxide dangerous?

Key points

- When hydrocarbon fuels are burnt in plenty of air the carbon and hydrogen in the fuel are completely oxidised. They produce carbon dioxide and water.
- Sulfur impurities in fuels burn to form sulfur dioxide, which can cause acid rain. Sulfur can be removed from fuels before burning them or sulfur dioxide can be removed from flue gases.
- Changing the conditions in which hydrocarbon fuels are burnt can change the products made.
- In insufficient oxygen, poisonous carbon monoxide gas is formed. We can also get particulates of carbon (soot) and unburnt hydrocarbons, especially if the fuel is diesel. These can cause global dimming.
- At the high temperatures in engines, nitrogen from the air reacts with oxygen to form oxides of nitrogen. These cause breathing problems and can also cause acid rain.

10.4 Alternative fuels

Learning objectives

After this topic, you should know:

- what biofuels are
- the advantages and disadvantages of using biofuels.

Biofuels

Biofuels are fuels that are made from plant or animal products (renewable resources). Examples are **biodiesel**, which is made from oils extracted from plants, and biogas, which is generated from animal waste. Biofuels will become more and more important as our supplies of crude oil diminish.

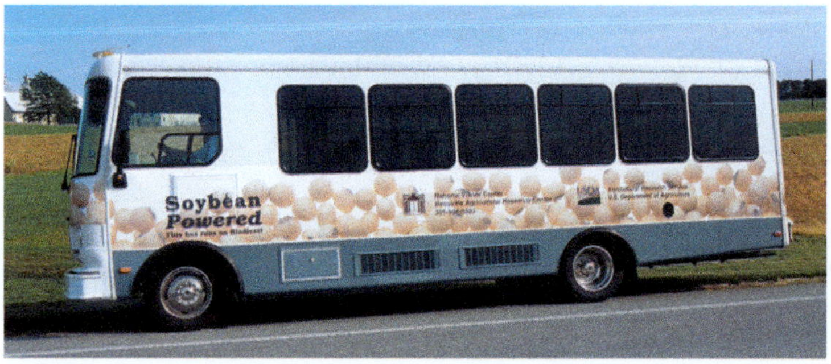

Figure 1 *This coach runs on biodiesel*

Advantages of biodiesel and other biofuels

There are advantages in using biodiesel and other biofuels as a fuel.

- Biodiesel is much less harmful to animals and plants if it is spilled than the diesel obtained from crude oil.
- When biodiesel is burnt in an engine it burns much more cleanly, reducing the particulates emitted. It also makes very little sulfur dioxide.
- As **non-renewable** fossil fuels, such as crude oil, run out, their price will increase and biofuels will become cheaper to use.
- Another really big advantage over fossil fuels is the fact that the crops used to make biofuels absorb carbon dioxide gas as they grow. So biofuels from plants are in theory 'CO_2 neutral'. That means the amount of carbon dioxide given off when the fuel burns is balanced by the amount absorbed as the plants it was made from grew. Therefore, biofuels make little contribution to the carbon dioxide in our atmosphere. We say that they have a 'reduced carbon footprint' as fuels compared with petrol and diesel.

However, we cannot claim that all biofuels make a ***zero*** contribution to carbon dioxide emissions. We should really take into account the CO_2 released when:

- fertilising and harvesting the crops
- extracting and processing the biofuel
- transporting the plant material and biofuel.

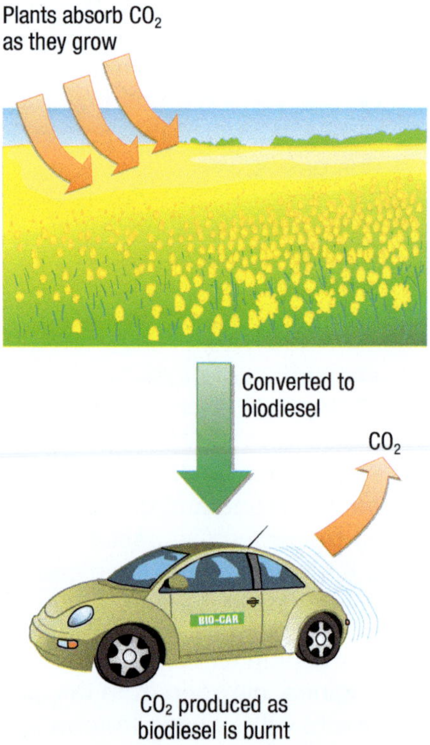

Figure 2 *Cars that run on biodiesel produce very little CO_2 overall, as CO_2 is absorbed by the plants used to make the biofuel*

Disadvantages of biofuels

There are also disadvantages in using biofuels.

- The use of large areas of farmland to produce biofuel instead of food could pose problems. If people start to rely on oil-producing crops for their fuel, farmers will turn land once used for food crops to land for growing biofuel crops.
- This could result in famine in poorer countries if the price of staple food crops rises as demand overtakes supply. Forests, which absorb lots of carbon dioxide, might also be cleared to grow the biofuel crops if they get more popular.
- People are also worried about endangered species because of the destruction of their habitats, such as tropical forests, cleared to grow biofuel crops.

Using ethanol as a biofuel

Another biofuel is ethanol. It can be made by fermenting sugar solution, extracted from sugar beet or sugar cane, using yeast (whose enzymes provide a natural catalyst). The **fermentation** is a slow batch process that takes place in large vats, at temperatures between 20 °C and 35 °C. It produces yields of up to 15% ethanol. The ethanol is then distilled from the aqueous solution for use as a biofuel. This fermentation process is:

$$\text{glucose} \rightarrow \text{ethanol} + \text{carbon dioxide}$$
$$C_6H_{12}O_6(aq) \rightarrow 2C_2H_5OH(aq) + 2CO_2(g)$$

Ethanol made by fermentation is known as 'bioethanol'.

As with other biofuels, the ethanol gives off carbon dioxide (a greenhouse gas) when it burns:

$$C_2H_5OH(l) + 3O_2(g) \rightarrow 2CO_2(g) + 3H_2O(g)$$

However, this should be balanced against the sugar cane absorbing CO_2 gas during photosynthesis.

In countries like Brazil, that have no natural oil supplies of their own, ethanol is manufactured on a large scale by fermentation. They have a climate that is ideal for growing sugar cane (renewable). So although the fermentation process is a slow reaction, it is the cheapest way for them to make ethanol to be used as a fuel.

The ethanol has to be made in batches and left to ferment, but can only produce yields of up to 15% ethanol in solution. However, the energy requirements cost less as the reaction mixture ferments at just warm temperatures (between 20 °C and 35 °C), and atmospheric pressure. Ethanol is distilled off, then used to run some Brazilian cars. This helps preserve fossil fuel supplies, as petrol and ethene come from crude oil. It also reduces carbon dioxide released into the atmosphere. On the other hand, lots of land that could be used for food crops are set aside for biofuel crops.

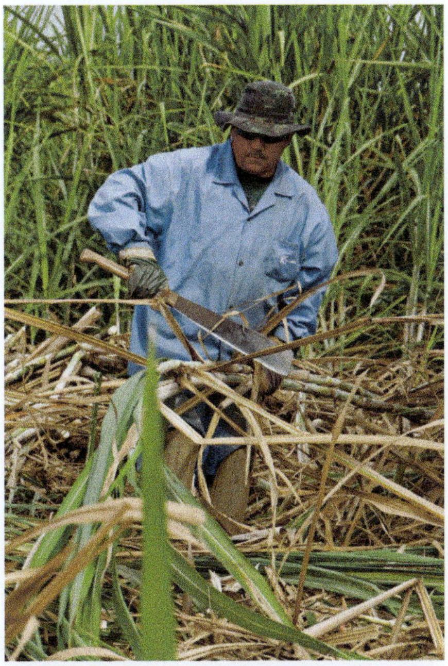

Figure 3 *Ethanol can be made from sugar cane. The growing and harvesting of the sugar cane crop is labour-intensive work.*

links

For more information on ethanol, see 12.2 Properties and uses of alcohols.

Summary questions

1. Why is burning ethanol a better choice of fuel than petrol if you want to reduce carbon dioxide emissions?
2. Explain where the energy in biodiesel comes from.
3. Explain why shifting from fossil fuels to biofuels could possibly cause food shortages.

Key points

- **Biofuels are a renewable source of energy that could be used to replace some fossil fuels.**
- **Biodiesel can be made from vegetable oils.**
- **There are advantages, and some disadvantages, in using biofuels.**
- **Ethanol is also a biofuel as it can be made from the sugar in plants.**

Chapter summary questions

1 **a** **i** Copy and complete this general formula for the alkanes:

C_nH

ii What is the formula of the alkane with 18 carbon atoms?

iii What is the formula of the alkane with 18 hydrogen atoms?

b Look at the boiling points in this table:

Alkane	Number of carbon atoms	Boiling point in °C
methane	1	–161
ethane	2	–88
propane	3	–42
butane	4	–0.5
pentane	5	
hexane	6	69

Draw a graph of the alkanes' boiling points (vertical axis) against the number of carbon atoms (horizontal axis).

c What is the general pattern you see from your graph?

d Use your graph to predict the boiling point of pentane.

2 **a** The alkanes are all 'saturated hydrocarbons'.

i What is a hydrocarbon?

ii What does 'saturated' mean when describing an alkane?

b **i** Give the name and formula of this alkane:

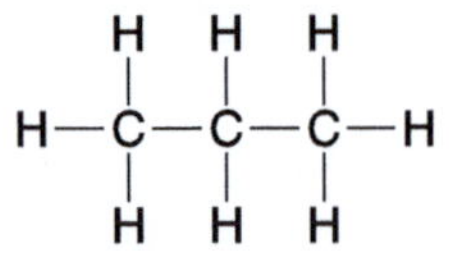

ii What do the letters represent in this displayed formula?

iii What do the lines between the letters represent?

3 One alkane, A, has a boiling point of 344 °C and another, B, has a boiling point of 126 °C.

a Which one will be collected nearer the top of a fractionating column in an oil refinery? Explain your choice.

b Which one will be the better fuel? Explain your choice.

c State the differences you would expect between A and B in terms of their:

i viscosity

ii volatility.

4 **a** What problem is associated with the increased levels of carbon dioxide gas in the atmosphere?

b **i** What gas is given off from fossil fuel power stations that can cause acid rain?

ii Give **two** ways of stopping this acidic gas getting into the atmosphere.

iii Name the other cause of acid rain which comes from car engines and how it arises.

5 Two students are testing the products formed when ethanol burns. They set up the experiment below:

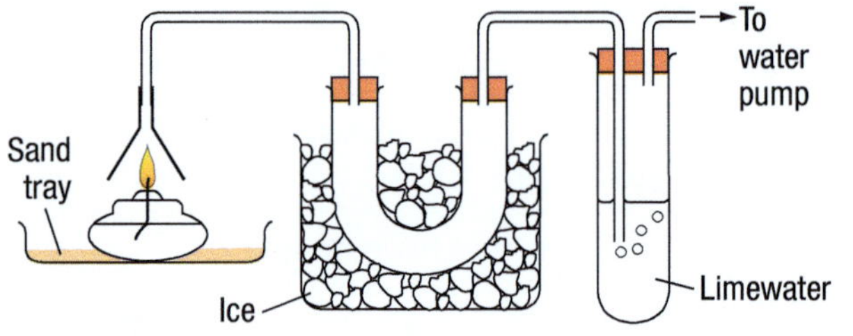

a Why do they put ice around the U-tube?

b How can they test for the substance formed in the U-tube?

c Explain what happens to the limewater.

d There is a small amount of carbon dioxide in the air. How can they show that the carbon dioxide they test for is not just the result of the carbon dioxide in the air?

e Write a word equation and balanced symbol equation for the complete combustion of ethanol.

f The students wanted to test the products of combustion of a hydrocarbon. Wax is made of hydrocarbons. How would the students change their experiment to carry out this test?

g Write a word equation and balanced symbol equation for the complete combustion of propane gas.

h Propane is used in portable gas heaters but there must be good ventilation in the room. Which toxic gas will be produced when the propane burns if there is a poor supply of air in the room?

6 **a** Which one of these fuels could be termed a 'biofuel'? Explain your choice.

Hydrogen Butane Ethanol Diesel Petrol

b Explain what is meant by the statement 'Biodiesel is potentially CO_2 neutral'.

c Why is the use of hydrogen as a fuel one way to tackle the problem of climate change?

d State **two** problems with the use of hydrogen as a fuel.

e Write a word equation and a balanced symbol equation to show the combustion of hydrogen.

Practice questions

1 Crude oil is a mixture of many compounds, most of which are saturated hydrocarbons. Most of these hydrocarbons are alkanes.

a **i** What is a hydrocarbon? (2)

ii What is the meaning of the term 'saturated'? (1)

b The formulae of the first two alkanes are CH_4 and C_2H_6

i What is the general formula of the alkanes? (1)

ii What is the molecular formula of the alkane with three carbon atoms in each molecule? (1)

iii Draw the displayed formula of the alkane with four carbon atoms in each molecule. (1)

c The compounds in crude oil are separated into fractions by fractional distillation. This process involves converting most of the crude oil into vapour, and then cooling it. The fraction that reaches the top of the fractionating column contains the smallest molecules.

i Name the changes of state involved in this process of fractional distillation. (2)

ii State **two** properties of the liquid fraction that leaves the column near the lowest part. (2)

2 Many of the smaller molecules obtained from crude oil are used as fuels.

a Name the **two** products of complete combustion of a hydrocarbon fuel. (2)

b Write the symbol equation for the complete combustion of methane. (2)

c If there is not enough oxygen, then a hydrocarbon may undergo incomplete combustion.

Name one solid product and one gaseous product that could form by incomplete combustion. (2)

d The combustion of hydrocarbon fuels can produce small amounts of oxides of nitrogen.

i What condition is needed for oxides of nitrogen to form? (1)

ii What is the main environmental problem caused by oxides of nitrogen? (1)

e Hydrocarbon fuels may contain small amounts of sulfur, which can release sulfur dioxide into the atmosphere during combustion.

i What is done to prevent the emission of sulfur dioxide from a car exhaust? (1)

ii What is done to prevent the emission of sulfur dioxide from a power station? (1)

3 Alternative fuels are increasingly used to replace fuels obtained from crude oil. Biofuels are one type of alternative fuel.

a One common biofuel that has been used for many centuries is wood.

Why is wood described as a biofuel? (1)

b Ethanol is another biofuel.

State the main source of ethanol and name the method used to convert it into ethanol. (2)

c **i** State **one** reason why biofuels are being increasingly used. (1)

ii State the main disadvantages of using large areas of land for biofuel production. (1)

d Hydrogen is another alternative fuel.
State why the combustion of hydrogen is less likely to cause climate change than burning a hydrocarbon fuel. (1)

11.1 Cracking hydrocarbons

Learning objectives

After this topic, you should know:

- how smaller, more useful hydrocarbon molecules are made from larger, less useful ones in crude oil
- what alkenes are and how they differ from alkanes.

Some of the heavier fractions that are produced in the fractional distillation of crude oil are not very useful. The hydrocarbons in them are made up of large molecules. They are thick liquids or solids with high boiling points. They are difficult to vaporise and do not burn easily – so they are poor fuels. Yet the main demand from crude oil is for fuels. Fortunately these large hydrocarbon molecules can be broken down in a process called **cracking**.

The process takes place at an oil refinery in a steel vessel called a cracker. In the cracker, a heavy fraction distilled from crude oil is heated to vaporise the hydrocarbons. The vapour is then either passed over a hot catalyst or mixed with steam and heated to a very high temperature. The hydrocarbons are cracked as thermal decomposition reactions take place. The large molecules split apart to form smaller, more useful ones.

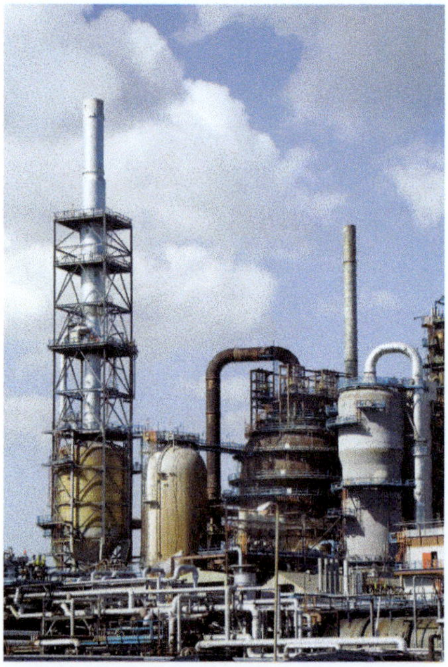

Figure 1 *In an oil refinery, huge crackers like this are used to break down large hydrocarbon molecules into smaller ones*

An example of cracking

Decane, $C_{10}H_{22}$, is a medium-sized alkane molecule. When heated to 500 °C with a catalyst, it breaks down. One of the molecules produced is pentane, which is used in petrol.

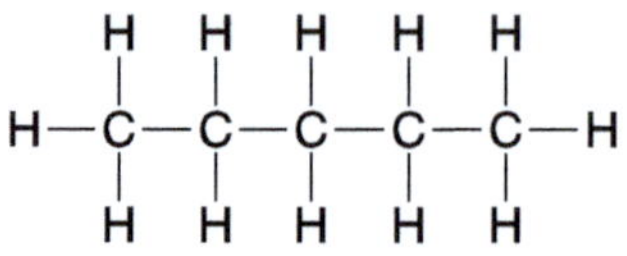

Figure 2 *Pentane (C_5H_{12}) can be used as a fuel. This is the displayed formula of pentane.*

We also get propene and ethene, which can be used to produce other chemicals.

$$\underset{\text{decane}}{C_{10}H_{22}} \xrightarrow{500\,°C\ +\ \text{catalyst}} \underset{\text{pentane}}{C_5H_{12}} + \underset{\text{propene}}{C_3H_6} + \underset{\text{ethene}}{C_2H_4}$$

This reaction is an example of thermal decomposition.

Notice how this cracking reaction produces different types of molecules. One of the molecules is pentane. The first part of its name tells us that it has five carbon atoms (*pent*-). The last part of its name (-*ane*) shows that it is an alkane. Like all other alkanes, pentane is a saturated hydrocarbon. Its molecules have as much hydrogen as possible in them.

The other molecules in this reaction have names that end slightly differently. They end in -*ene*. This type of molecule is called an **alkene**. The different ending tells us that these molecules are **unsaturated**. Unsaturated compounds contain at least one **double bond** between their carbon atoms. Look at Figure 3. You can see that these alkenes have one C=C double covalent bond and have the general formula $\mathbf{C_nH_{2n}}$.

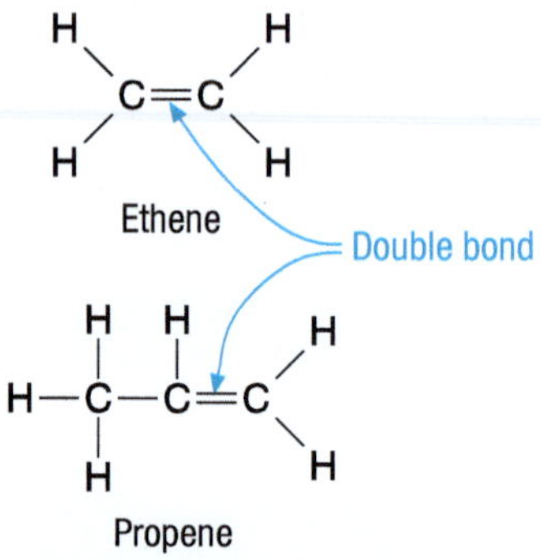

Figure 3 *The displayed formula of a molecule of ethene (C_2H_4) and a molecule of propene (C_3H_6). These are both alkenes – each molecule has a carbon–carbon (C=C) double bond in it.*

A simple experiment like the one on the next page shows that alkenes burn (but not as well as equivalent small alkanes which are used as fuels). Alkenes also react with bromine water, which is orange in colour. The products of this reaction are colourless so this gives you a good test to see if a compound contains a C=C double bond:

Positive test for an unsaturated hydrocarbon: orange bromine water turns colourless.

Practical

Cracking

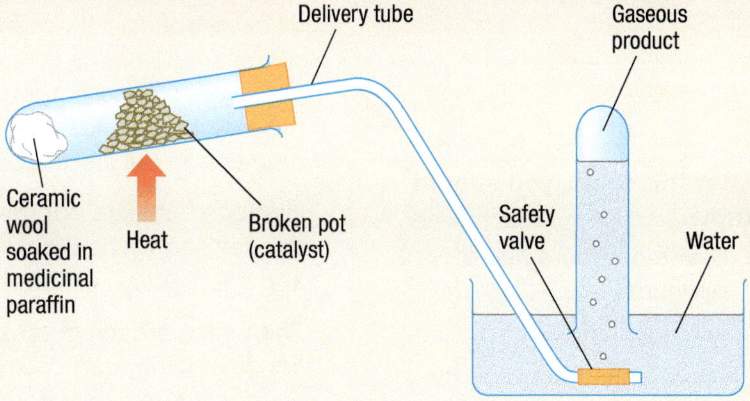

Medicinal paraffin is a mixture of hydrocarbon molecules. You can crack it by heating it and passing the vapour over hot pieces of broken pot. The broken pot acts as a catalyst.

- Why must you remove the end of the delivery tube from the water before you stop heating?

If you carry out this practical, collect at least two test tubes of gas.

Test the gas (or another unsaturated hydrocarbon) by shaking it with a few drops of bromine water (harmful).

- Record your observations and conclusions.

Safety: Avoid cold water being sucked back into the hot tube by removing the delivery tube from the water trough before you stop heating. Wear eye protection. Some gases collected may be harmful or even toxic.

Making ethanol from ethene (hydration)

Ethanol for industrial use as a fuel or solvent can be made from ethene gas instead of by fermentation. Ethene is the main by-product made in cracking. Ethene gas can react with steam to make ethanol.

$$\text{ethene} + \text{steam} \xrightarrow{\text{catalyst}} \text{ethanol}$$
$$C_2H_4 + H_2O \rightleftharpoons C_2H_5OH$$

This reaction is called **hydration**. The reaction requires energy to heat the gases and to generate a high pressure. The reaction is reversible so ethanol can break down back into ethene and steam. So unreacted ethene and steam are recycled over the concentrated phosphoric acid catalyst.

links

For more information on fermentation to make ethanol, look back to 10.4 Alternative fuels.

Summary questions

1 **a** Why is cracking so important?
 b How can large hydrocarbon molecules be cracked in an oil refinery?

2 Cracking a hydrocarbon makes two new hydrocarbons, A and B. When bromine water is added to A, nothing happens. Bromine water added to B turns from an orange solution to colourless.
 a i Which hydrocarbon, A or B, is unsaturated?
  ii What is an 'unsaturated' hydrocarbon?
  iii What do you call the type of unsaturated hydrocarbon formed in cracking?
 b i Which hydrocarbon, A or B, is used as a fuel?
  ii What do you call the type of saturated hydrocarbon formed in cracking?
 c What type of reaction is cracking an example of?

3 An alkene molecule with one double bond contains 12 carbon atoms. How many hydrogen atoms does it have? Write down its formula.

4 Dodecane (an alkane with 12 carbon atoms) can be cracked into octane (with 8 carbon atoms) and ethene. Write a balanced symbol equation for this reaction.

Key points

- **Large hydrocarbon molecules can be split up into smaller molecules by passing the vapours over a hot catalyst or by mixing them with steam and heating them to a very high temperature.**
- **Cracking produces saturated hydrocarbons which are used as fuels and unsaturated hydrocarbons (called alkenes).**
- **Alkenes (and other unsaturated compounds containing carbon–carbon double bonds) react with yellow-orange bromine water, turning it colourless.**

11.2 Making polymers from alkenes

Learning objectives

After this topic, you should know:

- how monomers make polymers
- how alkenes undergo polymerisation reactions
- how to represent polymerisation reactions by an equation.

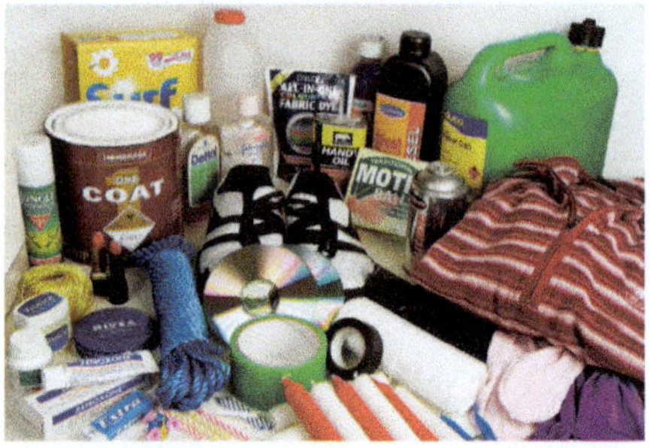

Figure 1 *All of these products were manufactured using chemicals originating from crude oil*

The fractional distillation of crude oil and cracking produces a large range of hydrocarbons. These are very important to our way of life. Products based on crude oil are all around us. It is difficult to imagine life without them.

Hydrocarbons are our main fuels. We use them in our transport and at home to cook and for heating. We also use them to generate electricity in oil-fired and gas-fired power stations.

Then there are the chemicals made from crude oil. They are used to make things ranging from cosmetics to explosives. But one of the most important ways that chemicals from crude oil are used is to make plastics.

Plastics

Plastics are made up of huge molecules made from lots of small molecules joined together. We call the small molecules **monomers**. We call the huge molecules they make **polymers**. (*Mono* means 'one' and *poly* means 'many'.) Engineers can make different types of plastics, which can have very different properties, by using different monomers.

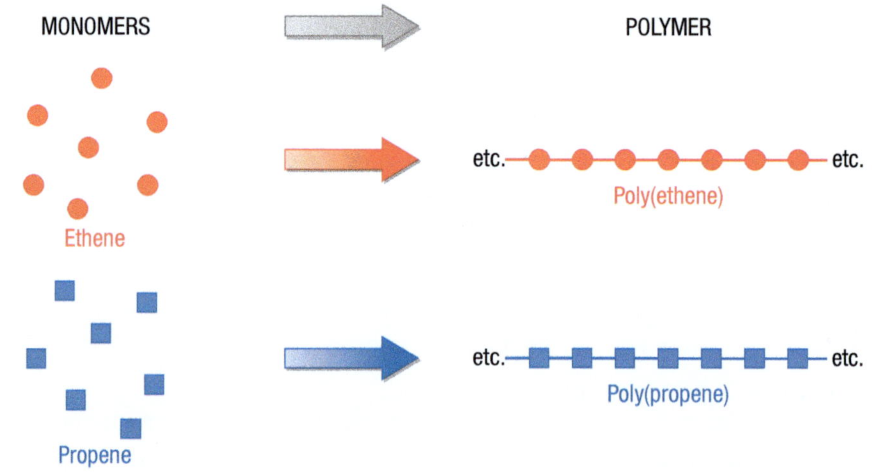

Figure 2 *Polymers are made from many smaller molecules called monomers*

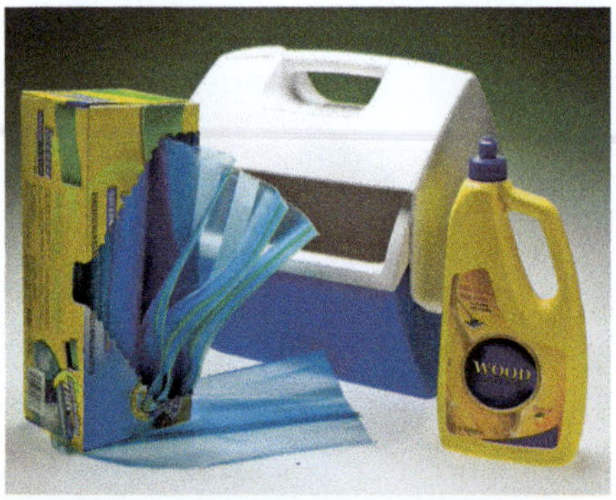

Figure 3 *Polymers produced from compounds derived from crude oil are all around us and are part of our everyday lives*

Ethene (C_2H_4) is the smallest unsaturated hydrocarbon molecule. It can be turned into a polymer known as poly(ethene) or polythene. Poly(ethene) is a really useful plastic as it is easy to shape, strong, and transparent (unless manufacturers add colouring material to it). 'Plastic' carrier bags, some drinks bottles, dustbins, washing-up bowls, and clingfilm are all examples of uses of poly(ethene).

Propene (C_3H_6) is another alkene. Engineers can also make polymers with propene as the monomer. The polymer formed is called poly(propene). It forms a very strong, tough plastic. Manufacturers can use it to make many things, including carpets, milk crates, and ropes.

How do monomers join together?

When alkene molecules join together, the double bond between the carbon atoms in each molecule 'opens up'. It is replaced by single bonds as thousands of molecules join together. The reaction is called **polymerisation**.

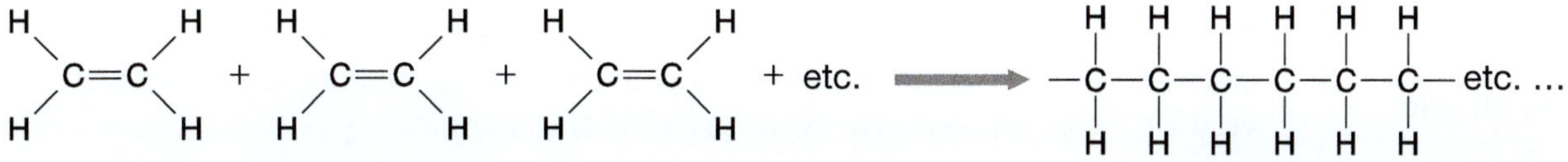

Ethene monomers

Poly(ethene)

You can also write this more simply as:

where *n* is a large number

Many single ethene monomers

Long chain of poly(ethene)

Activity

Modelling polymerisation

Use a molecular model kit to show how ethene molecules polymerise to form poly(ethene).

Make sure you can see how the equation shown above represents the polymerisation reaction you have modelled.

- Describe what happens to the bonds in the reaction.
- Think up a model to demonstrate the polymerisation of ethene, using people in your class as monomers.

Then evaluate the ideas of other groups.

Study tip

The C=C double bond in ethene (an alkene) makes it much more reactive than ethane (an alkane).

Summary questions

1 a Define a monomer and a polymer.
b What is the name for the reaction between a large number of monomers?
c Write an equation to represent the formation of poly(ethene) from ethene.
d State **two** uses of poly(ethene).

2 Why is ethene the smallest possible alkene molecule whereas methane is the smallest alkane?

3 a Draw the displayed formula of a propene molecule, showing all its bonds.
b Draw a diagram to show how propene molecules join together to form poly(propene).
c State **two** uses of poly(propene).
d Explain the polymerisation reaction in part **b**.

Key points

- Plastics are made of polymers.
- Polymers are large molecules made when many monomers (small, reactive molecules) join together.
- The reaction between monomers to form a polymer is called polymerisation.

11.3 The properties of polymers

Learning objectives

After this topic, you should know:

- that the properties of polymers depend on their monomers
- that changing reaction conditions can modify the polymers made
- the differences between thermosetting and thermosoftening polymers.

As you know, **polymers** are made from chemicals derived from crude oil. Small molecules called monomers join together to make much bigger molecules called polymers. As the monomers join together they produce a tangled web of very long chain molecules. Poly(ethene) is an example.

The properties of a polymer depend on:

- the monomers used to make it, and
- the conditions chosen to carry out the reaction.

Different monomers

Polymer chains can be made from many different monomers. The monomers chosen make a big difference to the properties of the polymer made. Consider the properties of the polymers in the bag in Figure 1 and the electrical socket in Figure 4.

Different reaction conditions

There are two types of poly(ethene). One is called high density (HD) and the other low density (LD) poly(ethene). Both are made from ethene monomers but they are formed under different reaction conditions.

- Using very high pressures and a trace of oxygen, ethene forms LD poly(ethene). The polymer chains are randomly branched and they cannot pack closely together so LD poly(ethene) has a lower density.
- Using a catalyst at 50 °C and a slightly raised pressure, ethene makes HD poly(ethene). This is made up of straighter poly(ethene) chains. They can pack more closely together than branched chains so HD poly(ethene) has a higher density. The HD poly(ethene) also has a higher softening temperature and is stronger than LD poly(ethene).

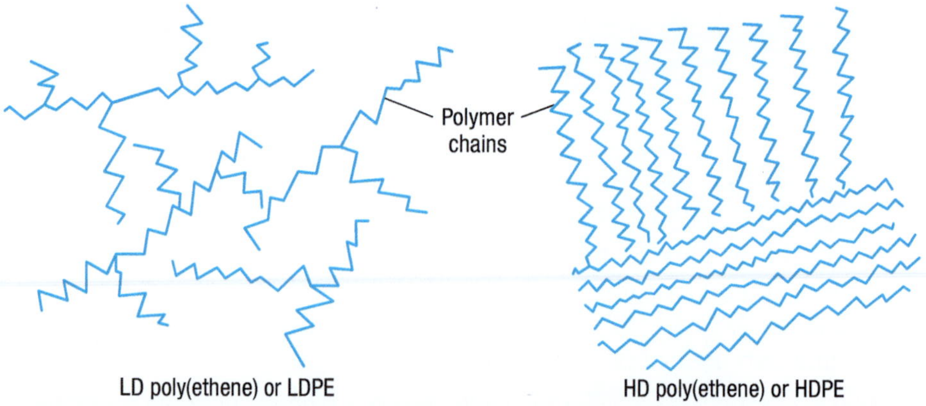

Figure 2 *The branched chains of LD poly(ethene) cannot pack as tightly together as the straighter chains in HD poly(ethene), giving the polymers different properties*

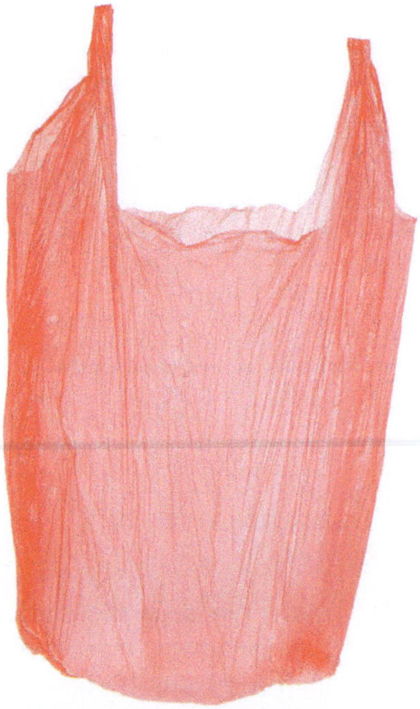

Figure 1 *The forces between the molecules in poly(ethene) are relatively weak as there are no strong covalent bonds (cross links) between the molecules. This means that this plastic softens fairly easily when heated.*

Thermosoftening and thermosetting polymers

It's useful to classify polymers by looking at what happens to them when they are heated. Some will soften quite easily. They will reset when they cool down. These are called **thermosoftening polymers**. They are made up of individual polymer chains that are tangled together.

Other polymers do not melt when heated. These are called **thermosetting polymers**. These have strong covalent bonds forming 'cross links' between their polymer chains (see Figure 3.)

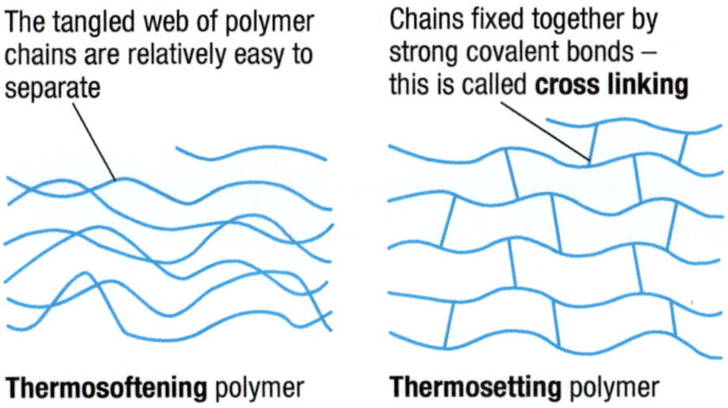

Figure 3 *Extensive cross linking by covalent bonds between polymer chains makes a thermosetting plastic that is heat-resistant and rigid*

Bonding in and between polymer chains

The atoms in polymer chains are held together by very strong covalent bonds. This is true for all plastics. But the size of the forces *between* polymer molecules in different plastics can be very different.

Ext

In thermosoftening polymers the forces between the polymer chains are weak. When the polymer is heated, these weak intermolecular forces are broken. The polymer becomes soft. When the polymer cools down, the intermolecular forces bring the polymer molecules back together. Then the polymer hardens again. This type of polymer can be remoulded.

However, thermosetting polymers are different. Their monomers make covalent bonds between the polymer chains when they are first heated in order to shape them. These covalent bonds are strong, and they stop the polymer from softening. The covalent 'cross links' between chains do not allow them to separate. Even if heated strongly, the polymer will still not soften. Eventually, the polymer will char at high enough temperatures.

Practical

Modifying a polymer

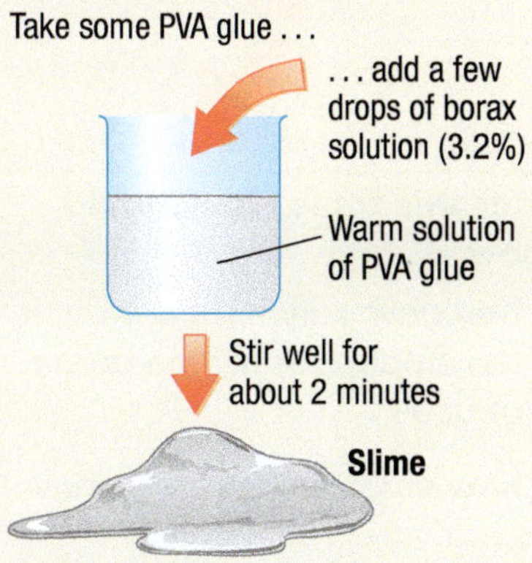

The glue becomes slimy because the borax makes the long polymer chains in the glue link together to form a jelly-like substance.

- How could you investigate if the properties of slime depend on how much borax you add?

Safety: Wear gloves and eye protection. Borax solution should not exceed 8%.

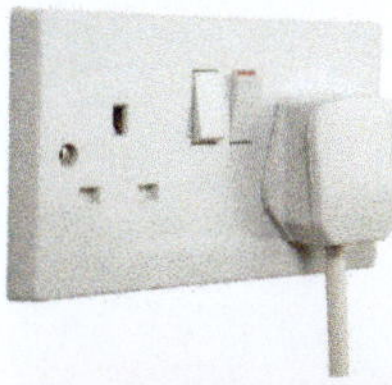

Figure 4 *Electrical sockets are made out of thermosetting polymers. If the plug or wires get hot, the socket will not soften.*

Summary questions

1 **a** How are the polymer chains arranged in a thermosoftening polymer?
b **i** What is the difference between the structures of a thermosoftening and a thermosetting polymer?
ii Give two differences in the properties of the two types of polymer.

2 Why do manufacturers use thermosetting rather than thermosoftening polymers to make the handles of pans?

Ext

3 Polymer A starts to soften at 100 °C whilst polymer B softens at 50 °C. Polymer C resists heat but eventually starts to char if heated to very high temperatures.
Explain this using ideas about intermolecular forces.

4 There are two types of poly(ethene), high density (HD) and low density (LD) poly(ethene).
a What is varied in order to produce the different types of poly(ethene)?
b Which statement is true?
HDPE is a thermosetting polymer and LDPE is thermosoftening polymer.
Both HDPE and LDPE are thermosoftening polymers.
c Explain the differing densities of HDPE and LDPE in terms of their structures.

Key points

- Monomers affect the properties of the polymers that they produce.
- Changing reaction conditions can also change the properties of the polymer that is produced.
- Thermosoftening polymers will soften or melt easily when heated because their intermolecular forces are relatively weak. Thermosetting polymers will not soften because of their 'cross linking' but will eventually char if heated very strongly.

Ext

11.4 New and useful polymers

Learning objectives

After this topic, you should know:

- that new polymers are being developed for a wide range of uses
- how smart polymers behave.

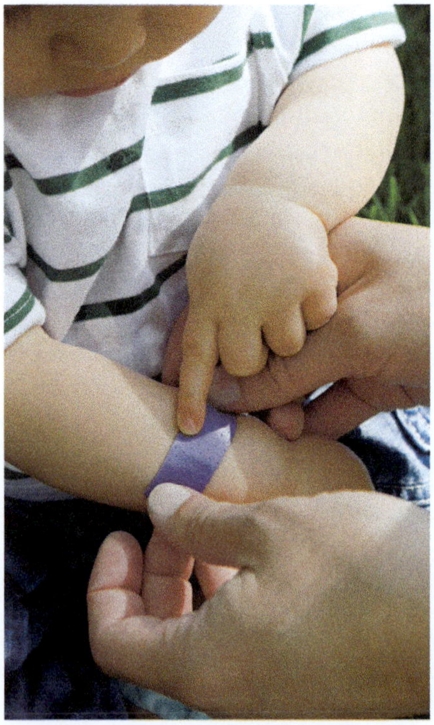

Figure 1 *A sticking plaster is often needed when you cut yourself, but taking the plaster off can be painful too*

Chemists can design new polymers to make materials with special properties to do particular jobs. Medicine is one area where we are beginning to see big benefits from these 'polymers made to order'.

New polymer materials will eventually take over from the current metal fillings for teeth, which contain mercury. Working with the toxic mercury every day is a potential hazard to dental workers.

Other developments include:

- new softer linings for dentures (false teeth)
- new packaging materials
- implants that can slowly release drugs into a patient.

Light-sensitive plasters

You probably know how uncomfortable pulling a plaster off your skin can be. But for some of us taking off a plaster is really painful. Both very old and very young people have quite fragile skin. But now a group of chemists has made a plaster where the 'stickiness' can be switched off before the plaster is removed. The plaster uses a light-sensitive polymer (see Figure 2 below).

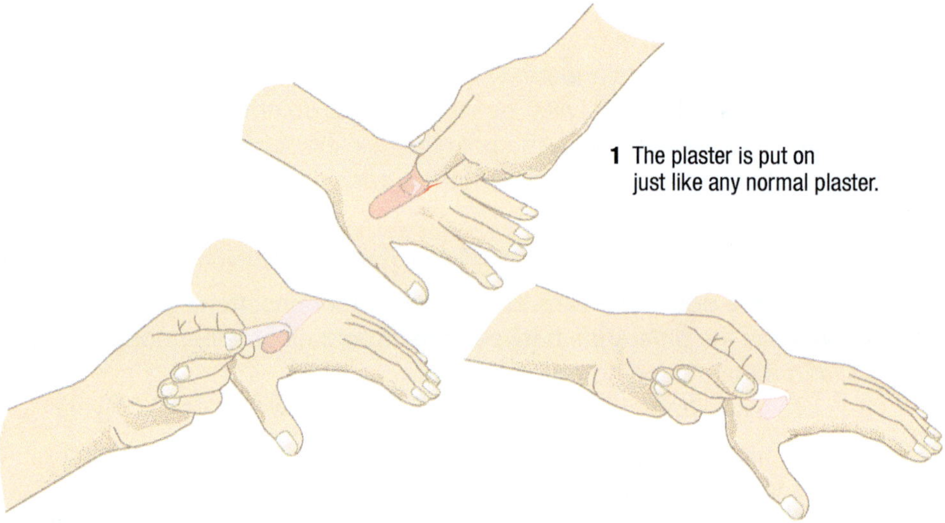

1 The plaster is put on just like any normal plaster.

2 To remove the plaster, the top layer is peeled away from the lower layer which stays stuck to the skin.

3 Once the lower layer is exposed to the light, the adhesive becomes less sticky, making it easy to peel off your skin.

Figure 2 *This plaster uses a light-sensitive polymer*

Hydrogels

Hydrogels are polymer chains with a few cross-linking units between chains. This makes a matrix (framework) that can trap water. These hydrogels can be used as wound dressings. They let the body heal in moist, sterile conditions. This makes them useful for treating burns.

The latest 'soft' contact lenses are also made from hydrogels. To change the properties of hydrogels, scientists can vary the amount of water in the matrix structure of the hydrogel.

Practical

Evaluating plastics

Plan an investigation to compare and evaluate the suitability of different plastics for a particular use.

For example, you might look at treated and untreated fabrics for waterproofing and 'breatheability' (gas permeability), or different types of packaging.

Shape memory polymers

A new 'shape memory polymer' is being developed for surgeons which will make stitching in awkward places easier. When a shape memory polymer is used to stitch a wound loosely, the temperature of the body makes the thread tighten and close the wound, applying just the right amount of force.

This is an example of a **smart polymer**, that is, one that changes in response to changes in its surroundings. In this case a change in temperature causes the polymer to change its shape. Later, after the wound is healed, the polymer is designed to dissolve and is harmlessly absorbed by the body. So, there will be no need to go back to hospital to have the stitches out.

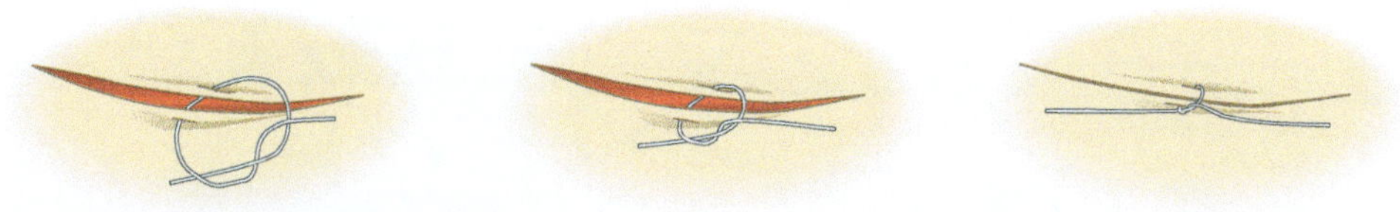

Figure 3 *A shape memory polymer uses the temperature of the body to make the thread tighten and close the wound*

New uses for old polymers

The bottles that people buy fizzy drinks in are a good example of using a plastic because of its properties. These bottles are made out of a plastic called PET.

The polymer it is made from is ideal for making drinks bottles. It produces a plastic that is very strong and tough, and which can be made transparent. The bottles made from this plastic are much lighter than glass bottles. This means that they cost less to transport and are easier for us to carry around.

The PET from recycled bottles is used to make polyester fibres for clothing, such as fleece jackets, and the filling for duvet covers. School uniforms and football shirts are now also made from recycled drinks bottles.

Did you know ... ?

PET is an abbreviation for poly(ethene terephthalate). It takes five 2-litre PET lemonade bottles to make one T-shirt.

Summary questions

1 a What is meant by:
- **i** a 'designer polymer'?
- **ii** a 'smart polymer'?

b i Why is PET used to make drinks bottles?
- **ii** State **two** uses of recycled PET.
- **iii** Is PET a thermosetting polymer or a thermosoftening polymer? How did you decide?

2 a What is a hydrogel?

b Give **two** uses of hydrogels.

3 Explain how a light-sensitive plaster works.

4 Explain how stitches made from smart polymers work.

Key points

- New polymers are being developed all the time. They are designed to have properties that make them specially suited for certain uses.
- Smart polymers may have their properties changed by light, temperature, or other changes in their surroundings.
- We are now recycling more plastics and finding new uses for them.

11.5 Plastic waste

Learning objectives

After this topic, you should know:

- the problems caused by the disposal of plastics
- what biodegradable polymers are
- how polymers can be made biodegradable.

One of the problems with plastics is what to do with them when you have finished with them. Too much plastic ends up as rubbish in our streets. Even the beaches in the most remote parts of the world can be polluted with the eyesore of plastic waste. Wildlife can also get trapped in the waste or eat the plastics and die.

Not only that, just think of all the plastic packaging that goes in the bin after shopping. Most of it ends up as rubbish in landfill sites. Other landfill rubbish rots away quite quickly as microorganisms in the soil break it down. However, many waste polymers last for hundreds of years before they are broken down completely, taking up valuable space in our landfill sites. So, what was a useful property during the working life of the plastic (its lack of reactivity) becomes a disadvantage in a landfill site.

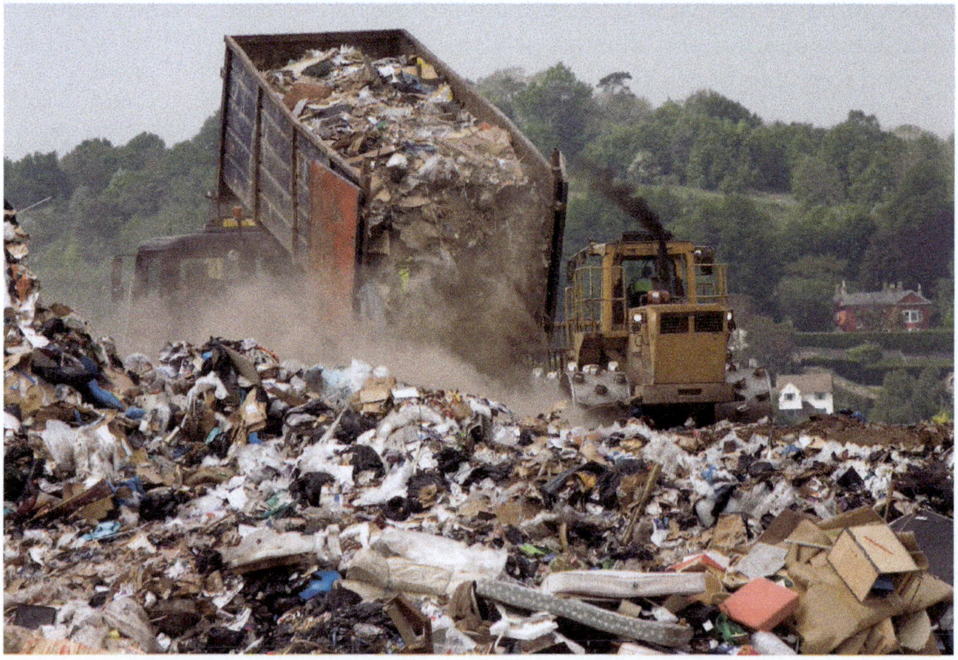

Figure 1 *Finding space to dump and bury our waste is becoming a big problem*

Biodegradable polymers

Scientists are working to solve the problems of plastic waste. Humans are now making more plastics that do rot away in the soil when dumped. The polymers in these plastics are called **biodegradable**. They can be broken down by microorganisms.

Scientists have found different ways to speed up the decomposition:

- One way uses granules of cornstarch built into a plastic. The microorganisms in soil feed on the starch. This breaks the plastic up into small pieces more quickly.
- Other types of polymer have been developed that are made from plant products.

A polymer called PLA, poly(lactic acid), can be made from cornstarch. The polymer is totally biodegradable. It is used in food packaging. However, it cannot be put in a microwave oven, which limits its use in ready-meal packaging.

Manufacturers can also make plastic carrier bags using PLA. In carrier bags the PLA is mixed with a traditional polymer. This makes sure the bag is strong enough but will still biodegrade a lot more quickly.

Using polymers such as PLA also helps preserve our supplies of crude oil. Remember that crude oil is the raw material for many traditional polymers, such as poly(ethene).

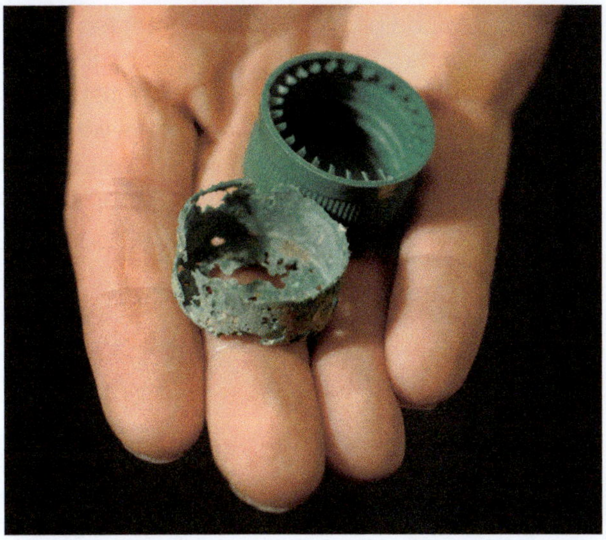

Figure 2 *The breakdown of a biodegradable polymer. PLA can be designed to break down in a few months.*

Disadvantages of biodegradable polymers

The use of a food crop like corn to make polymers can raise the same issues as biofuels. Farmers who sell their crops to be turned into fuel and plastics could cause higher food prices. The lack of basic food supplies could result in starvation in developing countries. Another problem is the destruction of tropical forests to create more farmland. This will destroy the habitats of wildlife and could affect climate change.

Other degradable polymers used for bags will break down in light. However, they will not decompose when buried in a landfill site. One of the best solutions is to reuse the same plastic carrier bags over and over again.

Summary questions

1 Why are waste plastics proving to be a problem for us?

2 Explain what is meant by a 'biodegradable' polymer.

3 **a** Why are plastics whose raw materials are plants becoming more popular?

b PLA is a biodegradable plastic. What is its monomer?

4 Non-biodegradable polymers such as poly(ethene) can be made to decompose more quickly by mixing them with additives. These enable the polymer chain to be broken down by reacting with oxygen.

a Why might this be a waste of money if the plastic is buried and compressed under other waste in a landfill site?

b What could be a disadvantage of using this type of degradable plastic?

c Explain how cornstarch can play a role in helping to solve the problems of plastic waste.

Practical

Investigating cornstarch

Cornstarch can be fermented to make the starting material for PLA. However, cornstarch itself also has some interesting properties. You can make your own plastic material directly from cornstarch.

- Investigate how varying the proportions of cornstarch and water affect the product.

Safety: Be aware of allergies and sensitisation.

links

For information on the issues of using biofuels, look back at 10.4 Alternative fuels.

Key points

- **Non-biodegradable polymers cause unsightly rubbish, can harm wildlife, and take up space in landfill sites.**
- **Biodegradable polymers are decomposed by the action of microorganisms in soil.**
- **Making plastics with starch granules in their structure helps the microorganisms break down a polymer.**
- **Scientists can make biodegradable polymers from plant material such as cornstarch.**

Chapter summary questions

1 Propene is a hydrocarbon molecule containing three carbon atoms and six hydrogen atoms.

a What is the chemical formula of propene?

b Draw the displayed formula of propene, showing all its bonds.

c Is propene a saturated molecule or an unsaturated molecule? Explain your answer.

d You are given two unlabelled test tubes. One test tube contains propane gas, whilst the other test tube contains propene gas.
Explain how you could test which tube contains which gas, stating clearly the results obtained in each case.

e Propene molecules will react together to form long chains.

i What is this type of reaction called?
ii Name the product of the reaction.
iii What is the general name given to the many propene molecules that react together?
iv Compare the properties of the reactants to those of the product.

2 Give a symbol equation to show the reaction of ethene to make poly(ethene).

3 **a** Write a word equation and a balanced symbol equation, including state symbols, for the reaction between ethene and steam.

b Give an advantage and a disadvantage of making ethanol from ethene compared with making it from sugar obtained from plant material.

4 Chemists have developed special waterproof materials made from polymers. It is easy to make plastic material that is waterproof but they tend to make the wearer hot and sweaty. However, there are now polymer materials that have pores 2000 times smaller than a drop of water. However, the tiny pores are 700 times larger than a water molecule.

a Explain why these materials are described as 'breathable'.

b Would you describe the 'breathable' polymer material as a smart polymer? Explain your answer.

5 Read the following information then answer the questions.

New biodegradable polymers are now being developed. They use normal crops as their starting material. They do not use up our decreasing supplies of crude oil. The crop is fermented with microorganisms which make a polymer called PHB, poly(hydroxybutyrate). In America, scientists have used genetic engineering to grow plants which make PHB themselves. They are continuing their research to increase the yield of the polymer in crops such as potatoes.

Look at this cycle for the plastic PHB:

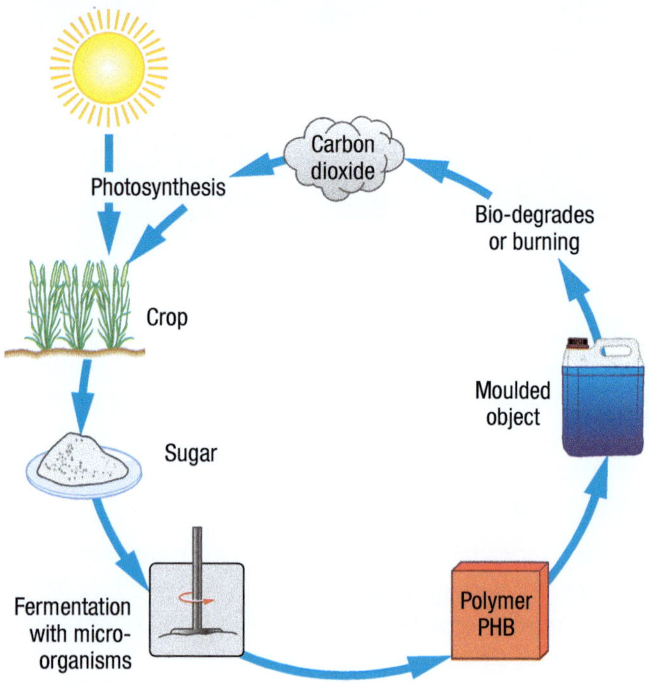

a Why might people object to the crops that make PHB directly?

b Does the use of PHB increase the amount of carbon dioxide in the air? Explain your answer.

c Why is it difficult to say whether PHB made directly by plants will be cheaper than the PHB shown in the cycle?

Practice questions

1 The fractions from crude oil that contain the biggest molecules have few uses. Cracking converts them into more useful substances, including alkenes.

a Describe the conditions used in **two** different types of cracking. (4)

b Unlike alkanes, alkenes are *unsaturated*.

i What feature is present in an alkene but not in an alkane? (1)

ii Give the displayed formula of the simplest alkene. (1)

iii Propene has the molecular formula C_3H_6.

Deduce the molecular formula of the alkene with four carbon atoms in each molecule. (1)

c Copy and complete this equation for a cracking reaction.

$C_{12}H_{26} \rightarrow C_8H_{18} +$ ------------ (1)

d Alkanes and alkenes can be distinguished by a simple chemical test.

State the reagent used and the result with each type of compound. (3)

e The traditional way to make ethanol is by fermentation.

State how it is made using one of the products of cracking. (3)

2 Most alkenes are used to make polymers.

a State **two** features of polymer molecules that alkenes do not have. (2)

b Poly(ethene) is made in two forms, depending on the conditions used for polymerisation. These are described as LD and HD forms.

i State the meanings of the terms 'LD' and 'HD'. (1)

ii Both forms are described as 'thermosoftening'. What is the meaning of this term? (1)

c Another type of polymer is described as thermosetting.

i How does a thermosetting polymer behave when heated? (1)

ii Describe how the bonding in a thermosetting polymer differs from the bonding in a thermosoftening polymer. (2)

d Some polymers are 'biodegradable'.

State the meaning of this term and **one** advantage of these polymers over non-biodegradable polymers. (2)

3 A manufacturer plans to produce objects made from two new polymers. Polymer 1 needs to withstand heat without changing shape. Polymer 2 needs to be able to change shape but does not need to withstand heat.

The diagrams show two types of polymer.

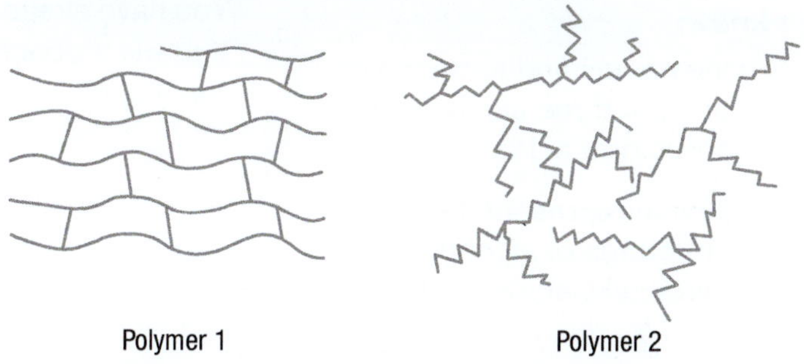

Use information from the diagrams and your knowledge and understanding of polymers to identify the types of polymer that could be used as Polymer 1 and Polymer 2. You should support your choices by referring to the properties, structure, and bonding in polymers. (6)

12.1 Structures of alcohols, carboxylic acids, and esters

Learning objectives

After this topic, you should know:

- the names and formulae of the first three alcohols and carboxylic acids
- how to represent the structures of alcohols, carboxylic acids, and esters.

The substances that form the basis of all living things, including ourselves, are organic compounds. Organic molecules all contain carbon atoms. The carbon atoms tend to form the 'backbone' of organic molecules.

You have already met some organic compounds in Chapters 10 and 11. You will probably recall how to draw molecules of alkanes and alkenes (see Figure 1):

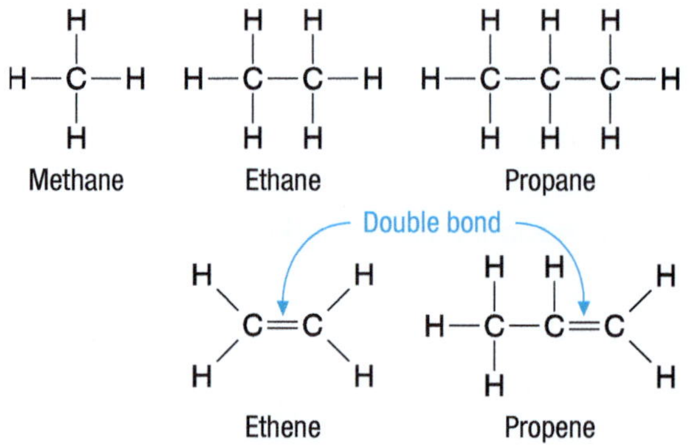

Figure 1 *The structures of the smallest alkane and alkene molecules. The lines between atoms represent covalent bonds. Notice the double bonds in ethene and propene. This type of 2D drawing to show the structure of a molecule is called a 'displayed formula'.*

Did you know ... ?

Not all carbon compounds are classified as organic compounds. The oxides of carbon and compounds containing carbonate and hydrogencarbonate ions are classified as inorganic compounds.

Both alkanes and alkenes are made of only carbon and hydrogen atoms. However, there are many more 'families' of organic compounds that also contain a few other types of atom.

In this chapter you will learn about some organic compounds made up of carbon, hydrogen, and oxygen. The two 'families' you will look at are called alcohols and carboxylic acids.

Alcohols

You have also met a member of the alcohol 'family' before. This was ethanol, which can be used as a biofuel. So what is an alcohol?

links

For more information on the use of ethanol as a biofuel, look back at 10.4 Alternative fuels.

Imagine removing an H atom from an alkane molecule and replacing it with an O–H group. This would give us an alcohol molecule. The –OH group of atoms is an example of a **functional group**.

A functional group gives a 'family' of organic compounds their characteristic reactions. A 'family' of compounds with the same functional group is called a **homologous series**.

You need to know the first three members of the homologous series of alcohols:

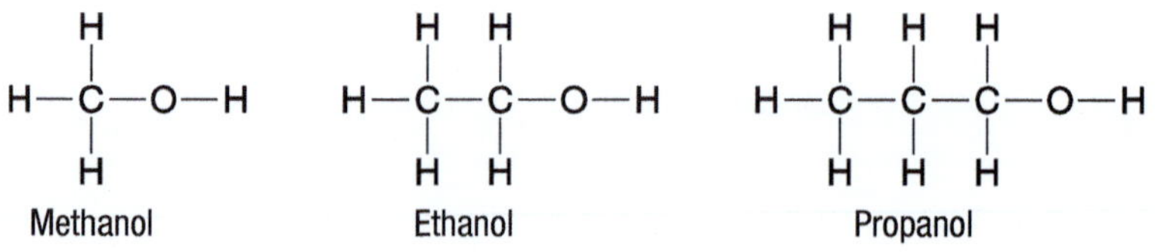

Figure 2 *The displayed formulae and names of the first three alcohol molecules. The alcohols are named from the alkane with the same number of carbon atoms. Just take the 'e' from the end of the alkane's name and replace it with 'ol'.*

Study tip

If you draw displayed formulae, make sure you show all the bonds, including those in the functional group (as lines between atoms) and all the atoms (as their chemical symbols).

If you were asked for the formula of ethanol, you might count the atoms in a molecule and write C_2H_6O. This is correct but chemists can give more information in a **structural formula**. This doesn't show all the bonds, as in a displayed formula, but shows what is bonded to each carbon atom. So for ethanol, a chemist will often show its formula as CH_3CH_2OH (often shortened to C_2H_5OH). Can you see how this relates to the structure of ethanol shown in Figure 2?

Carboxylic acids

You will certainly know of one carboxylic acid. Ethanoic acid is the main acid in vinegar. All carboxylic acids contain the –COOH functional group. Look at the first three members of the homologous series of carboxylic acids below:

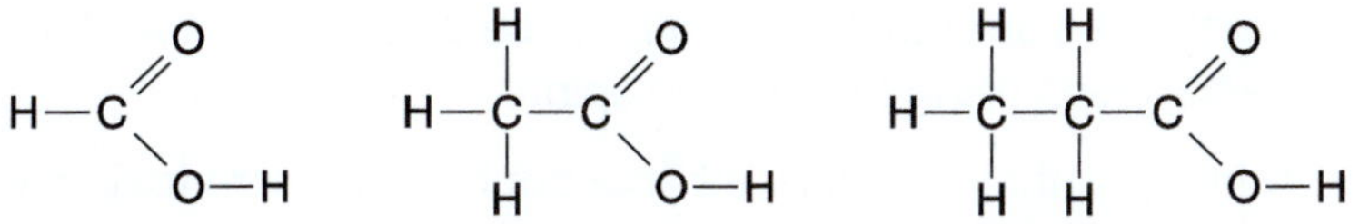

Methanoic acid   Ethanoic acid   Propanoic acid

Figure 3 *The displayed formulae and names of the first three carboxylic acid molecules*

You show the structural formula of each of the carboxylic acids in Figure 3 as HCOOH, CH_3COOH, and CH_3CH_2COOH (or C_2H_5COOH).

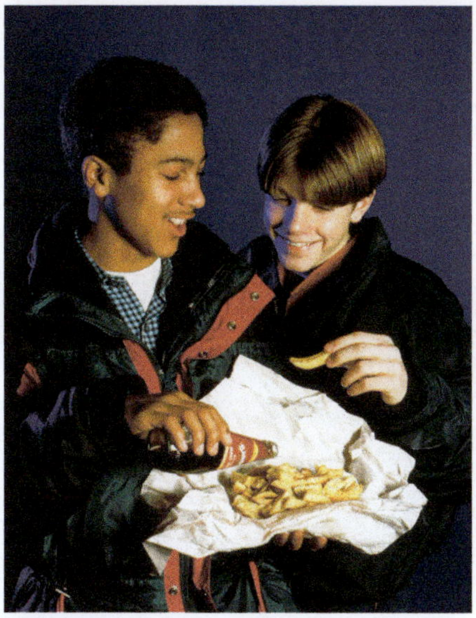

Figure 4 *Vinegar contains less than 10 per cent ethanoic acid in an aqueous solution but the acid provides the characteristic sharp taste and smell*

Esters

Esters are closely related to and can be made from carboxylic acids. If you replace the H atom in the –COOH group by a hydrocarbon (alkyl) group, such as $–CH_3$ or $–C_2H_5$, you get an ester. Here is the ester called ethyl ethanoate:

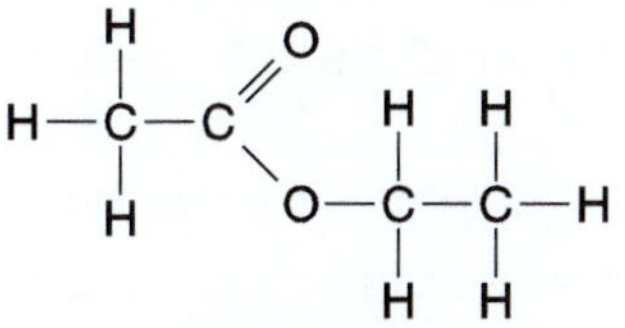

Ethyl ethanoate

Figure 5 *The displayed formulae of the ester ethyl ethanoate*

An ester's structural formula always has the –COO– functional group in it. The structural formula of ethyl ethanoate is $CH_3COOCH_2CH_3$ (or $CH_3COOC_2H_5$).

links

For information about the homologous series of carboxylic acids and esters, see 12.3 Carboxylic acids.

Summary questions

1 Which homologous series do the following compounds belong to?
   a $CH_3COOCH_2CH_2CH_3$
   b $CH_3CH_2CH_2CH_2CH_2CH_2OH$
   c $CH_3CH_2CH_2CH_2COOH$

2 Name the following compounds:
   a $CH_3CH_2CH_2OH$
   b $CH_3COOC_2H_5$
   c HCOOH

3 Draw a displayed formula showing all the bonds in:
   a ethanol
   b butanoic acid, which contains four carbon atoms.

Key points

- The homologous series of alcohols contain the –OH functional group.
- The homologous series of carboxylic acids contain the –COOH functional group.

12.2 Properties and uses of alcohols

Learning objectives

After this topic, you should know:

- some properties of alcohols
- the main uses of alcohols

links

For more information on how ethanol is manufactured by fermentation, look back to 10.4 Alternative fuels, and from ethene in 11.1 Cracking hydrocarbons.

Alcohols, especially ethanol, are commonly used in everyday products. Ethanol is the main alcohol in alcoholic drinks. It is made by fermenting sugars from plant material and is becoming an important alternative fuel to petrol and diesel. Ethanol can also be made in industry from ethene and steam in the presence of a catalyst.

Alcohols dissolve many of the same substances as water. In fact the alcohols with smaller molecules mix very well with water, giving neutral solutions. The alcohols can also dissolve many other organic compounds. This property makes them useful as solvents. For example, you can remove ink stains from permanent marker pens using methylated spirits.

Methylated spirits ('meths') is mainly ethanol but has the more toxic methanol mixed with it. It also has a purple dye and other substances added to make it unpleasant to drink. Alcohols are also used as solvents in products such as perfumes, aftershaves, and mouthwashes.

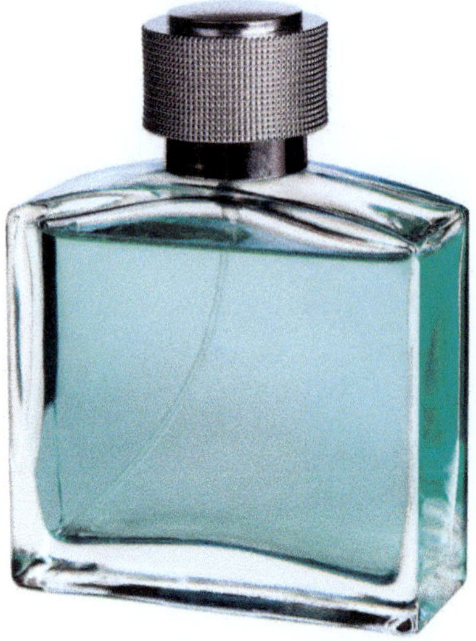

Figure 1 *Alcohols are used as solvents in perfumes*

Reactions of alcohols

Practical/Demonstration

Comparing the reactions of methanol, ethanol, and propanol

a Ignite and observe the flame in three spirit burners – one containing methanol, one ethanol, and the other propanol.
Compare the three combustion reactions.

b Watch your teacher add a small piece of sodium metal to each of the alcohols.
Compare the reactions. Which gas is given off?

c Watch your teacher boil some of each alcohol with acidified potassium dichromate(VI) solution.
What do you see happen in each reaction?

Safety: Ethanol is highly flammable and harmful. Methanol is highly flammable and toxic. Propanol is highly flammable and irritant. No naked flames. Wear chemical splashproof eye protection.

Did you know ... ?

Ethanol is the main solvent in many perfumes but a key ingredient in some perfumes is octanol. It evaporates more slowly and so holds the perfume on the skin for longer.

Combustion

The use of ethanol (and also methanol) as fuels shows that the alcohols are flammable. Ethanol is used in spirit burners and can be used as a biofuel in cars. It burns with a 'clean' blue flame:

$$\text{ethanol} + \text{oxygen} \rightarrow \text{carbon dioxide} + \text{water}$$
$$C_2H_5OH + 3O_2 \rightarrow 2CO_2 + 3H_2O$$

Reaction with sodium

The alcohols react in a similar way to water when sodium metal is added. The sodium effervesces (gives off bubbles of gas), producing hydrogen gas, and gets smaller and smaller as it forms a solution of sodium ethoxide in ethanol. The reactions of alcohols are not as vigorous as the reaction between sodium and water. For example, with ethanol:

$$\text{sodium} + \text{ethanol} \rightarrow \text{sodium ethoxide} + \text{hydrogen}$$
$$2Na + 2C_2H_5OH \rightarrow 2C_2H_5ONa + H_2$$

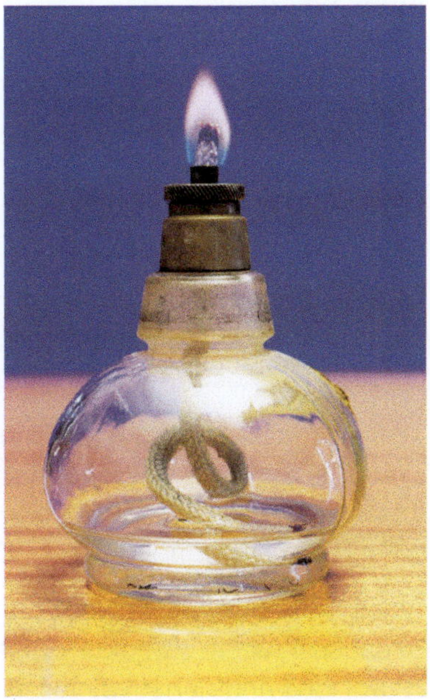

Figure 2 *Alcohols are flammable. They produce carbon dioxide and water in their combustion reactions.*

Summary questions

1. Give the name and structural formula of the main alcohol in alcoholic drinks.
2. List the main uses of alcohols.
3. **a** Write a word equation and a balanced symbol equation for the reaction between sodium metal and methanol.
   b Write a word equation and a balanced symbol equation for the complete combustion of methanol.
4. Methanol, ethanol, and propanol are all liquids at room temperature. Plan an investigation to see which alcohol – methanol, ethanol, or propanol – releases most energy per gram when it burns.

Key points

- Alcohols are used as solvents and fuels, and ethanol is the main alcohol in alcoholic drinks.
- Alcohols burn in air, forming carbon dioxide and water.
- With sodium metal, alcohols react to form a solution, and hydrogen gas is given off.

12.3 Carboxylic acids and esters

Learning objectives

After this topic, you should know:

- how to recognise carboxylic acids from their properties
- some uses of carboxylic acids and esters
- why carboxylic acids are described as weak acids
- how to make esters.

links

For more information on the structure of carboxylic acids, look back to 12.1 Structures of alcohols, carboxylic acids, and esters.

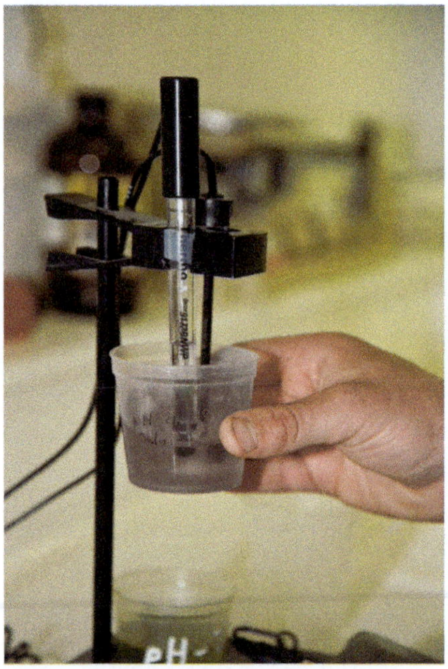

Figure 2 *Testing the pH of a solution using a pH sensor*

You have already learnt about the structure of carboxylic acids. The most well-known carboxylic acid is ethanoic acid.

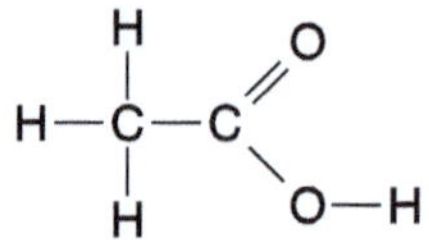

Figure 1 *Ethanoic acid, CH_3COOH, is the main acid in vinegar. Its old name was 'acetic acid'. Carboxylic acids are also used to make polyester fibres.*

Carboxylic acids, as their name suggests, form acidic solutions when they dissolve in water. You can look at one of their reactions in the practical on the next page.

Carboxylic acids have the typical reactions of all acids. For example, reaction with a metal carbonate forms a salt, water, and carbon dioxide. In the practical at the top of page 151:

$$\text{ethanoic acid} + \text{sodium carbonate} \rightarrow \text{sodium ethanoate} + \text{water} + \text{carbon dioxide}$$

$$2CH_3COOH(aq) + Na_2CO_3(s) \rightarrow 2CH_3COONa(aq) + H_2O(l) + CO_2(g)$$

Why are carboxylic acids called 'weak acids'?

You will see in the practical on the next page how CO_2 gas is given off more slowly when a metal carbonate reacts with a carboxylic acid as compared with hydrochloric acid of the same concentration. Carboxylic acids are called **weak** acids, as opposed to **strong** acids such as hydrochloric acid.

The pH of a 0.1 mol/dm^3 solution of hydrochloric acid (a strong acid) is 1.0. Yet a 0.1 mol/dm^3 solution of ethanoic acid (a weak acid) has a pH of only 2.9. The solution of ethanoic acid is not as acidic even though the two solutions have the same concentration. Why is this?

Acids must dissolve in water before they show their acidic properties. This is because in water all acids ionise (split up). Their molecules split up to form $H^+(aq)$ ions and negative ions. It is the $H^+(aq)$ ions that all acidic solutions have in common. For example, in hydrochloric acid, the HCl molecules all ionise in water:

$$HCl(aq) \xrightarrow{\text{water}} H^+(aq) + Cl^-(aq)$$

We say that strong acids ionise *completely* in solution. However, in weak acids most of the molecules stay as they are. Only some will ionise in their solutions. A position of **equilibrium** is reached in which both molecules and ions are present. So, in ethanoic acid:

$$\underset{\text{ethanoic acid}}{CH_3COOH(aq)} \overset{\text{water}}{\rightleftharpoons} \underset{\text{ethanoate ions}}{CH_3COO^-(aq)} + \underset{\text{hydrogen ions}}{H^+(aq)}$$

Therefore, given two aqueous solutions of equal concentration, the strong acid will have a higher concentration of $H^+(aq)$ ions than the solution of the weak acid. So, a weak acid has a higher pH (and therefore reacts more slowly with a metal carbonate).

Practical

Comparing ethanoic acid and hydrochloric acid

Write down your observations to compare ethanoic acid with hydrochloric acid of the same concentration.

a Take the pH of solutions of both acids.

b Add a little sodium carbonate to solutions of both acids.

Why did you use the same concentrations of each acid in the experiment?

Safety: Wear eye protection.

Making esters

Carboxylic acids also react with alcohols to make esters. Water is also formed in this reversible reaction. A strong acid, usually sulfuric acid, is used as a catalyst. For example:

$$\text{ethanoic acid} + \text{ethanol} \xrightleftharpoons{\text{sulfuric acid catalyst}} \text{ethyl ethanoate} + \text{water}$$

$$CH_3COOH + C_2H_5OH \rightleftharpoons CH_3COOC_2H_5 + H_2O$$

In general:

$$\textbf{carboxylic acid} + \textbf{alcohol} \xrightleftharpoons{\text{strong acid catalyst}} \textbf{ester} + \textbf{water}$$

Demonstration

Making esters

Your teacher will show you how to make different esters using carboxylic acids and alcohols.

After neutralising the acid with sodium hydrogencarbonate, carefully smell the test tubes containing the different esters formed.

- Write word equations for each reaction.

Summary questions

1 **a** Which gas is made when propanoic acid reacts with potassium carbonate?

b Name the salt formed.

c Write a balanced symbol equation for the reaction.

2 Write a word equation and balanced symbol equation, including the catalyst, to show the reversible reaction between ethanoic acid and ethanol.

3 Explain in detail why propanoic acid is described as a weak acid.

links

Look back to Chapter 7 to see the typical reactions of acids.

Ext

Key points

- Solutions of carboxylic acids have a pH value less than 7. Carbonates gently fizz in their acidic solutions, releasing carbon dioxide gas.
- Aqueous solutions of weak acids, such as carboxylic acids, have a higher pH value than solutions of strong acids with the same concentration.
- Esters are made by reacting a carboxylic acid and an alcohol together, with a strong acid catalyst.

Chapter summary questions

1 Look at the three organic molecules **A**, **B**, and **C** below:

A

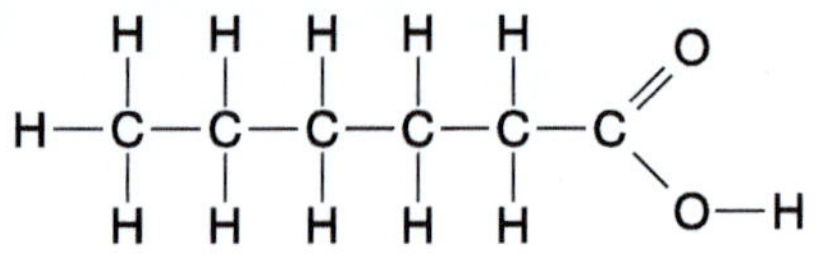

B

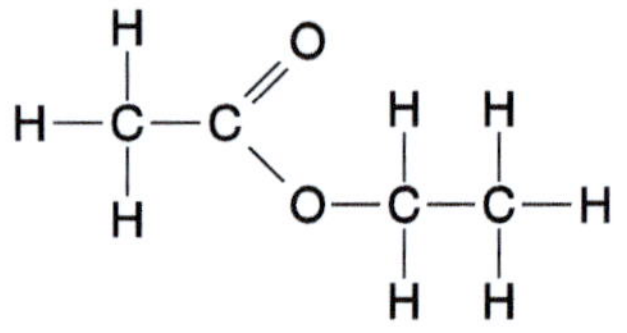

C

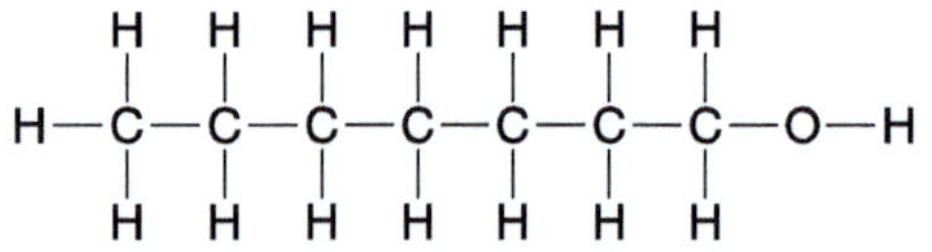

Answer these questions about **A**, **B**, and **C**:

a Which one is a carboxylic acid?

b Which one is an alcohol?

c Which homologous series of organic compounds does **B** belong to?

d Which of the compounds can be represented as the structural formula $CH_3COOCH_2CH_3$?

e Using a structural formula as shown in part **d**, give the structural formulae of the other two compounds.

2 **a** **i** Describe what you would ***see*** happen if a small piece of sodium metal was dropped into a beaker containing some ethanol.

ii Name the gas given off in this reaction.

iii Name the sodium compound formed in the reaction.

iv The sodium in the compound formed is present as ions. Give the formula of a sodium ion.

v Write a balanced symbol equation for the reaction of sodium with ethanol.

b Using your knowledge of the periodic table and trends in reactivity, suggest how ethanol's reaction with lithium metal would differ from its reaction with sodium.

3 **a** Draw the displayed formula of methanoic acid, showing all the atoms and bonds.

b **i** Some potassium carbonate powder is dropped into a test tube of a solution of methanoic acid. How would you positively identify the gas given off? Include a labelled diagram of the apparatus you could use.

ii Write a word equation and balanced symbol equation for the reaction.

c **i** Which aqueous solution of the following would you expect to have the highest pH value if they all had the same concentration?

A hydrochloric acid
B sulfuric acid
C methanoic acid
D nitric acid
E ethanol

ii Which of the five solutions listed above would have the second highest pH value? Explain your choice.

4 **a** What is the name of this compound?

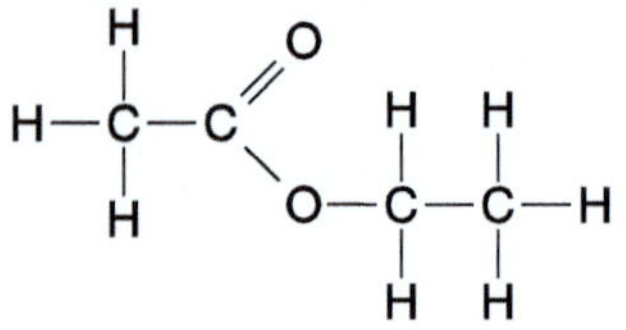

b Name the carboxylic acid and alcohol used to make the compound in part **a**.

c Write a word equation and a balanced symbol equation, showing how this compound can be made. Include the name of the catalyst.

d The compound shown in part **a** is volatile. What does this mean?

5 You are given a 0.5 mol/dm^3 solution of nitric acid, and a 0.5 mol/dm^3 solution of methanoic acid.

a What can you predict about the relative pH values of the two solutions?

b Explain in detail your answer to part **b**, including equations to show the ionisation of nitric acid and methanoic acid in aqueous solution.

Practice questions

1 Ethanol is often known as alcohol, but is just one member of a homologous series of alcohols. Methanol and propanol are two other members of the same homologous series.

a State **two** features that members of a homologous series have in common. (2)

b **i** What is the molecular formula of methanol? (1)

ii Draw the displayed formula of propanol. (1)

c A small piece of sodium is added to a beaker containing methanol.

Describe **two** observations you could make. (2)

d A sample of propanol burns completely in air.

Name the products formed. (2)

e Ethanol burns completely in air in an oxidation reaction.

Write a balanced symbol equation for this reaction. (2)

2 Carboxylic acids are compounds in a homologous series.

Like alcohols they dissolve in water to form colourless solutions.

a A student was given separate solutions of ethanol and ethanoic acid.

Describe how these could be distinguished by adding sodium carbonate. Include **one** observation for each compound. (2)

b The student was given separate solutions of ethanoic acid and nitric acid with the same concentration.

These solutions can be distinguished by using a pH meter.

Choose a possible pH value for each solution.

i The pH value of ethanoic acid is 1 5 7 9 13 (1)

ii The pH value of nitric acid is 1 5 7 9 13 (1)

c The student was shown these equations:

$CH_3COOH \rightleftharpoons CH_3COO^- + H^+$

$HNO_3 \rightarrow H^+ + NO_3^-$

Explain how the arrows show that ethanoic acid is weaker than nitric acid. (2)

3 Esters are organic compounds formed in the reaction between an alcohol and a carboxylic acid. A reaction of this type is known as esterification.

a An example of an esterification reaction is shown by this equation:

$HCOOH + CH_3CH_2CH_2OH \rightleftharpoons HCOOCH_2CH_2CH_3 + H_2O$

i Name the two reactants. (2)

ii Draw the displayed formula of the ester. (1)

b What is the name of the ester made from ethanol and ethanoic acid? (1)

Investigations

Learning objectives

After this topic, you should know:

- what 'continuous variables' and 'categoric variables' are
- what is meant by 'repeatable evidence', 'reproducible evidence' and 'valid evidence'
- what the link is between the independent and dependent variable
- what a 'hypothesis' and a 'prediction' are
- how to reduce risks in hazardous situations.

Science works for us all day, every day. Working as a scientist you will have knowledge of the world around you and particularly about the subject you are working with. You will observe the world around you. An enquiring mind will then lead you to start asking questions about what you have observed.

Science usually moves forward by slow, steady steps. Each small step is important in its own way. It builds on the body of knowledge that you already have.

Thinking scientifically

Deciding on what to measure

Variables can be one of two different types:

- A **categoric variable** is one that is best described by a label (usually a word). The type of metal is a categoric variable, for example, magnesium or zinc.
- A **continuous variable** is one that you measure, so its value could be any number. Temperature (as measured by a thermometer or temperature sensor) is a continuous variable, for example, 37.6 °C, 45.2 °C. Continuous variables can have values (called a quantity) that can be given by any measurements made (e.g., mass, volume).

When designing your investigation you should always try to measure continuous **data** whenever you can. If there is no way to measure your variable then you have to use a label (categoric variable).

Making your investigation repeatable, reproducible, and valid

When you are designing an investigation you must make sure that you check results are **repeatable** (using the same method), and then plan for somebody else to carry out the experiment, or use different apparatus, to check if results are **reproducible**.

You must also make sure you are measuring the actual thing you want to measure. If you do not, your data cannot be used to answer your original question. This seems very obvious but it is not always quite so easy. You need to make sure that you have controlled as many other variables as you can, so that no-one can say that your investigation is not **valid**.

How might an independent variable be linked to a dependent variable?

The **independent variable** is the one you choose to vary in your investigation.

The **dependent variable** is used to judge the effect of varying the independent variable.

These variables may be linked together. If there is a pattern to be seen (e.g., as one thing gets bigger the other also gets bigger), it may be that:

- changing one has caused the other to change
- the two are related, but one is not necessarily the cause of the other.

Starting an investigation

Observation

As scientists you use observations to ask questions. You can only ask useful questions if you know something about the observed event. You will not have all of the answers, but you know enough to start asking the correct questions.

When you are designing an investigation you have to observe carefully which variables are likely to have an effect.

What is a hypothesis?

A **hypothesis** is an idea based on observation that has some really good science to try to explain it.

When making hypotheses you can be very imaginative with your ideas. However, you should have some scientific reasoning behind those ideas so that they are not totally bizarre.

Remember, your explanation might not be correct, but you think it is. The only way you can check out your hypothesis is to make it into a prediction and then test it by carrying out an investigation.

observation + knowledge → hypothesis → prediction → investigation

Starting to design an investigation

An investigation starts with a question, followed by a **prediction**. You, as the scientist, predict that there is a **relationship** between two variables.

You should think about carrying out a preliminary investigation to find the most suitable range and interval for the independent variable.

Making your investigation safe

Remember that when you design your investigation, you must:

- look for any potential **hazards**
- decide how you will reduce any **risk**.

You will need to write these down in your plan:

- write down your plan
- make a risk assessment
- make a prediction
- draw a blank table ready for the results.

Study tip

Observations, backed up by creative thinking and good scientific knowledge can lead into a hypothesis.

Key points

- Continuous data can give you more information than other types of data.
- You must design investigations that produce repeatable, reproducible, and valid results if you are to be believed.
- Be aware that just because two variables are related, does not mean that there is a causal link.
- Hypotheses can lead to predictions and investigations.
- You must make a risk assessment, make a prediction, and write a plan.

Setting up investigations

Learning objectives

After this topic, you should know:

- what a 'fair test' is
- how to set up a valid investigation
- what a 'control group' is
- how to decide on the variables, range, and intervals
- how to ensure accuracy and precision
- the causes of error and anomalies.

Fair testing

A **fair test** is one in which only the independent variable affects the dependent variable. All other variables are controlled in order to carry out a valid investigation. They are known as **control variables**.

This is easy to set up in the laboratory, but almost impossible in fieldwork. Investigations in the environment are not that simple and easy to control. There are complex variables that are changing constantly.

So how can you set up the fieldwork investigations? The best you can do is to make sure that all of the many variables change in much the same way, except for the one you are investigating. Then at least the plants you might be monitoring for the effects of pollution are getting the same weather, even if it is constantly changing.

If you are investigating two variables in a large population then you will need to do a survey. Again, it is impossible to control all of the variables. Imagine scientists were investigating the effect of a new drug on diabetes. They would have to choose people of the same age and same family history to test. The larger the sample size tested, the more valid the results will be.

Control groups are used in these investigations to try to make sure that you are measuring the variable that you intend to measure. When investigating the effects of a new drug, the control group will be given a placebo. The control group think they are taking a drug but the placebo does not contain the drug. This way you can control the variable of 'thinking that the drug is working' and separate out the effect of the actual drug.

Study tip

Trial runs will tell you a lot about how your investigation might work out. They should get you to ask yourself:

- Do I have the correct conditions?
- Have I chosen a sensible range?
- Have I got enough readings that are close together?
- Will I need to repeat my readings?

Designing an investigation

Accuracy

Your investigation must provide **accurate** data. Accurate data is essential if your results are going to have any meaning.

How do you know if you have accurate data?

It is very difficult to be certain. Accurate results are very close to the true value. It is not always possible to know what that true value is.

- Sometimes you can calculate a theoretical value and check it against the experimental evidence. Close agreement between these two values could indicate accurate data.
- You can draw a graph of your results and see how close each result is to the line of best fit.
- Try repeating your measurements with a different instrument and see if you get the same readings.

How do you get accurate data?

- Using instruments that measure accurately will help.
- The more carefully you use the measuring instruments, the more accuracy you will get.

Study tip

Just because your results show precision does not mean your results are accurate.

Imagine you carry out an investigation into the energy value of a type of fuel. You get readings of the amount of energy released that are all about the same. This means that your data will have precision, but it doesn't mean that they are necessarily accurate.

Precision

Your investigation must provide data with sufficient **precision**. If it doesn't then you will not be able to make a valid conclusion.

How do you get precise and repeatable data?

- You have to repeat your tests as often as necessary to improve repeatability.
- You have to repeat your tests in exactly the same way each time.
- Use measuring instruments that have the appropriate scale divisions needed for a particular investigation. Smaller scale divisions have better **resolution**.

Making measurements

Using instruments

You cannot expect perfect results. When you choose an instrument you need to know that it will give you the accuracy that you want, that is, it will give you a true reading.

When you choose an instrument you need to decide how precise you need to be. Some instruments have smaller scale divisions than others. Instruments that measure the same thing can have different sensitivities. The resolution of an instrument refers to the smallest change in a value that can be detected. Choosing the wrong scale can cause you to miss important data or make silly conclusions.

You also need to be able to use an instrument properly.

Errors

Even when an instrument is used correctly, the results can still show differences. Results may differ because of a **random error**. This is most likely to be due to a poor measurement being made. It could be due to not carrying out the method consistently. The effects of random errors are reduced by taking sets of repeat readings and calculating their mean values.

The **error** may be a **systematic error**. This means that the method was carried out consistently but an error was being repeated. Measurements will be consistently high or consistently low as a result of systematic error.

Anomalies

Anomalies are results that are clearly out of line. They are not those that are due to the natural variation that you get from any measurement. These should be looked at carefully. There might be a very interesting reason why they are so different. If they are simply due to a random error then they should be ignored.

If anomalies can be identified whilst you are doing an investigation, then it is best to repeat that part of the investigation. If you find anomalies after you have finished collecting the data for an investigation, then they must be discarded.

Did you know ... ?

Imagine measuring the temperature after a set time when a fuel is used to heat a fixed volume of water.

Two students repeated this experiment, four times each. Their results are marked on the thermometer scales below:

- A **precise** set of results is grouped closely together.
- An accurate set of results will have a mean (average) close to the true value.

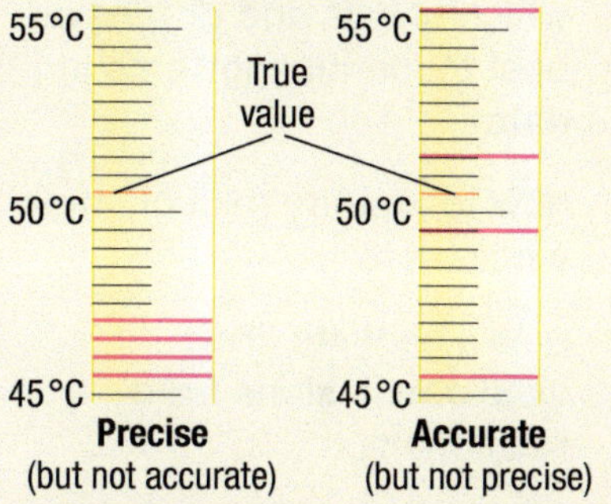

Key points

- Care must be taken to ensure fair testing.
- You can use a trial run to make sure that you choose the best values for your variables.
- Careful use of the correct equipment can improve accuracy.
- If you repeat your results carefully you can improve precision.
- Results will nearly always vary. Better instruments give more accurate results.
- Resolution in an instrument is the smallest change that it can detect.
- Human error can produce random and systematic errors.
- You must examine anomalies.

Using data

Learning objectives

After this topic, you should know:

- what is meant by the 'range' and the 'mean' of a set of data
- how data should be displayed
- which charts and graphs are best to identify patterns in data
- how to identify relationships within data
- how scientists draw valid conclusions from relationships
- how to evaluate the reproducibility of an investigation.

Presenting data

Tables

Tables are really good for getting your results down quickly and clearly. You should design your table before you start your investigation.

The range of the data

Pick out the maximum and the minimum values and you have the **range**. You should always quote these two numbers when asked for a range. For example, the range is between … (the lowest value) and … (the highest value) and don't forget to include the units!

The mean of the data

To find the **mean** of a set of data, add up all of the measurements and divide by how many there are.

Bar charts

If you have a categoric independent variable and a continuous dependent variable then you should use a **bar chart**.

Line graphs

If you have a continuous independent variable and a continuous dependent variable then use a **line graph**.

Scatter graphs

These are used in much the same way as a line graph, but you might not expect to be able to draw such a clear line of best fit. For example, to find out if the melting point of an element is related to its density you might draw a scatter graph of your results.

Using data to draw conclusions

Identifying patterns and relationships

Now you have a bar chart or a graph of your results you can begin looking for patterns in your results. You must have an open mind at this point.

Firstly, there could still be some anomalous results. You might not have picked these out earlier. How do you spot an anomaly? It must be a significant distance away from the pattern, not just within normal variation.

A line of best fit will help to identify any anomalies at this stage. Ask yourself – do the anomalies represent something important or were they just a mistake?

Secondly, remember a line of best fit can be a straight line or it can be a curve – you have to decide from your results.

The line of best fit will also lead you into thinking what the relationship is between your two variables. You need to consider whether your graph shows a linear relationship. This simply means can you be confident about drawing a straight line of best fit on your graph? If the answer is yes, then does this line have a positive or negative gradient?

A **directly proportional** relationship is shown by a straight line with a positive gradient that goes through the origin (0, 0).

Your results might also show a curved line of best fit. These can be predictable, complex, or very complex!

Drawing conclusions

Your graphs are designed to show the relationship between your two chosen variables. You need to consider what that relationship means for your conclusion. You must also take into account the repeatability, reproducibility, and the validity of the data you are considering.

You will continue to have an open mind about your conclusion.

You will have made a prediction. This could be supported by your results, it might not be supported, or it could be partly supported. It might suggest some other hypothesis to you.

You must be willing to think carefully about your results. Remember it is quite rare for a set of results to completely support a prediction and be completely repeatable.

Look for possible links between variables. It may be that:

- changing one has caused the other to change
- the two are related, but one is not necessarily the cause of the other.

You must decide which is the most likely. Remember a positive relationship does not always mean a causal link between the two variables.

Your conclusion must go no further than the **evidence** that you have. Any patterns you spot are only strictly valid in the range of values you tested. Further tests are needed to check whether the pattern continues beyond this range.

The purpose of the prediction was to test a hypothesis. The hypothesis can:

- be supported,
- be refuted, or
- lead to another hypothesis.

You have to decide which it is on the evidence available.

Evaluation

If you are still uncertain about a conclusion, it might be down to the repeatability, the reproducibility, and the validity of the results. You could check reproducibility by:

- looking for other similar work on the Internet or from others in your class
- getting somebody else to redo your investigation
- trying an alternative method to see if you get the same results.

Key points

- The range states the maximum and the minimum value.
- The mean is the sum of the values divided by how many values there are.
- Tables are best used during an investigation to record results.
- Bar charts are used when you have a categoric independent variable and a continuous dependent variable.
- Line graphs are used to display data that are continuous.
- Drawing lines of best fit helps us to study the relationship between variables. The possible relationships are linear, positive and negative; directly proportional; predictable and complex curves.
- Conclusions must go no further than the data available.
- The reproducibility of data can be checked by looking at other similar work done by others, perhaps on the Internet. It can also be checked by using a different method or by others checking your method.

Calcium carbonate reacts with dilute hydrochloric acid. The equation for the reaction is:

$$CaCO_3(s) + 2HCl(aq) \rightarrow CaCl_2(aq) + H_2O(l) + CO_2(g)$$

A student investigated how changing the concentration of dilute hydrochloric acid altered how quickly carbon dioxide gas was made.

The gas was collected over water and its volume measured every 20 seconds.

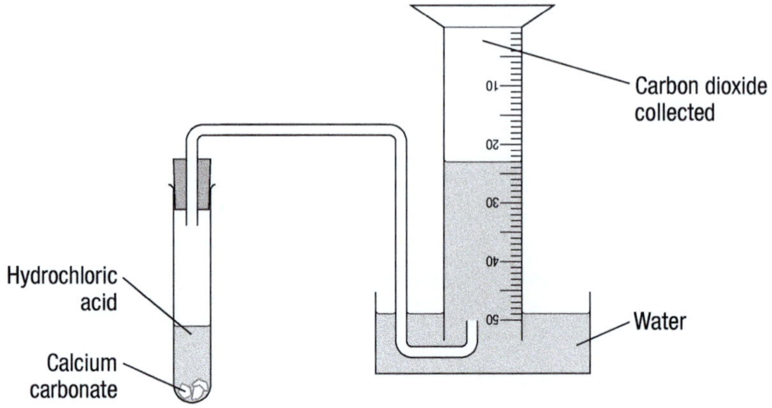

1 (a) The diagram shows the apparatus during one experiment.

What volume of carbon dioxide gas has been collected?

23 cm³

(1)

The volume is correct and units have been given. Level has been read to bottom of the meniscus.

The graph shows the results the student obtained.

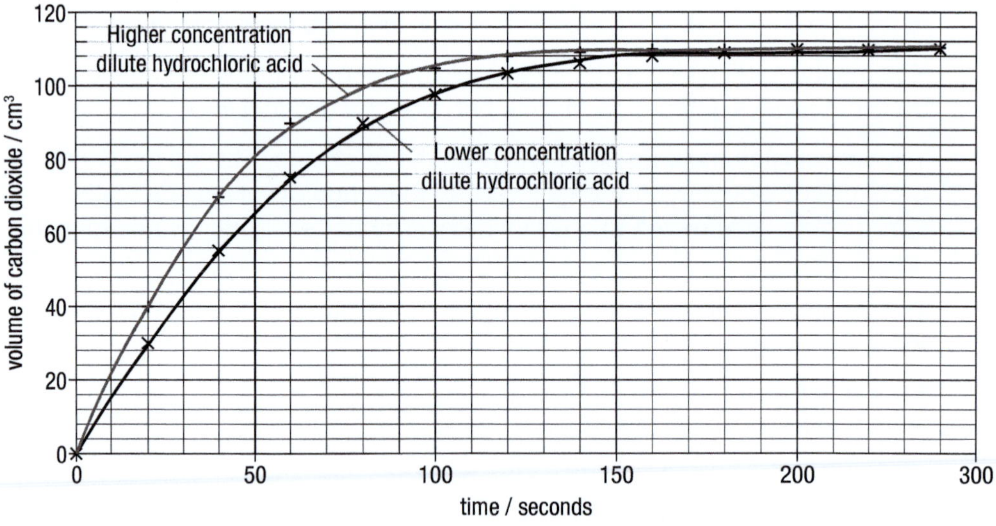

1 (b) Describe the effect of changing the concentration of the dilute hydrochloric acid on the volume of carbon dioxide collected during the experiment.

When the concentration of the acid is higher the gas is collected more quickly but the same final volume of gas is collected.

(2)

There are two marks available for the answer, so there will normally be two things that need to be said to gain full marks. This candidate has spotted that whilst the final volume of gas collected is the same (the graphs level off at the same height) the line for the more concentrated acid is steeper – this means that at any time before the reaction is complete, more gas has been collected when the more concentrated acid is used.

1 (c) Carbon dioxide gas is slightly soluble in water. What effect will this have on the volume of gas collected?

It will reduce the volume of gas collected.

(1)

Due to the fact that carbon dioxide is slightly soluble in water, a small amount of it will dissolve in the water in the water bath. This will reduce the volume of gas that can be collected in the measuring cylinder.

1 (d) The student carried out her investigation so that it was a fair test. Select one variable that must be kept constant for the experiment to be a fair test and explain why it must be kept constant.

The surface area of the calcium carbonate must be kept constant. If the surface area was higher, then there would be more collisions of hydrogen ions with calcium carbonate per second. This would make the reaction faster.

(3)

> A variable which must be controlled has been identified (other variables that must be controlled include the temperature of the acid). This scores one mark. The remaining two marks are awarded for explaining why changing the selected variable would change the results.

Another student investigated the mass of calcium carbonate used on the final volume of carbon dioxide gas collected. The method she followed was:

1. Place 25.0 cm^3 of dilute hydrochloric acid in a boiling tube.
2. Add a known mass of calcium carbonate to the dilute acid in the boiling tube.
3. Connect the boiling tube to a gas syringe as shown in the diagram.

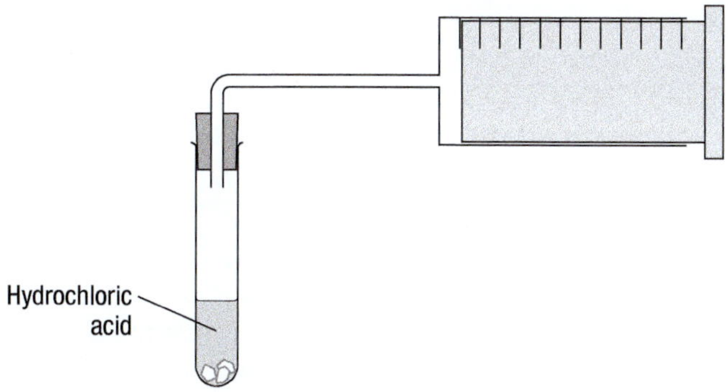

The graph shows the results she obtained.

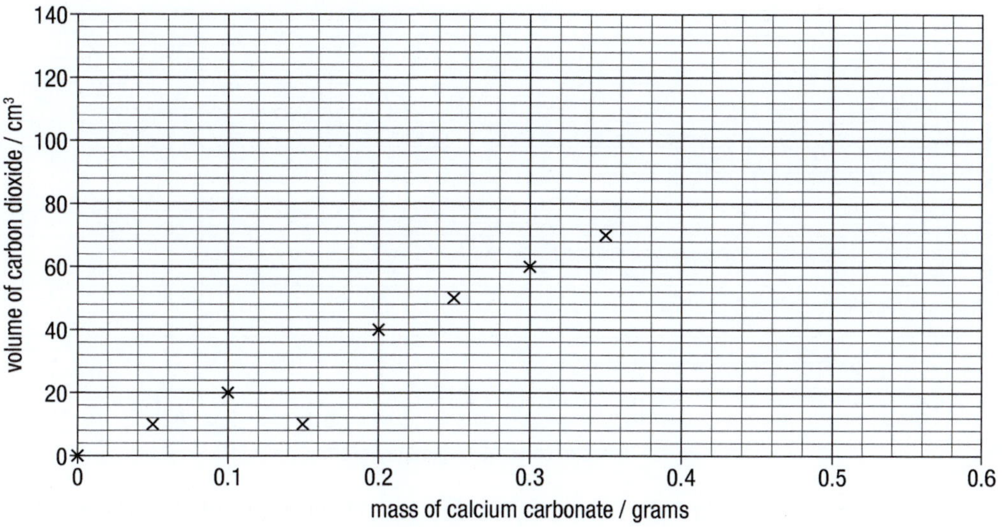

1 (e) Name an item of laboratory apparatus most suitable for measuring 25.0 cm^3 of hydrochloric acid.

A volumetric pipette could be used.

(1)

> A volumetric pipette is the best apparatus to measure a fixed volume such as 25.0 cm^3. A burette could also be used.

1 (f) Draw a line of best fit through the points on the graph.

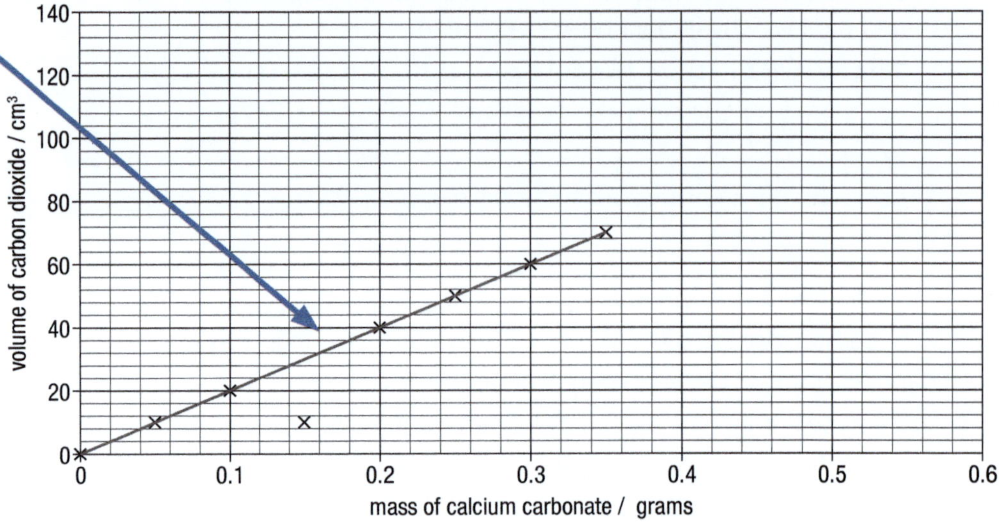

(1)

The line drawn is straight (it has been done with the aid of a rule) and it ignores the anomalous point.

1 (g) Describe the relationship between the mass of calcium carbonate used and the volume of carbon dioxide gas collected.

As the mass of calcium carbonate is doubled, the volume of gas collected also doubles.

(2)

An alternative way to say this is 'they are directly proportional'. A straight line through the origin shows a directly proportional relationship. If the line is straight but does not pass through the origin then you can say it is a linear relationship (but it is not directly proportional).

1 (h) There is an anomalous point on the graph. Circle the anomalous point and explain what could have happened to cause the anomalous point.

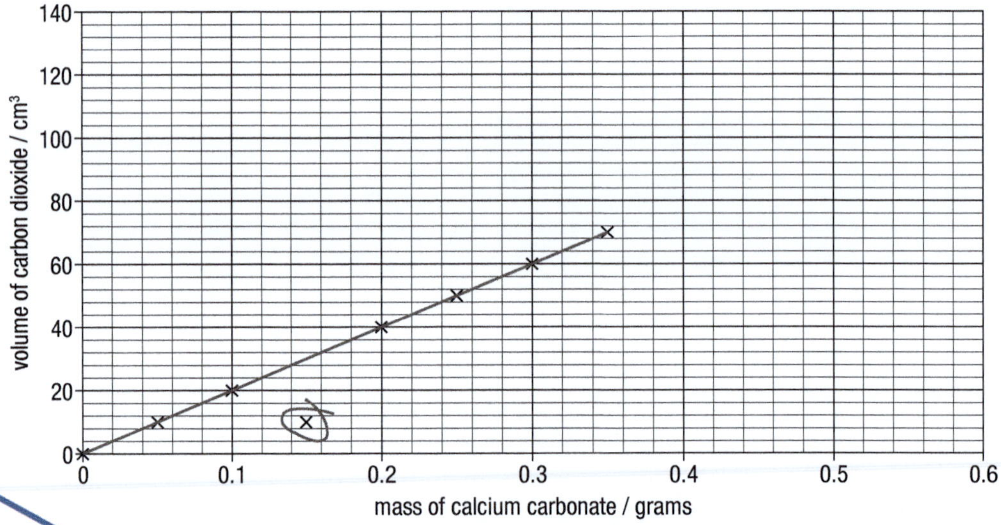

The bung may not have been replaced correctly. This would have allowed some of the gas to escape, and so less was collected.

(3)

The point that is some distance from the line has been correctly identified.
The explanation gives a correct reason why the volume of gas collected could have been too small and explains why the reason given would result in too small a volume. Other possible explanations include the mass of calcium carbonate being too small so less carbon dioxide would be made.

1 (i) What should the student have done to check the precision of her results and improve the accuracy of the data she has plotted?

The experiment should have been repeated at least three times and then a mean value calculated for the volume of gas collected for each mass of calcium carbonate.

(2)

Repeating the experiment does not necessarily make the results more accurate, but it does let us check to see if the results are precise. Calculating a mean using the repeated results will reduce any random errors and so the mean values should be more accurate.

1 (j) Use the graph to predict the volume of gas that would be collected if 0.55 g of calcium carbonate were used in the experiment. Show all of your working.

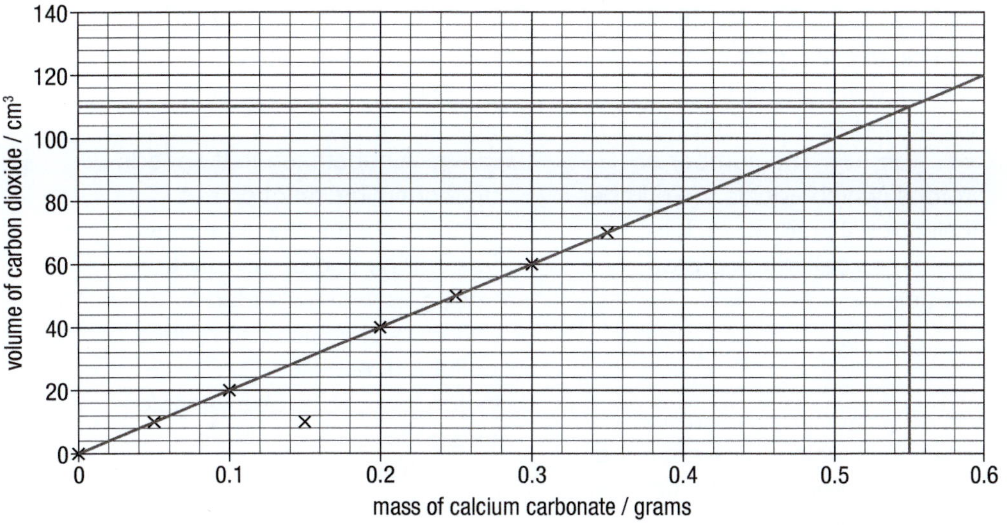

The volume of gas would be 110 cm³.

(2)

This scores both marks because the candidate has extrapolated the graph line and then read off the correct value from the graph. The value has been read from the graph accurately.

The student then repeated the experiment using 0.55 g of calcium carbonate. She obtained a much smaller volume of gas than she expected. Her teacher suggested that this was because she had not used enough acid to react with all the calcium carbonate.

1 (k) Explain how she could check whether her teacher's suggestion was correct.

She could repeat the experiment using a larger volume of acid.
If the teacher is correct then the volume of gas will increase.

(2)

This scores both marks as the candidate has said what should be done and the result that should be obtained if the teacher is correct.

The student calculated the volume of gas, at 25 °C, she should have made in some of the runs. The table shows the volumes she collected and how much should have been made.

Mass calcium carbonate / g	Volume carbon dioxide collected / cm^3	Theoretical volume of carbon dioxide / cm^3
0.10	20	24
0.20	40	48
0.30	60	72

All of the gas volumes are too small. This means there is a problem with the procedure being used.

1 (l) What type of error do her results show?

It is a systematic error.

(1)

1 (m) Explain how an error of this type could have occurred in each run.

As soon as the calcium carbonate has been added to the acid carbon dioxide gas is made. Some of this gas escapes before the bung is placed in the boiling tube connected to the gas syringe.

(2)

This answer scores both marks as it gives a problem that would cause a systematic error and explains how that error makes the gas volume too small. Another correct answer would be if the gas was being collected at a temperature below 25 °C as at a lower temperatures the gas will have a smaller volume.

Glossary

A

Accurate A measurement is considered accurate if it is judged to be close to the true value.

Acid A sour substance which can attack metal, clothing, or skin. When dissolved in water, its solution has a pH value less than 7. Acids are proton (H^+ ion) donors.

Activation energy The minimum energy needed for a reaction to take place.

Alkali metal Elements in Group 1 of the periodic table, e.g., lithium (Li), sodium (Na), potassium (K).

Alkali Its solution has a pH value more than 7.

Alkane Saturated hydrocarbon with the general formula C_nH_{2n+2}, e.g., methane, ethane, and propane.

Alkene Unsaturated hydrocarbon which contains a carbon–carbon double bond. Its general formula is C_nH_{2n}, e.g., ethene C_2H_4.

Alloy A mixture of two or more elements, at least one of which is a metal.

Aluminium A low density, corrosion-resistant metal used in many alloys, including those used in the aircraft industry.

Anhydrous Describes a substance that does not contain water.

Anode The positive electrode in electrolysis.

Anomalies Results that do not match the pattern seen in the other data collected or are well outside the range of other repeat readings. They should be retested and if necessary discarded.

Aqueous solution The mixture made by adding a soluble substance to water.

Atmosphere The relatively thin layer of gases that surround planet Earth.

Atom The smallest part of an element that can still be recognised as that element.

Atomic number The number of protons (which equals the number of electrons) in an atom. It is sometimes called the proton number.

B

Balanced (equation) A symbol equation in which there are equal numbers of each type of atom on either side of the equation.

Bar chart A chart with rectangular bars with lengths proportional to the values that they represent. The bars should be of equal width. Also called a bar graph.

Base The oxide, hydroxide, or carbonate of a metal that will react with an acid, forming a salt as one of the products. (If a base dissolves in water it is called an alkali.) Bases are proton (H^+ ion) acceptors.

Biodegradable Materials that can be broken down by microorganisms.

Biodiesel Fuel for cars made from plant oils.

Biofuel Fuel made from animal or plant products.

Bond dissociation energy The energy required to break a specific chemical bond.

Brine A solution of sodium chloride in water.

Burette A long glass tube with a tap at one end and markings to show volumes of liquid. It is used to add precisely known volumes of liquids to a solution in a conical flask below it.

C

Carbon monoxide A toxic gas whose formula is CO.

Carbon steel Alloy of iron containing controlled, small amounts of carbon.

Catalyst A substance that speeds up a chemical reaction but remains chemically unchanged itself at the end of the reaction.

Catalytic converter Fitted to exhausts of vehicles to reduce pollutants released.

Categoric variable See Variable – categoric.

Cathode The negative electrode in electrolysis.

Chromatography The process whereby small amounts of dissolved substances are separated by running a solvent along a material such as absorbent paper.

Climate change The change in global weather patterns that could be caused by excess levels of greenhouse gases in the atmosphere.

Closed system A system in which no matter enters or leaves.

Collision theory An explanation of chemical reactions in terms of reacting particles colliding with sufficient energy for a reaction to take place.

Compound A substance made when two or more elements are chemically bonded together. For example, water (H_2O) is a compound made from hydrogen and oxygen.

Continuous variable See Variable – continuous.

Control group If an experiment is to determine the effect of changing a single variable, a control is often set up in which the independent variable is not changed, therefore enabling a comparison to be made. If the investigation is of the survey type a control group is usually established to serve the same purpose.

Control variable See Variable – control.

Covalent bond The bond between two atoms that share one or more pairs of electrons.

Covalent bonding The attraction between two atoms that share one or more pairs of electrons.

Cracking The reaction used in the oil industry to break down large hydrocarbons into smaller, more useful ones. This occurs when the hydrocarbon vapour is either passed over a hot catalyst or mixed with steam and heated to a high temperature.

D

Data Information, either qualitative or quantitative, that has been collected.

Delocalised electron Bonding electron that is no longer associated with any one particular atom.

Dependent variable See Variable – dependent.

Diffusion The automatic mixing of liquids and gases as a result of the random motion of their particles.

Directly proportional A relationship that, when drawn on a line graph, shows a positive linear relationship that passes through the origin.

Displacement reaction A reaction in which a more reactive element takes the place of a less reactive element in one of its compounds or in solution.

Distillation Separation of a liquid from a mixture by evaporation followed by condensation.

Dot and cross diagram A drawing to show only the arrangement of the outer shell electrons of the atoms or ions in a substance.

Double bond A covalent bond made by the sharing of two pairs of electrons.

E

Electrolysis The breakdown of a substance containing ions into elements by electricity.

Electrolyte A liquid, containing free-moving ions, which is broken down by electricity in the process of electrolysis.

Electron A tiny particle with a negative charge. Electrons orbit the nucleus in atoms or ions.

Electronic structure A set of numbers to show the arrangement of electrons in their shells (or energy levels), e.g., the electronic structure of a potassium atom is 2,8,8,1.

Electroplating The process of depositing a thin layer of metal on an object during electrolysis.

Element A substance made up of only one type of atom. An element cannot be broken down chemically into any simpler substance.

Empirical formula The simplest ratio of atoms of each element in a compound.

End point The point in a titration where the reaction is complete and titration should stop.

Endothermic A reaction that *takes in* energy from the surroundings.

Energy level see Shell.

Equilibrium The point in a reversible reaction in which the forward and backward rates of reaction are the same. Therefore, the amounts of substances present in the reacting mixture remain constant.

Error Sometimes called an uncertainty.

Error – random Causes readings to be spread about the true value, due to results varying in an unpredictable way from one measurement to the next. Random errors are present when any measurement is made, and cannot be corrected. The effect of random errors can be reduced by making more measurements and calculating a new mean.

Error – systematic Causes readings to be spread about some value other than the true value, due to results differing from the true value by a consistent amount each time a measurement is made. Sources of systematic error can include the environment, methods of observation, or instruments used. Systematic errors cannot be dealt with by simple repeats. If a systematic error is suspected, the data collection should be repeated using a different technique or a different set of equipment, and the results compared.

Ethene An alkene with the formula C_2H_4.

Evidence Data which has been shown to be valid.

Exothermic A reaction that *gives out* energy to the surroundings.

F

Fair test A fair test is one in which only the independent variable has been allowed to affect the dependent variable.

Fermentation The reaction in which the enzymes in yeast turn glucose into ethanol and carbon dioxide.

Flammable Easily ignited and capable of burning rapidly.

Fraction Groups of hydrocarbons separated from crude oil. Each fraction contains molecules with a similar number of carbon atoms.

Fractional distillation A way to separate liquids from a mixture of liquids by boiling off the substances at different temperatures, then condensing and collecting the liquids.

Fullerene Form of the element carbon that can exist as large cage-like structures, based on hexagonal rings of carbon atoms.

Functional group An atom or group of atoms that give organic compounds their characteristic reactions.

G

Gas A state of matter.

Giant covalent structure A huge 3-D network of covalently-bonded atoms (e.g., the giant lattice of carbon atoms in diamond or graphite).

Giant lattice A huge 3-D network of atoms or ions (e.g., the giant ionic lattice in sodium chloride).

Giant structure See Giant lattice.

Global dimming The reflection of sunlight by tiny solid particles in the air.

Group All the elements in the columns (labelled 1 to 7 and 0) down the periodic table.

H

Half equation An equation that describes reduction (gain of electrons) or oxidation (loss of electrons), such as the reactions that take place at the electrodes during electrolysis. For example: $Na^+ + e^- \rightarrow Na$.

Halogens The elements found in Group 7 of the periodic table.

Hazard Something (e.g., an object, a property of a substance, or an activity) that can cause harm.

High-alloy steel Expensive alloy of iron mixed with relatively large proportions of other metals, e.g., stainless steel which contains nickel and chromium along with the iron.

Homologous series A group of related organic compounds that have the same functional group, e.g., the molecules of the homologous series of alcohols all contain the –OH group.

Hydrated Describes a substance that contains water in its crystals, e.g., hydrated copper sulfate.

Hydration A reaction in which water (H_2O) is chemically added to a compound.

Hydrocarbon A compound containing only hydrogen and carbon.

Hypothesis A proposal intended to explain certain facts or observations.

I

Incomplete combustion When a fuel burns in insufficient oxygen, producing carbon monoxide as a toxic product or carbon (soot) particles.

Independent variable See Variable – independent.

Inert Unreactive.

Intermolecular forces The attraction between the individual molecules in a covalently-bonded substance.

Interval The quantity between readings, for example, a set of 11 readings equally spaced over a distance of 1 m would have an interval of 10 cm.

Ion A charged particle produced by the loss or gain of electrons.

Ionic bond The electrostatic force of attraction between positively and negatively charged ions.

Ionic bonding The electrostatic force of attraction between positively and negatively charged ions.

Ionic equation An equation that shows only those ions or atoms that change in a chemical reaction.

Isotope Atoms that have the same number of protons but a different number of neutrons, i.e., they have the same atomic number but different mass numbers.

L

Limewater The common name for calcium hydroxide solution.

Line graph Used when both variables are continuous. The line should normally be a line of best fit, and may be straight or a smooth curve.

Liquid A state of matter.

Low-alloy steel Alloy of iron containing small amounts (1 to 5 per cent) of other metals.

M

Macromolecule Giant covalent structure.

Mass number The number of protons plus neutrons in the nucleus of an atom.

Mean The arithmetical average of a series of numbers.

Metal ore A rock in which there is sufficient metal compound (or occasionally metal) to make it economically viable to extract the metal.

Mixture When some elements or compounds are mixed together and intermingle but do not react together (i.e., no new substance is made). A mixture is not a pure substance.

Mole The amount of substance in the relative atomic or formula mass of a substance in grams.

Molecular formula The chemical formula that shows the actual numbers of atoms of each element in a particular molecule (e.g., C_2H_4).

Molecule A group of atoms bonded together, e.g., PCl_5.

Monomers Small reactive molecules that react together in repeating sequences to form a very large molecule (a polymer).

N

Nanoscience The study of very tiny particles or structures between 1 and 100 nanometres in size, where 1 nanometre = 10^{-9} metres.

Neutral A solution with a pH value of 7 which is neither acidic nor alkaline. Alternatively, something that carries no overall electrical charge, that is, neither positively nor negatively charged.

Neutralisation The chemical reaction of an acid with a base in which they cancel each other out, forming a salt and water. If the base is a carbonate or hydrogen carbonate, carbon dioxide is also produced in the reaction.

Neutron A dense particle found in the nucleus of an atom. It is electrically neutral, carrying no charge.

Nitrogen oxide Gaseous pollutant given off from motor vehicles. It is a cause of acid rain.

Noble gases The very unreactive gases found in Group 0 of the periodic table.

Non-renewable Something which cannot be replaced once it is used up.

Nucleus (of an atom) The very small and dense central part of an atom which contains protons and neutrons.

O

Oxidation The reaction when oxygen is added to a substance (or when electrons are lost).

Oxidised A reaction where oxygen is added to a substance (or when electrons are lost from a substance).

P

Particulate Small solid particle, e.g., carbon (soot), given off from motor vehicles as a result of incomplete combustion of its fuel.

Periodic table An arrangement of the elements in the order of their atomic numbers, forming groups and periods.

pH scale A number which shows how strongly acidic or alkaline a solution is. Acids have a pH value of less than 7 (pH 0 is strongly acidic). Alkalis have a pH value above 7 (pH 14 is strongly alkaline). A neutral liquid has a pH value of 7.

Pipette A glass tube used to measure accurate volumes of liquids.

Polymer A substance made from very large molecules made up of many repeating units, e.g., poly(ethene).

Polymerisation The reaction of monomers to make a polymer.

Precipitate An insoluble solid formed by a reaction taking place in solution.

Precise A precise measurement is one in which there is very little spread about the mean value. Precision depends only on the extent of random errors – it gives no indication of how close the results are to the true value.

Precision A precise set of repeat readings will be closely grouped together.

Prediction A forecast or statement about the way something will happen in the future. In science it is not just a simple guess, because it is based on some prior knowledge or on a hypothesis.

Product A substance made as a result of a chemical reaction.

Propene An alkene with the formula C_3H_6.

Proton A tiny positive particle found inside the nucleus of an atom.

R

Random error See Error – random.

Range The maximum and minimum values of the independent or dependent variables. It is important in ensuring that any pattern is detected.

Reactant A substance you start with before a chemical reaction takes place.

Reactivity series A list of elements in order of their reactivity. The most reactive element is put at the top of the list.

Reduction A reaction in which oxygen is removed (or electrons are gained).

Relationship The link between the variables that were investigated. These relationships may be: causal, i.e., changing *x* is the reason why *y* changes; by association, i.e., both *x* and *y* change at the same time, but the changes may both be caused by a third variable changing; by chance occurrence.

Relative atomic mass, A_r The average mass of the atoms of an element compared with carbon-12 (which is given a relative mass of exactly 12). The average mass must take into account the proportions of the naturally occurring isotopes of the element.

Repeatable A measurement is repeatable if the original experimenter repeats the investigation using the same method and equipment and obtains the same results.

Reproducible A measurement is reproducible if the investigation is repeated by another person, or by using different equipment or techniques, and the same results are obtained.

Resolution This is the smallest change in the quantity being measured (input) of a measuring instrument that gives a perceptible change in the reading.

Reversible reaction A reaction in which the products can re-form the reactants.

R_f (retention factor) A measurement from chromatography. It is the distance a spot of substance has been carried above the baseline divided by the distance of the solvent front.

Risk The likelihood that a hazard will actually cause harm. We can reduce risk by identifying the hazard and doing something to protect against that hazard.

Rusting The corrosion of iron.

S

Salt A compound formed when some or all of the hydrogen in an acid is replaced by a metal (or by an ammonium ion), for example, potassium nitrate, KNO_3 (from nitric acid).

Saturated hydrocarbon A hydrocarbon with only single bonds between its carbon atoms. This means that it contains as many hydrogen atoms as possible in each molecule.

Shell (or energy level) An area in an atom, around its nucleus, where electrons are found.

Smart polymer Polymers that change in response to changes in their environment.

Solid A state of matter.

Stainless steel A chromium-nickel alloy of steel which does not rust.

State symbol The abbreviations used in balanced symbol equations to show if reactants and products are solid (s), liquid (l), gas (g) or dissolved in water (aq).

State of matter Tells us whether a substance is a solid, a liquid, or a gas.

Steel An alloy of iron with small amounts of carbon or other metals, such as nickel and chromium, added.

Sulfur dioxide A toxic gas whose formula is SO_2. It causes acid rain.

Symbol equation A balanced chemical equation showing the formula of each reactant and product in the reaction, e.g., $H_2 + Cl_2 \rightarrow 2HCl$

Systematic error See Error – systematic.

T

Thermal decomposition The breakdown of a compound by heating it.

Thermosetting polymer Polymer that can form extensive cross-linking between chains, resulting in rigid materials which are heat-resistant.

Thermosoftening polymer Polymer that forms plastics which can be softened by heating, then remoulded into different shapes as they cool down and set.

Titration A method for measuring the volumes of two solutions that react together.

Transition metal Element from the central block of the periodic table. It has typical metallic properties and forms coloured compounds.

U

Universal indicator A mixture of indicators that can change through a range of colours depending on the pH of a solution. Its colour is matched to a pH number using a pH scale. It shows how strongly acidic or alkaline liquids and solutions are.

Unsaturated hydrocarbon A hydrocarbon whose molecules contains at least one carbon–carbon double bond.

V

Valid Suitability of the investigative procedure to answer the question being asked.

Variable Physical, chemical, or biological quantity or characteristic.

Variable – categoric Categoric variables have values that are labels. For example, names of plants or types of material.

Variable – continuous Can have values (called a quantity) that can be given by measurement (e.g., light intensity, flow rate, temperature).

Variable – control A variable which may, in addition to the independent variable, affect the outcome of the investigation and therefore has to be kept constant or at least monitored.

Variable – dependent The variable for which the value is measured for each and every change in the independent variable.

Variable – independent The variable for which values are changed or selected by the investigator.

Viscosity The resistance of a liquid to flowing or pouring; a liquid's 'thickness'.

W

Word equation A way of describing what happens in a chemical reaction by showing the names of all reactants and the products they form.

Answers

1 Atomic structure

1.1

1 E.g.

	General properties	Average distance between particles	Arrangement of particles	Movement of particles
Solid	Fixed shape; incompressible	Particles are touching	Regular pattern	Vibrate on the spot
Liquid	No fixed shape; can flow; very difficult to compress	Most particles are touching	Irregular, random	Slip and slide over and around each other
Gas	No fixed shape; spreads out to fill its container; easily compressed	Large distances	Irregular, random	Can move very quickly. In a random manner, between collisions

2 As the particles of gas are cooled down their average speed decreases until at its condensation point the particles become much closer together. They form a liquid in which the particles are moving randomly, slipping over and around each other. As the liquid is cooled, the average speed of the particles decreases until at its freezing point the particles stop moving around randomly and remain in fixed positions, vibrating on the spot. As the solid is cooled the average rate of the vibrations slows down.

3 **a** freeze/solidify
b condense
c melt
d boil/evaporate
e sublime

4 As the temperature is increased, the particles in a gas gain energy and their average speed is increased and they take up more space if the pressure remains constant. Therefore, the density decreases as the same mass of gas occupies a larger volume.
By compressing a gas the pressure is increased as particles collide with the walls of their container more frequently. So, the same mass of gas occupies a smaller volume and the density of the gas increases.

5 The strength of the attractive forces between particles varies in different substances so those with stronger forces of attraction will have higher melting points than those with weaker forces of attraction.

6 Plan a fair test varying one factor, e.g., temperature of the water or surface area of the paper towel, keeping all other variables constant. Monitor the rate of evaporation by measuring the mass of the wet paper towel on the electronic balance at regular time intervals.

1.2

1 **a** The food particles released from the hot food diffuse through the air outside the shop and passers-by detect these with their sense of smell.
b The particles of water move around faster in hot water than in cold water so they collide into the sugar particles in the solid more frequently and with more energy. This breaks down the regular arrangement of sugar particles in the solid and spreads them out more quickly as the sugar solution is formed.
c Hot water releases water particles into the air as its most energetic particles are moving fast enough to escape from their neighbouring water particles at the surface. The glass in the window is colder than the air so any water particles diffusing through the air to the window will cool down and slow down; then the vapour will condense back to liquid on the glass.
d Petrol is a volatile liquid so particles can evaporate from its surface quite easily. It is also flammable. In a petrol station there are likely to be particles from petrol diffusing through the air which could be ignited by any naked flame or a lighted cigarette.

2 **a** The movement of one substance through another due to the random motion of the particles in liquids or gases.
b The average speed of the particles in a gas is greater than that in a liquid so the mixing together of particles happens more quickly in gases.

3 The jittery movement of the pollen grains must be caused by collisions with the particles in liquid water which are too small to be seen under the microscope.

4 As hydrogen bromide is heavier than hydrogen chloride the white ring of smoke would form nearer the end of the tube releasing particles (molecules) of hydrogen bromide.

ammonia + hydrogen bromide → ammonium bromide
$NH_3(g)$ + $HBr(g)$ → $NH_4Br(s)$

1.3

1 **a** **C** Atoms are solid spheres that cannot be split into simpler particles.
b soda and lime

2 **a** The electron
b A diffuse cloud of positive charge with tiny negatively charged electrons spread throughout.

3 Rutherford said that the positive charge in an atom was concentrated into a very small volume at the centre of the atom (in the nucleus) and that the electrons were orbiting the centre of the atom/nucleus.

4 He found that energy emitted from electron transitions could only have certain fixed energies, so he refined the 'orbiting electrons' in Rutherford's nuclear model to 'orbiting electrons in energy levels (or shells) at fixed distances from the nucleus'.

1.4

1 **a**

Metals	Non-metals
Barium	Phosphorus
Vanadium	Krypton
Mercury	
Potassium	
Uranium	

b Non-metal because it does not have the physical properties of a metal, e.g., it does not conduct electricity.

2 A mixture of elements can be separated by physical means because atoms from the different elements are not chemically bonded to each other whereas they are if they have reacted together.

3 One diagram showing an element in which all the atoms present must of the same type and another showing a compound containing more than one type of atom chemically combined.

4 A tiny central nucleus surrounded by orbiting electrons.

5 **a** Na from Latin *natrium*
b Au from Latin *aurum*
c Pb from Latin *plumbum*
d K from Latin *kalium*

1.5

1 **a** Because no atoms are created or destroyed in a chemical reaction, equal numbers and types of atoms must appear on both sides of the equation.
b $H_2 + Cl_2 \rightarrow 2HCl$

2 **a** 17.6 g
b magnesium carbonate → magnesium oxide + carbon dioxide
$MgCO_3(s) \rightarrow MgO(s) + CO_2(g)$

3 **a** $2KNO_3 \rightarrow 2KNO_2 + O_2$
b $4Li + O_2 \rightarrow 2Li_2O$
c $4Fe + 3O_2 \rightarrow 2Fe_2O_3$

4 $2Na(s) + 2H_2O(l) \rightarrow 2NaOH(aq) + H_2(g)$

1.6

1

Sub-atomic particle	Location	Relative charge
Proton	In the nucleus	+1
Neutron	In the nucleus	0
Electron	Orbiting the nucleus	−1

2 **a** It increases by 1.
b It increases by 8.
c Metals – Li, Be, Na, Mg, Al
Non-metals – H, He, C, N, O, F, Ne, P, S, Cl, Ar
Metalloids – B, Si

3 Atoms contain an equal number of protons (carrying a relative charge of +1) and electrons (carrying a relative charge of −1) so the opposite charges cancel each other out.

4 Cobalt, Co, atomic number = 27, mass number = 59.

5 **a** 7 protons, 7 electrons, and 7 neutrons.
b 17 protons, 17 electrons, and 18 neutrons.
c 47 protons, 47 electrons, and 61 neutrons.
d 92 protons, 92 electrons, and 143 neutrons.

1.7

1 **a** The first or innermost shell.
b 2 in the first then 8 in the second.

2 a 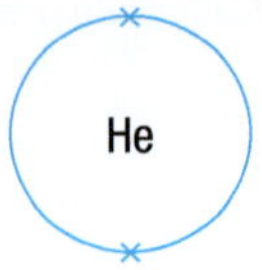

b 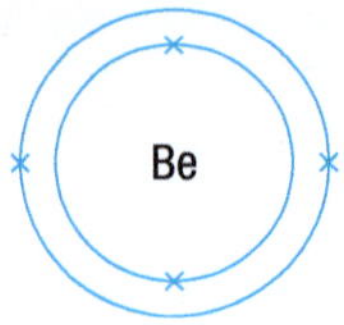

c 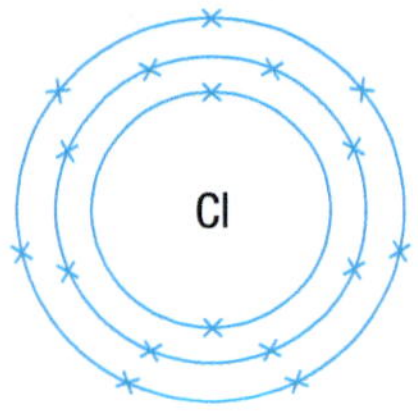

d 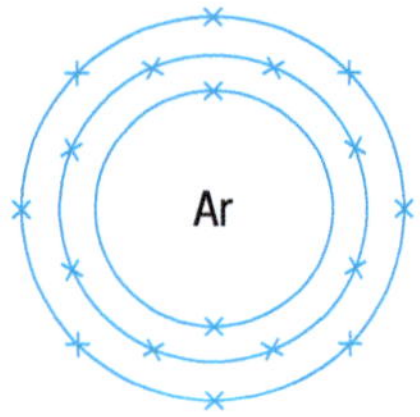

3 a 2,8,8,1 b 1 electron
4 phosphorus, P
5 a Because they all have one electron (the same number of electrons) in the highest energy level (outermost shell) of their atoms.
 b lithium + oxygen → lithium oxide
 sodium + oxygen → sodium oxide
 potassium + oxygen → potassium oxide

1.8

1

Sub-atomic particle	Relative mass	Relative charge
Proton	1	+1
Neutron	1	0
Electron	Very small $\left(\frac{1}{2000}\right)$	−1

2 a 5 protons and 6 neutrons
 b 7 protons and 7 neutrons
 c 12 protons and 12 neutrons
 d 17 protons and 20 neutrons
 e 53 protons and 74 neutrons
3 a 29
 b D
 c 35
 d $^{64}_{29}Cu$
 e i 79 ii 118 iii 79
4 Isotopes are the atoms of an element with different numbers of neutrons. They have the same proton number, but different mass numbers.
5 The relative atomic mass is the average mass of the atoms of an element compared with carbon-12 (which is given a relative mass of exactly 12). This average mass takes into account the proportions of the naturally occurring isotopes of the element.

Answers to end of chapter summary questions

1 a The change from a solid directly to a gas.
 b 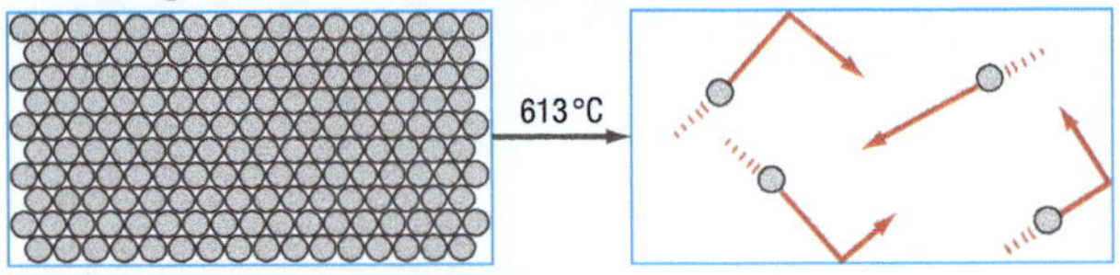

 c Boiling, melting, and sublimation
2 a Particles (molecules) of hydrogen sulfide and sulfur dioxide diffuse through the particles (molecules) of air in the long tube. Where they meet, they collide and react with each other to form the yellow powder.
 b Diffusion
 c Because the particles (molecules) of sulfur dioxide travel down the tube/diffuse more slowly than the particles (molecules) of hydrogen sulfide (showing sulfur dioxide molecules have a greater mass than hydrogen sulfide molecules).
 d A long tube showing a jagged, random path
 e The yellow powder would appear sooner because the molecules of gas move faster at higher temperatures.
3 a Bromine – liquid, Caesium – solid, Fluorine – gas, Strontium – solid, Xenon – gas
 b Caesium
 c The two gases have much lower densities because they have large spaces between their particles, unlike the solids and liquid whose particles are touching (so many more particles fit into the same volume compared with the gases).
 d Bromine – Br, Caesium – Cs, Fluorine – F, Strontium – Sr, Xenon – Xe
 e Bromine – non-metal, Caesium – metal, Fluorine – non-metal, Strontium – metal, Xenon – non-metal

4 a i Protons and neutrons
 ii 2 electrons in the first shell and 8 in the second
 b i It is neutral because the number of protons (+) and electrons (–) is the same in an atom so the charges cancel out.
 ii Atomic number is the number of protons.
 Mass number is the number of protons plus neutrons.
5 a i Non-metal
 ii Metals
 iii 10 protons
 iv 10 neutrons
 v Noble gases, Group 0
 vi Helium, Argon, Krypton, Xenon, Radon
 vii 2,8
 viii They are very stable arrangements of electrons.
 b i 88
 ii 2 electrons because it is in Group 2
 iii Metal
 iv 2,8,8,2

Answers to end of chapter practice questions

1 Solid *(1 mark)*
 Gas *(1 mark)*
 Liquid *(1 mark)*
2 a Element – all atoms are the same. *(1 mark)*
 Compound – two different atoms/elements combined together. *(1 mark)*
 b Ammonia is a compound because only one type of molecule, each containing two types of atom. *(1 mark)*
 Air is a mixture because more than one type of molecule. *(1 mark)*
 c i Condensation/liquefaction *(1 mark)*
 ii Evaporation/boiling *(1 mark)*
 iii Sublimation *(1 mark)*
3 a Blue *(1 mark)*
 Darker at bottom of beaker/lighter at top of beaker *(1 mark)*
 b Becomes smaller/disappears *(1 mark)*
 c Dissolving/solution *(1 mark)*
 Diffusion *(1 mark)*
4 a White solid/smoke *(1 mark)*
 Closer to ammonia end *(1 mark)*
 b g g s *(1 mark)*
 c They travel further than hydrogen chloride molecules. *(1 mark)*
5 a 2 *(1 mark)*
 b 8 *(1 mark)*
 c 3 *(1 mark)*
 d 5 *(1 mark)*
 e 16 *(1 mark)*
 f i 10 *(1 mark)* ii 10 *(1 mark)* iii 10 *(1 mark)* iv 22 *(4 marks)*

2 Structure and bonding

2.1

1 a Covalent bond
 b Ionic bond
2 The atoms of Group 1 lose their single electron in the outermost shell (highest energy level) by transferring it to a Group 7 atom, which has seven electrons in the outermost shell (highest energy level). The atoms become ions which have the stable electronic arrangements of a noble gas.
3 a 2,8 for the Al^{3+} ion (3 electrons lost)
 b 2,8 for the F^- ion (1 electron gained)
 c 2,8,8 for the K^+ ion (1 electron lost)
 d 2,8 for O^{2-} (2 electrons gained)

2.2

1

Atomic number	Atom	Electronic structure of atom	Ion	Electronic structure of ion
9	F	2,7	F^-	2,8
3	Li	2,1	Li^+	2
16	S	2,8,6	S^{2-}	2,8,8
20	Ca	2,8,8,2	Ca^{2+}	2,8,8

2 Metal atoms lose electrons when they form ions (therefore their ions have more positively-charged protons than negatively-charged electrons) resulting in positively-charged ions. Non-metal atoms gain electrons when they form ions (therefore their ions have more negatively-charged electrons than positively-charged protons) resulting in negatively-charged ions.
3 a Groups 1, 2, and 3; the charge on their ions = (group number)+
 b Groups 5, 6, and 7; the charge on their ions = (8 – group number)–
4 a In KBr the 1– charge on the Br^- ion is cancelled out by the 1+ charge on K^+ ion whereas two K^+ ions are needed to cancel out the 2– charge on an O^{2-} ion.
 b In MgO the 2– charge on the O^{2-} ion is cancelled out by the 2+ charge on Mg^{2+} ion whereas two Cl^- ions are needed to cancel out the 2+ charge on an Mg^{2+} ion.

5 a
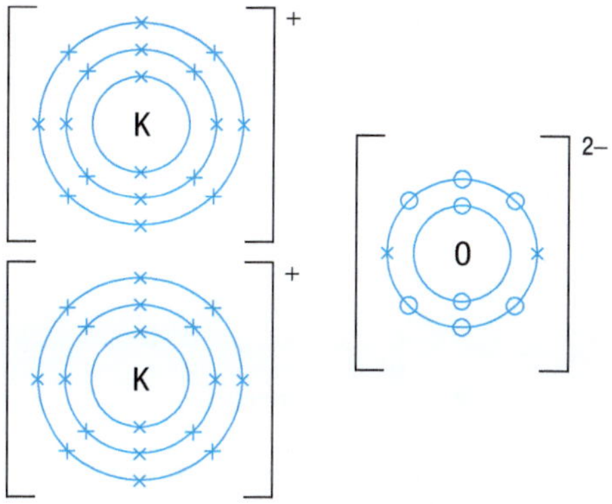

b
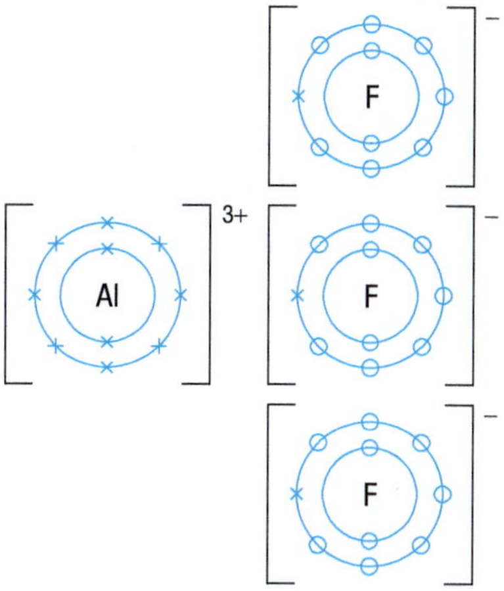

2.3

1 Hydrogen iodide, sulfur dioxide, and nitrogen(III) chloride because these contain only non-metallic elements.

2 a
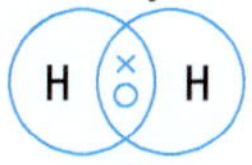

b
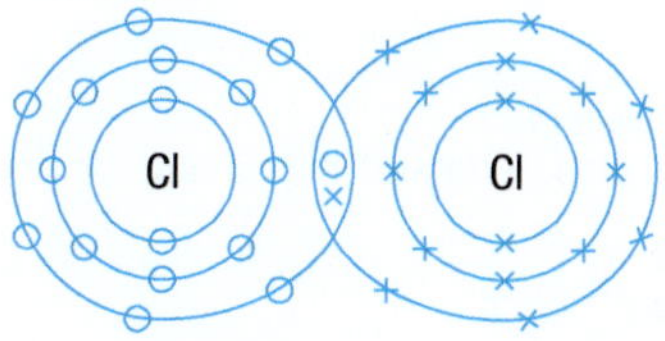

c
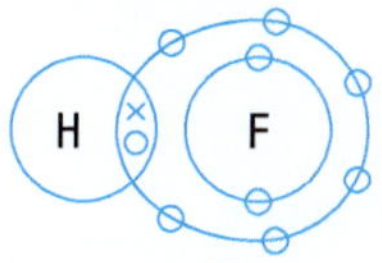

3 a
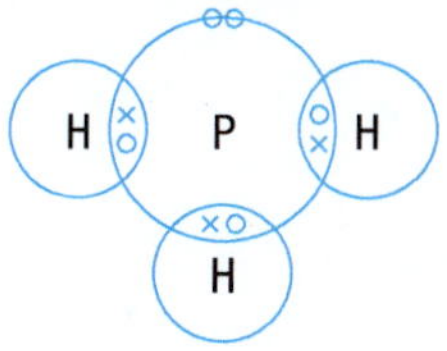

b
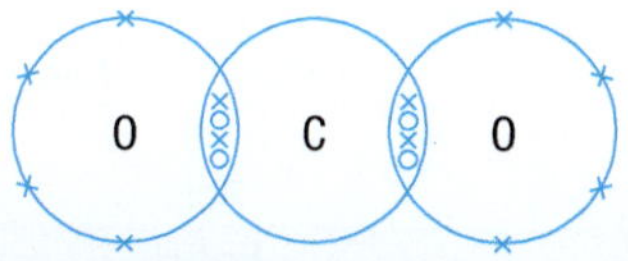

4 Hydrogen attains the electronic structure of helium.
Chlorine attains the electronic structure of argon.

5 The electrostatic attraction between the bonding pair of negatively charged electrons for each of the positively charged nuclei on either side of the pair hold the atoms together.

2.4

1 The particles are arranged in regular patterns.

2 a Because the metal atoms donate their outer shell electrons into a 'sea' of electrons so have more protons (+) than electrons (–).

b Electrons that are free-moving within a structure and are no longer associated with any particular atom.

3 Magnesium atoms have two electrons in their outer shell (highest energy level). These are donated into the 'sea' of delocalised electrons which are free to move around. The electrostatic attraction of the negatively charged delocalised electrons for the positively charged Mg^{2+} ions bonds the ions in the giant metallic lattice.

4 The 'glue' model can help us imagine the positively charged metal ions being stuck in position in the giant lattice but a glue itself becomes solid when it sets so is not helpful in visualising the fluid movement of the delocalised electrons throughout the structure.

2.5

1 There are strong electrostatic forces of attraction between the oppositely charged ions in the giant lattice, acting in all directions, which result in a lot of energy being required to separate the ions in the process of melting.

2 The ions in the solid are fixed in position and are only free to move (and carry their charge to electrodes) when they are molten or dissolved in water.

3 There is a higher concentration of ions from the dissolved salts in seawater than there are in freshwater.

4 Positive electrode – chloride ions, bromide ions, oxide ions, iodide ions
Negative electrode – lithium ions, calcium ions, sodium ions, zinc ions, barium ions

5 Aluminium oxide because it contains 3+ ions as opposed to the 1+ ions in sodium oxide so you can expect stronger electrostatic forces of attraction between the metal ions and the oxide ions (the smaller size of the aluminium ions also contributes towards this).

2.6

1 Forces of attraction between molecules

2 a Oxygen

b Chlorine

c Hydrogen sulfide; hydrogen; sulfur

3 a It has a giant covalent structure with strong covalent bonds holding the atoms strongly into the regular giant lattices.

b Nitrogen gas has a very strong triple covalent bond between its nitrogen atoms within each N_2 molecule but only very weak forces of attraction between the N_2 molecules/weak intermolecular forces between N_2 molecules. Therefore molecules easily separated from each other.

4 Good electrical insulator/does not conduct electricity as there is no overall charge on its molecules.

5 There are only weak intermolecular forces between HCl molecules whereas in the giant ionic lattice of sodium chloride, very strong ionic bonds are present, which form strong electrostatic forces of attraction in all directions.

2.7

1 a Diamond, graphite, fullerenes

b Allotropes

2 Very high melting point and boiling point, hard, insoluble in water, electrical insulator

3 a Delivering drugs to parts of the body where they are needed

b (long) tubes / tubular

b reinforcing materials (tennis racquets) / catalysts / lubricants

4 The layers of graphite atoms have weak forces between them so can slip and slide over each other to act as a lubricant.

5 The carbon atoms in graphite's layers are arranged in hexagons, with each carbon atom forming three strong covalent bonds to its nearest neighbours. As carbon atoms have four electrons in their outer shell available for bonding, this leaves one spare outer electron on each carbon atom. This electron is free to move along the layers of carbon atoms. So these free-moving delocalised electrons can drift along the layers enabling graphite to conduct electricity. In diamond all the outer shell electrons are involved in covalent bonding so there are no free electrons.

2.8

1 a Because the layers of atoms (positively charged ions) can slide over each other relatively easily

b i Malleable

ii Ductile

2 a The differently sized atoms inserted into the regular arrangement of metal atoms (positively charged ions) is disrupted, making it more difficult for the layers to slip past each other.

b A mixture of metals that once deformed will revert to its original shape at a certain temperature

3 Nitinol can apply a force to the teeth once it is warmed up in the mouth as it changes to its original shape whereas a traditional metal must be adjusted manually to change the force applied to the teeth.

4 They conduct electricity because the 'sea' of delocalised electrons can drift through the metal's giant structure because they are free-moving. They conduct heat because the free-moving delocalised electrons gain energy when heated and can move around more quickly within the metal, spreading the energy through the metal quickly.

Answers to end of chapter summary questions

1 a 1
b 2
c 7
d 6
e 4

2 a

Giant covalent	Giant ionic	Simple molecules
silicon dioxide	magnesium oxide	ammonia
graphite	lithium chloride	hydrogen bromide

b Ammonia, and hydrogen bromide
c Graphite because although it has a giant covalent structure it does conduct electricity
d

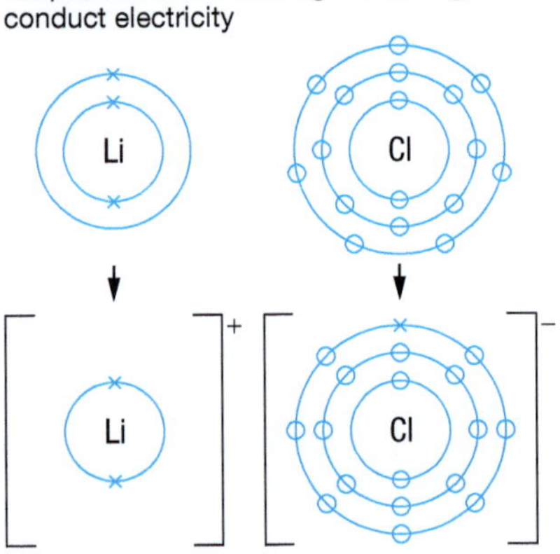

3 a Hydrogen iodide, chlorine(VII) oxide, phosphorus(V) fluoride
b They contain only non-metallic elements.
c Ionic bonding
d i HI
ii $CaBr_2$

4

	chloride, Cl^-	oxide, O^{2-}	sulfate, SO_4^{2-}	phosphate(V), PO_4^{3-}
potassium, K^+	KCl	K_2O	K_2SO_4	K_3PO_4
magnesium, Mg^{2+}	$MgCl_2$	MgO	$MgSO_4$	$Mg_3(PO_4)_2$
iron(III), Fe^{3+}	$FeCl_3$	Fe_2O_3	$Fe_2(SO_4)_3$	$FePO_4$

5 a

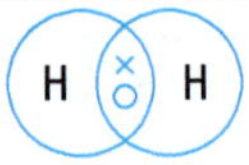

b

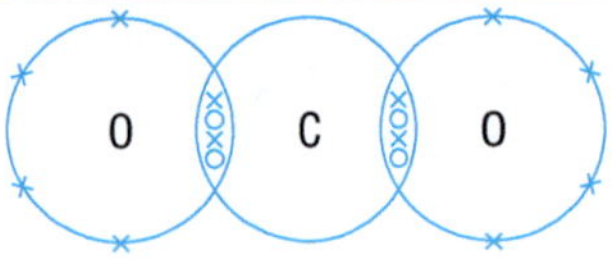

Answers to end of chapter practice questions

1 a Electrons transfer *(1 mark)*
From lithium to oxygen *(1 mark)*
Each lithium atoms loses one electron, each oxygen atom gains two electrons. *(1 mark)*
b Li^+ *(1 mark)*
O^{2-} *(1 mark)*
c Ions attract each other strongly. *(1 mark)*
Many bonds need to be broken. *(1 mark)*
d Ions cannot move when solid. *(1 mark)*
Ions move to the electrodes when molten. *(1 mark)*

2 a Diagram showing two electrons between H and F *(1 mark)*
Six more electrons in outer shell of F *(1 mark)*
b Covalent *(1 mark)*
c Attractions between molecules are weak. *(1 mark)*
Easily overcome/need little energy to break *(1 mark)*
d H–Br *(1 mark)*

3 a Covalent bonds *(1 mark)*
Many/strong bonds *(1 mark)*
Hard to overcome/need a lot of energy to break *(1 mark)*
b No ions *(1 mark)*
No electrons free to move *(1 mark)*

4 a Carbon *(1 mark)*
In hexagonal rings *(1 mark)*
b In drug delivery *(1 mark)*

5 a i Atoms/ions in layers *(1 mark)*
Layers slide *(1 mark)*
ii Delocalised/free electrons *(1 mark)*
Move *(1 mark)*
b i Alloy *(1 mark)*
ii Atoms of other metals are different in size *(1 mark)*
Make it harder for layers of copper atoms to slide *(1 mark)*

3 The periodic table

3.1

1 a Repeated at regular intervals
b i A vertical column of elements
ii A horizontal row of elements
2 There are many more metals.
3 They have the same number of electrons in the highest energy level (outermost shell).
4 a 2 b 3 c 1 d 2
e 8 f 2 g 8 h 7
5 Because of their very stable electron arrangements

3.2

1 To keep them out of contact with air/oxygen and water vapour
2 The melting point decreases with increasing atomic number/going down the group.
3 They all have one electron in their outermost shell (highest energy level) which they lose when forming ions.
4 The metal would explode on contact with water as hydrogen gas is liberated very quickly. The alkali metals get more reactive going down the group so caesium, being near the bottom of Group 1, is extremely reactive. (Alkaline caesium hydroxide would also be formed in the reaction.)

caesium + water → caesium hydroxide + hydrogen

$$2Cs(s) + 2H_2O(l) \rightarrow 2CsOH(aq) + H_2(g)$$

5 a $2Cs(s) + I_2(g) \rightarrow 2CsI(s)$
b $2Cs(s) + Br_2(g) \rightarrow 2CsBr(s)$

3.3

1 a Their melting points increase.
b Their reactivity decreases.
2 a Fluorine – gas; Chlorine – gas; Bromine – liquid; Iodine – solid
b The halogens
3 a

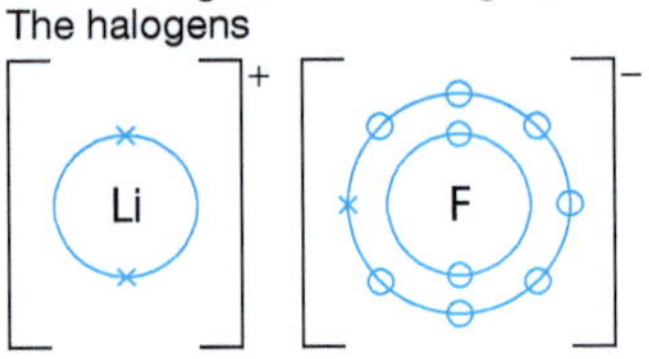

b

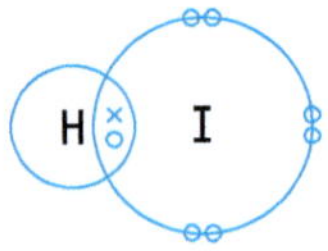

4 a Lithium + bromine → lithium bromide
b Bromine water + potassium iodide → potassium bromide + iodine solution
5 a $2Na(s) + I_2(g) \rightarrow 2NaI(s)$
b $Cl_2(aq) + 2NaI(aq) \rightarrow 2NaCl(aq) + I_2(aq)$

Answers to end of chapter summary questions

1 a i Group 7
ii Group 0
iii Group 1
b i Group 1/alkali metals
ii Group 0/noble gases
iii Group 7/halogens
2 a Seven electrons as it is in Group 7.
b Solid
c i Ionic
ii White
iii NaAt
iv $2Na + At_2 \rightarrow 2NaAt$
3 a i Soft
ii Good electrical conductivity
iii Low melting point
b i 1+
ii

Rubidium compound	Chemical formula
Rubidium iodide	RbI
Rubidium fluoride	RbF
Rubidium hydroxide	RbOH

iii White; they will all dissolve in water.
c i $2Rb(s) + 2H_2O(l) \rightarrow 2RbOH(aq) + H_2(g)$
ii $2Rb(s) + Cl_2(g) \rightarrow 2RbCl(s)$
d Rubidium will react more vigorously than potassium because it can lose its outer electron more easily as it is further from the nucleus than potassium's outer electron and it is shielded from the nuclear charge by one more inner shell of electrons than potassium.

4 a i
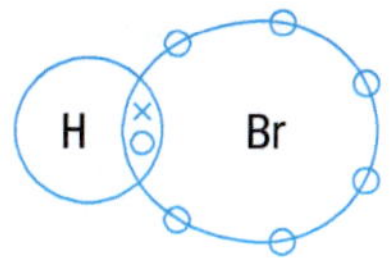

ii
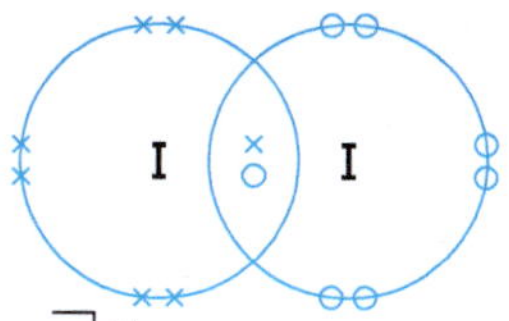

b
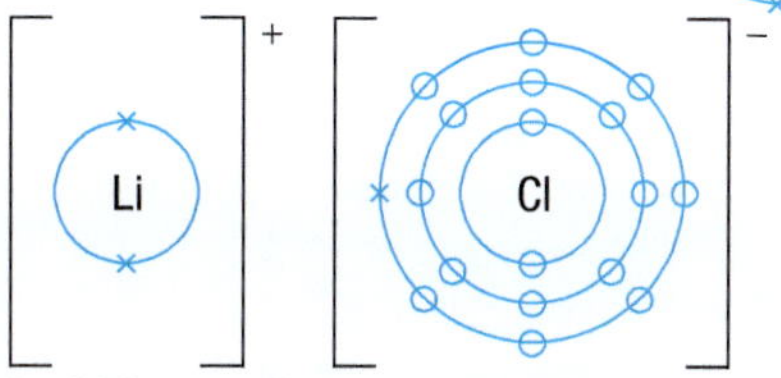

5 a i lithium, sodium and potassium
ii lithium
b i Br
ii fluorine / F_2

Answers to end of chapter practice questions

1 a Melting point/boiling point/density (any two of) *(2 marks)*
b i Fizzing/bubbles/effervescence
Metal floats or moves on the surface
Metal gets smaller or disappears
(any two) *(2 marks)*
ii Potassium melts. *(1 mark)*
Flame *(1 mark)*
iii Blue *(1 mark)*
Alkali present/OH^- ions formed. *(1 mark)*
iv $2K + 2H_2O \rightarrow 2KOH + H_2$
Four correct formulae *(1 mark)*
Balancing *(1 mark)*
c change '$NaOH_2$' to 'NaOH' *(1 mark)*
most sodium compounds are white, not pale yellow *(1 mark)*
and are soluble in water, not insoluble *(1 mark)*
hydrogen gas is given off, not oxygen *(1 mark)*
d colourless *(1 mark)*

2 a $Ca + Cl_2 \rightarrow CaCl_2$
Three correct formulae *(1 mark)*
Balancing *(1 mark)*
b iodine = 184, fluorine = –188, bromine = 59, chlorine = –34 *(2 mark)*
c i Fluorine *(1 mark)*
Because the halogens get more reactive going up the group / with decreasing atomic number *(1 mark)*
ii hydrogen fluoride *(1 mark)*
iii *(3 marks)*
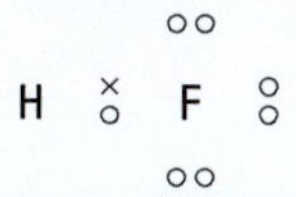

d Charge on lithium ion is 1+ / Li^+ *(1 mark)*
charge on fluoride ion in 1– / F– *(1 mark)*
all ionic compounds are neutral / charges cancel out *(1 mark)*
so the ratio of lithium to fluoride ions is 1 : 1 *(1 mark)*

4 Metals

4.1

1 a Good conductors of heat and electricity; high melting points, strong; high density
b The central block between Groups 2 and 3
c Aluminium
2 a It is very unreactive and is malleable.
b To make gold more hard-wearing
3 The silver and gold would be too expensive to use (except in small amounts in specialist uses).
4 They are 'light-weight' alloys due to the low density of aluminium, so more passengers and/or cargo can be carried on the aircraft; and the alloying makes them strong enough to withstand the high stresses put on an aeroplane in flight.
5 The copper alloys are harder-wearing so won't be worn away as quickly as softer coins made from pure copper. In alloying copper, differently-sized atoms of other metals are introduced into the regular layers of copper atoms, distorting the layers and making it more difficult for them to slide over each other.

4.2

1 a It contains too much carbon.
b Cast iron contains about 4% carbon whereas pure iron contains only iron. This makes cast iron very hard and brittle as opposed to pure iron which is relatively soft and malleable.
c For example, man-hole covers
2 a Haematite (iron ore/iron(III) oxide); coke (carbon); limestone (calcium carbonate); air
b Carbon monoxide
$CO_2(g) + C(s) \rightarrow 2CO(g)$
c Iron(III) oxide + carbon → iron + carbon dioxide
$2Fe_2O_3(s) + 3C(s) \rightarrow 4Fe(l) + 3CO_2(g)$
d As a gas, carbon monoxide can diffuse throughout the blast furnace and come into contact with lots of iron(III) oxide, as opposed to solid carbon which can only react with iron(III) oxide it is directly in contact with.
3

Type of steel	Main useful properties
Low carbon steel	Relatively soft and malleable
High carbon steel	Hard/strong
Chromium–nickel steel	Corrosion resistant

4 a They will not rust so are easier to sterilise and stay sharp.
b i Low carbon steel as it can be stamped into shapes
ii High carbon steel as it is very strong and hard

4.3

1 a lithium + water → lithium hydroxide + hydrogen
$2Li(s) + 2H_2O(l) \rightarrow 2LiOH(aq) + H_2(g)$
b zinc + steam → zinc oxide + hydrogen
$Zn(s) + H_2O(g) \rightarrow ZnO(s) + H_2(g)$
2 a Gas given off/fizzing; magnesium gets smaller and smaller then disappears; heat energy released/gets hot.
b metal + an acid → a salt + hydrogen
c magnesium + sulfuric acid → magnesium sulfate + hydrogen
$Mg(s) + H_2SO_4(aq) \rightarrow MgSO_4(aq) + H_2(g)$
3 a Because they are so unreactive they don't react with water at all.
b Because they are so reactive they will react with water vapour (and oxygen) in the air.
c Zinc will react with acidic foods whereas tin will not at room temperature.
4 Aluminium is protected by a tough/impervious layer of aluminium oxide.

4.4

1 a No reaction
b $Zn(s) + CuSO_4(aq) \rightarrow ZnSO_4(aq) + Cu(s)$
c $Mg(s) + FeCl_2(aq) \rightarrow MgCl_2(aq) + Fe(s)$
2 a Tungsten is below hydrogen in the reactivity series.
b $WO_3 + 3H_2 \rightarrow W + 3H_2O$
3 a $Zn(s) + Fe^{2+}(aq) \rightarrow Zn^{2+}(aq) + Fe(s)$
b Zinc atoms lose two electrons to form zinc(II) ions. Zinc atoms have been oxidised as oxidation is the loss of electrons. Iron(II) ions are reduced as they form iron atoms when they gain two electrons from zinc (and reduction is the gain of electrons).

4.5

1 A metal ore is a rock which contains enough of a metal or metal compound to make it worth extracting the metal.
2 It is a very unreactive metal.
3 Very low reactivity; used for jewellery.
4 a zinc oxide + carbon → zinc + carbon monoxide
b $ZnO(s) + C(s) \rightarrow Zn(l) + CO(g)$
5 a lead sulfide + oxygen → lead oxide + sulfur dioxide
b $2PbS(s) + 3O_2(g) \rightarrow 2PbO(s) + 2SO_2(g)$
c $2PbO + C \rightarrow 2Pb + CO_2$

4.6

1 It is used in electrical wiring to deliver the electricity we need to run our appliances.
2 a Smelting of copper ores; electrolysis of solutions containing copper ions.
b Copper can be extracted from lower-grade ores than would be economical by traditional methods of extraction.
c it is very unreactive/low in the reactivity series.
d Negative electrode/cathode because copper ions are positively charged (like all metal ions).
3 a $2CuS(s) + 3O_2(g) \rightarrow 2CuO(s) + 2SO_2(g)$
b $Fe(s) + CuSO_4(aq) \rightarrow FeSO_4(aq) + Cu(s)$

4 a At the negative copper electrode: $Cu^{2+}(aq) + 2e \rightarrow Cu(s)$
At the positive electrode: $Cu(s) \rightarrow Cu^{2+}(aq) + 2e$
b Reduction takes place at the negative electrode because copper ions gain electrons to become copper atoms.
Oxidation takes place at the positive electrode because copper atoms lose electrons to become copper ions.
5 In phytomining, plants can absorb copper ions from low-grade copper ore as they grow. Then plants are burned and the metals can be extracted from the ash by leaching copper ions in solution from the ash by adding sulfuric acid. Then we can use displacement by scrap iron and electrolysis to extract pure copper metal. This method will become more important as our copper-rich deposits become more scarce.

4.7

1 E.g. fill with water to create a recreational resource for fishing, sailing, wildlife reserve, etc./replace topsoil and replant vegetation.
2 56 hours.
3 The aluminum oxide from the ore must be molten and then electrolysed, using large amounts of energy compared with the energy required in the recycling process.
4 Copper is found in a variety of alloys with varying amounts of different metals, making the recycling of pure copper more difficult. Making new alloys is one solution or improving the percentage of copper in the recycled mixture by adding pure copper and then electrolysing to complete the purification process.
5 E.g. less scarring of the landscape from open cast mining; less pollution of water running through waste heaps; less fossil fuels burnt during extraction so reducing atmospheric pollution.

4.8

1 a metal carbonate + acid → a salt + water + carbon dioxide
b metal carbonate $\xrightarrow{\text{heat}}$ metal oxide + carbon dioxide
2 sodium carbonate + hydrochloric acid → sodium chloride + water + carbon dioxide
$Na_2CO_3(s) + 2HCl(aq) \rightarrow 2NaCl(aq) + H_2O(l) + CO_2(g)$
3 $CuCO_3(s) \rightarrow CuO(s) + CO_2(g)$
4 $CuCO_3(s) + 2HNO_3(aq) \rightarrow Cu(NO_3)_2(aq) + H_2O(l) + CO_2(g)$
5 Limewater is a solution of alkaline calcium hydroxide. Carbon dioxide is a weakly acidic gas so it reacts with the alkaline limewater, forming a suspension of solid particles of insoluble calcium carbonate which precipitates out of solution making it cloudy.
The reaction is:
calcium hydroxide (limewater) + carbon dioxide → calcium carbonate (an insoluble white precipitate) + water
$Ca(OH)_2(aq) + CO_2(g) \rightarrow CaCO_3(s) + H_2O(l)$

Answers to end of chapter summary questions

1 a Vigorous reaction, metal changes to metal oxide.
X + steam → X oxide + hydrogen
$X(s) + H_2O(g) \rightarrow XO(s) + H_2(g)$
b Fizzes readily, X gets smaller and eventually dissolves away completely into the acid.
X + sulfuric acid → X sulfate + hydrogen
$X(s) + H_2SO_4(aq) \rightarrow XSO_4(aq) + H_2(g)$
c Because we do not know how much less reactive than calcium and more reactive than magnesium X is, so bubbles of hydrogen may be given off too slowly to be seen immediately or they might be liberated slowly on contact with water.
d i You would expect the more reactive metal X to displace the less reactive copper from solution – so the solution will lose its blue colour, X will dissolve into solution, and copper metal will be deposited as a brown solid.
$X(s) + Cu(NO_3)_2(aq) \rightarrow X(NO_3)_2(aq) + Cu(s)$
ii $X(s) + Cu^{2+}(aq) \rightarrow X^{2+}(aq) + Cu(s)$
iii $X(s) \rightarrow X^{2+}(aq) + 2e^-$ X atoms lose two electrons so they are oxidised
$Cu^{2+}(aq) + 2e^- \rightarrow Cu(s)$ Cu^{2+}ions gain two electrons so they are reduced.
e i Just above copper
ii No change/no reaction as Y is less reactive than magnesium so cannot displace it from a solution of one of its compounds.
2 a zinc + copper(II) oxide → zinc oxide + copper
$Zn(s) + CuO(s) \rightarrow ZnO(s) + Cu(s)$
b Iron + zinc nitrate will not react.
c Iron + magnesium oxide will not react.
d Magnesium + copper(II) sulfate will react.
$Mg(s) + CuSO_4(aq) \rightarrow MgSO_4(aq) + Cu(s)$
3 a i aluminium + iron(III) oxide → aluminium oxide + iron
$2Al + Fe_2O_3 \rightarrow Al_2O_3 + 2Fe$
ii Displacement/redox reaction
b Aluminium and copper(II) oxide would react more vigorously than aluminium and iron(III) oxide.
c No change/no reaction
d You would expect it to react in air, water, and acid more readily than it does so you would not expect it to be used outdoors or for drinks cans.
4 a Gold
b Chromium
c Aluminium
d Copper
e Magnesium
5 a i Bioleaching
ii Phytomining
iii Smelting
iv Electrolysis
b Bioleaching and phytomining.

Answers to end of chapter practice questions

1 a	i Concentration/temperature/volume (any two of)	*(2 marks)*
	ii Surface area	*(1 mark)*
b	i Magnesium	*(1 mark)*
	ii X has the same observation.	*(1 mark)*
c	Timer	*(1 mark)*
	Gas syringe/measuring cylinder/boiling tube	*(1 mark)*
2 a	$Zn + CuSO_4 \rightarrow ZnSO_4 + Cu$	
	Reactants	*(1 mark)*
	Products	*(1 mark)*
b	$Fe + Cu^{2+} \rightarrow Fe^{2+} + Cu$	*(1 mark)*
c	i Reduction and oxidation occur.	*(1 mark)*
	ii Iron is oxidised	*(1 mark)*
	Because it loses electrons	*(1 mark)*
3 a	Aluminium alloys are much stronger than pure aluminium	*(1 mark)*
	because the other atoms mixed with it are different sizes / disrupt aluminium's regular arrangement of layers	*(1 mark)*
	so the layers of atoms / ions find it more difficult to slide over each other	*(1 mark)*
b	Good conductor of heat / thermal energy	*(1 mark)*
	High melting point	*(1 mark)*
c	i Al^{3+}	*(1 mark)*
	because Al is in Group 3 / has 3 electrons in its outermost shell	(1 mark)
	it loses those 3 outer electrons when its atoms form ions	*(1 mark)*
	ii Al2S3	*(1 mark)*
	iii because each atom in its (giant) structure donates 3 electrons into the cloud / sea of **delocalised** electrons	*(1 mark)*
	so there are more delocalised / mobile / free-moving electrons than in most metals	*(1 mark)*
	available to carry the charge through the metal	*(1 mark)*

5 Electrolysis

5.1

1 a The breakdown of a compound by electricity
b Electrolyte
c Ionic
2

	Cathode (–)	Anode (+)
a	zinc	iodine
b	lithium	bromine
c	iron	fluorine
d	sodium	oxygen
e	potassium	chlorine

3 $2NaCl(l) \rightarrow 2Na(l) + Cl_2(g)$
4 a $CuCl_2(aq)$ and $AgNO_3(aq)$
b Copper and silver are below hydrogen in the reactivity series.
5 In the solid, the ions are in fixed positions in the giant ionic lattice; but when molten or in aqueous solution the ions are free to move around within the liquid and can carry their charge to the oppositely charged electrode.

5.2

1 a i They lose electrons.
ii Oxidation
b i They gain electrons.
ii Reduction
2

	Cathode	Anode
a	lithium	oxygen
b	copper	chlorine
c	hydrogen	oxygen

3 a $2Cl^- \rightarrow Cl_2 + 2e^-$
b $2Br^- \rightarrow Br_2 + 2e^-$
c $Mg^{2+} + 2e^- \rightarrow Mg$
d $Al^{3+} + 3e^- \rightarrow Al$
e $K^+ + e^- \rightarrow K$
f $2H^+ + 2e^- \rightarrow H_2$
g $2O^{2-} \rightarrow O_2 + 4e^-$
h $4OH^- \rightarrow O_2 + 2H_2O + 4e^-$

5.3

1 a Because in solid aluminium oxide the ions are fixed in position in the giant lattice so can only move to electrodes if molten when they are free to move around within the liquid.
  b To lower the melting point of aluminium oxide and save energy.

2 Oxygen is produced at the hot carbon anodes and reacts with the carbon to produce carbon dioxide gas, in effect gradually burning away the anodes.

3 a Cathode: $Al^{3+}(l) + 3e^- \rightarrow Al(l)$
  Anode: $2O^{2-}(l) \rightarrow O_2(g) + 4e^-$
  b Oxide ions are oxidised as they lose electrons and aluminium ions are reduced as they gain electrons.

4 a Lots of energy is needed to purify the aluminium oxide which involves heating to decompose aluminium hydroxide formed in the process; melting the aluminium oxide/cryolite mixture; electrical energy in the electrolytic cells.
  b Aluminium in nature is combined/bonded to other elements in compounds that are difficult to break down. It was not until scientists could use electrical cells to pass electricity through substances that aluminium could be extracted from one of its molten compounds by electrolysis.

5.4

1 a Chlorine, hydrogen, and sodium hydroxide solution
  b Chlorine is used to make bleach and plastics;
  hydrogen is used to make margarine;
  sodium hydroxide is used to make bleach, paper, and soap.

2 a At anode: $2Cl^-(aq) \rightarrow Cl_2(g) + 2e^-$
  b At cathode: $2H^+(aq) + 2e^- \rightarrow H_2(g)$

3 a Molten sodium chloride will produce sodium metal and chlorine, whereas sodium chloride solution produces chlorine, hydrogen, and sodium hydroxide solution.
  b The difference at the cathode in aqueous solution is caused by the presence of $H^+(aq)$ ions from the ionisation of water, so hydrogen is produced and not sodium as with molten sodium chloride.
  Sodium hydroxide solution is formed from the excess aqueous sodium ions and hydroxide ions left in solution when aqueous hydrogen and chloride ions are discharged.

5.5

1 Nickel, chromium, silver, gold, tin, zinc, copper (any four)

2 To protect from corrosion; to improve appearance; to increase durability; to save money by using a thin layer of a precious metal

3 a At the anode/positive electrode
  b Aqueous zinc ions, $Zn^{2+}(aq)$

4

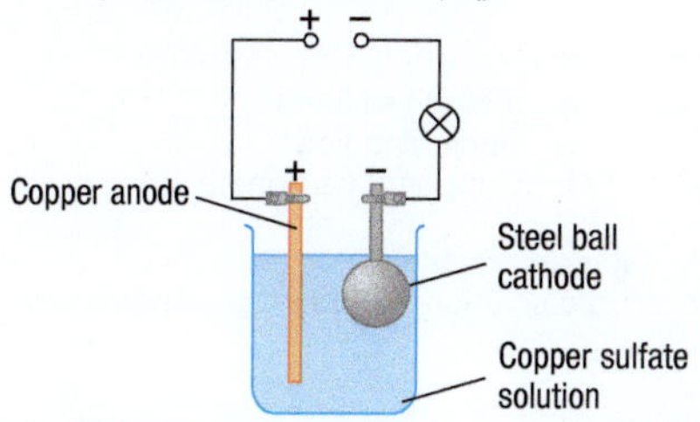

5 a $Ni^{2+}(aq) + 2e^- \rightarrow Ni(s)$ b $Cr^{3+}(aq) + 3e^- \rightarrow Cr(s)$

5.6

1

	At the cathode	At the anode
With copper electrodes	copper electrode becomes thicker/gains mass	copper electrode becomes thinner/loses mass
With carbon electrodes	copper deposited on surface of carbon electrode	bubbles of (oxygen) gas given off

2 With copper electrodes, the copper anode undergoes a chemical reaction turning into copper(II) ions so is known as 'active', whereas the carbon electrodes just carry electrons to and from the electrolyte and do not undergo any chemical change themselves so are known as 'inert'(meaning unreactive).

3 a At the cathode: $Cu^{2+}(aq) + 2e^- \rightarrow Cu(s)$
  At the anode: $Cu(s) \rightarrow Cu^{2+}(aq) + 2e^-$
  b Reduction occurs at the cathode as copper(II) ions **gain** electrons.
  Oxidation occurs at the anode as copper atoms **lose** electrons.

Answers to end of chapter summary questions

1 a B b A c B d A e B f A

2 a Anode: iodide, fluoride, oxide, bromide
  Cathode: potassium, calcium, magnesium, aluminium
  b i $Mg^{2+} + 2e^- \rightarrow Mg$ ii $2Br^- \rightarrow Br_2 + 2e^-$ or $2Br^- - 2e^- \rightarrow Br_2$

3 a **A** = chlorine, **B** = hydrogen, and **C** = sodium hydroxide solution
  b For example, making bleach and plastics, sterilising water
  c 11–14
  d Lighted spill burns with a 'pop'.
  e Anode: $2Cl^-(aq) \rightarrow Cl_2(g) + 2e^-$ or $2Cl^-(aq) - 2e^- \rightarrow Cl_2(g)$
  Cathode: $2H^+(aq) + 2e^- \rightarrow H_2(g)$

4 a $2H_2O(l) \rightarrow 2H_2(g) + O_2(g)$
  b $H_2O(l) \rightleftharpoons H^+(aq) + OH^-(aq)$
  c Anode: $4OH^-(aq) \rightarrow 2H_2O(l) + O_2(g) + 4e^-$
  Cathode: $2H^+(aq) + 2e^- \rightarrow H_2(g)$
  d Electrical supply/battery/cell/power pack

5 a $Li^+ + e^- \rightarrow Li$
  b $Sr^{2+} + 2e^- \rightarrow Sr$
  c $2F^- \rightarrow F_2 + 2e^-$ or $2F^- - 2e^- \rightarrow F_2$
  d $2O^{2-} \rightarrow O_2 + 4e^-$ or $2O^{2-} - 4e^- \rightarrow O_2$

6 Description to include:
Diagram of circuit with tin anode, iron cathode, and tin(II) nitrate solution
At anode: oxidation i.e., loss of electrons; $Sn \rightarrow Sn^{2+} + 2e^-$ or $Sn - 2e^- \rightarrow Sn^{2+}$
At cathode: reduction i.e., gain of electrons; $Sn^{2+} + 2e^- \rightarrow Sn$

7 a Beaker A – copper deposited on cathode (negative electrode); copper(II) ions released from anode (positive electrode).
  Beaker B – copper deposited on cathode (negative electrode); oxygen gas given off at anode (positive electrode).
  b Beaker A – at the cathode: $Cu^{2+} + 2e^- \rightarrow Cu$;
  at the anode: $Cu \rightarrow Cu^{2+} + 2e^-$
  Beaker B – at the cathode: $Cu^{2+} + 2e^- \rightarrow Cu$;
  at the anode: $4OH^- \rightarrow H_2O + O_2 + 4e^-$
  c Beaker A – when the copper anode is worn away completely and all the copper(II) ions in solution are converted to copper at the cathode
  Beaker B – when all the copper(II) ions have been removed from solution/deposited as copper atoms at the cathode

Answers to end of chapter practice questions

1 a Bromine *(1 mark)*
  $2Br^- \rightarrow Br_2 + 2e^-$
  Both formulae correct *(1 mark)*
  Balancing *(1 mark)*
  b Lead *(1 mark)*
  $Pb^{2+} + 2e^- \rightarrow Pb$
  Both formulae correct *(1 mark)*
  Balancing *(1 mark)*
  c Electrons move. *(1 mark)*
  d Ions cannot move when solid/ions move when molten. *(1 mark)*
  e Ions gain electrons. *(1 mark)*

2 a H^+ *(1 mark)*
  b $4OH^- \rightarrow 2H_2O + O_2 + 4e^-$
  All formulae correct *(1 mark)*
  Balancing *(1 mark)*
  c Sulfate/SO_4^{2-} *(1 mark)*
  d It increases. *(1 mark)*
  e It takes twice as many electrons to discharge the same volume of oxygen compared with hydrogen/same number of electrons discharges twice the volume of H^+ ions as OH^- ions, e.g., 2 moles of electrons give 1 mole of H_2 but only 0.5 mole of O_2. *(1 mark)*

3 a Hydrogen less reactive/sodium more reactive *(1 mark)*
  b Greater concentration of Cl^- ions *(1 mark)*
  c Sodium hydroxide *(1 mark)*
  d i Fuel/making margarine *(1 mark)*
  ii Bleach/making plastics *(1 mark)*

4 a i Nickel for the anode and copper spoon for the cathode *(1 mark)*
  ii Nickel chloride/nitrate/sulfate *(1 mark)*
  iii $Ni \rightarrow Ni^{2+} + 2e^-$ *(1 mark)*
  b Appearance/durability *(1 mark)*
  c Graphite conducts electricity/plastic does not conduct electricity *(1 mark)*

5 **0 marks** No relevant content
Level 1 (1–2 marks) There is a brief description of the electrolysis of aluminium oxide.
Level 2 (3–4 marks) There is some description of the electrolysis of aluminium oxide.
Level 3 (5–6 marks) There is a clear, balanced, and detailed description of the electrolysis of aluminium oxide.
Examples of chemistry points made in the response:
- aluminium oxide is melted/made liquid
- cryolite is used as a solvent/to decrease the amount of energy or electricity used
- carbon/graphite used as the positive electrode
- aluminium ions are attracted to the negative electrode
- at the negative electrode aluminium is formed or aluminium ions gain electrons
- oxide ions are attracted to the positive electrode
- oxygen is formed at the positive electrode or oxide ions lose electrons
- the oxygen reacts with carbon to make carbon dioxide or carbon dioxide formed at positive electrode
- $Al^{3+} + 3e^- \rightarrow Al$
- $2O^{2-} \rightarrow O_2 + 4e^-$

6 Chemical Analysis

6.1

1 A mixture is made up of two or more elements or compounds which are not chemically combined together.
2 The relative proportions of each substance/component of the mixture can be in any ratio (it is not fixed as in a compound).
3 a

Fractional distillation

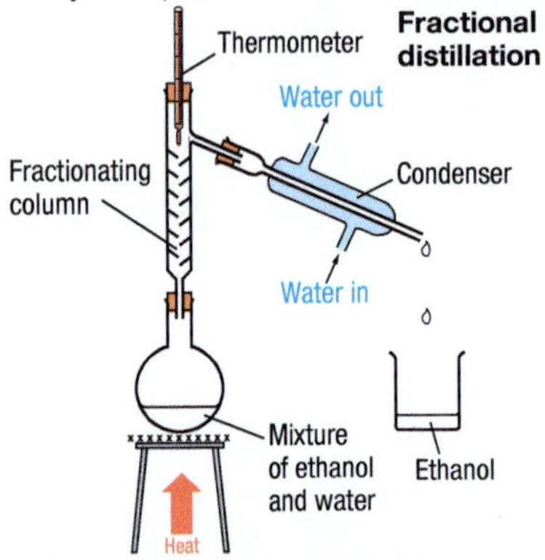

b At 78 °C/the boiling point of ethanol, much of the water vapour rising up the fractionating column would condense and return to the heated flask instead of entering the condenser to be collected with the ethanol.
4 Method A – Add water to the mixture, stir, and filter. Sulfur residue will be left on the filter paper. Wash with distilled water and leave sulfur to dry. Evaporate water from the filtrate of sodium nitrate solution on a water bath until the point of crystallization. Then leave the saturated solution to crystallise.
Method B – Add xylene to the mixture, stir, and filter. Sodium nitrate residue will be left on the filter paper. Wash with xylene and leave sodium nitrate to dry. Evaporate xylene from the filtrate of sulfur solution using water bath (electrically heated/no naked flame) in a fume cupboard to crystallise.

6.2

1 Allow the paper to dry and measure the distance from the pencil line to the solvent front and to each dye left on the paper. Divide the distance each dye moved by the distance of the solvent front to get the R_f values, then match the values against tables of data to identify the dyes.
2 0.77
3 The solubility of Z in the solvent is greater than the solubility of Y in the same solvent. To identify Y and Z, their R_f values are matched against values of known substances in the 50–50 water–ethanol solvent at 20 °C in a database or databook.
4 Because changing the solvent and the temperature both affect the attraction of the compound to the solvent (mobile phase) and paper (stationary phase)/its solubility in the solvent/its distribution between the mobile phase and the stationary phase, so the distance the spot travels along the paper will differ under different conditions, resulting in different R_f values.

6.3

1 a White
b Add sodium hydroxide solution – all will form a white precipitate but the aluminium hydroxide precipitate formed would dissolve in excess sodium hydroxide solution (Al^{3+} identified). Take the original magnesium and calcium compounds and carry out a flame test – the calcium ions will produce a brick red flame (Ca^{2+} identified) and the magnesium ions will not colour the flame (so Mg^{2+} identified).
c $Mg^{2+}(aq) + 2OH^-(aq) \rightarrow Mg(OH)_2(s)$
2 a Dip a wire loop in concentrated hydrochloric acid and heat to clean it → dip the loop into conc. acid again before dipping in the metal compound to be tested → hold the loop in the edge of a roaring Bunsen flame → match the colour of the flame to the known flame test colours of metal ions.
b (Apple) green flame
3 a brown precipitate
b nothing observed (no change)
c nothing observed (no change)
d nothing observed (no change)
e yellow
f K^+
g Ca^{2+}
h Al^{3+}
i Fe^{2+}
j Li^+

6.4

1 Dilute hydrochloric acid, limewater, dilute nitric acid, silver nitrate solution, barium chloride solution
2 Potassium iodide (potassium ions have a lilac flame test; and silver iodide, a pale yellow precipitate, is formed with silver nitrate solution.)
3 a magnesium chloride + silver nitrate → magnesium nitrate + silver chloride
$MgCl_2(aq) + 2AgNO_3(aq) \rightarrow Mg(NO_3)_2(aq) + 2AgCl(s)$
b potassium carbonate + hydrochloric acid → potassium chloride + water + carbon dioxide
$K_2CO_3(s) + 2HCl(aq) \rightarrow 2KCl(aq) + H_2O(l) + CO_2(g)$
c aluminium sulfate + barium chloride → aluminium chloride + barium sulfate
$Al_2(SO_4)_3(aq) + 3BaCl_2(aq) \rightarrow 2AlCl_3(aq) + 3BaSO_4(s)$
4 a $Ag^+(aq) + Br^-(aq) \rightarrow AgBr(s)$
b $Ba^{2+}(aq) + SO_4^{2-}(aq) \rightarrow BaSO_4(s)$
c $2H^+(aq) + CO_3^{2-}(s) \rightarrow CO_2(g) + H_2O(l)$
5 To dissolve the compound and to remove any carbonate ions as they would also form a precipitate with the silver ions, interfering with the test. Also, any other acids added would produce precipitates with silver nitrate solution, e.g., sulfuric acid would make a precipitate of silver sulfate.

Answers to end of chapter summary questions

1 a Nothing observed/dissolves.
b White precipitate forms.
c White precipitate forms.
d (Brick) red flame
e Sodium iodide
f Copper(II) carbonate
2 Lithium sulfate
3 a Lilac flame test to identify potassium ions
Add nitric acid, then silver nitrate solution – a cream precipitate will identify bromide ions.
b KBr
c Ionic
4 a Compounds have a fixed composition whereas mixtures do not (their proportions vary). Compounds cannot be easily separated into their elements/needing chemical reactions but mixtures can be separated by physical means, as there are no chemical bonds between different substances in a mixture.
b i Crystallisation
ii Filtration
iii (Simple) distillation
iv (Fractional) distillation
c $Pb(NO_3)_2(aq) + 2NaI(aq) \rightarrow PbI_2(s) + 2NaNO_3(aq)$
5 a i sodium - yellow;
ii potassium - lilac;
iii calcium - red;
iv barium - green
b i a white precipitate
ii $CaCl_2 + 2NaOH \rightarrow Ca(OH)_2 + 2NaCl$
$MgCl_2 + 2NaOH \rightarrow Mg(OH)2 + 2NaCl$
iii Precipitation
iv $Ca^{2+}(aq) + 2OH^-(aq) \rightarrow Ca(OH)_2(s)$
$Mg^{2+}(aq) + 2OH^-(aq) \rightarrow Mg(OH)_2(s)$
v Carry out a flame test - calcium chloride will give a red flame; magnesium chloride no colour / does not colour the flame
6 a R_f of X = 0.6
R_f of Y = 0.2
b X is more soluble in/has stronger attraction to ethanol than Y.
c Temperature

Answers to end of chapter practice questions

1 a i Lilac *(1 mark)*
ii K^+ *(1 mark)*
b i White precipitate *(1 mark)*
ii Aluminium hydroxide *(1 mark)*
c Too much added *(1 mark)*
So white precipitate dissolved *(1 mark)*
d Add dilute hydrochloric acid *(1 mark)*
And barium chloride solution *(1 mark)*
White precipitate forms *(1 mark)*
2 a i Carbon dioxide *(1 mark)*
ii Limewater *(1 mark)*
turns cloudy *(1 mark)*
b i Silver chloride *(1 mark)*
ii $Ag^+ + Cl^- \rightarrow AgCl$
Reactants *(1 mark)*
Products *(1 mark)*
c Sodium ions do not form a precipitate. *(1 mark)*
The two iron ions form a precipitate. *(1 mark)*
The colour is not green or brown/colour is a mixture of green and brown. *(1 mark)*
3 a Distillation *(1 mark)*
Difference in boiling point *(1 mark)*
b Filtration *(1 mark)*
Difference in solubility *(1 mark)*
c (Paper) chromatography *(1 mark)*
Difference in solubility in solvent/R_f values *(1 mark)*
4 **0 marks** No relevant content
Level 1 (1–2 marks) There is a brief description of how to do the chromatography experiment
Level 2 (3–4 marks) There is some description of how to do the chromatography experiment.
Level 3 (5–6 marks) There is a clear, balanced, and detailed description of how to do the chromatography experiment.
Examples of chemistry points made in the response:
- use chromatography paper
- draw pencil line near the bottom
- place drops of the drink and colours on the line
- pour some water into a large beaker or tank
- place the paper in the tank
- with the spots of colour above the water level
- fit the tank with a lid
- leave until the water reaches almost to the top
- leave to dry

5 a Pencil (1)
b Use a fine paint brush dipped in solvent to collect colouring *(1 mark)*
Dab onto the baseline on the chromatography paper *(1 mark)*
Allow to dry and repeat (to increase concentration of spot) *(1 mark)*
c Use a different solvent *(1 mark)*

7 Acids, bases, and salts

7.1

1 a An alkali is a base that dissolves in water.
b They dissolve in water to produce hydroxide ions.
c $KOH(s) \xrightarrow{\text{water}} K^+(aq) + OH^-(aq)$
2 a $H^+(aq)$ ions
b $HI(g) \xrightarrow{\text{water}} H^+(aq) + I^-(aq)$
3 Distilled water pH 7; sodium hydroxide solution pH above 7, e.g., 14; ethanoic acid pH below 7, e.g., 4
4 A pH sensor and datalogger would be more accurate as the matching of colours against a pH chart by eye is subjective and difficult to judge. A pH sensor is more likely to produce more repeatable measurements over a narrower range than using universal indicator paper.

7.2

1 a acid + a base → a salt + water
b acid + a metal → a salt + hydrogen
2 Copper sulfate solution is heated in an evaporating dish on a water bath. Some of the water is evaporated off from the copper sulfate solution until the point of crystallisation when crystals appear at the edge of the solution. The copper sulfate solution is then left at room temperature for the remaining water to evaporate off slowly, leaving crystals in the dish.
3 a Copper metal does not react with dilute acid.
b Potassium metal is so reactive it will explode in dilute acid.
4 a $Mg(s) + 2HCl(aq) \rightarrow MgCl_2(aq) + H_2(g)$
b $Li_2O(s) + H_2SO_4(aq) \rightarrow Li_2SO_4(aq) + H_2O(l)$

7.3

1 a acid + alkali → a salt + water **b** $H^+(aq) + OH^-(aq) \rightarrow H_2O(l)$
2 a Ammonium nitrate
b It is used as a fertiliser to provide plants with nitrogen.
c $NH_4OH + HNO_3 \rightarrow NH_4NO_3 + H_2O$ or $NH_3 + HNO_3 \rightarrow NH_4NO_3$
3 $LiOH(aq) + HCl(aq) \rightarrow LiCl(aq) + H_2O(l)$
Add a known volume of dilute hydrochloric acid (e.g., from a burette) to a measured volume of lithium hydroxide solution which has a few drops of an indicator added (e.g., methyl orange) until the indicator just changes colour. Note how much acid is needed to neutralise a known volume of lithium hydroxide solution. Repeat until consistent volumes of acid are used. Then repeat without the indicator and evaporate off water from the lithium chloride solution by heating until the point of crystallisation is reached. Then leave at room temperature for the rest of the water to evaporate off.
4 a Add solutions of lead nitrate and, e.g., sodium chloride, filter, wash the precipitate of lead chloride collected on the filter paper with distilled water and leave in a warm oven or leave to dry at room temperature.
b For example: $Pb(NO_3)_2(aq) + 2NaCl(aq) \rightarrow PbCl_2(s) + 2NaNO_3(aq)$
c Ionic bonding
5 Add an alkali (e.g., sodium hydroxide or lime) and filter off the precipitate of chromium(III) hydroxide formed.

7.4

1 Precise
2 a Meniscus
b i (Volumetric) pipette and burette
ii Read to the bottom of the meniscus, with the eye level with that point.
3 a Measure a known volume of sodium hydroxide solution into a conical flask using a pipette, and add a few drops of an acid/base indicator. Then pour the dilute nitric acid into a burette, recording the reading on the burette. Then slowly add small amounts of acid into the flask, swirling it to make sure that the two solutions are mixed. Continue until the indicator in the flask changes colour. Repeat the titration until you get two identical results.
b $NaOH(aq) + HNO_3(aq) \rightarrow NaNO_3(aq) + H_2O(l)$
4 a For example, methyl orange, phenolphthalein
b Two distinctly different colours in acidic and alkaline conditions in order to make the end point clear to the experimenter

Answers to end of chapter summary questions

1 a i Nickel(II) oxide
ii $NiO(s) + H_2SO_4(aq) \rightarrow NiSO_4(aq) + H_2O(l)$
iii Neutralisation
b Add excess nickel(II) oxide to warm sulfuric acid and filter off the excess solid. Then heat the nickel(II) sulfate solution in an evaporating dish on a water bath until the point of crystallisation is reached. Stop heating and allow the remaining water to evaporate from the solution at room temperature to leave the crystals of nickel(II) sulfate.
2 a $2LiOH(aq) + H_2SO_4(aq) \rightarrow Li_2SO_4(aq) + 2H_2O(l)$
b $Fe_2O_3(s) + 6HNO_3(aq) \rightarrow 2Fe(NO_3)_3(aq) + 3H_2O(l)$
c $Zn(s) + 2HCl(aq) \rightarrow ZnCl_2(aq) + H_2(g)$
d $Ba(NO_3)_2(aq) + K_2SO_4(aq) \rightarrow BaSO_4(s) + 2KNO_3(aq)$
3 a $CaCO_3$
b i $CaCO_3(s) + 2HCl(aq) \rightarrow CaCl_2(aq) + H_2O(l) + CO_2(g)$
ii

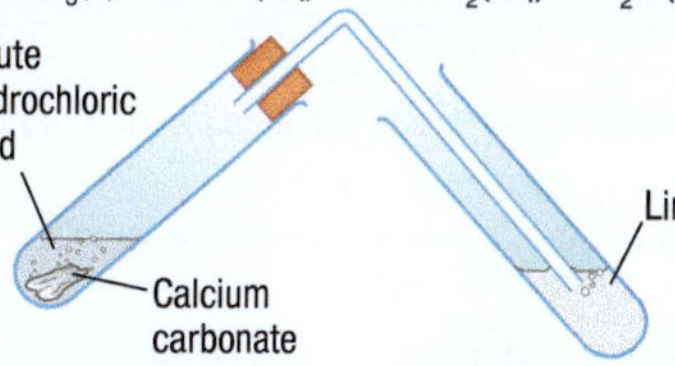

iii calcium hydroxide + carbon dioxide → calcium carbonate + water
$Ca(OH)_2(aq) + CO_2(g) \rightarrow CaCO_3(s) + H_2O(l)$
c i calcium carbonate → calcium oxide + carbon dioxide
$CaCO_3(s) \rightarrow CaO(s) + CO_2(g)$
ii Thermal decomposition
iii 5.5 tonnes
iv Making cement; glass; extracting iron from its ore; building material; raising pH of acidic soil or lakes

Answers to end of chapter practice questions

1 a Solution 1 pH = 2
Solution 2 pH = 7
Solution 3 pH = 12 *(1 mark)*
b Universal indicator *(1 mark)*
It has more colours/it indicates pH values. *(1 mark)*
c Solution 4 *(1 mark)*

2 a i Magnesium chloride (1 mark)
Hydrogen (1 mark)
ii Zinc nitrate (1 mark)
Water (1 mark)
iii Copper(II) sulfate (1 mark)
Water + carbon dioxide (1 mark)
b Bubbles (1 mark)
c To make sure all the acid reacts (1 mark)
d i Magnesium chloride (1 mark)
ii Zinc oxide (1 mark)
iii Blue (1 mark)
e Evaporate some of the water (on a water bath). (1 mark)
Cool the liquid/heat to the point of crystallisation. (1 mark)
Filter off the crystals/then leave at room temperature. (1 mark)
Dry them on filter paper/until all water has evaporated. (1 mark)
3 a $MgCl_2(aq) + 2NaF(aq) \rightarrow MgF_2(s) + 2NaCl(aq)$
All four formulae (1 mark)
Balancing (1 mark)
All four state symbols (1 mark)
b i Lead nitrate (1 mark)
Sodium sulfate/other soluble sulfate or sulfuric acid (1 mark)
ii To remove soluble reactant. (1 mark)

8 Rates of reaction

8.1

1 a calcium carbonate + hydrochloric acid → calcium chloride + water + carbon dioxide
$CaCO_3(s) + 2HCl(aq) \rightarrow CaCl_2(aq) + H_2O(l) + CO_2(g)$
b All the acid had been used up in the reaction.
c The line will be horizontal.
2 a i

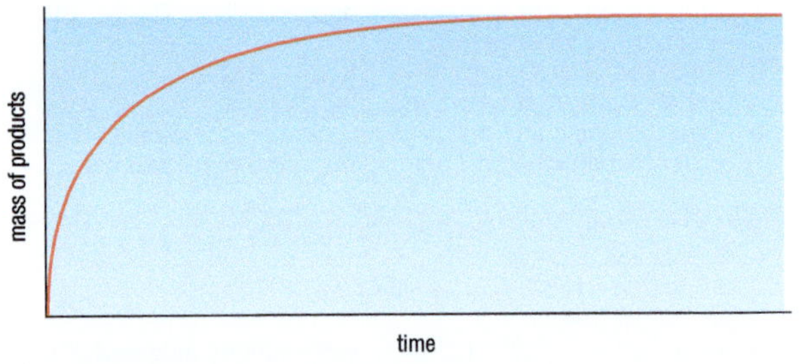

ii

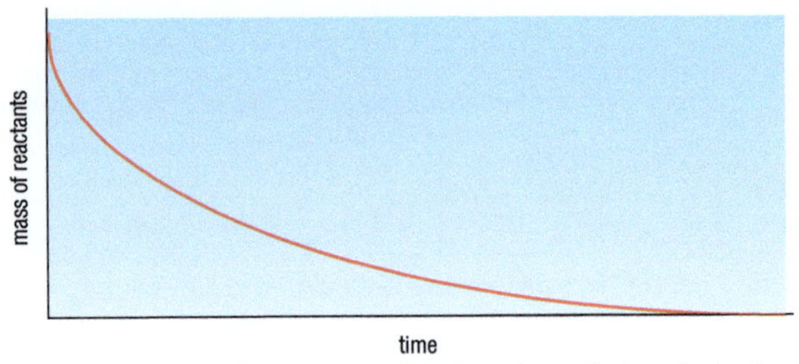

b The slope of the line tells us the rate of the reaction at that particular time.

8.2

1 Temperature, concentration, surface area, pressure (if gases involved), catalyst (some reactions affected by light)
2 a

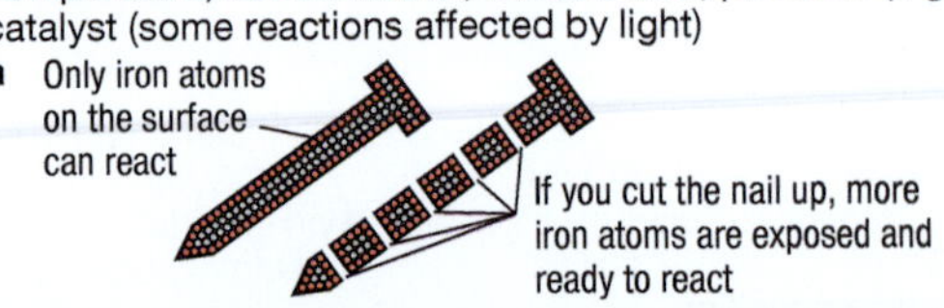

b To control all the other variables/keep the other variables constant in order to make it a fair test
3 The 'activation energy' is the minimum energy needed for reactant particles to react so any collisions with insufficient energy will not react so having no effect on the rate of reaction; only those colliding particles with the activation energy will react.
4 Well-chewed food will be in smaller pieces so will have a greater surface area. Therefore it will have more food molecules exposed to attack by the acid particles in your stomach than unchewed food.

8.3

1 a Because the frequency of collisions increases and more particles collide with energy greater than the activation energy
b By a factor of 2/doubles/twice the rate
2 a carbon dioxide
b It gets shorter.
c The reactant hydrogencarbonate and acid particles move around more quickly so they collide more often and there is a higher proportion of collisions with energy greater than the activation energy needed for a reaction to take place/for effective collisions to occur.
3 The chemical reactions that take place in the cooking process will occur more quickly as the water under pressure can be heated to a higher temperature than 100 °C.

8.4

1 a The lowest (yellow) line/highest concentration because its slope is steepest.
b To stop any acid spray escaping whilst allowing the carbon dioxide gas to escape/a rubber bung would trap the carbon dioxide gas given off until the bung blew off under the increasing pressure as the reaction proceeded.
c The electronic balance responds to small changes in mass.
2

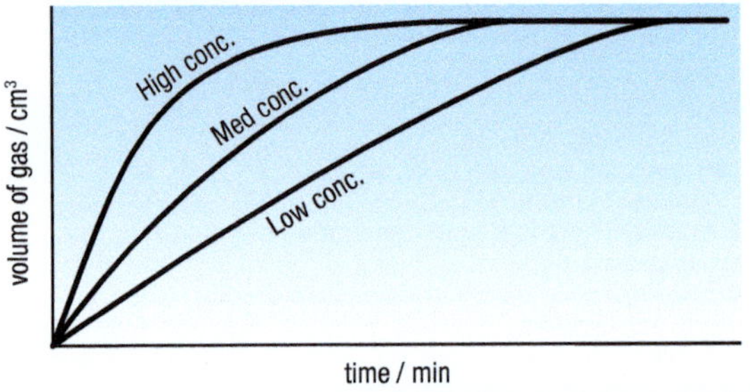

3 The higher the concentration of a gas, the more particles there are in a given volume and each particle of gas will contribute to the overall pressure exerted by the gas. If you double the concentration of a gas, you double the number of particles in a given volume. The particles are moving randomly at high speeds so the force per unit area caused by their collisions with the walls of the container will also double.
4 There are many more collisions between the particles of acid in the undiluted cleaner and the limescale (calcium carbonate) in a given time resulting in a faster reaction than with diluted cleaner. This is because the number of acid particles in a given volume is far higher in the undiluted cleaner than in a diluted cleaning solution.

8.5

1 It remains chemically unchanged.
2 To make them as effective as possible by increasing their surface area as much as possible
3 The reactants are used up as they turn into products but catalysts remain chemically unchanged at the end of a reaction. So catalysts can go on to catalyse further conversion of reactants to products (eventually they do become 'poisoned' by impurities and need to be replaced, but not often).
4 For example – Manufacture of ammonia/Haber process:
nitrogen + hydrogen ⇌ ammonia (uses an iron catalyst)
Manufacture of sulfuric acid/Contact process:
sulfur dioxide + oxygen ⇌ sulfur trioxide (uses a vanadium(V) oxide catalyst)
Manufacture of nitric acid:
ammonia + oxygen ⇌ nitrogen(II) oxide (nitrogen monoxide) + water (uses platinum/rhodium as a catalyst)
Manufacture of margarine:
unsaturated oil + hydrogen → hydrogenated fat (uses nickel as a catalyst)
5 They speed up the production process, making it more economical; save energy; reduce pollution from, and save limited resources of, fossil fuels.

Answers to end of chapter summary questions

1 a For example – Measuring the mass of the reaction mixture over time/measuring the volume of gas given off in a gas syringe (or measuring cylinder over water) over time.
b Use more concentrated acid; increase the temperature of the acid; use a larger surface area of magnesium (e.g., cut the magnesium ribbon up into smaller pieces).
c i The student could repeat the reaction at different temperatures, keeping the other variables constant i.e., concentration and volume of acid, mass and surface area of magnesium ribbon.
ii The higher the temperature of acid, the greater the rate of reaction/faster the reaction.

iii As the temperature of the acid is increased the particles of acid (hydrogen ions) in solution gain more energy and move around more quickly (on average). Therefore they will collide with particles (atoms) of the magnesium ribbon more frequently. Not only that, a higher proportion of the collisions will have energy greater than the activation energy so more collisions in any given time will be successful/result in a reaction.

2 a Carbon dioxide; limewater turns cloudy.
b i calcium carbonate + nitric acid → calcium nitrate + water + carbon dioxide
ii $CaCO_3(s) + 2HNO_3(aq) \rightarrow Ca(NO_3)_2(aq) + H_2O(l) + CO_2(g)$
c They used two solutions of nitric acid with different concentrations, keeping all other variables constant, in a conical flask. This was placed on an electronic balance, marble chips added, with a cotton wool plug in the mouth of the flask and the loss in mass (which is equivalent to the mass of gas produced) was monitored for 2.5 minutes, taking readings every 30 seconds.
d Student graphs (both lines drawn as smooth curves and labelled)
e The rate of reaction in Investigation B is half that in Investigation A.
f The final mass of gas produced in Investigation B is half of that produced in Investigation A.
g The initial concentration of the acid in Investigation A is twice/double the concentration of acid in Investigation B.
h In Investigation A there are twice as many acid particles ($H^+(aq)$ ions) as in Investigation B in the same volume of acid. So, there will be twice the number of collisions in a given time between the acid particles in solution and particles at the surface of the marble chips. Therefore the rate of reaction in Investigation A is twice the rate in Investigation B.

3 a They kept the temperature, concentration of acid, volume of acid, and mass of zinc constant and only varied the surface area of the zinc in each different test.
b Hydrogen; a lighted spill pops.
c $Zn(s) + H_2SO_4(aq) \rightarrow ZnSO_4(aq) + H_2(g)$
d Line 1
e The largest pieces of zinc
f The line would be the steepest, rising to the same level as the other three lines, levelling off before them.
g The smaller the pieces of zinc, the larger its surface area and the more zinc particles (atoms) are exposed to react with the acid particles ($H^+(aq)$ ions) moving around randomly in the solution. Therefore the frequency of collision between reactant particles increases, causing an increase in the rate of reaction.

4 a A substance that increases the rate of a reaction but remains chemically unchanged at the end of the reaction
b $2H_2O_2(aq) \rightarrow 2H_2O(l) + O_2(g)$
c For example – Measure the time to collect a fixed volume of oxygen gas using the same mass of potential catalyst (with the same surface area) in the same concentration of hydrogen peroxide solution at the same temperature in each test.
d Filter off the insoluble metal oxides after the reaction, wash with distilled water, and dry in a warm oven/leave to dry/dab with filter paper to dry.

Answers to end of chapter practice questions

1	a	Acid concentration	*(1 mark)*
		Temperature	*(1 mark)*
	b	Curve is steeper.	*(1 mark)*
		Curve becomes horizontal before the others.	*(1 mark)*
	c	Greater surface area	*(1 mark)*
	d i	Student 1	*(1 mark)*
		Bigger (%) error in recording short times	*(1 mark)*
	ii	1 ÷ 11	*(1 mark)*
		= 0.09	*(1 mark)*
	iii	Rate increases as concentration increases	*(1 mark)*
		In direct proportion	*(1 mark)*
	iv	Concentration doubled/twice as many (acid) particles	*(1 mark)*
		More collisions between (acid) particles	*(1 mark)*
		In a given time/more frequent	*(1 mark)*
2	a	S/sulfur	*(1 mark)*
		Does not dissolve/appears as a precipitate	*(1 mark)*
	b i	They move more quickly.	*(1 mark)*
	ii	Collisions are more energetic.	*(1 mark)*
3	a	A substance that speeds up a chemical reaction	*(1 mark)*
		But is not used up during the reaction	*(1 mark)*
	b	They reduce costs/they last a long time/they help to make a lot of products in a shorter time.	*(1 mark)*
	c	Greater surface area	*(1 mark)*

9 Energy changes in chemical reactions

9.1

1 a Exothermic
b Endothermic
c For example, oxidation, combustion, neutralisation, respiration
d For example, any thermal decomposition, photosynthesis

2 The beaker would feel cold as the process of dissolving absorbed energy from its surroundings which included the beaker and your hand holding it.

3 The enthalpy of the reactants was greater/higher than the products, with the difference released as energy which raised the temperature of the surroundings. ΔH would have a negative value.

4 a $MgCO_3(s) \rightarrow MgO(s) + CO_2(g)$
b +117 kJ/mol

9.2

1 a It uses the energy released in the oxidation of iron, forming hydrated iron(III) oxide in an exothermic reaction. Sodium chloride (common salt) is used as a catalyst.
b A supersaturated solution is made to crystallise by pressing a small metal disc. The crystals spread throughout the solution, releasing energy. The crystals are re-dissolved in hot water, ready to use again.
c The disposable hand warmer lasts longer when activated than the reusable one. However, it can only be used once. Opposite applies to reusable hand warmers.
d Self-heating cans

2 a To treat injuries with cold packs; to chill drinks in cans
b Dissolving ammonium nitrate in water
c i NH_4NO_3 ii For example, fertiliser

3 a Calcium oxide
b $CaO(s) + H_2O(l) \rightarrow Ca(OH)_2(aq)$
c It would form a harmful alkaline solution.

9.3

1 a Their size/numerical value/magnitude is the same but they have opposite signs.
b Water
c It reacts with water vapour in the air.
d Energy is released.

2 a $W + X \rightleftharpoons Y + Z$
b It will absorb 50 kJ (+50 kJ/mol).

3 a 4 moles
b $CoCl_2{\cdot}2H_2O + 4H_2O \rightleftharpoons CoCl_2{\cdot}6H_2O$
c Warm them up.

9.4

1 a

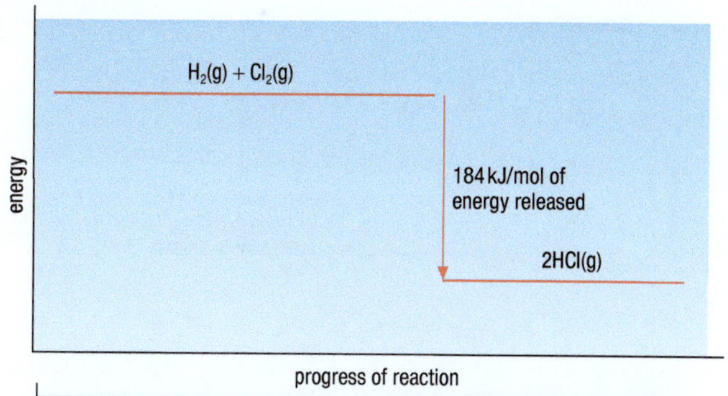

b

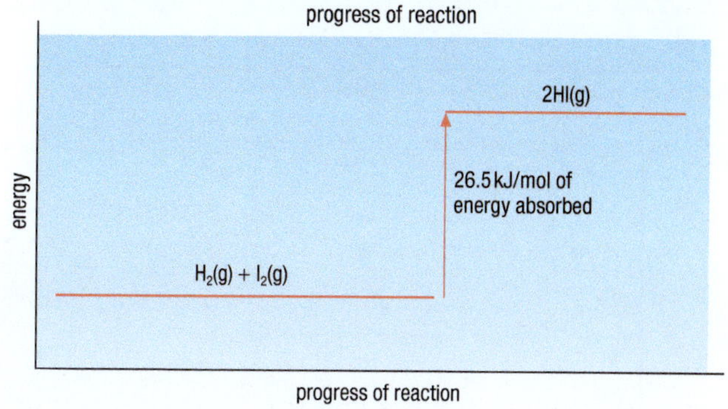

2 a and **b**

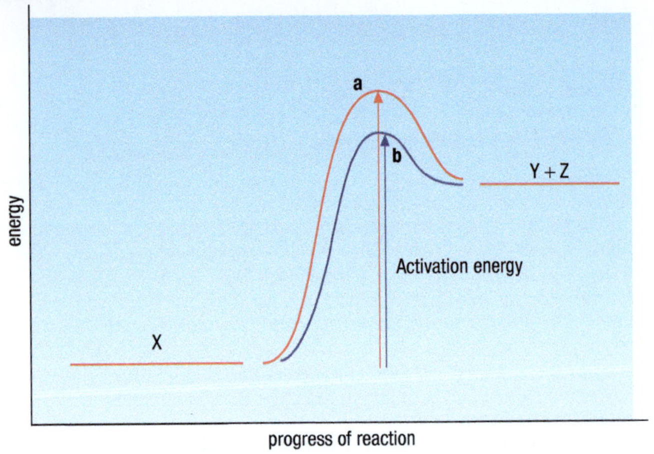

c It reduces the activation energy/energy needed for colliding particles to react so increasing the proportion of collisions in a sample with sufficient energy to cause a reaction and therefore increases the rate of reaction.

3 a Energy must be supplied from the surroundings and absorbed by the molecule whose bonds are being broken to overcome the attraction between atoms. So the separated atoms formed will have a higher energy content than the original molecule.

b

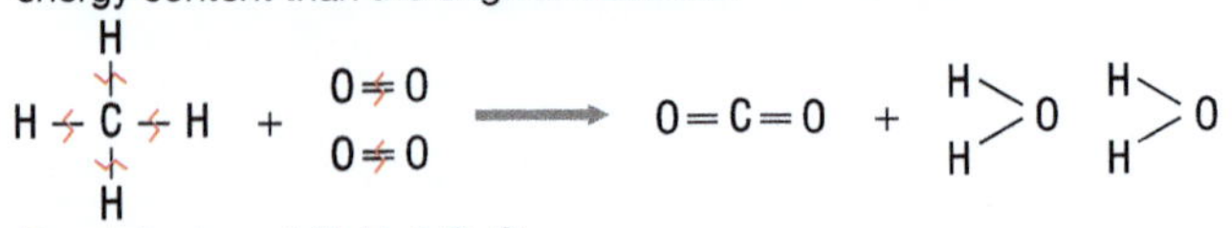

c Bonds broken: 4 C–H; 2 O=O
Bonds made: 2 C=O; 4 O–H

9.5

1 Endothermic
2 The energy required to break a specific bond.
3 **a** $H_2 + Cl_2 \rightarrow 2HCl \quad \Delta H = -185\,kJ/mol$
b $2H_2 + O_2 \rightarrow 2H_2O \quad \Delta H = -486\,kJ/mol$

Answers to end of chapter summary questions

1 a and **b**

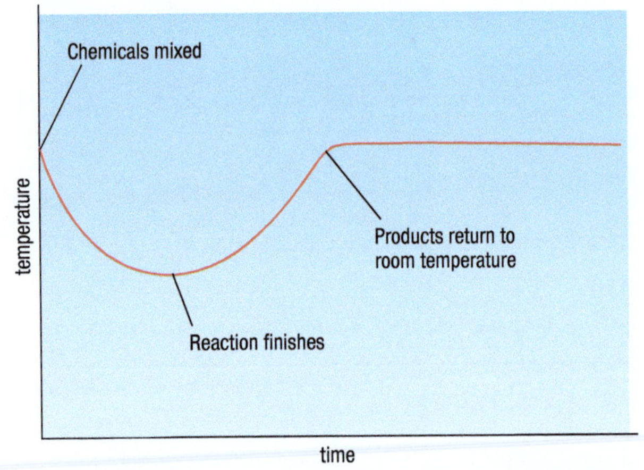

2 a

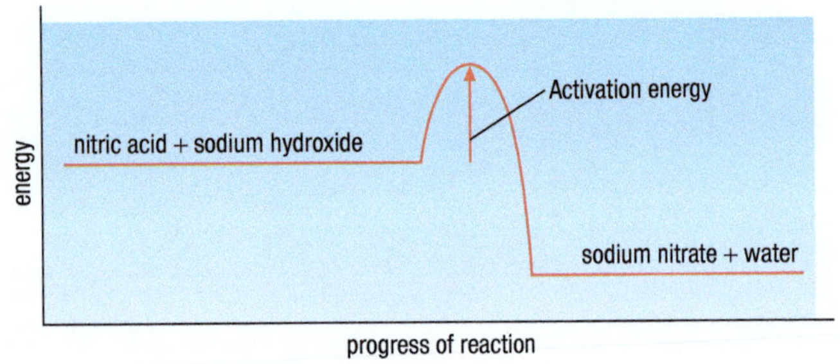

b

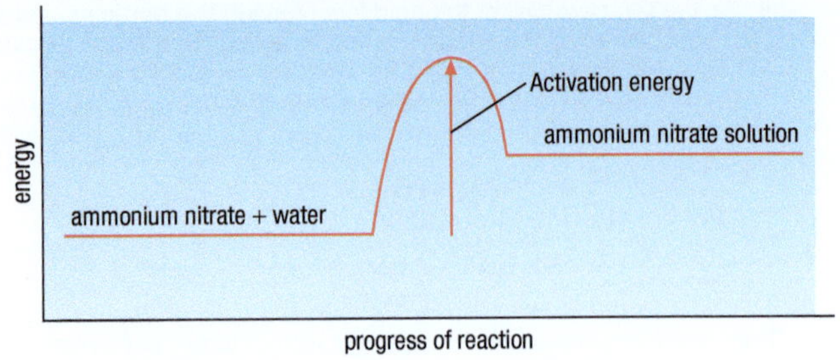

c

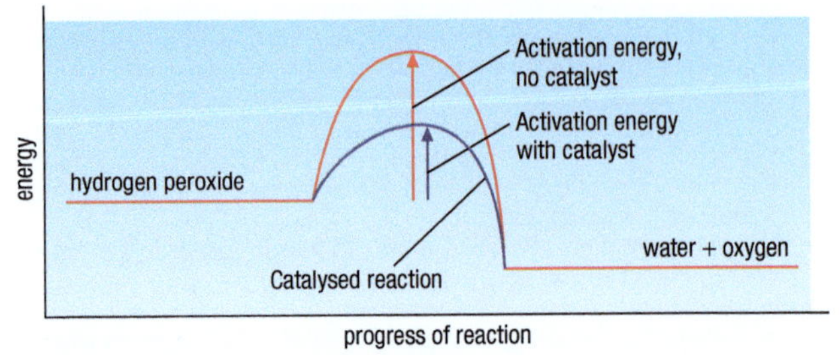

3 a $C_{12}H_{22}O_{11} + 12O_2 \rightarrow 12CO_2 + 11H_2O$
b To break the bonds in reactants/to supply the activation energy
c The process of making new bonds in carbon dioxide and water releases energy
d 85 kJ

4 a –210 kJ/mol
b The energy absorbed in breaking the bonds in hydrogen peroxide is less than the energy released when the new bonds in water and oxygen are made.

5 a E.g. The larger the volume of copper(II) sulfate solution used, the lower the temperature rise - because the same energy is transferred in each test but the it requires more energy to raise the temperature of a larger volume of solution by the same amount as the rise in a smaller volume
b volume of (copper(II) sulfate) solution
c temperature change / rise
d iron + copper(II) sulfate → iron(II) sulfate + copper
$Fe(s) + CuSO_4(aq) \rightarrow FeSO_4(aq) + Cu$
e i rise
ii because energy was transferred to the surroundings (from the reaction mixture)

Answers to end of chapter practice questions

1 a i Exothermic reactions give out heat/produce temperature rise.
Endothermic reactions take in heat/produce temperature fall. *(2 marks)*
ii Enthalpy change *(1 mark)*
iii Negative sign means exothermic/positive sign means endothermic. *(1 mark)*
b i Energy of reactants is higher than energy of products. *(1 mark)*
ii Activation energy *(1 mark)*
iii Catalyst used (in B) *(1 mark)*
iv C *(1 mark)*
c –31 kJ/mol *(1 mark)*

2 a i calorimeter *(1 mark)*
ii Polystyrene / poly(phenylethene) *(1 mark)*
it is a thermal insulator / poor conductor of thermal energy *(1 mark)*
so minimises energy transfer to from the reaction mixture to the surroundings or from the surroundings to the reaction mixture *(1 mark)*
iii 0.2 oC (1) – looking at the results in the table, you can read the temperature to 0.1 oC / half the interval with this thermometer
b A, B, D – exothermic *(1 mark)*
C – endothermic *(1 mark)*
c B / magnesium + iron(II) sulfate *(1 mark)*
d i $HCl(aq) + NaOH(aq) \rightarrow NaCl(aq) + H_2O(l)$ *(3 mark)*
ii 4.1 oC / same as Reaction A *(1 mark)*
because both are neutralization reactions *(1 mark)*
In which the overall change is $H^+(aq) + OH^-(aq) \rightarrow H_2O(l)$ *(1 mark)*

e **i** Displacement / redox *(1 mark)*
ii Order of reactivity Mg, Zn, Fe (most reactive first) *(1 mark)*
Iron is the least reactive of the three metals because both magnesium and zinc can displace iron(II) ions from solution *(1 mark)*
Magnesium is more reactive than zinc as the Reaction B is more vigorous / transfers more energy to the surroundings than Reaction D. *(1 mark)*

3 **a** $(4 \times 412) + (2 \times 496)$ *(1 mark)*
$= 2640$ *(1 mark)*
b $(2 \times 743) + (4 \times 463)$ *(1 mark)*
$= 3338$ *(1 mark)*
c −698 kJ/mol *(1 mark)*

10 Carbon compounds as fuels

10.1

1 **a** A mixture of hydrocarbons
b We rely on fractions from crude oil for most of our fuels, as well as many other products made from them.
c Because it is a mixture of different substances with different boiling points

2 As a mixture, crude oil contains a wide range of hydrocarbons. Its components all have differing properties, such as boiling points, so it is better to separate the crude oil into fractions which can have different specific uses.

3 **a** $C_nH_{(2n+2)}$
b hexane, C_6H_{14}; heptane, C_7H_{16}; octane, C_8H_{18}; nonane, C_9H_{20}; decane, $C_{10}H_{22}$

4 **a**

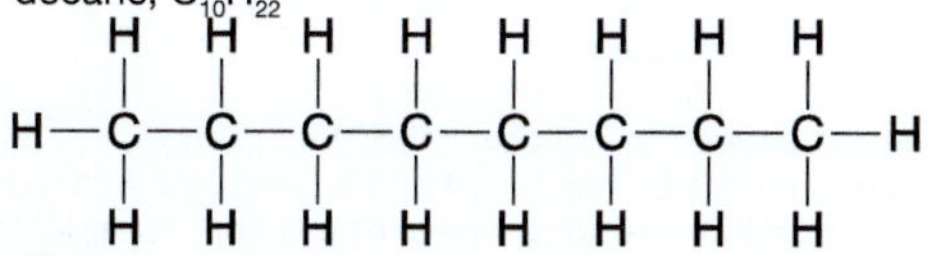

b 46
c 15
d Because they are compounds of hydrogen and carbon atoms only which have the maximum number of hydrogen atoms possible in their molecules/contain only single covalent C–C bonds.

10.2

1 **a** **i** The larger the hydrocarbon, the higher the boiling point
ii The larger the hydrocarbon, the lower the volatility
iii The larger the hydrocarbon, the higher the viscosity
b Short-chain hydrocarbon molecules – it will burn with a clean flame/not smoky.

2 Student table that effectively shows the patterns in the boiling points (gets higher), volatility (gets lower), viscosity (gets more viscous), and flammability (gets less flammable) as the size of the hydrocarbon molecules increase.

3 Hot crude oil is heated and enters a fractionating column near the bottom as a vapour. The temperature decreases going up the column. The gases condense when they reach the temperature of their boiling points so different fractions are collected as liquids at different levels in a continuous process. The hydrocarbons with the smallest molecules have the lowest boiling points and are collected at the top of the column where the temperature is lower. Nearer the bottom of the fractionating column, the fractions with the higher boiling points are collected.

10.3

1 **a** Carbon dioxide and water **b** Sulfur
2 **a** Acid rain **b** Oxides of nitrogen
3 **a** From oxidation of sulfur impurities when fuels burn
b When nitrogen in the air is oxidised in the very high temperatures inside a vehicle engine
c When fuel, such as diesel, undergoes incomplete combustion
4 **a** $CH_4(g) + 2O_2(g) \rightarrow CO_2(g) + 2H_2O(l)$
b $2CH_4(g) + 3O_2(g) \rightarrow 2CO(g) + 4H_2O(l)$
c Carbon monoxide is a highly toxic gas. As it is colourless and odourless, people cannot detect it and so become poisoned.

10.4

1 Because ethanol can be made from plants which actually absorb carbon dioxide as they photosynthesise which offsets the carbon dioxide released when it is burnt, whereas burning petrol is releasing carbon dioxide from hydrocarbons trapped beneath the surface for millions of years.

2 The energy comes from the Sun, which is used by the plants, such as oilseed rape, in the process of photosynthesis as the biofuel crop is growing.

3 If farmers switch from producing food crops to growing crops for biofuels, there will be less land available to grow food or raise animals. This could result in food shortages and higher food prices.

Answers to end of chapter summary questions

1 **a** **i** $C_nH_{(2n+2)}$ **ii** $C_{18}H_{38}$ **iii** C_8H_{18}
b Student graph
c The higher the number of carbon atoms (the larger the alkane molecule), the higher its boiling point.
d Actual boiling point of pentane is 36 °C – see student graph for accuracy.

2 **a** **i** A compound made up of hydrogen and carbon atoms only
ii They have the maximum number of hydrogen atoms possible in their molecules/contain only single covalent bonds between carbon atoms.
b **i** Propane, C_3H_8
ii Atoms of carbon and hydrogen
iii Single covalent bonds

3 **a** B, because a fractionating column gets cooler nearer the top and the vapour of B will condense at a lower temperature than A.
b B as it is made up of smaller alkane molecules than A because it has a lower boiling point – and smaller hydrocarbons are more flammable.
c **i** A is more viscous than B.
ii B is more volatile than A.

4 **a** Climate change
b **i** Sulfur dioxide
ii Remove sulfur impurities before burning the fossil fuel or prevent the sulfur dioxide gas formed from entering the atmosphere.
iii Oxides of nitrogen – formed when nitrogen in the air inside a combustion engine is oxidised at very high temperatures.

5 **a** To condense the steam formed in the combustion of ethanol and collect it as a liquid
b Blue cobalt chloride paper turns pink/white anhydrous copper(II) sulfate turns blue.
c It turns cloudy as carbon dioxide is produced when the carbon atoms in ethanol are oxidised.
d Compare the time it takes for the limewater to turn cloudy when ethanol burns with the time it takes with just air being drawn through the apparatus.
e ethanol + oxygen → carbon dioxide + water
$C_2H_5OH + 3O_2 \rightarrow 2CO_2 + 3H_2O$
f Swap the spirit burner with ethanol in for a wax candle.
g propane + oxygen → carbon dioxide + water
$C_3H_8 + 5O_2 \rightarrow 3CO_2 + 4H_2O$
h Carbon monoxide

6 **a** Ethanol, because it can be made from plants, e.g., sugar cane and sugar beet
b The carbon dioxide released when it burns was taken in from the atmosphere as it grew.
c Water is the only product of combustion so no more carbon dioxide is added to the atmosphere when it burns.
d How to store the gas (large volume or very high pressures in cylinders);
explosive with oxygen in an accident;
how to generate the hydrogen.
e hydrogen + oxygen → water
$2H_2 + O_2 \rightarrow 2H_2O$

Answers to end of chapter practice questions

1 **a** **i** (Compound containing) hydrogen and carbon *(1 mark)*
only/but no other elements *(1 mark)*
ii Only single bonds/no double bonds *(1 mark)*
b **i** C_nH_{2n+2} *(1 mark)*
ii C_3H_8 *(1 mark)*
iii

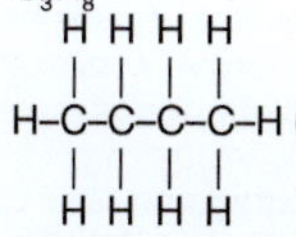

(or displayed formula for methylpropane) *(1 mark)*

c **i** (Liquid to vapour) evaporation/boiling *(1 mark)*
(Vapour to liquid) condensation *(1 mark)*
ii Viscous *(1 mark)*
High boiling point *(1 mark)*

2 a Carbon dioxide (1 mark)
Water (1 mark)
b $CH_4 + 2O_2 \rightarrow CO_2 + 2H_2O$
Four formulae correct (1 mark)
Balancing (1 mark)
c (Solid) carbon (1 mark)
(Gaseous) carbon monoxide (1 mark)
d i High temperature (1 mark)
ii Acid rain (1 mark)
e i Remove it before fuel is burnt. (1 mark)
ii Remove it before it enters the atmosphere. (1 mark)
3 a It comes from plants. (1 mark)
b Sugar (cane) (1 mark)
Fermentation (1 mark)
c i Crude oil/fossil fuels are becoming depleted. (1 mark)
ii Less food can be grown. (1 mark)
d i No carbon dioxide formed (1 mark)

11 Other products from crude oil

11.1

1 a To meet our demands for fuels (petrol and diesel) from crude oil
b The hydrocarbon vapours are passed over a hot catalyst or mixed with steam at very high temperatures.
2 a i B
ii A hydrocarbon that contains at least one C=C double bond
iii Alkene
b i A **ii** Alkane
c Thermal decomposition
3 24 hydrogen atoms in $C_{12}H_{24}$
4 $C_{12}H_{26} \rightarrow C_8H_{18} + 2C_2H_4$

11.2

1 a A monomer is a small reactive molecule that joins together with other monomers to form a polymer.
A polymer is a very large molecule made up of many repeating units.
b Polymerisation
c
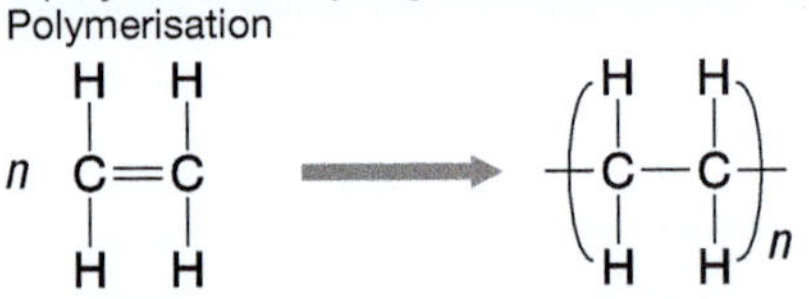
Ethene Poly(ethene)

d For example, carrier bags, dustbins, clingfilm, bottles, washing-up bowls
2 Two carbon atoms are needed for a hydrocarbon to have a C=C double bond whereas in alkanes only one carbon atom is needed to form a saturated hydrocarbon as in CH_4.
3 a
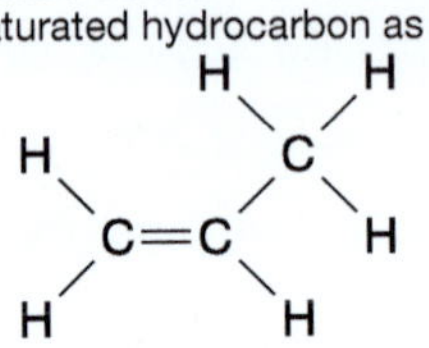

b
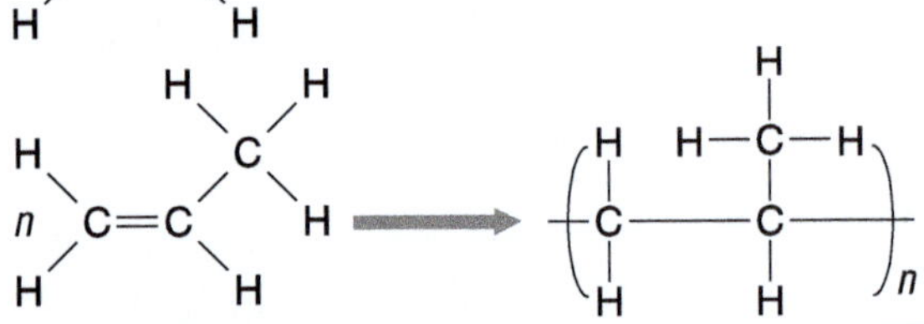

c For example, carpets, milk crates, ropes
d The C=C double bond 'opens up' in neighbouring propene molecules and forms single bonds, joining the monomers together in a long chain.

11.3

1 a In a tangled mess
b i Thermosoftening polymers have their individual chains held in place by relatively weak intermolecular forces whereas thermosetting polymers have strong covalent bonds (cross links) between the chains.
ii Thermosoftening plastics soften when heated and tend to be soft but thermosetting polymers are heat-resistant (eventually charring at high enough temperatures) and rigid.
2 The handles would soften if thermosoftening polymers were used as heat is conducted through the metal pan to its handle.
3 Polymer A has stronger intermolecular forces than polymer B so it takes more energy to soften it. Polymer C has strong covalent bonds holding its chains in position so it will not soften on heating.
4 a The reaction conditions are different (temperature, pressure, catalyst).
b Both HDPE and LDPE are thermosoftening polymers.
c HDPE has straighter chains which can pack more closely together so it has a higher density, whereas LDPE has randomly branched chains so the chains cannot pack regularly together so there is more space in its structure so it has a lower density.

11.4

1 a i A polymer that is developed with a specific use in mind
ii A polymer which changes in response to changes in its surroundings
b i It is light, tough, and transparent
ii For example, clothing, duvet filling
iii Thermosoftening polymer because it can be melted and re-worked.
2 a A loose network of cross-linked polymers with water trapped in its structure
b Dressings for burns, contact lenses
3 Once the top layer is peeled off, the light-sensitive polymer beneath loses its stickiness when in contact with light so can easily be removed from the skin.
4 The stitches are inserted loosely and tighten when warmed to body temperature.

11.5

1 Waste plastic mostly ends up in landfill sites where it takes many years to break down.
2 Polymers that can be broken down by microbes in the soil.
3 a Because they are biodegradable
b Lactic acid
4 a Little or not enough oxygen to aid decomposition process
b Decomposition might start before the plastic's useful life has expired.
c It can be incorporated into the structure of non-biodegradable plastics so that microbes feed on it once disposed of and speed up decomposition.
Polymers derived from cornstarch are themselves biodegradable.

Answers to end of chapter summary questions

1 a C_3H_6
b
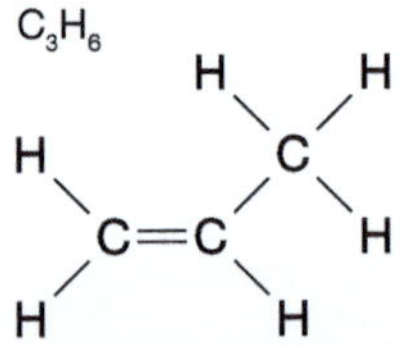

c Unsaturated molecule as it contains a C=C double bond
d Add bromine water, stopper, and shake – the propene will decolourise the bromine water whereas the propane has no effect/bromine water remains orange in colour.
e i Polymerisation
ii Poly(propene)
iii Monomers
iv The poly(propene) is a solid at room temperature whereas propene is a gas.
2 $n\,C_2H_4 \rightarrow -CH_2\text{–}CH_{2n}-$
3 a ethene + steam ⇌ ethanol
$C_2H_4(g) + H_2O(g) \rightleftharpoons C_2H_5OH$
b Advantage – it is a continuous process and a quicker process.
Disadvantage – it uses a non-renewable resource as its raw material (crude oil) and uses more energy in the process.
4 a Water molecules can pass out of the tiny pores in the material (as when we breathe out water vapour) so the wearer does not get clammy.
b No, because it does not change in response to changes in its environment.
5 a The crops have been genetically modified.
b Not in theory as it absorbs the same amount of carbon dioxide when the crop grows as it releases when it decomposes. However, processing and transporting the crop to extract the polymer will use fossil fuels which will result in some excess carbon dioxide being released.
c Probably as the recycling bypasses the processing/fermentation stages but it would itself require some costs in terms of extracting the polymer.

Answers to end of chapter practice questions

1 a (Type 1)
Heat *(1 mark)*
With a catalyst *(1 mark)*
(Type 2)
Mix with steam *(1 mark)*
Very high temperature *(1 mark)*
b i (Carbon–carbon) double (covalent) bond *(1 mark)*
ii
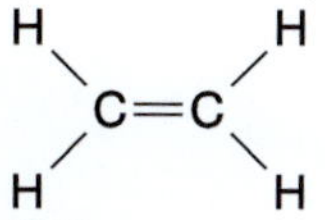
(1 mark)
iii C_4H_8 *(1 mark)*
c C_4H_8 or $2C_2H_4$ *(1 mark)*
d Bromine (water) *(1 mark)*
Alkanes show no change in colour. *(1 mark)*
Alkenes decolourise it. *(1 mark)*
e Ethene *(1 mark)*
Steam *(1 mark)*
Heat/catalyst *(1 mark)*

2 a No double bonds/saturated *(1 mark)*
Much bigger/long chains *(1 mark)*
b i LD = low density and HD = high density *(1 mark)*
ii Melt when heated *(1 mark)*
c i Does not melt/decompose *(1 mark)*
ii Cross links/chains joined together *(1 mark)*
d Broken down by microbes *(1 mark)*
Reduce space taken up in landfill *(1 mark)*

3 **0 marks** No relevant content
Level 1 (1–2 marks) One type of polymer is correctly identified and there is a brief account of the properties, structure, and bonding of polymers.
Level 2 (3–4 marks) Both types of polymer are correctly identified and there are some references to the properties, structure, and bonding of polymers.
Level 3 (5–6 marks) Both types of polymer are correctly identified and there is a clear, balanced, and detailed account of the properties, structure, and bonding of polymers.
Examples of chemistry points made in the response:
- Polymer 2 should be made using low-density thermosoftening polymer
- Polymer 1 should be made using thermosetting polymer
- low-density (thermosoftening) polymer chains have many branches
- high-density (thermosoftening) polymer chains have no/few branches
- thermosetting polymer chains have cross links/covalent bonds between the chains
- HD polymer chains can pack closely together
- LD polymer chains do not pack closely together
- thermosetting polymers cannot change shape because the cross links do not break when heated

12 Alcohols and carboxylic

12.1

1 a Esters
b Alcohols
c Carboxylic acids

2 a Propanol
b Ethyl ethanoate
c Methanoic acid

3 a
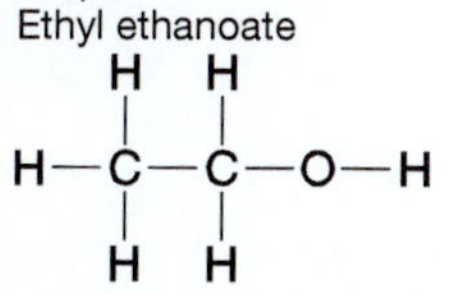

b
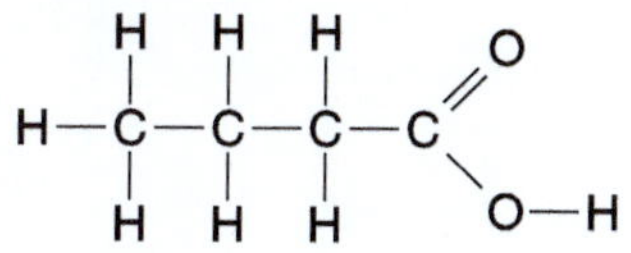

12.2

1 Ethanol, CH_3CH_2OH or C_2H_5OH
2 Fuels, solvents, and ethanol in alcoholic drinks
3 a sodium + methanol → sodium methoxide + hydrogen
$2Na + 2CH_3OH \rightarrow 2CH_3ONa + H_2$
b methanol + oxygen → carbon dioxide + water
$2CH_3OH + 3O_2 \rightarrow 2CO_2 + 4H_2O$

4 Place methanol, ethanol, and propanol in separate spirit burners and weigh then accurately. Heat a known volume of water for a set time and record the rise in temperature of the water. Re-weigh the spirit burners with their remaining alcohols. Calculate the rise in temperature that would have been produced if one gram of each alcohol had burnt. The alcohol with the largest temperature rise per gram is the one that releases most energy when it burns.

12.3

1 a Carbon dioxide
b Potassium propanoate
c $2C_2H_5COOH + K_2CO_3 \rightarrow 2C_2H_5COOK + H_2O + CO_2$

2 methanoic acid + ethanol $\overset{\text{sulfuric acid catalyst}}{\rightleftharpoons}$ ethyl methanoate + water

3 Propanoic acid is a weak acid because it does not ionise completely when added to water. The majority of its molecules remain intact and only a fraction form $H^+(aq)$ ions and propanoate (negative) ions. Therefore propanoic acid does not produce as high a concentration of $H^+(aq)$ ions in its solution as a solution of a strong acid of equal concentration.

Answers to end of chapter summary questions

1 a A
b C
c Esters
d B
e A is $CH_3CH_2CH_2CH_2CH_2COOH$
C is $CH_3CH_2CH_2CH_2CH_2CH_2CH_2OH$

2 a i Sodium fizzes/effervesces/gives off bubbles of gas, and gets smaller and smaller as a solution is formed.
ii Hydrogen
iii Sodium ethoxide
iv Na^+
v $2Na + 2C_2H_5OH \rightarrow 2C_2H_5ONa + H_2$
b The reaction with lithium would be slower/gas given off more slowly/longer for lithium to dissolve into the solution.

3 a
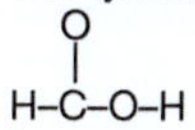

b i
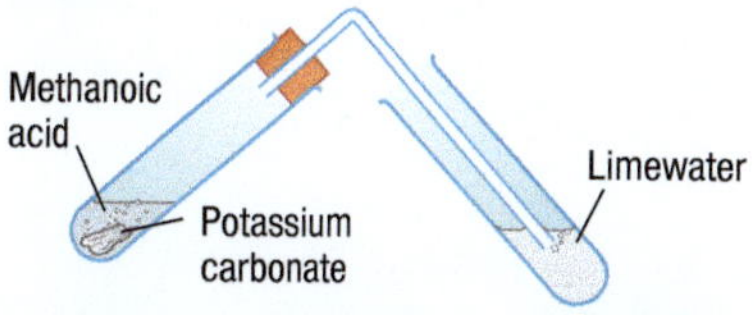

ii methanoic acid + potassium carbonate → potassium methanoate + water + carbon dioxide
$2HCOOH + K_2CO_3 \rightarrow 2HCOOK + H_2O + CO_2$
c i **E** ethanol
ii **C** methanoic acid, because ethanol is neutral so has the highest pH of 7. The rest are acids so have a pH below 7, but methanoic acid is the only weak acid. The other three being strong acids will have lower pH values.

4 a Ethyl ethanoate
b Ethanol and ethanoic acid
c ethanoic acid + ethanol $\overset{\text{sulfuric acid catalyst}}{\rightleftharpoons}$ ethyl ethanoate + water
$CH_3COOH + C_2H_5OH \rightleftharpoons CH_3COOC_2H_5 + H_2O$

5 a Methanoic acid will have a higher pH value than nitric acid.
b Nitric acid is a strong acid. The HNO_3 molecules all ionise in water:
$$HNO_3(aq) \rightarrow H^+(aq) + NO_3^-(aq)$$
However, methanoic acid is a weak acid so most of its molecules stay un-ionised. Only a few molecules will ionise and split up in their solutions in a reversible reaction.
$$HCOOH(aq) \rightleftharpoons HCOO^-(aq) + H^+(aq)$$
So there are fewer $H^+(aq)$ ions in a given volume of methanoic acid solution compared with the same volume of nitric acid solution.

Answers to end of chapter practice questions

1 a (Any two of)
Same general formula
Same functional group
Same/similar chemical reactions *(2 marks)*

b i CH_3OH/CH_4O *(1 mark)*

ii 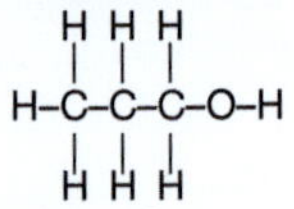 *(1 mark)*

c (Any two of)
Bubbles
Sodium disappears/gets smaller
Solid moves around *(2 marks)*

d Carbon dioxide *(1 mark)*
Water *(1 mark)*

e $CH_3CH_2OH + 3O_2 \rightarrow 2CO_2 + 3H_2O$
All formulae correct *(1 mark)*
Balancing *(1 mark)*

2 a (Ethanol) – no change *(1 mark)*
(Ethanoic acid) – bubbles *(1 mark)*

b i 5 *(1 mark)*

ii 1 *(1 mark)*

c Ethanoic acid is weaker because the ionisation is not complete/fewer H^+ ions are formed. *(1 mark)*
Nitric acid is stronger because ionisation is complete/more H^+ ions are formed. *(1 mark)*

3 a i Methanoic acid *(1 mark)*
Propanol *(1 mark)*

ii 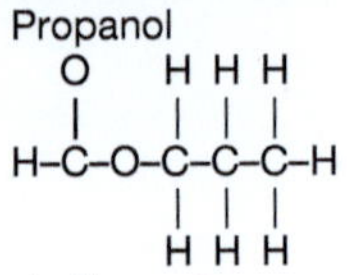 *(1 mark)*

b Ethyl ethanoate *(1 mark)*

Index

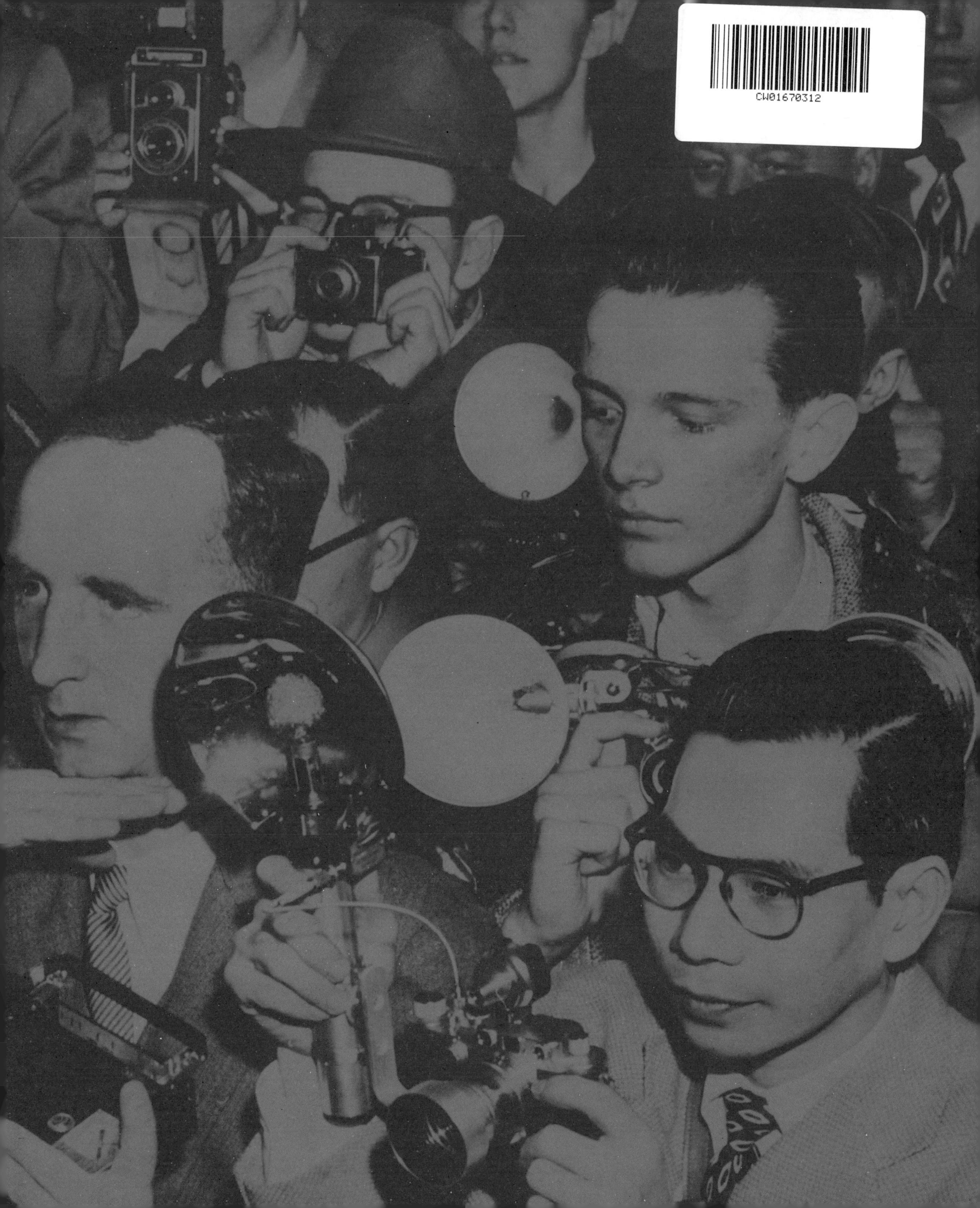

WITNESS

THIS IS A SEVENOAKS BOOK

Published in 2005 by Sevenoaks
An imprint of the Carlton Publishing Group
20 Mortimer Street
London W1T 3JW

A catalogue record for this book is available from the British Library.

ISBN 1 86200 245 2

Executive Editor: Stella Caldwell
Art Director: Clare Baggaley
Book Design: SMITH
Art Editors: Vicky Holmes and Emma Wicks
Picture Research: Sarah Edwards
Production: Lisa Moore

Printed and bound in Dubai

PHOTOGRAPH OVERLEAF: A volunteer educator from the Africa Directions Centre performs a play in a crowded Lusaka market. The plays performed by the centre's drama groups aim to educate about HIV and AIDS. Photograph by Gideon Mendel, 2003.

PHOTOGRAPH ON PAGES 6 AND 7: Children of a migrant worker from Oklahoma in a labour camp in California during America's Great Depression. Photograph by Dorothea Lange, 1936.

WITNESS
THE WORLD'S GREATEST NEWS PHOTOGRAPHERS

REUEL GOLDEN

SEVENOAKS

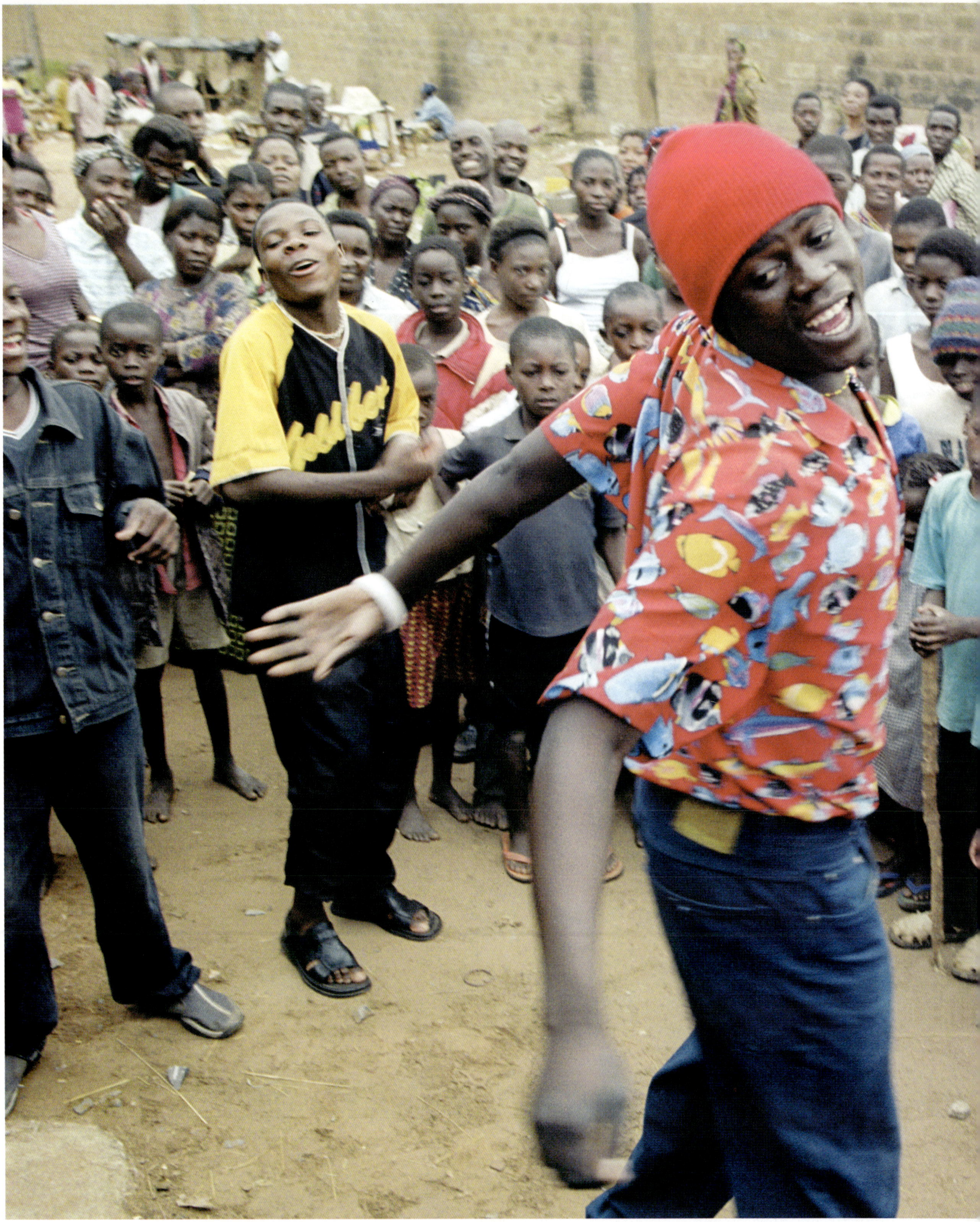

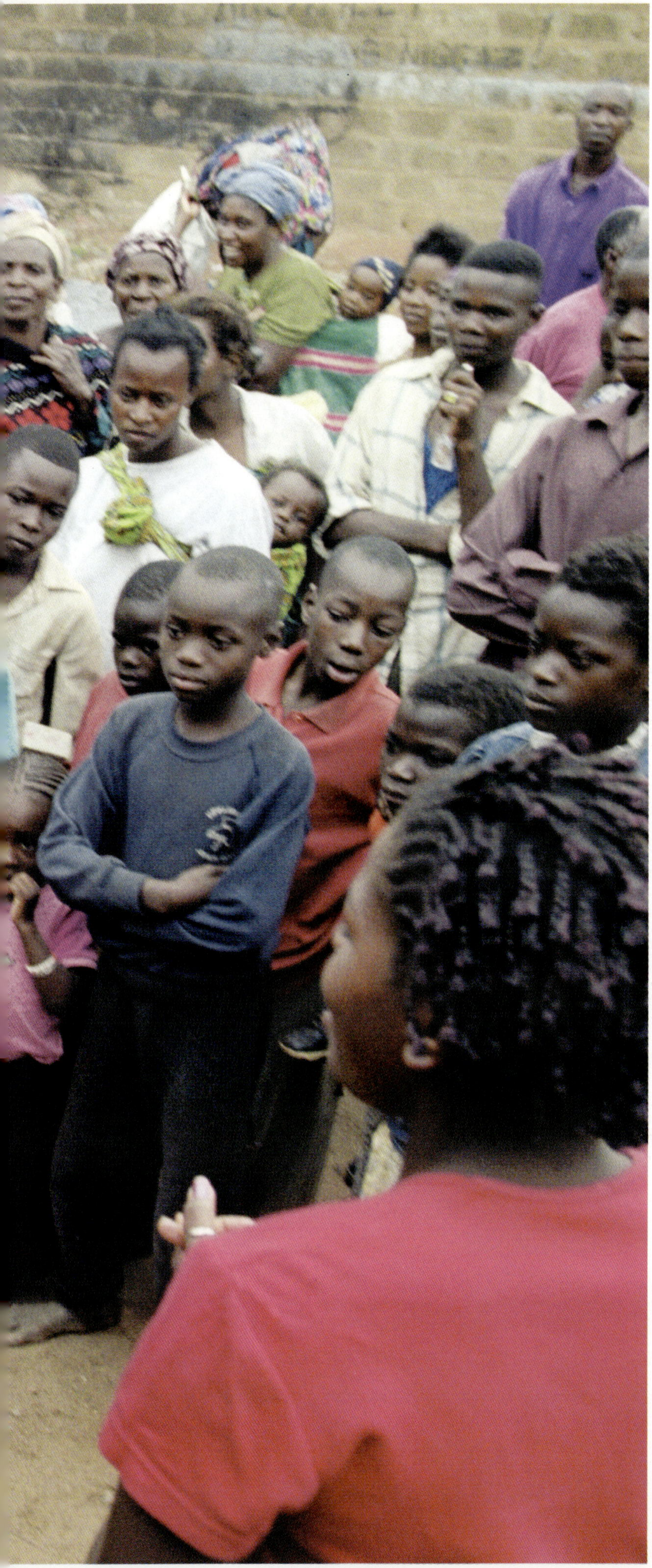

CONTENTS

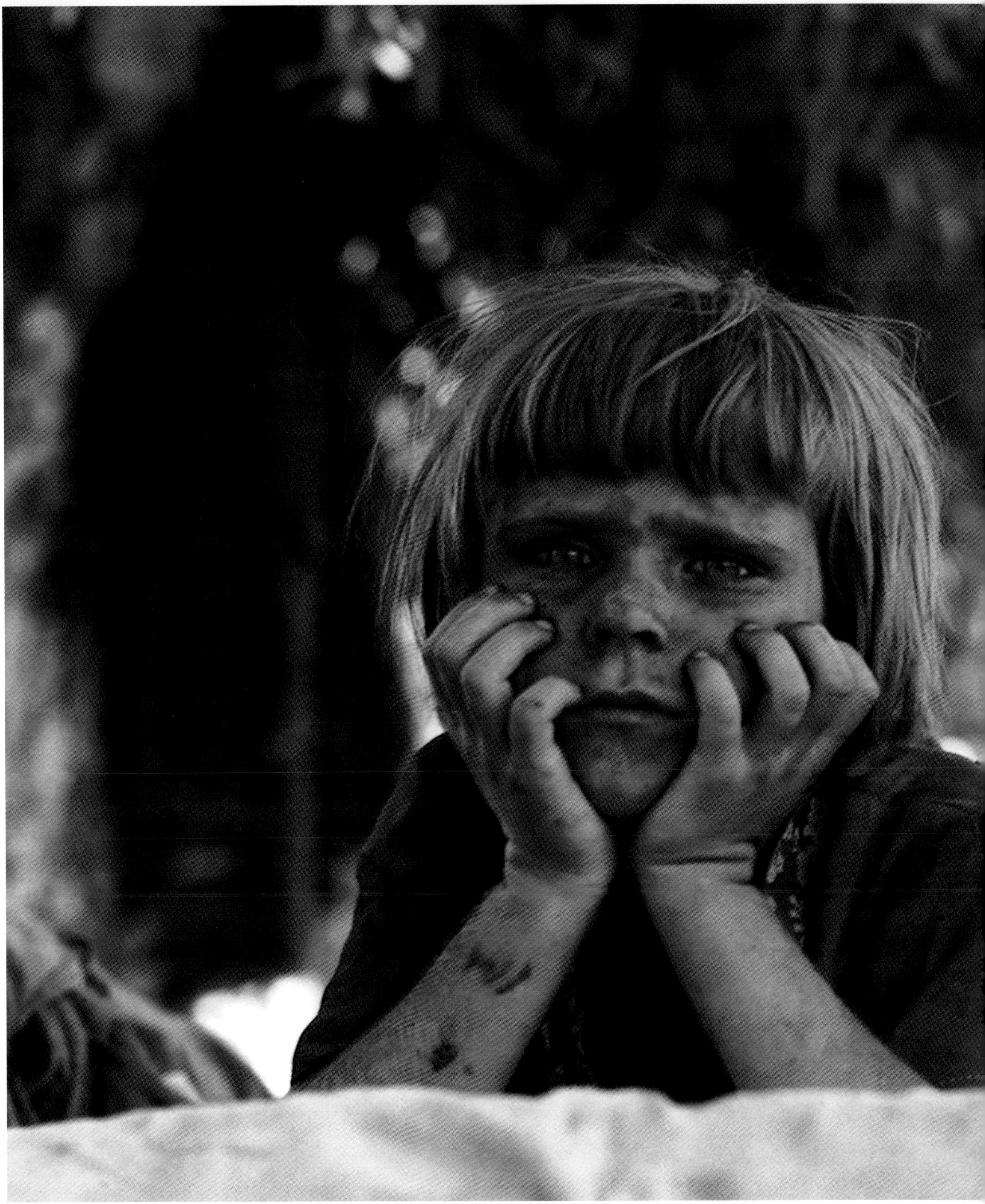

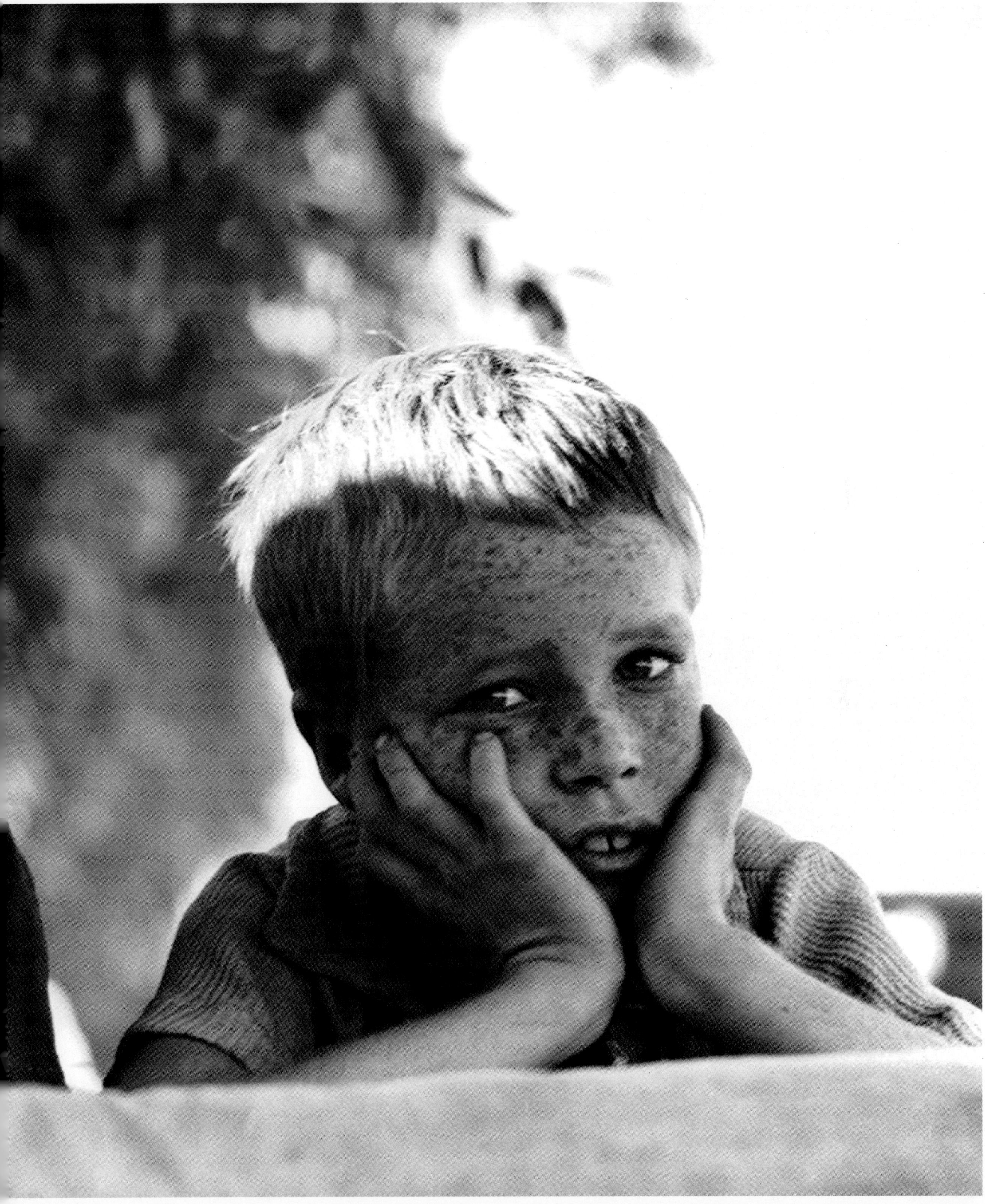

INTRODUCTION

The war in Iraq and its aftermath were relentlessly covered by thousands of television channels from all over the world. Journalists filed reports from burnt-out rooftops, from inside American tanks making their way toward Baghdad, from refugee camps. It was a big story, as war always is, and the 24-hour news channels were anxious not to miss anything – yet invariably they did. From all the hours, days and weeks of moving footage, there is nothing that really lingers in the memory from this strange time. The television coverage was immediate, dramatic and neverending. It showed us a lot, but taught us very little. It is the still photographs of the conflict that are memorable. The famous image of a statue of Saddam Hussein being toppled over by a jubilant crowd was a powerful symbol of repression and subsequent liberation. On the flip side of that, there were the chilling images taken by an anonymous American soldier with a cheap digital camera of Iraqi prisoners being abused by their US captors in the hellhole of Abu Ghraib. When historians look back at this period and try to make sense of what happened, it is these images, as well as photographs taken by people such as Luc Delahaye, Tom Stoddart, Jerry Lampen, James Nachtwey and dozens of others, that will be used as evidence.

Photojournalism's perspective

These photojournalists and all the others featured in this book were the key witnesses to a series of events that together make up recent history. They are our eyes on the world. Great photojournalism witnesses events that we wouldn't necessarily see or be allowed to see, or even want to think about. At its most basic definition, photojournalism is the presentation of stories through photographs – photojournalists are journalists with cameras. Since the inception of the medium, when Roger Fenton photographed the Crimean War in the mid-nineteenth century, photojournalists have been preoccupied with photographing humanity at the extreme edge of existence. War, civil unrest, famine, disease, natural disasters, poverty, homelessness: these are the grim stories told by photojournalists for more than 150 years.

Some critics resent this narrow, bleak viewpoint and continually question why photojournalists focus only on the negative. These are valid criticisms, but they can be rebutted. First, photojournalists are working in a commercial environment where there has always been a demand for this kind of image and story. Sadly, good news has never helped sell newspapers. Second, photographing a harrowing or dangerous event presents the photojournalist with a series of logistical, aesthetic and moral challenges. By challenging themselves, they in turn challenge the viewer on an emotional and intellectual level. The best photojournalism gets us to see and feel what is happening and more importantly forces us to ask "Why?".

The logistical challenge is to get the photograph in the first place; the aesthetic challenge is to make the image as compelling as possible. Often this means beautifying misery and suffering, and the more enlightened photojournalists are conscious of this dilemma. Yet they also realize that a well-composed, attractively toned and perfectly lit print is the most effective way of connecting and engaging an often indifferent audience.

The other moral challenge facing photojournalists is the notion of conveying an objective truth. As bystanders, they are supposed to merely record events and not influence them in any way. In this book there are controversial examples where the photographer supposedly "set up" the shot - the more extreme cases of a photojournalist tampering with the truth. Yet the notion of objectivity is ambiguous, and every time the photojournalist takes a photograph subjective judgements are being made, starting with the fundamental decision about what to photograph and equally importantly what to leave alone. Many factors will influence how the image is perceived and interpreted: how the image is composed and cropped; whether it is shot in colour or black-and-white; the detail that is included; whether the photograph is shot in close-up or the camera is pulled back; the accompanying caption. This doesn't mean that the photographer is not telling the truth; it is just one version of the truth. Click the shutter again and the viewer is confronted with a new version.

The evolution of the genre

There were some remarkable photojournalists in the nineteenth century: the pioneering Roger Fenton, the enigmatic Felice Beato, and Alexander Gardner, who photographed the American Civil War. (He, rather than the more famous Matthew Brady, makes it into this book, since there has always been some controversy over Brady, who claimed sole copyright from all the photographers who worked under him.) Yet overall two factors hindered the development of the medium. Firstly, cameras were extremely bulky and unwieldy contraptions involving glass plates and long exposure times, fine for formal portraiture, but not suited to the spontaneous nature of photojournalism. Secondly, there was no demand for journalistic images, apart from private collectors and museums.

This was to change in the first 20 years of the twentieth century. In 1910 the rotary printing cylinder was invented, which meant that text could now be combined with photographs. Following on from that was the development of the small hand-held camera, the Leica, which was to change the genre forever. Armed with a Leica, a photojournalist could get close to the action, taking photographs in quick succession, as the camera followed the movements of the human eye. These twin developments propelled photojournalism into people's consciousness and homes with a spate of photo-led publications.

This "golden age of photojournalism", as it became known, was roughly to last from the mid-1930s, when *Life* magazine started, to the mid-1950s, with the advent of television. At one point, *Life* was selling by the millions and even by today's standards photographers were being paid a lot of money to shoot stories, $20,000 in the case of the legendary Robert Capa. *Life* magazine loyally served its readers with its use of extended photo essays, where the photographer was

RIGHT: Children cool down in the spray from a fire hydrant during a hot summer on New York's Lower East Side. Photograph by Weegee, 1937.

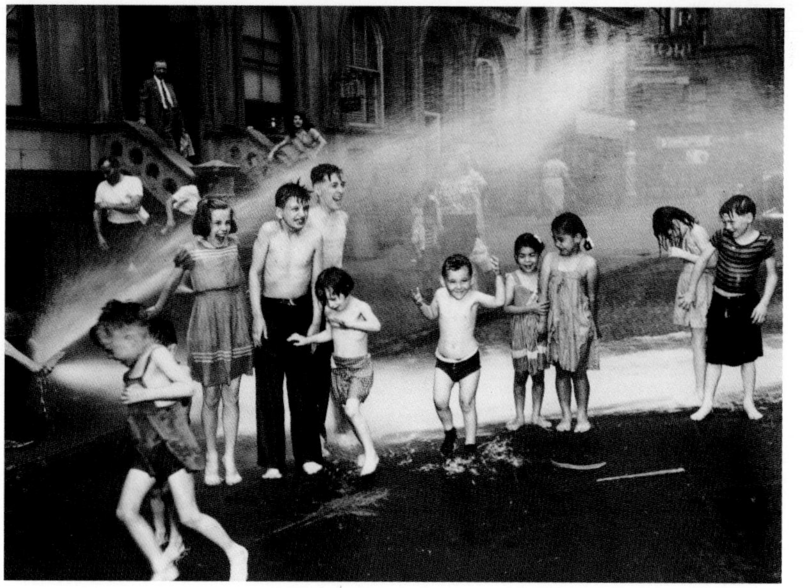

given sufficient space to develop a coherent narrative over page after page.

Photojournalism was perceived as glamorous and the photographers, led by those such as Capa and Cartier-Bresson, had a high self-regard. What they lacked, however, was power. This was to change with the formation of the Magnum photo cooperative in the late 1940s. Magnum established the principle that the copyright of the photograph belonged to the creator. Since one of its founders was Cartier-Bresson, Magnum also played a significant role in elevating the genre from a craft into an art form, and in time photojournalism would be displayed in galleries and reproduced in glossy books. Magnum also created an infrastructure that allowed its members to spend a long time on stories, to reflect, rather than just react to news.

The Second World War shaped the careers of a generation of legendary photographers, such as Robert Capa and W. Eugene Smith. Similarly, the Vietnam War around 20 years later established a new kind of photojournalism, which produced its own legends – photographers such as Larry Burrows, Don McCullin, Gilles Caron and Philip Jones Griffiths. These (sometimes colour) images were brutal in their depiction of war. They were graphic and technically very sharp, since the quality of film and cameras had improved significantly. While Capa saw war in heroic terms, these men clearly identified with the victims of war, rather than with the occupying force. They wanted their photographs to bring about change and to a large extent they succeeded.

Their sensibility, dedication and moral responsibility was adopted by the third generation of war photographers who covered the conflicts in the Middle East in the 1970s and 1980s and in particular the civil war in the former Yugoslavia in the 1990s. Photographers such as Gilles Peress, Luc Delahaye, Roger Hutchings, James Nachtwey, Tom Stoddart, Carol Guzy, Eli Reed and many others were committed, brave and passionate, but less idealistic than their 1960s counterparts. Sceptical and at times distrustful of both their role and the media in general, these photographers also now had digital technology at their fingertips, which revolutionized the taking and transmission of photographs. Images could be taken in a war zone, transmitted down the wire in a matter of just a few seconds and, make it on to the front pages of a newspaper within minutes.

The witnesses

Most of the photographers featured in this book are traditional photojournalists who report from the front-line. Their images of major world events were, and are, seen on the front pages of newspapers. The selection process for a book of this nature is never easy, and inevitably great photographers are going to be omitted. There is not one criterion that justified selection but rather a combination of many factors: technique, originality, consistency, versatility, dedication to the point of obsession to a particular story, political awareness. Above all else, however, everyone in this book has produced memorable and compelling photographs that move us in some way.

There are also photographers here like Martin Parr, Zed Nelson, Sebastião Salgado, W. Eugene Smith and Lewis Hine who are as remarkable as any photojournalist, even though their work falls within the genre of social documentary. This is photography that moves away from the purely dramatic news event and focuses on how we live and interact with each other. These photographers are included in the book because almost all of them started out as "hard news" photographers who then evolved into a different type of storyteller. Boundaries are never clear-cut, and history is not just the unfolding of dramatic events. Social, economic and cultural issues like gun control, migration and tourism are also part of what form, in the words of Henri Cartier-Bresson, the "decisive moments" of history.

The future of photojournalism

People have been writing about the death of photojournalism since the invention of television. Fifty years on, in our celebrity-obsessed world, there might appear to be little room for serious stories and photographs. But even in the "golden age" of *Life* magazine, most of its covers featured film stars and even W. Eugene Smith's seminal essay on the country doctor wasn't a cover story. As long as there are newspapers,current affairs magazines and web sites, there will always be a space for serious news photographs.

There are genuine concerns that the ease with which a photograph can be digitally manipulated means that the camera can indeed lie. Yet photographers have always had the ability to manipulate an image, either by setting a shot up or by making alterations in the darkroom. True, clicking a mouse in Photoshop is a lot easier than spending hours changing a print in the darkroom, but this has made both viewers and the newspapers themselves much more alert to the possibility of anything underhand going on. During the last war in Iraq, the *LA Times* sacked one of its more distinguished photographers for digitally altering the perspective of an image.

Everyone these days has a digital camera or an image-taking device on his or her cell phone. As a result, whatever is going on in the world, there will be someone present who will be able to record it and then sell his or her images to a newspaper or web site. The barriers are therefore being broken down between the committed photojournalist and the amateur snap shooter. There are billions of photographs pinging around in cyberspace and there is a danger of image overload, where we are jaded and feel that we have seen everything there is to see.

Will photojournalism still have an important function in the years to come? The war in Iraq gave us a glimpse into a future where serious photojournalism will simply work in tandem with the amateur opportunist, like the aforementioned American soldier who took those deeply disturbing photographs from the Abu Ghraib prison. If the twenty-first century is as bloody and violent as the century that preceded it, then photojournalism will still have a role to play as an observer and a witness. That is both the bad and good news.

Reuel Golden

PHOTOGRAPHER BIOGRAPHIES

DMITRI BALTERMANTS

RUSSIAN

BORN: POLAND, 1912; DIED: RUSSIA, 1990

Baltermants was born in Poland when it was still a part of Imperial Russia. In 1914, when his father was killed at the beginning of the First World War, he moved with his mother to Moscow. As a child he experienced the turbulent period of the revolution and the civil war. Part of a cultured family, he studied mathematics from 1928 to 1933, and then taught geometry in an artillery school. Self-taught in photography, he worked part-time for *Investia* during this time, then was sent (or "drafted" as he later described it) by the newspaper, official organ of the Communist Party, to photograph the Russian invasion of eastern Poland in 1939. He was active on many of the fronts of the "great patriotic war" and in 1945 he became a photographer on the leading weekly news publication *Ogonyok*. He was the official photographer for Nikita Krushchev's visit to China and for Leonid Brezhnev's visit to the USA.

Key book: *Faces of a Nation: The Rise and Fall of the Soviet Union, 1917–1991* (1996)

LETIZIA BATTAGLIA

ITALIAN

BORN: SICILY, 1935

A journalist by trade, Battaglia turned to photography initially as a means of supplementing her income from writing, then more seriously in the early 1970s when the Palermo communist newspaper for which she worked, *l'Ora*, asked her to become its photo editor. Her work has largely focused on the impact of the Mafia on Sicilian society, although it also contains much more about the daily life of the Sicilian people. She has founded a feminist publishing firm, and became a local municipal councillor for the Green Party, in addition to pursuing a career as a photographer. She is a former winner of the W. Eugene Smith Award.

Key publication: *Passion Justice Freedom: Photographs of Sicily* (1999)

FELICE BEATO

BORN: ITALY OR CORFU C. 1825; DIED: PROBABLY BURMA, C. 1907–08

Beato learnt photography, along with his brother Antoine, from James Robertson (1813–88) in around 1850. He became Robertson's assistant in Malta, then a partner in their work in the Near East, then in Crimea (where they replaced Roger Fenton in 1855) and in India until 1862, before working independently. He was the first Western photographer to reside in Japan from 1863 until 1884, when the failure of his business there led him to the Sudan, then to India and finally Burma, where he established a curio and furniture business.

Key publication: *Of Battle and Beauty: Felice Beato's Photographs of China* (2000)

IAN BERRY

BRITISH

BORN: ENGLAND, 1934

On leaving school, Berry travelled to South Africa in 1952 to work for a family acquaintance, the photographer Roger Madden, who had been an assistant to Ansel Adams. Berry carried out commercial photography, and then began work as a photojournalist. He was a staff photographer on the *Rand Daily News* and then the black *Drum* magazine in 1960, where his political conscience was sharpened. The only photographer at the Sharpeville massacre of 1960, his pictures were not used by *Drum* for fear that the government would close down the magazine. Berry managed somehow to get the pictures to London. He left South Africa in 1961 and joined Magnum in 1962. Assignments have taken him worldwide, documenting Russia's invasion of Czechoslovakia, conflict in Israel, Ireland, Vietnam and Congo, famine in Ethiopia and a long-term project on water.

Key publication: *Living Apart* (1996)

MARGARET BOURKE-WHITE

AMERICAN

BORN: USA,1904; DIED: USA, 1971

In her day, Bourke-White was one of the world's most famous photojournalists, and was immortalized in the Oscar-winning film *Gandhi* (where she was played by Candice Bergman). She took up photography seriously in the mid-1920s while studying at Cornell. Later she moved to Cleveland and started a successful studio, shooting dramatic industrial photographs at night and elegant homes and gardens during the day. She was appointed chief staff photographer of *Fortune* magazine in 1929 after impressing owner Henry Luce. In 1936 she signed on as one of five staff photographers for the new magazine *Life*, a working relationship that would last until the 1960s. During her career she covered everything from the Great Depression to the Second World War and the liberation of the concentration camps. After the war, she worked in Pakistan, South Africa and India and took the last photograph of Mahatma Gandhi before he was assassinated.

Key publication: *You Have Seen Their Faces* (text by Erskine Caldwell), 1937

RENE BURRI

SWISS

BORN: SWITZERLAND, 1933

Burri originally studied design in Zurich, his hometown, taking up photography during his military service between 1953 and 1955. At around this period he came to the attention of Magnum members and was taken under the wing of Cartier-Bresson. He travelled extensively in Europe and the Middle East and in 1959 became a full-time member of Magnum. He then spent six months in South America photographing the gauchos. In the late 1950s and early 1960s he produced two of most famous photo-essays, intimate studies of Picasso and Che Guevara. The latter includes the famous shot of the charismatic revolutionary smoking a cigar. Throughout the 1960s and 1970s he reported from a number of war zones including Vietnam and Cambodia and in the 1980s he went to Beirut.

Key publication: *Photographs* (2004)

LARRY BURROWS

BRITISH

BORN: ENGLAND,1926; DIED: SOUTH-EAST ASIA, 1971

Part of a generation of war photographers who made their name covering the conflict in Vietnam, Burrows worked almost exclusively in the region from 1962 until his death, while on assignment, in 1971. Burrows started his photographic career aged 16 as a lab-room technician in the London offices of *Life*, eventually working his way up to the position of staff photographer on the magazine. Prior to Vietnam, he covered conflicts in the Middle East and the Congo, as well as more gentle assignments such as photographing the Taj

Mahal and British society. During his lifetime he won many awards, including Magazine Photographer of the Year in 1967, and his work appeared on no fewer than 15 *Life* magazine covers.
Key publication: *Larry Burrows: Vietnam* (2002)

ROBERT CAPA

HUNGARIAN (NATURALIZED AMERICAN)

BORN: AUSTRO-HUNGARY, 1913; DIED: INDOCHINA, 1954

Endre Friedman (Robert Capa) was brought up in what was then the Austro-Hungarian Empire. Alienated by the right wing and anti-Semitic Horthy regime, he left for Germany in 1930 to follow studies in political science. Penniless, he found work as a darkroom technician at the Dephot agency. Its editor, Simon Guttman, taught him the emergent techniques of photojournalism, its business principles and the importance of the picture story. He scored his first scoop with his pictures of the Russian Communist, Leon Trotsky. After the rise of Nazism in 1933, he migrated to Paris. He made his name during the Spanish Civil War (1936–39), when *Life* magazine described him as "The world's greatest war photographer". He carried on working through most of the Second World War, and co-founded the Magnum agency in 1947. While photographing "one last war", he was killed when he stepped on a landmine in French Indochina on 25 May, 1954.
Key publication: *Robert Capa: The Definitive Collection* (2001)

GILLES CARON

FRENCH

BORN: FRANCE, 1939; DIED: CAMBODIA, C. 1970

Caron first experienced war during military service in the Algerian colonial war of 1958–61. After working as an assistant to photographer Patrice Molinard, he took up photojournalism first as a member of the Apis agency in 1966, then as co-founder (with Raymond Depardon) of Gamma photo agency in 1967. Dubbed "the French Robert Capa", he covered the Six-Day War in Israel in 1967, conflicts in Vietnam and Biafra (Nigeria) in 1968, the May 1968 student demonstrations in Paris, riots in Northern Ireland in 1969, anti-Soviet demonstrations in Prague in 1969, and the Toubou uprising against the central government in Chad in 1970. On 4 April of that same year his meteoric career was cut short when he went missing in a Khmer Rouge-controlled area of Cambodia. His fate is unknown to this day.
Key publication: *Gilles Caron* (1998)

HENRI CARTIER-BRESSON

FRENCH

BORN: FRANCE, 1908; DIED: FRANCE, 2004

Born to an extremely wealthy family, Cartier-Bresson originally trained as a painter. His decisive moment came in the 1930s, when he discovered the Leica, a light and portable 35mm camera that liberated the composing and taking of photographs. He started out by taking surreal art-based images, but with the rise of fascism his pictures became more photojournalistic and politically motivated. In 1947 he co-founded Magnum, the highly influential photographic agency. He is best known for his concept of "the decisive moment" in photography, a philosophy and working method that is still influencing the way people take photographs today. A tireless traveller, he spent much of the 1940s, 1950s and 1960s working in places such as China, India, the USA, Cuba and the USSR. By the late 1960s, his interest in photography had waned and he returned to his original love of drawing and painting. He remained a somewhat enigmatic semi-recluse until his death in 2004.
Key publication: *The Decisive Moment* (1952)

LUC DELAHAYE

FRENCH

BORN: FRANCE, 1962

One of the most skilled and versatile photojournalists of the past 20 years, Delahaye has constantly reinvented himself and his audience. Throughout the 1980s and 1990s he worked in Lebanon, Rwanda, Chechnya and Bosnia. In the past few years he has covered the conflicts in Iraq and Afghanistan and been extensively exhibited in the USA and Europe. A member of Magnum for 10 years until 2004, his work has been published all over the world and he is also a contract photographer with *Newsweek*. He has had six books published and won every major award going, including The Robert Capa Gold Medal (twice), the ICP Infinity award, and first prize at the World Press Photo Awards (three times). In 2005 he was the winner of the Inaugural Fine Art Deutsche Borse Photography Prize.
Key publication: *Luc Delahaye: History* (2003)

ALFRED EISENSTAEDT

AMERICAN

BORN: WEST PRUSSIA, 1898; DIED: USA, 1995

A photographer with the Associated Press in Berlin in the early 1930s, Eisenstaedt fled Nazi persecution to start a new life in the USA. He joined *Life* magazine in 1935 as one of five staff photographers when it was still known as "project X". "Eisie" was synonymous with the very best of *Life* and during a career spanning 50 years with the highly influential magazine he shot 80 covers and worked on over 2,500 assignments. He took the photograph of a couple celebrating the end of the Second World War with a passionate embrace in Times Square, which became one of the most famous images of the twentieth century.
Key publication: *Eisenstaedt: Remembrances* (1999)

ROGER FENTON

BRITISH

BORN: ENGLAND, 1819; DIED: 1869

Born into a family of bankers and mill-owners, Fenton initially studied law before turning to painting, receiving an academic training in Paris. Inspired by the Pre-Raphaelites on his return to Britain around 1847–48, he exhibited work in this style at the Royal Academy in 1850–51, but soon thereafter took up photography. From 1852 to 1860 Fenton was enormously active, both as a photographer and as promoter of the new art and profession. He was a founder member of the Photographic Society of London, and the first official photographer of the British Museum. He gave up the medium in 1862, returning to the practice of law until his death.
Key publication: *All the Mighty World: The photographs of Roger Fenton, 1852–60* (2004)

ALEXANDER GARDNER

BRITISH

BORN: SCOTLAND, 1821; DIED: USA, 1882

One of the pioneers of unflinching war photography, Gardner began experimenting with photography in 1851 after seeing an exhibition of Matthew Brady's work. He moved to New York a few years later and started working for Brady's studio. He became an expert in the new collodion (wet-plate) process that was replacing the daguerreotype, gaining a reputation as an outstanding portrait photographer. In 1861 he was part of a team of around 20 photographers sent by Brady to cover the American Civil War. Although Brady did not actually take the photographs, he signed them in his name, a practice that alienated Gardner, who went on to open his own studio in Washington, DC. He later became the official photographer of the Union Pacific Railroad.
Key publication: *Gardner's Photographic Sketchbook of the War* (1866)

JAN GRARUP

DANISH

BORN: DENMARK, 1968

At the age of 15, Grarup began freelancing after school for a local newspaper. In the late 1980s he studied photography at the Danish School of Journalism. While still a student, he began covering various conflicts, beginning with the fall of Romania's communist regime in 1989. After graduating in 1991, Grarup joined the staff of the daily newspaper *Ekstra Bladet*, where he began covering war, conflict and genocide in Europe and the Middle East. Currently a staff photographer for the daily *Politiken*, Grarup is represented by the Rapho agency in Paris. In 2000 he won first place in the World Press Photo awards for his coverage of the war in Kosovo. He is a two-time winner of the UNICEF Children's Award, and a two-time finalist in the W. Eugene Smith memorial fund for humanistic photography.

CAROL GUZY

AMERICAN

BORN: USA, 1956

Guzy originally trained as a nurse, but after graduating she decided to pursue a career in photography. While attending the Art Institute at Fort Lauderdale in Florida, she did an internship at the *Miami Herald* and joined the paper full-time in 1980, working there until 1988. At the paper, she received her first Pulitzer Prize for her work covering mudslides in Colombia. In 1988 she moved to the *Washington Post*, where she still works. Guzy has since won two more Pulitzer Prizes for her coverage in 1995 of the American intervention in Haiti and more recently in 2000 for her work on the plight of refugees from Kosovo.

BERT HARDY

BRITISH

BORN: ENGLAND, 1913; DIED: 1995

A true Cockney, Hardy came from a poor working-class family of seven children. Leaving school at 14 to work in a darkroom for 10 shillings (50p) a week, he wanted to be a successful photographer. A keen cyclist, he managed to acquire an early Leica to take pictures of races, and began to work for picture agencies. From 1940 he worked for *Picture Post*, then was mobilized as an Army war photographer until 1945, during which time he covered major campaigns such as D-Day, the liberation of Paris and the invasion of Germany, as well as the opening of the Nazi concentration camps. He continued with *Picture Post* until its demise in 1957, when he turned to advertising photography and printing.
Key publication: *Bert Hardy: My Life* (1985)

LEWIS HINE

AMERICAN

BORN: USA, 1874; DIED: USA, 1940

Hine took up the camera seriously in around 1904 to document the life of immigrants on Ellis Island in New York. After meeting Paul Strand in 1905, who encouraged his "sociological" photography, he began to document child labourers in 1907, and shortly after was appointed photographer to the Pittsburgh Survey, a major investigation of living and working conditions in the heavily industrialized city. From 1908 he served as staff photographer for the National Child Labor Committee, travelling the southern and eastern states to document working conditions in factories, mines and farms. From 1917 to 1920 the Red Cross sent Hine to photograph wartime conditions in Europe. In 1920 he began as series of Work Portraits, and in 1930–31 he photographed the last stages of construction of the Empire State Building.
Key publication: *America and Lewis Hine: Photographs 1904–1940* (1997)

HEINRICH HOFFMAN

GERMAN

BORN: GERMANY, 1885; DIED: GERMANY, 1957

The son of a photographer, Hoffman worked in his father's photography shop until 1914 when he joined the German Army as an official photographer. His first book of photographs, based on his experiences in the First World War, was published in 1919. In 1920 Hoffman joined the Nazi Party, (NSDAP) and became friendly with Adolf Hitler. Named as Hitler's official photographer, he was a close associate and travelled widely with him. Between 1920 and 1945 he took hundreds of thousands of photographs of the Nazi leader. Hoffman became extremely wealthy and politically influential, and was elected to the Reichstag in 1940. Arrested in 1945 by the Allies, he was sentenced to 10 years' imprisonment in 1947 for war profiteering.
Key publication: *Hitler Was My Friend* (1955)

FRANK HURLEY

AUSTRALIAN

BORN: AUSTRALIA; 1885; DIED: AUSTRALIA, 1962

Australia's most famous photojournalist, Hurley was present at some of the key moments of twentieth-century history, including both world wars and as the official photographer for Ernest Shackleton's expedition to Antarctica, aboard the *Endurance*. He originally ran away to work on the docks aged 14, and at 17 bought his first camera. In 1910, aged 25, he went on his first trip to the Antarctic with the Australian explorer Douglas Mawson, and this was the start of a career of relentless travelling. Almost immediately afterward, he went on his most famous voyage accompanying Shackleton for 22 months between 1914 and 1916. In 1917, he became official photographer for the Australian army during the First World War and was a witness to the third battle of Ypres. Between the wars he returned to Antarctica and worked in New Guinea, the Middle East, Europe and the USA. He was also a keen filmmaker. During the Second World War he repeated his role as a photographer for the Australian army.
Key publication: *South with "Endurance": The Antarctic Photographs of Frank Hurley* (2001)

ROGER HUTCHINGS

BRITISH

BORN: ENGLAND, 1952

After studying documentary photography at Newport, Wales, Hutchings started freelancing for the *Observer* in 1983, and a year later joined Network Photographers. Between 1986 and 1990 he worked in Sudan, Sri Lanka and India and covered the fall of communism in Eastern Europe. Between 1992 and 1997 he worked extensively in Bosnia and Croatia documenting the conflict and break-up of Yugoslavia. He has also photographed stories from Haiti, Turkey and Berlin. In recent years he has moved away from traditional market-led photojournalism and turned his attention to the fashion industry, leading to a book collaboration with Giorgio Armani in 2002. He is presently working on another book, *Armani in China*. A winner of every major photojournalism award, he has also chaired the World Press Photo awards.

Key publication: *Bosnia* (2001)

PHILIP JONES GRIFFITHS

BRITISH

BORN: WALES, 1936

Jones Griffiths started his career freelancing for the Manchester *Guardian* and the *Observer*. In 1962 he covered the Algerian War, which started a life-long career documenting conflict. He photographed the Vietnam War from 1966 to 1968, returning in 1970. In 1971 he published *Vietnam Inc*, the definitive photographic account of the war, which mobilized public opinion and helped bring the conflict to an end. He has also worked extensively in the Middle East, Cambodia, Thailand and Northern Ireland. An associate member of Magnum since 1967, he was also President of the cooperative for five years. His work has appeared in every major magazine in the world and he has shot assignments in 120 countries.

Key publication: *Vietnam Inc* (1971)

YEVGENY KHALDEI

RUSSIAN

BORN: UKRAINE, 1917; DIED: RUSSIA, 1997

Khaldei was fascinated by photography from childhood, and at the age of 15 made his first camera from a cardboard box and his grandmother's spectacles. In 1936 he joined the official Soviet press agency TASS, and his work took him to all the major theatres of war – from 1941 to 1945 as a member of the Red Army. Despite the popularity of his work among the Soviet leaders, from Stalin to Gorbachev, his career suffered on a number of occasions because of anti-Semitism, and he was forced to retire in 1972. It was only after the collapse of communism in 1991 that Khaldei's work became known in the West.

Key publication: *Witness to History: The Photographs of Yevgeny Khaldei* (1997)

JOSEF KOUDELKA

CZECH (FRENCH CITIZEN FROM 1979)

BORN: MORAVIA, 1938

Koudelka took up photography as an adolescent, when he befriended a local baker who was an enthusiastic amateur photographer. At this stage of his life he was also obsessed with aeroplanes and trained as an aviation engineer, a career he followed from 1961 until 1967, when he became a full-time photographer. Active as a freelance from 1961, in theatre and in a long-term project on Slovakian gypsies,he took pictures of the Soviet invasion of Prague in 1968 that were smuggled to the West and published to great acclaim. He left Czechoslovakia in 1970 and was officially stateless until 1979, though he had political asylum in the UK. Koudelka became a member of Magnum in 1974. He has worked long-term on a project about gypsies throughout Europe.

Key publication: *Exiles* (1988)

JOACHIM LADEFOGED

DANISH

BORN: GERMANY, 1971

After his original dream of becoming a professional football player was curtailed by injury, Ladefoged studied at the prestigious state-run Danish School of Journalism. His first job was on a small regional newspaper in Denmark. In 1995 he moved on to become a staff photographer at the national newspaper *Politiken*. Between 1997 and 1999 he worked extensively in Albania, Japan, China and the Yemen; he covered the 2004 Olympic Games and most recently the tsunami in South-East Asia. He is the newest member of the prestigious photo collective VII and in a short career has already won three World Press Photo awards, the first ever Dane to do so, and the Essie Award/LIFE Magazine award for Best Photo Essay in 2000.

Key publication: *Albanians* (2000)

JERRY LAMPEN

DUTCH

BORN: HOLLAND, 1961

Lampen's first career was as a professional actor, but after meeting a photographer in 1981 who gave him an idea for a photo, which was published a week later in a newspaper, Lampen gave up the stage for good. He started working for various Dutch agencies and two of the country's biggest newspapers, shooting a variety of domestic stories. In 1990 he started freelancing for Reuters and in 1992 joined the agency on a full-time basis. Now one of its star photographers, he has covered the Olympics and the World Cup, and has shot in Gaza, Pakistan and Iraq. A World Press Photo award winner, he has also won the Photographer of the Year award in the Netherlands.

DOROTHEA LANGE

AMERICAN

BORN: USA, 1895; DIED: USA, 1965

Lange, who had studied under the pictorialist Clarence White and worked for a time with Arnold Genthe, started her own successful portrait studio in San Francisco in 1918 and married painter Maynard Dixon two years later. She abandoned portraiture in the early 1930s after discovering documentary photography. In 1935 she divorced Dixon to marry the economist Paul Taylor, with whom she collaborated for the rest of her life. She took photographs for various government agencies, most notably the Farm Security Administration, between 1934 and 1945. With Taylor, she published *An American Exodus* in 1939, and in 1940 became the first woman to win a Guggenheim Fellowship for photography. Sidelined by health problems after the war, she resumed work in the early 1950s, co-founding *Aperture* magazine with Ansel Adams and others, shooting for *Life* magazine and travelling the world with Taylor.

Key publication: *Dorothea Lange: Photographs of a Lifetime* (1998)

GERD LUDWIG

GERMAN

BORN: GERMANY, 1947

After studying photography in Essen, Ludwig graduated in 1972. The following year he co-founded VISUM, Germany's first photographer-owned photo agency. In 1975 he moved to Hamburg and started working for *Stern*, *Geo*, *Spiegel*, *Time* and *Life*. In 1984 he moved to New York and continued shooting travel stories for all the major publications. In the early 1990s he signed as a contracted photographer for the *National Geographic*, focusing on the social changes in Germany and Eastern Europe. Now based in Los Angeles, Ludwig has photographed in over 70 countries and his work has been exhibited extensively in Europe and the USA.
Key publication: *Broken Empire: After the Fall of the USSR* (2002)

DON McCULLIN

BRITISH

BORN: ENGLAND, 1935

Brought up in a working-class district of north London, McCullin worked initially in a commercial art studio, and learnt photography in the RAF during National Service, 1953–55. His pictures of a North London gang (first published in 1959) brought him acclaim, and he began a freelance career for the London press until 1966, when he joined the *Sunday Times Magazine* as a staff photographer, a post he held until 1983. Since 1961 he has photographed conflicts, famines and human disasters throughout Europe, Africa, Asia, the Middle East and South America – interspersed with travel and landscape photography.
Key publication: *Sleeping with Ghosts: A Life's Work in Photography* (1996)

PETER MAGUBANE

SOUTH AFRICAN

BORN: SOUTH AFRICA,1932

Magubane started working for the influential *Drum* magazine in 1954, first as a driver, then as a darkroom assistant. A year later he got his first assignment covering the ANC convention. He later covered the Treason Trials and the Sharpeville massacre in 1960. Between 1963 and 1964 he worked in London as a freelance, returning to South Africa in 1966. From 1967 to 1980 he worked for the *Rand Daily Mail*. In 1976 he documented the Soweto student uprisings, which brought him international recognition and a number of awards. He was there to photograph the release of Nelson Mandela, but now has moved away from photojournalism and concentrates on travel and fine art photography.
Key publication: *Magubane South Africa* (1978)

ALEX MAJOLI

ITALIAN

BORN: ITALY, 1971

A full-time photographer since 1986, Majoli joined the Grazia Neri agency, Italy's leading photographic agency, in 1990, and remained there until 1995. In that period he covered religions in Italy, as well as the new Republic of Macedonia and post-communist Albania. He also went to Yugoslavia several times to cover the conflict. In 1994 and 1995 he produced his most famous project, documenting the closure of the notorious Leros mental asylum in Greece. He has worked in Brazil, China, Congo, Iraq and all over Europe. His photographs have appeared in *Newsweek*, *National Geographic*, the *New York Times* and *Vanity Fair*. Since 1997 he has been shooting a long-term essay on port cities in various parts of the world. At the time of going to press, he was working on a book on the US Democratic National Convention of 2004. He has been a full-time member of Magnum since 2001.
Key publication: *Leros* (2004)

MARY ELLEN MARK

AMERICAN

BORN: USA, 1940

After graduating in 1964 with a Masters degree in photography, Mark spent the next two yeas working in Europe and New York. In the late 1960s and early 1970s she started supplementing her photojournalism with shooting production stills on the sets of Hollywood movies. Working on *One Flew Over the Cuckoo's Nest* inspired her to produce her famous essay on a mental hospital, called *Ward 81*. In the 1970s she started working in India and completed a project on prostitutes in Bombay called *Falkland Road*. In the 1980s she shot a seminal essay on Seattle's street children called *Streetwise* and spent several years photographing the troubled Damm family of Los Angeles. Her work has appeared in the world's leading publications and she has won many photographic prizes including the Cornell Capa Award from the International Center of Photography. She has also published 14 books.
Key publication: *Mark Ellen Mark: American Odyssey* (1999)

PETER MARLOW

BRITISH

BORN: ENGLAND, 1952

Marlow graduated with a degree in psychology. His first job as a professional photographer was working for Cunard on a cruise ship. He later joined the prestigious Paris-based photographic agency Sygma and covered the war in Lebanon and the revolution in Iran. In 1980 he joined Magnum and moved away from war photography toward more social documentary work. During the 1980s he worked on his epic project on Liverpool and in 1991 was given an assignment by the French government to photograph Amiens. During the 1990s he was also working on *Non Places*, a body of work on fragmentary landscapes. His work has appeared in *GQ*, the *Sunday Times*, *Arena* and the *Independent*. He has also had solo shows in Japan, Liverpool and London.
Key publication: *Liverpool – Looking out to Sea* (1993)

SUSAN MEISELAS

AMERICAN

BORN: USA, 1948

Meiselas first studied photography while at Harvard, where she received her MA in visual communication. Between 1972 and 1973 she ran workshops for teachers and children in the South Bronx. Her first major photography project was *Carnival Strippers*, for which she spent three summers travelling with her subjects across the USA. She spent two years covering the civil war in Nicaragua and became a full member of Magnum in 1980. In the 1980s she also documented the civil war in El Salvador, where she photographed the unmarked graves of four American nuns, which prompted a US congressional investigation. Throughout much of the 1990s she worked on a visual history of Kurdistan including starting a web site dedicated to the cause of the Kurdish refugees.
Key publication: *Nicaragua* (1981)

GIDEON MENDEL

SOUTH AFRICAN

BORN: SOUTH AFRICA, 1959

A multi-award-winning documentary photographer, Gideon Mendel is best known for his epic project (he has been working on it for the past ten years and it is still ongoing) on the social, cultural and economic impact of the AIDS epidemic in Africa. He began his career as a photographer on the *Johannesburg Star* in 1983, focusing in particular on the popular widespread grassroots campaigns against apartheid. In 1985 he joined the prestigious Agence France-Presse photographic agency and began freelancing for international publications such as *Stern Geo* and the *Guardian*. In 1990 he moved to London and joined the Network Photographers agency. Over the past 10 years Mendel's work has earned six World Press Photo awards, the W Eugene Smith Award for Humanistic Photography and the Nikon Feature Photographer of the Year award.

Key publication: *A Broken Landscape: HIV & AIDS in Africa* (2003)

BERTRAND MEUNIER

FRENCH

BORN: FRANCE, 1965

Meunier is part of a new generation of French photojournalists who are following in the footsteps of Marc Riboud and Cartier-Bresson. Like these two legends, he is a relentless traveller who is fascinated with documenting Asia and in particular China. Self-taught, he first visited China 15 years ago and in 1997 he began documenting the country's changing economic and social landscape. He has also worked in Pakistan, Mexico and Iran. He has been a member of the VU agency since 2000. His work has been exhibited at the festival of photojournalism in Perpignan in France, and in Italy. His images have also been published in some of the world's leading publications such as *Newsweek* and *Paris Match*.

DAVID MODELL

BRITISH

BORN: ENGLAND, 1969

After leaving school at 16, David Modell began taking photographs of local news events, which he then tried to sell to magazines and newspapers. After building up a portfolio, he started working for the *Sunday Telegraph* at the age of 18 and continued to shoot for that newspaper on a regular basis for the next two years. He moved on to the UK colour supplement magazines such as the *Sunday Times Magazine* and the *Independent Magazine* and started working on longer-term assignments. His photo essays have won many national and international awards and he has been extensively exhibited. He has also branched out into making documentary films and his work has been acclaimed at the Royal Television Society awards.

RALPH MORSE

AMERICAN

BORN: USA, 1918

Morse's first job after graduating from high school was working for a photographer as an assistant. A quick learner, by 1939 he was shooting for *Life* after being spotted by Alfred Eisenstaedt. His first assignment in a 30-year career for the magazine was to cover Thornton Wilder making *Our Town*. During the Second World War he covered the US marines at Guadalcanal, the Doolittle raid in Tokyo and General Patton's drive across France. Morse was the only civilian photographer who recorded the surrender of the German armies to General Eisenhower and he also covered the Nuremberg War Trials. In 1958 he began a 15-year period of covering the space programme. During a varied career for *Life*, he shot numerous sports, arts and science stories.

Key publication: *Life Photographers: What They Saw* (1998)

CARL MYDANS

AMERICAN

BORN: USA, 1907; DIED: USA, 2004

Mydans started out on the *Boston Globe* as a reporter, but by the mid-1930s he had started taking a camera with him on assignments. He was hired by the Farm Security Administration, to take photographs of impoverished farm workers. He became the new *Life* magazine's fifth photographer in 1935. In 1937 he met the *Life* journalist Shelly Smith, who become his wife, and together they formed a formidable writer-photographer team. They covered the Second World War together in the Far East and were interned by the Japanese for 22 months. After his release, Mydans went on to shoot some of his most famous images of the Allied invasion of Europe and General MacArthur landing in the Philippines. He carried on working for *Life* until the early 1970s.

Key publication: *More Than Meets the Eye* (1959)

JAMES NACHTWEY

AMERICAN

BORN: USA, 1948

Nachtwey grew up in Massachusetts, studied art history and political science at Dartmouth College, then taught himself photography. In 1980 he moved to New York City to pursue magazine photography. Since then, Nachtwey has ventured to most of the world's bloodiest conflicts, including wars in Central America, the Middle East, Africa, the Balkans and the former Soviet republics. A *Time* magazine contract photographer since 1984, Nachtwey was a member of Magnum (1986–2001) and became a founding member of the photo agency VII. He has won numerous awards, including the Robert Capa gold medal five times, POY's Magazine Photographer of the Year seven times, the World Press Photo award, several ICP Infinity awards and the W. Eugene Smith Memorial Grant.

Key publication: *Inferno* (1999)

ZED NELSON

BRITISH

BORN: UGANDA, 1966

A graduate of Westminster University, with a BA Honours in photography, Nelson has spent the past 15 years on magazine assignments and, when possible, pursuing his own long-term projects and themes. His work in the early to mid-1990s took him to Somalia, Afghanistan and Angola where he covered war, famine and political turmoil. Over a period of three years he documented America's gun culture and the project known as *Gun Nation* brought him widespread international acclaim and five major photography awards. Since then, he has produced essays on the porn industry, obesity in the USA, plastic surgery in Iran and *Toxic Texas – The Environmental Legacy of George W Bush*. His work has been widely exhibited and published in every major magazine.

Key publication: *Gun Nation* (2001)

MARTIN PARR

BRITISH

BORN: ENGLAND, 1952

Parr studied photography at Manchester Polytechnic in the early 1970s and gained early recognition in the UK and Europe when he won three successive awards from The Arts Council in the late 1970s. He became a member of Magnum in 1994 and is now one of England's most prolific and high profile photographers whose idiosyncratic style is instantly recognizable the world over. His work has appeared in all the major magazines and been exhibited at some of the world's most important museums including the Tate Modern and New York's Metropolitan Museum of Modern Art. He has also directed commercials and made television documentary films both for the BBC and in Europe. Parr has also curated photographic festivals, written about photography and had close to 20 books on his work published.

Key publication: *Martin Parr* (2002)

JUDAH PASSOW

ISRAELI/AMERICAN

BORN: ISRAEL, 1949

A graduate of Boston University, Judah Passow has been working on assignments for American and European magazines and newspapers since 1978, specializing in the Middle East. He is also one of the co-founders of Network Photographers, the influential British picture agency dedicated to pure photojournalism. His extensive work on the Israeli-Palestinian conflict has earned him four World Press Photo awards. *Days of Rage*, his CD-ROM brought out in 1995 and based on his work in Beirut from 1982 to 1985, received critical acclaim for its journalistic integrity and technical innovation. In 1998 he was artist in residence at the ICA. His photographs have been exhibited in Europe, Israel and the USA.

GILLES PERESS

FRENCH

BORN: FRANCE, 1946

Originally a philosophy student, Peress's worldview was shaped by the Paris riots of the late 1960s. In 1970 he embarked on his first photography project, a portrait of a French coal-mining village, which brought him to the attention of Henri Cartier-Bresson and an invitation to join Magnum. He next went to Northern Ireland where he made his international name with images of Bloody Sunday. Since then, he has embarked on an ongoing project called *Hate Thy Brother*, which has taken him to some of the most bloody conflicts in recent times including Bosnia and the genocide in Rwanda. He has also produced major bodies of work on Iran, the fall of the Berlin Wall and 9/11.

Key publication: *Telex: Iran* (1997)

RAGHU RAI

INDIAN

BORN: INDIA, 1942

Originally trained as an engineer, Rai joined the staff of the *Hindustan Times* in 1965. In 1966 he became chief photographer for *The Statesman*. In 1976 he quit the paper and became a freelance, joining Magnum a year later. Between 1982 and 1992 he was director of photography for India's leading news magazine, *India Today*. During this period he produced his seminal work on the Bhopal tragedy, which brought him international acclaim. His images have appeared in most of the world's leading publications including *Time*, *Geo*, *Paris Match*, the *Sunday Times* and *National Geographic*. He has served on the jury of the World Press Photo awards and his photographs have also been widely exhibited all over the world.

Key publication: *Exposure: Portrait Of A Corporate Crime* (2004)

ELI REED

AMERICAN

BORN: USA, 1946

Reed studied pictorial illustration at the Newark School of Fine and Industrial Arts, graduating in 1969. After freelancing for several years, he was a staff photographer for newspapers including the *Detroit News* (1978) and the *San Francisco Examiner* (1980). A Nieman Fellow at Harvard University in 1982, Reed joined Magnum as a nominee in 1983 and became a full member in 1988. He completed assignments for *National Geographic*, *Life*, *Time* and other publications. Major projects include his documentation of the African-American experience in the USA from the 1970s onward and a long-term study on Beirut (1983–87). Reed has published several books and won major awards including the W. Eugene Smith Memorial Grant in 1992.

Key publication: *Black in America* (1997)

EUGENE RICHARDS

AMERICAN.

BORN: USA, 1944

Richards studied photography in the late 1960s at MIT and began his career working in eastern Arkansas for the Volunteers in Service to America. Within two years he had helped start a social services organization and community newspaper for which he shot stories. He later joined Magnum, carrying on its best tradition of concerned social photography. He has spent most of his career documenting the underprivileged and suffering within American society. Some of his photo essays have resulted in books, including *Exploding into Life* (1986), *Below the Line: Living Poor in America* (1987) and *Cocaine True Cocaine Blue* (1994). He has won all the major photojournalism awards and his work has appeared in *Newsweek*, the *New York Times* and countless other publications.

Key publication: *Cocaine True Cocaine Blue* (1994)

HENRYK ROSS

POLISH-ISRAELI

BORN: POLAND, 1910; DIED: ISRAEL, 1991

Before the Second World War, Ross worked as a press photographer in Lodz, Poland, until he went into war service during the brief campaign that ended in Polish defeat in October 1939. Confined to the Lodz ghetto in 1940, he became one of two official photographers. Later he went into hiding, buried his negatives, and was in Auschwitz when it was liberated by Soviet forces in January 1945. Emigrating to Israel in 1950, he worked as a photographer and engraver. During his lifetime Ross released only a certain proportion of the surviving photographs from the 6,000 or so he had made during 1940–44.

Key publication: *Lodz Ghetto Album* (2004)

SEBASTIAO SALGADO

BRAZILIAN

BORN: BRAZIL, 1944

Originally Salgado trained as an economist, becoming interested in photography in the early 1970s when he was working for the International Coffee Organization. He first made his name while on assignment for the *New York Times Magazine* and photographed at close hand the assassination attempt on President Reagan. In 1984–85 he produced his famous essay on famine in the African Sahel. Between 1986 and 1992 he shot *Workers*, one of the greatest photo essays of all time. Between 1993 and 1999 he photographed *Migrations*, which is also a seminal and groundbreaking piece of work. His work has been extensively exhibited and published all over the world and he has also won all the major photography prizes.

Key publication: *Workers* (1993)

W. EUGENE SMITH

AMERICAN

BORN, USA, 1918; DIED: USA, 1978

Smith took his first images at the age of 15 and shortly after started selling them to newspapers. He moved to New York to study photography and started working for *Newsweek* magazine in 1937. Between 1938 and 1943 he worked for the famous Black Star photo agency. In 1939 he started shooting for *Life*, with whom he would have a stormy relationship throughout his career. While covering the Second World War for the magazine, he shot some of his most famous images, but he also suffered severe injuries. After a two-year break, he rejoined the magazine from 1947 to 1955. He also joined Magnum in the 1950s, resigning a few years later. His popularity waned in the 1960s and 1970s, but he continued to work on significant projects including extensive essays from Japan where he lived for a year. After his death, his work was rediscovered and he is now revered as the USA's greatest ever photojournalist.

Key publication: *Let Truth be the Prejudice: W. Eugene Smith His Life, and Photographs* (1984)

JOHN STANMEYER

AMERICAN

BORN: USA, 1964

Stanmeyer attended the Florida Art Institute, majoring in art and fashion photography. After graduating in 1983, he moved to Milan and began shooting fashion for *Interview*, *Vanity Fair*, *Harper's Bazaar* and other magazines. While on sabbatical in 1987 he took up street photography in Madrid. In 1989, after returning to the USA, Stanmeyer began pursuing photojournalism as a staff photographer for the *Tampa Tribune*. From there he began documenting international stories including the Sudanese civil war, conditions in Eastern Europe after the end of communism, and unrest in Haiti. He moved to Hong Kong in 1996 and now resides in Bali, Indonesia. A *Time* contract photographer since 1998 and a co-founding member of VII, Stanmeyer has won the Robert Capa Gold Medal (2000) and was named POY's Magazine Photographer of the Year in 1999.

Key publication: *Tsunami: a Document of Devastation* (2005)

TOM STODDART

BRITISH

BORN: ENGLAND, 1953

Stoddart's first job was working for the Berwick-on-Tweed *Advertiser* in the photography department at the age of 16. Since then he has travelled to more than 50 countries shooting virtually every big story of the past 20 years. In 1989 he covered the fall of the Berlin Wall, Rwanda, and the election of Nelson Mandela, and he spent four years in the early 1990s documenting the conflict in Saravejo. In 1997 he was given exclusive access by Tony Blair to photograph his victorious election campaign. In 1998 he shot famine-ravaged Sudan and he was embedded with the British troops in the last Gulf War. His images have appeared in the world's leading publications and he has also won several important photography awards including the World Press Photo award and the Visa d'or Perpignan.

Key book: *iWitness* (2004)

WEEGEE (ARTHUR FELLIG)

HUNGARIAN (NATURALIZED AMERICAN)

BORN: AUSTRO-HUNGARY, 1899; DIED: USA, 1969

Weegee's photographic career began in New York in 1913, where he had a series of jobs as a portrait and street photographer. In 1921 he began press work for the *New York Times*, moving to Acme Photos in New York in 1924, and working there until 1935, after which he freelanced. He specialized in crime photography and from 1938 he was allowed to use a police radio in his car so that he could get to crime scenes rapidly. For the next 10 years he built a career as a publicity-seeking photographer of lurid events – murders, fires and bizarre accidents. In 1947 he left New York for Hollywood to work on a film about his life, and he remained there as extra and photographer until 1952. After his return to New York, he made several short films and experimented with optical distortions, a subject that absorbed him until his death in 1969.

Key publication: *Weegee's New York Photographs 1935-1960* (2000)

LI ZHENSHENG

CHINESE

BORN: CHINA, 1940

The Sino-Japanese War, and the subsequent civil war between communists and nationalists in which his 17-year-old brother was killed, disrupted Li's early life. He was a trained cinematographer but was appointed a news photographer by the government, and from 1963 to 1982 worked on a daily paper in Harbin, capital of the province nearest to the USSR. He photographed the early stages of the Cultural Revolution (1966–76), hiding negatives that the authorities would have destroyed. Denounced in 1968 as "bourgeois", he was sent to the countryside for "rectification" – two years' hard labour. From 1982 he began to teach photography at Beijing University. His work came to light again in 1988, during the beginnings of the liberalization of the Chinese communist regime.

Key publication: *Red-color News Soldier* (2003)

DMITRI BALTERMANTS

Baltermants made several of the most telling pictures of the Russian side of the Second World War. His best-known images show the human suffering associated with events like the battle around Kerch in the Crimea (176,000 Russian dead) in 1942 with a stark yet humanist depiction. The horror of the savagery wreaked upon these people by the Nazi war machine is curiously mitigated by images of mourners tending to the bodies of their family or friends, supplicants to their suffering. It is clear that Baltermants had a pacifist vision, but that his place in the front-line, as a soldier-reporter, took him to scenes of unbelievably brutal carnage. Like so many of his peers, Baltermants's work is steeped in the great Russian photographic tradition, particularly in the struggles between formalism and socialist realism that raged in the 1920s and 1930s. Composed with immense graphic power and yet replete with a strongly humanist perspective, the photographs justify Baltermants's reputation as the "Soviet Capa". The dramatic construction of Baltermants's images, such as the extraordinary *Attack* of 1941, may have served an important propaganda function as well as making their points as evidence of the sheer barbarism of the war in Russia.

One of the problems of reviewing the work of photojournalists who were active during the Soviet era is that their pictures are refracted through the ways in which Soviet media represented the great historical events of the period. They photographed much else besides the horrors of war, but how many of their pictures remain? And when were they seen, and by whom? The history of this photography could only begin to be written after 1991, and the quality of the work is only now beginning to be appreciated. For as Baltermants would write much later, "We photographers make magnificent shots of wars, fires, earthquakes, and murder: the grief of humanity. We would like to see photographs about joy, happiness and love, but on the same level of quality. I realize, though, that this is difficult."

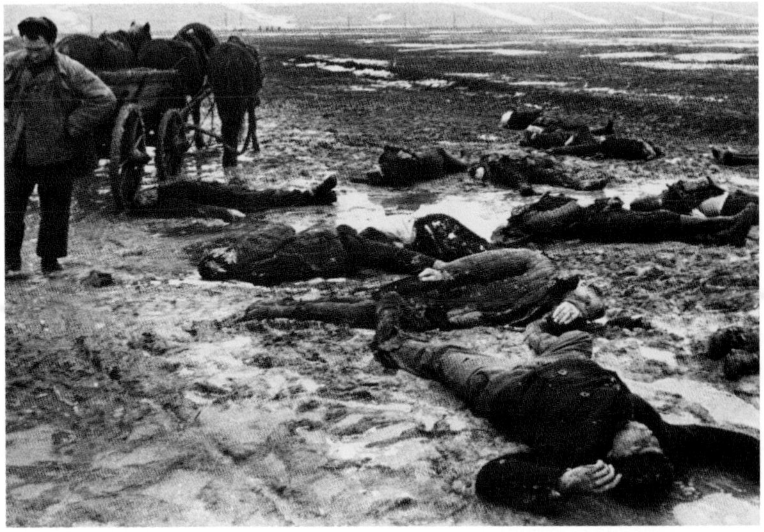

RIGHT: Baltermants constructed dramatic images, such as this one showing Russian soldiers going into action near Kerch in 1942, probably as a means of ensuring that the picture would be used in a newspaper or magazine. This could be a still from a war film.

LEFT: This classic image shows the heavy civilian losses during the battle of Kerch in May 1942. This really does look like a very muddy valley of death.

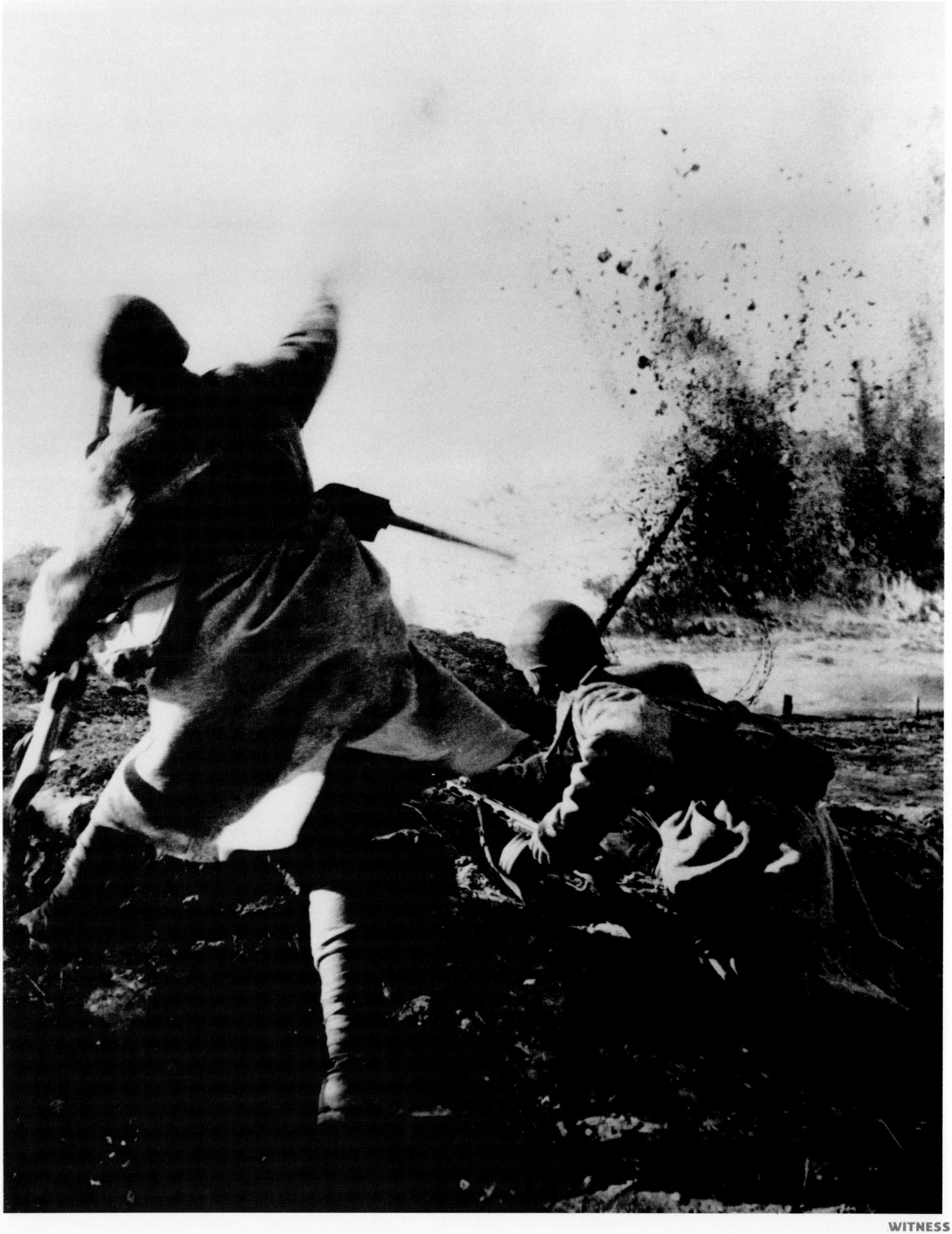

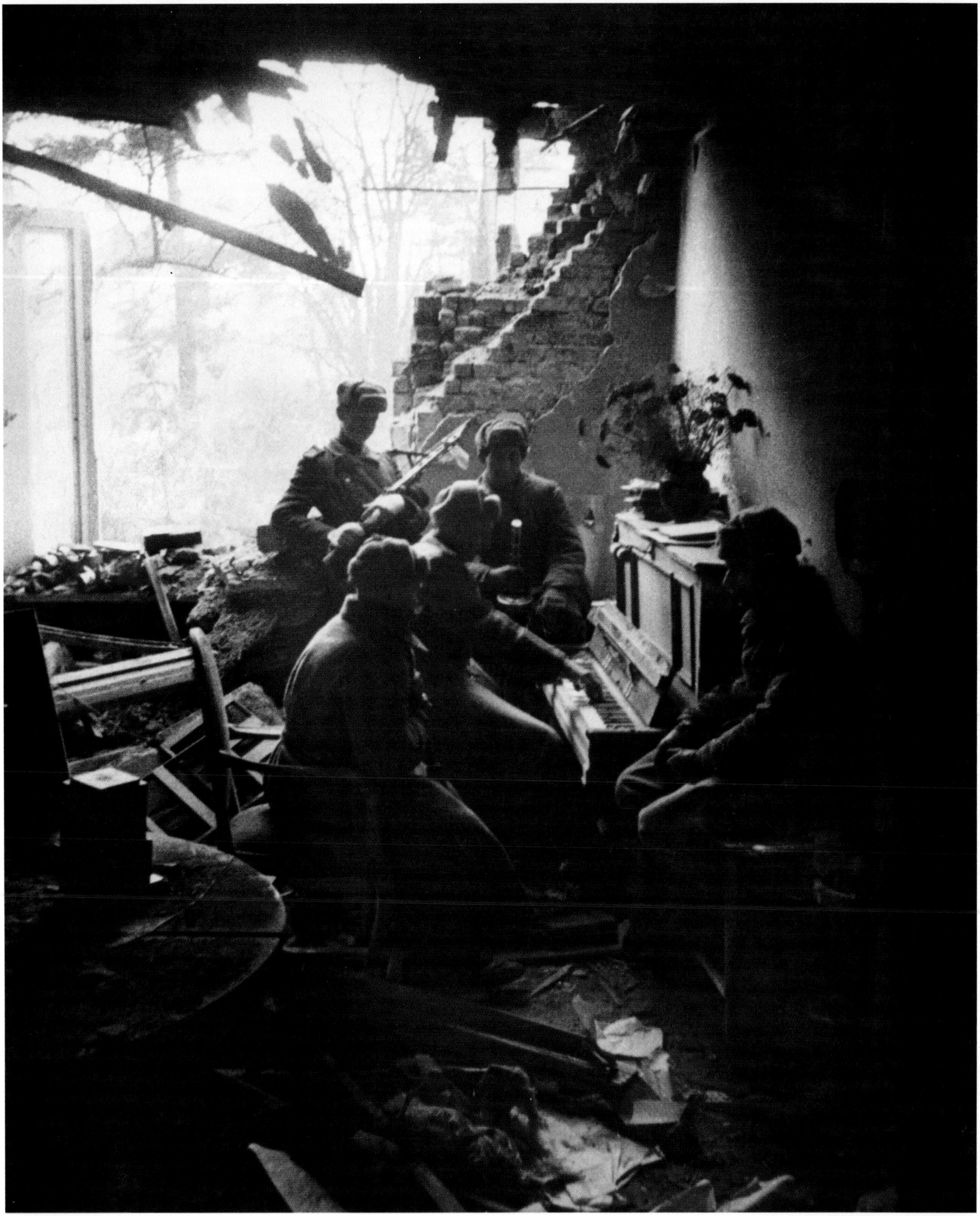

LEFT: By photographing these Russian soldiers playing Tchaikovsky on a piano in a German house in 1945, Baltermants humanizes the scene of devastation. There is something a little staged and sentimental about this image, but it is so adeptly composed that we want to believe that the photographer just stumbled upon the scene.

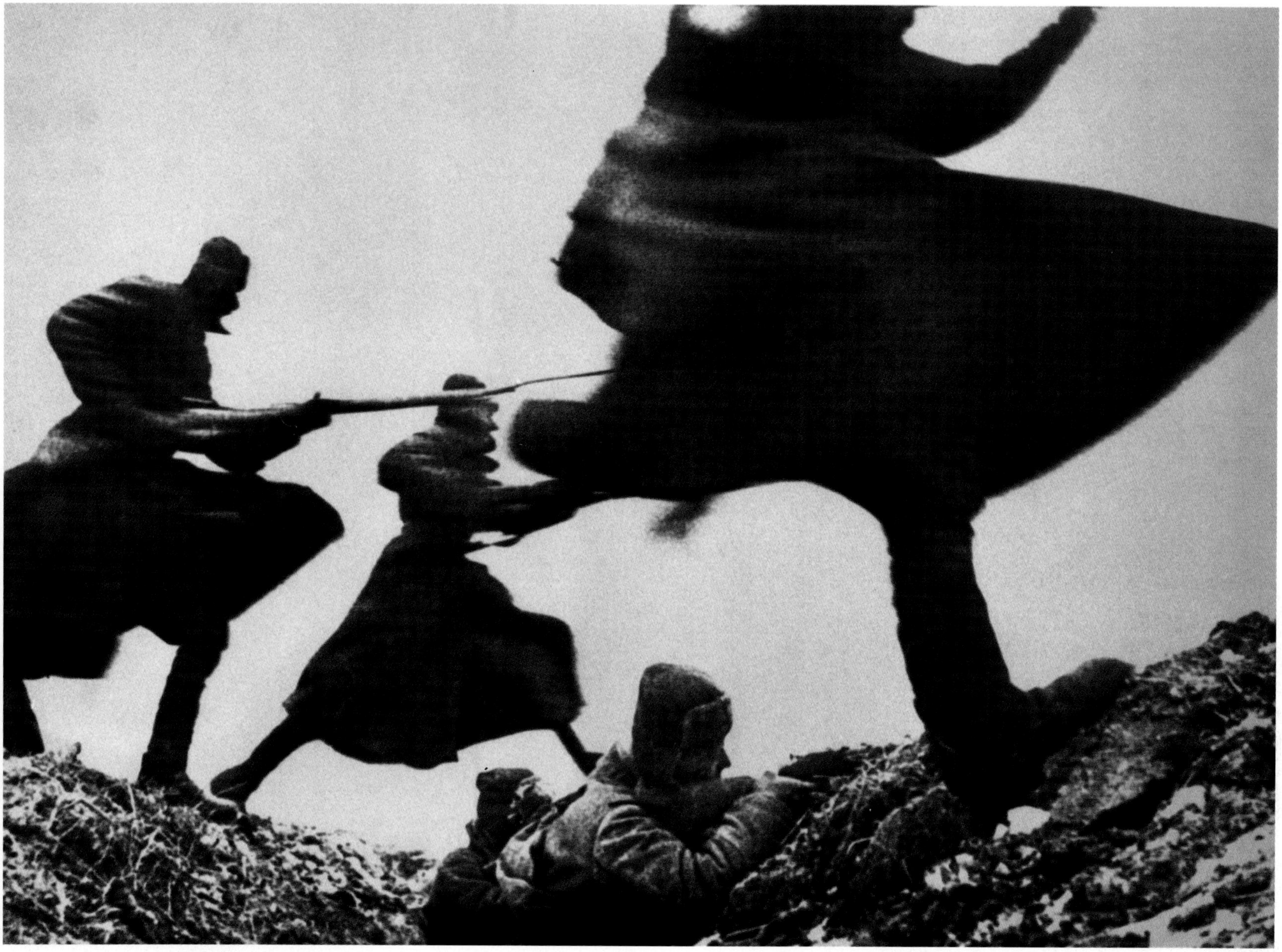

ABOVE: In his semi-abstract *Attack* of 1941, Baltermants uses some of the key pictorial elements of Russian modernist photography, such as the blurring of motion and a low viewpoint, to generate an image of dynamism that is both instantly recognizable as a war photograph, but at the same time vague as to time and place.

RIGHT: *Grief*, a picture from Baltermants's series on the civilian losses during the battle for the Crimea, near Kerch, 1942. Beautifully constructed as an image, the picture seems almost a *tableau*, made even more dramatic by the overprinting of the sky to emphasize the heavy clouds of war. While some photographers from the West tended to glamourize the Second World War, Baltermants had no qualms about presenting the full horrors of conflict.

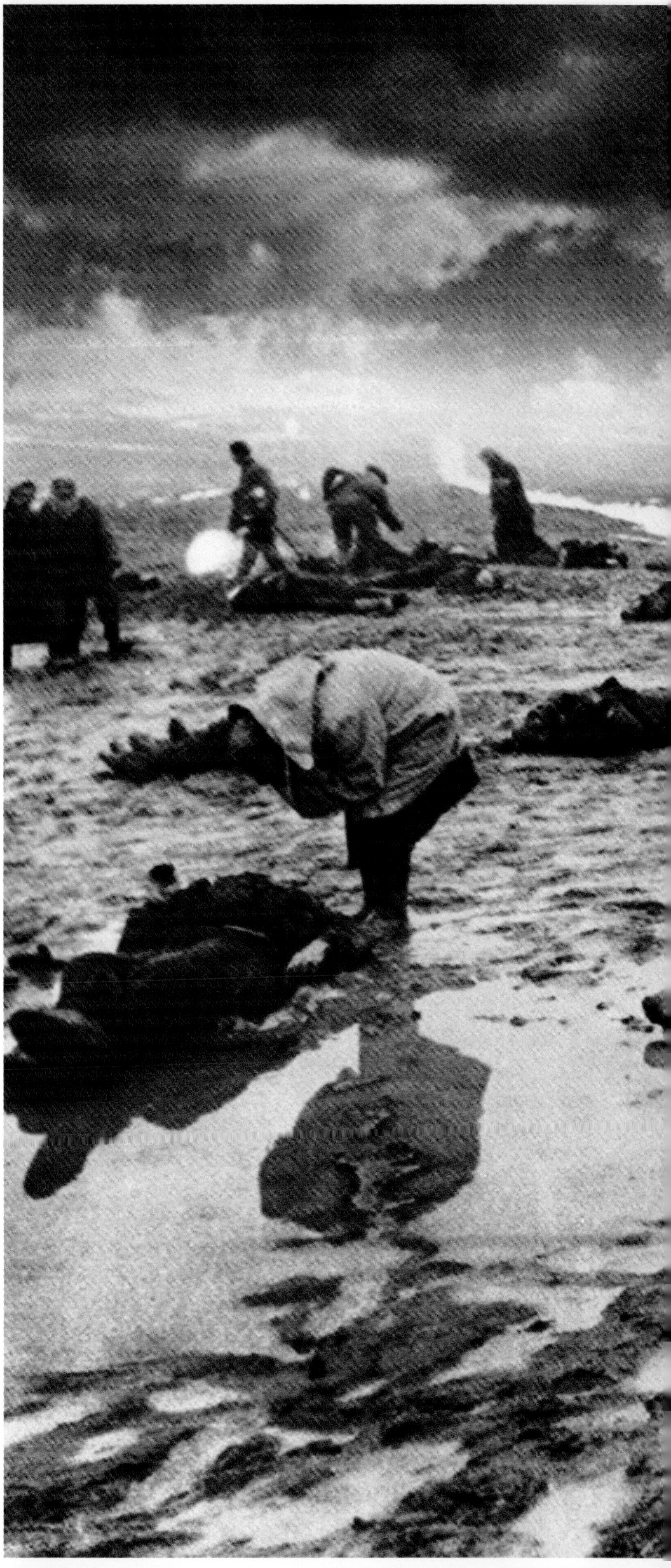

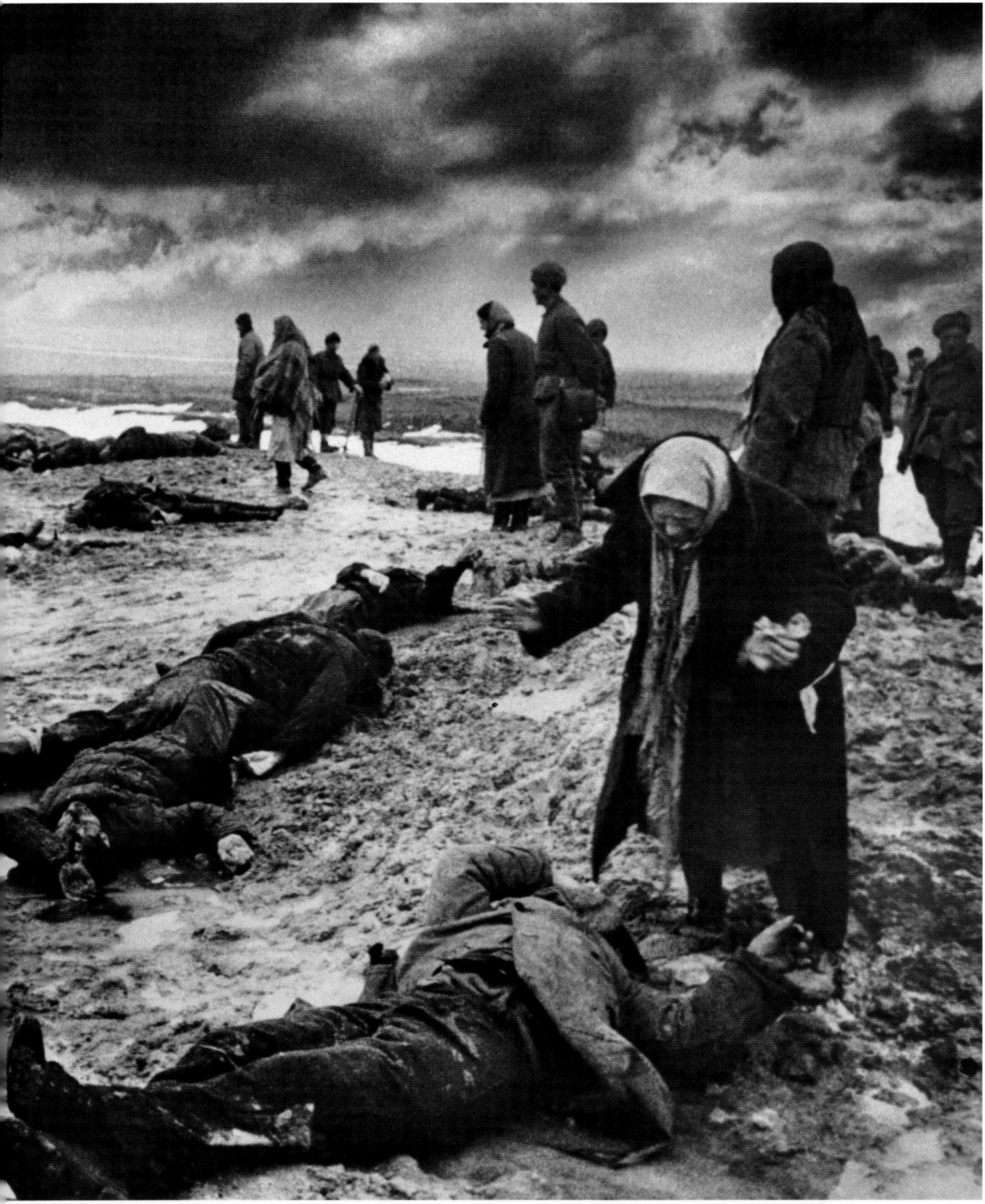

LETIZIA BATTAGLIA

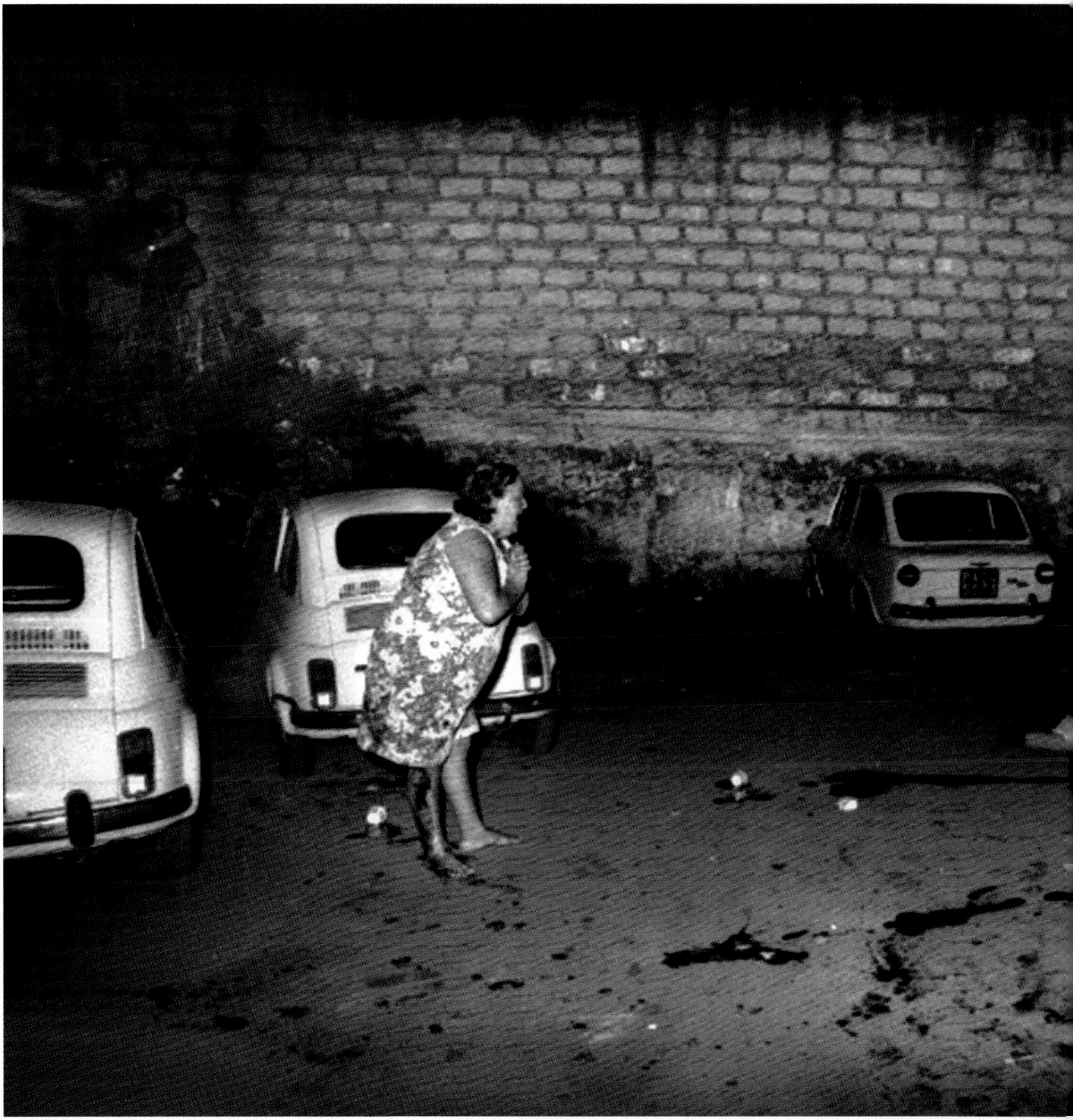

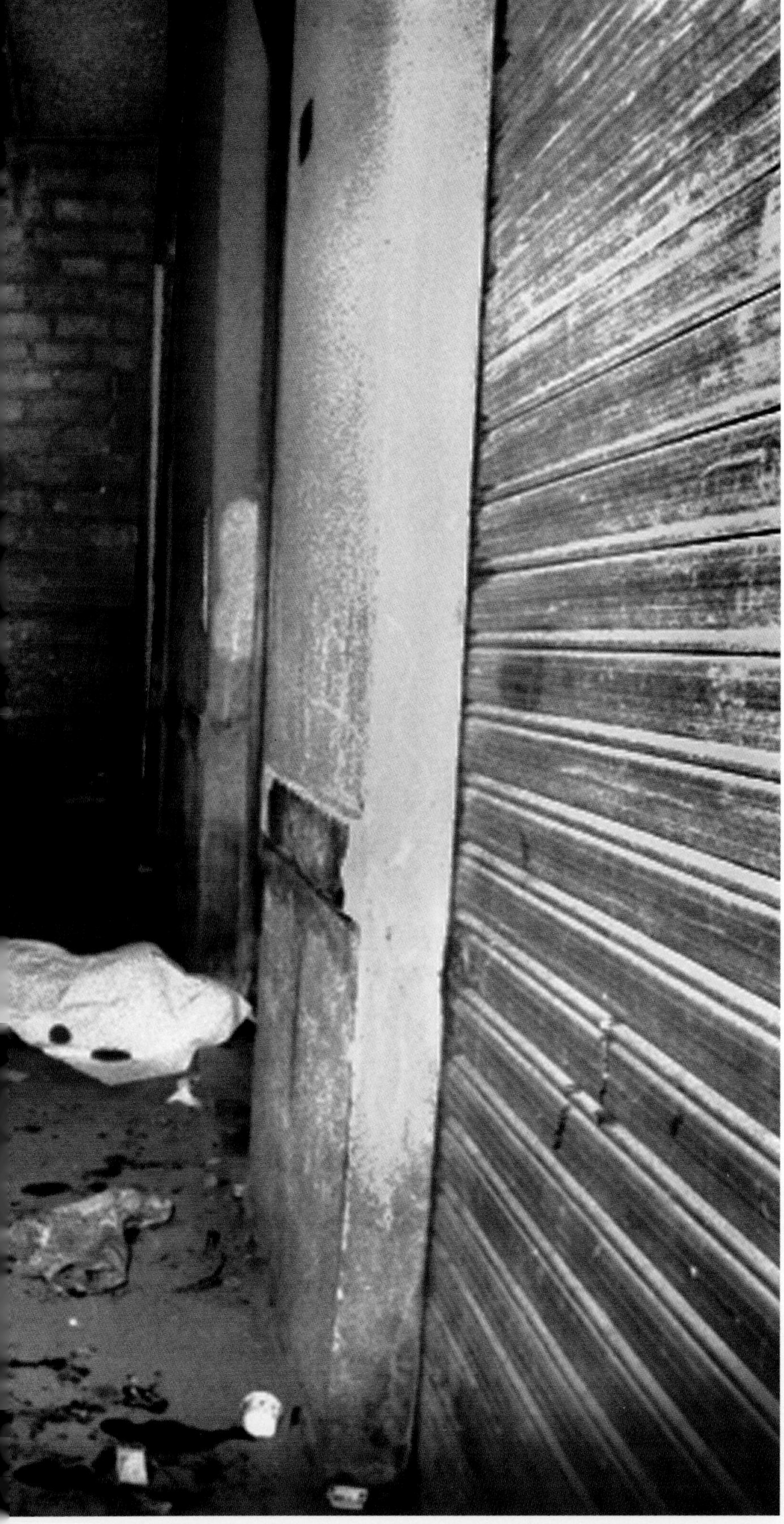

Letizia Battaglia has never covered a war, at least not a conventional one, but she is as courageous and committed as any of the war photographers featured in this book, if not more so. For just under 20 years, she relentlessly exposed the impact of the Mafia on her hometown of Palermo in Sicily. With a grim determination, she photographed the endless cycle of crime and violence, the arrests, the funerals, the trials, the grief, the outrage and the literally vice-like grip that the Mafia has on Sicilian society. She had a Weegee-like knack of being present at a murder scene while the bodies were still warm. Unlike Weegee, however, she was not motivated by a voyeuristic urge or personal glory. Battaglia took these often gory and visceral images because she wanted to change things; the camera is her weapon in her fight for justice. As she says in her book, "I felt it was my responsibility, as a part of the Sicilian people, to fight ... And so with my camera, it turned into a madness, a desperate life where in a single day I might see five men killed, men with families."

Remarkably in such a vendetta-driven society, Battaglia survived, while judges and prosecutors were ruthlessly murdered. Her survival is not just down to luck. The Mafia clans came to respect her because she didn't just take photos of murders, she also documented the living conditions in Palermo, the poverty and social deprivation, as well as the aristocracy, the local rituals, the religious processions and the city's surrounding hills and fields. The Mafia recognized her commitment and love for Sicily and chose to leave her alone. By the early 1990s, Battaglia had moved away from obsessively photographing the Mafia. While organized crime is still thriving, its power had been curtailed by a new generation of prosecutors and it is no longer front-page news. These days Battaglia is very much a hands-on local politician, striving to change the living conditions of ordinary Sicilians. Rumour has it that she is just itching to start taking photos again, which is very good news indeed.

LEFT: His name was Vincenzo Battaglia (we are assuming no relation to the photographer) and he was killed in the dark amid the garbage. His wife tried to help him, but it was too late. Sad and sordid, this photograph was taken in Palermo, 1976.

BELOW: Seconds after this photo was taken in Palermo, 1980, the house collapsed. The Mafia has a stronghold over every aspect of the local Palermo infrastructure and the photographer says that this house was subsequently going to be rebuilt for wealthy people by a mob-tied construction company.

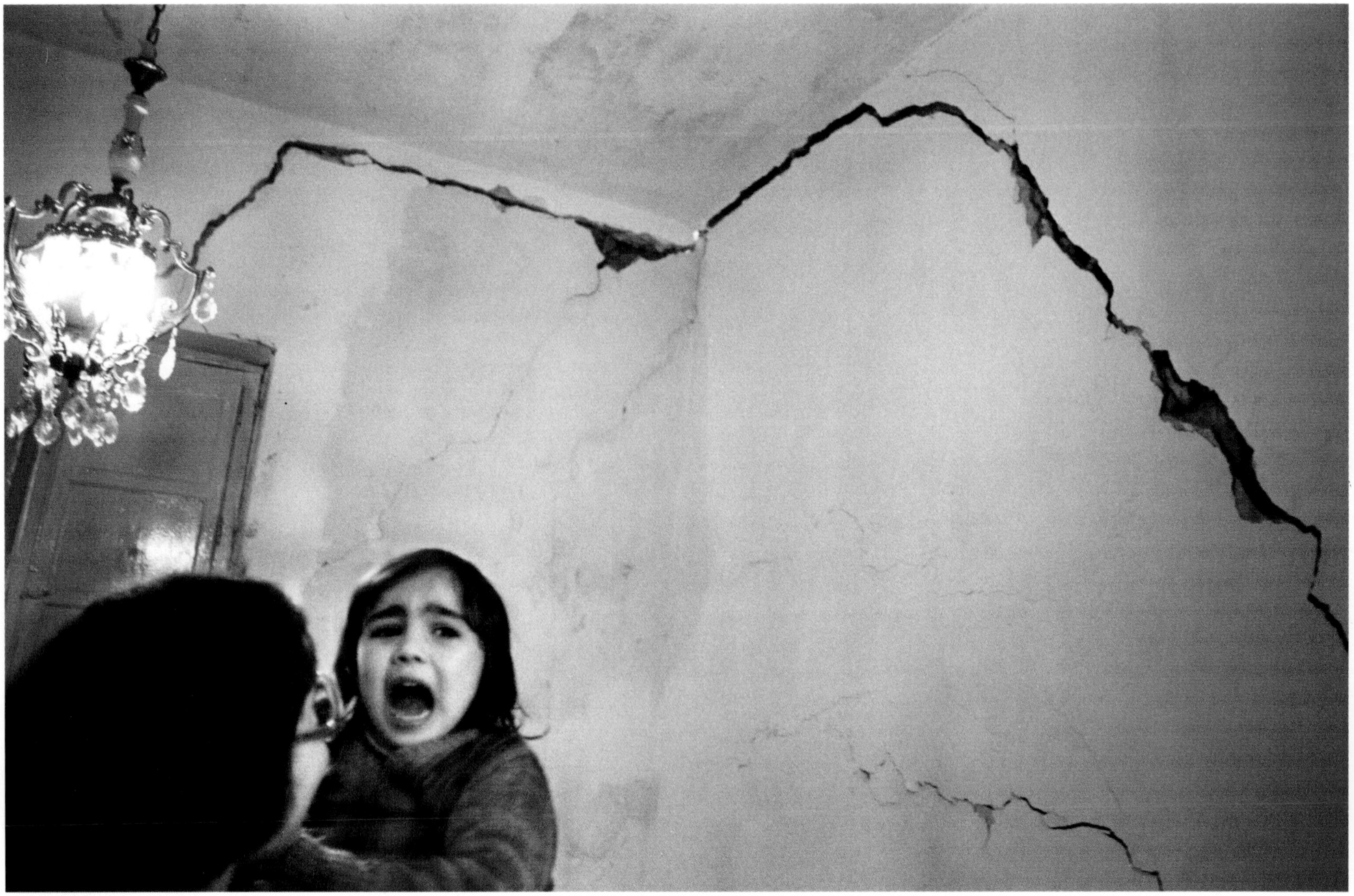

RIGHT: Battaglia says of this image take in 1986, "They put the dead father in the entrance hall so that everyone who passed by could honour the death with a greeting." When she met the boy again some years later, he was looking for work – honest work, he specified.

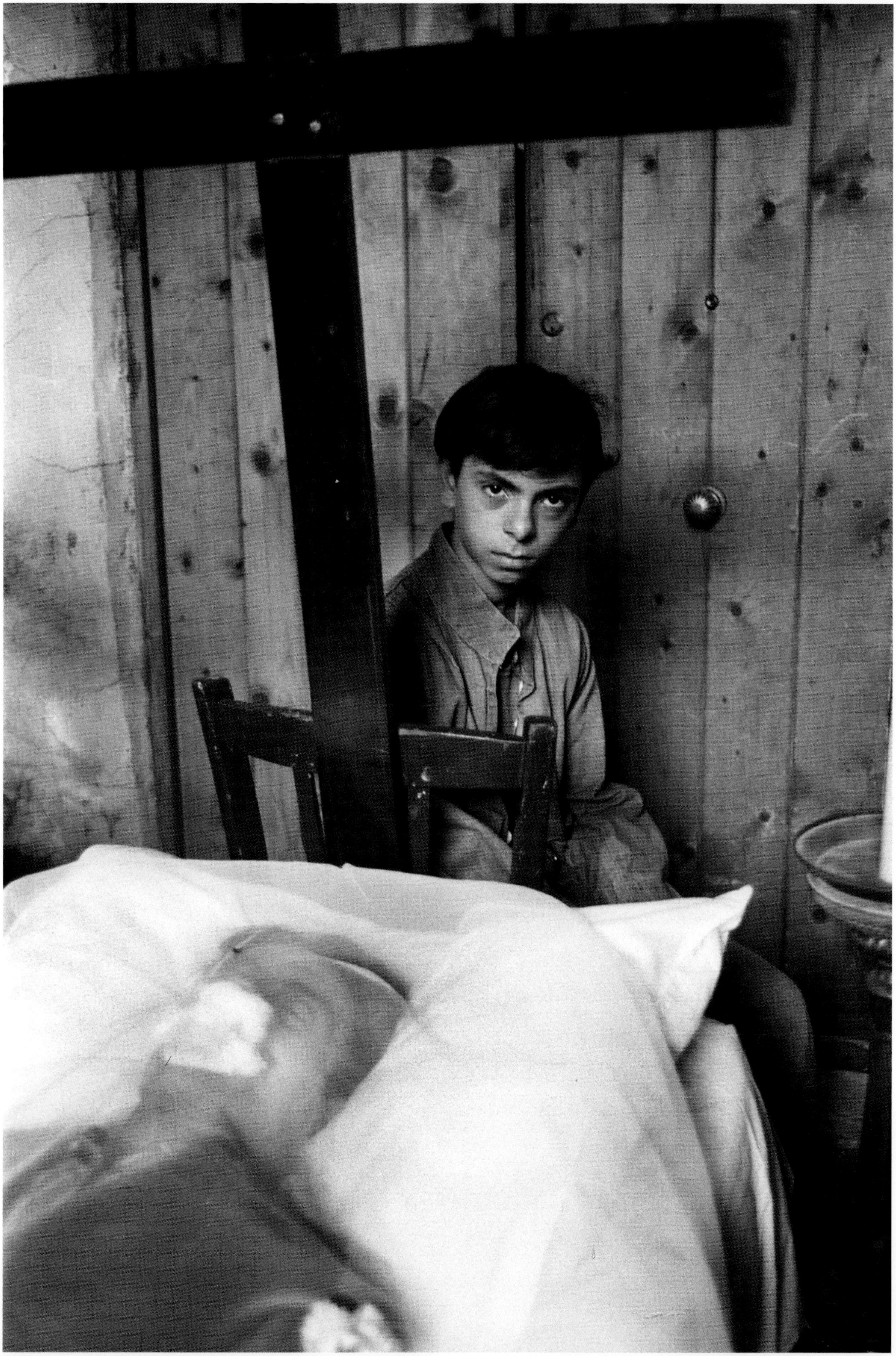

FELICE BEATO

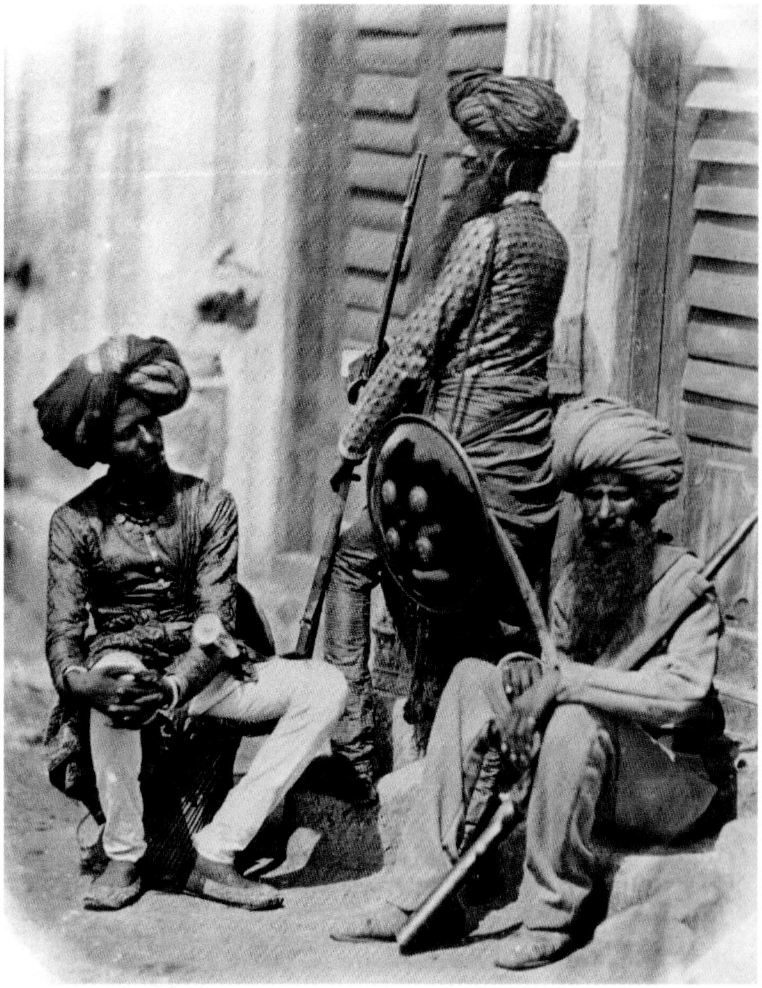

It is possible that Felice Beato was the first photographer to have recorded a military campaign. He may also have been the first (with his brother-in-law James Robertson) to have photographed dead soldiers on a battlefield. Whatever the truth of these claims, there is no doubt that his photographic career was advanced by his presence at a series of conflicts: the Crimean War in 1855; the Indian Mutiny of 1857–58; the Opium War of 1860; the American expedition to Korea in 1871; and the Sudan war in 1885. As a result, Beato, rather than Roger Fenton, is often considered the first of the war photographers, although such a title gives little idea of the huge scope of his work.

Beato made most of his war photographs on a large wet-collodion plate camera of 10 in x 12 in (25 cm x 30 cm). They were produced as individual albumen prints (and sometimes in the form of album collections) to be sold to those who had an interest in their subject matter: soldiers, colonial administrators, the general public. Their commercial and documentary functions are thus neatly dovetailed. There was no photographically illustrated press to reproduce them except when they were copied as engravings. Nonetheless, Beato's pictures served as remarkable records of a period when the West began to impose its rule on the great empires of the East. They are also images that attest to his abiding fascination with exploration and discovery. His work in China during the Opium Wars, for instance, is remarkable not only for the somewhat static scenes of the aftermath of battle, or for his great "joiner" panoramas of the British fleet in Hong Kong and of a captured Chinese fortification, but for the extraordinary beauty of his views of the secret city of Beijing and of a land opened up to outside scrutiny for the first time in its history. Beato's images are poignant records of the imperialism of this era, made at a time when British and French forces were in the process of destroying Chinese military and civil installations such as the Emperor's Summer Palace, and compelling the empire to accept their terms.

ABOVE: Part of Beato's coverage of the Indian Mutiny and its aftermath, this portrait of a group of Sikh officers in 1858 emphasizes their heroic pose, probably because they remained loyal to the British during the Mutiny.

RIGHT: Begum Zenal Mahat, wife of the Shah of Delhi, was exiled to Rangoon after the Indian Mutiny in 1857–58. She stares defiantly at the viewer in this masterful portrait by Beato.

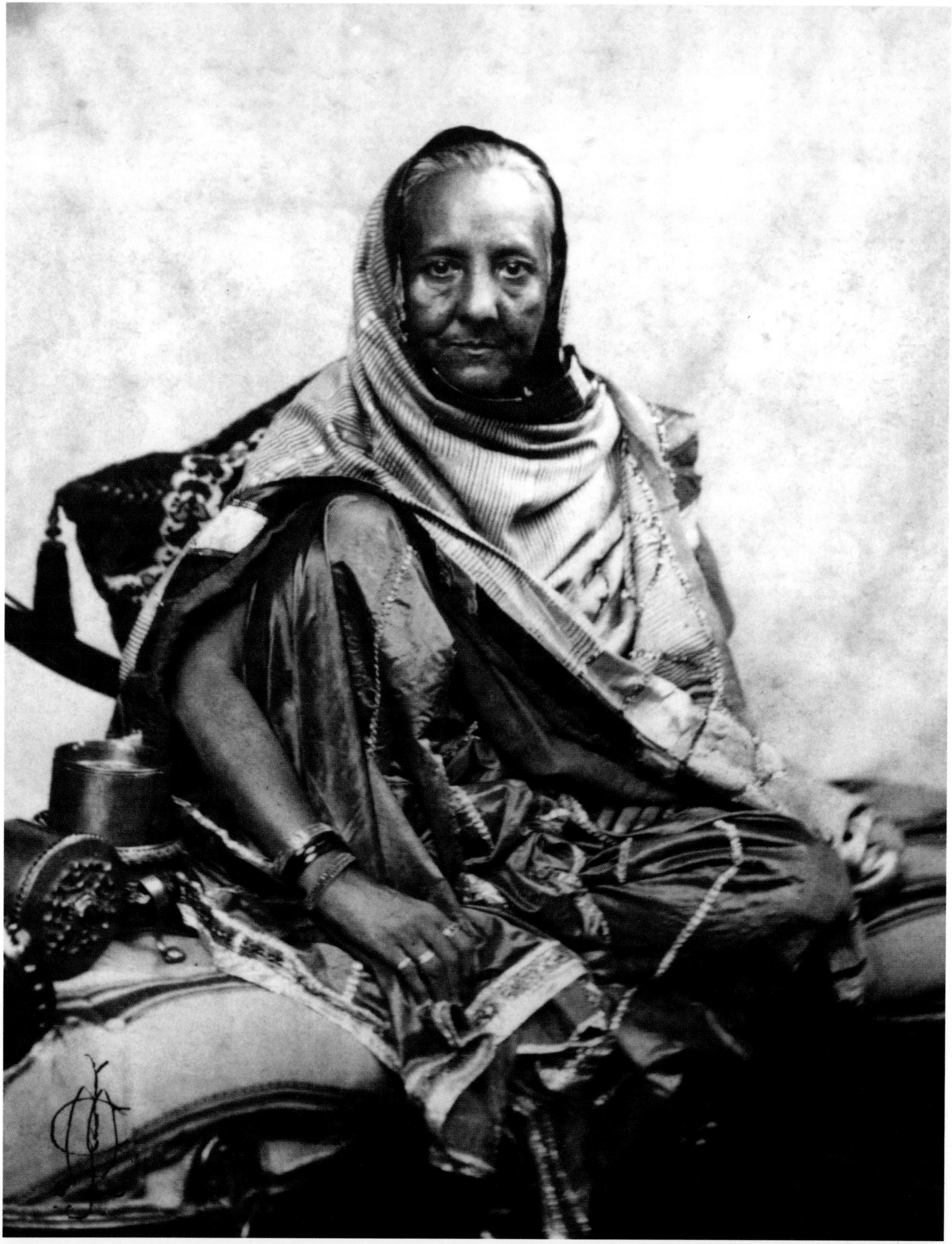

BELOW: **At Lucknow 2,000 rebel sepoys were slaughtered by the 93rd Highlanders and 4th Punjab Regiment in 1858. This image of Martimere and Brasyer Sikhs at Lucknow could be seen as underlining the imperial dominance of the British in India.**

RIGHT: **Hodson's Horse was a mixed troop of British and Indian soldiers, and this photograph of native officers is one of a series of this formation taken by Beato in 1858. The loyal Indian horsemen of Hodson's Horse wore distinctive uniforms, which included scarlet turbans and shoulder sashes over beige tunics. Hodson was also head of the intelligence department, and his spies enabled him to keep the British headquarters accurately informed of events in Delhi, of troop movements and of the damage done by British guns.**

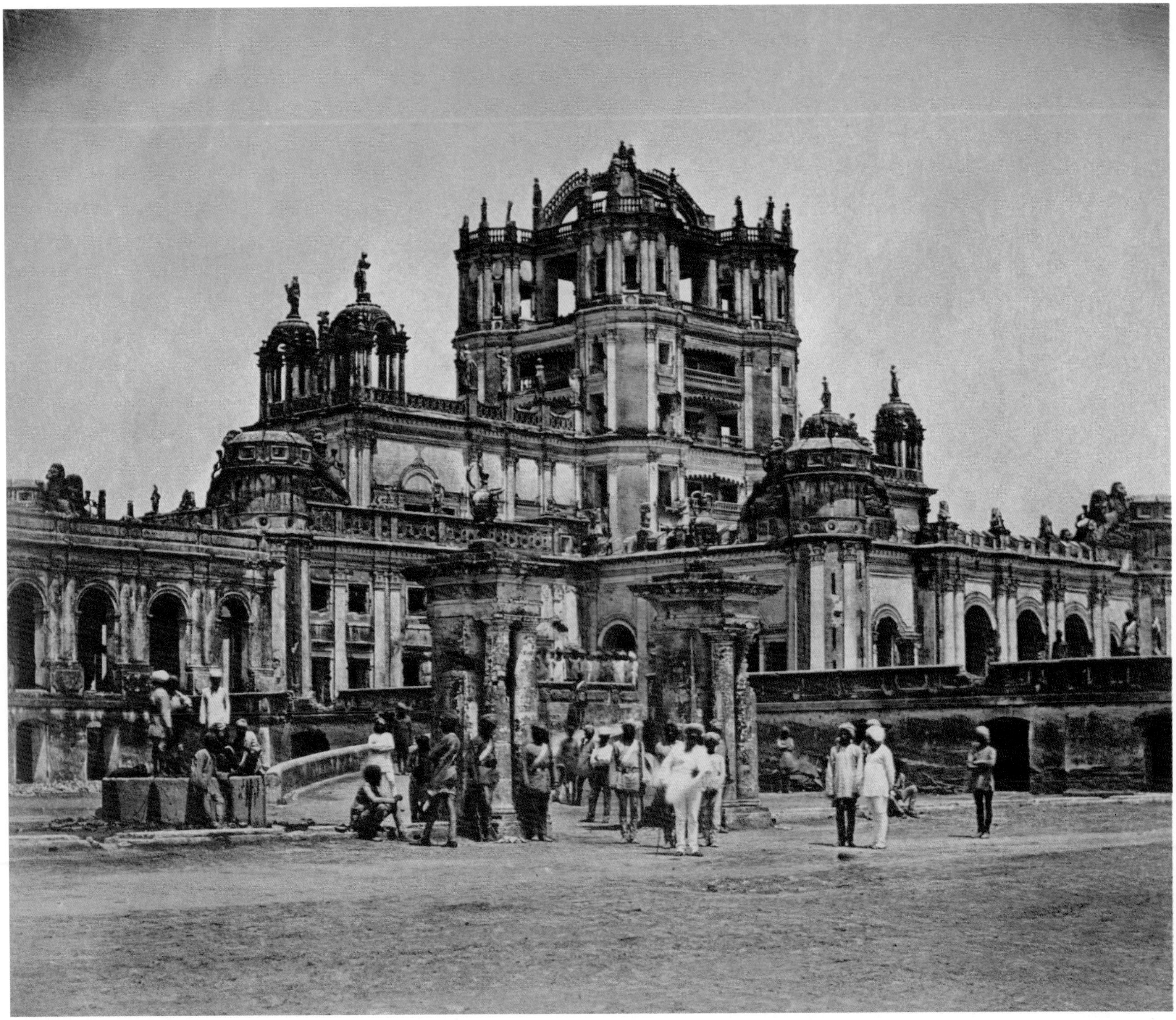

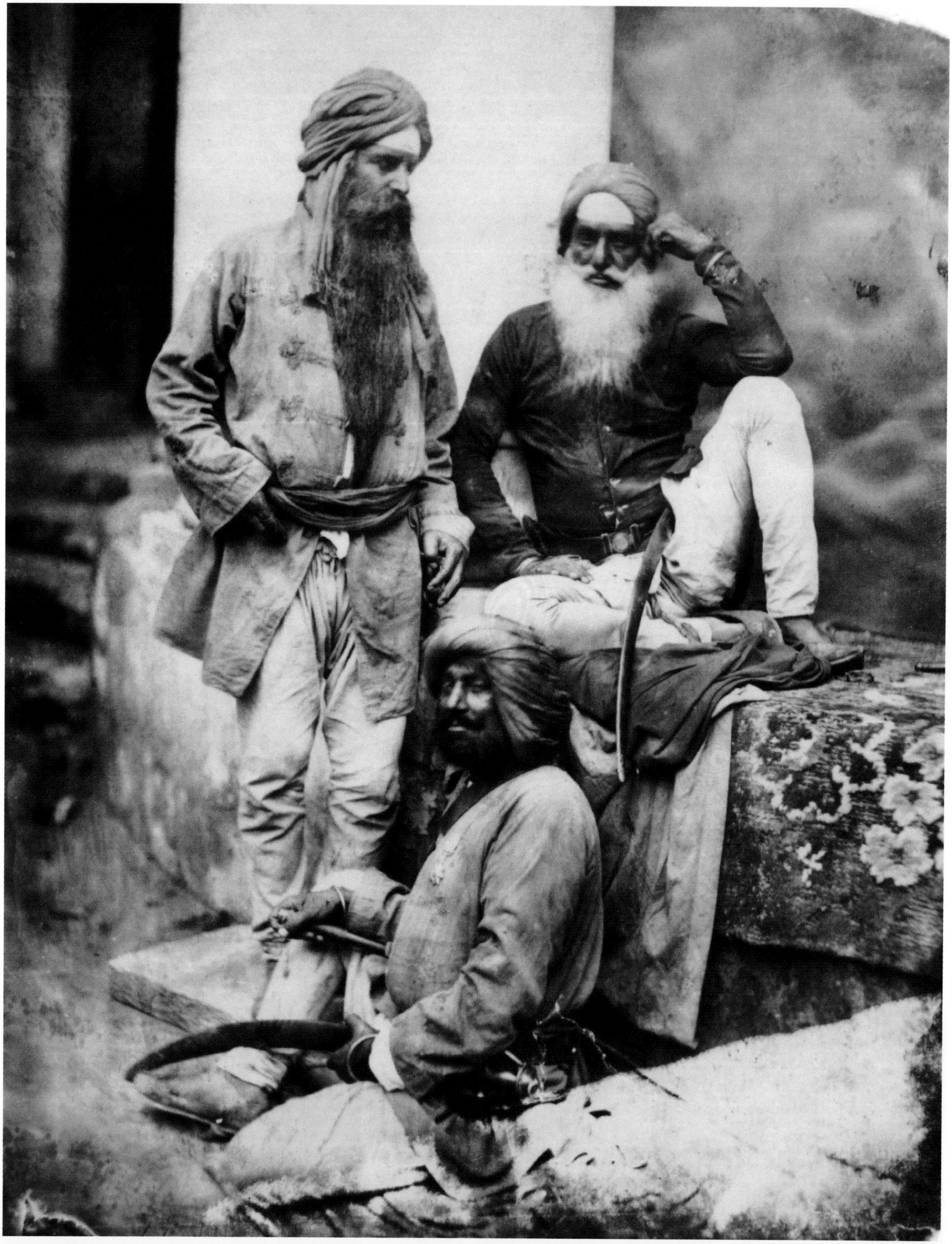

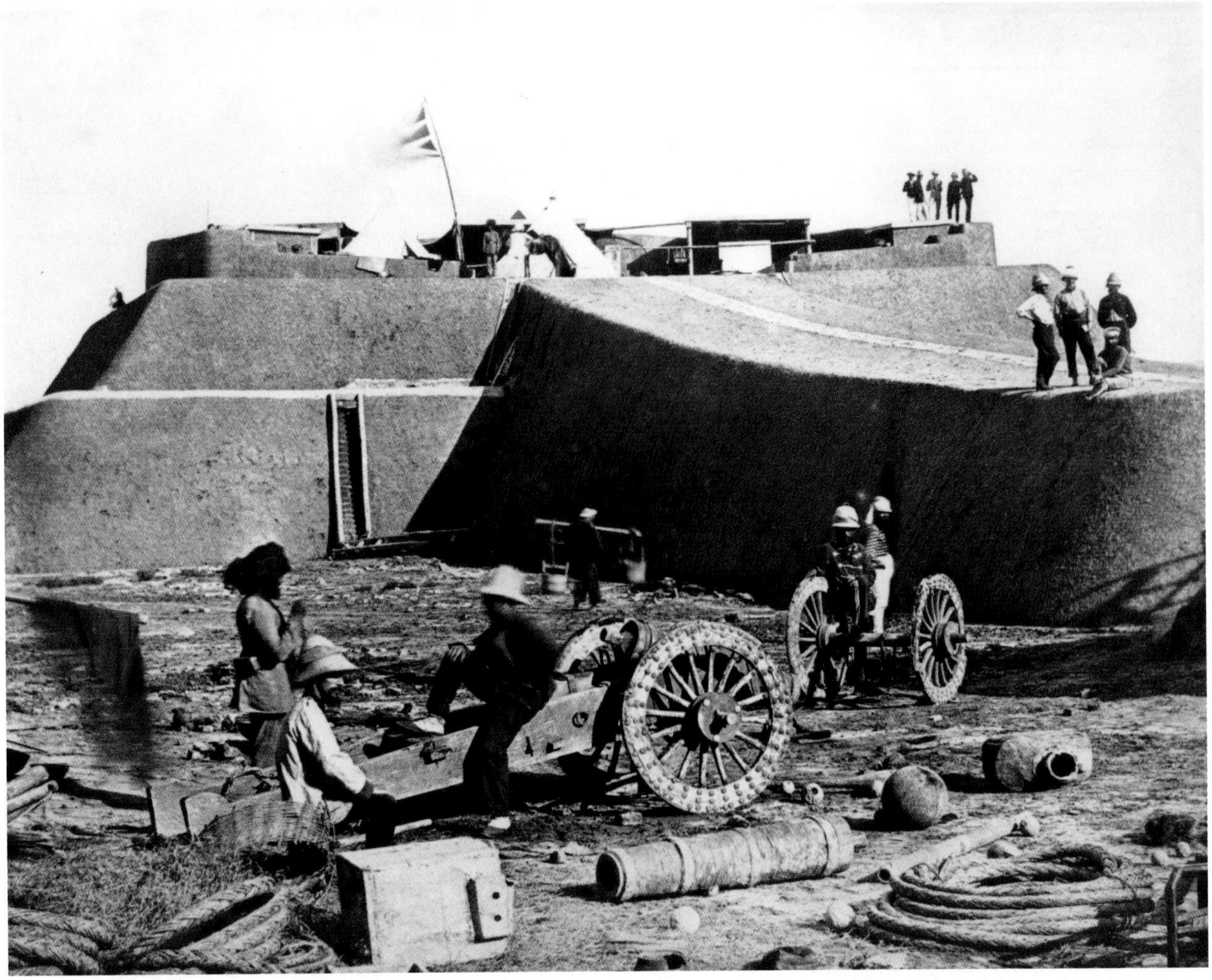

LEFT: British artillery at Pehtang Fort, one of the Taku Forts, shortly after its capture during the Opium Wars in 1860. Beato's views of the aftermath of such actions are carefully delineated documentary images of the scenes, with precisely posed participants who make the image seem like a *tableau vivant*.

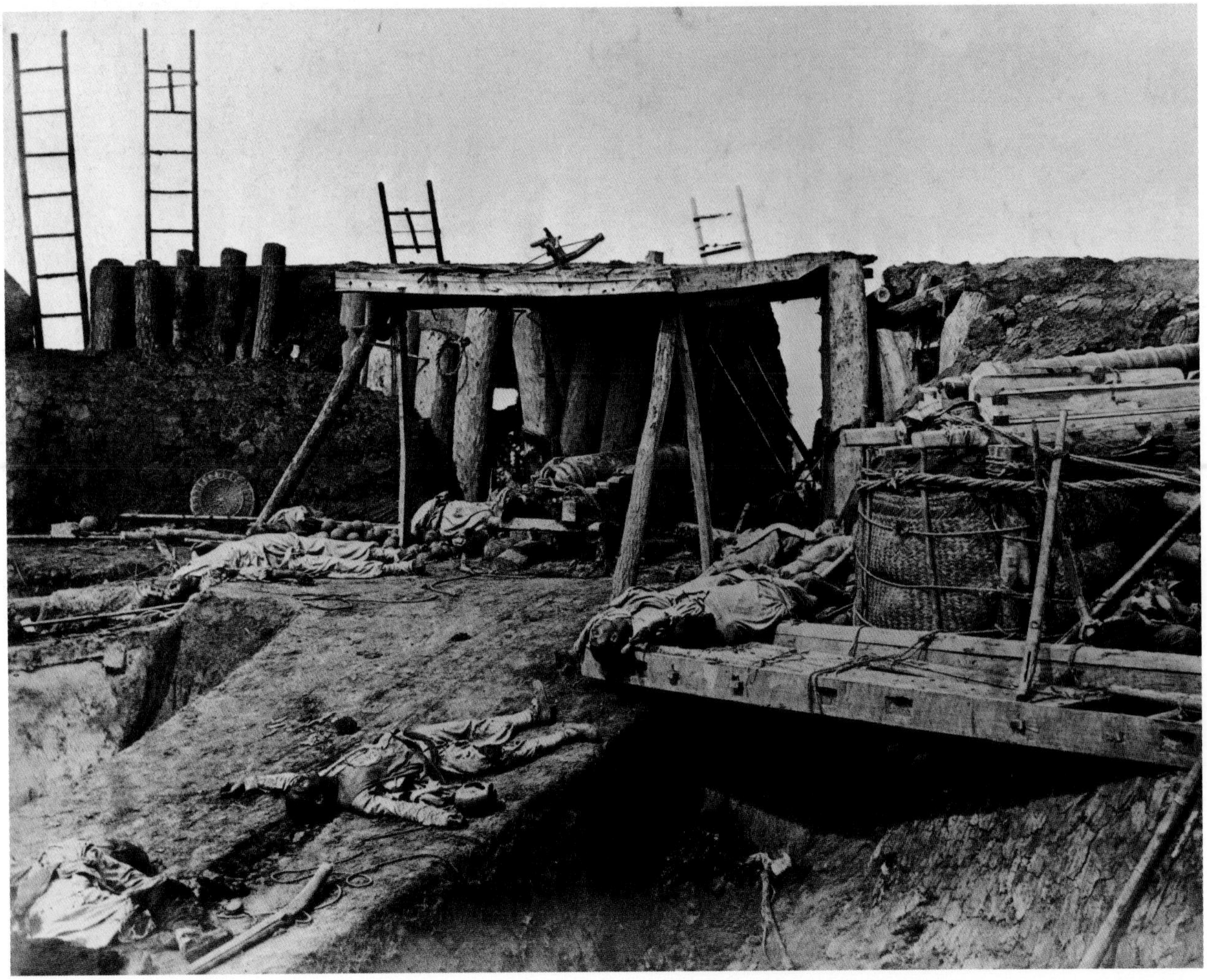

LEFT: The dead bodies of Chinese soldiers lie in the northernmost of the Taku Forts shortly after it was taken by the British and French on 21 August 1860.

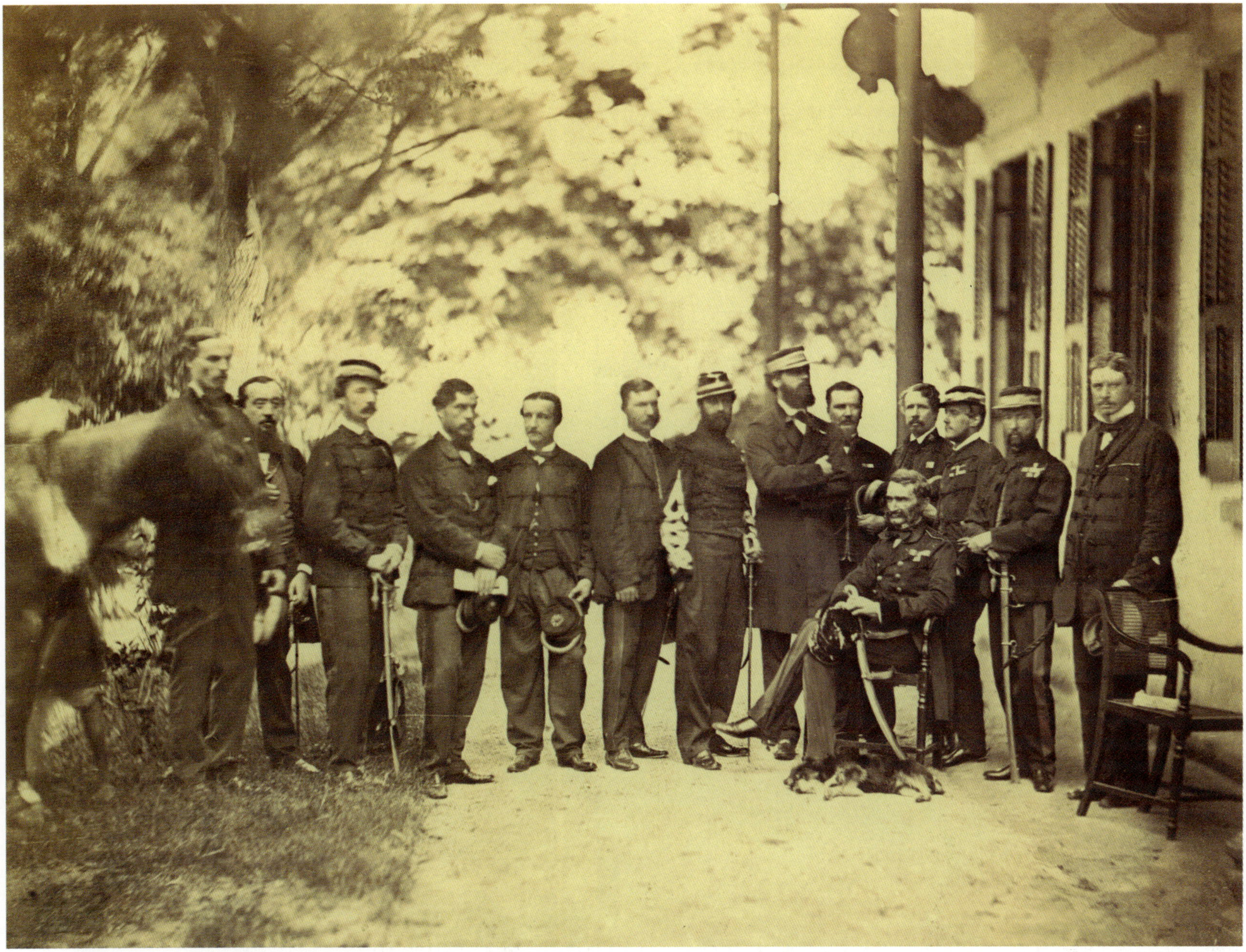

ABOVE: Beato covered the Anglo-French expedition to China in 1860 in depth. This group portrait of British officers is typical of Beato's informally posed groups, a picture made before the stiffer conventions of neatly assembled ranks had become more common.

IAN BERRY

Ian Berry conceives his role as being "to inform, to convey as accurately as one is able to as wide an audience as is possible, the reality of the situation confronting the photographer. The truth is that one will inevitably carry bias or prejudice in any given situation but one should maintain an open mind."

Since the time when he made the historic pictures of life in a South Africa dominated by apartheid, he has seen his subject not in terms just of events to be recorded, but as an exploration of the society that produces them. His survey of the recent history of South Africa is only one of several long-term projects. His work on the politics and social conflicts of water is shown here. It has taken him all over the world but in the case of Bangladesh he had particular interests: "The monsoon, how people adjust annually to being flooded and learn to live with an ever worsening situation." With extensive experience of the problems and dangers of photojournalism, Berry often has to weigh up the cost versus the benefit of photographing politically sensitive situations, as in Bangladesh, where the pollution of drinking water wells with arsenic is an acute problem. "Shooting in such situations is always the photojournalist's dilemma. As a Westerner with a bunch of Leicas one runs the risk of being perceived as a voyeuristic tourist. At the same time, one wishes to keep a low profile because governments invariably dislike being seen to have shortcomings." In all the situations where he has worked, Berry's ability to construct memorable images has been prominent. "For me the great strength of the camera over the brush is the ability to seize a moment, to combine the peak of a situation and meld it into a graphic shape."

BELOW, LEFT AND RIGHT: Ian Berry's current project focuses on the developing water crisis that is affecting people all over the world, as here in Bangladesh, where a village has been left as an island by floods. All travel is done by boat between villages and even between parts of villages. Berry presents us with two perspectives of the same scene.

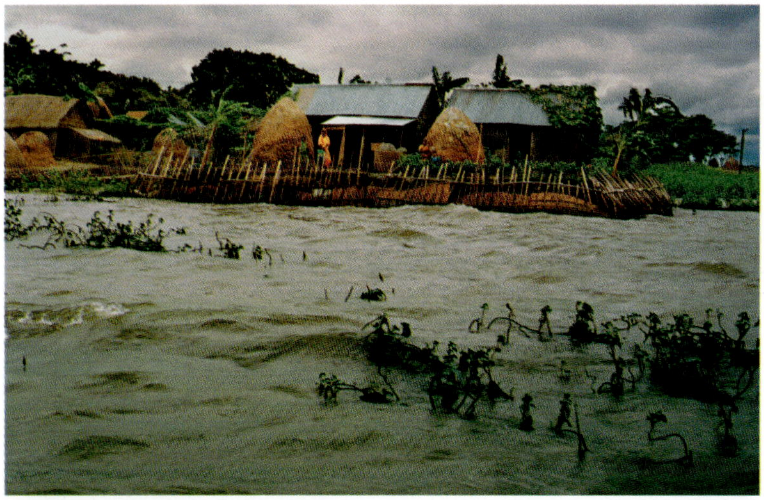

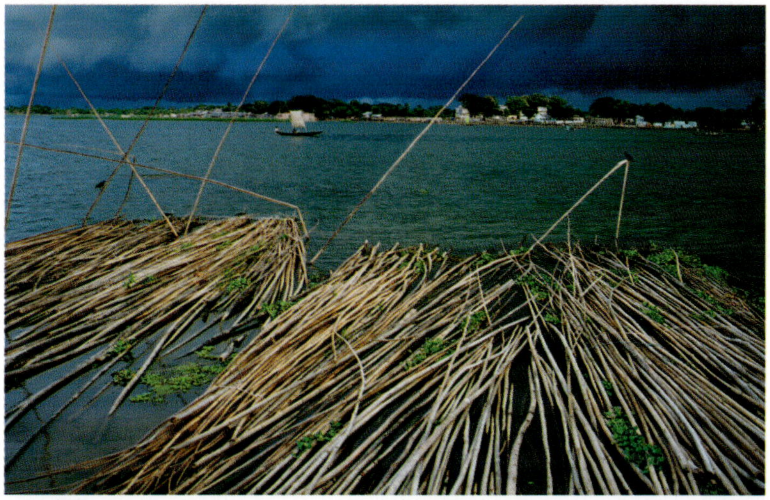

BELOW: Fishermen stand for hours on bamboo poles in the floodwaters, raising and lowering a huge net every few minutes to catch talapia, a small fish. These photos were taken in 2000.

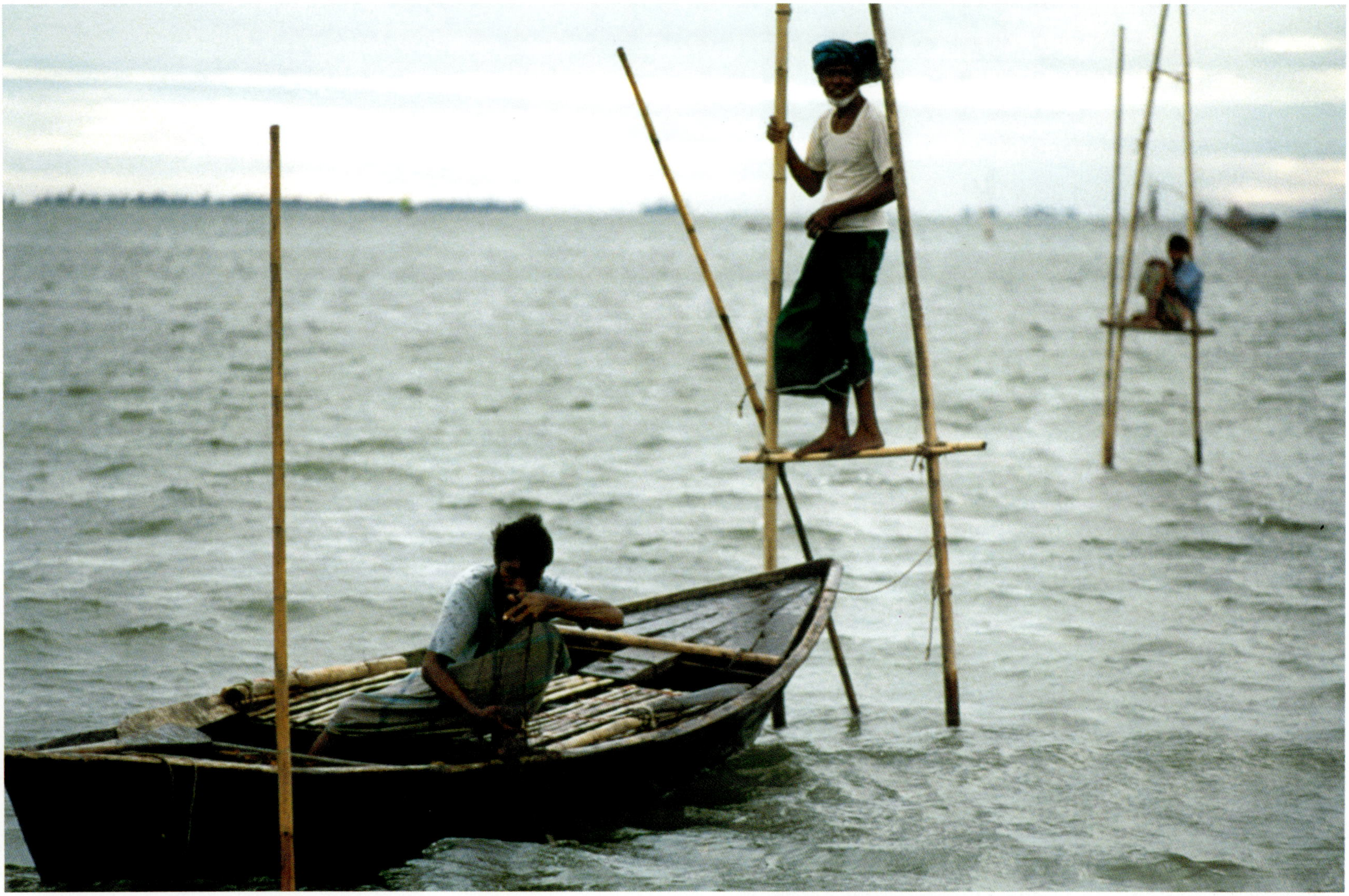

OVERLEAF: Berry's work documents the social consequences of both natural and manmade situations. In Bangladesh the monsoon brings flooding that often lasts for a considerable part of every year. When the village of Khaliajuri (in north-east Bangladesh) floods, locals must travel by water taxi from one part of the village to another – here they return to their homes from the market with their purchases.

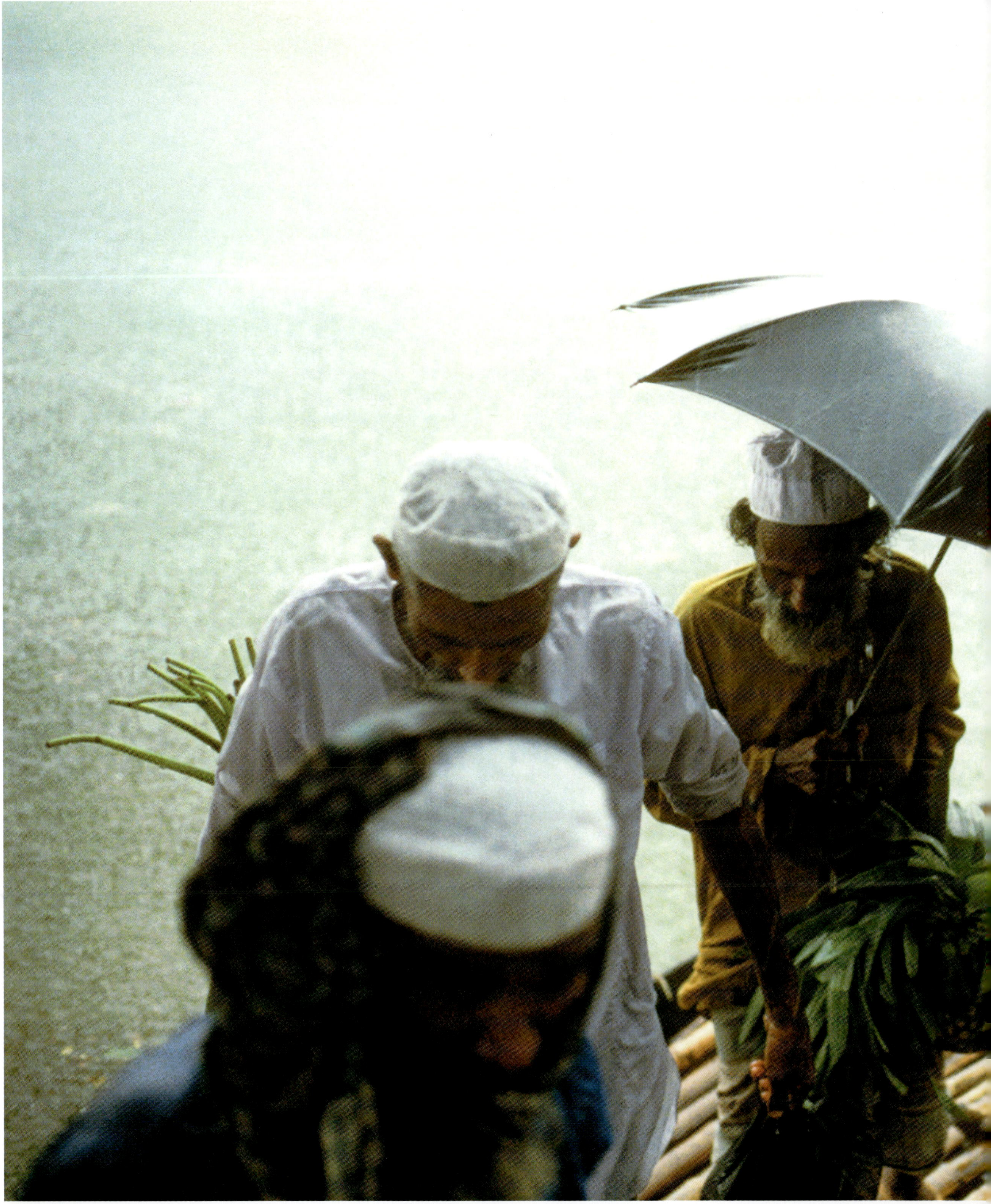

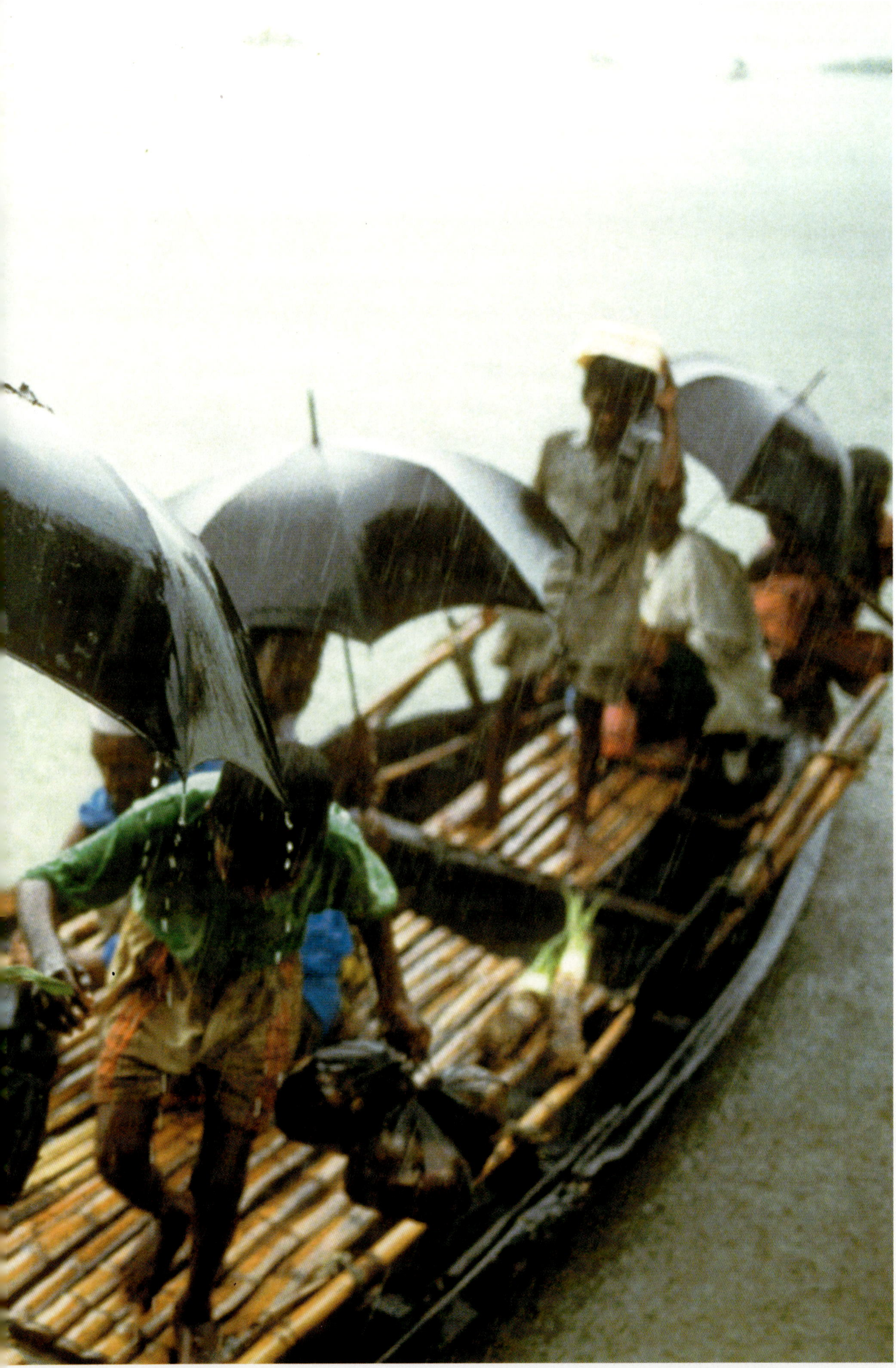

MARGARET BOURKE-WHITE

Margaret Bourke-White has never been given the credit she deserves for taking some of the most memorable images of the twentieth century. She was a formidable and tireless photographer, who was prepared to use whatever was at her disposal, in particular her beauty and charisma, to get a shot. Photojournalism is still very much a boys' club, and Bourke-White was seen as manipulative. The readers of *Life*, however, did not care about how the images ended up in the magazine, they just wanted to experience something different. While most of the other *Life* photographers shot on the more flexible 35mm format, Bourke-White stuck to the larger-format cameras that had served her so well as an industrial photographer. She was not keen on experimentation and instead favoured visually simple, but strongly composed and dramatic images.

This more formal industrial style worked best when, early in her career as chief staff photographer for *Fortune* magazine, she travelled to the Soviet Union in 1930 and completed the first major project on the newly emerging communist dictatorship by a Western photographer. She later made a name for herself as a concerned social documentary photographer, touring the southern states and documenting the rural poor who were still in the midst of the Great Depression. Despite her Yankee and Ivy League background, Bourke-White showed great sensitivity for her subjects, resulting in a book collaboration with the writer Arsine Caldwell (whom she later married); images from the project featured in the first-ever issue of *Life* magazine, including the cover. She did lasting damage to her reputation when she smuggled in a camera to shoot the grieving family and friends gathered round a dying Gandhi. She actually took a shot using a flashbulb, and the family were so outraged that they chased her out of the house and smashed her camera. Astonishingly, Bourke-White was far from contrite and tried to talk her way back in. While some would find her actions highly insensitive, others would argue that she had the instincts of a true professional.

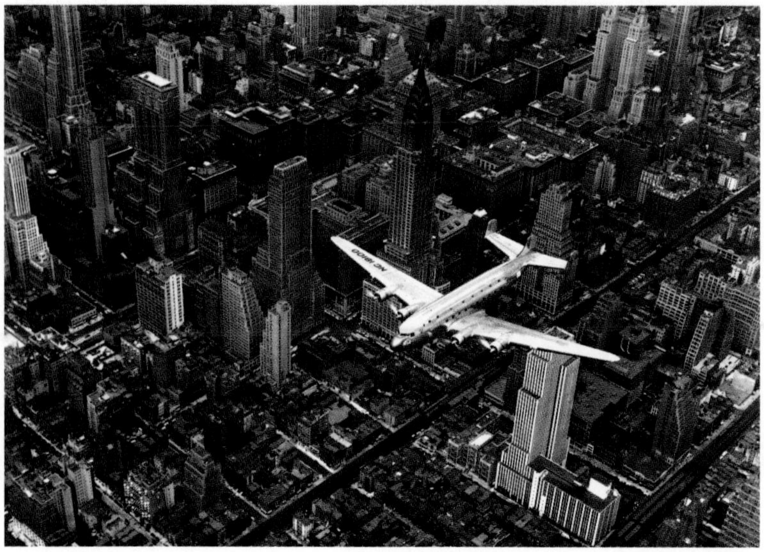

ABOVE: It is hard to identify the vantage point from which Bourke-White took this image of a DC4 over New York in 1939; the assumption is that she is in another plane.

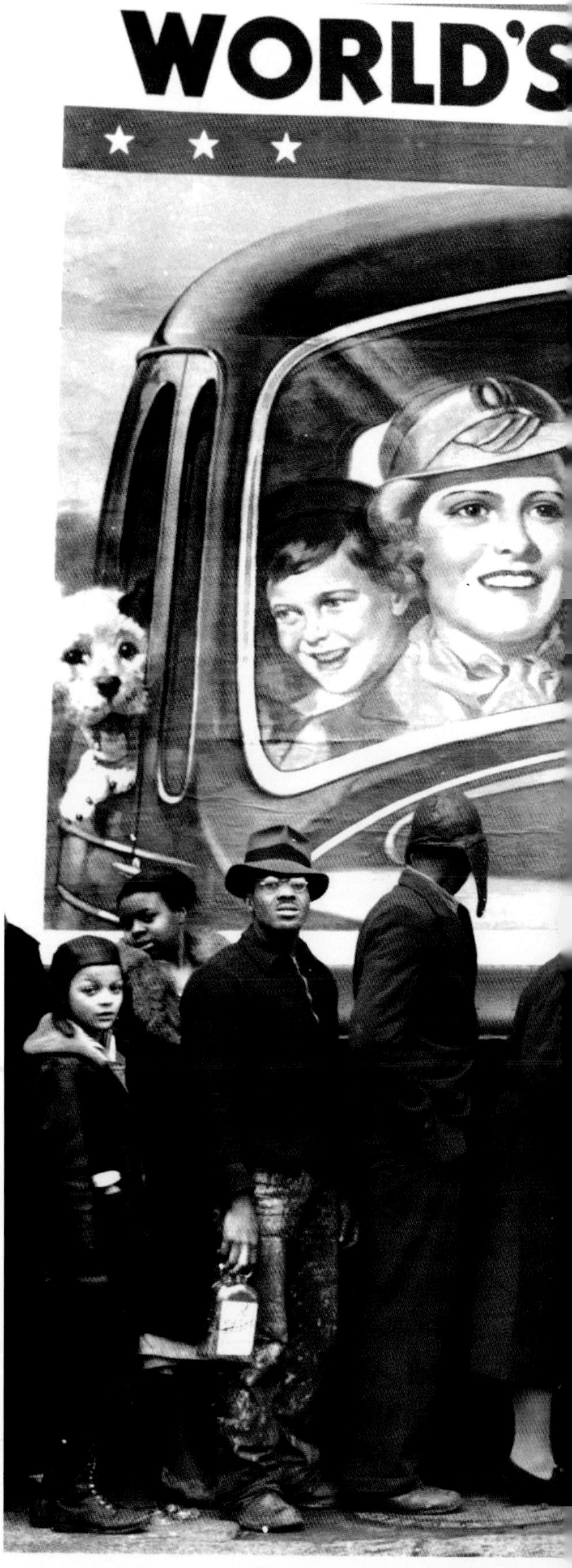

BELOW: This photograph, taken at the time of the Louisville, Kentucky, flood in 1937, is such a perfect juxtaposition of fact and fiction that it almost looks like a set-up. Of course, it isn't. It is rather a timeless statement about the inequalities of society and is still relevant today.

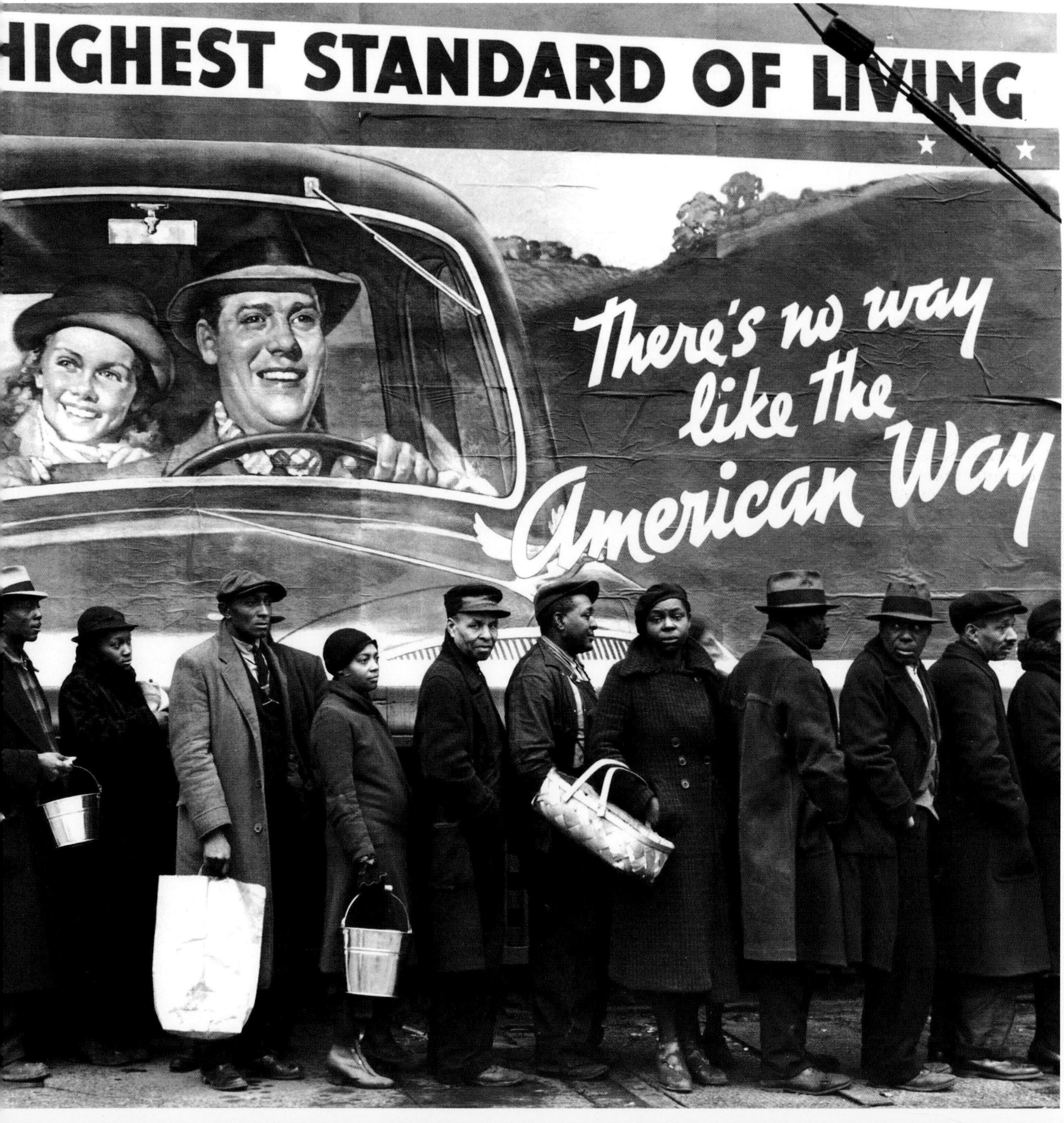

BELOW: Indian leader Mahatma Gandhi reading at home next to a spinning wheel, which looms in the foreground as a symbol of India's struggle for independence. This photograph taken in 1946 is one of the most famous portraits of the twentieth century. Gandhi got on well with Bourke-White, thus allowing her such intimate access. She didn't quite break the enigma, but she certainly tried.

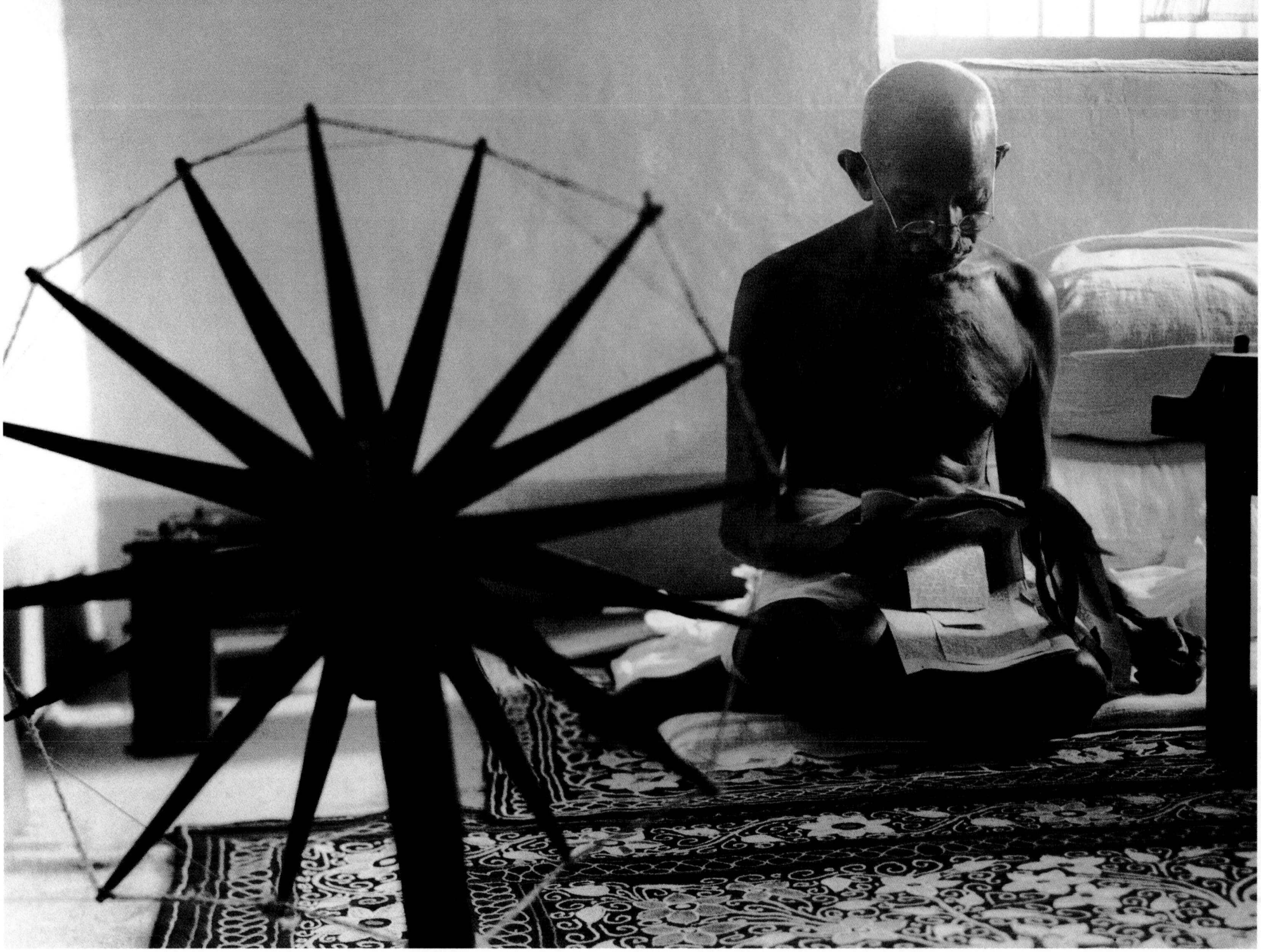

BELOW: Mourners in New Delhi in 1948 climb a telephone pole to view the funeral procession of their assassinated Indian leader, Gandhi. The sheer number of people is overwhelming.

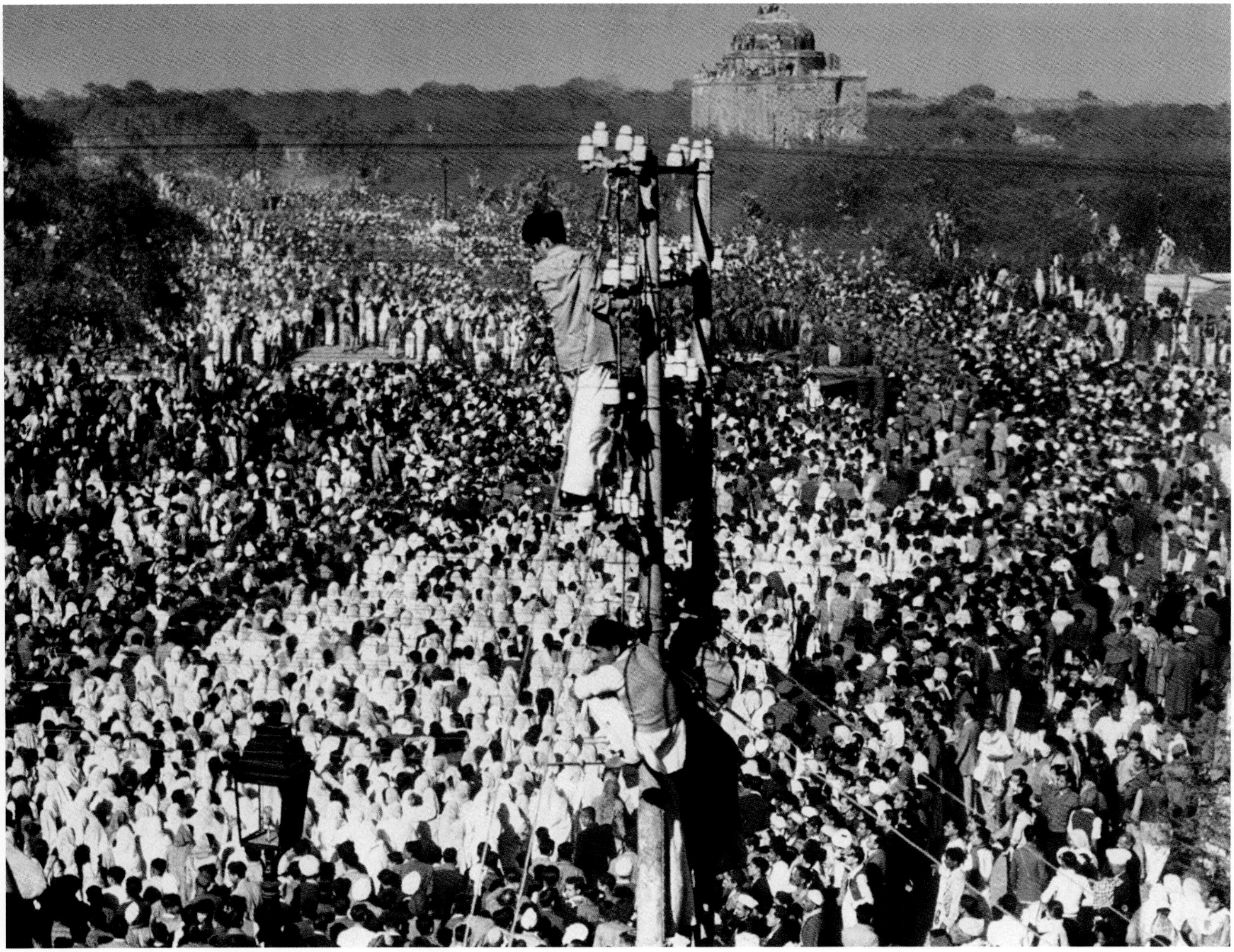

RENE BURRI

An Internet search on René Burri will inevitably lead to one of the thousands of Che Guevara sites out there in cyberspace. The founder of revolutionary chic is as popular as ever, thanks to the hit film *The Motorcycle Diaries* (2004), and, inevitably, because of "that" photograph Burri has also been propelled back into the spotlight. The photograph is, of course, the iconic shot of Che smoking a cigar (in the sequence published here, it is the middle shot in the top row) looking cocky and very handsome. Che Guevara was at the time Minister of Industry in Cuba under Castro. Burri took these photographs to accompany an interview with Che for *Look* magazine, just after the Cuban Missile Crisis. In the book *Magnum – Fifty Years at the Frontline of History* by Russell Miller, Burri recalls Che arguing furiously with the reporter about American politics. He tells Miller, "He was like a caged tiger, pacing up and down, and every now and then he would bite the end off another cigar. I didn't really have any sense that I was in the presence of someone who would become a legend or any idea how significant that picture would become to me." Burri might not have been aware of what his subject would become, but Che is in no doubt, so every pose and gesture is being made with an eye for posterity.

It would be unfair, however, to judge Burri' s career in the context of just one photograph. He built up an impressive portfolio prior to this assignment and continued to thrive throughout the next three decades. He first studied design, and a fondness for clean and crisp graphics permeates his photography. By his own admission, he went out of his way to copy Henri Cartier-Bresson. The great man's influence can be seen in Burri's best images, which combine clinical composition with the movement and vibrancy of real life. Like Cartier-Bresson, he was, and still is, an obsessive traveller, and his best photographs celebrate the world's diversity, ethnicity, culture and traditions with insight and sensitivity.

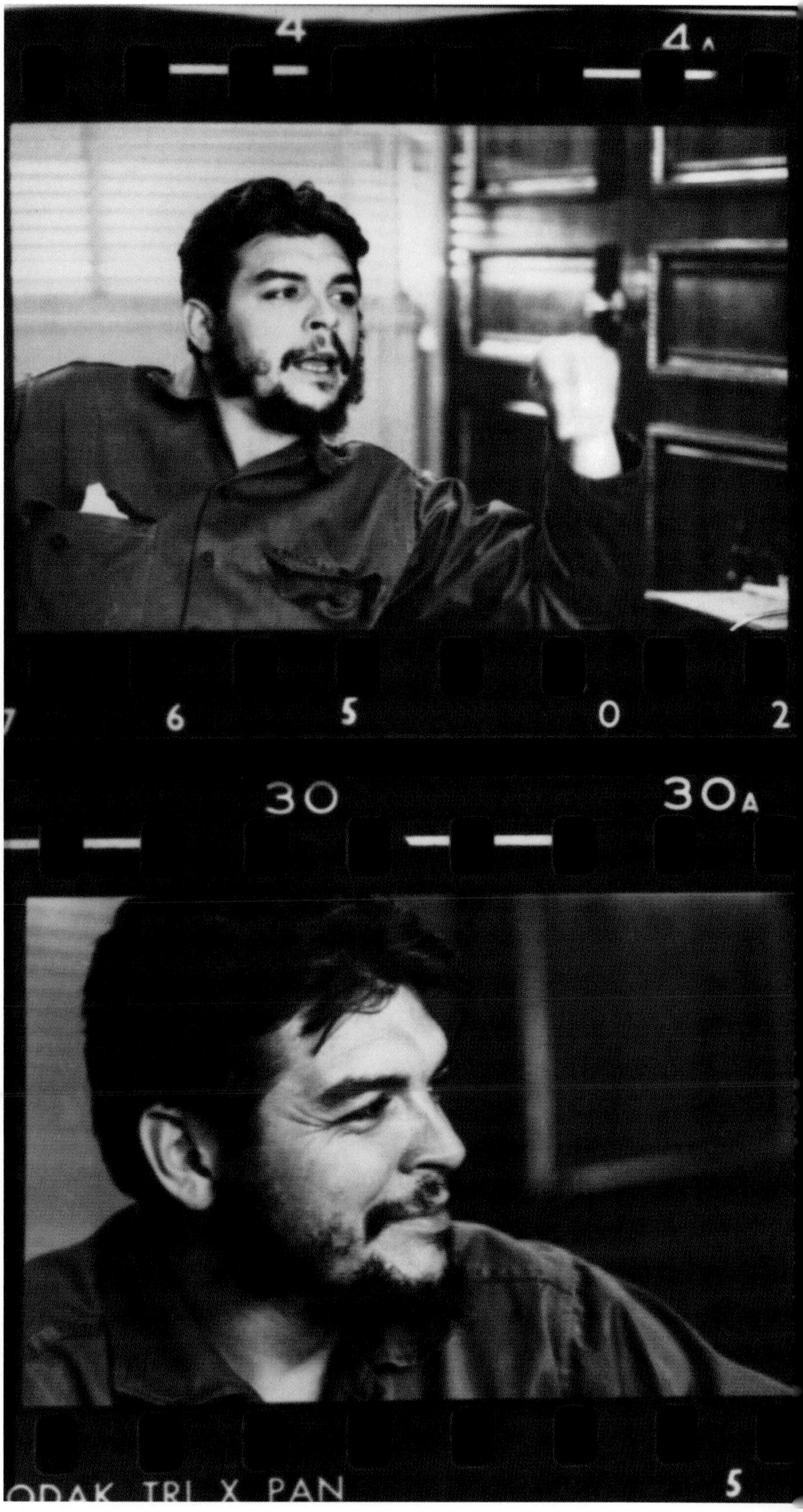

RIGHT: Politics never looked so sexy as in this mesmerizing portrait of Ernesto Guevara (Che), Argentinean politician (1928–67). At the time, Che was Minister of Industry in revolutionary Cuba and this sequence of photographs was taken in his somewhat cramped office. Che refused to look directly at the camera, but his eyes were very much on history. He was a handsome man and well aware of the power of his own image. The fine Cuban cigar is the perfect macho prop and the top middle image is one of the most iconic shots of all time.

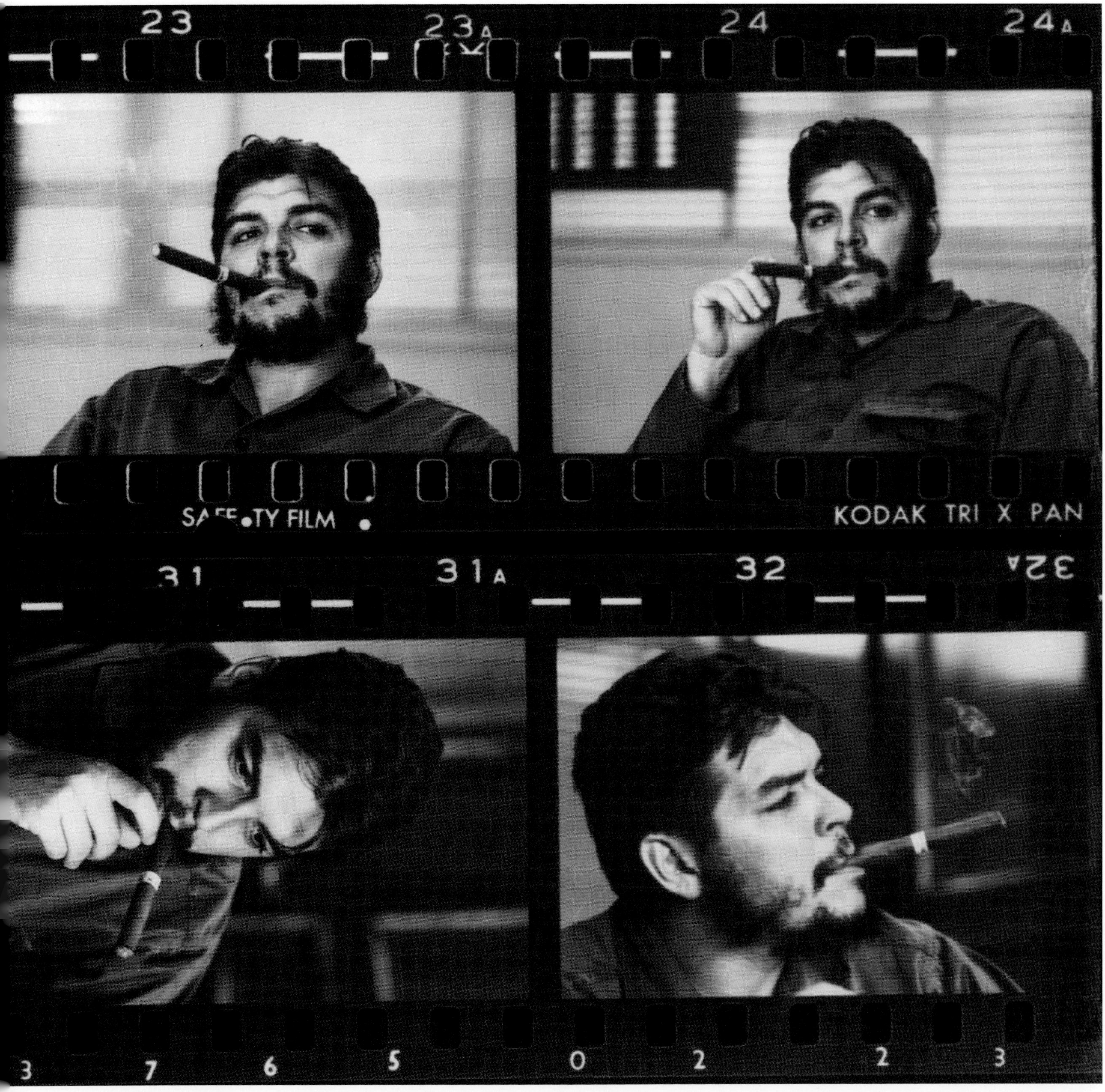
23
23A
24
24A
SAFETY FILM
KODAK TRI X PAN
31
31A
32
32A

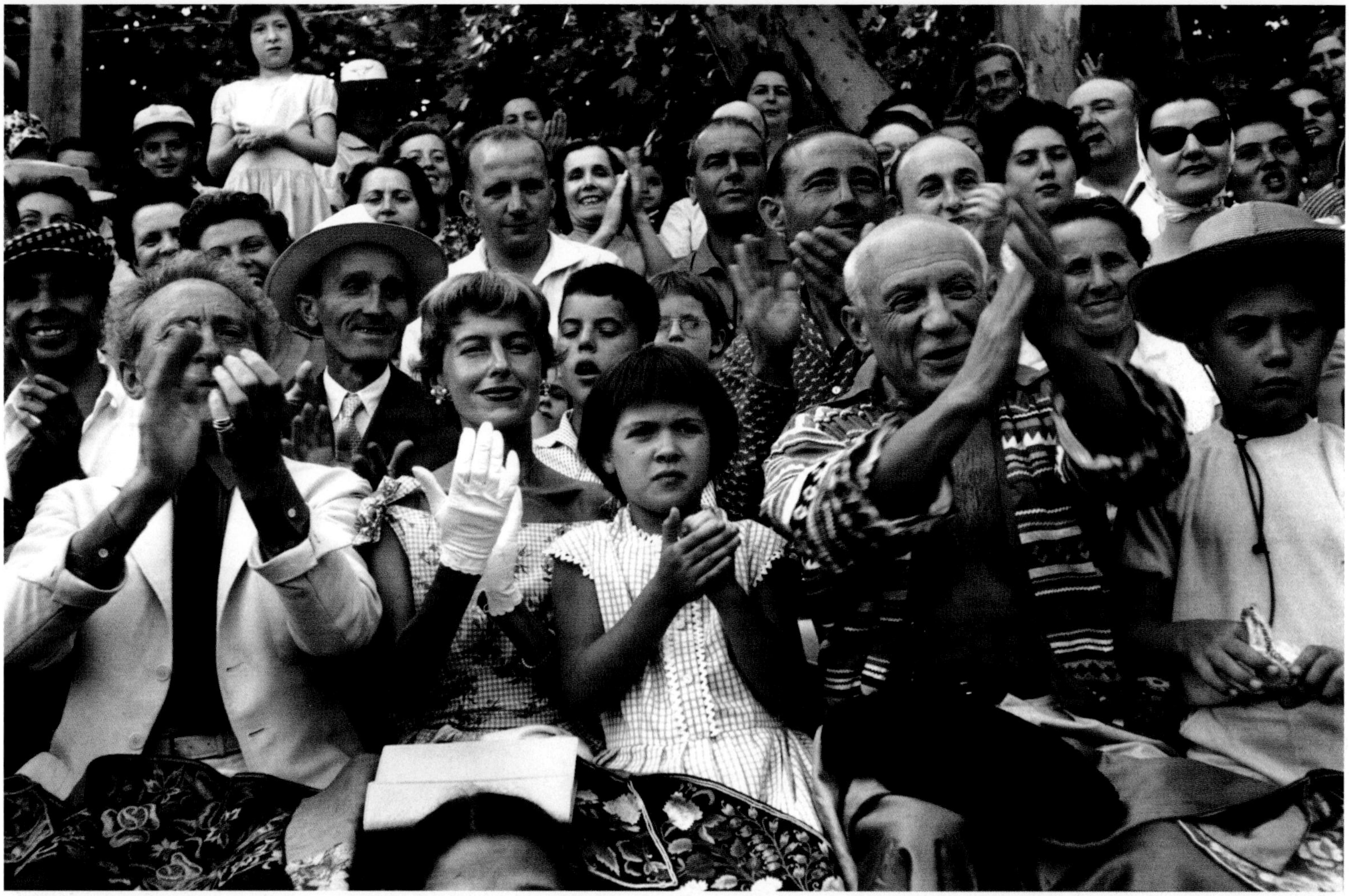

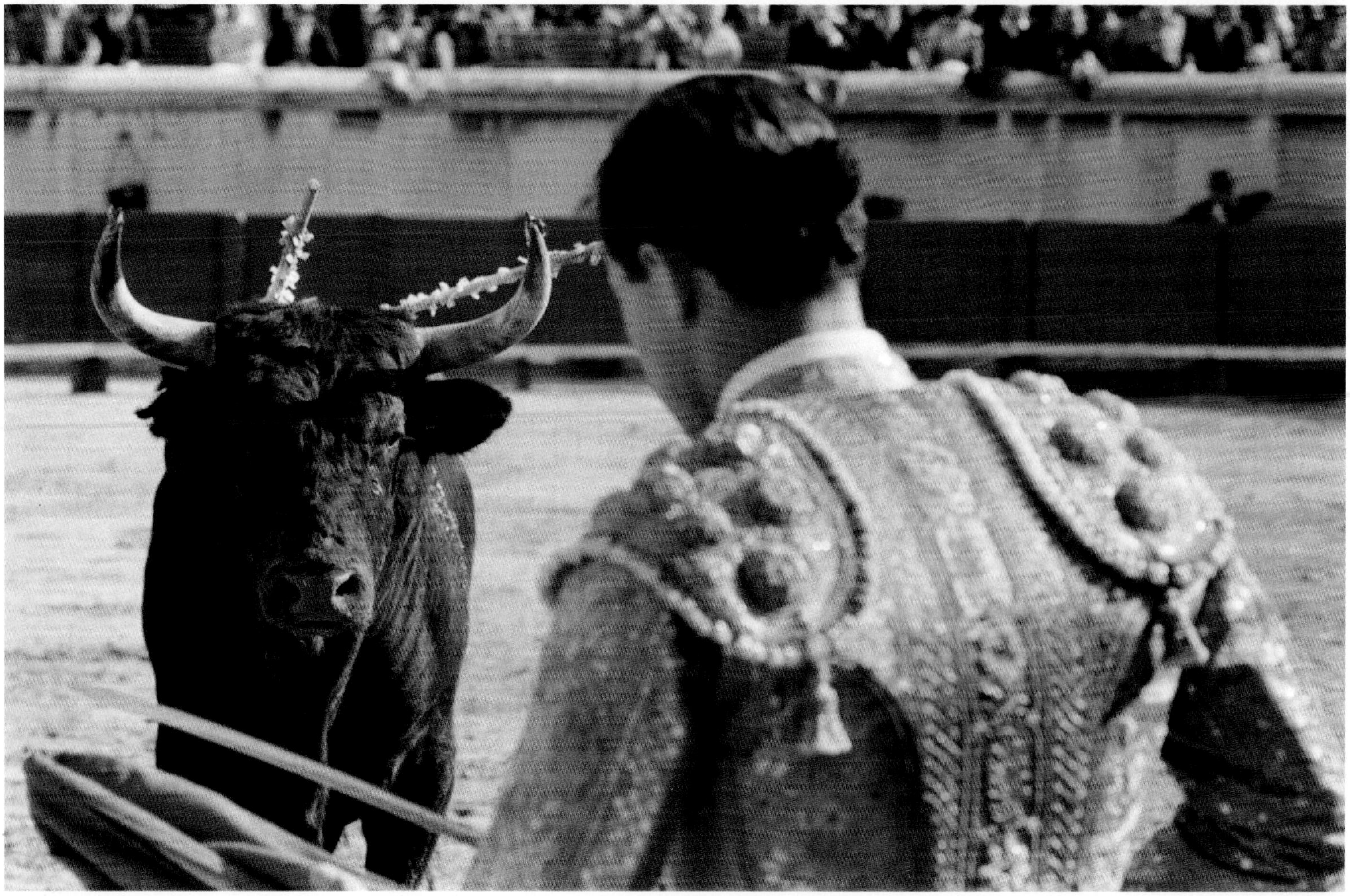

BELOW: Pablo Picasso, Spanish painter and sculptor, at his villa, "La Californie", in Cannes, France, 1957. Burri's essay on Picasso helped to cement the painter's myth and also introduced him to a wider audience. The strength and total self-assurance of Picasso really leaps out of this photograph.

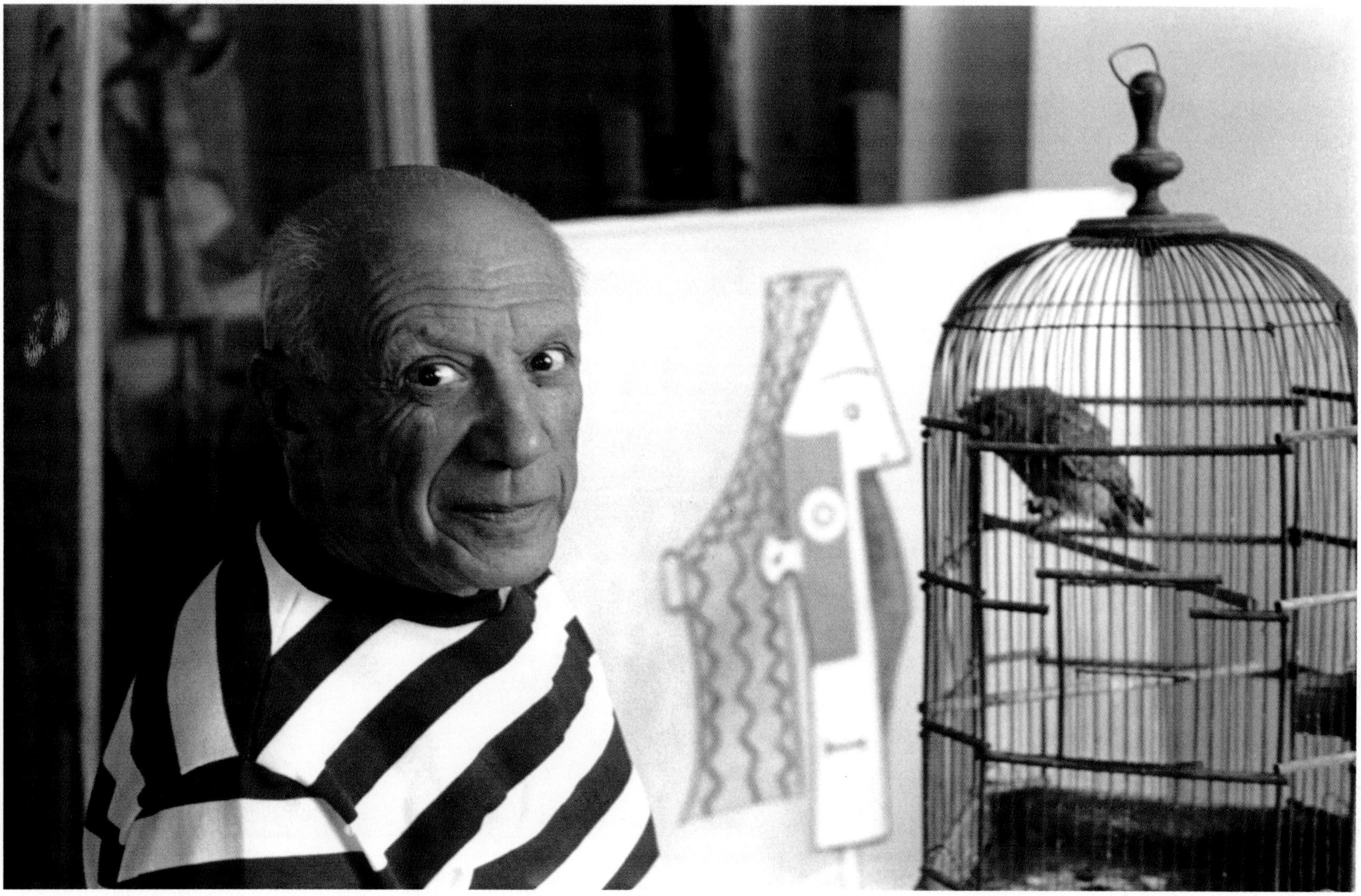

LEFT TOP: Picasso is seen with the French poet Jean Cocteau (far left) and with his own children, Paloma and Claude, in Corrida. It is evident from this photograph that Picasso wished to be portrayed as a doting parent and family man.

LEFT BOTTOM: Part of the same essay, this photograph captures the drama of a bull fight. Picasso was a traditional Spaniard who loved the excitement and cruelty of bull fighting.

LARRY BURROWS

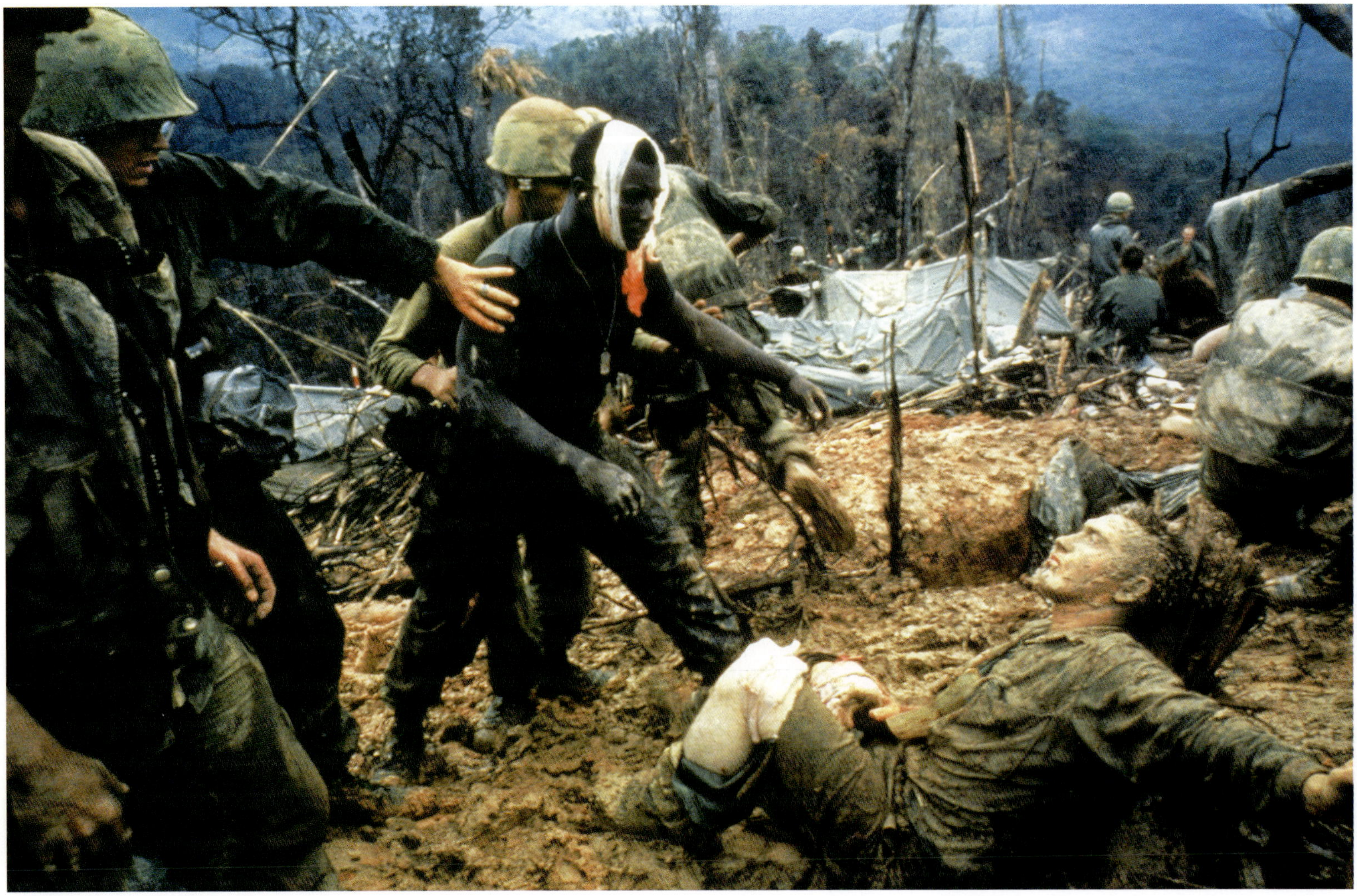

Larry Burrows's work is the most complete photographic record we have of the Vietnam War. When he arrived in the region for the first time in 1962, most Americans were blissfully unaware that Vietnam was a trouble spot whose problems had the potential to become America's problems. In a few years that was all to change, and Burrows should be given credit for educating people about what was really going on. Burrows became embedded in the battle zone before anyone else and he had the foresight to realize that this was not only an important conflict, but one that was going to escalate and probably go badly wrong. Tall and elegant, he was something of a gentleman and the antithesis of the macho war photographer. He was also somewhat aloof and preferred to work alone. Vietnam was very much his story and tragically he gave his life to it.

In the war against Iraq, the access of photographers was carefully monitored by the military, and American news sources were reluctant to publish images of dead Iraqis and wounded American soldiers. In the early 1960s Burrows had complete freedom to photograph the theatre of war and its bloody consequences. Ironically, this access was originally granted because the military believed that on-the-spot photographers would help the public relations effort in selling the war to the folks back home. For months Burrows consorted with small US fighting units, shooting photographs from helicopters and planes and photographing blood-spattered wounded soldiers, bewildered and lost. He was also deeply sympathetic to the plight of the Vietnamese and saw them as innocents caught in the crossfire. He was repelled by much of what he saw and it made him angry, yet he felt morally compelled to photograph it all, much of it in vivid colour. *Life* magazine was under pressure from the new medium of colour television and Burrows's coverage was in direct competition with the television networks. At a time when colour film was not as reliable and sharp as it is today, his years in the darkroom paid off. Burrows's colour images of the Vietnam War changed not just what we saw, but how we saw it – war photography would never be the same again.

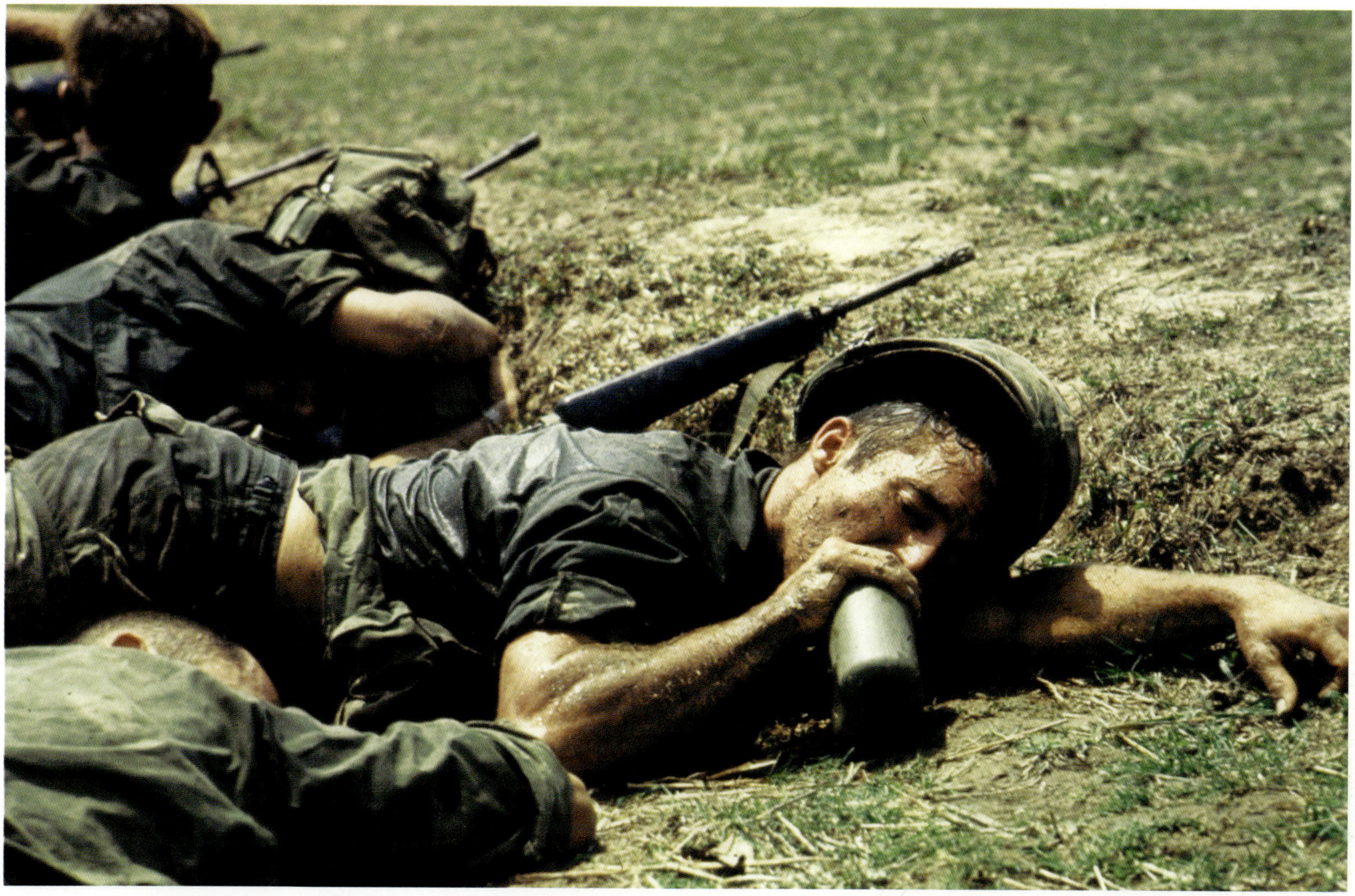

LEFT: In one of the most famous images of the Vietnam War, and one of the most powerful war photographs of all time, wounded Marine Gunnery Sgt Jeremiah Purdie is led past a stricken comrade after a fierce firefight for control of Hill 484 in South Vietnam, in 1966. The facial expressions of the two injured soldiers elevate this image into something beyond an action shot. Although one is caked in mud, unable to move, and the other is bleeding and stunned, they are still trying to help and reach out for each other. The fact that one is black and the other white gives the photograph even more resonance.

ABOVE: A US infantryman on the Cambodia/Vietnam frontier overcome by heat and fatigue drinks from a canteen while others lie about on the ground. Burrows has a unique ability to place the viewer right at the heart of the action. The low angle accentuates the soldier's predicament and the sense that these men are trapped.

OVERLEAF LEFT: US marines are pictured on patrol in 1966. The soldier has a gentle and sensitive face, at odds with his heavy combat gear. He seems uncertain about why he is there and what he is doing.

OVERLEAF RIGHT: Although he made his name shooting in colour, Burrows was also adept at photographing in black-and-white, as in this image of marines searching for Vietcong in the Delta 1967.

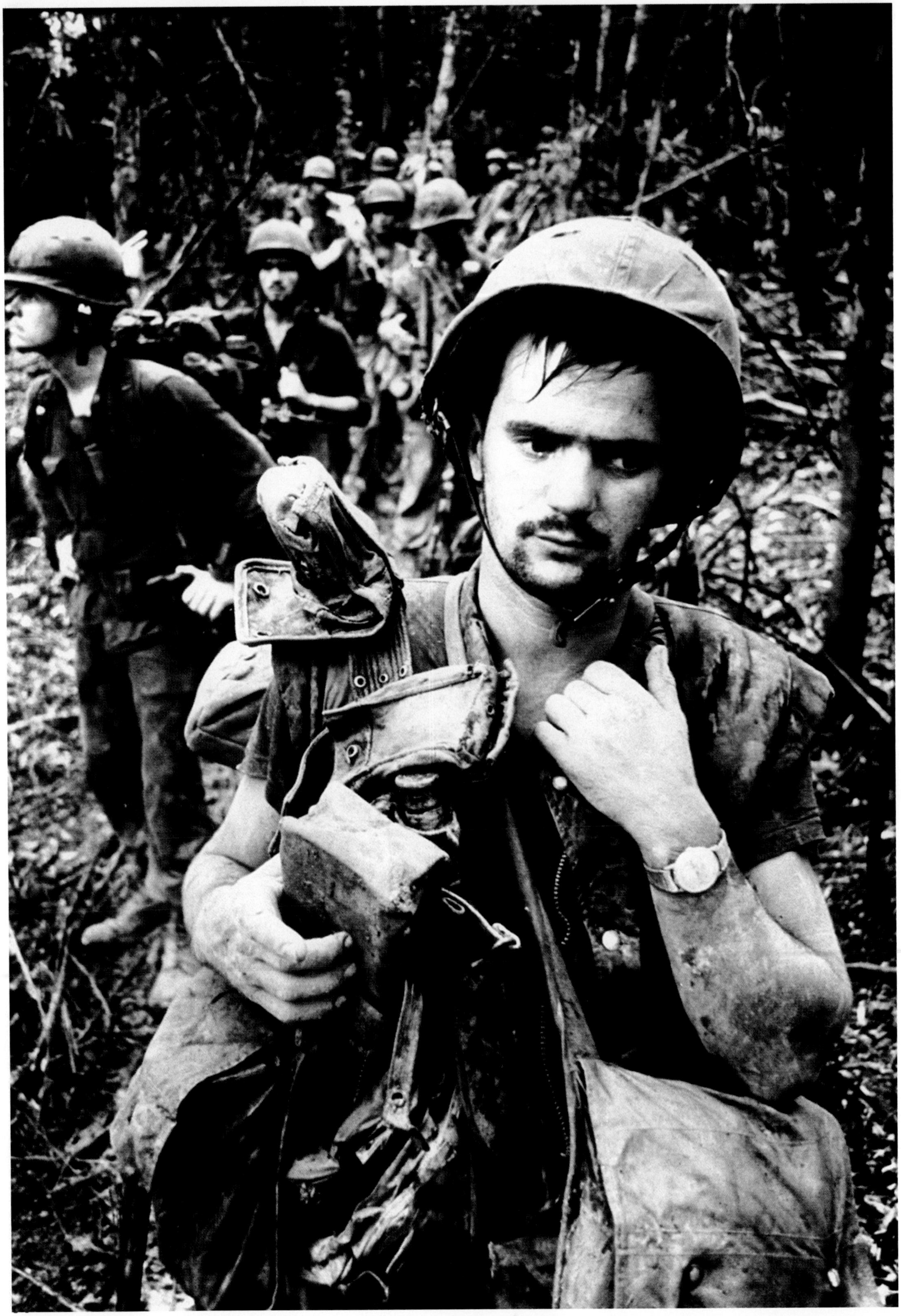

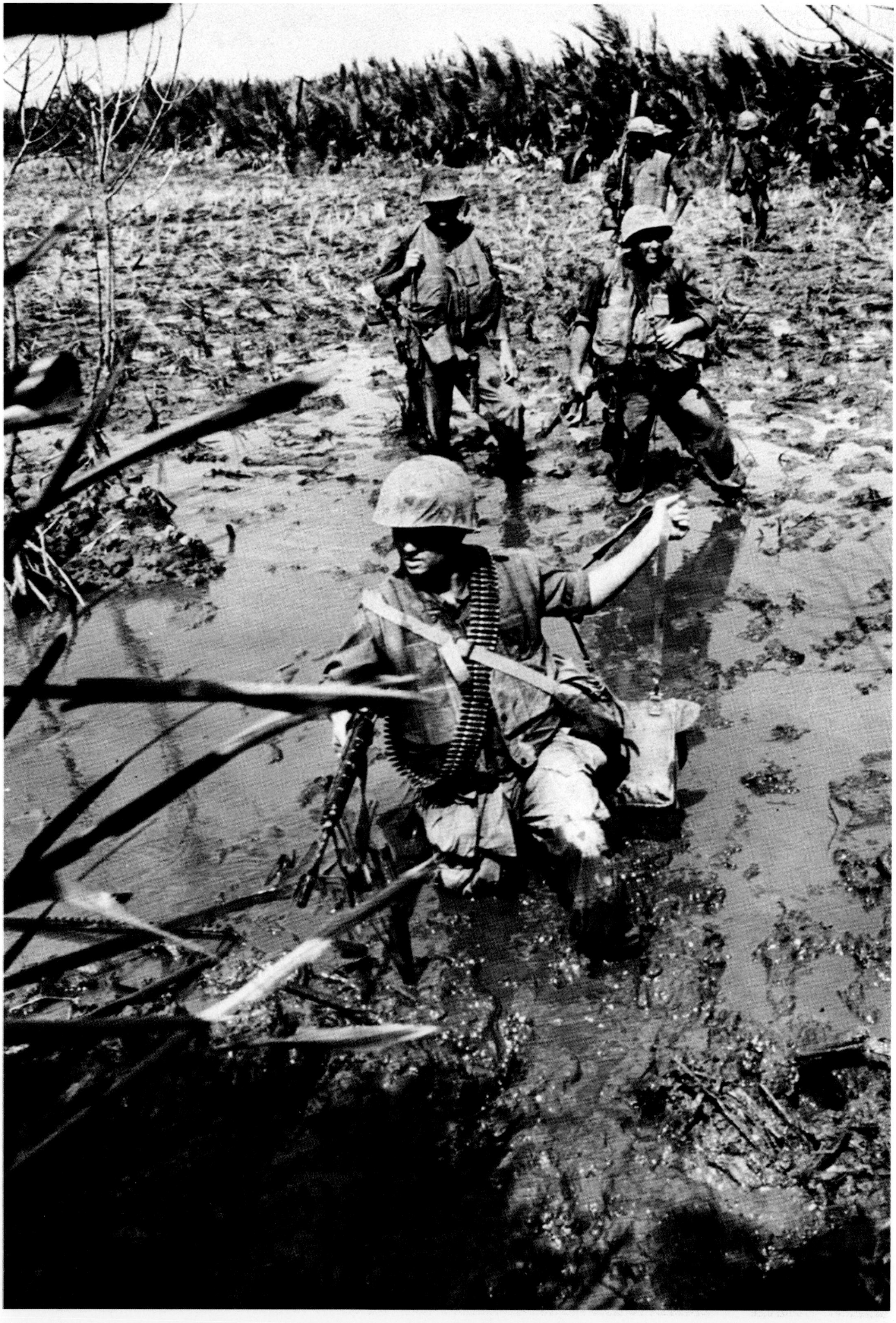

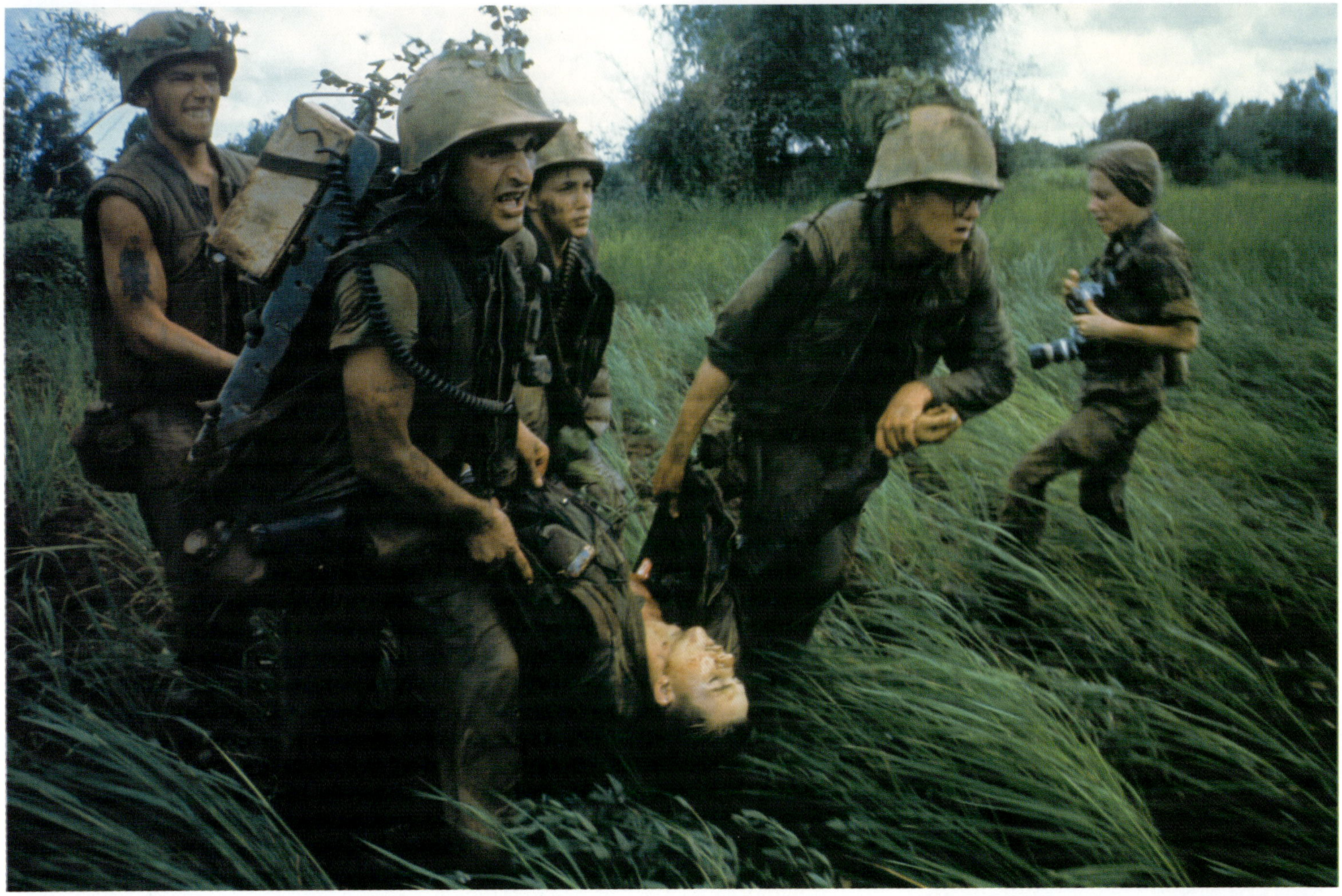

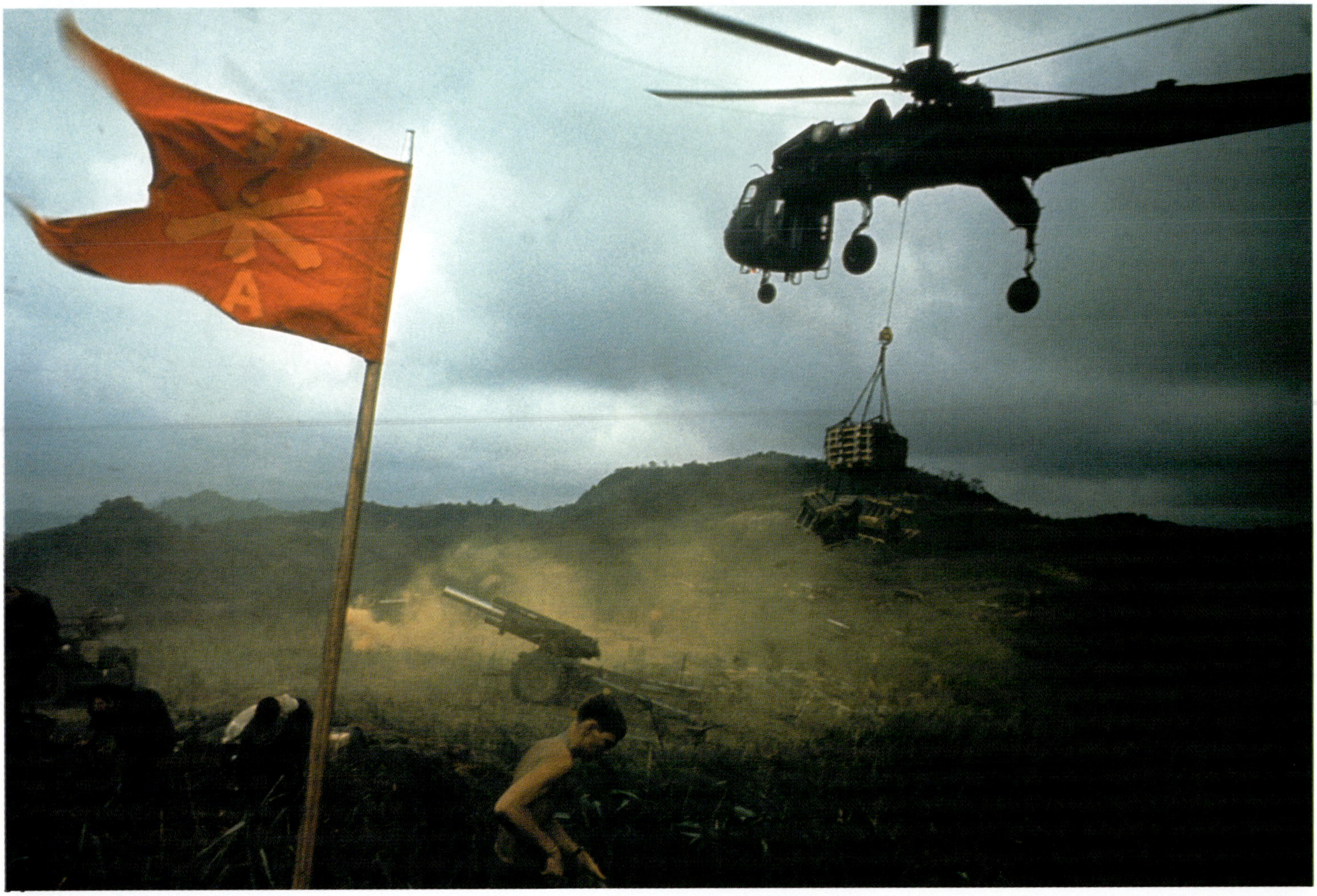
A

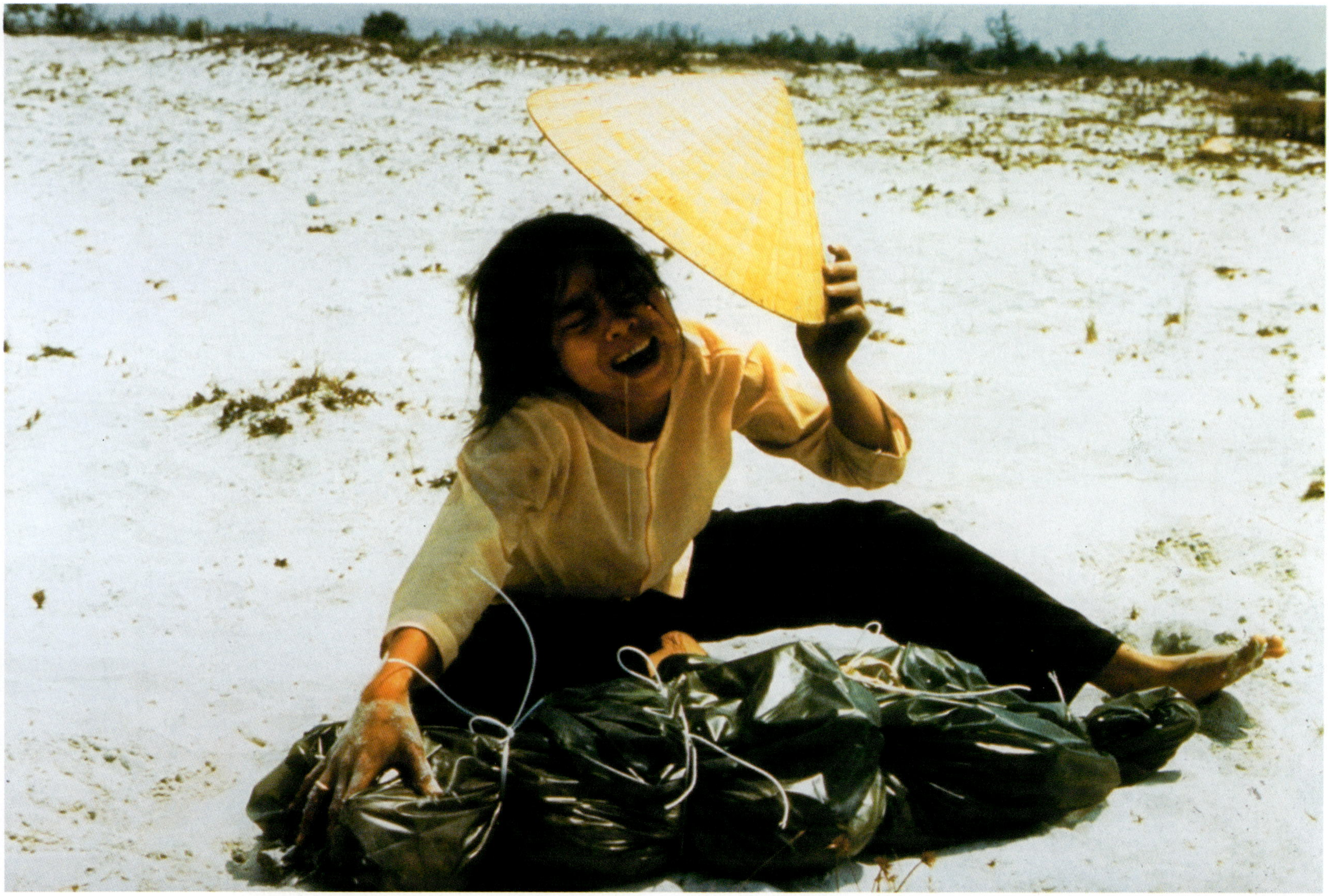

LEFT TOP: Burrows's visceral photography had a profound impact on some of the subsequent films made about the Vietnam War. This image of marines recovering the body of a comrade while under fire from the North Vietnamese could be a still from *Platoon*.

LEFT BOTTOM: During a persistent North Vietnamese attack in 1968, a US 1st Air Cavalry helicopter airlifts ammunition into a marine outpost.

ABOVE: In this harrowing image of raw and absolute grief, a distraught widow cries over a plastic bag that contains the remains of her husband, killed in the 1968 Tet offensive, and recently found in a mass grave. Burrows was the supreme war photographer who could document all sides of the conflict and who had a natural empathy with the Vietnamese people.

ROBERT CAPA

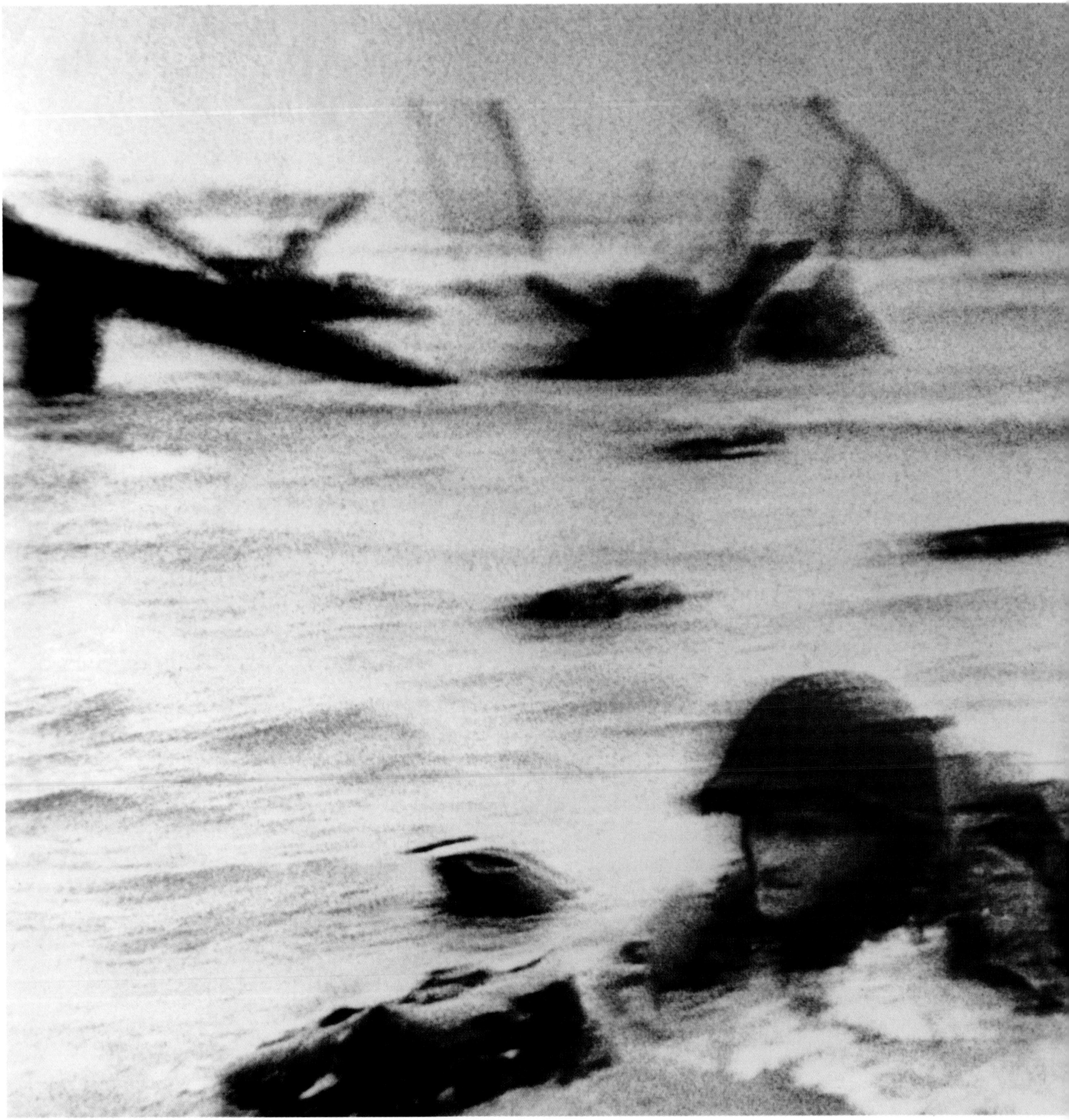

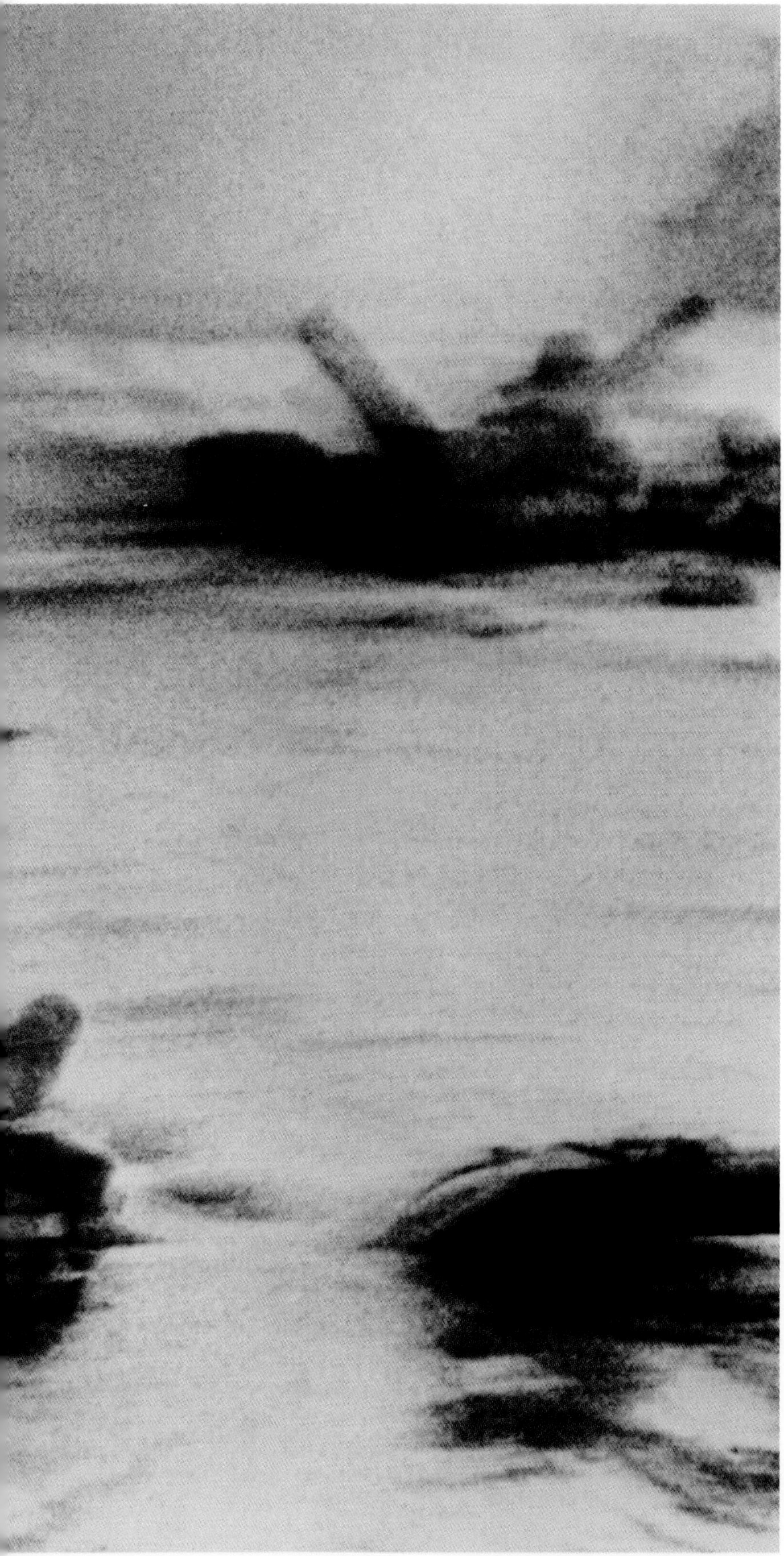

Capa's romantic and heroic reputation hides another side to his work. His dictum "If your pictures aren't good enough it's because you're not close enough" has a double meaning, because it implies that involvement and sympathy with the subject are equally as crucial as being close to the action. He was to draw on his sense of empathy to make important pictures about the situations and people with whom he came into contact. His notoriety – as gambler, drinker, *bon viveur*, serial seducer of beautiful women – was carefully nurtured by him to increase the value of his work.

While covering the Spanish Civil War in 1936, he took the iconic image of the conflict and one of the most important of the twentieth century, the Republican soldier at the moment of death. There has been controversy about it ever since: was it set up? (His biographer Richard Whelan succeeded in putting all doubts about this image to rest in 2002, following a positive identification of the subject and the action in which he died.) After the fall of France in 1940, Capa was in the USA and managed to gain assignments from the leading American magazines *Collier's* and *Life*. His reputation as "the greatest war photographer" was finally confirmed by his pictures of D-Day. He photographed under heavy fire on the American beachhead, and his four films were rushed back to England where a hapless darkroom assistant at *Life* managed to destroy all but 11 frames (out of a total 108) of his film in an overheated drying cabinet. Yet the heavy grain and distortions of the negatives made the pictures graphically powerful. When published, they were immediately seen as defining records of the battle, though *Life* hid its mistake by saying they were "slightly out of focus". His romantic life (which included many friends in Hollywood) and early death made Capa a star known far beyond the narrow confines of photography. But he left a vast photographic legacy, a body of work that showed him to be a perceptive humanist photographer, an outstanding portraitist and masterful at capturing the complexity of a military action. He was also an inspired innovator in the field of photojournalism, creating and nurturing the Magnum cooperative.

LEFT: "The war correspondent has his stake – his life – in his own hands, and he can put it on this horse or that horse, or he can put it back in his pocket at the very last minute ... I am a gambler. I decided to go in with Company E in the first wave." This photograph of Omaha Beach, Normandy, 6 June 1944, was one of 11 surviving pictures from the four films Capa shot on his Contax. His D-Day images have become the enduring symbol of the struggle for the beachhead.

BELOW: This photograph of a Spanish Republican soldier at the moment of death, on the Aragon Front in September 1936, made Capa's name. Uncertainty about whether the photograph was "set-up" was finally resolved only when several witnesses to the action in which the soldier was killed were located in 2002.

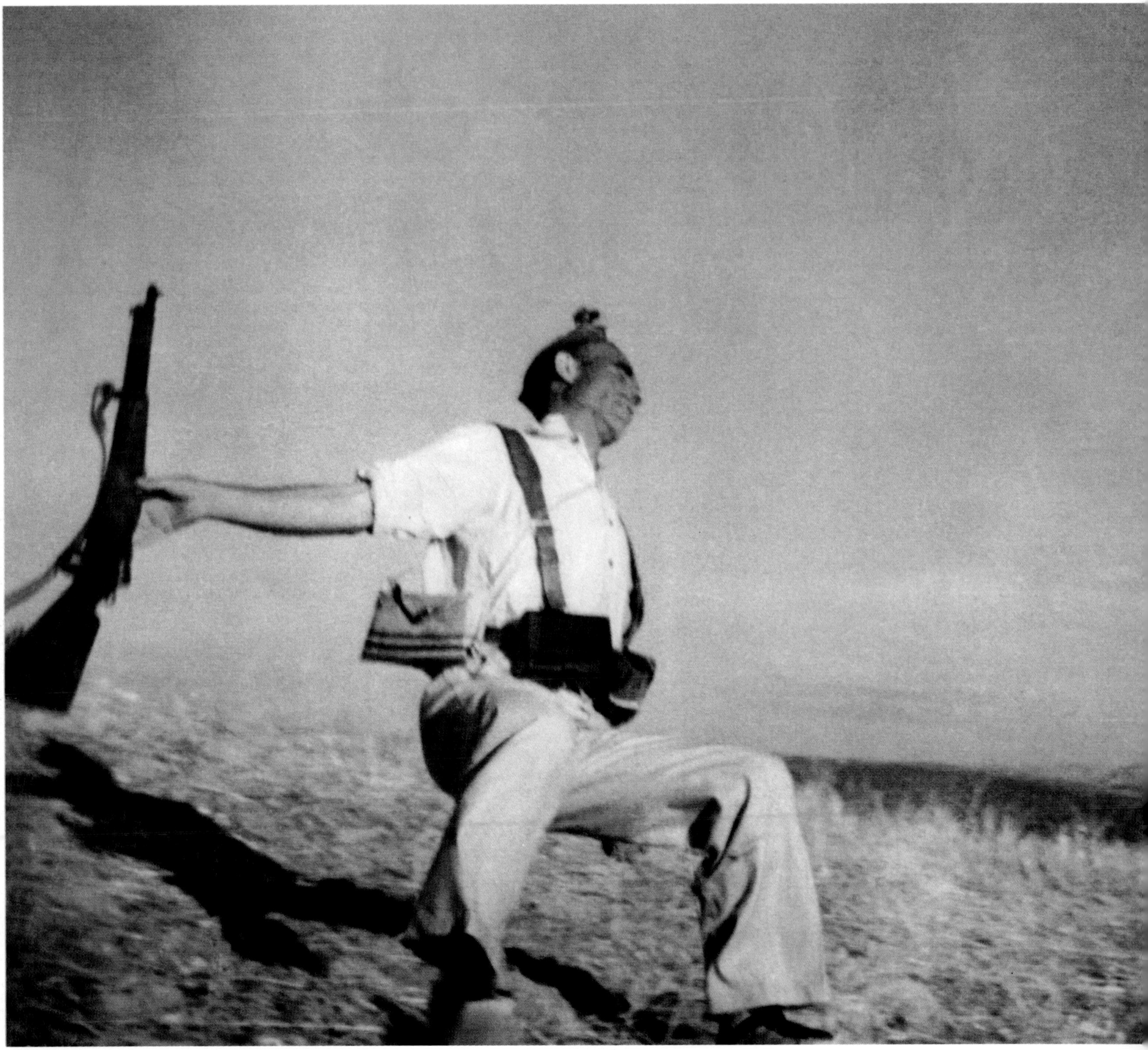

BELOW: **Capa chose to show this Spanish Republican soldier on the Aragon Front (August–September 1936) in a heroic pose, which is accentuated by the viewpoint.**

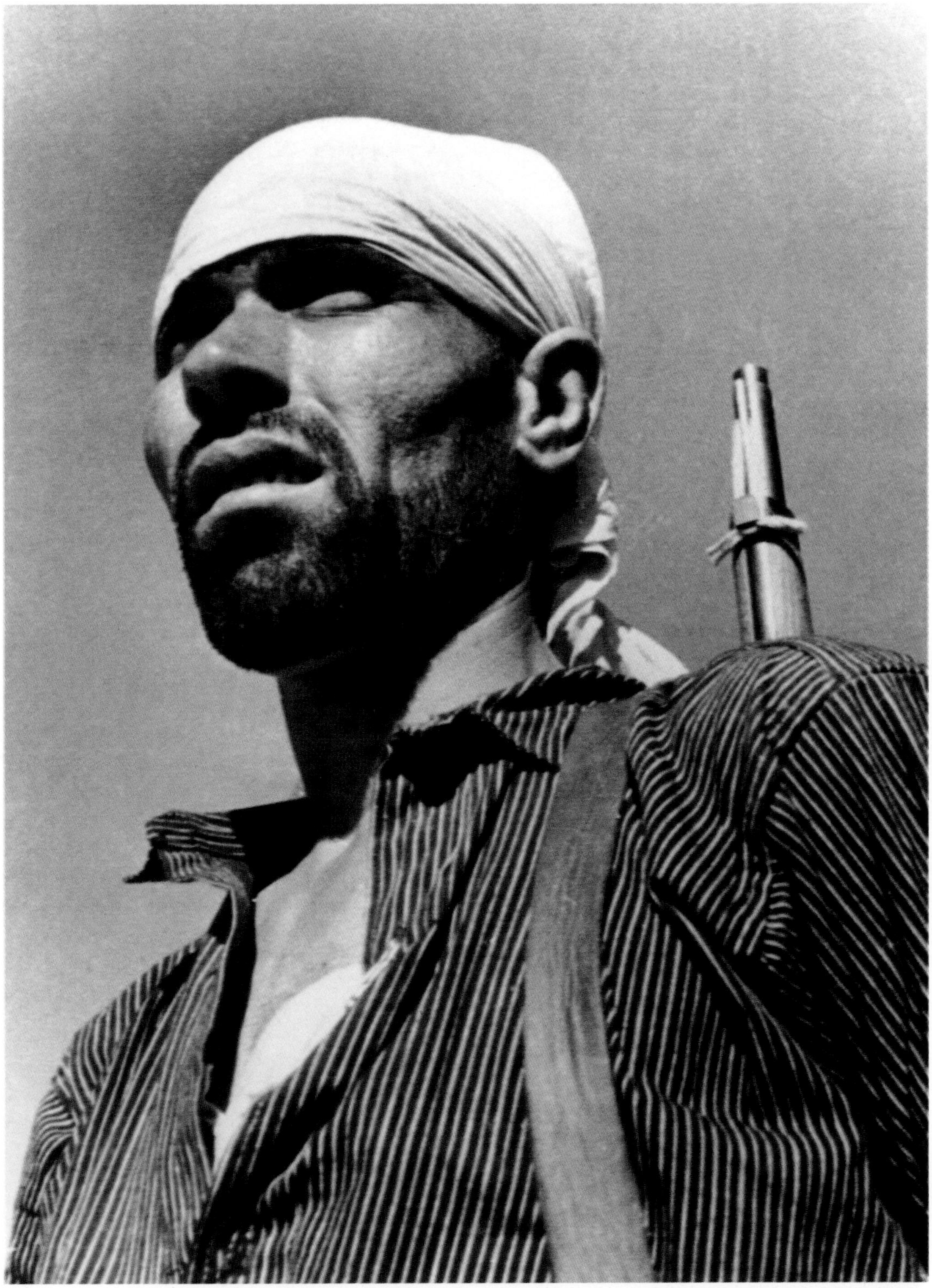

GILLES CARON

The power and beauty of Caron's work as a photojournalist probably owes a great deal to his experiences in Algeria. According to his friend Robert Pledge, photographer and founder of Contact Press Images, Caron's 24 months as a paratrooper were recounted in the almost daily letters he wrote to his mother. They contain remarkable observations on what was going on around him and his feelings and distress about the violence and the horror that took place. It led him to photography. As he wrote, he "felt the need to be there and be a witness and tell the world what was going on".

When he returned to France, he decided to become a photographer and a witness to world events. Caron's pictures of Paris in May 1968 are remarkable for the way they capture the riots as street theatre, like staged and pitched battles in a civil war (not unlike the photos of the insurrection that brought the German occupation to an end in August 1944). All his experience as a soldier and as a war photographer was brought to bear on them. The same turn in world events that had taken Caron to wars in Africa and Indochina brought him back to France and on to the streets of Paris, before he was whisked away to South-East Asia. Don McCullin, a friend and a competitor for the same picture stories, recalled the moment he learnt of Caron's disappearance. "The tragedy about Gilles was that when the Cambodian conflict broke out in a very serious way, being French of course, he was that much closer to the culture. He got there very quick and I got there a week later, and by the time I got there Gilles had already been captured and disappeared out of our lives."

RIGHT: Caron's knack of capturing the beauty of the balletic stone thrower in the Rue St Jacques emphasizes the theatrical character of so much of what occurred during May 1968.

BELOW: This is one of the most enduring images from the 1960s, with the riot policeman representing the full force of repression. It is a surreal isolated moment from a strange time and we certainly feel the demonstrator's pain.

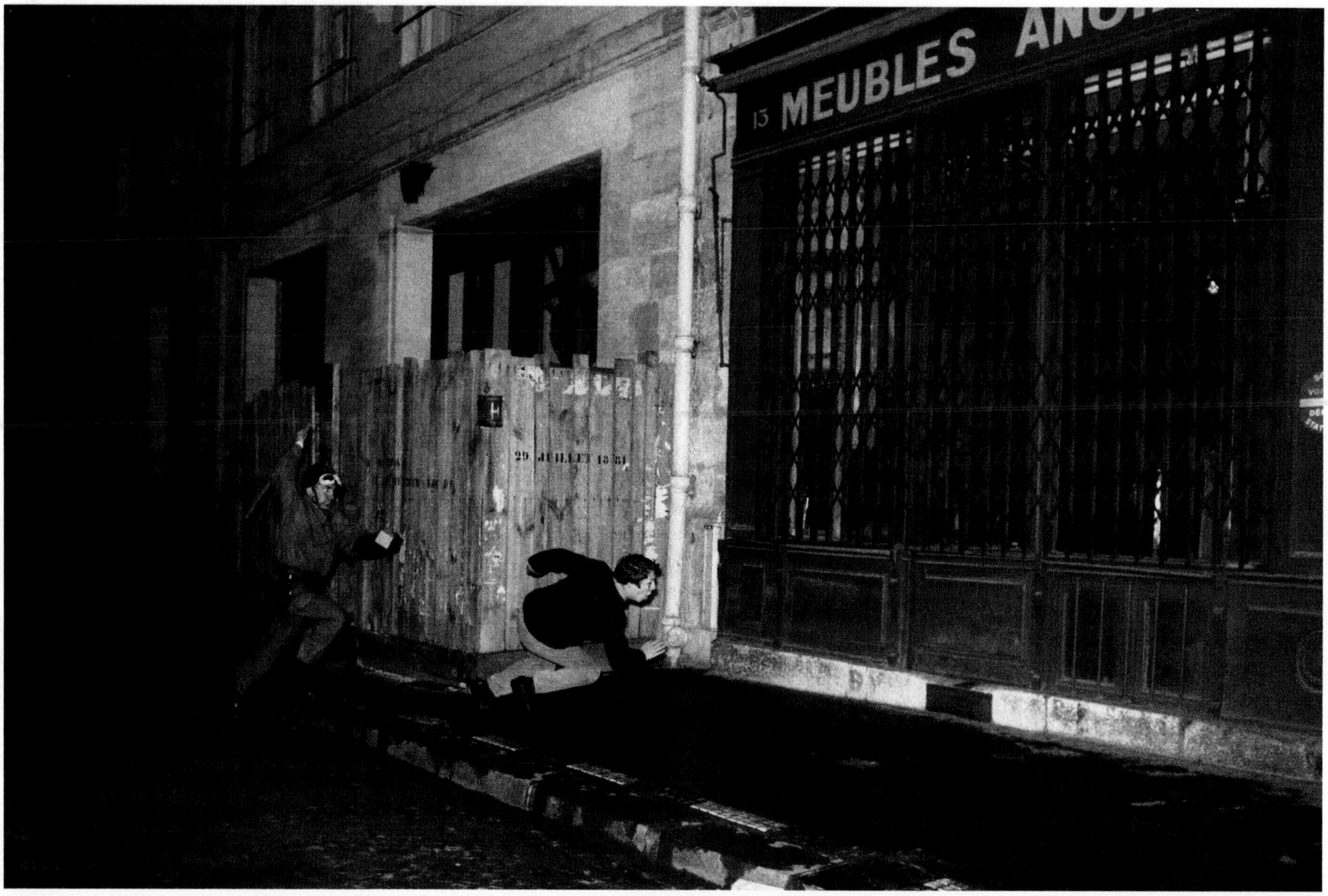

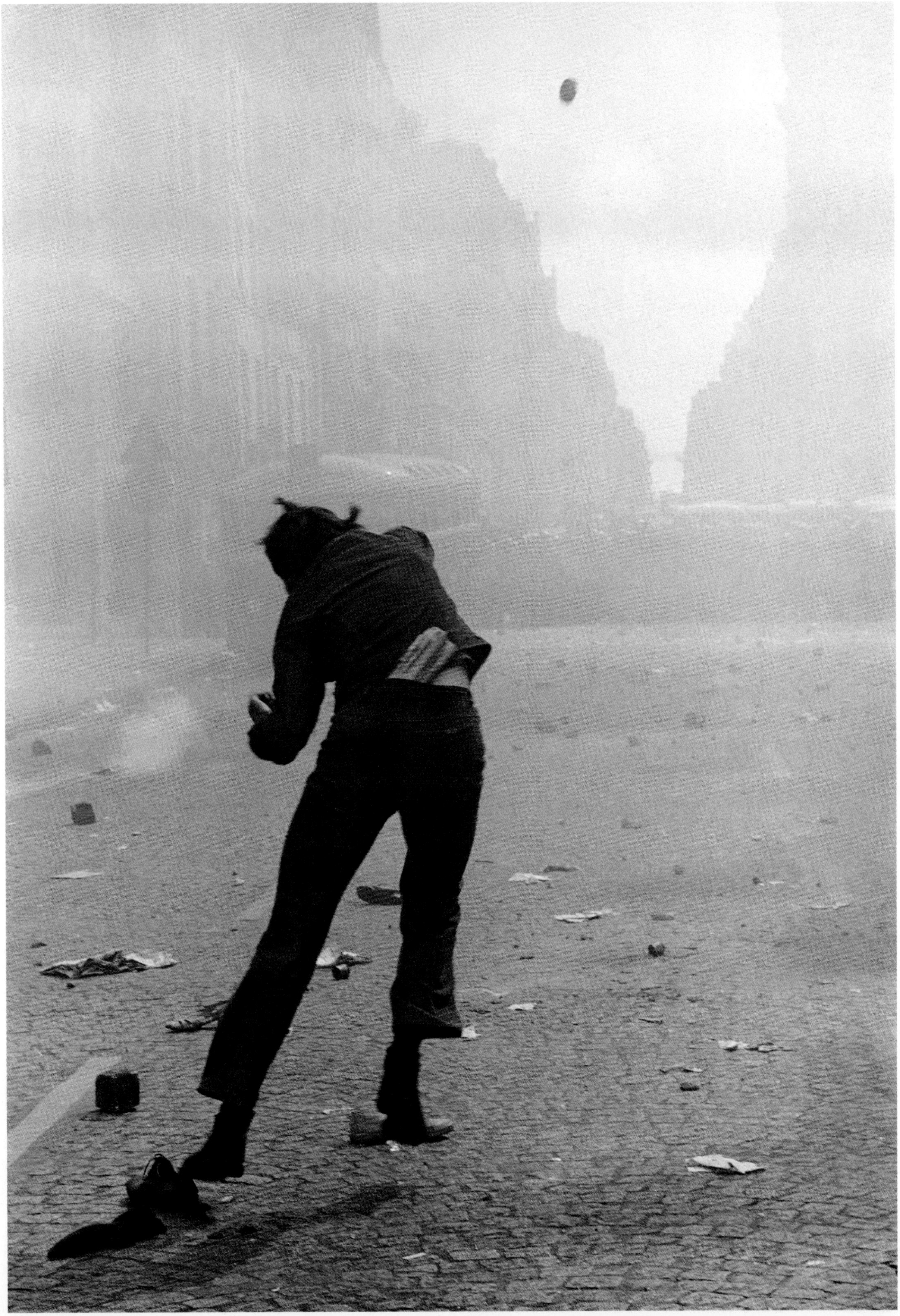

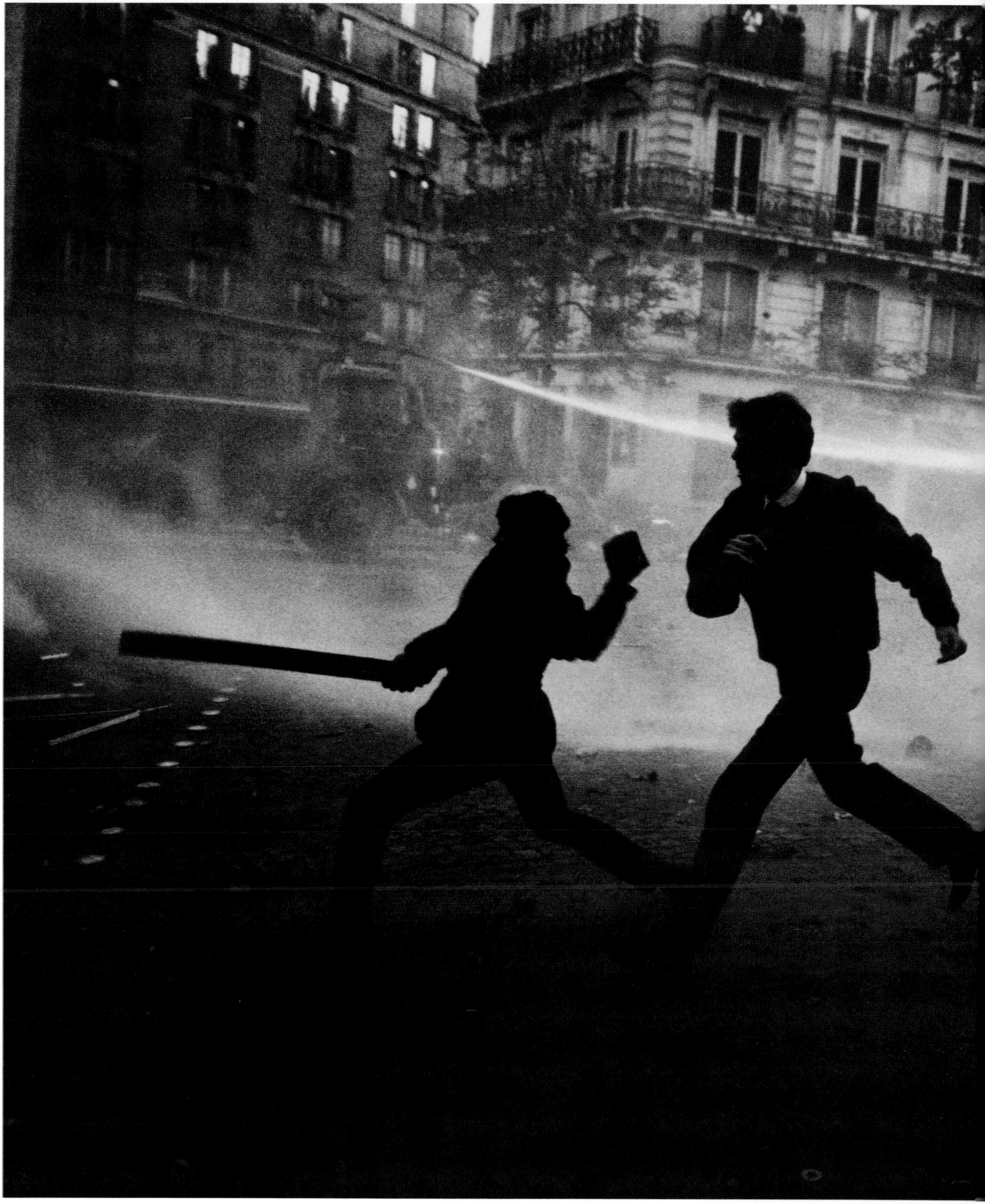

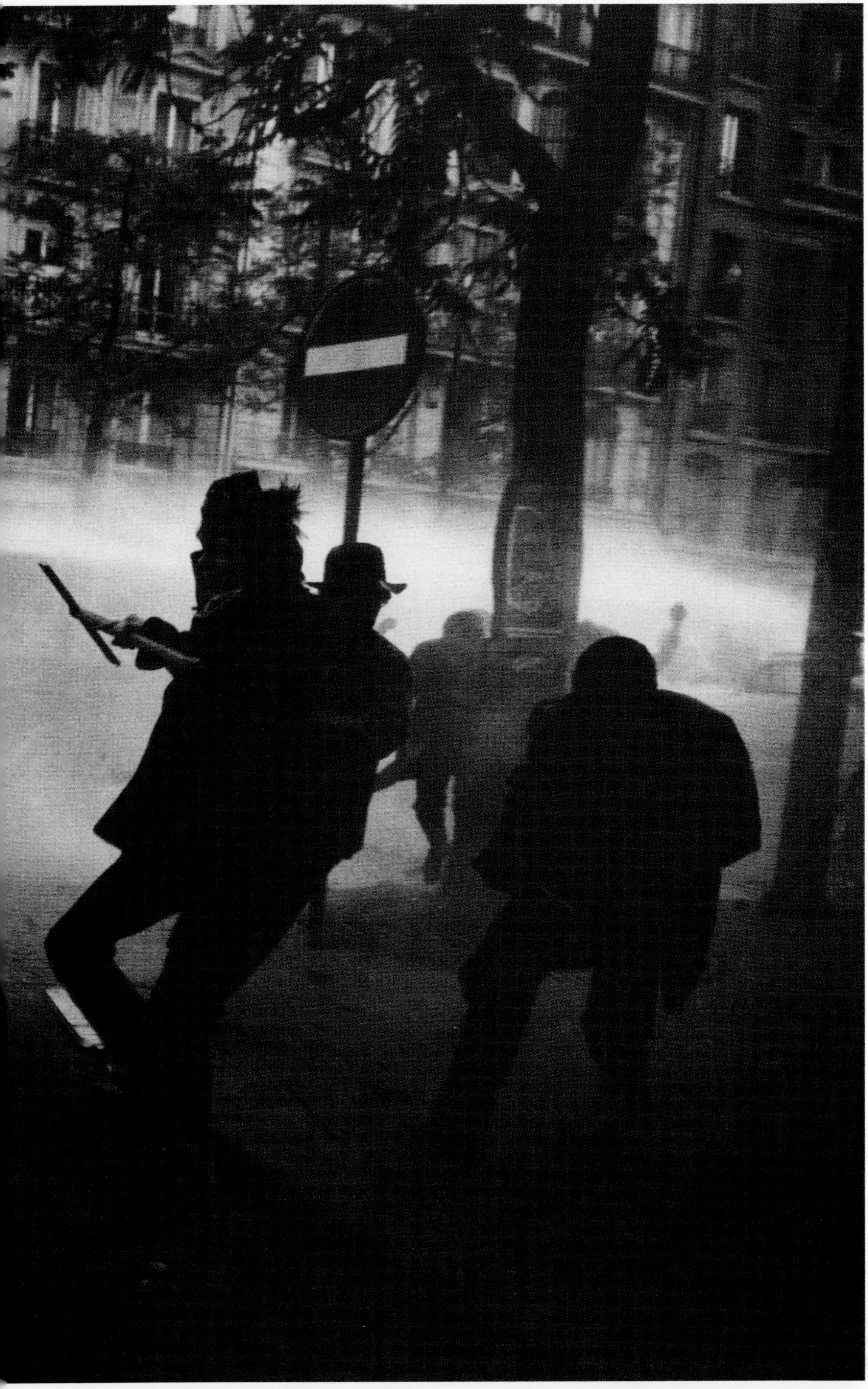

LEFT: A group of demonstrators in action during the pitched battles fought along the streets of the Latin quarter, an echo of the struggles waged in August 1944 when Paris was liberated from the Germans.

HENRI CARTIER-BRESSON

It is ironic that the greatest photojournalist of the twentieth century was somewhat disdainful of the term and in the latter part of his lifetime appeared to be bored with photography itself. But Cartier-Bresson was always something of a contradiction: an upper-class left-wing bohemian; a photojournalist who worked for magazines, yet who regarded himself as an incorruptible artist; and an idealist who was also very much a shrewd businessman with a great sense of his own worth and legacy. In *The Decisive Moment* he writes: "I prowled the streets all day ... ready to pounce, determined to 'trap' life – to preserve life in the art of living. Above all I craved to seize the whole essence, in the confines of a single photograph, of some situation that was in the process of unrolling itself before my eyes."

This "whole essence" comes together when the hand, eye and heart are working in perfect tandem. Cartier-Bresson would study his photographs upside down in order to better assess the lines and composition, in much the same way a painter looks at his canvas. Cartier-Bresson perpetuated his own myths, and one of them was that he would take few photographs, preferring instead to merge into the background, observe a situation through his Leica until the Zen moment and then click the shutter. The reality was somewhat different; Cartier-Bresson probably shot as many rolls of film as some of his Magnum colleagues – he simply had a higher hit rate and was also a very efficient editor of his own work. For all his high-art ideals, he was also an extremely capable and brave frontline news photographer who knew how to jolt his viewers. His experiences had been partly shaped by being imprisoned by the Nazis during the Second World War and his subsequent escape and time in the French Resistance. It is against this background that the famous photograph shown here should be judged. Prior to Cartier-Bresson, photojournalism was considered a trade; he elevated the medium into an art form. A true visionary and a genius, we shall probably never see the like of him again.

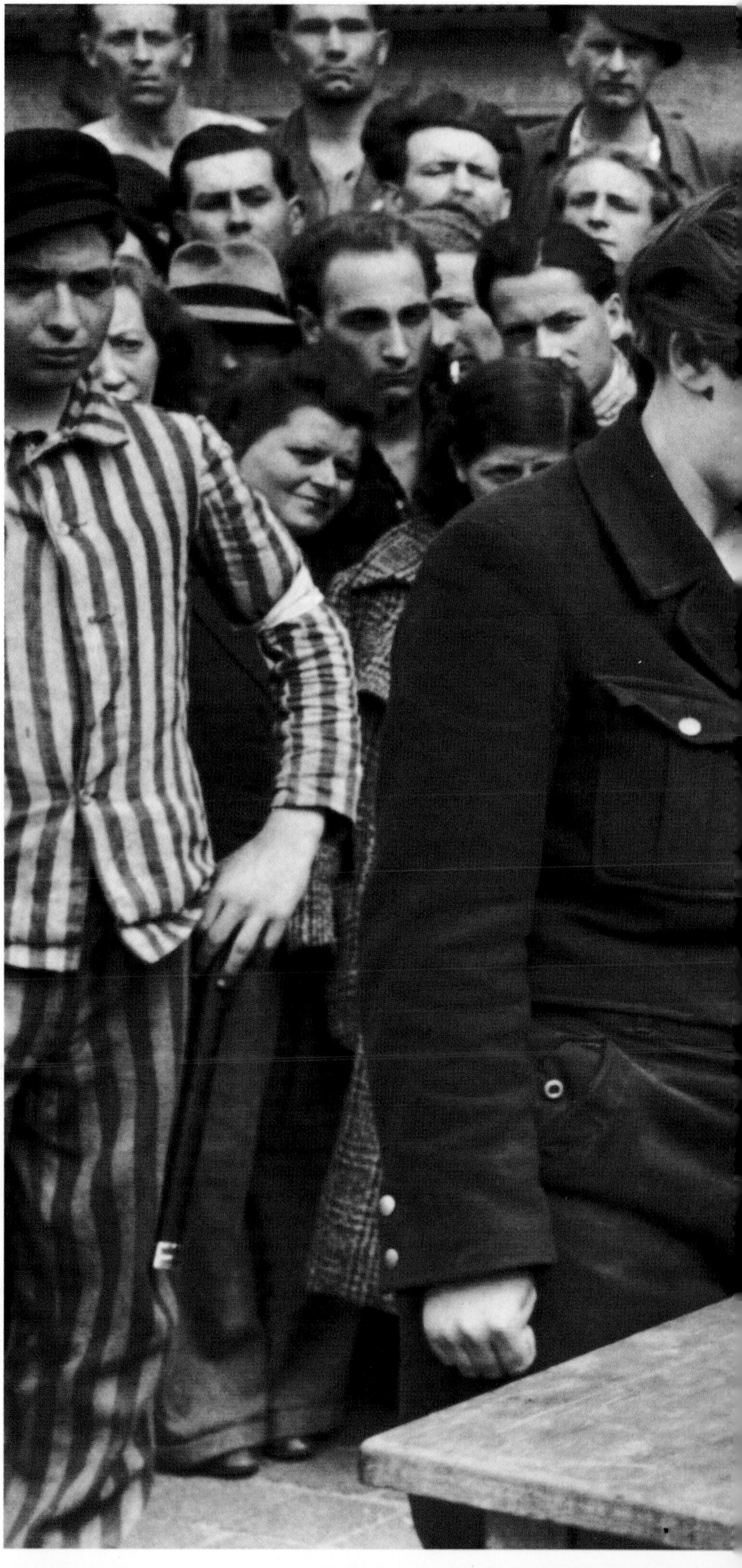

RIGHT: A young Belgian woman and former Gestapo informer is identified as she tried to hide in the crowd in what is probably Cartier-Bresson's most famous on-the-spot news photograph. Cartier-Bresson brilliantly captures the harsh emotions evoked by the scene – anger, shame, curiosity, revenge – and no one comes out of this photograph particularly well.

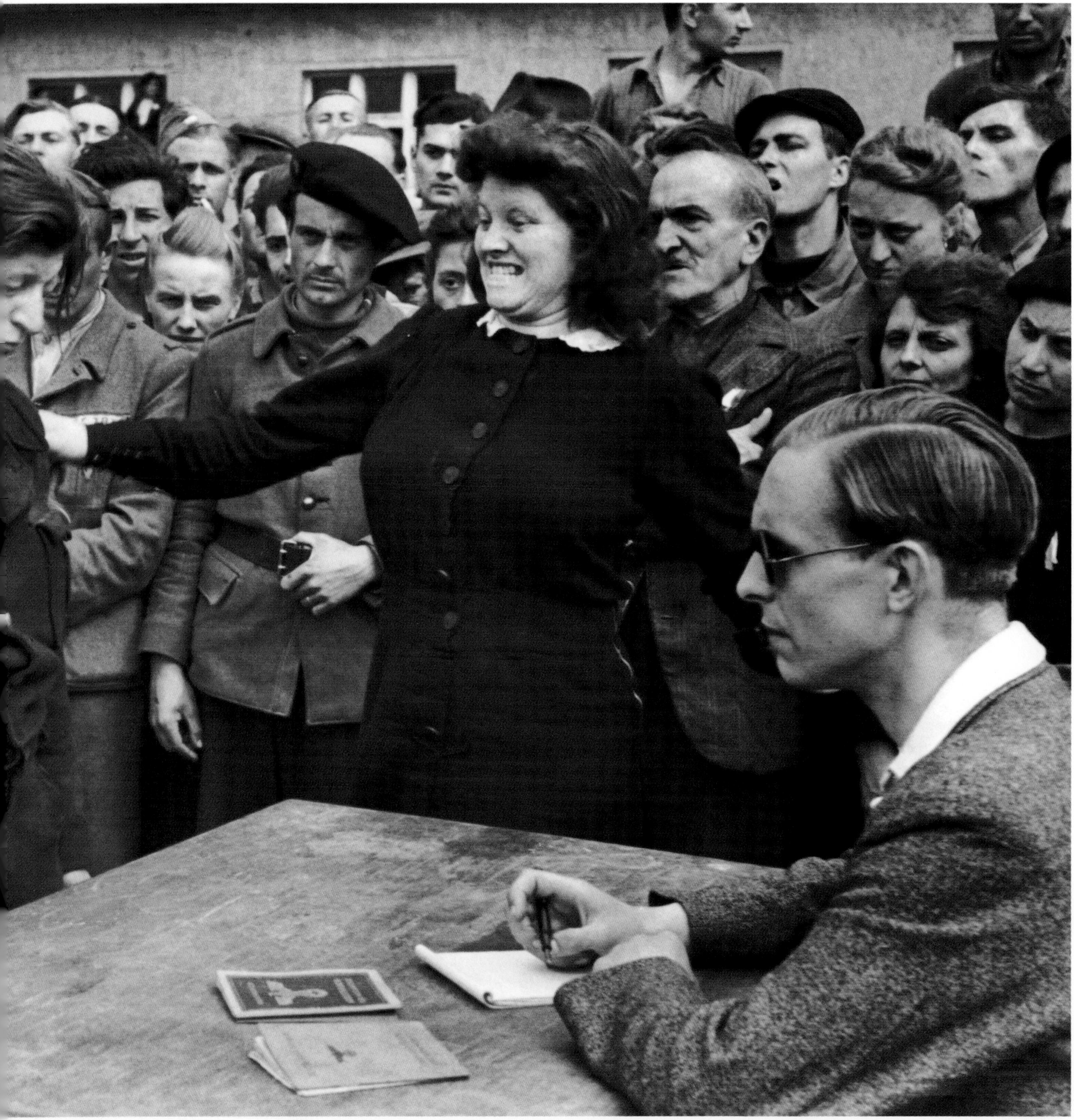

BELOW AND RIGHT: **Two views of the crowds waiting in Trafalgar Square, London, in 1937 for the coronation parade of King George VI. This was a strange period in English history because the true heir, the King's brother Edward VIII (the Duke of Windsor), had abdicated in order to marry Wallis Simpson. There is a sense of anticipation, but also uncertainty. Both images show Cartier-Bresson's absolute mastery of conveying an event through human emotion.**

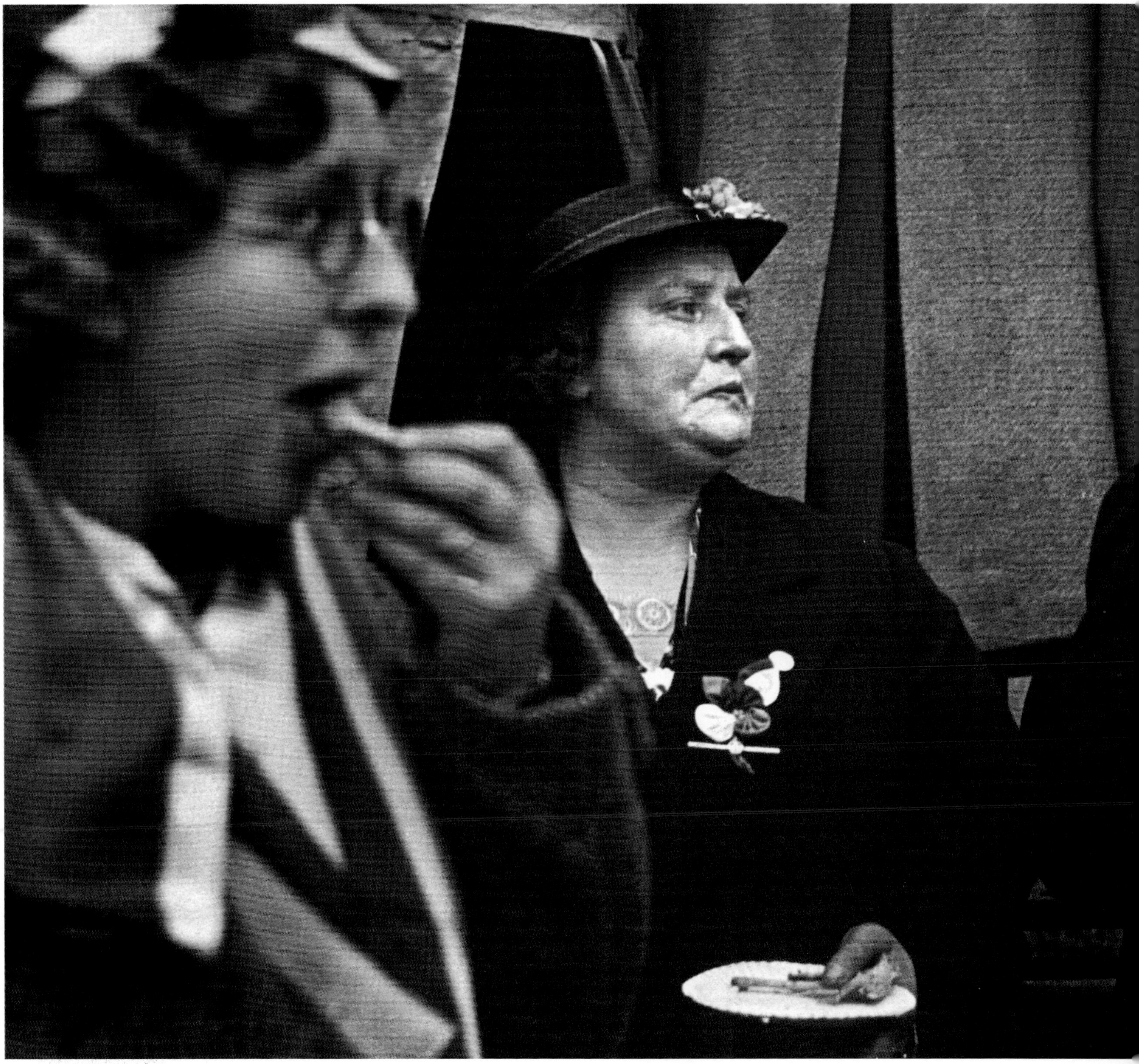

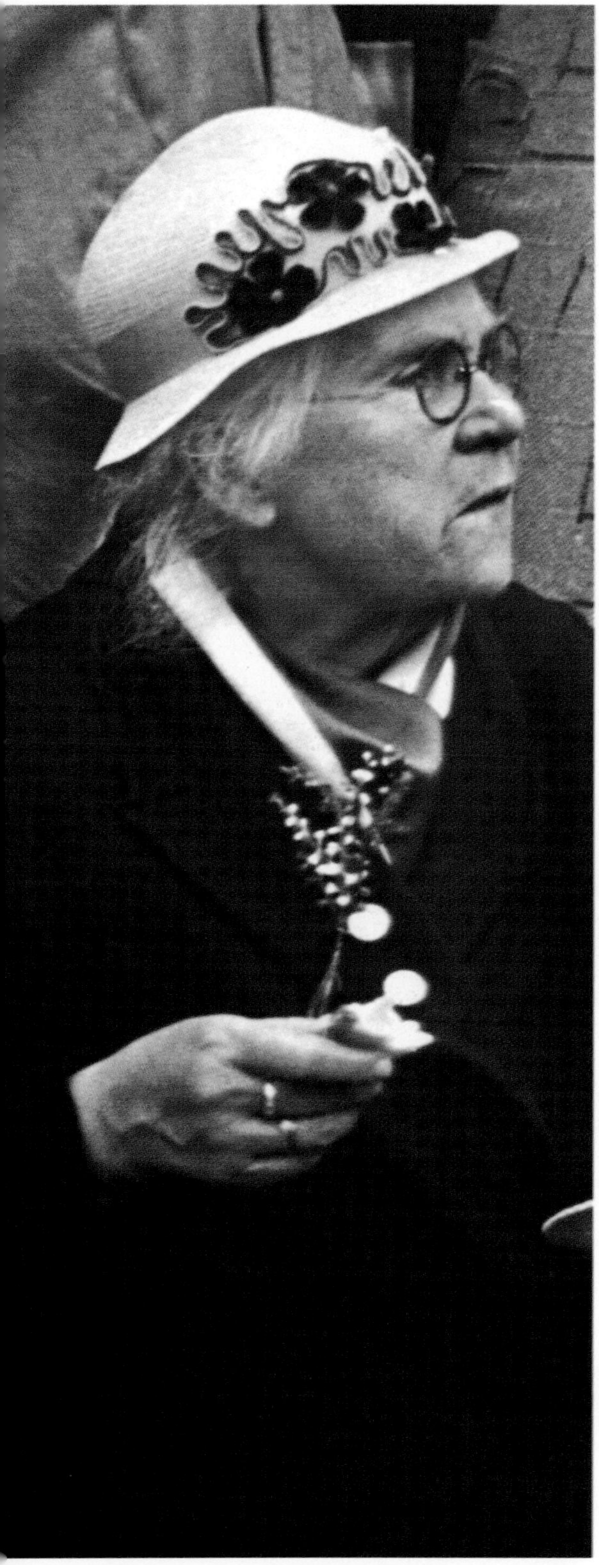

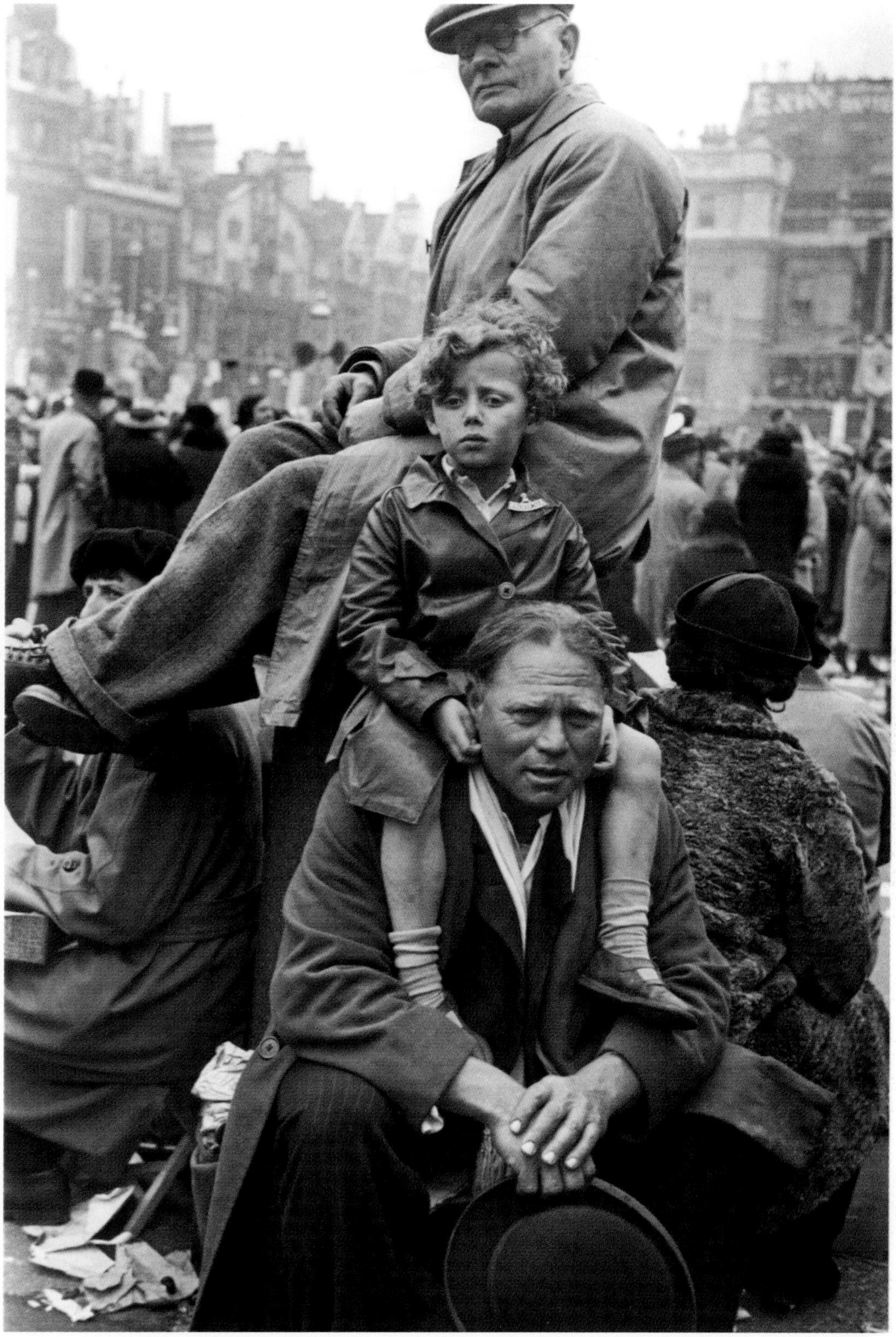

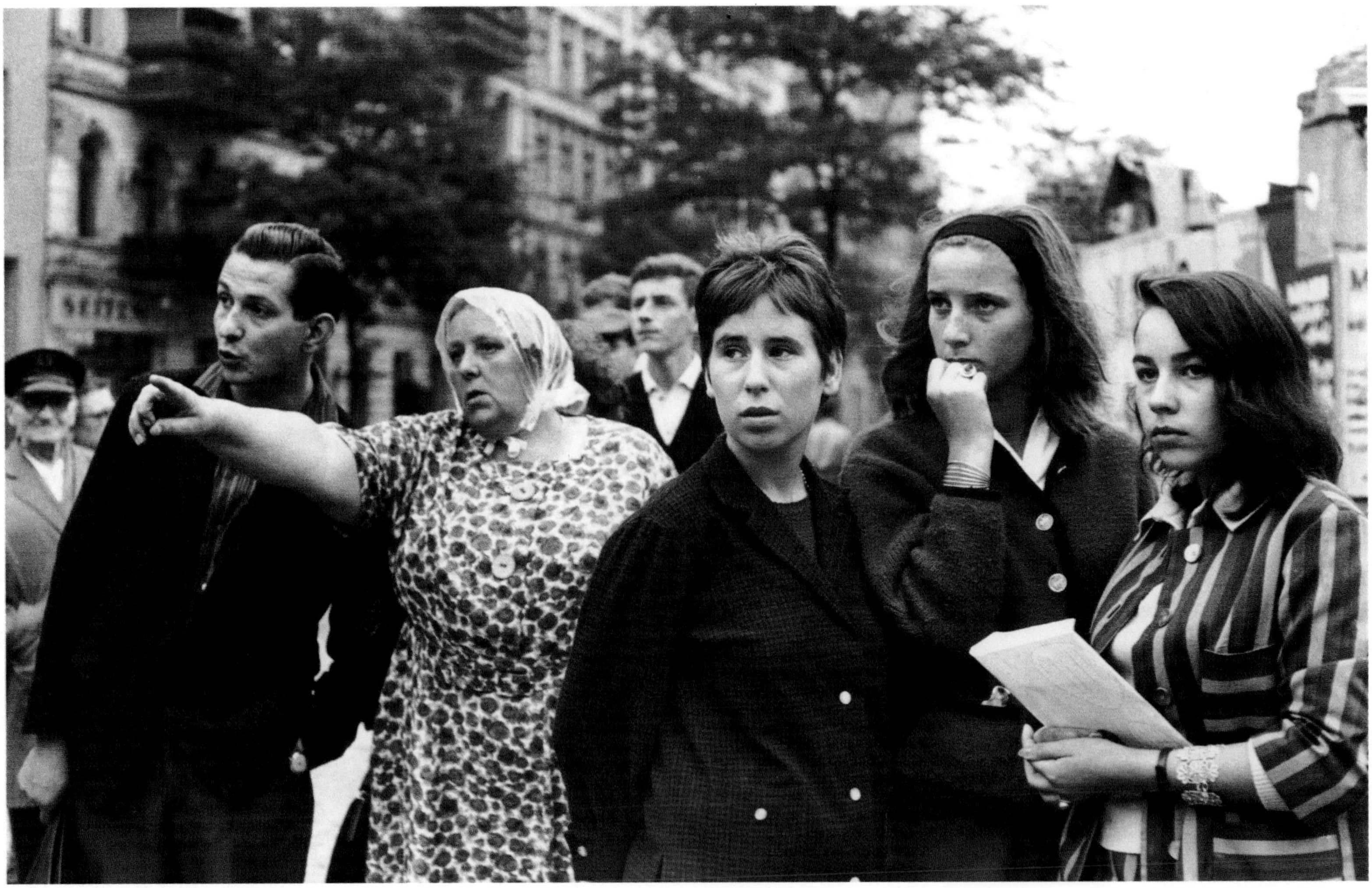

ABOVE: Again Cartier-Bresson applies his trademark technique of revealing an event through human emotion to his essay on the building of the Berlin Wall in 1961-62. We see the drama unfold through the eyes and nervous gestures of the small group of onlookers wondering what is going to happen next.

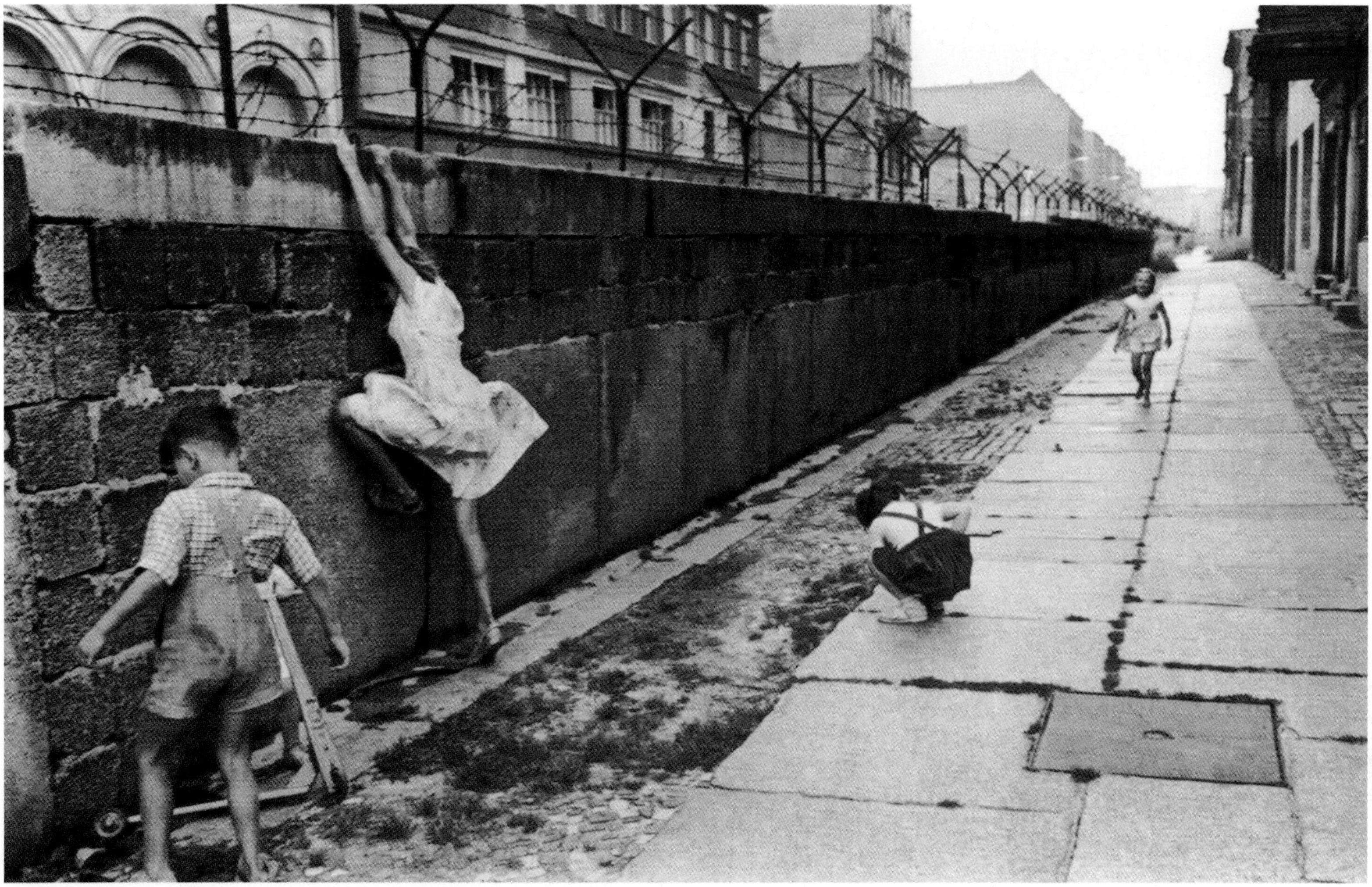

ABOVE: Cartier-Bresson was also very skilful at telling a story through contrasts. Part of the same Berlin Wall essay, this shot completely encapsulates the conflicting elements of the Wall's bleakness and the innocent acceptance of its existence by these children playing in the West Berlin sector.

LUC DELAHAYE

BELOW: **Delahaye's most famous image, which was exhibited on a huge scale in a gallery in New York, depicts a Taliban soldier, killed during the offensive of the Northern Alliance on Kabul in 2001. Despite his violent death, the photograph is oddly serene.**

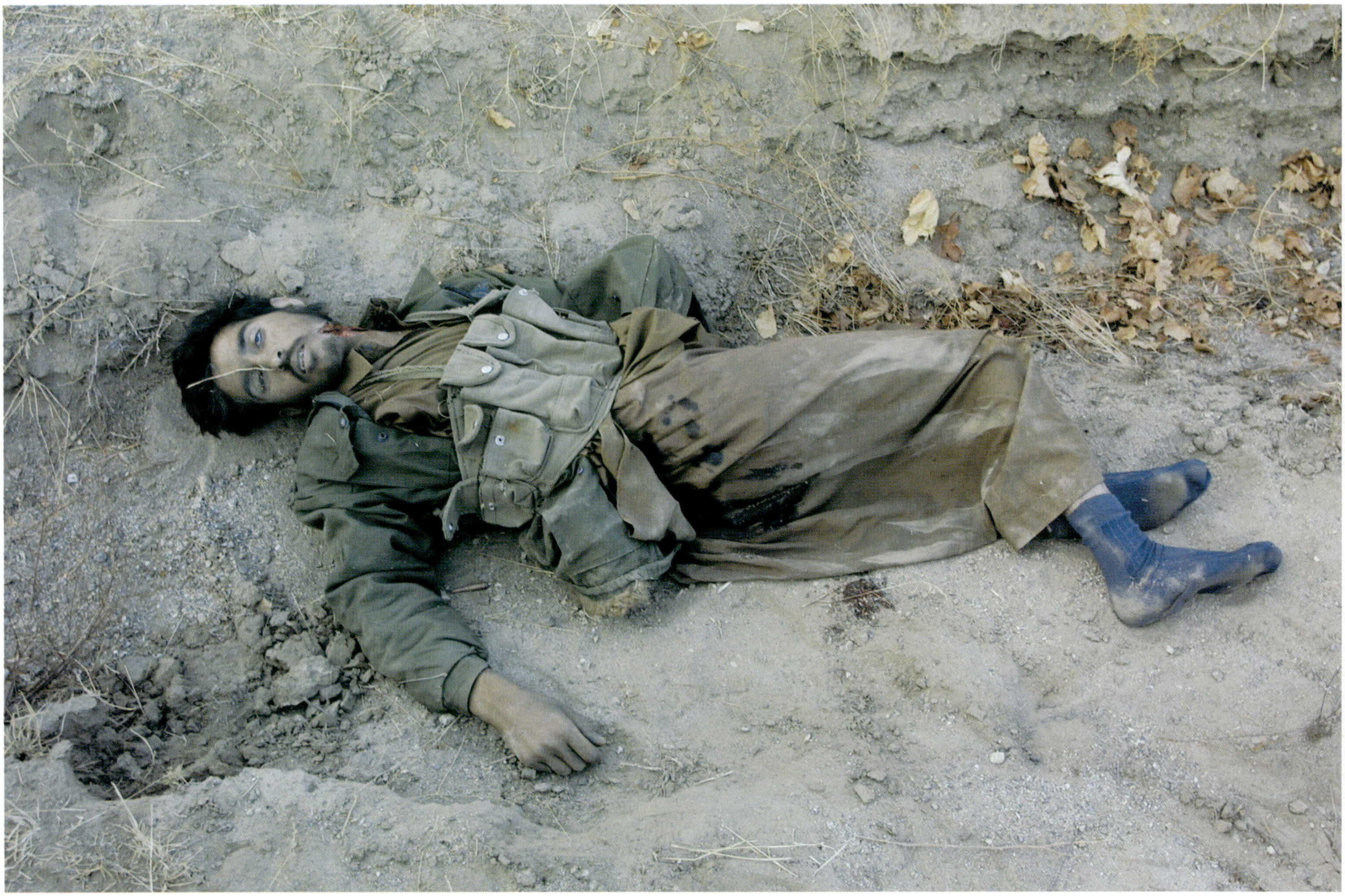

Luc Delahaye is part of a select group of outstanding photojournalists who came of age during the war in the former Yugoslavia. He started out as a more traditional war photographer, intent on getting as near as possible to the action, so close that you can almost hear the bullets whizzing around in his photographs. Yet Delahaye has always been prepared to also take artistic risks as well as personal risks. In the words of Jamie Wellford, International Photo Editor of *Newsweek*,"He challenges himself consistently to define the image as opposed to fulfilling the expectations of what an image should or is expected to be." By challenging himself, he is reinventing the conventions of photojournalism and how conflict should be presented. So for example, he took the unusual decision to photograph the US invasion of Iraq using a larger-format camera, as opposed to the more traditional 35mm. Such a method produced vast panoramas, giving the viewer a literally wider view. Depicted in this way, the story of the invasion was now not just a news event, but an epic struggle. These all-encompassing and sweeping views are closer in spirit to eighteenth- and nineteenth-century historical paintings, than to modern confrontational war photography.

This conflation of fine art photography and reportage was also used while covering the US invasion of Afghanistan in 2001. The most famous image from this period is Delahaye's photograph of the sprawled figure of a dead Taliban soldier lying in a ditch. No detail is omitted and everything is presented in graphic clarity. It might seem morbid, but in the hands of such a skilled craftsman it is an extremely beautiful photograph. This image was shown on a huge scale at one of New York's most prestigious private galleries and subsequently sold for thousands of dollars. Yet for all his fine art pretensions – Delahaye no longer considers himself a photojournalist, but rather an artist – his work will, according to Wellford, "remain definitive in the world of photojournalism and be recognized as a body of work that redefines, addresses, exposes and ultimately illuminates the medium".

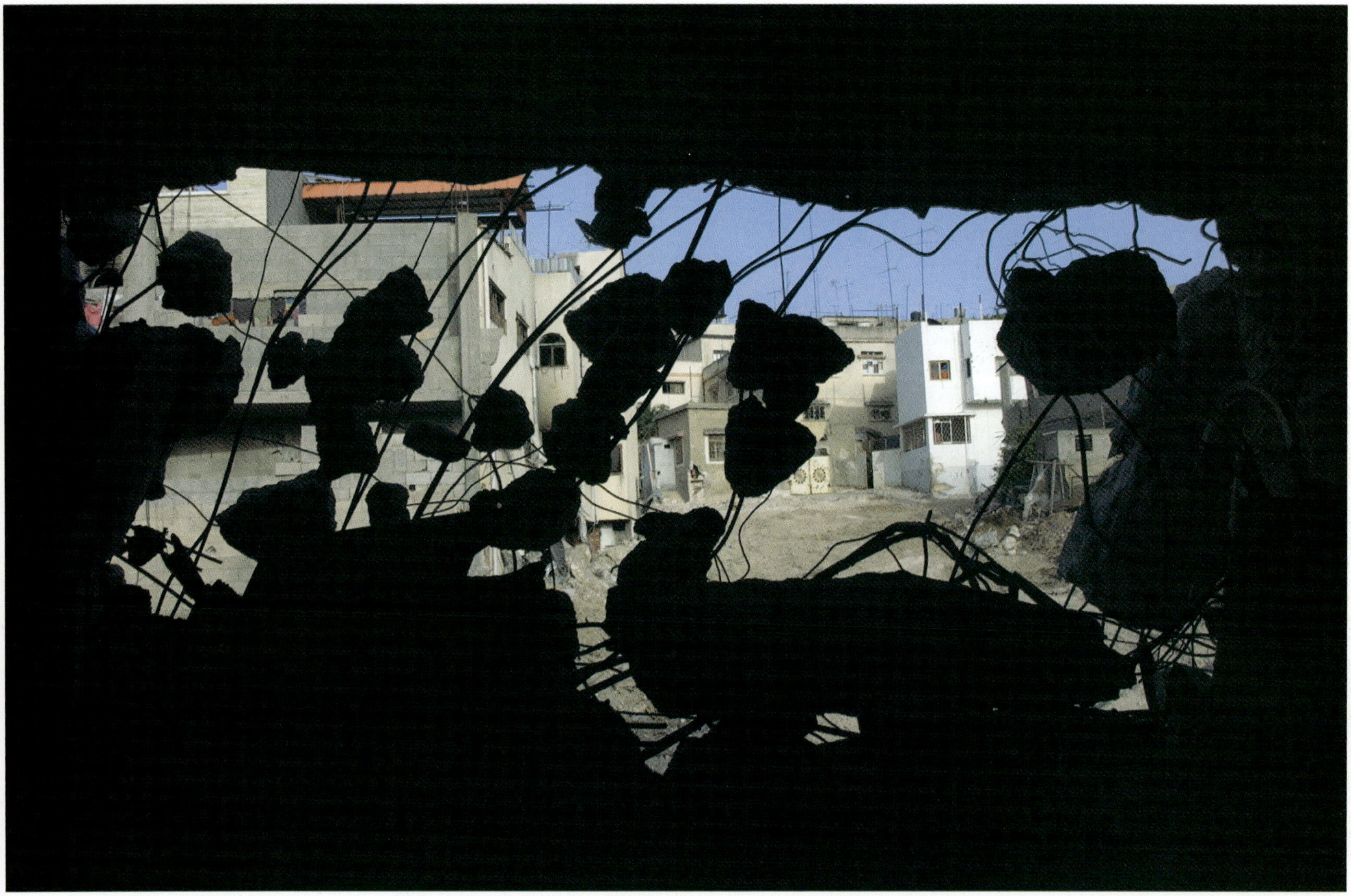

ABOVE: A clever composition conveys the bleakness of the Palestinian situation at the Jenin refugee camp on the West Bank/Israel in 2002.

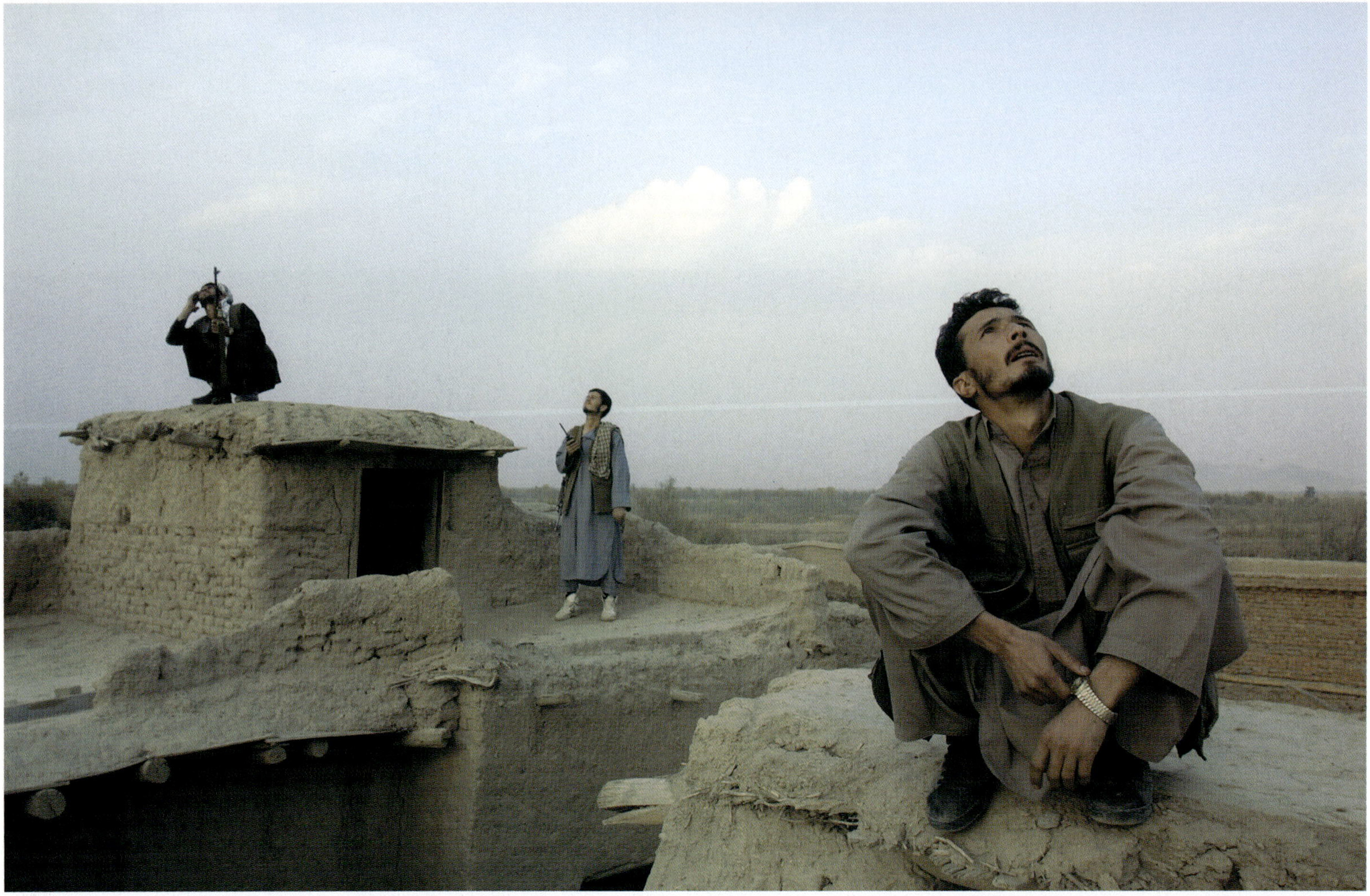

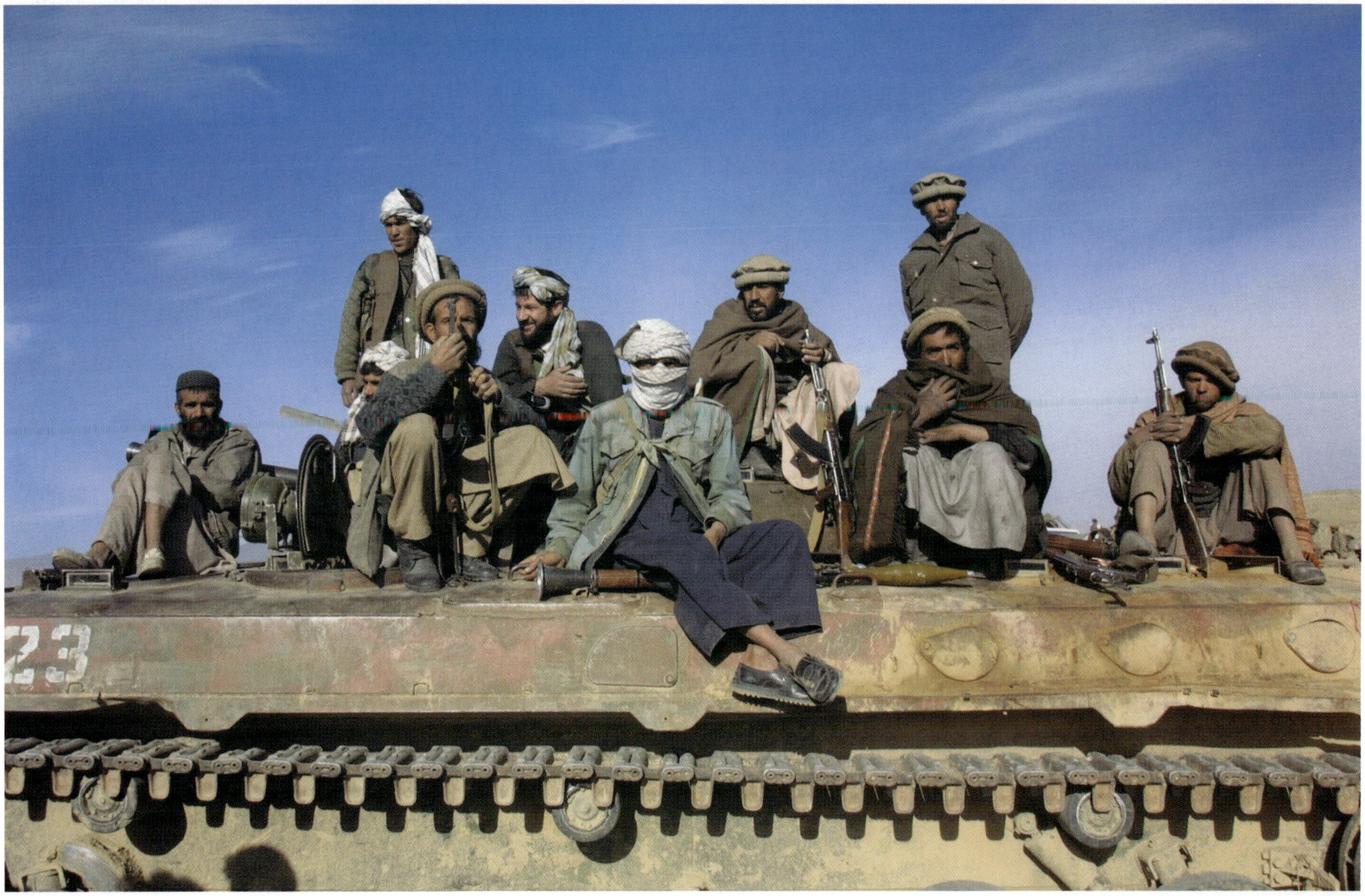
23

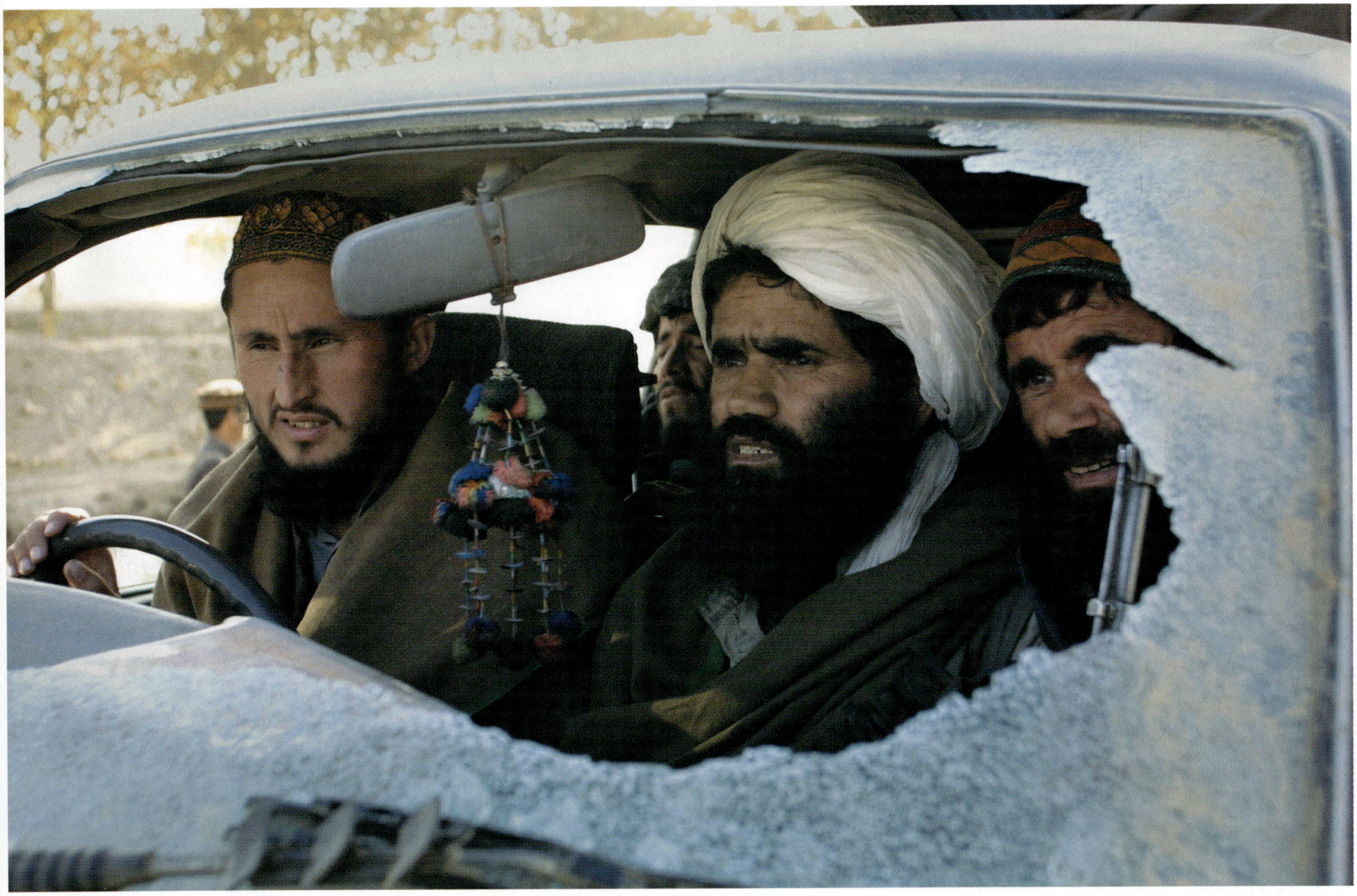

ABOVE: Delahaye captures the uncertainty of surrendering Taliban fighters in Afghanistan 2001. They are arriving by car in Northern Alliance territory near Kunduz and they are clearly fearful about what lies ahead.

LEFT TOP: From the rooftop of the command post of the Bagram military airbase, 12 miles (20 km) north of Kabul in Afghanistan, Northern Alliance soldiers watch the jets bombing nearby Taliban defence lines in 2001. Delahaye combines the lyrical with the dramatic, a fine art sensibility with a hard news edge.

LEFT BOTTOM: It is 6 am, and Northern Alliance forces, intent on the liberation of Kabul, are shown on the outskirts of the city in 2001.

ALFRED EISENSTAEDT

RIGHT: In one of the most famous images of the twentieth century, a jubilant sailor celebrates a long-awaited victory over Japan in 1945, bending a nurse over backward in a passionate embrace. In the background celebrants jam Times Square, New York. For years after the image was published, a succession of people came forward, claiming to be the original subjects. Eisie revealed that he saw the scene unfolding out of the corner of his eye. He took the one shot and then the couple disappeared.

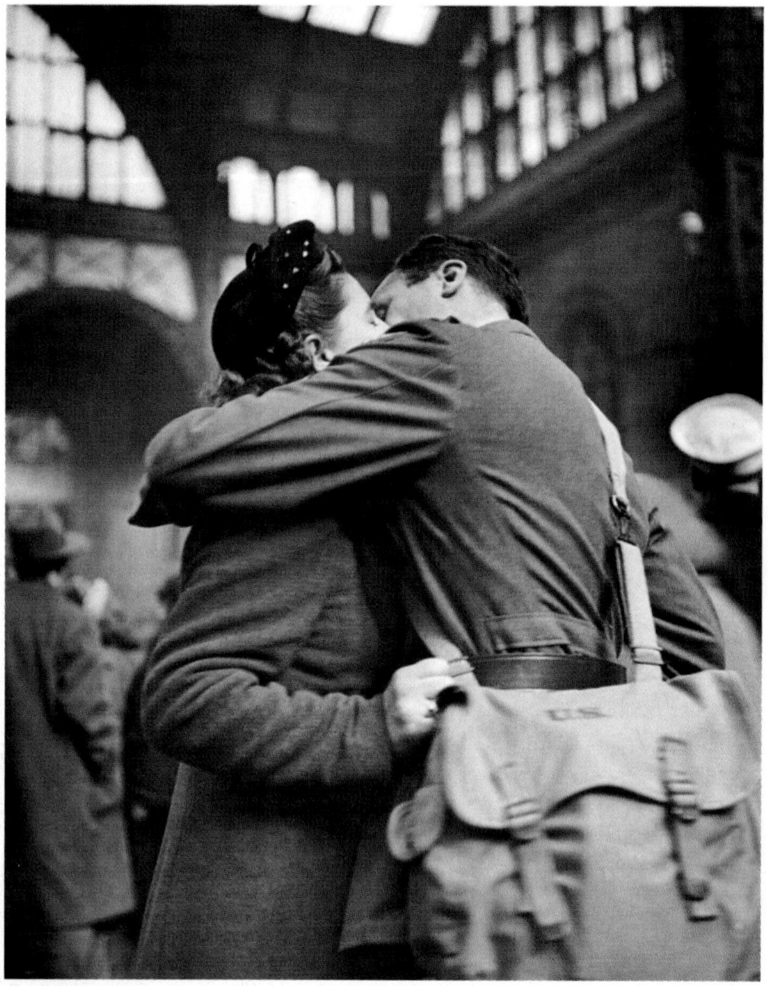

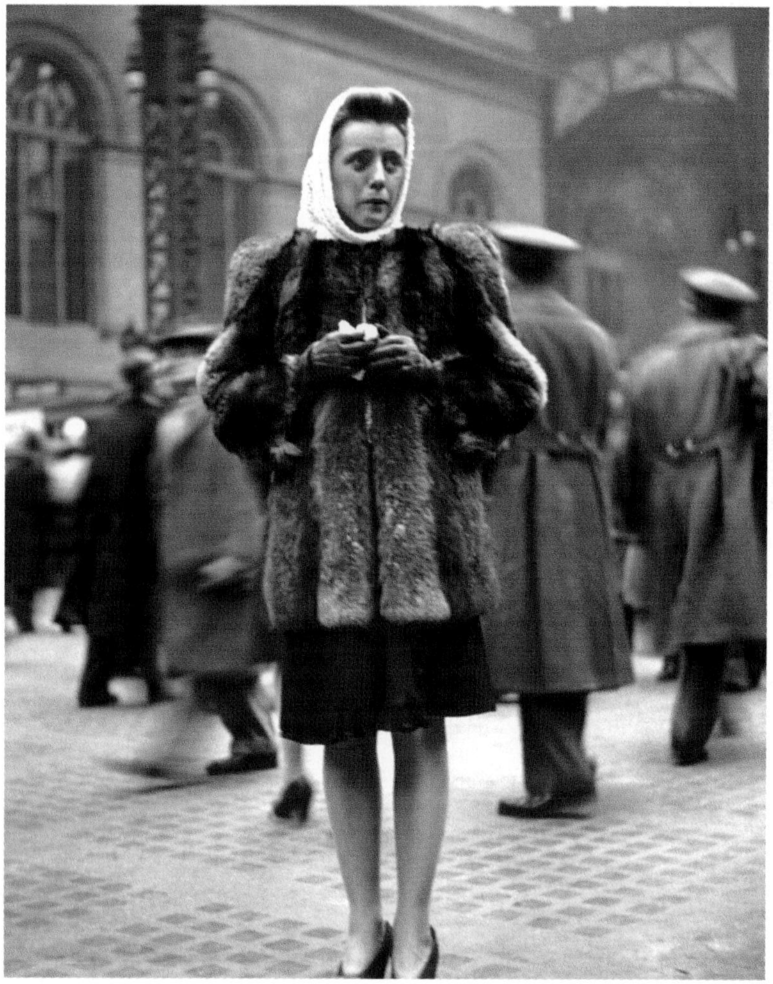

Alfred Eisenstaedt was chosen "Photojournalist of the Century" by the influential web magazine *The Digital Journalist*, beating candidates such as Robert Capa, Cartier-Bresson and W. Eugene Smith. Justifying his choice, the editor Dirk Halstead writes, "He had the most profound impact and leaves the greatest legacy." While he lacked the charisma of Capa, and his work never reached the artistic heights of Cartier-Bresson, he did have a great gift for storytelling, especially when the story was unfolding on the pages of *Life* magazine. In these days of the Internet and 24-hour cable television, it is hard to imagine the power and influence of *Life* magazine during its golden years from the mid-1930s to the mid-1950s. To many Americans it was their only window to a world beyond their front lawns and small towns. Eisie dutifully guided these readers through some of the key moments of the twentieth century, as well as photographing virtually every icon of the past 100 years, including Churchill, Marilyn Monroe and JFK. Eisie was a small man with boundless energy and curiosity about people. He described his technique as "naïve" and argued that "every professional should remain always in his heart an amateur". This meant that Eisie approached every assignment with fresh-faced enthusiasm and a hunger to tell his loyal readers at *Life* about the world. Despite the competitiveness and cynicism of the magazine world, he never became jaded or lost his love of taking pictures. He also kept it simple and his photographs always cut through the clutter and resonate with the viewer. There are no strange angles, or abstract compositions, there is no ego, or even a sense that Eisie has a point of view – his function is to record it all with great clarity and incisiveness. He made it look very easy and therefore some critics have dismissed his photography as the visual equivalent of easy listening. That description does both the man and his impressive career a great disservice.

ABOVE LEFT: On New Year's Day 1944, a soldier gives his girlfriend a smothering kiss goodbye at Penn Station, New York before returning to duty after a brief furlough. This was the kind of image that would resonate with *Life* readers, and it has all of Eisie's signatures – straightforward composition with little to distract the viewer from the main storyline.

ABOVE RIGHT: The same day, but a different scenario. A distraught woman clutches a tear-sodden handkerchief as she watches her soldier boyfriend walk away after saying goodbye in Penn Station, as he, too, returns to duty.

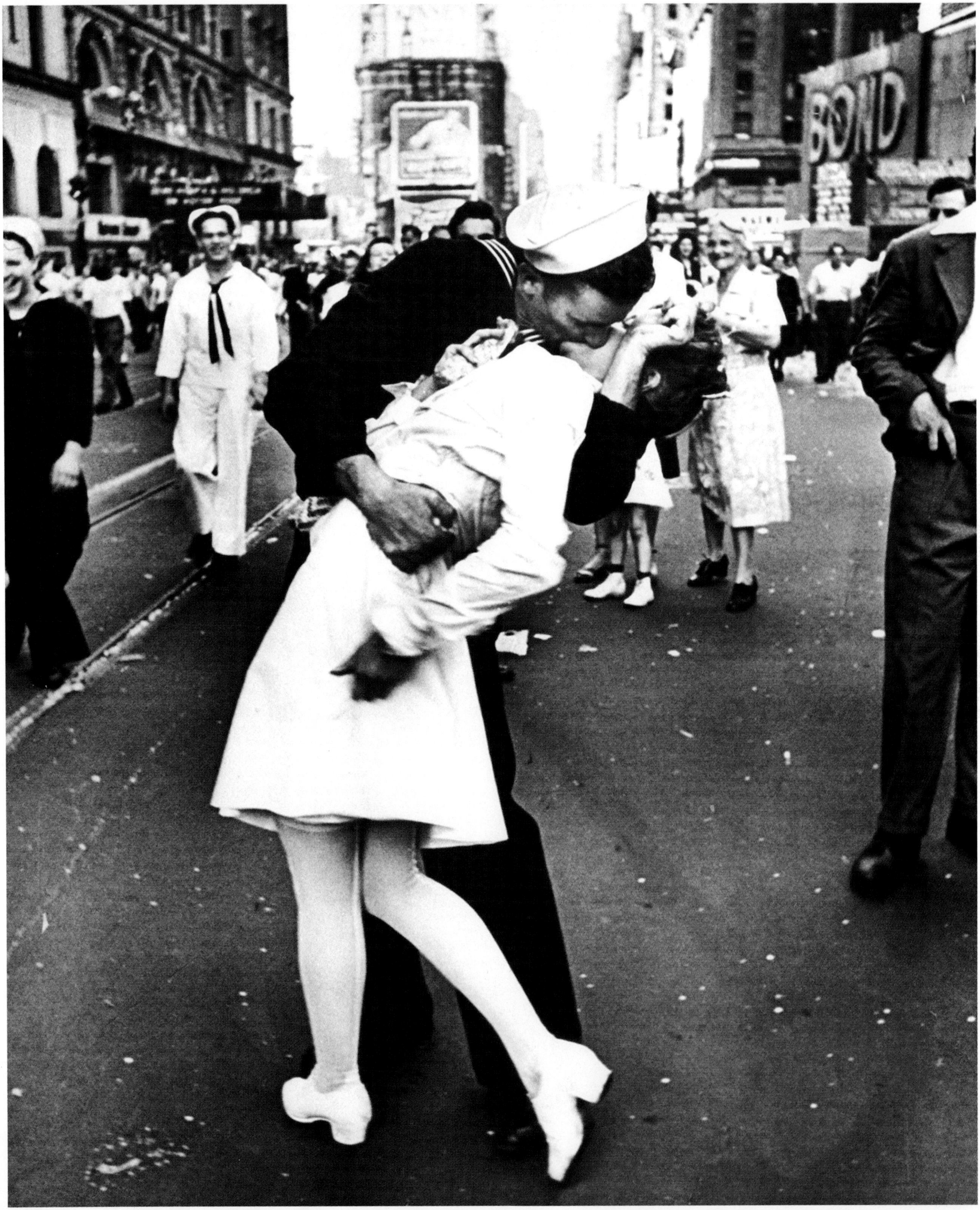
BOND

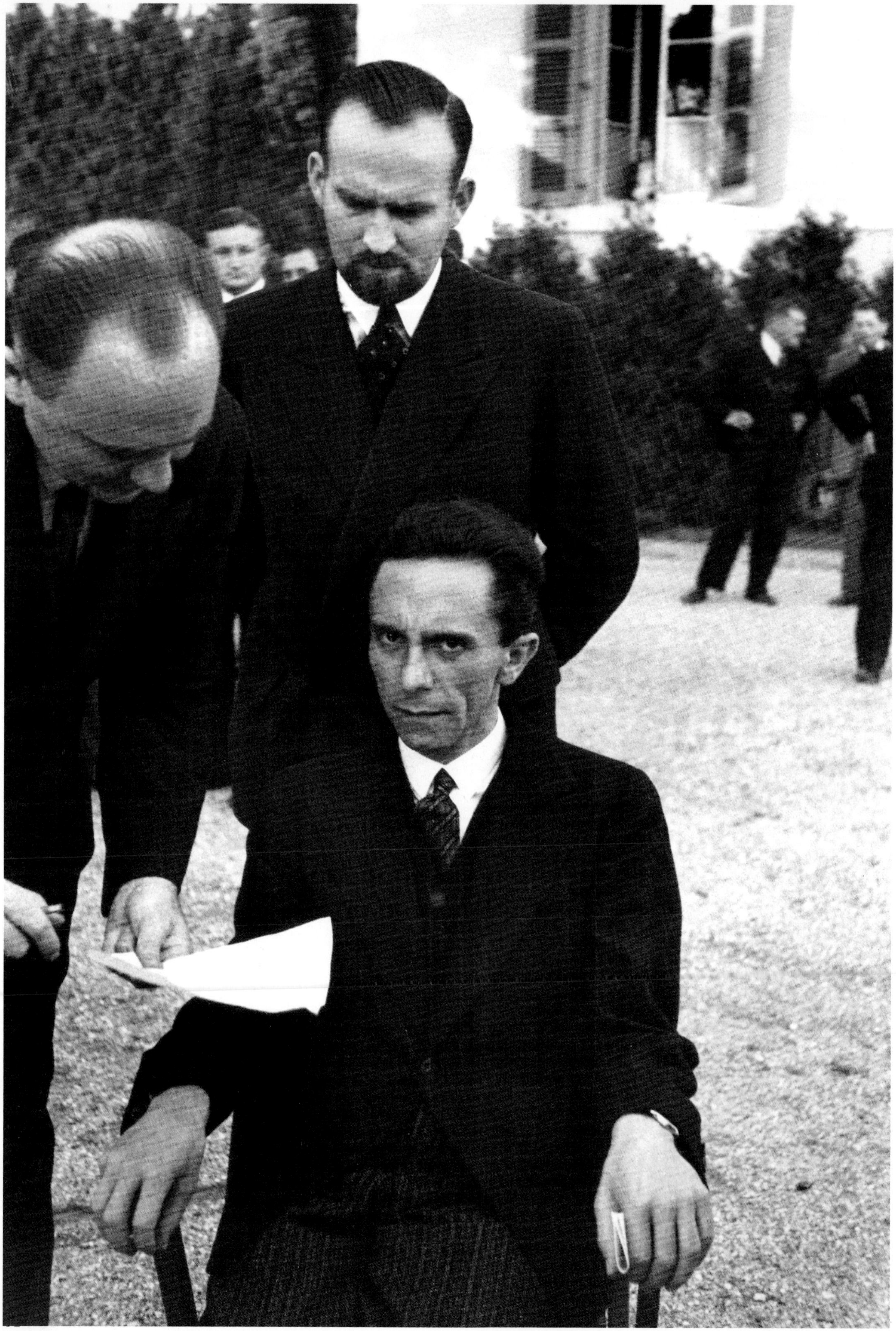

LEFT: During his first trip abroad to attend the League of Nations, in 1933, Hitler's Minister of Culture, Dr Joseph Goebbels, glowers at he sits in the garden of the Carlton Hotel in Geneva. At that time, the National Socialists were still perceived as an unknown quantity and the Europeans felt that they could do business with them. Goebbels's expression suggests not. Eisie was Jewish and Goebbels's eyes reveal what he thinks of the photographer, and what he would like to do to him.

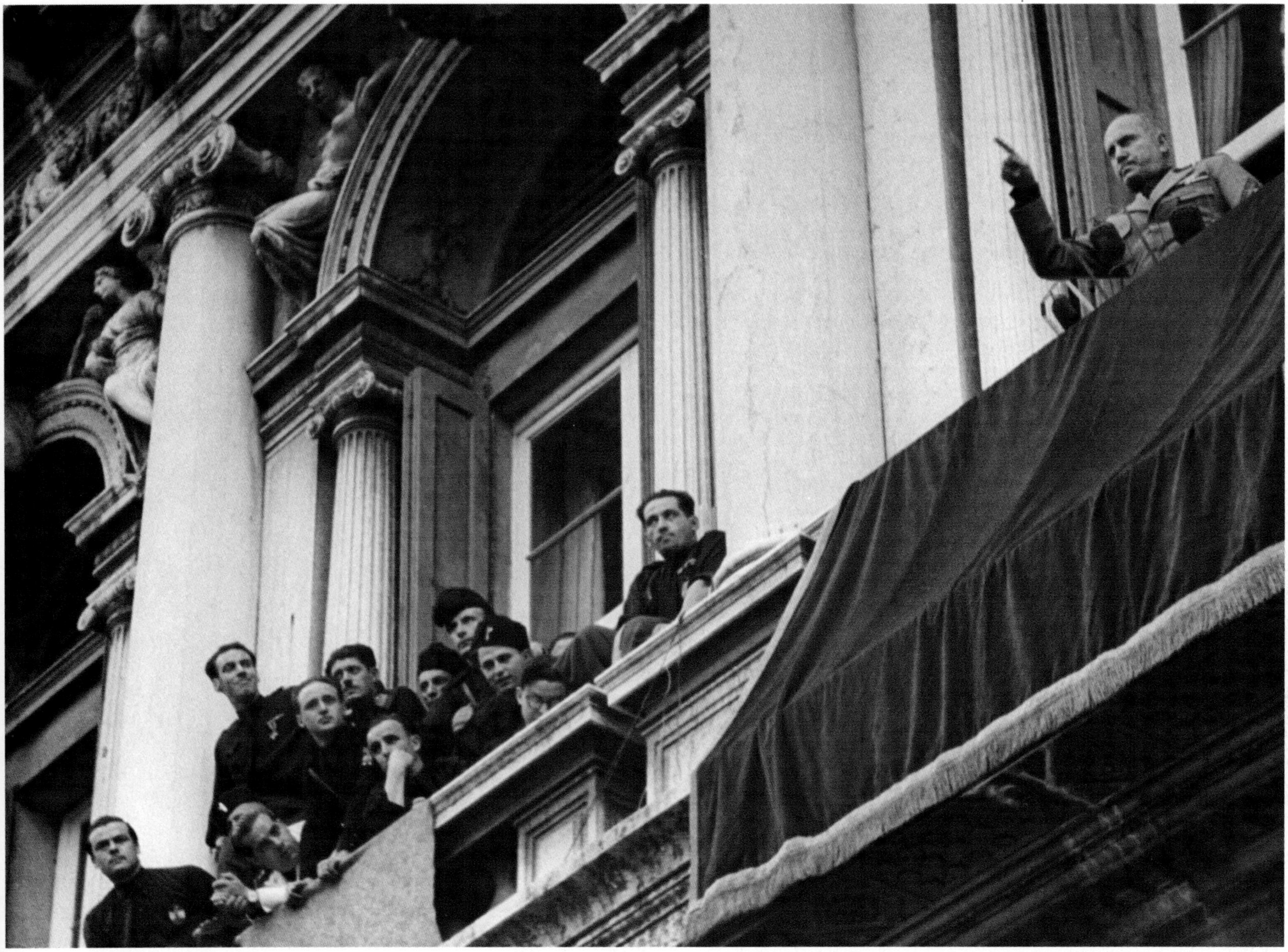

ABOVE: In 1934 Eisie captured the Italian fascist dictator Benito Mussolini giving a speech from a balcony in St Mark's Square, Venice, as a group of Black Shirts looked on. There is a notable contrast between the splendour of the Renaissance architecture and the posturing of Mussolini and his band of thugs. The jabbing, insistent finger reveals something about the nature of the man.

ROGER FENTON

As a photographer, Roger Fenton's chief source of income was from the sale of prints. He benefited greatly from a privileged relationship with the celebrity family of the day, the Royal Family, producing fascinating photographs of Queen Victoria, Prince Albert and their children from 1854. Fenton found favour with them because he was the leading photographer of the era, exhibiting more work over the decade 1852–62 than any other photographer, perhaps as many as a thousand images. Since his pictures were made by labour-intensive methods, initially using wax-paper negatives and then wet-collodion, this output is certainly substantial, particularly as it covered architecture, museum collections, still life, genre studies and portraiture.

Fenton also seems modern in his ceaseless self-promotion, and he derived considerable personal celebrity from his photographs of the Crimean War in 1855 (the commission for which may have been thanks to the influence of Prince Albert). His war images are mostly portraits of officers and notables, made as part of a commercial deal with the London print-seller Agnews, and they seem hardly akin to "war-photography" in the modern sense. Fenton photographed the leading figures of all the Allied armies, as well as the most notable officers in the British regiments. He also made interesting views of military camp life, which included the more exotic combatants – Zouaves, Croats, Turks and of course Highlanders in their kilts. Among the small numbers of landscape views is his photograph of the deserted "Valley of the Shadow of Death", taken shortly after the charge of the Light Brigade, which swiftly became an iconic image of this conflict. Yet it is a picture almost bereft of information about the battle itself, with just a scattering of cannon balls lying on the ground to indicate that anything significant may have happened. Pictures of dead bodies or the chaos of war would not have been considered acceptable. His commission was an attempt to make the war acceptable to the influential classes, many of whom had lost family and friends in the Crimea, by promoting the idea that their loved ones had been sacrificed to a noble cause.

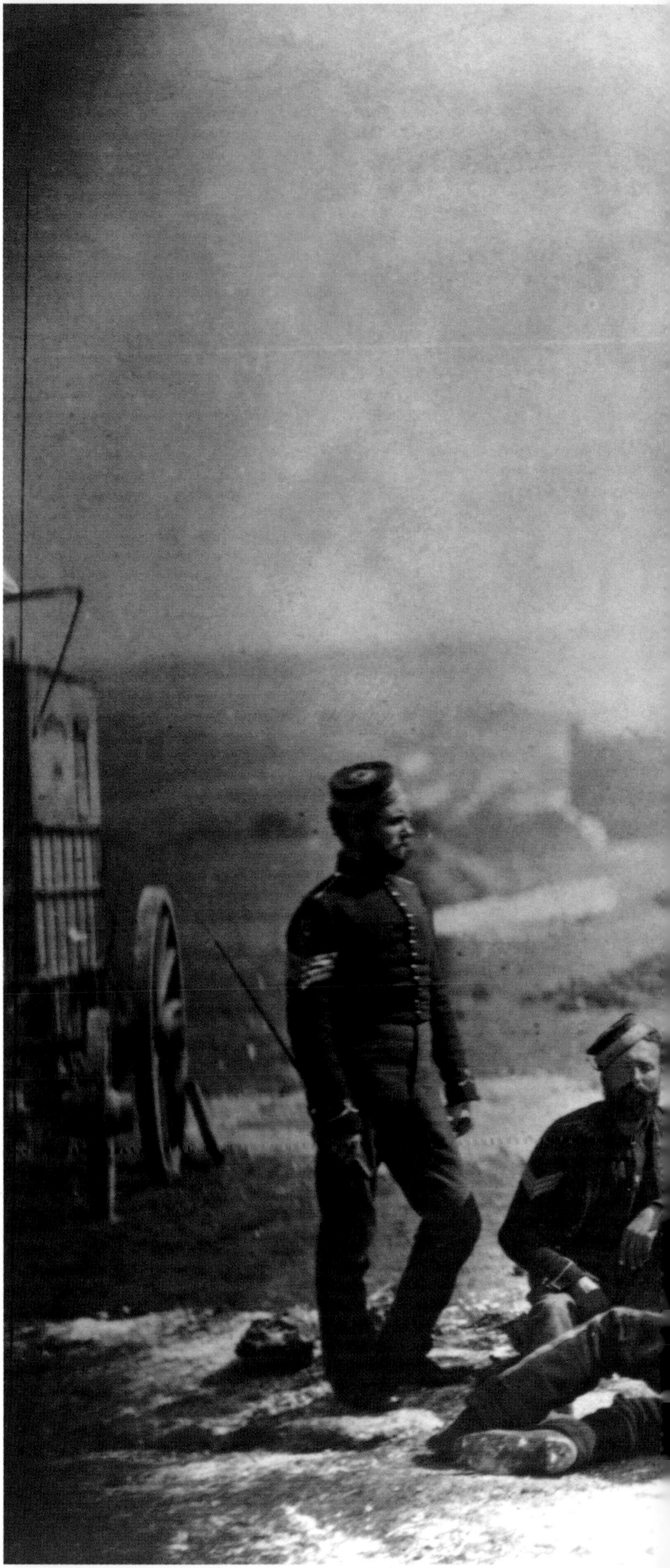

RIGHT: Fenton's group portraits during the Crimean War were loosely posed because the conventions about such military portraits were still being formulated. Civilian and military groups generally look quite similar around this period, the mid-1850s, as in this case, which shows members of the 8th Hussars gathering around their cookhouse. Note how some soldiers are more aware of the camera than others.

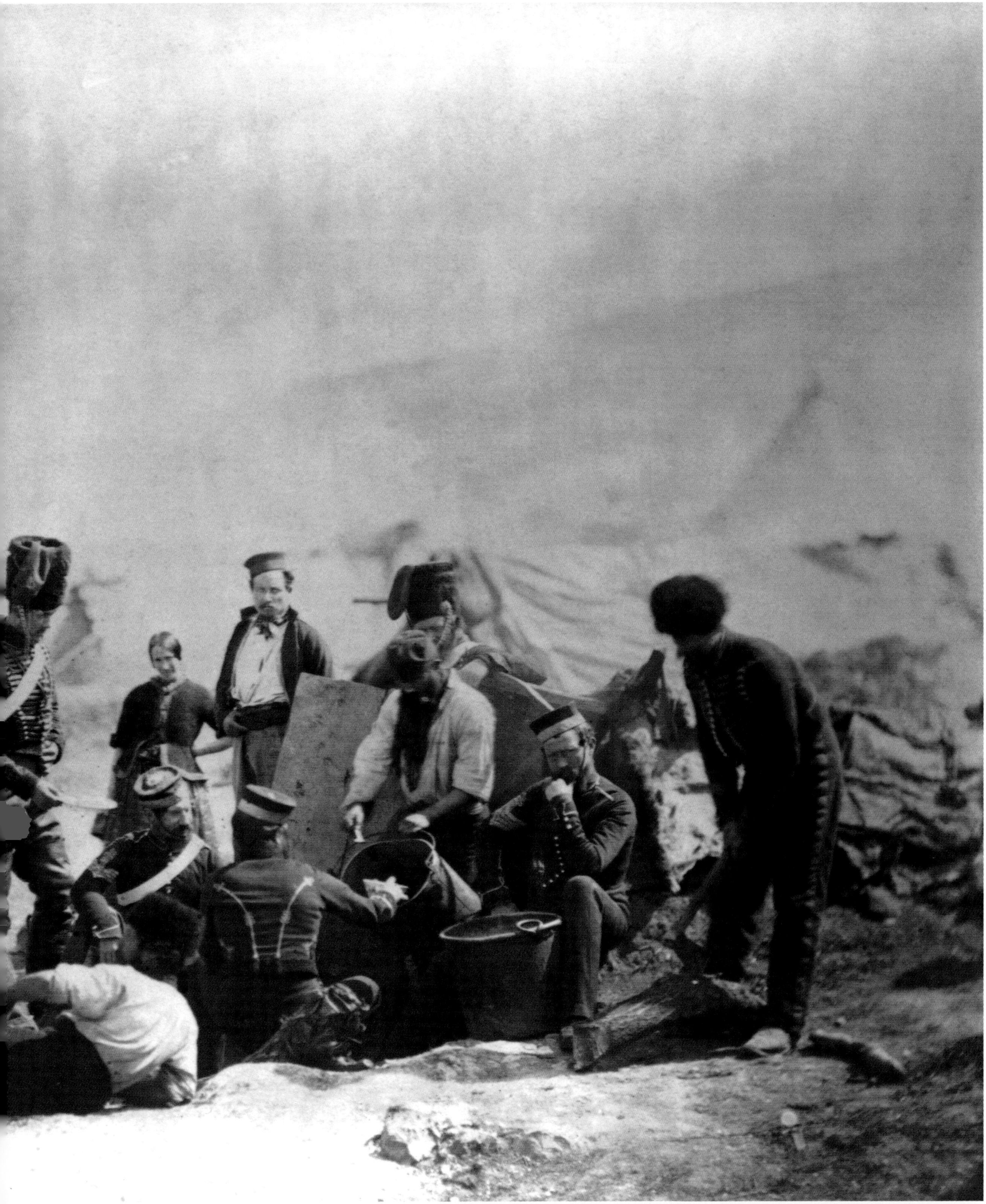

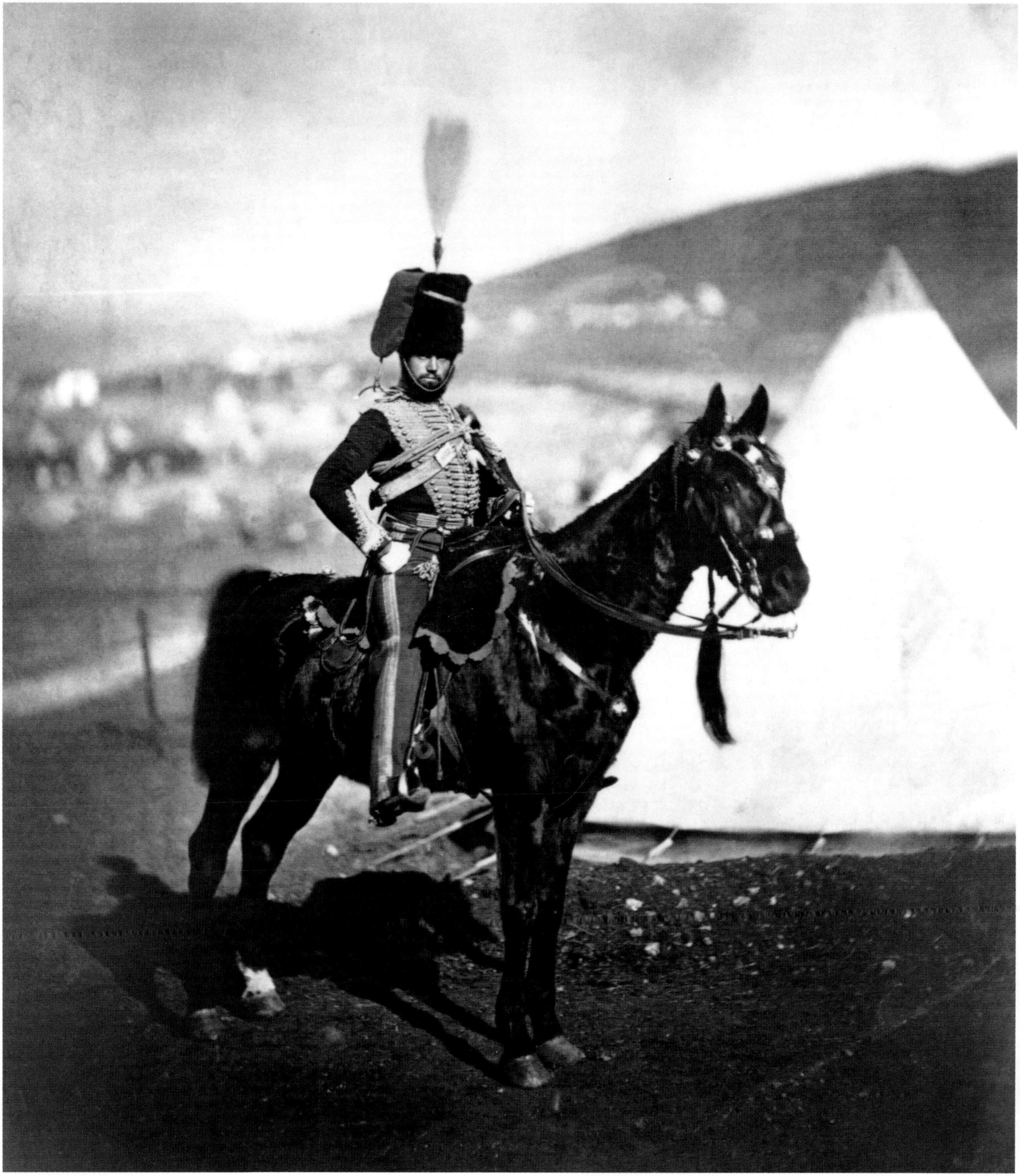

LEFT: The main reason for Fenton's photographic journey to the Crimea was to assemble a series of portraits and views that his client, Agnews, could sell as part of an album or as individual prints. This portrait of Cornet Wilkin of the 8th Hussars is a carefully posed image that would be likely to find a commercial market back in England.

BELOW: The "Valley of the Shadow of Death" on the plain of Balaklava, a photograph taken shortly after the famous Charge of the Light Brigade, and showing spent cannon balls littered along the path of the cavalry charge. This is probably Fenton's most famous image from the campaign.

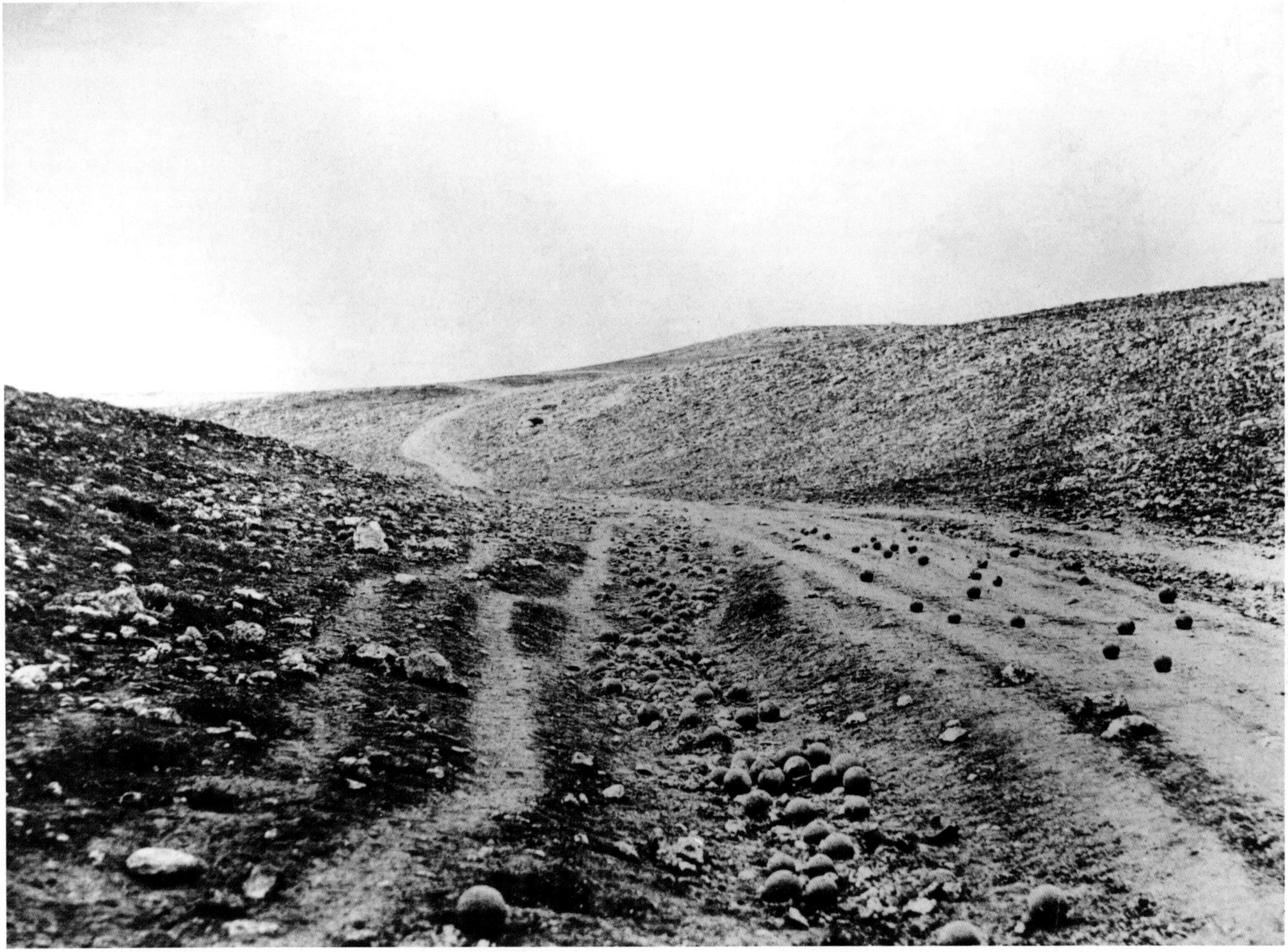

OVERLEAF TOP LEFT: In his search for interesting images to complement the portraits that make up most of his work, Fenton sought out scenes such as this one showing the camp of the 5th Dragoon Guards looking toward Kadioki in 1855.

OVERLEAF BOTTOM LEFT: A group shot, although it is not clear whether the men are preparing for battle or if this is a respite from the fighting.

OVERLEAF RIGHT: Taken in 1855, this beautifully posed portrait of Major Butler, 28th regiment, is typical of Fenton's work in the Crimea. It is probable that the soldier's family would want to buy a number of prints from the sitting.

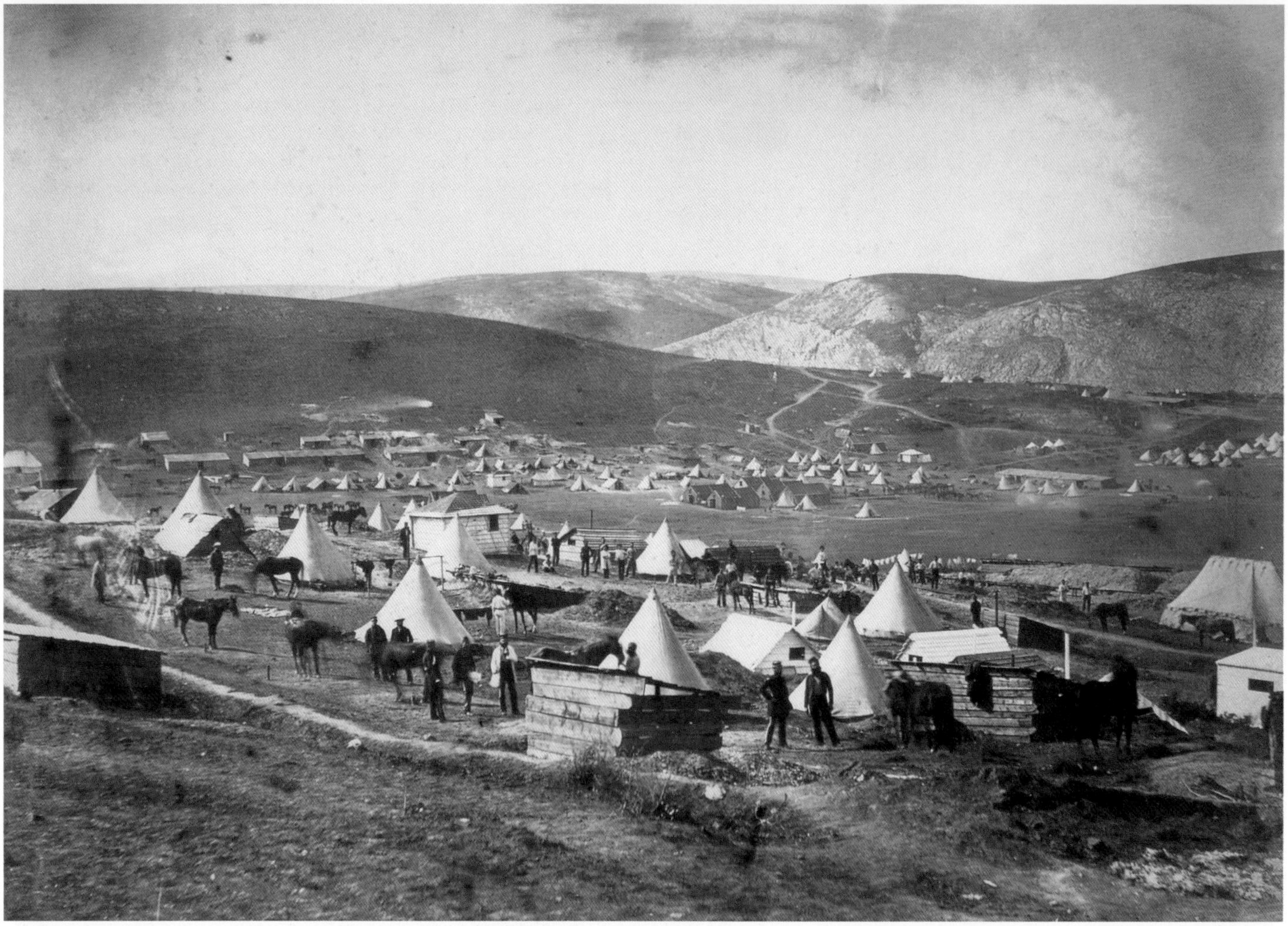

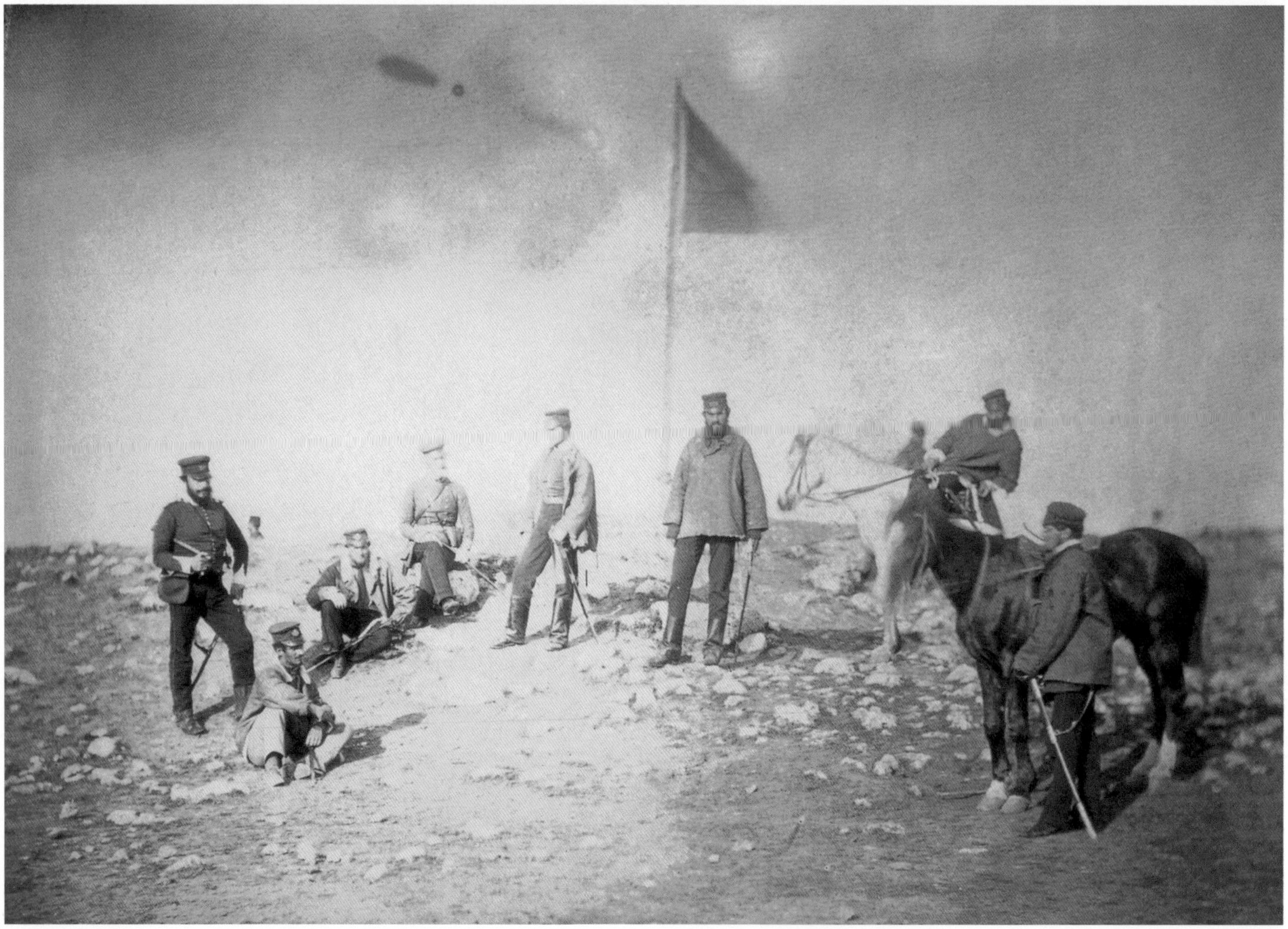

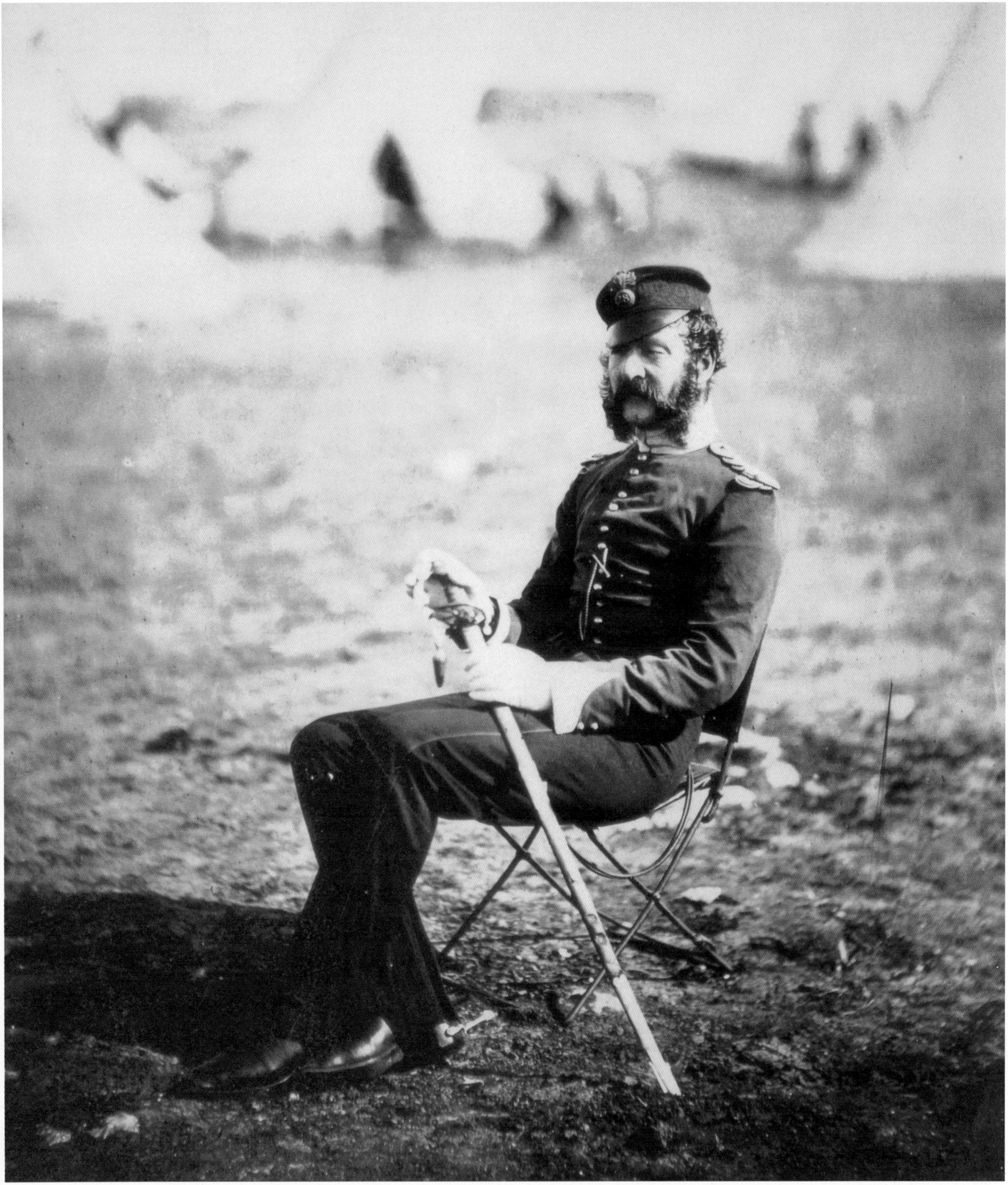

ALEXANDER GARDNER

RIGHT: **In 1862, in the midst of the Civil War, Gardner captured (from left to right) Major Allan Pinkerton, US President Abraham Lincoln and General John A. McClernand, standing in front of a pitched tent on a battlefield. The photograph poses the obvious question – what is the President doing so close to the heat of the battle?**

BELOW: **An overview of the Second Inauguration of Lincoln, 4 March 1864.**

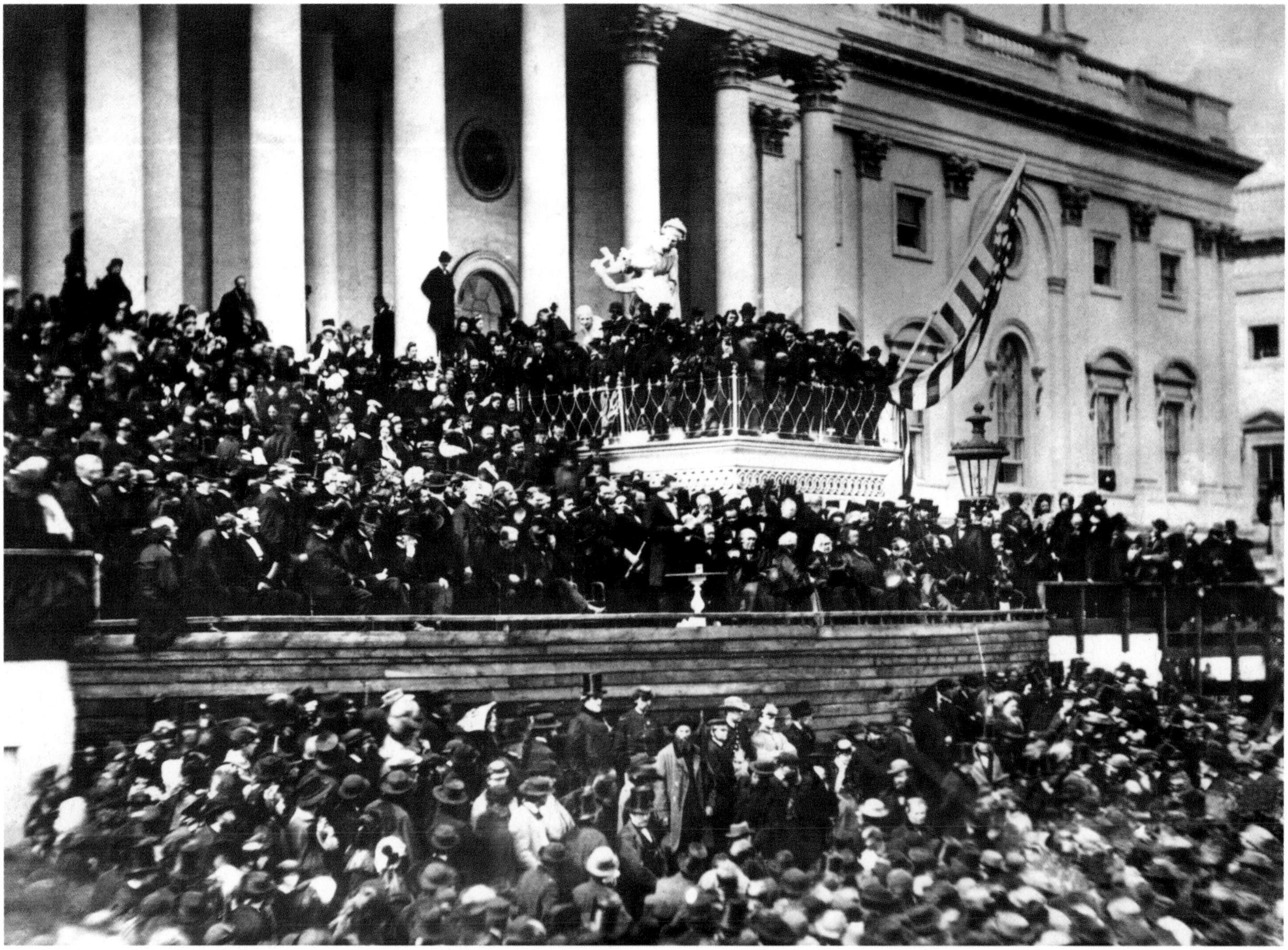

On seeing one of Alexander Gardner's photographs from the American Civil War, the famous American writer Oliver Wendell Holmes wrote, "It is so nearly like visiting the battlefield to look at these views that all the emotions excited by the actual sight of the stained and sordid scene, stewed with rags and wrecks, come back to us." Indeed they do. The government gave Gardner and his colleagues complete access to document the Union troops during the campaigns and Gardner set about his task with particular relish. Until then, his photographic experience had been within the more rigid confines of shooting studio portraits, but he had a natural instinct for the demands and rigours of working out in the field. He not only took the photographs, but also had his own travelling darkroom, so that the collodion plates could be processed on the spot. Gardner's images caused a sensation; the public was simply not used to seeing such an accurate representation of war. The scenes of carnage were vivid, macabre and relentless. Unfortunately, for all his ideals and photographic skills, Gardner was also prepared to tamper with the truth in pursuit of a good story. William Frassanito, the writer of *Gettysburg: A Journey In Time*, concludes, after painstaking research, that one of Gardner's more famous photographs, *The Home of a Rebel Sharpshooter, Gettysburg*, is a fake. He suggests that Gardner and his colleague, Timothy O' Sullivan, started by taking photographs of a body in a field. When they noticed a more picturesque sharpshooter's den, they dragged the body some 40 yards away, placed a rifle (probably Gardner's) as a prop, turned the corpse's face toward the camera and took the picture. The soldier is no longer just a body in a field among thousands, but a man who had suffered a lonely and painful death, and the drama of the image is intensified. This one photograph, however, should not diminish his whole legacy. Gardner took more than a thousand images of the American Civil War and as far as we know they are genuine. He was a genius of his day, albeit a flawed one.

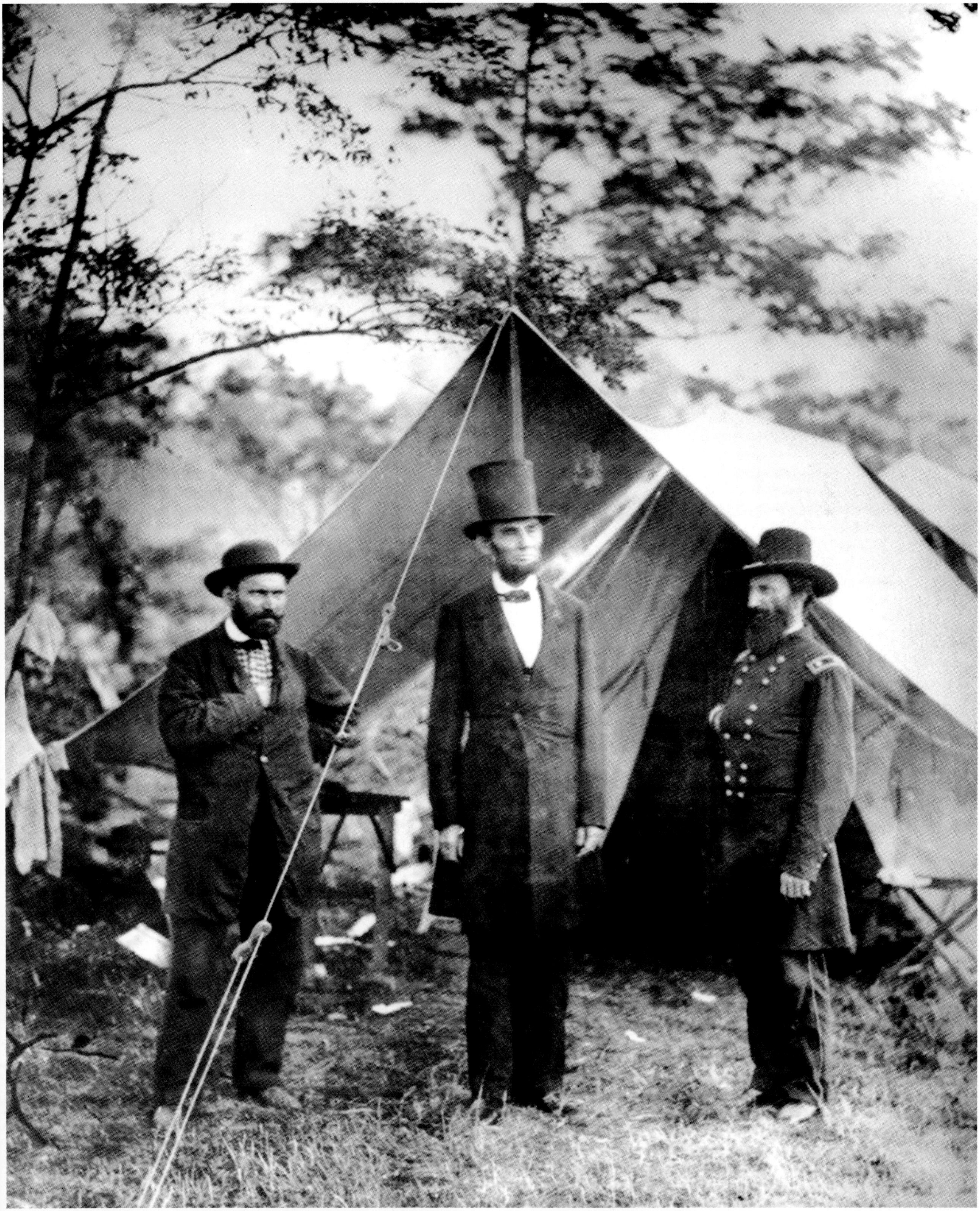

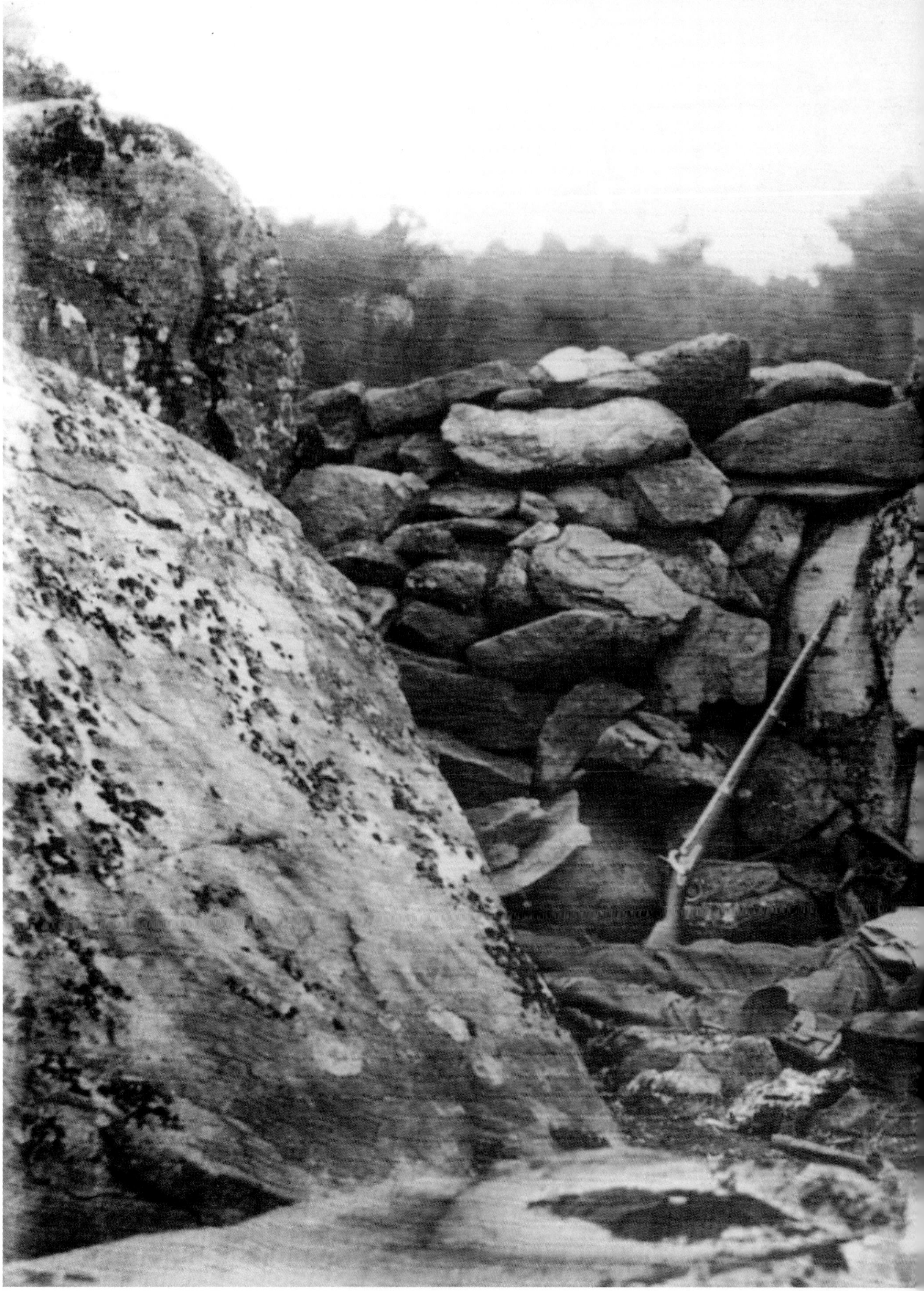

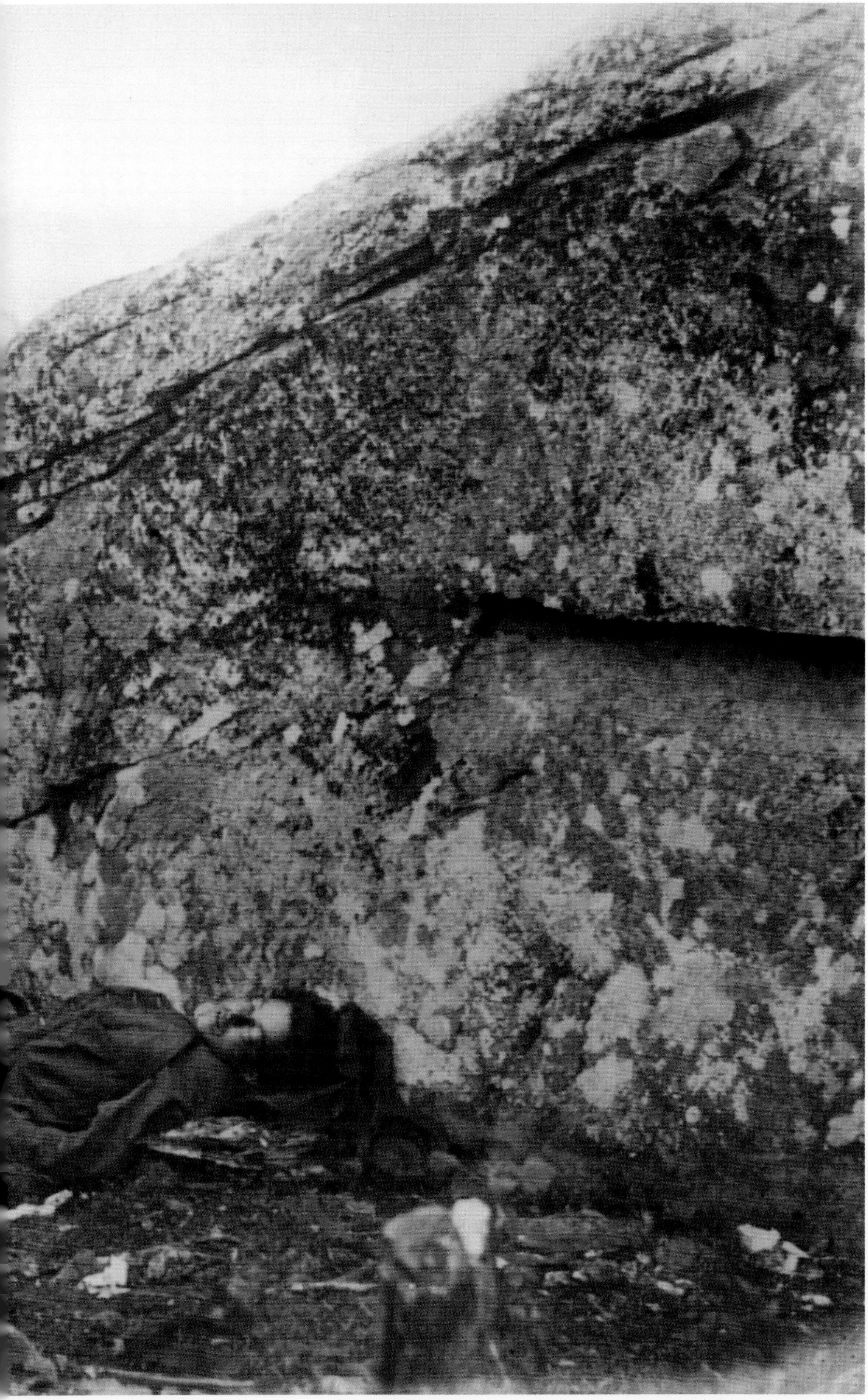

LEFT: Extensive research has shown that this image, ***The Home of A Rebel Sharpshooter, Gettysburg, 1863***, is not as it seems. It does not actually portray the "home" of the soldier, who had in fact been dragged by Gardner and a colleague from a nearby meadow and photographed in this more poignant setting. In his ***Photographic Sketchbook of the Civil War***, Gardner writes that he came across this dead man, still with his rifle, in the aftermath of battle, but in reality the gun would have been looted long before this picture was taken. It is actually a prop provided by Gardner.

JAN GRARUP

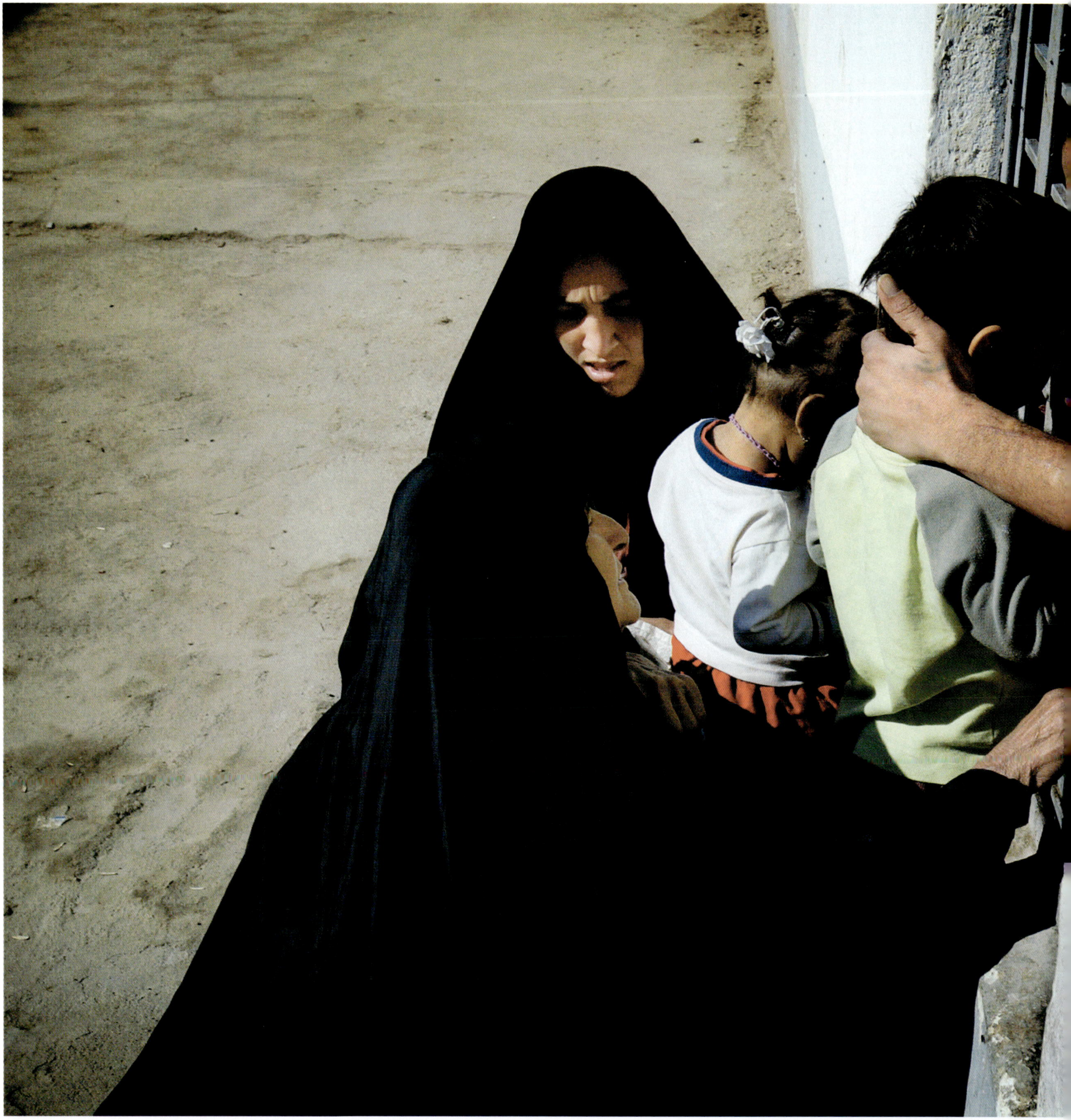

BELOW: Family members visit a relative at the Al-Maaqal prison near Basra, Iraq, where some 300 prisoners have been detained. The framing, featureless foreground and background, and gestures of the subjects – particularly the hand of the prisoner drawing the boy closer to the window – focus viewer attention on the emotionally charged encounter and lend it a clandestine feel.

Jan Grarup began his career as a hard news photographer, but soon found himself in Bosnia and other dangerous places doing work "that didn't have any impact on anyone," he says, "so I had to restructure my whole identity as a photographer." Taking inspiration from W. Eugene Smith, Sebastião Salgado, Gilles Peress and others, Grarup embraced a humanistic documentary approach to exploring social upheaval. "I always keep their work in the back of my mind" Grarup says. "If you take the best of them and put it in a pot and mix it with a little bit of yourself, you come out with a very personalized expression in your own work, and that's very important." The influence of Peress's seminal book, *Telex: Iran*, is strikingly obvious. Tilted horizons, the blur of motion and frames broken by jutting limbs are the clichés of Peress's imitators, but Grarup's use of these techniques is informed and effective, never self-conscious or gratuitous. And the more you look, the more there is to see. He puts every image element to work, achieving balance and tension in the foreground, middle and background. Grarup is also adept at making subtle but powerful use of symbolism.

His work shines with clarity and emotional resonance. "The more simple an image, but still nicely composed and structured, the more impact it will have," he says. Some of the best examples of his work to date include *The Boys of Ramallah* (2000–01), a classic narrative about the undertow of violence in Palestinian society, and his impressionistic take on the aftermath of the 2003 earthquake in Bam, Iran: "What struck me most was the silence. What came out were very dark, very calm pictures of the situation." He is currently at work on projects about the forgotten refugees of Chechnya, Liberia and other war zones, as well as Slovakia's Roma culture. Grarup has no illusions that photojournalism will change the world, however. "I don't believe in that. Photojournalists have an obligation to keep informing the rest of the world," he says. "The fact that people reflect on my work is the most important thing of all."

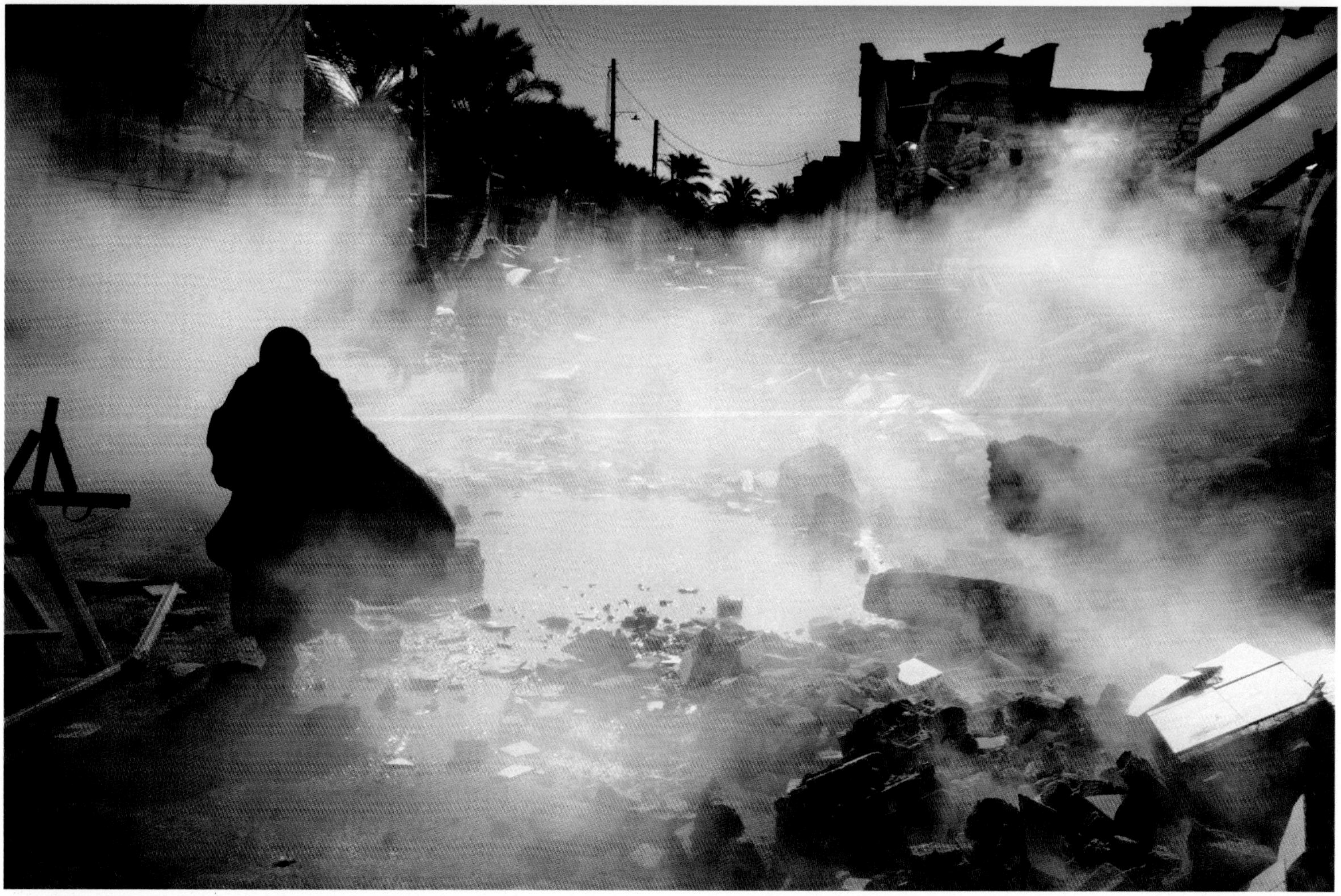

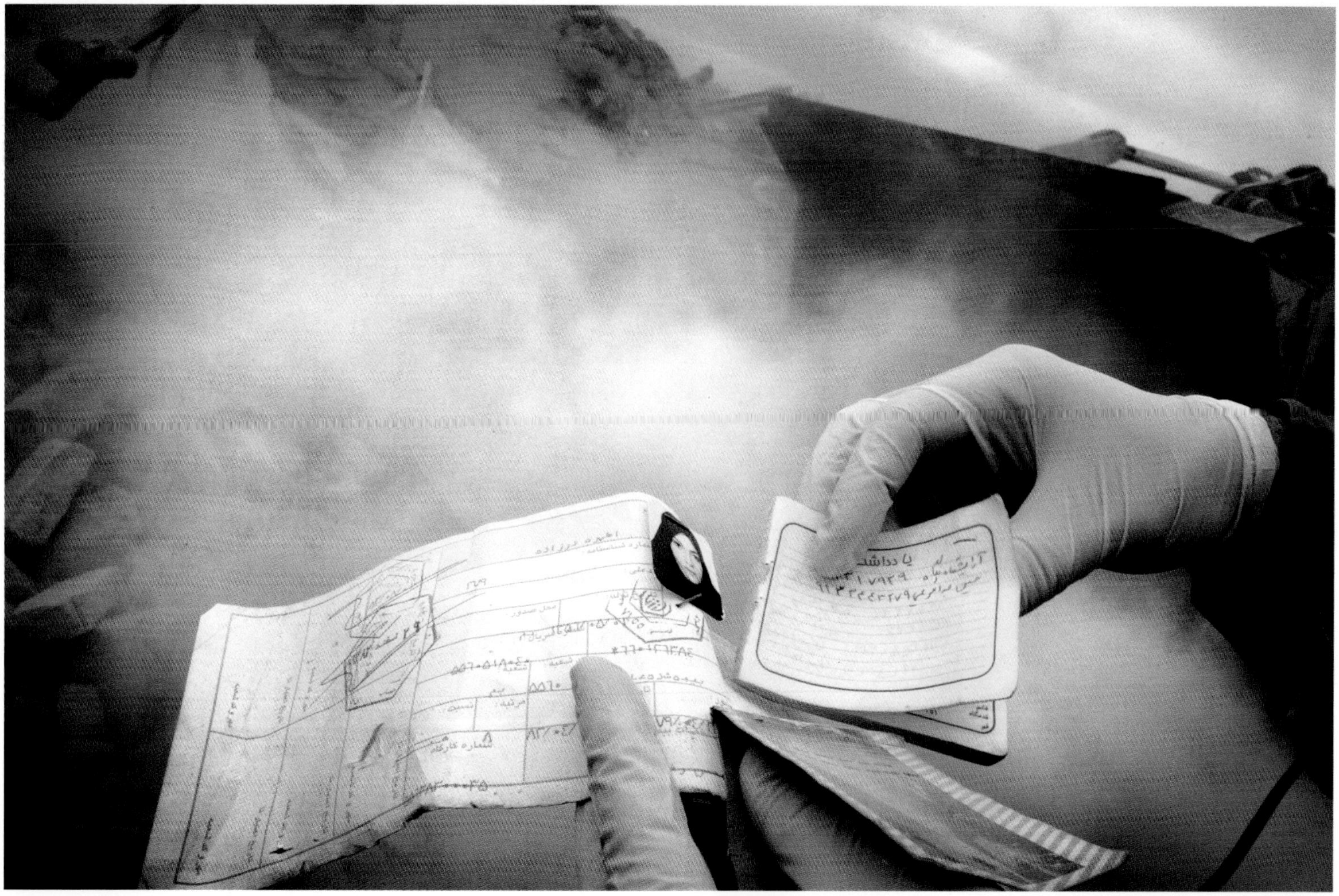

یادداشت
محل صدور
مرتبه
نسبت
شماره کارگاه

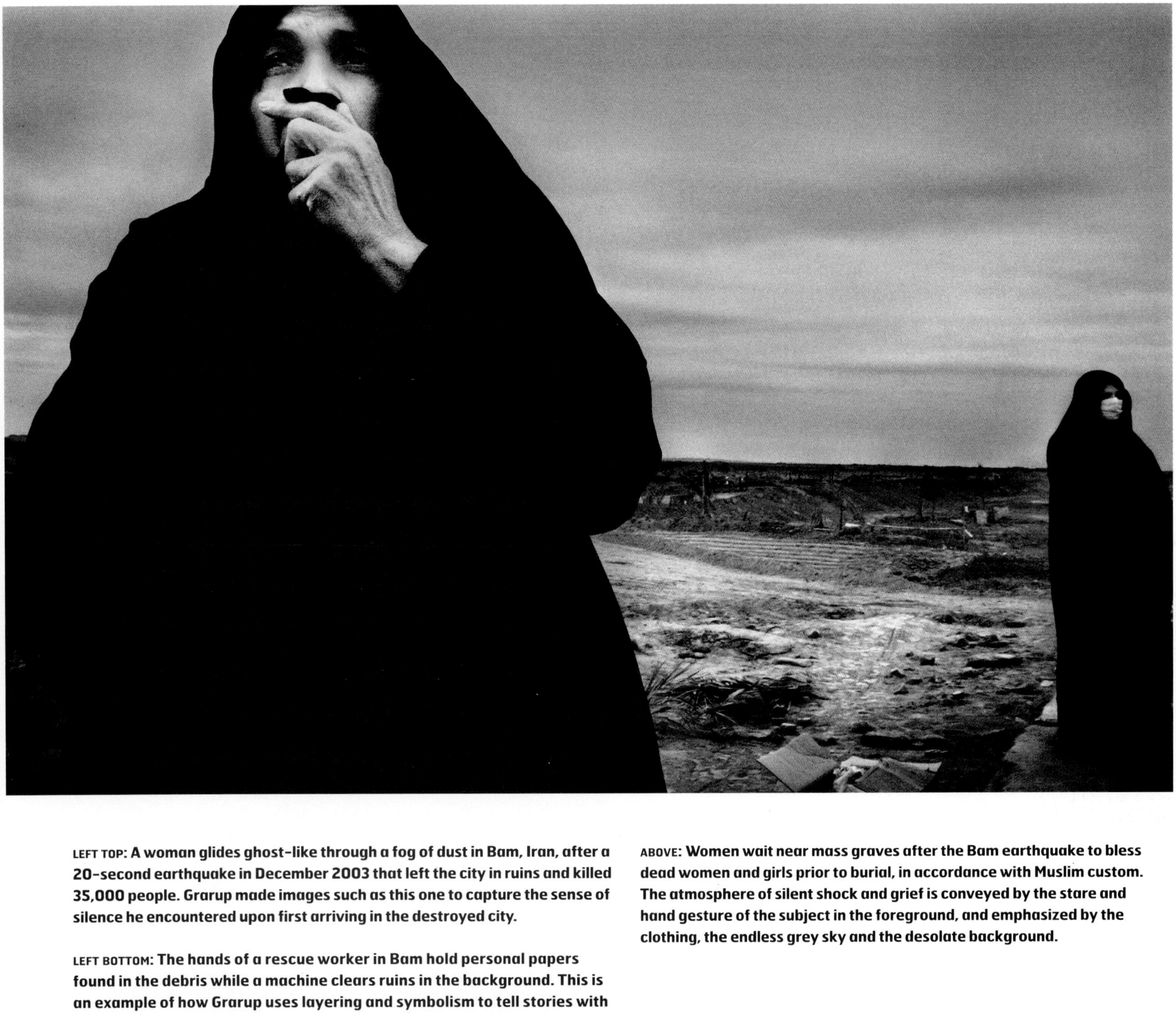

LEFT TOP: A woman glides ghost-like through a fog of dust in Bam, Iran, after a 20-second earthquake in December 2003 that left the city in ruins and killed 35,000 people. Grarup made images such as this one to capture the sense of silence he encountered upon first arriving in the destroyed city.

LEFT BOTTOM: The hands of a rescue worker in Bam hold personal papers found in the debris while a machine clears ruins in the background. This is an example of how Grarup uses layering and symbolism to tell stories with single images: rather than show a victim directly, he engages the viewer's imagination with a remnant of a life that probably ended in sudden, tragic death.

ABOVE: Women wait near mass graves after the Bam earthquake to bless dead women and girls prior to burial, in accordance with Muslim custom. The atmosphere of silent shock and grief is conveyed by the stare and hand gesture of the subject in the foreground, and emphasized by the clothing, the endless grey sky and the desolate background.

CARAROL GUZY

Carol Guzy is one of the USA's most high-profile photojournalists who combines an eye for edgy hard news with a sensitive heart. Guzy is both consistent and extremely versatile. She can photograph domestic social issues, political turmoil like the fall of the Berlin Wall, natural disasters like the mudslides in Colombia, the aftermath of 9/11, and the civil conflicts in the former Yugoslavia, Rwanda and Haiti. If there is any place in the world that is currently engulfed by chaos, violence and grief, Guzy is probably there working for the *Washington Post*. She is capable of photographing news images for the front pages, or more feature-based assignments, both in colour and black-and-white, and all for a daily newspaper with demanding editorial standards and a discerning readership.

Guzy has said that her original training in nursing endowed her with a deep level of compassion that might not otherwise have been there. Perhaps, but this degree of empathy with subjects cannot be taught – it is something instinctive that all great photojournalists must have before they ever pick up a camera. When her sense of compassion is combined with her technical proficiency, it is easy to see why she has been so widely acclaimed. There is never a sense that she is exploiting, or even intruding upon, her subjects. She is just trying to relate their terrible and distressing stories in a way that will capture our attention. Often the photographer is the only voice these people have, so Guzy will speak quietly on their behalf and pull back her camera. She will focus on the crowds caught up in terrible situations or take a general scene from a distance. At other times she will shout a little more, jolting us as she captures an individual close up at a moment of grief or despair. She is especially strong on conveying how war and conflicts impact on the innocent. Her photographs enlighten, captivate and inform and, it is to be hoped, spur people and, more importantly, governments into action. It may not be nursing, but a photojournalist as committed as Guzy is performing an equally valid public service.

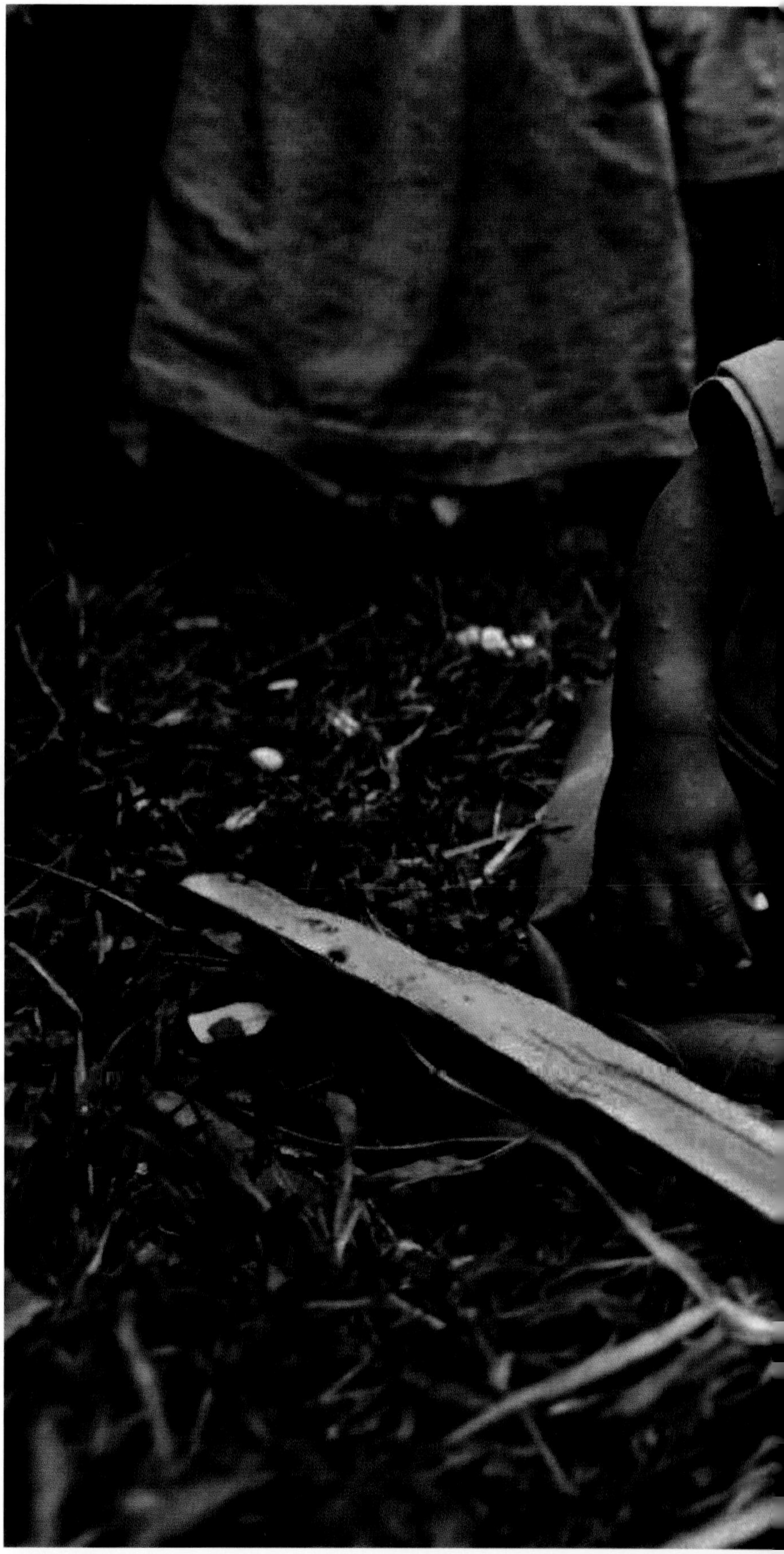

BELOW: This photograph was taken in Rwanda, some time between November and December 1996. A baby sits next to his mother, who became gravely ill during their journey from Gisenyi to Kigali. This is a haunting image and demonstrates Guzy's instinctive empathy with people in distress, especially women and children.

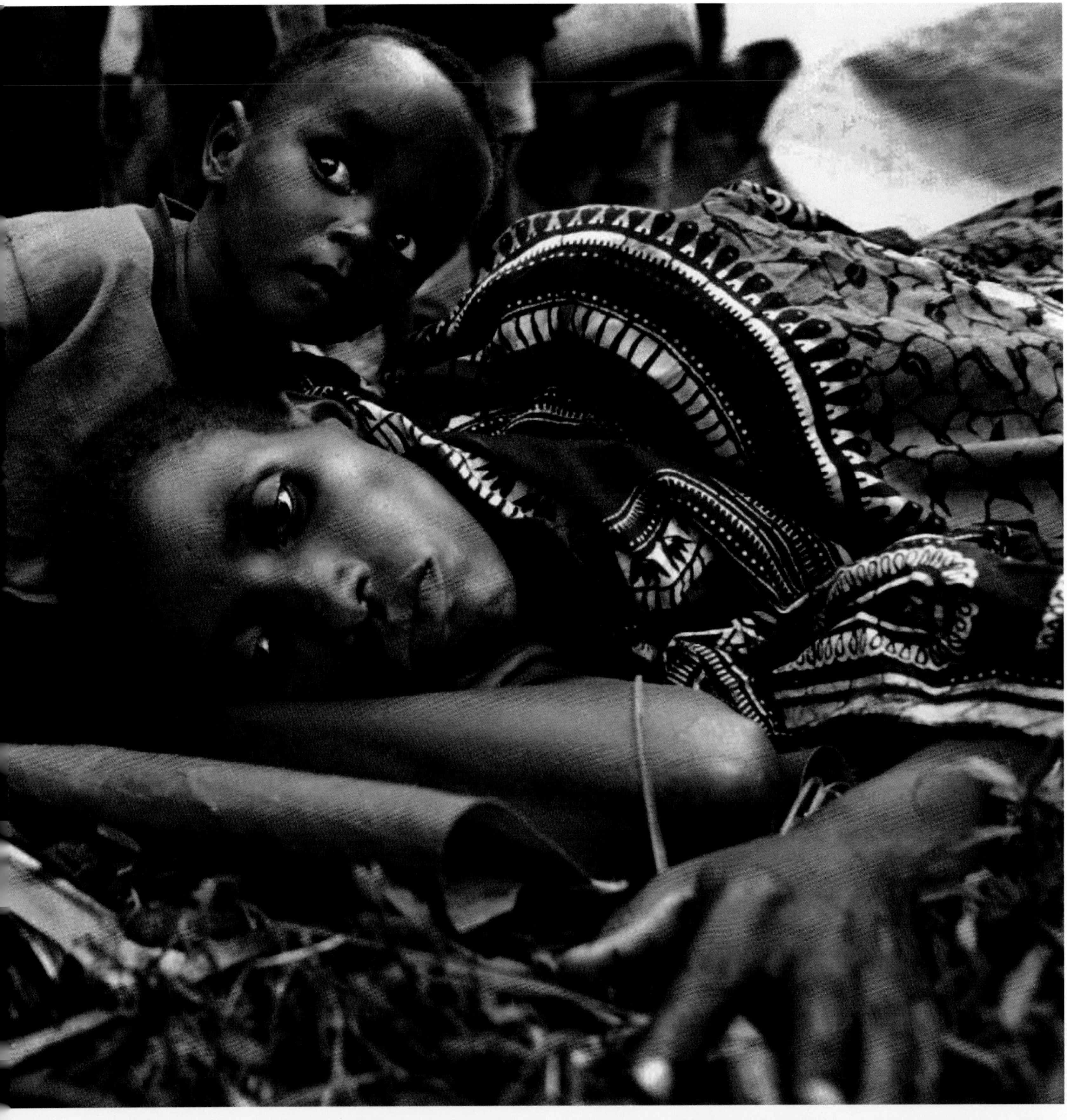

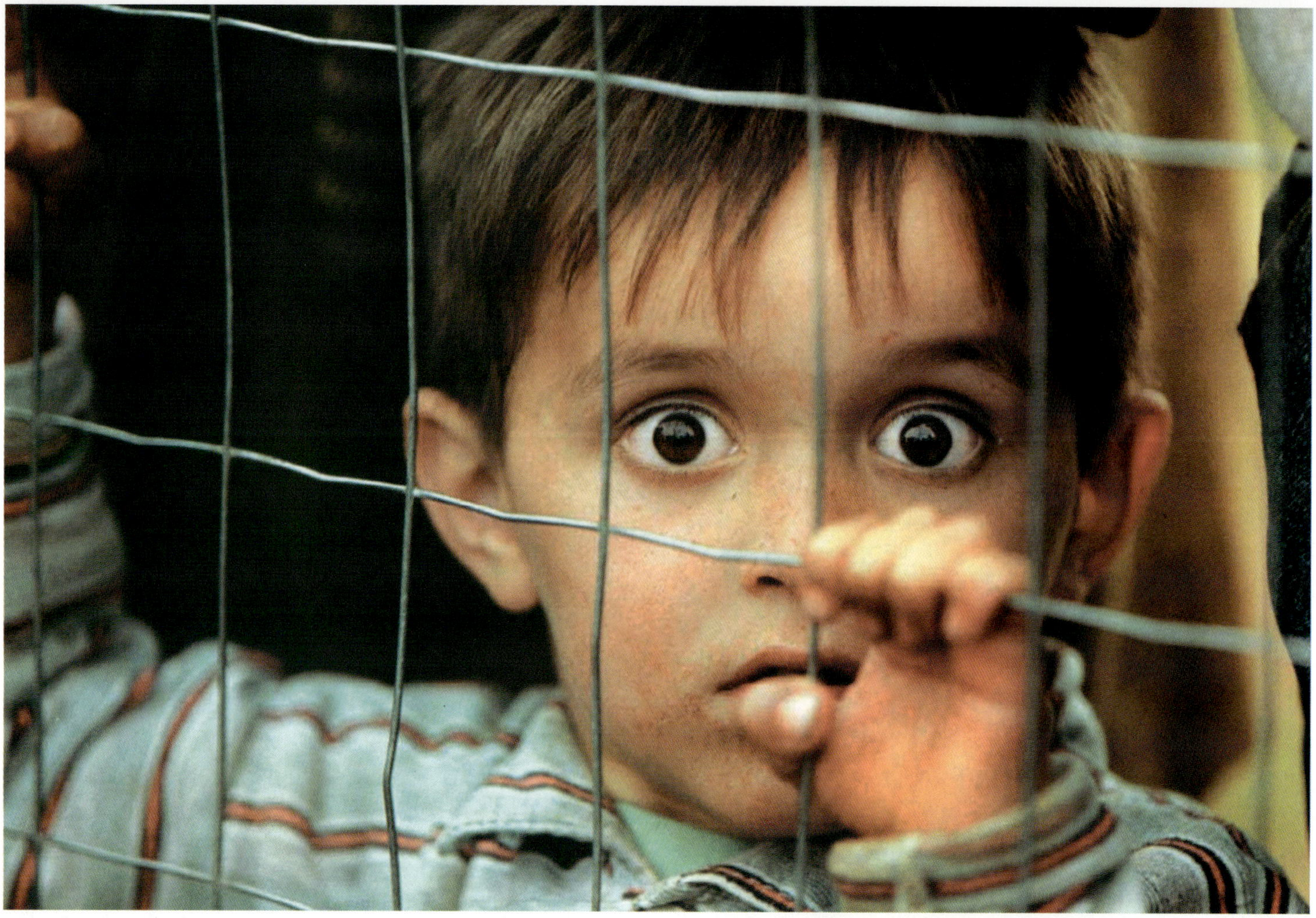

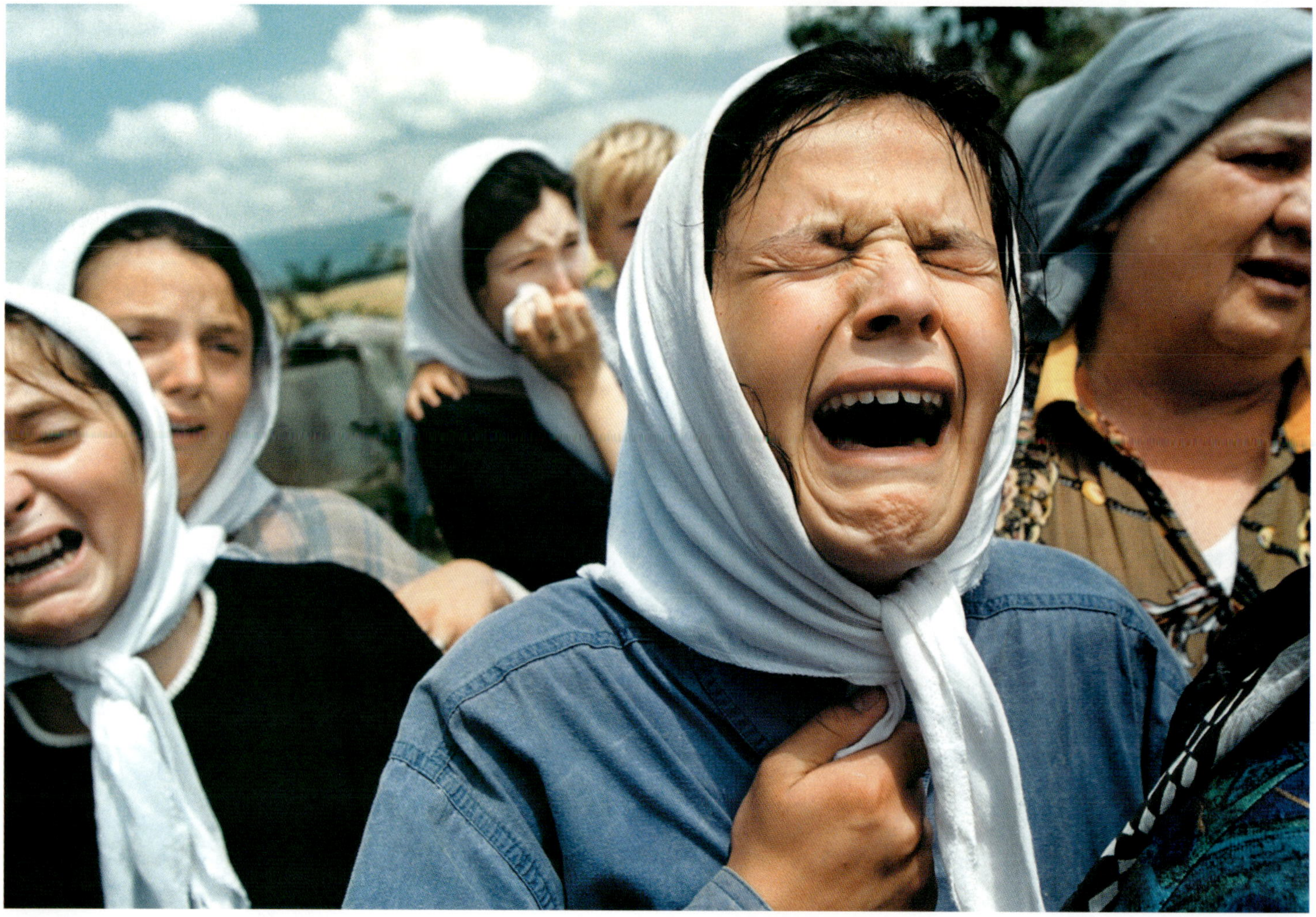

LEFT: **Life in exile: Bekir Shala, four years old, peers through the barbed-wire fence with a wide-eyed expression at the camp run by the United Arab Emirates in Kukes, Albania, in 1999. Once again, we see Guzy's signature style in expertly conveying the chaos and uncertainty of a situation though the eyes of a child.**

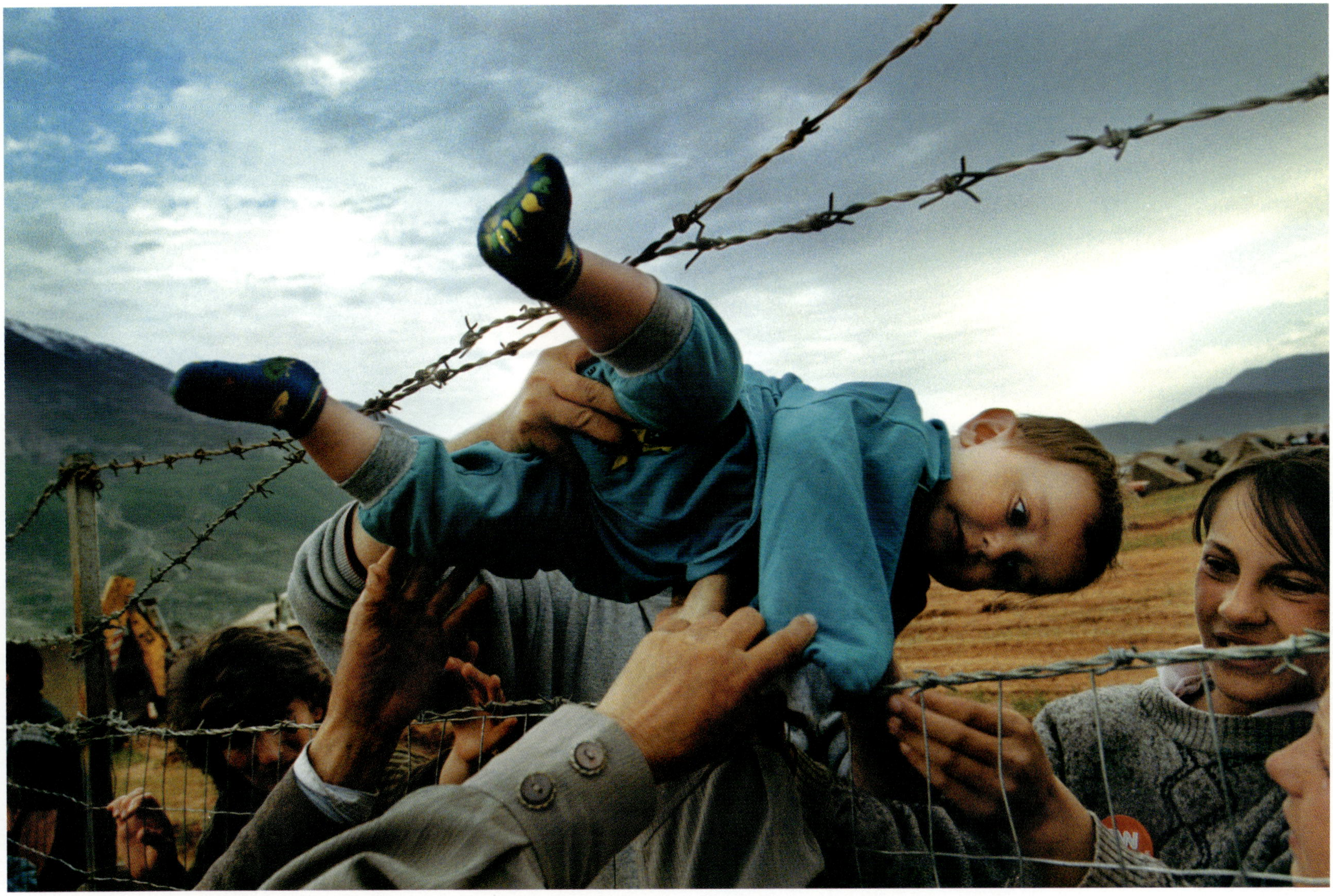

ABOVE: **A two-year-old boy is passed into the hands of his grandparents through the barbed wire at a refugee camp in Albania. The members of the family were reunited in 1999 after fleeing Kosovo during the conflict. This is a simply stunning image from Guzy's very powerful essay on the plight of the refugees, work that won her a deserved Pulitzer Prize for Features.**

LEFT: **A woman wails in grief after the death of her uncle in Kosovo in 1999. His body was found with the body of his daughter. Apparently, Serbs shot them as they tried to reach their family in the mountains.**

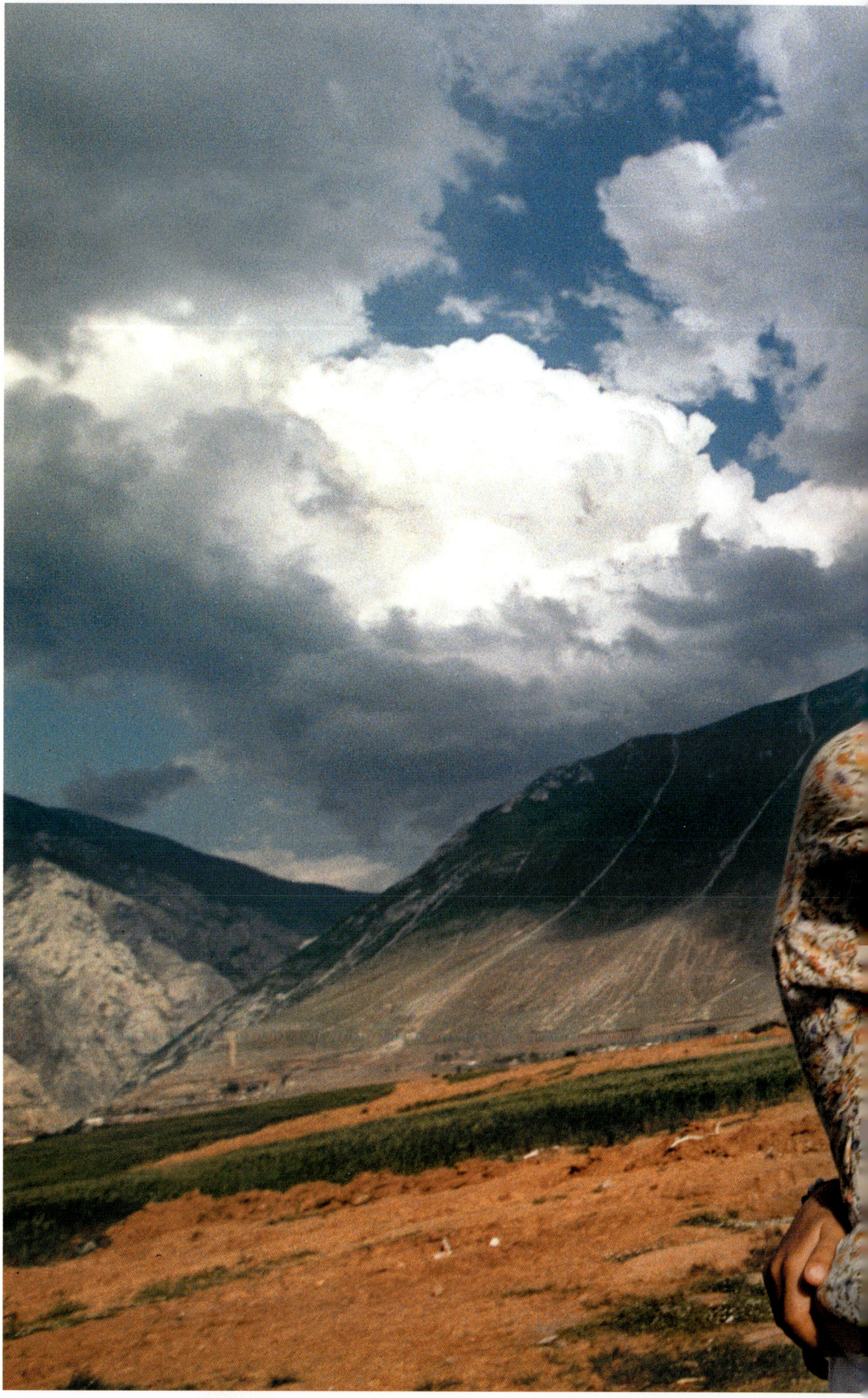

RIGHT: This is aptly called *Children's Joy* and it was taken at a UNICEF-run camp in Albania for refugee children. At the camp the children are counselled to help them deal with the trauma of their ordeal. This image has it all: beautiful composition, bold colours, a dramatic landscape and most of all hope.

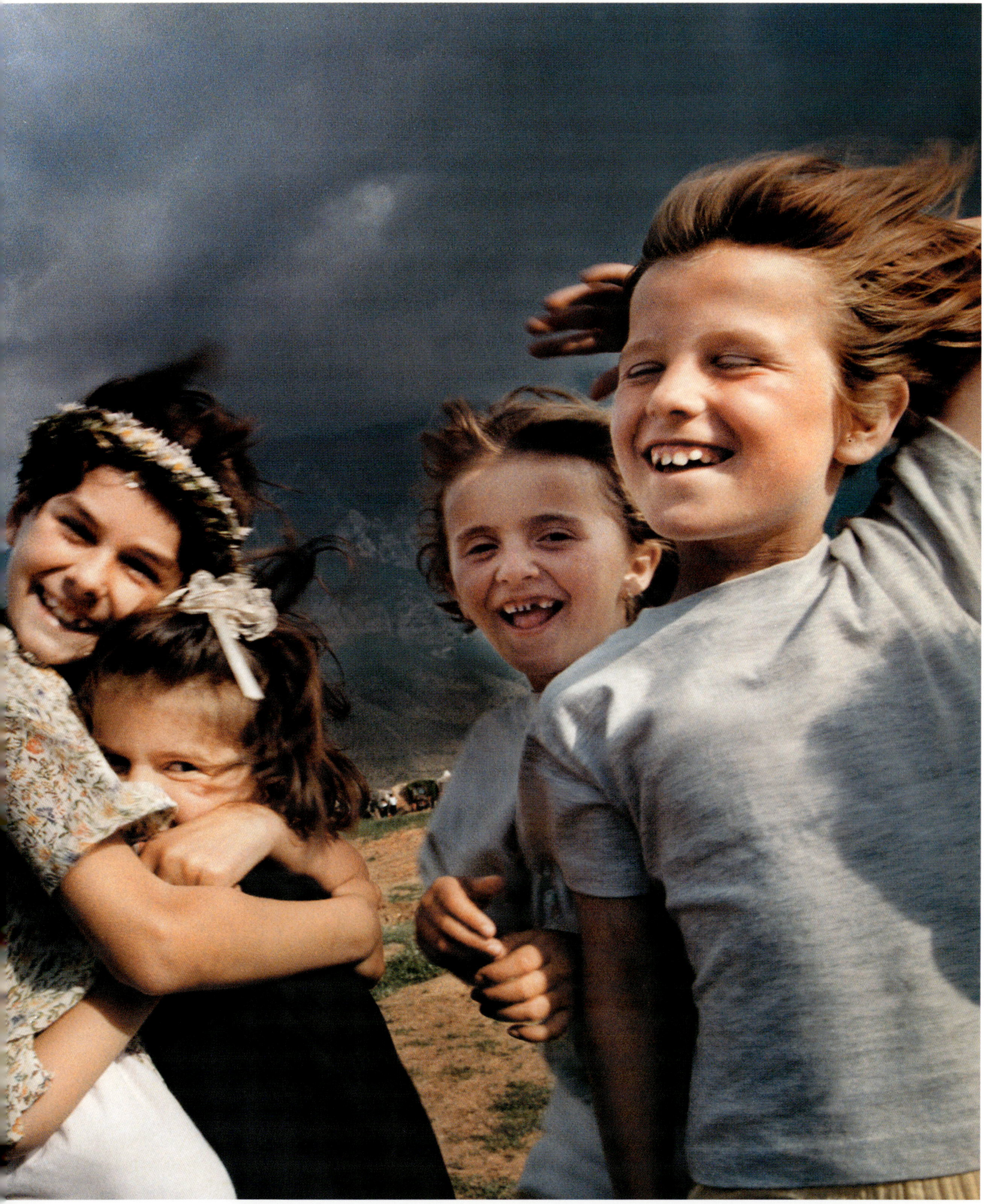

BERT HARDY

RIGHT: **One of the subjects of Bert Hardy's work in Northern Ireland during 1955 was the retired lion-tamer Alec Robinson, pictured here in Belfast.**

BELOW: **As part of his work for the 1955 *Picture Post* story, "One Man in Five is out of Work", Bert Hardy included this picture of an unemployed man and his family in Northern Ireland. Hardy's forte was the reportage of social conditions, and his empathy with his subjects is always apparent.**

Bert Hardy's work is one of the high points of British photojournalism. He acquired his first Leica in the 1930s, when Fleet Street smudgers still wedded to the large-format press camera considered it a "toy". But Hardy's Leica pictures were so well made and emotive that they convinced many a picture editor that a new sort of photojournalism was emerging. The photographer's ability to get close to the subject and make intimate and revealing images that seem like a slice of life was becoming all-important. His pictures of the people and communities of working-class districts are touching and realistic evocations of a lost sense of British solidarity. Hardy's Cockney background, his ability to communicate with ordinary people and his genuine affection for his fellow man were as essential to the pictures he could take as his total mastery of the 35mm camera. Hardy's photography fully embraced the humanist spirit, and he was greatly concerned with his role as a witness. Covering the Korean War in 1950, he and the journalist James Cameron sent back a story to *Picture Post* about how the South Koreans were treating their own political prisoners. The owner of the magazine, Edward Hulton, decided the article was "communist propaganda" and the editor, Tom Hopkinson, was forced to resign. Cameron later wrote about Hardy's evident bravery under fire during their coverage of the decisive Allied landing on Inchon: "it was long ago established that one way you cannot take pictures is lying face-down in a hole. I spent considerable periods of time doing that. Bert, on the other hand, was plying his trade upright in the open, cursing the military exigencies that had organized this invasion in the middle of the night. One of my enduring memories of that strange occasion is of Bert Hardy on the seawall of Blue Beach, blaspheming among the impossible din, and timing his exposures to the momentary flash of the rockets."

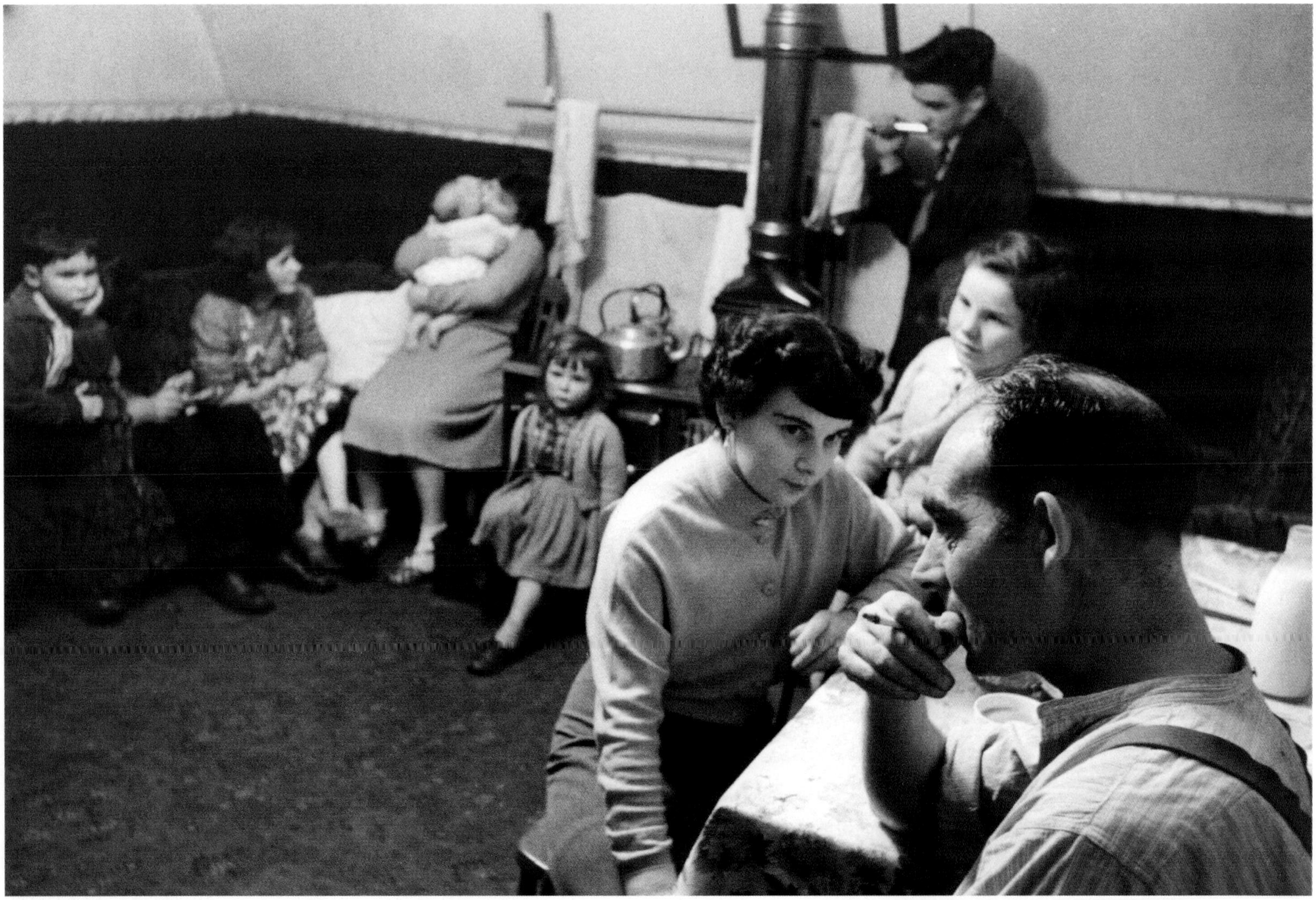

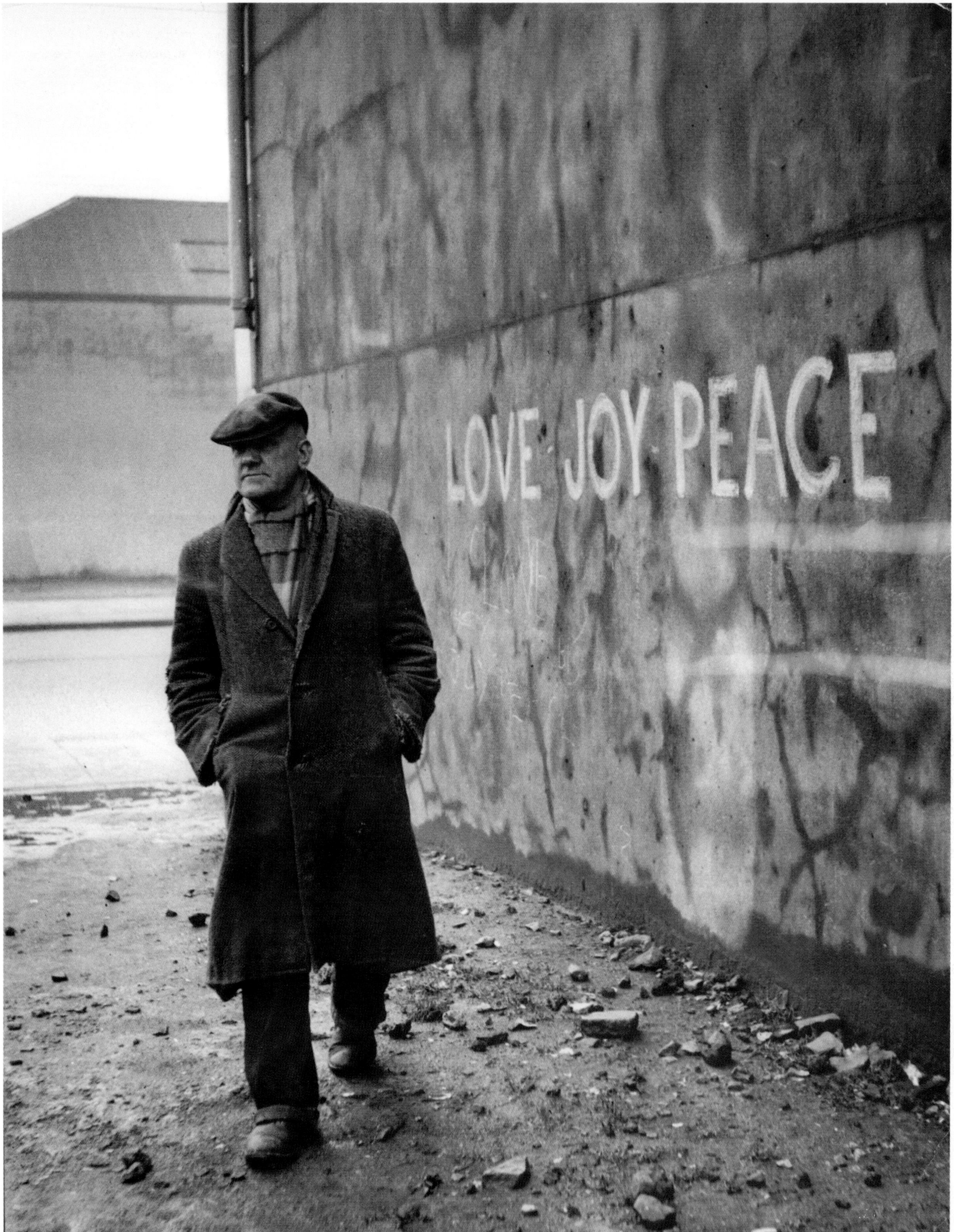
LOVE JOY PEACE

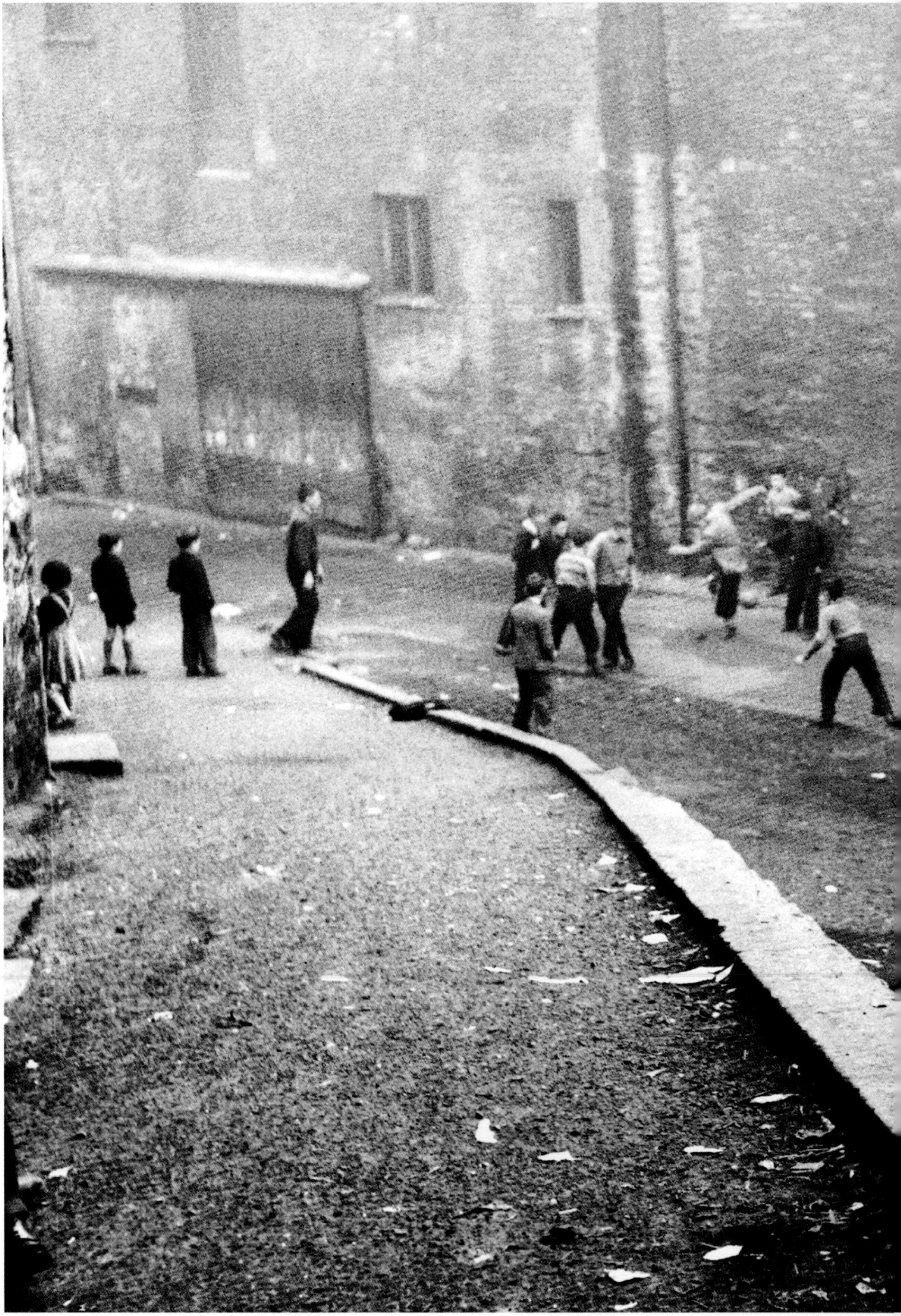

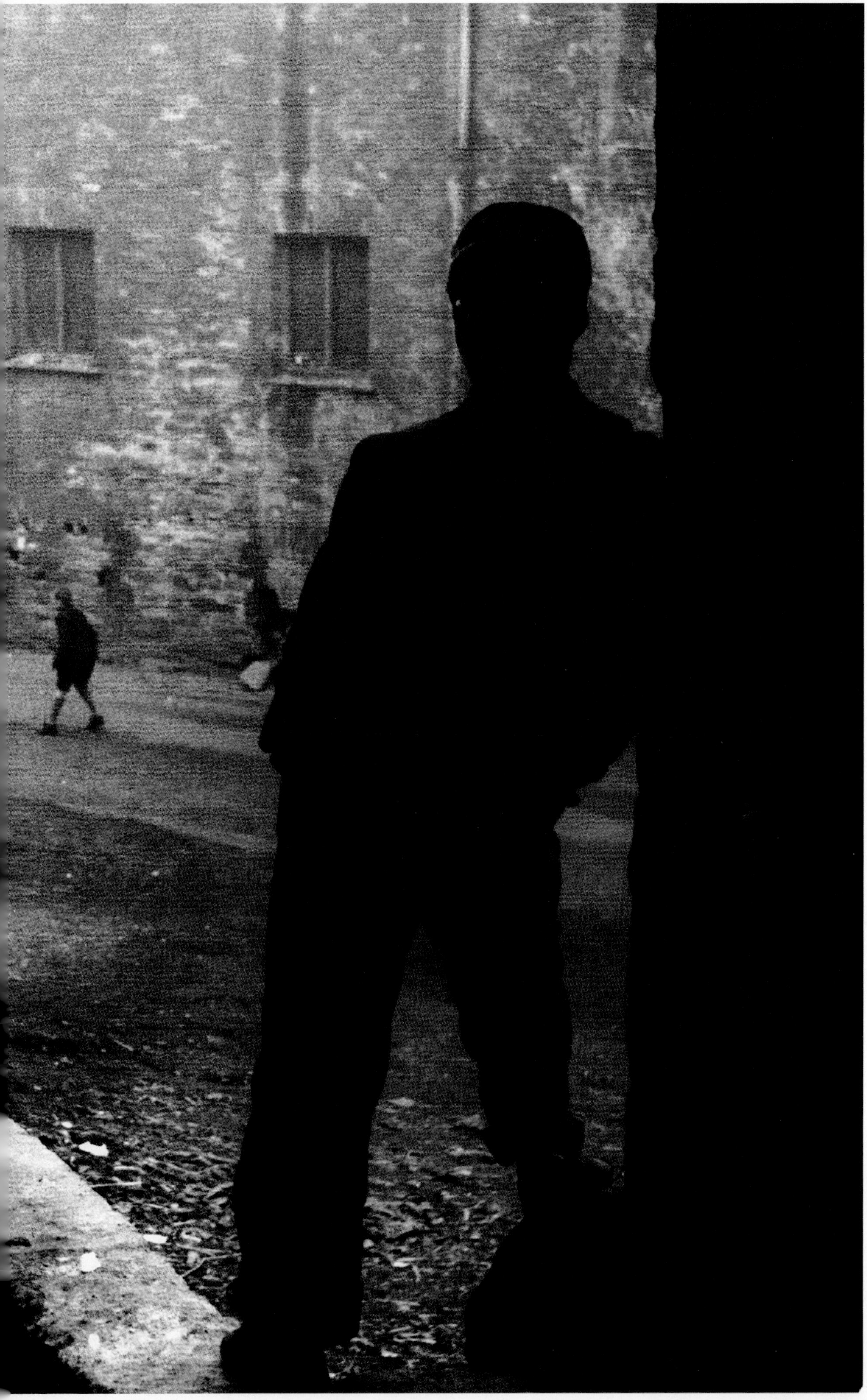

LEFT: In 1955 Bert Hardy took a series of pictures for *Picture Post*, including this photograph of unemployed people and children on the streets of Derry (Londonderry) in Northern Ireland. The characteristically strong composition of Hardy's images focuses attention on the subjects, emphasizing their social conditions. The shadowed figure of the unemployed man in the foreground lends the image a haunting quality. Will the same fate befall the children?

LEWIS HINE

Hine's basic photographic motivations were strongly humanist and sociological, although his work is increasingly appreciated now for its aesthetic qualities. So powerful were his early pictures of the terrible conditions suffered by child workers that they led to a public outcry when published and displayed, and thus directly to changes in American law. This extraordinary body of work, much of it made in difficult circumstances and despite the inconvenience of working with a large-format 5 in x 7 in (12 cm x 18 cm) camera, a tripod and open flash, shows Hine's evident interest in "witnessing" the social conditions of his subjects. His photographs of the early years of the twentieth century seem closer in spirit to contemporary humanist photojournalism than some of his projects of the 1920s and 1930s. In this later work, Hine's fascination with making heroic portraits of the working man is evidently driven by more aesthetic concerns. Perhaps his acquaintance with Alfred Stieglitz in the early 1920s persuaded him that he should temper his reformist zeal with a more careful attention to the pictorial qualities of his work. Some commentators have even found evidence of a desire to make a striking image out of the misery of his subjects in his early projects, such as his records of newly arrived immigrants on Ellis Island. His portrait of the young Russian Jewess on Ellis Island in 1905 (far right) might fall into this category, for her wan beauty can still transfix the viewer. Although he sometimes experimented with art photography, he worked consistently to the end of his life to document, in as truthful a manner as possible, the realities of life for the poor and the oppressed. Hine's later work was made when his early fame seemed no longer able to generate sufficient commissions to support him. Yet the series on the construction of the Empire State Building remains one of his most masterful achievements. Persuaded that technology could now offer better working conditions to the worker, Hine produced a series that became a hymn to manual labour and the new forms of construction that the famous skyscraper embodied.

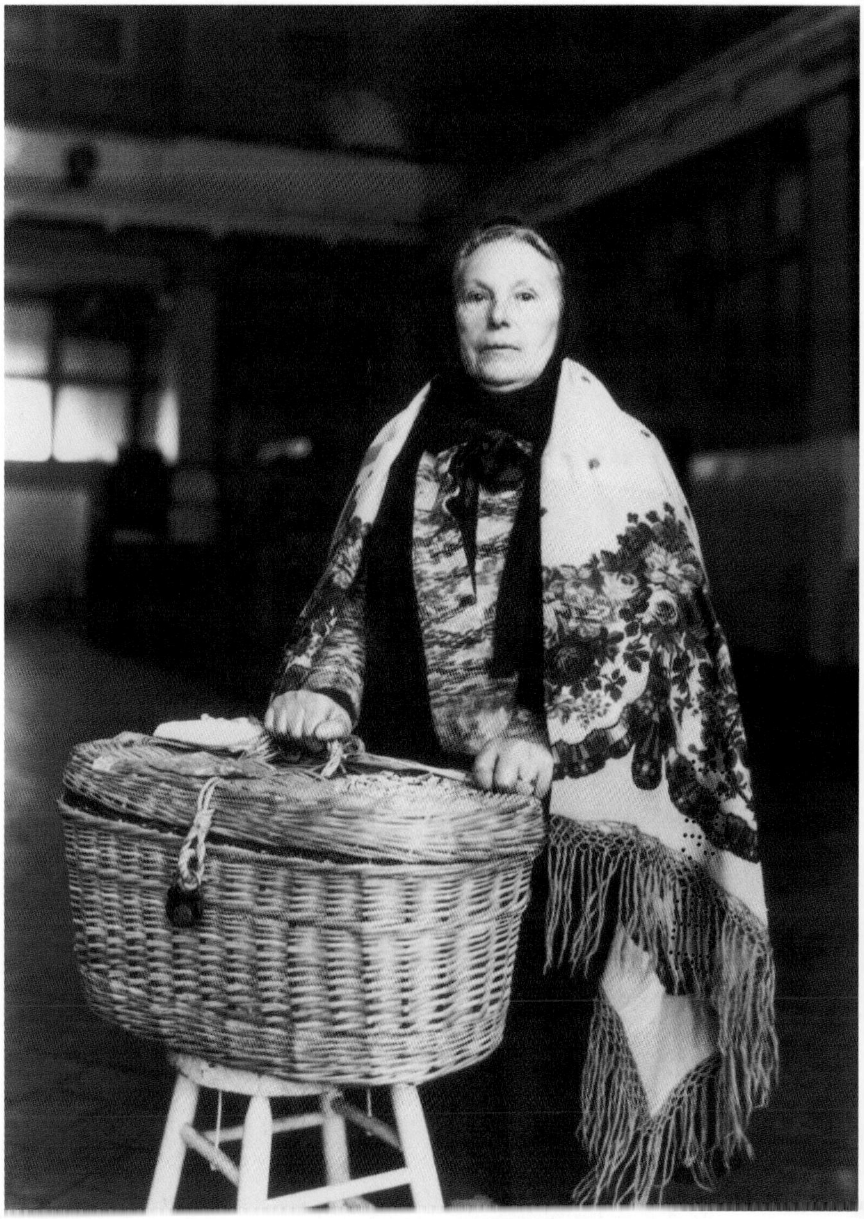

ABOVE: In this carefully posed portrait, Hine depicts an elderly Jewish woman, recently arrived from Russia at Ellis Island in 1905, no doubt a victim of one of the innumerable pogroms against the Jews then raging in Russia. She is shown with the wicker basket that contains all her worldly goods.

RIGHT: A young Jewish woman at Ellis Island in 1905 is shown in a proud and defiant pose.

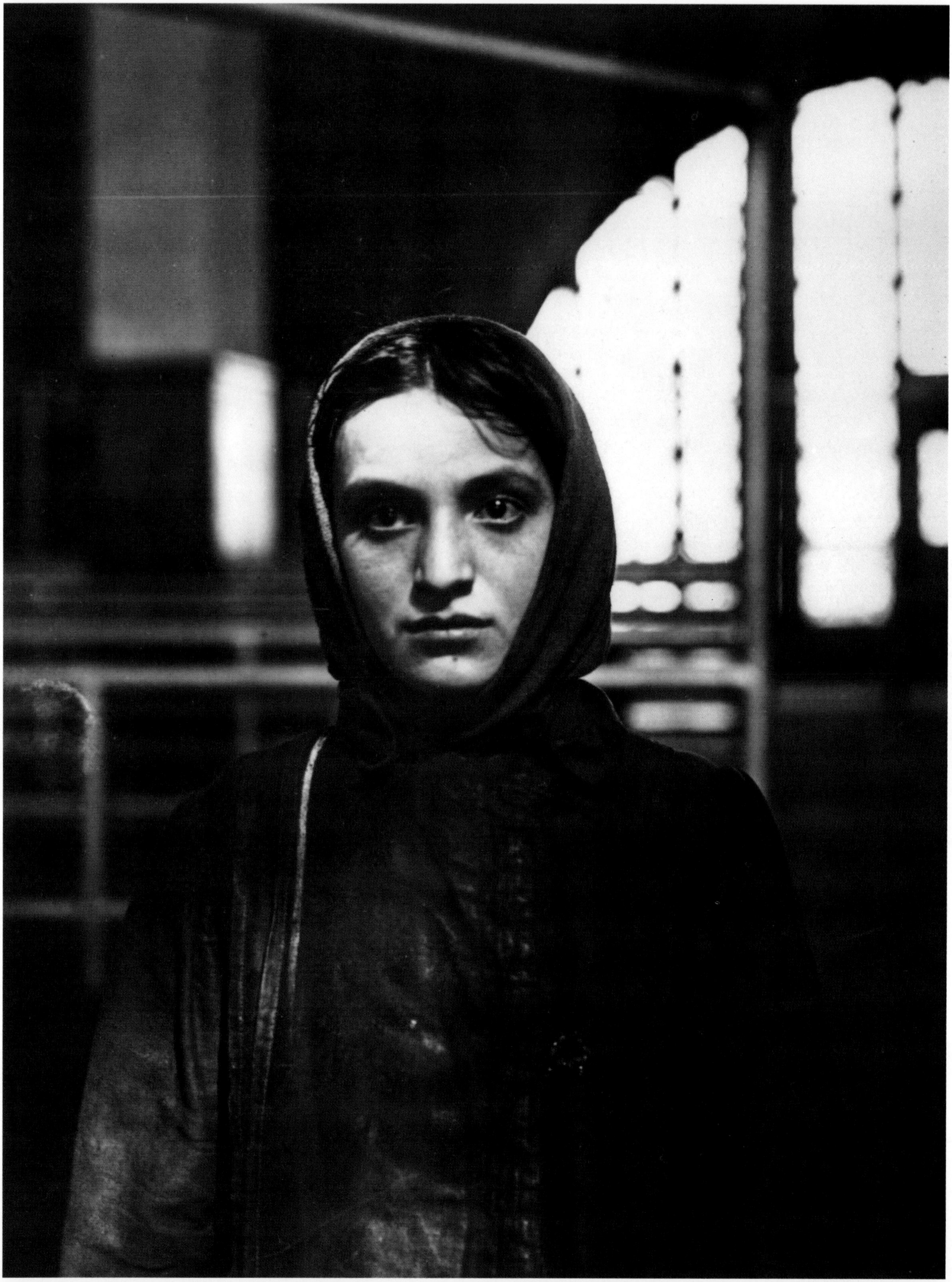

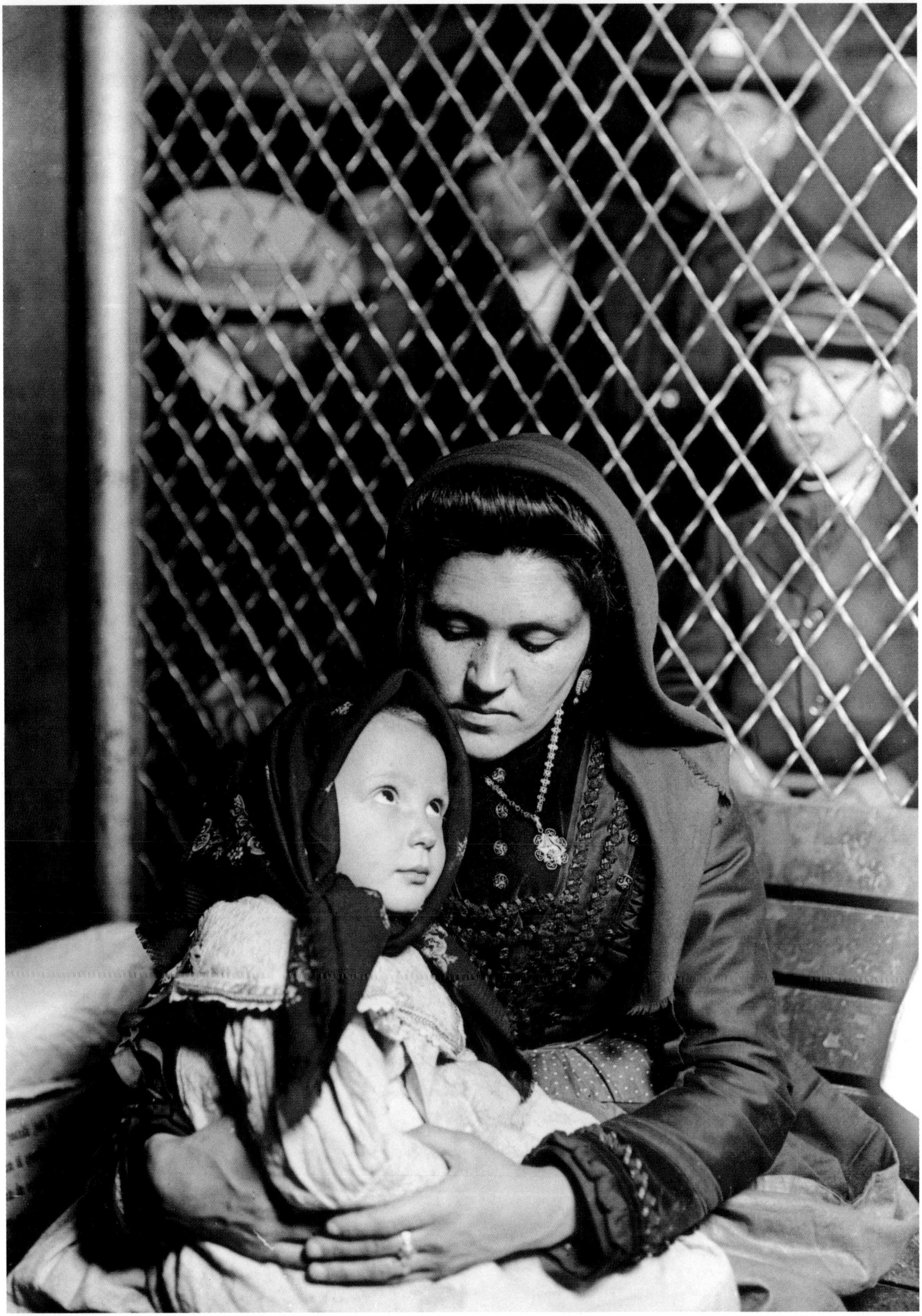

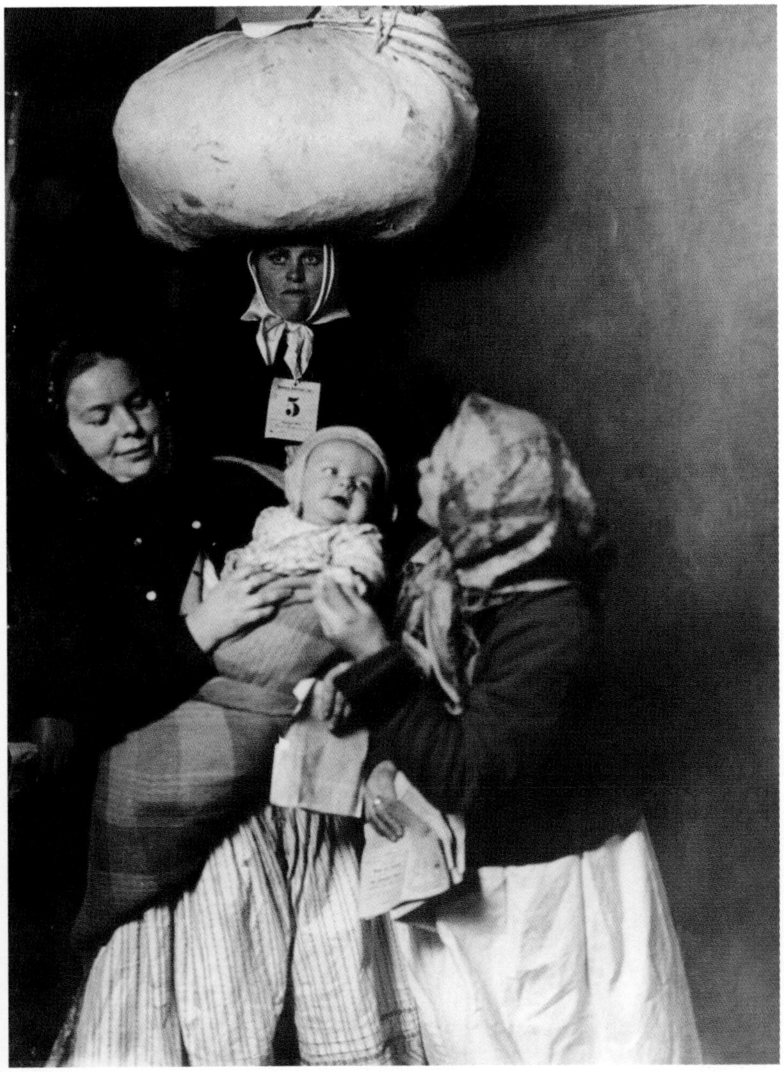

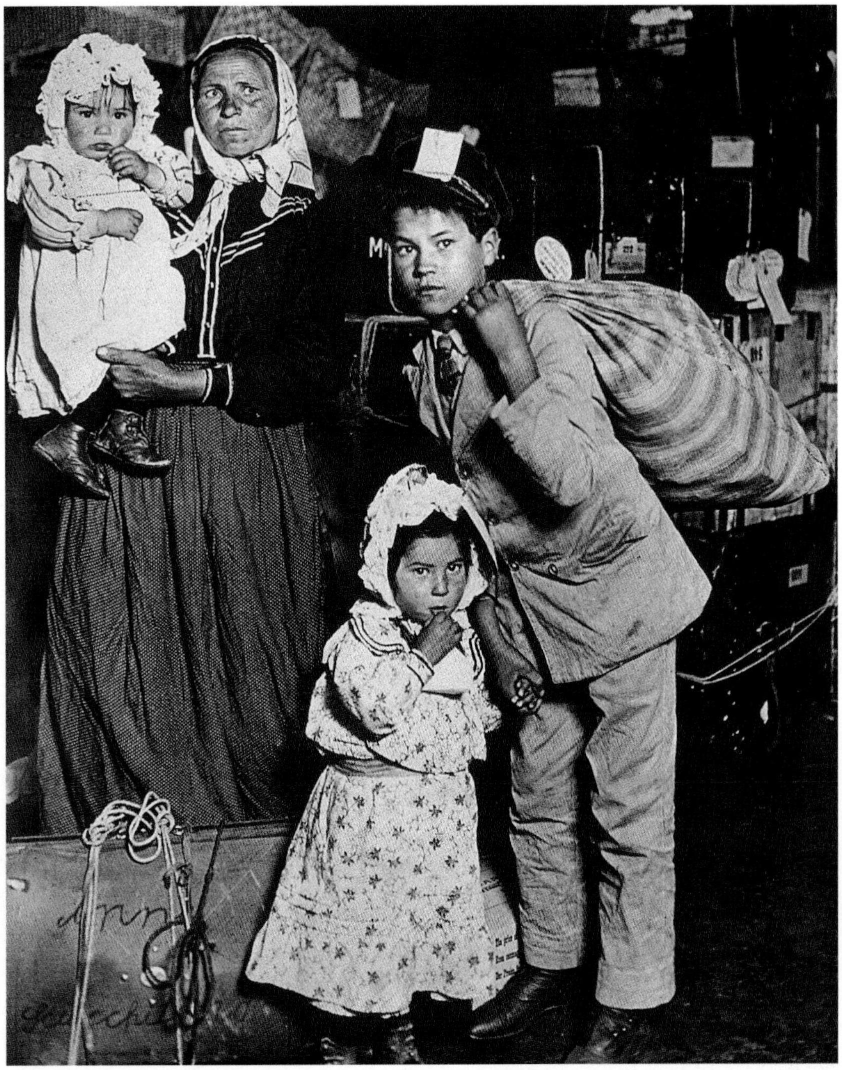

ABOVE: **Presented with honesty and compassion, this well-constructed composition portrays three Eastern European women and a baby at Ellis Island in 1905.**

LEFT: **Hine's framing of this picture, taken in 1905, with the newly arrived Italian immigrant and child so gently captured in front of a grille, emphasizes the way in which immigrants were wrongly seen as dangerous people who needed to be confined, despite their evident innocence.**

ABOVE: **The careful and straightforward depiction of the newly arrived immigrants at Ellis Island, such as this woman and her children in 1905, presents them as if they were refugees from a distant conflict or disaster, people who require help rather than condemnation.**

HEINRICH HOFFMAN

Although Leni Riefenstahl may be better known as Hitler's film-maker, Hoffman was almost certainly much more important as the key image-maker in the fascist leader's rise to power. A close personal friend from 1920, he persuaded Hitler to embrace photography as a central element in his political campaigns, to create the image of celebrity and of malevolent energy that sustains the Hitler myth to this day. In addition, Hoffman managed to acquire the exclusive rights to photograph Hitler as *Reichsbildberichterstatter der NSDAP* (Official State Photographer). His exclusive photographs made him (and Hitler, whom he persuaded to insist on a royalty on every photographic portrait stamp sold by the German Post Office) very wealthy. He also played a key role in Hitler's personal life, for Hoffman's assistant Eva Braun became the Führer's mistress and, during the very last days of the Third Reich, his wife.

Hoffman's photography has two clear purposes: one is to show Hitler as a natural leader, symbolizing the "power of the will" that would eventually make him Führer. But a second aim was to "humanize" the leader. Hoffman's book, *The Hitler Nobody Knows*, published in 1933, shows both sides. It eventually sold half a million copies, and was followed by several other small photo-books that fed the Hitler myth. During the Second World War Hoffman went almost everywhere with his leader, and the huge body of photographs that resulted is an important part of the historical record of the rise, decline and fall of the Third Reich. Hoffman continued to take two distinct approaches to his main subject. His monumental portraits were lit in a way that seemed to endow the Führer with superhuman attributes. Alternatively, he was depicted as a man of the people, attentive despite his great task to their needs. He was shown listening to a carefully posed group of SA stormtroopers, talking to a child, or quietly watching while some farmers went about their work in an idealized Black Forest setting. Despite the propaganda functions of Hoffman's Hitler pictures, they are also instructive about the role of the photograph in the era of totalitarian states, when the mass circulation of such images played such a central part in the creation of leader-myths.

RIGHT: Hoffman shows Hitler posing alongside members of the *Reichswehr* in 1930, General Ludendorff in the centre. Although he is not in uniform, Hoffman has caught Hitler's attempt to make his bearing seem, as befits a veteran of the Great War, entirely military in stance.

OVERLEAF LEFT: Hoffman's construction of this image of Hitler at a Nazi rally places him in a dominant position, the photograph emphasizing his position of "natural" power and authority.

OVERLEAF RIGHT: Hoffman followed Hitler throughout his career, and this photo shows Goering and Hitler discussing the blast that nearly killed the Führer only two hours after the attempt on his life of 20 July 1944. Hitler personally banned the picture because of the expressions on his and Goering's faces.

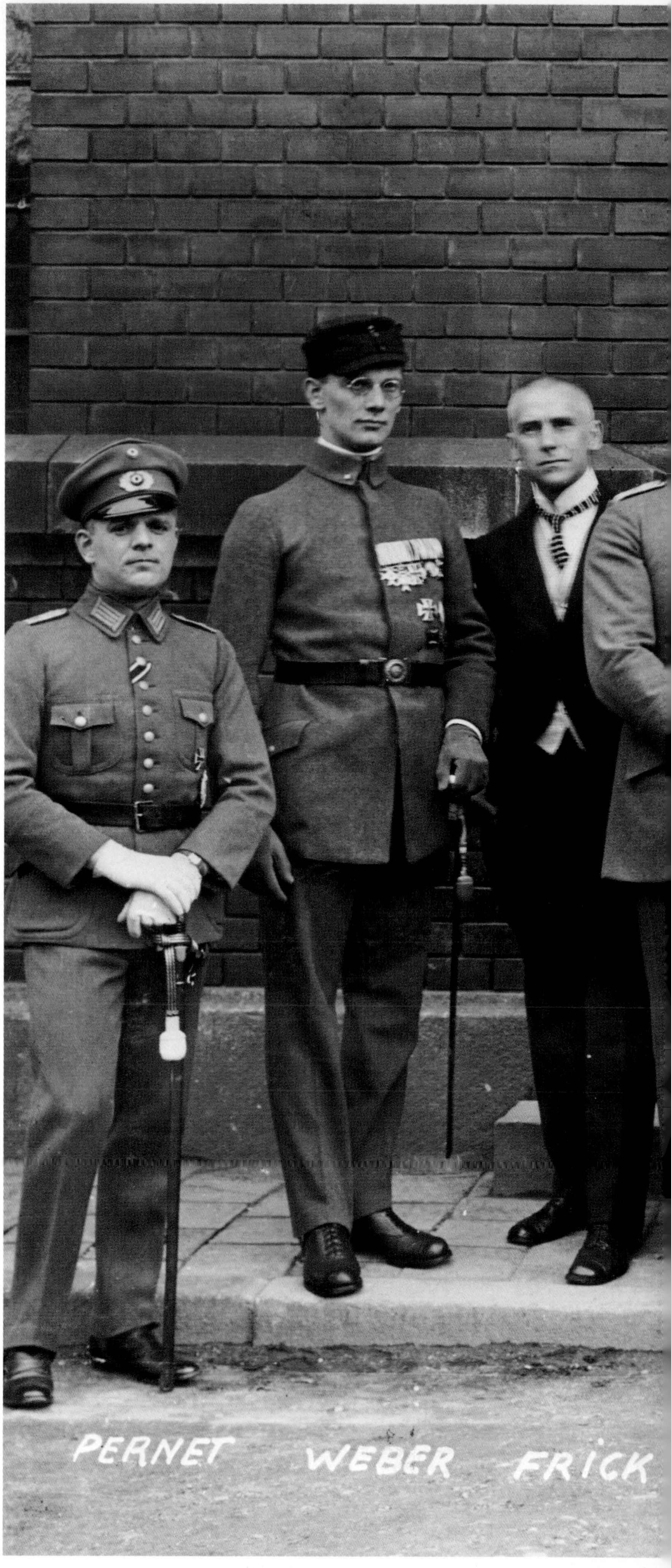

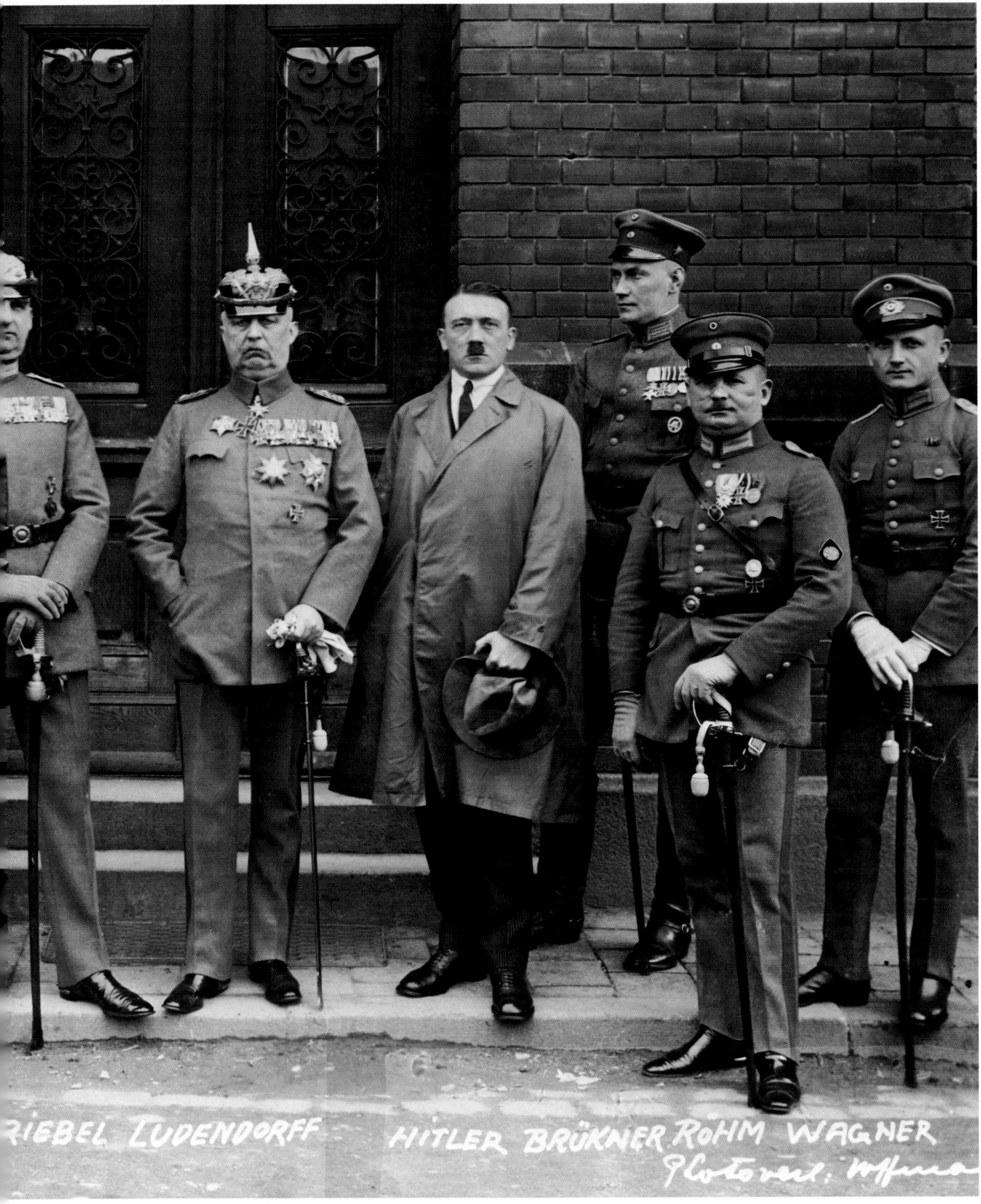
RIEBEL LUDENDORFF HITLER BRÜKNER RÖHM WAGNER

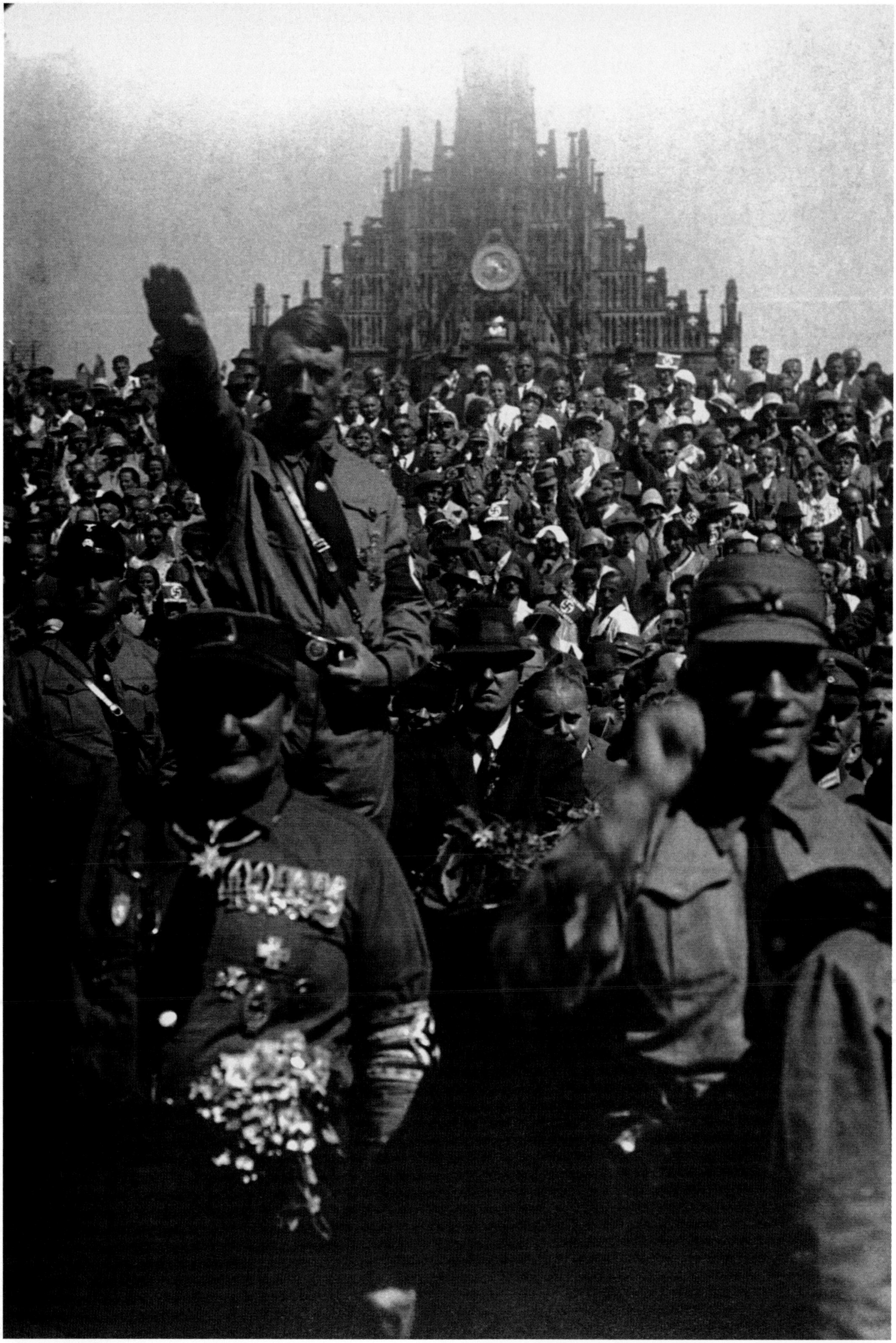

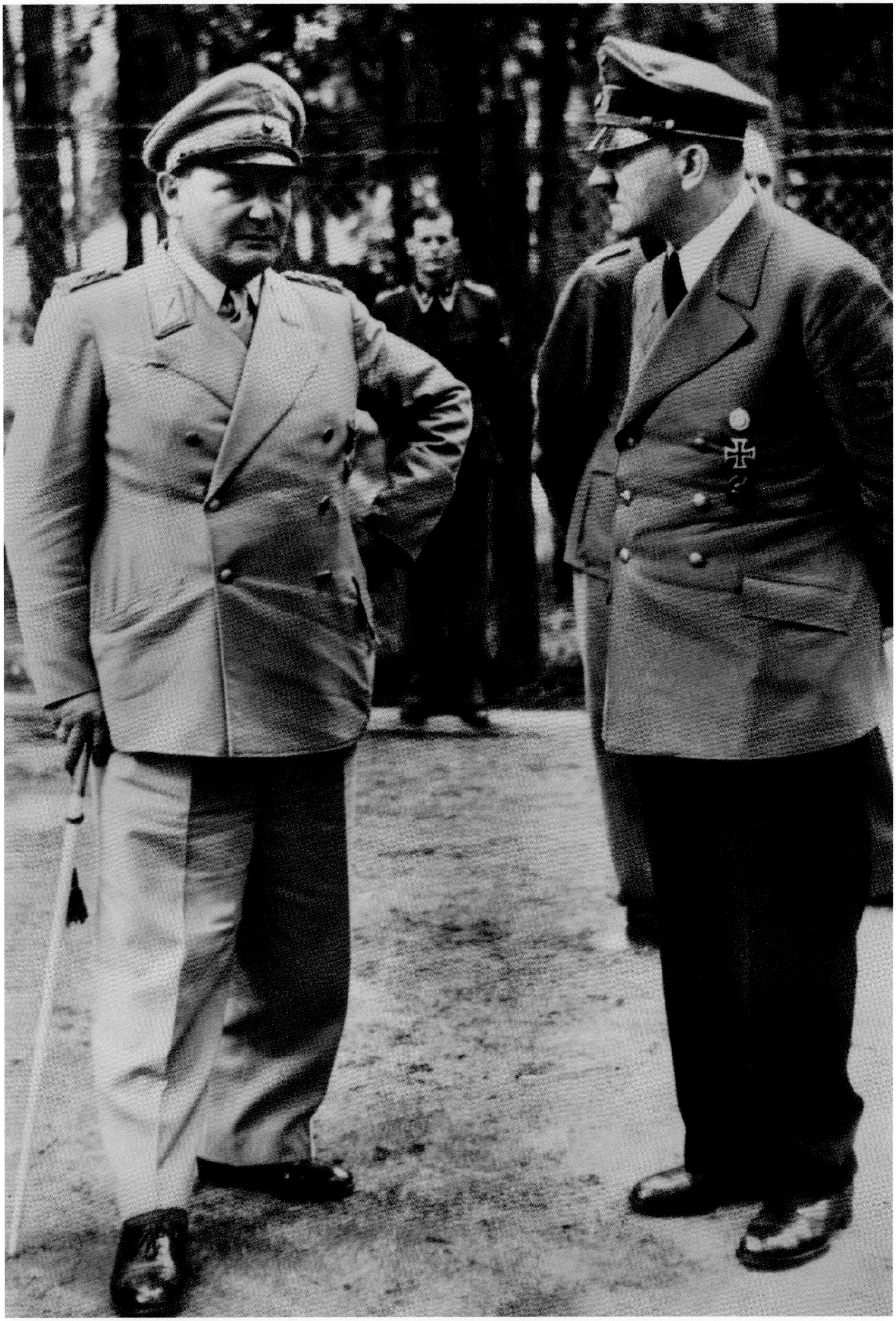

FRANK HURLEY

BELOW: **Australian wounded on the Menin Road, near Birr Cross Road on 20 September 1917. Photographing the suffering of his compatriots must have been tough for Hurley, but he handled this assignment with consummate professionalism. The image is packed with incident and detail: there is the overturned truck, the walking wounded slowly making their way in the mud, and the supine men who are too injured to stand. In the middle of the frame a soldier stares imploringly at the camera.**

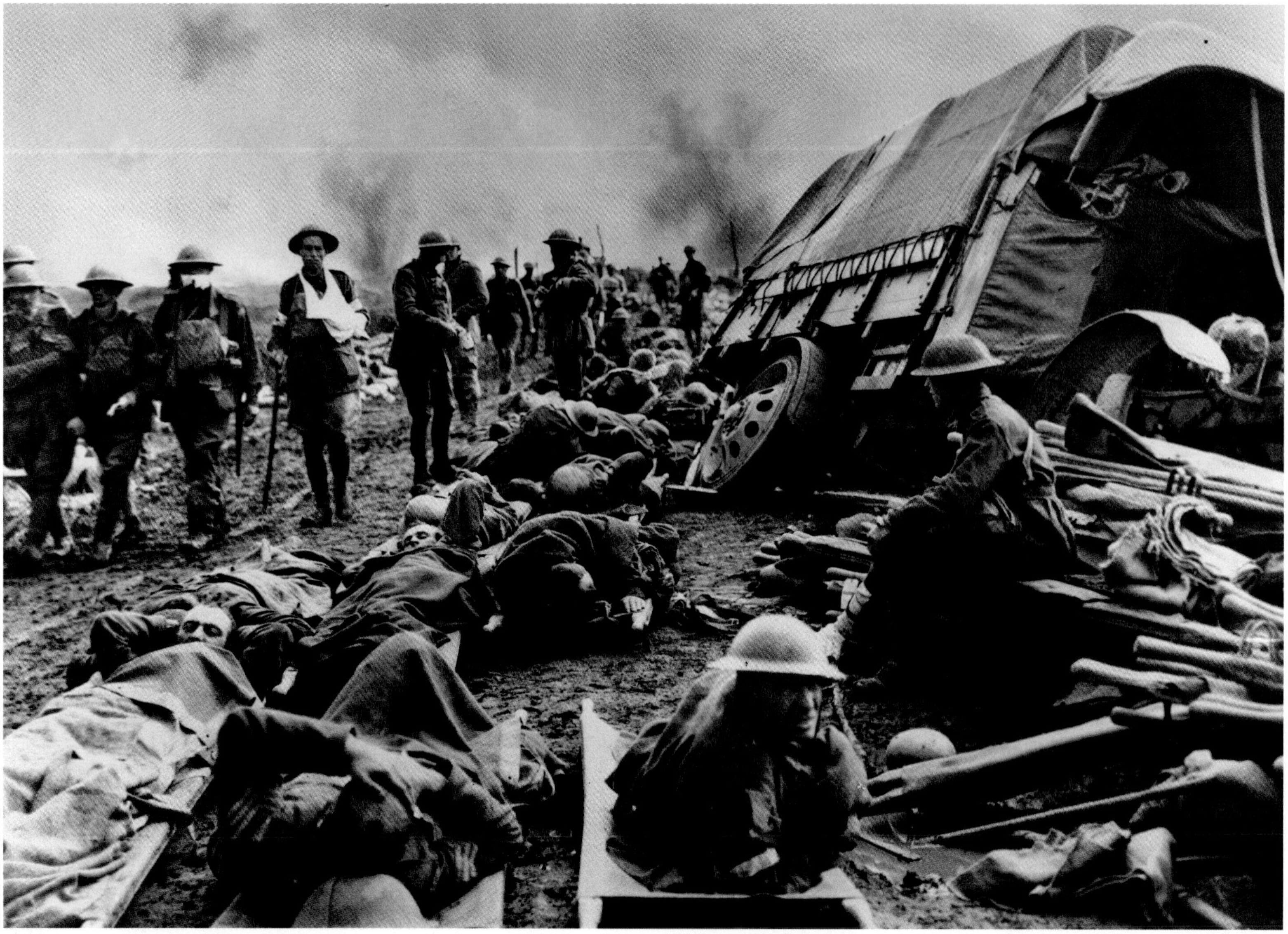

Famed for his photographs of Ernest Shackleton's legendary Antarctic expedition, Frank Hurley was dubbed "hard as nails" by one of Shackleton's crew, because he wouldn't wear a hat and gloves when he photographed. Legend has it that when the *Endurance* started to sink, taking with it Hurley's invaluable glass plates, he jumped into the freezing water shirtless to retrieve them. Yet Hurley was much more than a "warrior with a camera", as another shipmate described him. He was a self-taught highly accomplished photographer with an unusual eye, who also had a great sense of how to compose a picture. In his expedition photographs he often pulls his camera back from the standard shot of explorers looking heroic, and focuses instead on the cruel and unrelenting polar landscape. His diaries reveal that while he wasn't particularly impressed with his fellow explorers, he had a great respect for and affinity with the natural world.

During the ill-fated voyage he also experimented with colour. These colour experiments were to continue with his groundbreaking shots taken during the First World War. Photographs of the war were subject to strict censorship and Hurley reinforced his reputation as a fearless man when he attempted to smuggle his glass plates out of France. His work from the Western Front is again far from the heroic photography typical of the time. Although he admired the soldiers and was fascinated by the ebb and flow of battle, he photographed the reality of the war: mud, misery, chaos, destroyed landscapes, mangled machinery and inevitably death – the British offensive at Ypres alone led to half a million casualties. Fortunately, despite taking great risks, Hurley survived the carnage, and his work is striking evidence of one of the bloodiest periods in history.

BELOW: This is the morning after the first battle of Passchendaele on the Western Front and wounded Australian infantry are still in the mud seeking assistance. This photograph is almost a homage to a Renaissance painting depicting some gruesome biblical scene. Hurley presents the complete picture: in the foreground we see the consequences of the battle for the men, while in the background there is the bleak landscape and the ominous sky. It really is a photograph of hell on earth.

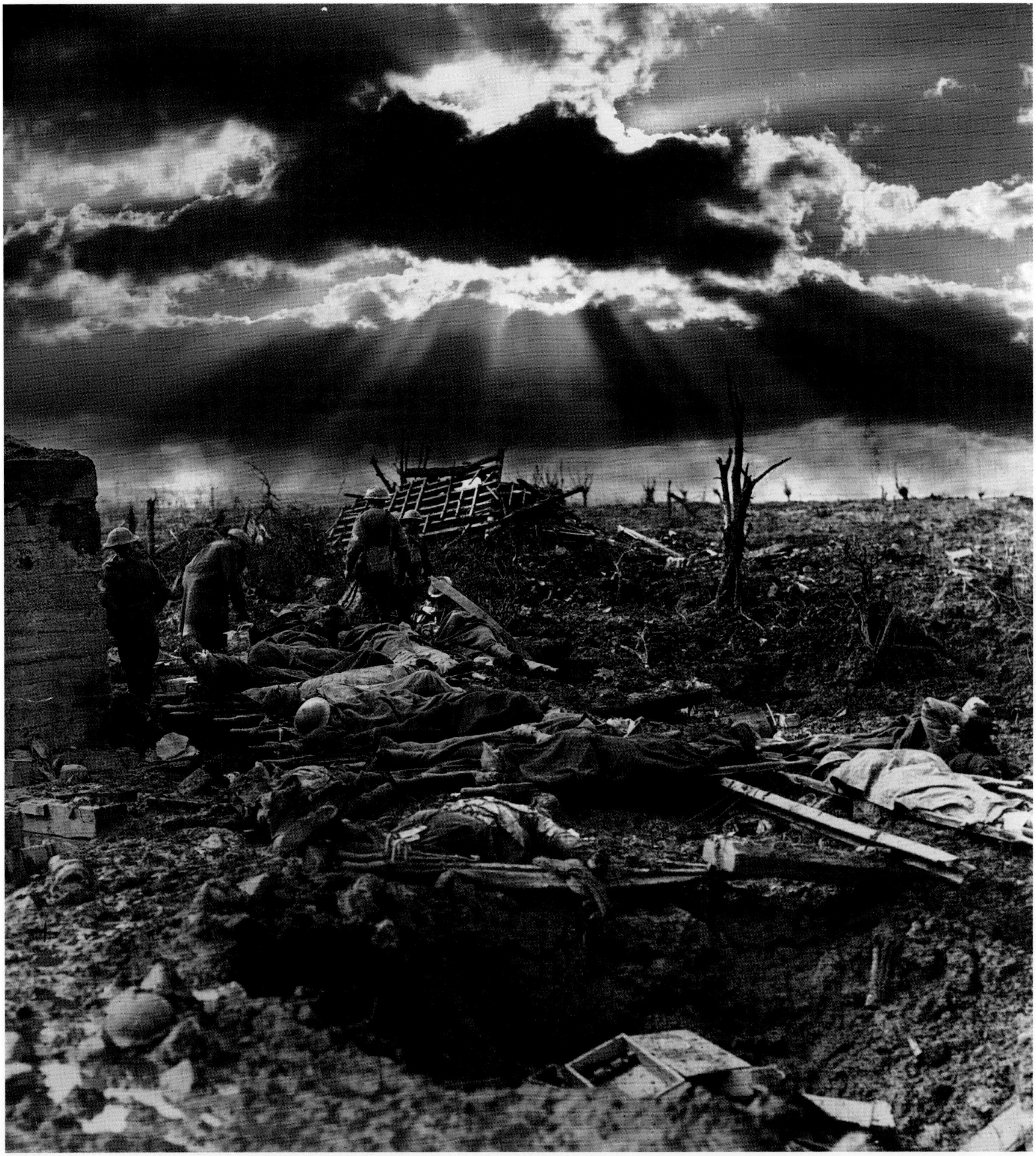

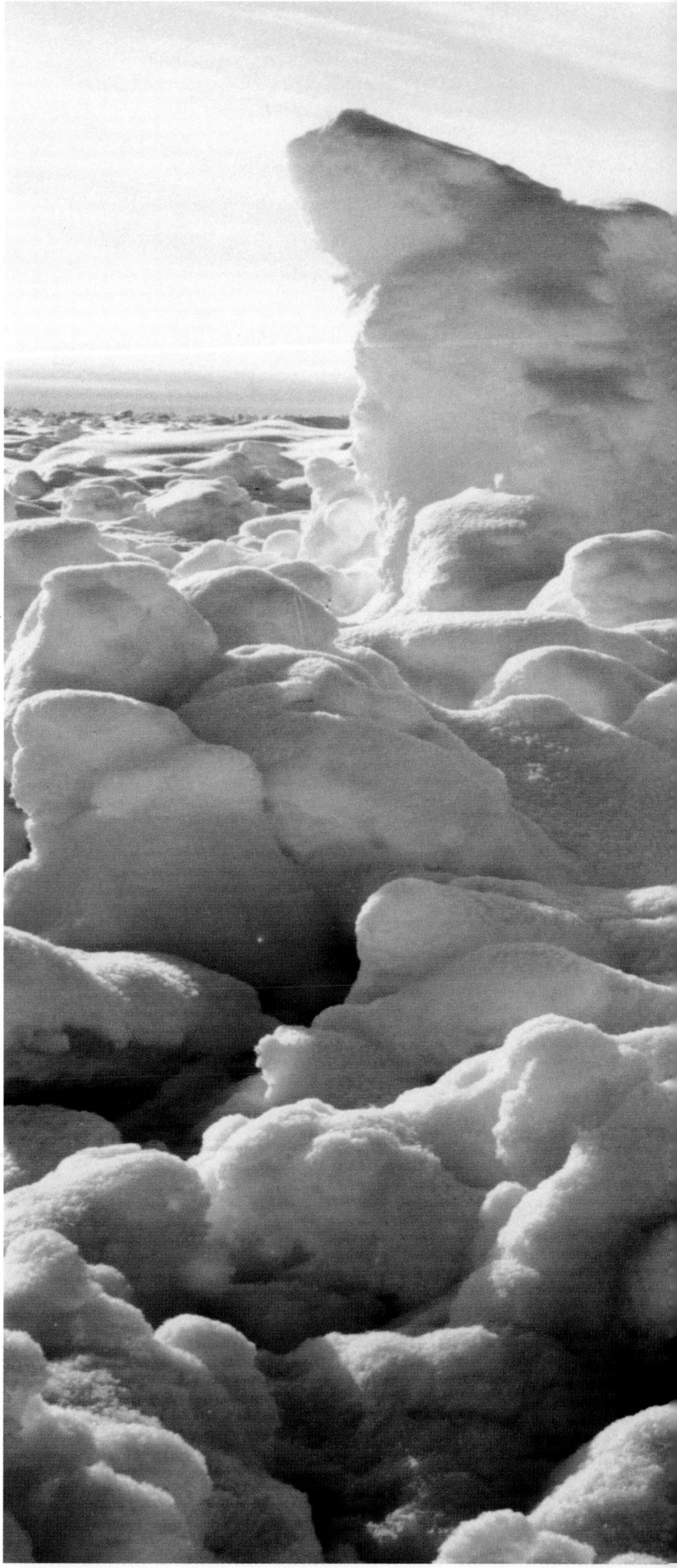

RIGHT: The *Endurance* in full sail amid the ice. Hurley was the official photographer on the Trans Antarctic Expedition 1914–17. He was fascinated by the snowscapes and his diaries seem to suggest that he had more time for the dramatic scenery than for the ship and the crew. Dragging all his camera equipment along the ice was a feat in itself.

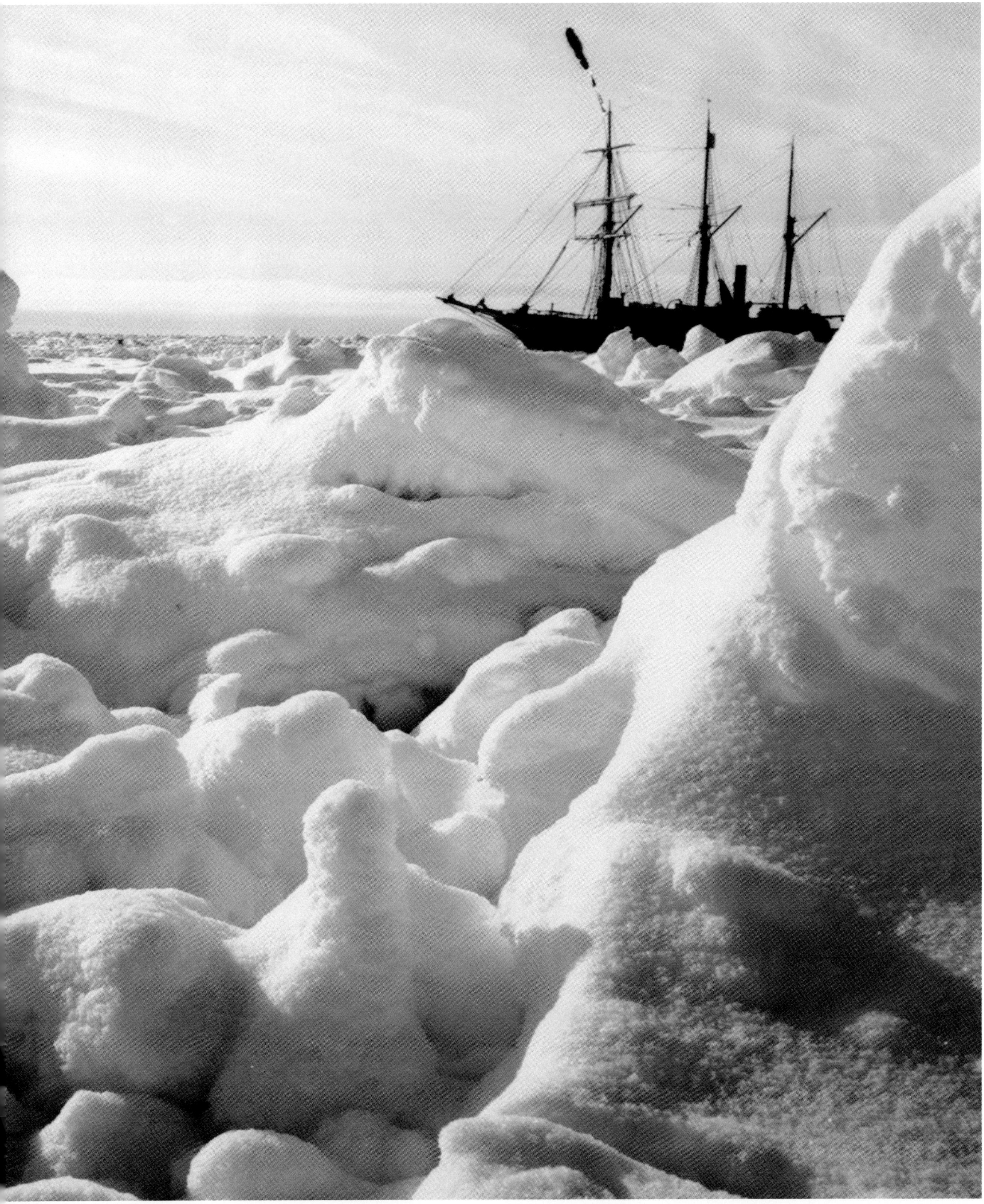

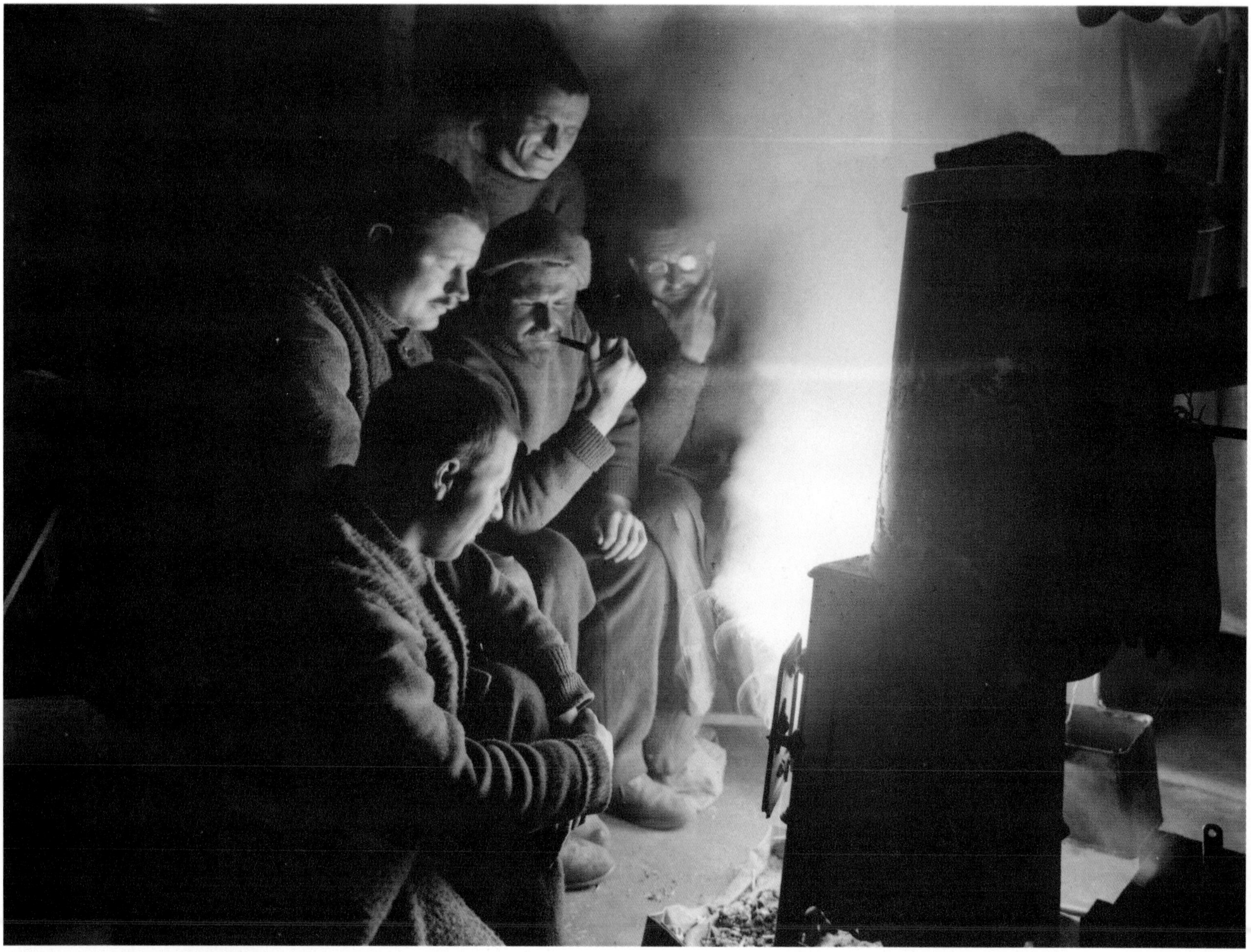

ABOVE: Trying to keep warm in the night watchman's room in the *Endurance*. The scene is skilfully lit and it's as if Hurley has stumbled upon these sea dogs exchanging tales. The men and Hurley, however, seem somewhat detached from each other.

RIGHT: The end for the *Endurance*, crushed in the ice with the dogs looking on. A poignant image where even the dogs look morose and downbeat. It also conveys the sense of man's helplessness in the face of nature.

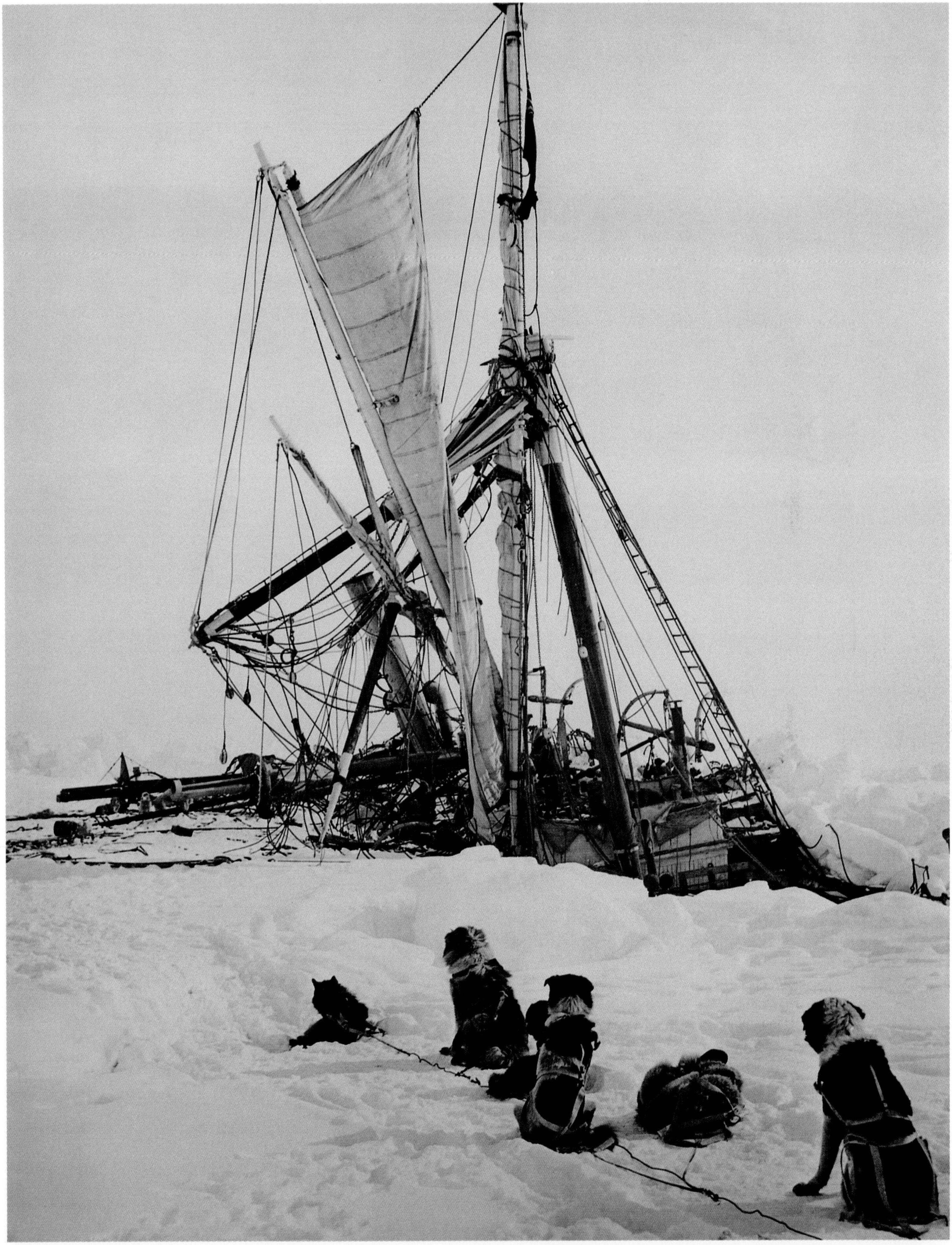

ROGER HUTCHINGS

Roger Hutchings is best known for his remarkable images from war-torn Bosnia: "My aim was to tell the stories of ordinary people caught in this bloody civil war. I was angry at what was happening to the innocent: the civilians, the kids and the elderly." Hutchings is the heir apparent to Philip Jones Griffiths, sharing his lack of interest in photographing the ebbs and flows of combat. Instead, his subjects are people to whom we can relate; they could be us, but for the fact that they are caught up in something terrible and extreme. Yet while Jones Griffiths saw the Vietnam War in imperialist terms, Hutchings sees the civil war in the former Yugoslavia as something more nebulous, preventable and ultimately somewhat absurd. His photographs from that period reflect this ambiguity. Hutchings is frequently angry and he says that he took photographs a lot of the time with "the spineless European politicians and UN bureaucracy in mind", but he is too intelligent a photojournalist to be inspired just by rage. He also has a poet's eye for those idiosyncratic and whimsical moments that unroll in front of him, moments that he describes as "the banality of war, that is, the violence becomes so commonplace that people treat it as normal behaviour". On this page, for example, there is an image of a woman having her hair done. She is serene and at peace, yet sitting in the middle of a war zone. Her insistence that life must go on is admirable, but also slightly preposterous.

In recent years Hutchings has moved away from traditional conflict and concentrated on documenting the fashion industry, often from behind the scenes. This is also a highly charged and absurd environment, which Hutchings appears to both embrace and mock. When asked what is the role of the photojournalist, Hutchings responds, "It may sound like a cliché, but to tell the truth." This is not always an easy task, especially when the subject is a confusing civil war, but Roger Hutchings rises to the challenge.

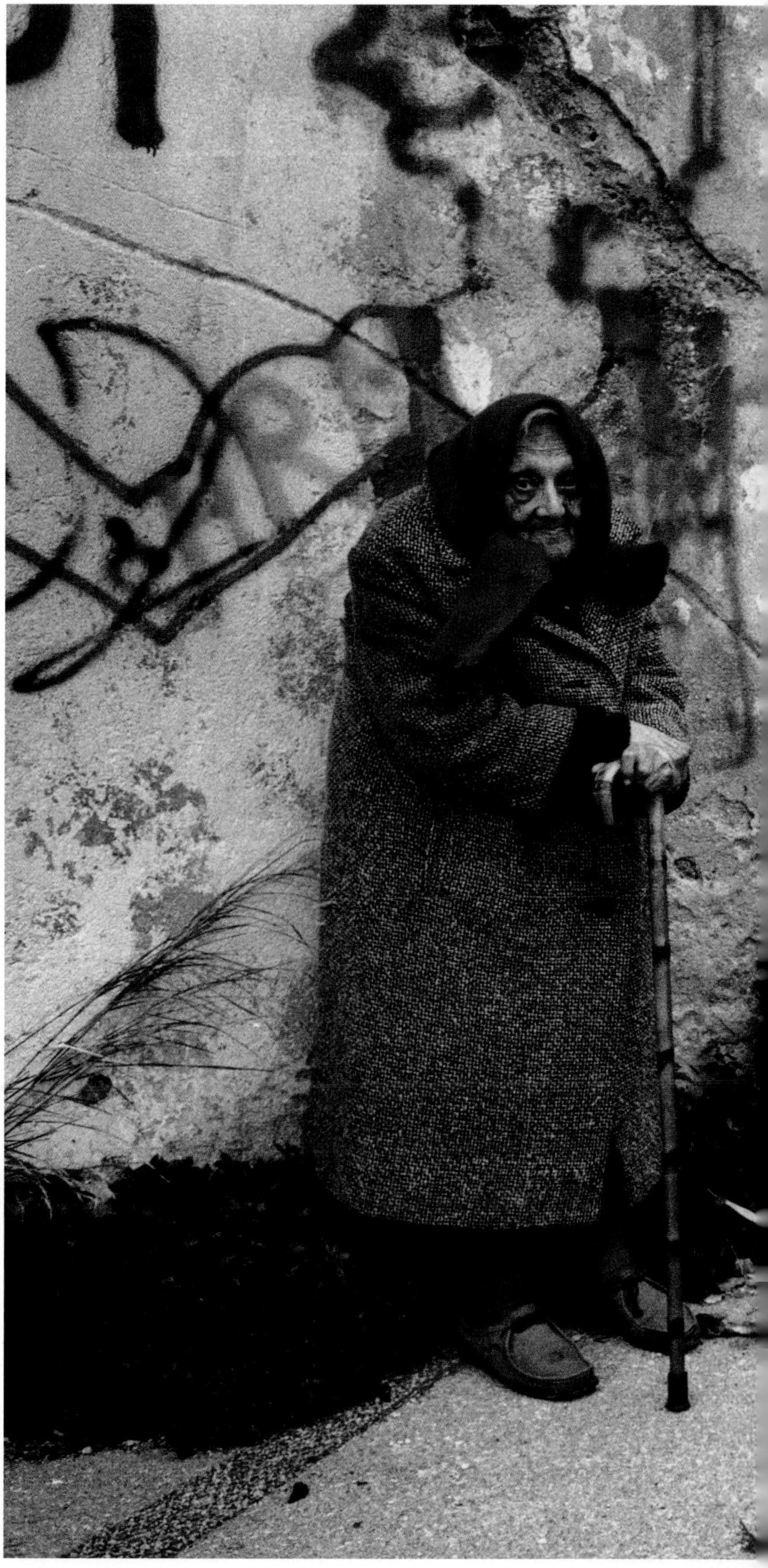

BELOW: Residents struggle to maintain their self-respect and their appearance in the middle of a war zone in Sarajevo, Bosnia. There is something very engaging and original about this image. Hutchings is using humour to convey the absurdity of war – not a typical approach.

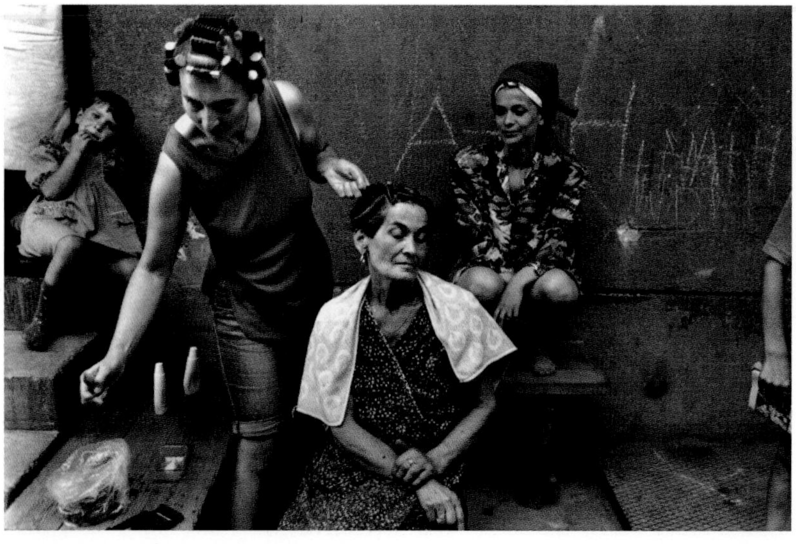

BELOW: Refugees from Sarajevo arriving in Split, Bosnia. The older woman is a university professor and her daughter a doctor. The older woman's expression says it all. A conflict has reduced two well-educated people to standing in a grim street with everything they own packed into a few suitcases. Hutchings's war stories always offer something a little different.

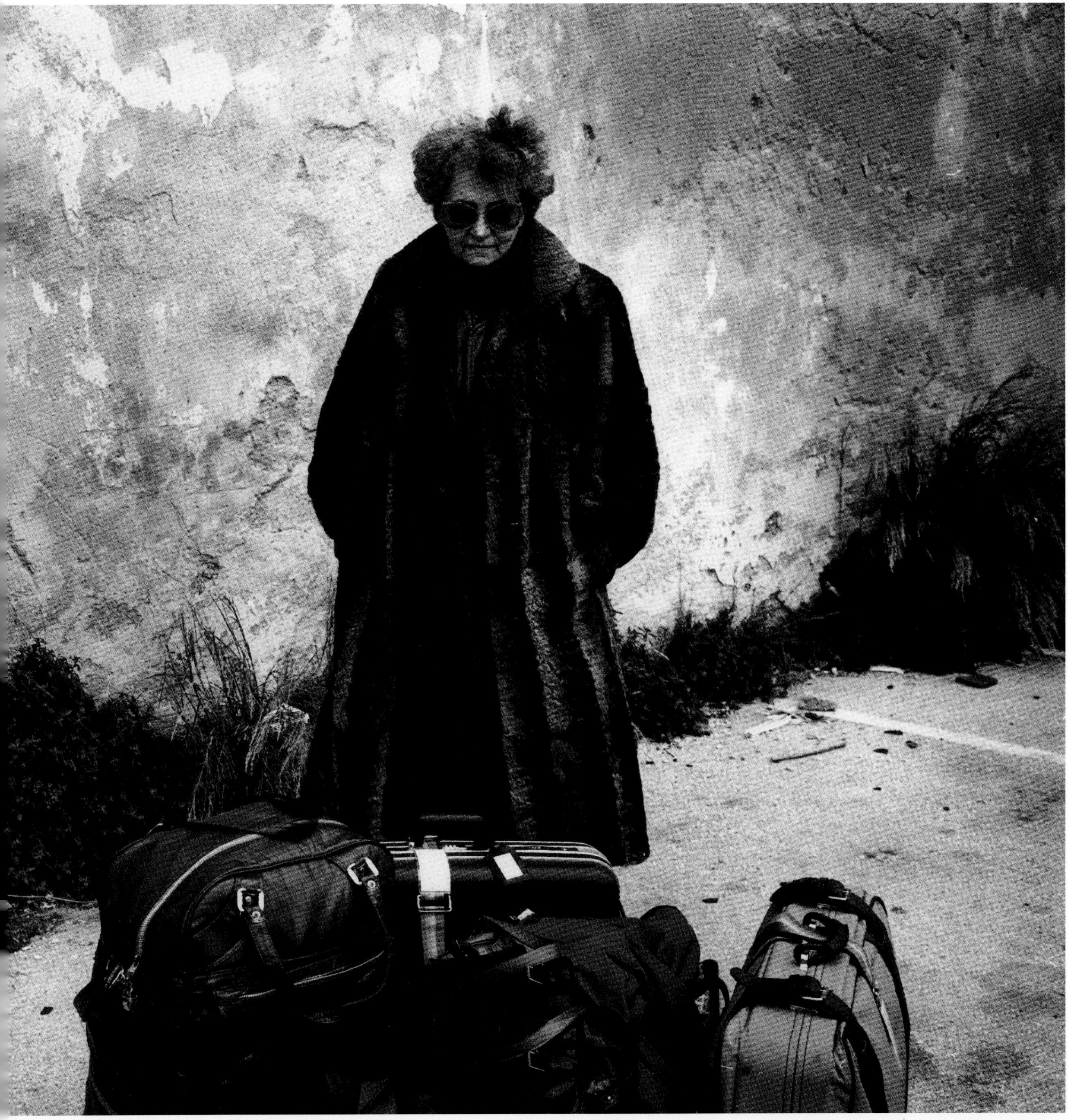

BELOW: Backstage, Fashion in Milan model Alek Wek before the Moschino Cheap and Chic show. Hutchings is usually associated with black-and-white photography, but only colour could convey the sheer lush red of the model's lipstick.

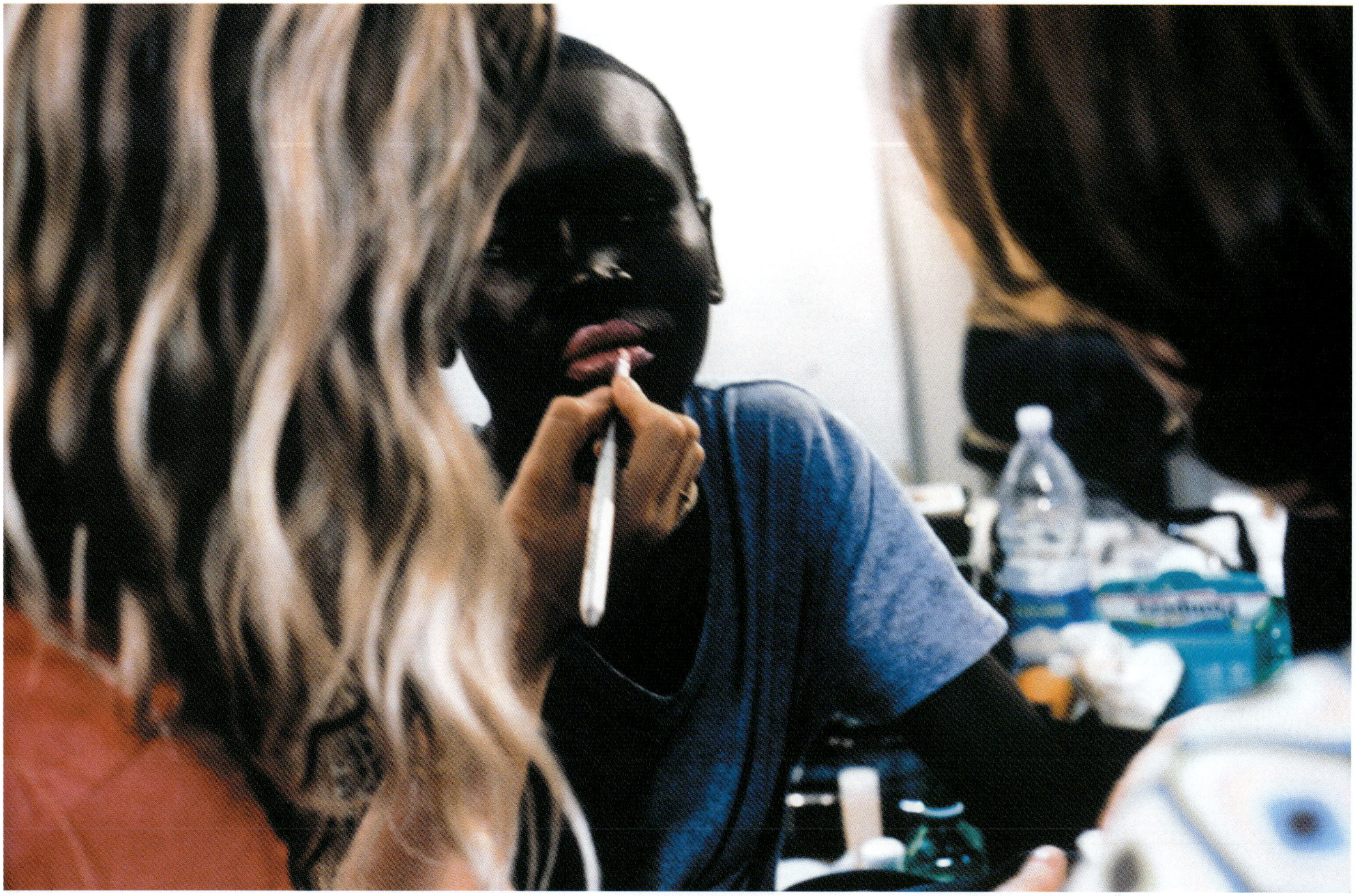

RIGHT TOP: Models backstage at the Krizia fashion show, Milan, Italy. "Pretty vacant" is the phrase that springs to mind.

RIGHT BOTTOM: A photographer works to get the right shot as a model pauses to turn on the catwalk at London Fashion Week. Hutchings is, of course, photographing the photographer, so who is watching who?

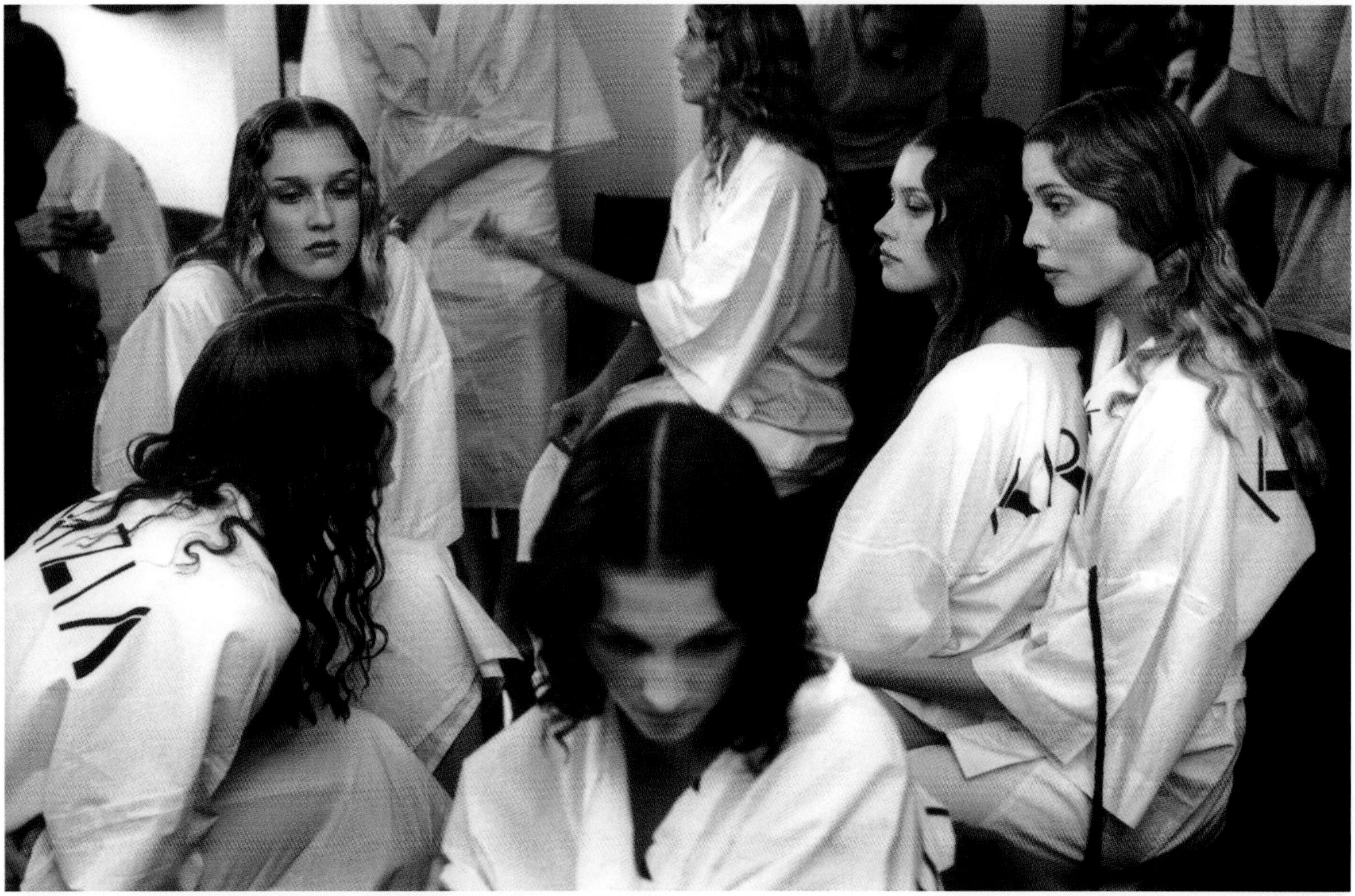

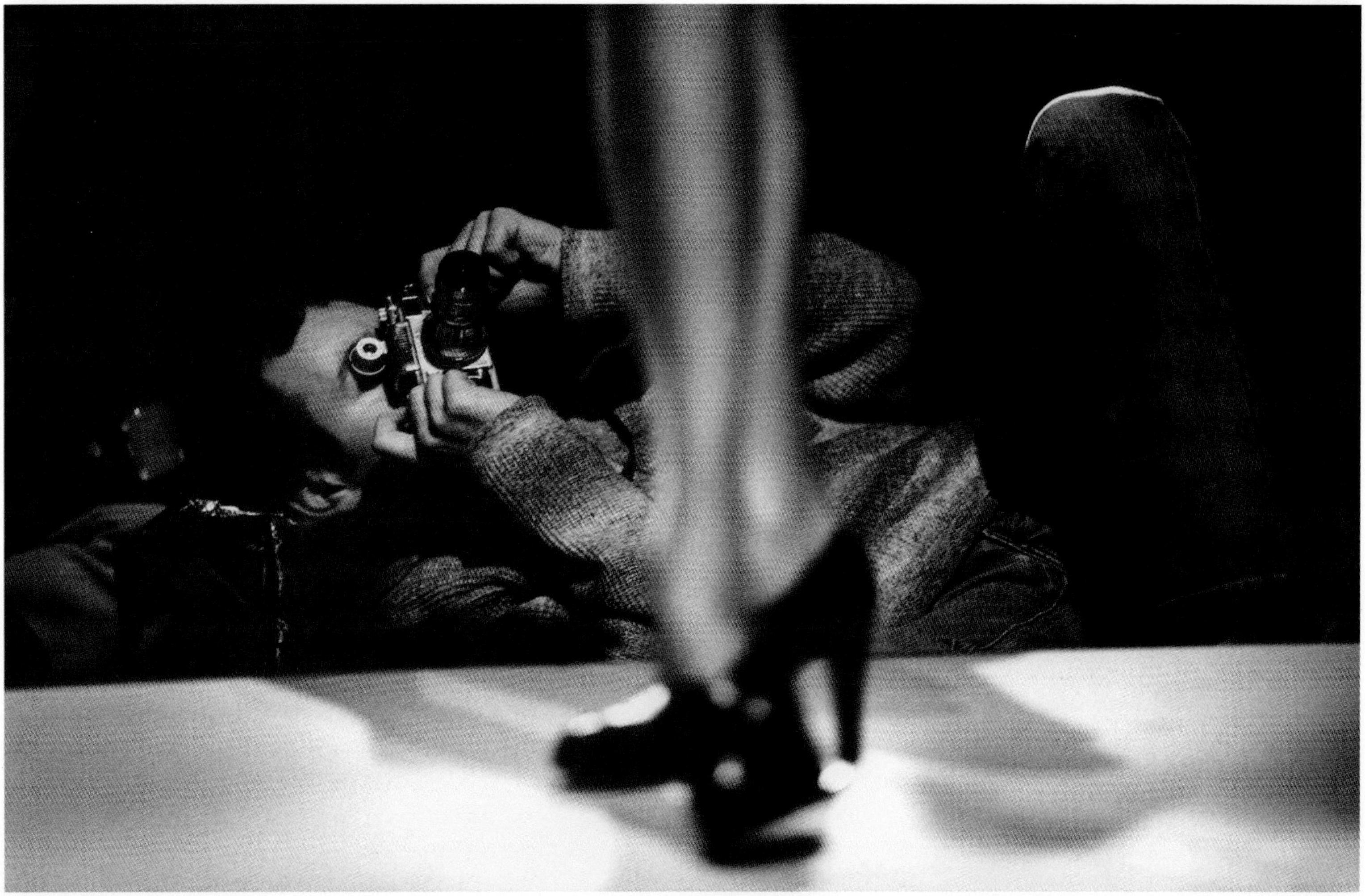

PHILIP JONES GRIFFITHS

Philip Jones Griffiths has said that what motivates him as a photographer is trying to answer the question "Why?". Jones Griffiths has spent the past five decades trying to find an answer to two urgent questions; why terrible wars and conflicts happen, and why they have such a terrible impact on innocent people. He is part of that exclusive club of legendary Vietnam photojournalists, which also includes Larry Burrows and Don McCullin, who redefined the way war is photographed. A fierce Welsh nationalist, to him the Vietnam War was a clear case of one country trying to impose its will on another. In classic black-and-white he photographed the often crass attempts by American soldiers to endear themselves to the locals, demonstrating how the beautiful Vietnamese landscape and its 2,000 years of tradition were the real casualties of war. He saw the conflict in Vietnam in imperialist terms and not surprisingly his images were perceived as being anti-American. Consequently, Jones Griffiths found himself being shunned by the media and his images went largely unseen at the time. He responded by publishing *Vietnam Inc*, which not only helped change the course of the conflict, but also empowered both Jones Griffiths and photojournalism itself. He took all the photographs, designed a very personal layout and wrote a commentary and captions, which veered from the matter of fact to the ironic and sardonic. W. Eugene Smith would have approved. The book proved that photojournalism didn't have to be subservient to the agenda of magazines and it could thrive in a different medium. From that moment onward, every self-respecting photojournalist aspired to get his or her own book published.

In his coverage of Northern Ireland, there is also the sense that Jones Griffiths clearly sees the British as the occupying force. Yet again, he is drawn to ask what kind of an impact the conflict is having on the civilian population and, in a wider context, questions why the occupying force is there in the first place. As a war photographer, he demands more from his viewer than a knee-jerk response to blood and gore; he wants you to think and question what you are seeing.

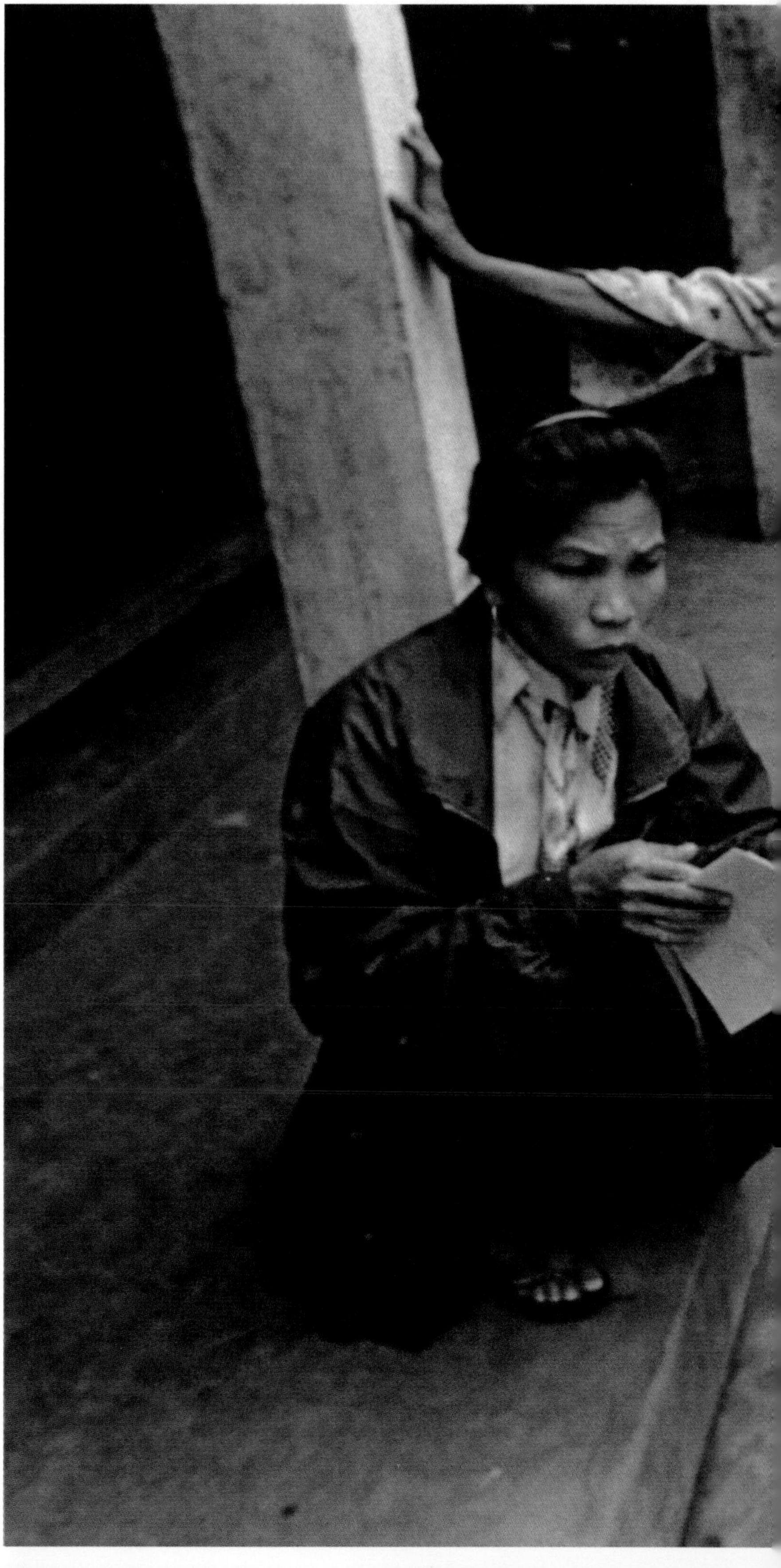

RIGHT: This photograph taken in Cam Nghia, Vietnam, in 1998, shows Pham Hong Quy, 24, who has several epileptic fits a day. During the war his father was in the South where much Agent Orange was sprayed. Jones Griffiths has dedicated his professional life to photographing every facet of the conflict in Vietnam and its grim epilogue. His style is always direct and unflinching.

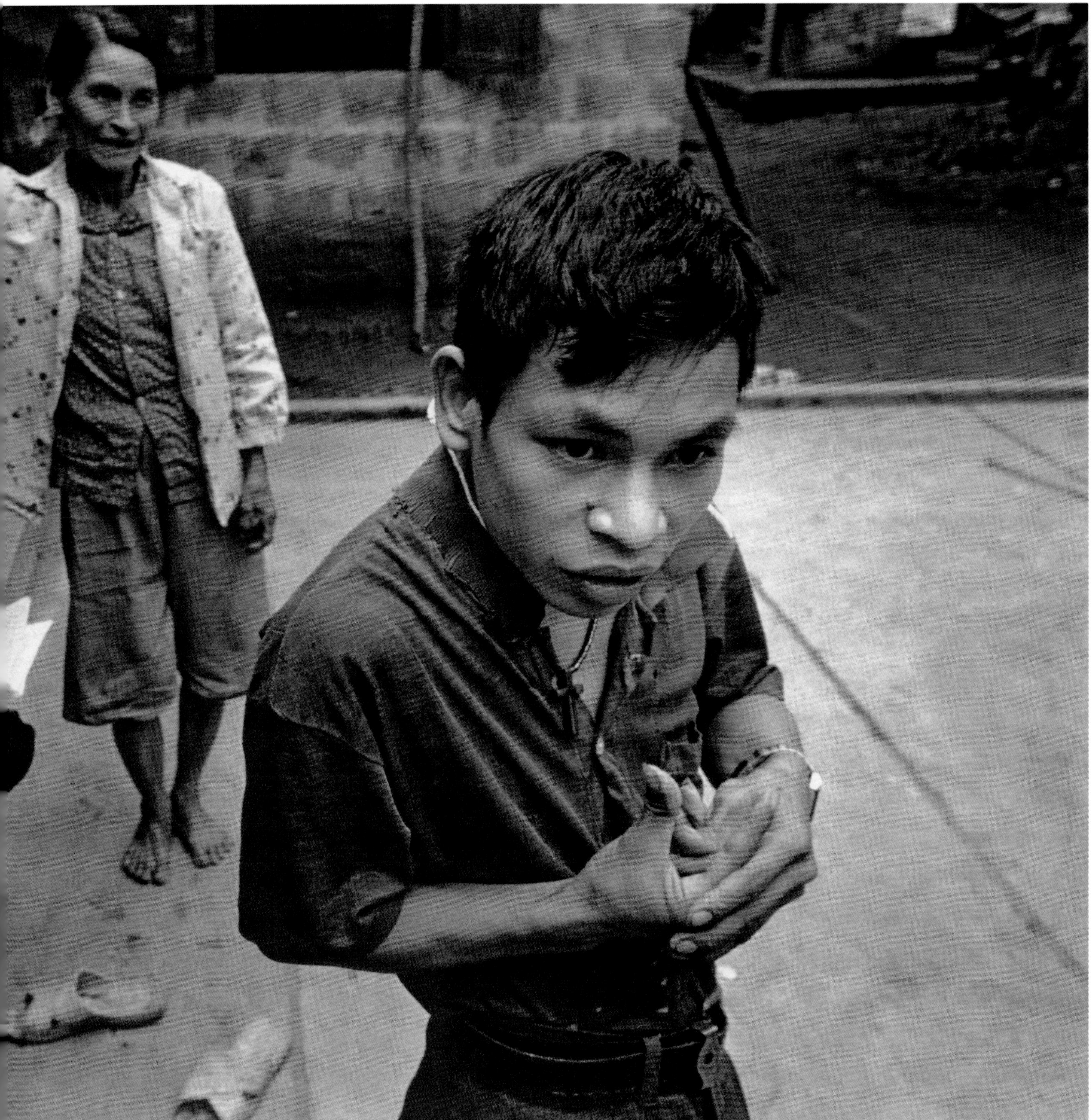

BELOW: "In the narrow terraced streets of working-class Northern Ireland, 1965 (every house except the last needs only three walls), the closely-knit communities of differing religious persuasions are encouraged to battle with one another." As well as being a great photographer, Jones Griffiths is an eloquent and sardonic writer, who provides the captions for his photos, giving them his own cynical and illuminating spin.

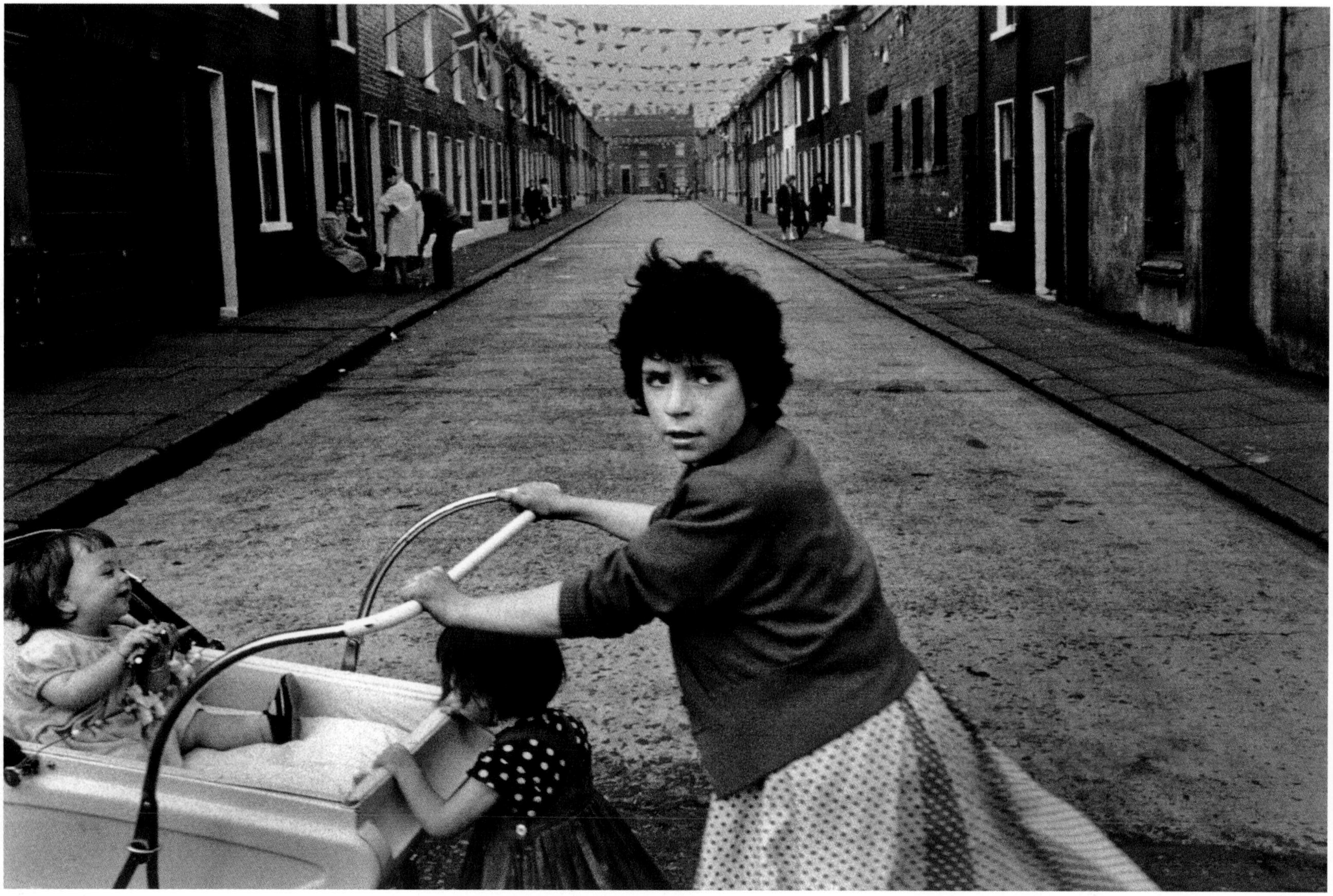

RIGHT: This abstract portrait of a British soldier was taken in Northern Ireland in 1973. What he thought about Jones Griffiths we will never know, but it is the photo's ambiguity that holds our attention.

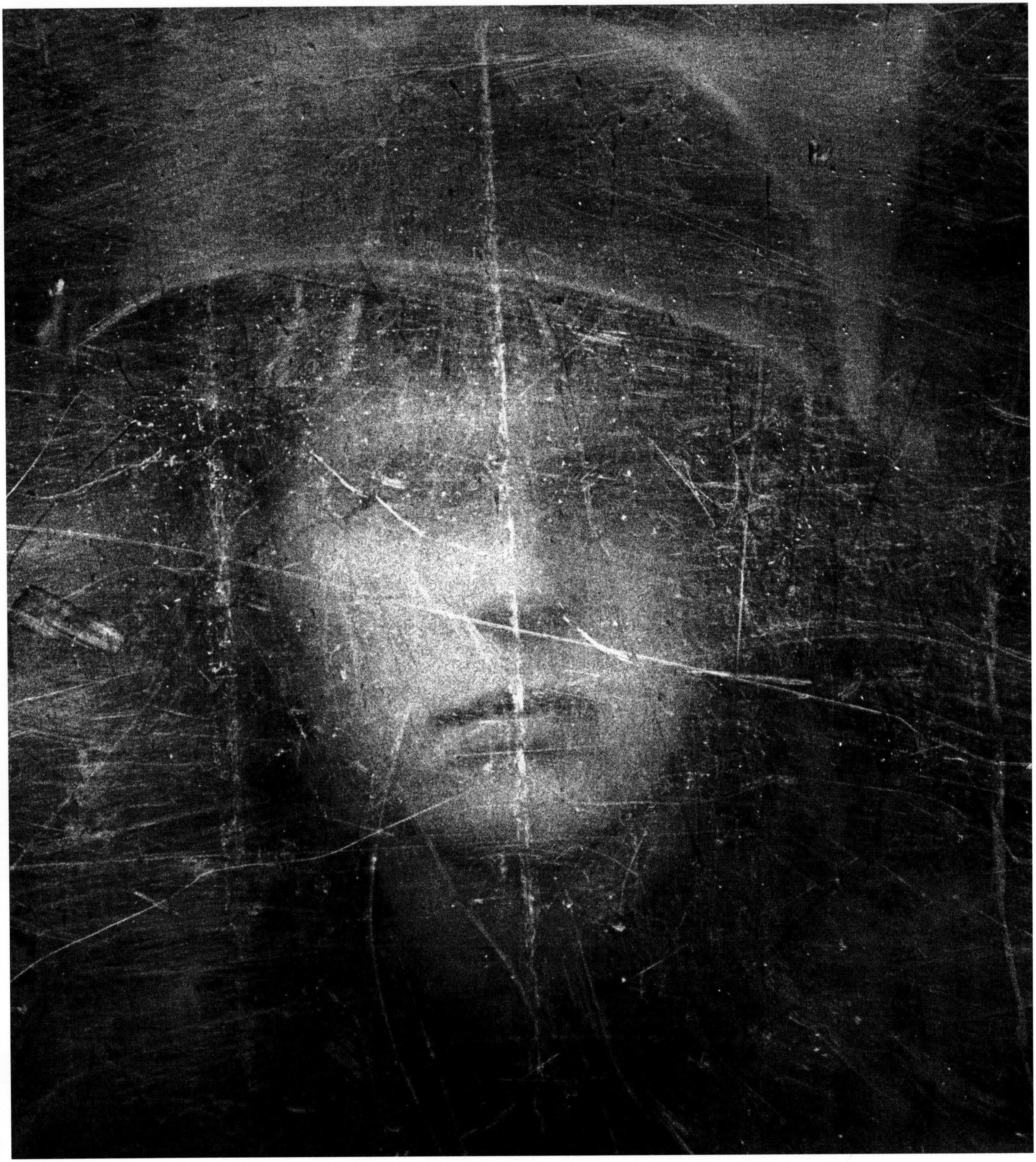

YEVGENY KHALDEI

Yevgeny Khaldei's most famous photograph is of a Russian soldier waving the Red Flag over the Reichstag during the battle for Berlin in May 1945. The soldier is wearing at least two wristwatches, possibly the result of looting – a fact retouched out in later uses of this "patriotic" image. Although the picture was staged, its composition and setting are dramatic and dynamic, hallmarks of Khaldei's work. As a TASS photographer, he had every opportunity to be present at the turning-points of history, and he made the most of them. He was at the Potsdam conference where he photographed the "Big Three" – Stalin, Churchill and Roosevelt – and at the Nuremberg War Crimes Trials in 1945–46. As he said about the latter, "I photographed the atrocities wrought by the Fascists in the Soviet Union. Now I am photographing the vengeance."

Khaldei was an invaluable witness to some of the key events of the twentieth century. But there is another aspect to his work, which was much informed by the cultural currents that raged around photography, constructivism and socialist realism in Russia during the 1920s and 1930s. This has only recently come to light through the rediscovery of the early personal work he made while learning the craft of photography, his *Photo Album Devoted to the Happy Life of a Young Man*, c. 1934. It shows just how much his photojournalism relies on his experiments with form, collage and dynamic points of view. His early work for *Pravda* emphasizes the image of the heroic worker – a strong element of Soviet iconography in the 1930s – for Khaldei always thought that a good picture should be strong, easily understood and capable of communicating directly with the viewer. The great importance of photography to the Soviet regime, its role as a medium of propaganda and communication, allowed Khaldei freer rein to make striking and beautiful images, but it came with a heavy price. Despite his great achievements, his mistreatment by the Soviet regime because of his Jewish origins must have been a bitter pill to swallow.

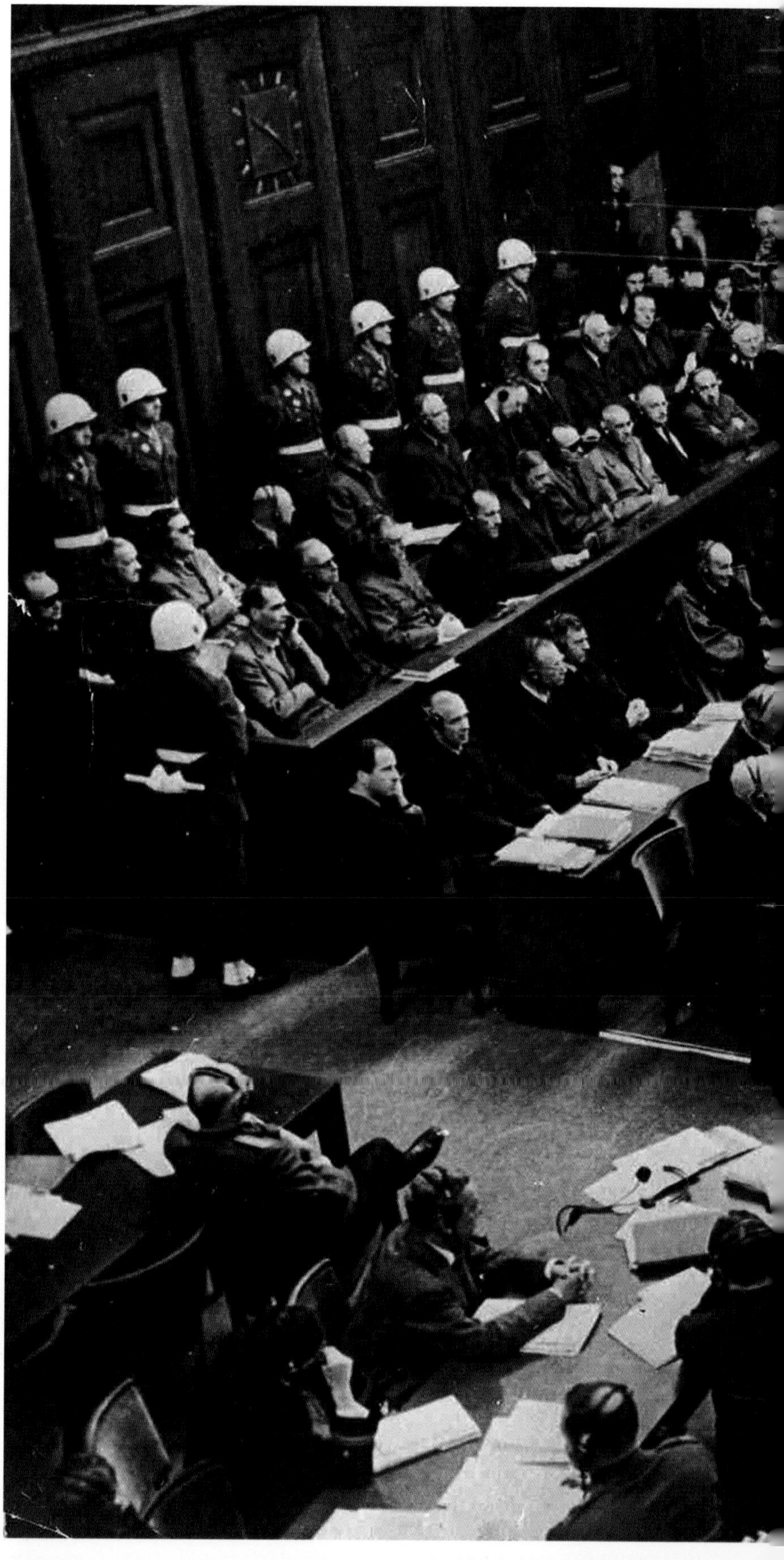

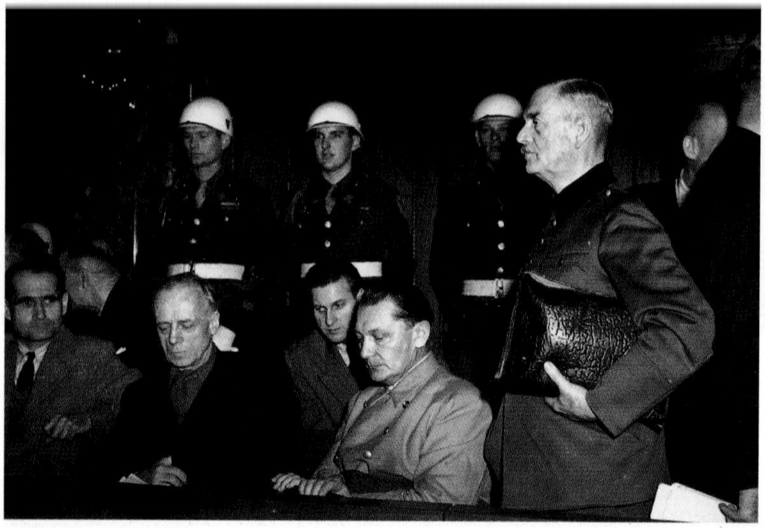

BELOW LEFT AND RIGHT: **As well as taking part in many of the biggest actions of the "Great Patriotic War", Khaldei also photographed the Nuremberg War Crimes Trials in 1945, taking a particular delight in annoying one of the senior Nazi leaders, Herman Goering.**

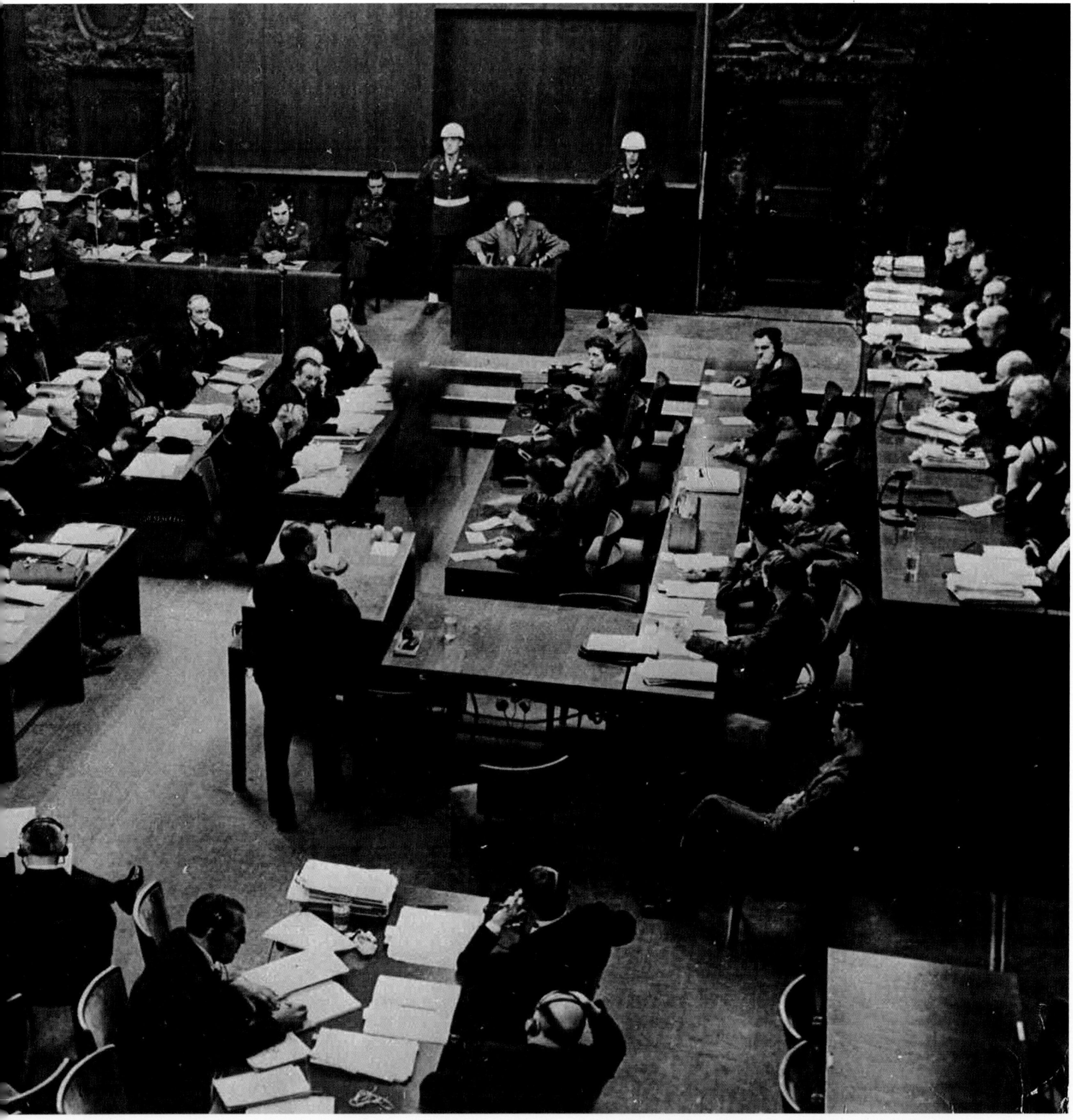

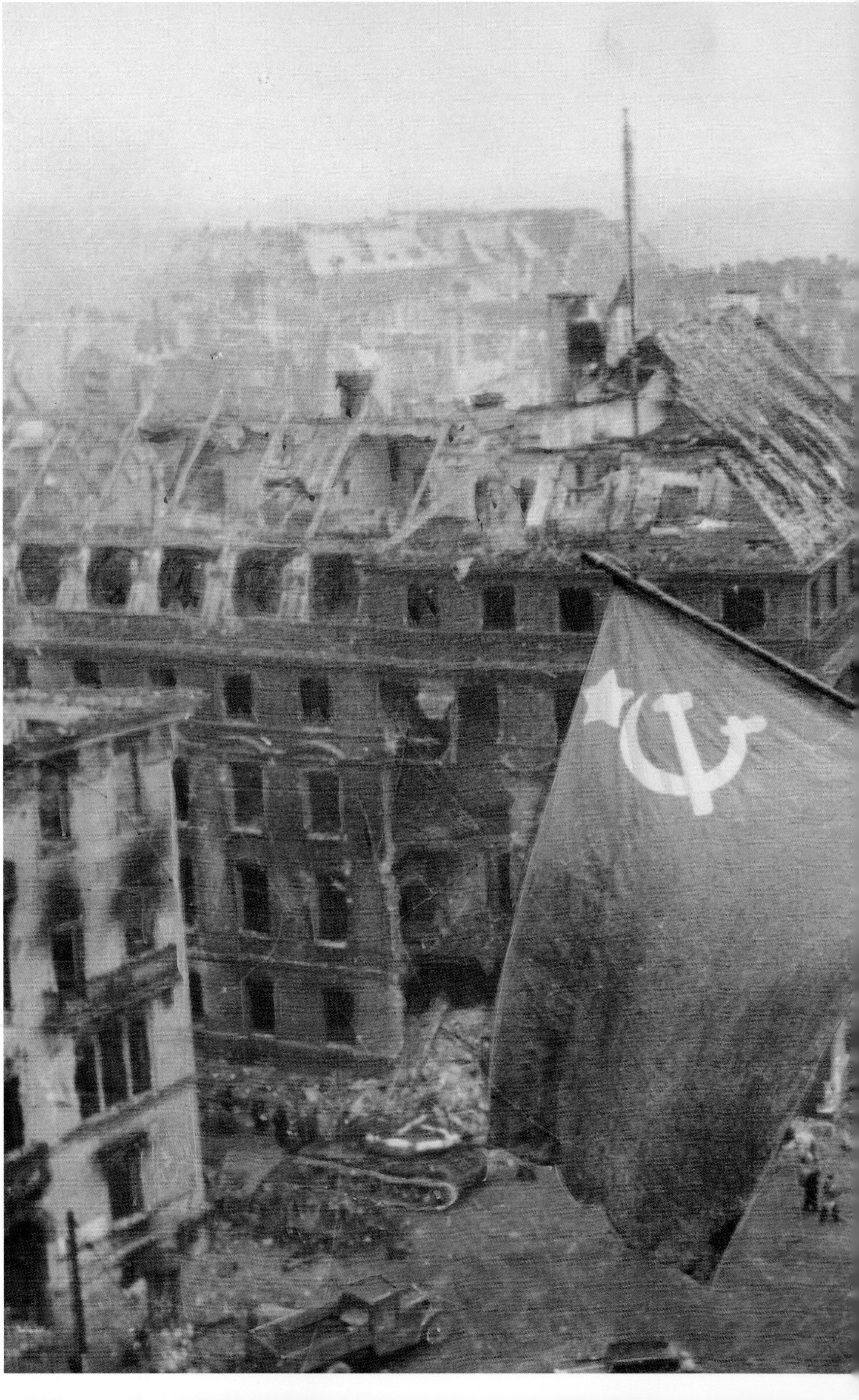

RIGHT: **Khaldei's war culminated in the fall of Berlin in 1945, when he raced to the roof of the burning Reichstag to capture this monumental photograph of a soldier hoisting the Soviet flag. From the various versions of the picture, we know that Khaldei asked the soldier to perform the action several times. When it was used at the time, the fact that the soldier appears to be wearing at least two wristwatches was retouched out of the photograph, for accounts of Russian soldiers looting German civilians were rife.**

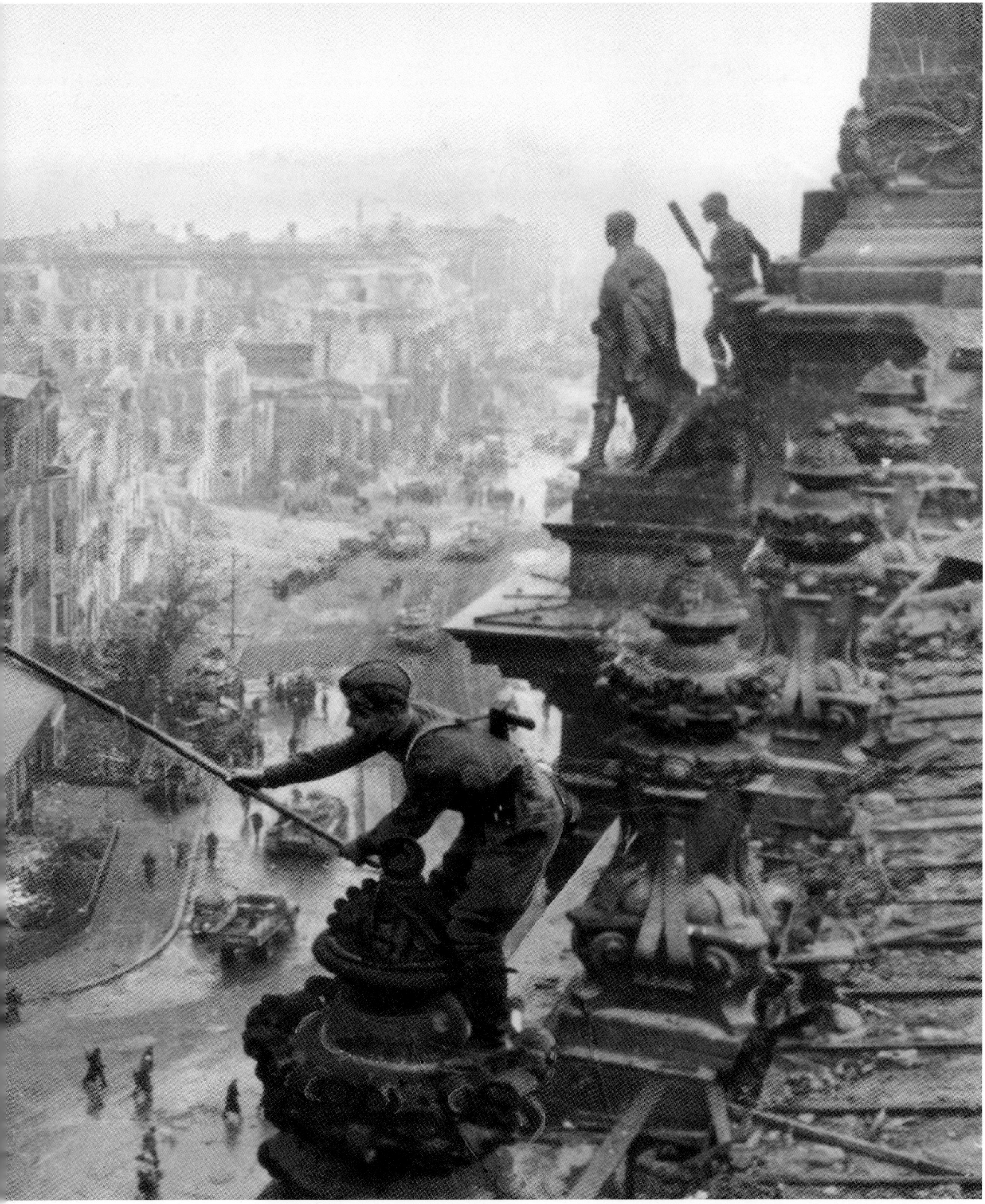

JOSEF KOUDELKA

BELOW: As in so many of Koudelka's pictures of the August 1968 invasion of Czechoslovakia by Warsaw Pact troops, the precise context of the images remains unclear. This group of people are demonstrating against the invasion in a clearly peaceful way.

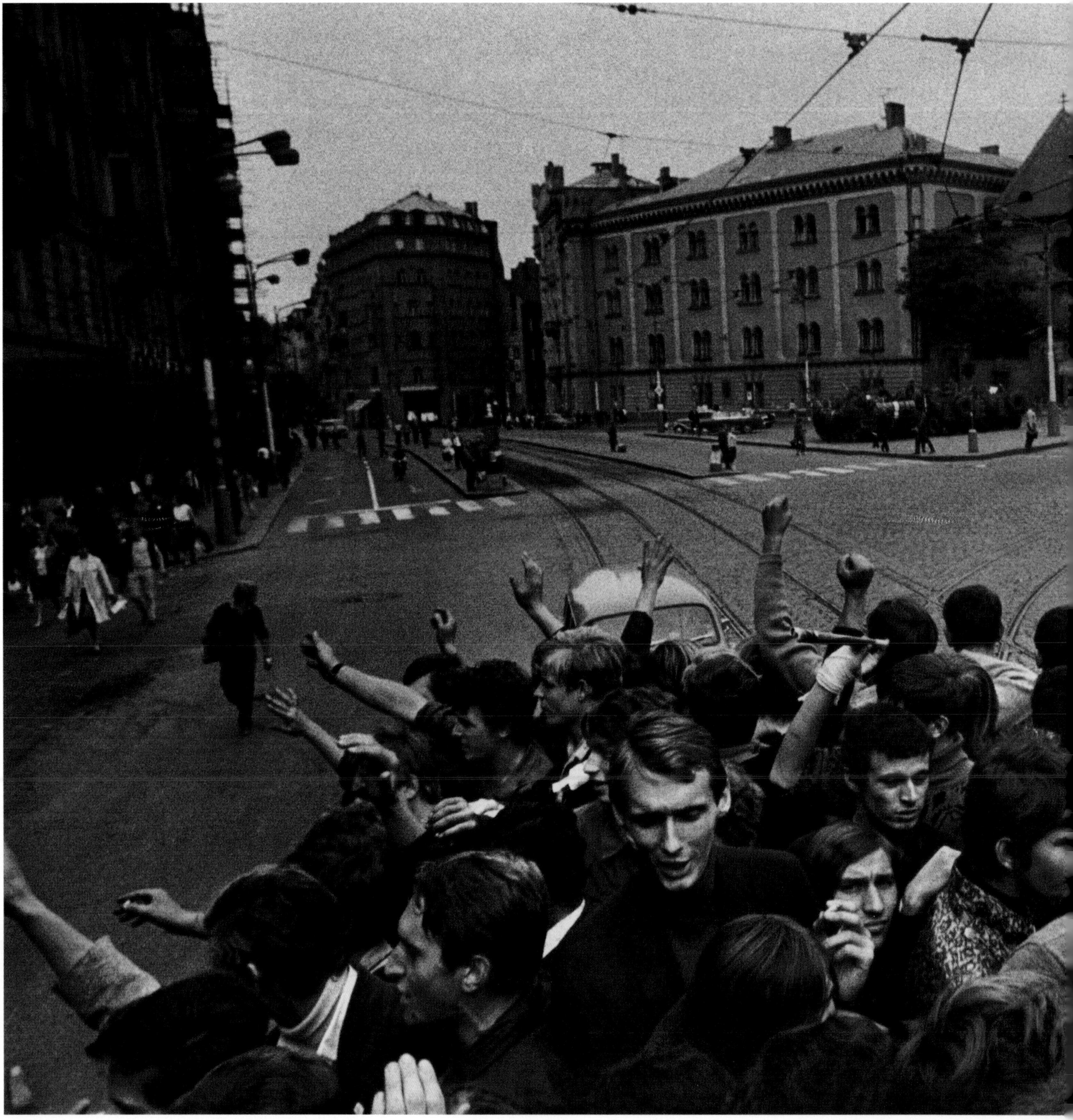

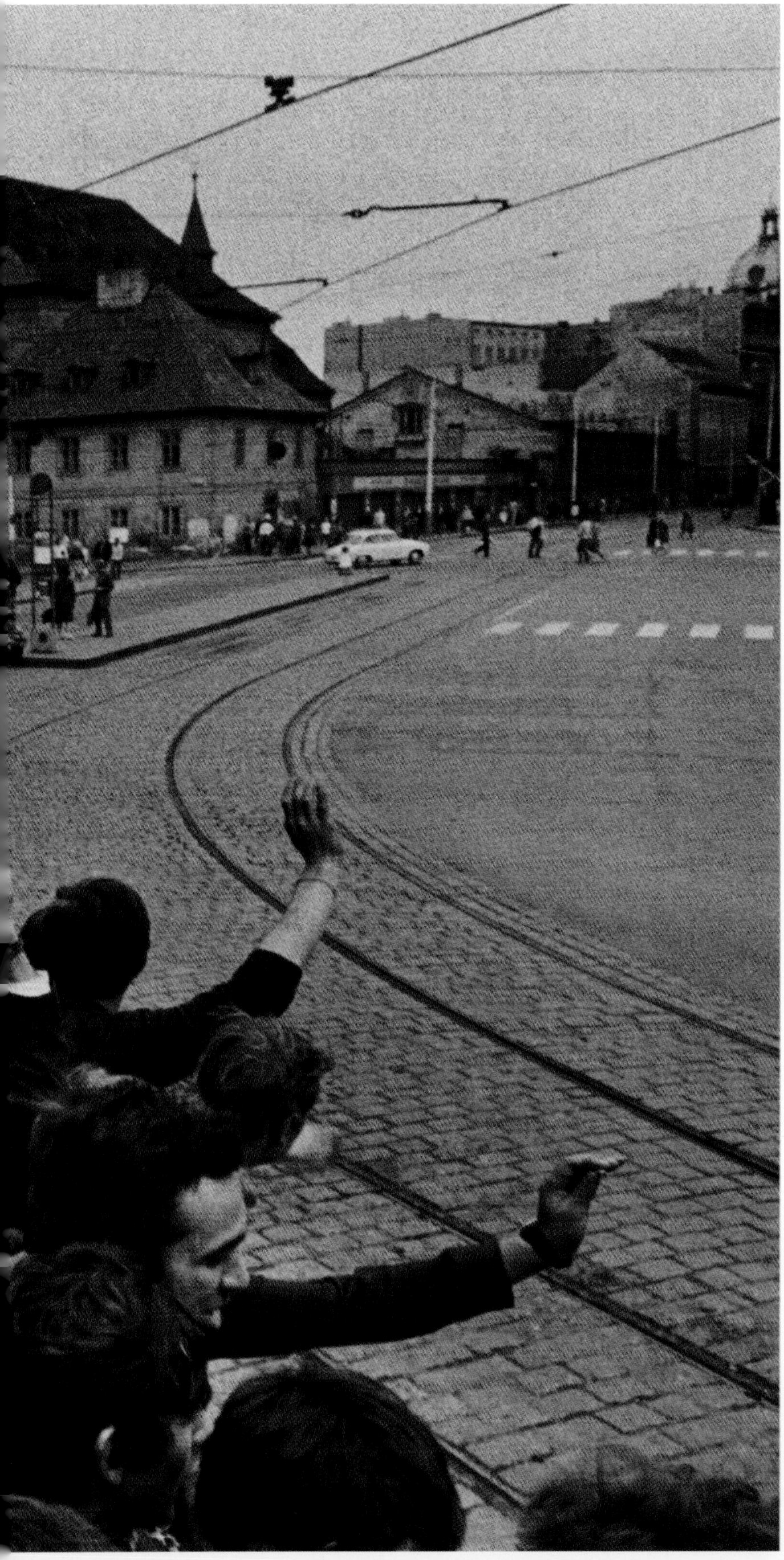

Josef Koudelka cemented his international reputation in the Prague Spring of 1968. Ian Berry, the only Western photographer in the city to cover the Warsaw Pact's invasion of Czechoslovakia, remembered, "I was walking around hiding a couple of Leicas under my coat, taking the occasional picture, because the Russians would shoot at anybody with a camera. I came across this lunatic, with two Exaktas on strings round his neck and a cardboard box as a camera case, taking photographs in full view of the Russians, with the support of the crowd!"

The "lunatic" was Koudelka, who produced the definitive, highly dramatic images of the end of Dubcek's brave attempt to introduce "communism with a human face". Koudelka takes us into the action of the Russian invasion: we feel so close to the reaction of the Czechs to their oppressors and invaders because, as in all of Josef Koudelka's work, we see his life through his eyes. His pictures are powerful, strongly composed and beautifully made. Yet Koudelka, though evidently a brave and committed witness to these terrible events, was working in much the same way as he had during his earlier project on the oppression of the Slovakian gypsies. Although credited anonymously as P.P. (Prague Photographer) until 1984, Koudelka could not stay in his homeland: "Everybody knew it was me who made the pictures. I got afraid. I asked Magnum to send me a letter inviting me to photograph gypsies. I still had a few friends in the Ministry of Culture, so I got the letter signed there, and then I was given permission to leave the country for three months to photograph the gypsies. I took my best negatives with me." He thus began a long period of exile and ceaseless movement between the only two anchor points for his nomadic life, London and Paris, until the Velvet Revolution in 1989. He would travel throughout the summer months, often sleeping rough, and spend the winters in a friend's darkroom, processing and printing the work. It was a life not unlike that of the gypsies who have been his constant subject.

BELOW: In this, the best known of Koudelka's photographs of the invasion of Czechoslovakia by Warsaw Pact troops, the image is made more poignant by the outstretched arm of the demonstrator, his gesture imitating both the Nazi and the Soviet salute.

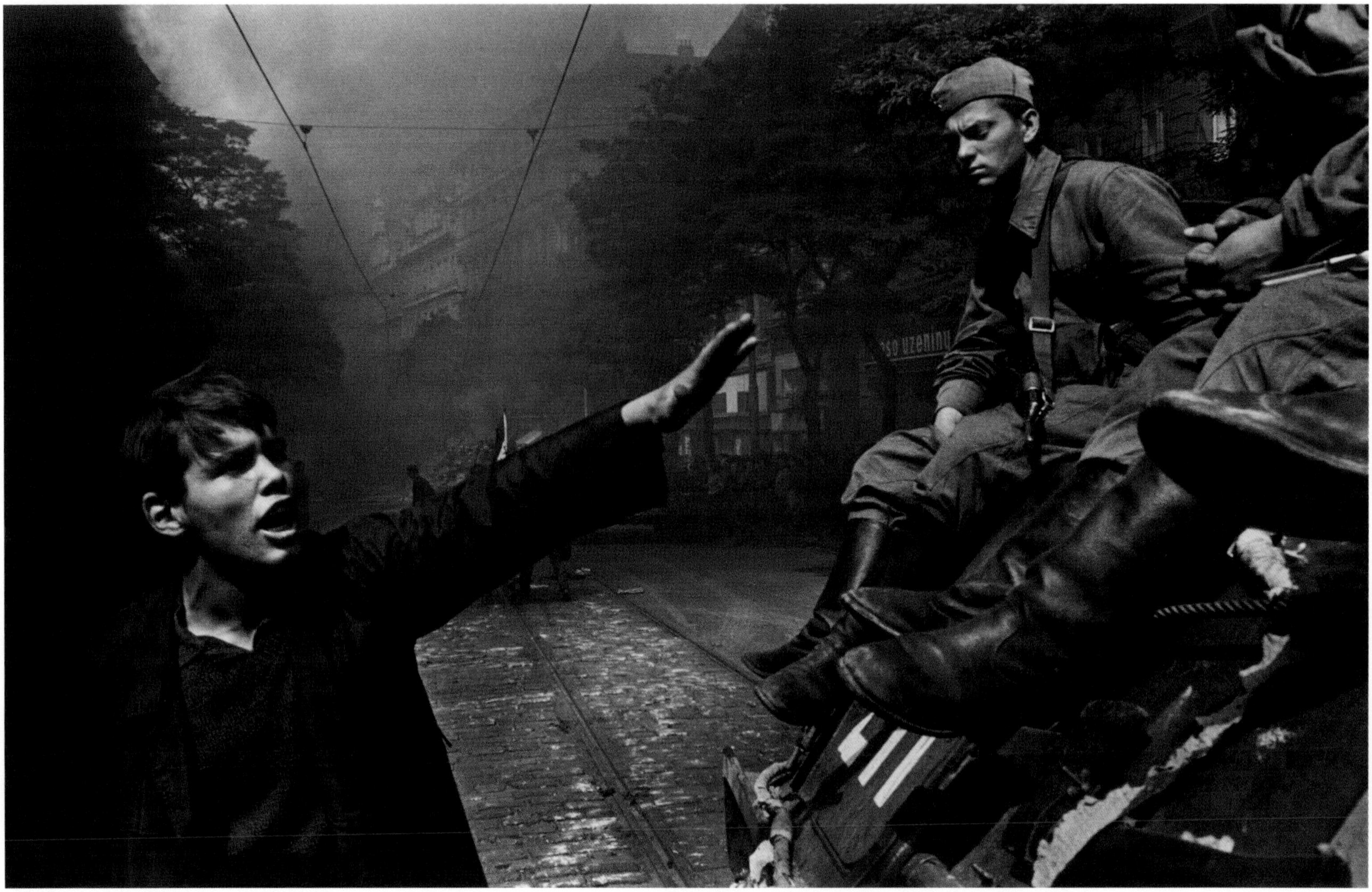

RIGHT: From the angle of the photograph it looks as if the foolhardy Koudelka has jumped on to the tank in order to achieve this menacing perspective of Prague, 1968. Perhaps the crowd is waving at him.

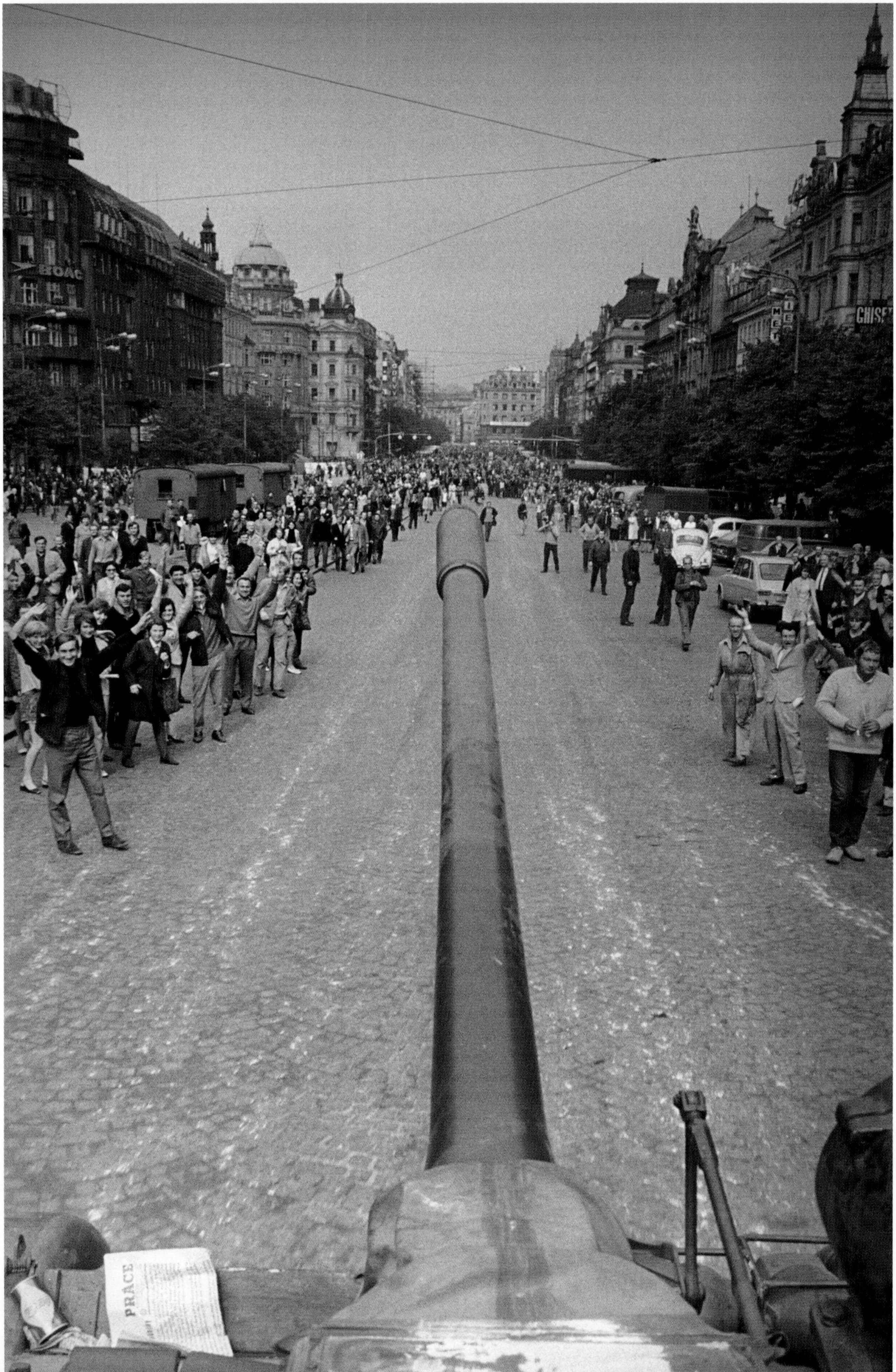
BOAC
PRACE

JOACHIM LADEFOGED

BELOW: **The trailer camp in the Kreutzberg district of Berlin, otherwise known as the Wagon Camp, in 1993. None of the residents worked full-time and their days were spent hanging out, drinking and partying. These men might be Ladefoged's subjects, but it is the feet in the foreground that we really want to know about.**

Joachim Ladefoged is part of a generation of outstanding Danish photojournalists who have gained international recognition in the past five years. So far, in an eventful career, he has alternated between shooting social documentary stories and more traditional hard news. Ladefoged has also varied his style, veering between bold colour and graphic black-and-white; he is equally at home photographing sports and travel assignments. This essay on the Wagon Camp in Berlin was taken in the early 1990s, when Ladefoged was just 22. In the 1990s New Age travellers/hippies were very much in the news and their somewhat casual, feckless, drug-influenced lifestyle was seen as a threat to Europe's middle classes. This is the first story that Ladefoged shot outside Denmark and his curiosity was aroused when driving past the camp while vacationing with his father in Berlin. He says his aim was threefold: "I wanted to record history, give a very honest image of the life in the camp and learn how to shoot in colour."

The work is certainly honest. It is also engaging and a notable document of a sub-culture from a particular era. In the photographs these people are not threatening at all; they may need a bath and perhaps a stylist, but they also have a certain poise. Says Ladefoged, "I hope that these photos will help people to understand a different way of life and that people even if they are dirty, drink, smoke dope and have no jobs, still have dignity and a right to live their life the way they want to". Ladefoged spent a long time in the camp, gaining the trust of his subjects and earning their respect. In time he had complete access to photograph whatever he wanted; he is present during private and intimate moments between the camp dwellers; he shoots them when they are frankly a little out of it, chatting and just playing with their pets. The camp does not exist any more, so Ladefoged achieved his aim of recording a strange little chapter in late twentieth-century European history.

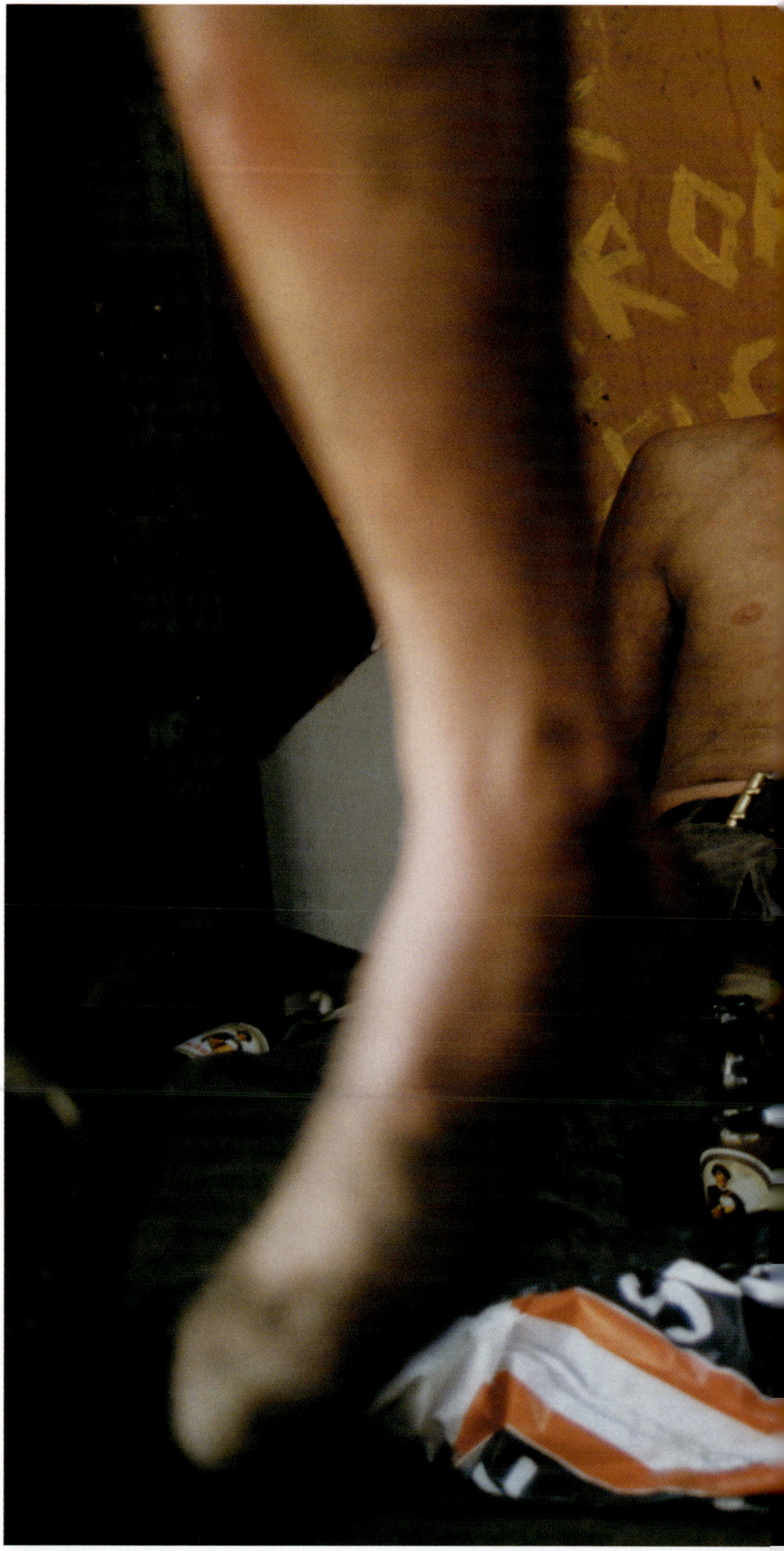

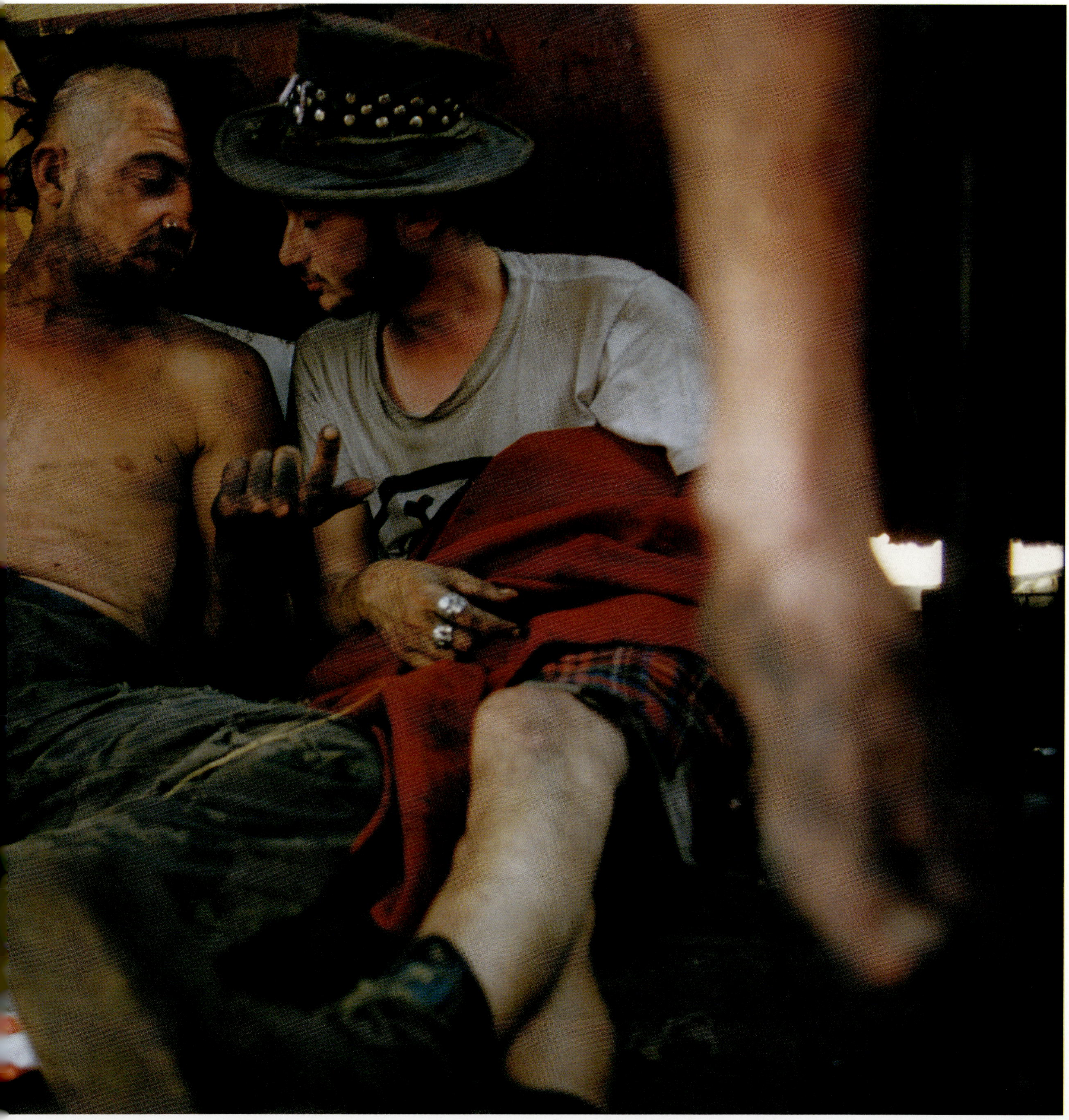

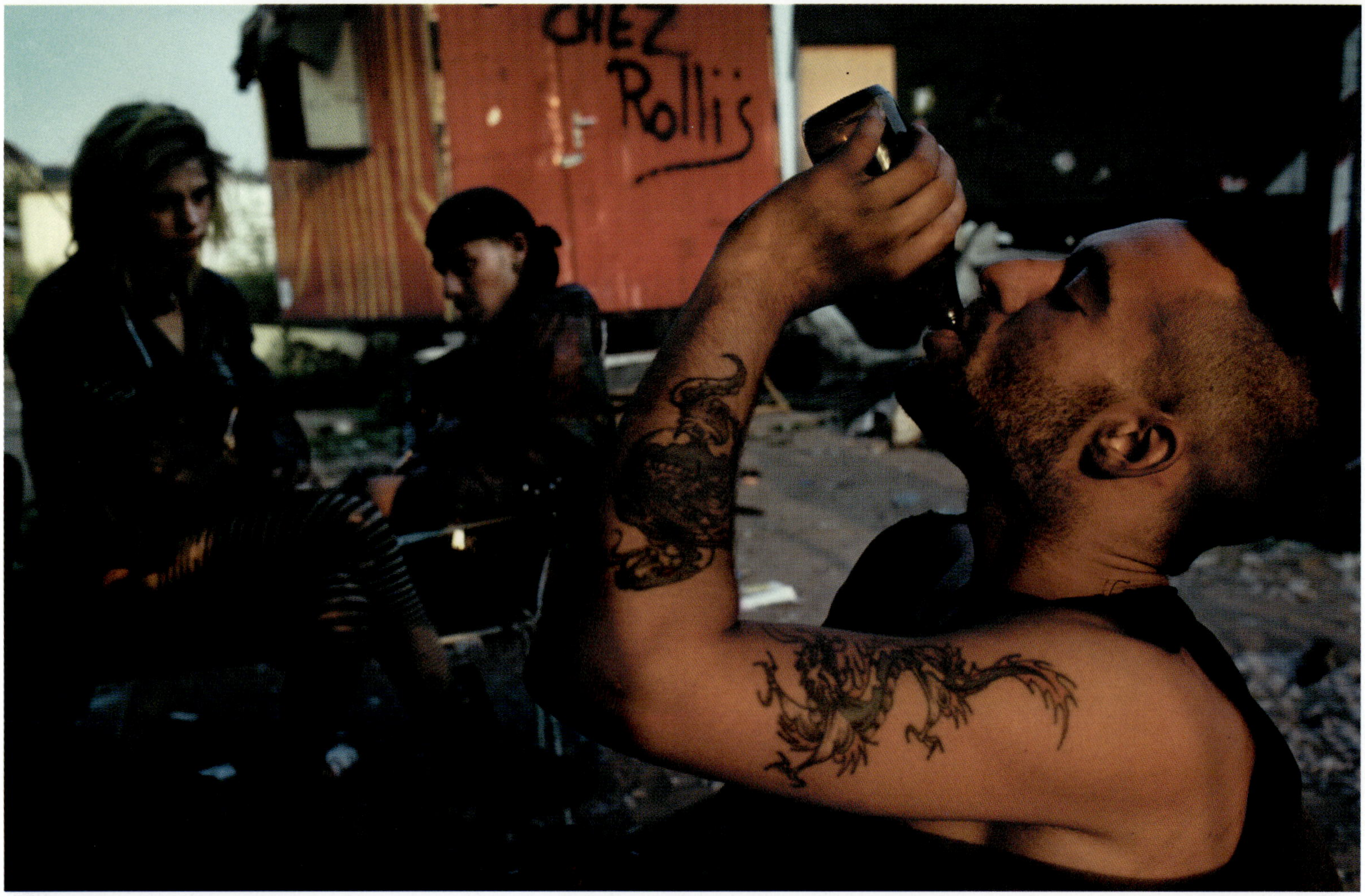
CHEZ
Rolli's

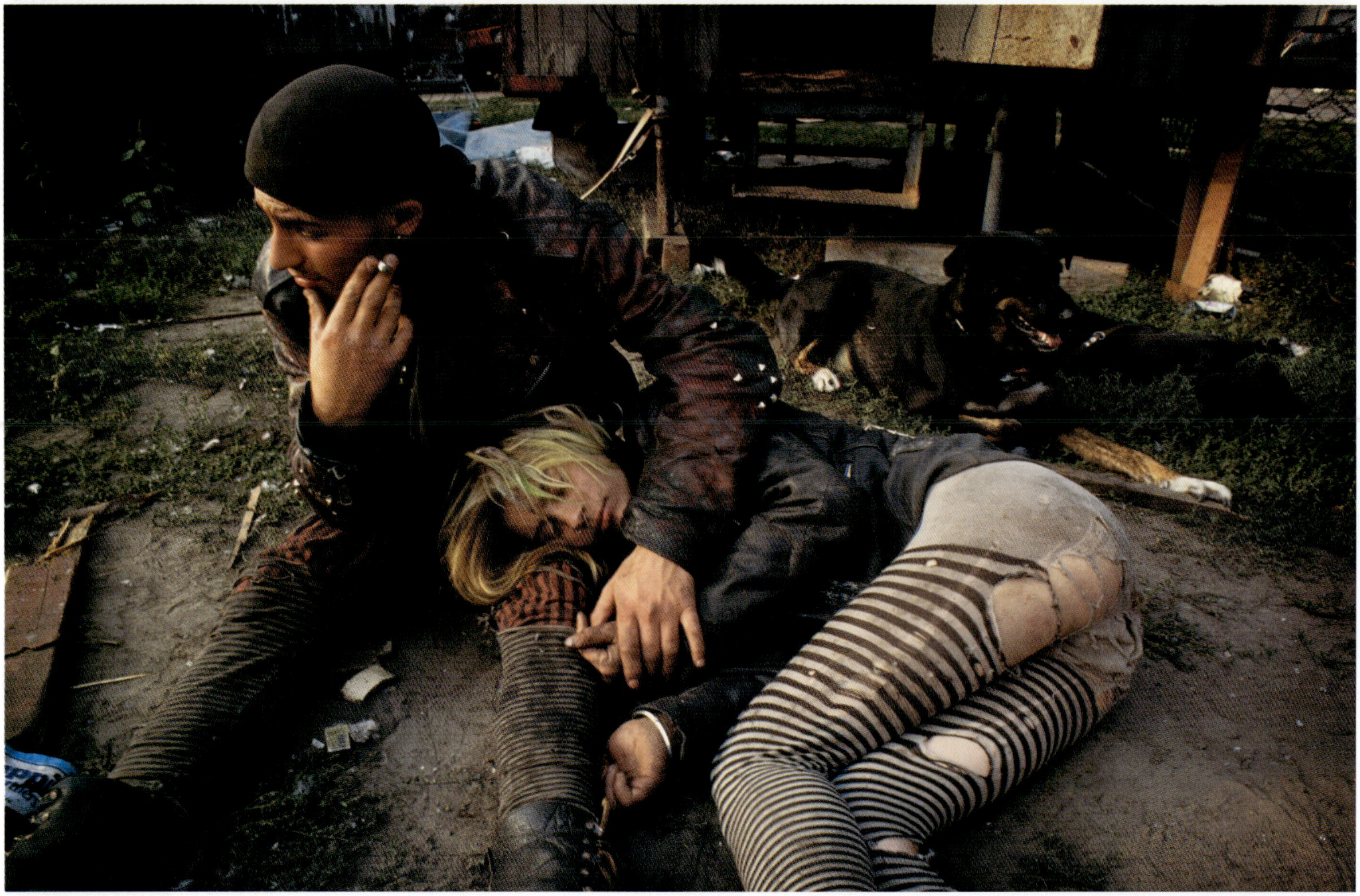

LEFT AND BELOW: **Ladefoged spent a long time with his subjects, so he eventually just blended into the ramshackle scenery. He photographs quiet moments of contemplation, but also drunken, riotous behaviour. It is amazing to think that he was only in his early twenties when he completed this essay – perhaps that is why he was able to earn the trust of these New Age hippies.**

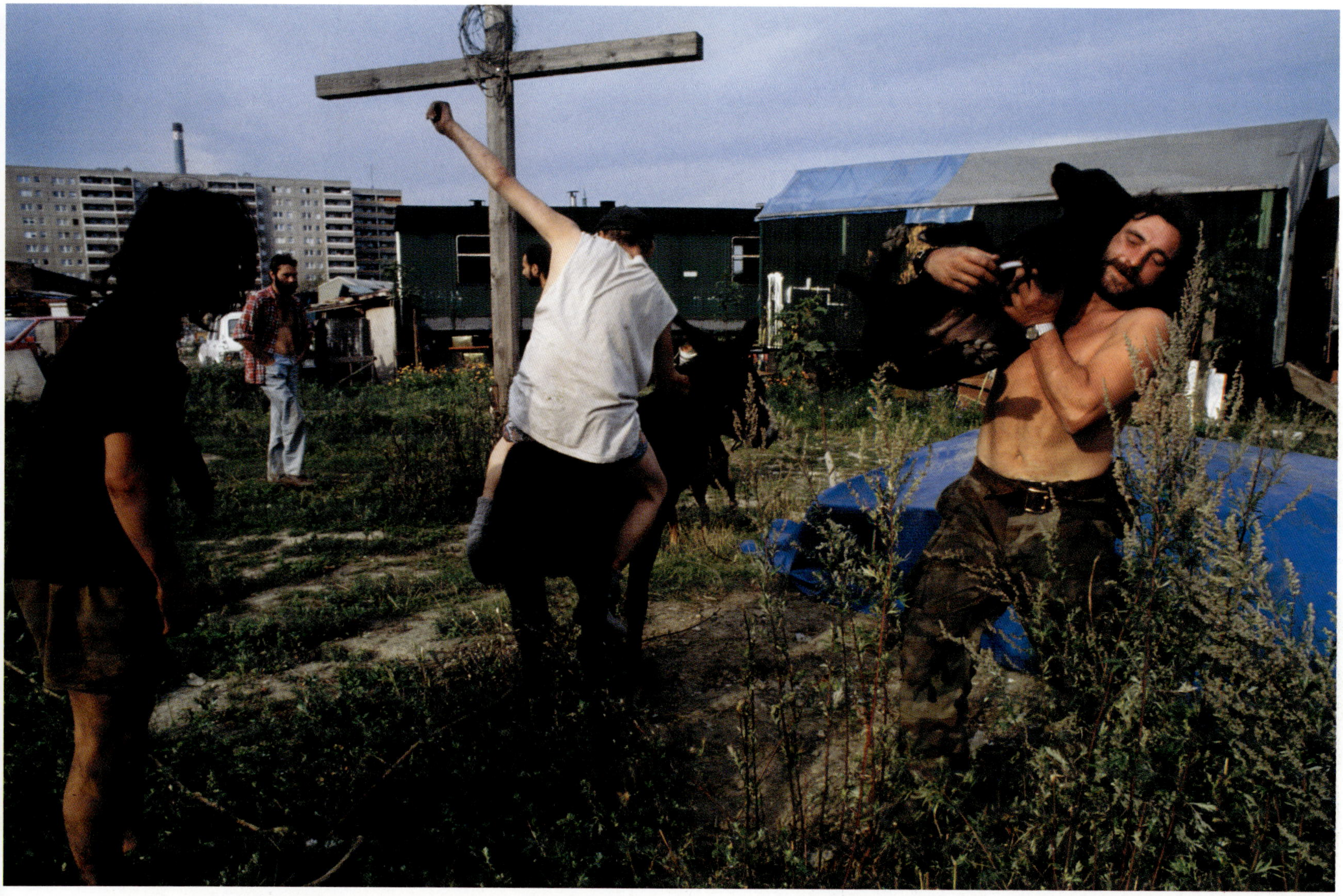

JERRY LAMPEN

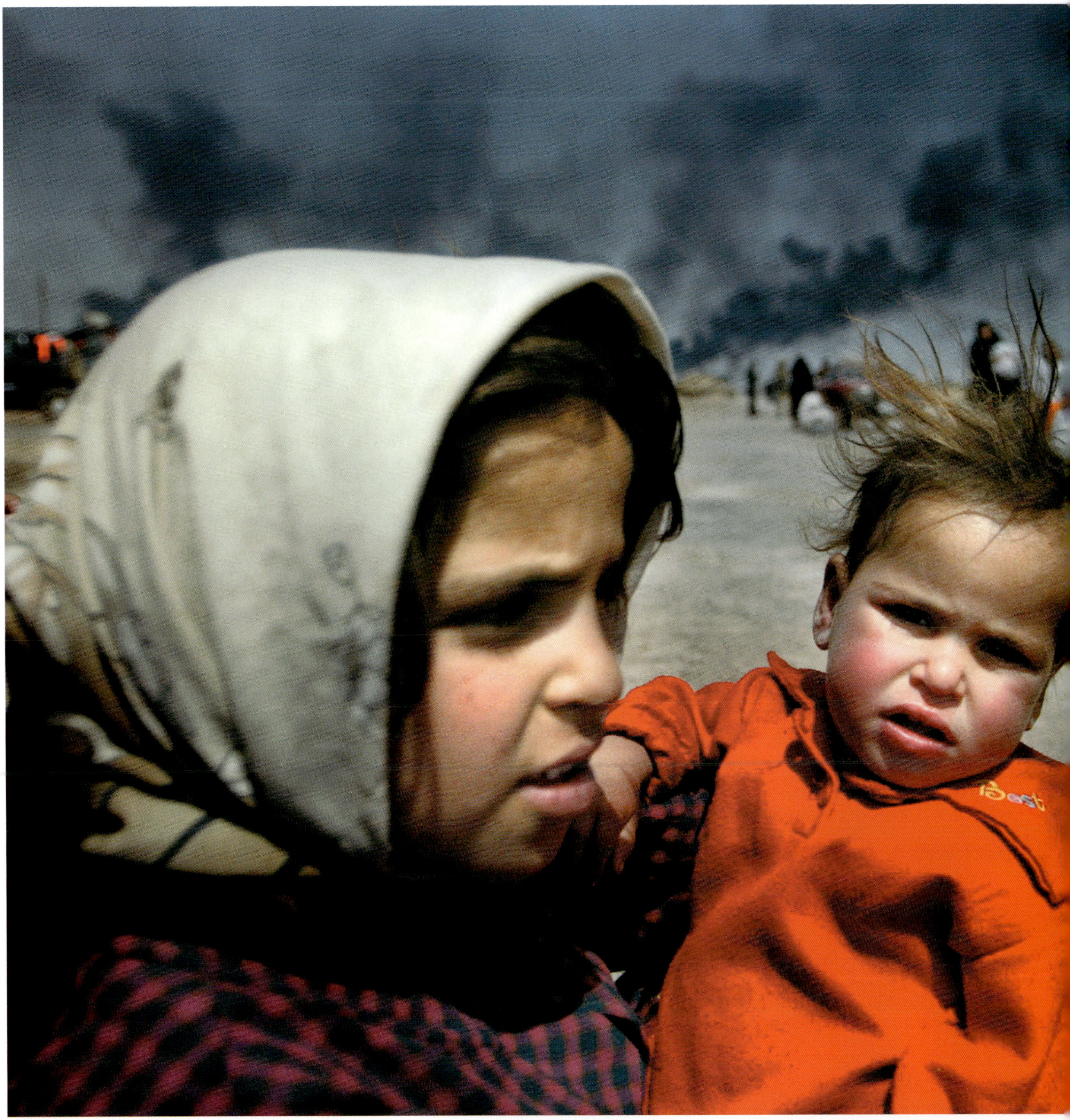

BELOW: **An Iraqi girl holds her sister as she waits for her mother to bring food bought in Basra. This photograph taken in 2003 has a sweeping epic quality with despairing figures in the background as far as the eye can see, while in the foreground the little girl's glazed expression is just heart-wrenching.**

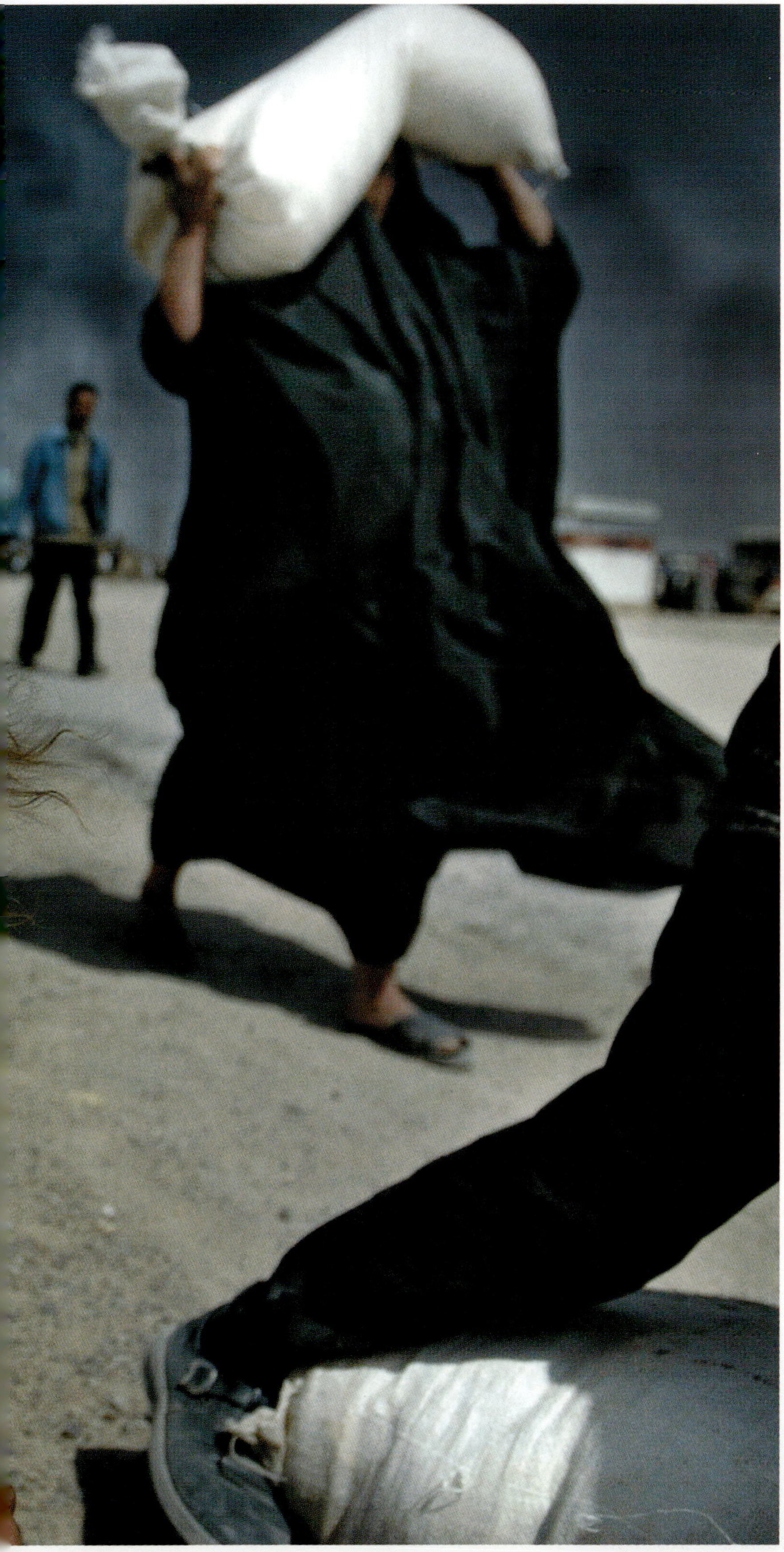

Photographing a war is never straightforward, but the recent conflict in Iraq was a particular logistical and ideological challenge. The photographers were embedded within military units, so their access and thus their ability to present a different viewpoint was limited. While the military was not censoring their images, it was clear that, in the early stages at least, there was an unspoken agreement between the allies and their respective media outlets that the conflict should be portrayed as one of liberation. This is certainly how the Iraqi people initially saw it, but very quickly disillusionment set in. "One moment people felt liberated, and in particular the older people were thanking the American soldiers, but within a matter of a few days, people's attitudes were changing. There was no water and electricity and they were asking me what was going on," recalls the highly accomplished Jerry Lampen. Working for Reuters, he says, he had a duty to remain objective. Yet at the same time, it was clear that the war was an ambiguous one and innocent people were suffering. "I tried to focus on the victims and in particular the children because they get forgotten. It is the adults fighting over land, religion, oil, but all the kids want to do is play football and play with their dolls," he says.

Shooting for a newswire means that the photographer's greatest enemy is the ever-present deadline, but Lampen's images, all shot on digital cameras, never appear rushed or hackneyed. He may be engulfed by chaos, but it never interferes with his ability to calmly compose a photograph that gives equal weight to the foreground and middle ground. Lampen also has the knack of getting right into his subject's space, yet somehow remaining unobtrusive. He says that his photographs are never going to change the world, but if they make people think a little more about what is going on, he feels that he has accomplished something. On that score he need be in no doubt. Many very big names covered this story, but few with as much distinction as Lampen.

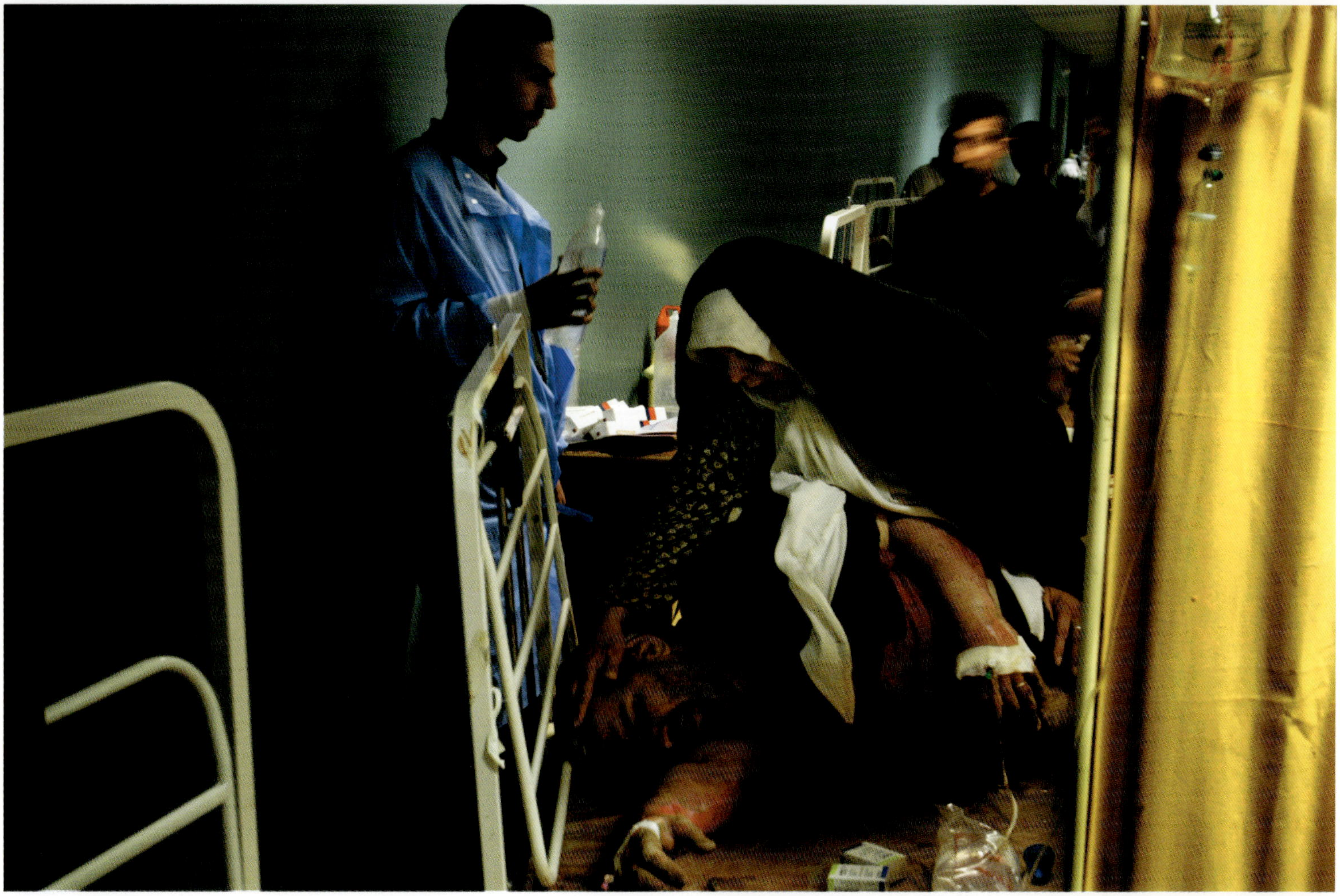

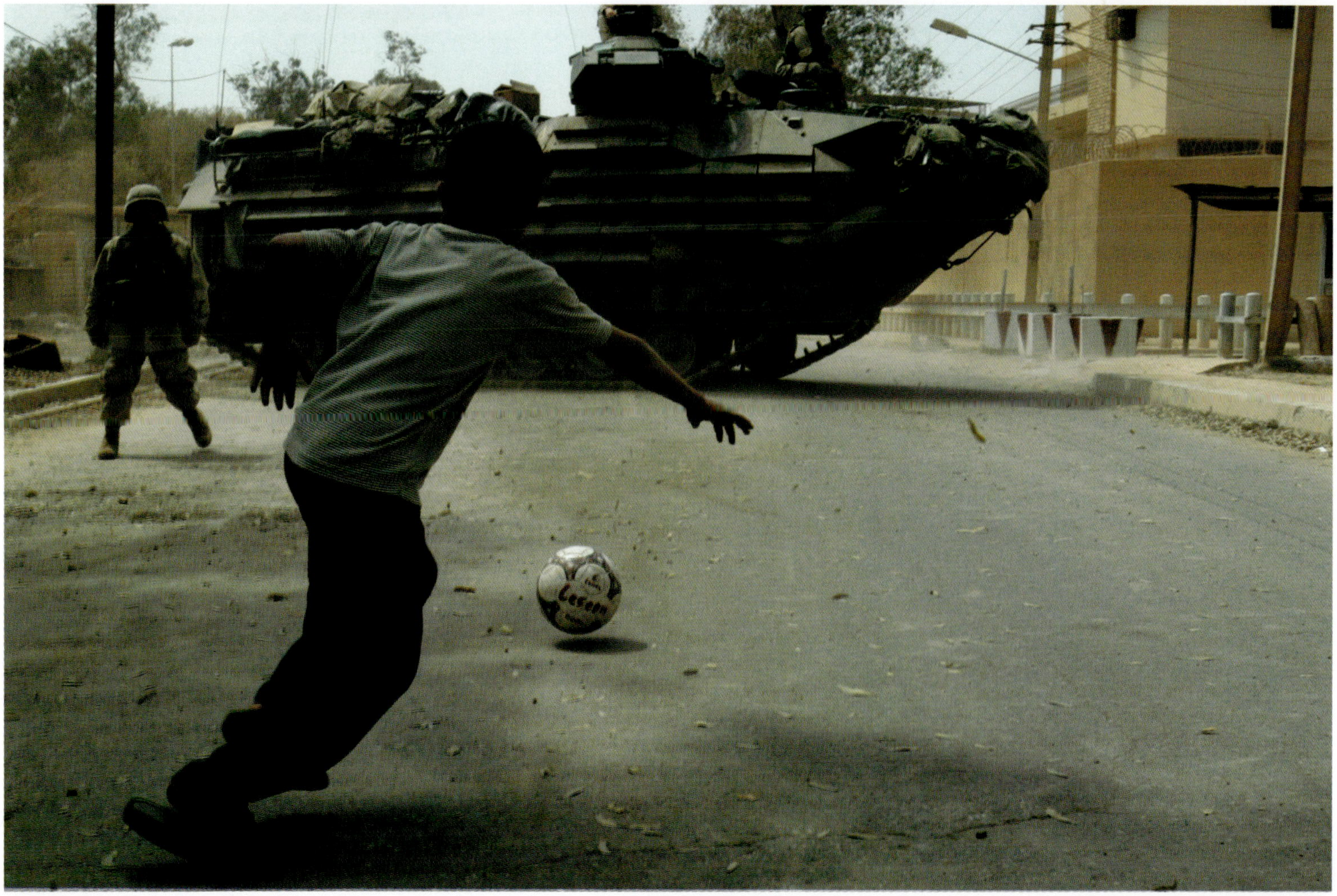

LEFT: A woman and her husband with severe burns at a ramshackle and chaotic hospital in central Baghdad, April 2003. This is an unsettling image with the photographer close, almost too close, to the pain.

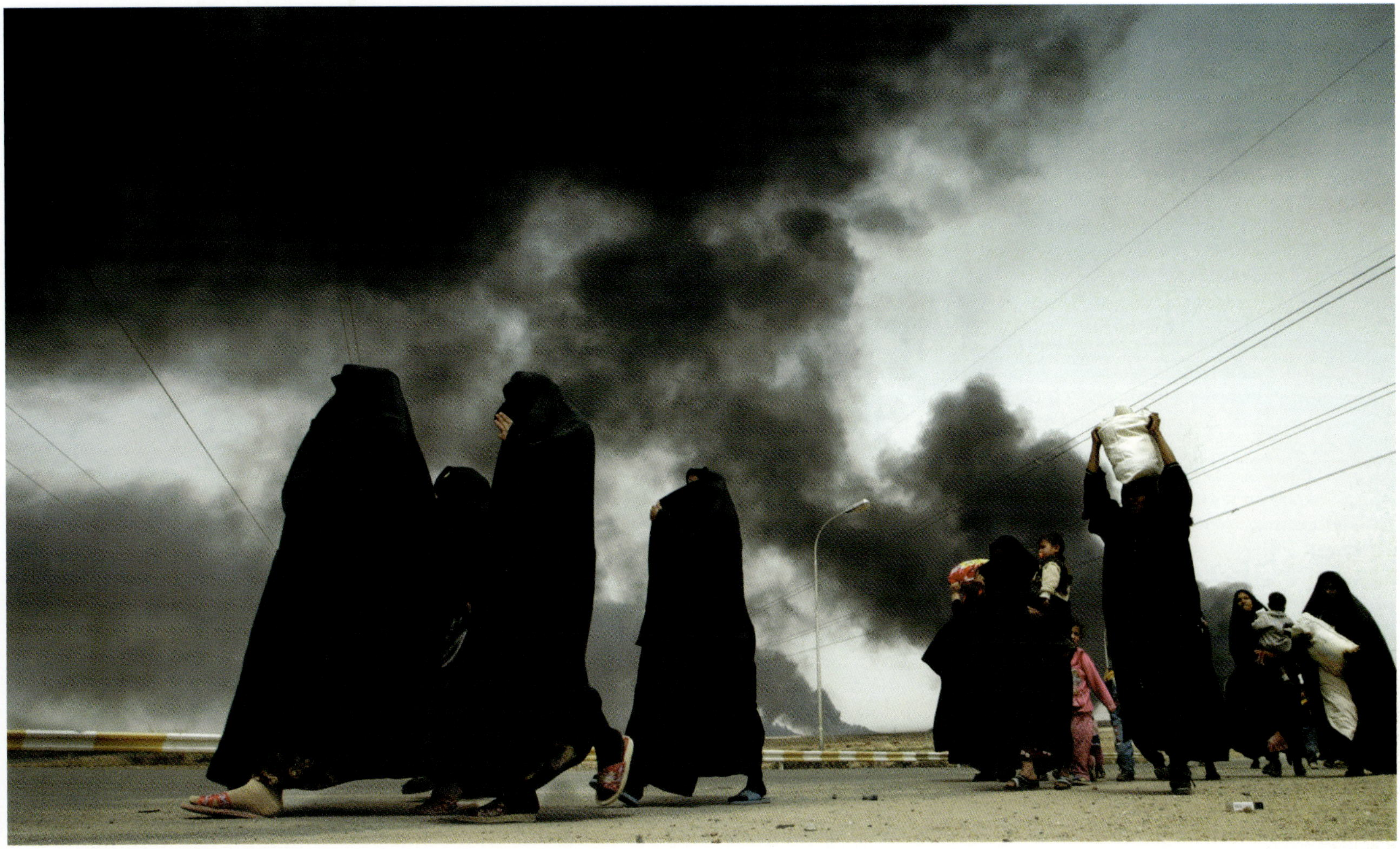

ABOVE: Iraqi women leave the besieged city of Basra. Once again, we see the consequences of war – the suffering of the innocent fleeing under a shroud of black smoke.

LEFT: An Iraqi boy plays football with a US soldier at a checkpoint in central Baghdad. This is a welcome respite from the fighting and the scene suggests that perhaps a better and more peaceful Iraq might emerge from the conflict. Note the soldier sitting on the tank staring into the distance at the top of the frame.

DOROTHEA LANGE

BELOW: **The family of an Alabama turpentine worker who earns $1 per day. Lange appeals for help on behalf of her subjects by emphasizing the obvious signs of their poverty, such as shoeless feet, and tattered clothing and window screens. But the faces connect viewers emotionally, and elevate images such as this beyond mere government documents.**

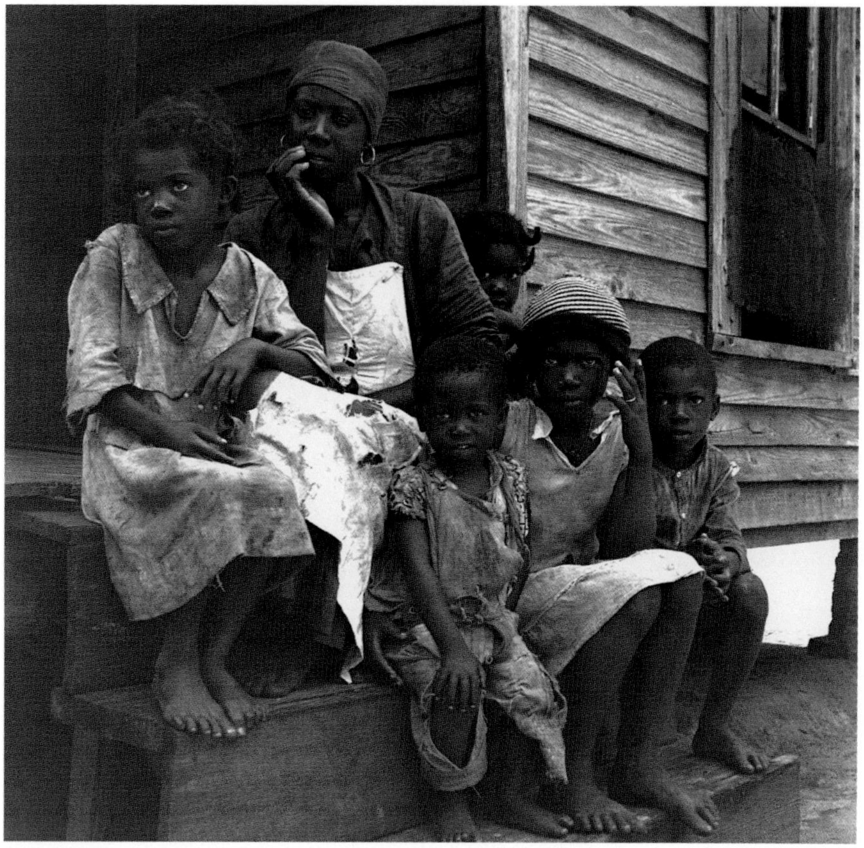

A seminal figure in social documentary photography, Dorothea Lange gave voice to the "everyman" (and woman), convinced that arresting images of society's disadvantaged people could compel government officials to intervene. Although Lange never considered herself an artist, her photographs are highly subjective and resonate with emotion. Her instantly recognizable photograph, *Migrant Mother, Nipomo, California* (1936), is the iconic image of America's Great Depression and the touchstone of her *oeuvre*. Talking about the subject of that photograph, Lange once told an interviewer, "[She] seemed to know that my pictures might help her, and so she helped me. There was a sort of equality about it."

Lange ran a portrait studio catering to a wealthy clientele during the 1920s, but began dabbling with documentary work when she photographed Native Americans while travelling with her first husband, Maynard Dixon, in 1923. By the early 1930s, she was restless; portrait work seemed static and increasingly irrelevant after the 1929 stock market crash. "It came to me that what I had to do," she later recalled to an interviewer, "was concentrate on people, all kinds of people, people who paid me and people who didn't." In the tradition of Lewis Hine and Jacob Riis, Lange took her camera to the streets and started photographing the throngs of unemployed in bread lines and striking dock-workers along the San Francisco waterfront. Lange's strong personality informed her work. Biographers have described her as egotistical, domineering and contentious, but also kind-hearted and empathetic. She approached her subjects with simple questions about their routines and activities, asked permission to photograph them, then lingered until they stopped trying to pose. Although best known for images of the destitute farmers whom she shot in the 1930s for the Farm Security Administration, Lange also worked for government agencies during the Second World War. She documented women and minorities working in wartime industries and also the internment camps for Japanese Americans. The latter work was at times scathingly critical of US Government policies, portraying the prisoners' spirit and hope against a backdrop of their oppressive living conditions. In the 1950s she turned her attention to the rapid cultural changes in post-war America, for example the relentless spread of the suburbs.

RIGHT: **This image of the *Migrant Mother, Nipomo, California* taken in 1936 is an icon of America's Great Depression and stands for the personal tragedy of millions of ordinary citizens suffering from economic forces beyond their control. The mother's burdens are written in the sleeping baby in her lap, the children leaning listlessly on her shoulders, the worry on her face and the pensive gesture of her right hand. But her demeanour also reflects strength and determination. The image makes a powerful appeal for public sympathy and assistance, which was Lange's intent.**

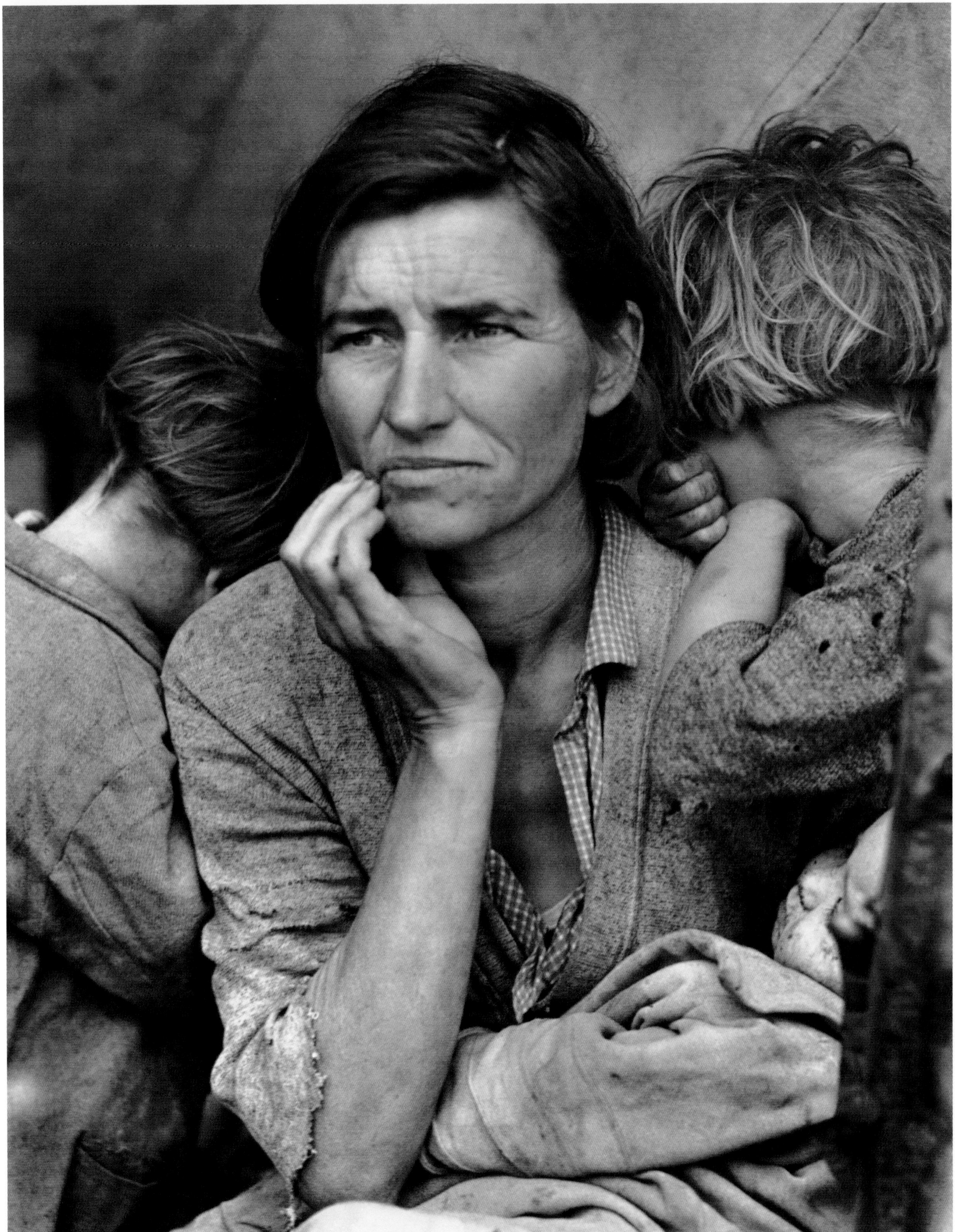

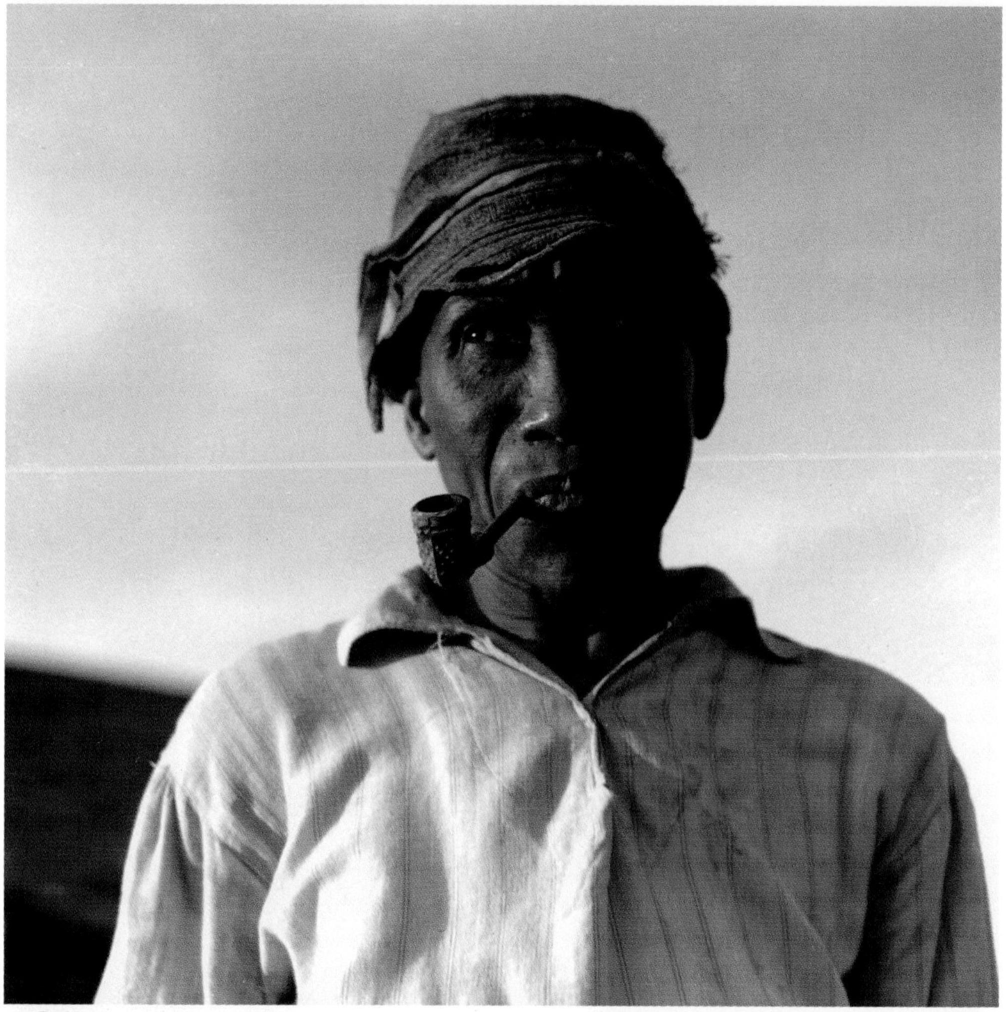

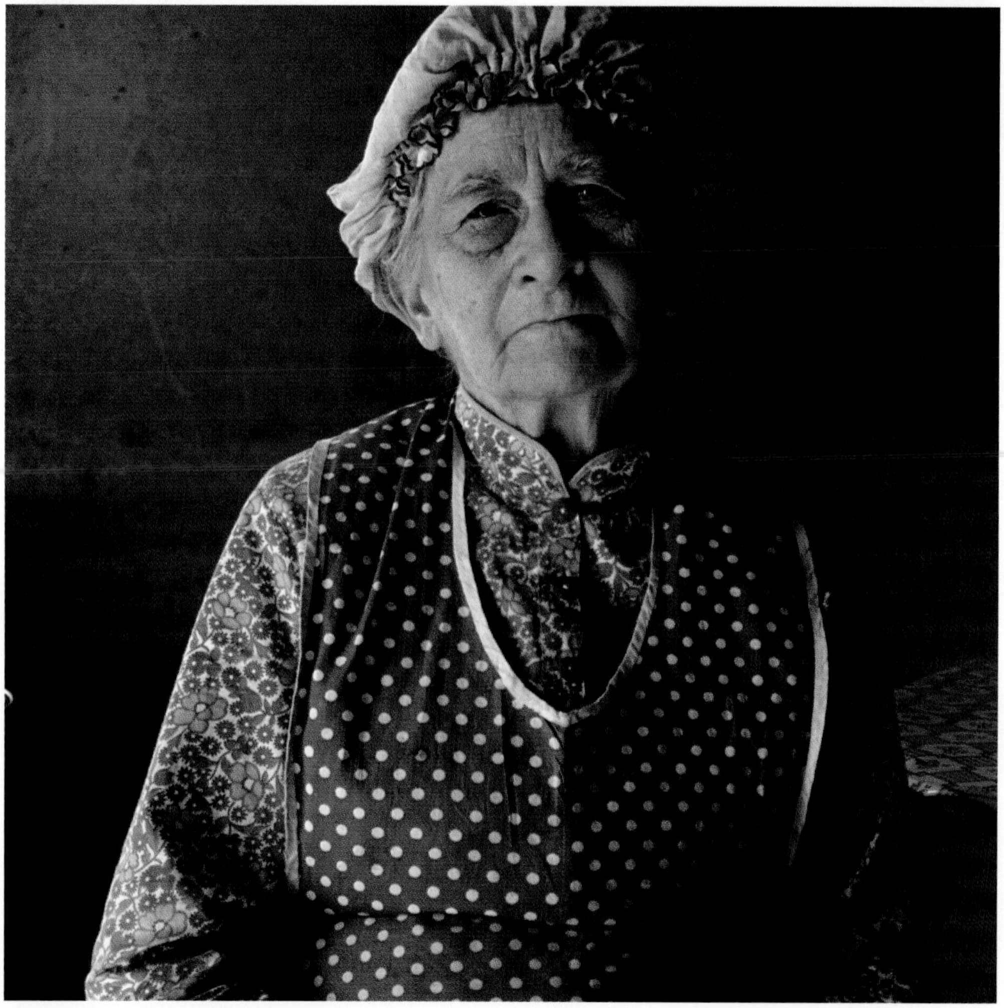

LEFT: A tattered hat, leathery skin and a wary glance convey the hard life of this Mississippi plantation resident. But the pipe, combined with Lange's low camera angle, lend her subject an air of dignity and pride.

LEFT: This 1939 portrait of an irrigation project resident in Oregon endorses government social intervention with its subtle suggestion that this woman is a deserving beneficiary: her dress and demeanour suggest poverty, but also a determination to work, and her face reflects a ray of guarded hope.

BELOW: **Drought refugees from Abilene, Texas, are following the crops to California. The trepidation on the faces of the subjects and the household effects tied to the automobile convey the desperation of Dust Bowl farm families during the Great Depression.**

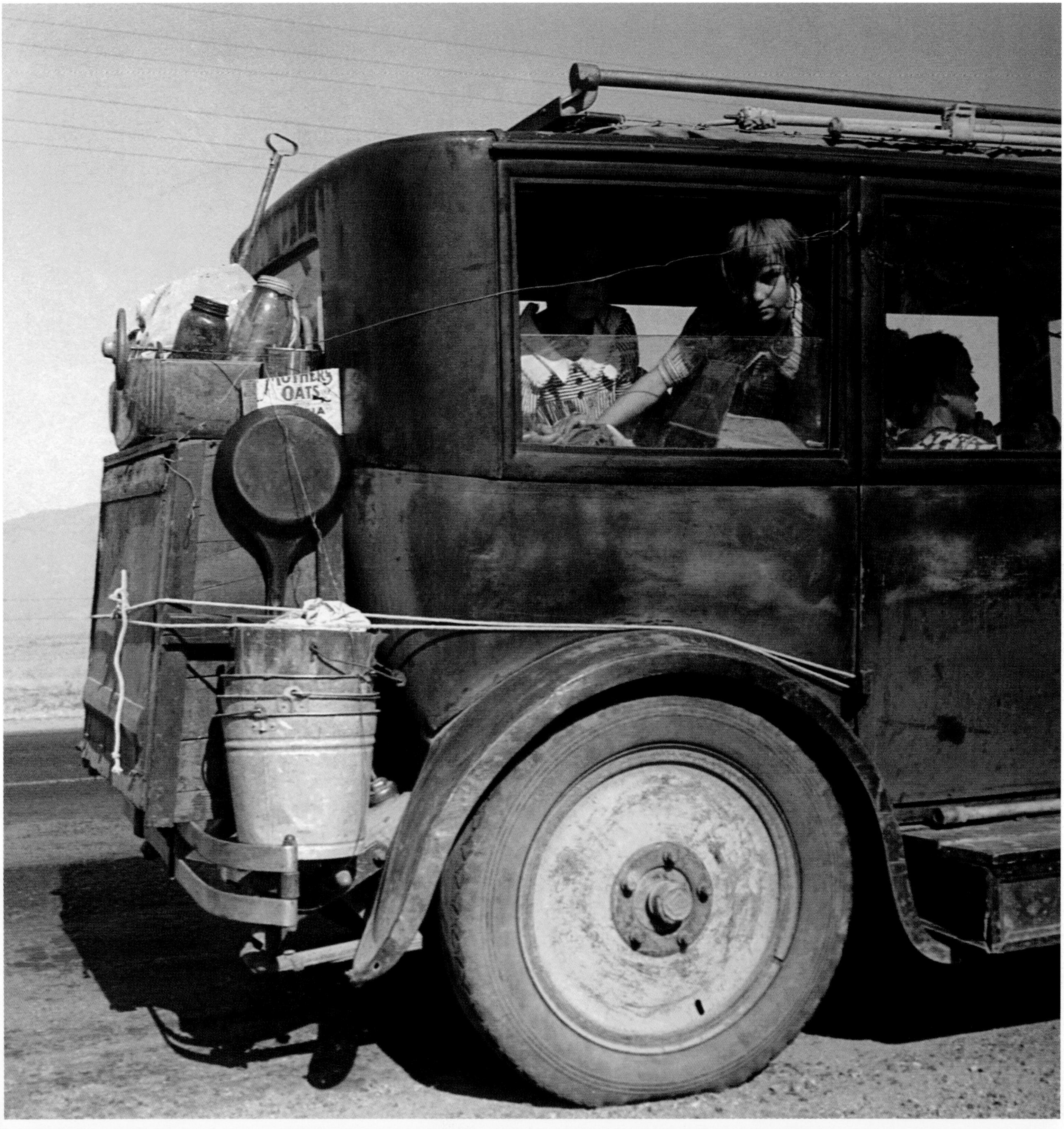

GERD LUDWIG

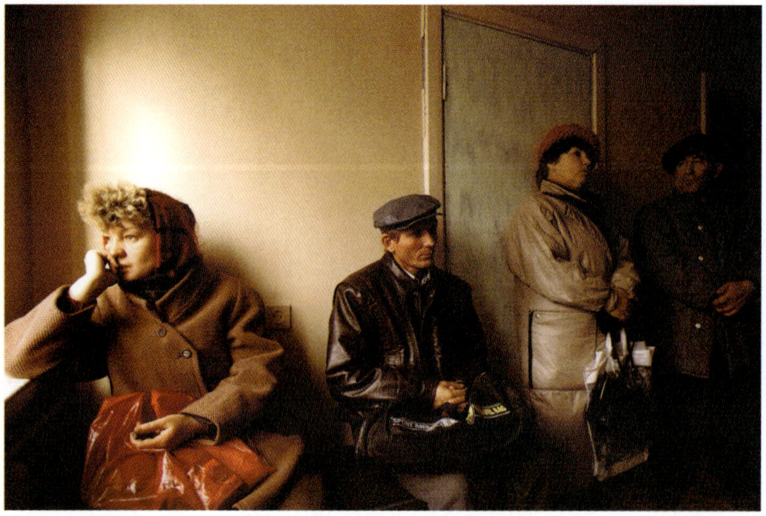

RIGHT: Like this Muscovite, many of Russia's elderly live in poorly maintained, communal flats, where they are forced to share kitchens and bathrooms. The composition of this photograph cleverly captures this lady from the old Russia sitting between the younger, more Westernized women on the wall calendar and on the television.

LEFT: Victims of the nuclear fallout from the 1986 Chernobyl nuclear disaster line up to register in Kiev. The seriousness of their side effects – measured on a scale of one to four – will determine the compensation awarded to them.

Gerd Ludwig's personal relationship with Russia began as a young boy, when he was growing up in post-war Germany. His father was drafted into the Germany Sixth Army that invaded the USSR in 1942 and was lucky to survive the disastrous campaign. The young Ludwig would listen to his father's harrowing tales of the endless winter landscapes and soldiers battling their way through bitter snowstorms. Later, as a member of the first post-war generation of Germans, filled with guilt, Ludwig compensated by glorifying everything Germany had tried to destroy. So when he went on his first assignment to the USSR in 1980, he was more than a merely curious observer, he was a photographer embarking on his own personal journey.

His journey also coincided with the gradual thawing of the communist regime. Glasnost offered Ludwig a chance to document just what kind of impact this new call for openness was having on ordinary Russians. Ludwig's images catch the Russian people at something of a crossroads. We see glimpses of the new USSR and its accompanying material benefits, yet he also reveals people living in grim social and economic conditions that for generations have been hidden from Western eyes. Often these two worlds collide in the same image. Yet despite these harsh realities, Ludwig's photographs are imbued with an infectious optimism. Many photojournalists succumb to a slightly clichéd view of Russia and photograph the country in stark monochrome. Ludwig takes a more bold and colourful approach, which makes his subjects appear more human and less one-dimensional. He has a marvellous eye for the surreal juxtaposition of subject matter and a sure touch in the way he composes and crops his images. The optimism also comes from something within the Russian soul, known as "Dasha". Ludwig explains: "It does not acknowledge harsh reality. It is the antithesis of everyday modern Western life. It is forgiveness, empathy, conscience and the ability of humans to partake in the Divine." Gerd Ludwig is part travel photographer, part social documentarian and part classic photojournalist. His images tell us something about the human condition in an accessible, yet always challenging way. Dasha indeed.

OVERLEAF TOP LEFT: Illicit distillers from the Caucasus sell their homemade wine to thirsty Muscovites on Krasnopresnenskaya Square.

OVERLEAF BOTTOM LEFT: A young soldier-to-be is fitted for his uniform at the Royal Cossack Cadet Academy.

OVERLEAF TOP RIGHT: A Benetton megastore replaced the state-run NATASHA department store. Again, this is a surreal combination of images.

OVERLEAF BOTTOM RIGHT: Some of the new, rich Russians, probably part of the affluent mafia crowd, have gathered to wine and dine at the grave of a deceased relative at Sochi cemetery on Parents' Day. Although Ludwig works for the conventional *National Geographic*, he has the eye of a fine art photographer, and is always looking for an oblique viewpoint.

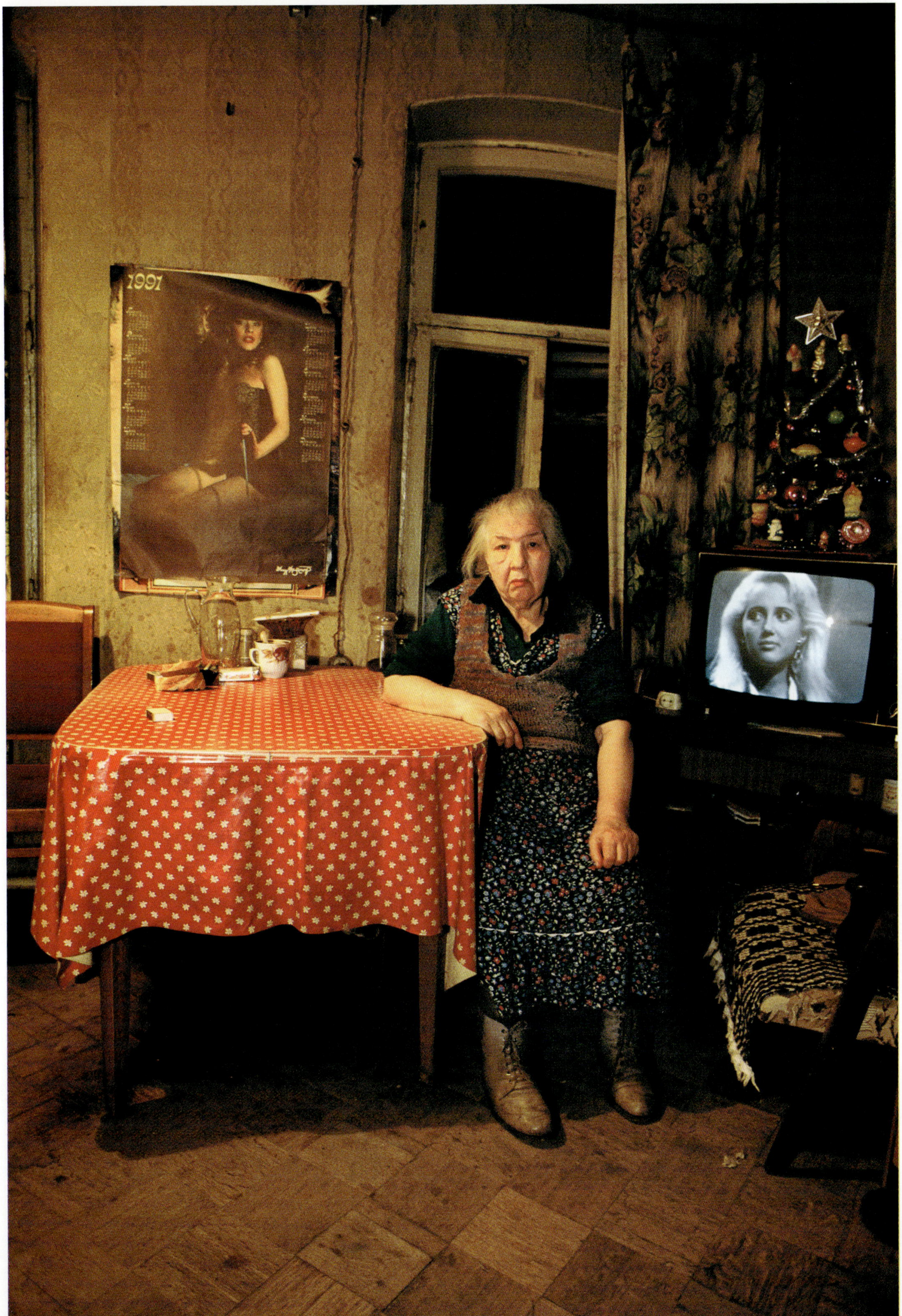
1991

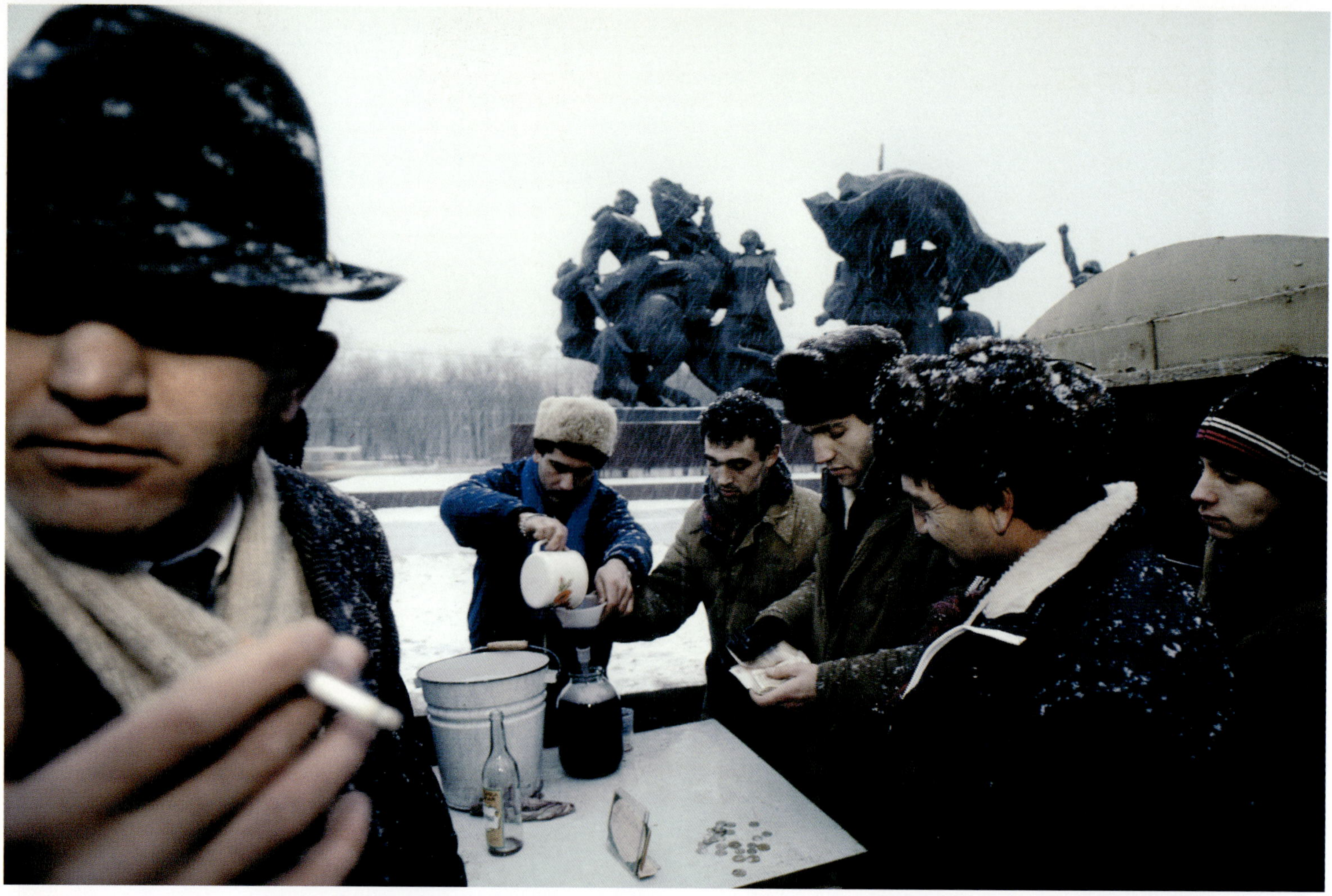

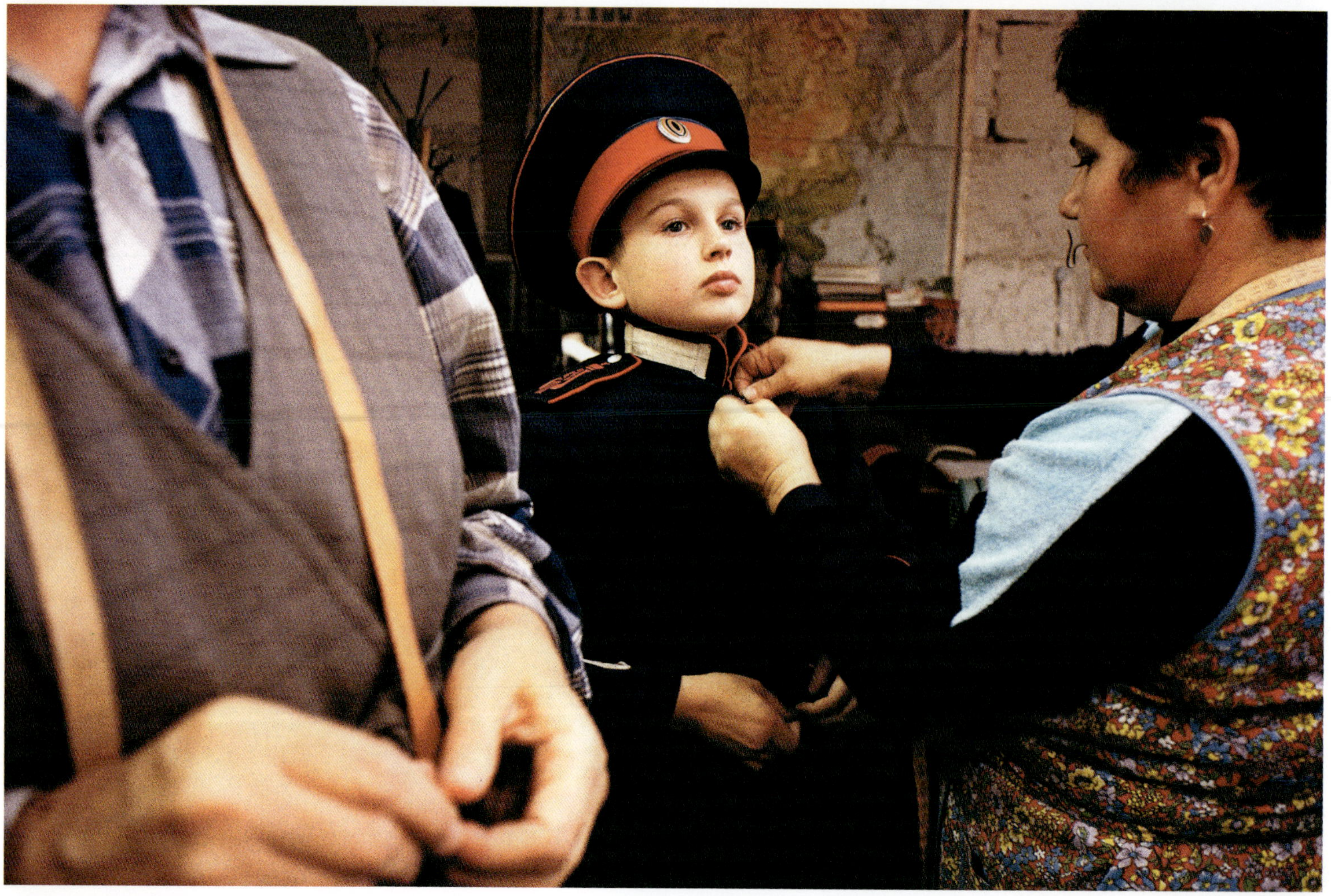

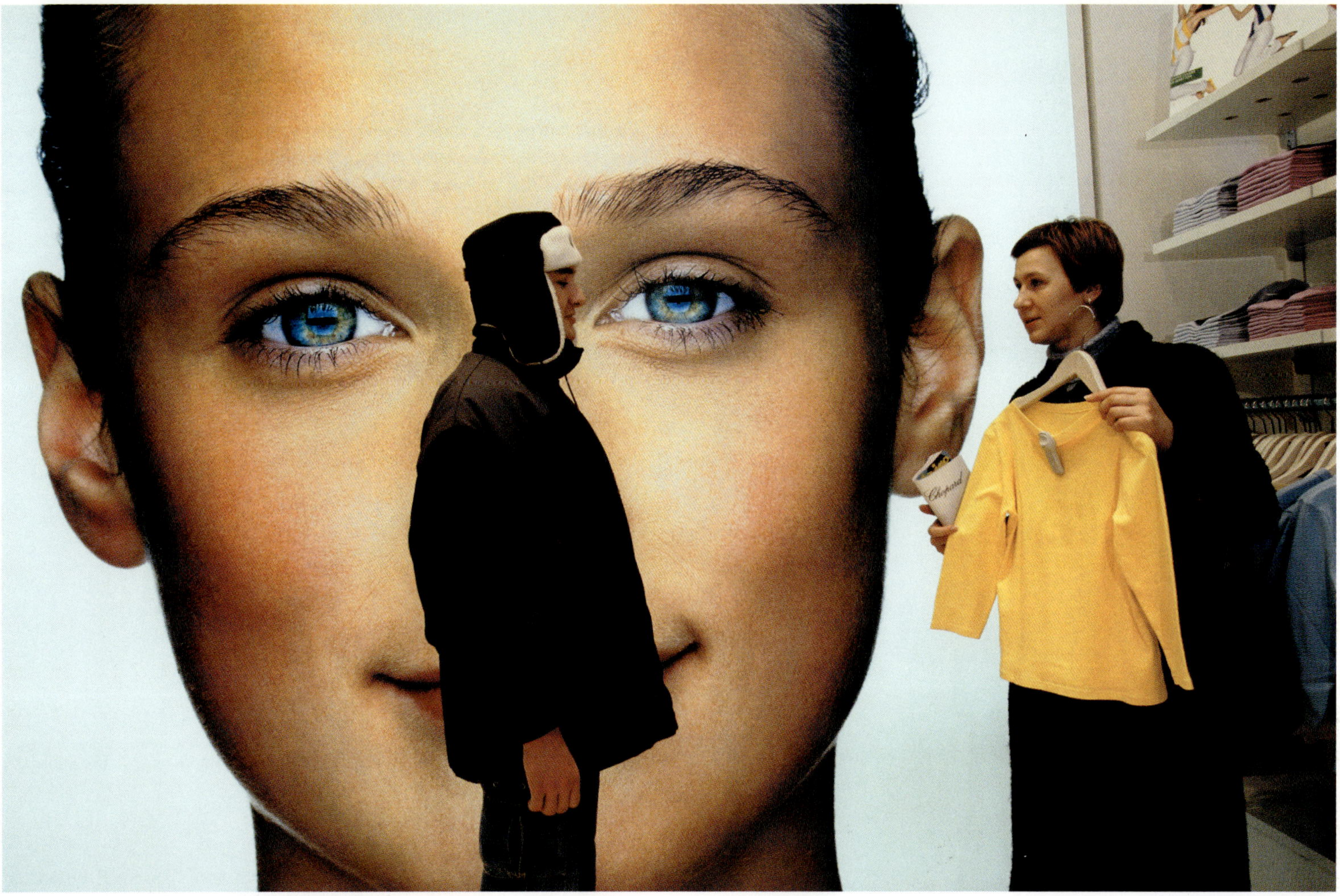
Chopard

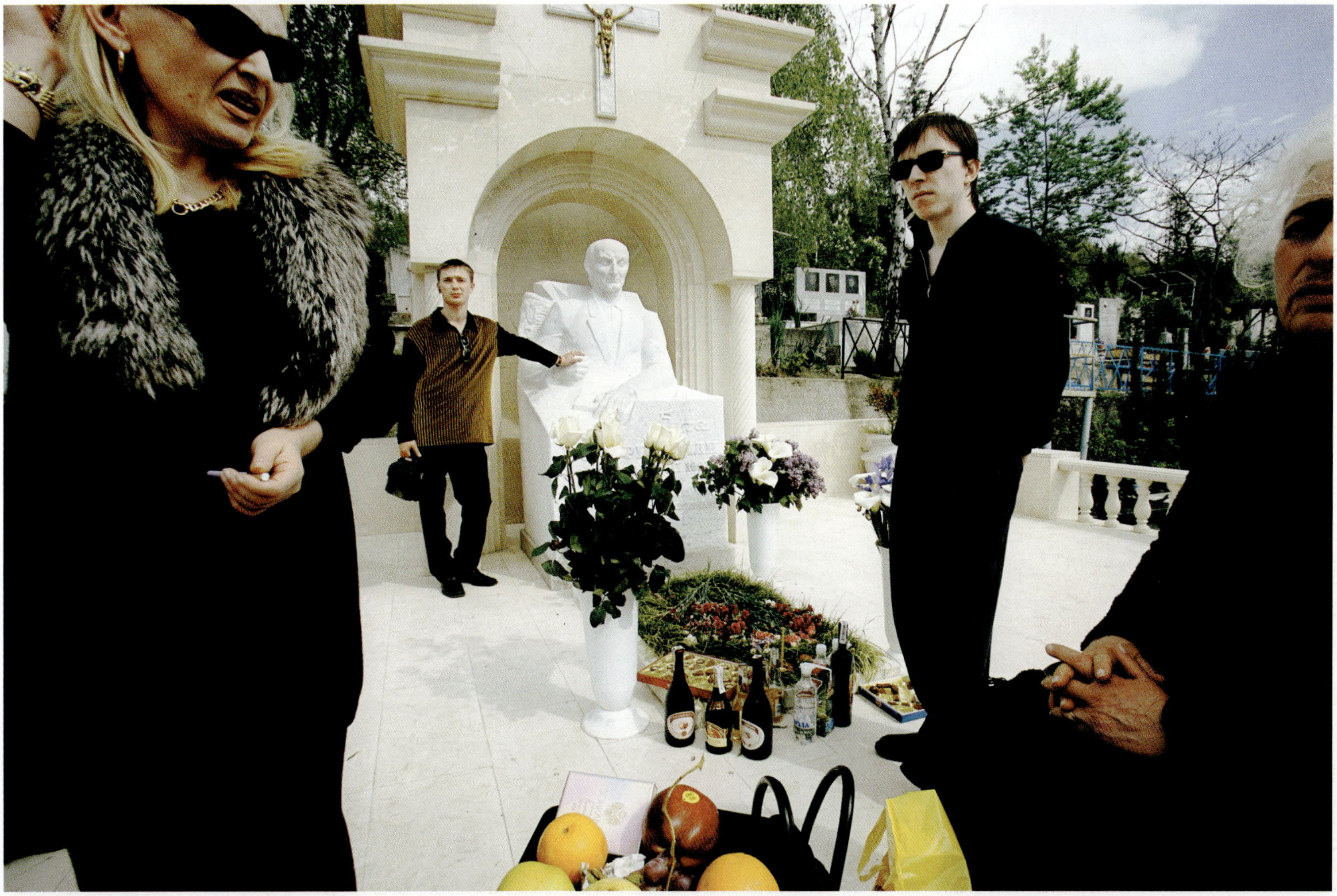

DON McCULLIN

BELOW: **In Don McCullin's war scenes there is often a photograph that has an almost lyrical quality, a beautiful moment amid the carnage of battle, such as in this image of a US marine throwing a hand grenade in 1968 during the Tet offensive in Hue, Vietnam.**

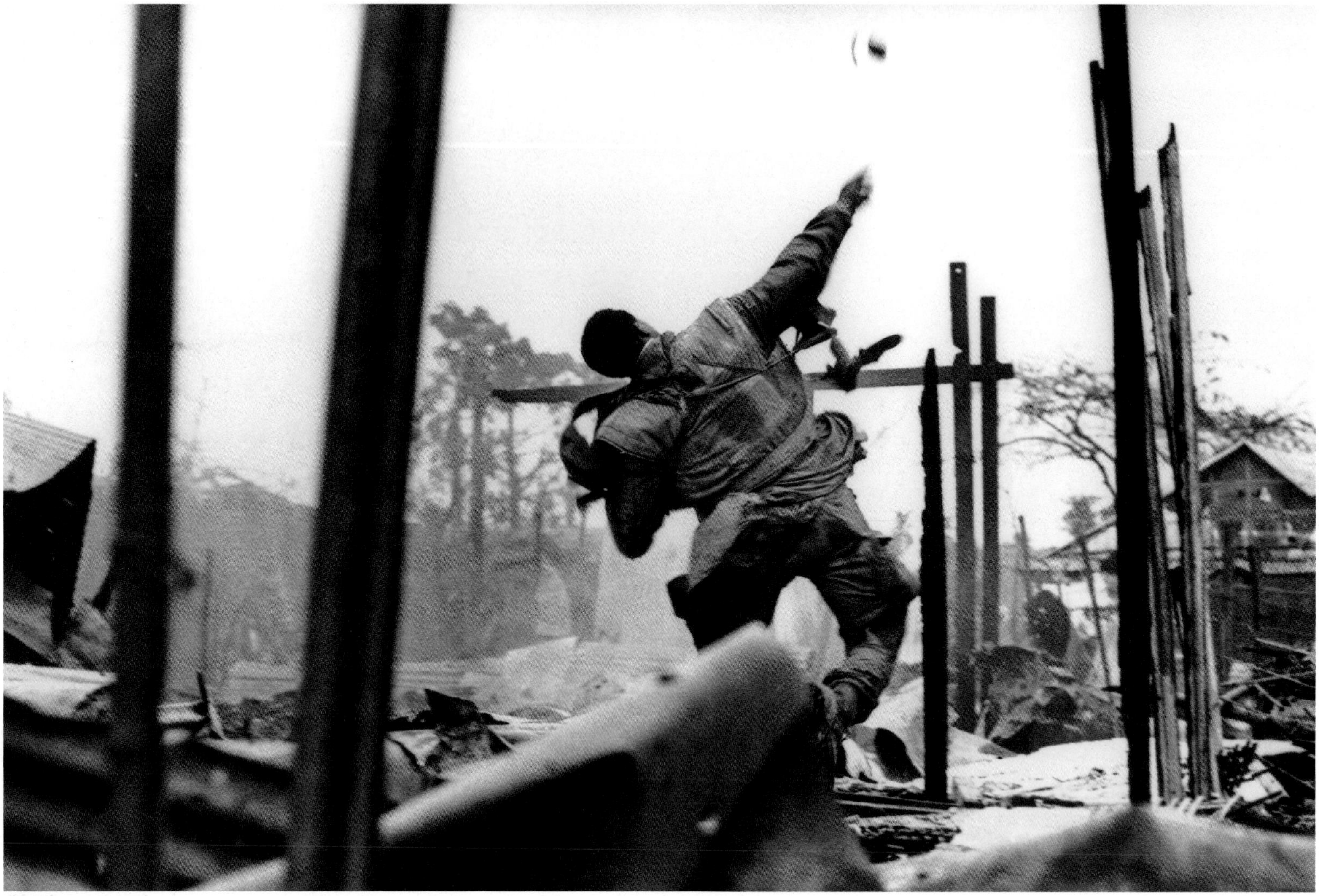

Don McCullin's photographs combine a sense of pictorial drama with humanist concern. Heir to the great pictorialist tradition, he has combined an eye for the beautifully constructed image with an acute social conscience. No greater tribute could have been paid to him than Cartier-Bresson's term "Goya with a camera", to describe his war photographs. McCullin is an obsessive photographer who also claims that he "hates carrying a camera". He was the creator of several pictures that have come to define in a single image some key conflicts of the second half of the twentieth century, from the Nigerian civil war of the 1960s, to Vietnam, Bangladesh, Northern Ireland, the Lebanon and Paraguay. His desire to get as close as possible to scenes of conflict and suffering reflected a deeply felt need to "witness" these events on the behalf of humanity, an urge that is present more generally in his social reportage.

His extraordinary study of the British underclass, *Homecoming* (1971) is a dark and disturbing view of a nation that ignores the social problems of its disadvantaged groups, a particularly poignant portrait at a time when the magazines for which he worked were becoming increasingly obsessed with "lifestyle" consumerism.

McCullin bears the scars of his numerous close brushes with death, yet ironically his remarkable record worked against him when he was denied access to the Gulf War in 1991 because of the heavy censorship employed by the military authorities. He has continued to report on the other great struggles of modern times, on poverty, AIDS and deprivation in the Third World. Yet McCullin's reportage on situations of conflict and deprivation has always been interspersed with projects dedicated to seeking out settings in which to renew his faith in humanity and nature. His pictures of New Guinea tribes (1985) and of Indian people and places (since 1988), his dark and beautiful and wintry Somerset landscapes, and the classically constructed large-format still lifes made in the coal shed of his Somerset home may indeed play a redemptive role in his life. Without a doubt, he is Britain's greatest ever photojournalist.

BELOW: This photograph of a shell-shocked US marine during the battle for Hue in February 1968 has become an iconic image of the Vietnam War, symbolizing both the power and the impotence of American military might against its enemy, and the failure of American society to support the war.

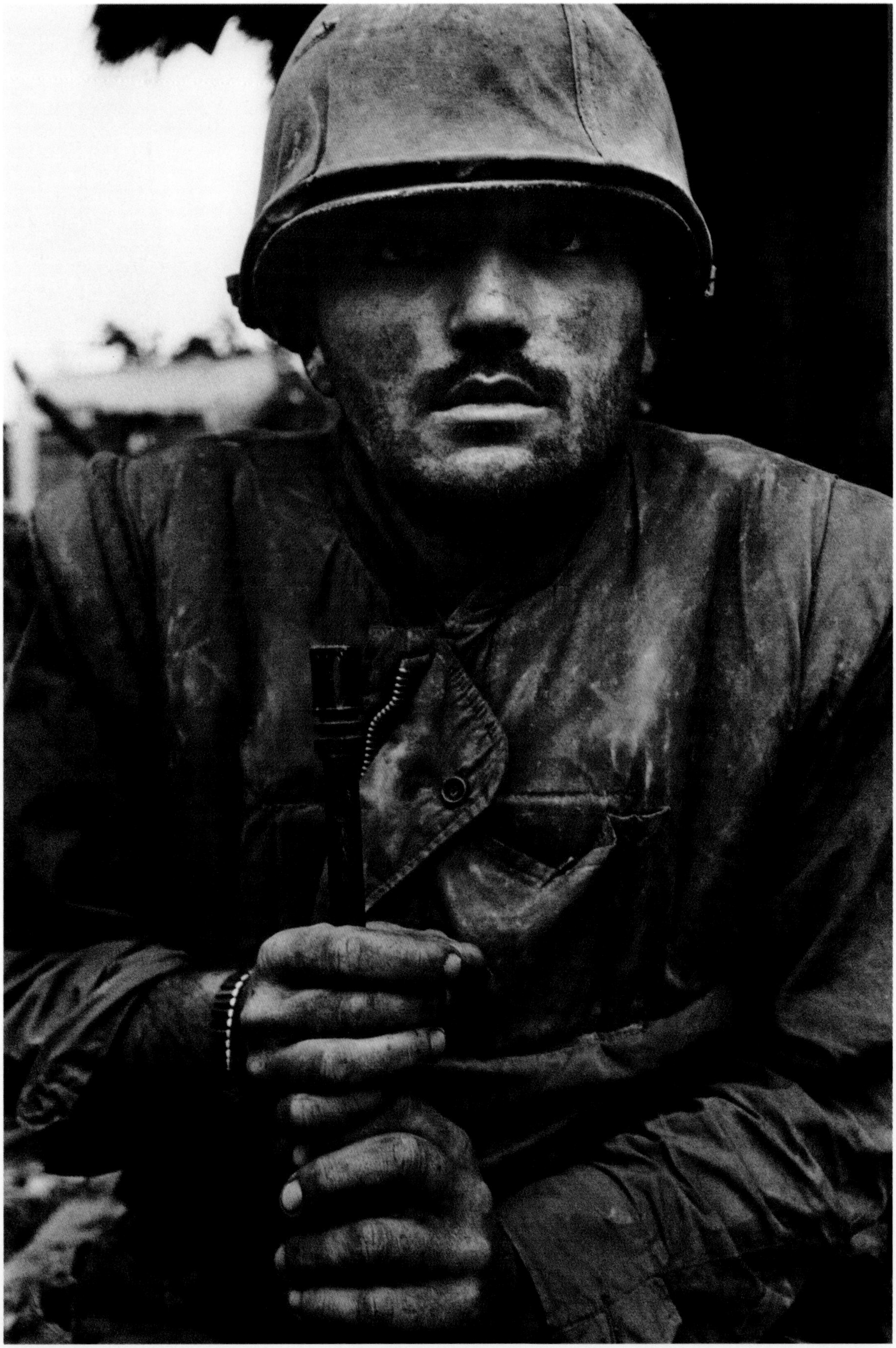

BELOW: The sheer pathos of this image of an albino boy clutching an empty corned beef tin in Biafra in 1968 is a mark of McCullin's acute concern to make pictures of such events that both witness the horror of what people can do to each other and involve us as viewers in the scene.

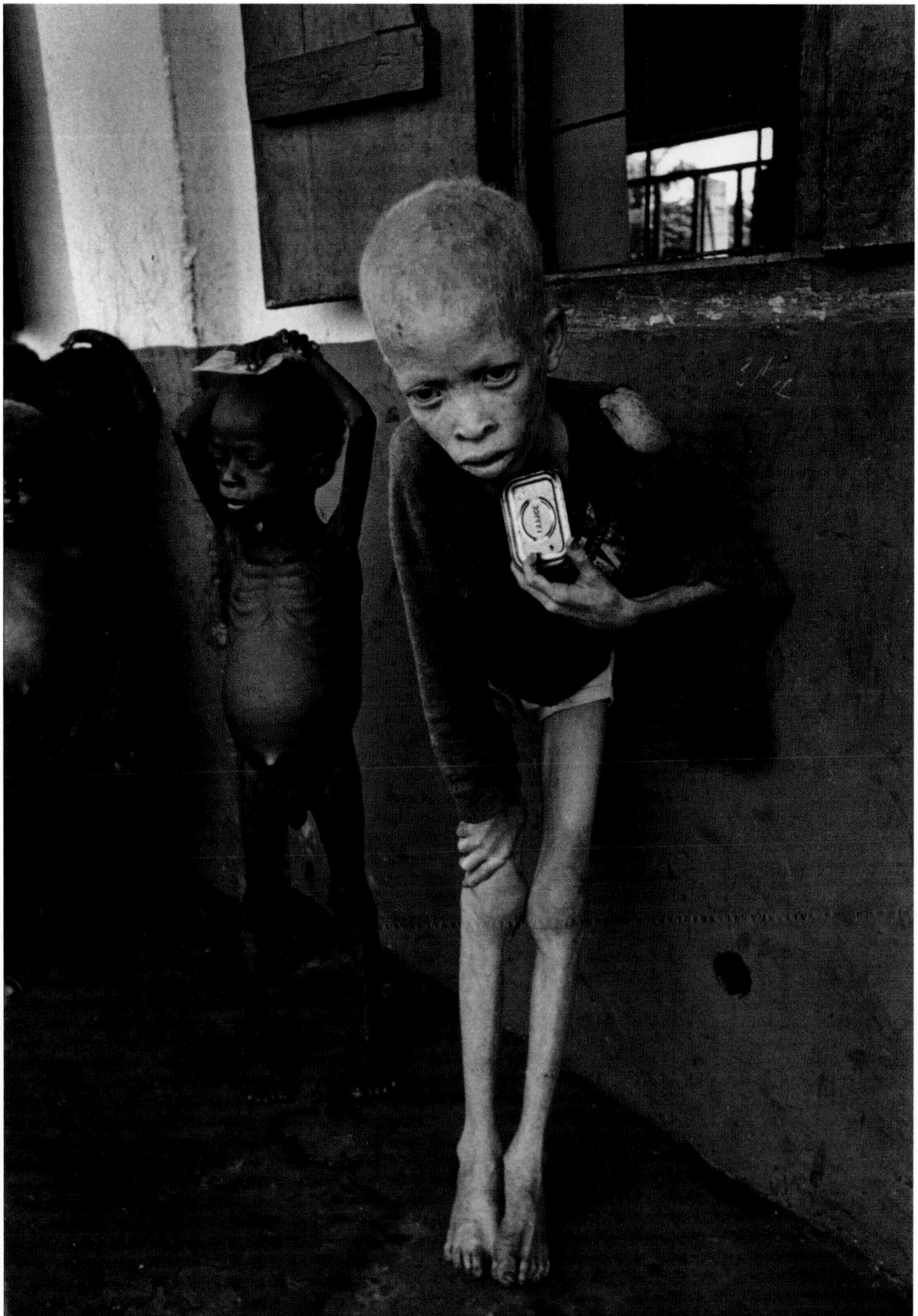

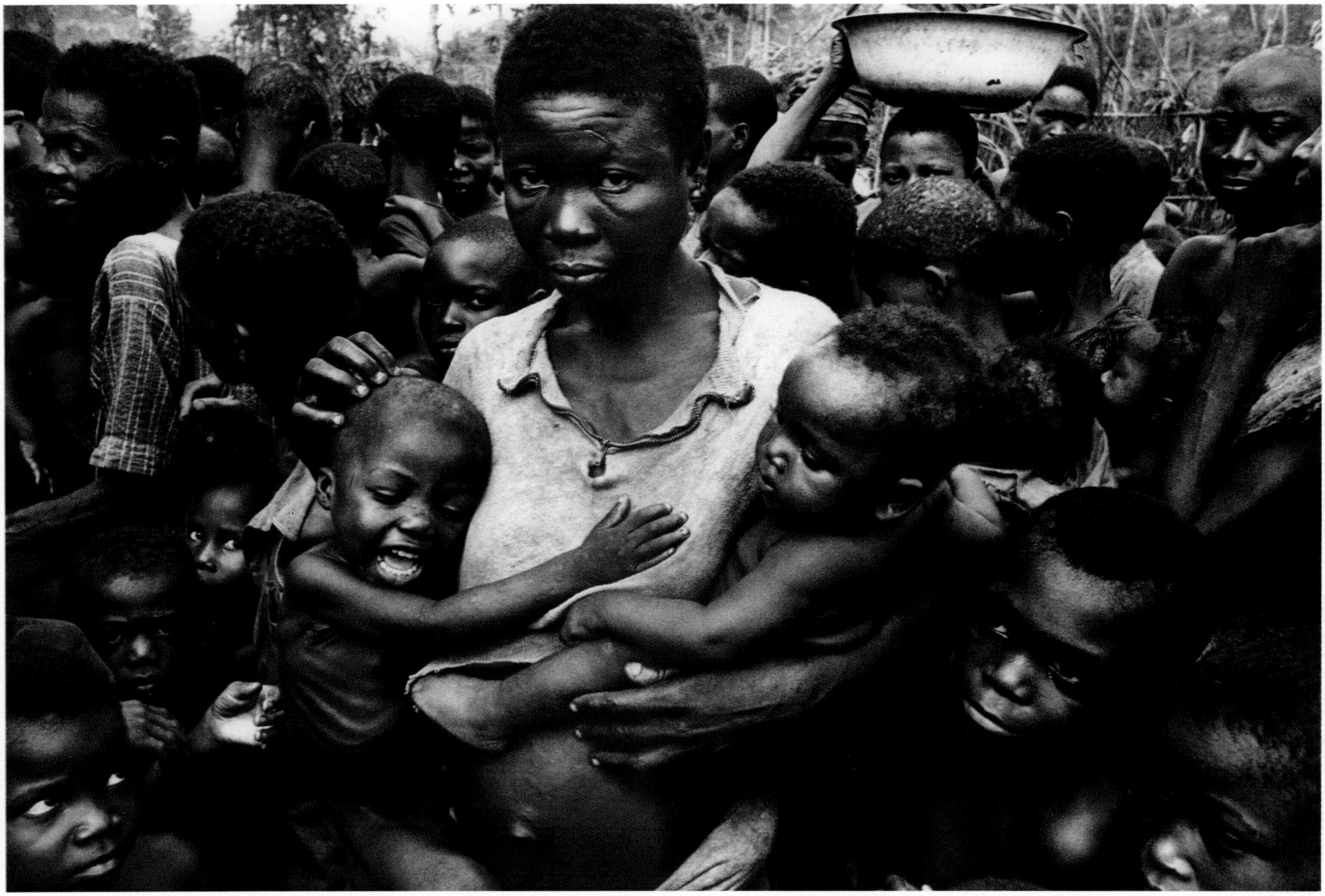

ABOVE: A food distribution centre in Biafra during the failed secession war with Nigeria in 1968.

PETER MAGUBANE

Peter Magubane once said, "I knew I could use my camera to tell the world how apartheid operated. I was demonstrating with the camera." Throughout a long career he has paid a high price, more than once, for being prepared to observe and record the harsh realties of life under apartheid. He has spent long periods in solitary confinement, been shot at, been badly beaten up by the South African police on several occasions and in 1969 was banned from taking pictures for five years. Yet Magubane was never deterred from carrying out what he regards as his mission. When he was prohibited from carrying a camera, he took pictures with his trusted Leica, which he hid in a hollowed-out Bible. On another occasion he smuggled his camera into a trial concealed inside a loaf of bread.

Despite his treatment by what were in effect white oppressors, his photographs are always balanced. He documents the brutality of the black kangaroo courts, which often resulted in burnt corpses of supposed informers, and he also took sympathetic photographs of ordinary Afrikaners. He has been present at most of the key moments in the post-war South Africa and his images are part of the country's dark history. Thankfully, light does emerge toward the end of Magubane's photojournalistic career with the release of Nelson Mandela and the emergence of a new South Africa. Technically, Magubane was solid, rather than outstanding, but in terms of commitment, resourcefulness and sheer courage, he is one of the key figures in post-war photojournalism. Steven Sack, Director of Arts, Culture and Heritage for the City of Johannesburg, says of his legacy, "Every attempt at documenting the daily lives and regular confrontations endured by black South Africans was a risky and dangerous activity. Peter Magubane placed himself between the apartheid state and the black majority in order to report on and capture the many instances of the ongoing abuse. These photographs kept the spirit of resistance alive. They inspired many others to resist by giving a face to the courageous."

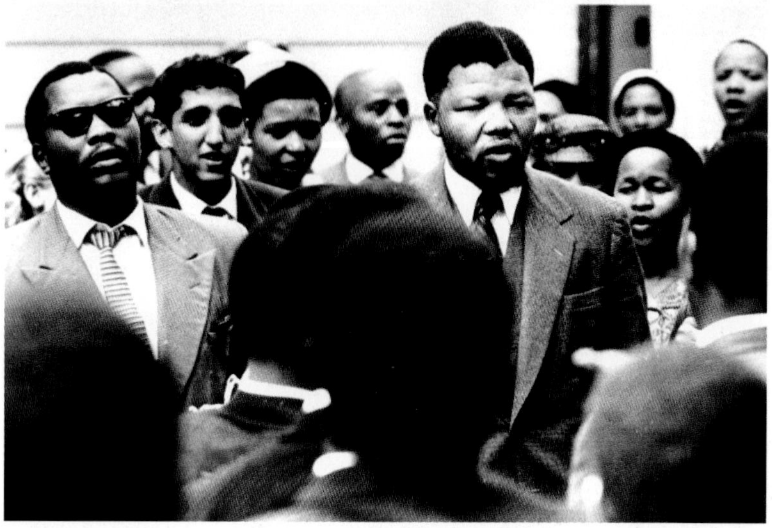

ABOVE: During the first treason trial in Johannesburg, South Africa, in 1956, the attorney Nelson Mandela (centre), with his wife Winnie behind him, stands singing in the midst of a group of his co-defendants. These trials made Mandela an international figure. His charismatic presence dominates this image.

RIGHT: This photograph of ranks of coffins at the mass funeral for victims killed in demonstrations in Sharpeville, South Africa, in 1960 is one of the most famous images from this era and it alerted the world to the horrors of the apartheid regime.

BELOW LEFT: Magubane, always on the front-line, captured this image of black South Africans setting up a barricade by setting fire to tyres in the street during a protest against apartheid during Election Day in 1989.

BELOW RIGHT: On Election Day in 1989 South African police killed 14-year-old Patric Mueller. In this photograph throngs of mourners, including South African clergy, comfort the distraught mother at the funeral.

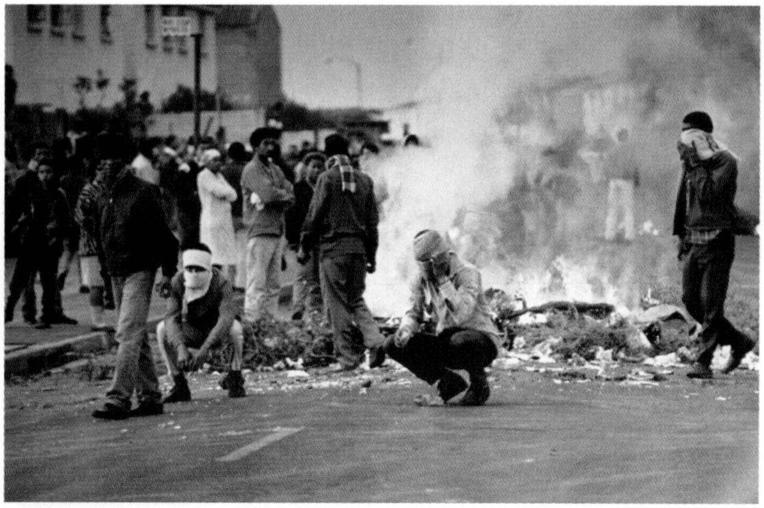

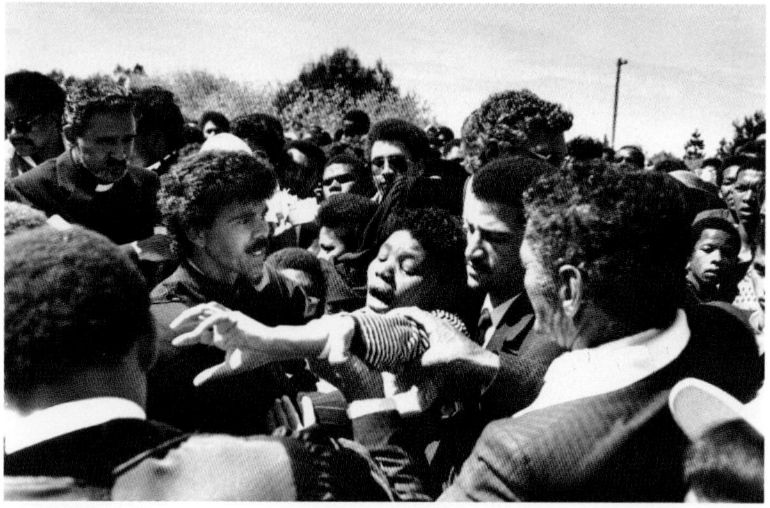

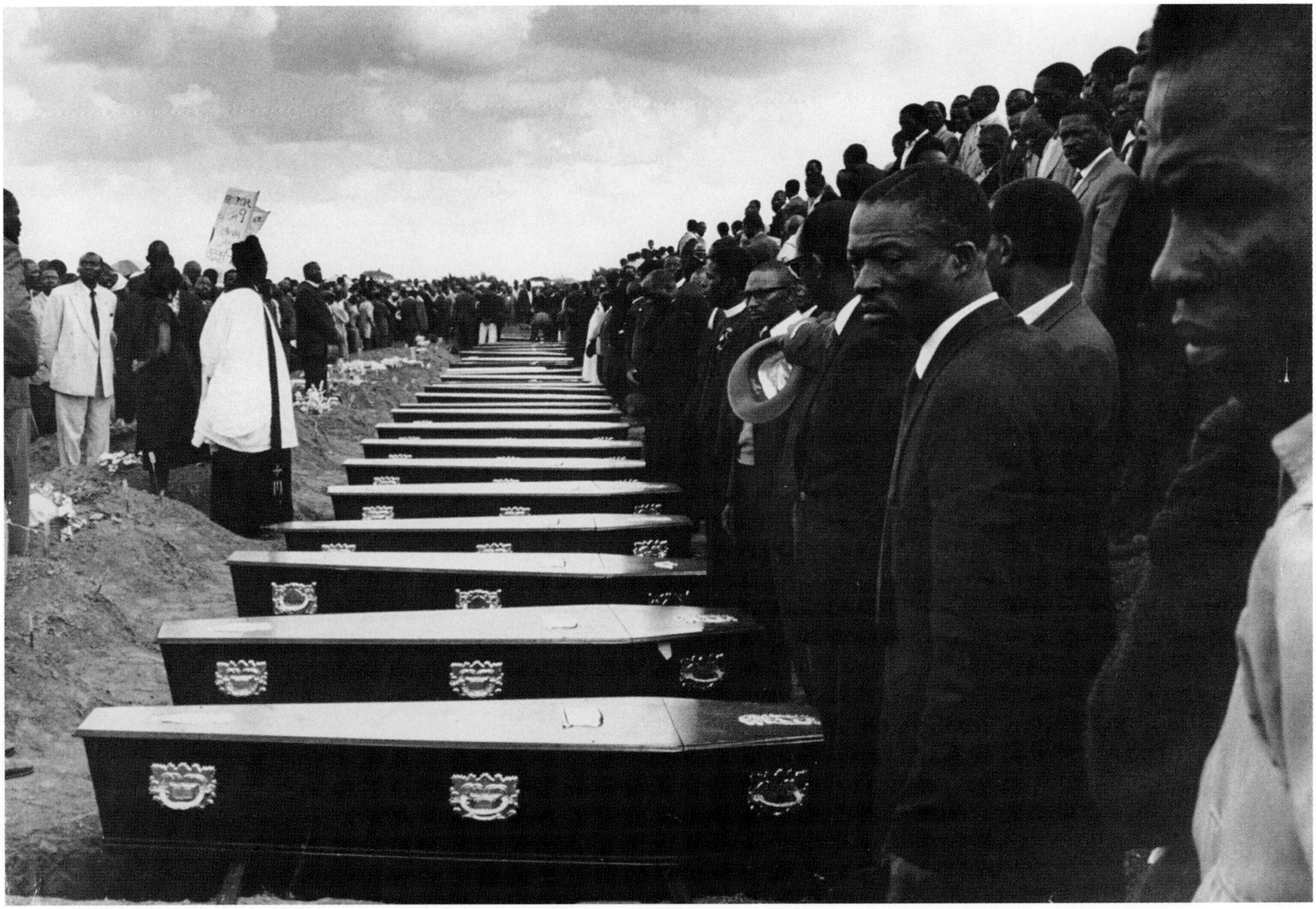

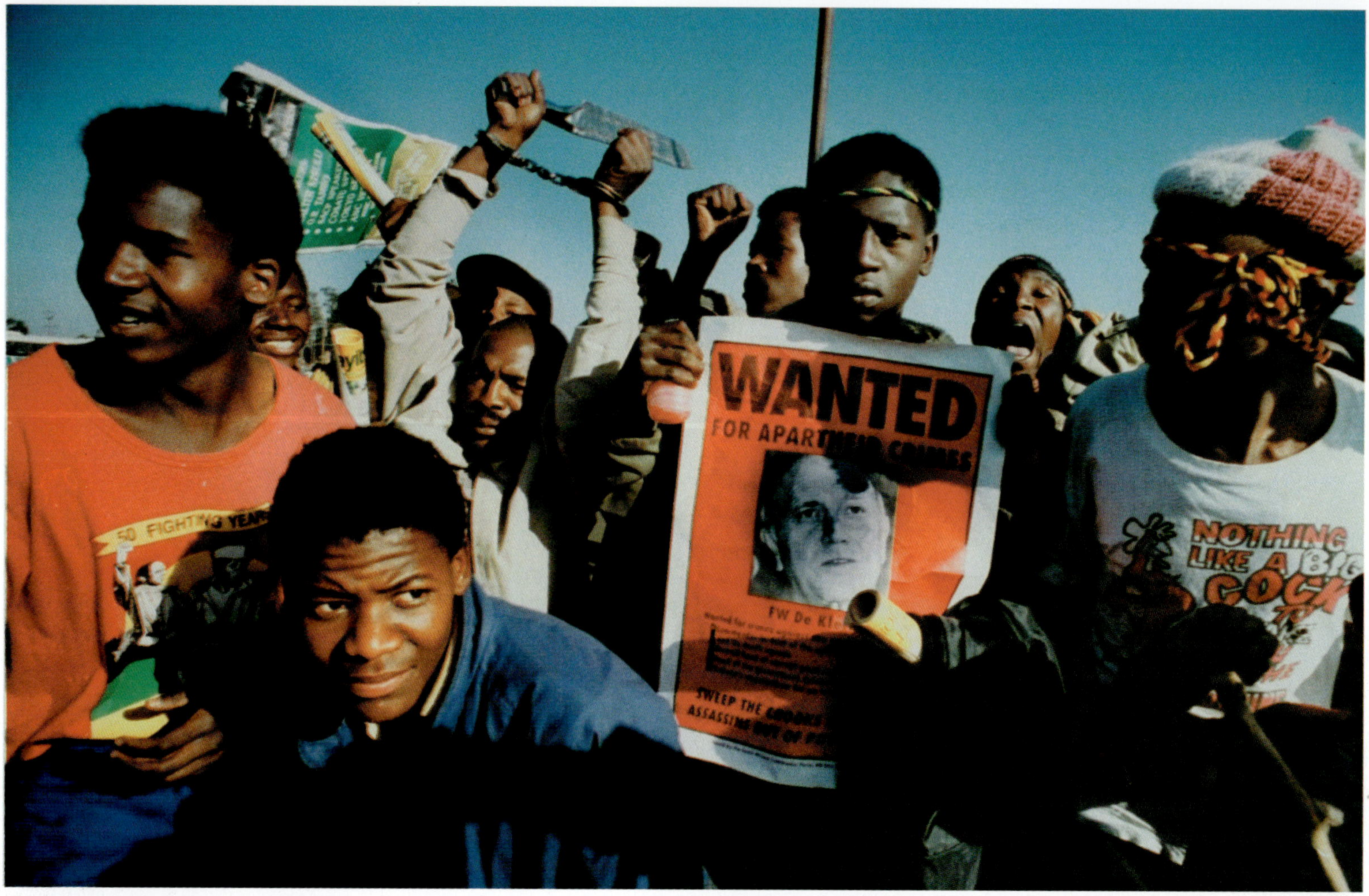
WANTED
50 FIGHTING YEARS
NOTHING

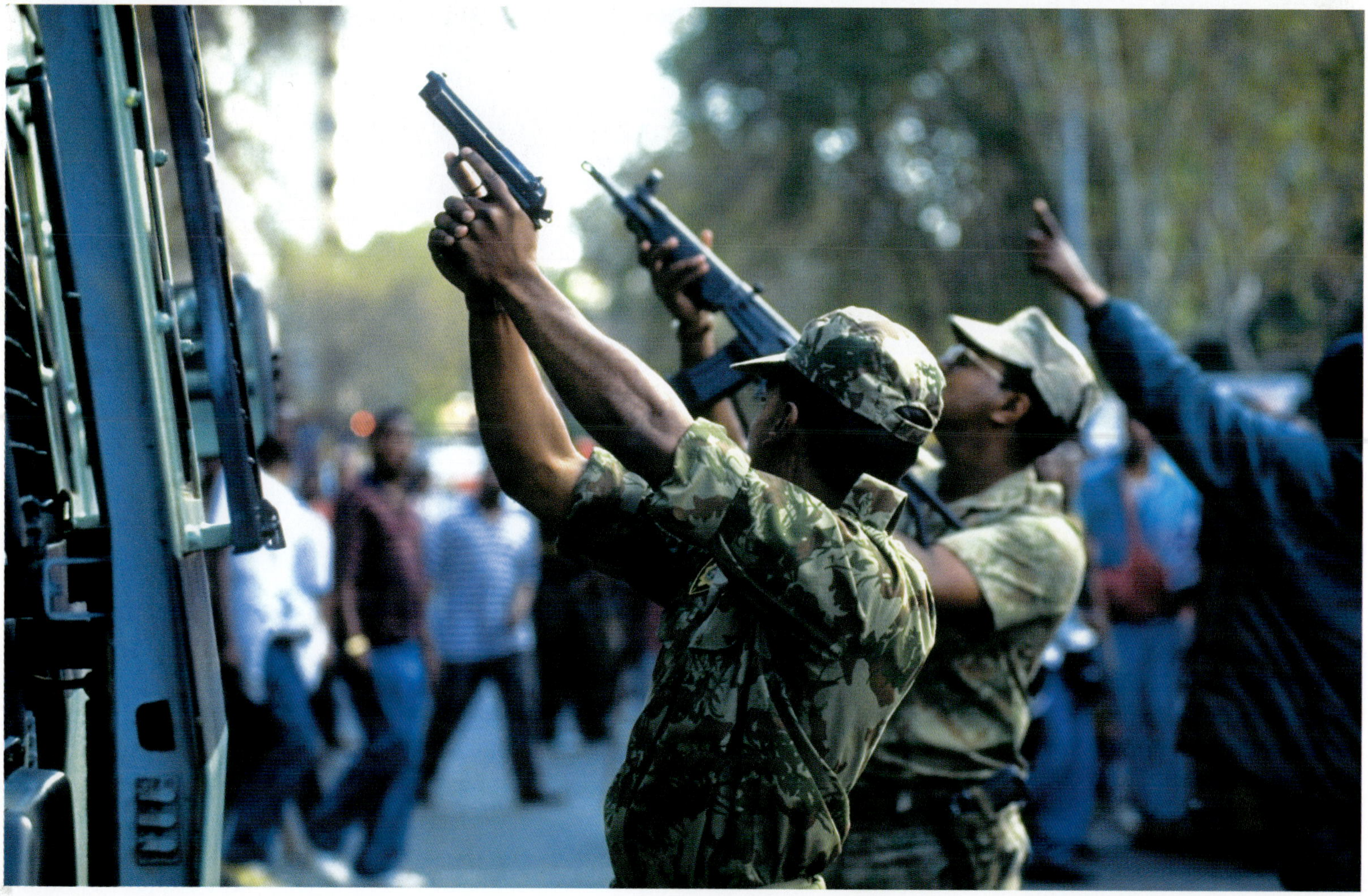

LEFT: On 17 June 1992 armed KwaMadal Zulu hostel residents – enraged by persistent attacks on Inkatha Freedom Party supporters – fell upon the Vaal Triangle township of Boipatong and massacred some 45 men, women and children. In this photograph we see people protesting against the massacre. Magubane expertly captures their anger and sense of injustice. He never sanitized the struggle for freedom and always saw it in grey terms.

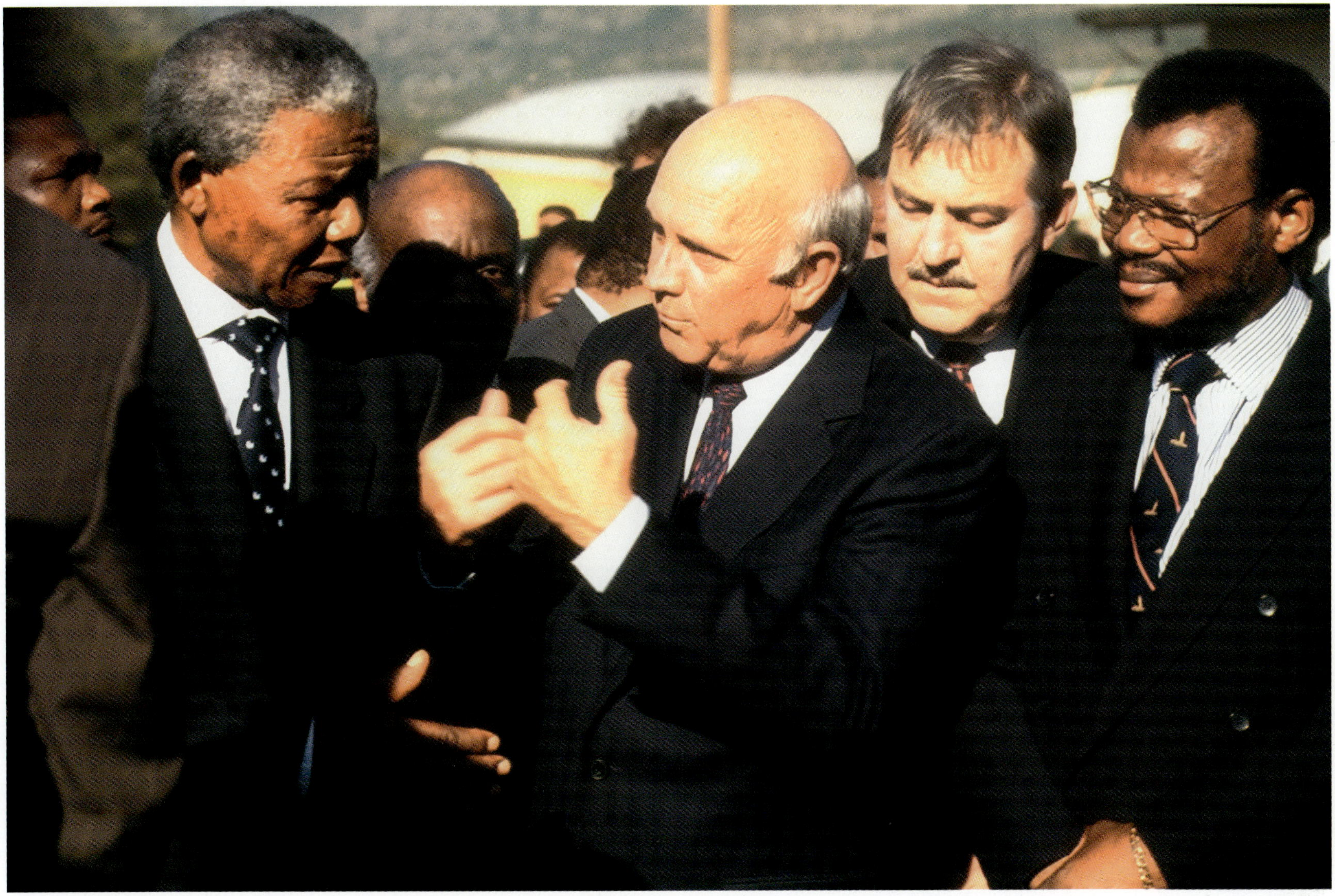

LEFT: In Johannesburg, South Africa, 1994, police return fire during a deadly mêlée started by gunmen firing on protesting Zulus, with ensuing gun battles between Zulus, ANC and the police.

ABOVE: It was a major coup for Magubane to capture all these men from different ends of the political spectrum and tribes in one image during the election campaign of 1994. The rival candidates are from left to right, ANC leader Nelson Mandela, President de Klerk, Inkatha Zulu leader Buthelezi, with former minister Pik Botha behind them.

ALEX MAJOLI

BELOW AND RIGHT: These extremely disturbing photographs are from Majoli's most famous project, *Leros*. These seriously mentally ill people are being left to fend for themselves in a squalid and inhumane environment. Despite the religious iconography in the main photograph, it is clear that no charity or compassion has ever touched this man. The starkness of the room accentuates the man's despair. In the portrait on the right, the composition conveys a sense of claustrophobia.

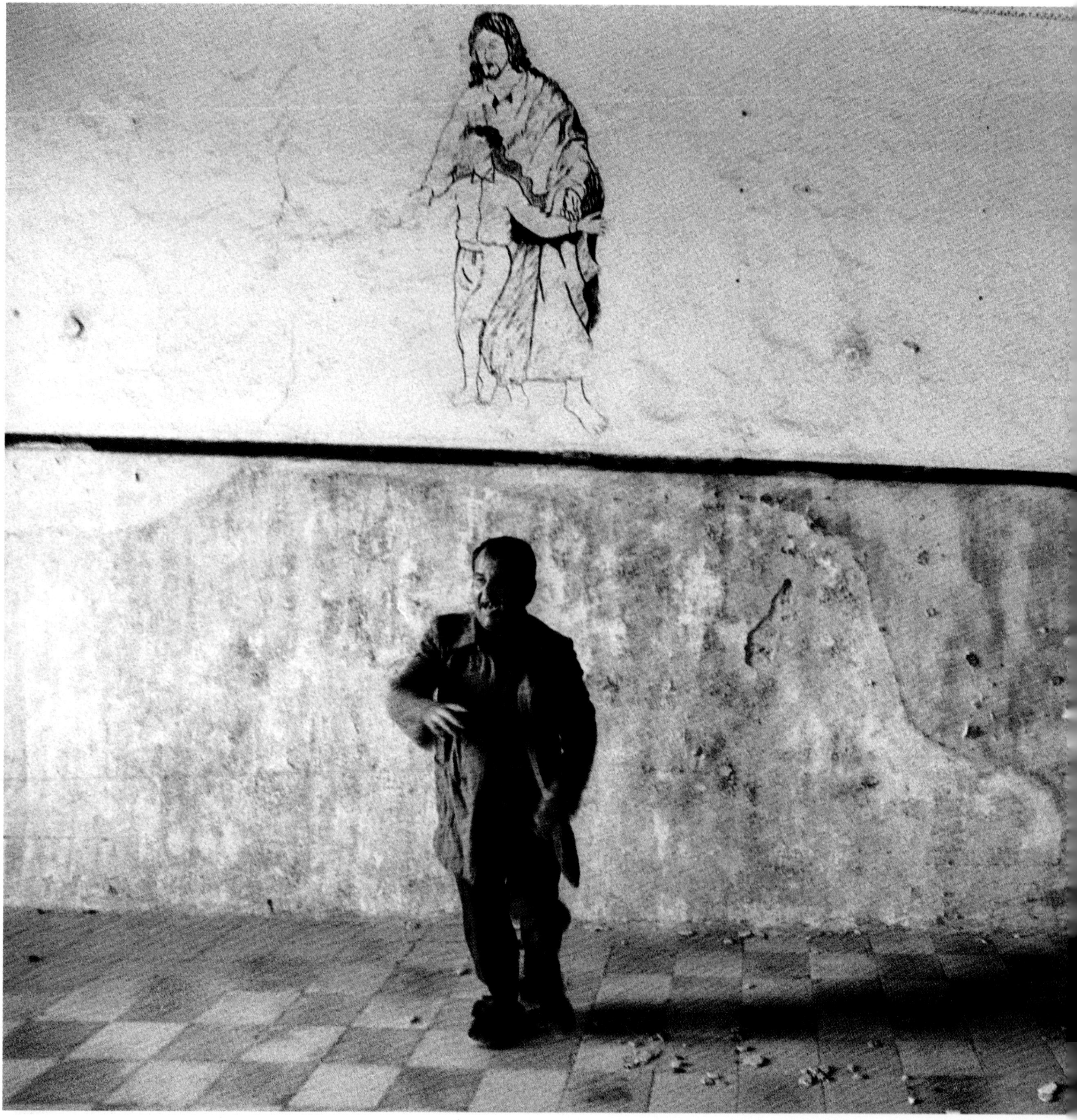

A Greek Island is normally associated with beauty and serenity. The Greek island that Alex Majoli came across in the mid-1990s, however, was so extreme and barbaric that it compares with Stalin's Gulags, albeit on a smaller scale. Leros was home to an asylum for the insane that, in a former life, had been a political prison. Its occupants were now Greece's most seriously mentally disturbed cases, casually shipped by the psychiatric hospitals to this squalid and inhumane hellhole. Majoli arrived at the point when the European Union was looking to close down Leros. His project looks at the conditions in which these poor people lived and their subsequent, gradual rehabilitation back into island life. In various shades of black and grey, Majoli documents their physical and mental anguish, the squalor, the cruelty of the staff (local goat herders, rather than doctors or nurses) who controlled the patients with brute terror. His images are so claustrophobic, unflinching and relentless that they hit the senses at full tilt. You don't just see the asylum, you smell the stench and hear the screams. Chinks of light, however, start to illuminate some of the photographs, as the hospital closes down and the patients start on their unsteady journey back into society.

Since this project, Majoli has covered most of the key events of the past 10 years. Everywhere he goes, he produces remarkable stories, but he seems to be at his best when he is working in the more wild and uncompromising parts of Europe: Albania, the former Yugoslavia and of course Leros. *Newsweek*'s International Photo Editor, Jamie Wellford, calls Majoli a visionary, but a modest one: "Alex has never claimed to have the absolute photograph when I have spoken to him about an assignment. On the contrary, he has frequently apologized for not having that moment, which must be understood as his continuing search for the picture, for the story and for the eternal." Long may Majoli search.

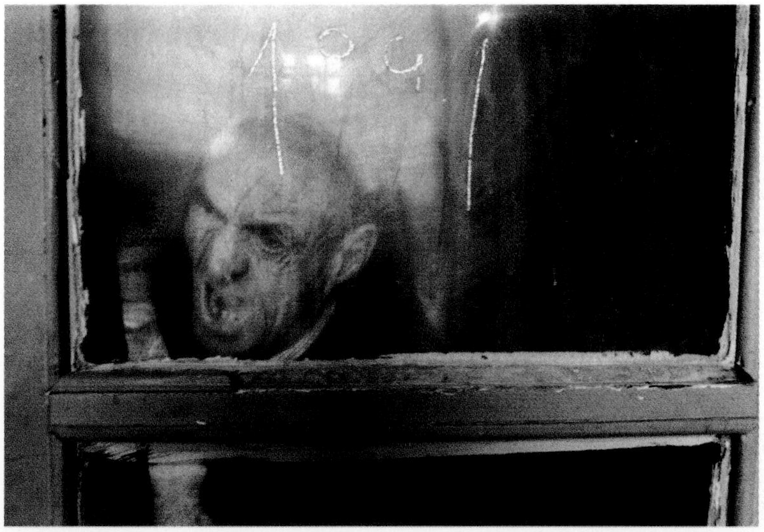

BELOW: In 1997 this 10-year-old boy, photographed in Scutari hospital, Albania, lost a leg after stepping on a landmine near the town's military barracks. In the words of a photo editor who works with Majoli, "He strikes the chord of humility every time he makes a picture".

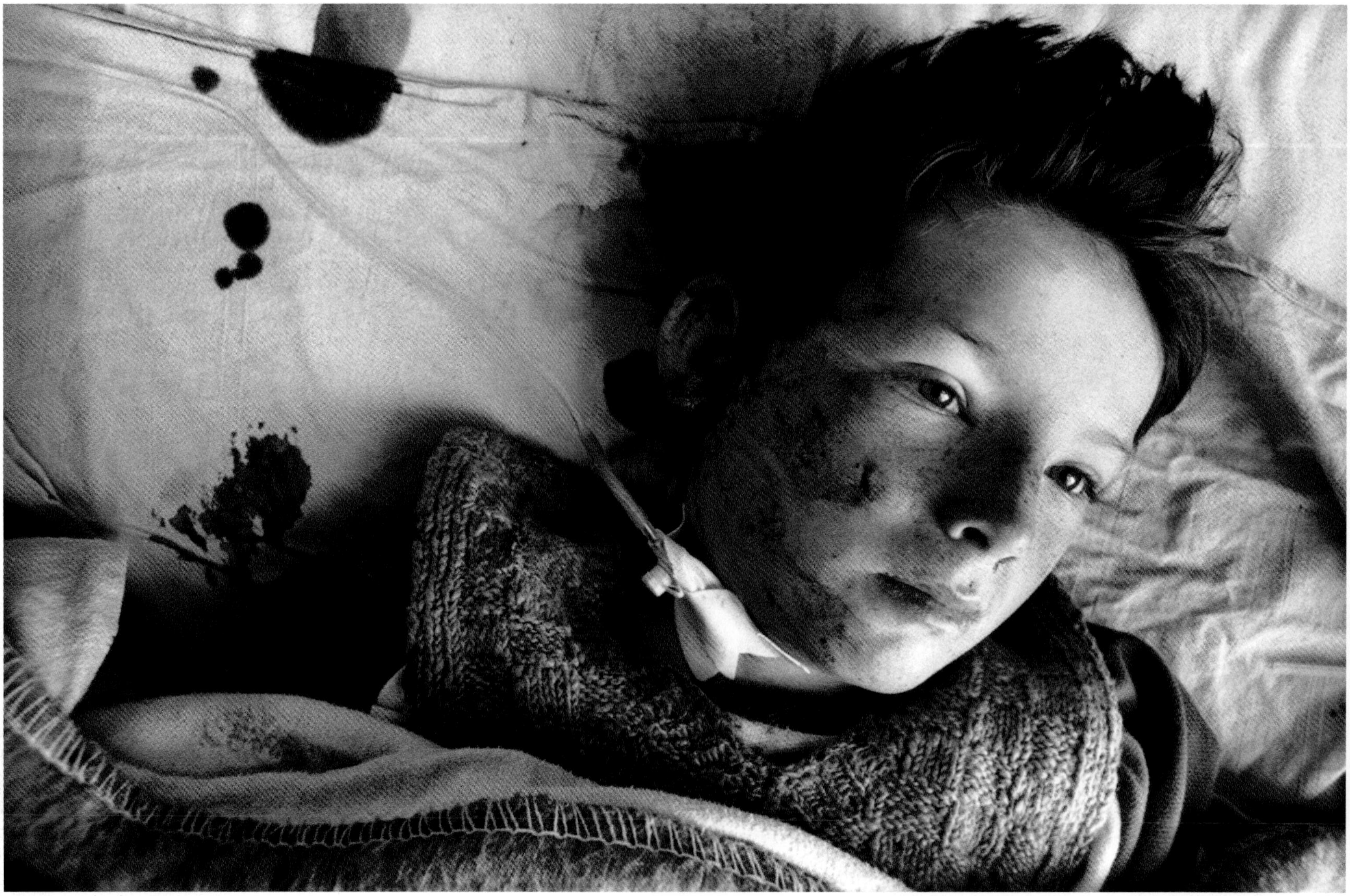

RIGHT TOP: After two attempts, a train carrying thousands of refugees from Albania crosses the Macedonian border in 1999. While there is hope for the refugees on the train, the reflection of the refugees still awaiting their fate is heart-wrenching, a fine example of Majoli's ability to extract something unique from a situation.

RIGHT BOTTOM: A mother and son battle the elements and the landscape as they return from work in Albania,1998. There is a tension between the subjects' stoicism and the dramatic, ominous sky.

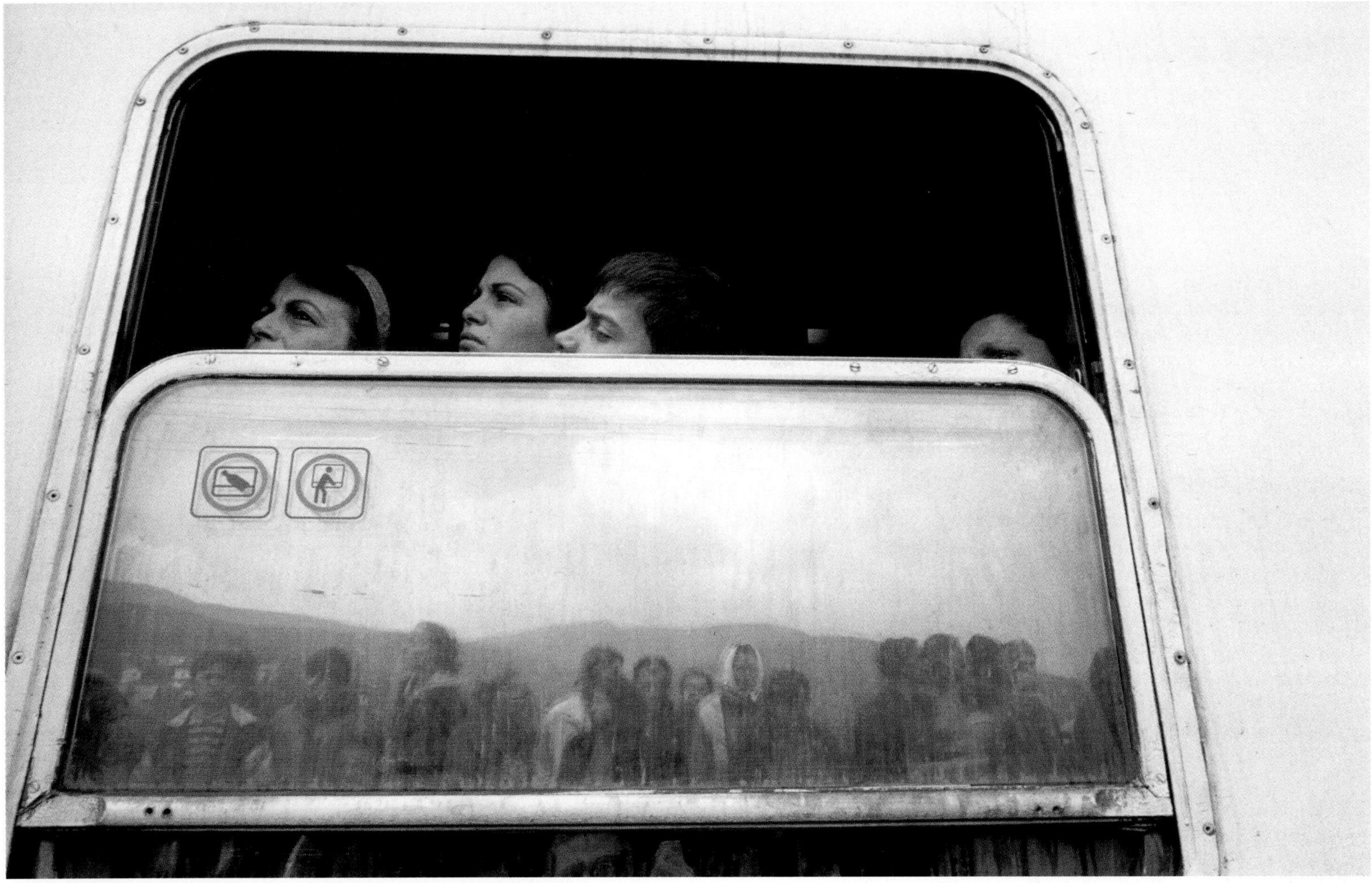

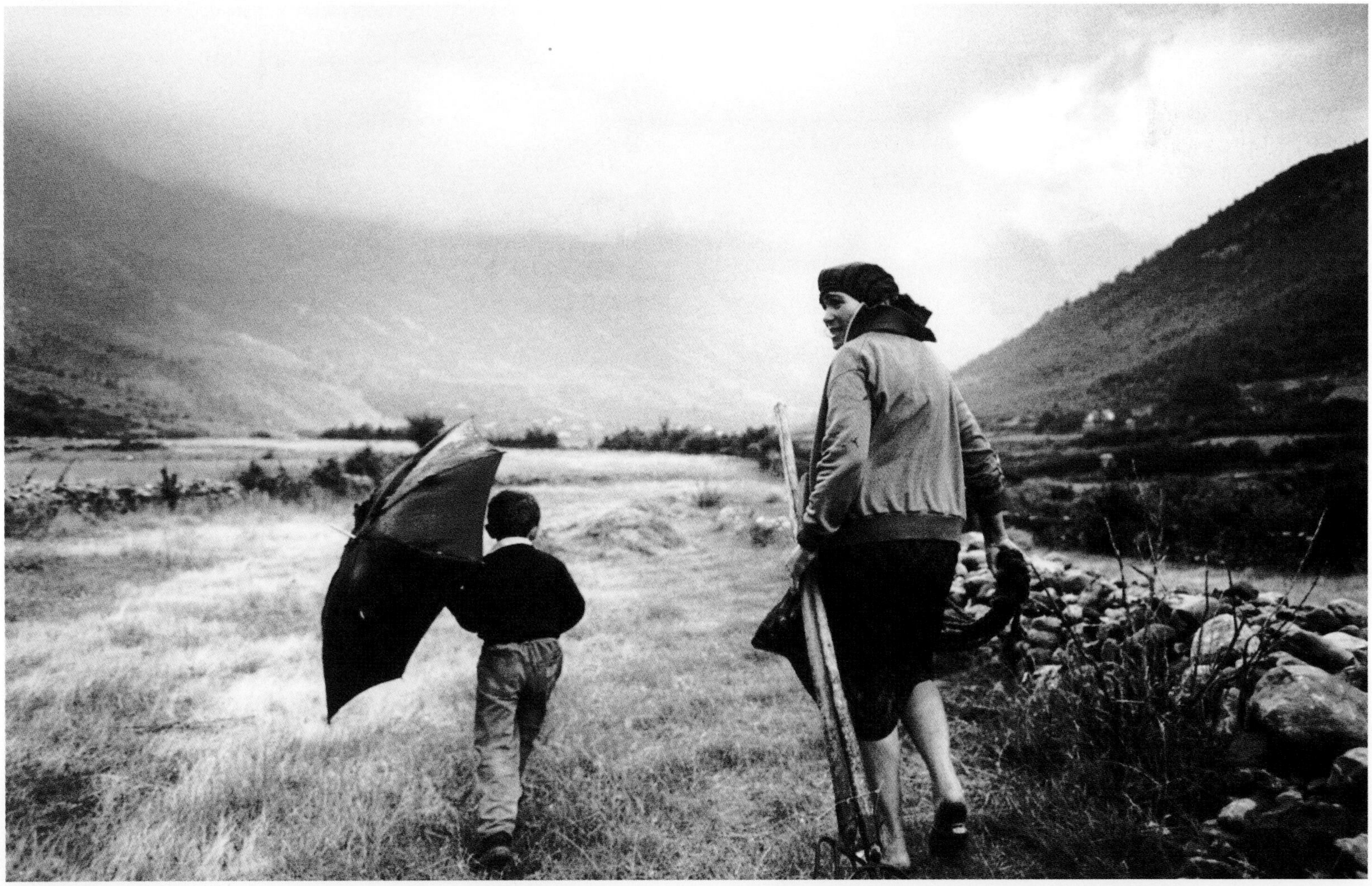

MARY ELLEN MARK

BELOW: Lillie with her rag doll in Pike Street, Seattle, Washington. Taken in 1983, this is from Mark's seminal essay on the troubled homeless children who survive through hustling, stealing and prostitution. The girl is probably not much older than 12, but there is a look in her eyes of an innocence lost, despite the fact that she is clutching a doll.

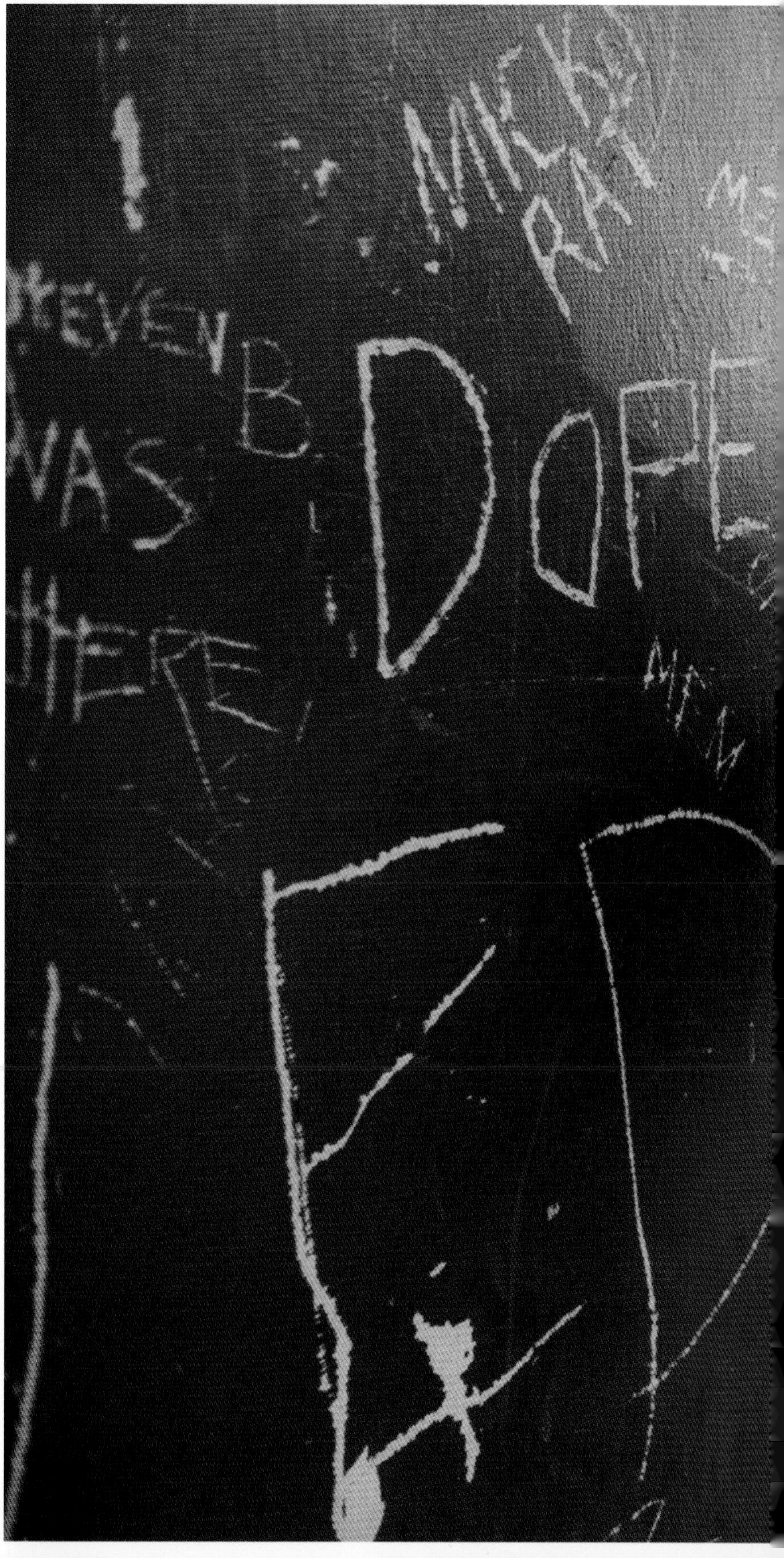

Mary Ellen Mark has been the USA's leading female photojournalist for the past 25 years. She does not so much simply photograph a story, but immerses herself in it, like a method actor tackling a difficult role. In the late 1970s, for example, she lived in a mental hospital in Oregon with the patients, while she worked on a photo essay about the institution. Throughout her career she has been attracted to photographing people on the fringes of society: prostitutes, the mentally ill, the homeless, the helpless, drug addicts and the people who simply do not get the breaks. In her unflinching black-and-white beautifully composed images, she asks us to acknowledge, but never to sentimentalize, her subjects' harsh lives. Her photographs are often stark, with little to distract the viewer from the stories they tell. She is very much the antithesis of the overly complex or "arty" photographer, and her best images combine reportage with classic portraiture, relying on strong eye contact between the viewer and the subject.

She has produced so many remarkable essays over the years that it is hard to pinpoint one, but it is perhaps her story on Seattle's street children that is her greatest. These children were surviving on the streets through hustling, pimping and prostitution, so potentially it is a subject that could be mishandled and exploited. Mark, however, pitches it just perfectly. She got to know the children, they trusted her and the result is a melancholy and soulful collaboration between the kids and a photojournalist at the height of her powers. These images never flinch from the grim reality, but they are also filled with beauty. Buzz Hartson, head of the International Photography Center in New York, which has shown a huge retrospective of her photographs, says of Mark, "Her work is documentary with all of the social awareness and immediacy that implies, and it is also remarkably personal in its feel. It is clear from her work that her subjects are comfortable with her and this gives an intimacy that is rare in all but the best photography."

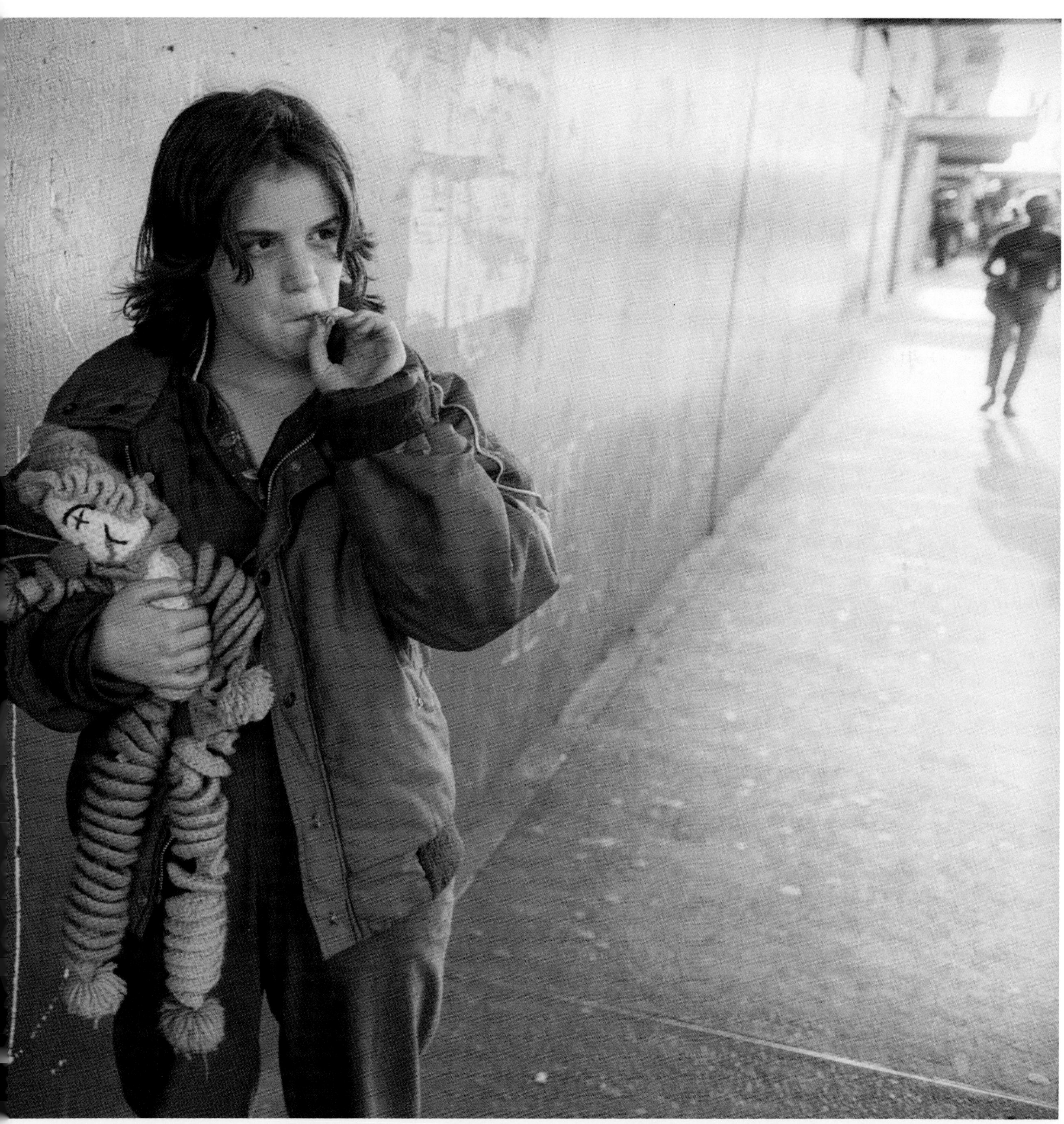

BELOW: The Damm family in their car in Los Angeles, 1987. Mark photographed this family for several years as the parents drifted in and out of various degrees of addiction and homelessness. This image became a symbol for an American underclass forgotten and largely ignored in the Reagan years.

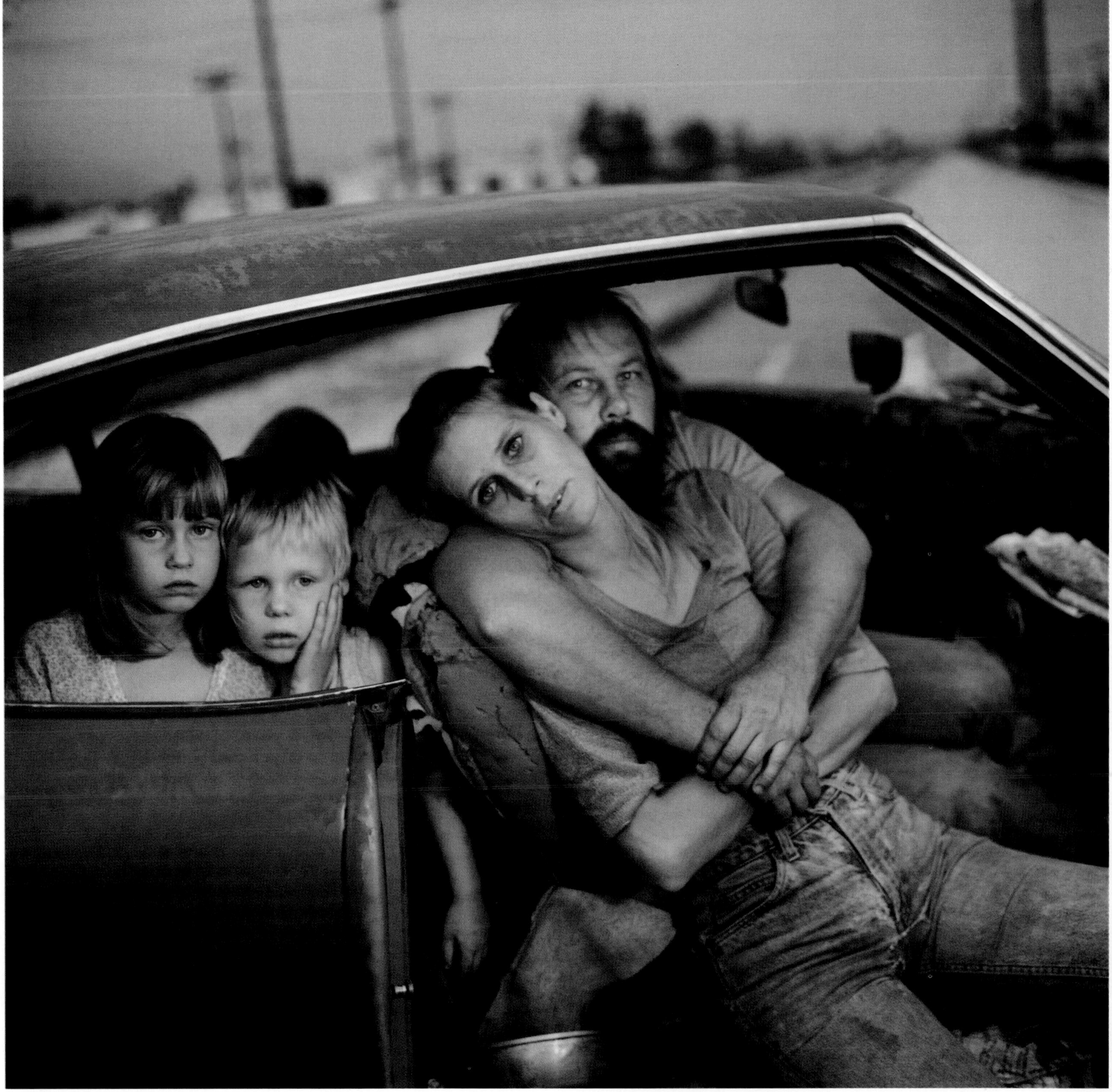

BELOW: This image, titled *Christopher with his Kitten, Sandgap*, was taken in Kentucky in 1990. Mark has always favoured strong and direct eye contact in her portraiture. This is taken from the essay *Rural Poverty*.

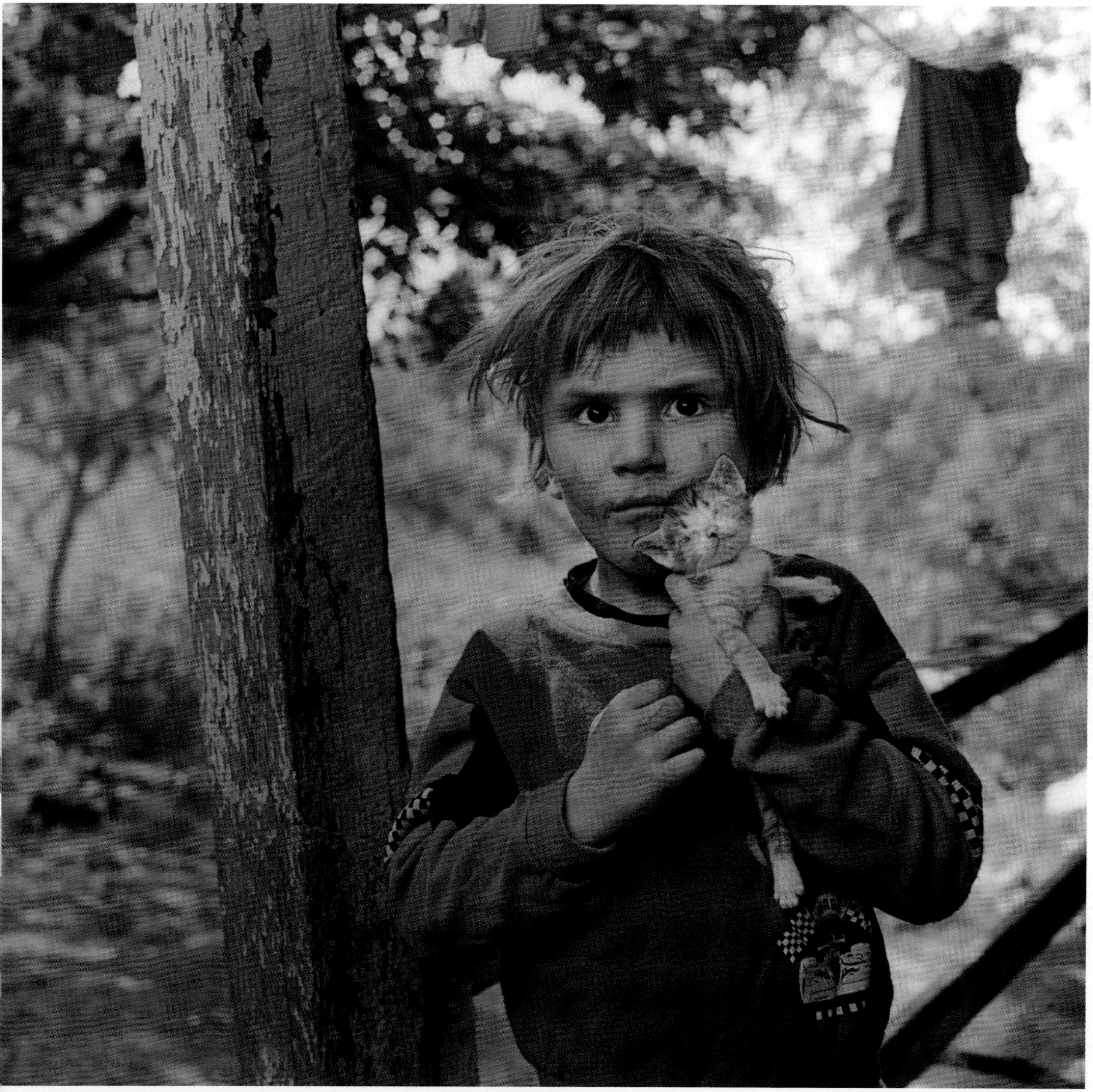

PETER MARLOW

BELOW: Marlow was sent on assignment to photograph the destruction of the rainforest in Borneo, Malaysia, in 1990. There is an arresting contrast between the innocent expression on the man's face and the havoc he has wreaked behind him.

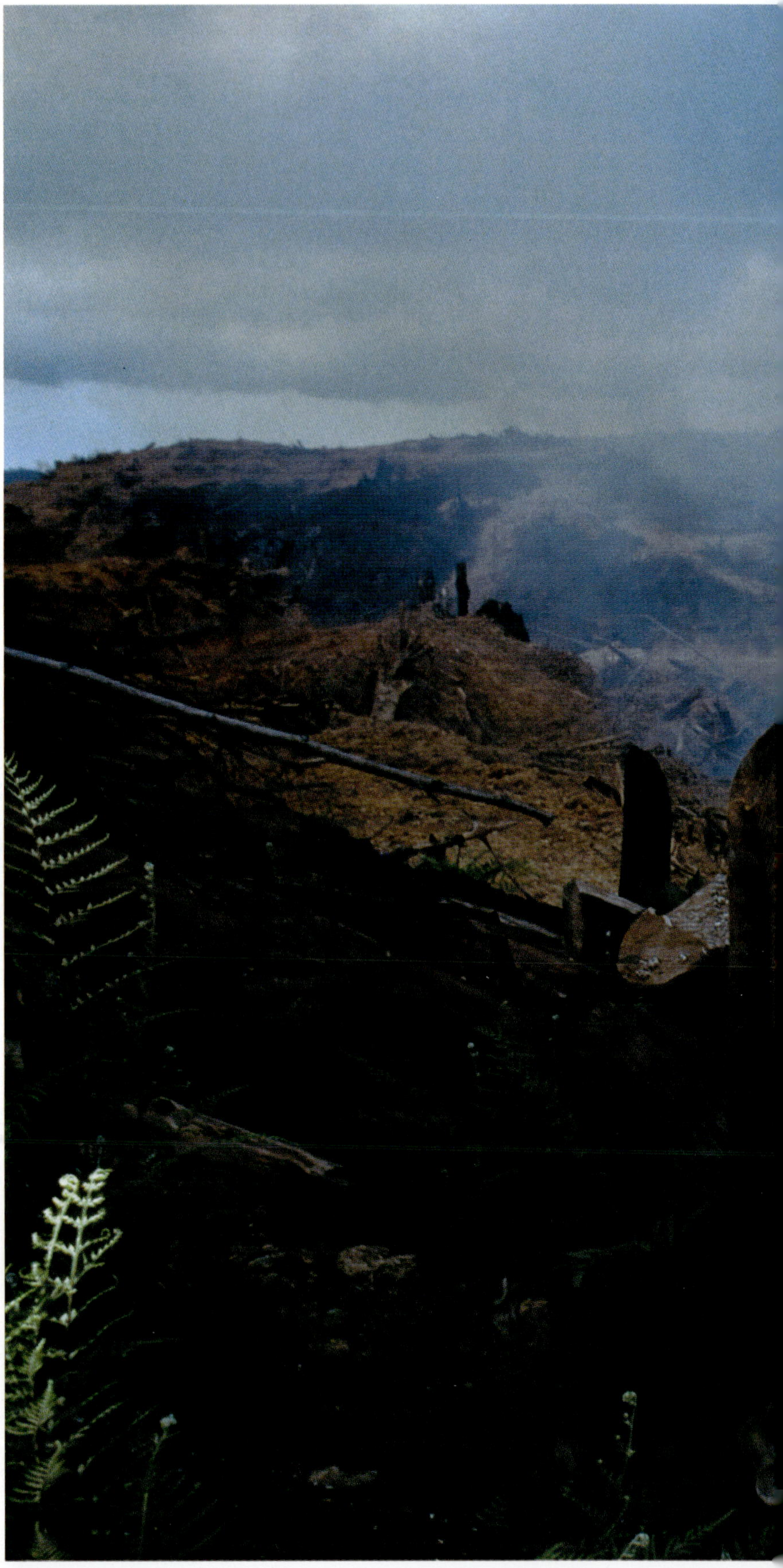

"A photojournalist's role is not to wear his or her heart on their sleeve, but respond to the world and then find their own response through photography, in a way that works for them," says Peter Marlow. What works for him are quiet and understated images that are finely balanced between informing the viewers and leaving them wanting to know more. He started out as a more traditional war photographer, but by his own admission he didn't fit in. The next phase in his career was humanist social documentary. He displayed compassion and soul in his project on the decline of Liverpool in the 1980s. The images here, from 1990, are part of an essay on the destruction of the rainforests of Northern Borneo, Malaysia, an assignment for the *Telegraph Magazine*. They were taken when his career was at something of a crossroads, when his Liverpool project had reached its natural conclusion. The brief he gave himself was to record what he saw using contrasting juxtaposition: "Rich versus poor, lush virgin rainforests versus forest burnt out by settlers to create palm oil plantations on land owned by Malaysian cabinet ministers who operated above the law," as he explains.

Marlow has an innate sense of how to narrate a story, when to make his points subtly and when to jolt the viewer. Loud or quiet, his photographs always resonate. In these images we see not just the physical destruction of this beautiful landscape, but also the erosion of the traditional hunter-gatherer lifestyle of the Penan Indian. The images are therefore dreadfully poignant; as Marlow says, "The loggers had moved in and cut down the Indians' world. They were being taught how to be farmers, they were trying so hard, but in the end you could sense that it was not going to work out." Marlow says that for him photojournalism does not have to be dramatic or dangerous. "It could be mundane, boring, undramatic and still have more to say about life than the more macho style of many lauded exponents of the genre." In Marlow's world, less is definitely more.

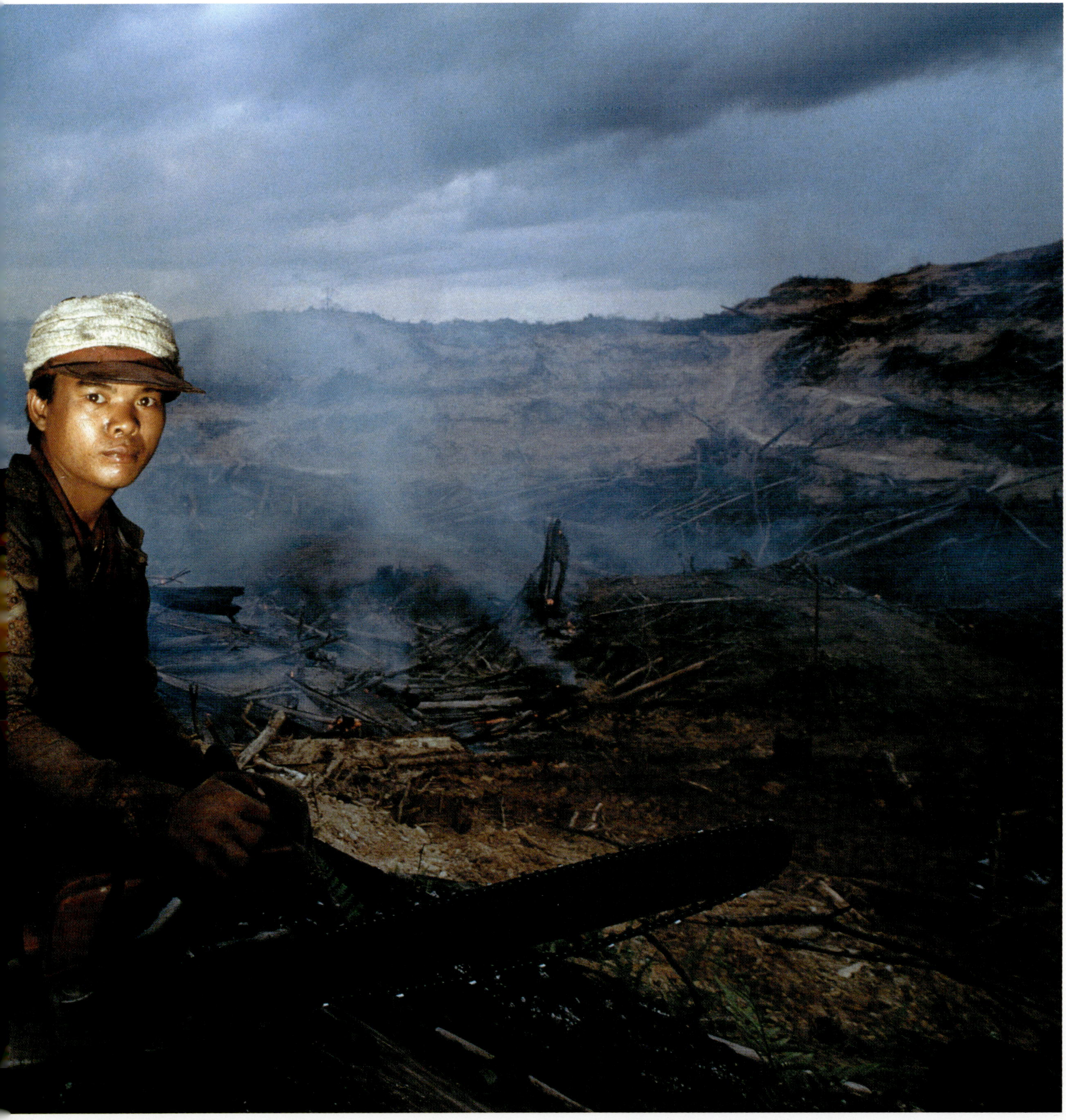

BELOW: These are members of the Penan tribe whose way of life is under threat from the rainforest devastation. Marlow has posed them formally against their natural habitat. The man on the right with his more Western dress style has already been sucked into the new world.

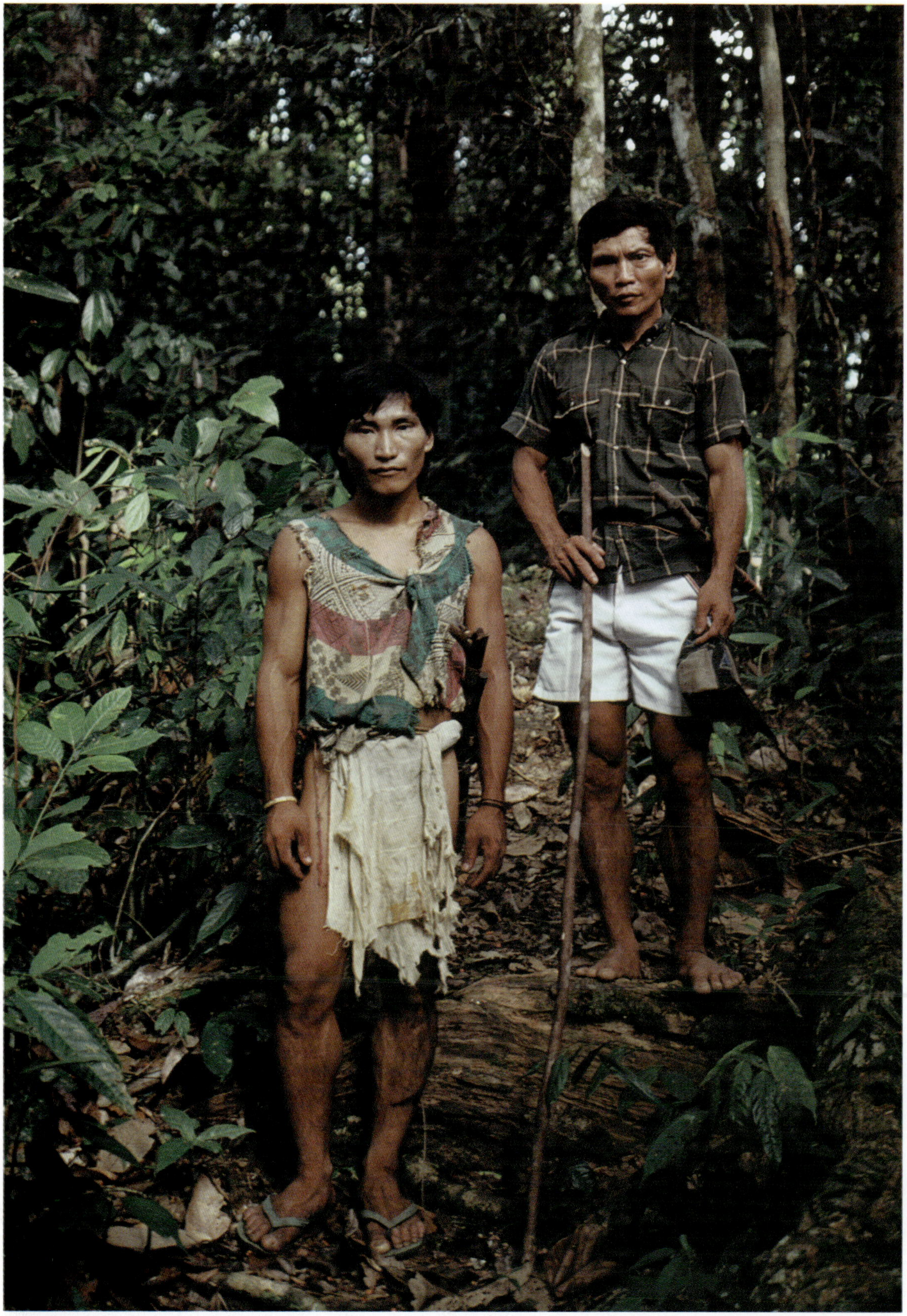

RIGHT TOP: The sheer scale and majesty of the trees being destroyed in the Baram River region of Borneo, Malaysia, is enhanced by this angle with the camera looking skywards.

RIGHT BOTTOM: Here the lowland forests are being burnt off before they are planted with cash crops.

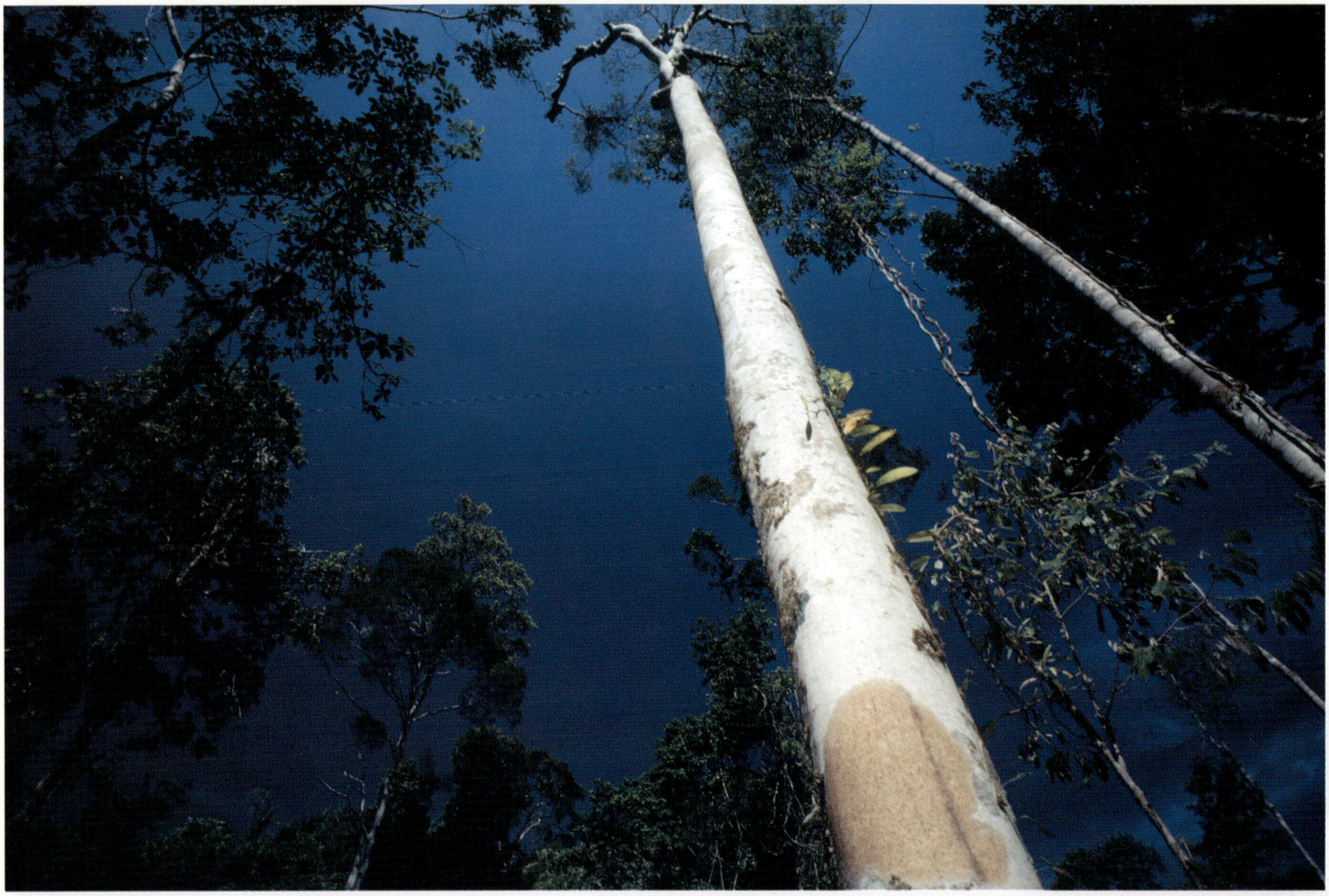

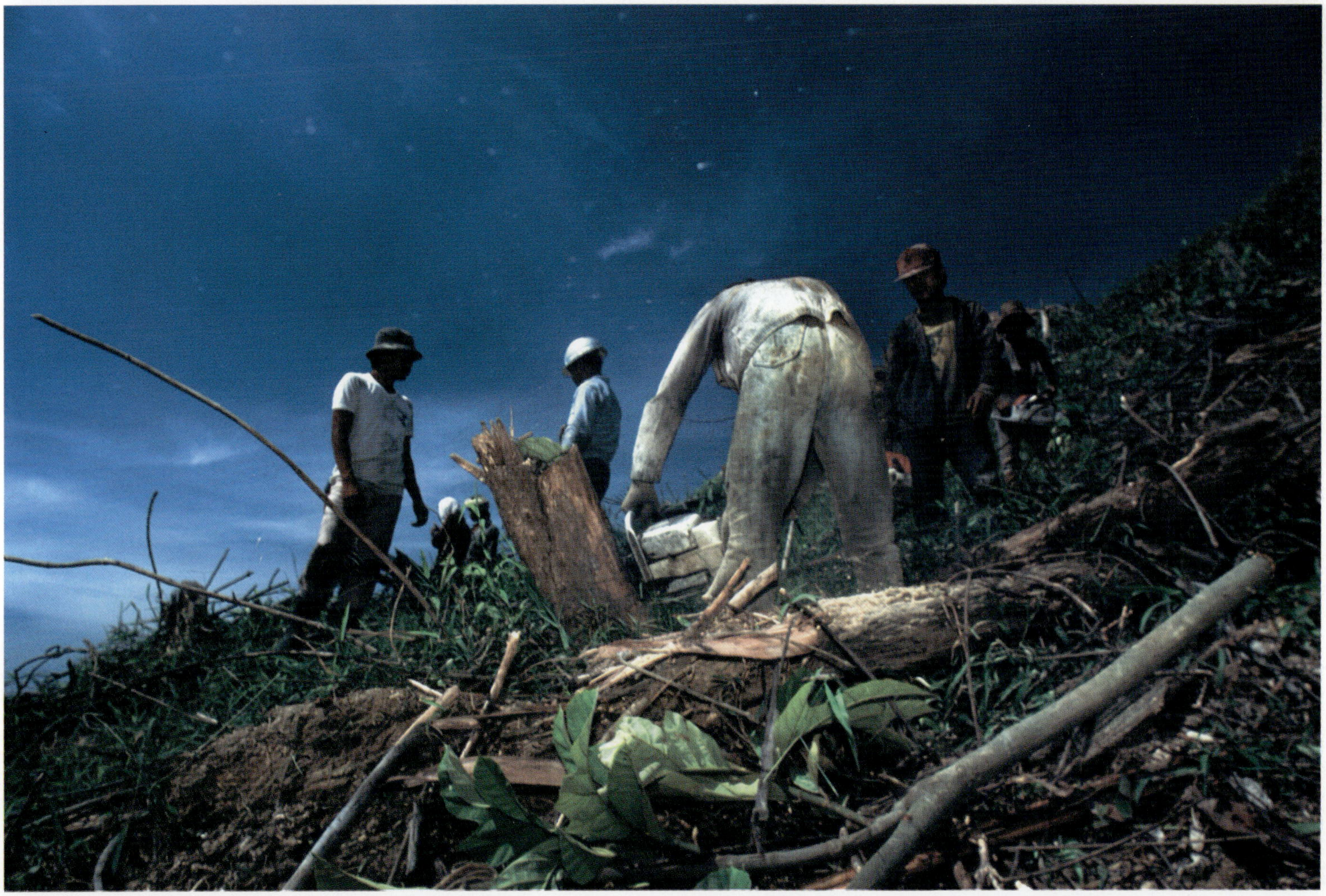

SUSAN MEISELAS

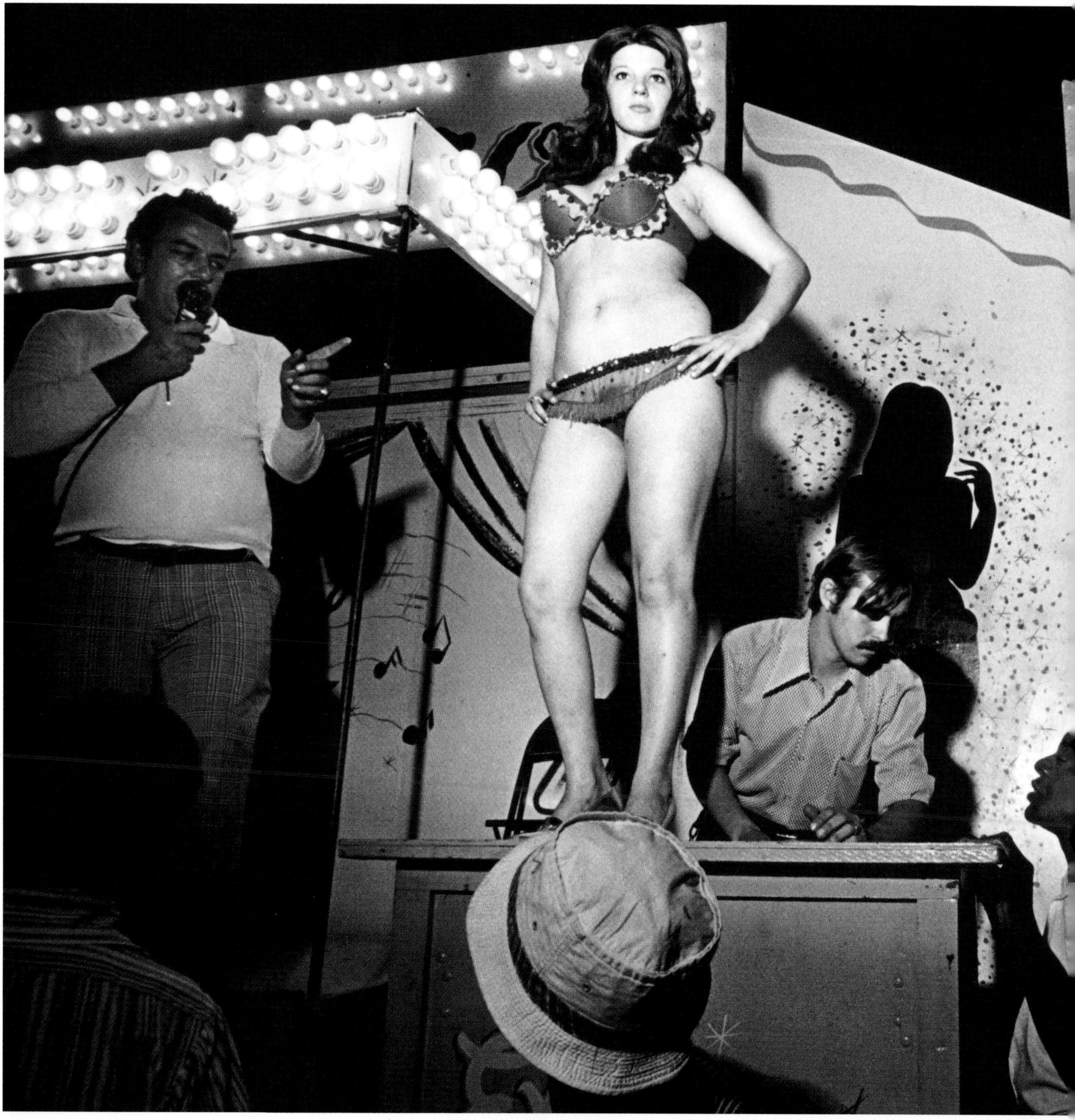

BELOW: This photograph of *Lena on the Bally Box* (Vermont, USA, 1973) is not so much about sex, as boredom. The only person in the photograph who looks vaguely animated is the man to the right of the frame who clearly doesn't want his photograph taken. His posture and look suggest that he is either the manager or the boyfriend of the stripper, maybe both.

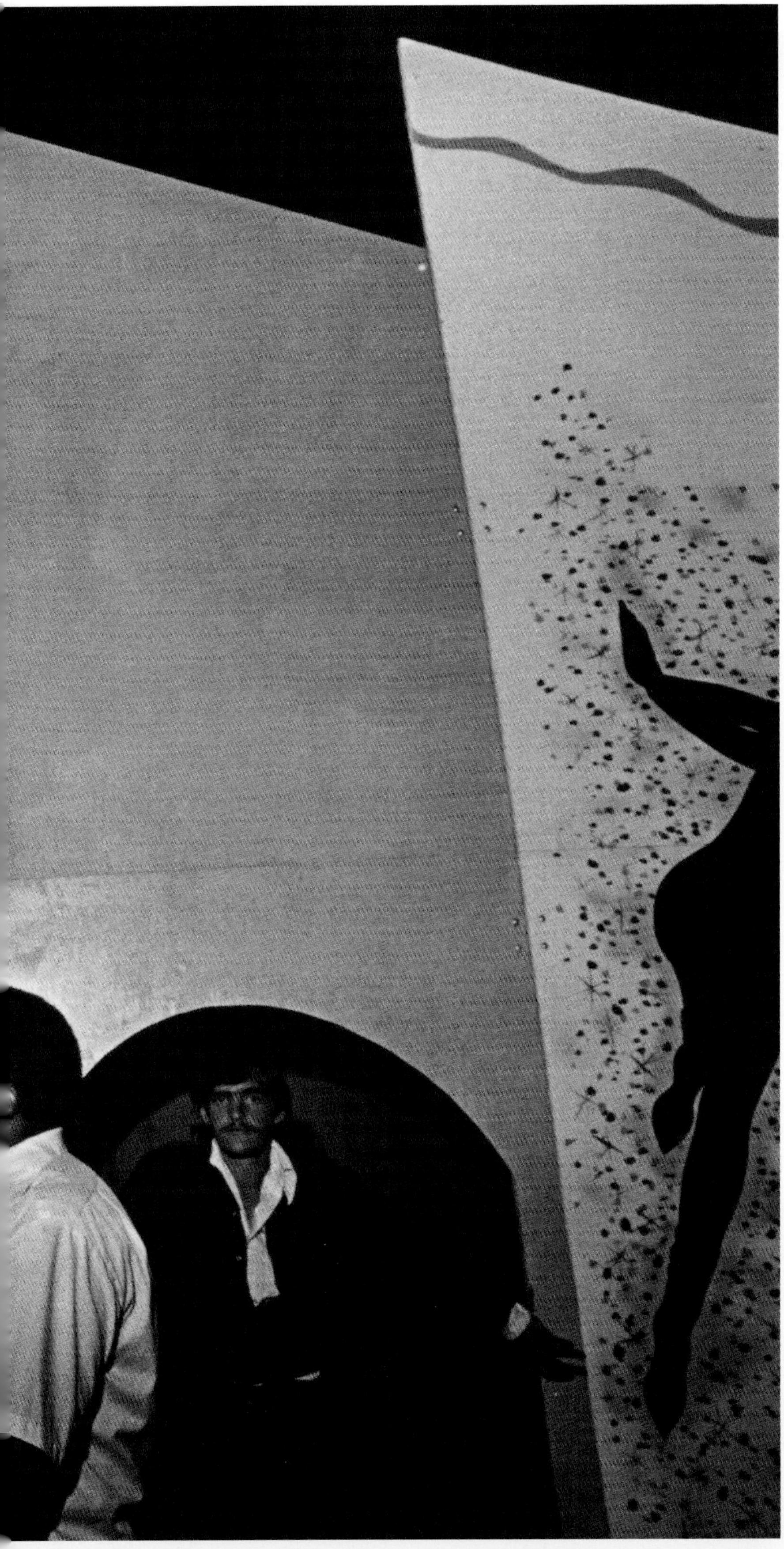

When Susan Meiselas flew to Nicaragua in 1978, she had never covered a major political story, she had little money, couldn't speak Spanish and had no prospects of any major commissions. Yet despite all of these things, Meiselas had a lot going for her. Her previous project, *Carnival Strippers*, although very different in content from a civil war, showed that she could present a coherent and complete narrative of a unique way of life. She was observant and unassuming. She could quietly watch the more mundane moments of carnival life, but also be alert to the strange, the quirky and the sleazy. Nicaragua presented a whole different set of challenges, including staying alive, but her methodology remained the same. She embedded herself in the story and used the virtues of time and patience to get the photographs. The brief that she gave herself was to document the struggle between the Sandinista rebels and the despised regime of President Somoza and its wider impact on a country that she grew to love. The story is very much told from the point of view of the rebels and Meiselas is clearly sympathetic to their cause. She spent months with the Sandinistas, training, eating and marching with them through the jungle, and subsequently recording the street fighting, where she gets perilously close to the action. Her use of colour is so vibrant and some of the fighters are so photogenic with their beards, scarves, hats and guns, that at times it seems like the struggle is being a touch glamorized. But Meiselas is too much of an intelligent photographer to fall into this trap for long, and we also see the inevitable consequences of war, the chaos and the suffering of the innocent. What also emerges from Nicaragua is the affection she has for the people, culture and landscape of the country. It is this affection that ultimately elevates her work to a level beyond straightforward war photography. She has created a complete portrait of a country in crisis, but her photographs suggest that a new Nicaragua, perhaps even a better one, will emerge from the devastation.

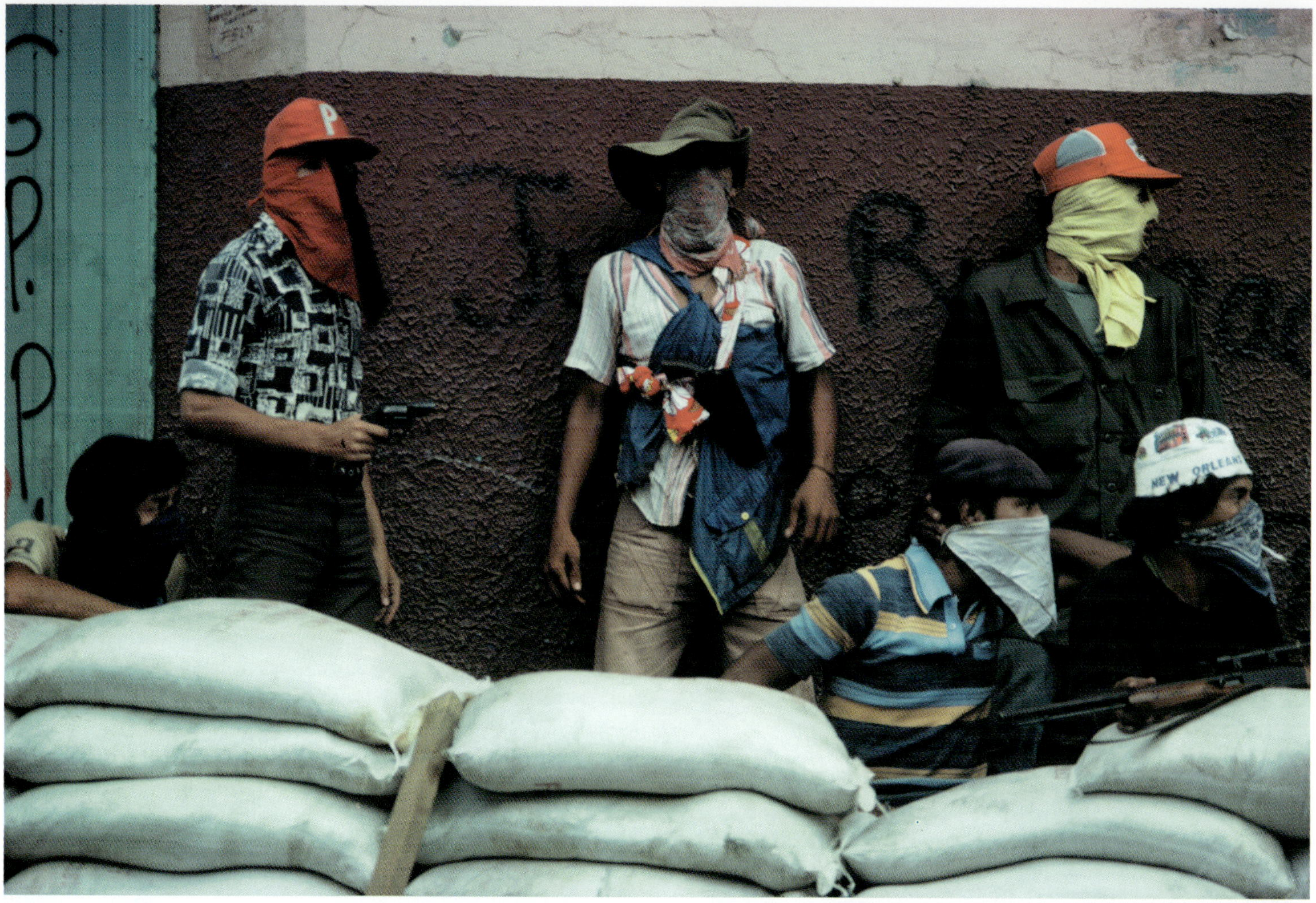

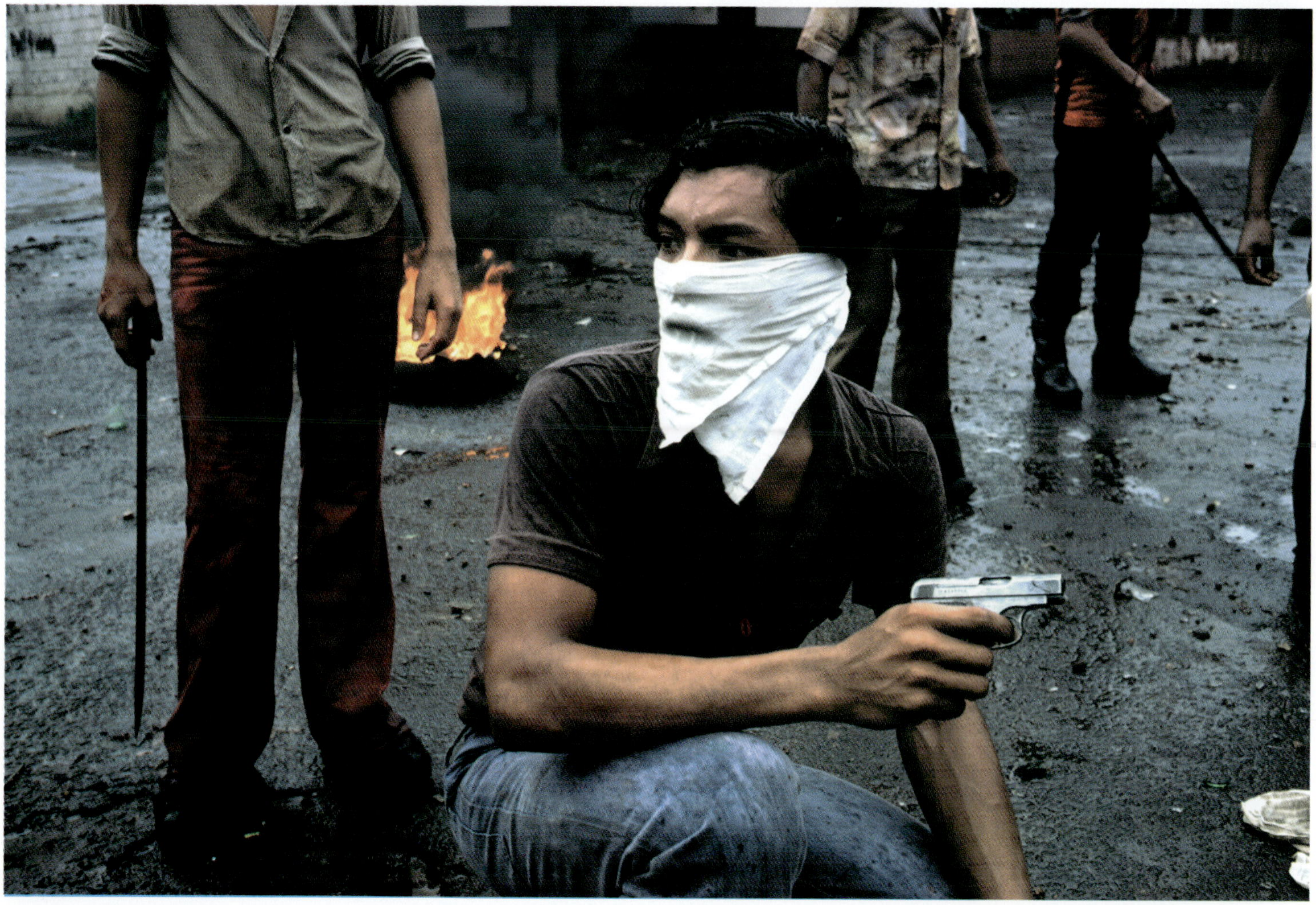

LEFT TOP: As Sandinista comrades await counterattack by the Guard in Nicaragua in 1978, there is a strong sense of anticipation, a moment of calm before explosive action.

LEFT BOTTOM: The crouching figure of a Nicaraguan streetfighter dominates the photograph (1979), but our eyes are also drawn to the anonymous cropped figures in the background who look somewhat menacing.

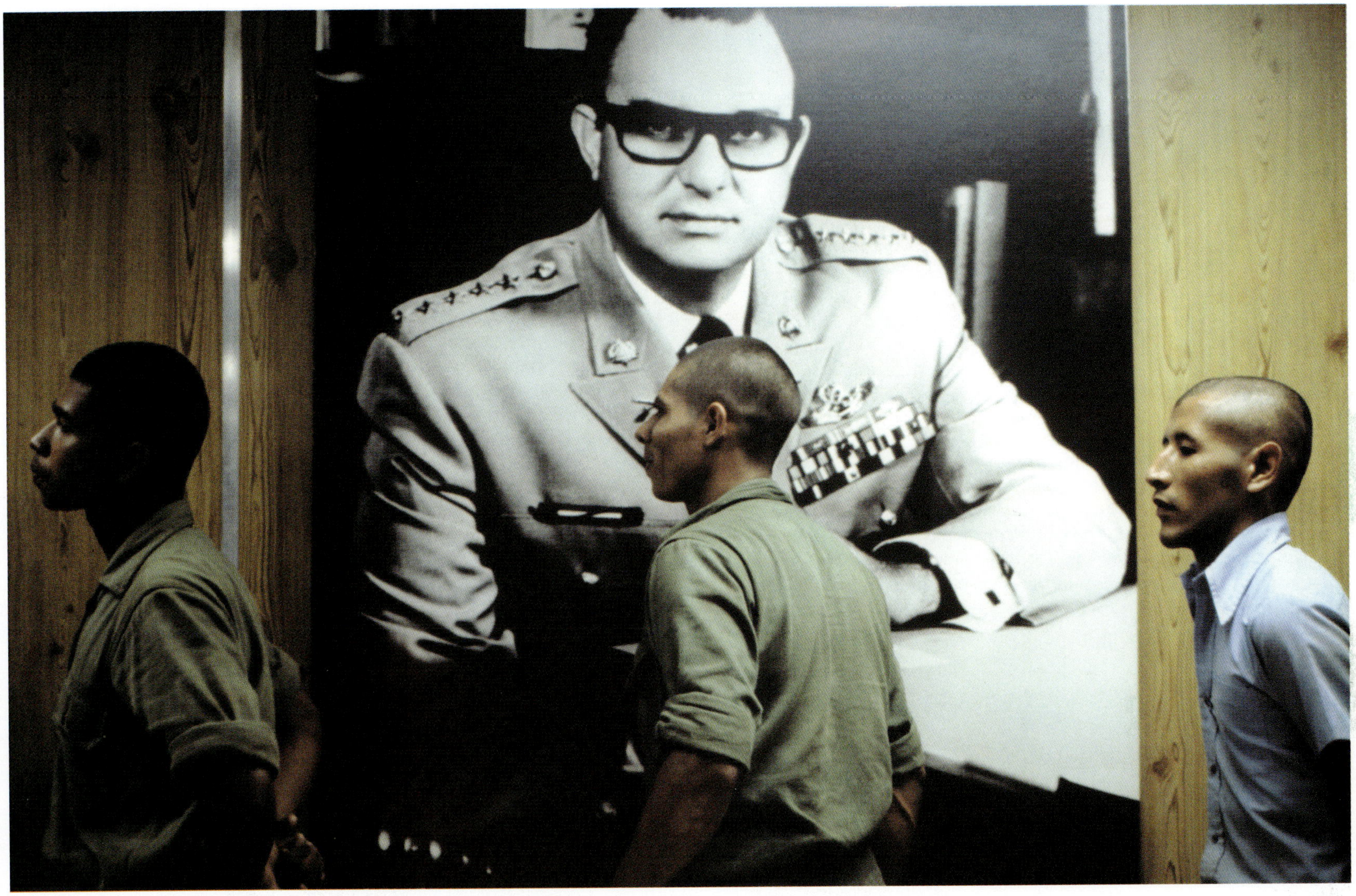

ABOVE: In an understated photograph, recruits pass by an official state portrait of Anastasio Somoza Debayle as President and Commander-in-Chief of the armed forces, Nicaragua, 1978. The photograph makes the point that the President is out of touch with this people – none of the recruits seem even to notice him – and that he is not a man to be trusted.

GIDEON MENDEL

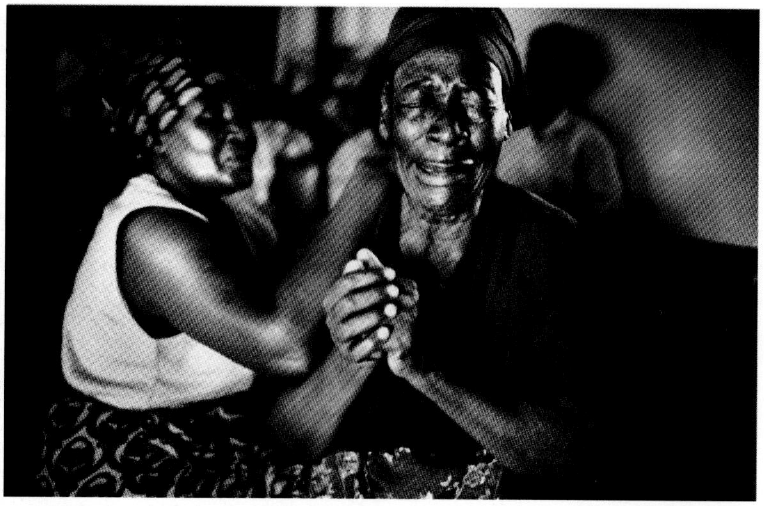

ABOVE: **This is taken from Mendel's epic project *A Broken Landscape* and was photographed in Malawi in 2000. The woman is weeping for her daughter Mary who had died the previous night in hospital, her sixth child to die of AIDS. This picture might be regarded as intrusive if it had been taken by someone else, but Mendel is so committed to both the issues and his subjects (and they clearly trust him), that you feel that he has a right to be there.**

Many photographers have shot stories on AIDS, but Gideon Mendel has concentrated and focused on this devastating disease more than any other, producing over a decade a body of work that is without parallel. His first exposure to the issue was photographing an AIDS ward in London in 1993. He says that the situation was different from any he had experienced as a photojournalist, and describes it as 10 per cent photography and 90 per cent communication. From that assignment, Mendel felt that as an African photographer he needed to find a way to respond to the AIDS crisis that was clearly developing on the continent and so he began this groundbreaking work. His former agent Neil Burgess says of his AIDS photographs, "It is the continuity of concern and the depth of knowledge and understanding of the issues which make him and his work unique." Mendel's work on AIDS is more than just a project, it is a campaign of which he is no longer an impartial observer, but an activist with a camera. Mendel has repeatedly returned to places such as Tanzania, Malawi, Zambia and Zimbabwe, allowing him to develop meaningful relations with his subjects. This in turn has produced photographs that have depth, humanity, and most importantly of all, compassion. He is not just interested in showing the horror, but also proving that there are 30 million people living with AIDS in Africa who can still lead productive lives. For example, one of his favourite subjects is an inspirational priest in Uganda who is HIV-positive and who plays an active role in educational work and campaigning about AIDS. The way the "campaign" has been photographed has also evolved over time. It started with Mendel shooting in traditional black-and-white, but in recent years he has been using colour, video and panoramic photography. He has also been incorporating the images online into a multi-media experience accompanied by his own moving audio commentary. In his own words, "Photographs can be powerful weapons, they can convey intimacy, tragedy, passion and hope." Mendel's work does all of this and more.

RIGHT: **This truck is used by the AIDS and HIV home-care team as they drive around the villages of Zambia offering much-needed medical supplies and aid. It is not clear in this instance whether the children are in dire need of help or just having fun. What makes this picture so compelling is the hand that almost floats into the frame – the hand of salvation, perhaps? That and the child's great grin make it a photograph of hope.**

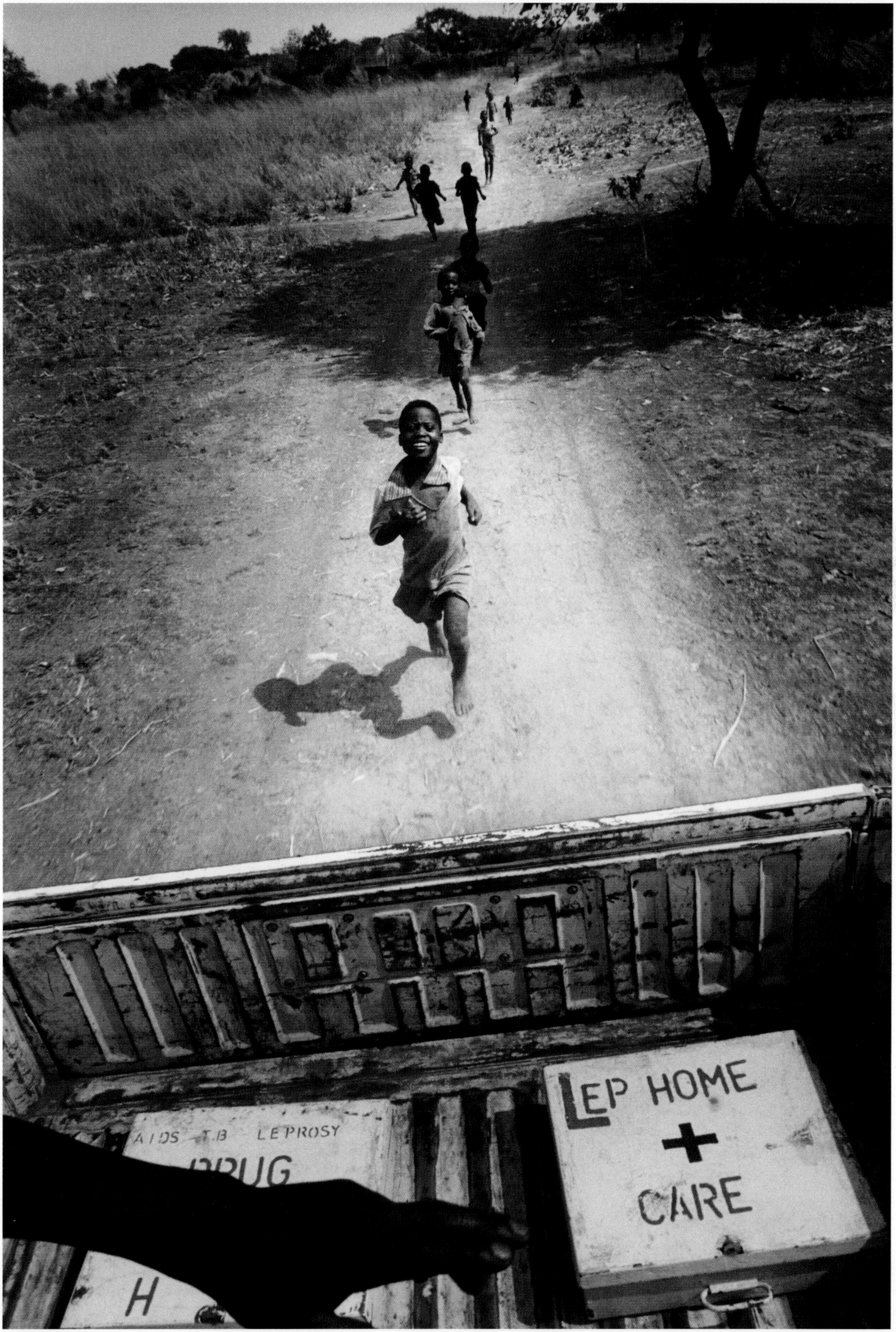
AIDS T.B LEPROSY
LEP HOME
+
CARE

BELOW: This image was photographed at an orphanage for abandoned children with HIV or AIDS in Cape Town, South Africa, in 1995. The little boy Josaphat is receiving an aromatherapy massage, but he died shortly after this picture was taken. There is a dramatic contrast between the tender hands of the masseuse and the tiny, fungal-infected hands of the boy. Just pitiful.

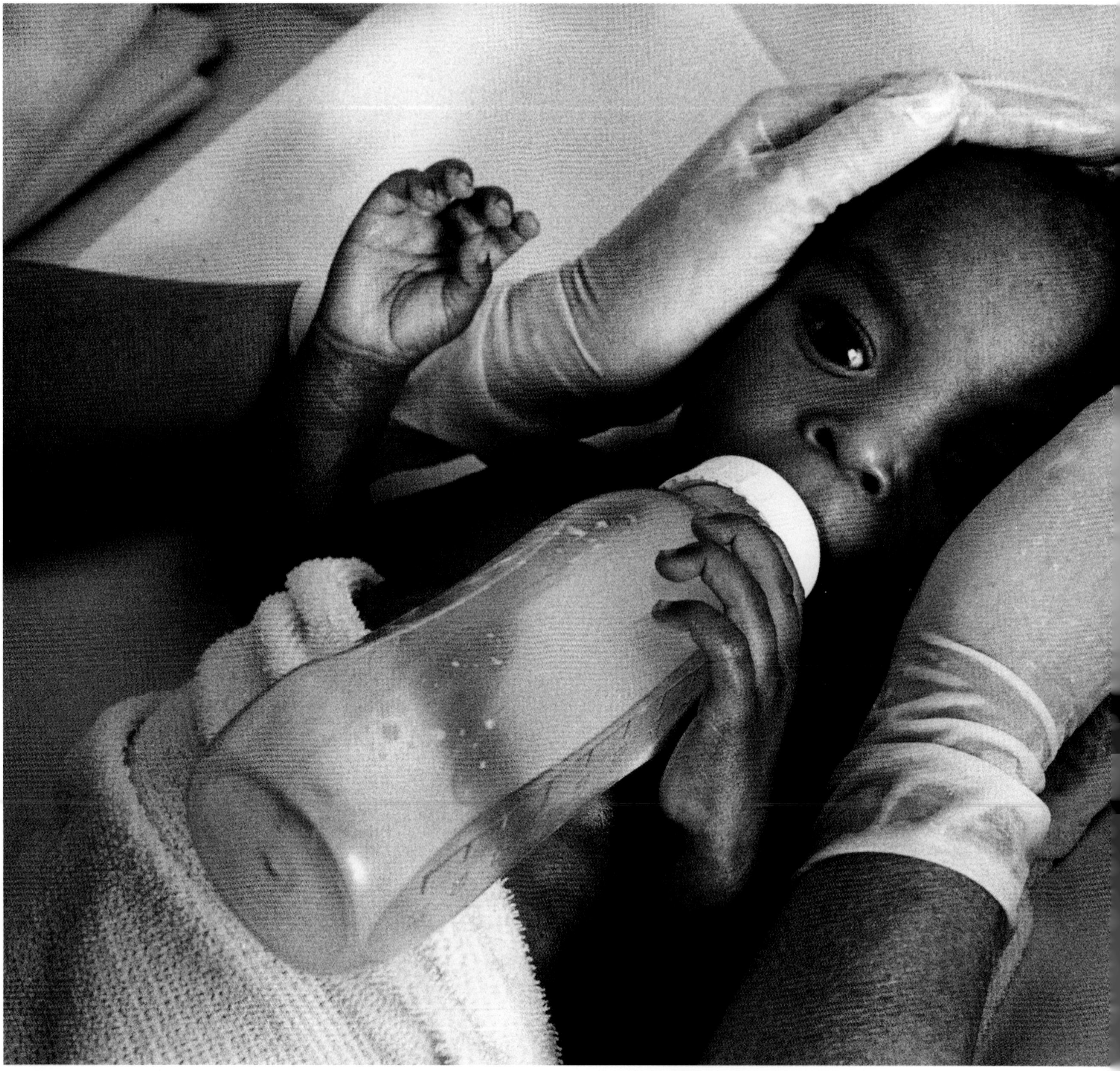

BELOW: Eliza is being supported by her aunt so that her other aunt can try to feed her in an AIDS hospital ward in Malawi. Eliza died later that night, so this may well have been the last shot of her alive. Despite her frailty and suffering, she remains defiant. This is another example of Mendel's photography humanizing such a destructive disease. For him it is not about facts and figures, but raw emotion; naturally there is suffering, but there is also great love and tenderness.

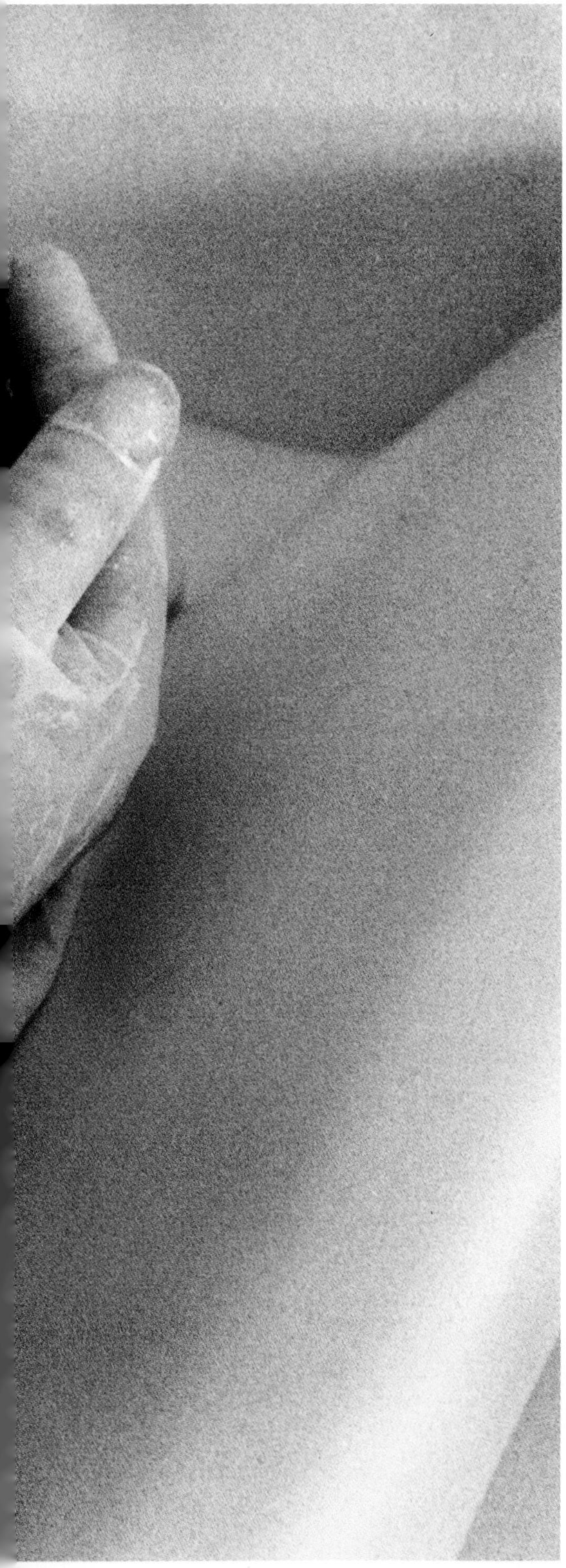

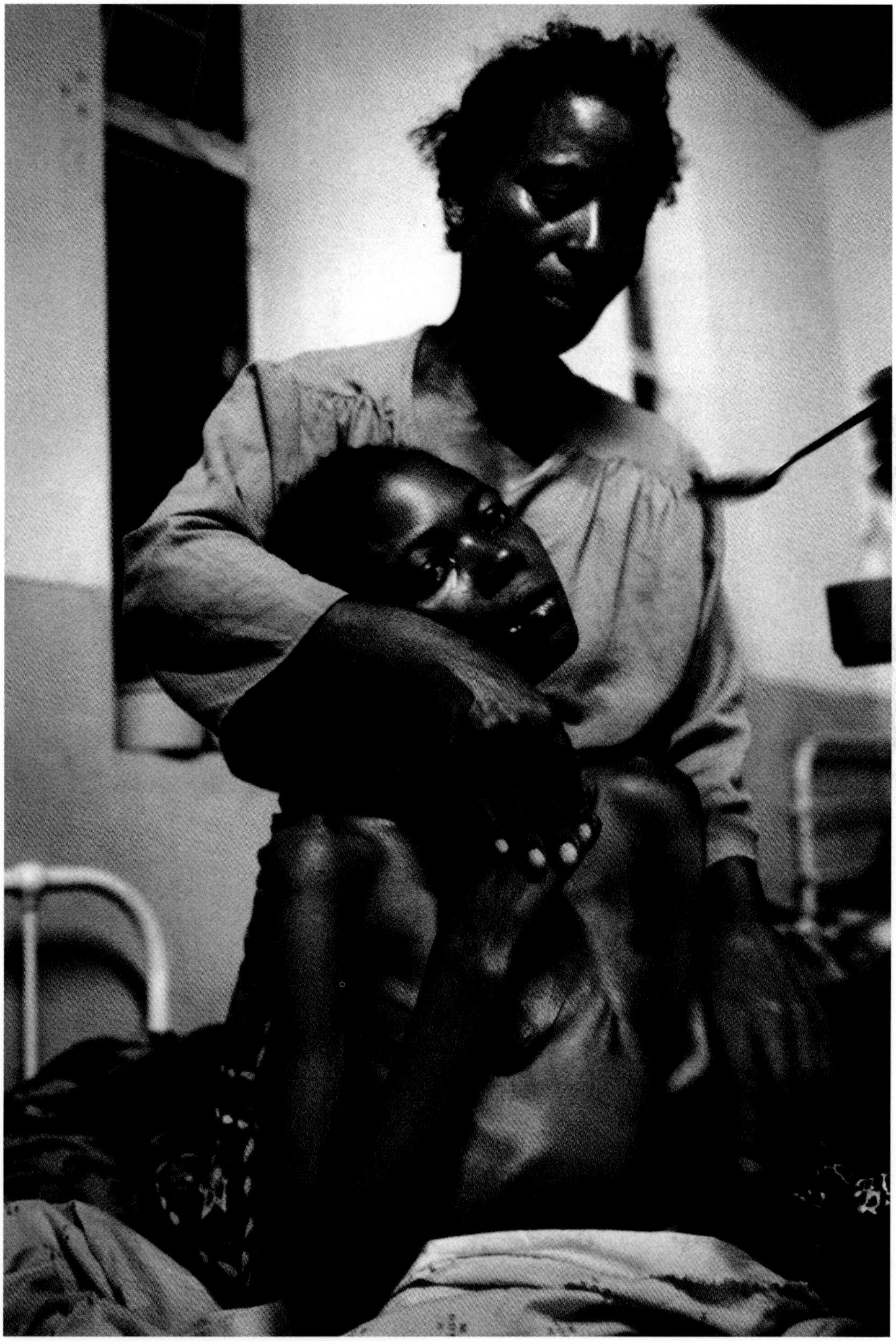

RIGHT: Mendel has adopted different shooting styles over the years for his AIDS project, moving from traditional black-and-white to these colour panoramas. This is more recent work from 2004 and was photographed in collaboration with The International HIV/AIDS Alliance. Seven orphans from the Muroemba family walk the long distance (approximately four-and-a-half miles) through the bush from their school to the home of their grandfather where they live.

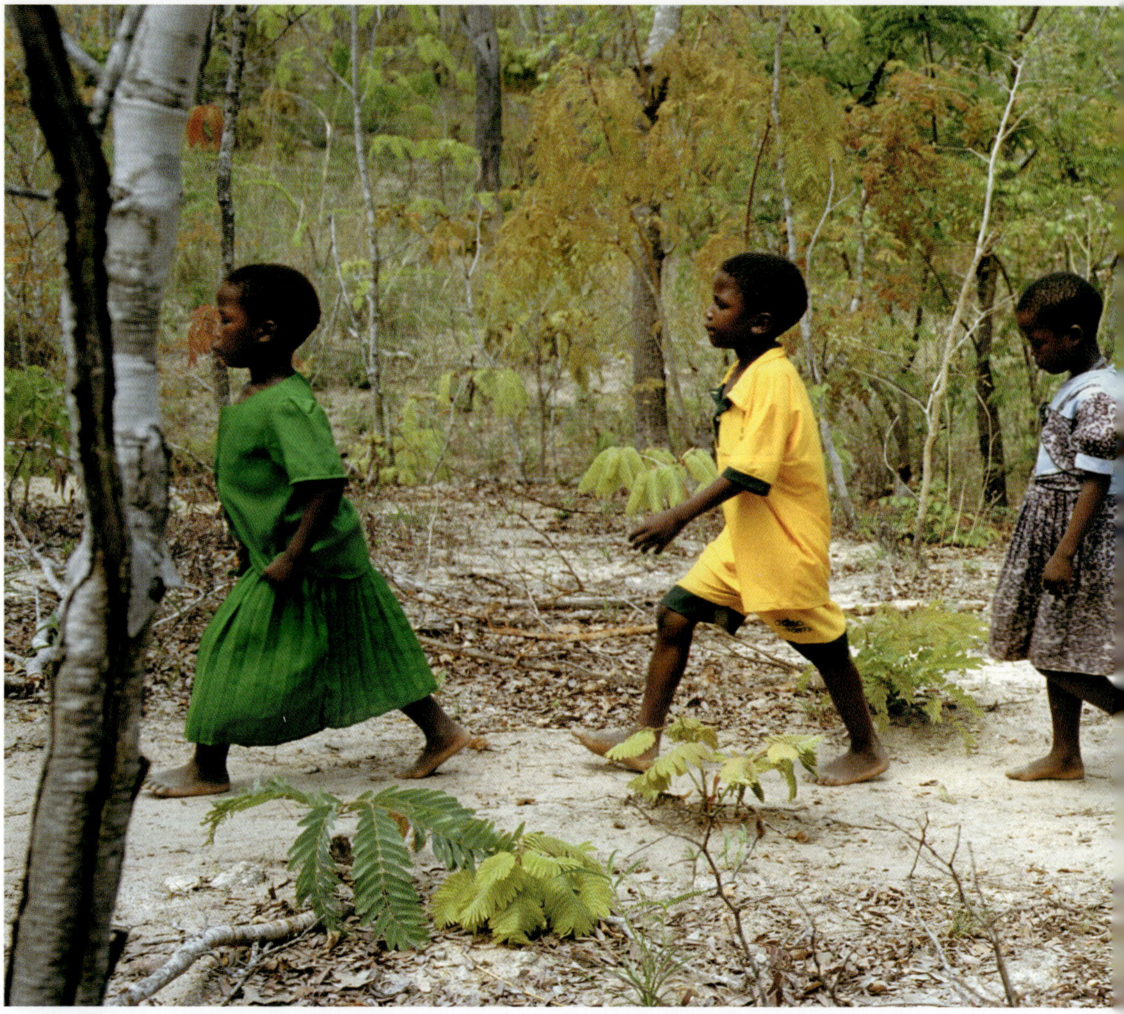

RIGHT: Elisa Tomas (12) takes care of her brother, eight-year-old Tomas Tomas, in the village of Penhalonga near the border with Zimbabwe. Both their parents are dead. Mendel skilfully lights his subjects and makes them dominate the frame.

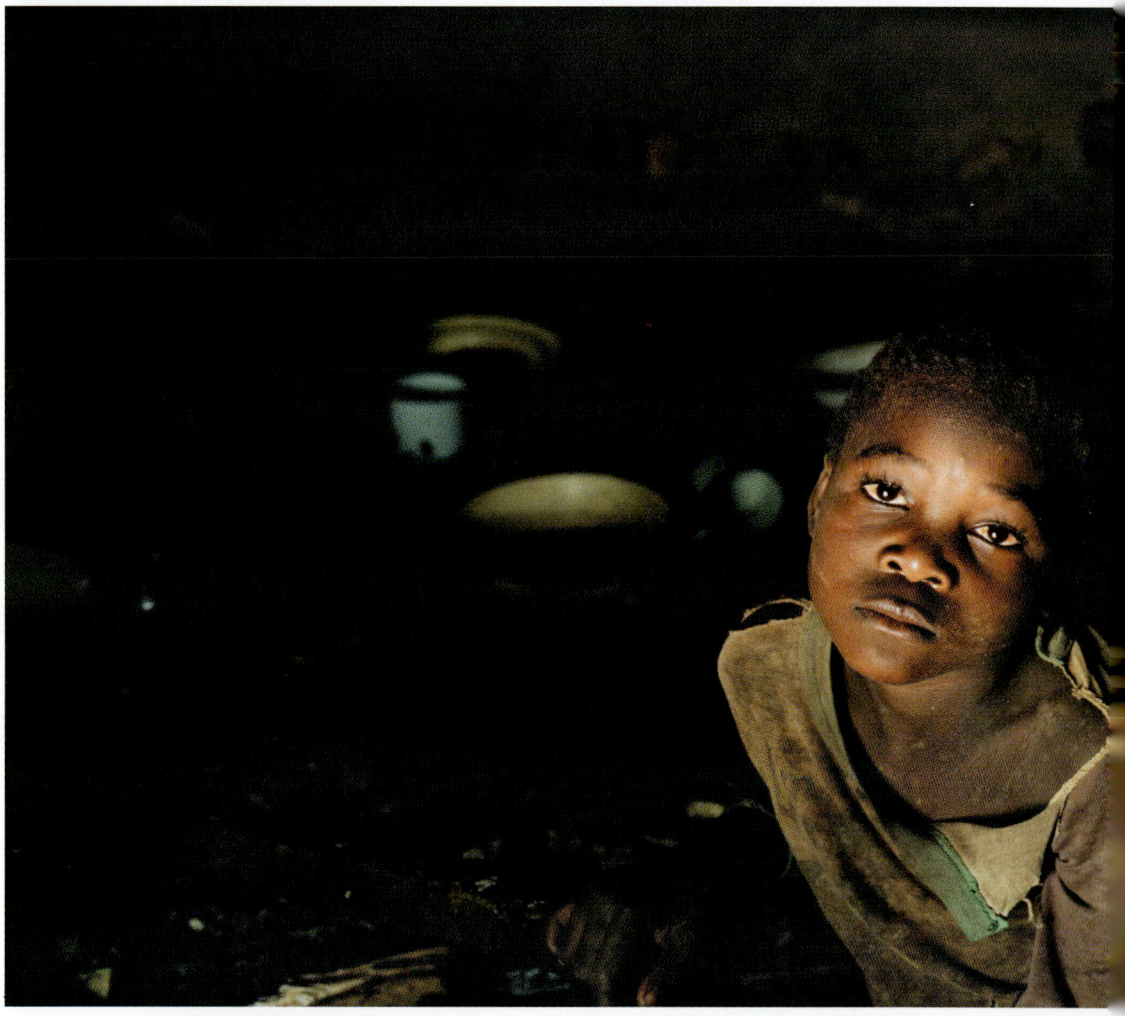

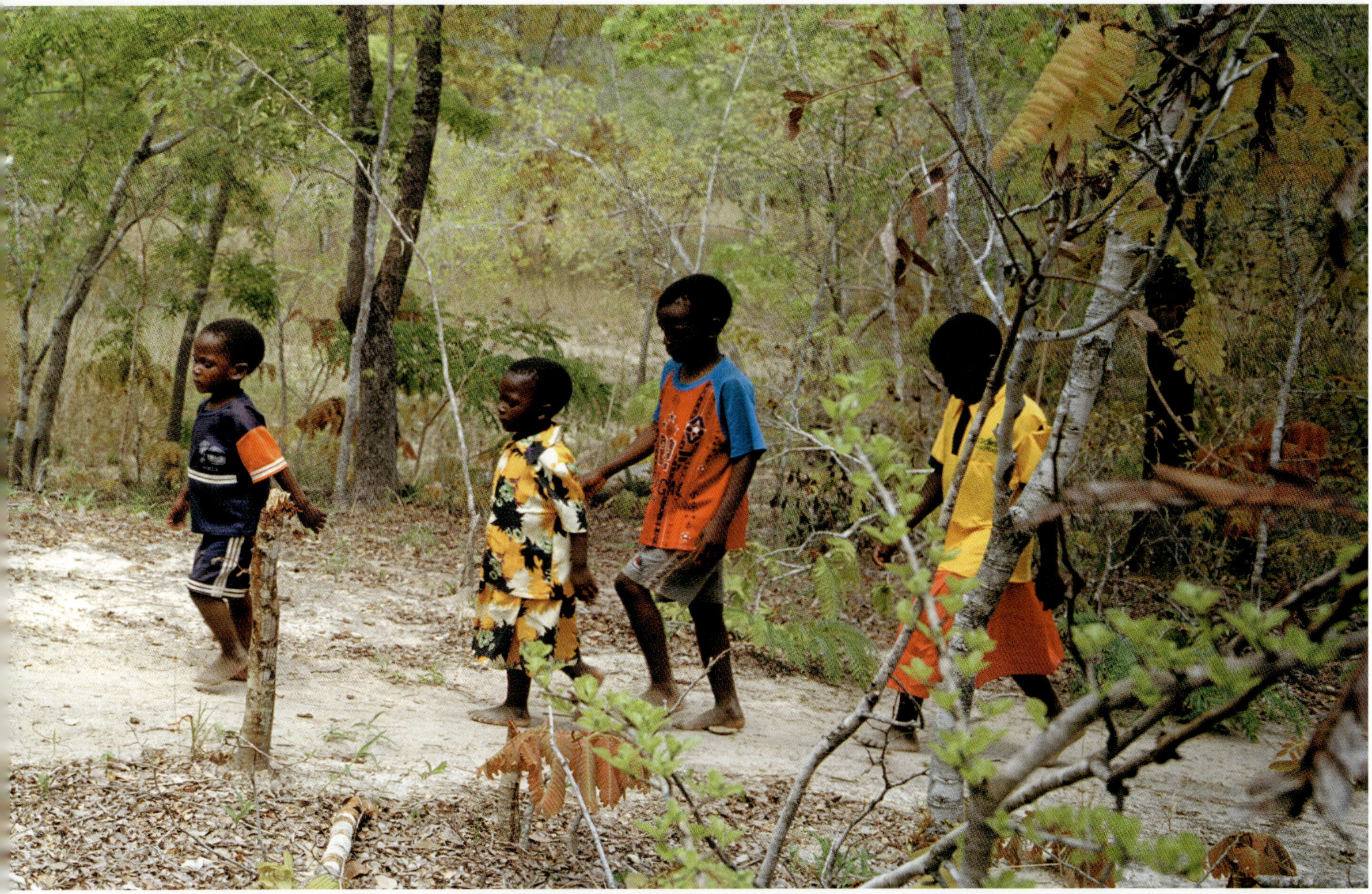

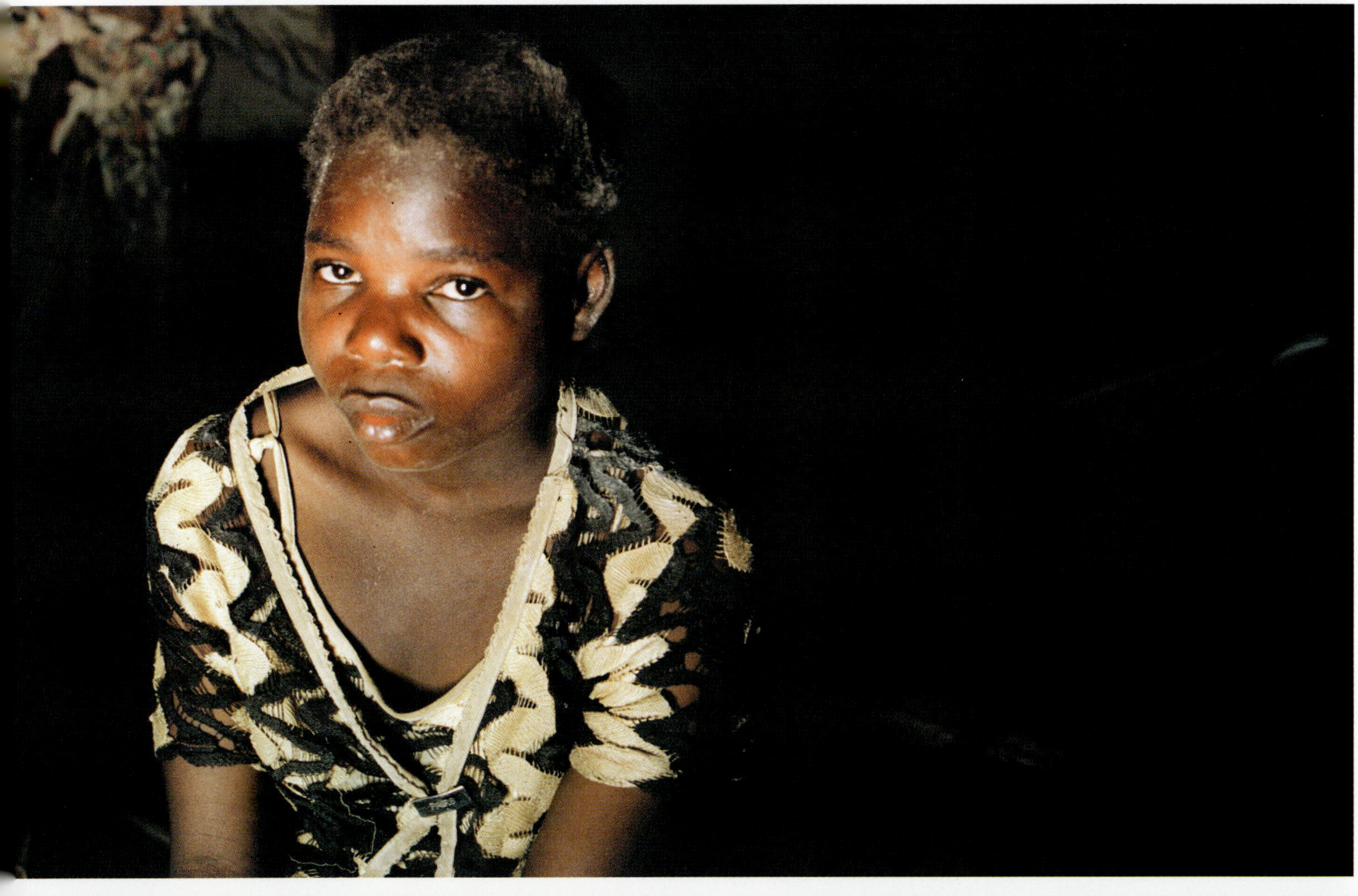

BERTRAND MEUNIER

BELOW: **In Chinese mythology Fengdu is called the "City of Devils" or the "Gates of Hell". Economic development does not seem to have changed the heart of this town, which will soon be erased from the map, blown-up and drowned beneath the waters. That is the grim reality, but in the meantime people go about their everyday business. All these images were taken between December 2000 and January 2001.**

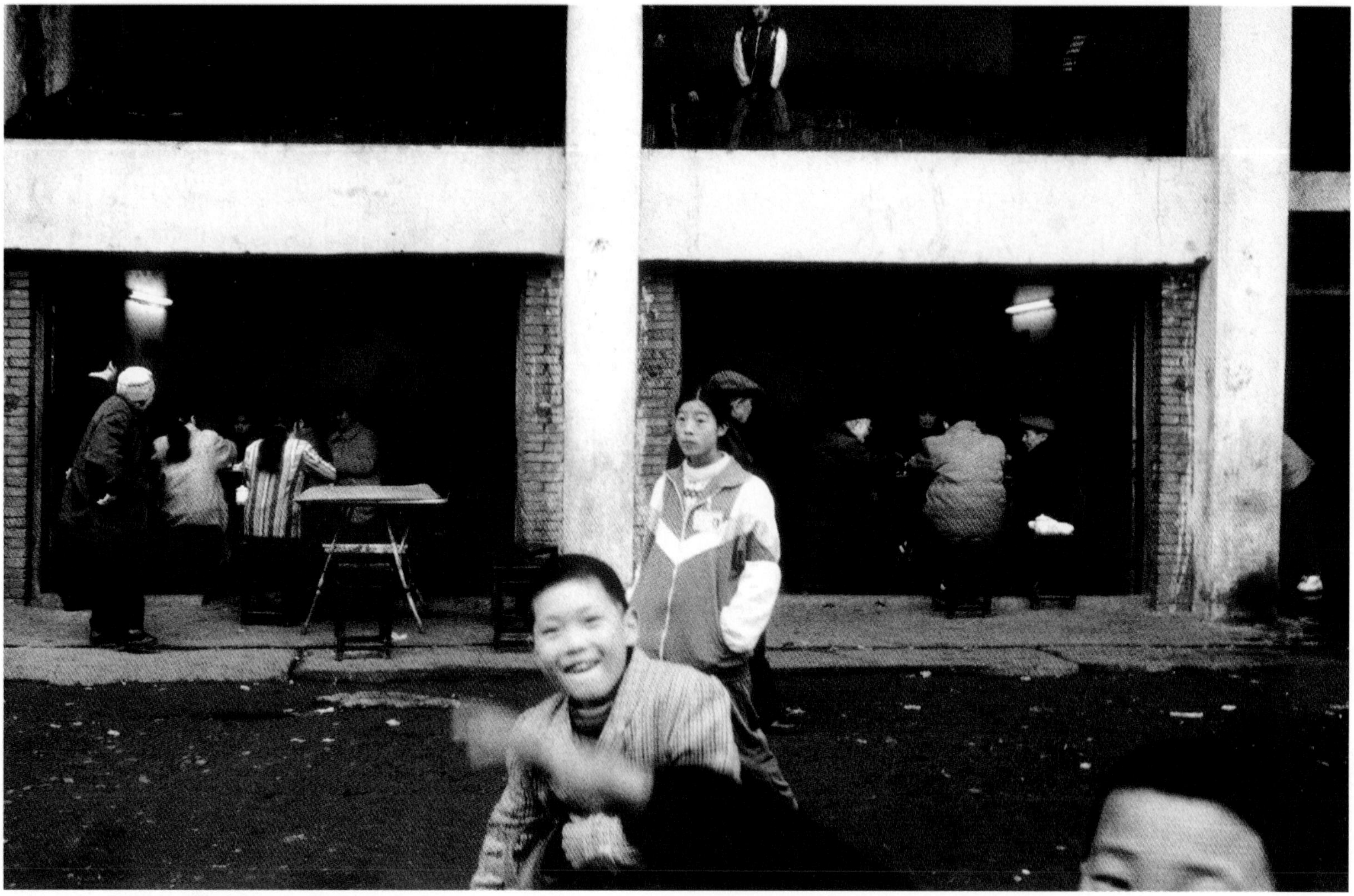

In the highly competitive world of photojournalism, tenacity and technical brilliance is not enough. To make work that is really outstanding, the big story has to be approached from a different angle, and Bertrand Meunier is a case in point. In the late 1990s, the West became fixated with China's so-called economic boom under Deng Xiaoping, who had introduced a series of reforms that were transforming parts of the country as it started to lurch toward capitalism. Meunier, however, had a different story to tell: "I discovered the great industrial centres of the north of China. The cities were living through the full impact of the reforms, with apocalyptic effects on the social landscape. Everyone's eyes were turned toward the coast, so it seemed to me, therefore, that it was crucial to work on an unknown aspect of contemporary China."

In his carefully constructed black-and-white photographs, the word "contemporary" is almost ironic. These grainy photographs might have been taken in the last few years or so, but they do not depict a Chinese economic boom – far from it. They capture a bleak, developing urban landscape, which is more reminiscent of communist China under Mao. Meunier's subjects are not thriving, but enduring and struggling. Life here is very hard and development is slow and labour-intensive. It is a story that is so close to Meunier's heart that he never veers from absolute respect for his subjects and empathy with them. His images are also highly evocative , and the dust, grime and pollution of these half-built cities are almost tangible. Above all, perhaps his greatest strength is his innate grasp of what a photograph should do. As Amy Pereira-Frears, a photo editor at *Newsweek* explains, "Bertrand gives you so much more than simply relaying information; he sees the poetry of what it means to be human. He tells the story of suffering and sadness, all in the quiet, subtle moments of time, and in those fleeting seconds he finds the texture of the scene that makes you understand."

RIGHT: **This 11-year-old girl was found as a newborn baby in the public toilets of their quarter by an old couple in Wanxian City. As well as living with them, she does all their housework. Meunier has caught the girl in rapt concentration, but our eyes are more drawn to the urban squalor behind her. It really is the gate to hell.**

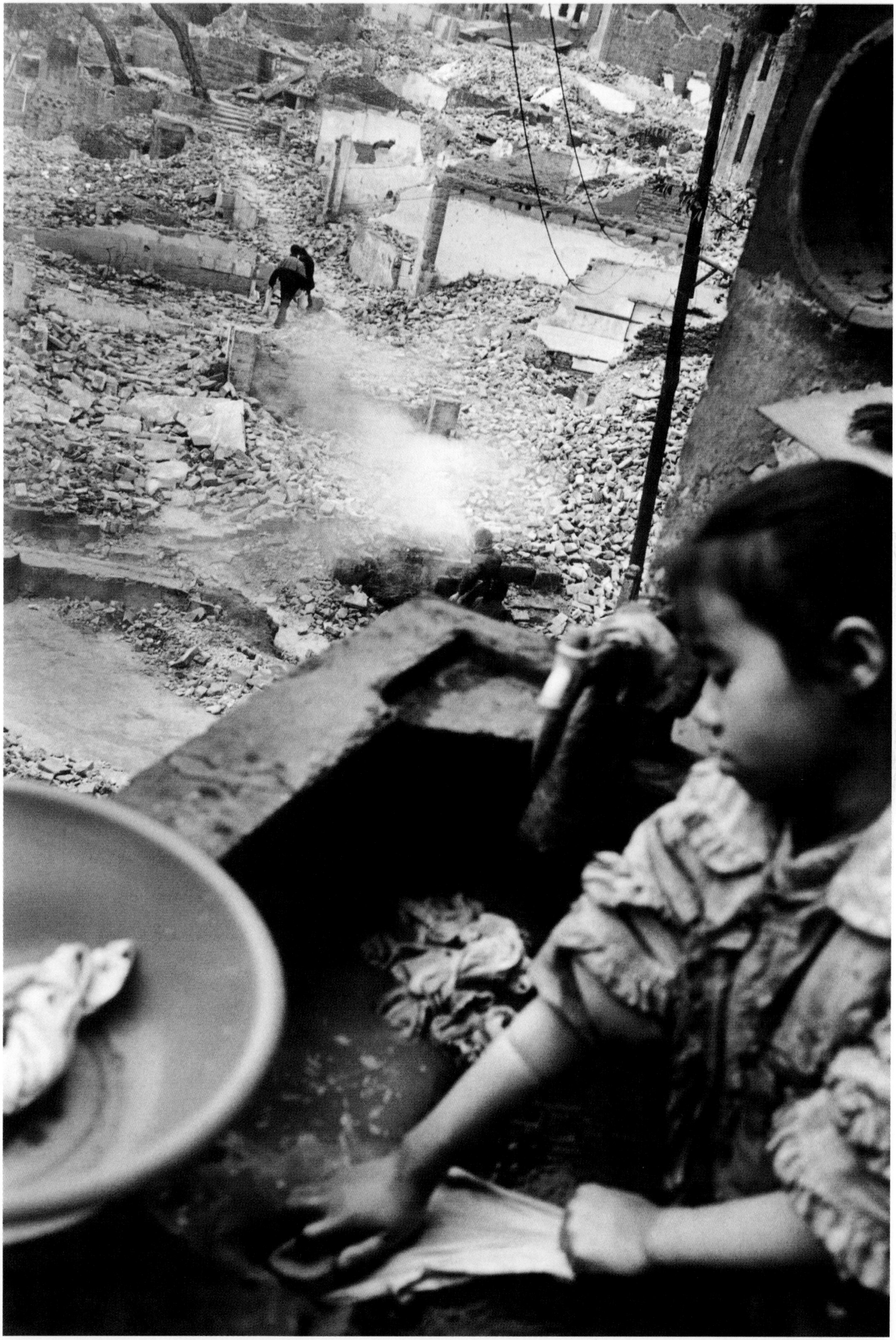

BELOW: Here we have an overview of the construction of a dam. As in the previous image of the little girl, Meunier shows himself to be very adept at juxtaposing people against their environment.

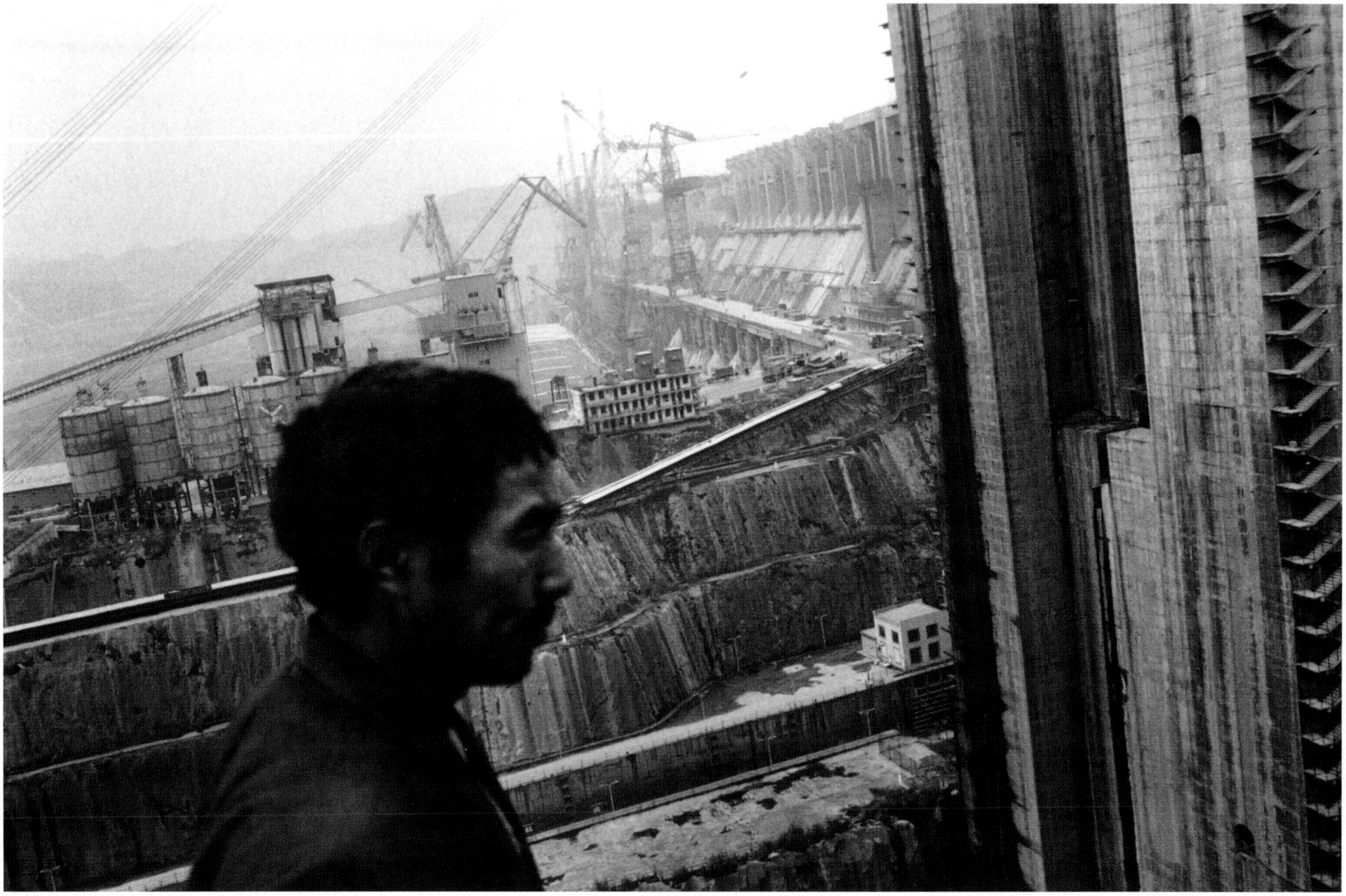

RIGHT TOP: This is almost a parody of a communist propaganda poster with the macho worker swinging a hammer. Again we are made aware of contrast, but this time it is between the manmade environment and the natural landscape.

RIGHT BOTTOM: At Wushan, coal porters carry their burdens all the way to the barges that deliver to the factories upstream. Coal is one of the principal sources of energy in China. The porters are paid three centimes for each trip over a distance of 164 yards (150m) carrying about 154 pounds (70kg) on their shoulders. The blur on the photo intensifies the experience and gives a sense of motion.

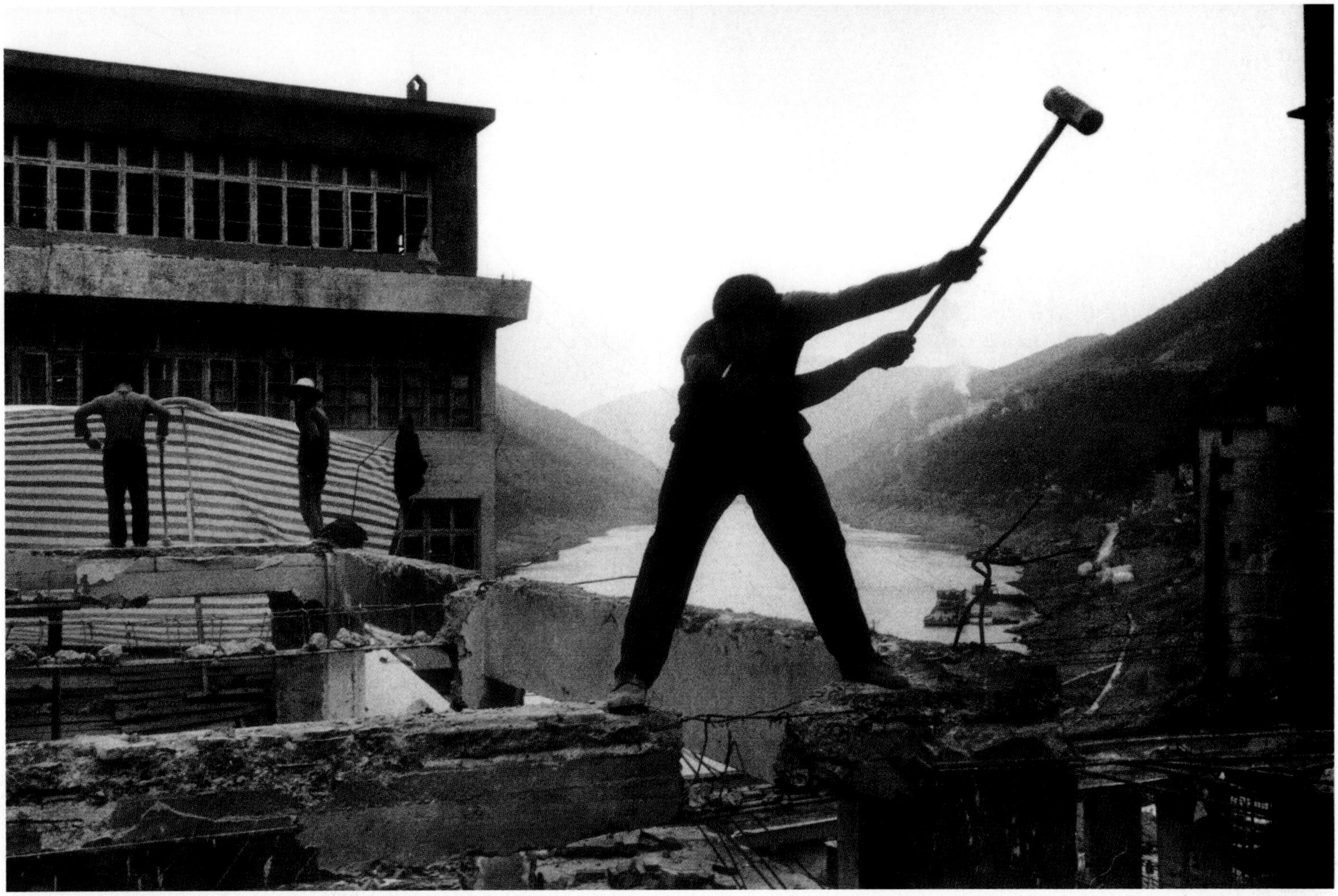

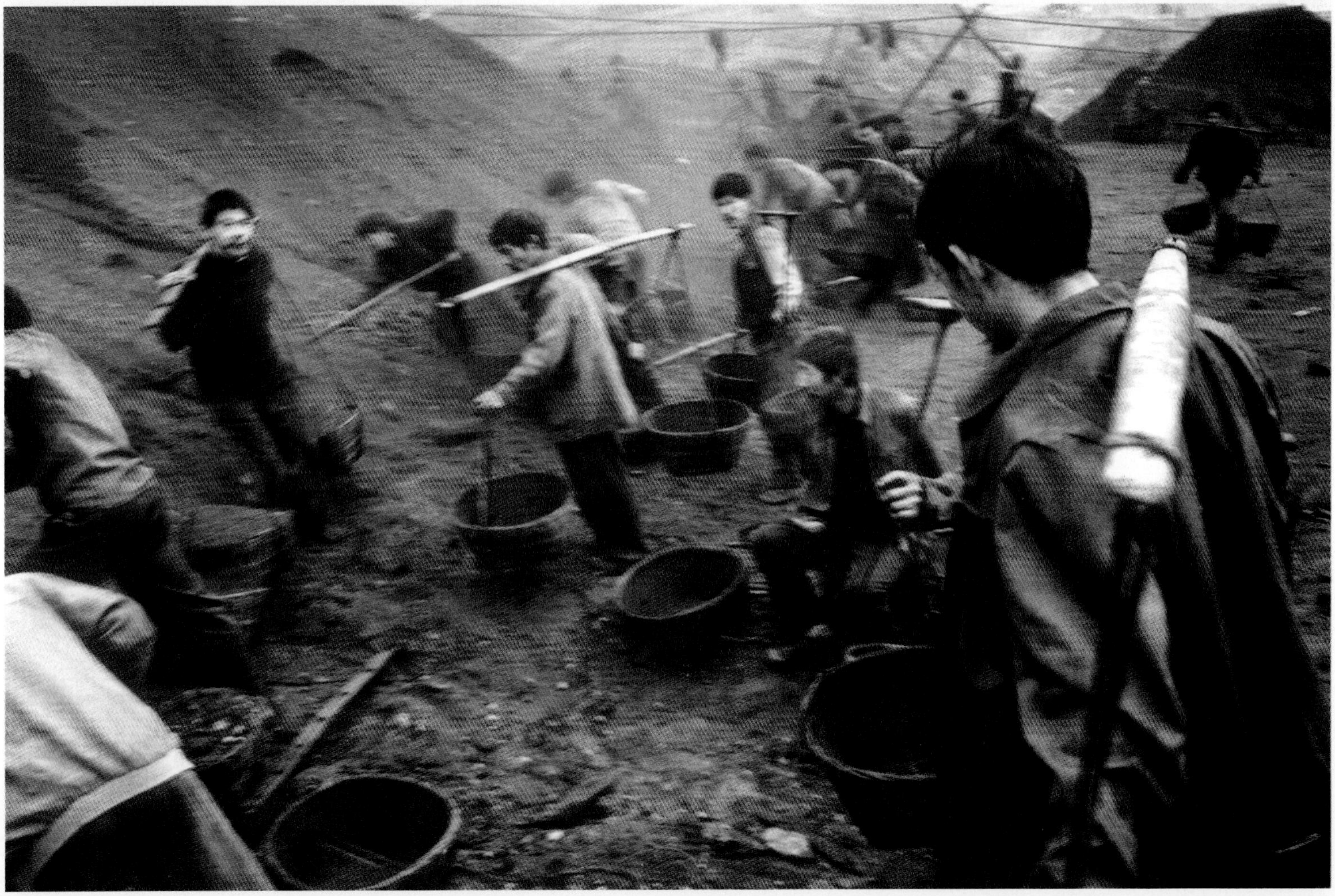

DAVID MODELL

David Modell has lived in London all his life and has an insider's knowledge of how his countrymen behave and interact with each other. He is not so much concerned with the differences in class (a particular British obsession), but rather the post-Thatcher notion of the classless society. He can photograph the mundane and the routine – for instance, a photographic essay on train commuting – but more often he looks for those moments of high emotion and drama that unite people across different social boundaries. These moments occur at political rallies (recorded in his seminal work *Tory Story*), at office Christmas parties, at betting tracks or in his essay *Diana is Dead*. He defines his style as "observational and non-interventionist. I use small cameras and try not to influence the events that I'm photographing in any way. That's not to say that I'm trying to be 'invisible'. As a photographer, you can't ignore your presence in any scene – but I do all I can to blend in and allow people to behave as they would if I wasn't there."

The English have a reputation for keeping their emotions in check, but when Princess Diana died in such a horrific and pointless way there was an unprecedented, almost irrational, outpouring of national grief. Modell's images of this strange time really capture the English behaving in a most extraordinary way. He describes the brief he gave himself: "When I went out to shoot the Diana pictures I was simply reacting to a big story in the only way that I felt was natural, which was to get out to the streets and see how people were responding. What I found was quite bizarre; a monumental expression of grief for a person that no one knew, but clearly felt that they had a connection with." Modell's images make an emotional association with the people caught up in the drama and this in turn forms a connection with the viewer. His deceptively simple and arresting style makes us feel as if we were present – one of the hallmarks of a great photojournalist.

BELOW: An England fan during the 1994 World Cup. Modell always tries to tell a story from a slightly different point of view. The cropping of the image enhances the raw and very likely drunken emotion of the fan who is confronting the photographer with his rage/joy/frustration – we shall never know. As a side note England never qualified for the 1994 World Cup.

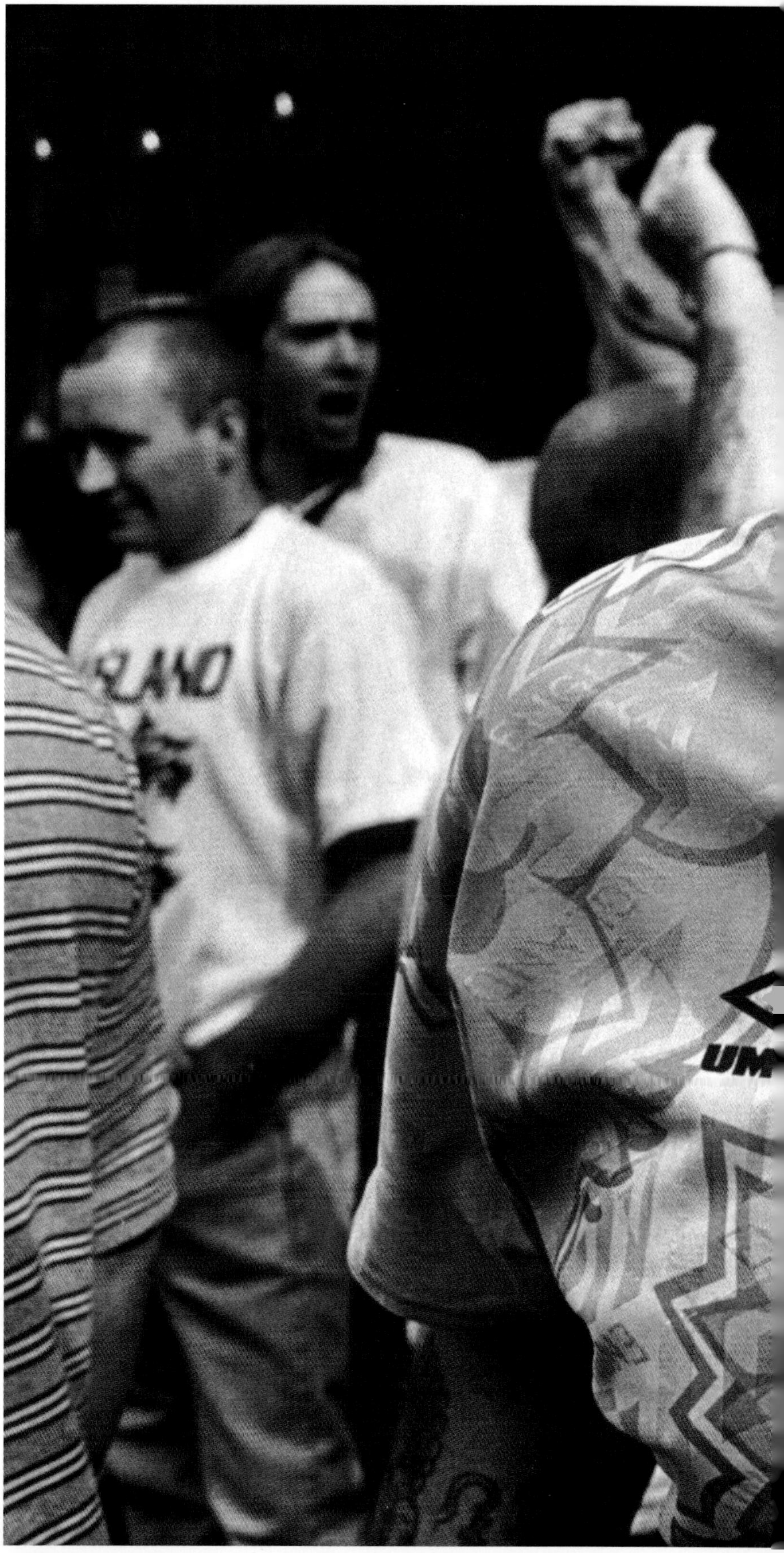

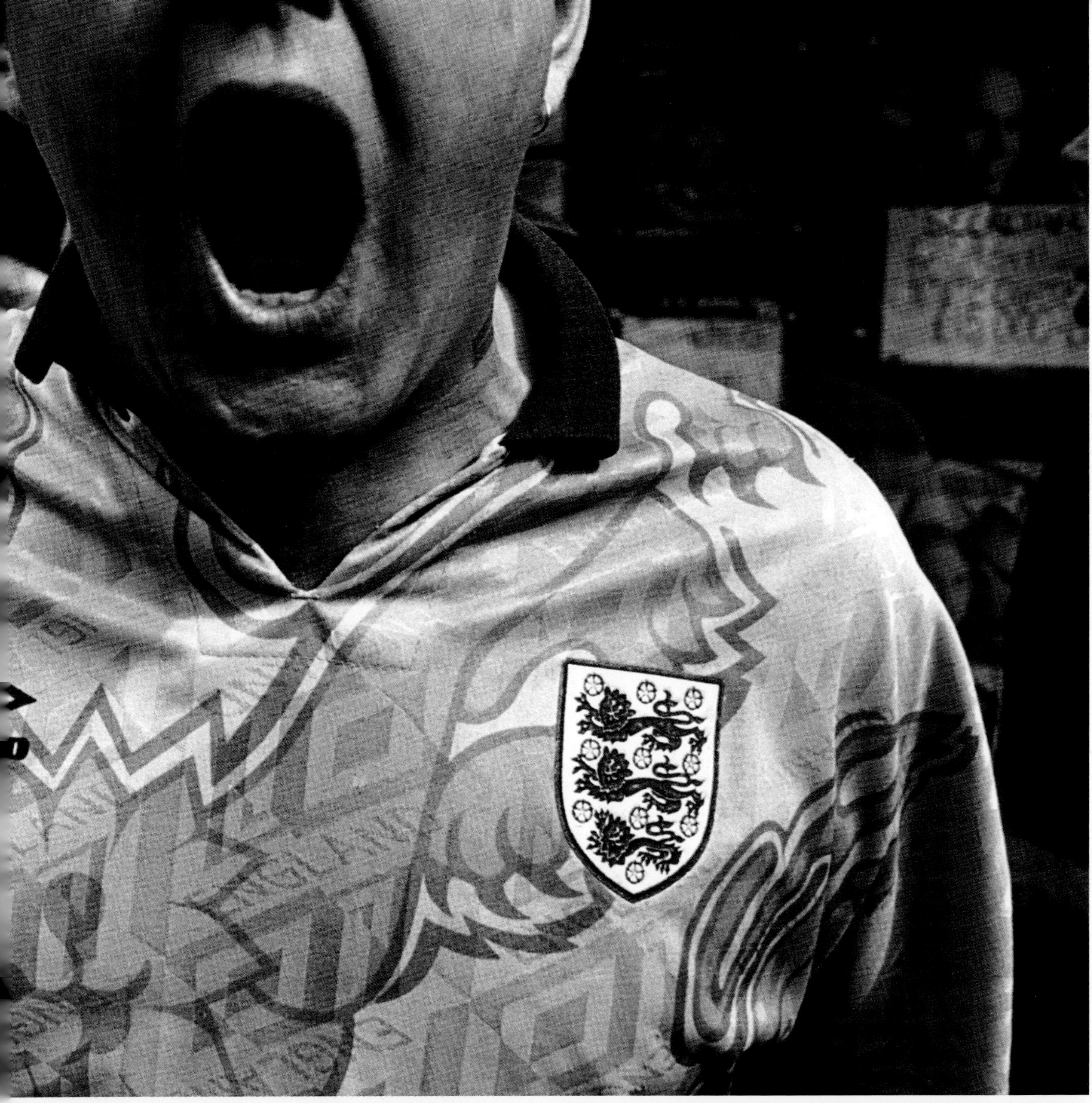

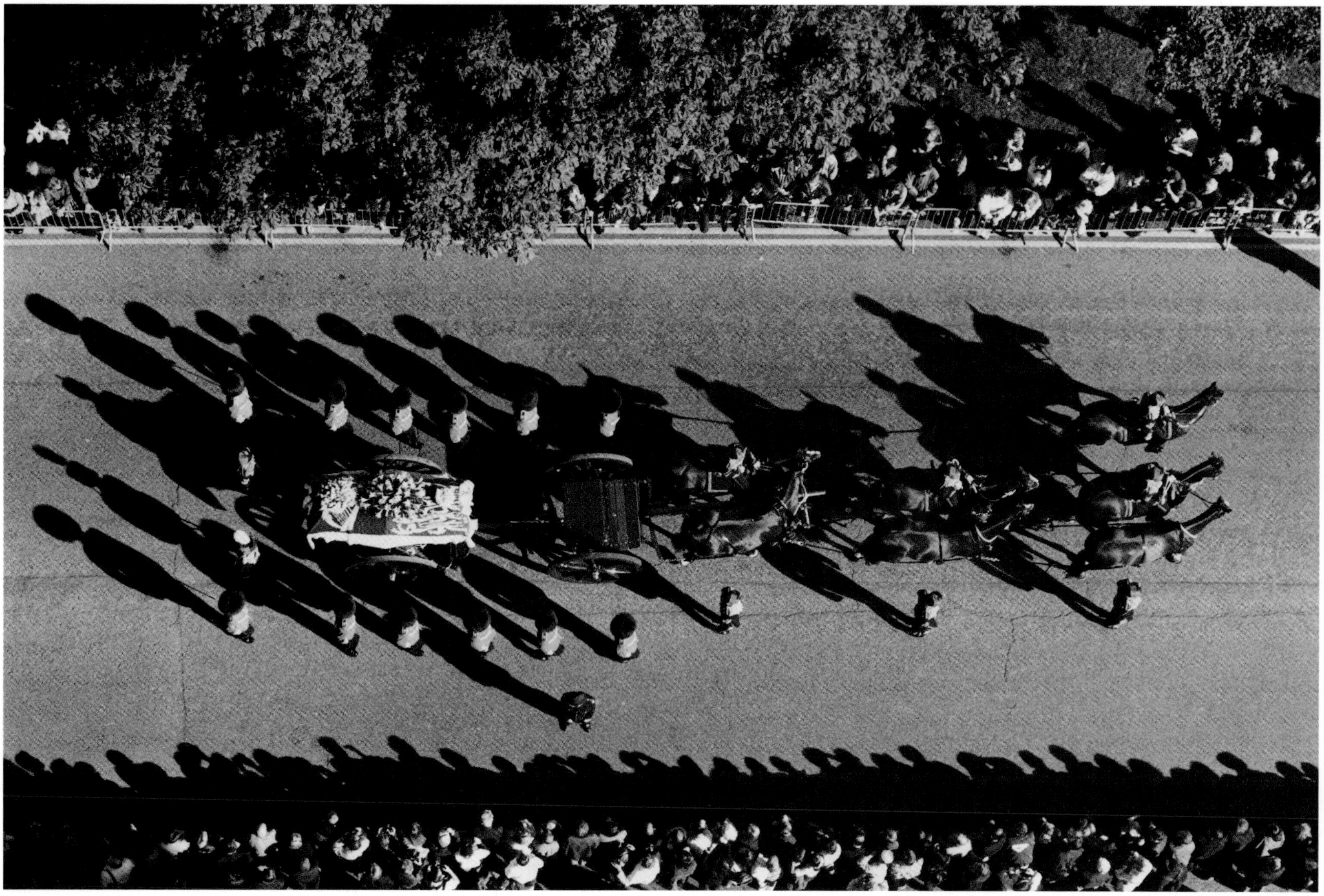

ABOVE: This aerial shot of Princess Diana's funeral in 1997 puts this poignant moment of recent British history in some kind of universal, almost spiritual, context. Modell says that it was a lucky shot, but the best photojournalism nearly always is. The shadows emphasize the deep sense of loss.

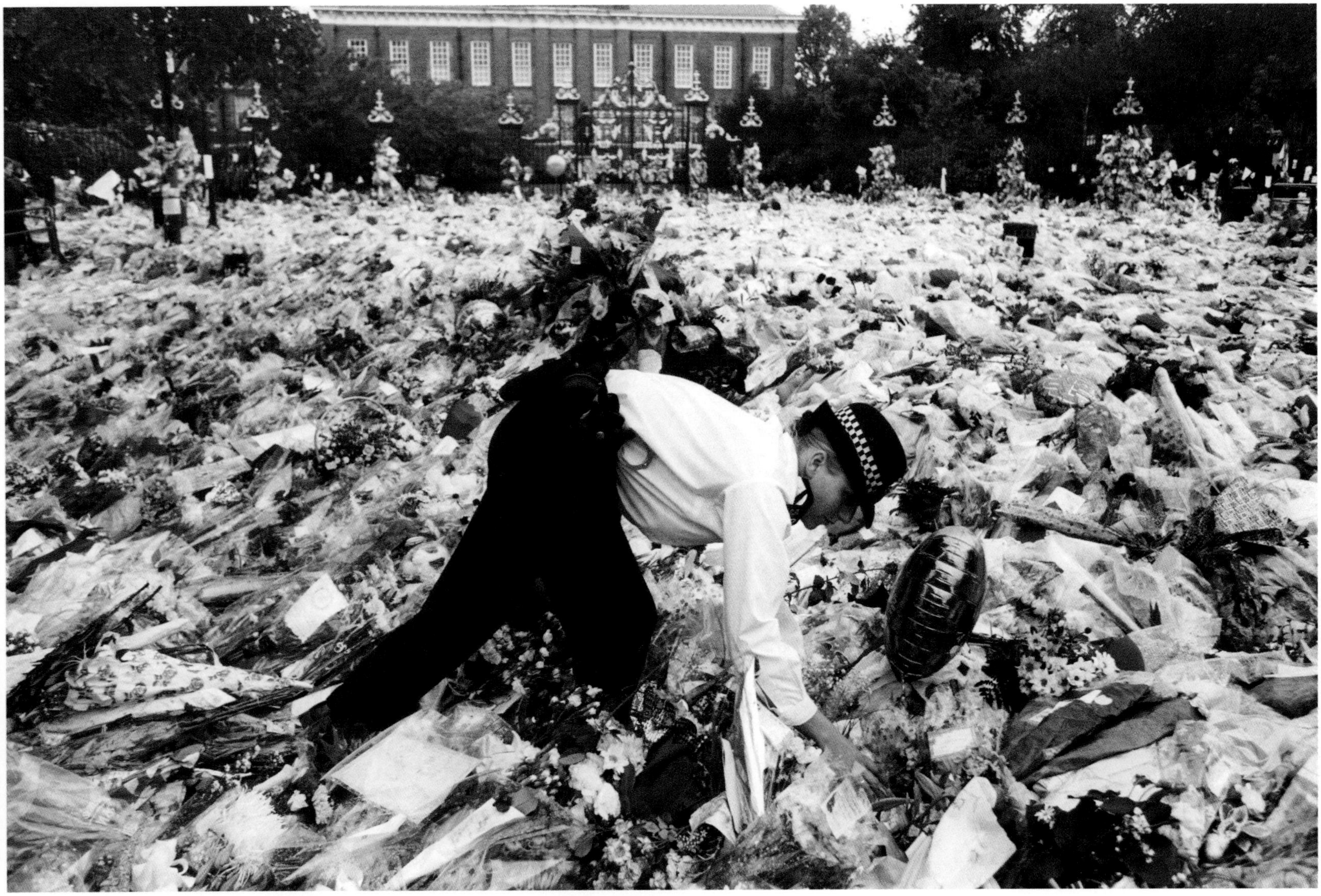

ABOVE: A sea of flowers placed outside Kensington Palace, Princess Diana's residence, in central London. Her death led to an unprecedented outpouring of national grief. The fact that the policewoman looks a little like the late princess makes the photograph somewhat eerie.

RALPH MORSE

The golden age of the space programme of the 1950s and 1960s was not just about exploring the "final frontier". It was also a major front in the Cold War against the Soviet Union. The editors at *Life* magazine sensed that the space race was a compelling story that had it all: science, politics, danger and human interest. They signed an exclusive contract with the astronauts and NASA in the late 1950s, just in time for the first manned space flight. Ralph Morse was an obvious candidate for the assignment. He had the right macho credentials, which he had earned during the Second World War. He was also fascinated by the mechanics of photography, with a scientific ability to adapt and experiment with cameras, lighting and shooting techniques. Morse also bonded easily with people and in time one of the team of the *Mercury Seven* dubbed Morse "the Eighth Astronaut".

Morse's brief was twofold. He had to convey to *Life* readers the magnitude and significance of space travel, yet his role was also to humanize the astronauts. They were the new breed of supermen carrying the hopes of America, but *Life* also rightly felt that they should be portrayed as regular guys – family men with children. As a result, Morse photographed them in their homes, bonding with their children, reading, eating and being doted on by their adoring wives, as well as seated at the controls of the rockets that would launch them on the ultimate voyage. His images of astronauts at home are prototypes for the celebrity spreads of *Hello!* magazine, and for readers in the 1950s they were just as addictive. Morse shows great skill in capturing these moments and since he was in effect living with the astronauts, the images never appear too posed. He was also highly adept at documenting space travel using such practices as multiple exposures, or firing off remote cameras under very difficult conditions with sometimes less than a second to get the shot. Over the years, he became known as the dean of space photography. No wonder one of his former managing editors said, "If *Life* magazine could afford only one photographer, it would have to be Ralph Morse."

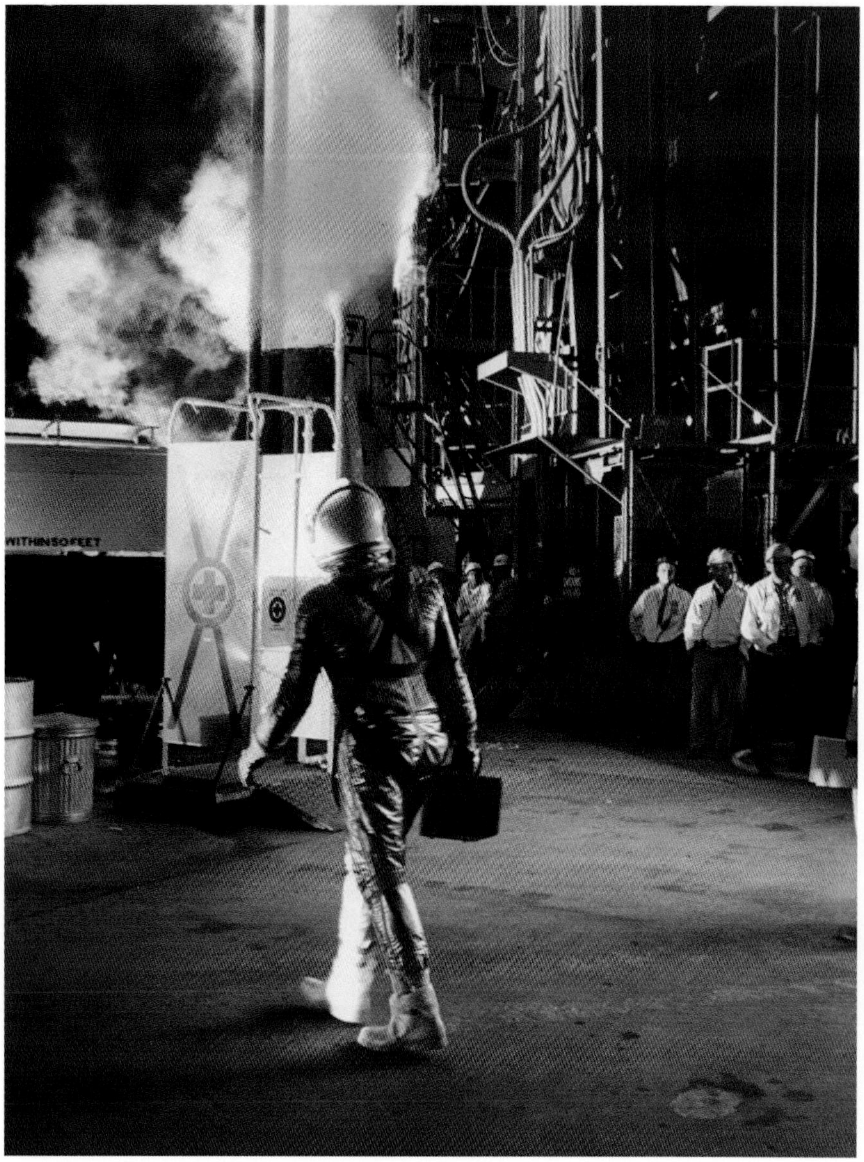

ABOVE: This is the astronaut Alan Shephard in an air suit heading toward the capsule for the first manned space flight in 1961. It is photographed as if it is just another day at the office for the astronaut, as he carries his "briefcase". Morse was such a part of their lives that he was dubbed the "Eighth Astronaut".

RIGHT: The *Apollo* spaceship lifting off on its historic flight during which astronauts Edwin Aldrin and Neil Armstrong walked on the surface of the moon in 1969. It is not clear from where Morse took this photograph, but his contacts within NASA probably secured him the best vantage point.

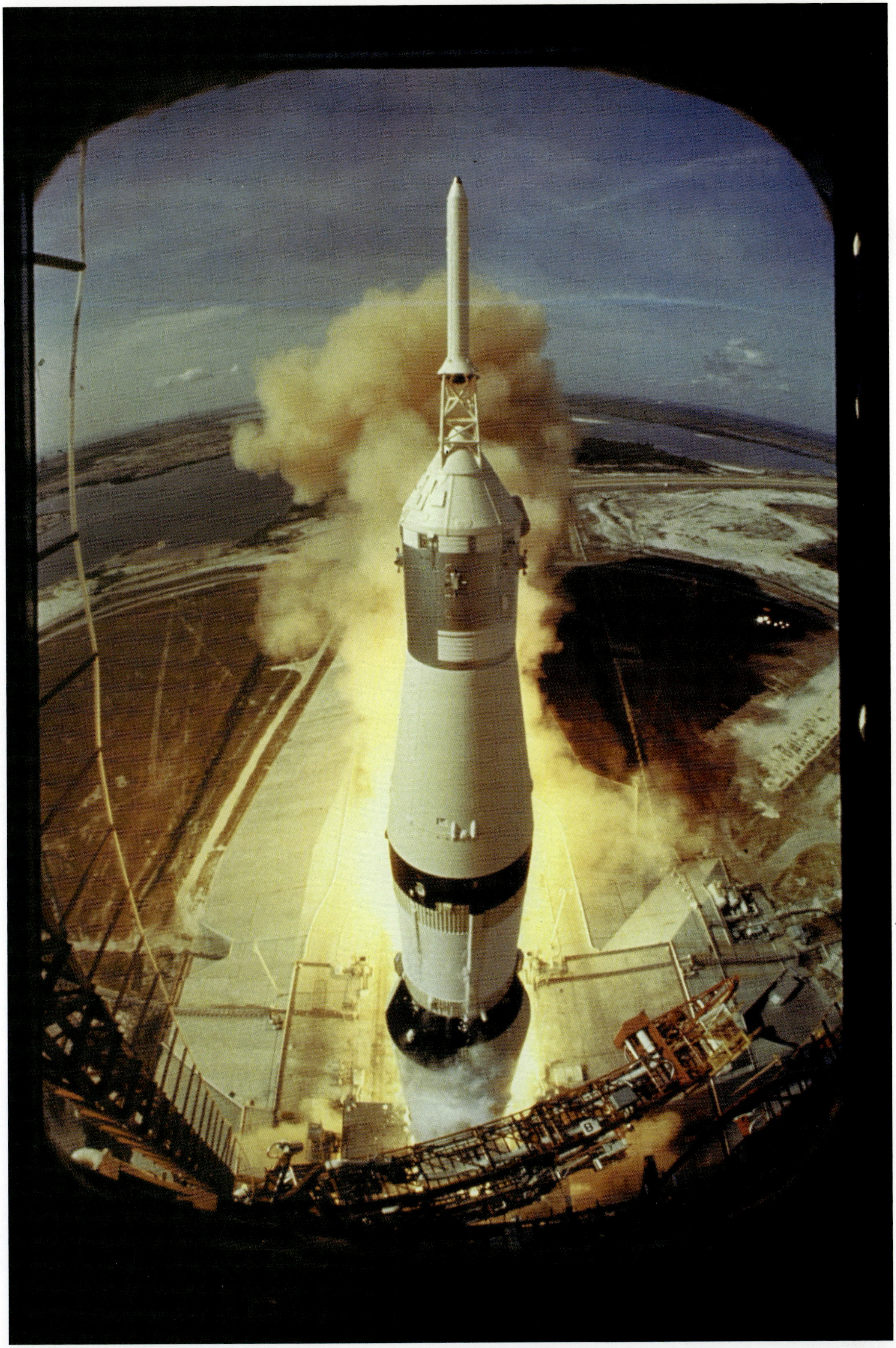

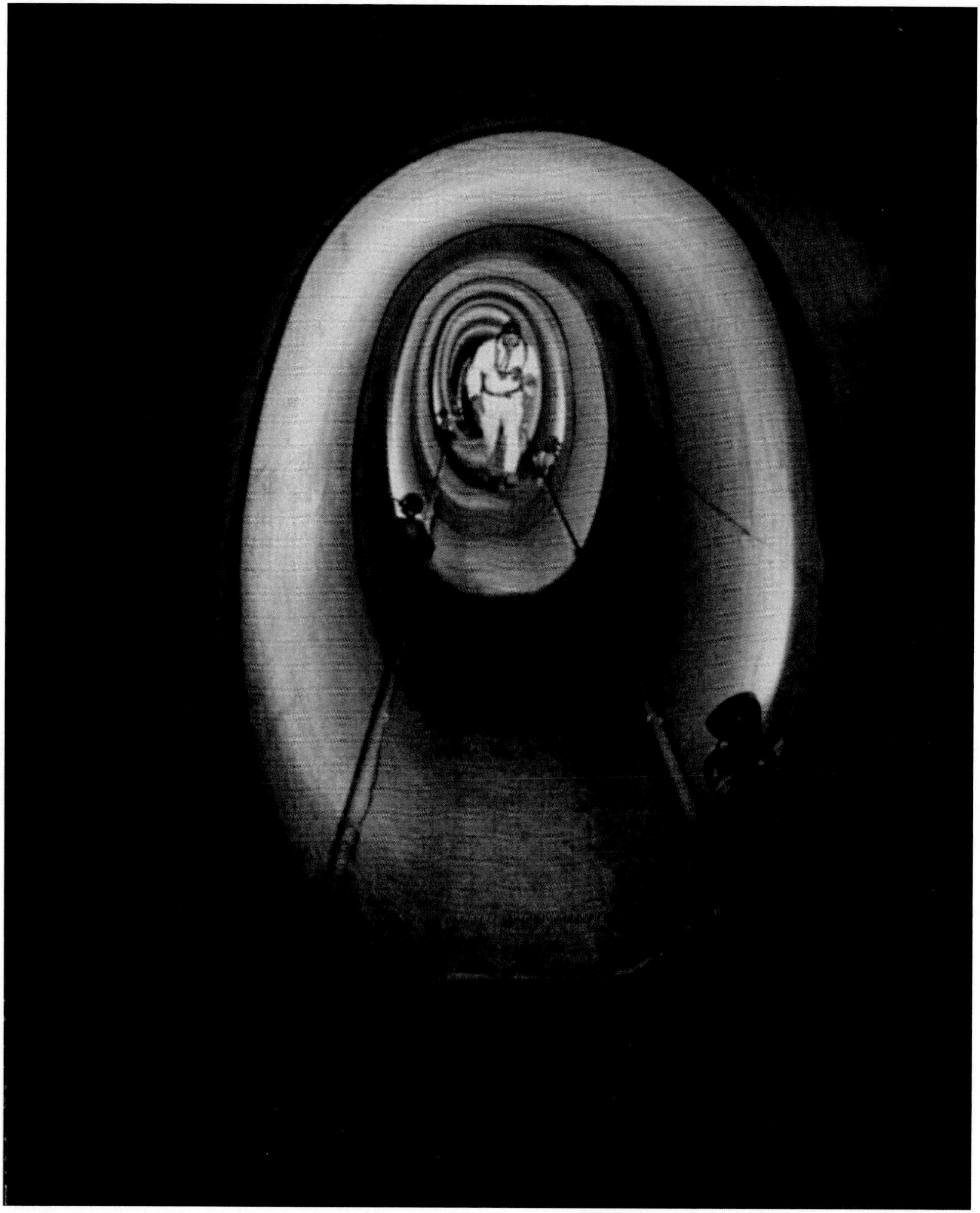

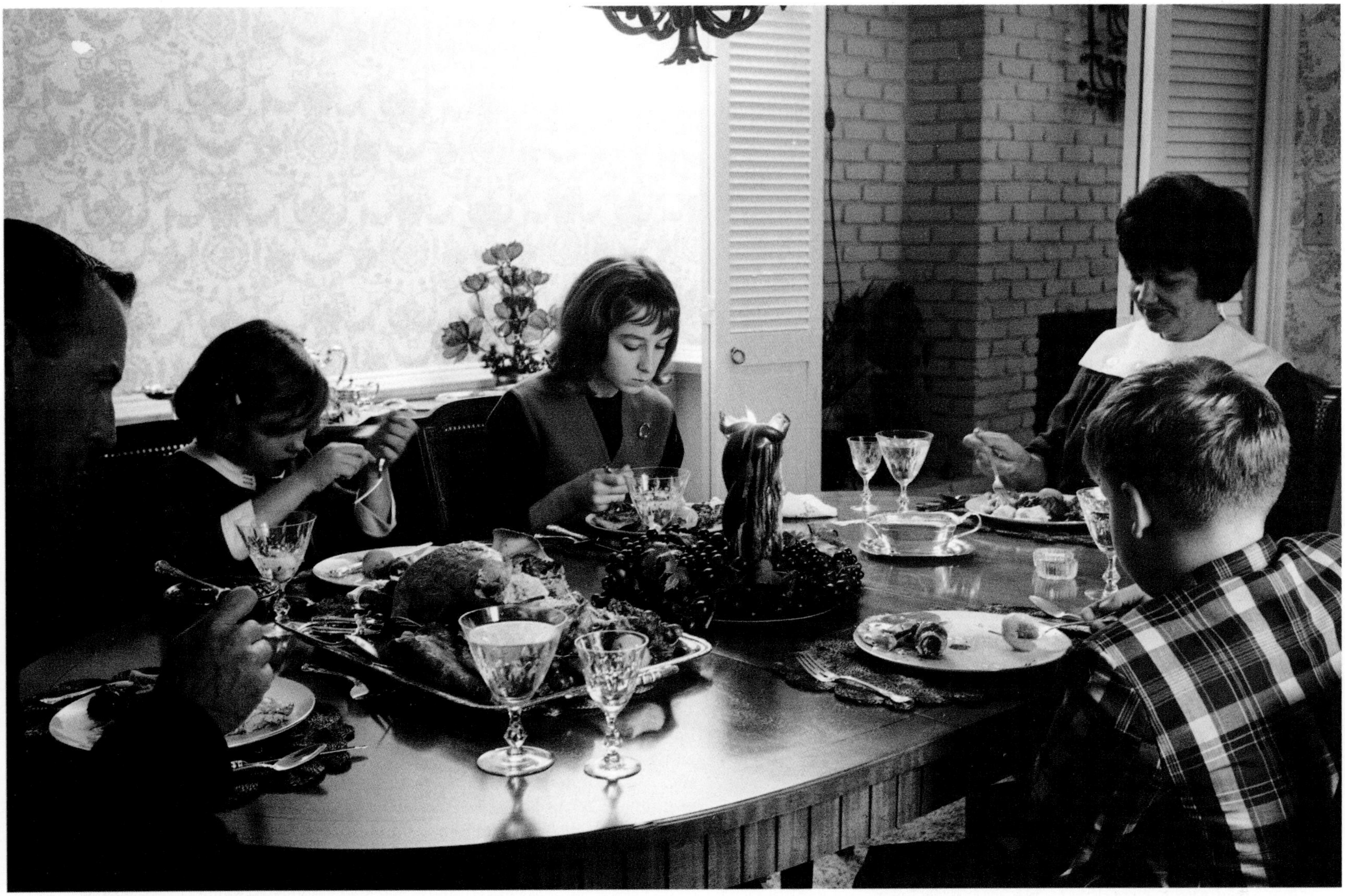

LEFT: A concrete air duct that acts as an escape route for astronauts, photographed in 1968. This was the sort of image beloved of *Life* readers who were intrigued by the marvel and mystery of space travel.

ABOVE: American astronaut Jim Lovell eating a turkey dinner with his wife and three children, Houston, 1965. It was important that the astronauts were seen as "regular guys" with families who just happened to have extraordinary talents – Morse was therefore given complete access to photograph them in their homes. The image is intimate, but also somewhat stiff.

CARL MYDANS

Carl Mydans is not as well known as two of the other original *Life* photographers, Margaret Bourke-White and Alfred Eisenstaedt, yet he had the charm of "Eisie" and the tenacity of Bourke-White, combined with a perfect hard news sensibility. Mydans was not an especially stylish photojournalist (he was a more talented portrait photographer), but he had a natural instinct for taking powerful images that would transport the viewer to the heart of the action. In 1948, for instance, he produced a dramatic and terrifying photo-essay on the Japanese earthquake in Fakui. The story of how Mydans got to be there in the first place reveals much about the forgiving and easygoing nature of the man. Despite his internment by the Japanese during the war, he bore them no ill will and, together with his wife, he jumped at the opportunity in 1946 to become *Life*'s bureau chief in Tokyo. He just happened to be the only journalist in Fakui when the tumultuous earthquake struck and he ran out into the street shooting pictures as buildings collapsed around him. These incredible images of devastation are perhaps the most powerful record ever of an unfolding earthquake. It is incredible to think that Mydans was able to compose a photograph and develop a narrative under such fraught circumstances. At the time of this earthquake, Americans were still ambivalent about the Japanese, but these images shifted attitudes, arousing sympathy and empathy toward the perceived enemy. In his book *More Than Meets the Eye*, an eloquent discussion of his profession that contains no photographs, he says, "All of us live in history, whether we are aware of it or not." Mydans was very aware of history, was an authoritative witness to it, understood it and recognized, without any pomposity, his own important role in recording what he called "the great flowing river of time and humanity." Since his death in 2004, his work is receiving renewed acclaim.

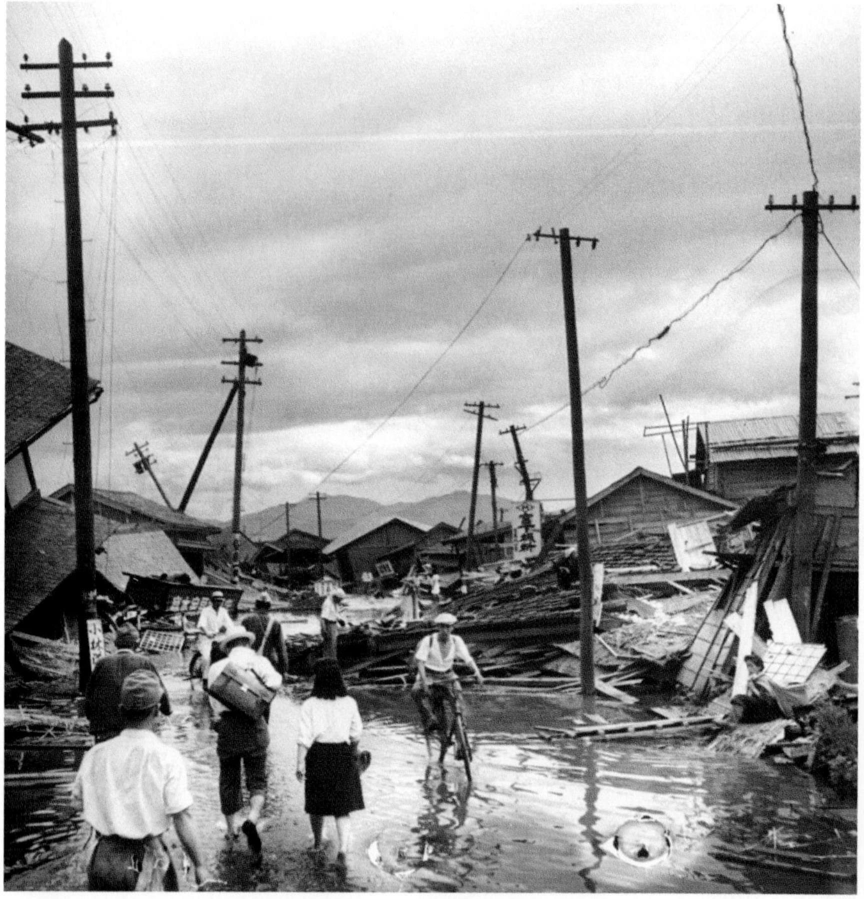

ABOVE: In 1948 the manmade landscape was devastated by the Fakui earthquake. In the background of this image, the mountains are unchanged, suggesting the precarious nature of these people's existence. As well as the mountains, our eyes are drawn toward the cyclist who appears in the frame, as if he is guiding us through the chaos.

RIGHT: During the earthquake buildings crumble and break apart.

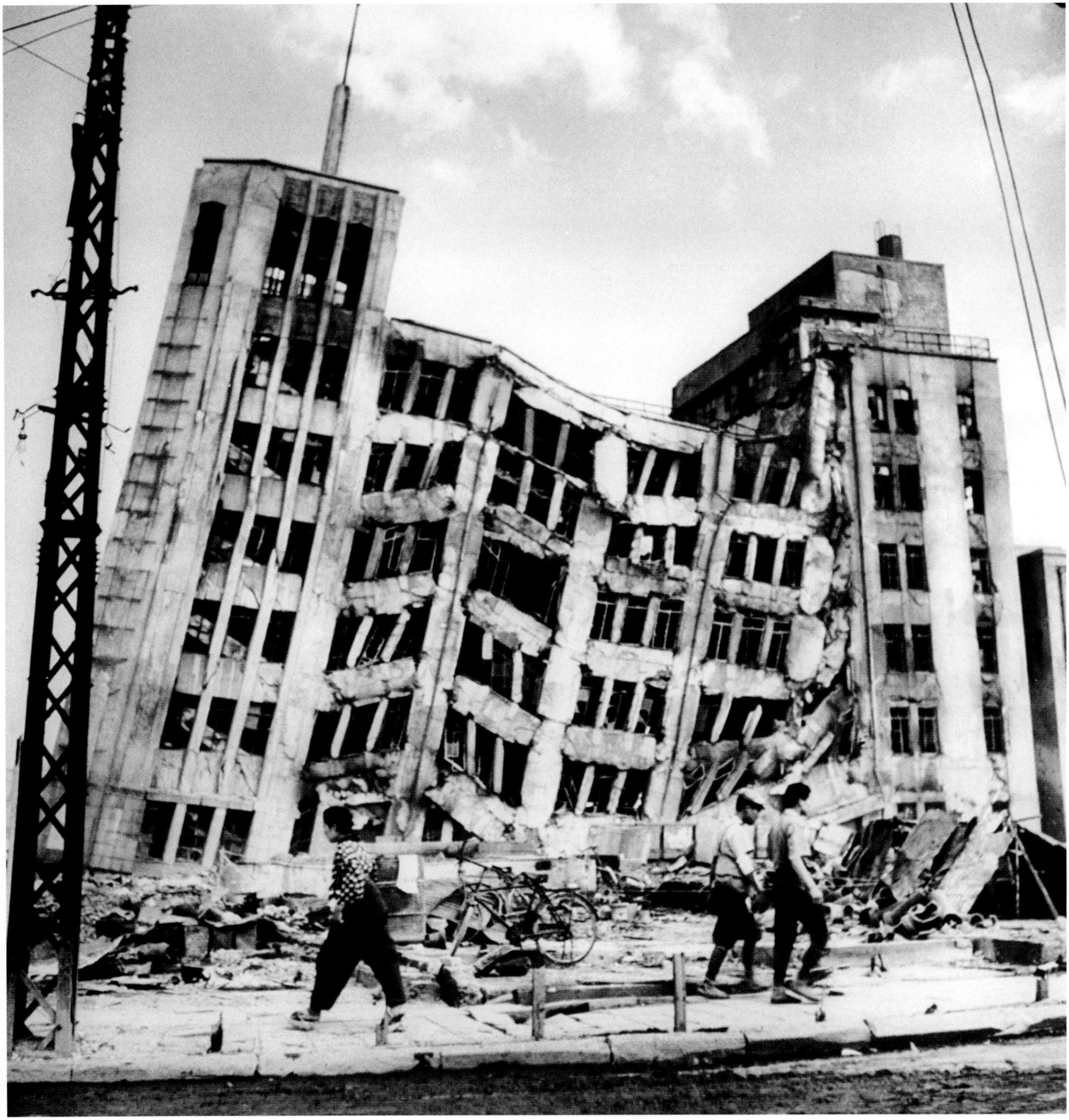

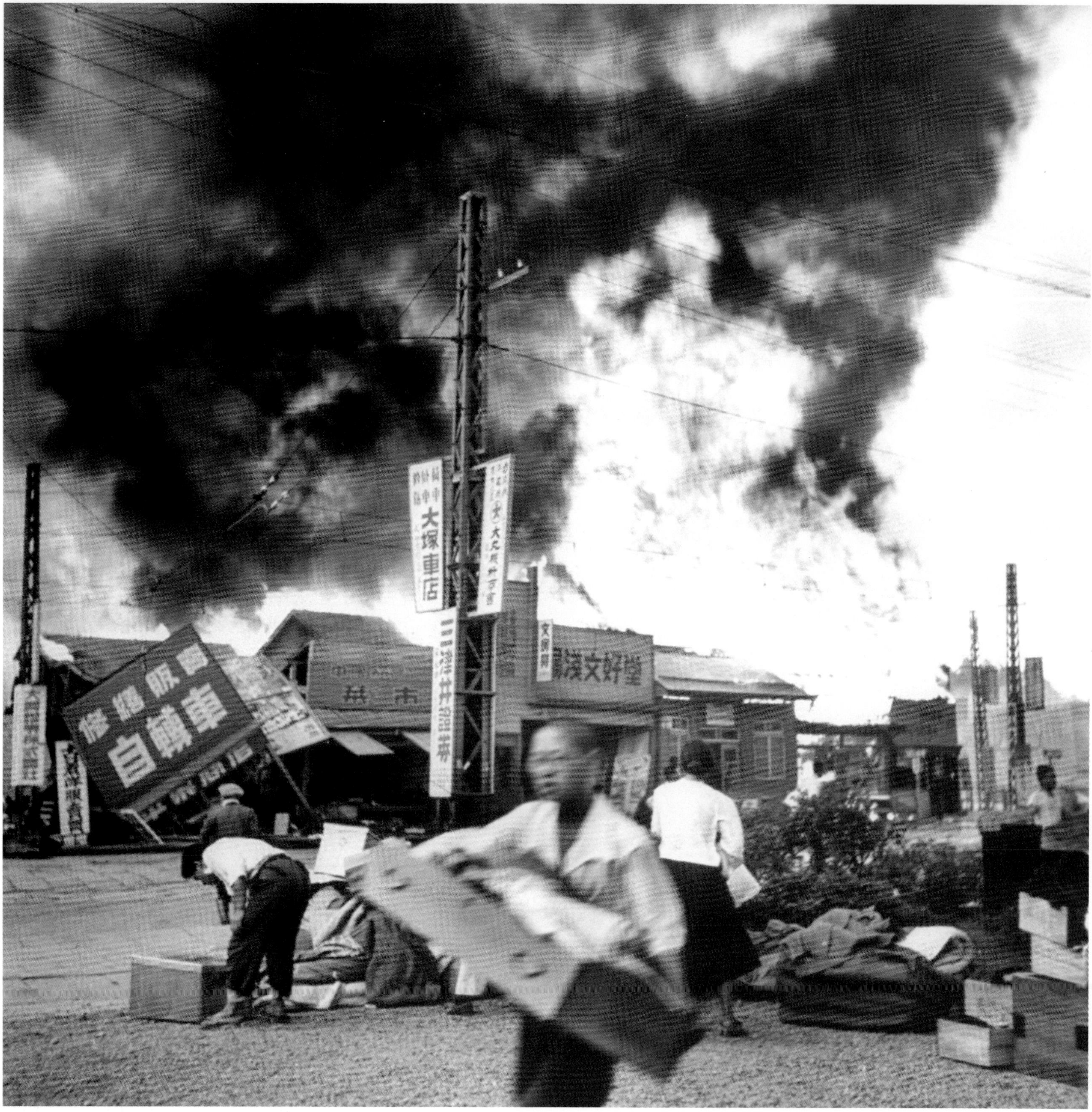

ABOVE: **After the Fakui earthquake in 1948, Mydans captured scenes of ruin and devastation, as people fled burning buildings.**

RIGHT: **A wounded man, his body contorted with pain, is stretchered to safety during the Fakui earthquake.**

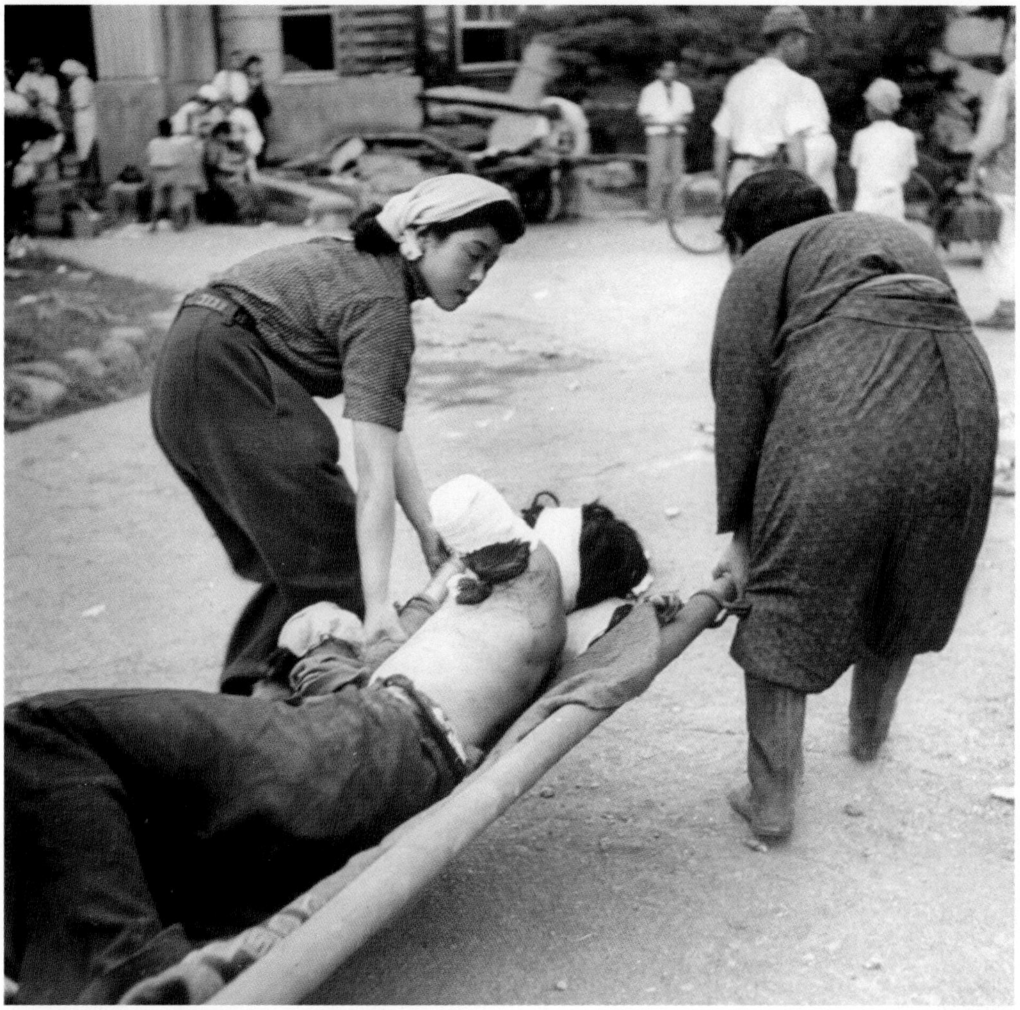

RIGHT: **American GIs were drafted in to administer first aid to victims of the Fakui earthquake. Everywhere you look in this photograph, there is ruin and suffering, with the ever-present smoke billowing in the distance, suggesting that this scene is just a small detail of a terrible whole. *Life* readers would have also appreciated the patriotic subtext, with the American GI a central, composed figure in the midst of the crisis.**

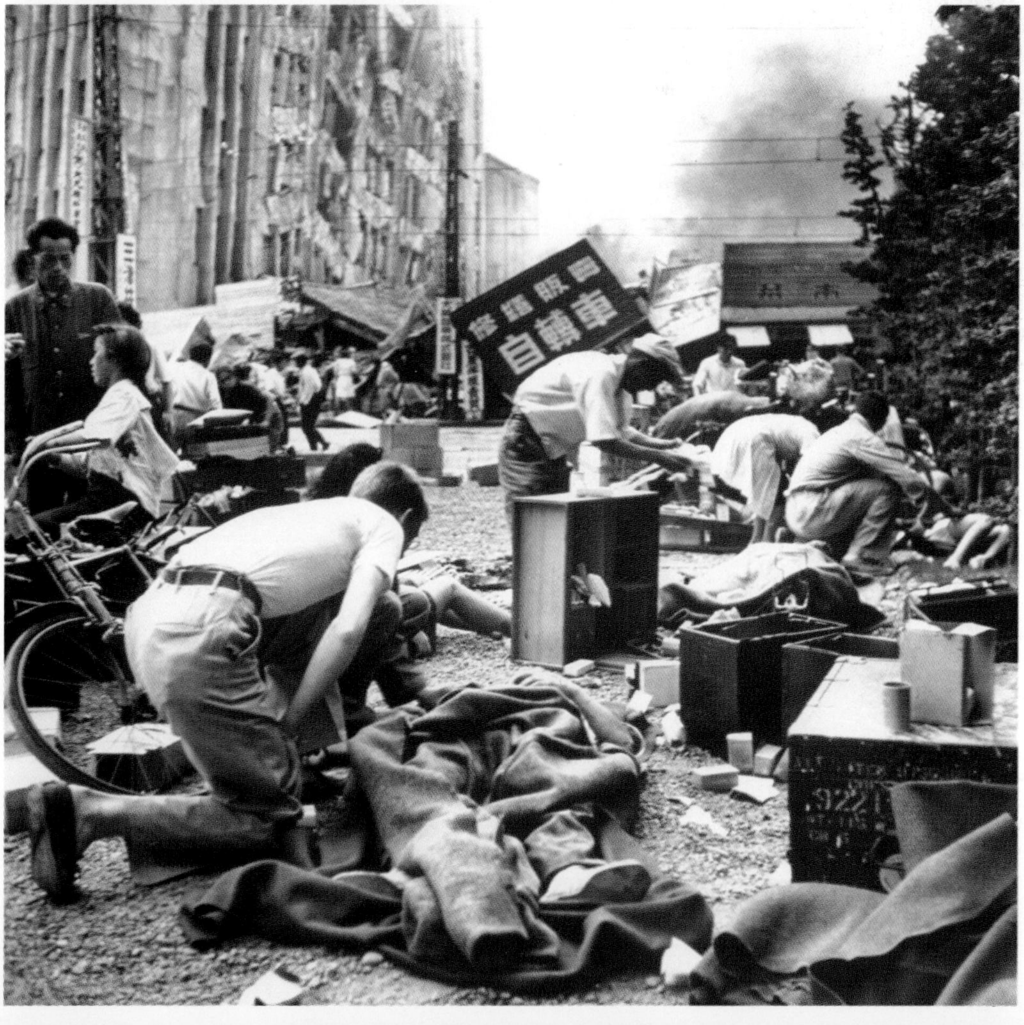

JAMES NACHTWEY

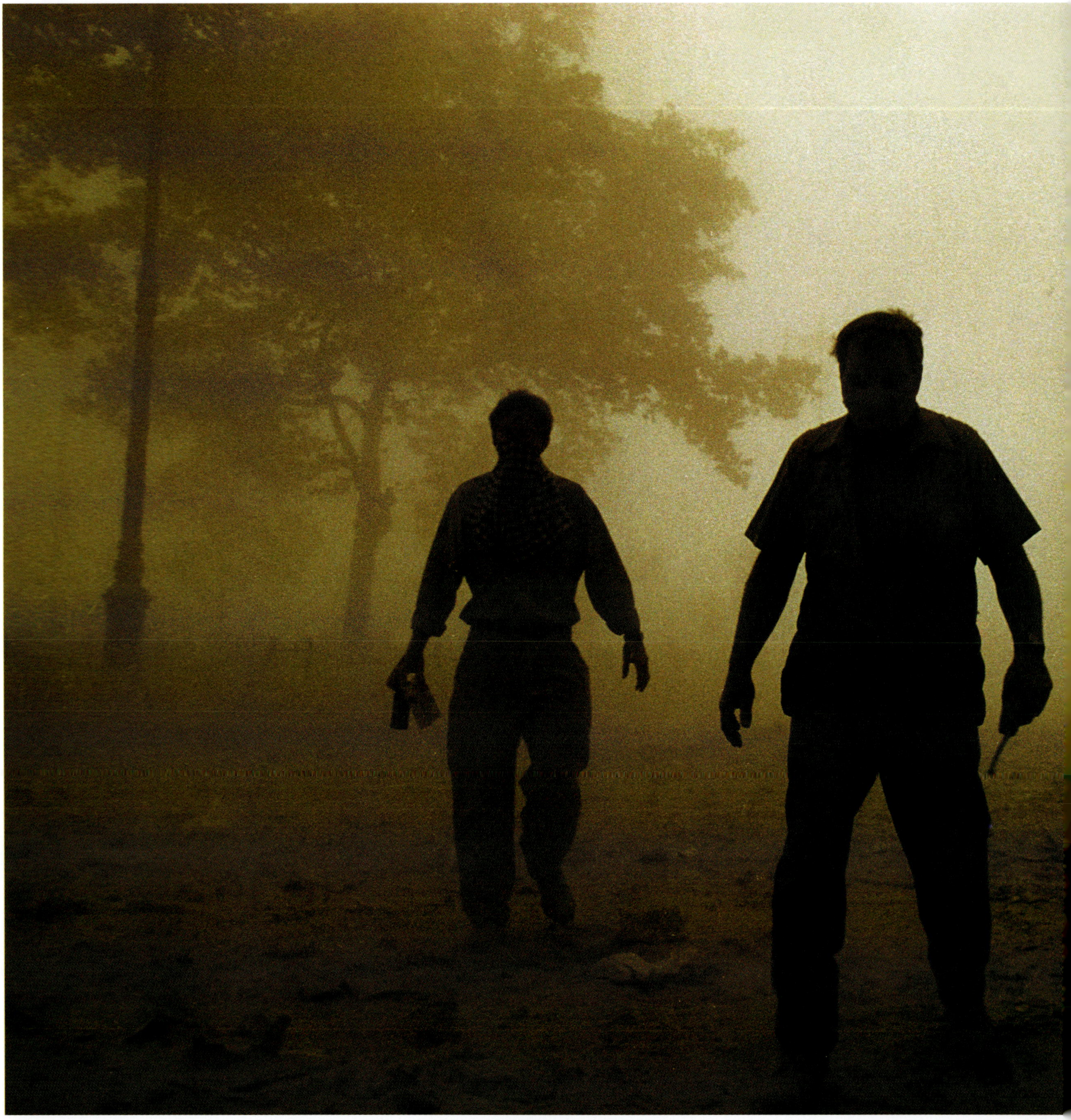

BELOW: Dazed survivors and a police officer walk through an apocalyptic landscape in lower Manhattan after the collapse of the World Trade Center Twin Towers on 11 September, 2001. The formal composition and ethereal beauty of the image are typical of Nachtwey's style.

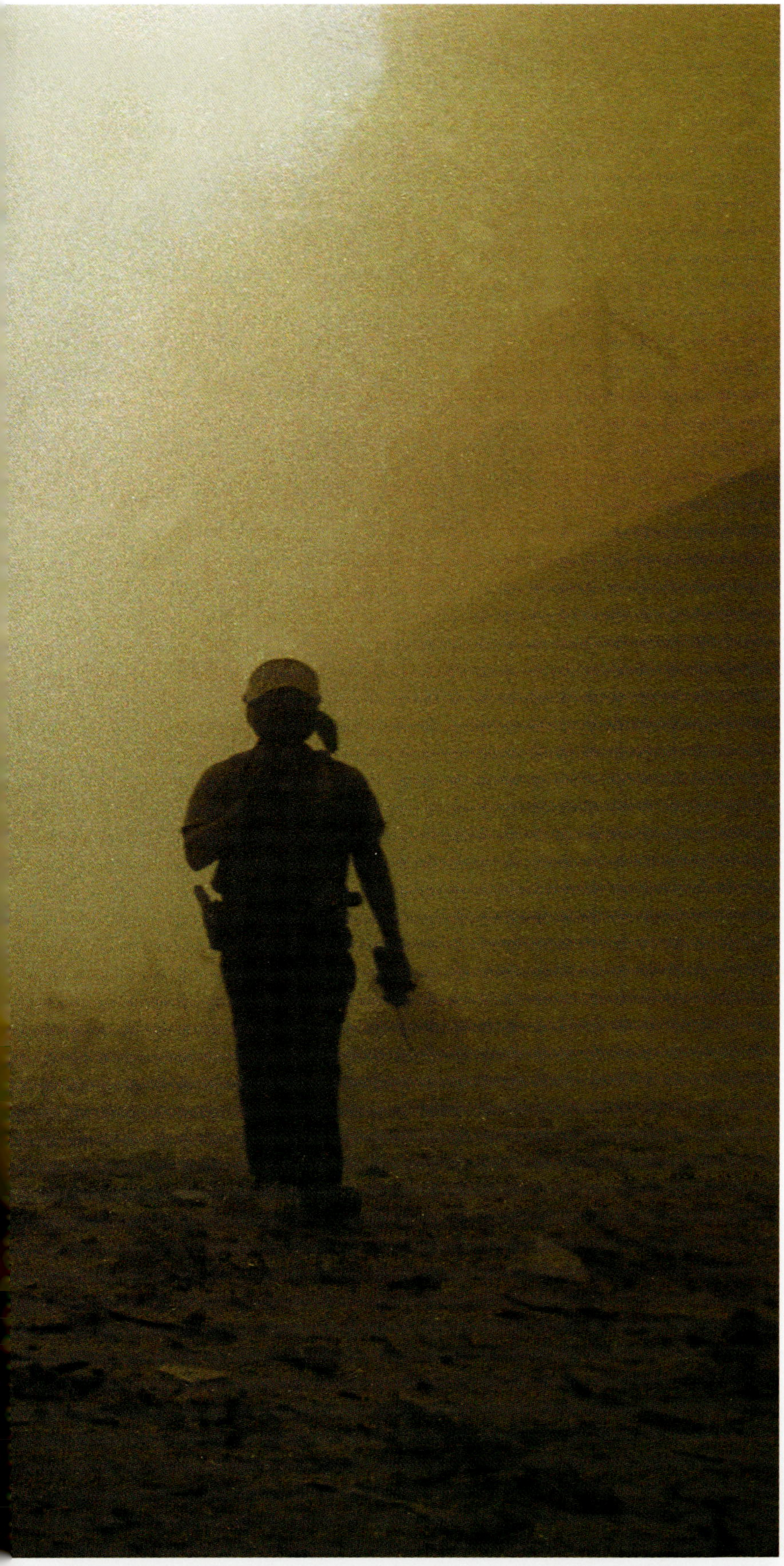

Nachtwey is one of the most renowned and enigmatic of contemporary photojournalists. Inspired in the 1960s by images of the Vietnam War and civil rights movement, he trained himself to become a war photographer with near-religious zeal and single-mindedness. Among photographers, Nachtwey is very much a loner, and discipline, self-control and a deliberate style are his hallmarks. He seems to have a limitless capacity for fear, anger and grief – emotions that he says he channels back into his work. Nachtwey is known for getting physically closer to his subjects than other photojournalists, and has explained to various interviewers that he likes to work within the same space that his subjects inhabit, so that viewers can connect viscerally. His daring and risk-taking have nearly cost Nachtwey his life on several occasions – in 2003, for instance, he was badly wounded in Iraq by a grenade thrown into a vehicle in which he was riding. His personality and working style stir plenty of curiosity, but Nachtwey is an extremely private person who deflects questions about himself, insisting over and over again that he wants his audience to concern themselves with his subjects instead.

To draw attention to his subject matter, he shoots images that are formally composed and strikingly beautiful. His book *Inferno*, a collection of photographs he shot during the 1990s, features 480 pages of the most graphic, gruesome and beautifully photographed horrors of humanity. Not surprisingly, he has been criticized for creating objects of beauty out of other people's misery, but he counters that images need to be compelling to draw the attention and outrage that his subjects need and deserve. Nachtwey has also been criticized for giving short shrift to the context of the horrors he photographs, but he's less concerned with explaining situations than stirring an instinctive reaction. To accusations that he is a war junkie, Nachtwey admits an attraction, but if it were a mere addiction, he has asserted, he would have burnt out long ago. In recent years, he has taken to referring to himself as an "anti-war" photographer with a mission to sway public opinion and pressure politicians and policy-makers into redressing injustices.

OVERLEAF LEFT: A businessman stops amid dust and detritus to stare up at the burning World Trade Center Towers in Lower Manhattan after the terrorist attacks. Nachtwey's impeccable composition and the subject's pose convey the awe-inspiring magnitude of the horror.

OVERLEAF TOP RIGHT: Firemen and rescue workers stand in the wreckage of the World Trade Center Towers after their collapse. By framing the scene in a jagged, broken panel of an adjacent building, Nachtwey suggests the violence of the attacks that precipitated the disaster.

OVERLEAF BOTTOM RIGHT: A stairwell near the World Trade Center in Lower Manhattan is littered with paper and dust following the attacks. Nachtwey uses the light, debris, and the lone figure at the top of the left-hand staircase to portray a post-apocalyptic scene.

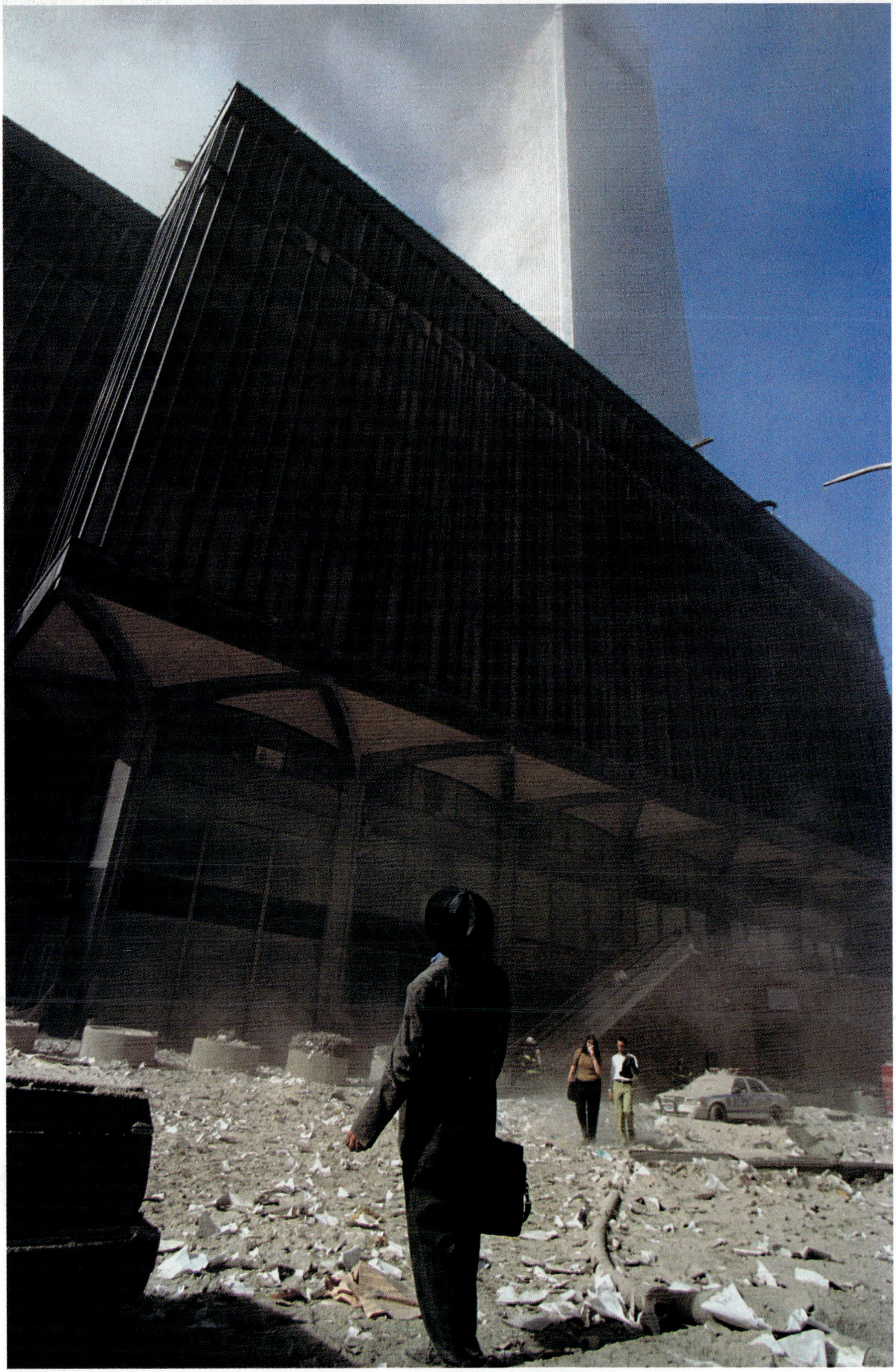

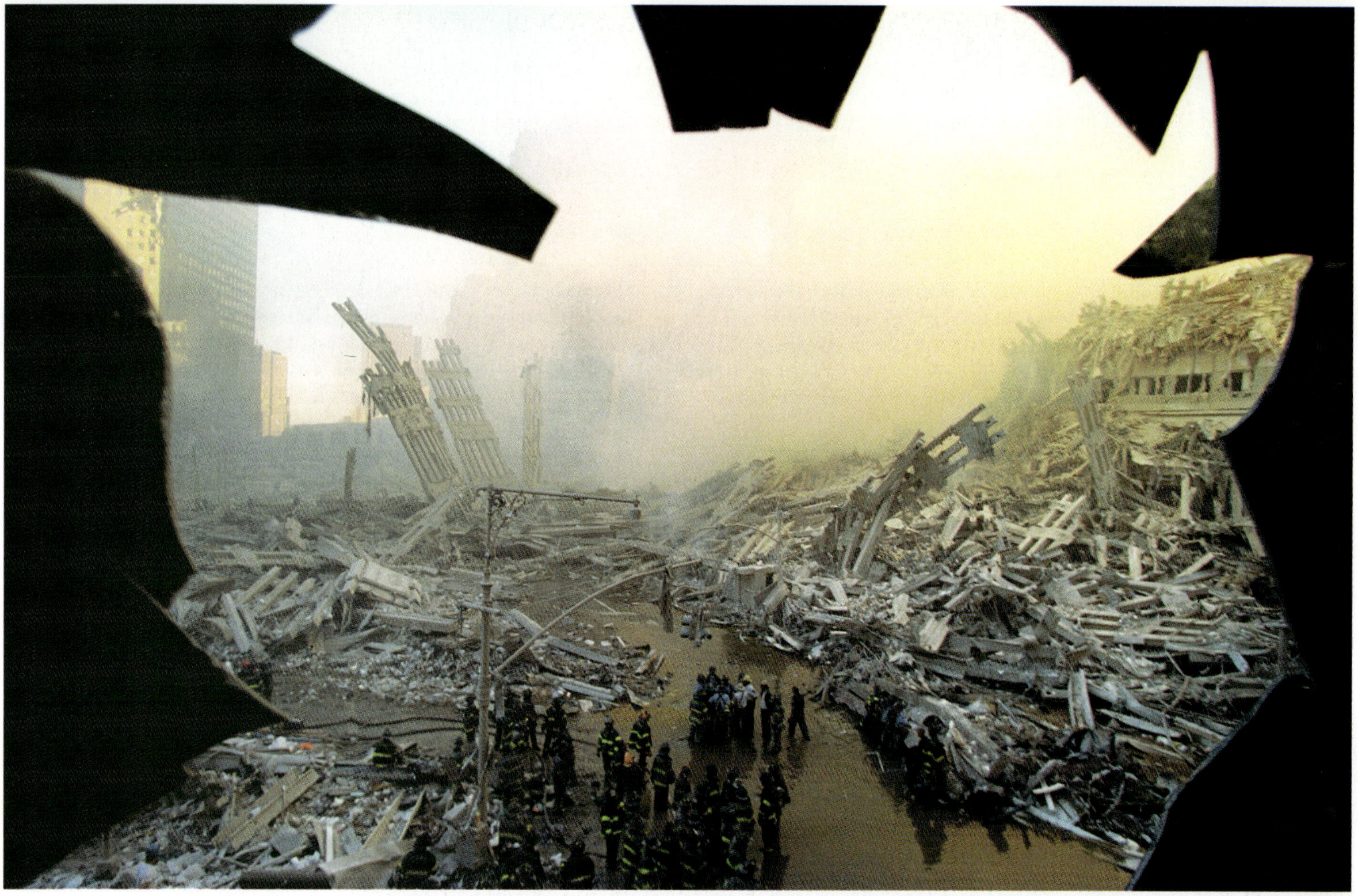

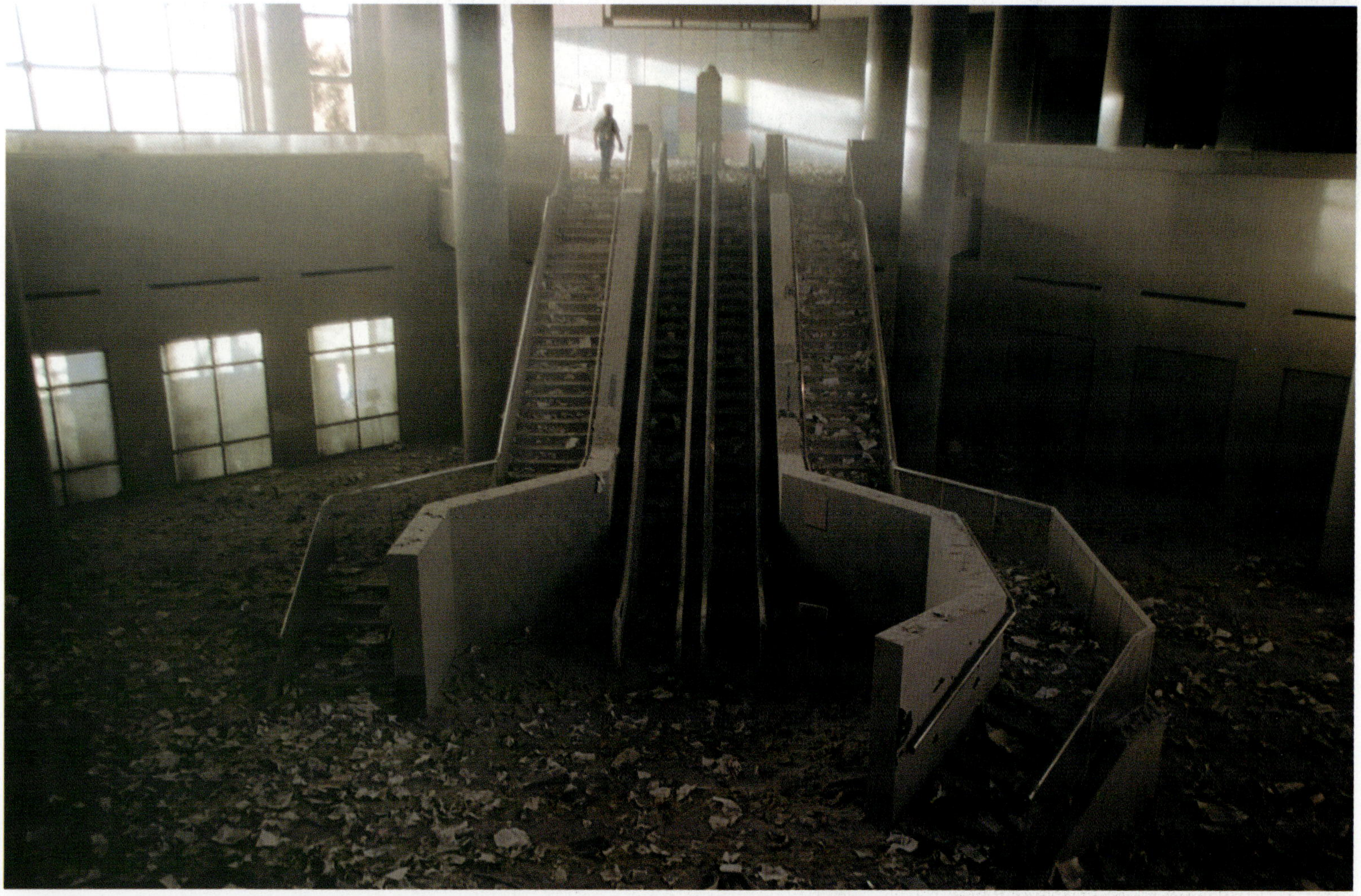

ZED NELSON

Zed Nelson is part of a select group of photographers who can seamlessly combine dynamic 35mm spot-news photojournalism, medium-format portraiture and social documentary. This straddling of genres was displayed to devastating effect in his seminal essay *Gun Nation*. The project, he says, was in many ways a spin-off of spending years working in war zones where violence is the natural law. Nelson himself came very close to becoming a victim while on assignment in Afghanistan, when his car came under fire, and his driver and a close friend were shot and badly injured. Weapons and guns were at the crux of this tragedy, and this revelation led to a career change when Nelson abandoned the path of war photography. "I decided to document America's example, of a nation that had accepted, embraced and even popularized gun ownership and where a nation is in denial of a problem that allows 30,000 people to be killed by gunfire every year," he says. Rather than photographing the usual stereotypical groups normally associated with guns – right-wing extremists or gang members – Nelson documents, in a matter-of-fact way, the normal citizens who see guns as part of their social landscape, in much the same way as baseball and apple pie. We see these law-abiding middle-class and (almost exclusively) white folks at gun shops and conventions, in living rooms, emergency rooms and school yards. It is the banality of it all that makes it so chilling. The project created such a stir in the USA that after a television interview on *Good Morning America* Nelson received death threats.

Since this essay, Nelson has continued looking for projects that, in his words, "investigate our own obsessions and weaknesses". Guns are one obsession; food is another. In *Obesity in the USA* Nelson photographs extremely overweight people at leisure with a satirical eye and in unforgiving colour. Hidden beneath the frivolity is the serious message that too much wrong food is as potent a killer as a gun. Zed Nelson is an astute social commentator. Whatever the project, he consistently emerges with original and thoughtful-provoking images.

RIGHT AND BELOW: The line between celebrating and exploiting your subjects can be a thin one, but Nelson here manages to stay on the right side of respecting who he is photographing. These people at a Fat Convention in the USA are happy in their skin and therefore relishing the attention.

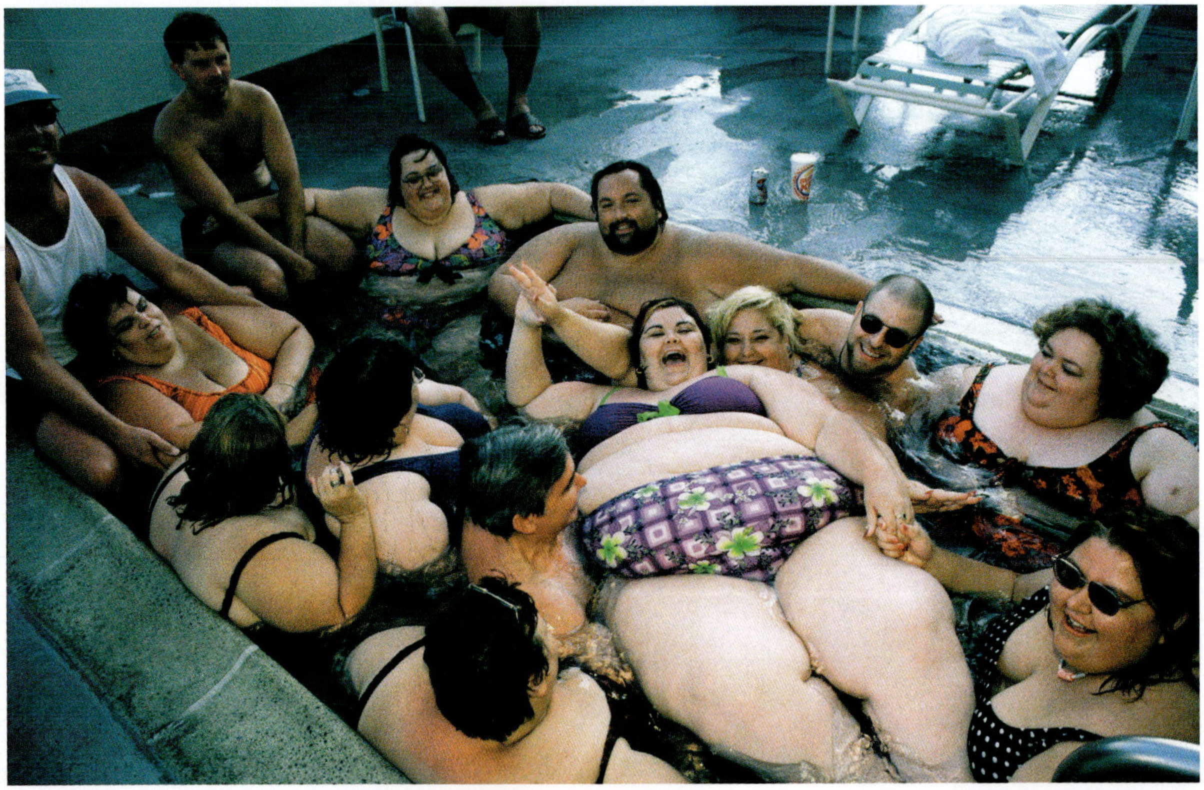

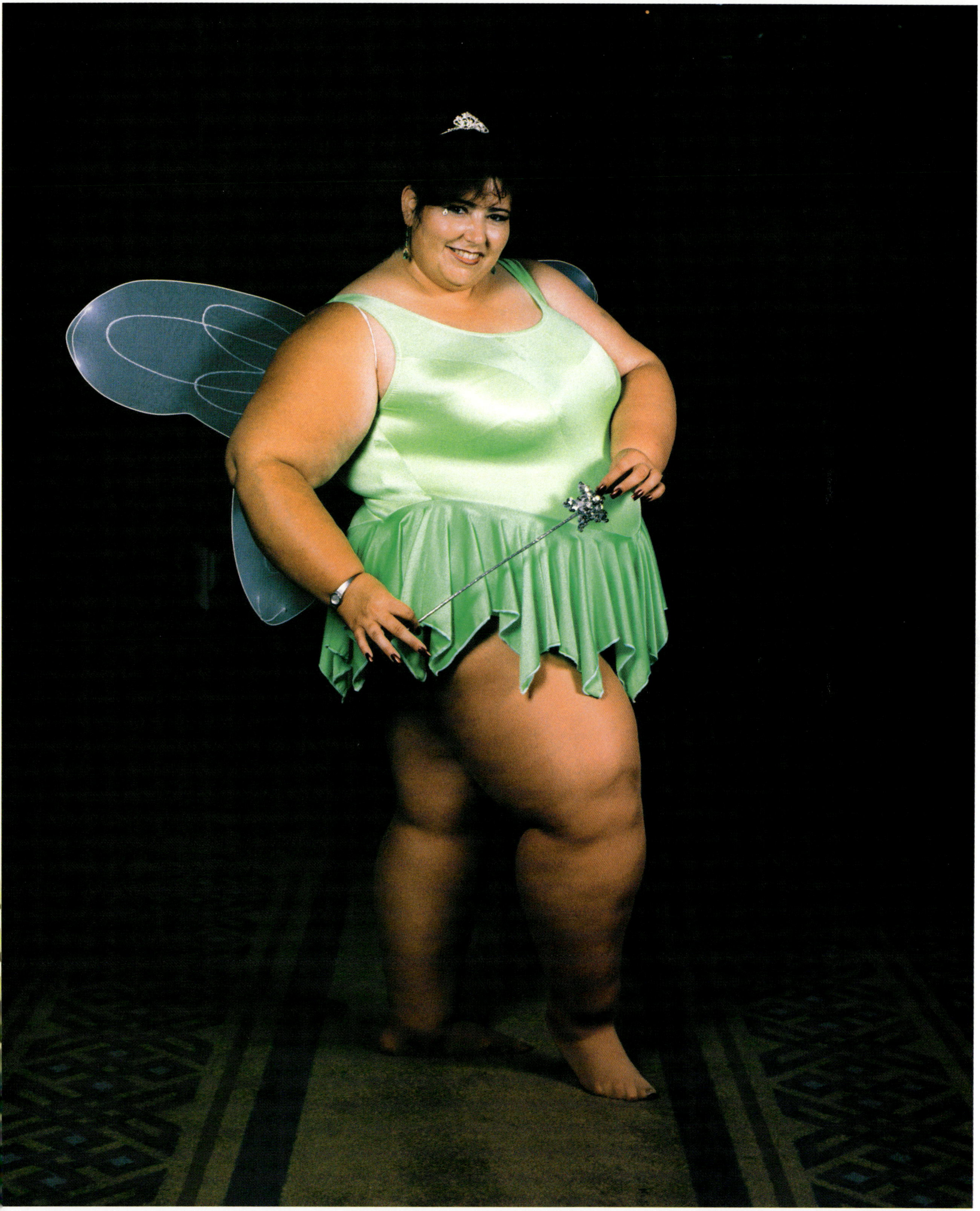

BELOW: A cowboy shows his gun to young admirers at Universal Studios, Hollywood, Los Angeles. Nelson shows how the cycle of gun worship can start in very conventional ways – this seemingly harmless sheriff with his friendly grin is perhaps a man to be avoided. Subtle and sinister.

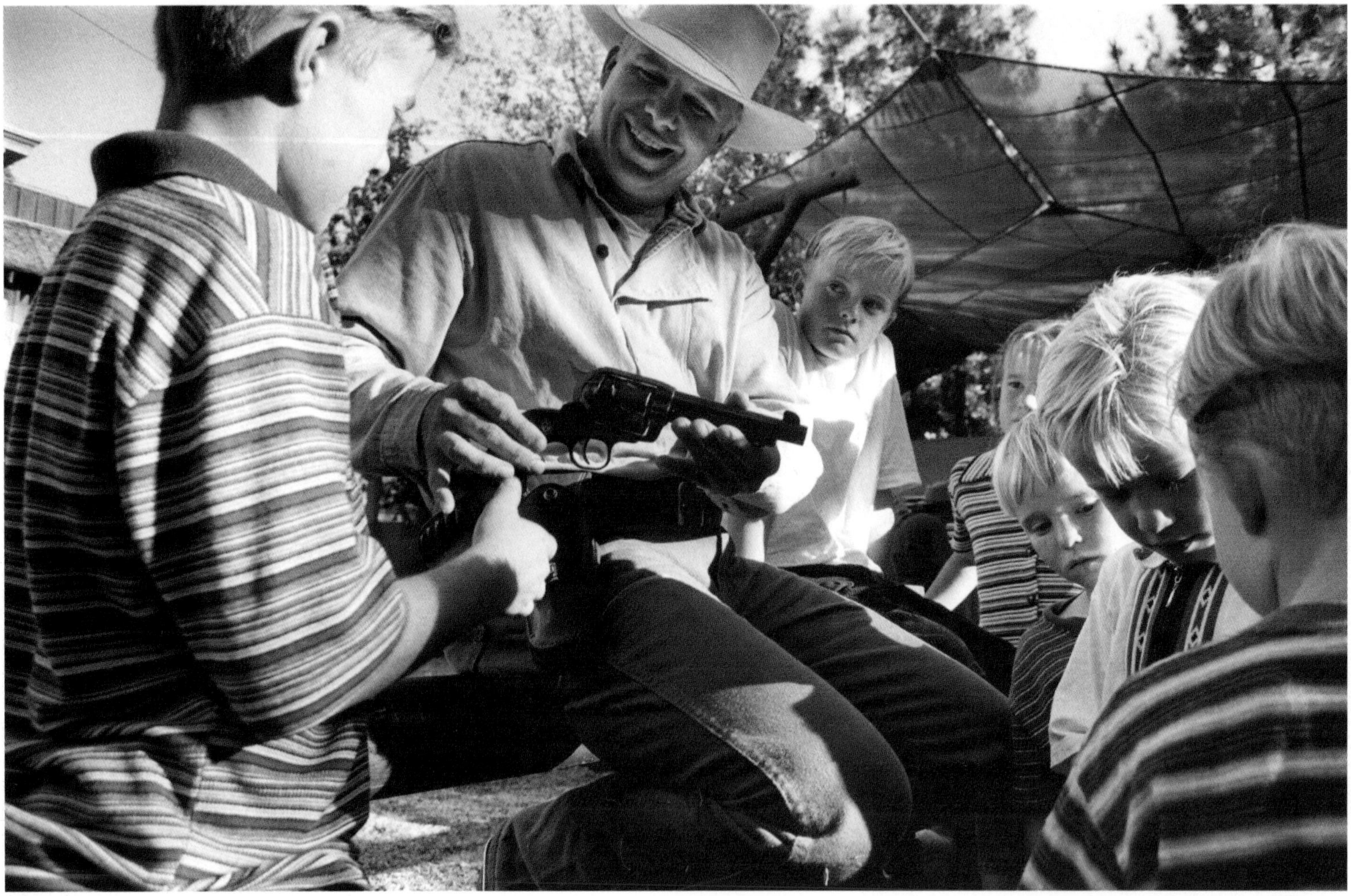

RIGHT: "It's my constitutional right to own a gun and protect my family," says Mike, a father and gun owner. This photograph is really terrifying; the man's expression alone is reason enough to look away. It is also ironic that he is talking about protecting his family and yet pointing the gun in the direction of his child.

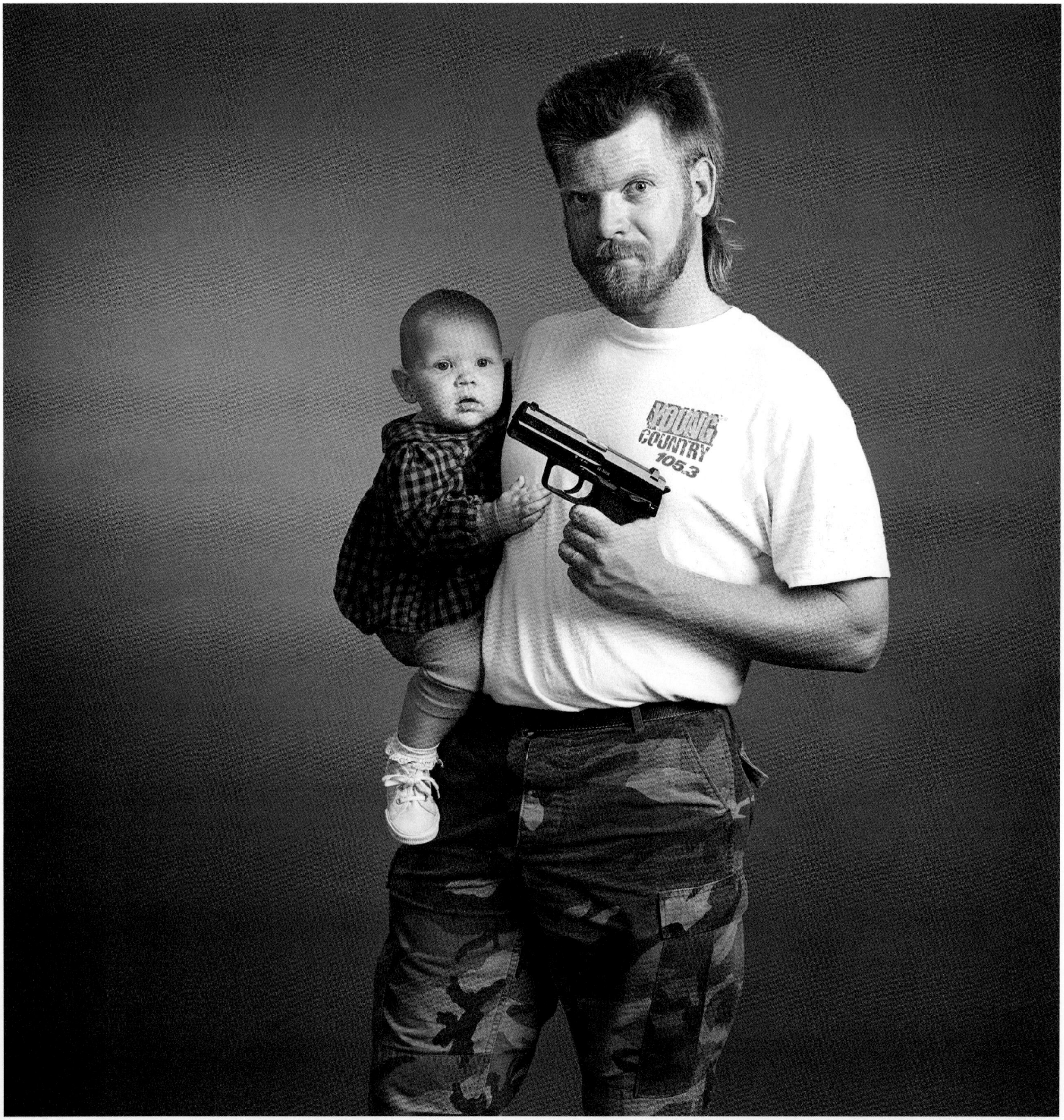
YOUNG
COUNTRY
105.3

MARTIN PARR

BELOW: This photograph, along with those on the opposite page, are taken from Parr's essay on New Brighton, an English resort just outside Liverpool, 1984–85. Parr photographed with cheap amateur colour film to make everything look even more gaudy and tacky. Named *The Last Resort*, the essay depicts the resort as dirty, overcrowded, bleak and grim. This work is unforgiving, but also very funny.

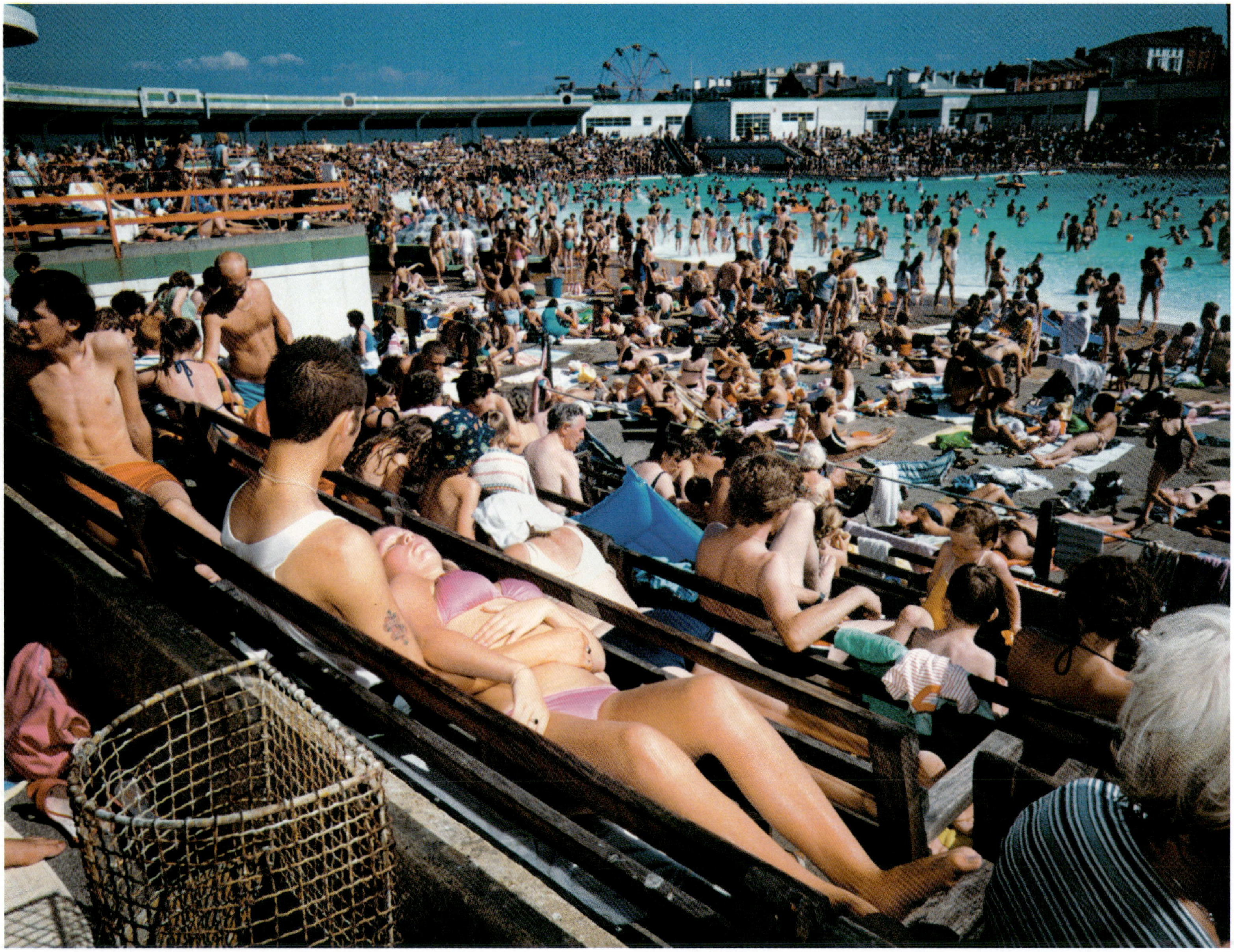

Photojournalism and documentary photography have always had a strong element of exploitation and voyeurism. Humanistic photojournalists led by Cartier-Bresson, however, have always rejected this charge of exploitation, saying that their images celebrate life. At the other end of the spectrum is the equally brilliant Martin Parr, who acknowledges that his photographs are unashamedly voyeuristic. Parr was a controversial choice to be admitted into the Magnum cooperative in the 1990s, yet ironically he is one of the most commercially successful photographers in Magnum's history. When he met Parr for the first time, Cartier-Bresson allegedly expressed his unease to the British photographer: "I have only one thing to say to you. You are from a completely different planet to me." Parr's reputation, or infamy, depending on your viewpoint, was established in the 1980s with his seminal essay on New Brighton, a seaside town just outside Liverpool. This body of work, *The Last Resort,* is aptly named because in Parr's somewhat cruel and brutal view it is a grim place of pink and overweight people sunbathing next to rubbish and eating greasy food. Parr photographs in saturated and unforgiving colour and has a surreal sense of composition. His work was seen as unflinching to the point of reactionary; the photographer defended the work from his mainly middle-class critics, saying that their comments confirmed their bourgeois prejudices.

Since then, Parr, although still cynical, has become more humorous with the passing of time. He has dealt with such themes as the absurdity of global tourism, relentless mass consumerism and the homogenization of culture. Often he likes to get in very close, using a macro lens, in order to convey the horror of a particular tacky item of clothing or inedible food. Parr is relentless in his quest to document how we live, what we buy and how we look – a unique British talent.

RIGHT: This image could have been taken at any time in the past 50 years – the woman fiddling nervously with her hands and the man's pained expression say it all.

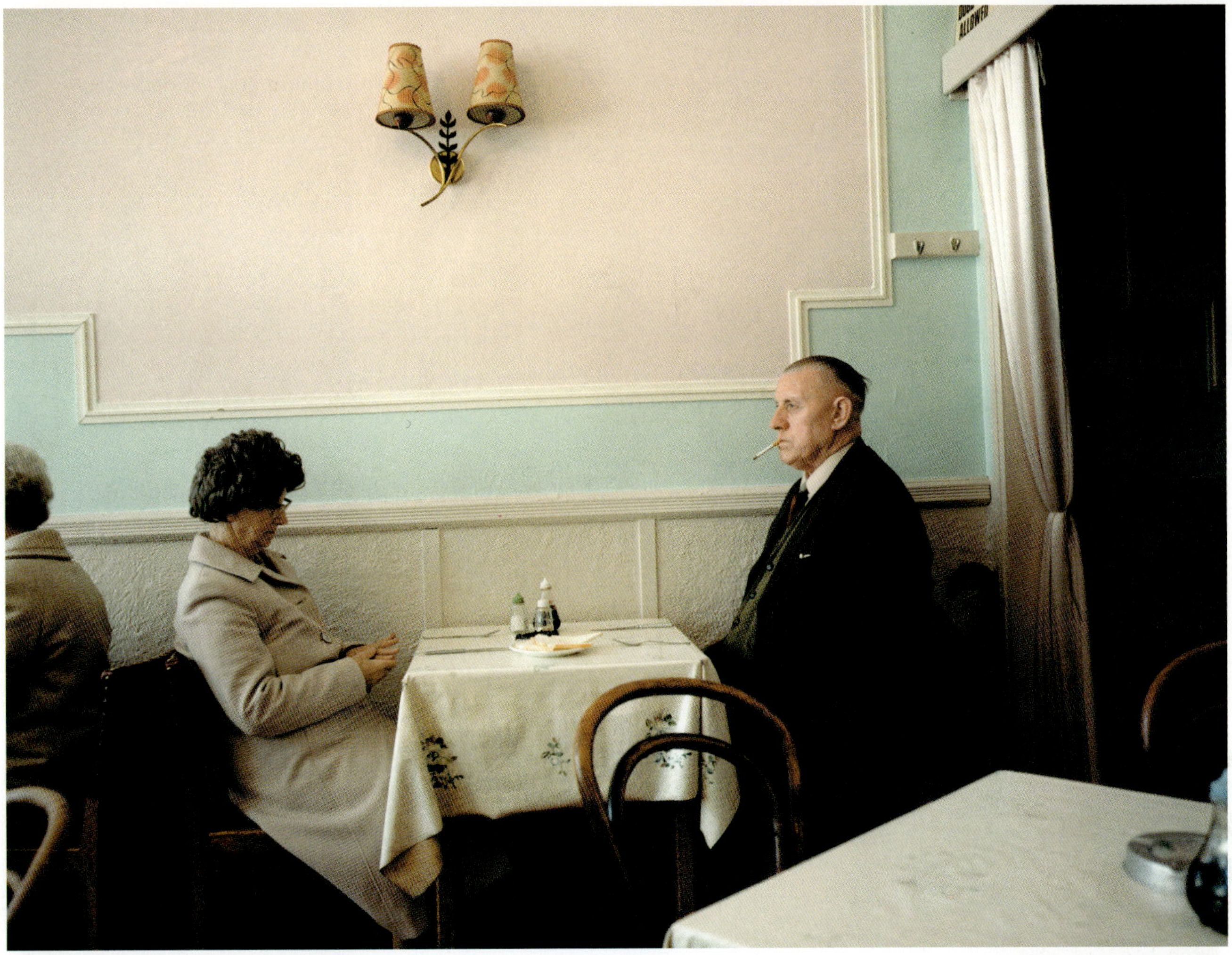

RIGHT: A woman and her child sunbathe forlornly on concrete. Parr's surreal sense of composition and colour makes the bleak appear absurd.

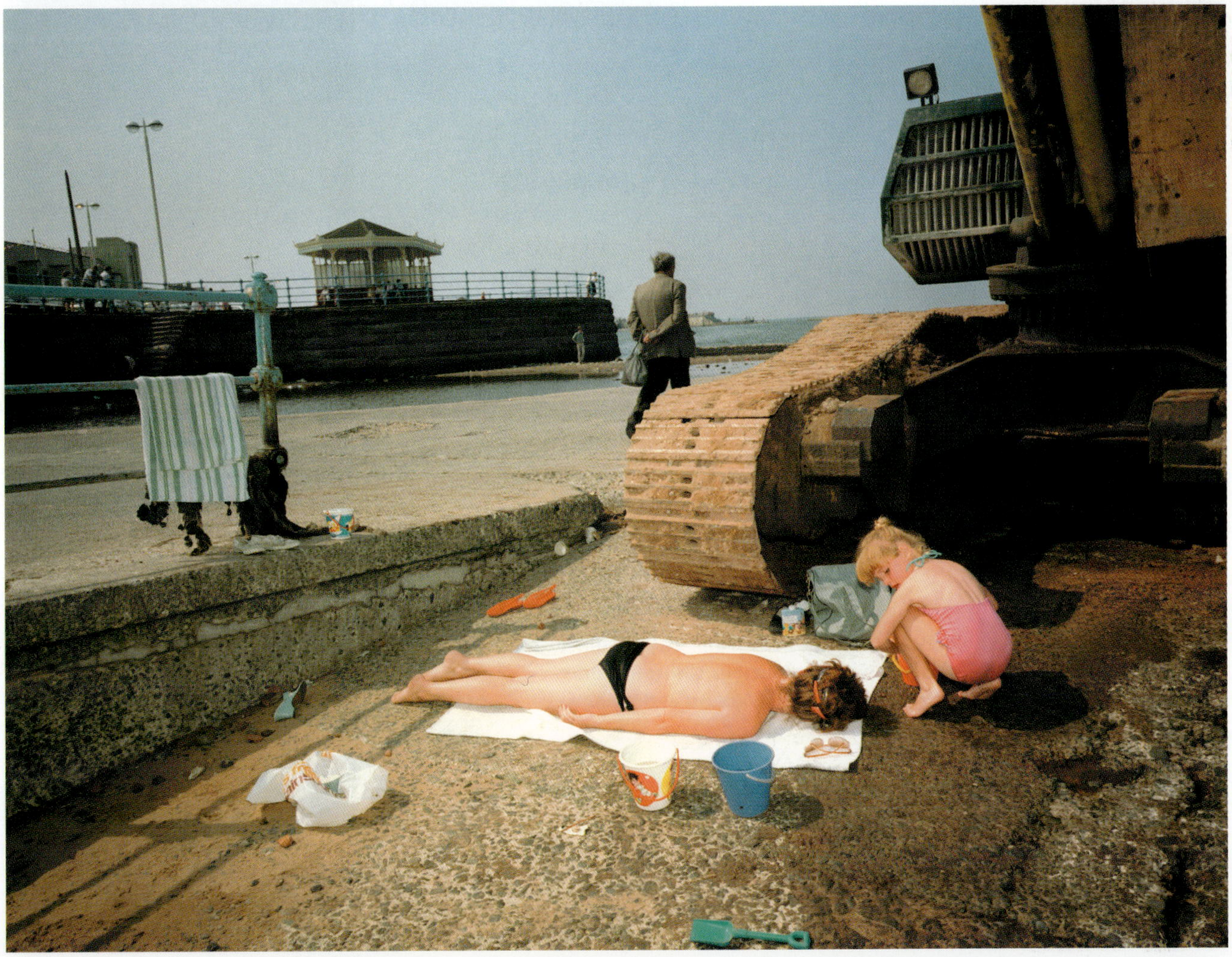

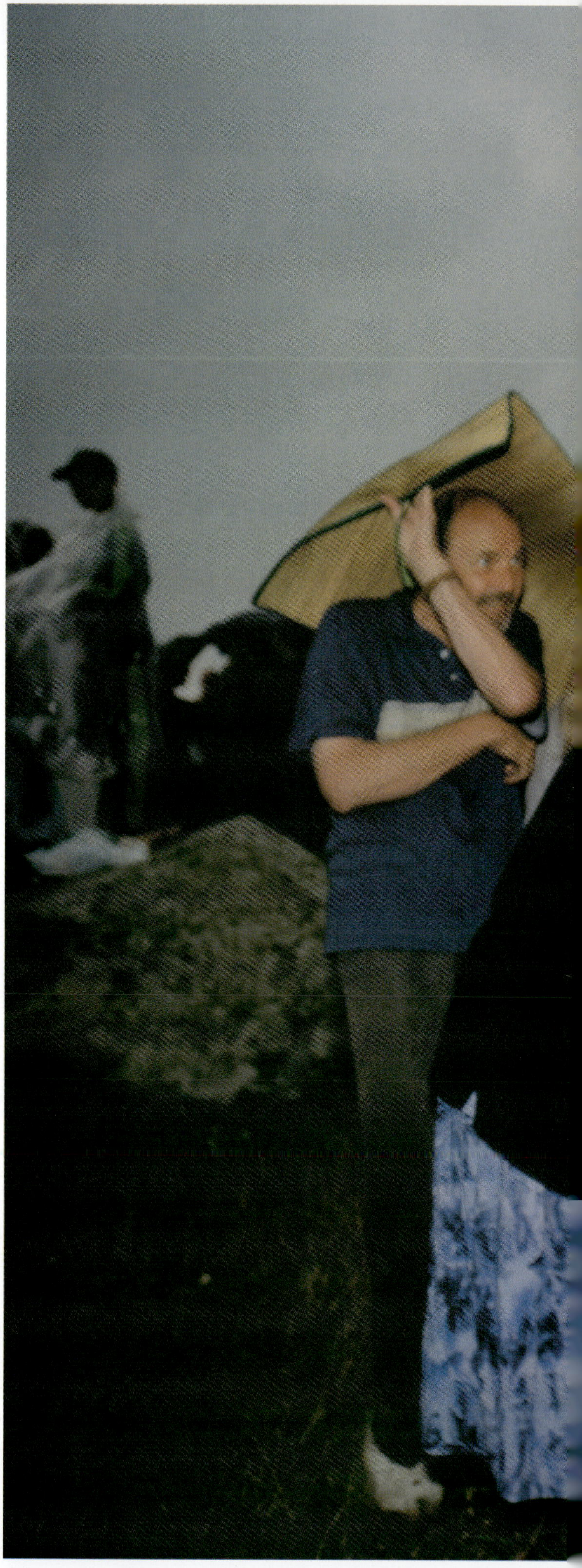

RIGHT: In the summer of 1999, more than half a million people flocked to St Ives in Cornwall, England, to witness a total eclipse of the sun. Parr is more interested in the somewhat tacky human celebration and forced jollity than the cosmic phenomenon. Weather and its impact upon us is a recurring theme in Parr's work.

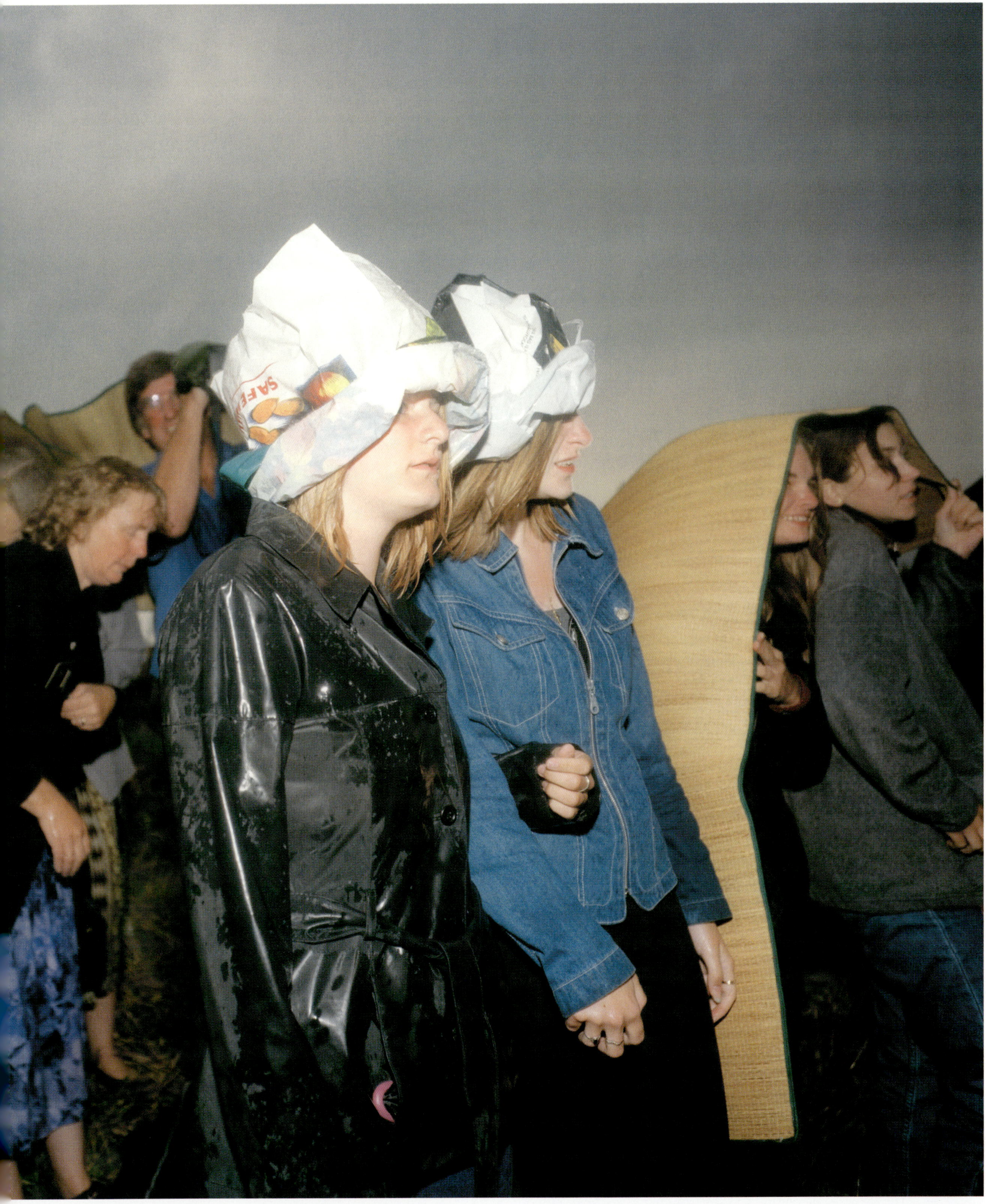

JUDAH PASSOW

BELOW: Palestinian children in the village of Fahme playing "Intifada". They are acting out a scene they have seen in the streets of neighbouring Jenin – Israeli troops arresting Palestinian men. It is a provocative image combining a painful reality with a kind of absurdity.

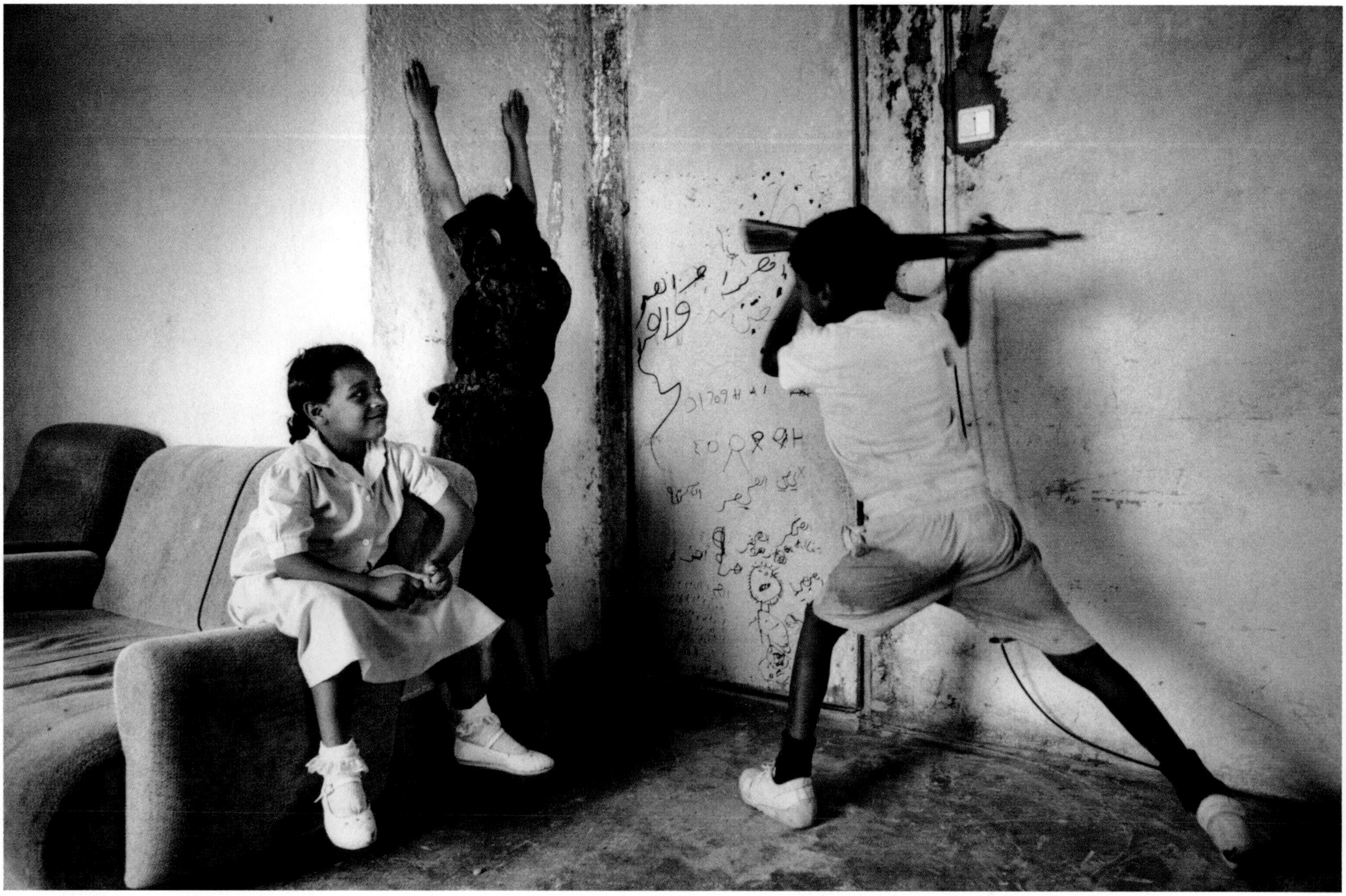

The Middle East, and in particular the Israeli-Palestinian conflict, has proved irresistible to many of the famous photojournalists featured in this book. For Judah Passow, however, the Middle East is not a tour of duty, but a life's work. It is an intricate religious, nationalist and ideological conflict with many shades of grey and it needs a photographer with Passow's integrity, dedication and intellect to try make sense of it all. "The conflict is complex and requires a nuanced reading of history and the abandoning of dogma to understand," he says. "My photographs reflect hopefully the lack of preconceived notions from which I approach both sides of the ideological divide."

Despite being Jewish and born in Israel, Passow – especially in his work in the West Bank and in Beirut (1982–85) – is clearly not portraying the Israeli occupation sympathetically. The Palestinians in these deceptively simple images are very much photographed as the victims. We see in these images the young, stripped of their youth, and the elderly, divested of their dignity, while the Israeli soldiers alternate between empathy, arrogance and confusion. Steven Mayes, formerly head of Network Photographers and secretary to the jury of the World Press Photo awards, says that Passow has the ability to "produce clean graphic frames that combine metaphor and actuality". Mayes adds, "His signature black-and-white technique has cut-glass clarity and beauty with a sensual quality that seduces the viewer to engage with even the grimmest reality." Yet these images are far more than simply a journalistic record of conflict and turmoil. They are also quite intimate personal statements from Passow. As Passow himself says of his work, "It is an exploration across the battered emotional landscape of the neighbourhood I grew up in and keep returning to out of a sense of longing and belonging. The streets have names like Lebanon, Israel, West Bank and Gaza." Judah Passow is very much a photojournalist from the old school. He is not motivated by personal glory or the adrenaline rush of working in a war zone, but rather a quest for meaning.

RIGHT: This photograph is from *Days of Rage*, and shows the abandoned headquarters of the PLO, West Beirut, in 1982. Arafat is now dead and the effectiveness of his legacy is still being determined. In the early 1980s, he was a dominant figurehead at his peak, and his presence was felt everywhere.

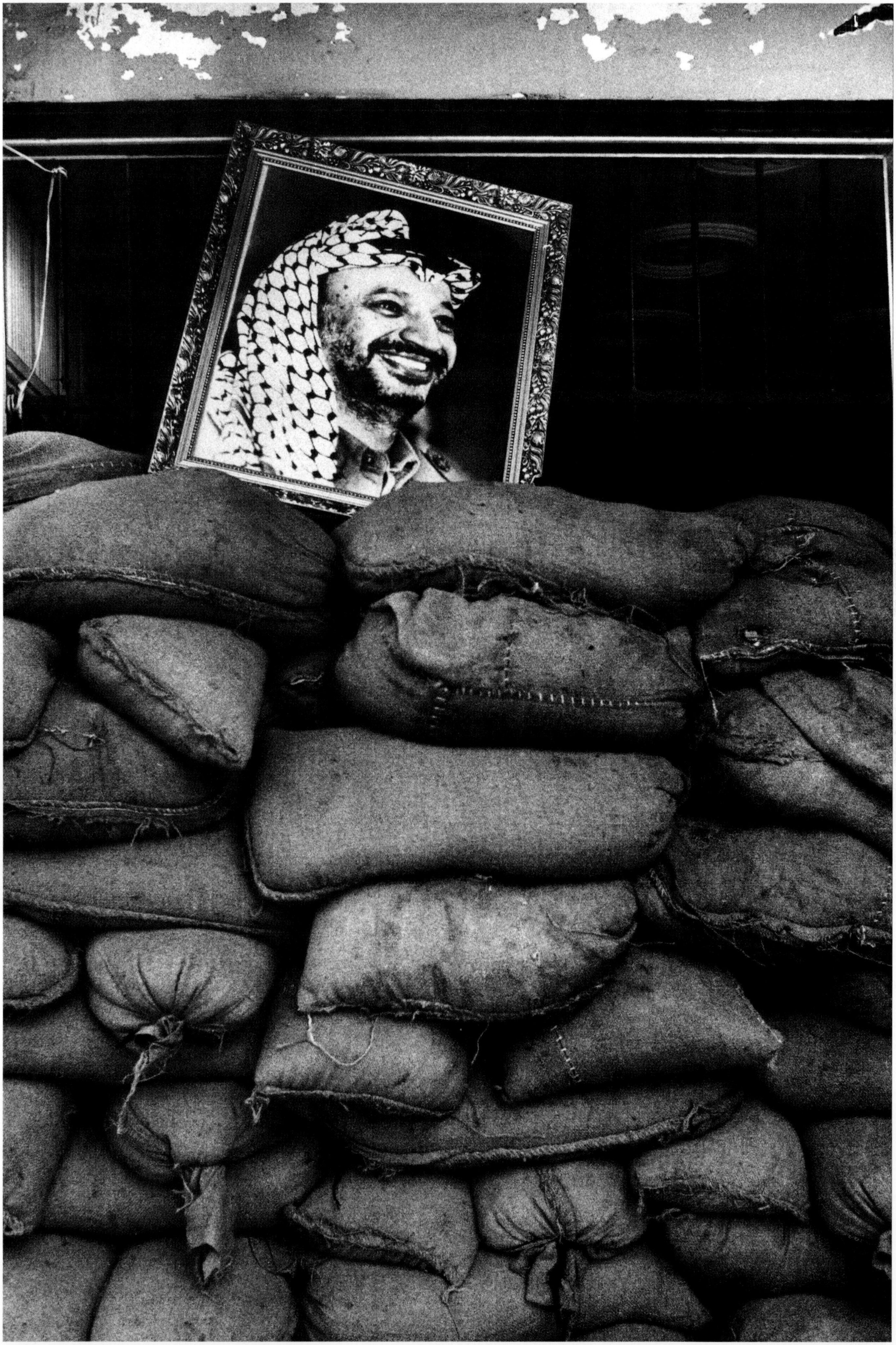

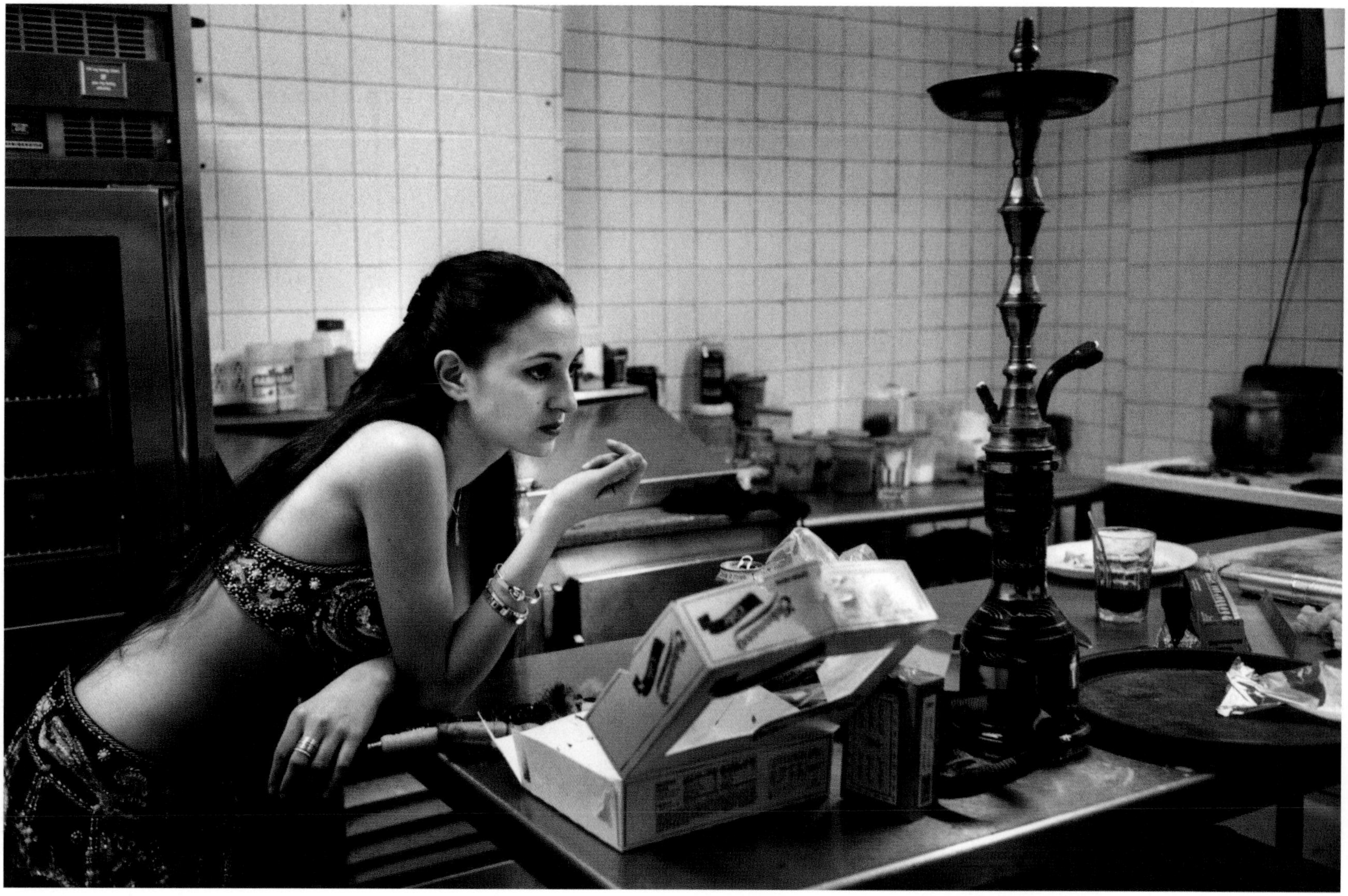

ABOVE: Brooklyn, New York has a huge Muslim and Arab population. In this essay Passow was attempting to discover the impact of 9/11 on the community that immediately after the terrorist attacks was being singled out by angry Americans. This is a belly dancer during a break between sessions in an Arab nightclub in Brooklyn, 2001.

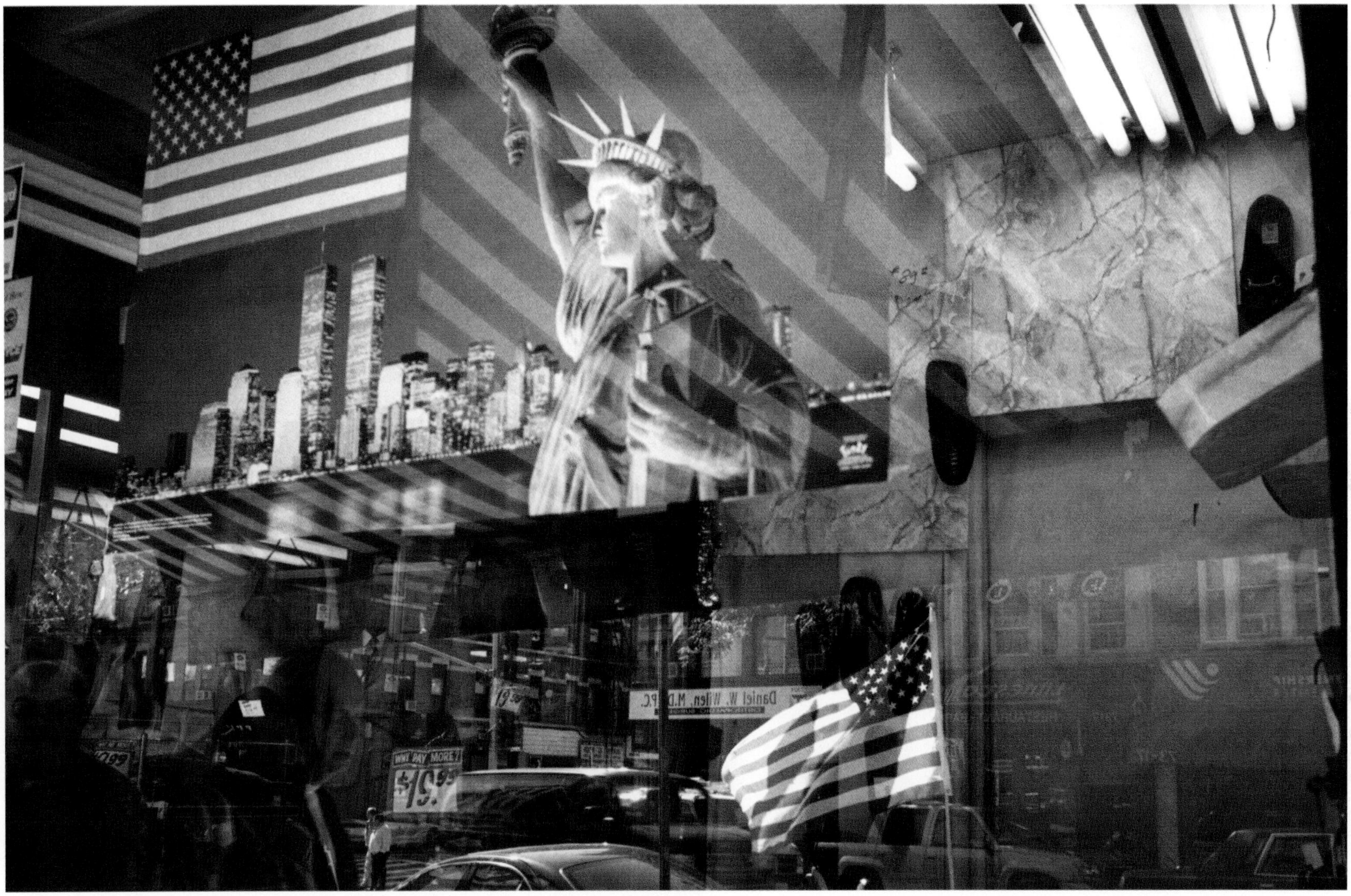

ABOVE: Reflections of the USA in the window of a Muslim-owned shoe store in Bay Ridge, Brooklyn, New York, 2001. Passow is a photojournalist who favours quiet observation and uses symbolism to reach his viewer.

GILLES PERESS

In a French-Canadian documentary about war photographers made in the late 1990s, a somewhat shell-shocked Gilles Peress says at one point that "photography is part of human memory". If that is the case, then Peress has enough bad memories to last several lifetimes. For the past 35 years, he has been faithfully documenting some of the darkest moments of the late twentieth century, what he himself has called the "curse of history". Peress was active in the student riots in Paris in the late 1960s and he comes from a generation of people who grew up mistrusting the media. This is something of a paradox for a photographer who is employed by newspapers and magazines, yet in the same film he says, "You cannot define yourself and your reality through your relationship to the press." One way he defines himself is by getting books of his work published. He was also one of the earliest photojournalists to explore the interactive storytelling potential of the Internet.

So what is his reality? He prefers to shoot with an open mind, rather than having a preconceived notion of what he should be photographing. He says that his primary goal on assignment is to photograph something so that he will have a better perception of what is actually going on. It is a voyage of self-enlightenment which the viewer is compelled to join. He has also said that it is difficult to maintain total objectivity while shooting, but it can be achieved at the editing stage. Technically Peress has everything. He can compose a photograph like Cartier-Bresson and can capture the essence of an unfolding scene in just one image with telling precision, often using visual metaphors and symbols. Yet he also has a perfect sense of drama and knows how to develop a haunting narrative from a series of pictures in the best traditions of W. Eugene Smith. He is also sensitive to what, and who, he is photographing and has the intellect to grasp the magnitude of his role. He is a worthy heir to some of the great Magnum photographers of the past.

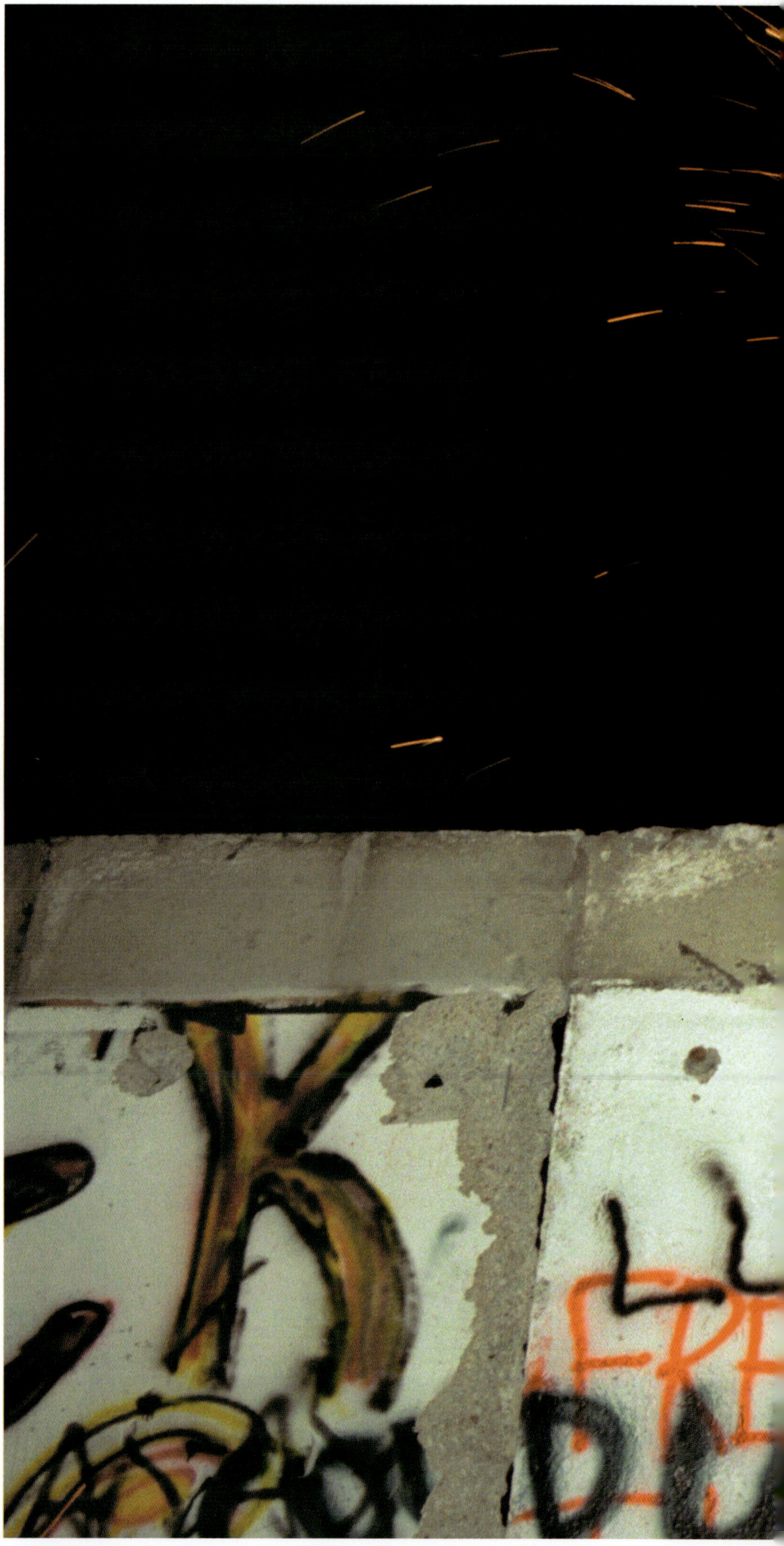

BELOW: Peress is usually associated with classic black-and-white photography, but for this more uplifting story on the fall of the Berlin Wall, Germany, he decided to use colour film. The sparks coming out of the wall have an almost supernatural and ethereal quality, contrasting against the black backdrop of night. If you look closely at the wall, there is some bizarre graffiti: "Boys on Tour" next to the names of Hitler and Stalin.

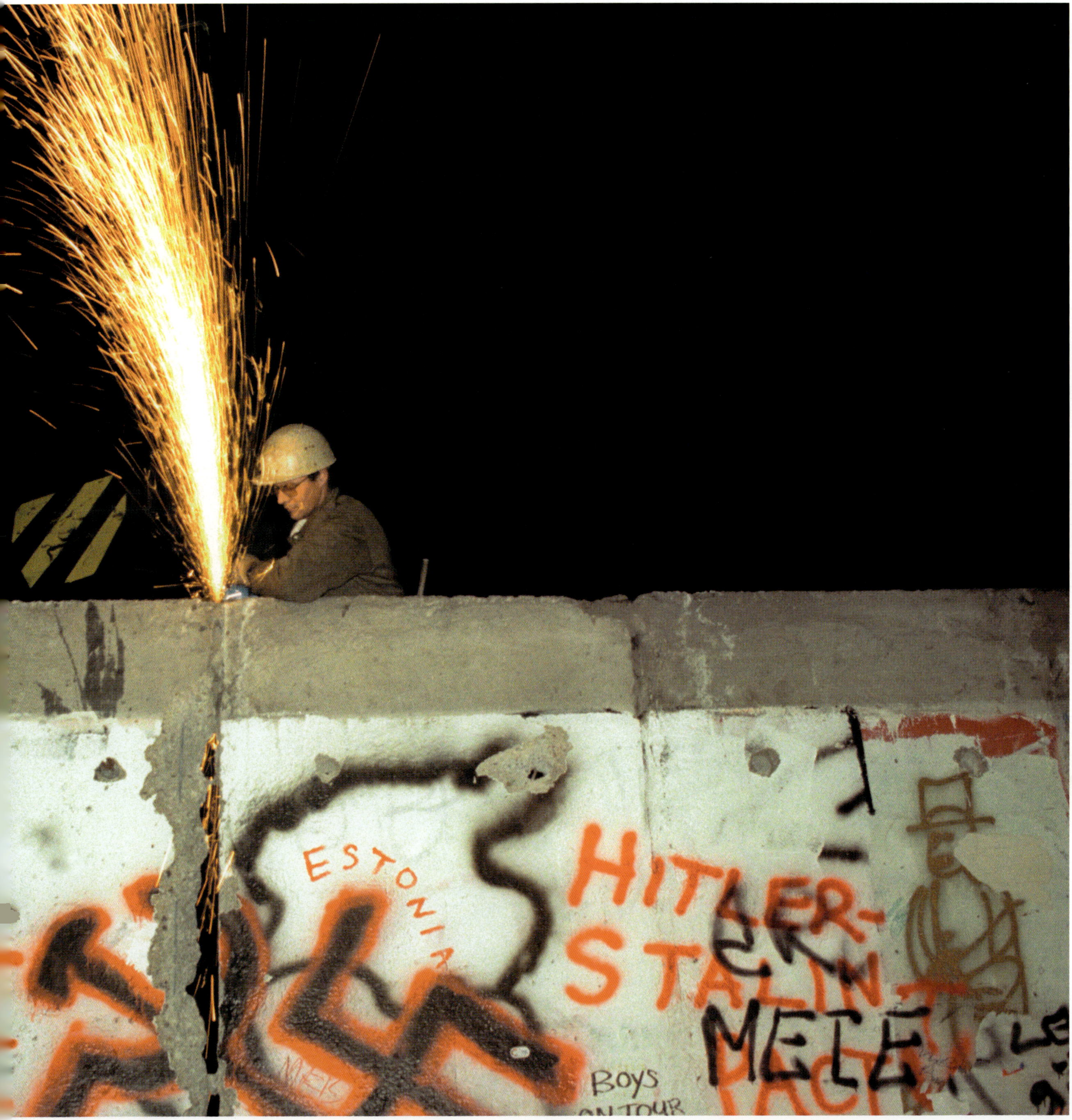

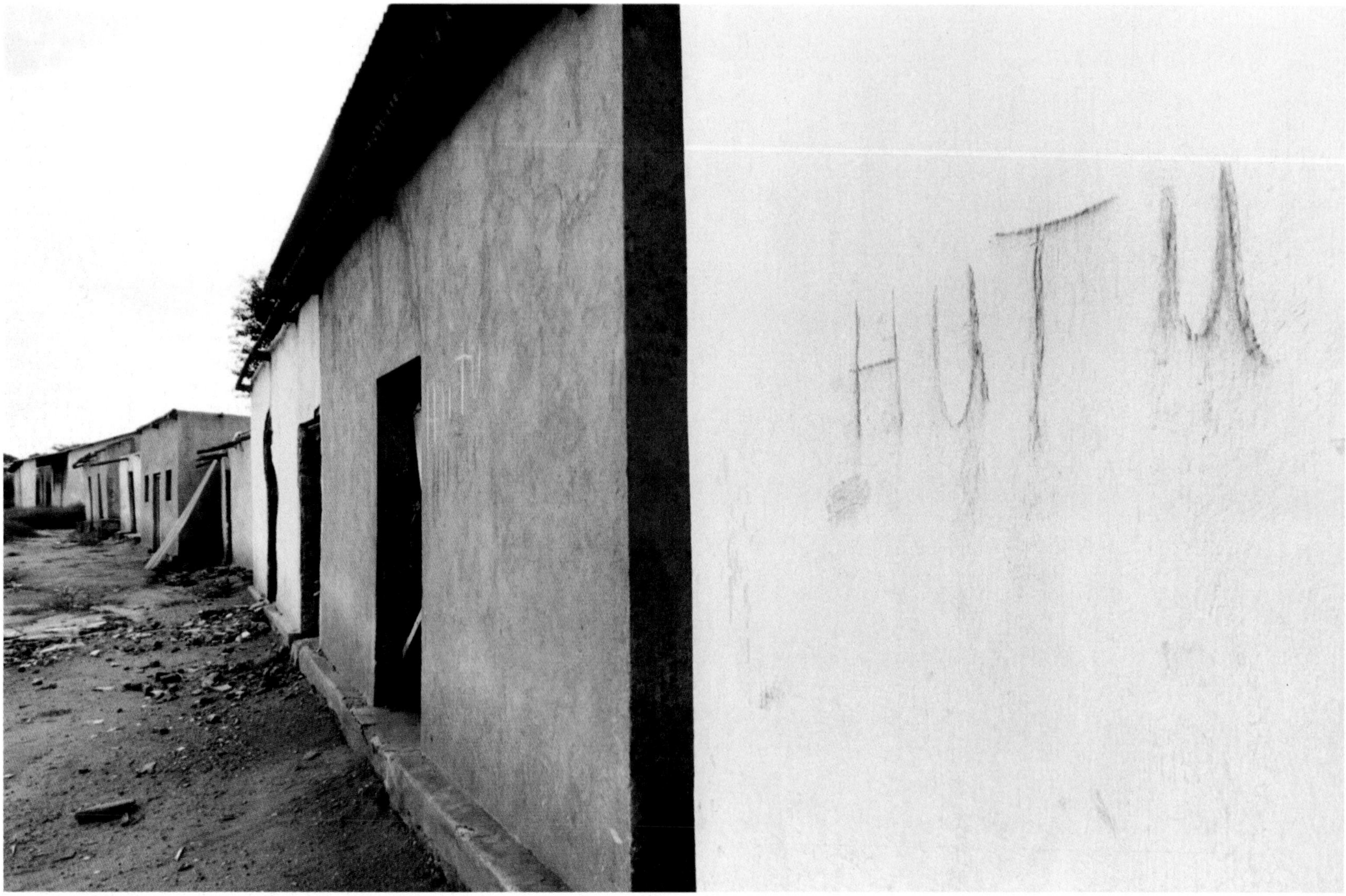

ABOVE: Hutus living in this house in Rwanda in 1994 scrawled their ethnicity on the wall to prevent looting. The advance of the rebel Rwandan Patriotic Army caused the Hutus to flee in turn. The Western press portrayed the Rwandan tragedy as a typically disorganized and chaotic African conflict, but it was in fact a highly systematic and regimented genocide. Peress is a remarkably subtle photojournalist who thinks deeply about what he is photographing and what impact his images will have on the viewers. He has the ability to be direct without always being graphic.

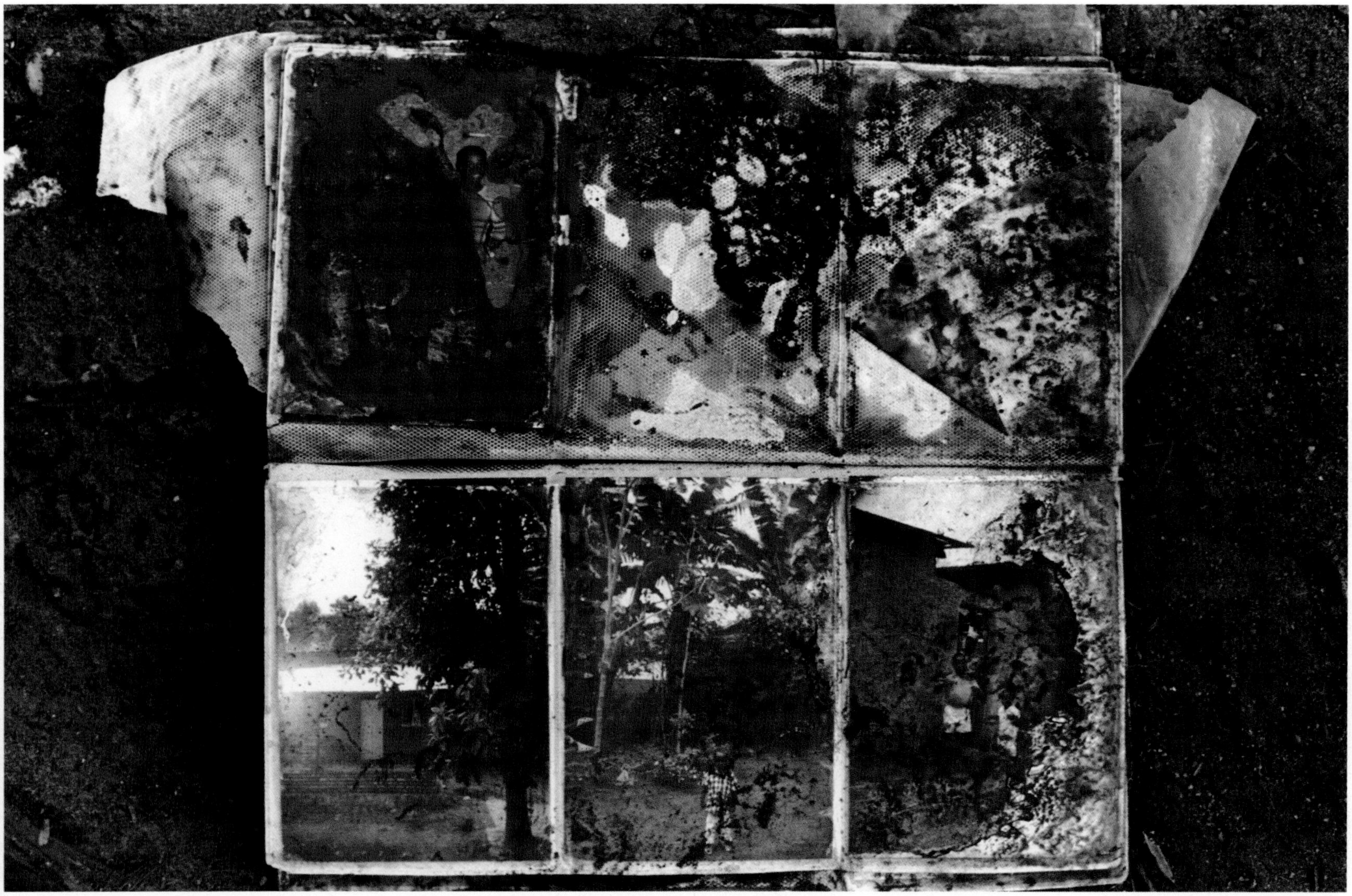

ABOVE: A photo album found at a massacre site at Nyamata in Rwanda, 1994. Sometimes it is this kind of poignant image that has the power to get the viewer to really feel and question what they are seeing, as opposed to a photograph of a blood-strewn corpse. The stains on the photos are dramatic and emotional symbols. A classic Peress image.

RAGHU RAI

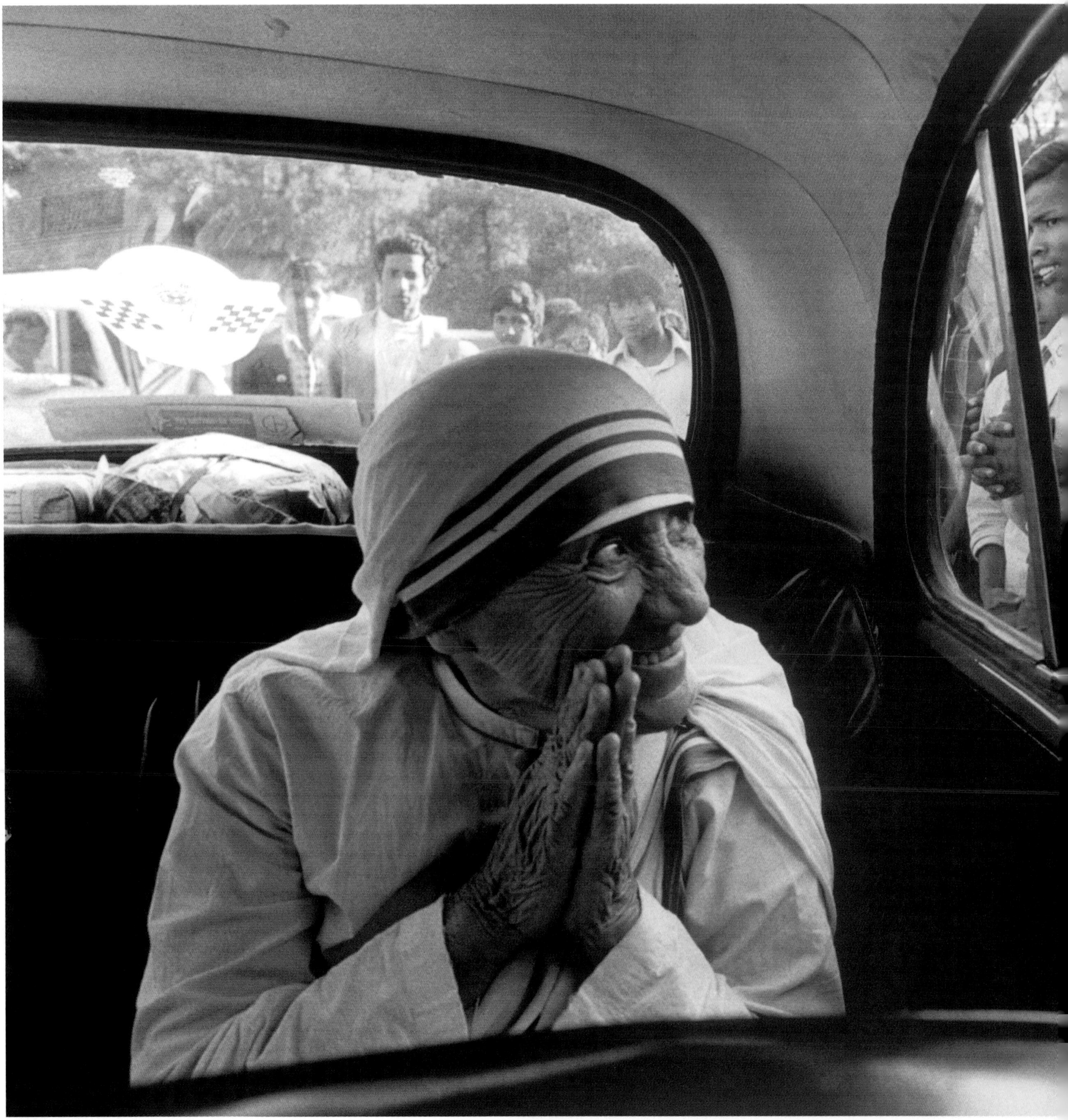

BELOW: Mother Teresa being greeted during a visit to one of her missions in Shillom, Assam, India. This image is one of pure joy and manages to humanize the saint-like figure. Rai must have been sitting at the front of the car in order to get such a complete view. The boys' expressions are also a sight to behold.

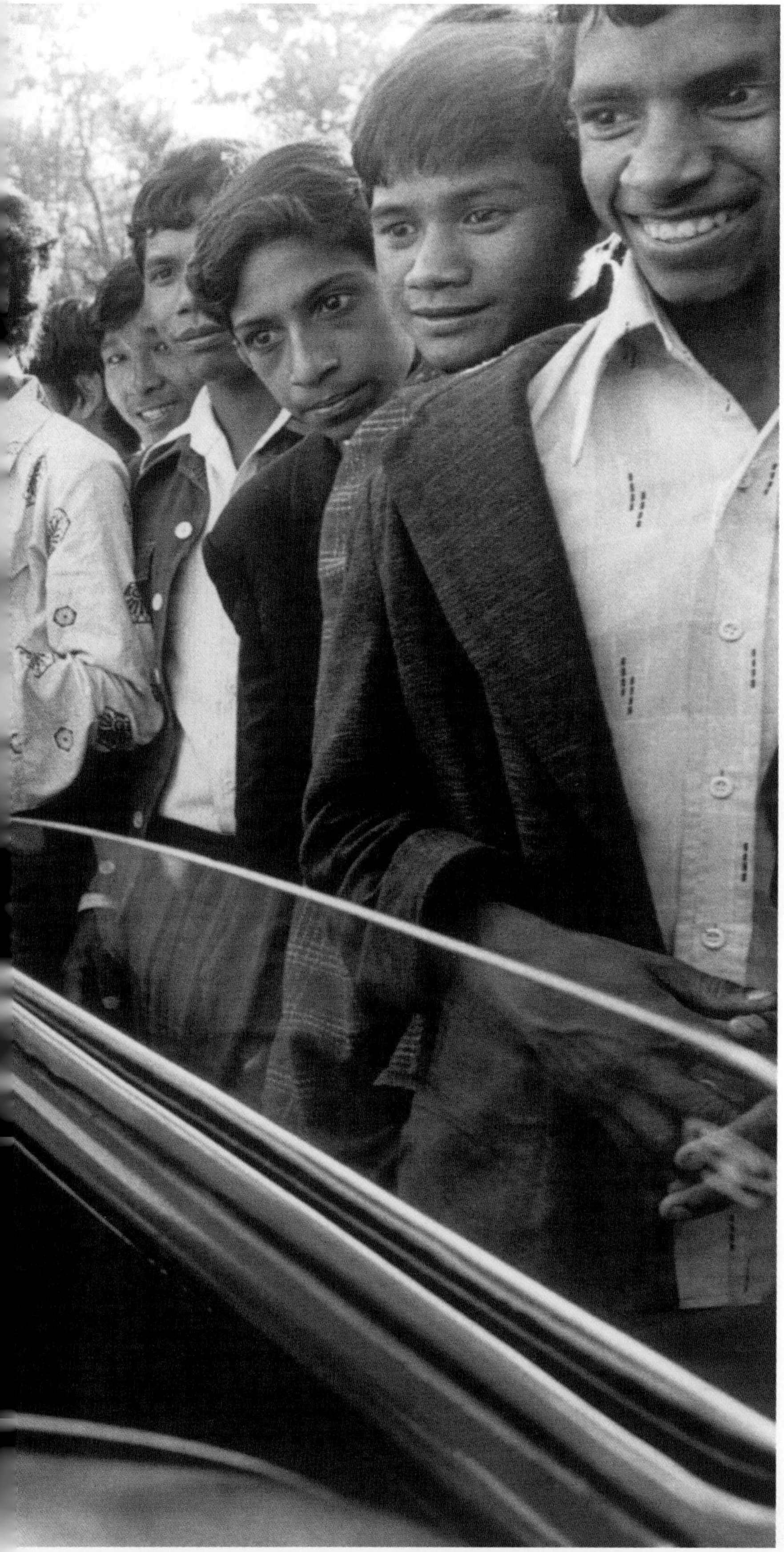

In December 1984, 27 tons of a deadly gas began to leak out of a Union Carbide plant in Bhopal, India. None of the six safety systems was working, resulting in 20,000 deaths, with more than 100,000 people still suffering from a variety of serious ailments. It was a "corporate crime" (the title of Rai's book) on an epic scale – the worst in history – and it is a crime that its perpetrators still refuse to acknowledge fully. The victims, however, do have India's greatest photojournalist, Raghu Rai, fighting their cause. He was there the morning after the tragedy photographing what he called "the silence of death." He shot the mass cremations, the overflowing hospitals, the grieving and the confused. He has also repeatedly returned to Bhopal over the past 20 years, photographing the slow death of thousands of people, while also documenting in steady and unrelenting black-and-white the survivors' struggle to lead normal, healthy and productive lives. He also shows the victims still fighting for justice and compensation from an essentially indifferent West.

One person who could never be accused of being indifferent to suffering in India is Mother Teresa who, like the tragedy at Bhopal, had a profound effect on Rai's personal and professional life. Mother Teresa granted Rai unlimited access to photograph her work with the Mission of Charity, an order devoted to helping Calcutta's poor and needy. The result is a powerful and moving portrait of both her spiritual commitment and a gruelling daily routine – being a saint is clearly hard work. Mother Teresa was initially reluctant to allow Rai into her inner sanctum, but his persistence, conviction and absolute respect for her work won her over. In the early stages of their relationship, however, there were some tricky moments. At one point Rai photographed three sisters at prayer. Mother Teresa saw this and thundered up to him asking, "What the hell on earth are you doing here?" Rai told her that they looked like angels and the moment was too good to miss. She relented and from that moment their relationship gelled, resulting in a remarkable essay.

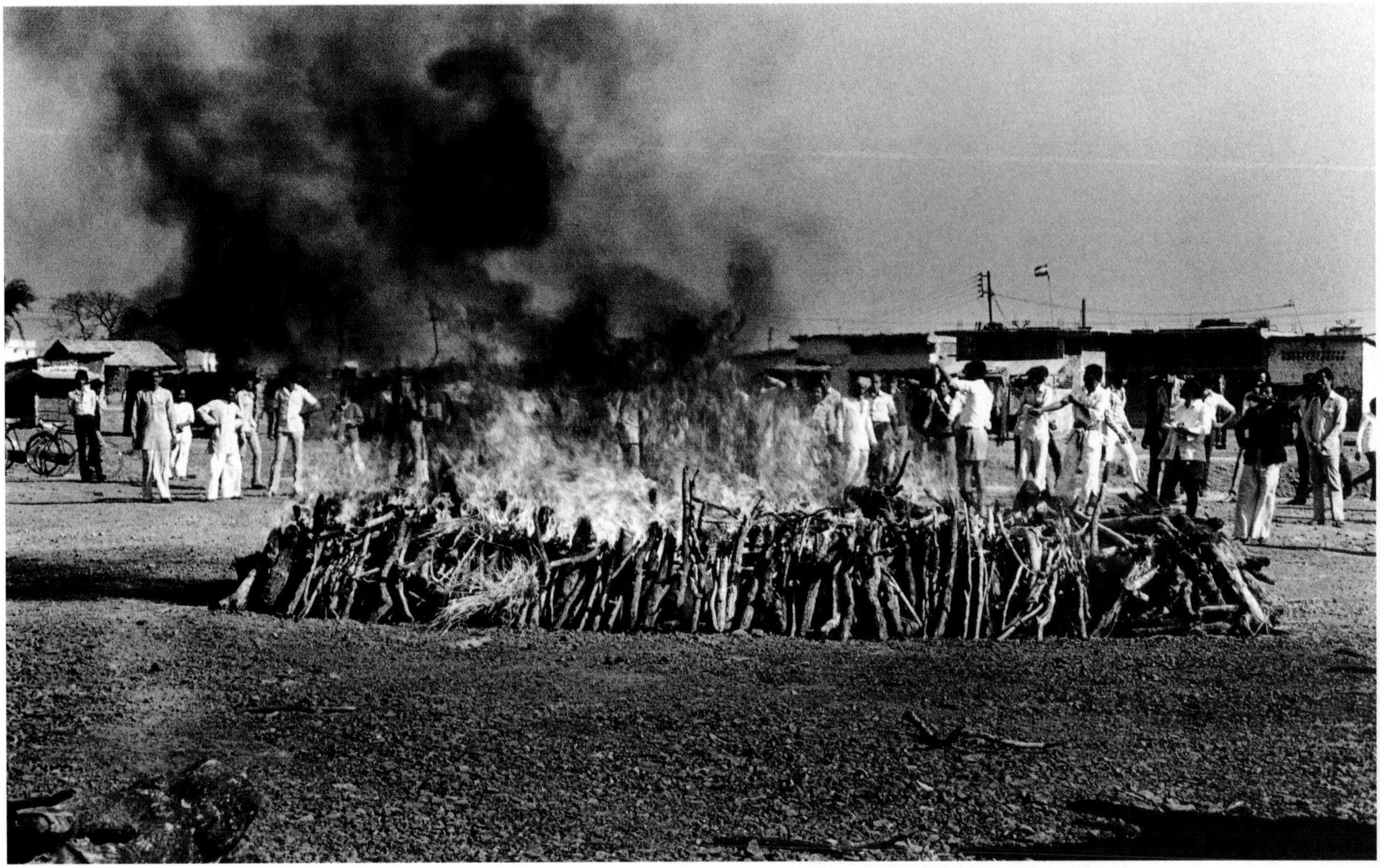

ABOVE: Rai has been documenting the Indian Bhopal disaster of 1984 for the past 20 years, from the morning after the disaster to the present; thousands of people still bear physical and emotional scars. Here we see the mass cremation of victims held alongside the communal graves.

RIGHT TOP: Dr Sathpathy is the forensic expert at the Hamida hospital. He has performed more than 20,000 autopsies so far. No relative of a gas victim can claim compensation for a death without his certificate. This powerful portrait was taken in 2002.

RIGHT BOTTOM: A family suffering from serious eye and lung damage after the Bhopal tragedy.

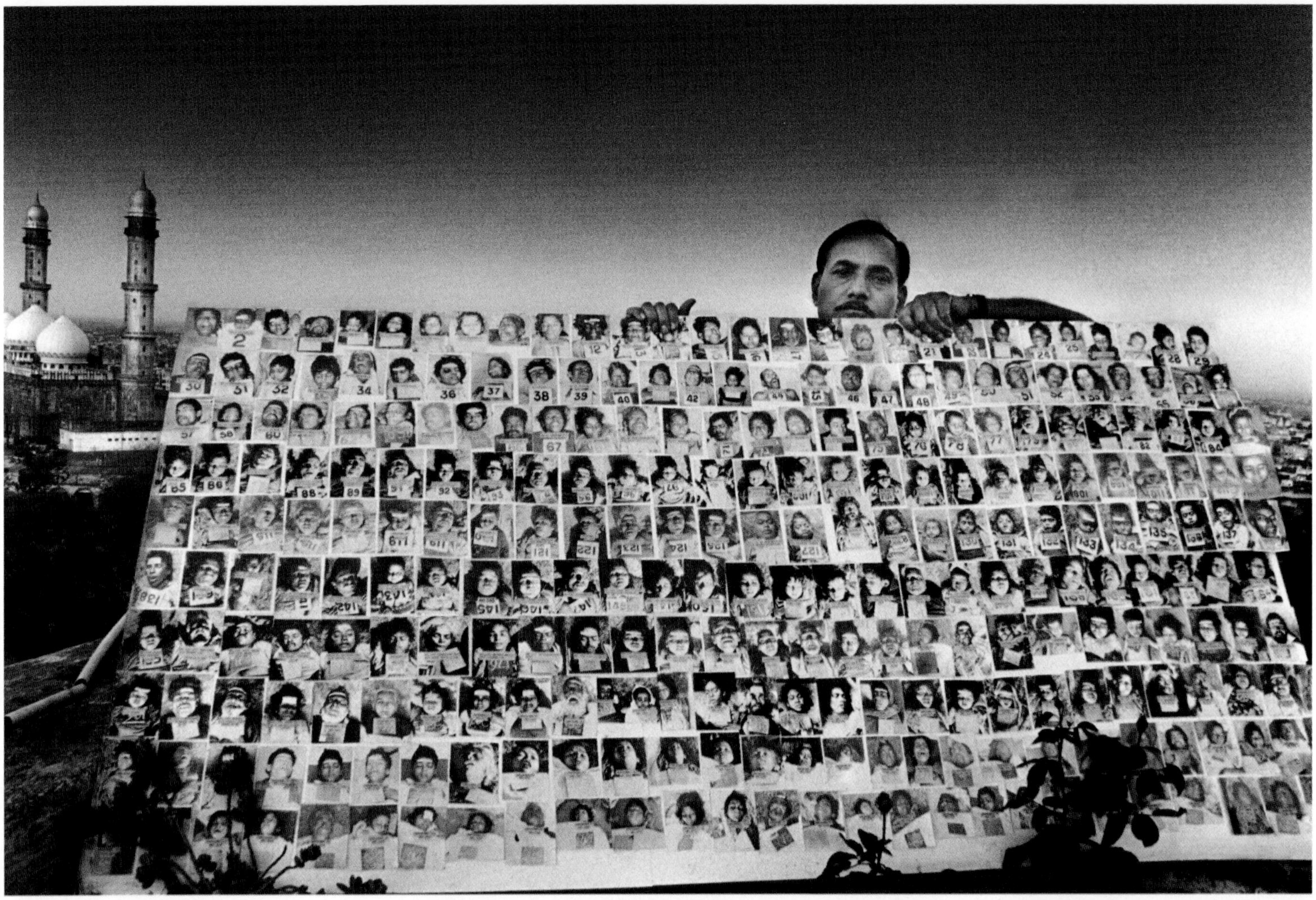

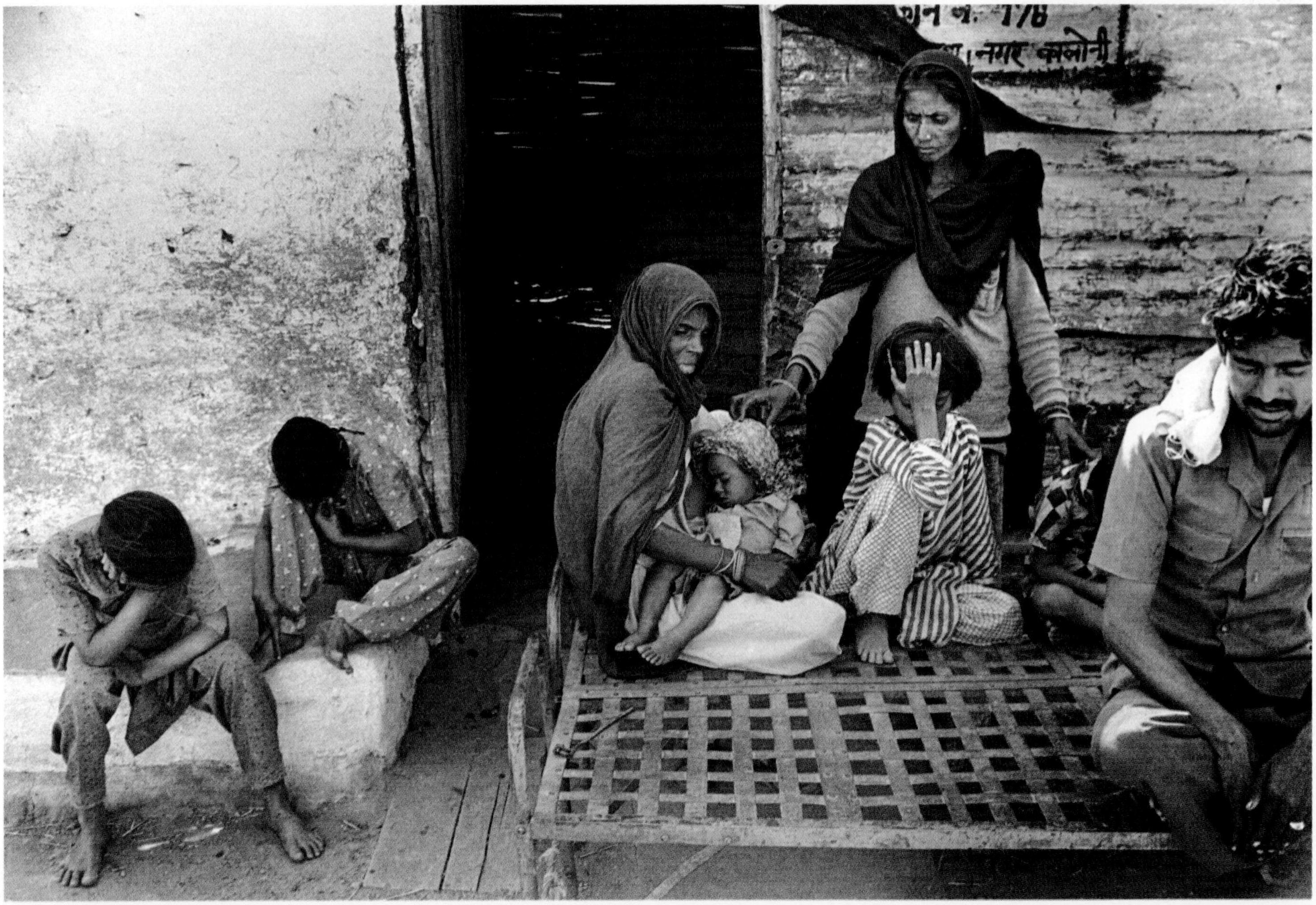
नगर कालोनी

ELI REED

BELOW: Three faces and three contrasting reactions among attendees of the Million Man March on the Washington Mall. This image epitomizes Reed's sensitivity to the emotional range of his subjects and to understated interactions between them.

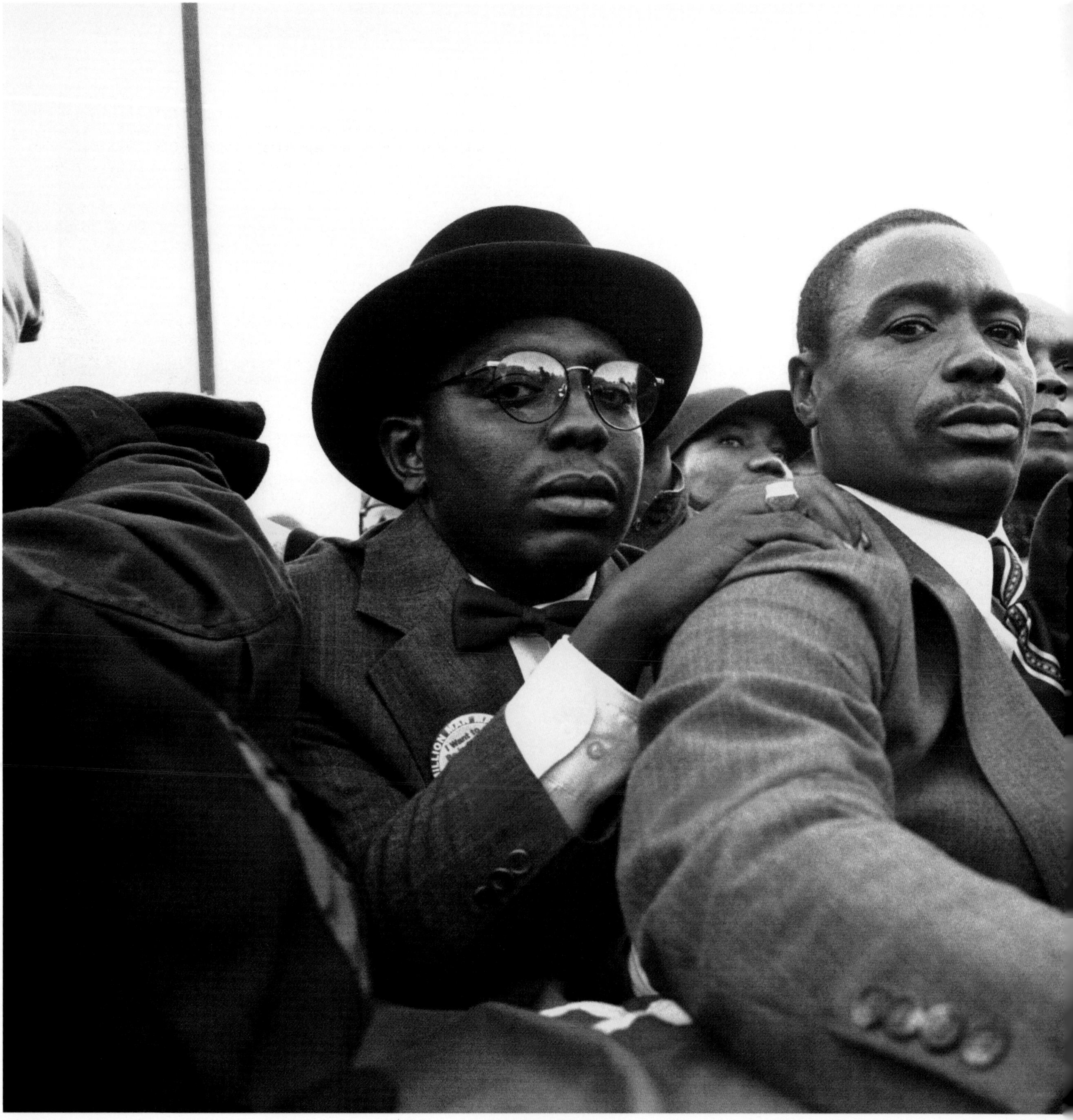

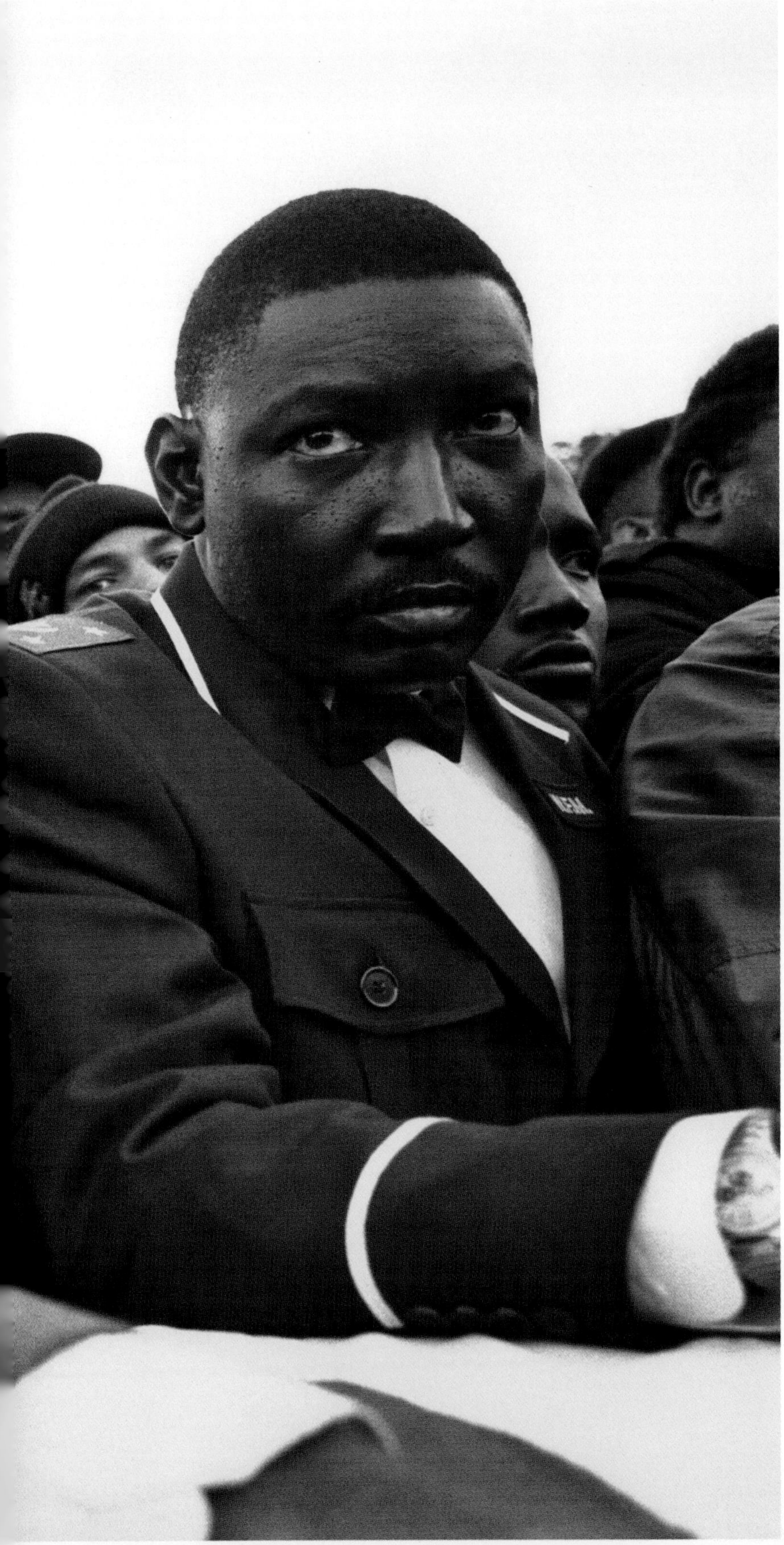

Eli Reed's defining work is *Black in America*, his 1997 collection of impressionistic images of the experience of African Americans from the 1970s onward. "*Black in America* is my favourite work because it is from the heart," he said in a television interview. "I just try to go in quietly and I try to see things from all the different angles." The book reflects the compassion, sensitivity and optimism apparent in all of his work, but his anger over lingering injustice is also present in a quiet way. Reed juxtaposes images of what he describes as "the beat of life" – a moment from a wedding, a father looking lovingly at his infant – with scenes from the Los Angeles riots, the Million Man March and other events. He has said that he is a painter at heart, drawn particularly to the Impressionists and their use of light and shadow to interpret everyday life. But he came of age in the tumultuous 1960s, and the work of Larry Burrows, W. Eugene Smith and others stirred his interest in photography. "It seemed like the guy with the camera knew what was going to happen next," he told one interviewer. Over the years, he has done in-depth stories on Central America, Haiti, Beirut, Africa and other locations. His work shows a keen eye for universal emotion in quotidian interaction, and Reed never objectifies his subjects. While others tend to depict Africans as victims in a wasteland of war, poverty and disease, for instance, Reed emphasizes their dignity and strength and focuses on how they go about life under abject conditions. "Africa is ignored in a lot of ways until a disaster happens, but there is other life in Africa," he said in a magazine interview. That isn't to say that Reed romanticizes his subjects, though. For a project on refugees called *The Lost Boys of Sudan*, he followed his subjects to the USA, where he saw past the trappings of their new middle-class lives to capture their lingering trauma and loss. "If you don't fear the unknown," he told an interviewer, "you can go a lot of places you can't imagine. And that's what I've tried to do all my life."

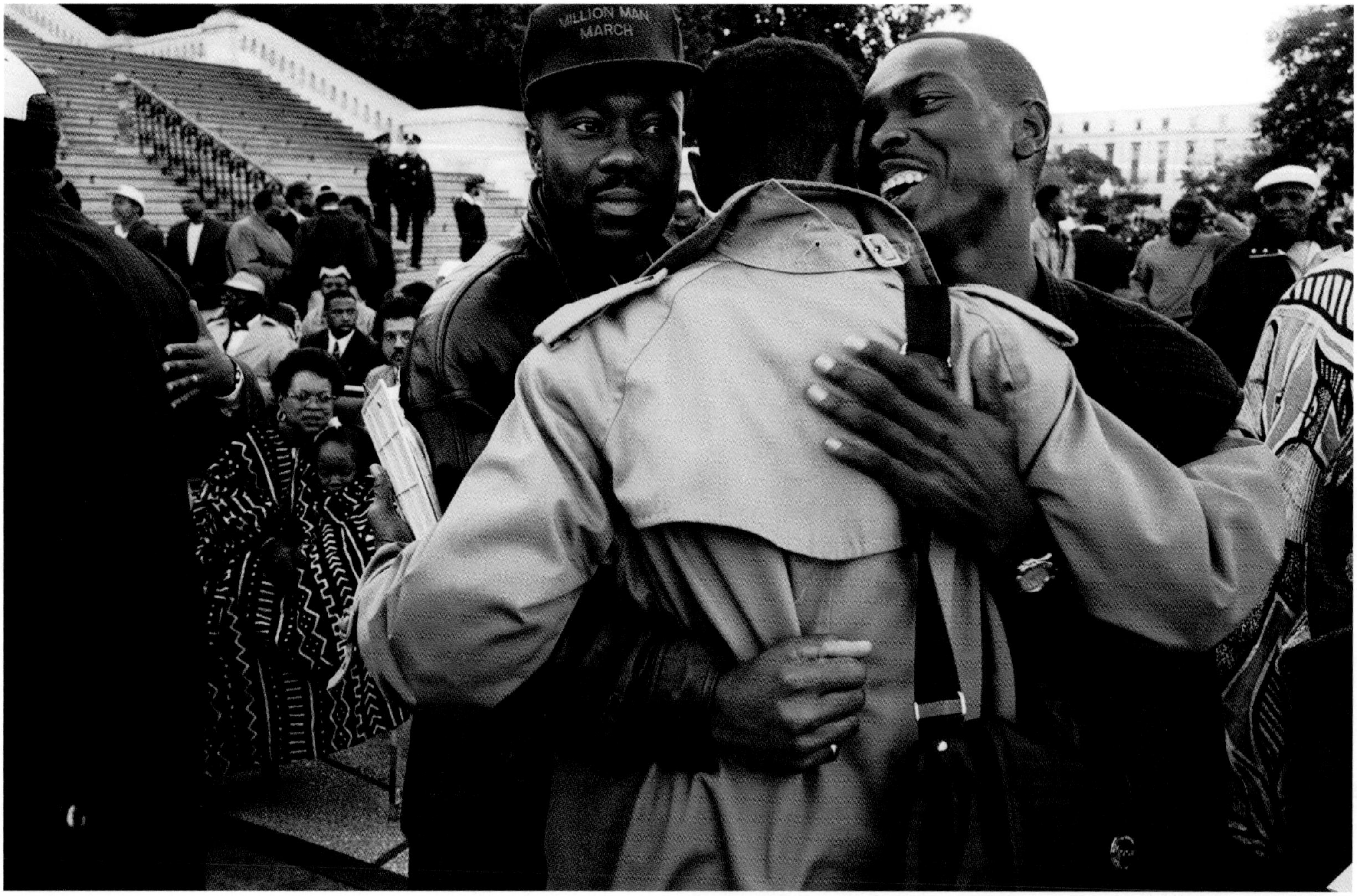

ABOVE: Attendees of the Million Man March embrace on the steps of the Capitol Building. The tension of this image arises from the contrast between the emotional reserve and restraint of the man on the left and the warmth and intimacy exhibited by the man on the right.

RIGHT: The focal point of this image from the Million Man March – a raised fist against a placard reading "America" – harks back to the Black Power movement of the 1960s, although the defiance and anger that characterized that movement are less evident in the faces here.

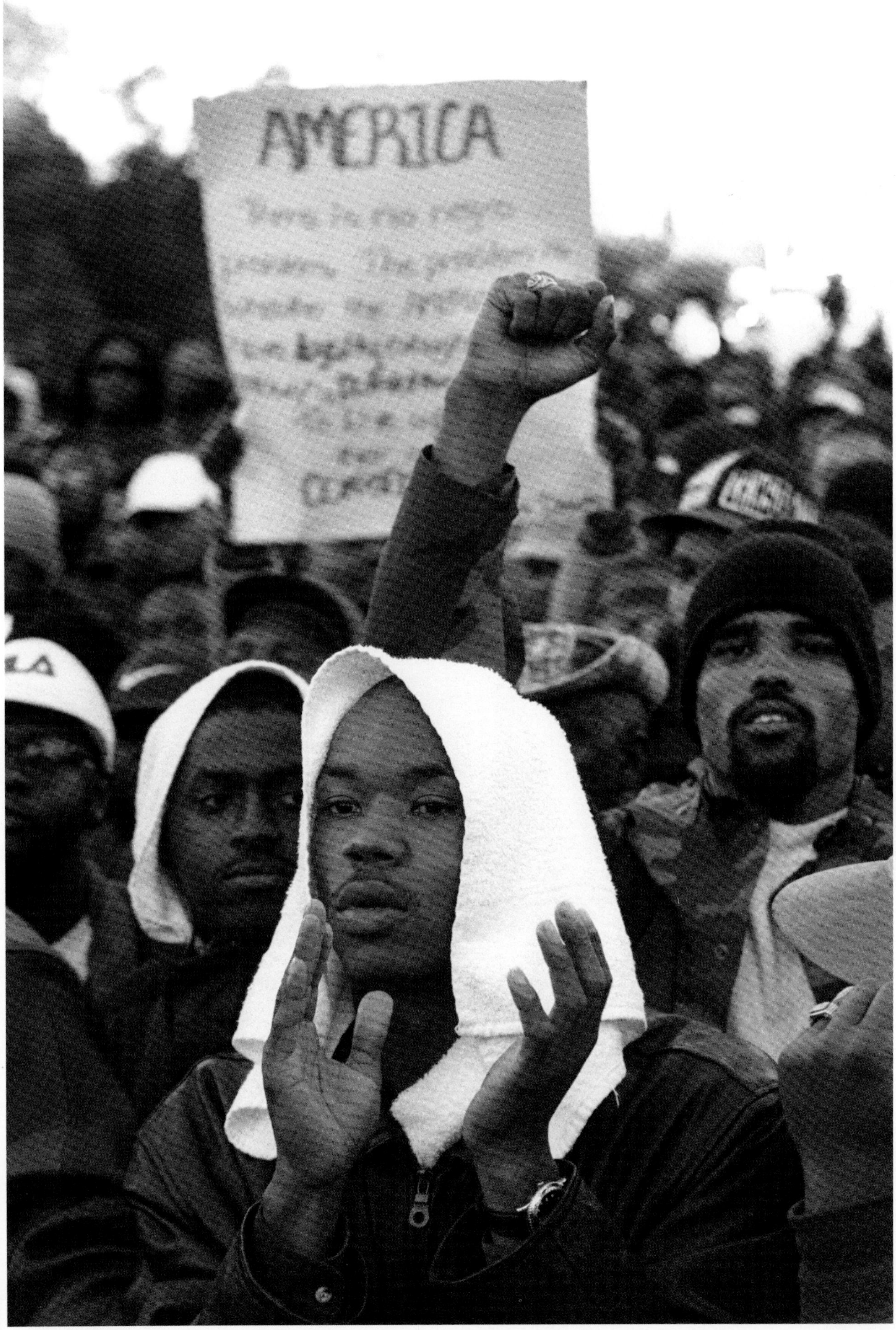
AMERICA

EUGENE RICHARDS

BELOW: In North Philadelphia, Pennsylvania, two men, one with a needle still in his leg, died moments after shooting too-pure cocaine. This photograph, taken in 1989, might look like an episode from *Law and Order*, but it is a vivid record of the painful reality of two pointless and public deaths.

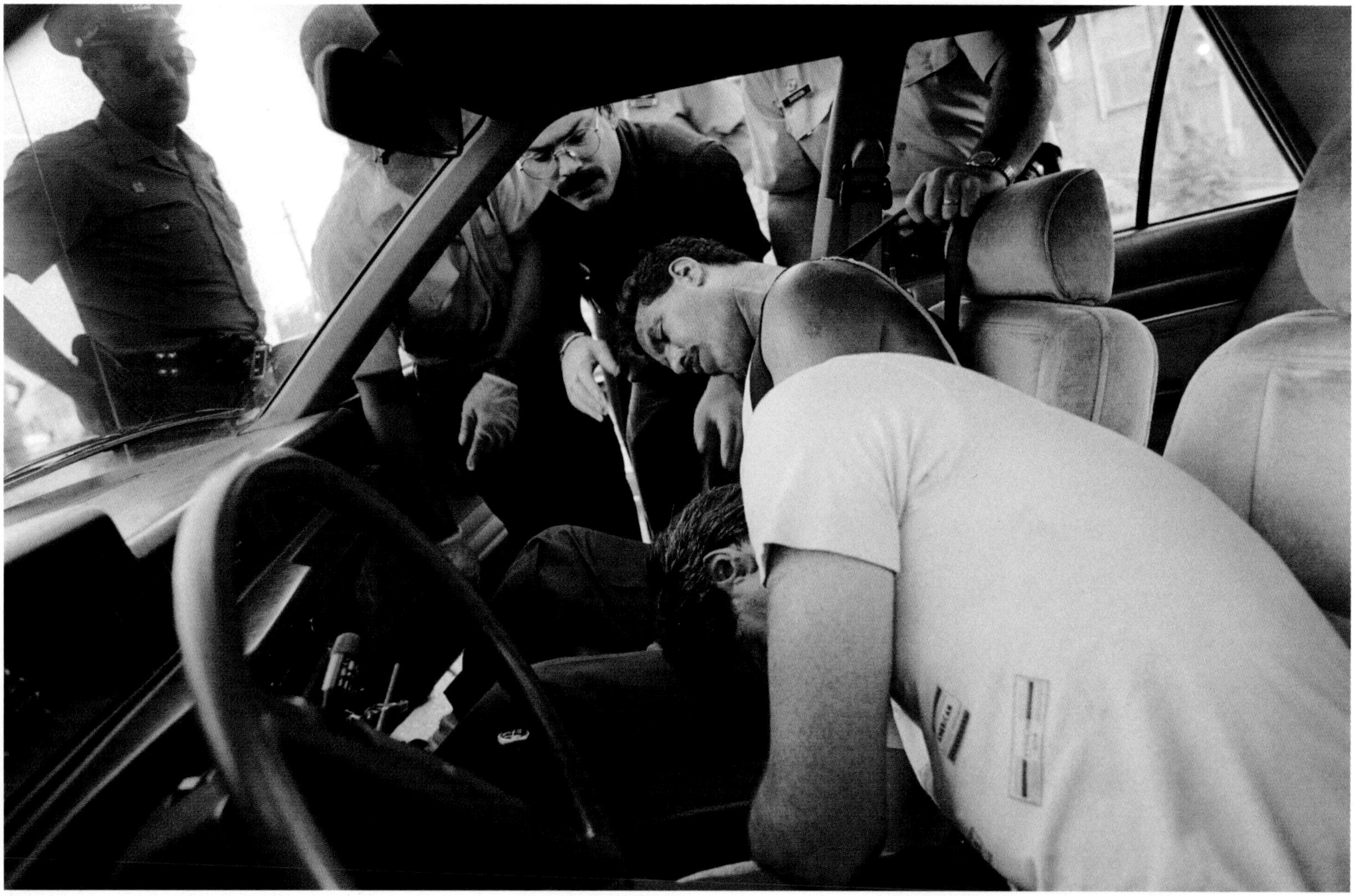

The legendary photojournalist Don McCullin is not known for being especially effusive, but in the twentieth anniversary issue of *Photo District News* magazine, he said of Eugene Richards, "He brings tremendous pain into his vision, and he makes you very aware of what you are looking at .... At the moment, he's possibly the best walking, living photographer in the world." Richards's sense of outrage at the injustices of the world was partly shaped by the previous generation of photojournalists, typified by people such as McCullin. Richards is very much carrying on their tradition, but for him the front-line is not to be found in a foreign conflict, but within the USA itself. He prefers to turn his camera on the pain and suffering brought about by poverty, drug addiction, bad housing and education. He tells stories about the blight of the inner cities where the so-called American Dream is barely alive.

Richards is a straightforward man who appears to be free of any artistic pretension or ego. His mission is simply to tell it like it is and if it is going to take him a few years to get to the core of the subject, he is prepared to dedicate time to his work. He spent four years on his epic project on the impact of crack-cocaine and heroin within sections of the African-American and Hispanic communities. He photographed in seriously deprived areas, mainly Brooklyn, New York, which had been ravaged by the drugs and inevitably their side effects of violence, death, prostitution and AIDS. Richards quietly, but with compassion and a non-judgemental eye, photographs it all. His subjects allow him to focus very closely, trusting him to tell their story, to tell the truth. This is clearly collaboration, and yet when the book came out, certain curators and magazine editors deemed Richards's work racist and exploitative. His critics said that a white photographer had no right to be there and even less right to present a one-dimensional and negative view of black and Hispanic society. Indeed, very few photographers came to Richards's defence, but the few that did were mainly African-American. They pointed out, as is obvious, that Eugene Richards is a photographer with a rare insight and integrity.

RIGHT: In an example of Richards's ability to quietly observe and record, a mother of one child, now pregnant with twins, smokes crack in Red Hook Houses, Brooklyn, New York, 1988. The woman has a blissful look on her face as she takes a hit, but it is momentary. The future is bleak for her and her unborn twins.

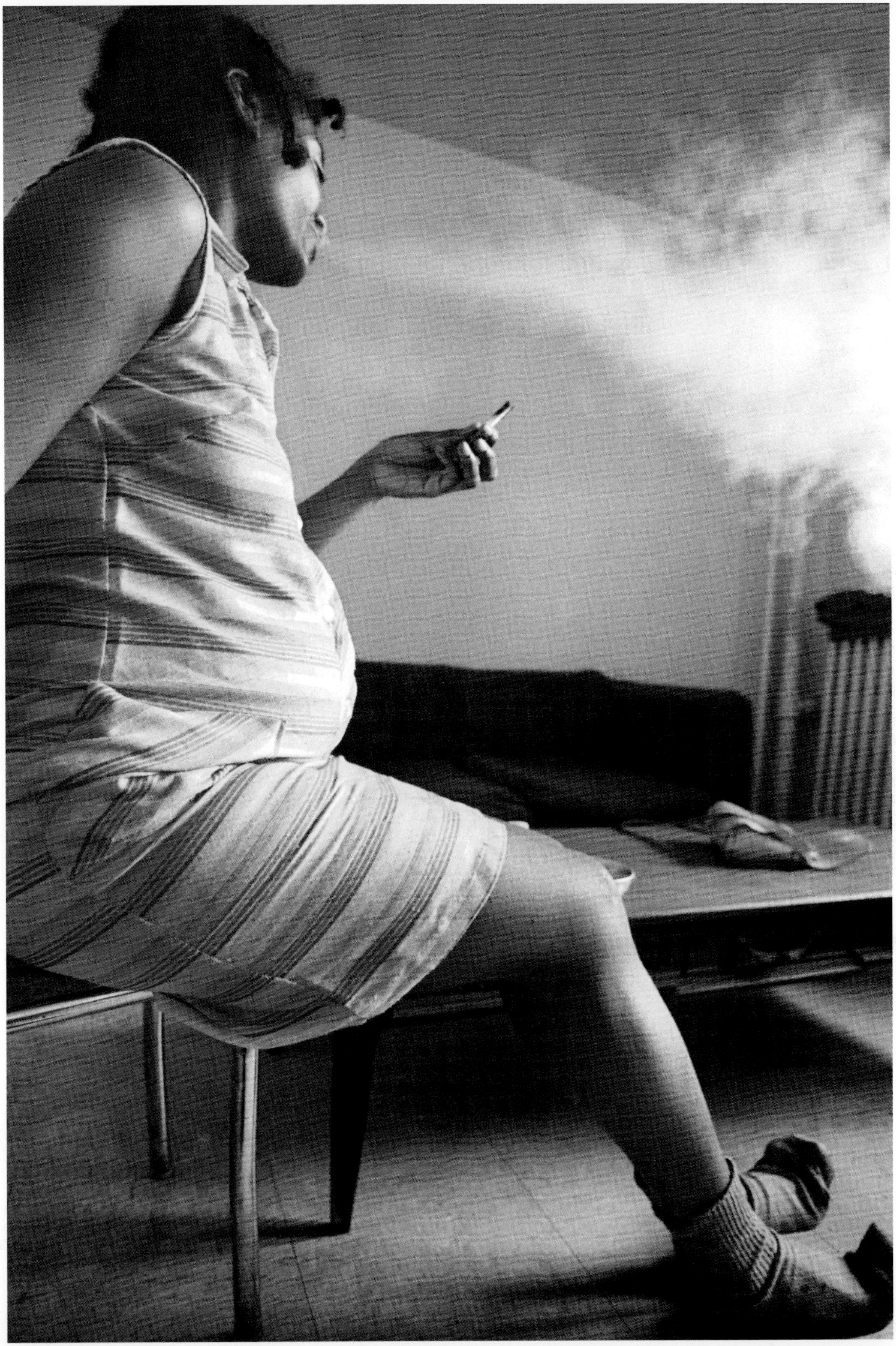

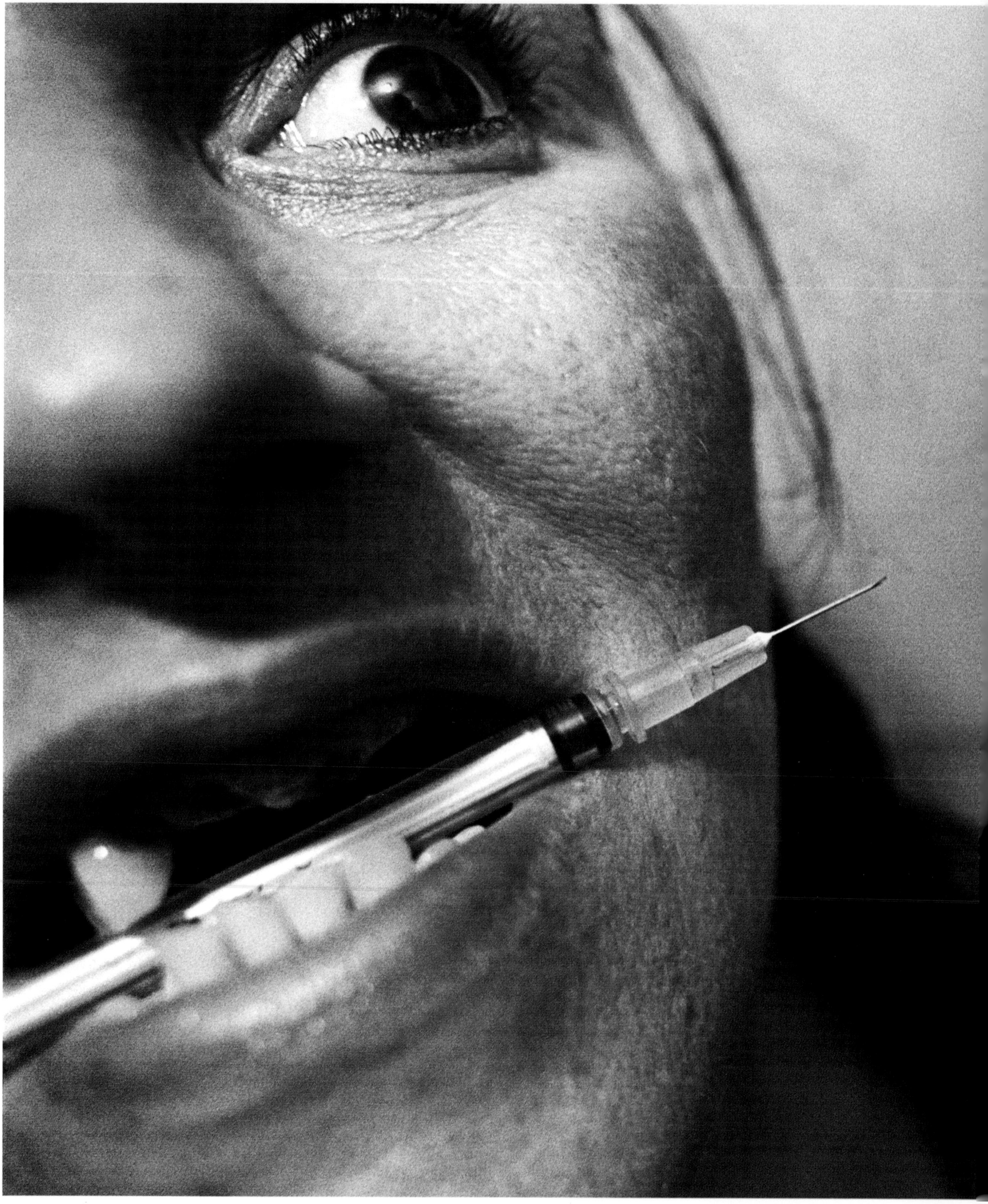

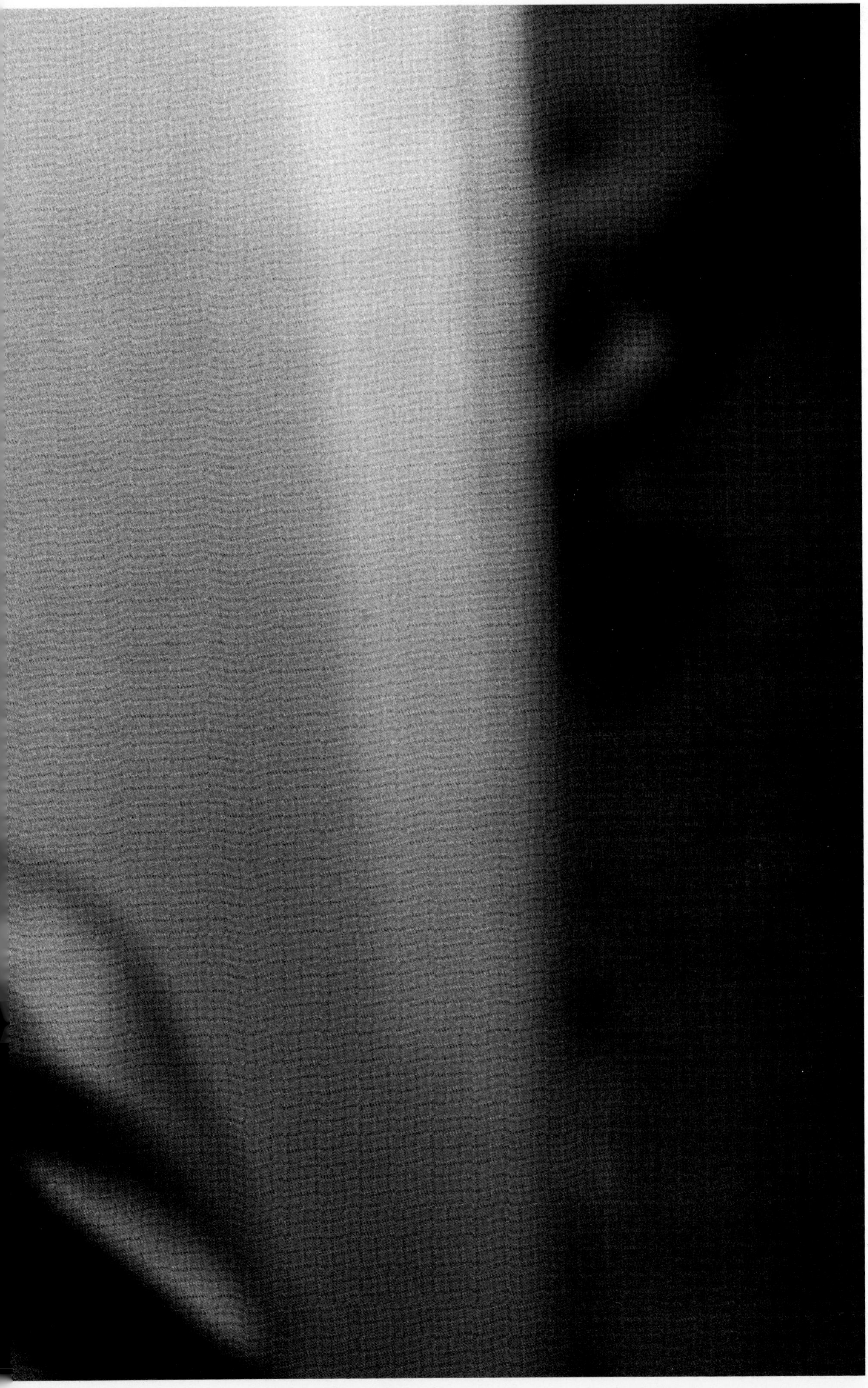

LEFT: This shot, which shows "Mariella" just before shooting up cocaine in Brooklyn, New York, was used for the cover of Richards's seminal book *Cocaine True Cocaine Blue*. It is one of the most forceful photos ever taken of someone in the grip of an addiction.

HENRYK ROSS

BELOW: Children of the ghetto playing as ghetto policemen. The Lodz ghetto was self-administering to a degree, with its own security force. The chubby child at the end of the line features in a significant number of Ross's pictures and may perhaps have been the son of a policeman himself, for he seems to wear an authentic cap and brassard. The picture is dated 22 October 1943, more than a year after the majority of ghetto children were deported.

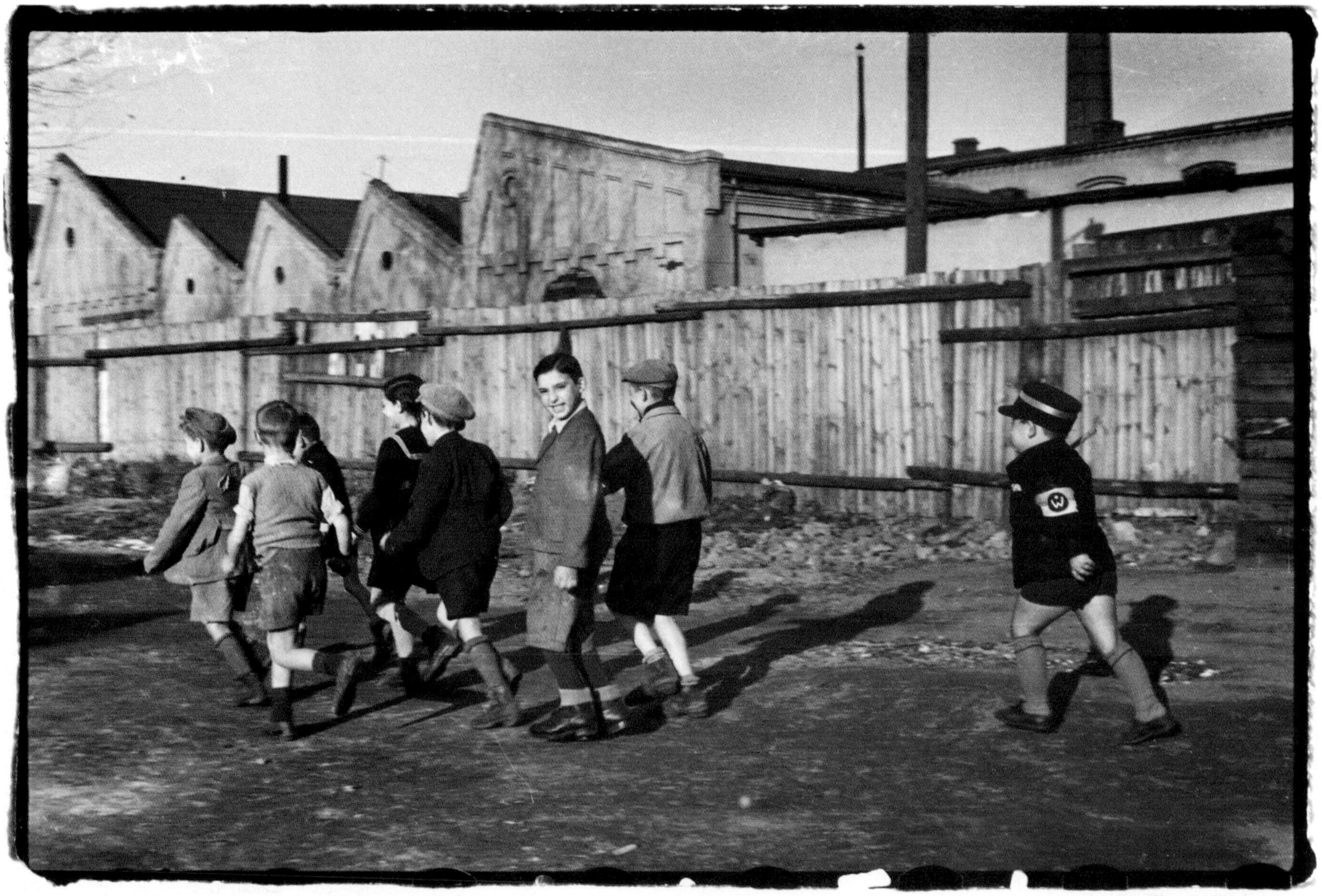

Henryk Ross was a witness to one of the worst episodes in history, in Aushchwitz and before that the Lodz ghetto. The ghetto served as a forced labour camp and as a prison for Jews in transit toward the Final Solution, their destinies sealed by a trip to the gas lorries of Chelmno or the sham showers of Auschwitz. Ross had been trained as a photojournalist, and this may have helped him turn his camera into a tool in the desperate task of recording a truth that the German state wished to obliterate. Yet he was the "official" photographer in Lodz, a role assigned him by a Jewish body, the Department of Statistics, that kept records for its German overlords. The ghetto was run by the notorious Chaim Rumkowski, who believed that by conforming to German requirements he could save the majority of its denizens. Ross and Mendel Grossman, the other "official" ghetto photographer, took thousands of images of living conditions in the ghetto. Of the 170,000 people in the ghetto, 95 per cent died, either in Lodz or in the concentration camps, and Ross himself survived only because he was one of those whom the Germans kept back to clean up the ghetto after they had removed its last remaining occupants to Auschwitz in August 1944. Ross photographed the worst and the best of the ghetto: starvation on the one hand, but also the celebrations of those who managed to find enough to eat; executions and deportations, but also embracing couples and smiling children. The Ross archive offers a complex picture of a complex tragedy, much of it kept out of public view until after Ross's death, perhaps for fear that it told too difficult a tale, particularly about those who managed to create a quasi-normal existence under German oppression as opposed to those who were starved, beaten, executed or deported. A brave and committed photojournalist who was part of this terrible story.

RIGHT TOP: One of the ghetto's garment factories, with feathers being attached to hats, photographed by Ross in a style that would not have been out of place in a fashion magazine of the 1930s.

RIGHT BOTTOM: Captioned by Ross *Ghetto life*, this picture shows a ghetto policeman, his wife and his child. Although the 35mm negative is badly damaged, the gentle charm of the image has not been lost.

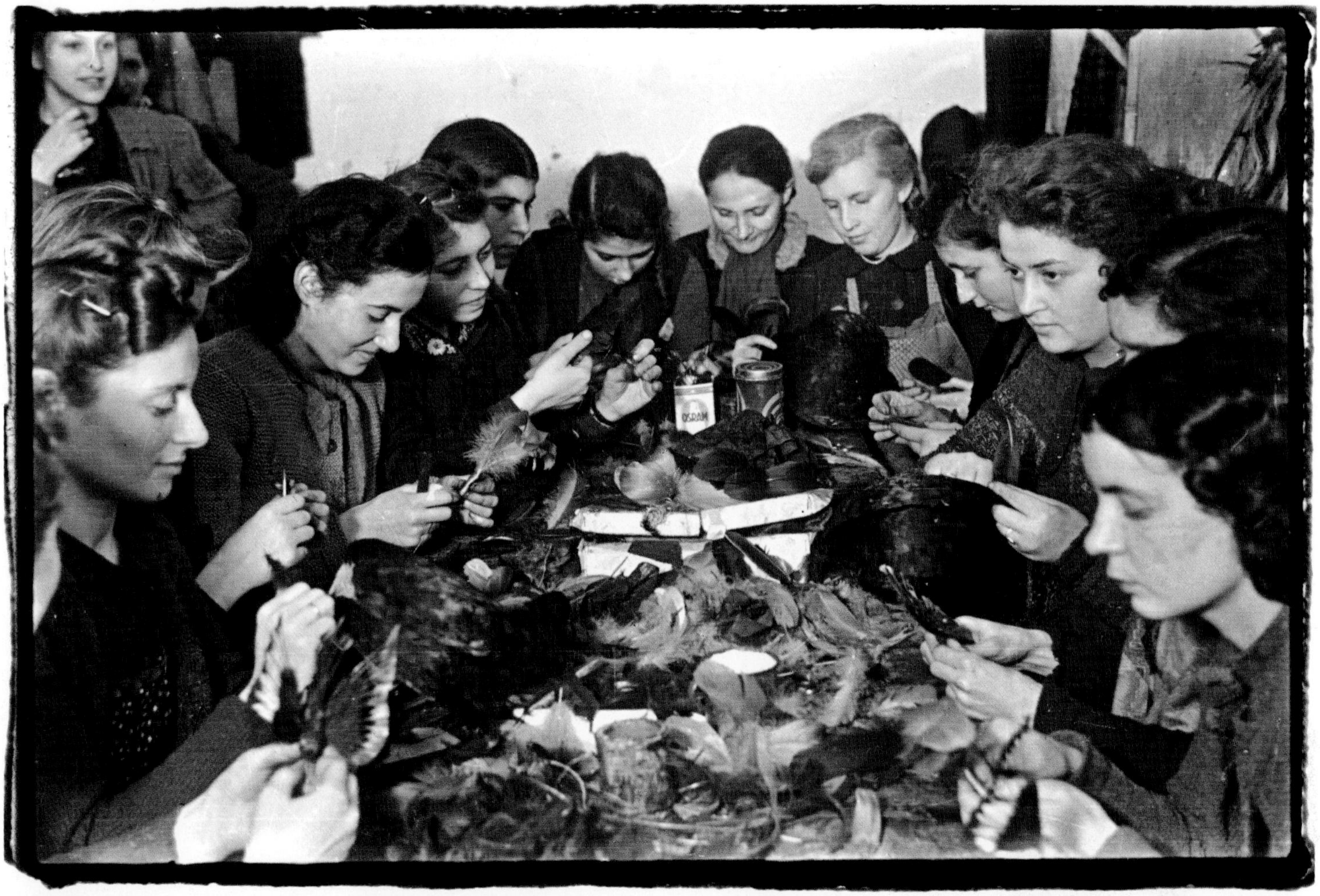
OSRAM

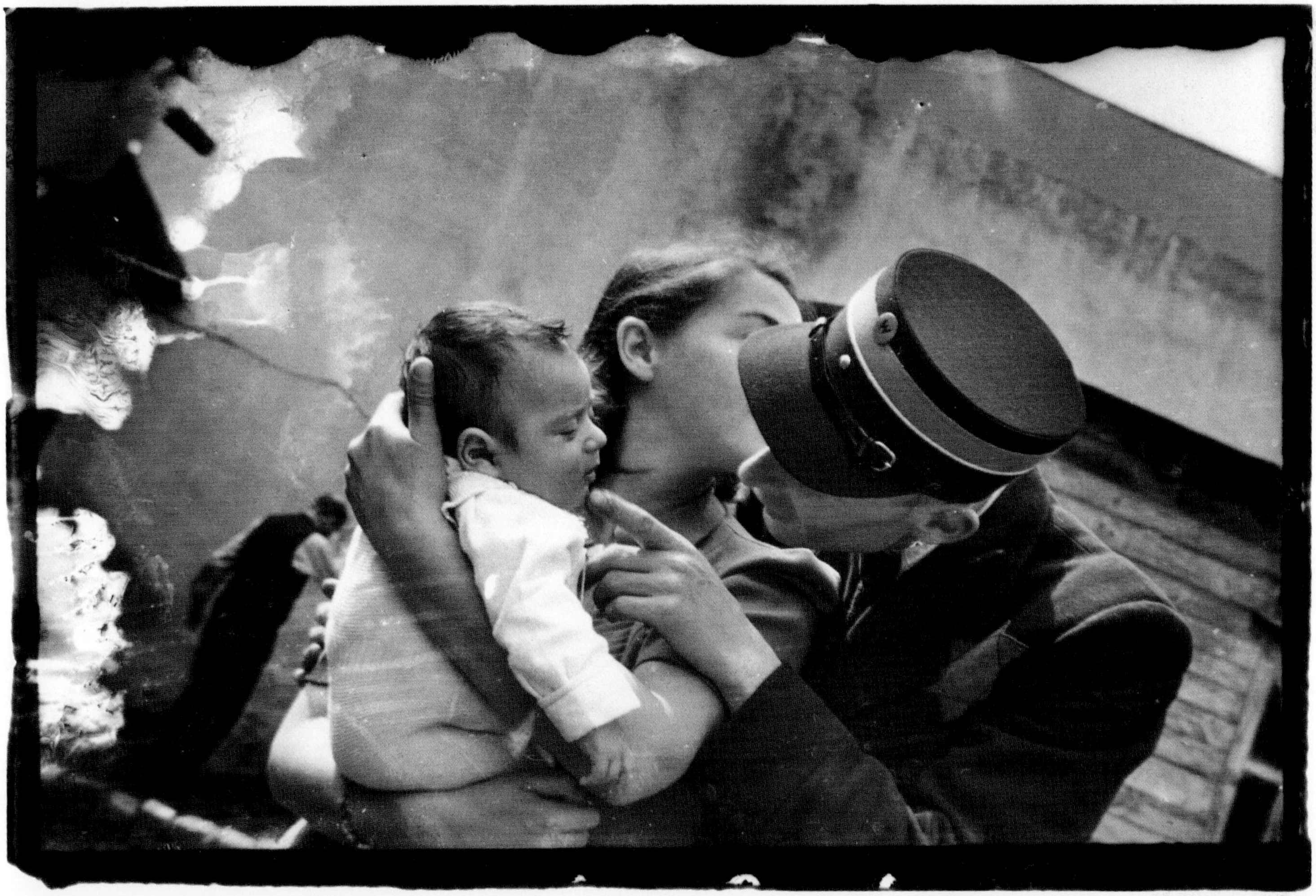

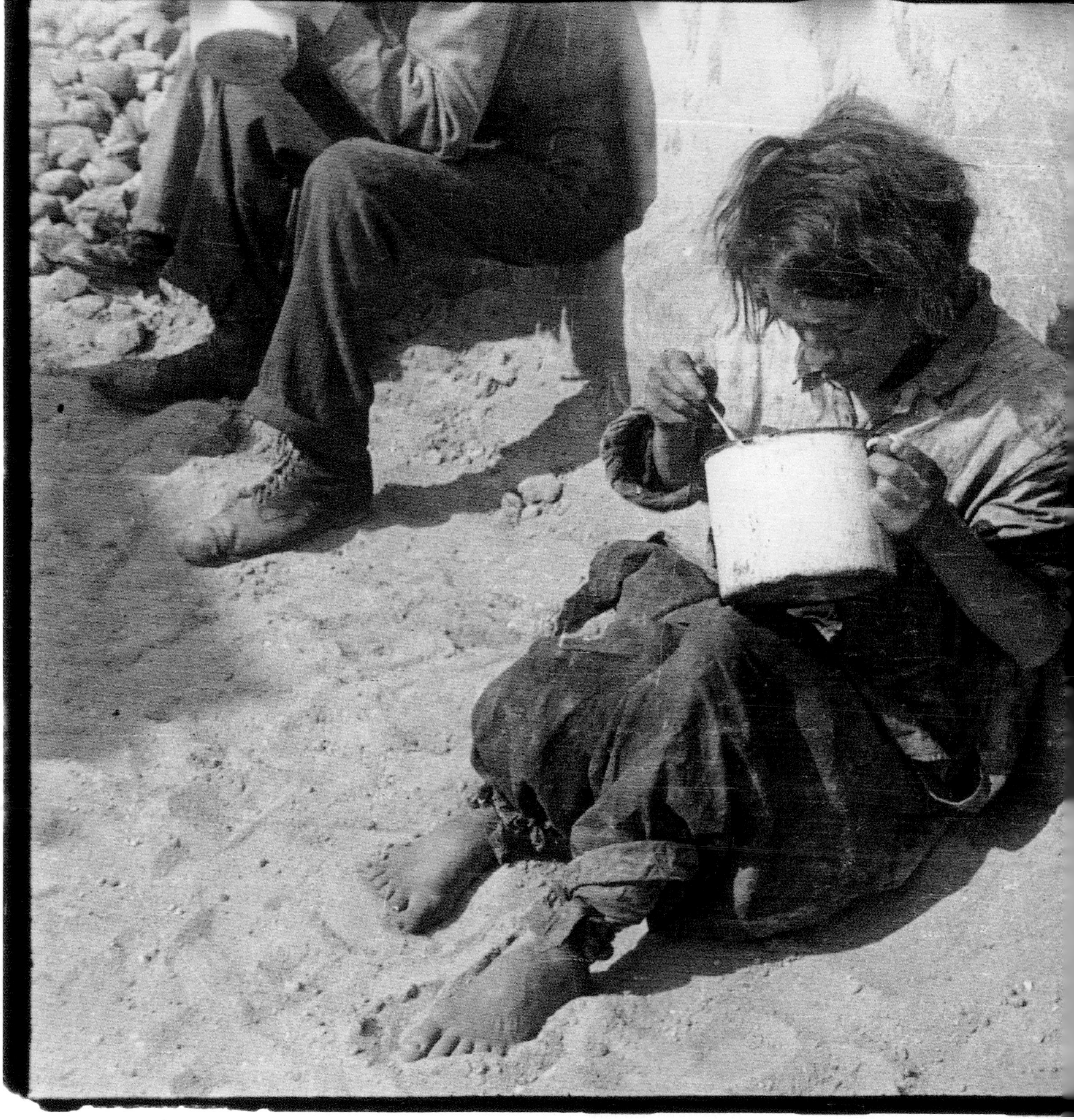

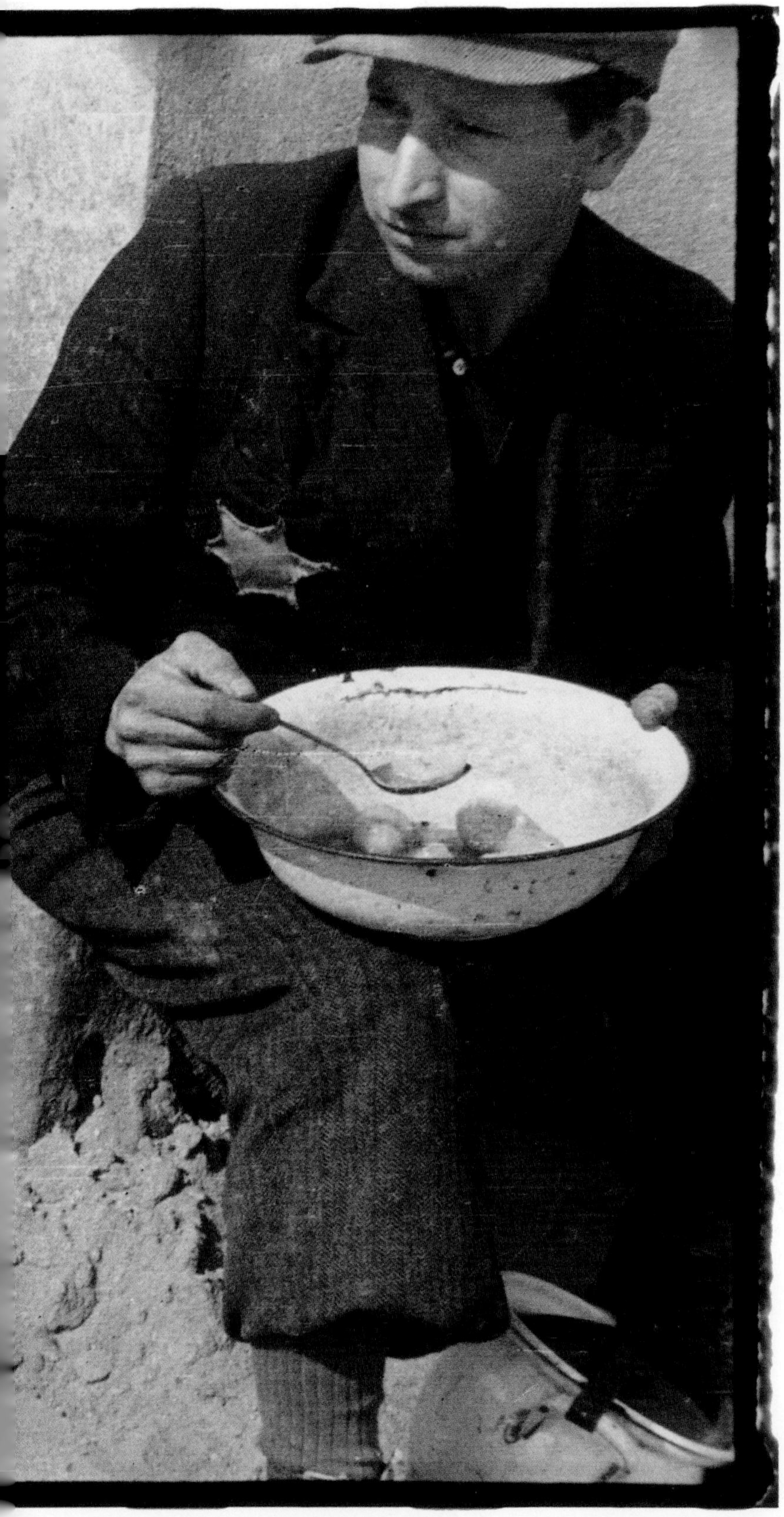

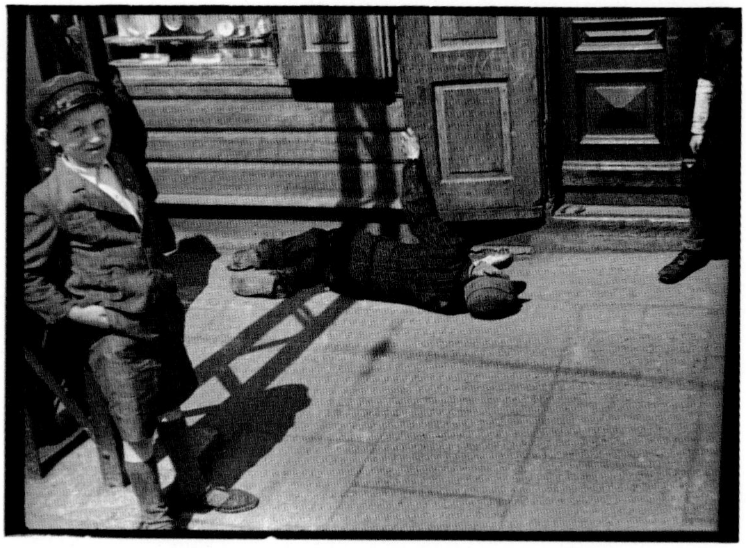

ABOVE: Shortage of food and its effects is one of the most poignant aspects of Ross's photographs of the Lodz ghetto, where the poorest inhabitants were literally starved to death. This man has fallen in the street from hunger.

LEFT: Ross captioned this photograph *Lunch break – Soup for Lunch* and it is part of a series that focuses on the distribution of soup from a public kitchen to the poorest members of the ghetto, those able to survive only through what was handed out to them by the community.

SEBASTIAO SALGADO

Sebastião Salgado does not do small projects. He produces only epic masterpieces, which take years to shoot and are huge in scope and ambition. His first great body of work was *Workers*, which is both a homage to and critique of manual labour. Salgado went to the mines, the oil wells, the factories, the fisheries, the car plants and the fields, photographing men and women as they toiled and sweated. In these stunningly composed prints, which veer from sweeping panoramas to more detailed studies, we see human experience on both the smallest and grandest of scales. Salgado is a passionate photographer who has a clear ideological affinity with his subjects, yet he has the intelligence not to allow this sympathy to cloud his vision. Perhaps it is the economist in him, but his photographs remain detached and objective. Salgado has in the past been condemned for beautifying his subject matter and some people have found his images just too crisp and perfect. He is, rightly, not concerned with these quibbles, arguing that he just wants to engage as many people as he can and why not do that with a beautiful photograph?

He describes *Migrations* as the second chapter to *Workers*. This, too, has a socio-economic viewpoint, but here Salgado looks at "Humanity in Transition" (the subtitle of the book). He photographs desperate migrants leaving rural areas to look for work, as well as displaced people and refugees. This huge and complex body of work involved Salgado criss-crossing the globe trying to make sense of an issue that is permanently in a state of flux. Perhaps the most memorable section of this project is "Megacities", for which Salgado travelled to the urban centres of Brazil, Mexico, India, China and Indonesia. Here he photographed the chronic overcrowding, poor sanitation, pollution and sheer mass of people that characterize these sprawling cities. Salgado has now had a change of direction and is working on what he says will be his last project, *Genesis*, photographing the parts of the earth and the wildlife that have been untainted by man. We can't wait to see the results from this master photographer.

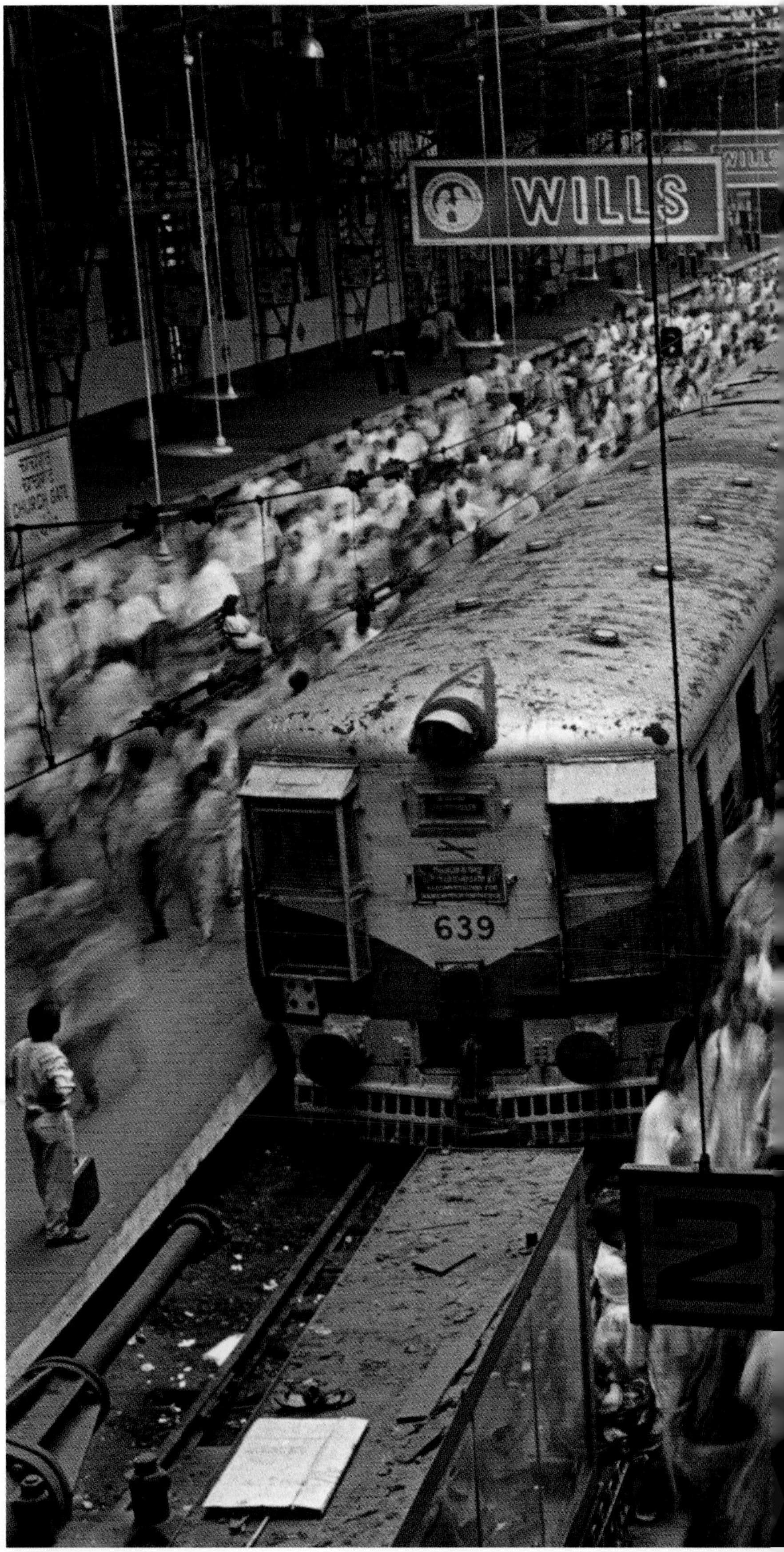

RIGHT: This image of the Church Gate railway station, Bombay, taken in 1995, is from Salgado's essay "Megacities", just one chapter in his epic project *Migrations*. In one remarkable image, Salgado has managed to capture the density of human traffic that passes through the station; around 2.7 million people flow through every day. Salgado used blur to intensify the experience and the effect also dehumanizes the individualism of the commuters, turning them into one struggling mass.

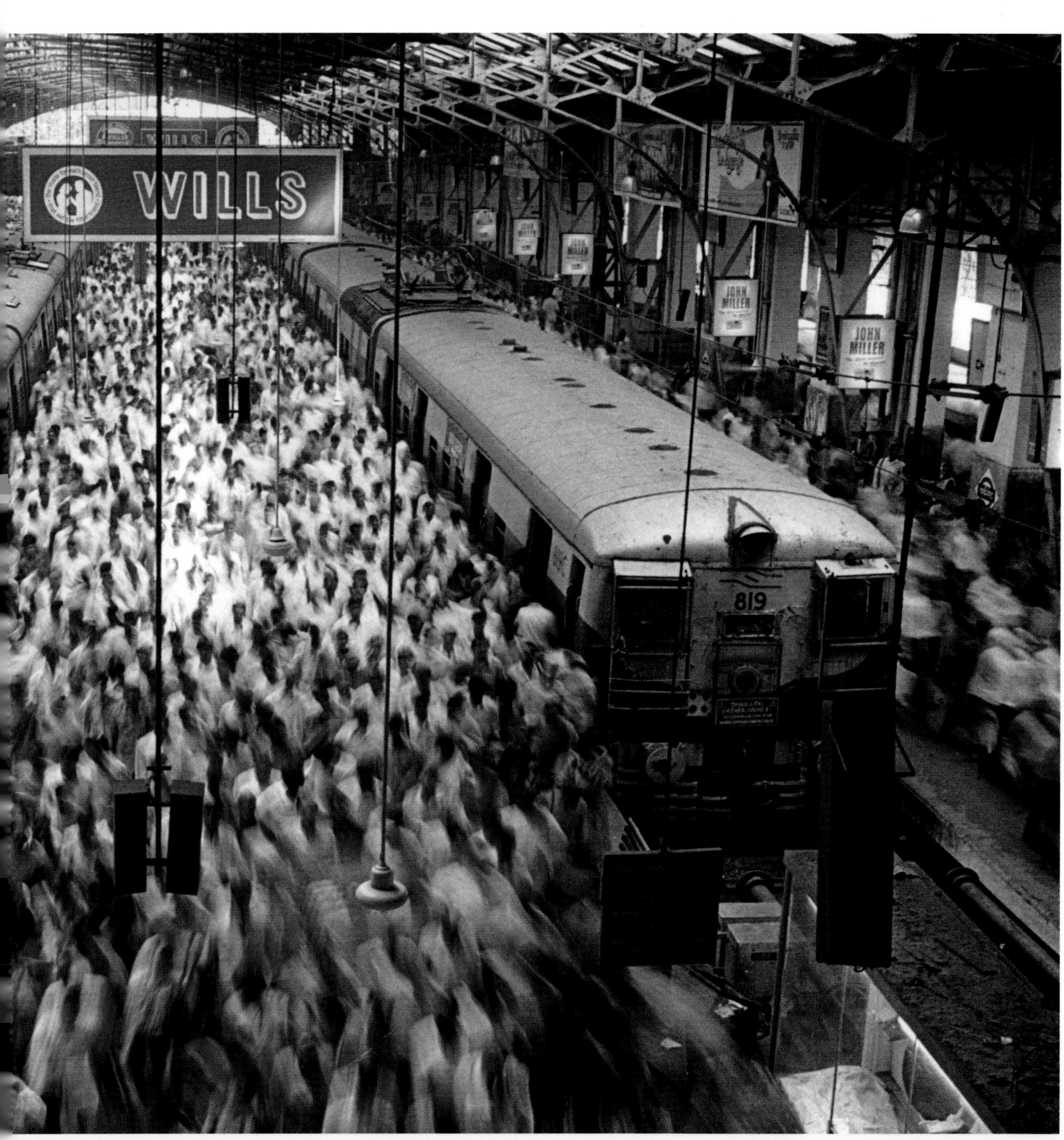
WILLS
JOHN MILLER
819

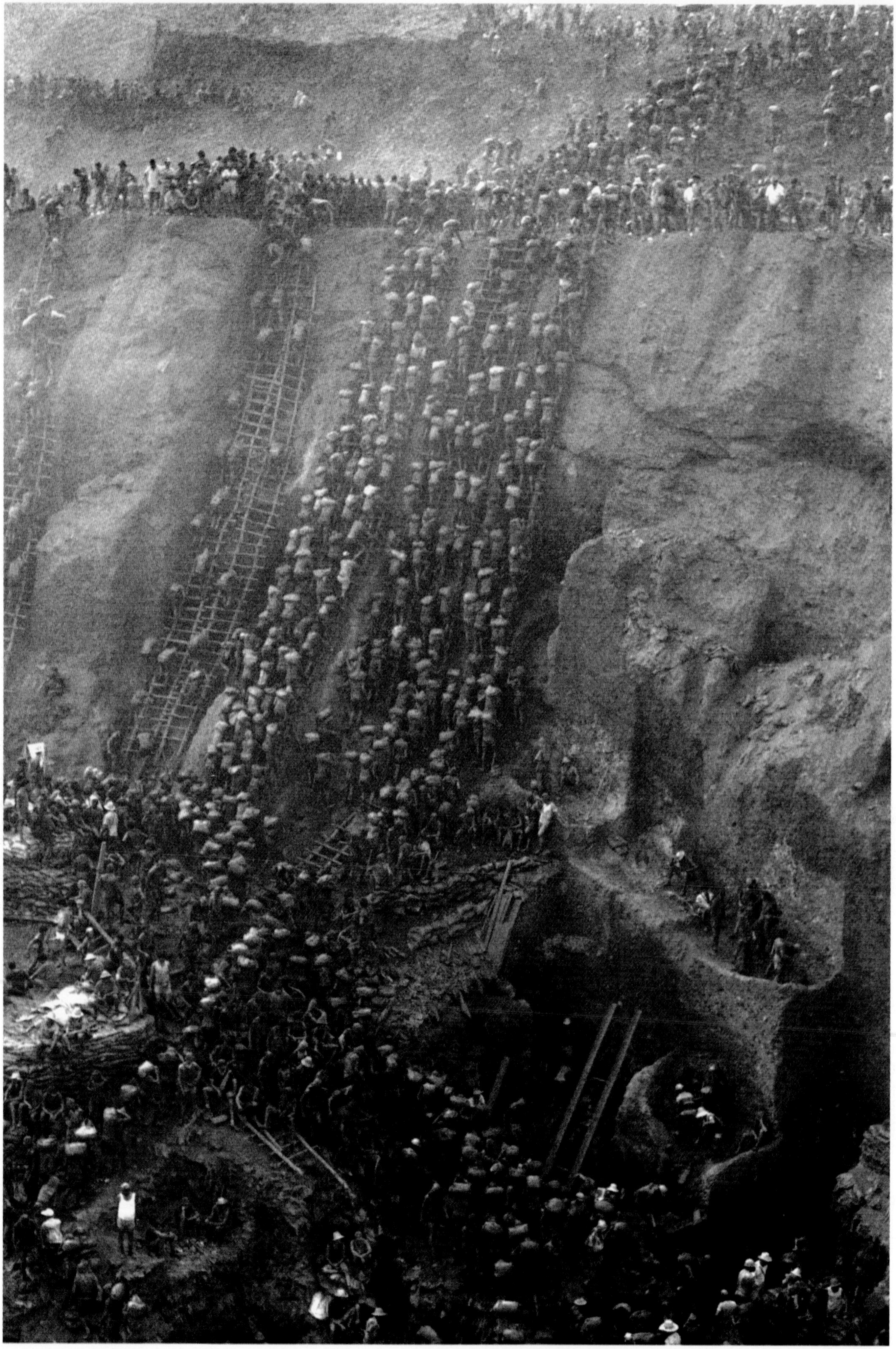

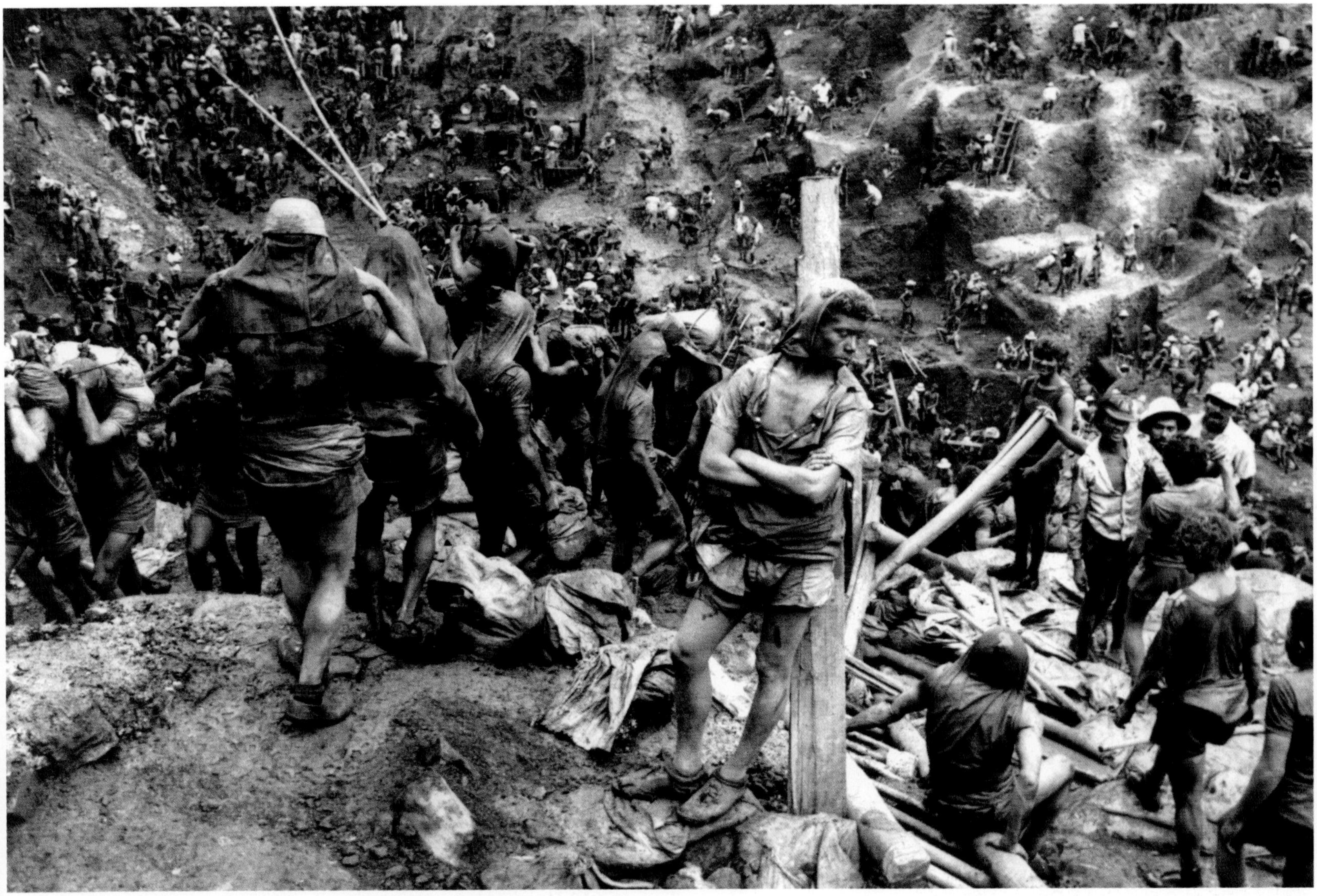

LEFT AND ABOVE: Every day 50,000 *garimpeiros* (gold diggers) descend Sierra Pelada's open-top mine in Brazil. The gold diggers are called mud hogs, as they wade in the dirt and slime. These two images from 1980 are part of Salgado's seminal epic project *Workers*,a documentation of manual labour throughout the world. The religious symbolism jumps out of these majestic photos. The image on the left could be a photographic record of Dante's *Inferno*, while in the photograph above, the man leaning against the wooden stake has a saint-like presence amid the dirt and the sweat. Photography has never been so powerful.

W. EUGENE SMITH

W. Eugene Smith did not invent the photo essay, but he revolutionized both its aesthetic and the role of the photographer in relation to it. Until Smith, photo essays were just stories, and the photographer was merely the objective commentator. Smith had loftier ideas. He believed that he was there not just to document, but also to interpret and offer moral judgement on what he was photographing. Smith's relationship with his subject becomes the story and through that dynamic photojournalism redefines itself and becomes art. For the true artist to realize their vision, therefore, they must have absolute mastery over every stage of the artistic process.

These are lofty ideals, but Smith was operating in a commercial environment and being assigned stories by photographic editors with budgets and deadlines. The dogmatic photographer, however, fought them every inch of the way. He felt that it was his job to come up with the stories, and to shoot as many pictures as he wanted in the format of his choice, time and money being no object. Moreover, only he would see the contact sheets, edit the work, write the captions, allocate the pages to his story and have absolute control over the layout. His essay on Pittsburgh virtually destroyed him both personally (Smith was a heavy drinker and highly strung) and professionally, and almost sank Magnum. He had been assigned to spend a couple of weeks in the city shooting about 100 photos. Instead, he spent five months there taking over 13,000 images and then spent a further 18 months printing them. For his most famous essay, *The Country Doctor*, he also went AWOL and fell out with *Life* after it ran the story to his inevitable dissatisfaction. Yet in this case the ends certainly justified the (increasingly difficult) means. Through his dramatic composition and lighting, we learn not just what the doctor does, but what he represents and in turn something about Smith himself. This is a masterpiece of story-telling and was a blueprint for a new kind of photo essay. It is an exaggerated, often a staged, reality, but it is absolutely enthralling nonetheless. Smith was truly a genius who redefined his craft.

RIGHT: Dr Ernest C. Ceriani, a country doctor, going to visit his patients in their remote villages around rural Colorado in 1948. Smith shadowed the doctor for weeks, learning everything he could about the man and his routine. In Smith's essay he becomes an understated but true American hero, selflessly devoting himself to the community. He is also highly photogenic, which helped Smith get his point across. Note how he is perfectly framed in the middle of the image, while the brooding sky gives him even more gravitas.

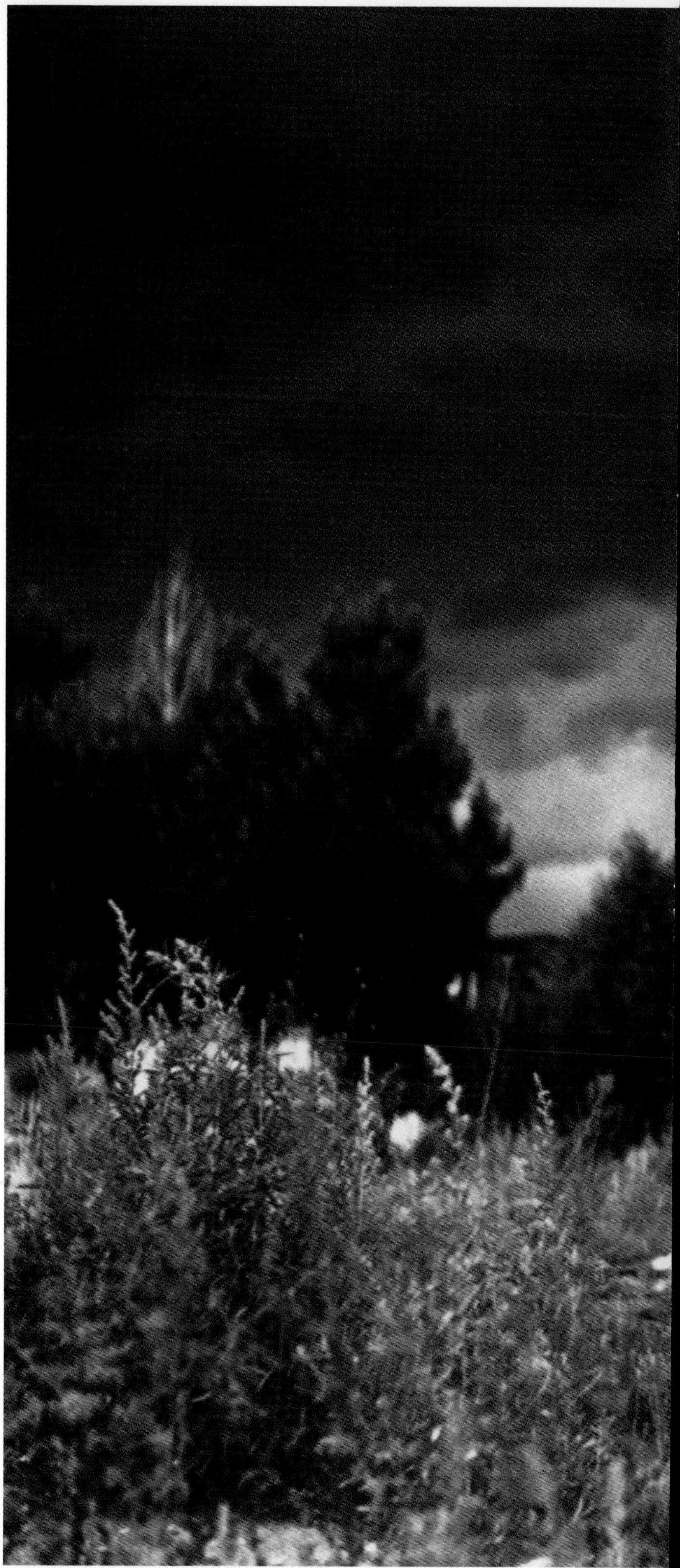

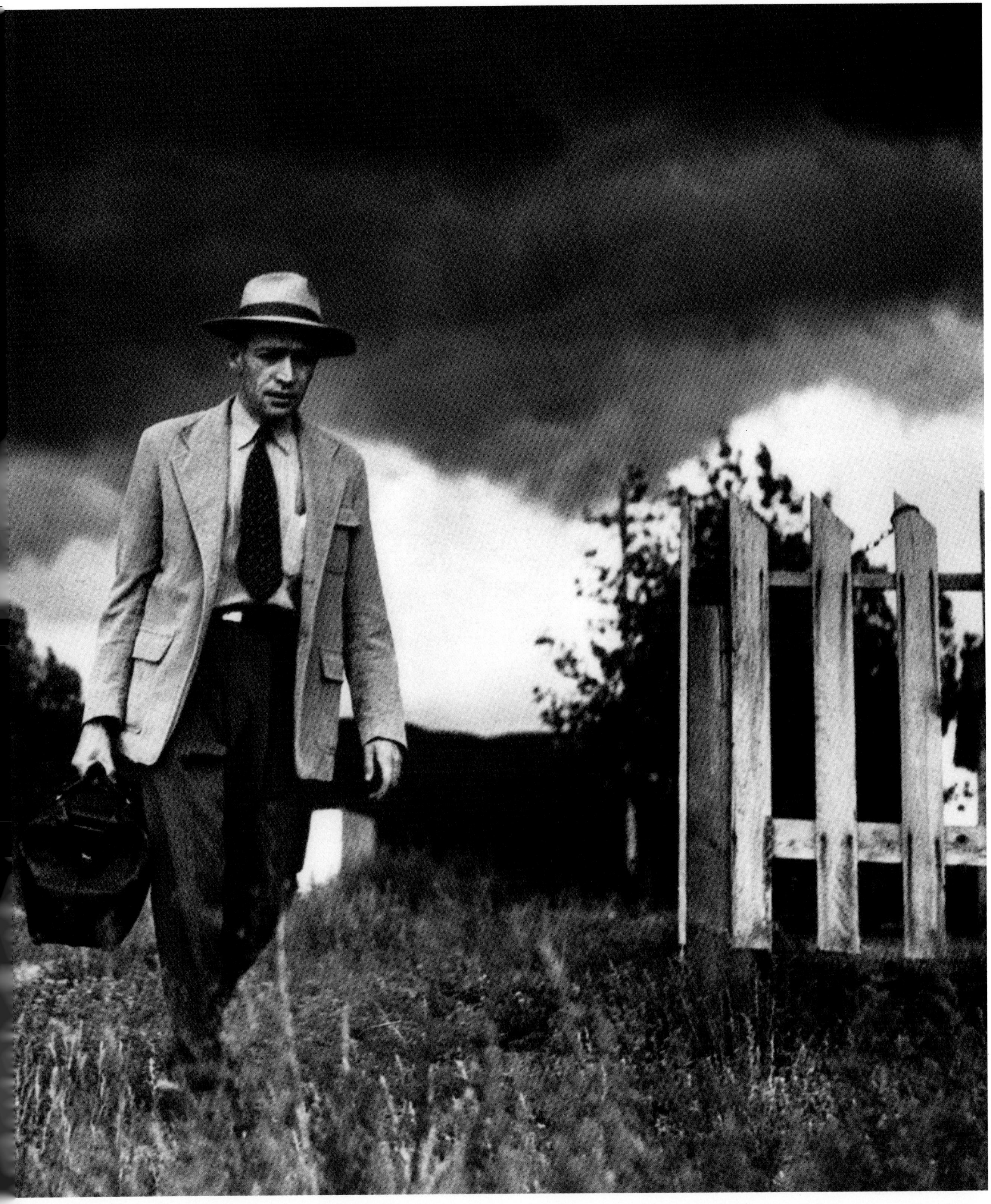

BELOW: The doctor attends to a child who has been kicked by a horse as the family watch on anxiously. Smith has pulled back the camera to quietly observe the scene unfolding before his eyes. The light coming through the shutters somehow suggests that the child will make a recovery.

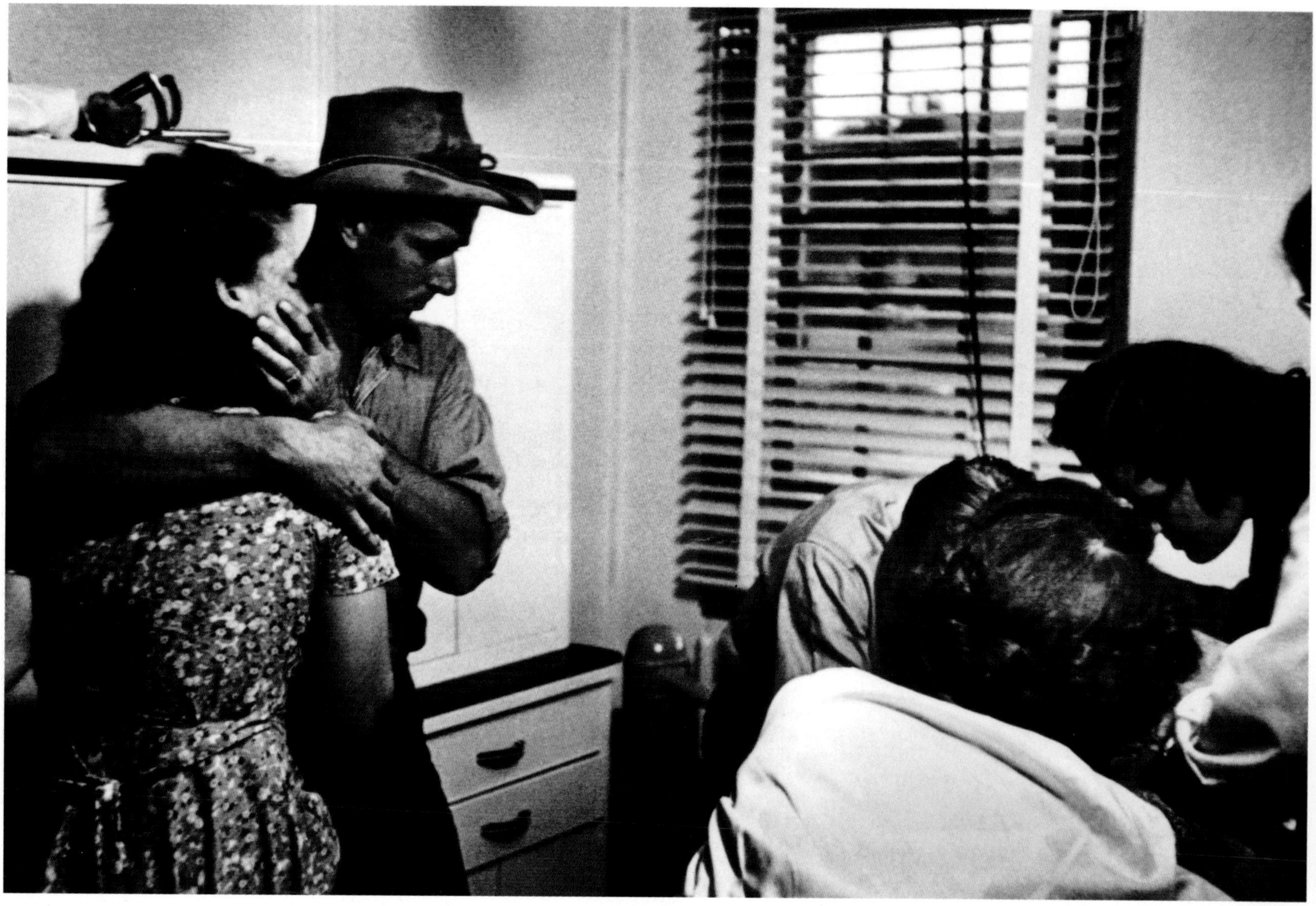

RIGHT: This is a second view of the incident shown above. Here Smith has gone for the tight crop and we see the doctor calm and composed. It is actually quite a graphic photograph, but there is something oddly stilted about the image, as if it is from a movie. Smith was known to construct his photos occasionally, and although there is a genuine injury, you do wonder why the doctor seems to be posing at such a moment.

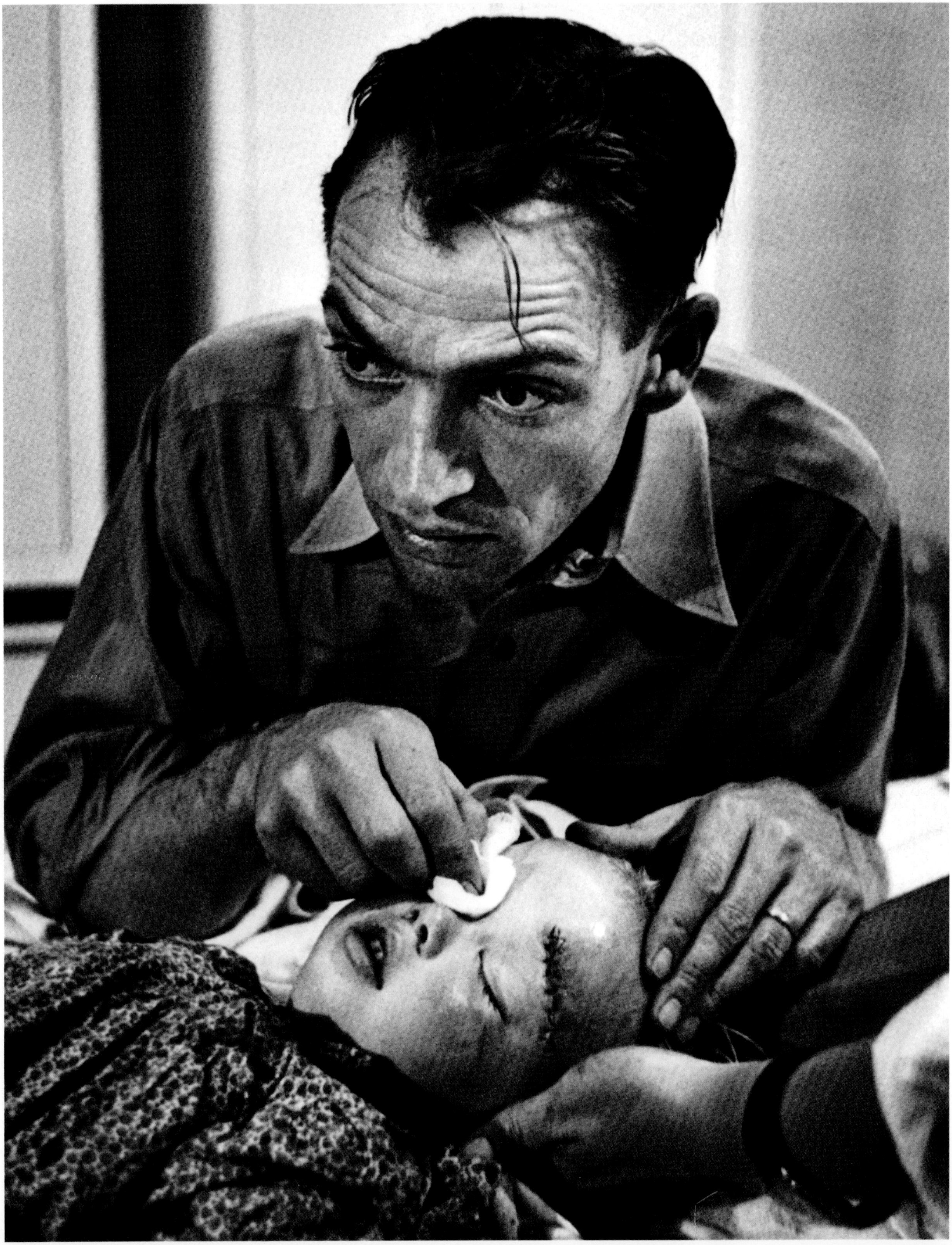

JOHN STANMEYER

BELOW: **A Sri Lankan woman salvages a few possessions from her tsunami-destroyed house in the city of Batticaloa. On the surface, this image is straightforward and simple, but it gives viewers a sense of the power of the tsunami, and personalizes the devastating losses.**

One of the first photographers to arrive in Sri Lanka after the tsunami on 26 December, 2004, John Stanmeyer conveyed a sense of the disaster's magnitude with a dramatic series of images shot for *Time* magazine. His take interspersed aerial images of widespread destruction with close-ups of the human toll: a water-scoured cemetery where a drowning victim had come to rest atop a tomb, residents of a decimated village scrounging for scraps to build shelters, mass burials ... "No matter how difficult a situation is, you know John will get where he has to go and get what you need," says photo editor Robert Stevens of *Time* magazine. "His tsunami pictures were amazing." Stanmeyer is not so easily satisfied. "I feel I've only touched the surface," he said shortly after the disaster. "It's beyond words and visually what I can see framed in my cameras. I am simply too small." Stanmeyer, who doesn't let stories go easily, plans to spend at least a year documenting the tsunami recovery efforts.

He has spent the past seven years documenting the growing AIDS crisis in Asia, and exploring stories about the children of Asian sex workers and the state of mental health care in the region. "I am fascinated by the [Asian] people, the history, the culture, the music, the literature, the progress and the lack thereof, the movements forward and the movements backward," he explains. Stanmeyer says that his parents encouraged his interest in photography from a young age, but his journey into photojournalism was an unlikely one. "I didn't have any solid enlightenment whatsoever in photojournalism. I was mostly inspired by the work of Helmut Newton, Arthur Elgort, Peter Lindbergh, Albert Watson and Nadar," he says. After art school, where he failed all three photojournalism courses that he took, Stanmeyer gained immediate success as a fashion photographer. But he soon grew disillusioned, and lost interest. "I woke up and realized the greatest power of all: reality photography."

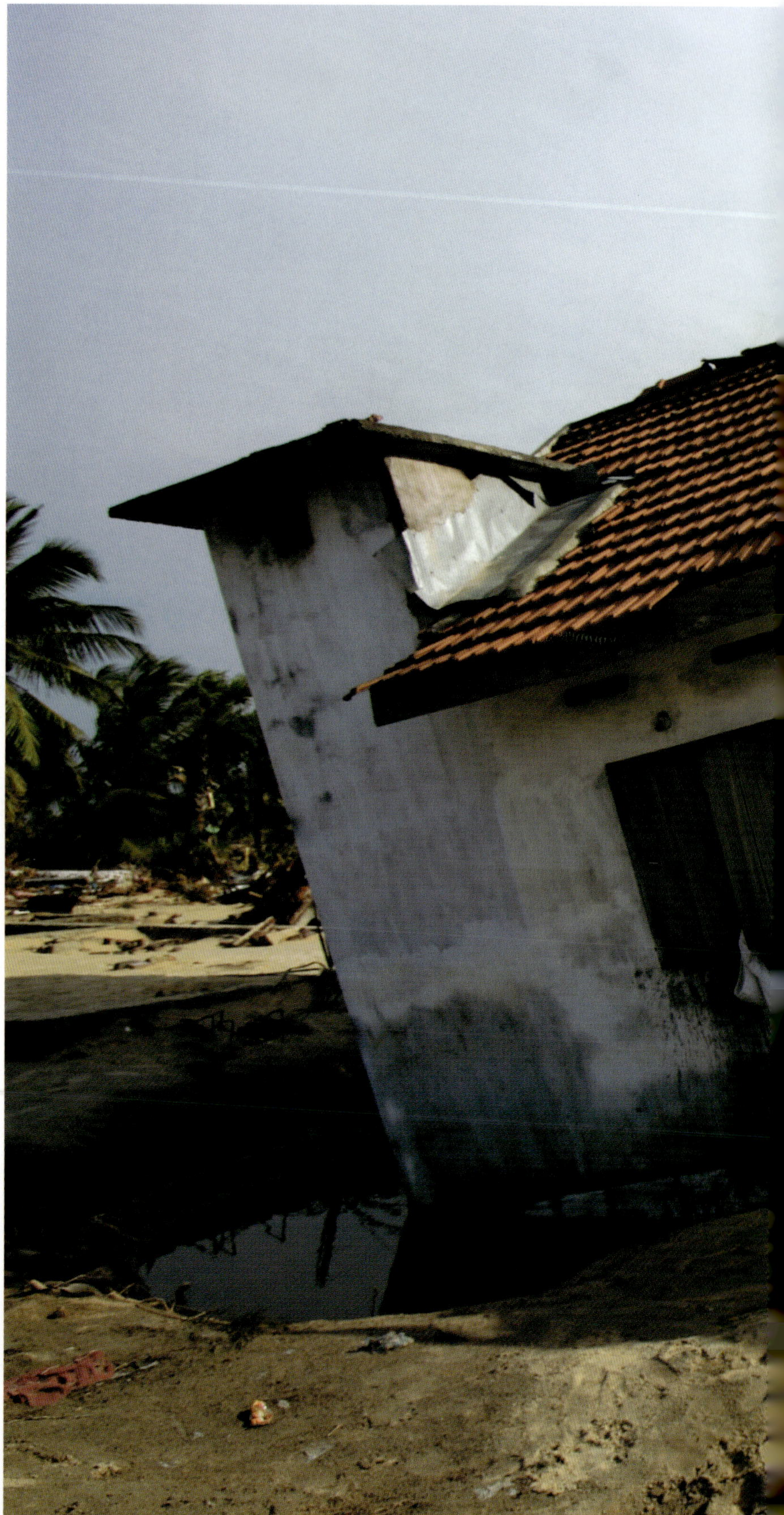

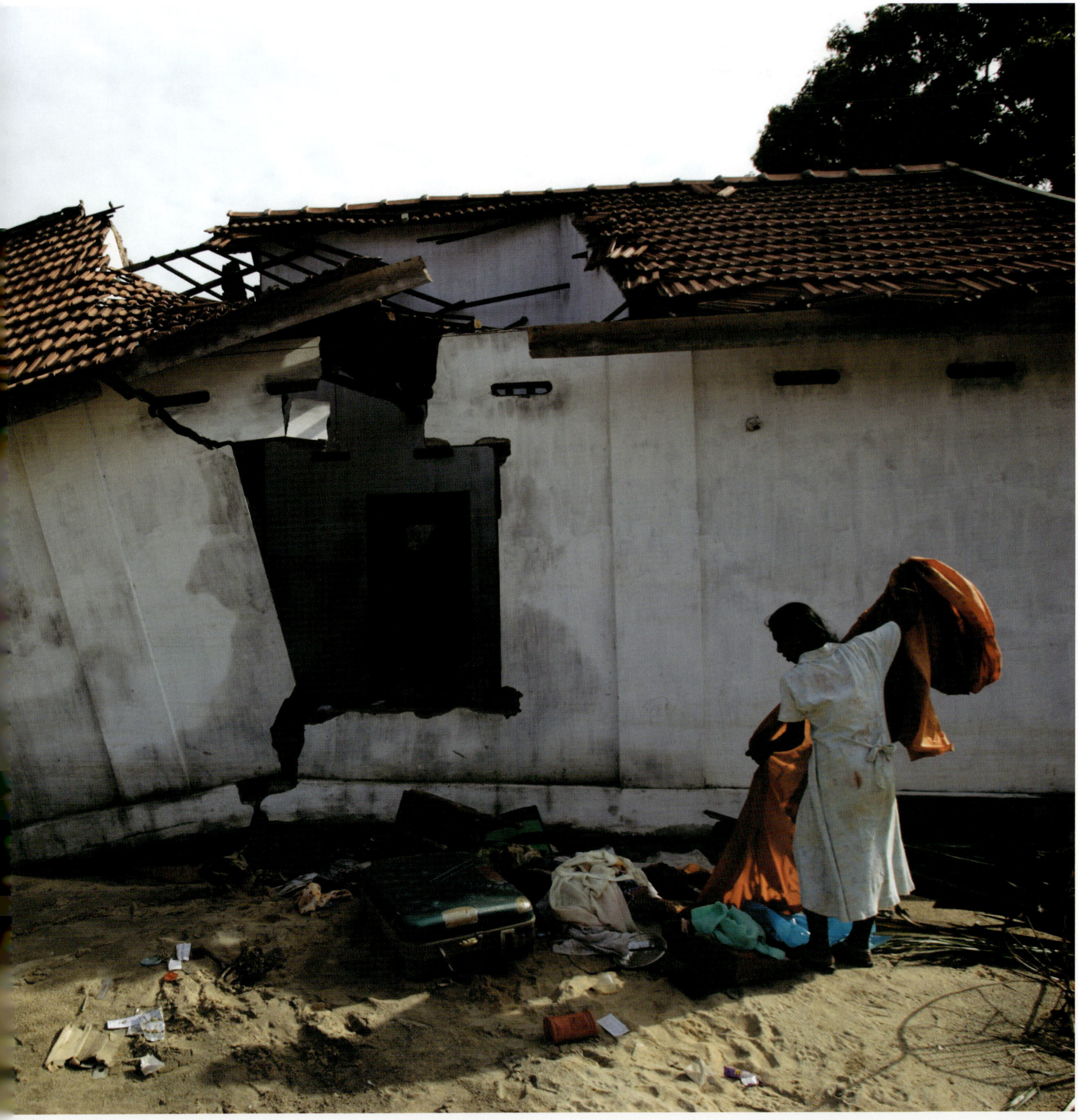

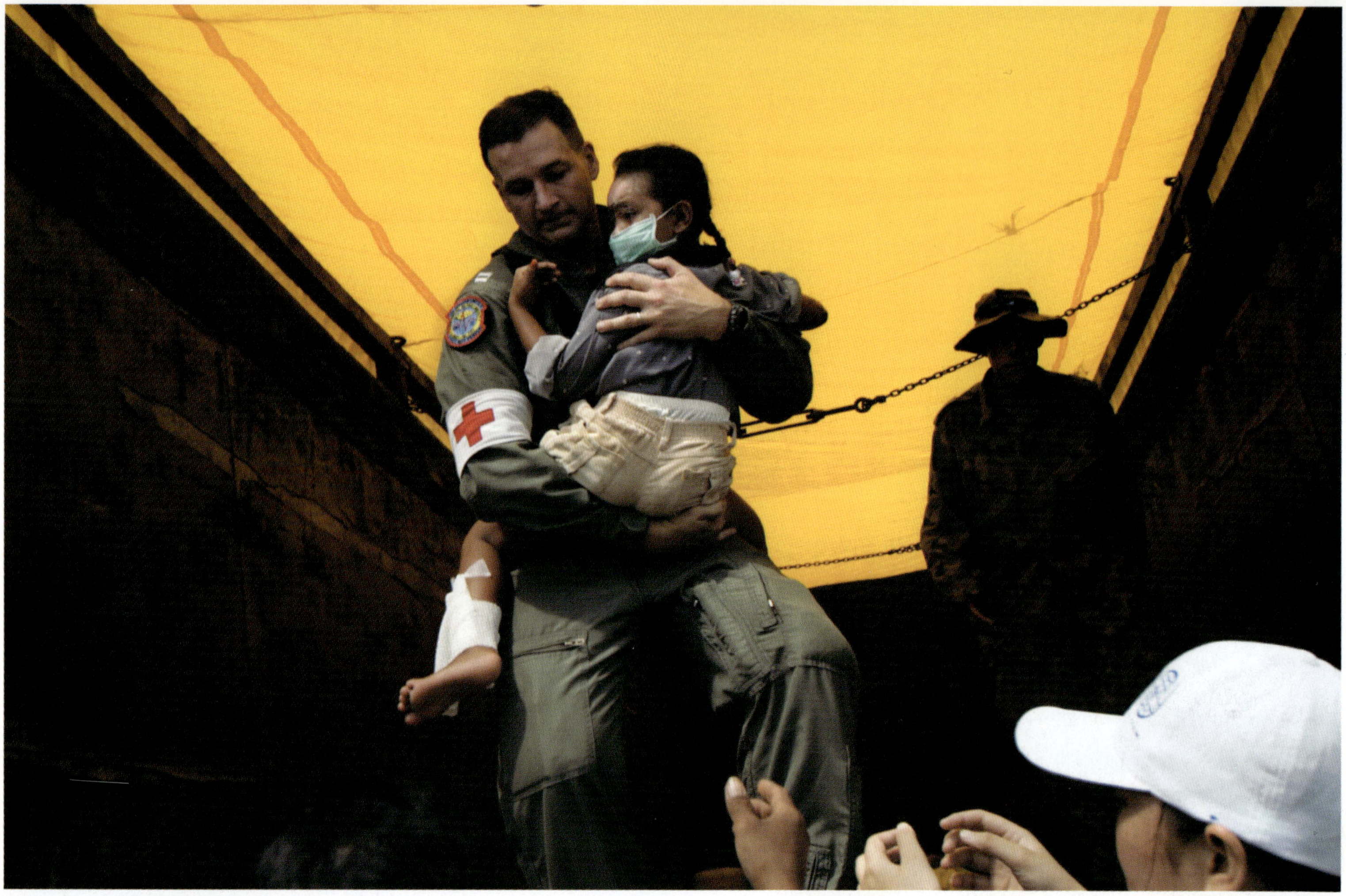

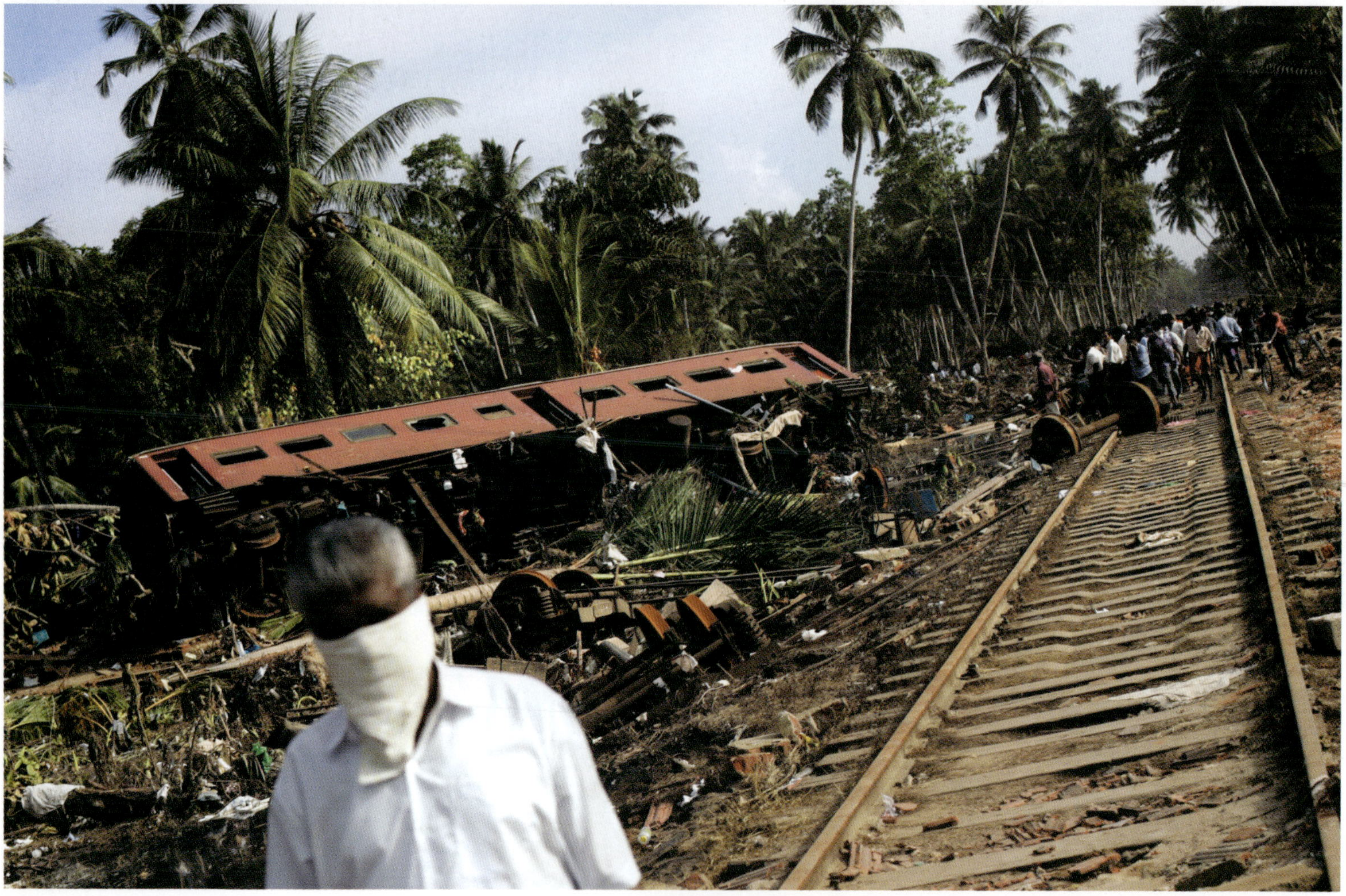

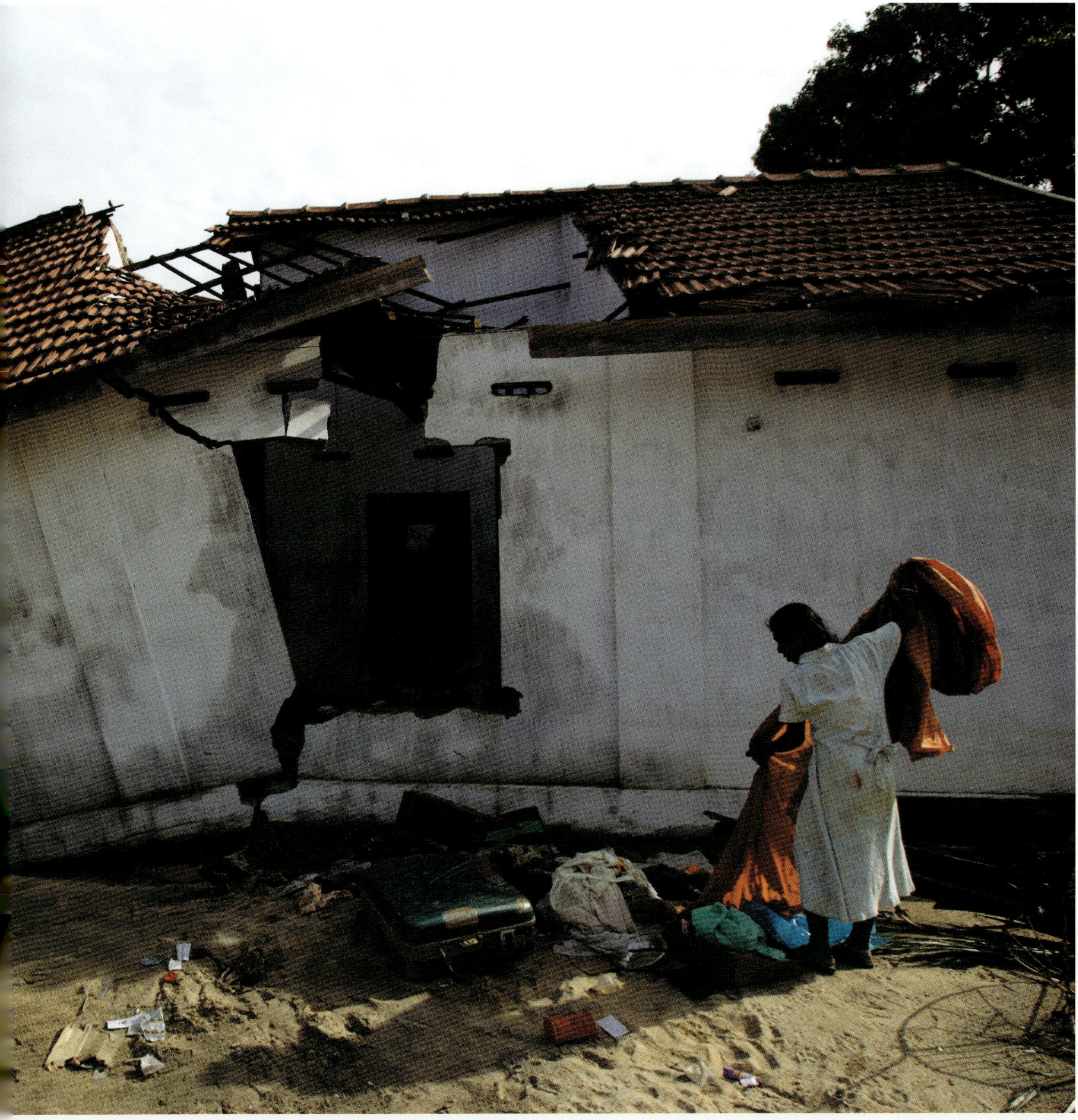

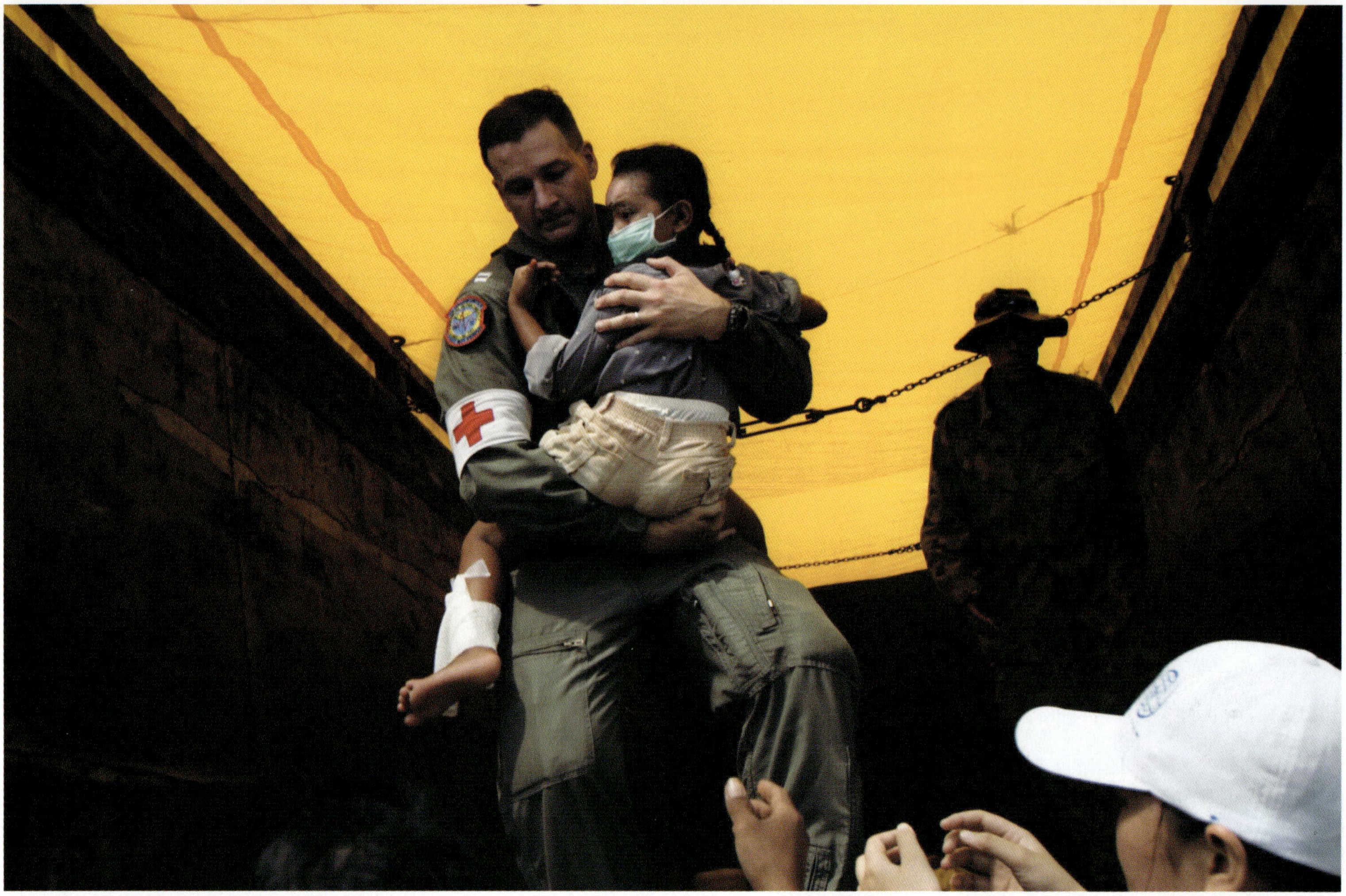

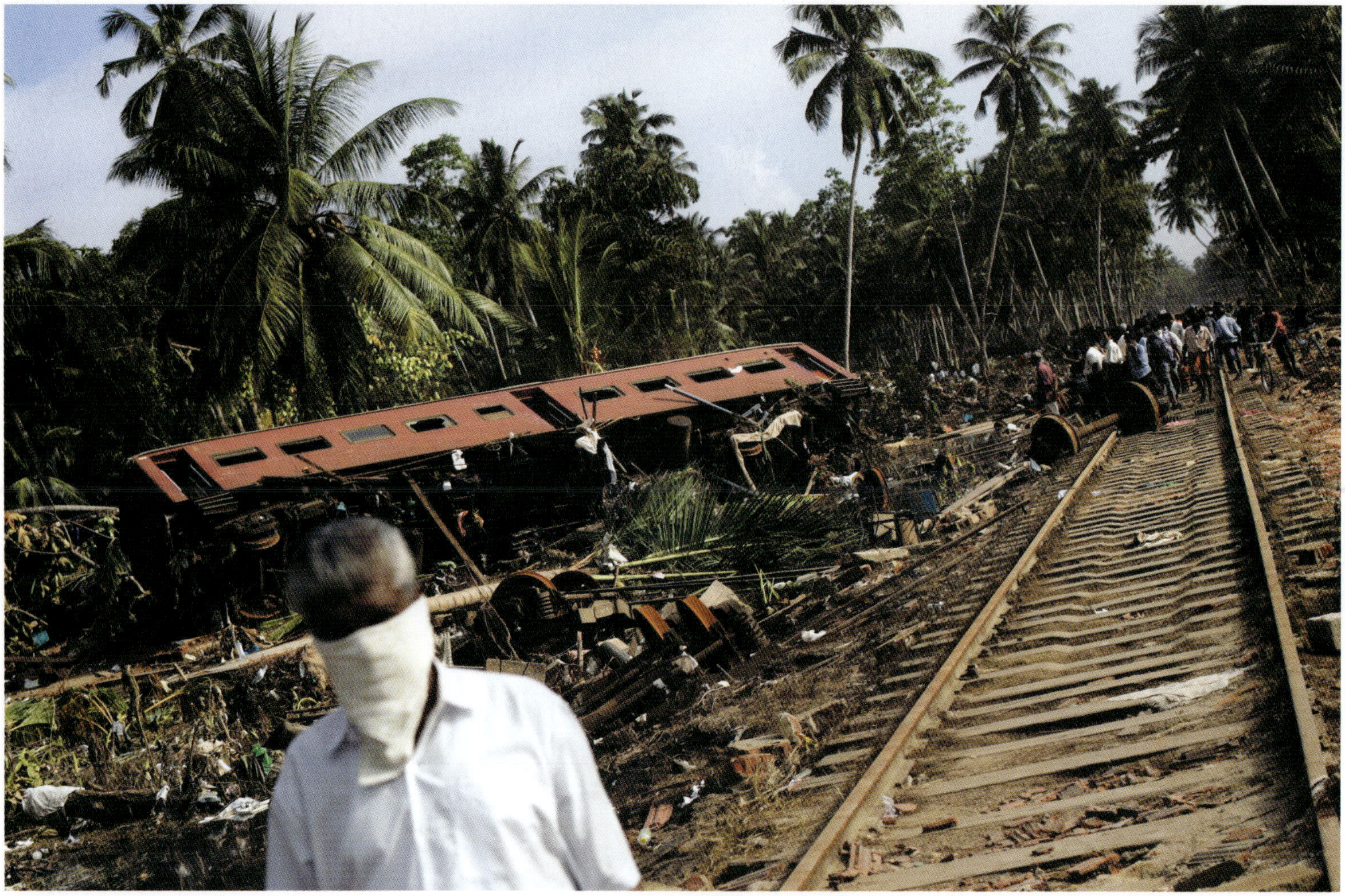

BELOW: Desperate tsunami victims from the remote city of Krueng Raya pulling food supplies from a US Navy helicopter moments after it landed. Stanmeyer's use of a tilted frame focuses attention on the woman in the foreground, but also helps impart a sense of urgency and chaos to the scene.

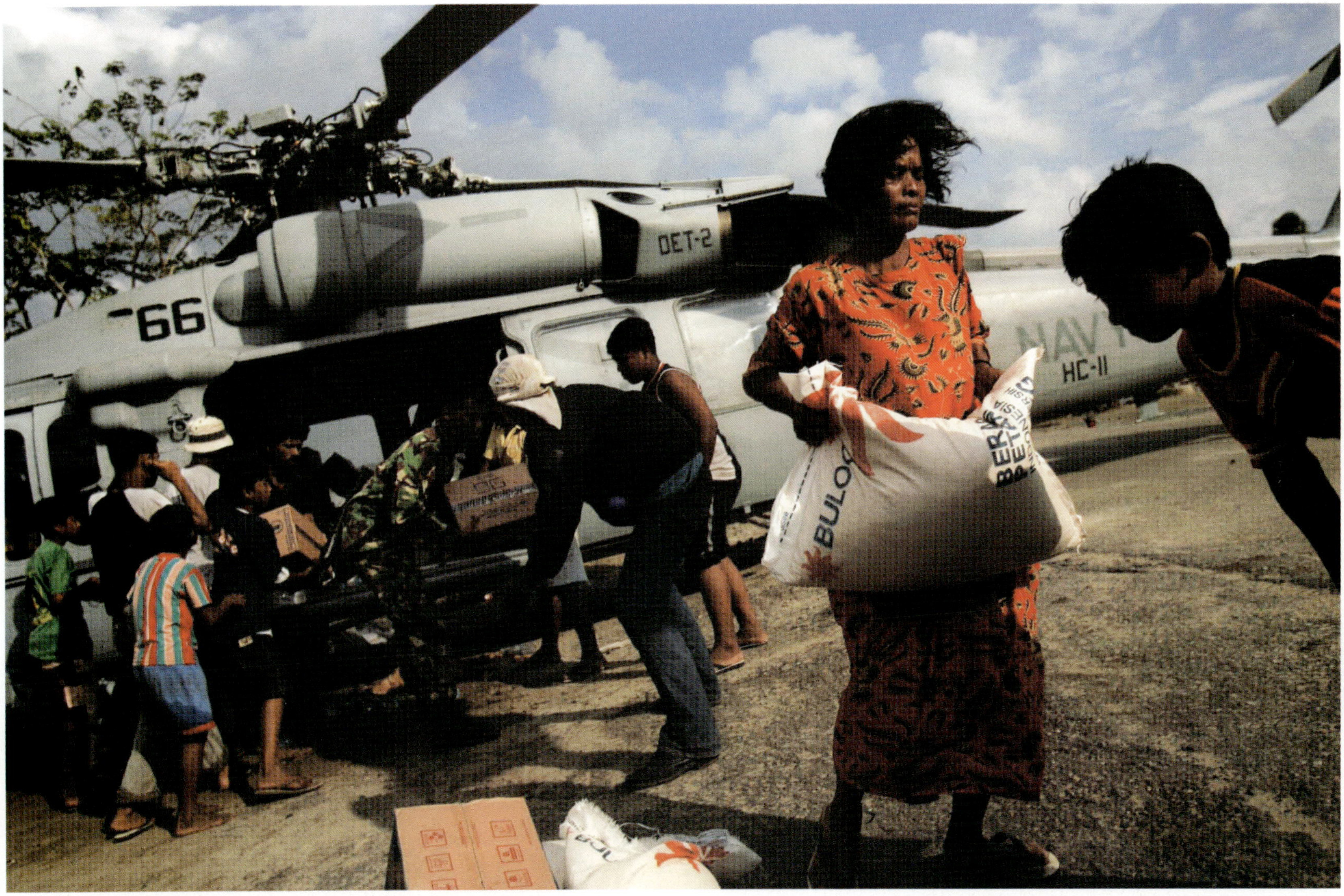

LEFT TOP: US troops evacuate injured children from Banda Aceh after a giant tsunami struck the Indonesian province on 26 December, 2004. This image symbolizes the fragility and innocence of survivors, particularly the youngest.

LEFT BOTTOM: This photograph shows the sheer scale and devastation of the tsunami and its impact on both the people and the landscape. Here we see the crumpled wreckage of a passenger train after the tsunami hit Galle in southern Sri Lanka, littering bodies everywhere.

TOM STODDART

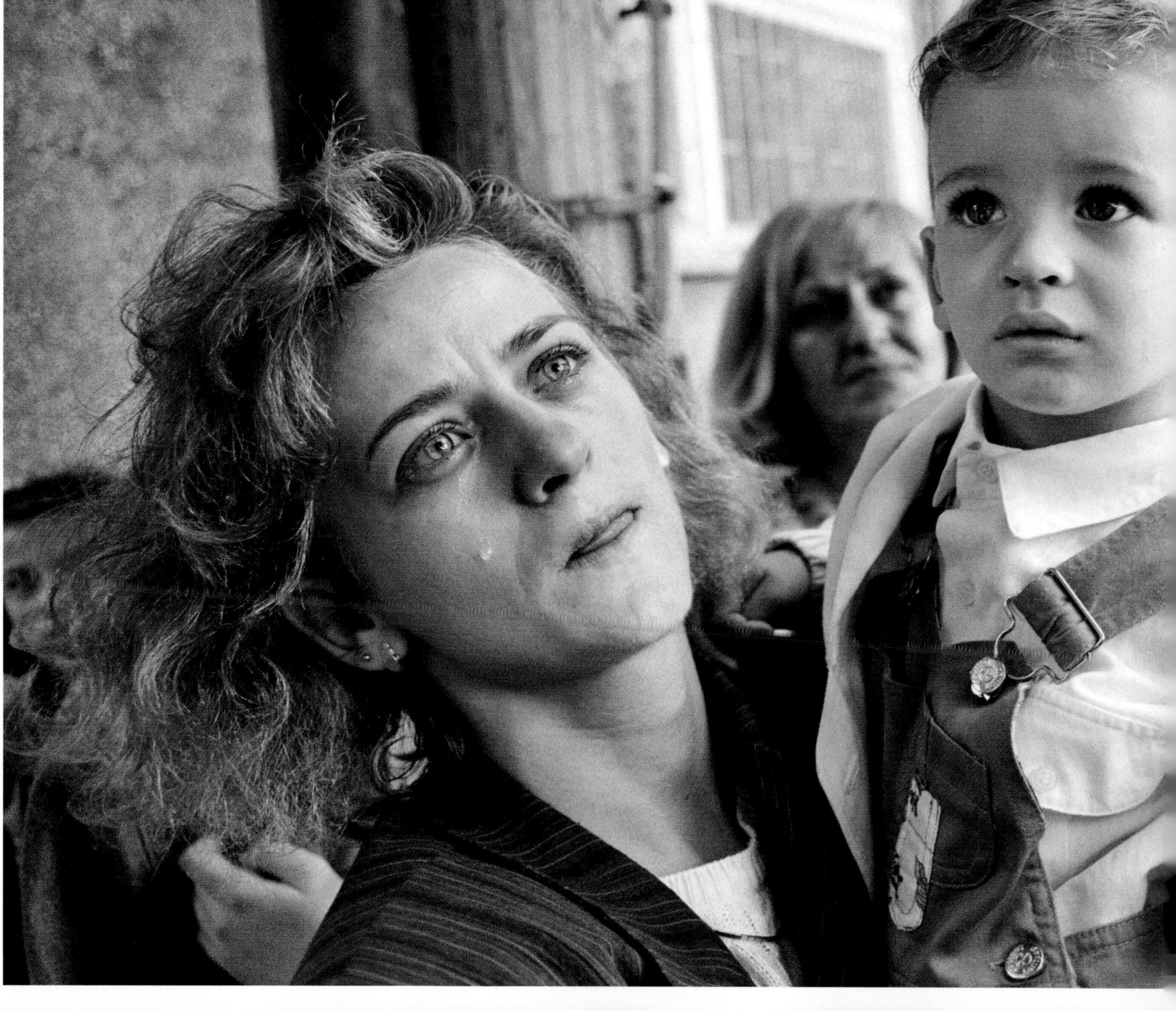

BELOW: Tears of anguish for a mother as she prepares to send her confused child out of Sarajevo on a bus promised safe passage by the Serb forces, during the siege of Sarajevo 1992–96. This photo opens Stoddart's website, so it is clear that he rightly holds this image in high regard. Both the mother and her son face an uncertain future, encapsulated by the single tear running down the woman's face.

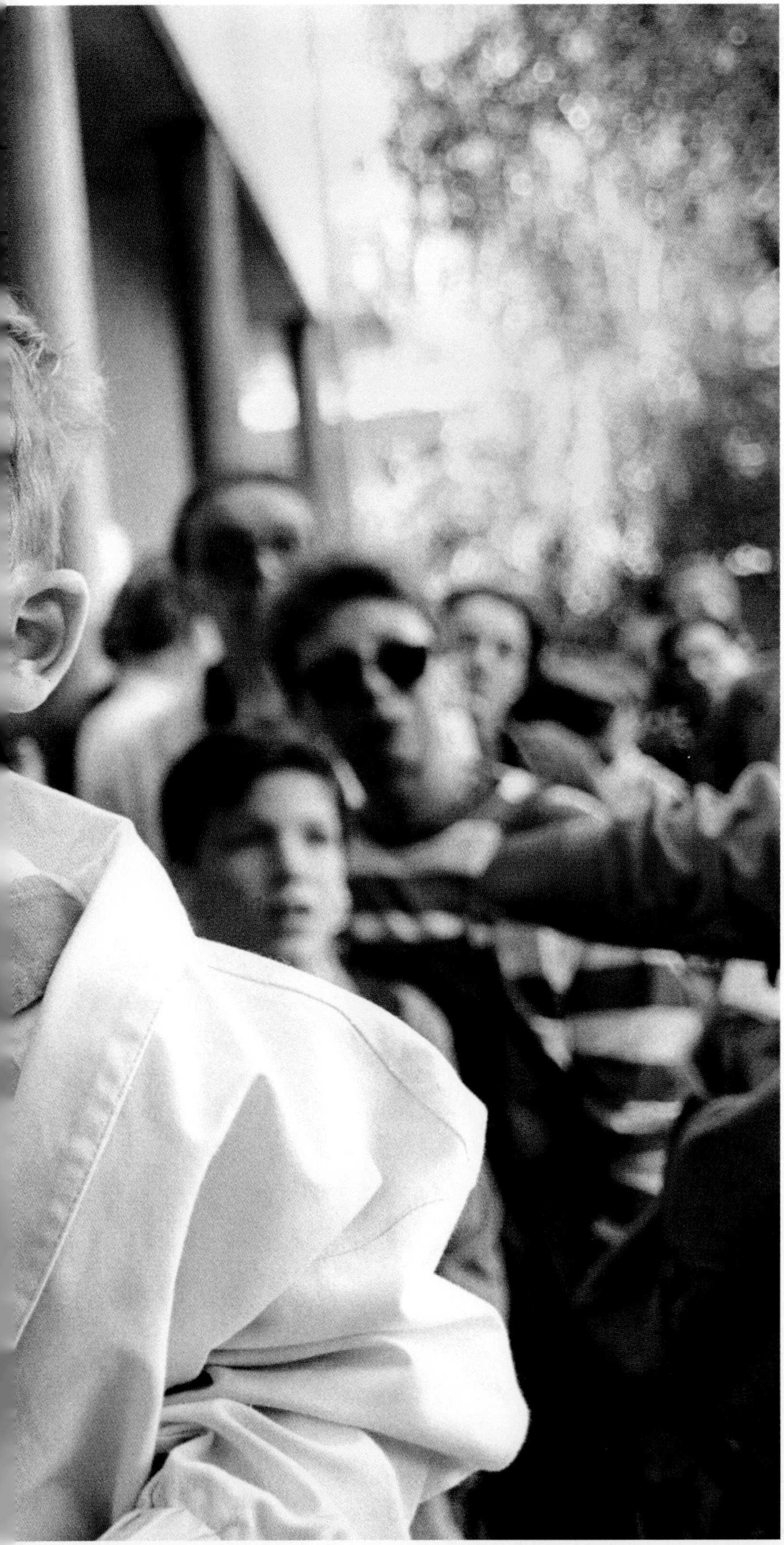

On the home page of Tom Stoddart's website, he quotes from one of the greatest and most controversial figures in the history of photojournalism, the American Civil War photographer Matthew Brady: "A spirit in my feet said 'go' and I went." Stoddart has certainly followed in his mentor's footsteps. He is a relentless, multi-prizewinning and much travelled photojournalist who says that the "real prize has been the privilege of witnessing history unfolding in front of my cameras". A modest, softly spoken man from the north of England, Stoddart is not only an extremely sensitive photographer, but also a very brave one, who was shot in the leg while working in the besieged city of Sarajevo. His most famous photographs are often of women and their children, caught in the middle of a conflict or a natural disaster, trying to not only survive, but to get on with their lives with stoicism and dignity.

Stoddart is one of the old school of photojournalists, who prefers to spend time, often years, with his subjects, living side by side with them. This intimacy is reflected in his images, which get up so close, both physically and mentally, that you get the sense that Stoddart is there for his subjects, speaking for them and letting the world know of their plight. Yet he doesn't just photograph victims, and some of his most powerful work is from the last Gulf War when Stoddart was embedded with the Royal Marines. Whatever the subject matter, the images always resonate, since he is such a technically accomplished photographer. Working almost exclusively in black-and-white, it seems that Stoddart always manages to produce an image that is akin to fine art photography, no matter how terrible the circumstances. In fact, he once said that he is often in something of a moral quandary while on assignment. People might be suffering and there he is, in the centre of all the chaos, looking through the viewfinder and trying to get his composition just right. Yet at the same time, he is professional enough to know that if he didn't worry about the look of an image, he wouldn't be doing his job.

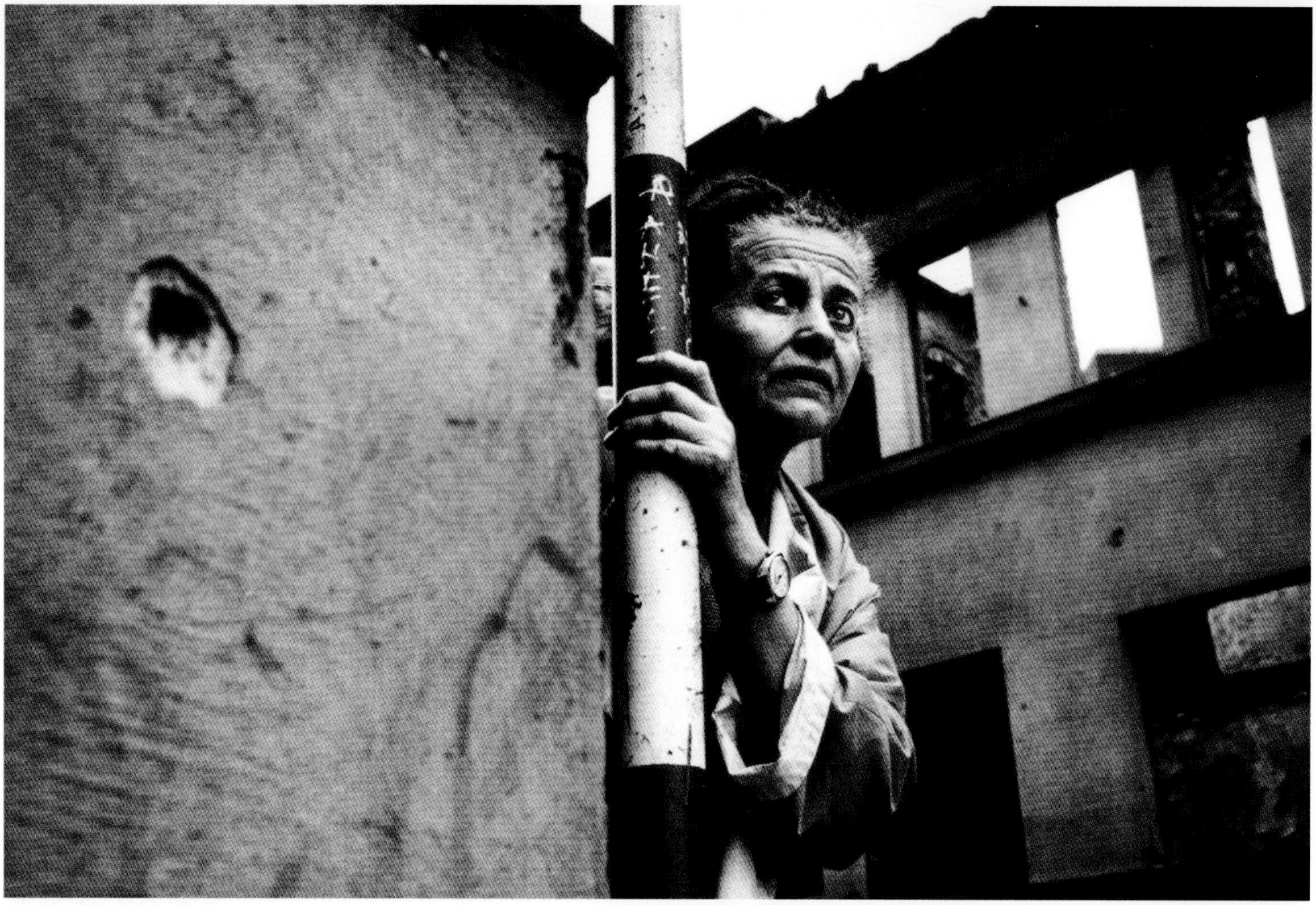

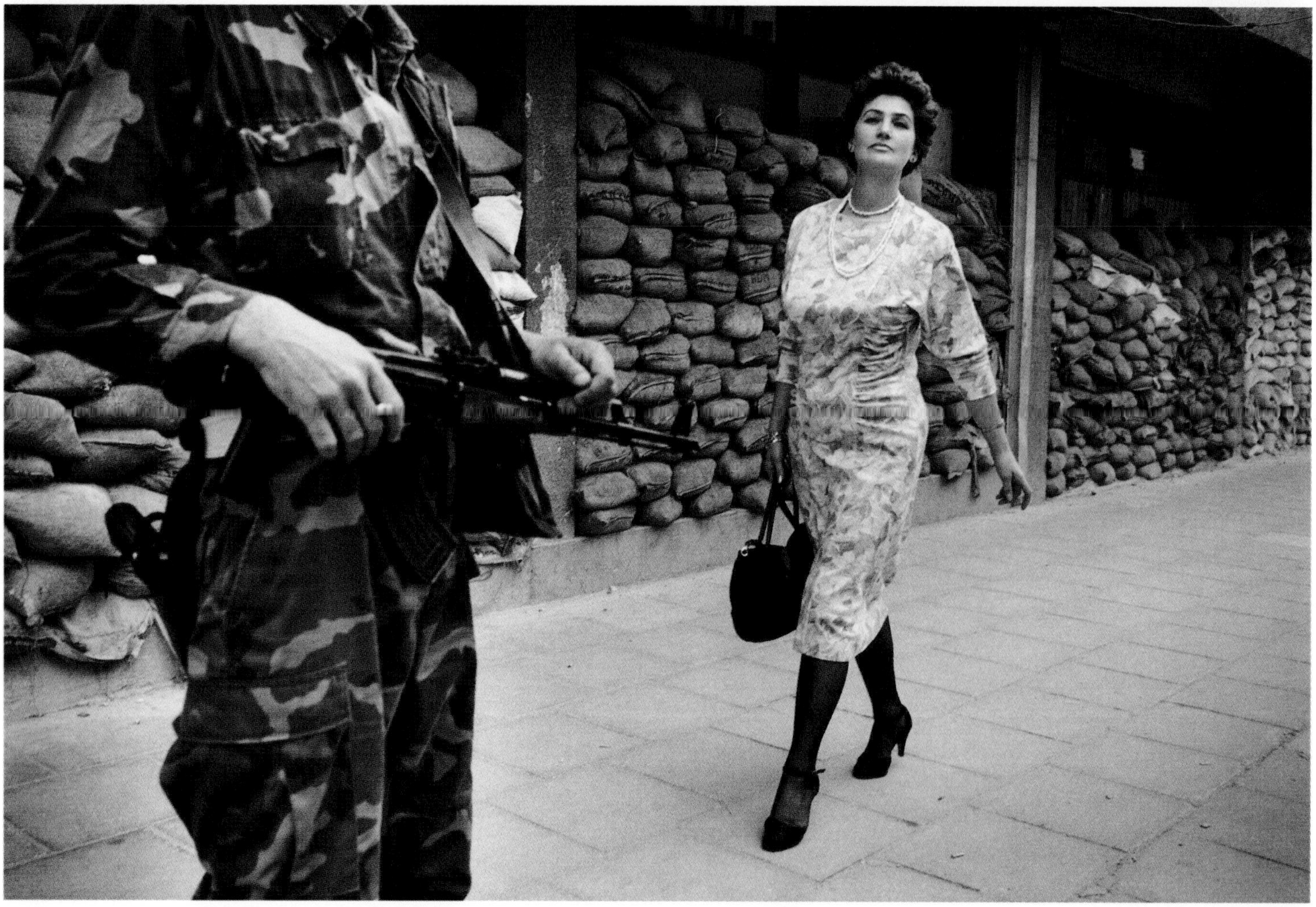

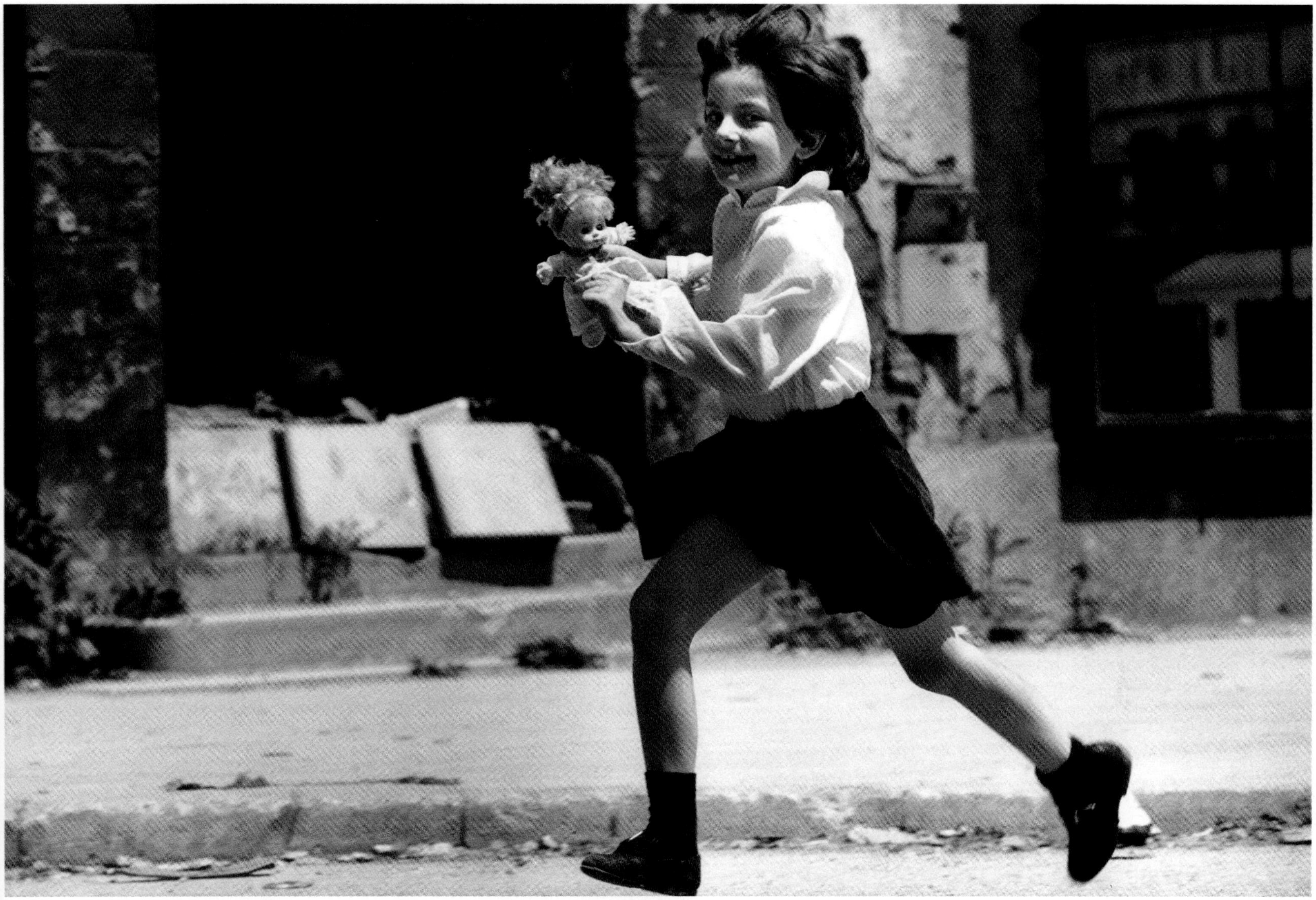

LEFT AND ABOVE: Three images from the notorious "sniper alley" in Sarajevo, Bosnia. Stoddart, no matter, how dangerous the situation, has the ability to compose his images calmly and make them resonate with the viewer. In the photograph top left, the woman is trying to summon the courage to venture out as the Serbs shoot people indiscriminately. The wall, the woman and the burnt-out building in the background are all working in tandem. In the photograph bottom left, Meliha Vareshanovic walks proudly and defiantly to work in a gesture of defiance towards the seen and unseen tormentors responsible for the terrible plight of her city. The photograph above is one of the most famous images from this whole period. It is the ultimate photograph of an innocent caught in the crossfire, and the fact that the girl has the inclination to grin at the camera while running for her life makes her adorable.

WEEGEE

Weegee was originally named Arthur Fellig. His pseudonym, adopted by him in around 1938, comes from the Ouija board. The girls at Acme Photos gave him the name because he always seemed to know where to find the best stories. Although he is best known for his striking crime pictures, Weegee's photography seems now to be much more about character and caricature than it is about murder, robbery and mayhem. Arthur Fellig began his photographic career as a portraitist. He worked for small studios in New York, and even, from around 1915–17, as a street photographer on the Lower East Side, taking pictures of children with a 5 in x 7 in (12 cm x 18 cm) camera and a pony called Hypo. A relentless, brash and hyperbolic self-publicist, self-titled "Weegee the world's most famous photographer", he was also consumed by an overwhelming obsession with his work. This is borne out by the car he used as a crime reporter, which was equipped with every requirement for his photographic work on the streets of the "Naked City", including a police radio, cigars, salami and a change of clothes. "I was no longer glued to the Teletype machine at police headquarters. I had my wings. I no longer had to wait for crime to come to me; I could go after it. The police radio was my lifeline. My camera ... my life and my love ... was my Aladdin's lamp" (*Weegee by Weegee*, 1961).

Weegee's pictures exerted a great influence on several photographers of the "New York School", particularly William Klein, Helen Levitt and Lisette Model, and this may have been because they eschew style in favour of content, a sort of visual truth that requires no cultural wrapping. Iconoclastic and self-taught, Weegee learnt his craft in a hard commercial environment where if his picture could hit the editor's desk before anybody else's he got the credit and the fee. Yet the truth and power of his images were quickly recognized as having a value beyond their ephemeral use in the tabloids. A few were acquired by the Museum of Modern Art in 1943, and his reputation was assured for ever after.

RIGHT: Gunman Anthony Esposito, accused of the murder of a businessman and a policeman in the "Battle of Fifth Avenue", is captured in the line-up room in police headquarters, New York, 1941. The harsh lighting of Weegee's picture, created by the direct flash on his camera, both delineates and caricatures the scene.

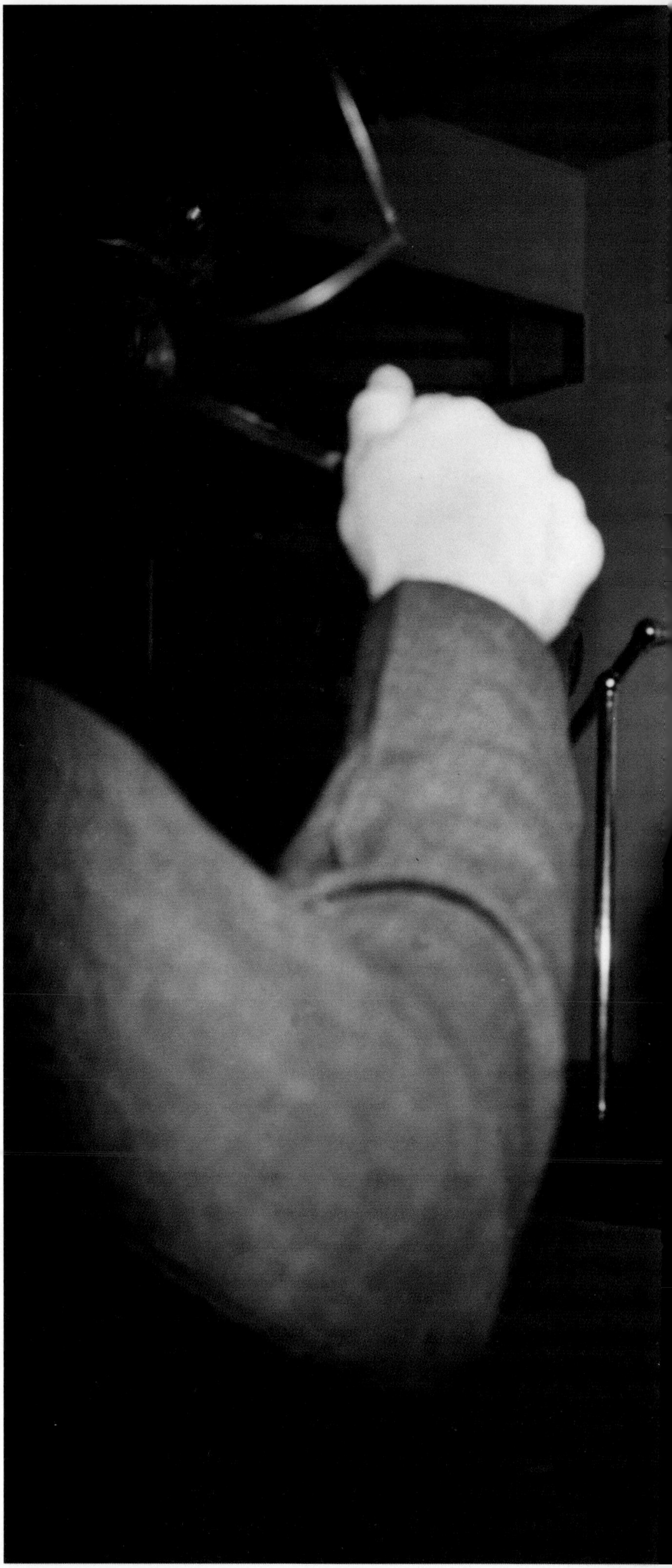

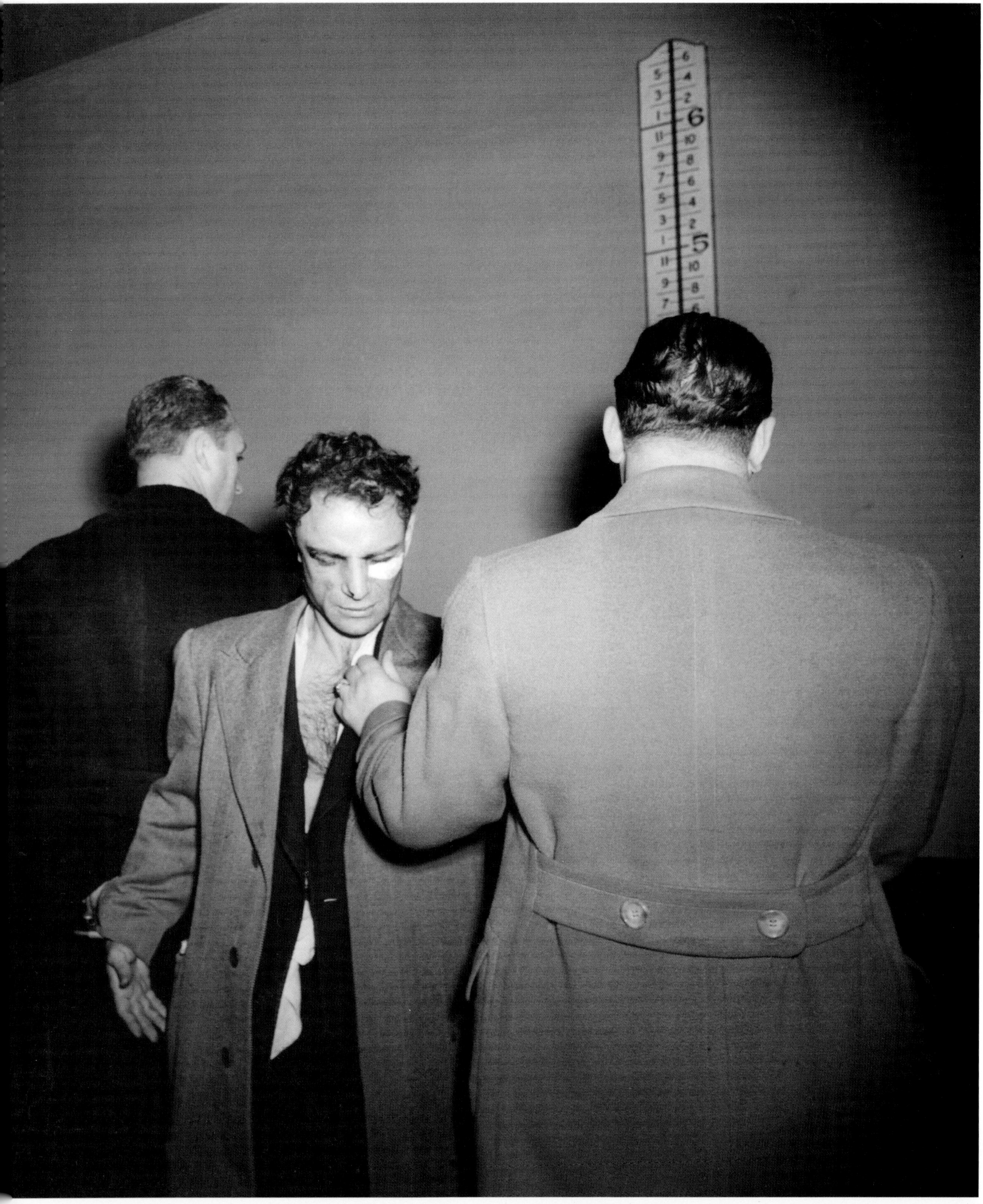
6
5

BELOW: Charles Sodokoff and Arthur Webber use their top hats to hide their faces as a police van takes them away, New York, 1942. Weegee's image of the two Brooklynites, arrested for being drunk and disorderly, perfectly captures their abject shame and attests to the power of the camera's role as a witness to delinquency and social disorder.

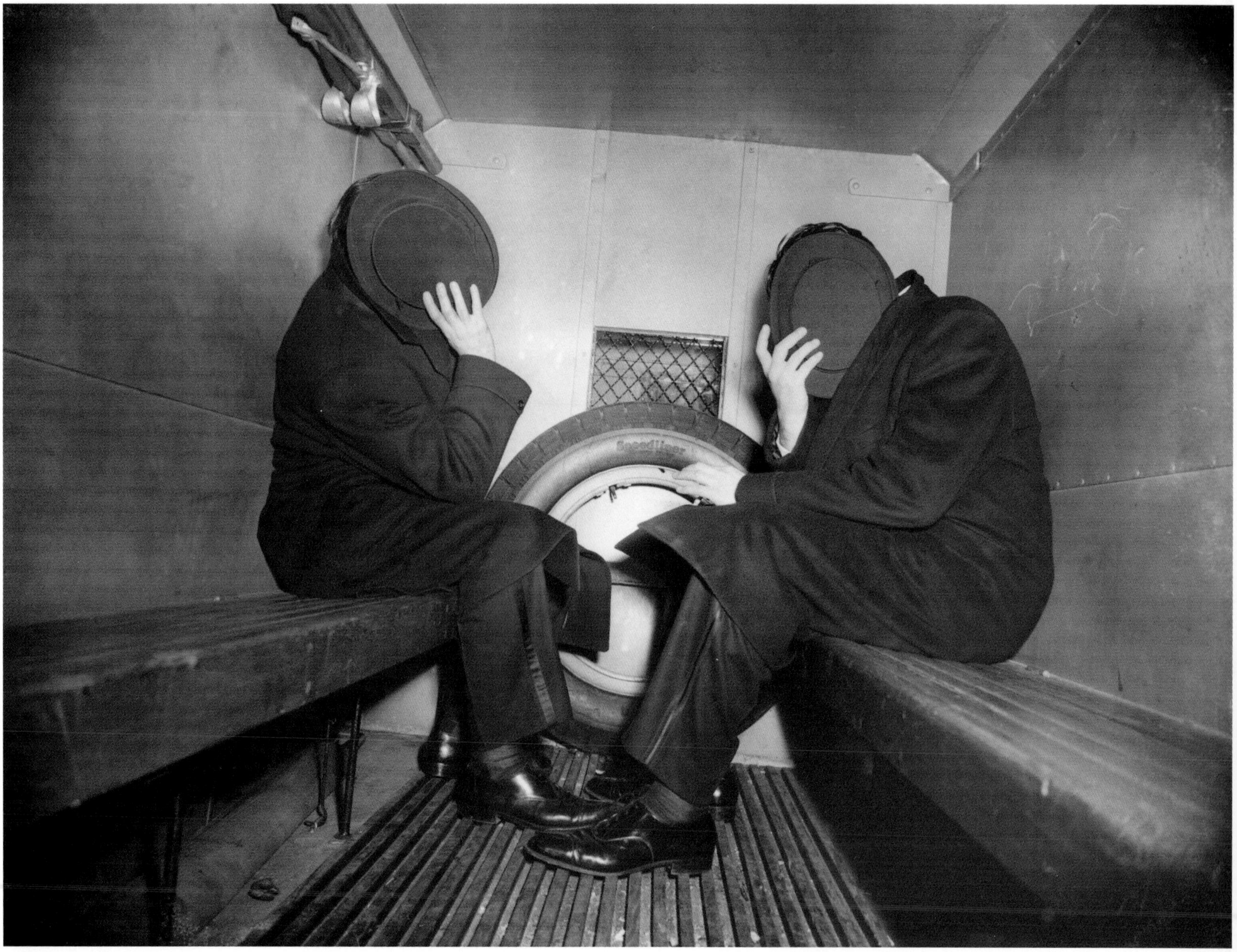

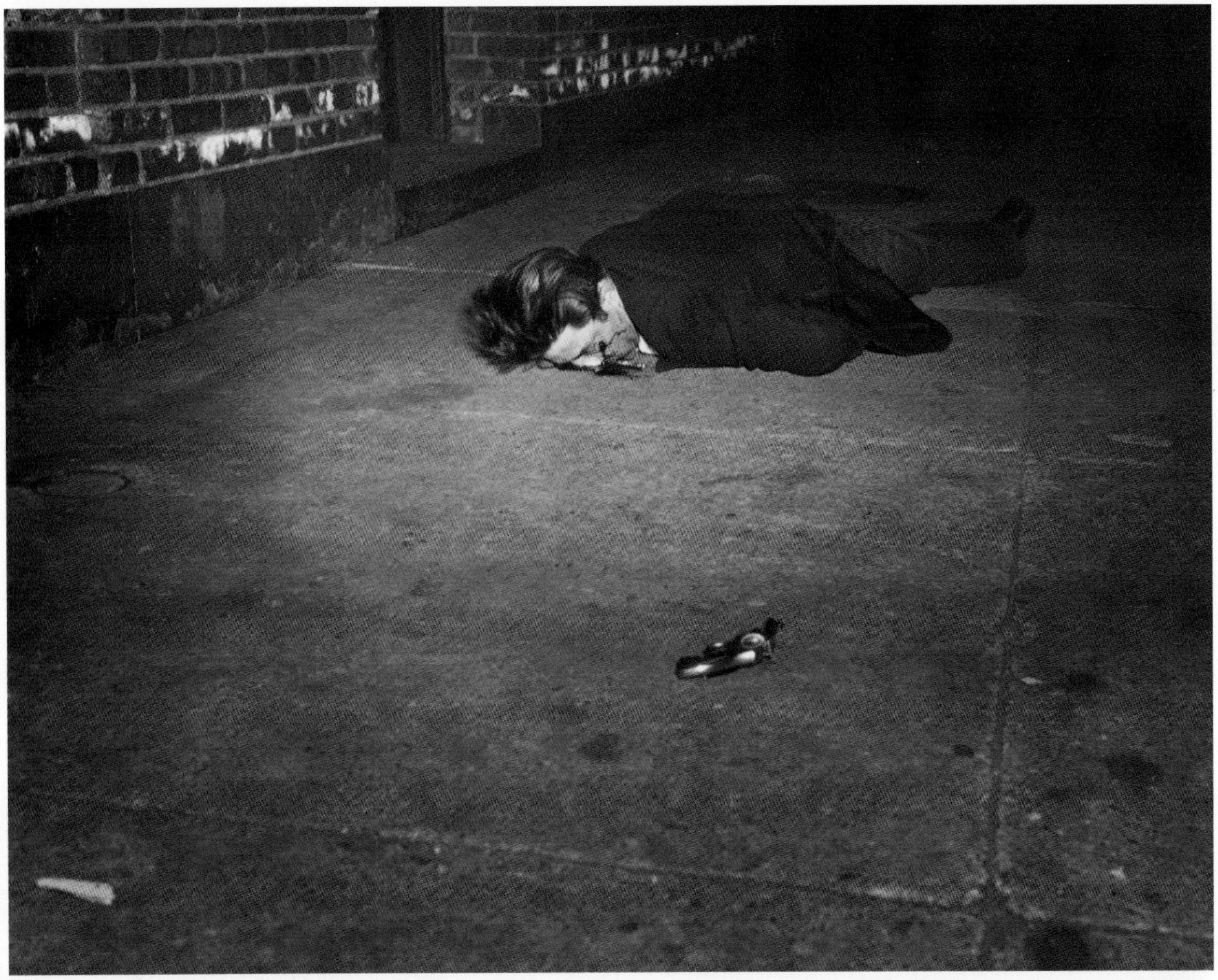

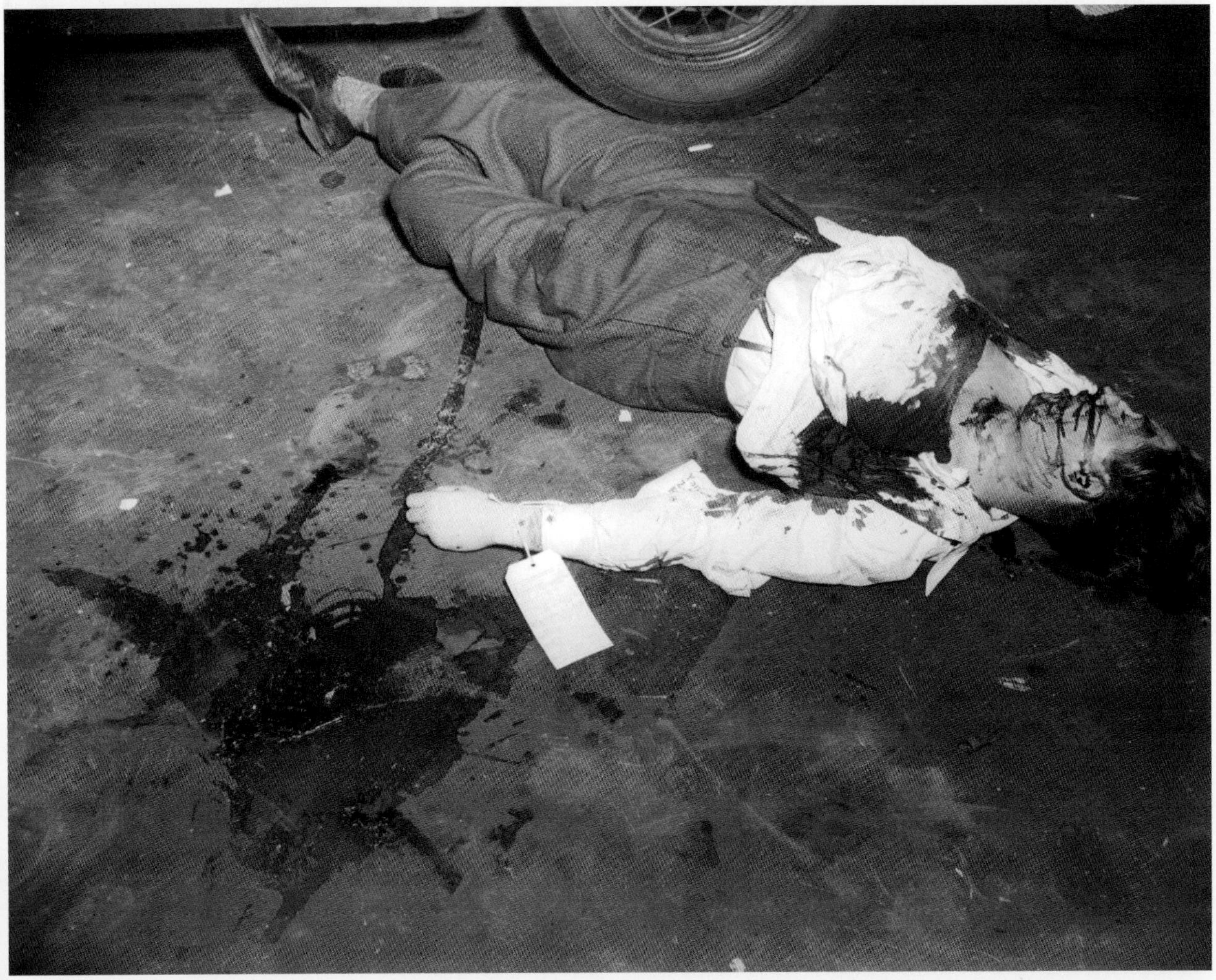

LEFT: **When a gunman attempted a hold-up at the Spring Arrow Social and Athletic Club in New York City, 1942, he was shot by off-duty policeman, Eligio Sarro, who was at the scene by chance. The circle of light in which the gunman's torso and head are placed has undoubtedly been accentuated for dramatic effect by Weegee's printing of the negative.**

BELOW: **"Here he is as he was left in the gutter, in a pool of his own blood." The body of a young man, with DOA (Dead on Arrival) tag already fixed to his right arm, lies in a New York Street, 1941.**

OVERLEAF LEFT: **This image of firemen extinguishing a fire in the Ameko American Kitchen Products Company building in New York, 1937, is a classic example of Weegee's ability to find images that are both documentary reportage and ironic commentary on the events depicted. The sign "Simply add boiling water" is an advertisement for a brand of frankfurter.**

OVERLEAF RIGHT: **A New York fireman holds a hose at the scene of a fire in New York, 1940. Weegee's work, much of it made at night with a 4 x 5 inch (10 cm x 12 cm) press camera and a powerful flashbulb, plays with the caricature qualities of black-and-white photography.**

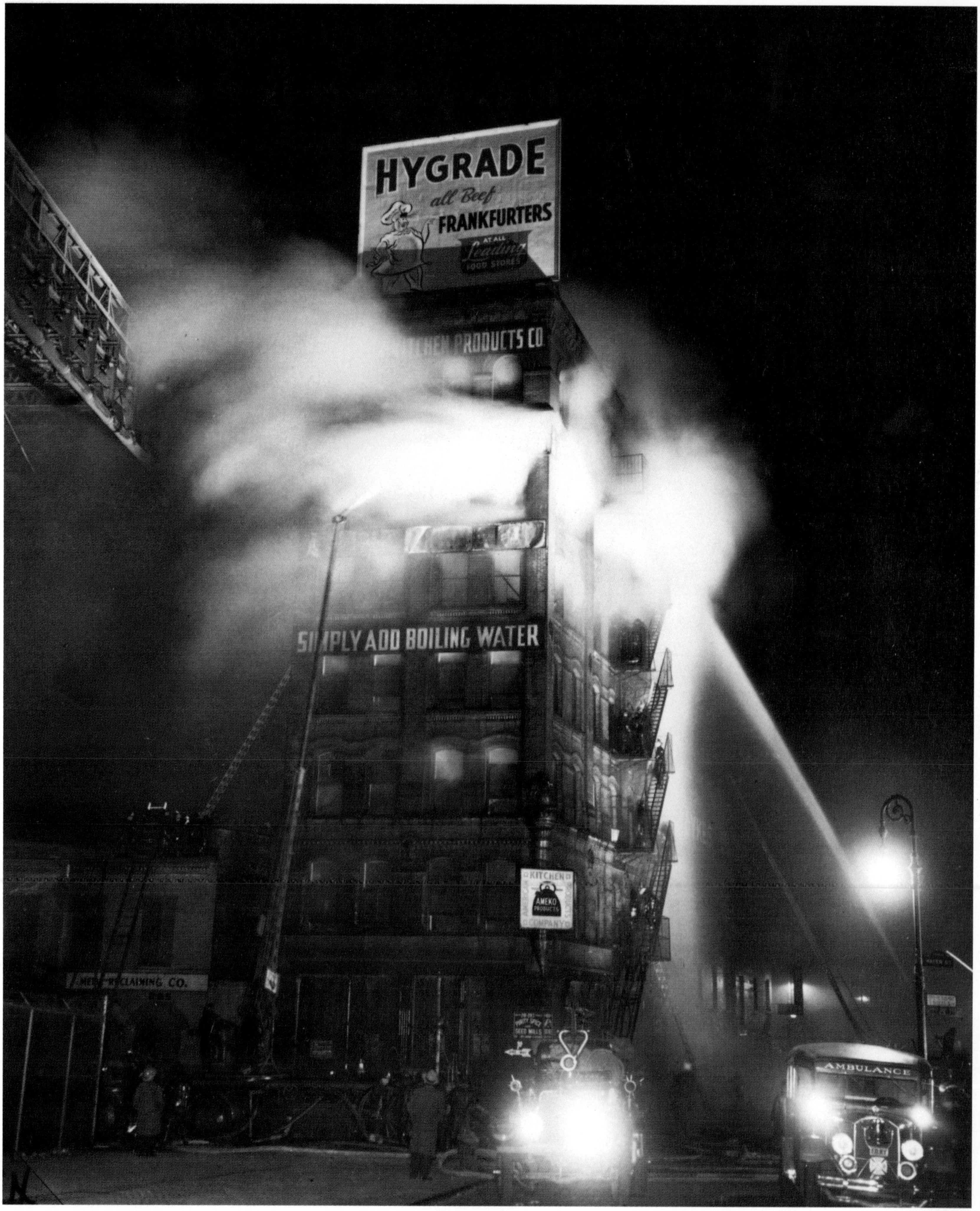
HYGRADE
all Beef
FRANKFURTERS
AT ALL
Leading
FOOD STORES
PRODUCTS CO.
SIMPLY ADD BOILING WATER
KITCHEN
AMEKO PRODUCTS
COMPANY
RECLAIMING CO.
AMBULANCE

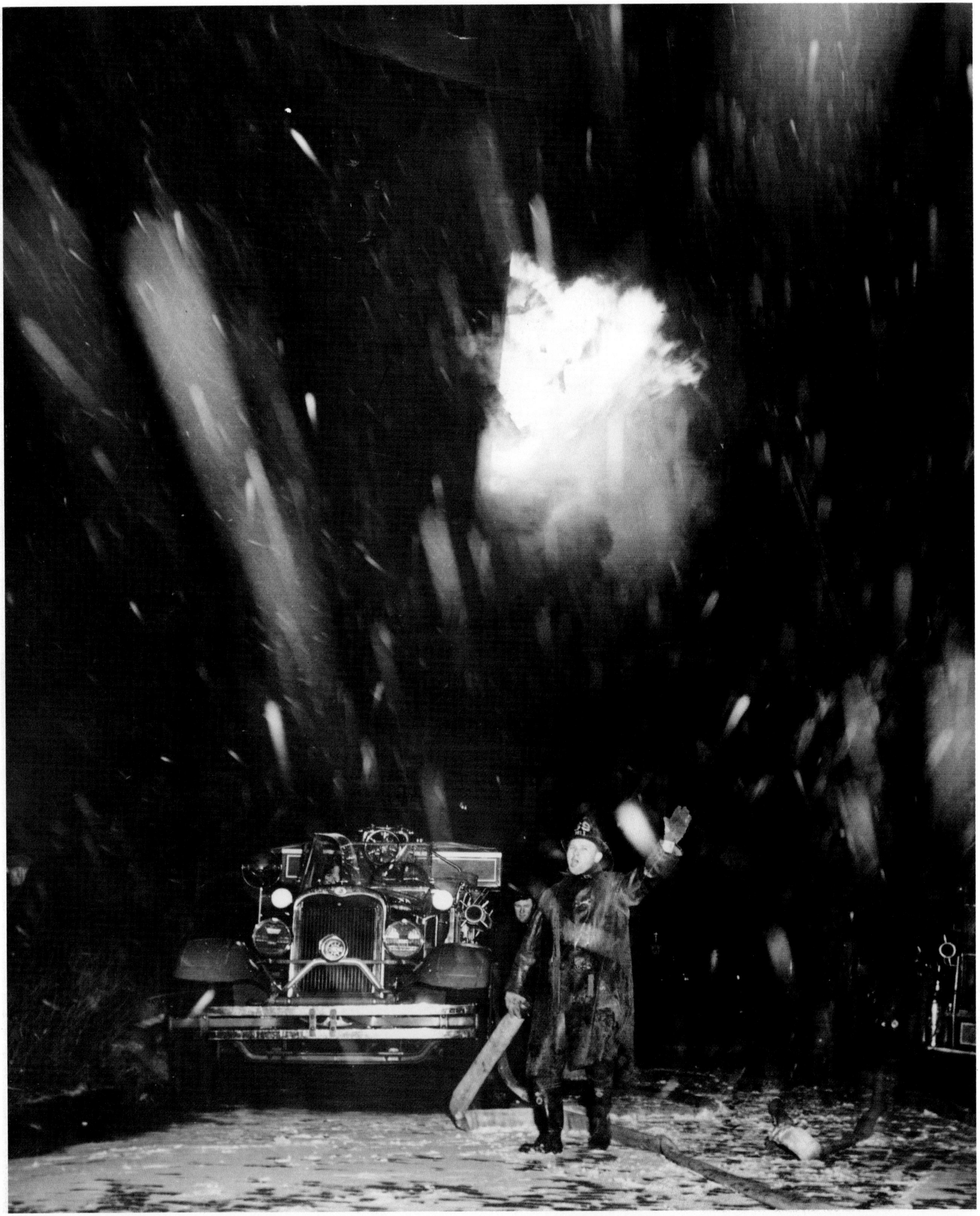

LI ZHENSHENG

BELOW: **By taking a low angle and making the photographic frame of the 35mm camera shape the heroic aspects of this image, Li is able to create a strong picture of teams of female workers sent to retrieve cartloads of mud to enrich the heavily salinated soil in Chaoyang Commune, Shuangcheng County, 1974.**

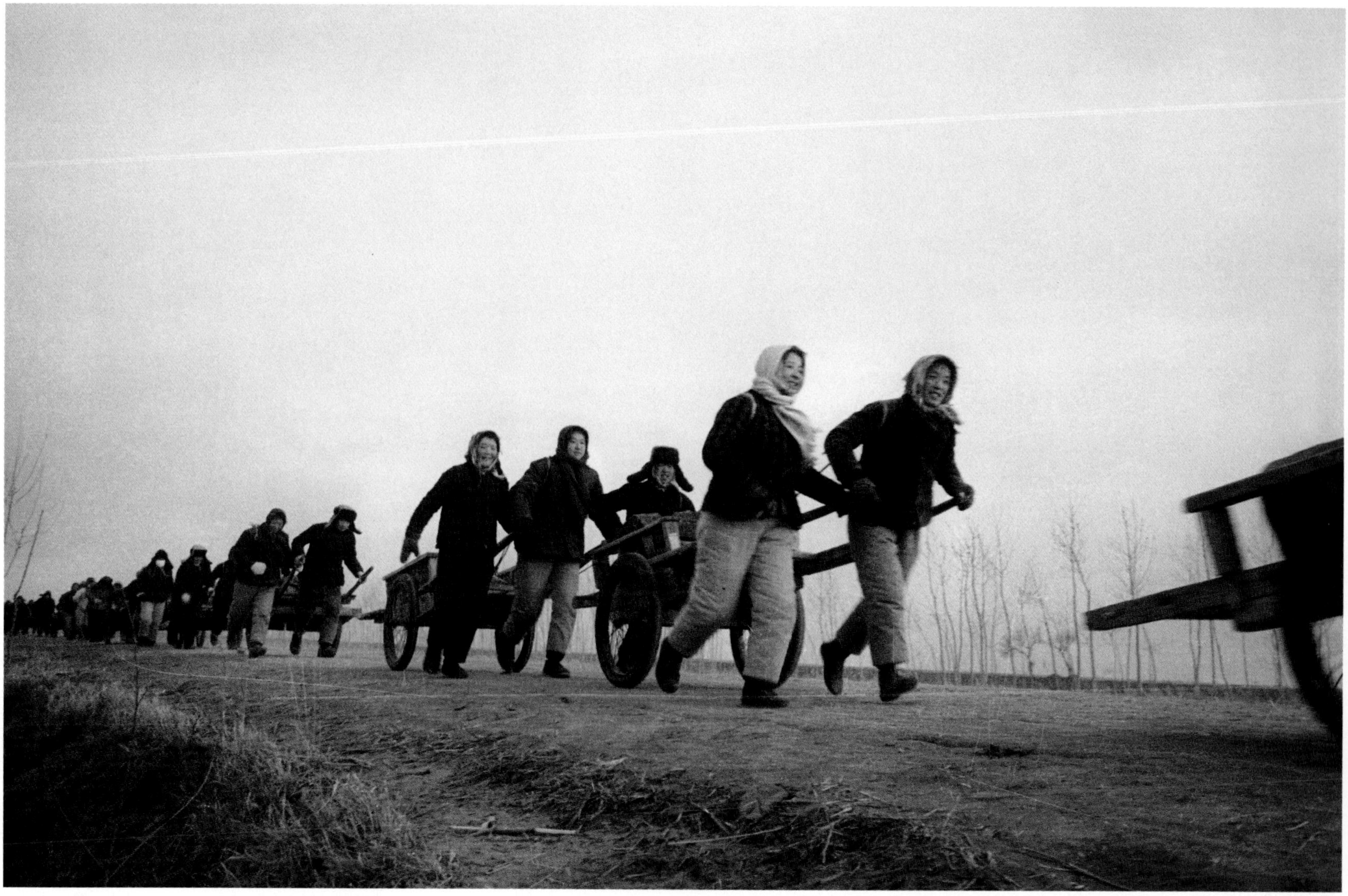

Li's photographs are a rare, and possibly unique, pictorial record of the horror, absurdity and brutality that accompanied Mao's Cultural Revolution. Published as *Red-color News Soldier* (2003), the book also contains much of the sort of imagery distributed as propaganda during this era, which showed the parades, demonstrations and processions that were part and parcel of this extraordinary moment in Chinese history. Li's pictures also reveal the ritual humiliations of those denounced as bourgeois speculators. Their meagre possessions are organized into a still life, bearing witness to their decadence – a wristwatch, a handbag or a pair of foreign-made shoes are displayed as the paltry evidence of their counter-revolutionary nature.

There is a much darker side to this work, for Li also photographed executions, and the grisly sequences of events leading up to them. In one of his photographs, taken in 1967, the Chinese leader Chairman Mao appears, crossing Beijing's Tiananmen Square in a jeep that speeds through a crowd of admirers. Although Li got only one chance to capture Mao in person, his image is omnipresent in many of Li's photographs, carried by the rebel groups and political zealots on banners or large framed portraits, shown on massive posters, or blazoned across cinema screens saluted by Red Guards.

The most remarkable aspect of Li's work is that he managed to safeguard so much of it. He had been, in 1966 and 1967, a supporter of the revolution, so his access to many of the events that marked this period was privileged, and in due course it rebounded upon him. To retain the negatives of these pictures was highly subversive. They show that Li was visually gifted, and was interested in making a good picture. They reveal how he tried to compose these photographs to dramatic effect, and how he surmounted the limitations of his equipment (Russian 35mm cameras and a Rolleiflex 6x6cm). The "joiners" (overlapping 35mm or 6x6cm negatives) that were used by Li to make a panorama, sometines 6–7 frames wide, capture the wider view of a political rally or a group pasting posters on a billboard, and offer another perspective on this troubled era.

BELOW: Many of Li's pictures emphasize the iconography of Mao; here swimmers reading Mao's *Little Red Book* prepare themselves to plunge into the Songhua River to commemorate the second anniversary of Mao's swim in the Yangtze, in Heilongjiang Province, 1968.

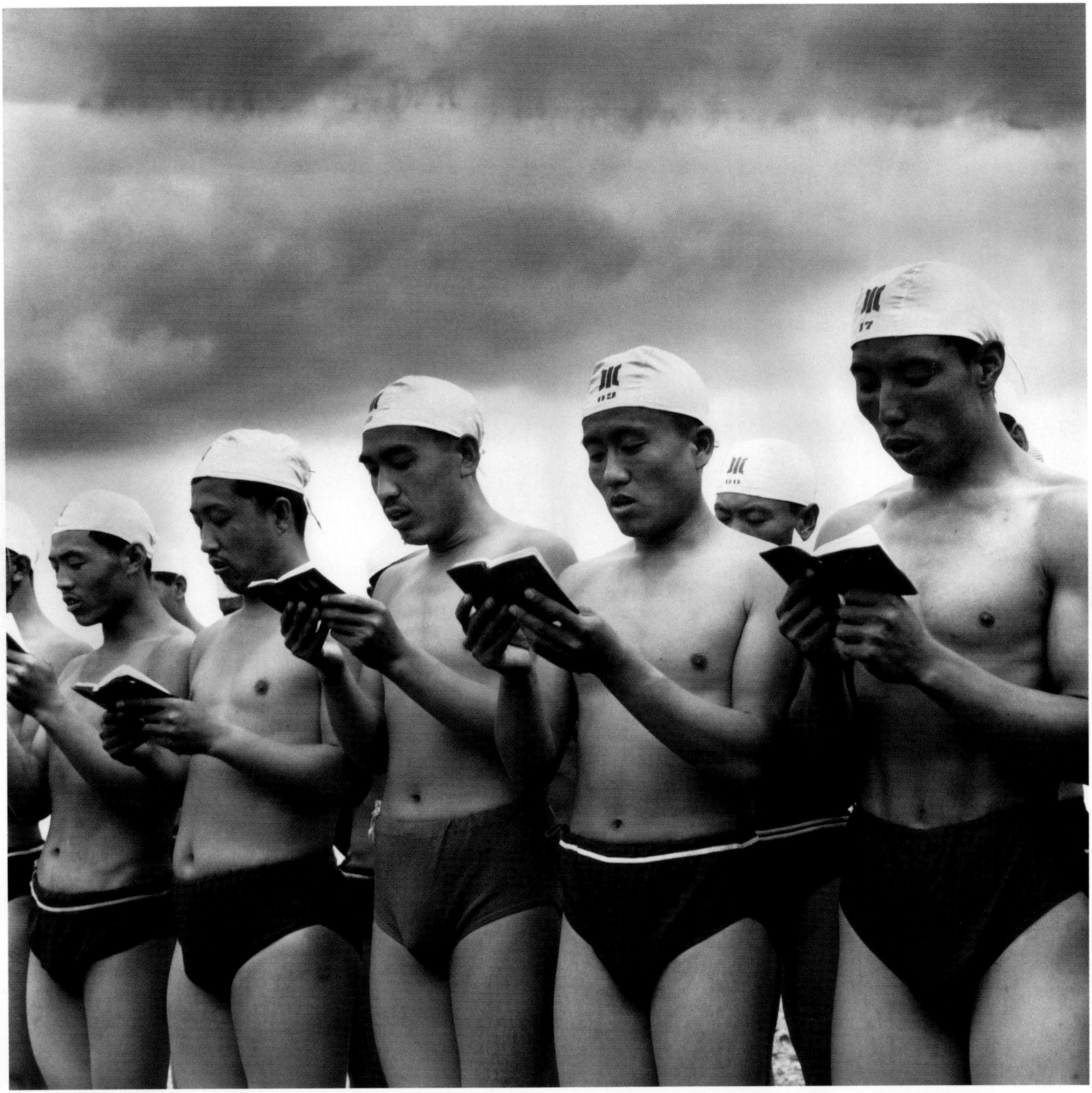

BELOW: Li makes the square frame of his Rolleiflex camera emphasize the dynamism of his picture of Red Guards performing the "It is Right to Rebel" song and dance, in Harbin, August 1966.

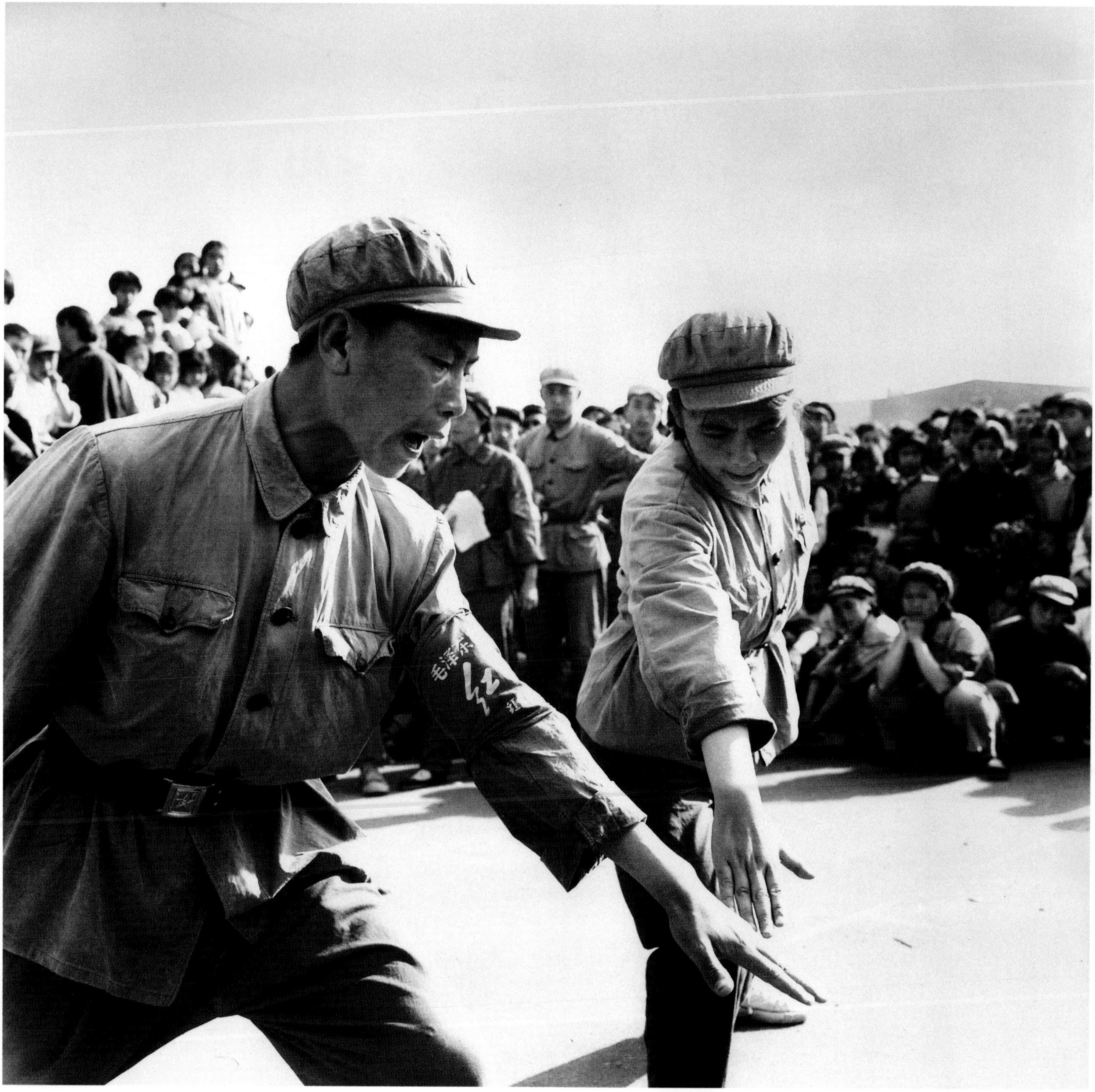

BELOW: Li focuses on the head of Mao, no doubt for political reasons, in his picture showing Red Guards at Harbin's University of Industry inscribe big character posters with slogans such as "Upsurge Revolutionary Criticism", in Harbin, 1967.

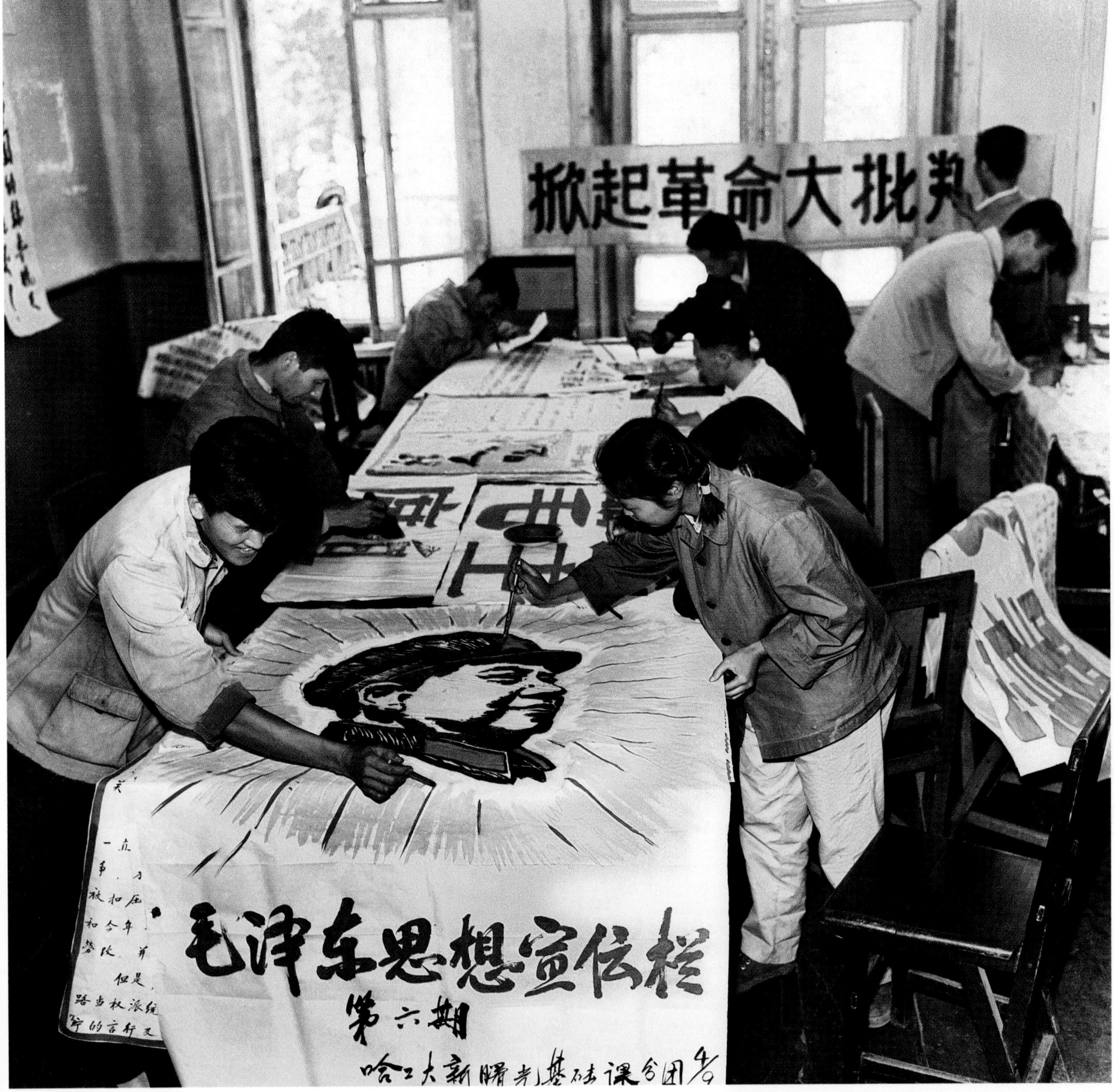

INDEX

Note: page numbers in **bold** refer to picture captions.

CREDITS

The publishers would like to thank the following sources for their kind permission to reproduce the pictures in this book.

Agence VU:
Bertrand Meunier: 174, 175, 176, 177

Archive of Modern Conflict 2004:
Henryk Ross/Courtesy Chris Boot Ltd: 222, 223, 224, 225

Letizia Battaglia:
24–5, 26, 27

Corbis Images:
Roger Fenton: 74–5, 76; /Alexander Gardner/Bettmann: 80; /Heinrich Hoffman/Bettmann: 102–3, 104, 105; /Jerry Lampen/Reuters: 132–3, 134, 135; /Dorothea Lange: 6–7, 136, 137, 138, 139; /Gideon Mendel for the International HIV/AIDS Alliance: 4–5; /Gideon Mendel: 168, 169, 170, 171, 172–3

Getty Images:
Felice Beato: 28, 29, 30, 31, 32, 33; /Margaret Bourke-White/Time Life Pictures: 38, 38–9, 40, 41; /Larry Burrows/Time Life Pictures: 46, 47, 48, 49, 50, 51; /Alfred Eisenstaedt/Pix Inc./Time LifePictures: 70, 71, 72, 73; /Roger Fenton: 77; /Alexander Gardner/Mathew Brady Collection/National Archives/Time Life Pictures: 8; /Alexander Gardner: 82–3; /Bert Hardy: 6, 94, 95, 96–7; /Lewis W. Hine: 99; /Lewis W. Hine/George Eastman House: 98, 100, 101; /Lewis W. Hine/Museum of City of N. York: 101; /Ralph Morse/Time Life Pictures: 182, 183, 184, 185; /Peter Mugabane/Time Life Pictures: 148, 149,150, 151; /Carl Mydans/Time Life Pictures: 186, 187, 188, 189; /Weegee (Arthur Fellig) International Centre of Photography: 9, Endpapers

Katz Pictures/IPG:
David Modell: 178–9, 180, 181; /Zed Nelson: 194, 195, 196, 197; /Tom Stoddart: 238–9, 240, 241

Library of Congress Prints & Photographs Division:
Roger Fenton: 78, 79

Magnum Photos Ltd:
Ian Berry: 34, 35, 36–7; /Rene Burri: 42–3, 44, 45; /Cornell Capa Photos by Robert Capa: 52–3, 54, 55; /Henri Cartier-Bresson: 60–1, 62, 63, 64, 65; /Luc Delahaye: 66, 67, 68, 69; /Philip Jones Griffiths: 116–17, 118, 119; /Josef Koudelka: 124–5, 126, 127; /Alex Majoli: 152, 153, 154, 155; /Peter Marlow: 160–1, 162, 163; /Susan Meiselas: 164–5, 166, 167; /Martin Parr: 198. 199, 200–1; /Gilles Peress: 206–7, 208, 209; /Raghu Rai: 210–11, 212, 213; /Eli Reed: 214–15, 216, 217; /Eugene W. Smith: 230–1, 232; 233

Mary Ellen Mark:
156–7, 158, 159

Moscow House of Photography:
Dmitri Baltermants: 18, 19, 20, 21, 22–3

National Library of Australia:
Frank Hurley: 106, 107

nbpictures:
Gilles Caron/Contact Press Images: 56, 57, 58–9; /Don McCullin/Contact Press Images: 144, 145, 146, 147; /Sebastião Salgado/Amazanos: 226–7, 228, 229; /Li Zhensheng/Contact Press Images: 248, 249, 250, 251

Network Photographers:
Roger Hutchings: 112, 113, 114, 115; /Judah Passow: 202, 203, 204, 205

Novosti Picture Library:
Yevgney Khaldei: 120, 120–1, 122–3

Panos Pictures:
Gerd Ludwig: 140, 141, 142, 143

Rapho:
Top/Jan Grarup: 84–5, 86, 87

Royal Geographical Society:
Frank Hurley: 108–9, 110, 111

VII:
Joachim Ladefoged: 128–9, 130, 131; /James Nachtwey: 190–1, 192, 193; /John Stanmeyer: 234–5, 236, 237

Washington Post Writer's Group:
Carol Guzy: 88–9, 90, 91, 92–3

Every effort has been made to acknowledge correctly and contact the source and/or copyright holder of each picture and Carlton Books Limited apologizes for any unintentional errors or omissions that will be corrected in future editions of this book.

Author's Acknowledgements

This book could not have turned out the way it did and on schedule without the invaluable help of my co-writers, Peter Hamilton and David Walker, who are friends as well as colleagues. Peter wrote the profiles on the following photographers: Dmitri Baltermants, Felice Beato, Ian Berry, Robert Capa, Gilles Caron, Roger Fenton, Bert Hardy, Lewis Hine, Heinrich Hoffman, Yevgeny Khaldei, Josef Koudelka, Don McCullin, Henry Ross, Weegee and Li Zhensheng, David wrote the profiles for the following five photographers: Jan Grarup, Dorothea Lange, James Nachtwey, Eli Reed and John Stanmeyer.

I would also like to thank my editor at Carlton Books, Stella Caldwell, who originally approved my idea for such a book and then intelligently and coolly brought the project together from concept to execution. Thanks also to Sarah Edwards for photo research and to the design team of Stuart Smith, Anita Ruddell and Emma Wicks.

I would also like to thank Jeanine Fijol, my colleague at *Photo District News* for her help with the initial photo research. Thanks also to Holly Stuart Hughes, my editor in chief at PDN, for her insights and suggestions. Also at PDN, Darren Ching, Jay DeFoore, John Gimenez, Michelle Golden, Jane Helmick, Anthony LaSala, Jacqueline Tobin and Michael Goesele were all helpful in different ways and always encouraging.

Steve Mayes at Art Commerce, Paul Moakley at *Newsweek*, Neil Burgess at NB Pictures and Nadja Masri at Geo all came up with some great photographers for possible inclusion in the book. Thanks also to Chris Boot, Abby Johnson and Michelle Franklin at Getty, Jackie Ching and Gideon Rachman.

I would also like to thank some of the photographers featured in this book who took the time to answer my questions about their work. Interviews were conducted both by phone and e-mail. Thanks also to the various experts and photo editors for their critical judgments, in particular Jamie Wellford at *Newsweek*.

Finally, I would also like to thank my wife Emma for her love, assistance and wisdom. This book is dedicated to you.

Reuel Golden

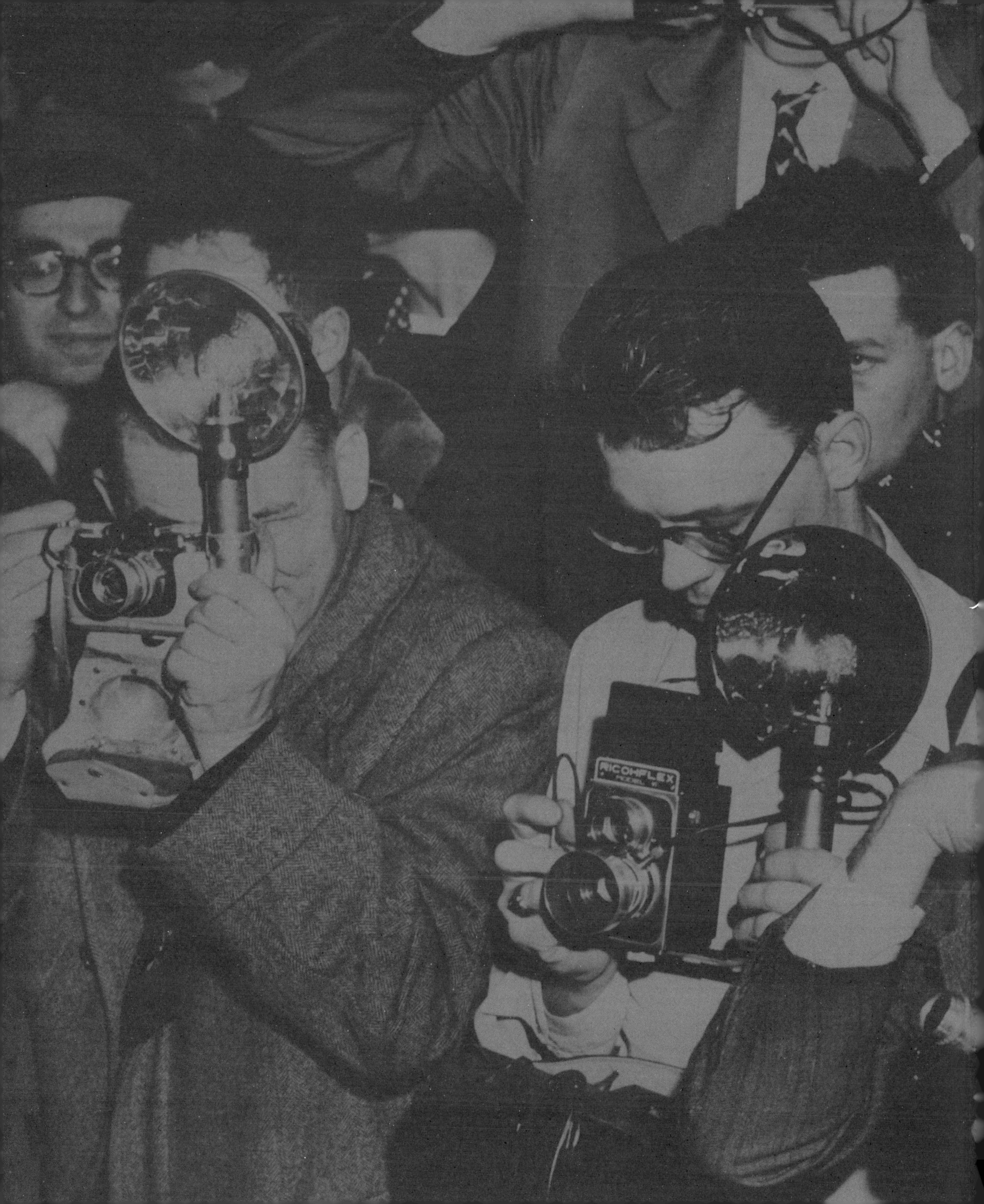
RICOHFLEX